ROGET'S THESAURUS

Existence

Ens, entity, being, exist^ce | Nonentity, nullity, nihility

Essence, quintess.^ce quiddess^ce | nonexist.^ce noth^g nought

Nature thing substance | void zero, cypher blank
course world frame | empty
position constitution

Reality, (v.truth) actual | unsubstantial
exist^ce — fact, | Unreal, ideal, imaginary
course of things, under ; sun | visionary, fabulous
extant, present | fictitious, supposititious
| absent, shadow. dream
| phantom, phantasm

Positive, affirmative absolute | Negative, virtual, extrinsic
intrinsic, substantive | potential. adjective
inherent

To be; exist, obtain, stand

pass, subsist, prevail, lie

— on foot, on ; tapis

to constitute, form, compose | to consist of
| scope, habitude, temperament

State, mode of exist.^ce condition, nature, constitut.^on habit
| place
Affection, predicament, situat.^on posit.^on posture, contingency

Circumstances, case, plight, Trim, tune, — point, degree

juncture, conjuncture pass, emergency, exigency.

— Mode, manner, style, cast, fashion, form shape
| tenor
Strain, way, degree. — tenure, terms,

footing, character, capacity

Relation, ship affinity, alliance, analogy, filiat.^on fv.Connect.^on

Reference, about respect? regard? concerning, touching
in point of, as to — pertaining to, belong? applicable to
relatively, according to
Comparable commensurate, incomp.^ble incommens.^te — ble,
correspondent — able. irreconcilable, discordant.
account

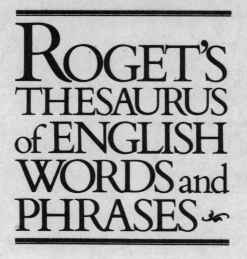

ROGET'S THESAURUS of ENGLISH WORDS and PHRASES

CLASSIFIED AND ARRANGED

SO AS TO FACILITATE THE EXPRESSION OF IDEAS
AND TO ASSIST IN LITERARY COMPOSITION

BY

PETER MARK ROGET, M.D., F.R.S.

ENLARGED BY

JOHN LEWIS ROGET, M.A.

*THIS CLASSIC AMERICAN EDITION WAS ORIGINALLY
REVISED AND ENLARGED BY*

SAMUEL ROMILLY ROGET, M.A.

CHATHAM RIVER PRESS
New York

This edition is published by Chatham River Press, a division of
Arlington House, Inc., distributed by Crown Publishers, Inc.,
One Park Avenue, New York, New York, 10016.

Manufactured in the United States of America

Library of Congress Cataloging in Publication Data

Roget, Peter Mark, 1779-1869.
    Roget's Thesaurus of English Words and Phrases.

    "This classic American edition was originally revised and
enlarged by Samuel Romilly Roget."
    Reprint. Originally published: Thesaurus of English words and
phrases. New York : Avenel Books, 1979.
    Includes index.
    1. English language—Synonyms and antonyms.   I. Roget,
John Lewis, 1828-1908.   II. Roget, Samuel Romilly, 1875-
III. Title.   IV. Title: Thesaurus of English words and phrases.
PE1591.R7 1984   423'.1   83-26270
ISBN 0-517-436248

i h g f e d c b

FOREWORD
TO THE
1979 EDITION

FOR over three generations, *Roget's Thesaurus* has served the needs of writers, speakers, students, and translators. Peter Mark Roget first compiled and organized his guide to English words and phrases in 1805; the work was published in 1852 and was immediately recognized as a valuable tool for anyone concerned with the proper and creative use of the English language. Three generations of Rogets have worked to keep the thesaurus up to date, preserving Peter Mark Roget's original concept, organization, and format, while adapting the work to contemporary needs.

Roget recognized that writing and speaking difficulties are not necessarily the result of a poor vocabulary or ill-formed ideas. He grasped what many writers, orators, and translators had long had to contend with: the necessity of finding the exactly appropriate word or phrase from a group of synonyms. In every language, words are subject to a variety of shadings and implications. A living, growing language contains words that have specific meanings—meanings either embedded in the root of a word or that have developed in the course of history and usage. Words that at first seem synonymous and therefore completely interchangeable, prove otherwise in certain contexts. The word first chosen on impulse may interrupt the mood of a piece of writing or a speech and may jar the reader or the listener by its lack of specificity, or, more seriously, may imply a completely different intent than that which the author had in mind.

The translator is especially concerned with the problems of mood and intent, for even the most formal scholarly works depend on the idiomatic expressions of a language. The richness of poetry and fiction sometimes depends totally on an exact and idiomatic turn of phrase. These expressions are inaccessible to literal translation; a translator must find a matching idiom to retain the author's original sense.

A standard dictionary provides little assistance in these situations. Dictionaries serve only to define words, giving little indication of their use within a language. More importantly, dictionaries are not designed to allow the playing with words that is so important to creating individual nuance.

With the thesaurus, a whole new approach to creative expression is possible, because the thesaurus stresses the importance of the *idea* first. It functions almost as a reverse dictionary: as a dictionary goes from word to idea, a thesaurus starts with a concept and leads to specific words. In this way, the thesaurus becomes both thought-expressing and thought-provoking. A writer or speaker who has a general idea in mind must find the word or phrase that will convey his meaning most clearly and succinctly. The thesaurus, with its exhaustive compilation of synonyms, permits on-the-spot, rapid comparisons of similar words. In addition, while glancing over the list of words, one may decide to modify or strengthen his initial concept. The thesaurus user may come upon an expression or word that had not occurred to him before. And, finally, the selection of a word may start off new trains of thoughts and ideas.

THE DESIGN OF THE THESAURUS

The format of *Roget's Thesaurus* is well adapted to the needs of the user. It is organized by general categories that reflect the most common patterns of words and their usage in the English language. The six general categories are:

1) Abstract relations
2) Space
3) Matter
4) Intellect
5) Volition
6) Affections

Of course, many words fit under more than one of these categories, and they will be found in each relevant one. For example, *work*, because of its multiple meanings, has a place in "abstract relations," "space," "intellect," "volition" and "affections." An introductory synopsis of the general categories describes in detail the subcategories within each general category, making it easy for the thesaurus user to pinpoint and clarify in his own mind the precise meaning he is looking for.

The format of the thesaurus embodies the principle that form must follow function. And the function of the thesaurus is to facilitate the precise expression of ideas; it encourages the exploration of shades of meaning, of comparing directly one word with another that is almost synonymous. In addition, each subcategory is printed beside the subcategory that most nearly reflects its antithesis. For example, *superiority* and *inferiority* appear in parallel columns, as do *safety* and *danger*, *vanity* and *modesty*, and so on.

The thesaurus functions in another way also. The index at the back of the book is arranged by individual words. Within the entry, each word is further broken down into its various meanings, with references to the subcategory in the text proper. When the thought is clear, but the word is missing, the index functions as a quick, easy guide. The index is so specific that a word may have as many as twenty different references. *Rude*, for example, is broken down into ten possible contexts, reflecting the variety of meanings it may assume— "violent," "shapeless," "inelegant," "uncivil," and so on.

The arrangement of words and phrases within each subcategory remains constant throughout the book, and is again designed for easy use. The keyword of each subcategory is printed in bold-faced type. It is followed by a list of synonymous nouns, then verbs, adjectives, adverbs, etc. Under each part of speech, the most closely related synonyms are grouped together in paragraphs. Finally, there is a list of phrases and idiomatic expressions, for often a phrase is the only way to get at the true thought. Slang expressions (indicated as such) that have become a part of the language are also given. Foreign words that have been naturalized are included, as are those foreign words that have no literal translation in English and serve a distinctive role in the English language.

Because further refinements may be necessary, all entries are internally cross-referenced. For example, under *disobedience*, one finds references to *disorder, resistance, defy.*

The Thesaurus as an Indispensable Tool

The aim of *Roget's Thesaurus* is twofold. It is a quick reference of synonyms for someone looking for a fresh word or a word with a slightly different meaning than the word in the writer's mind. These thesaurus users will depend heavily on the index, where they will find references to the literal, figurative, and derivative senses of any word. Others might depend more on the general categories. These are the users who immerse themselves in the rich lists of words and phrases, thereby getting a total feeling of the concept under consideration and all its ramifications.

The purpose of the thesaurus is not to regulate word usage in the English language. Rather, it expands anyone's appreciation of English, supplying a rich vocabulary and suggesting new forms of expression, possibly even new ideas.

Ellen Leventhal

PREFACE

TO

THE FIRST EDITION

(1852)

It is now nearly fifty years since I first projected a system of verbal classification similar to that on which the present Work is founded. Conceiving that such a compilation might help to supply my own deficiencies, I had, in the year 1805, completed a classed catalogue of words on a small scale, but on the same principle, and nearly in the same form, as the Thesaurus now published.* I had often during that long interval found this little collection, scanty and imperfect as it was, of much use to me in literary composition, and often contemplated its extension and improvement; but a sense of the magnitude of the task, amidst a multitude of other avocations, deterred me from the attempt. Since my retirement from the duties of Secretary of the Royal Society, however, finding myself possessed of more leisure, and believing that a repertory of which I had myself experienced the advantage might, when amplified, prove useful to others, I resolved to embark in an undertaking which, for the last three or four years, has given me incessant occupation, and has, indeed, imposed upon me an amount of labour very much greater than I had anticipated. Notwithstanding all the pains I have bestowed on its execution, I am fully aware of its numerous deficiencies and imperfections, and of its falling far short of the degree of excellence that might be attained. But, in a Work of this nature, where perfection is placed at so great a distance, I have thought it best to limit my ambition to that moderate share of merit which it may claim in its present form; trusting to the indulgence of those for whose benefit it is intended, and to the candour of critics who, while they find it easy to detect faults, can at the same time duly appreciate difficulties.

P. M. Roget

April 29th, 1852

* A facsimile of the first page of this little manuscript book which is the original form of the Thesaurus is given in the frontispiece.

EDITOR'S PREFACE

(1879)

(*Slightly Abridged*)

THE FIRST EDITION of Dr. Roget's Thesaurus was published in the year 1852, and a second in the ensuing spring. On the issue of the third, in 1855, the volume was stereotyped. Since that time until now, the work has been reprinted in the same form and with little alteration, in rapidly succeeding editions, the printing of which has worn out the original plates.

During the last years of the author's life, which closed, at a very advanced age, in the month of September, 1869, he was engaged in the task of collecting additional words and phrases, for an enlarged edition which he had long projected. This he did not live to complete, and it became my duty, as his son, to attempt to carry the design into execution.

The result of the author's labours was embodied in a copy of the Thesaurus, in which the margins and spaces about the letterpress were closely covered with written words and phrases, without any very precise indication of the places in the text where additions or alterations were intended to be made. On a careful examination of these *addenda*, I came to the conclusion that, in order to introduce them with advantage, it would be necessary to make some slight changes; without, however, interfering at all with the framework of the book, and but little with the details of its system. In this proceeding my course has been mainly determined by the following considerations.

Any attempt at a philosophical arrangement under categories of the words of our language must reveal the fact that it is impossible to separate and circumscribe the several groups by absolutely distinct boundary lines. Many words, originally employed to express simple conceptions, are found to be capable, with perhaps a very slight modification of meaning, of being applied in many varied associations. Connecting links, thus formed, induce an approach between the categories; and a danger arises that the outlines of our classification may, by their means, become confused and eventually merged. Were we to disengage these interwoven ramifications, and seek to confine every word to its main or original import, we should find some secondary meaning has become so firmly associated with many words and phrases, that to sever the alliance would be to deprive our language of the richness due to an infinity of natural adaptations.

Were we, on the other hand, to attempt to include, in each category of the Thesaurus, every word and phrase which could by any possibility be appropriately used in relation to the leading idea for which that category was designed, we should impair, if not destroy, the whole use and value of the book. For, in the endeavour to enrich our treasury of expression, we might easily allow ourselves to be led imperceptibly onward by the natural association of one word with another, and to add word after word, until group after group would successively be absorbed under some single heading, and the fundamental divisions of the system be effaced. The small cluster of nearly synonymous words, which had formed the nucleus of a category, would be lost in a sea of phrases, and it would become difficult to recognize those which were peculiarly adapted to express the leading ideas.

These considerations were material in dealing with the new and multitudinous store of words and phrases which the author had accumulated. Many of these were altogether new to the Thesaurus. Many were merely repetitions in new places of words already included in its pages. With reference to cases similar to the latter, the author had declared it to have been a general rule with him 'to place words and phrases which appertain more especially to one head, also under other heads to which they have a relation,' whenever it appeared to him 'that this repetition would suit the convenience of the inquirer and spare him the trouble of turning to other parts of the work.' But, with the now increased mass of words, it became a question, in many cases, whether such repetition would still prove convenient. Where categories might by that course be unduly swollen, or where they might, by reason of their being separated from each other by subtile distinctions or faint lines of demarcation, be thereby too nearly assimilated, I thought it would often be better to confine words of the kind referred to to their primary headings. The necessity of keeping the book within reasonable dimensions had also to be borne in mind.

Under these circumstances, the best method of ensuring the ready accessibility of the multitude of words now to be dealt with, and at the same time preserving unimpaired the unity of the several categories, appeared to me to lie in the copious use of references from one place in the book to another. Relying on this contrivance as a means of opening more widely the resources of the collection, by making the groups of words mutually suggestive, and thereby leading not only to more varied forms of expression, but to kindred ideas, I have added largely to the references already inserted by the author. I have also ventured occasionally to substitute a reference for a group of words, when the identical group existed in another place, and could thus be made immediately available.

In order, at the same time, to make the value of the references more appreciable, I have (whenever it has appeared to me to be necessary) inserted, in a parenthesis, a word indicating the nature of the group or category referred to. Any one using the book will thereby be enabled to judge whether it will be worth his while to turn to the place in question.

The cross references may also be looked upon as indicating in some degree the natural points of connection between the categories, and the ramification of the ideas which they embody. As would be the case under any classification of language, a large proportion of the expressions, to find which recourse is had to the Thesaurus, lie on an ill-defined border land between one category and another; and it is not always easy, even with the aid of a carefully compiled index, to determine under which of several allied headings they should be sought. In the present edition, when the inquirer has once started on his voyage of discovery, the references enable him to pass freely from one division to another without recurring to the Index.

Many new words have also been inserted which were not contained in the author's manuscript.

Except in a very few cases, where distinct ideas were obviously united under one head, I have not had the presumption to meddle with the author's division into categories; but, within each category, I have endeavoured to carry somewhat further the sorting of words according to the ideas which they convey.

With these objects in view, I have supplied the work with a new and elaborate Index, much more complete than that which was appended to the previous editions. Although, in the original design of his work, the author appears to have conceived the process of search for a required expression as one in which the system of classification would be first consulted, and the Index afterwards called in aid if necessary, I believe that almost everyone who uses the book finds it more convenient to have recourse to the Index first.

From the peculiar nature and use of the Thesaurus, its Index will be found to differ, in some of its essential functions, from an alphabetical table of contents. The present Index does not merely afford an indication of the place where every given word or topic occurs or is dealt with in the text; but it is intended as a guide to other expressions which may be found there. The word we look out in this Index is not that which we require, but that which we wish to avoid. It is, therefore, not necessary that every word there given should be a repetition of one in the text. It may even happen that the word selected as a guide, though suggestive of the group wanted, is wholly unfit to be comprised within it.

The new Index contains not only all the *words* in the book (without needless repetition of conjugate forms), but likewise the *phrases,* all of which had been excluded from the Index to the previous editions. It is hoped that these additions, although they increase the bulk of the book, will have the effect of extending its usefulness in at least a corresponding degree.

Some changes of detail have also been made, where the form of the work seemed susceptible of improvement, and there was no reason to suppose that the author would have disapproved of the alteration. In the previous editions, the *phrases* were in general placed in separate paragraphs, under the heading **Phr.**, in each of the subdivisions assigned to the different grammatical parts of speech. In the present edition, *words* and *phrases* are placed together, and the heading **Phr.** is only employed in the case of phrases which have no convenient place in such an arrangement. Much space has been saved, and many repetitions have been avoided, by the use of lines and hyphens, where words or phrases in the same group have syllables or parts in common, and by references from one part of speech to another. These abbreviations may, be best explained by examples, of which the following are a few:—

'with -relation, – reference, – respect, – regard- to'; is meant to include the phrases 'with relation to,' 'with reference to,' 'with respect to,' 'with regard to.'

'root –, weed –, grub –, rake- -up, – out;' includes 'root up,' 'root out,' 'weed up,' 'weed out,' 'grub up,' 'grub out,' 'rake up,' 'rake out.'

'away from –, foreign to –, beside- the -purpose, – question, – transaction, – point;' includes 'away from the purpose,' 'foreign to the purpose,' 'beside the purpose,' 'away from the question,' 'foreign to the question,' 'foreign to the transaction,' 'beside the question,' 'away from the point,' 'beside the transaction,' 'foreign to the point,' 'away from the transaction,' 'beside the point.'

'raze – to the ground'; includes 'raze,' and 'raze to the ground.'

'campan-iform, -ulate, -iliform;' includes 'campaniform,' 'campanulate,' and 'campaniliform.'

'goodness &c. *adj.*'; 'badly &c. *adj.*'; 'hindred &c. *v.*'; include all words similarly formed from synonyms of 'good,' 'bad,' and 'hinder,' respectively, given under the headings **Adj.** and **V.** in the same categories where the abbreviations occur.

The participle 'to' before a verb has in all cases been rejected, the heading **V.** being thought sufficiently distinctive; the use of capitals for the initial letters of the first words of paragraphs has been abandoned, as giving those words undue importance; and the title of each category has been kept distinct from the collection of words under its heading.

I should be ungrateful were I not to acknowledge the assistance derived, both by my father and myself, from various suggestions made by well-wishers to the work, some of whom have been personally unknown to either of us; and also to record my thanks to several kind friends, and to Messrs. Spottiswoode and Co.'s careful reader, for valuable aid during the passage of the sheets through the press.

JOHN L. ROGET

March 17th, 1879.

INTRODUCTION

[Notes within brackets are by the editors.]

THE present Work is intended to supply, with respect to the English language, a desideratum hitherto unsupplied in any language; namely, a collection of the words it contains and of the idiomatic combinations peculiar to it, arranged, not in alphabetical order as they are in a Dictionary, but according to the *ideas* which they express.* The purpose of an ordinary dictionary is simply to explain the meaning of the words; and the problem of which it professes to furnish the solution may be stated thus:—The word being given, to find its signification, or the idea it is intended to convey. The object aimed at in the present undertaking is exactly the converse of this: namely,—The idea being given, to find the word, or words, by which that idea may be most fitly and aptly expressed. For this purpose, the words and phrases of the language are here classed, not according to their sound or their orthography, but strictly according to their *signification*.

The communication of our thoughts by means of language, whether spoken or written, like every other object of mental exertion, constitutes a peculiar art, which, like other arts, cannot be acquired in any perfection but by long and continued practice. Some, indeed, there are more highly gifted than others with a facility of expression, and naturally endowed with the power of eloquence; but to none is it at all times an easy process to embody, in exact and appropriate language, the various trains of ideas that are passing through the mind, or to depict in their true colours and proportions, the diversified and nicer shades of feeling which accompany them. To those who are unpractised in the art of composition, or unused to extempore speaking, these difficulties present themselves in their most formidable aspect. However distinct may be our views, however vivid our conceptions, or however fervent our emotions, we cannot but be often conscious that the phraseology we have at our command is inadequate to do them justice. We seek in vain the words we need, and strive ineffectually to devise forms of expression which shall faithfully portray our thoughts and sentiments. The appropriate terms, notwithstanding our utmost efforts, cannot be conjured up at will. Like 'spirits from the vasty deep,' they come not when we call; and we are driven to the employment of a set of words and phrases either too general or too

* See note in p. xxi.

limited, too strong or too feeble, which suit not the occasion, which hit not the mark we aim at; and the result of our prolonged exertion is a style at once laboured and obscure, vapid and redundant, or vitiated by the still graver faults of affectation or ambiguity.

It is to those who are thus painfully groping their way and struggling with the difficulties of composition, that this Work professes to hold out a helping hand. The assistance it gives is that of furnishing on every topic a copious store of words and phrases, adapted to express all the recognizable shades and modifications of the general idea under which those words and phrases are arranged. The inquirer can readily select, out of the ample collection spread out before his eyes in the following pages, those expressions which are best suited to his purpose, and which might not have occurred to him without such assistance. In order to make this selection, he scarcely ever need engage in any critical or elaborate study of the subtle distinction existing between synonymous terms; for if the materials set before him be sufficiently abundant, an instinctive tact will rarely fail to lead him to the proper choice. Even while glancing over the columns of this Work, his eye may chance to light upon a particular term, which may save the cost of a clumsy paraphrase, or spare the labour of a tortuous circumlocution. Some felicitous turn of expression thus introduced will frequently open to the mind of the reader a whole vista of collateral ideas, which could not, without an extended and obtrusive episode, have been unfolded to his view; and often will the judicious insertion of a happy epithet, like a beam of sunshine in a landscape, illumine and adorn the subject which it touches, imparting new grace and giving life and spirit to the picture.

Every workman in the exercise of his art should be provided with proper implements. For the fabrication of complicated and curious pieces of mechanism, the artisan requires a corresponding assortment of various tools and instruments. For giving proper effect to the fictions of the drama, the actor should have at his disposal a well-furnished wardrobe, supplying the costumes best suited to the personages he is to represent. For the perfect delineation of the beauties of nature, the painter should have within reach of his pencil every variety and combination of hues and tints. Now, the writer, as well as the orator, employs for the accomplishment of his purposes the instrumentality of words; it is in words that he clothes his thoughts; it is by means of words that he depicts his feelings. It is therefore essential to his success that he be provided with a copious vocabulary, and that he possess an entire command of all the resources and appliances of his language. To the acquisition of this power no procedure appears more directly conducive than the study of a methodized system such as that now offered to his use.

The utility of the present Work will be appreciated more especially by those who are engaged in the arduous process of translating into English a work written in another language. Simple as the operation may appear, on a superficial view, of rendering into English each of its sentences, the task of transfusing, with perfect exactness, the sense of the original, preserving at the same time the style and character of its composition, and reflecting with fidelity the mind and the spirit of the author, is a task of extreme difficulty. The cultivation of this useful department of literature was in ancient times strongly recommended both by Cicero and by Quintilian, as essential to the formation of a good writer and accomplished orator. Regarded simply as a mental exercise, the practice of translation is the best training for the attainment of that mastery of language and felicity of diction, which are the sources of the highest oratory, and are requisite for the possession of a graceful and persuasive eloquence. By rendering ourselves the faithful interpreters of the thoughts and feelings of others, we are rewarded with the acquisition of greater readiness and facility in correctly expressing our own; as he who has best learned to execute the orders of a commander, becomes himself best qualified to command.

In the earliest periods of civilization, translators have been the agents for propagating knowledge from nation to nation, and the value of their labours has been inestimable; but, in the present age, when so many different languages have become the depositories of the vast treasures of literature and of science which have been accumulating for centuries, the utility of accurate translations has greatly increased, and it has become a more important object to attain perfection in the art.

The use of language is not confined to its being the medium through which we communicate our ideas to one another; it fulfils a no less important function as an *instrument of thought*; not being merely its vehicle, but giving it wings for flight. Metaphysicians are agreed that scarcely any of our intellectual operations could be carried on to any considerable extent, without the agency of words. None but those who are conversant with the philosophy of mental phenomena, can be aware of the immense influence that is exercised by language in promoting the development of our ideas, in fixing them in the mind, and in detaining them for steady contemplation. Into every process of reasoning, language enters as an essential element. Words are the instruments by which we form all our abstractions, by which we fashion and embody our ideas, and by which we are enabled to glide along a series of premises and conclusions with a rapidity so great as to leave in the memory no trace of the successive steps of the process; and we remain unconscious how much we owe to this potent auxiliary of the reasoning faculty. It is on this ground, also, that the present Work founds a claim to utility. The review of a catalogue of words of analogous signification, will often suggest by association other trains of thought, which, presenting the subject under new and varied aspects, will vastly expand the sphere of our mental vision. Amidst the many objects thus brought within the range of our contemplation, some striking similitude or appropriate image, some excursive flight or brilliant conception, may flash on the mind, giving point and force to our arguments, awakening a responsive chord in the imagination or sensibility of the reader, and procuring for our reasonings a more ready access both to his understanding and to his heart.

It is of the utmost consequence that strict accuracy should regulate our use of language, and that every one should acquire the power and the habit of expressing his thoughts with perspicuity and correctness. Few, indeed, can appreciate the real extent and importance of that influence which language has always exercised on human affairs, or can be aware how often these are determined by causes much slighter than are apparent to a superficial observer. False logic, disguised under specious phraseology, too often gains the assent of the unthinking multitude, disseminating far and wide the seeds of prejudice and error. Truisms pass current, and wear the semblance of profound wisdom, when dressed up in the tinsel garb of antithetical phrases, or set off by an imposing pomp of paradox. By a confused jargon of involved and mystical sentences, the imagination is easily inveigled into a transcendental region of clouds, and the understanding beguiled into the belief that it is acquiring knowledge and approaching truth. A misapplied or misapprehended term is sufficient to give rise to fierce and interminable disputes; a misnomer has turned the tide of popular opinion; a verbal sophism has decided a party question; an artful watchword, thrown among combustible materials, has kindled the flame of deadly warfare, and changed the destiny of an empire.

In constructing the following system of classification of the ideas which are expressible by language, my chief aim has been to obtain the greatest amount of practical utility. I have accordingly adopted such principles of arrangement as appeared to me to be the simplest and most natural, and which would not require, either for their comprehension or application, any disciplined acumen, or depth of metaphysical or antiquarian lore. Eschewing all needless refinements and subtleties, I have taken as my guide the more obvious characters of the ideas for which expressions were to be tabulated, arranging them under such classes and categories as reflection and experience had taught me would conduct the inquirer most readily and quickly to the object of his search. Commencing with the ideas expressing abstract relations, I proceeded to those which relate to space and to the phenomena of the material world, and lastly to those in which the mind is concerned, and which comprehend intellect, volition, and feeling; thus establishing six primary Classes of Categories.

1. The first of these classes comprehends ideas derived from the more general and ABSTRACT RELATIONS among things, such as *Existence, Resemblance, Quantity, Order, Number, Time, Power*.

2. The second class refers to SPACE and its various relations, including *Motion,* or change of place.

3. The third class includes all ideas that relate to the MATERIAL WORLD; namely, the *Properties of Matter,* such as *Solidity, Fluidity, Heat, Sound, Light,* and the *Phenomena* they present, as well as the simple *Perceptions* to which they give rise.

4. The fourth class embraces all ideas of phenomena relating to the INTELLECT and its operations; comprising the *Acquisition,* the *Retention,* and the *Communication of Ideas.*

5. The fifth class includes the ideas derived from the exercise of VOLITION; embracing the phenomena and results of our *Voluntary and Active Powers;* such as *Choice, Intention, Utility, Action, Antagonism, Authority, Compact, Property,* &c.

6. The sixth and last class comprehends all ideas derived from the operation of our SENTIENT AND MORAL POWERS; including our *Feelings, Emotions, Passions,* and *Moral and Religious Sentiments.**

The further subdivisions and minuter details will be best understood from an inspection of the Tabular Synopsis of Categories prefixed to the Work, in which are specified the several *topics* or *heads of signification,* under which the words have been arranged. By the aid of this table the reader will, with a little practice, readily discover the place which the particular topic he is in search of occupies in the series; and on turning to the page in the body of the Work which contains it, he will find the group of expressions he requires, out of which he may cull those that are most appropriate to his purpose. For the convenience of reference, I have designated each separate group or heading by a particular number; so that if, during the search, any doubt or difficulty should occur, recourse may be had to the copious alphabetical Index of words at the end of the volume, which will at once indicate the number of the required group.†

---

* It must necessarily happen in every system of classification framed with this view, that ideas and expressions arranged under one class must include also ideas relating to another class; for the operations of the *Intellect* generally involve also those of the *Will,* and *vice versâ;* and our *Affections* and *Emotions,* in like manner, generally imply the agency both of the *Intellect* and of the *Will.* All that can be effected, therefore, is to arrange the words according to the principal or dominant idea they convey. *Teaching,* for example, although a Voluntary act, relates primarily to the Communication of Ideas, and is accordingly placed at No. 537, under Class IV Division (II). On the other hand, *Choice, Conduct, Skill,* &c., although implying the co-operation of Voluntary with Intellectual acts, relate principally to the former, and are therefore arranged under Class V.

† It often happens that the same word admits of various applications, or may be used in different senses. In consulting the Index the reader will be guided to the number of the heading under which that word, in each particular acceptation, will be found, by means of *supplementary words* printed in Italics; which words, however, are not to be understood as explaining the meaning of the word to which they are annexed, but only as assisting in the required reference. I have also, for shortness' sake, generally omitted words immediately derived from the primary one inserted, which sufficiently represents the whole group of correlative words referable to the same heading. Thus the number affixed to *Beauty* applies to all its derivatives, such as *Beautiful, Beauteous, Beautifulness, Beautifully,* &c., the insertion of which was therefore needless. [In compiling the new Index the editor has adopted this principle as a general rule, from which, however, he has not scrupled to depart where he has deemed it expedient to do so.]

The object I have proposed to myself in this Work would have been put imperfectly attained if I had confined myself to a mere catalogue of words, and had omitted the numerous phrases and forms of expression composed of several words, which are of such frequent use as to entitle them to rank among the constituent parts of the language.* Very few of these verbal combinations, so essential to the knowledge of our native tongue, and so profusely abounding in its daily use, are to be met with in ordinary dictionaries. These phrases and forms of expression I have endeavoured diligently to collect and to insert in their proper places, under the general ideas that they are designed to convey. Some of these conventional forms, indeed, partake of the nature of proverbial expressions; but actual proverbs, as such, being wholly of a didactic character, do not come within the scope of the present Work; and the reader must therefore not expect to find them here inserted.†

For the purpose of exhibiting with greater distinctness the relations between words expressing opposite and correlative ideas, I have, whenever the subject admitted of such an arrangement, placed them in two parallel columns in the same page, so that each group of expressions may be readily contrasted with those which occupy the adjacent column, and constitute their antithesis. By carrying the eye from the one to the other, the inquirer may often discover forms of expression, of which he may avail himself advantageously, to diversify and infuse vigour into his phraseology. Rhetoricians, indeed, are well aware of the power derived from the skilful introduction of antitheses in giving point to an argument, and imparting force and brilliancy to the diction. A too frequent and indiscreet employment of this figure of rhetoric may, it is true, give rise to a vicious and affected style; but it is unreasonable to condemn indiscriminately the occasional and moderate use of a practice on account of its possible abuse.

The study of correlative terms existing in a particular language, may often throw valuable light on the manners and customs of the nations using it. Thus, Hume has drawn important inferences with regard to the state of society among the ancient Romans, from certain deficiencies which he remarked in the Latin language.‡

* For example:—To take time by the forelock;—to turn over a new leaf;—to show the white feather;—to have a finger in the pie;—to let the cat out of the bag;—to take care of number one;—to kill two birds with one stone, &c., &c.

† See Trench, *On the Lessons in Proverbs*.

‡ 'It is an universal observation,' he remarks, 'which we may form upon language, that where two related parts of a whole bear any proportion to each other, in numbers, rank, or consideration, there are always correlative terms invented which answer to both the parts, and express their mutual relation. If they bear no proportion to each other, the term is only invented for the less, and marks its distinction from the whole. Thus, *man* and *woman*, *master* and *servant*, *father* and *son*, *prince* and *subject*, *stranger* and *citizen*, are correlative terms. But the words *seaman*, *carpenter*, *smith*, *tailor*, &c., have no correspondent terms, which express those who are no seamen, no carpenters, &c. Languages differ very much with regard to the particular words where this distinction obtains; and may thence afford very strong inferences concerning the manners and customs of different nations. The military government of the

In many cases, two ideas which are completely opposed to each other, admit of an intermediate or neutral idea, equidistant from both; all these being expressible by corresponding definite terms. Thus, in the following examples, the words in the first and third columns, which express opposite ideas, admit of the intermediate terms contained in the middle column, having a neutral sense with reference to the former.

Identity	*Difference*	*Contrariety*
Beginning	*Middle*	*End*
Past	*Present*	*Future*

In other cases, the intermediate word is simply the negative to each of two opposite positions; as, for example—

Convexity	*Flatness*	*Concavity*
Desire	*Indifference*	*Aversion*

Sometimes the intermediate word is properly the standard with which each of the extremes is compared; as in the case of

Insufficiency	*Sufficiency*	*Redundance*

for here the middle term, *Sufficiency*, is equally opposed, on the one hand to *Insufficiency*, and on the other to *Redundance*.*

These forms of correlative expressions would suggest the use of triple, instead of double, columns, for tabulating this threefold order of words; but the practical inconvenience attending such an arrangement would probably overbalance its advantages.

It often happens that the same word has several correlative terms, according to the different relations in which it is considered. Thus, to the word *Giving* are opposed both *Receiving* and *Taking*; the former

Roman emperors had exalted the soldiery so high that they balanced all the other orders of the state: hence *miles* and *paganus* became relative terms; a thing, till then, unknown to ancient, and still so to modern languages.'—'The term for a slave, born and bred in the family, was *verna*. As *servus* was the name of the genius, and *verna* of the species without any correlative, this forms a strong presumption that the latter were by far the least numerous: and from the same principles I infer that if the number of slaves brought by the Romans from foreign countries had not extremely exceeded those which were bred at home, *verna* would have had a correlative, which would have expressed the former species of slaves. But these, it would seem, composed the main body of the ancient slaves, and the latter were but a few exceptions'.— HUME, *Essay on the Populousness of Ancient Nations*.

The warlike propensity of the same nation may, in like manner, be inferred from the use of the word *hostis* to denote both *a foreigner* and *an enemy*.

* [In the following cases, the intermediate word signifies an imperfect degree of each of the qualities set in opposition—

Light	*Dimness*	*Darkness*
Transparency	*Semitransparency*	*Opacity*
Vision	*Dimsightedness*	*Blindness*]

correlation having reference to the *persons* concerned in the transfer, while the latter relates to the *mode* of transfer. *Old* has for opposite both *New* and *Young*, according as it is applied to *things* or to *living things*. *Attack* and *Defence* are correlative terms; as are also *Attack* and *Resistance*. *Resistance*, again, has for its other correlative *Submission*. *Truth in the abstract* is opposed to *Error*; but the opposite of *Truth communicated* is *Falsehood*. *Acquisition* is contrasted both with *Deprivation* and with *Loss*. *Refusal* is the counterpart both of *Offer* and of *Consent*. *Disuse* and *Misuse* may either of them be considered as the correlative of *Use*. *Teaching* with reference to what is taught, is opposed to *Misteaching*; but with reference to the act itself, its proper reciprocal is *Learning*.

Words contrasted in form do not always bear the same contrast in their meaning. The word *Malefactor*, for example, would, from its derivation, appear to be exactly the opposite of *Benefactor*: but the ideas attached to these two words are far from being directly opposed; for while the latter expresses one who confers a benefit, the former denotes one who has violated the laws.

Independently of the immediate practical uses derivable from the arrangement of words in double columns, many considerations, interesting in a philosophical point of view, are presented by the study of correlative expressions. It will be found, on strict examination, that there seldom exists an exact opposition between two words which may at first sight appear to be the counterparts of one another; for in general, the one will be found to possess in reality more force or extent of meaning than the other with which it is contrasted. The correlative term sometimes assumes the form of a mere negative, although it is really endowed with a considerable positive force. Thus *Disrespect* is not merely the absence of *Respect*; its signification trenches on the opposite idea, namely, *Contempt*. In like manner, *Untruth* is not merely the negative of *Truth*; it involves a degree of *Falsehood*. *Irreligion*, which is properly *the want of Religion*, is understood as being nearly synonymous with *Impiety*. For these reasons, the reader must not expect that all the words which stand side by side in the two columns shall be the precise correlatives of each other; for the nature of the subject, as well as the imperfections of language, renders it impossible always to preserve such an exactness of correlation.

There exist comparatively few words of a general character to which no correlative term, either of negation or of opposition, can be assigned, and which therefore require no corresponding second column. The correlative idea, especially that which constitutes a sense negative to the primary one, may, indeed, be formed or conceived; but, from its occurring rarely, no word has been framed to represent it; for, in language, as in other matters, the supply fails when there is no probability of a demand. Occasionally we find this deficiency provided for by the contrivance of prefixing the syllable *non*; as, for instance, the negatives of *existence, performance, payment,* &c., are expressed by the compound words, *non-existence, non-performance, non-payment,* &c. Functions of a similar kind are performed by the prefixes *dis-*, anti-, contra-, mis-, in-,* and *un-.†* With respect to all these, and especially the last, great latitude is allowed according to the necessities of the case; a latitude which is limited only by the taste and discretion of the writer.

On the other hand, it is hardly possible to find two words having in all respects the same meaning, and being therefore interchangeable; that is, admitting of being employed indiscriminately, the one or the other, in all their applications. The investigation of the distinctions to be drawn between words apparently synonymous, forms a separate branch of inquiry, which I have not presumed here to enter upon; for the subject has already occupied the attention of much abler critics than myself, and its complete exhaustion would require the devotion of a whole life. The purpose of this Work, it must be borne in mind, is, not to explain the signification of words, but simply to classify and arrange them according to the sense in which they are now used, and which I presume to be already known to the reader. I enter into no inquiry into the changes of meaning they may have undergone in the course of time.‡ I am content to accept them at the value of their present currency, and have no concern with their etymologies, or with the history of their transformations; far less do I venture to thrid the mazes of the vast labyrinth into which I should be led by any attempt at a general discrimination of synonyms. The difficulties I have had to contend with have already been sufficiently great, without this addition to my labours.

The most cursory glance over the pages of a Dictionary will show that a great number of words are used in various senses, sometimes distinguished by slight shades of difference, but often diverging widely from their primary signification, and even, in some cases, bearing to it no perceptible relation. It may even happen that the very same word has two significations quite opposite to one another. This is the case with the verb *to cleave,* which means *to adhere tenaciously,* and also *to separate by a blow. To propugn* sometimes expressed *to attack*; at other times *to defend. To let* is *to hinder,* as well as *to permit. To*

---

* The words *disannul* and *dissever,* however, have the same meaning as *annul* and *sever; to unloose* is the same as *to loose,* and *inebrity* is synonymous with *ebriety.*

† In the case of adjectives, the addition to a substantive of the terminal syllable *less,* gives it a negative meaning: as *taste, tasteless; care, careless; hope, hopeless; friend, friendless; fault, faultless;* &c.

‡ Such changes are innumerable: for instance, the words *tyrant, parasite, sophist, churl, knave, villain,* anciently conveyed no opprobrious meaning. *Impertinent* merely expressed *irrelative,* and implied neither *rudeness* nor *intrusion,* as it does at present. *Indifferent* originally meant *impartial; extravagant* was simply *digressive;* and *to prevent* was properly *to precede* and *assist.* The old translations of the Scriptures furnish many striking examples of the alterations which time has brought in the signification of words. Much curious information on this subject is contained in Trench's *Lectures on the Study of Words.*

ravel means both *to entangle* and *to disentangle*. *Shameful* and *shameless* are nearly synonymous. *Priceless* may either mean *invaluable* or *of no value*. *Nervous* is used sometimes for *strong*, at other times for *weak*. The alphabetical Index at the end of this Work sufficiently shows the multiplicity of uses to which, by the elasticity of language, the meaning of words has been stretched, so as to adapt them to a great variety of modified significations in subservience to the nicer shades of thought, which, under peculiarity of circumstances, require corresponding expression. Words thus admitting of different meanings have therefore to be arranged under each of the respective heads corresponding to these various acceptations. There are many words, again, which express ideas compounded of two elementary ideas belonging to different classes. It is therefore necessary to place these words respectively under each of the generic heads to which they relate. The necessity of these repetitions is increased by the circumstance, that ideas included under one class are often connected by relations of the same kind as the ideas which belong to another class. Thus we find the same relations of *order* and of *quantity* existing among the ideas of *Time* as well as those of *Space*. Sequence in the one is denoted by the same terms as sequence in the other; and the measures of time also express the measures of space. The cause and the effect are often designated by the same word. The word *Sound*, for instance, denotes both the impression made upon the ear by sonorous vibrations, and also the vibrations themselves, which are the cause or source of that impression. *Mixture* is used for the act of mixing, as well as for the product of that operation. *Taste* and *Smell* express both the sensations and the qualities of material bodies giving rise to them. *Thought* is the act of thinking; but the same word denotes also the idea resulting from that act. *Judgment* is the act of deciding, and also the decision come to. *Purchase* is the acquisition of a thing by payment, as well as the thing itself so acquired. *Speech* is both the act of speaking and the words spoken; and so on with regard to an endless multiplicity of words. Mind is essentially distinct from Matter; and yet, in all languages, the attributes of the one are metaphorically transferred to those of the other. Matter, in all its forms, is endowed by the figurative genius of every language with the functions which pertain to intellect; and we perpetually talk of its phenomena and of its powers, as if they resulted from the voluntary influence of one body on another, acting and reacting, impelling and being impelled, controlling and being controlled, as if animated by spontaneous energies and guided by specific intentions. On the other hand, expressions, of which the primary signification refers exclusively to the properties and actions of matter, are metaphorically applied to the phenomena of thought and volition, and even to the feelings and passions of the soul; and in speaking of a *ray of hope*, a *shade of doubt*, a *flight of fancy*, a *flash of wit*, the *warmth of emotion*, or the *ebullitions of anger*, we are scarcely conscious that we are employing metaphors which have this material origin.

As a general rule, I have deemed it incumbent on me to place words and phrases which appertain more especially to one head, also under the other heads to which they have a relation, whenever it appeared to me that this repetition would suit the convenience of the inquirer, and spare him the trouble of turning to other parts of the work; for I have always preferred to subject myself to the imputation of redundance, rather than incur the reproach of insufficiency.* When, however, the divergence of the associated from the primary idea is sufficiently marked, I have contented myself with making a reference to the place where the modified signification will be found.† But in order to prevent needless extension, I have, in general, omitted *conjugate words,*‡ which are so obviously derivable from those that are given in the same place, that the reader may safely be left to form them for himself. This is the case with adverbs derived from adjectives by the simple addition of the terminal syllable *-ly*; such as *closely, carefully, safely,* &c., from *close, careful, safe,* &c., and also with adjectives or participles immediately derived from the verbs which are already given. In all such cases, an '&c.' indicates that reference is understood to be made to these roots.§ I have observed the same rule in compiling the Index; retaining only the primary or more simple word, and omitting the conjugate words obviously derived from them. Thus I assume the word *short* as the representative of its immediate derivatives *shortness, shorten, shortening, shortened, shorter, shortly,* which would have had the same references, and which the reader can readily supply. ||

The same verb is frequently used indiscriminately either in the active or transitive, or in the neuter or intransitive sense. In these cases, I have generally not thought it worth while to increase the bulk of the Work by the needless repetition of that word; for the reader, whom I suppose

---

* Frequent repetitions of the same series of expressions, accordingly, will be met with under various headings. For example, the word *Relinquishment* with its synonyms, occurs as a heading at No. 624, where it applies to *intention,* and also at No. 782, where it refers to *property.* The word *Chance* has two significations, distinct from one another: the one implying the *absence of an assignable cause;* in which case it comes under the category of the relation of Causation, and occupies the No. 156: the other, the *absence of design,* in which latter sense it ranks under the operations of the Will, and has assigned to it the place No. 621. I have, in like manner, distinguished *Sensibility, Pleasure, Pain, Taste,* &c., according as they relate to *Physical,* or to *Moral Affections;* the fomer being found at Nos. 375, 377, 378, 390, &c., and the latter at Nos. 822, 827, 828, 850, &c.

† [See Editor's Preface, p. x.]

‡ By '*conjugate* or *paronymous* words is meant, correctly speaking, different parts of speech from the same root, which exactly corresponds in point of meaning.'— *A Selection of English Synonyms,* edited by Archbishop Whately.

§ [The author's practice, in this respect, has been followed in the present edition, and a reference to the group of adjectives, verbs, or other roots, has been added, where such suggestion has been thought expedient.]

|| [See note in p. xvii.]

to understand the use of the words, must also be presumed to be competent to apply them correctly.

There are a multitude of words of a specific character which, although they properly occupy places in the columns of a dictionary, yet, having no relation to general ideas, do not come within the scope of this compilation, and are consequently omitted.* The names of objects in Natural History, and technical terms belonging exclusively to Science or to Art, or relating to particular operations, and of which the signification is restricted to those specific objects, come under this category. Exceptions must, however, be made in favor of such words as admit of metaphorical application to general subjects, with which custom has associated them, and of which they may be cited as being typical or illustrative. Thus, the word *Lion* will find a place under the head of *Courage*, of which it is regarded as the type. *Anchor*, being emblematic of *Hope*, is introduced among the words expressing that emotion; and in like manner, *butterfly* and *weathercock*, which are suggestive of fickleness, are included in the category of *Irresolution*.

With regard to the admission of many words and expressions, which the classical reader might be disposed to condemn as vulgarisms, or which he, perhaps, might stigmatize as pertaining rather to the slang than to the legitimate language of the day, I would beg to observe, that, having due regard to the uses to which this Work was to be adapted, I did not feel myself justified in excluding them solely on that ground, if they possessed an acknowledged currency in general intercourse. It is obvious that, with respect to degrees of conventionality, I could not have attempted to draw any strict lines of demarcation; and far less could I have presumed to erect any absolute standard of purity. My object, be it remembered, is not to regulate the use of words, but simply to supply and to suggest such as may be wanted on occasion, leaving the proper selection entirely to the discretion and taste of the employer.† If a novelist or a dramatist, for example, proposed to delineate some vulgar personage, he would wish to have the power of putting into the mouth of the speaker expressions that would accord with his character; just as the actor, to revert to a former comparison, who had to personate a peasant, would choose for his attire the most homely garb, and would have just reason to complain if the theatrical wardrobe furnished him with no suitable costume.

Words which have, in process of time, become obsolete, are of course

* [The author did not in all cases rigidly adhere to this rule; and the editors have thought themselves justified both in retaining and in adding some words of the specific character here mentioned, which may be occasionally in request by general writers, although in categories of this nature no attempt at completeness has been made.]

† [It may be added that the Thesaurus is an aid not only in the choice of appropriate forms of expression, but in the rejection of those which are unfit; and that a vulgar phrase may often furnish a convenient clue to the group of classic synonyms among which it is placed. Moreover, the slang expressions admitted into the work bear but a small proportion to those in constant use by English writers and speakers.]

rejected from this collection.* On the other hand, I have admitted a considerable number of words and phrases borrowed from other languages, chiefly the French and Latin, some of which may be considered as already naturalized; while others, though avowedly foreign, are frequently employed in English composition, particularly in familiar style, on account of their being peculiarly expressive, and because we have no corresponding words of equal force in our own language.† The rapid advances which are being made in scientific knowledge, and consequent improvement in all the arts of life, and the extension of those arts and sciences to so many new purposes and objects, create a continual demand for the formation of new terms to express new agencies, new wants, and new combinations. Such terms, from being at first merely technical, are rendered, by more general use, familiar to the multitude, and having a well-defined acceptation, are eventually incorporated into the language, which they contribute to enlarge and to enrich. *Neologies* of this kind are perfectly legitimate, and highly advantageous; and they necessarily introduce those gradual and progressive changes which every language is destined to undergo.‡ Some modern writers, however, have indulged in a habit of arbitrarily fabricating new words and a new-fangled phraseology, without any necessity, and with manifest injury to the purity of the language. This vicious practice, the offspring of indolence or conceit, implies an ignorance or neglect of the riches in which the English language already abounds, and which would have supplied them with words of recognized legitimacy, conveying precisely the same meaning as those they so recklessly coin in the illegal mint of their own fancy.

A work constructed on the plan of classification I have proposed might, if ably executed, be of great value, in tending to limit the fluctuations to which language has always been subject, by establishing an authoritative standard for its regulation. Future historians, philologists, and lexicographers, when investigating the period when new words were introduced, or discussing the import given at the present time to the old, might find their labours lightened by being enabled to appeal to such a standard, instead of having to search for data among the scattered writings of the

---

* [A few apparently obsolete words have nevertheless found their way into the Thesaurus. In justification of their admission, it may be contended that well-known words, though no longer current, give occasional point by an archaic form of expression, and are of value to the novelist or dramatist who has to depict a bygone age.]

† All these words and phrases are printed in Italics. [A few of these expressions, although widely used by writers of English, are of a form which is really incorrect or unusual in their own language, in some more extreme cases of this kind, the more widely used or incorrect form has been given.]

‡ Thus, in framing the present classification, I have frequently felt the want of substantive terms corresponding to abstract qualities or ideas denoted by certain adjectives, and have been often tempted to invent words that might express these abstractions; but I have yielded to this temptation only in the four following instances, having framed from the adjectives *irrelative, amorphous, sinistral,* and *gaseous,* the abstract nouns *irrelation, amorphism, sinistrality,* and *gaseity.* I have ventured also to introduce the adjective *intersocial* to express the active voluntary relations between man and man.

age. Nor would its utility be confined to a single language; for the principles of its construction are universally applicable to all languages, whether living or dead. On the same plan of classification there might be formed a French, a German, a Latin, or a Greek Thesaurus, possessing, in their respective spheres, the same advantages as those of the English model.* Still more useful would be a conjunction of these methodized compilations in two languages, the French and English, for instance; the columns of each being placed in parallel juxtaposition. No means yet devised would so greatly facilitate the acquisition of the one language, by those who are acquainted with the other: none would afford such ample assistance to the translator in either language; and none would supply such ready and effectual means of instituting an accurate comparison between them, and of fairly appreciating their respective merits and defects. In a still higher degree would all those advantages be combined and multiplied in a *Polyglot Lexicon* constructed on this system.

Metaphysicians engaged in the more profound investigation of the Philosophy of Language will be materially assisted by having the ground thus prepared for them, in a previous analysis and classification of our ideas; for such classification of ideas is the true basis on which words, which are their symbols, should be classified.† It is by such analysis alone that we can arrive at a clear perception of the relation which these

* [This suggestion has been followed, in French, in a *'Dictionnaire Idéologique'* by T. Robertson (Paris, 1859); and, in German, in a *'Deutscher Sprachschatz'* by D. Sanders (Hamburg, 1878), and *'Deutscher Wortschatz oder Der passende Ausdruck'* by A. Schelling (Stuttgart, 1829).]

† The principle by which I have been guided in framing my verbal classification is the same as that which is employed in the various departments of Natural History. Thus the sectional divisions I have formed, correspond to Natural Families in Botany and Zoology, and the filiation of words presents a network analogous to the natural filiation of plants or animals.

The following are the only publications that have come to my knowledge in which any attempt has been made to construct a systematic arrangement of ideas with a view to their expression. The earliest of these, supposed to be at least nine hundred years old, is the AMERA CÓSHA, or *Vocabulary of the Sanscrit Language*, by Amera Sinha, of which an English translation, by the late Henry T. Colebrooke, was printed at Serampoor, in the year 1808. The classification of words is there, as might be expected, exceedingly imperfect and confused, especially in all that relates to abstract ideas or mental operations. This will be apparent from the very title of the first section, which comprehends *'Heaven, Gods, Demons, Fire, Air, Velocity, Eternity, Much;'* while *Sin, Virtue, Happiness, Destiny, Cause, Nature, Intellect, Reasoning, Knowledge, Senses, Tastes, Odours, Colours*, are all included and jumbled together in the fourth section. A more logical order, however, pervades the sections relating to natural objects, such as *Seas, Earth, Towns, Plants*, and *Animals*, which form separate classes; exhibiting a remarkable effort at analysis at so remote a period of Indian literature.

The well-known work of Bishop Wilkins entitled *'An Essay towards a Real Character and a Philosophical Language,'* published in 1668, had for its object the formation of a system of symbols which might serve as a universal language. It professed to be founded on a 'scheme of analysis of the things or notions to which names were to be assigned'; but notwithstanding the immense labour and ingenuity expended in the construction of this system, it was soon found to be far too abstruse and recondite for practical application.

In the year 1797, there appeared in Paris an anonymous work, entitled 'PASIGRAPHIE, *ou Premiers Eléments du nouvel Art-Science d'écrire et d'imprimer une langue*

symbols bear to their corresponding ideas, or can obtain a correct knowledge of the elements which enter into the formation of compound ideas, and of the exclusions by which we arrive at the abstractions so perpetually resorted to in the process of reasoning, and in the communication of our thoughts.

Lastly, such analysis alone can determine the principles on which a strictly *Philosophical Language* might be constructed. The probable result of the construction of such a language would be its eventual adoption by every civilized nation; thus realizing that splendid aspiration of philanthropists—the establishment of a Universal Language. However utopian such a project may appear to the present generation, and however abortive may have been the former endeavours of Bishop Wilkins and others to realize it,* its accomplishment is surely not beset with greater difficulties than have impeded the progress to many other beneficial objects, which in former times appeared to be no less visionary, and which yet were successfully achieved, in later ages, by the continued and persevering exertions of the human intellect. Is there at the present day, then, any ground for despair, that at some future stage of that higher civilization to which we trust the world is gradually tending, some new and bolder effort of genius towards the solution of this great problem may be crowned with success, and compass an object of such vast and paramount utility? Nothing, indeed, would conduce more directly to bring about a golden age of union and harmony among the several nations and races of mankind than the removal of that barrier to the interchange of thought and mutual good understanding between man and man, which is now interposed by the diversity of their respective languages.

de maniere a etre lu et entendu dans toute autre langue sans traduction,' of which an edition in German was also published. It contains a great number of tabular schemes of categories; all of which appear to be excessively arbitrary and artificial, and extremely difficult of application, as well as of apprehension. [Systems of grouping with relation to ideas are also adopted in an '*Analytical Dictionary of the English Language*' by David Booth (London, 1835), a '*Dictionnaire Analogique de la Langue Française*' by P. Boissière (Paris), and a '*Dictionnaire Logique de la Langue Française*' by L'Abbé Elie Blanc (Paris, 1882).]

* 'The Languages,' observes Horne Tooke, 'which are commonly used throughout the world, are much more simple and easy, convenient and philosophical, than Wilkins' scheme for a *real character;* or than any other scheme that has been at any other time imagined or proposed for the purpose.'—''Επεα Πτερόεντα, p. 125.

PLAN OF CLASSIFICATION

TABULAR SYNOPSIS OF CATEGORIES

Class I. ABSTRACT RELATIONS

I. EXISTENCE

1°. ABSTRACT..........	1. Existence.	2. Inexistence.
2°. CONCRETE.........	3. Substantiality.	4. Unsubstantiality.
3°. FORMAL........... {	*Internal.*	*External.*
	5. Intrinsicality.	6. Extrinsicality.
4°. MODAL........... {	*Absolute.*	*Relative.*
	7. State.	8. Circumstance.

II. RELATION

	9. Relation.	10. Irrelation.
	11. Consanguinity.	
1°. ABSOLUTE......... {	12. Correlation.	
	13. Identity.	14. Contrariety.
	15. Difference.	
2°. CONTINUOUS........	16. Uniformity.	16a. Non-uniformity.
	17. Similarity.	18. Dissimilarity.
	19. Imitation.	20. Non-imitation.
3°. PARTIAL........... {	20a. Variation.	
	21. Copy.	22. Prototype.
4°. GENERAL...........	23. Agreement.	24. Disagreement.

III. QUANTITY

	Absolute.	*Relative.*
1°. SIMPLE.............	25. Quantity.	26. Degree.
	27. Equality.	28. Inequality.
	29. Mean.	
	30. Compensation.	
	By Comparison with a Standard.	
2°. COMPARATIVE....... {	31. Greatness.	32. Smallness.
	By Comparison with a similar Object.	
	33. Superiority.	34. Inferiority.
	Changes in Quantity.	
	35. Increase.	36. Decrease.
	37. Addition.	38. { Non-addition. / Subduction.
	39. Adjunct.	40. Remainder.
		40a. Decrement.
3°. CONJUNCTIVE....... {	41. Mixture.	42. Simpleness.
	43. Junction.	44. Disjunction.
	45. Vinculum.	
	46. Coherence.	47. Incoherence.
	48. Combination.	49. Decomposition.

2°. SENSATION

(1) General

375. Sensibility.   376. Insensibility.
377. Pleasure.   378. Pain.
379. Touch.

1. Touch

380. { Sensations of Touch.   381. Numbness.

2. Heat

382. Heat.   383. Cold.
384. Calefaction.   385. Refrigeration.
386. Furnace.   387. Refrigeratory.
388. Fuel.
389. Thermometer.

3. Taste

390. Taste.   391. Insipidity.
392. Pungency.
393. Condiment.
394. Savouriness.   395. Unsavouriness.
396. Sweetness.   397. Sourness.

4. Odour

398. Odour.   399. Inodorousness.
400. Fragrance.   401. Fœtor.

(2) Special

5. Sound

(i.) *Sound in General.*
402. Sound.   403. Silence.
404. Loudness.   405. Faintness.

(ii.) *Specific Sounds.*
406. Snap.   407. Roll.
408. Resonance.   408a. Non-resonance.
     409. Sibilation.
410. Stridor.
411. Cry.   412. Ululation.

(iii.) *Musical Sounds.*
413. { Melody.   414. Discord.
     Concord.
415. Music.
416. Musician.
417. Musical Instruments.

(iv.) *Perception of Sound.*
418. Hearing.   419. Deafness.

6. Light

(i.) *Light in General.*
420. Light.   421. Darkness.
     422. Dimness.
423. Luminary.   424. Shade.
425. Transparency.   426. Opacity.
     427. Semitransparency.

(ii.) *Specific Light.*
428. Colour.   429. Achromatism.
430. Whiteness.   431. Blackness.
432. Gray.   433. Brown.
434. Redness.   435. Greenness.
436. Yellowness.   437. Purple.
438. Blueness.   439. Orange.
440. Variegation.

(iii.) *Perceptions of Light.*
441. Vision.   442. Blindness.
     443. Dimsightedness.
444. Spectator.
445. Optical Instruments.
446. Visibility.   447. Invisibility.
448. Appearance.   449. Disappearance.

Class IV. INTELLECT

Division (I.). Formation of Ideas

Division (II.). COMMUNICATION OF IDEAS

Class V. VOLITION

Division (I.). Individual Volition

I. Volition in General

1°. Acts....

600. Will.	601. Necessity.
602. Willingness.	603. Unwillingness.
604. Resolution.	605. Irresolution.
604a. Perseverance. }	607. Tergiversation.
606. Obstinacy. }	
	608. Caprice.
609. Choice.	⎰609a. Absence of Choice.
	⎱610. Rejection.
611. Predetermination.	612. Impulse.
613. Habit.	614. Desuetude.

2°. Causes..

615. Motive.	⎰615a. Absence of Motive.
	⎱616. Dissuasion.
617. Plea.	

3°. Objects..

618. Good.	619. Evil.

II. Prospective Volition.......

620. Intention.	621. Chance.
622. Pursuit.	623. Avoidance.
	624. Relinquishment.

1°. Conceptional..

625. Business.
626. Plan.
627. Method.
628. Mid-Course.   629. Circuit.
630. Requirement.

2°. Subservience to Ends...

1. *Actual Subservience.*

631. Instrumentality.
632. Means.
633. Instrument.
634. Substitute.
635. Materials.
636. Store.
637. Provision.   638. Waste.
    639. Sufficiency.
641. Redundance.   640. Insufficiency.

2. *Degree of Subservience.*

642. Importance.	643. Unimportance.
644. Utility.	645. Inutility.
646. Expedience.	647. Inexpedience.
648. Goodness.	649. Badness.
650. Perfection.	651. Imperfection.
652. Cleanness.	653. Uncleanness.
654. Health.	655. Disease.
656. Salubrity.	657. Insalubrity.
658. Improvement.	659. Deterioration.
660. Restoration.	661. Relapse.
662. Remedy.	663. Bane.

3. *Contingent Subservience.*

664. Safety.	665. Danger.
666. Refuge.	667. Pitfall.
668. Warning.	
669. Alarm.	
670. Preservation.	
671. Escape.	
672. Deliverance.	

Class VI. AFFECTIONS

II. PERSONAL

1°. PASSIVE

827. Pleasure.	828. Pain.
829. Pleasureableness.	830. Painfulness.
831. Content.	832. Discontent.
	833. Regret.
834. Relief.	835. Aggravation.
836. Cheerfulness.	837. Dejection.
838. Rejoicing.	839. Lamentation.
840. Amusement.	841. Weariness.
842. Wit.	843. Dulness.
844. Humorist.	

2°. DISCRIMINATIVE

845. Beauty.	846. Ugliness.
847. Ornament.	848. Blemish.
	849. Simplicity.
850. Taste.	851. Vulgarity.
852. Fashion.	
	853. Ridiculousness.
	854. Fop.
	855. Affection.
	856. Ridicule.
	857. Laughing-stock.

3°. PROSPECTIVE

858. Hope.	859. Hopelessness.
	860. Fear.
861. Courage.	862. Cowardice.
863. Rashness.	864. Caution.
865. Desire.	867. Dislike.
866. Indifference.	
	868. Fastidiousness.
	869. Satiety.

4°. CONTEMPLATIVE

870. Wonder.	871. Expectance.
872. Prodigy.	

5°. EXTRINSIC

873. Repute.	874. Disrepute.
875. Nobility.	876. Commonalty.
877. Title.	
878. Pride.	879. Humility.
880. Vanity.	881. Modesty.
882. Ostentation.	
883. Celebration.	
884. Boasting.	
885. Insolence.	886. Servility.
887. Blusterer.	

III. SYMPATHETIC

1°. SOCIAL

888. Friendship.	889. Enmity.
890. Friend.	891. Enemy.
892. Sociality.	893. Seclusion.
894. Courtesy.	895. Discourtesy.
896. Congratulation.	
897. Love.	898. Hate.
899. Favourite.	
	900. Resentment.
	901. Irascibility.
	901a. Sullenness.
902. Endearment.	
903. Marriage.	904. Celibacy.
	905. Divorce.

2°. DIFFUSIVE......... {
906. Benevolence.
907. Malevolence.
908. Malediction.
909. Threat.
910. Philanthropy.
911. Misanthropy.
912. Benefactor.
913. Evil doer.

3°. SPECIAL.......... {
914. Pity.
914a. Pitilessness.
915. Condolence.

4°. RETROSPECTIVE.... {
916. Gratitude.
917. Ingratitude.
918. Forgiveness.
919. Revenge.
920. Jealousy.
921. Envy.

IV. MORAL

1°. OBLIGATIONS....... {
922. Right.
923. Wrong.
924. Dueness.
925. Undueness.
926. Duty.
{ 927. Dereliction.
927a. Exemption.

2°. SENTIMENTS........ {
928. Respect.
929. Disrespect.
930. Contempt.
931. Approbation.
932. Disapprobation.
933. Flattery.
934. Detraction.
935. Flatterer.
936. Detractor.
937. Vindication.
938. Accusation.
939. Probity.
940. Improbity.
941. Knave.

3°. CONDITIONS........ {
942. Disinterestedness.
943. Selfishness.
944. Virtue.
945. Vice.
946. Innocence.
947. Guilt.
948. Good Man.
949. Bad Man.
950. Penitence.
951. Impenitence.
952. Atonement.
953. Temperance.
954. Intemperance.
954a. Sensualist.

4°. PRACTICE.......... {
955. Asceticism.
956. Fasting.
957. Gluttony.
958. Sobriety.
959. Drunkenness.
960. Purity.
961. Impurity.
962. Libertine.
963. Legality.
964. Illegality.

5°. INSTITUTIONS...... {
965. Jurisprudence.
966. Tribunal.
967. Judge.
968. Lawyer.
969. Lawsuit.
970. Acquittal.
971. Condemnation.
973. Reward.
{ 972. Punishment.
974. Penalty.
975. Scourge.

V. RELIGIOUS

1°. SUPERHUMAN BE-
INGS AND REGIONS.. {
976. Deity.
977. Angel.
978. Satan.
979. Jupiter.
980. Demon.
981. Heaven.
982. Hell.

2°. DOCTRINES........ {
983. Theology.
983a. Orthodoxy.
984. Heterodoxy.
985. Revelation.
986. Pseudo-revelation.

3°. SENTIMENTS........
987. Piety.
988. Impiety.
989. Irreligion.

4°. ACTS...............
- 990. Worship.
- 991. Idolatry
- 992. Sorcery.
- 993. Spell.
- 994. Sorcerer.

5°. INSTITUTIONS......
- 995. Churchdom.
- 996. Clergy.
- 997. Laity.
- 998. Rite.
- 999. Canonicals.
- 1000. Temple.

ABBREVIATIONS, &c.

Adj.	*adj.*	Adjectives, Participles, and Words having the power of Adjectives.
Adv.	*adv.*	Adverbs and Adverbial Expressions.
Int.	*int.*	Interjections.
Phr.	*phr.*	Phrases.
V.	*v.*	Verbs.

The numbers are those of the headings, or Categories.

Words in italics within parentheses are not intended to explain the meanings of the words which precede them, but to indicate the nature of allied group of words under the numbers which follow them.

See also the Editor's Preface, p. xi.

CLASS I
WORDS EXPRESSING ABSTRACT RELATIONS

THESAURUS

OF

ENGLISH WORDS AND PHRASES

CLASS I

Words expressing ABSTRACT RELATIONS

Section I. EXISTENCE

1°. Being, in the Abstract

1. Existence.—N. existence, being, entity, *ens, esse*, subsistence, quiddity.

reality, realness, actuality; positiveness &c. *adj.*; fact, matter of fact, sober reality; truth &c. 494; actual existence.

presence &c. (*existence in space*) 186; coexistence &c. 120.

stubborn fact; not a -dream &c. 515; no joke.

substance, essence, prime constituent, hypostatis.

[Science of existence], ontology.

V. exist, be; have -being &c. *n.*; subsist, live, breathe, stand, obtain, be the case; occur &c. (*event*) 151; have place, rank, prevail; find oneself, pass the time, vegetate.

consist in, lie in, reside in, inhere in.

come into -existence &c. *n.*; arise &c. (*begin*) 66; come forth &c. (*appear*) 446.

become &c. (*be converted*) 144; bring into existence &c. 161; coexist, pre-exist, endure &c. 141.

Adj. existing &c. *v.*; existent, subsistent, under the sun; in -existence &c. *n.*; extant; afloat, on foot, current, prevalent, rife, in force, -vogue; undestroyed.

real, actual, positive, absolute; true &c. 494; substan-tial, -tive; self-existing, -ent.

2. Inexistence.—N. inexistence; non-existence, -subsistence; nonentity, *nil*; negativeness &c. *adj.*; nullity; nihil-ity, -ism; *tabula rasa*, blank; abeyance; absence &c. 187; no such thing &c. 4; nothingness, oblivion, *non esse*.

annihilation; extinction &c. (*destruction*) 162.

V. not -exist &c. 1; have no -existence &c. 1; be null and void; cease to -exist &c. 1; pass away, perish; be –, become- extinct &c. *adj.*; die out; disappear &c. 449; melt away, dissolve, leave not a rack behind, leave no trace; go, be no more; die &c. 360.

annihilate, render null, nullify; abrogate &c. 756; destroy &c. 162; take away; remove &c. (*displace*) 185.

Adj. inexistent, non-existent &c. 1; negative, blank, null and void; missing, omitted; absent &c. 187; visionary &c. 515.

unreal, potential, virtual; baseless, *in nubibus*; unsubstantial &c. 4; vain.

un-born, -created, -begotten, -conceived, -produced, -made.

perished, annihilated &c. *v.*; extinct, exhausted, gone, lost, departed; defunct &c. (*dead*) 360; *spurlos versenkt.*

fabulous, ideal &c. (*imaginary*) 515; suppositious &c. 514.

Adv. negatively, virtually, &c. *adj.*

well-founded, -grounded; un-ideal, -imagined; not -potential &c. 2.

Adv. actually &c. *adj.*; in -fact, – point of fact, – reality; indeed; *de –, ipso-facto.*

2°. BEING, IN THE CONCRETE

3. Substantiality.—N. substantiality, *hypostasis*; person, thing, object, article; something, a being, an existence; creature, body, substance, flesh and blood, stuff, *substratum*; matter &c. 316; physical nature.

[Totality of existences], world &c. 318; *plenum.*

Adj. substan-tive, -tial, concrete; hypostatic; personal, bodily; tangible &c. (*material*) 316; real, corporeal, evident.

Adv. substantially &c. *adj.*; bodily, essentially.

---

4. Unsubstantiality.—N. un-, in-substantiality; nothingness, nihility.

nothing, naught, *nil*, nullity, zero, cipher, no one, nobody; never –, ne'er -a one; no such thing, none in the world; nothing -whatever, – at all, – on earth; not a -particle &c. (*smallness*) 32; all -talk, – moonshine, – stuff and nonsense, matter of no import.

thing of naught, man of straw, John Doe and Richard Roe; *nominis umbra*, nonentity, figurehead, lay figure; flash in the pan, *vox et præterea nihil.*

shadow; phantasm, phantom &c. (*fallacy of vision*) 443; dream &c. (*imagination*) 515; *ignis fatuus* &c.

(luminary) 423; 'such stuff as dreams are made of'; air, thin air; bubble &c. 353; 'baseless fabric of a vision'; mockery.

hollowness, blank; vacuity, void &c. (*absence*) 187.

inanity, fool's paradise, fatuity, stupidity, emptiness of mind.

V. vanish, evaporate, fade, sink, fly –, die –, melt- away, dissolve, disappear &c. 449, become extinct, become invisible.

Adj. unsubstantial; fleeting; base-, ground-less; ungrounded; without –, having no- foundation.

visionary &c. (*imaginary*) 515; immaterial &c. 317; spectral &c. 980; dreamy; shadowy; ethereal, airy, imponderable, tenuous, vague.

vacant, vacuous; empty &c. 187; eviscerated; blank, hollow; nominal; null; inane.

Phr. there's nothing in it.

3°. FORMAL EXISTENCE

Internal conditions

5. Intrinsicality.—N. intrinsicality, inbeing, inherence, inhesion, immanence; subjectiveness; *ego*; essence; essentialness &c. *adj.*; essential part, essential stuff, substance, quintessence, incarnation, quiddity, gist, pith, core, kernel, marrow, sap, life-blood, backbone, heart, soul, life, flower; important part &c. (*importance*) 642.

principle, nature, constitution, character, ethos, type, quality, crasis, *diathesis.*

habit; temper, -ament; spirit, humour, grain, disposition, streak, tendency &c. 176.

External conditions

6. Extrinsicality.—N. extrinsicality, objectiveness, *non ego*; extraneousness &c. 57; accident; letter of the law.

Adj. derived from without; objective; extrin-sic, -sical; extraneous &c. (*foreign*) 57; modal, adventitious, additional, supervenient, fortuitous; a-, ad-scititious; incidental, casual, accidental, unessential, non-essential, accessory.

implanted, ingrafted, instilled, inculcated.

outward &c. (*external*) 220.

Adv. extrinsically &c. *adj.*

endowment, capacity; capability &c. (*power*) 157; moods, declensions, features, aspects; peculiarities &c. (*specialty*) 79; idiosyncrasy; idiocrasy; diagnostics.

V. be –, run- in the blood; be born so; be -intrinsic &c. *adj.*

Adj. derived from within, subjective; idiocratic, idiosyncratic, intrin-sic, -sical; fundamental, cardinal, normal; inherent, essential, natural; in-nate, -born, -bred, -dwelling, -grained, -wrought; radical, incarnate, thoroughbred, hereditary, inherited, immanent; congen-ital, -ite; connate, running in the blood; coeval with birth, genetic, ingenerate, -genite; indigenous; in the -grain &c. *n.*; bred in the bone, instinctive; inward, internal &c. 221; to the manner born; virtual.

characteristic &c. (*special*) 79, (*indicative*) 550; invariable, incurable, ineradicable, fixed, settled, constant, unchanging.

Adv. intrinsically &c. *adj.*; at bottom, in the main, in effect, essentially, practically, virtually, substantially, *au fond*; fairly.

4°. Modal Existence

Absolute

7. State.—N. state, condition, category, estate, lot, case, trim, mood, pickle, plight &c. 704; temper; aspect &c. (*appearance*) 448.

constitution, habitude, *diathesis*; frame, fabric &c. 329; stamp, set, fit, mould.

mode, modality, schesis; fettle; form &c. (*shape*) 240.

tone, tenor, turn; trim, guise, fashion, light, complexion, style, character.

V. be in –, possess –, enjoy –, labour under- a -state &c. *n.*; be on a footing, do, fare; come to pass.

Adj. conditional, modal, formal; structural, organic.

Adv. conditionally &c. *adj.*; as -the matter stands, – things are; such being the case &c. 8.

Relative

8. Circumstance.—N. circumstance, situation, phase, position, posture, attitude, place, point; terms; *régime*; footing, standing, status.

occasion, juncture, conjuncture; contingency &c. (*event*) 151.

predicament; emergen-ce, -cy; exigency, crisis, pinch, pass, push; turning point; crossroads.

bearings, how the land lies.

Adj. circumstantial; given, conditional, provisional; critical; modal; contingent, incidental; adventitious &c. (*extrinsic*) 6.

Adv. in the circumstances &c. *n.*, under the conditions &c. 7; thus, in such wise.

accordingly; that –, such- being the case; that being so, since, seeing that. as matters stand; as -things, – times- go.

conditionally, provided, if, in case; if -so, – so be, – it be so; if it so -happen, – turn out; in the event of; in such a -contingency, – case, – event; provisionally, unless, without.

according to -circumstances, – the occasion; as it may -happen, – turn out, – be; as the -case may be, – wind blows; *pro re natâ.*

Section II. RELATION

1°. Absolute Relation

9. Relation.—N. relation, bearing, reference, connection, apposition, interconnection, concern, cognation; applicability, appositeness; correlation

10. [Want, or absence of relation.] **Irrelation.—N.** irrelation, dissociation; inapplicability; inconnection; multifariousness; disconnection &c. (*dis-*

&c. 12; analogy; similarity &c. 17; affinity, intimacy, friendship; homology, alliance, homogeneity, association, rapport; approximation &c. (*nearness*) 197; filiation &c. (*consanguinity*) 11; interest; relevancy &c. 23; relationship, relative position; relativity; interrelation &c. 12.

comparison &c. 464; ratio, proportion.

link, tie, bond, bond of union.

V. be-related &c. *adj.*; have a relation &c. *n.*; relate –, refer- to; bear upon, regard, concern, touch, affect, have to do with; pertain –, belong –, appertain- to; have respect to; answer to; interest.

bring -into relation with, – to bear upon; connect, associate, draw a parallel; link &c. 43.

Adj. relative; correlative &c. 12; cognate; relating to &c. *v.*; relative to, in relation with, referable *or* referrible to; belonging to &c. *v.*; appurtenant to, in common with.

related, connected; implicated, associated, affiliated, akin, allied to; collateral, cognate, congenial, kindred, affinitive, *en rapport*, in touch with.

approxima-tive, -ting; approaching; proportion-al, -ate, -able; allusive, comparable.

in the same -category &c. 75; like &c. 17; relevant &c. (*apt*) 23.

Adv. relatively &c. *adj.*; pertinently &c. 23.

thereof; as -to, – for, – respects, – regards; about; concerning &c. *v.*; anent; relating –, as relates- to; with -relation, – reference, – respect, – regard- to; in respect of; while speaking –, *à propos-* of; in connection with; by the -way, – by; whereas; for –, in -as much as; in point of, as far as; on the -part, – score- of; *quoad hoc*; *pro re natâ*; under the -head &c. (*class*) 75- of; in the matter of, *in re*.

Phr. 'thereby hangs a tale.'

junction) 44; inconsequence, independence; incommensurability; irreconcilableness &c. (*disagreement*) 24; heterogeneity; unconformity &c. 83; irrelevancy, impertinence, *nihil ad rem*; intrusion &c. 24.

V. have no -relation &c. 9 to, – bearing upon, – concern &c. 9 with, – business with; not -concern &c. 9; have -nothing to do with, – no business there; intrude, &c. 24.

bring –, drag –, haul –, lug- in head and shoulders.

Adj. irrelative, irrespective, unrelated, irrelated; arbitrary; independent, unallied; un-, dis-connected; adrift, isolated, insular; extraneous, strange, alien, foreign, outlandish, exotic.

not comparable, incommensurable, heterogeneous; unconformable &c. 83.

irrelevant; rambling &c. 279; inapplicable; not -pertinent, – to the purpose; impertinent, inapposite, beside the mark, *à propos de bottes*; away from –, foreign to –, beside- the -purpose, – question, – transaction, – point; misplaced &c. (*intrusive*) 24.

remote, far fetched, out of the way, forced, neither here nor there, quite another thing; detached, segregated, segregate.

multifarious; discordant &c. 24.

incidental, parenthetical, *obiter dictum*, episodic.

Adv. parenthetically &c. *adj.*; by the -way, – by; *en passant*, incidentally; irrespectively &c. *adj.*; without reference, – regard- to; in the abstract &c. 87; *a se*.

---

11. [Relations of kindred.] **Consanguinity.—N.** consanguinity, relationship, kindred, blood; parentage &c. (*paternity*) 166; filiation, affiliation; lineage, agnation, connection, cognation, alliance; family -connection, – tie; ties of blood; blood relationship; nepotism.

kins-man, -folk; people; kith and kin; rela-tion, -tive; connection; sib; next of kin; uncle, aunt, nephew, niece; cousin, -german; first –, second- cousin; cousin -once, – twice &c.- removed; near –, distant-relation; brother, sister, one's own flesh and blood.

family, patriarch, matriarch; fraternity; brother-, sister-, cousin-hood.

race, stock, generation; sept &c. 166; stirps, side; strain; breed, clan, tribe.

V. be -related &c. *adj.* – to; claim -relationship &c. *n.*- with.

Adj. related, akin, consanguineous, matrilinear, patrilineal, of the blood, family, allied, collateral; cog-, ag-, con-nate; kindred; affiliated, affine; fraternal, avuncular.

intimately –, nearly –, closely –, remotely –, distantly- related, – allied; german.

12. [Double or reciprocal relation.] **Correlation.—N.** reciprocalness &c. *adj.*; recipro-city, -cality, -cation; mutuality, correlation, correspondence, interdependence; interchange &c. 148; exchange, barter; interrelation, interconnection; alternation, see-saw.

V. reciprocate, alternate; interchange &c. 148; exchange; counterchange; interact, correspond, mutualize, give and take.

Adj. reciprocal, mutual, commutual, correlative; alternate; interchangeable; international; correspondent, complementary, analogous.

Adv. *mutatis mutandis*; *vice versâ*; each other; by turns &c. 148; reciprocally &c. *adj.*; to and fro &c. 314.

---

13. Identity.—N. identity, sameness, oneness, ditto, homogeneity; unity, coincidence, coalescence; convertibility; equality &c. 27; selfness, self, oneself; identification.

monotony, tautology &c. (*repetition*) 104.

synonym.

fac-simile &c. (*copy*) 21; *alter ego* &c. (*similar*) 17; *ipsissima verba* &c. (*exactness*) 494; same; self –, very –, one and the- same; very –, actual- thing; no other.

V. be -identical &c. *adj.*; match, coincide, coalesce.

treat as –, render- -the same, –identical; identify; recognize the identity of.

Adj. identical; self, ilk; the -same &c. *n.*; self same; synonymous; one and the same.

coincid-, coalesc-ent, -ing; indistinguishable; one; equivalent &c. (*equal*) 27; much -the same, – of a muchness; unaltered.

Adv. identically &c. *adj.*; on all fours; *ibid-*, *-em.*

---

14. [Non-coincidence.] **Contrariety.
—N.** contrariety, contrast, foil, antithesis, oppositeness; counterpole; contradiction; antagonism &c. (*opposition*) 708; counteraction &c. 179.

inversion &c. 218; the -opposite, – reverse, – inverse, – converse, – antipodes, – other extreme &c. 237.

antonym.

V. be -contrary &c. *adj.*; contrast with, oppose; differ *toto cœlo*.

invert, reverse, turn the tables &c. 218.

contra-dict, -vene; antagonize &c. 708.

Adj. contrar-y, -ious, -iant; opposite, counter, dead against; ad-, con-, reverse; opposed, antithetical, contrasted, antipodean, antagonistic, opposing; conflicting, inconsistent, contradictory, at cross purposes; negative; hostile &c. 708.

differing *toto cœlo*; diametrically opposite; as opposite as -black and white, – light and darkness, – fire and water, – the poles, as different as chalk from cheese; 'Hyperion to a satyr'; quite the -contrary, – reverse; no such thing, just the other way, *tout au contraire*.

Adv. contrarily &c. *adj.*; *contra*, contrariwise, *per contra*, on the contrary, nay rather; topsy-turvy; *vice versâ*; on the other hand &c. (*in compensation*) 30.

15. Difference.—N. difference, unlikeness; heterogeneity; vari-ance, -ation, -ety; diversity, dissimilarity &c. 18; disagreement &c. 24; disparity &c. (*inequality*) 28; distinction, contradistinction; distinctness; discrepancy, divergence, contrast &c. 18; nonconformity, incompatibility, antithesis.

discord &c. 713.

modification, moods and tenses.

nice -, fine -, delicate -, subtle- distinction; shade of difference, *nuance;* discrimination &c. 465; *differentia.*

different thing, something else, variant, apple off another tree, horse of another colour, another pair of shoes; this that or the other.

V. be -different &c. *adj.*; differ, vary, ablude, mismatch, contrast; diverge -, depart -, deviate- -from; divaricate; differ *-toto cœlo, - longo intervallo.*

disagree &c. 713.

vary, modify &c. (*change*) 140.

discriminate &c. 465.

Adj. differing &c. *v.*; different, diverse, divided, heterogeneous; distinguishable; varied, modified; divergent, incongruous, diversified, various; discrepant, dissentient, differential; divers, all manner of; variform &c. 81; discordant &c. 713.

other, another, not the same; unequal &c. 28; unmatched; widely apart.

distinctive, characteristic; discriminative; distinguishing.

Adv. differently &c. *adj.*

Phr. *il y a fagots et fagots; tot nomines tot sententiæ;* one man's meat is another man's poison.

2°. Continuous Relation

16.   Uniformity. — N. uniformity; homogene-ity, -ousness; continuity, stability, consistency; connatural-ity, -ness; homology; accordance; conformity &c. 82; agreement &c. 23.

regularity, constancy, even tenor, routine; monotony, evenness, sameness, dead level; steadiness, equability, unity.

V. be -uniform &c. *adj.*; accord with &c. 23; run through.

become -uniform &c. *adj.*; conform to &c. 82.

render uniform &c. *adj.*; assimilate, level, smooth, dress.

16a. [Absence or want of uniformity.] **Non-uniformity. — N.** diversity irregularity, unevenness; multiformity &c. 81; unconformity &c. 83; roughness &c. 256; heterogeneity, heteromorphism.

Adj. diversified, varied, irregular, uneven, rough &c. 256; multifarious; multiform &c. 81; of various kinds; all -manner, - sorts, - kinds- of.

Adv. in all manner of ways, here there and everywhere.

Adj. uniform; homo-geneous, -logous; of a piece, consistent, steady; connatural; monotonous, changeless, dreary, even, invariable, equable, level, regular, stereotyped, unchanged, unvarying; methodical &c. 60; habitual &c. 613.

Adv. uniformly &c. *adj.*; uniformly with &c. (*conformably*) 82; in harmony with &c. (*agreeing*) 23; in a -rut, - groove.

always, ever &c. 112; invariably, without exception, never otherwise; by clock-work; endlessly &c. 112.

Phr. *ab uno disce omnes.*

3°. Partial Relation

17.   Similarity.—N. similarity, resemblance, likeness, similitude, sem-

18.   Dissimilarity.—N. dissimil-arity, -itude; unlikeness, diversity, disparity,

blance; affinity, approximation, parallelism; parity; agreement &c. 23; ana-logy, -logicalness; correspondence, equality &c.

connatural-ness, -ity; brotherhood, family likeness.

alliteration, rhyme, pun.

repetition &c. 104; sameness &c. (*identity*) 13; uniformity &c. 16.

analogue; the like; match, *pendant*, fellow, companion, pair, mate, twin, double, counterpart, brother, sister; one's second self, *alter ego*, chip of the old block, *par nobile fratrum, Arcades ambo*, birds of a feather, *et hoc genus omne*.

parallel; simile; type &c. (*metaphor*) 521; image &c. (*representation*) 554; photograph; close –, striking –, speaking –, faithful &c. *adj.* – likeness, – resemblance.

V. be -similar &c. *adj.*; look like, resemble, bear resemblance, favour; savour –, smack- of; approximate; parallel, match, rhyme with; take after; imitate &c. 19; run in pairs.

render -similar &c. *adj.*; assimilate, approximate, bring near; connaturalize, make alike; rhyme, pun.

Adj. similar; resembling &c. *v.*; like, alike; twin.

analog-ous, -ical; parallel, of a piece; such as, so.

connatural, congeneric, allied to; corresponding, cognate; akin to &c. (*consanguineous*) 11.

approximate, much the same, near, close, something like, such like; a show of; mock, *pseudo*, simulating, representing.

exact &c. (*true*) 494; lifelike, faithful, realistic; true to -nature, – the life; the -very image – picture- of; for all the world like, *comme deux gouttes d'eau*; as like as -two peas, – it can stare; *instar omnium*, cast in the same mould, ridiculously like.

Adv. as if, so to speak; as –, as if- it were; *quasi*, just as, *veluti in speculum*.

dissemblance; divergence, inequality, difference &c. 15; novelty; variation, variety, originality, disguise.

V. be -unlike &c. *adj.*; vary &c. (*differ*) 15; bear no resemblance to, differ *toto cœlo*.

render -unlike &c. *adj.*; vary &c. (*diversify*) 140.

Adj. dissimilar, unlike, disparate; of a different kind &c. (*class*) 75; unmatched, unique; new, novel; unprecedented &c. 83; original.

nothing of the kind; no such –, quite another- thing; far from it, other than, cast in a different mould, *tertium quid*, as like a dock as a daisy, 'very like a whale'; as different as -chalk from cheese, – Macedon and Monmouth; *lucus a non lucendo*.

diversified &c. 16a.

Adv. otherwise, *alias*.

---

19. Imitation.—N. imitation; copying &c. *v.*; transcription; repetition, mimeograph, mimeotype, duplication, reduplication; quotation; reproduction.

mockery, mimicry, mime, simulation, personation; representation &c. 554; semblance, simulacrum; pretence; copy &c. 21; assimilation.

paraphrase, parody &c. 21.

plagiarism; forgery &c. (*falsehood*) 544.

imitator, echo, cuckoo, parrot, ape, monkey, mocking-bird, mimic, impersonator; copyist.

V. imitate, copy, mirror, reflect, reproduce, repeat, borrow; do like, echo, re-echo, catch; transcribe; match, parallel.

20. Non-Imitation.—N. no imitation, genuineness, originality; creativeness.

Adj. unimitated, uncopied; unmatched, unparalleled; inimitable &c. 33; *unique*, original, primordial, primary, pristine, underived, first-hand, archetypal, prototypal.

---

mock, take off, mimic, ape, simulate, personate, impersonate; forge; act &c. (*drama*) 599; represent &c. 554; counterfeit, duplicate; portray, parody, travesty, caricature, burlesque.

follow –, tread- in the- -steps, – footsteps, – wake- of; pattern after, take pattern by; follow -suit, – the example of; walk in the shoes of, take a leaf out of another's book, strike in with; take –, model -after; emulate.

Adj. imitated &c. *v.*; mock, mimic; counterfeit, false, pseudo; modelled after, moulded on, paraphrastic; literal; imitative, apish; second-hand; imitable; sham &c. 545.

Adv. literally, to the letter, strictly, precisely, *verbatim, literatim, sic, totidem verbis*, word for word, *mot à mot.*

Phr. like master like man.

20a. Variation.—N. variation; alteration &c. (*change*) 140. modification, moods and tenses; modulation.
divergency &c. 291; deviation &c. 279; aberration; innovation.
V. vary &c. (*change*) 140; deviate &c. 279; diverge &c. 291.
Adj. varied &c. *v.*; modified; dissimilar &c. 18; diversified &c. 16*a.*

21. [Result of imitation.] Copy.—N. copy, fac-simile, counterpart, *effigies*, effigy, symbol, image, form, likeness, similitude, semblance, resemblance, cast, electrotype, stereotype, tracing, ectype; imitation &c. 19; model, representation, adumbration, study; counterfeit presentment, portrait &c. (*representment*) 554.

duplicate; transcript, -ion; reflex, -ion; shadow, echo; chip of the old block; reprint, reproduction, casting, engraving, replica; transfer; second edition &c. (*repetition*) 104; *réchauffé*; apograph, fair copy, revise.

22. [Thing copied.] Prototype.—N. prototype, original, model, pattern, founding, precedent, standard, scantling, type, arche-, anti-type; protoplast, copy-book, module, exemplar, example, ensample, specimen; paradigm; guide; templet; lay-figure.

text, copy, manuscript, MS., design; fugleman, keynote.

die, mould; matrix, engraving, last, plasm; pro-, proto-plasm; mint; seal, punch, *intaglio*, negative, stamp.

V. be –, set- an example; set a copy; standardize.

_____

parody, caricature, cartoon, burlesque, travesty, paraphrase.
servile -copy, – imitation; counterfeit &c. (*deception*) 545; *pasticcio*.
Adj. faithful; lifelike &c. (*similar*) 17.

4°. GENERAL RELATION

23. Agreement. — N. agreement; ac-cord, -cordance; unison, harmony, syntony; concord &c. 714; concordance, concert, understanding, convention, *entente -cordiale, consortium,* consensus of opinion, pact, mutual understanding, unanimity.

conformity &c. 82; conformance; uniformity &c. 16; consonance, consentaneousness, consistency; congruity, -ence; keeping; congeniality; correspondence, concinnity, parallelism, apposition, union.

fitness, aptness &c. *adj.*; relevancy;

24. Disagreement. — N. disagreement; dis-cord, -cordance; disunion, dissonance, dissidence, discrepancy; unconformity &c. 83; incongru-ity, -ence; discongruity, *mésalliance, oxymoron*; jarring &c. *v.*; clash, collision, dissension &c. 713; conflict &c. (*opposition*) 708; controversy &c. 720; falling out, wrangle, argument.

disparity, mismatch, misfit, disproportion; disproportionateness &c. *adj.*; variance, divergence, repugnance.

unfitness &c. *adj.*; inaptitude, impropriety; inapplicability &c. *adj.*; in-

pertinen-ce, -cy; sortance; case in point; aptitude, coaptation, propriety, applicability, admissibility, commensurability, compatibility, suitability; cognation &c. (*relation*) 9.

adaptation, adjustment, arrangement, graduation, accommodation; reconcil-iation -ement; assimilation; attunement.

consent &c. (*assent*) 448; concurrence &c. 178; co-operation &c. 709.

right man in the right place, very thing; quite –, just- the thing.

V. be -accordant &c. *adj.*; agree, accord, harmonize; correspond, tally, respond; meet, suit, fit, befit, do, adapt itself to; fall in –, chime in –, square –, quadrate –, consort –, comport- with; dovetail, assimilate; fit like a glove; fit to a -tittle, – T; match &c. 17; become one.

consent &c. (*assent*) 488.

render -accordant &c. *adj.*; fit, suit, adapt, accommodate; graduate; adjust &c. (*render equal*) 27; dress, regulate, readjust; accord, harmonize, reconcile; fadge, dovetail, square.

Adj. agreeing, suiting &c. *v.*; in accord, accordant, concordant, consonant, congruous, consentaneous, correspondent, corresponding, homologous, congenial; becoming; harmonious, reconcilable, conformable; in -accordance, – harmony, – keeping, – unison, &c. *n.*- with; at one with, of one mind, of a piece; consistent, compatible, proportionate, answerable; commensurate; on all fours.

apt, apposite, pertinent, pat; to the -point, – purpose; happy, felicitous, germane, *ad rem*, in point, bearing upon, applicable, relevant, admissible.

fit, adapted, *in loco*, *à propos*, appropriate, seasonable, sortable, suitable, idoneous, deft; meet &c. (*expedient*) 646.

at home, in one's proper element.

Adv. *à propos of*; pertinently &c. adj.; *pro rata*.

Phr. *rem acu tetigisti*, the cap fits.

consistency, inconcinnity; irrelevancy &c. (*irrelation*) 10.

misjoin-ing, -der; syncretism, intrusion, interference; *concordia discors*.

fish out of water.

V. disagree; clash, quarrel, jar &c. (*discord*) 713; interfere, intrude, come amiss; not concern &c. 10; mismatch; *hymano capiti cervicem jungere equinam*.

Adj. disagreeing &c. *v.*; discordant, discrepant; at -variance, – war; hostile, antagonistic, repugnant, factious, contradictory, dissentious, incompatible, irreconcilable, inconsistent with; unconformable, exceptional &c. 83; intrusive, incongruous; disproportionate, -ed; unharmonious; unconsonant; divergent, repugnant to.

inapt, unapt, inappropriate, inept, infelicitous, improper; unsuit-ed, -able; inapplicable; un-fit, -fitting, -befitting; unbecoming; ill-timed, ill-adapted, unseasonable, *mal à propos*, inadmissible; inapposite &c. (*irrelevant*) 10.

uncongenial; ill-assorted, -sorted, -matched; mis-matched, -mated, -joined, -placed; unaccommodating, irreducible, uncommensurable, unsympathetic.

out of -character, – keeping, – proportion, – joint, – tune, – place, – season, – its element; at -odds, – variance with.

Adv. in -defiance, – contempt, – spite-of; discordantly &c. *adj.*; *à tort et à travers*.

Section III. QUANTITY

1°. Simple Quantity

25. [Absolute quantity.] **Quantity.—** **N.** quantity, magnitude; size &c. (*dimensions*) 192; amplitude, mass,

26. [Relative quantity.] **Degree.—** **N.** degree, grade, extent, measure, proportion, amount, ratio, stint, standard, amount, *quantum*, measure, measurement, substance, strength.

[Science of quantity.] Mathematics, Mathesis.

[Definite or finite quantity] arm-, hand-, mouth-, spoon-, thimble-, capful; stock, batch, lot, dose, ration, quotum, quota, pittance, driblet, part, portion &c. 51.

Adj. quantitative, some, any, more or less.

Adv. to the tune of.

———

height, pitch; reach, amplitude, range, scope, size, calibre; gradation, shade; tenor, compass; sphere, station, rank, standing; rate, way, sort.

point, mark, step, stage &c. (*term*) 71; intensity, strength &c. (*greatness*) 31.

V. compare, graduate, calibrate, measure.

Adj. comparative; gradual, shading off, gradational; within the bounds &c. (*limit*), 233.

Adv. by degrees, gradually, inasmuch, *pro tanto*; how-ever, -soever; step by step, bit by bit, little by little, inch by inch, drop by drop, gradatim; by -inches, – slow degrees, – little and little; in some -degree, – measure; to some extent; just a bit.

2°. Comparative Quantity

27. [Sameness of quantity or degree.] **Equality.—N.** equality, parity, co-extension, symmetry, balance, poise; evenness, monotony, level.

equivalence; equi-pollence, -poise, -librium, -ponderance; par, quits; not a pin to choose; distinction without a difference, six of one and half a dozen of the other; identity &c. 13; similarity &c. 17; isotropism; coequality.

equalization, equation; equilibration, co-ordination, adjustment, readjustment.

drawn -game, -battle, draw, stalemate; neck and neck race; tie, dead heat.

match, peer, compeer, equal, mate, fellow, brother; equivalent.

V. be -equal &c. *adj.*; equal, match,

28. [Difference of quantity or degree.] **Inequality.—N.** inequality; dis-, im-parity; odds; difference &c. 15; ill-balanced; unevenness; inclination of the balance, partiality; shortcoming; casting – make- weight; superiority &c. 33; inferiority &c. 34.

V. be -unequal &c. *adj.*; countervail; have –, give- the advantage; turn the scale; kick the beam; topple, -over; over-match &c. 33; not come up to &c. 34.

Adj. unequal, uneven, disparate, partial; un-, over-balanced; top-heavy, lop-sided.

Adv. *haud passibus æquis.*

———

reach, keep pace with, run abreast; come –, amount –, come up-to; be –, lie- on a level with; balance; cope with; come to the same thing; level off.

render -equal &c. *adj.*; equalize, level, dress, balance, equate, handicap, give points, trim, adjust, poise; fit, accommodate; adapt &c. (*render accordant*) 23; strike a balance; establish –, restore-equality, – equilibrium; readjust; stretch on the bed of Procrustes.

Adj. equal, even, level, monotonous, coequal, symmetrical, co-ordinate; on a -par, – level, – footing- with; up to the mark; equiparant.

equivalent, tantamount; quits; homologous; synonymous &c. 522; resolvable into, convertible, much at one, as broad as long, neither more nor less; much the same –, the same thing –, as good-as; all -one, – the same; equi-pollent, -ponderant, -ponderous, -balanced; equalized &c. *v.*; drawn; half and half; isochronous; isoperimetrical.

Adv. equally &c. *adj.*; *pari passu, ad eundem, cæteris paribus*; *in equilibrio*; to all intents and purposes.

Phr. it -comes, -adds up, – amounts- to the same thing.

29. Mean.—N. mean, medium, intermedium, average, run of the mill, normal, balance; mediocrity, generality, rule, ordinary -run, -ruck; golden mean &c. (*mid-course*) 628; middle &c. 68; compromise &c. 774; neutrality; middle point, middle course.

V. split the difference; take the -average &c. *n.*; reduce to a -mean &c. *n.*; strike a balance, pair off.

Adj. mean, intermediate; medial; middle &c. 68; average, normal, standard; neutral; middling, moderate.

médiocre, middle-class; *bourgeois*, commonplace &c. (*unimportant*) 643.

Adv. on an average, in the long run; taking -one with another, – all things together, – it for all in all; *communibus annis*, in round numbers.

30. Compensation.—N. compensation, equation; commutation; indemnification; compromise &c. 774; neutralization, nullification; counteraction &c. 179; reaction; measure for measure; retaliation &c. 718; equalization &c. 27; redemption, recoupment, recompense.

set-off, offset; make- casting-weight; counterpoise, equipoise, ballast; indemnity, reparation &c. 790; equivalent, *quid pro quo*; bribe, hush-money, tribute &c. 784; amends &c. (*atonement*) 952; counterclaim, counterbalance, equiponderance, countervail, cross demand.

V. make -amends, – compensation; com-pensate, -pense; indemnify; counter-act, -vail, -poise; equiponderate; balance; out-, over-, counter-balance; set off, offset, cancel; hedge, square, give and take; make up -for, – lee way; cover, fill up, neutralize, nullify; equalize &c. 27; make good; redeem &c. (*atone*) 952; recoup, pay &c. 973.

Adj. compensat-ing, -ory; amendatory, reparative, countervailing &c. *v.*; in the opposite scale; equivalent &c. (*equal*) 27.

Adv. in -return, – consideration; but, however, yet, still, notwithstanding; neverthe-, nath-less; although, though; al-, how-beit; in spite of, despite; maugre; at -all events, – any rate; be that as it may, for all that, even so, on the other hand, at the same time, *quoad minus*, *quand même*, however that may be; after all, – is said and done; taking one thing with another &c. (*average*) 29.

Quantity by Comparison with a Standard

31. Greatness.—N. greatness &c. *adj.*; magnitude; size &c. (*dimensions*) 192; multitude &c. (*number*) 102; immensity, enormity; infinity &c. 105; might, strength, intensity, fulness; importance &c. 642; fame &c. 873.

great quantity, quantity, deal, power, sight, pot, volume, world; mass, heap &c. (*assemblage*) 72; stock &c. (*store*) 636; peck, bushel, load, cargo; cart -, wagon -, car -, truck -, ship- load; flood, spring tide; abundance &c. (*sufficiency*) 639.

principal -, chief -, main -, greater -,

32. Smallness.—N. smallness &c. *adj.*; littleness &c. (*small size*) 193; tenuity; paucity; fewness &c. (*small number*) 103; meanness, insignificance &c. (*unimportance*) 643; mediocrity, moderation.

small quantity, *modicum, minimum*; vanishing point; material point, electron, atom, particle, molecule, corpuscle, point, dab, fleck, speck, dot, mote, jot, iota, ace; *minutiæ*, details; look, thought, idea, *soupçon*, whit, tittle, shade, shadow; spark, *scintilla*, gleam; touch, cast; grain, scruple,

major –, best –, essential- part; bulk, mass &c. (*whole*) 50.

V. be -great &c. *adj.*; run high, soar, loom up, tower, bulk large, transcend; rise –, carry- to a great height; know no bounds; scale, overtop, ascend.

enlarge &c. (*increase*) 35, (*expand*) 194.

Adj. great; greater &c. 33; large, considerable, fair, above par; big, massive, huge &c. (*large in size*) 192; ample; abundant &c. (*enough*) 639; Herculean &c. 159; full, intense, strong, sound, passing, heavy, plenary, deep, high; signal, at its height, in the zenith.

world-wide, wide-spread, extensive; wholesale; many &c. 102.

goodly, noble, precious, mighty; sad, grave, serious; far gone, arrant, downright; utter, -most; crass, gross, arch, profound, intense, consummate; rank, unmitigated, red-hot, desperate; glaring, flagrant, stark staring; thorough-paced, -going; roaring, thumping, thundering, strapping, whacking; extraordinary; important &c. 642; unsurpassed &c. (*supreme*) 33; complete &c. 52.

vast, immense, enormous, extreme; inordinate, excessive, extravagant, exorbitant, outrageous, preposterous, unconscionable, swinging, monstrous, over-grown; towering, stupendous, prodigious, astonishing, incredible; terrific, frightful; marvellous &c. (*wonder*) 870; grand.

unlimited &c. (*infinite*) 105; unapproachable, unutterable, indescribable, ineffable, unspeakable, inexpressible, beyond expression, fabulous.

un-diminished, -abated, -reduced, -restricted.

absolute, positive, stark, decided, unequivocal, essential, perfect, finished.

remarkable, of mark, marked, pointed, veriest; noticeable, uncommon, noteworthy, eminent &c. 873.

Adv. [in a positive degree] truly &c. (*truth*) 494; decidedly, unequivocally, purely, absolutely, seriously, essentially, fundamentally, radically, downright, in all conscience; for the most part, in the main.

[in a complete degree] entirely &c. (*completely*) 52; abundantly, &c. (*suf-*

granule, globule, minim, sup, sip, sop, spice, drop, droplet, sprinkling, dash, smack, tinge, tincture; inch, patch, scantling, dole; scrap, shred, tag, splinter, rag, tatter, cantlet, flitter, gobbet, mite, bit, morsel, crumb, seed, fritter, shive; snip, -pet; snick, snack, snatch, slip, scrag; chip, -ping; shiver, sliver, driblet, clipping, paring, shaving, hair.

nutshell; thimble-, spoon-, hand-, cap-, mouth-ful; fragment; fraction &c. (*part*) 51; drop in the ocean, drop in the bucket.

animalcule &c. 193.

trifle &c. (*unimportant thing*) 643; mere –, next to- nothing; hardly anything; just enough to swear by; the shadow of a shade.

finiteness, finite quantity.

V. be -small &c. *adj.*; lie in a nutshell.

diminish &c. (*decrease*) 36, (*contract*) 195.

Adj. small, little, tiny, weeny; diminutive &c. (*small in size*) 193; minute; minikin, fine, inconsiderable, dribbling, paltry &c. (*unimportant*) 643; faint &c. (*weak*) 160; slender, light, slight, scanty, scant, limited; meagre &c. (*insufficient*) 640; sparing; few &c. 103; low, so-so, middling, tolerable, no great shakes; below –, under-par, – the mark; at a low ebb; halfway; moderate, modest; tender, subtle; petty, shallow, skin-deep.

inappreciable, evanescent, infinitesimal, homœopathic, very small, atomic, molecular, ultra-, -microscopic.

petty, shallow &c. 499.

mere, simple, sheer, stark, bare; near run.

Adv. [in a small degree] to a small extent, on a small scale; a -little, – wee, – tiny bit; slightly &c. *adj.*; imperceptibly; miserably, wretchedly; insufficiently &c. 640; imperfectly; faintly &c. 160; passably, pretty well, well enough.

[in a certain or limited degree] partially, in part; in –, to a certain degree; to a certain extent; comparatively; some, rather; in some -degree, -measure; some-thing, -what; simply, only, purely, merely; at –, at the- -least,

ficiently) 639; widely, far and wide.

[in a great or high degree] greatly
&c. *adj.*; much, muckle, well, indeed,
very, very much, a deal, no end of,
most not a little; pretty, – well;
enough, in a great measure, passing
richly; to a -large, – great, – gigantic-
extent; on a large scale; so; never –,
ever- so; ever so much; by wholesale;
mightily, mighty, powerfully; with a
witness, *ultra*, in the extreme, extremely, exceedingly, intensely, ex-
quisitely, acutely, indefinitely, im-
measurably; beyond -compare, –
comparison, – measure, – all bounds;
incalculably, infinitely.

[in a supreme degree] pre-eminently,
superlatively &c. (*superiority*) 33.

[in a too great degree] immoderately,

– most; ever so little, as little as may
be, *tant soit peu*, in ever so small a
degree; thus far, *pro tanto*, within
bounds, in a manner, after a fashion.

almost, nearly, well nigh, short of,
not quite, all but; near –, close- upon;
peu s'en faut, near the mark; within an
-ace, – inch- of; on the brink of;
scarcely, hardly, barely, only just, no
more than.

[in an uncertain degree] about, there-
abouts, somewhere about, nearly, say;
be the same -more, – little more- or less.

[in no degree] no- ways, – wise; not
-at all, – in the least, – a bit, – a bit of
it, – a whit, – a jot, – a shadow; in no
-wise, – respect; by no -means, – manner of means; on no account, at no
hand.

unduly, monstrously, grossly, prepos-
terously, inordinately, exorbitantly, excessively, enormously, out of
all proportion, with a vengeance.

[in a marked degree] particularly, remarkably, singularly, curi-
ously, uncommonly, unusually, peculiarly, notably, signally,
strikingly, pointedly, mainly, chiefly; famously, egregiously, prominently, glaringly, emphatically, strangely, wonderfully, amazingly,
surprisingly, astonishingly, incredibly, marvellously, awfully,
stupendously.

[in an exceptional degree] peculiarly &c. (*unconformity*) 83.

[in a violent degree] furiously &c. (*violence*) 173; severely, des-
perately, tremendously, extravagantly, confoundedly, deucedly,
devilishly, with a vengeance; *à –, à toute- outrance*.

[in a painful degree] painfully, sadly, grossly, sorely, bitterly,
piteously, grievously, miserably, cruelly, woefully, lamentably,
shockingly, frightfully, dreadfully, fearfully, terribly, horribly,
distressingly, balefully.

QUANTITY BY COMPARISON WITH A SIMILAR OBJECT

33. Superiority.—N. supremacy,
superiority, majority; greatness &c.
31; advantage, odds, pull; preponderance, -ation; predominance, vantage
ground, coign of vantage, prevalence,
partiality; personal superiority; sovereignty &c. 737; nobility &c. (*rank*)
875; Triton among the minnows,
primus inter pares, nulli secundus,
superman; captain &c. 475.

supremacy, pre-eminence; primacy,
lead, *maximum*; record; climax, crest,
top; culmination &c. (*summit*) 210;
transcendence; *ne plus ultra*; lion's
share, Benjamin's mess; excess; bisque,

34. Inferiority.—N. inferiority, minority, subordinancy; shortcoming, deficiency; handicap; *minimum*; smallness
&c. 32; imperfection, shabbiness.

[personal inferiority] commonalty
&c. 876; subordinate, substitute, sub.

V. be -inferior &c. *adj.*; fall –,
come- short of; not -pass, – come up
to; want.

become –, render- smaller &c.
(*decrease*) 36, (*contract*) 195; hide its
diminished head, retire into the shade,
yield the palm, play second fiddle,
take a back seat; bow.

Adj. inferior, smaller; small &c. 32;

surplus &c. (*remainder*) 40, (*redundance*) 641.

V. be -superior &c. *adj.*; exceed, excel, transcend; out-do, -balance, -weigh, -rival, -Herod, outrank, pass, surpass, surmount, get ahead of; overtop, -ride, -pass, -balance, -weigh, -match; top, o'er-top, cap, beat, win out, cut out; beat hollow; outstrip &c. 303; eclipse, throw into the shade, take the shine out of, put one's nose out of joint; have the -upper hand, – whip hand of, – advantage; turn the scale, play first fiddle &c. (*importance*) 642; preponderate, predominate, prevail; precede, take precedence, come first; come to a head, culminate; beat &c. all others, bear the palm; break the record, take the cake.

become –, render- -larger, &c. (*increase*) 35, (*expand*) 194.

Adj. superior, greater, major, higher; exceeding &c. *v.*; great &c. 31; distinguished, *ultra*; vaulting; more than a match for.

supreme, greatest, maximal, maximum, utmost, paramount, pre-eminent, foremost, crowning; first-rate &c. (*important*) 642, (*excellent*) 648; unrivalled; peer-, match-less; none such, second to none, *sans pareil*; un-paragoned, -paralleled, -equalled, -approached, -surpassed; superlative, inimitable, *facile princeps*, incomparable, sovereign, without parallel, *nulli secundus, ne plus ultra*; beyond -compare, – comparison; culminating &c. (*topmost*) 210; transcendent, -ental; *plus royaliste que le Roi*.

increased &c. (*added to*) 35; enlarged &c. (*expanded*) 194.

Adv. beyond, more, over; over –, above- the mark; above par; upwards –, in advance- of; over and above; at the top of the scale, on the crest, at its height.

[in a superior or supreme degree] eminently, egregiously, pre-eminently, surpassing, prominently, superlatively, supremely, above all, of all things, the most, to crown all, *par excellence*, principally, especially, particularly, peculiarly, *a fortiori*, even, yea, still more.

Phr. 'we shall not look upon his like again.'

minor, less, lesser, deficient, minus, lower, subordinate, secondary; second-rate &c. (*imperfect*) 651; sub, subaltern; thrown into the shade; weighed in the balance and found wanting; not fit to hold a candle to.

least, smallest &c. (*see* little, small &c. 193); lowest.

diminished &c. (*decreased*) 36; reduced &c. (*contracted*) 195; unimportant &c. 643.

Adv. less; under –, below- -the mark, – par; at -the bottom of the scale, – a low ebb, – a disadvantage; short of, under.

Changes in Quantity

35. Increase—N. increase, augmentation, addition, enlargement, extension; dilatation &c. (*expansion*) 194; multiplication; increment, accretion; accession &c. 37; production &c. 161; development, growth; aggrandizement, aggravation, intensification; rise; ascent &c. 305; anabasis; ex-aggeration, -acerbation; spread &c. (*dispersion*) 73; flood-, spring-, -tide; gain, produce, profit &c. 618; booty, plunder &c. 793.

V. increase, augment, add to, enlarge; dilate &c. (*expand*) 194; grow,

36. Non-Increase, Decrease.—N. decrease, diminution; lessening &c. *v.*; subtraction &c. 38; reduction, abatement, declension; shrinkage &c. (*contraction*) 195; coarctation; abridgment &c. (*shortening*) 201; extenuation.

subsidence, catabasis, wane, ebb-, neap-tide, decline; descent &c. 306; decrement, reflux, depreciation; erosion, wear and tear, deterioration &c. 659; anticlimax; mitigation &c. (*moderation*) 174.

V. decrease, diminish, lessen; abridge

wax, mount, swell, get ahead, gain strength; advance; run -, shoot- up; rise; ascend &c. 305; sprout &c. 194.

aggrandize; raise, exalt; deepen, heighten; lengthen; thicken; strengthen; intensify, enhance, inflate, magnify, double, redouble; multiply; aggravate, exaggerate; ex-asperate, -acerbate; add fuel to the flame, *oleum addere camino*, superadd &c. (*add*) 37; spread &c. (*disperse*) 73.

Adj. increased &c. *v.*; on the increase, undiminished; additional &c. (*added*) 37; increasing &c. *v.*; growing, crescent, intensive, cumulative.

Adv. *crescendo*, increasingly.

Phr. *vires acquirit eundo.*

&c. (*shorten*) 201; shrink &c. (*contract*) 195; drop -, fall -, tail- off; fall away, waste, wear, erode; wane, ebb, decline; descend &c. 306; subside; deliquesce, melt -, die -away; retire into the shade, hide its diminished head, fall to a low ebb, run low, languish, decay, crumble, consume away.

bate, abate, dequantitate; discount; depreciate; extenuate, lower, weaken, attenuate, fritter away; mitigate &c. (*moderate*) 174; belittle, minimize; dwarf, throw into the shade; keep down, reduce &c. 195; shorten &c. 201; subtract &c. 38.

Adj. unincreased &c. (*see* increase &c. 35); decreased &c. *v.*; decreasing &c. *v.*; on the -wane &c. *n.*; deliquescent.

Adv. *diminuendo, decrescendo*, decreasingly.

3°. Conjunctive Quantity

37. Addition.—N. addition, annexation, adjection; junction &c. 43; super-position, -addition, -junction, -fetation; accession, reinforcement; increase &c. 35; increment, supplement; accompaniment &c. 88; interposition &c. 228; insertion &c. 300; summation &c. 85; adjunct &c. 39.

V. add, annex, adject, affix, attach, superadd, subjoin, superpose; clap -, saddle- on; tack to, postfix, append, tag; ingraft; saddle with; sprinkle; introduce &c. (*interpose*) 228; insert &c. 300.

become added, accrue; ad-, supervene; add up &c. 85.

reinforce, strengthen, swell the ranks of; augment &c. 35.

Adj. added &c. *v.*; additional; supplement, -al, -ary; suppletory, subjunctive; adjec-, adsci-, asci-titious; additive, extra, spare, further, fresh, more, new, ulterior, other, auxiliary, supernumerary, accessory.

Adv. in addition, more, plus, extra; and, also, likewise, too, furthermore, further, item; and -also, - eke; else, besides, to boot, *et cætera*; &c.; and bargain, *cum multis aliis*, over and above, moreover.

38. Non-Addition. Subduction.—N. sub-traction, -duction; deduction, retrenchment; removal; ab-, sub-lation; abstraction &c. (*taking*) 789; garbling &c. *v.*; mutilation, detruncation; amputation, severance; abs-, ex-, re-cision; curtailment &c. 201; minuend, subtrahend; decrease &c. 36; abrasion.

V. sub-tract, -duct; rebate, de-duct, -duce; bate, retrench; remove, withdraw; take -from, - away; detract.

garble, mutilate, amputate, sever, detruncate; cut -off, - away, - out; expurgate; abscind, excise; pare, thin, prune, decimate; abrade, scrape, file; geld, castrate, emasculate, unman, spay, caponize; eliminate.

diminish &c. 36; curtail &c. (*shorten*) 201; deprive of &c. (*take*) 789; weaken.

Adj. subtracted &c. *v.*; subtractive. tailless, acaudal.

Adv. in -deduction &c. *n.*; less; short of; minus, without, except, excepting, with the exception of, barring, bar, save, exclusive of, save and except, with a reservation.

so -on, - forth; into the

with, withal; including, inclusive, as well as, not to mention, let alone; together –, along –, coupled –, in conjunction- with; conjointly; jointly &c. 43.

39. [Thing added.] **Adjunct.—N.** adjunct; addit-ion, -ament; *additum*, affix, appendage, annex; augment, -ation; increment, reinforcement, supernumerary, accessory, item; garnish, sauce; accompaniment &c. 88; adjective, *addendum*, accession, complement; supplement; continuation; extension, subscript, tag, appendix, postscript, interlineation, interpolation, insertion.

rider, codicil, off-shoot, episode, side issue, corollary; piece; flap, lapel, label, tab, strip, fold, lappet, apron, skirt, embroidery, trappings, *cortège*; tail, suffix &c. (*sequel*) 65; wing.

Adj. additional &c. 37.

Adv. in addition &c. 37.

40. [Thing remaining.] **Remainder·**—**N.** remainder, residue; remains, *remanet*, remnant, rest, relic, relict; leavings, heel-tap, odds and ends, cheese-parings, candle ends, orts; *residuum*; dottle, dregs &c. (*dirt*) 653; refuse &c. (*useless*) 645; stubble, result, educt; fag-end, stub; ruins, wreck, skeleton, stump; *alluvium*.

surplus, overplus, excess; balance, complement; superfluity &c. (*redundance*) 641; surviv-al, -ance; afterglow.

V. remain; be -left &c. *adj.*; exceed, survive; leave.

Adj. remaining, left; left -behind, – over; residu-al, -ary; over, odd; unconsumed, sedimentary; surviving; net; exceeding, over and above; outlying, -standing; cast off &c. 782; superfluous &c. (*redundant*) 641.

40a. [Thing deducted.] **Decrement.—N.** decrement, discount, rebate, defect, loss, deduction, eduction, tare; drawback; waste, wastage; reprise.

41. [Forming a whole without coherence.] **Mixture.—N.** mix-, admix-, commix-ture, -tion, mingling; commixion, immixture, interfusion, intermixture, alloyage, matrimony; junction &c. 43; combination &c. 48; entanglement, interlacing; miscegenation, interbreeding.

impregnation; in-, dif-, suf-, transfusion; infiltration; seasoning, sprinkling, interlarding; interpolation &c. 228; adulteration, sophistication.

[Thing mixed] tinge, tincture, touch, dash, smack, sprinkling, spice, seasoning, infusion, *soupçon*.

[Compound resulting from mixture] alloy, brass, bronze, pewter &c.; amalgam, *magma*, blend, half-and-half, *mélange, tertium, quid*, miscellany, *ambigu*, medley, mess, hash, hotchpotch, hodgepodge, *pasticcio*, patchwork, odds and ends, all sorts; jumble &c. (*disorder*) 59; salad, sauce, mash, *omnium gatherum*, gallimaufry, ragout, *olla podrida, olio*, salmagundi, *potpourri*, Noah's ark; texture, mingled yarn; mosaic &c. (*variegation*) 440.

half-blood, -caste, -breed, Eurasian; mulatto; terc-, quart-, quinteron &c.; quad-, octo-roon; *griffo, zambo*; cross, hybrid, mongrel &c. 83.

42. [Freedom from mixture.] **Simpleness.—N.** simpleness &c. *adj.*; purity, homogeneity.

elimination; sifting &c. *v.*; purification &c. (*cleanness*) 652.

V. render -simple &c. *adj.*; simplify. sift, winnow, bolt, eliminate; narrow down; get rid of, exclude &c. 55; clear; purify &c. (*clean*) 652; disentangle &c. (*disjoin*) 44.

Adj. simple, uniform, of a piece, homogeneous, single, pure, clear, sheer, neat; Attic.

un-mixed, -mingled, -blended, -combined, -compounded; elementary, undecomposed; un-adulterated, -sophisticated, -alloyed, -tinged, -fortified; pure and simple.

free –, exempt- from; exclusive.

Adv. simply &c. *adj.*; only.

V. mix; join &c. 43; combine &c. 48; com-, im-, inter-mix; mix up with, mingle; com-, inter-, be-mingle; shuffle &c. (*derange*) 61; pound together; hash –, stir- up; knead, brew; impregnate with; interlard &c. (*interpolate*) 228; inter-twine, -weave &c. 219; associate with, miscegenate, interbreed.

be mixed &c.; get among, be entangled with.

instil, imbue; in-, suf-, trans-fuse; infiltrate, dash, tinge, tincture, season, sprinkle, besprinkle, attemper, medicate, blend, cross; alloy, amalgamate, compound, adulterate, sophisticate, infect.

Adj. mixed &c. *v.*; implex, composite, half-and-half, linsey-wolsey, hybrid, mongrel, heterogeneous; motley &c. (*variegated*) 440; miscellaneous, promiscuous, indiscriminate; miscible.

Adv. among, amongst, amid, amidst, with; in the midst of, in the crowd.

43. Junction.—N. junction; joining &c. *v.*; joinder, union; con-nection, -junction, -jugation, compendency, annex-ion, -ation, -ment; coalition; astriction, attachment, compagination, vincture, ligation, alligation; accouplement; marriage &c. (*wedlock*) 903; infibulation, inosculation, symphysis, anastomosis, confluence, communication, concatenation; concurrence, meeting, reunion; assemblage &c. 72.

copulation, coition, intercourse.

joint, joining, juncture, chiasma, pivot, hinge, articulation, commissure, seam, suture, gusset, stitch, splice; link &c. 45; mitre, mortise.

closeness, tightness &c. *adj.*; coherence &c. 46; combination &c. 48.

V. join, unite; con-join, -nect; associate; put –, lay –, clap –, hang –, lump –, hold –, piece –, tack –, fix –, bind up- together; embody, re-embody; roll into one.

attach, fix, affix, saddle on, fasten, bind, secure, clinch, twist, make -fast &c. *adj.*; tie, pinion, string, strap, sew, lace, stitch, tack, paste, knit, button, buckle, hitch, lash, truss, bandage, braid, splice, swathe, gird, tether, moor, picket, harness, chain; fetter &c. (*restrain*) 751; lock, latch, belay, brace, hook, grapple, leash, couple, accouple, link, yoke, bracket; marry &c. (*wed*) 903; bridge over, span.

pin, nail, bolt, hasp, clasp, clamp, screw, rivet; impact, solder, braze, cement, set; weld –, fuse- together; wedge, rabbet, mortise, mitre, jam, dovetail, enchase; graft, ingraft, inosculate; en-, in-twine; inter-link, -lace,

44. Disjunction.—N. dis-junction, -connection, -unity, -union, -association, -engagement, -sociation; discontinuity &c. 70; inconnection; abstraction, -edness; isolation; insul-arity, -ation; oasis; separateness &c. *adj.*; severalty; *disjecta membra*; dispersion &c. 73; apportionment &c. 786.

separation; parting &c. *v.*; detachment, segregation; divorce, sejunction, seposition, diduction, diremption, discerption; elision; *cæsura*, division, subdivision, break, fracture, rupture; compartition; dis-memberment, -integration, -location; luxation; sever-, dis-sever-ance; scission; re-, ab-scission; circumcision; lacer-, dilacer-ation; dis-, ab-ruption; avulsion, divulsion; section, resection, cleavage; fission; separability; separatism.

fissure, breach, rent, split, rift, crack, slit, slot, incision.

dissection, anatomy; decomposition &c. 49; cutting instrument &c. (*sharpness*) 253; saw.

V. be -disjoined &c.; come –, fall- -off, – to pieces; peel off; get loose.

dis-join, -connect, -engage, -unite, -sociate, -pair; divorce, part, dispart, detach, uncouple, separate, cut off, rescind, segregate; set –, keep- apart; insulate, isolate; throw out of gear; cut adrift; loose; un-loose, -do, -bind, -tie, -hitch, -chain, -lock &c. (*fix*) 43, -pack, -ravel; disentangle; set free &c. (*liberate*) 750.

sunder, divide, subdivide, sectionalize, sever, dissever, abscind; cut; segment; in-cide, -cise; circumcise; saw, snip, nib, nip, cleave, rive, rend, slit,

-twine, -twist, -weave; entangle; twine round, belay; tighten; trice –, screw-up.

be -joined &c.; hang –, hold- together; cohere &c. 46.

Adj. joined &c. v.; joint; con-joint, -junct; corporate, compact; hand in hand.

firm, fast, close, tight, taut, taught, tense, secure, set, intervolved; in-separable, -dissoluble, -secable, -severable.

Adv. jointly &c. adj.; in conjunction with &c. (in addition to) 37; fast, firmly &c. adj.; intimately.

split, splinter, chip, crack, snap, break, tear, burst; rend &c. -asunder, – in twain; wrench, rupture, shatter, shiver, cranch, crunch, craunch, chop; rip up; hack, hew, slash; whittle; haggle, hackle, discind, lacerate, scamble, mangle, gash, hash, slice.

cut up, carve, quarter, dissect, anatomize; take –, pull –, pick –, tear- to pieces; tear to tatters, – piecemeal; divellicate; skin &c. 226; dis-integrate, -member, -branch, -band; disperse &c. 73; dis-locate, -joint; break up; mince; comminute &c. (pulverize) 330; distribute, apportion &c. 786.

part, – company; separate, leave; alienate, estrange.

Adj. disjoined &c. v.; discontinuous &c. 70; bipartite, multipartite, abstract; digitate; disjunctive; isolated &c. v.; insular, separate, disparate, discrete, apart, asunder, far between, loose, free; unattached, -annexed, -associated, -connected; distinct; adrift; straggling; rift, reft, cleft, split.

[capable of being divided] scissile, partible, divisible, separable, severable, detachable.

Adv. separately &c. adj.; one by one, severally, apart; adrift, asunder, in twain; in the abstract, abstractedly.

45. [Connecting medium.] **Vinculum.—N.** vinculum, link, *nexus*; connec-tive, -tion; junction &c. 43; bond of union, copula, intermedium, hyphen; bracket; bridge, stepping-stone, isthmus.

bond, tendon, tendril; fibre; cord, -age; riband, ribbon, rope, guy, cable, line, halser, hawser, painter, moorings, wire, chain; string &c. (*filament*) 205.

fastening, tie; liga-ment, -ture; strap; bowline, halliard, tackle, lanyard, rigging, shrouds; standing –, running- rigging; traces, harness; yoke; band, -age; brace, roller, fillet; inkle; with, withe, withy; thong, braid; girder, tie-beam; girt, cinch, girth, girdle, cestus, garter, braces, suspenders, halter, noose, lasso, lariat, surcingle, knot, hitch, running knot, frog.

pin, corking pin, nail, brad, tack, skewer, staple, cleat, clamp; cramp, screw, button, buckle, clasp, hasp, hinge, hank, catch, latch, bolt, ring, latchet, pawl, tag; tooth; stud; hook, – and eye; morse, lock, holdfast, padlock, rivet; anchor, grappling-iron, drawbar, coupler, drawhead, coupling, treenail, trennel, stake, pale, pile, post, bollard.

cement, glue, gum, paste, size, wafer, solder, lute, putty, bird-lime, mortar, stucco, plaster, grout.

shackle, rein &c. (*means of restraint*) 752; suspender &c. 214; prop &c. (*support*) 215.

V. bridge over, span; connect &c. 43; hang &c. 214.

46. Coherence.—N. co-, ad-herence, -hesion, -hesiveness; concretion, accretion; con-, ag-glutination, -glomeration; aggregation; consolidation, set, cementation; sticking, soldering &c. v.; connection.

47. [Want of adhesion, non-adhesion, immiscibility.] **Incoherence.—N.** non-adhesion; immiscibility; incoherence; looseness &c. adj.; laxity; relaxation; loosening &c. v.; freedom; disjunction &c. 44; rope of sand.

tenacity, toughness; stickiness &c. 352; insepara-bility, -bleness; bur, remora.

conglomerate, concrete &c. (*density*) 321.

V. cohere, adhere, stick, cling, cleave, hold, take hold of, hold fast, close with, embrace, clasp, hug; grow –, hang-together; twine round &c. (*join*) 43.

stick like -a leech, – wax; stick close; cling like -ivy, – a bur; adhere like -a remora, – Dejanira's shirt.

glue; ag-, con-glutinate; cement, lute, paste, gum; solder, weld; cake, coagulate, consolidate &c. (*solidify*) 321; agglomerate.

Adj. co-, ad-hesive, -hering &c. *v.*; tenacious, tough; sticky &c. 352.

united, unseparated, sessile, inseparable, inextricable, infrangible; compact &c. (*dense*) 321.

48. Combination.—N. combination; mixture &c. 41; alloy; junction &c. 43; union, unification, synthesis, incorporation, amalgamation, embodiment, coalescence, crasis, fusion, blend, blending, absorption, centralization, federation.

compound, amalgam, composition, *tertium quid*; resultant, impregnation.

V. combine, unite, incorporate, alloy, intertwine &c. 41; amalgamate, embody, absorb, re-embody, blend, merge, fuse, melt into one, consolidate, coalesce, centralize, impregnate; put –, lump- together; federate, associate; fraternize; cement a union, marry, wed, couple, pair, ally.

Adj. combined &c. *v.*; conjunctive, conjugate, conjoint, allied, confederate; impregnated with, ingrained, inoculated.

V. make -loose &c. *adj.*; loosen slacken, relax; un-glue &c. 46; detach &c. (*disjoin*) 44.

Adj. non-adhesive, immiscible; incoherent, detached, loose, slack, baggy, lax, relaxed, flapping, streaming; dishevelled; segregated, like grains of sand; un-consolidated &c. 321, -combined &c. 48; non-cohesive.

49. Decomposition.—N. decomposition, analysis, diæresis, dissection, resolution, catalysis, electrolysis, hydrolysis, photolysis, dissolution; dispersion &c. 73; disjunction &c. 44; disintegration, decay, rot, putrefaction, putrescence, caries, necrosis, corruption &c. (*uncleanness*) 653.

V. decom-pose, -pound; analyze, disembody, dissolve; resolve –, separate-into its elements; electrolyze; dissect, decentralize, break up; disintegrate; disperse &c. 73; unravel &c. (*unroll*) 313; crumble into dust; decay &c. *n.*; deteriorate &c. 659.

Adj. decomposed &c. *v.*; catalytic, analytical.

4°. Concrete Quantity

50. Whole. [Principal part.]**—N.** whole, totality, integrity; totalness &c. *adj.*; entirety, *ensemble*, collectiveness; unity &c. 87; completeness &c. 52; indivisibility, indiscerptibility; integration, embodiment; integer, integral.

all, the whole, total, aggregate, one and all, gross amount, sum, sum-total, *tout ensemble*, length and breadth of, Alpha and Omega, 'be all and end all,' lock, stock and barrel.

bulk, mass, lump, tissue, staple, body, torso, *compages*; trunk, bole, hull, hulk, skeleton; greater –, major

51. Part.—N. part, portion; dose; item, particular; aught, any; division, ward; subdivision, section; chapter, verse; article, clause, count, paragraph, passage; phrase; number, volume, book, fascicule; sector, segment; fraction, fragment; cantle, -t; frustum; detachment, parcel, unit, class &c. 75.

piece, lump, bit; cut, -ting; chip, chunk, collop, slice, scale, shard; lamina &c. 204; moiety; small part; morsel, scrap, crumb; particle &c. (*smallness*) 32; instalment, dividend; share &c. (*allotment*) 786.

–, best –, principal –, main- part; essential part &c. (*importance*) 642; lion's share, Benjamin's mess; the long and the short; nearly –, almost- all.

V. form –, constitute- a whole; integrate, embody, amass; aggregate &c. (*assemble*) 72; amount to, come to.

Adj. whole, total, integral, entire; complete &c. 52; one, individual.

un-broken, -cut, -divided, -severed, -clipped, -cropped, -shorn; seamless; undiminished; un-demolished, -dissolved, -destroyed, -bruised.

in-divisible, -dissoluble, -dissolvable, -discerptible.

wholesale, sweeping, comprehensive.

Adv. wholly, altogether; totally &c. (*completely*) 52; entirely, all, all in all, considering all things, in a body, collectively, all put together; in the -aggregate, – lump, – mass, – gross, – main, – long run; *en masse*, on the whole, as a whole, bodily, *en bloc*, *in extenso*, throughout, every inch; substantially.

débris, odds and ends, oddments, *detritus*; *excerpta*; member, limb, lobe, lobule, arm, wing, scion, branch, bough, joint, link, offshoot, ramification, twig, stipule, tendril, bush, spray, sprig; runner; leaf, -let; stump; constituent, ingredient, component part &c. 56.

compartment; department &c. (*class*) 75; county &c. (*region*) 181.

V. part, divide, break &c. (*disjoin*) 44; partition &c. (*apportion*) 786.

Adj. fractional, fragmentary; sectional, aliquot; divided &c. *v.*; in compartments, multifid, incomplete, partial, divided &c. 44.

Adv. partly, in part, partially; piecemeal, part by part; by -instalments, – snatches, – inches, – driblets; bit by bit, inch by inch, foot by foot, drop by drop; in -detail, – lots.

---

52. Completeness.—N. completeness &c. *adj.*; completion &c. 729; integration; integrality.

entirety; universality; totality; perfection &c. 650; solid-ity, -arity; unity; all; *ne plus ultra*, ideal, limit.

complement, supplement, make-weight; filling up &c. *v.*

impletion; satur-ation, -ity; high water; high –, flood –, spring- tide; fill, load, bumper, bellyful; brimmer; sufficiency &c. 639.

V. be -complete &c. *adj.*; come to a head.

render -complete &c. *adj.*; complete &c. (*accomplish*) 729; fill, charge, load, replenish; make-up, – good; piece –, eke- out; supply deficiencies; fill -up, – in, – to the brim, – the measure of; saturate &c. 869.

go the whole -hog, – length, go all lengths.

Adj. complete, entire; whole &c. 50; perfect &c. 650; full, good, absolute, thorough, plenary; solid, undivided; with all its parts.

exhaustive, radical, sweeping, thorough-going; dead.

regular, consummate, unmitigated, sheer, unqualified, unconditional, free; abundant &c. (*sufficient*) 639.

53. Incompleteness.—N. incompleteness &c. *adj.*; deficiency, short -measure, – weight; shortcoming &c. 304; insufficiency &c. 640; imperfection &c. 651; immaturity &c. (*non-preparation*) 674; half measures.

[part wanting] defect, deficit, shortage, ullage, defalcation, omission, *caret*; interval &c. 198; break &c. (*discontinuity*) 70; non-completion &c. 730; missing link.

V. be -incomplete &c. *adj.*; fall short of &c. 304; lack &c. (*be insufficient*) 640; neglect &c. 460.

Adj. incomplete; imperfect &c. 651; unfinished; uncompleted &c. (*see* complete &c. 729); defective, deficient, wanting; failing; in -default, – arrear; short, – of; hollow, meagre, lame, half-and-half, perfunctory, sketchy; crude &c. (*unprepared*) 674.

mutilated, garbled, mangled, docked, lopped, truncated; bobtailed, cropped, bobbed, shingled.

in -progress, – hand; going on, proceeding.

Adv. incompletely &c. *adj.*; by halves.

Phr. *cætera desunt*; *caret*.

---

brimming; brim-, top-ful; chock –, choke- full; as full as -an egg is of meat, – a vetch, – a tick; saturated, crammed; replete &c. (*redundant*) 641; fraught, laden; full-laden, -fraught, -charged; heavy laden.

completing &c. *v.*; supplement-al, -ary; ascititious.

Adv. completely &c. *adj.*; altogether, outright, wholly, totally, *in toto*, quite; over head and ears; effectually, for good and all, nicely, fully, through thick and thin, head and shoulders; neck and -heel, – crop; all out; in -all respects, – every respect; at all points, out and out, to all intents and purposes; *toto cælo*; utterly, clean, – as a whistle; to the -full, – utmost, – backbone; hollow, stark; heart and soul, root and branch; down to the ground.

to the top of one's bent, as far as possible, *à outrance*.

throughout; from -first to last, – beginning to end, – end to end, – one end to the other, – Dan to Beersheba, – head to foot, – head to heels, – top to toe, – top to bottom; *de fond en comble*; *à fond, a capite ad calcem, ab ovo usque ad mala*, fore and aft; every -whit, – inch; *cap-à-pie*, to the end of the chapter; up to the -brim, – ears, – eyes; as . . . as can be.

on all accounts; *sous tous les rapports*; with a -vengeance, – witness.

---

54. Composition.—N. composition, constitution, crasis, synthesis; make-up; combination &c. 48; inclusion, admission, comprehension, reception; embodiment, formation, conformation, production.

compilation &c. 72; (*musical*) composition &c. 415; painting &c. 556; writing &c. 590; typography &c. 591.

V. be -composed, – made, – formed, – made up- of; consist of, be resolved into.

include &c. (*in a class*) 76; subsume; synthesize; contain, hold, comprehend, take in, admit, embrace, embody; involve; implicate, drag into.

compose, constitute, form, make; make –, fill –, build- up; weave, construct, fabricate; compile; write, draw; set up (*printing*); enter into the composition of &c. (*be a component*) 56.

Adj. containing, constituting &c. *v.*

---

56. Component.—N. component; component –, integral –, integrant- part; element, constituent, ingredient, leaven; part and parcel; contents; appurtenance; feature; member &c. (*part*) 51; personnel.

V. enter into, – the composition of; be a -component &c. *n.*; be –, form-part of; merge –, be merged- in; be

55. Exclusion.—N. exclusion, non-admission, omission, exception, rejection, repudiation; exile &c. (*seclusion*) 893; preclusion, lock out, ostracism, prohibition; disbarment, expulsion, ban.

separation, segregation, seposition, elimination, coffer-dam.

V. be excluded from &c.

exclude, bar, ban; leave –, shut –, thrust –, bar- out; reject, repudiate, spurn, blackball; ostracize, boycott; lay –, put –, set -apart, – aside; relegate, segregate; throw overboard; strike -off, – out; neglect &c. 460; banish &c. (*seclude*) 893; separate &c. (*disjoin*) 44.

pass over, omit; garble; eliminate, weed, winnow.

Adj. excluding &c. *v.*; exclusive.

excluded &c. *v.*; unrecounted, not included in; inadmissible; preventive, interdictive.

Adv. exclusive of, barring; except; with the exception of; save, bating.

---

57. Extraneousness.—N. extraneous-ness &c. *adj.*; extrinsicality &c. 6; exteriority &c. 220; alienism.

foreign -body, – substance, – element; alien, stranger, intruder, interloper, foreigner, tramontane, *novus homo*, new comer, immi-, emi-grant; creole, Afrikander; outsider, outlander, tenderfoot.

implicated in; share in &c. (*participate*) 778; belong –, appertain- to.

form, make, constitute, compose.

Adj. forming &c. *v.*; inclusive; inherent &c. 5.

Adj. extraneous, foreign, alien, ulterior; exterior, external, outside, outlandish; oversea; tra-, ultra-montane.

excluded &c. 55; inadmissible; exceptional.

Adv. in foreign -parts, – lands; abroad, beyond seas, overseas.

Section IV. ORDER

1°. Order in General

58. Order.—**N.** order, regularity &c. 80; uniformity, symmetry, *lucidus ordo*; harmony, music of the spheres.

gradation, progression; series &c. (*continuity*) 69.

subordination; course, even tenor, routine; method, disposition, arrangement, array, system, economy, discipline; orderliness &c. *adj.*

rank, place, &c. (*term*) 71.

V. be –, become- in order &c. *adj.*; form, fall in, draw up; arrange –, range –, place- itself; adjust; fall into –, take- -one's place, – rank; rally round; arrange &c. 60.

Adj. orderly, regular; in -order, – trim, – apple-pie order, according to Cocker, – its proper place, neat, neat as a pin, tidy, *en règle*, well regulated, correct, methodical, uniform, symmetrical, ship-shape, business-like, systematic; habitual; unconfused &c. (*see* confuse &c. 61) arranged &c. 60.

Adv. in order; methodically &c. *adj.*; in -turn, – its turn; step by step; by regular -steps, – gradations, – stages, – intervals; *seriatim*, systematically, by clockwork, *gradatim*; at stated periods &c. (*periodically*) 138.

---

59. [Absence, or want of Order, &c.; **Disorder.**—**N.** disorder; derangement &c. 61; irregularity; anomaly &c. (*unconformity*) 83; anar-chy, -chism; want of method; dishevelment, untidiness &c. *adj.*; disunion; discord &c. 24.

confusion; confusedness &c. *adj.*; disarray, jumble, mix-up, huddle, litter, lumber; *cahotage*; farrago; mess, muss, mash, muddle, hash; hotchpotch; *imbroglio*, chaos, *omnium gatherum*, medley; mere -mixture &c. 41; fortuitous concourse of atoms, *disjecta membra*, *rudis indigestaque moles*.

complexity; complexness &c. *adj.*; com-, im-plication; intri-cacy, -cation; perplexity; network, maze, labyrinth; wilderness, jungle; involution, ravelling, entanglement; coil &c. (*convolution*) 248; sleave, tangled skein, knot, Gordian knot, kink, web; wheels within wheels.

turmoil; ferment, &c. (*agitation*) 315; to do, trouble, pudder, pother, row, disturbance, convulsion, tumult, pandemonium, uproar, riot, rumpus, stour, scramble, *fracas*, embroilment, *mêlée*, spill and pelt, rough and tumble; whirlwind &c. 349; bear garden, Babel, Saturnalia, Donnybrook Fair, confusion worse confounded, most admired disorder, *concordia discors*; Bedlam –,

hell- broke loose; bull in a china shop; all the fat in the fire, *diable à quatre*, Devil to pay; pretty kettle of fish; pretty piece of -work, – business.

slattern, slut, sloven, draggle-tail.

V. be -disorderly &c. *adj.*; ferment, play at cross purposes.

put out of order; derange &c. 61; ravel &c. 219; ruffle, rumple; bungle, botch.

Adj. disorderly, orderless; out of -order, – place, – gear, – whack; irregular, desultory; anomalous &c. (*unconformable*) 83; acephalous, disorganized, straggling; un-, im-methodical; unsymmetric; unsystematic; untidy, slovenly, bedraggled, messy; dislocated; out of sorts; promiscuous, indiscriminate; chaotic, anarchical, lawless; unarranged &c. 60; confused, tumultuous, turbulent, tempestuous; deranged &c. 61; topsy turvy &c. (*inverted*) 218; shapeless &c. 241; disjointed, out of joint.

com-plex, -plexed; intricate, complicated, perplexed, involved, ravelled, entangled, knotted, tangled, inextricable; irreducible.

troublous; riotous &c. (*violent*) 173.

Adv. irregularly &c. *adj.*; by fits and -snatches, – starts; pell-mell; higgledy-piggledy; helter-skelter, harum-scarum; in a ferment; at -sixes and sevens, – cross purposes; upside down &c. 218.

Phr. the cart before the horse, chaos is come again.

---

60. [Reduction to Order.] **Arrangement.—N.** arrangement; plan &c. 626; preparation &c. 673; dispos-al, -ition; col-, al-location; distribution; sorting &c. *v.*; assortment, allotment; grouping; apportionment, *taxis*, taxonomy, *syn-taxis*, graduation, organization, grading; re-organization, rationalization.

analysis, classification, division, digestion; systematism.

[Result of arrangement] order, orderliness, form, array; digest, synopsis &c. (*compendium*) 596; *syntagma*, table, atlas; register &c. (*record*) 551; score &c. 415; cosmos, organism, architecture.

[Instrument for sorting] sieve &c. 260; file, card index.

V. reduce to –, bring into- order; introduce order into; rally.

arrange, dispose, place, form; put –, set –, place- in order; straighten up, tidy up; set out, collocate, allocate, pack, marshal, range, size, rank, array, group, parcel out, allot, space, distribute, deal; cast –, assign- the parts; dispose of, assign places to; assort, sort; sift, riddle; put –, set- -to rights, – into shape, – in trim, – in array.

class, -ify; divide; file, string together, thread; register &c. (*record*) 551; list, catalogue, tabulate, index, alphabeticize, graduate, digest, grade, codify; orchestrate, score.

methodize, regulate, systematize, standardize, co-ordinate, organize, settle, fix.

unravel, disentangle, ravel, card; disembroil.

Adj. arranged &c. *v.*; embattled, in battle array; cut and dried; methodical, orderly, regular, systematic, tabular.

61. [Subversion of Order; bringing into disorder.] **Derangement.—N.** derangement &c. *v.*; disorder &c. 59; evection, discomposure, disturbance; dis-, de-organization; involvement; dislocation; perturbation, interruption; shuffling &c. *v.*; inversion &c. 218; corrugation &c. (*fold*) 258; insanity &c. 503.

V. derange; dis-, mis-arrange; dis-, mis-place; mislay, discompose, disorder, de-, dis-organize; embroil, unsettle, disturb, confuse, trouble, perturb, jumble, tumble; huddle, shuffle, muddle, toss, hustle, fumble, riot; bring –, put –, throw- into -disorder &c. 59; break the ranks, disconcert, convulse; break in upon.

unhinge, dislocate, put out of joint, throw out of gear.

turn topsy-turvy &c. (*invert*) 218; bedevil; complicate, involve, perplex, confound; im-, em-brangle; tangle, en-tangle, ravel, tousle, dishevel, ruffle, rumple &c. (*fold*) 258; dement.

litter, scatter; mix &c. 41.

Adj. deranged &c. *v.*; syncre-tic, -tistic.

---

[23]

2°. Consecutive Order

62. Precedence.—N. precedence; coming before &c. *v.*; the lead, *le pas*; superiority &c. 33; importance &c. 642; anteced-ence, -ency; anteriority &c. (*front*) 234; precursor &c. 64; priority &c. 116; precession &c. 280; anteposition, preference.

V. precede; come -before, – first; forerun, head, lead, take the lead; lead the -way, – dance; introduce, usher in; have the *pas*; set the fashion &c. (*influence*) 175; lead off, kick off, open the ball; take –, have- precedence; outrank; have the start &c. (*get before*) 280.

place before; prefix; premise, prelude, preface.

Adj. preceding &c. *v.*; pre-, antecedent; anterior; prior &c. 116; before; former, foregoing; before-, above-mentioned; aforesaid, said; precurs-ory, -ive; prevenient, preliminary, prefatory, introductory; prelus-ive, -ory; proemial, preparatory.

Adv. before; in advance &c. (*precession*) 280.

Phr. *seniores priores.*

64. Precursor.—N. precursor, antecedent, precedent, predecessor; forerunner, van-courier, *avant-coureur*, pioneer, prodrome, *prodromos*, outrider; leader, bell-wether; herald, harbinger; dawn.

prelude, preamble, preface, prologue, foreword, *avant-propos*, *protasis*, prolusion, proem, *prolepsis*, *prolegomena*, prefix, introduction; lead, heading, frontispiece, groundwork; preparation &c. 673; overture, voluntary, *exordium*, symphony, *ritornello*; premises.

prefigurement &c. 511; omen &c. 512.

Adj. precursory; prelu-sive, -sory, -dious; proemial, introductory, prefatory, prodromous, inaugural, preliminary; precedent &c. (*prior*) 116.

66. Beginning.—N. beginning, commencement, opening, outset, incipience, inception, inchoation; introduction &c. (*precursor*) 64; *alpha*; initial; foundation; inauguration, *début*, *le premier pas*, embarcation, rising of the curtain; zero hour; exordium, curtain raiser; maiden speech; prelude; outbreak, onset, brunt; initiative, move, first move; gambit, narrow –, thin-

63. Sequence.—N. sequence, coming after; going after &c. (*following*) 281; consecution, succession; posteriority &c. 117.

continuation; prolongation, order of succession; successiveness; Elijah's mantle.

secondariness; subordinancy &c. (*inferiority*) 34.

V. succeed; come -after, – on, – next; follow, ensue, step into the shoes of; alternate.

place after, suffix, append.

Adj. succeeding &c. *v.*; sequent; sub-, con-sequent; sequacious, proximate, next; consecutive &c. (*continuity*) 69; alternate, amœbæan.

latter; posterior &c. 117.

Adv. after, subsequently; behind &c. (*rear*) 235.

_____

65. Sequel.—N. sequel, suffix, successor; tail, *queue*, train, wake, trail, rear; retinue, suite; appendix, postscript, subscript; epilogue; conclusion; peroration; codicil; continuation, *sequela*; appendage &c. 39; tail –, heelpiece; tag, more last words; *colophon*.

follower, after-glow, -growth, -crop, -taste, -math.

after-part, -piece, -course, -thought, -game; *arrière pensée*, second thoughts.

_____

67. End.—N. end, close, termination; desinence, conclusion, *finis*, *finale*, period, term, *terminus*, last, *omega*; extreme, -tremity; gable –, butt –, fagend; tip, nib, point; tail &c. (*rear*) 235; verge &c. (*edge*) 231; tag, epilogue, peroration; *bonne bouche*; bitter end, tail end; terminal; *apodosis*; appendix.

consummation, *dénouement*; finish &c. (*completion*) 729; fate; doom, -sday;

end of the wedge; fresh start, new departure; forefront.

origin &c. (*cause*) 153; source, rise; bud, germ &c. 153; egg, rudiment; genesis, birth, nativity, cradle, infancy, incunabula; start, starting-point &c. 293; dawn &c. (*morning*) 125.

title-page; head, -ing, caption; van &c. (*front*) 234.

en-trance, -try; inlet, orifice, mouth, chops, lips, porch, portal, portico, *propylon*, door; gate, -way; postern, wicket, threshold, vestibule; skirts, border &c. (*edge*) 231; tee.

first -stage, – blush, – glance, – impression, – sight.

rudiments, elements, outlines, *principia*, grammar, *protasis*; alphabet, ABC.

V. begin, commence, inchoate, rise, arise, originate, institute, conceive, initiate, open, dawn, set in, take its rise, enter upon, start; enter; set out &c. (*depart*) 293; embark in.

usher in; lead -off, – the way; take the -lead, – initiative; inaugurate, head; stand -at the head, – first, – for; lay the foundations &c. (*prepare*) 673; found &c. (*cause*) 153; set -up, – on foot, – agoing, – abroach, – the ball in motion; apply the match to a train; launch, broach; open -up, – the door to; set -about, – to work; make a -beginning, – start; handsel; take the first step, lay the first stone, cut the first turf; break -ground, – the ice, – cover; pass –, cross- the Rubicon; open -fire, – the ball; ventilate, air; undertake &c. 676.

come into -existence, – the world; make one's *début*, take birth; burst forth, break out; spring –, crop- up.

begin -at the beginning, – *ab ovo*, – again, – *de novo*; start afresh, make a fresh start, shuffle the cards, resume, recommence.

Adj. beginning &c. *v.*; initi-al, -atory, -ative; inceptive, introductory, incipient; proemial, inaugural; incho-ate, -ative; embryonic, rudimental; primogenial; primeval &c. (*old*) 124; rudimentary, aboriginal; natal, nascent.

first, foremost, front, leading, head; maiden.

begun &c. *v.*; just -begun &c. *v.*

Adv. at –, in- the beginning &c. *n.*; first, in the first place, *imprimis*, first and foremost; *in limine*; in -the bud, – embryo, – its infancy; from -the beginning, – its birth; *ab -initio*, – *ovo*, – *incunabilis*, primarily, originally.

crack of doom, day of Judgment, fall of the curtain, wind-up; goal, destination; limit, stoppage, end all, determination; expiration, expiry; death &c. 360; end of all things; finality; eschatology.

break up, *commencement de la fin*, last stage, turning point; *coup de grâce*, death-blow; knock-out.

V. end, close, finish, terminate, conclude, be all over; expire; die &c. 360; come –, draw- to a -close &c. *n.*; have run its course; run out, pass away.

bring to an -end &c. *n.*; put an end to, make an end of; determine; get through; achieve &c. (*complete*) 729; stop &c. (*make to cease*) 142; shut up shop.

Adj. ending &c. *v.*; final, terminal, definitive, conclusive; crowning &c. (*completing*) 729; last, ultimate; hindermost; rear &c. 235; caudal.

contermin-ate, -ous, -able.

ended &c. *v.*; at an end; settled, decided, over, played out, set at rest.

penultimate; last but -one, – two, &c.

unbegun, uncommenced; fresh.

Adv. finally &c. *adj.*; in fine; at the last; once for all.

---

68. Middle.—N. middle, midst, mediety; mean &c. 29; medium, middle term; centre &c. 222, mid-course &c. 628; *mezzo termine*; *juste milieu* &c. 628; half-way house, nave, navel, omphalos; nucle-us, -olus.

equidistance, bisection, half-distance; equator, diaphragm, midriff; interjacence &c. 228.

Adj. middle, medial, mesial, mean, mid; middle-, mid-most; middling; mediate; intermediate &c. (*interjacent*) 228; equidistant; central &c. 222; mediterranean, equatorial.

Adv. in the middle; in the thick; mid-, half-way; midships, *in medias res.*

69. [Uninterrupted sequence.] **Continuity.**—**N.** continuity; consecu-tion, -tiveness &c. *adj.*; succession, round, suite, progression, series, train, chain; cat-, concat-enation; catena; scale; gradation, course, constant flow, perpetuity.

procession, column; retinue, *cortège*, cavalcade, rank and file, line of battle, array.

pedigree, genealogy, lineage, race &c. 166.

rank, file, line, row, range, tier, string, thread, team; suit; colonnade.

V. follow in –, form- a series &c. *n.*; fall in.

arrange in a -series &c. *n.*; string together, catenate, file, thread, gradu-ate, tabulate.

Adj. continu-ous, -ed; consecutive; progressive, gradual; serial, successive; immediate, unbroken, entire; linear; in a -line, – row &c. *n.*; uninter-rupted, -mitting; unremitting; perennial, ever-green; constant.

Adv. continuously &c. *adj.*; *seriatim*; in a -line &c. *n.*; in -succession, – turn; running, gradually, step by step, *gradatim*, at a stretch; in -file, – column, – single file, – Indian file.

70. [Interrupted sequence.] **Discon-tinuity.**—**N.** discontinuity; disjunction &c. 44; anacoluthon; interruption, break, fracture, flaw, fault, split, crack, cut; gap &c. (*interval*) 198; solution of continuity, *cæsura*; broken thread; parenthesis, episode; rhapsody, patch-work; intermission; alternation &c. (*periodicity*) 138; dropping fire.

V. be -discontinuous &c. *adj.*; alter-nate, intermit.

discontinue, pause, interrupt; inter-vene; break, – in upon; interpose &c. 228; break –, snap- the thread; dis-connect &c. (*disjoin*) 44.

Adj. discontinuous, unsuccessive, broken, interrupted, *décousu*; dis-, un-connected, discrete, disjunctive; fitful &c. (*irregular*) 139; spasmodic, desultory, intermit-ting &c. *v.*, -tent; alternate; recurrent &c. (*periodic*) 138; few and far between.

Adv. at intervals; by -snatches, – jerks, – skips, – catches, – fits and starts; skippingly, *per saltum*; *longo intervallo.*

71. Term.—**N.** term, rank, station, stage, step; degree &c. 26; scale, remove, grade, link, peg, round –, rung- of the ladder, *status*, position, place, point, mark, *pas*, period, pitch; stand, -ing; footing, range.

V. hold –, occupy –, fall into- a place &c. *n.*

3°. COLLECTIVE ORDER

72. Assemblage.—**N.** assemblage; col-lection, -location, -ligation; com-pilation, levy, gathering, ingathering, mobilization, meet, foregathering, mus-ter, *attroupement*; con-course, -flux, -gregation, -tesseration, -vergence &c. 290; meeting, *levée*, *réunion*, drawing room, at home; conversazione &c. (*social gathering*) 892; assembly, con-gress, eisteddfod; conven-tion, -ticle;

73. Non-assemblage. Dispersion.—**N.** dispersion; disjunction &c. 44; divergence &c. 291; scattering &c. *v.*; dissemination, broadcasting, diffusion, dissipation, distribution; apportion-ment &c. 786; spread, respersion, cir-cumfusion, interspersion, spargefaction.

waifs and estrays, flotsam and jet-sam, *disjecta membra.*

V. disperse, scatter, sow, dissemi-

gemote; conclave, &c. (*council*) 696; posse, *posse comitatûs*; Noah's ark.

miscellany, *collectanea*, symposium; museum, menagerie, &c. (*store*) 636.

crowd, throng, multitude; flood, rush, deluge; rout, rabble, mob, press, crush, *cohue*, jam, horde, body, tribe; crew, gang, knot, squad, band, party; swarm, shoal, school, covey, flock, herd, drove, kennel; array, bevy, galaxy; *corps*, company, troop, *troupe*; army, force, regiment, &c. (*combatants*) 726; host &c. (*multitude*) 102; populousness.

clan, brotherhood, association &c. (*party*) 712.

volley, shower, storm, cloud.

group, cluster, Pleiades, clump, pencil; set, batch, lot, pack; budget, *dossier*, assortment, bunch; parcel; pack-et, -age; bundle, *fasciculus*, fascine, bale; ser-on, -oon; faggot, wisp, truss, tuft; shock, rick, fardel, stack, sheaf, swath, gavel, haycock, stook.

accumulation &c. (*store*) 636; congeries, heap, lump, pile, *rouleau*, tissue, mass, pyramid; drift; snow-ball, -drift; acervation, cumulation; amassment, glom-, agglom-eration; conglobation; conglomeration, -ate; coacervation, coagmentation, aggregation, concentration, congestion, *omnium gatherum*, *spicilegium*, black hole of Calcutta; quantity &c. (*greatness*) 31.

collector, gatherer; whip, -per in.

V. [be or come together] assemble, collect, muster; meet, unite, join, rejoin; cluster, flock, swarm, surge, stream, herd, crowd, throng, associate; con-gregate, -glomerate, -centrate; centre round, *rendezvous*, resort; come –, flock –, get –, pig- together; forgather; huddle; reassemble.

[get or bring together] assemble, muster, mobilize; bring –, get –, put –, draw –, scrape –, lump- together; col-lect, -locate, -ligate; get –, whip- in; gather; hold a meeting; con-vene, -voke, -vocate; rake up, dredge; heap, mass, pile; pack, put up, truss, cram; acervate; ag-glomerate, -gregate; compile; group, aggroup, concentrate, unite; collect –, bring- into a focus; amass, accumulate &c. (*store*) 636; collect in a drag-net; heap Ossa upon Pelion.

Adj. assembled &c. *v.*; closely packed, dense, serried, crowded to suffocation, teeming, swarming, populous; as thick as hops; all of a heap, fasciculated; cumulative.

Phr. the plot thickens.

74. [Place of meeting.] **Focus.**—**N.** focus; point of- convergence &c. 290; corradiation; centre &c. 222; gathering-place, resort; haunt; retreat; *venue, rendezvous*; rallying point, head-quarters, home, club; *dépôt* &c. (*store*) 636; tryst, trysting-place; place of -meeting, – resort, – assignation; *point de –, lieu de- réunion*; issue.

V. bring to- a point, – a focus, – an issue; focus.

4°. Distributive Order

75. Class.—**N.** class, category, *categorema*, head, order, sec-

nate, radiate, diffuse, shed, spread, ted, bestrew, overspread, dispense, disband, disembody, demobilize, dismember, distribute; apportion &c. 786; blow off, let out, dispel, cast forth, draught off; strew, straw, strow; spirtle, cast, sprinkle, shatter; issue, deal out, retail, utter; re-, inter-sperse; set abroach, circumfuse.

turn –, cast- adrift; scatter to the winds; sow broadcast.

spread like wildfire, disperse themselves.

Adj. unassembled &c. (*see* assemble &c. 72); dispersed &c. *v.*; sparse, dispread, broadcast, sporadic, widespread; far-flung; epidemic &c. (*general*) 78; adrift, stray; dishevelled, streaming.

Adv. *sparsim*, here and there, *passim*.

tion; division, subdivision; department, province, domain, sphere.

kind, sort, genus, species, variety, branch, family, race, tribe, caste, sept, clan, breed; *clique, coterie*; type, kit, sect, set; assortment; feather, kidney; suit; range; gender, sex, kin.

manner, description, denomination, persuasion, connection, designation, character, stamp; predicament; conviction &c. 484.

similarity &c. 17.

76. Inclusion. [Comprehension under, or reference to a class.]—**N.** inclusion, admission, incorporation, comprehension, reception.

composition &c. (*inclusion in a compound*) 54.

V. be -included in &c.; come –, fall –, range- under; belong –, pertain- to; range with; merge in.

include, compromise, comprehend, contain, admit, embrace, receive; enclose &c. (*circumscribe*) 229; incorporate, cover, embody, encircle.

reckon –, enumerate –, number- among; refer to; place –, arrange- under, – with; take into account.

Adj. includ-ed, -ing &c. *v.*; inclusive; comprehensive, all-embracing; congen-er, -erous: of the same -class &c. 75.

Phr. *et hoc genus omne*, &c.; *et cætera*.

77. Exclusion.*—N. exclusion &c. 55.

_____

78. Generality. — N. general-ity, -ization; universality; catholic-ity, -ism; miscel-lany, -laneousness; drag-net.

every-one, -body; all hands, all the world and his wife; any body, N or M, all sorts; *tout le monde*.

prevalence, run.

V. be -general &c. *adj.*; prevail, obtain, be going about, stalk abroad.

render -general &c. *adj.*; generalize; spread, broadcast.

Adj. general, usual, current, generic, collective; broad, comprehensive, sweeping; encyclopedical, panoramic, widespread &c. (*dispersed*) 73.

universal; catho-lic, -lical; common, world-wide; œ-, e-cumenical; transcendental; prevalent, prevailing, rife, epidemic, besetting; all over, covered with.

every, all; indeterminate, indefinite, unspecified, impersonal.

customary &c. (*habitual*) 613.

Adv. what-ever, -soever; to a man, one and all, without exception.

generally &c. *adj.*; always, for better

79. Speciality.—N. speciality, *spécialité*; individ-uality, -uity; particularity, peculiarity; idiocrasy &c. (*tendency*) 176; personality, characteristic, mannerism, idiosyncrasy, attribute specific-ness &c. *adj.*; singularity &c. (*unconformity*) 83; reading, version, lection; state; *trait*; distinctive feature; technicality; *differentia*.

particulars, details, minutiæ, items, counts.

I, self, I myself, *ego*; my-, him-, her-, it-self.

V. specify, particularize, individualize, realize, specialize, designate, differentiate, determine, define, denote, indicate, itemize, detail.

descend to particulars, enter into detail, come to the point.

Adj. special, particular, individual, specific, proper, personal, intimate, original, private, respective, definite, concrete, determinate, especial, certain, esoteric, endemic, partial, party, peculiar, marked, appropriate, several, characteristic, diagnostic, exact, exclusive; singular &c. (*exceptional*) 83;

_____

* The same set of words is used to express *Exclusion from a class* and *Exclusion from a compound.* Reference is therefore made to the former at 55. This identity does not occur with regard to *Inclusion*, which therefore constitutes a separate category.

for worse; in general, generally speaking; speaking generally; for the most part; in the long run &c. (*on an average*) 29.

---

idiomatic; typical, representative, distinctive.

this, that; yon, -der.

Adv. specially &c. *adj.*; in particular, *in propriâ personâ*; *ad hominem*; for my part.

each, apiece, one by one; severally, respectively, each to each; *seriatim*, in detail, bit by bit; *pro hac vice, – re natâ*.

namely, that is to say, *videlicet*, viz.; to wit.

5°. Order as regards Categories

80. Rule.—N. regularity, uniformity &c. 16; clock-work precision; punctuality &c. (*exactness*) 494; routine &c. (*custom*) 613; formula; system; rut; canon, convention, maxim; rule &c. (*form, regulation*) 697; key-note, standard, model; precedent &c. (*prototype*) 22; conformity &c. 82.

nature, principle; law; order of things; normal -, natural -, ordinary -, model- -state, - condition; standing -dish, - order; normality; Procrustean law; law of the Medes and Persians; hard and fast rule.

Adj. regular, uniform, symmetrical, constant, steady; according to rule &c. (*conformable*) 82; customary &c. 613; orderly &c. 58.

81. Multiformity.—N. multi-, omniformity; variety, diversity; multifariousness &c. *adj.*

Adj. multi-form, -fold, -farious, -generous; multiplex, variform, manifold, many-sided, multiplicate; omni-form, -genous, -farious; polymorphic; protean; heterogeneous, motley, mosaic; epicene, indiscriminate, desultory, irregular, diversified, different, divers; all manner of; of -every description, - all sorts and kinds; *et hoc genus omne*; and what not? *de omnibus rebus et quibusdam aliis*.

82. Conformity.—N. conform-ity, -ance; observance.

naturalization; conventionality &c. (*custom*) 613; agreement &c. 23.

example, instance, specimen, sample, quotation; exemplification, illustration, case in point; object lesson.

conventionalist, formalist, Philistine.

pattern &c. (*prototype*) 22.

V. conform to, - rule; accommodate -, adapt- oneself to; rub off corners.

be -regular &c. *adj.*; move in a groove; follow -, observe -, go by -, bend to -, obey- -rules, - precedents; comply -, tally -, chime in -, fall in with; be -guided, - regulated- by; fall into a -custom, - usage; follow the -fashion, - multitude; pass muster, do as others do, *hurler avec les loups*; do at Rome as the Romans do; go -, swim- with the -stream, - current, - tide; tread the beaten track &c. (*habit*) 613; rubber-stamp; keep one in countenance.

exemplify, illustrate, cite, quote, put

83. Unconformity.—N. non-conformity &c. 82; un-, dis-conformity; unconventionality, informality, abnormity, anomaly; anomalousness &c. *adj.*; exception, peculiarity, &c. 79; infraction -, breach -, violation -, infringement- of -law, - custom, - usage; eccentricity, *bizarrerie*, oddity, *je ne sais quoi*, monstrosity, rarity; freak of Nature.

individuality, idiosyncrasy, singularity, originality, mannerism.

aberration; irregularity; variety; singularity; exemption; salvo &c. (*qualification*) 469.

nonconformist; nondescript, character, original, nonsuch, monster, prodigy, wonder, miracle, curiosity, missing link, flying fish, black swan, *lusus naturæ*, *rara avis*, queer fish; mongrel; half-caste, -blood, -breed; *métis*, cross breed, hybrid, mule, mulatto, sacatra, marabou; *tertium quid*, hermaphrodite, gynander, androgyn.

phœnix, chimera, hydra, sphinx, minotaur; griff-in, -on; centaur; hippo-

a case; produce an- instance &c. *n.*

Adj. conformable to rule, adaptable, compliant, consistent, agreeable; regular &c. 80; according to -regulation, – rule, – Cocker; *en règle, selon les règles,* well regulated, orderly; symmetric &c. 242.

conventional, commonplace &c. (*customary*) 613; of -daily, – every day-occurrence; in the natural order of things; ordinary, common, – or garden, prosaic, habitual, usual.

in the order of the day; naturalized.

typical, normal, formal; canonical, orthodox, sound, strict, rigid, positive, uncompromising, Procrustean; point device.

secundum artem, ship-shape, technical. exemplary, illustrative, in point.

Adv. conformably &c. *adj.*; by rule; agreeably to; in -conformity, – accordance, – keeping- with; according to; consistently with; as usual, *ad instar, instar omnium; more -solito,* – *majorum.*

for the sake of conformity; of –, as a matter of- course; *pro formâ,* for form's sake, by the card; according to plan.

invariably &c. (*uniformly*) 16.

for -example, – instance; *exempli gratiâ; e.g.; inter alia.*

Phr. *cela va sans dire; ex pede Herculem, noscitur a sociis.*

griff, -centaur; sagittary; kraken, cockatrice, wyvern, roc, liver, dragon, sea-serpent; mermaid; unicorn; Cyclops, 'men whose heads do grow beneath their shoulders'; Teratology.

fish out of water; neither -one thing nor another, – fish flesh nor fowl nor good red herring; one in a -way, – thousand; out-cast, -law; Ishmael, pariah; oasis.

V. be -unconformable &c. *adj.*; leave the beaten -track, – path; infringe –, break –, violate- a -law, – habit, – usage, – custom; drive a coach and six through; stretch a point; have no business there; baffle –, beggar- all description.

Adj. unconformable, exceptional; abnorm-al, -ous; anomal-ous, -istic; out of -order, – place, – keeping, – tune, – one's element; irregular, arbitrary; lawless, informal, aberrant, stray, wandering, wanton; peculiar, exclusive, unnatural, eccentric, crotchety, egregious; out of the -beaten track, – common, – common run, – pale of; misplaced; funny.

un-usual, -accustomed, -customary, -wonted, -common; rare, singular, *unique,* curious, odd, extraordinary, strange, monstrous; wonderful &c. 870; unexpected, unaccountable; *outré,* out of the way, remarkable, noteworthy; queer, quaint, nondescript, none such, *sui generis;* original, unconventional, Bohemian, unfashionable; un-described, -precedented, -paralleled, -exampled, -heard of, -familiar; fantastic, new-fangled, grotesque, *bizarre;* outlandish, exotic, *tombé des nues,* preternatural; denaturalized.

heterogeneous, heteroclite, amorphous, mongrel, amphibious, epicene, half-blood, hybrid; androgyn-ous, -al; unsymmetric &c. 243.

qualified &c. 469.

Adv. unconformably &c. *adj.*; except, unless, save, barring, beside, without, save and except, let alone.

however, yet, but.

Int. what -on earth! – in the world!

Phr. never was -seen, – heard, – known- the like.

Section V. NUMBER

1°. Number, in the Abstract

84. Number.—N. number, symbol, numeral, figure, cipher, digit, integer; counter; round number; formula; function; series.

sum, total, aggregate, difference, complement, subtrahend; product; multipli-cand, -er, -cator; coefficient, multiple; dividend, divisor, factor, quotient, sub-multiple, fraction; mixed number; numerator, denominator; decimal, circulating decimal, repetend; common measure, aliquot part; reciprocal; prime number; totitive, totient.

permutation, combination, variation; election.

ratio, proportion; progression; arithmetical –, geometrical –, harmonical- progression; percentage.

figurate –, pyramidal –, polygonal- numbers.

power, root, exponent, index, logarithm, antilogarithm; modulus.

differential, integral, fluxion, fluent.

Adj. numeral, complementary, divisible, aliquot, reciprocal, prime, fractional, decimal, figurate, incommensurable.

proportional, exponential, logarithmic, logometric, differential, fluxional, integral.

positive, negative; rational, irrational; surd, radical, real, imaginary, impossible.

85. Numeration.—**N.** numeration; numbering &c. *v.*; pagination; tale, tally, recension, enumeration, summation, reckoning, computation, supputation; calcu-lation, -lus; algorithm, rhabdology, dactylonomy; measurement &c. 466; statistics.

arithmetic, analysis, algebra, fluxions; differential –, integral –, infinitesimal- calculus; calculus of differences.

[Statistics] dead reckoning, muster, poll, census, capitation, roll-call, recapitulation; account &c. (*list*) 86.

[Operations] notation, addition, subtraction, multiplication, division, proportion, rule of three, practice, equations, extraction of roots, reduction, involution, evolution, approximation, interpolation, differentiation, integration.

[Instruments] abacus, swan-pan, logometer, sliding –, slide- rule, tallies, Napier's bones, calculating –, adding- machine, difference engine; cash register.

arithmetician, calculator, abacist; mathematician, actuary, statistician, surveyor, geodesist.

V. number, count, tell; call –, run- over, take an account of, enumerate, call the roll, muster, poll, recite, recapitulate; sum; sum –, cast- up; tell off, score, cipher, compute, calculate, set a price, reckon, – up, estimate; suppute, add, subtract, multiply, divide, extract roots.

check, prove, demonstrate, balance, audit, overhaul, take stock; affix numbers to, page, foliate, paginate.

amount –, come- to.

Adj. numer-al, -ical; arithmetical, analytic, algebraic, statistical, numerable, computable, calculable; commensur-able, -ate; incommensur-able, -ate.

86. List.—**N.** list, catalogue, enumeration, inventory, schedule; register &c. (*record*) 551; account; bill, – of costs; syllabus; terrier, tally, file; almanac, calendar, index, table, atlas, contents, card index; rota, ticket; book, ledger; synopsis, *catalogue raisonné*; *tableau*; scroll, manifest, invoice, bill of lading; prospectus, *programme*; bill of fare, *menu*, *carte*; score, census, statistics, returns; Red –, Blue –, Domesday- book; *cadastre*; directory, gazetteer, dictionary, glossary, lexicon, thesaurus, gradus.

roll; check –, chequer –, bead- roll, – of honour; muster -roll, – book; roster, panel; cartulary, diptych.

V. list, enrol, schedule, register &c. *n.*; indent, post, docket; matriculate.

Adj. cadastral, listed &c. *v.*

2°. Determinate Number

87. Unity.—N. unity; oneness &c. *adj.*; individuality; solitude &c. (*seclusion*) 893; isolation &c. (*disjunction*) 44; unification &c. 48.

one, unit, ace; item; individual; solo, none else, no other, naught beside.

V. be -one, – alone &c. *adj.*; dine with Duke Humphrey.

isolate &c. (*disjoin*) 44.

render one; unite &c. (*join*) 43, (*combine*) 48.

Adj. one, sole, single, solitary, only-begotten; individual, apart, alone; kithless.

un-accompanied, -attended; *solus*, single-handed; singular, odd, unique, unrepeated, azygous, first and last; isolated &c. (*disjoined*) 44; insular; unitary.

lone; lone-ly, -some; desolate, dreary.

in-secable, -severable, -discerptible; compact, irresolvable.

Adv. singly &c. *adj.*; alone, by itself, *per se*, only, apart, in the singular number, in the abstract; one -by one, – at a time; simply; one and a half, *sesqui-*.

Phr. *natura il fece, e poi roppe la stampa.*

88. Accompaniment.—N. accompaniment; appurtenance, adjunct &c. 39; context.

coexistence, concomitance, company, association, companionship; part-, co-part-nership; coefficiency.

concomitant, accessory, coefficient; companion, attendant, fellow, associate, consort, spouse, colleague, *fidus Achates*; part-, co-part-ner; satellite, hanger on, shadow; escort, *entourage*, suite, *cortège*; convoy, follower &c. 65; attribute.

V. accompany, coexist, attend, convoy, chaperon; hang –, wait- on; go hand in hand with; synchronize &c. 120; bear –, keep- company; row in the same boat; bring in its train, associate –, couple- with.

Adj. accompanying &c. *v.*; concomitant, fellow, twin, joint; associated –, coupled- with; accessory, attendant, *obbligato.*

Adv. with, withal; together –, along –, in company- with; hand in hand, side by side; cheek by -jowl, – jole; arm in arm; there-, here-with; and &c. (*addition*) 37.

together, in a body, collectively.

---

89. Duality.—N. dual-ity, -ism; duplicity; bi-plicity, -formity; span, polarity.

two, deuce, couple, couplet, doublet, brace, pair, cheeks, twins, Castor and Pollux, *gemini*, Siamese twins; fellows; yoke, conjugation, dyad, distich.

V. [unite in pairs] pair, couple, bracket, yoke; conduplicate, mate.

Adj. two, twain; dual, -istic; binary, binomial; twin, biparous; dyadic; conduplicate; duplex &c. 90; *tête-à-tête*; paired; dihedral.

coupled &c. *v.*; conjugate.

both, – the one and the other.

90. Duplication.—N. duplication; doubling &c. *v.*; gemi-, ingemi-nation; reduplication; iteration &c. (*repetition*) 104; renewal.

V. double; re-double, -duplicate; geminate; repeat &c. 104; renew &c. 660; duplicate, copy &c. 21.

Adj. double; doubled &c. *v.*; bicameral, bicapital, bi-fold, -form, -lateral,

91. [Division into two parts.] **Bisection.—N.** bi-section, -partition; di-, subdi-chotomy; halving &c. *v.*; dimidiation; *hendiadis*.

bifurcation, forking, branching, furcation, ramification, divarication; fork, prong; fold.

half, moiety.

V. bisect, halve, divide, split, cut in

-farious, -facial; two-fold, -sided, -headed, -edged &c.; duplex; double-faced; twin, duplicate, ingeminate; second; dual &c. 29.

Adv. twice, once more; over again &c. (*repeatedly*) 104; as much again, twofold.

secondly, in the second place, again.

two, cleave, dimidiate, dichotomize, divaricate.

go halves, divide with.

separate, fork, bifurcate; branch -off, – out; ramify.

Adj. bisected &c. *v.*; cloven, cleft; bipartite, biconjugate, bicuspid, bifid; bifur-cous, -cate, -cated; semi-, demi-, hemi-.

92. Triality.—N. triality, trinity,* triplicity.

three, triad, triplet, trey, trio, ternion, trinomial, leash; tierce; triennium; trefoil, triangle, trident, tripod, triumvirate, *troika*.

third power, cube.

Adj. three; tri-form, -nal, -nomial; tertiary; triune.

93. Triplication.—N. tripli-cation, -city; trebleness, trine, trilogy.

V. treble, triple, triplicate, cube.

Adj. treble, triple; tern, -ary; triplex, triplicate, threefold, trilogistic; third; trinal; trihedral.

Adv. three -times, – fold; thrice, in the third place, thirdly; trebly &c. *adj.*

94. [Division into three parts.] Trisection. — N. tri-section, -partition, -chotomy; third, – part.

V. trisect, divide into three parts, trifurcate.

Adj. trifid; trisected &c. *v.*; tripartite, -chotomous, -sulcate.

95. Quaternity.—N. quaternity, four, tetrad, quartet, quaternion, square, quadrature, quarter, quadruplet; quadrilateral, quadrangle, quatrefoil; *quadriga*.

V. reduce to a square, square.

Adj. four; quat-ernary, -ernal; quadratic; quartile, quartic, tetractic, tetrad, tetrahedral; quadrennial; quadrivalent.

96. Quadruplication.—N. quadruplication.

V. multiply by four, quadruplicate, biquadrate.

Adj. fourfold; quad-ruple, -ruplicate, -rible; quadruplex; fourth.

Adv. four times; in the fourth place, fourthly.

97. [Division into four parts.] Quadrisection.—N. quadri-section, -partition; quartering &c. *v.*; fourth; quart, -er, -ern; farthing (*i.e.* fourthing); quarto.

V. quarter, divide into four parts, quadrisect.

Adj. quartered &c. *v.*; quadri-fid, -partite.

98. Five, &c.—N. five, cinque, quint, quincunx, quintuplet, quintet, pentagon, pentameter, Pentateuch; six, half-a-dozen, sextet, hexagon, hexameter; seven, Heptarchy; eight, octet, octagon, octave; nine, three times three; ten, decade; eleven; twelve, dozen; thirteen; long -, baker's- dozen.

twenty, score; twenty-four, four and twenty, two dozen; twenty-five, five and twenty, quarter of a hundred; forty, two score; fifty, half a hundred; sixty, three score, sexagenarian; seventy, three score and ten, septuagenarian; eighty, four score, octogenarian; ninety, four score and ten, nonagenarian.

99. Quinquesection, &c.—N. division by -five &c. 98; quinquesection &c.; fifth &c.; decimation.

V. decimate, quinquesect.

Adj. quinque-fid, -partite; quinquarticular; octifid; decimal, tenth, tithe, teind; duodecimal, twelfth; sexagesimal, -genary; hundredth, centesimal; millesimal &c.

* *Trinity* is hardly ever used except in a theological sense; *see* Deity 976.

hundred, centenary, hecatomb, century; hundredweight, cwt.; one hundred and forty-four, gross; bicentenary, tercentenary &c.

thousand, chiliad; myriad, millennium, ten thousand; lac, lakh, one hundred thousand, plum; million; thousand million, *milliard*.

billion, trillion &c.

V. centuriate.

Adj. five, quinary, quintuple; fifth; senary, sextuple; sixth; seventh; octuple; eighth; ninefold, ninth; tenfold, decimal, denary, decuple, tenth; eleventh; duo-denary, -denal; twelfth; in one's 'teens, thirteenth.

vices-, viges-imal; twentieth; twenty-fourth &c. *n.*

cent-uple, -uplicate, -ennial, -enary, -urial; secular, hundredth; thousandth; millenary &c.

3°. Indeterminate Number

100. [More than one.] **Plurality.—N.** plurality; a -number, – certain number; one or two, two or three &c.; a few, several; multitude &c. 102.

Adj. plural, more than one, upwards of, some, certain; not -alone &c. 87.

Adv. *et cætera,* &c., etc.

Phr. *non deficit alter.*

100a. [Less than one.] **Fraction.—N.** fraction, fractional part, fragment; part &c. 51.

Adj. fractional, fragmentary, partial.

101. Zero.—N. zero, nothing naught, nought, duck's egg, goose egg; cipher, none, nobody; not a soul; *âme qui vive*; absence &c. 187; unsubstantiality &c. 4.

Adj. not -one, – any.

102. Multitude.—N. multitude; numerousness &c. *adj.*; numer-osity, -ality; multiplicity; profusion &c. (*plenty*) 639; legion; host; great –, large –, round –, enormous- number; a quantity, numbers, array, sight, army, sea, galaxy; scores, peck, bushel, school, shoal, swarm, draft, bevy, cloud, flock, herd, drove, flight, covey, hive, brood, litter, farrow, fry, nest; mob, crowd &c. (*assemblage*) 72; lots, loads, heaps; all the world and his wife.

[Increase of number] greater number, majority; multiplication, multiple.

V. be -numerous &c. *adj.*; swarm –, teem –, crawl –, creep -with; crowd, swarm, come thick upon; outnumber, multiply; people; swarm like -locusts, – bees.

Adj. many, several, sundry, divers, various, not a few; a -hundred, – thousand, – myriad, – million, – thousand and one; some -ten or a dozen, – forty or fifty &c.; half a -dozen, – hundred &c.; very –, full –, ever so- many; numer-ous, -ose; profuse, in profusion; manifold, multiplied, multitudinous, multiferous, multiple, multinomial, teeming, crawling, populous, peopled, crowded, thick, studded; galore.

thick coming, many more, more than one can tell, a world of; no end -of, – to; *cum multis aliis*; thick as -hops, – hail; plenty as blackberries; numerous as the -stars in the firmament, – sands on

103. Fewness.—N. fewness &c. *adj.*; paucity, small number; small quantity &c. 32; scarcity, sparsity; rarity; infrequency &c. 137; handful; maniple; minority, exiguity.

[Diminution of number] reduction; weeding &c. *v.*; elimination, sarculation, decimation.

V. be -few &c. *adj.*

render -few &c. *adj.*; reduce, diminish the number, weed, eliminate, thin decimate.

Adj. few; scarce; scant, -y; thin, rare, thinly scattered, few and far between; exiguous; infrequent &c. 137; *rari nantes*; hardly –, scarcely- any; to be counted on one's fingers; reduced &c. *v.*; unrepeated.

Adv. here and there.

the sea-shore, – hairs on the head; and -what not, – heaven knows what; endless &c. (*infinite*) 105.

Phr. their name is 'Legion.'

104. Repetition.—N. repetition, iteration, reiteration, duplication, ding-dong, alliteration; *epistrophe*; harping, recurrence, succession, run; batto-, tauto-logy; monotony, tautophony; rhythm &c. 138; pleonasm, redundancy, diffuseness.

chimes, repetend, echo, *ritornello*, burden of a song, *refrain*; rehearsal; encore; *réchauffé, rifacimento*, recapitulation.

cuckoo &c. (*imitation*) 19; reverberation &c. 408; drumming &c. (*roll*) 407; renewal &c. (*restoration*) 660.

twice-told tale; old -story, – song, chestnut; second –, new- edition; reprint, new impression; return game, return match, reappearance, reproduction; periodicity &c. 138.

V. repeat, iterate, reiterate, reproduce, parrot, echo, re-echo, drum, harp upon, battologize, hammer, redouble.

recur, revert, return, reappear; renew &c. (*restore*) 660.

rehearse; do –, say- over again; ring the changes on; harp on the same string; din –, drum- in the ear; conjugate in all its moods, tenses and inflexions, begin again, go over the same ground, go the same round, never hear the last of; resume, return to, recapitulate, reword.

Adj. repeated &c. *v.*; repetition-al, -ary; recur-rent, -ring; ever recurring, thick coming; frequent, incessant, redundant, pleonastic, tautological.

monotonous, harping, iterative; mocking, chiming; retold; aforesaid, -named; above-mentioned, said; habitual &c. 613; another.

Adv. repeatedly, often, again, afresh, anew, over again, once more; ditto, *encore, de novo, bis, da capo*.

again and again; over and over, – again; many times over; time- and again, – after time; year after year; day by day &c.; many –, several –, a number of- times; many –, full many- a time; times out of number, year in and year out, morning, noon and night; frequently &c. 136.

Phr. *ecce iterum Crispinus, toujours perdrix,* cut and come again; 'tomorrow and tomorrow.'

105. Infinity.—N. infini-ty, -tude, -teness &c. *adj.*; perpetuity &c. 112.

V. be -infinite &c. *adj.*; know –, have- no -limits, – bounds; go on for ever.

Adj. infinite; immense; number-, count-, sum-, measure-less; in-numer-, immeasur-, incalcul-, illimit-, intermin-, unfathom-, unap-proach-able; exhaustless, inexhaustible, indefinite; without -number, – measure, – limit, – end; incomprehensible; limit-, end-, bound-, term-less; un-told, -numbered, -measured, -bounded, -limited; illimited; perpetual &c. 112.

Adv. infinitely &c. *adj.*; *ad infinitum*.

Section VI. Time

1°. Absolute Time

106. Time.—N. time, duration; period, term, stage, space, span, spell, season; the whole -time, – period; course &c. 109.

107. Neverness.*—N. 'neverness'; absence of time, no time; *dies non*; Tib's eve; Greek Kalends.

Adv. never; at no -time, – period;

* A term introduced by Bishop Wilkins.

intermediate time, while, *interim*, interval, bit, pendency; inter-vention, -mission, -mittence, -regnum, -lude; respite.

era, epoch, æon, cycle; time of life, age, year, date; decade &c. (*period*) 108; moment, &c. (*instant*) 113; reign &c. 737.

glass –, ravages –, whirligig –, noiseless foot- of time; scythe.

V. continue, last, endure, go on, hold out, remain, stay, persist, abide, run; intervene; elapse &c. 109.

take –, take up –, fill –, occupy- time.

pass –, pass away –, spend –, while away –, consume –, talk against –, kill- time; tide over; use –, employ- time; tarry &c. 110; seize an opportunity &c. 134; waste time &c. (*be inactive*) 683.

Adj. continuing &c. *v.*; on foot; permanent &c. (*durable*) 110.

Adv. while, whilst, during, pending; during the -time, – interval; in the course of; for the time being, day by day; in the time of, when; mean-time, -while; in the -meantime, – *interim*; *ad interim*, *pendente lite*; *de die in diem*; from -day to day, – hour to hour &c.; hourly, always; for a -time, – season; till, until, up to, yet; the whole –, all the- time; all along; throughout &c. (*completely*) 52; for good &c. (*diuturnity*) 110.

here-, there-, where-upon; then; *anno*, – *Domini*; A.D.; *ante Christum*; A.C.; before Christ; B.C.; *anno urbis conditæ*; A.U.C.; *anno regni*; A.R.; once upon a time, one fine morning.

Phr. time -runs, – runs against; *tempus fugit*.

on no occasion, never in all one's born days, nevermore, *sine die*.

---

108. [Definite duration, or portion of time.] **Period.**—**N.** period; second, minute, hour, day, week, sennight, octave, month, moon, quarter, semester, year, *lustrum*, *quinquennium*, decade, *decennium*, indiction, lifetime, generation, epoch, era, cycle.

century, age, *millennium*; *annus magnus*.

Adj. horary; hourly, annual &c. (*periodical*) 138.

108a. Contingent Duration.—Adv. during -pleasure, – good behaviour; *quamdiu se bene gesserit*.

---

109. [Indefinite duration.] **Course.** —**N.** course –, progress –, process –, succession –, lapse –, flow –, flux –, effluxion, stream –, tract –, current –, sweep –, tide –, march –, step –, flight- of time; duration &c. 106.

[Indefinite time] aorist.

V. elapse, lapse, flow, run, proceed, advance, pass; roll –, wear –, press –, drag- on; flit, fly, slip, slide, glide, crawl; run -its course.

out; expire; go –, pass- by; be -past &c. 122.

Adj. elapsing &c. *v.*; aoristic; pro-gressive, transient &c. 111.

Adv. in due -time, – season; in -course, – process, – the fulness- of time; in time.

Phr. *labitur et labetur*; *truditur dies die*; *fugaces labuntur anni*; 'tomorrow and tomorrow and tomorrow creeps in this petty pace from day to day.'

---

110. [Long duration.] **Diuturnity.** —**N.** diuturnity; a -long –, length of- time; an age, a century, an eternity,

111. [Short duration.] **Transientness.** —**N.** transientness &c. *adj.*; evanes-cence, impermanence, fugacity, transi-

æons; slowness &c. 275; perpetuity &c. 112; blue moon.

dura-bleness, -bility; persistence, lastingness &c. *adj.*; continuance, assiduity, endurance, standing; permanence &c. (*stability*) 150; survi-val, -vance; longevity &c. (*age*) 128; distance of time.

protraction –, prolongation –, extension- of time; delay &c. (*lateness*) 133.

V. last, endure, stand, remain, abide, continue, brave a thousand years.

tarry &c. (*be late*) 133; drag -on, – its slow length along, – a lengthening chain; protract, prolong; spin –, eke –, draw –, lengthen- out; temporize; gain –, make –, talk against- time.

out-last, -live; survive; live to fight again.

Adj. durable; perdurable; lasting &c. *v.*; of long -duration, – standing; permanent, chronic, long-standing; intransi-ent, -tive; intransmutable, persistent; life-, live-long; longeval, long-lived, macrobiotic, diuturnal, sempervirent, evergreen, perennial; unin-, ter-, unre-mitting; perpetual &c. 112.

lingering, protracted, prolonged, spun out &c. *v.*; long-pending, -winded; slow &c. 275.

Adv. long; for -a long time, – an age, – ages, – ever so long, – many a long day; long ago &c. (*in a past time*) 122; *longo intervallo*.

all the -day long, – year round; the livelong day, as the day is long, morning, noon and night; hour after hour, day after day, &c.; for good; permanently &c. *adj.*

112. [Endless duration.] **Perpetuity.** —**N.** perpetuity, eternity, timelessness; everness,* aye, sempiternity, immortality, athanasia; everlastingness &c. *adj.*; perpetuation; infinite duration.

V. last –, endure –, go on- for ever; have no end.

eternize, eternify, perpetuate, immortalize.

Adj. perpetual, eternal, eterne; everlasting, -living, -flowing; continual, constant, sempiternal; co-eternal; endless, unending; ceaseless, incessant, uninterrupted, indesinent, unceasing; interminable, having no end; unfad-

toriness, volatility, caducity, mortality, span; flash in the pan, nine days' wonder, bubble, May-fly; spurt; temporary arrangement, interregnum.

velocity &c. 274; suddenness &c. 113; changeableness &c. 149.

V. be -transient &c. *adj.*; flit, pass away, fly, gallop, vanish, fade, fleet, melt away, evaporate; pass away like a -cloud, – summer cloud, – shadow, – dream.

Adj. transi-ent, -tory, -tive; passing, evanescent, fleeting; flying &c. *v.*; fug-acious, -itive; shifting, slippery; spasmodic.

tempor-al, -ary; provis-ional, -ory; cursory, short-lived, ephemeral, deciduous; perishable, mortal, precarious; impermanent.

brief, quick, brisk; cometary, meteoric, extemporaneous, summary; pressed for time &c. (*haste*) 684; sudden, momentary &c. (*instantaneous*) 113.

Adv. temporarily &c. *adj.*; *pro tempore*; for -the moment, – a time; awhile, *en passant, in transitu*; in a short time; soon &c. (*early*) 132; briefly &c. *adj.*; at short notice; on the -point, – eve -of; *in articulo*; between cup and lip.

Phr. one's days are numbered; the time is up; here to-day and gone to-morrow; *non semper erit æstas; eheu! fugaces labuntur anni; sic transit gloria mundi.*

113. [Point of time.] **Instantaneity.** —**N.** instantane-ity, -ousness; sudden-, abrupt-ness.

moment, instant, second, minute; twinkling, trice, flash, breath, crack, jiffy, *coup*, burst, flash of lightning, stroke of time.

epoch, time; time of -day, – night; hour, minute; very -minute &c., – time, – hour; present –, right –, true –, exact –, correct- time.

V. be -instantaneous &c. *adj.*; twinkle, flash.

Adj. instantaneous, momentary, extempore, sudden, instant, abrupt;

* Bishop Wilkins.

ing, evergreen, amaranthine; never-ending, -dying, -fading; deathless, immortal, undying, imperishable.

Adv. perpetually &c. *adj.*; always, ever, evermore, aye; for -ever, – aye, – evermore, – ever and a day, – ever and ever; in all ages, from age to age; without end; world –, time- without end; *in sæcula sæculorum*; to the -end of time, – crack of doom, – 'last syllable of recorded time'; till dooms-day; constantly &c. (*very frequently*) 136.

Phr. *esto perpetuum*; *labitur et labetur in omne volubilis ævum*.

subitaneous, hasty; quick as -thought,* – lightning, – a flash; rapid as electricity.

Adv. instantaneously &c. *adj.*; in –, in less than- no time; *presto, subito, instanter*, suddenly, at a stroke, like- a shot, – greased lightning; in a trice, in a moment &c. *n.*; eftsoons, in the twinkling of -an eye, – a bed post; at one jump, in the same breath, *per saltum, uno saltu*; at –, all at- once; in one's tracks; plump, slap; 'at one fell swoop'; at the same -instant &c. *n.*; immediately &c. (*early*) 132; *ex tempore*, on the -spot, – spur of the moment, – dot; just then; slap- dash &c. (*haste*) 684; before you could -turn

round, – say -knife, – Jack Robinson.

Phr. touch and go; no sooner said than done.

---

114. [Estimation, measurement, and record of time.] **Chronometry.—N.** chrono-, horo-metry, -logy; date, epoch; style, era.

almanac, calendar, ephemeris; register, -try; chronicle, annals, journal, diary, chronogram.

[Instruments for the measurement of time] clock, watch; chrono-meter, -scope, -graph; repeater, alarum; time-keeper, -piece; dial, sun-dial, *gnomon, pendule*, horologe, pendulum, hour-glass, water clock, clepsydra.

mean –, Greenwich –, solar –, sidereal –, local –, summer- time; daylight saving.

chrono-grapher, -loger, -logist; annalist.

V. fix –, mark- the time; date, register, chronicle; measure –, beat –, mark- time; bear date.

Adj. chrono-logical, -metrical, -grammatical; isochronal.

Adv. o'clock; *a.m., p.m.*

115. [False estimate of time.] **Anachronism.—N.** ana-, meta-, para-, pro-chronism; *prolepsis*, misdate; anticipation, antichronism.

disregard –, neglect –, oblivion- of time.

intempestivity &c. 135.

V. mis-, ante-, post-, over-date; anticipate; take no note of time.

Adj. misdated &c. *v.*; undated; overdue; out of date; anachronous &c. *n.*

2°. RELATIVE TIME

1. *Time with reference to Succession*

116. Priority.—N. priority, antecedence, anteriority, pre-existence, precedence &c. 62; precession &c. 280; precursor &c. 64; the past &c. 122; premises.

V. precede, come before; forerun; antecede, go before &c. (*lead*) 280; pre-exist; dawn; premise, presage &c. 511.

be -beforehand &c. (*be early*) 132;

117. Posteriority.—N. posteriority; succession, sequence; following &c. 281; subsequence, supervention; futurity &c. 121; successor; sequel &c. 65; remainder, reversion.

V. follow &c. 281 –, come –, go-after; ensue, result; succeed, supervene; step into the shoes of.

Adj. subsequent, posterior, following, after, later, succeeding, postliminious,

* See note on 264.

steal a march upon, anticipate, forestall; have –, gain- the start.

Adj. prior, previous; preced-ing, -ent; anterior, antecedent; pre-existing, -existent; foresighted; former, foregoing; afore –, before-, above-mentioned; aforesaid, said; introductory &c. (*precursory*) 64; pre-war.

Adv. before, prior to; earlier; previously &c. *adj.*; afore, ere, theretofore, erewhile; ere –, before- -then, – now; erewhile, already, yet, beforehand; aforetime, on the eve of, in anticipation.

118. The Present Time.—N. the present -time, – day, – moment, – juncture, – occasion; the times, existing time, time being; twentieth century; nonce, crisis, epoch, day, hour.

age, time of life.

Adj. present, actual, instant, current, latest, existing, that is.

Adv. at this -time, – moment &c. 113; at the -present time &c. *n.*; now, at present.

at this time of day, to-day, now-a-days; already; even –, but –, just-now; on the present occasion; for the -time being, – nonce; *pro hâc vice*; on the -nail, – spot; on the spur of the -moment, – occasion.

until now; to -this, – the present day.

postnate; successive &c. 63; postdiluvial, -an; *puisné*; posthumous; post-war, future &c. 121.

Adv. subsequently, after, afterwards, since, later; at a -subsequent, – later- period; next, in the sequel, close upon, thereafter, thereupon, upon which, eftsoons; from that -time, – moment; after a -while, – time; in process of time.

postcenal, postcibal, postprandial, after-dinner.

___

119. [Time different from the present.] **Different Time.—N.** different –, other- time.

[Indefinite time] aorist.

Adj. aoristic.

Adv. at that –, at which- -time, – moment, – instant; then, on that occasion, upon.

when; when-ever, -soever; upon which, on which occasion; at -another, – a different, – some other, – any- time; at various times; some –, one- -of these days, – fine morning, – day; sooner or later; some time or other; once upon a time, once.

___

120. Synchronism.—N. synchronism; coexistence, coincidence; simultaneousness &c. *adj.*; concurrence, concomitance, unity of time, interim.

[Having equal times] isochronism, syntony.

contemporary, coetanian.

V. coexist, concur, accompany, go hand in hand, keep pace with; synchronize, isochronize.

Adj. synchron-ous, -al, -ical, -istical; simultaneous, coexisting, coincident, concomitant, concurrent; coev-al, -ous; contempora-ry, -neous; coetaneous; coterminous, coeternal; isochronous.

Adv. at the same time; simultaneously &c. *adj.*; together, in concert, during the same time; in the same breath; *pari passu*; in the interim.

at the -very moment &c. 113; just as, as soon as; meanwhile &c. (*while*) 106.

121. [Prospective time.] **Futurity. —N.** futur-ity, -ition; future, hereafter, time to come; approaching –, coming –, after- -time, – age, – days, – hours, – years, – ages, – life; morrow, to-morrow, by and by; millennium, doomsday, day of judgment, crack of doom, remote future.

122. [Retrospective time.] **Preterition.—N.** preterition; priority &c. 116; the past, past time; days –, times- -of yore, – of old, – past, – gone by; bygone days, good old days; old –, ancient –, former -times; fore time; yesterdays; the olden –, good old- time; auld lang syne; eld.

approach of time, advent, time drawing on, womb of time; destiny &c. 152;
eventuality.

heritage, heirs, posterity, descendants.

prospect &c. (*expectation*) 507; foresight &c. 510.

V. look forwards; anticipate &c. (*expect*) 507, (*foresee*) 510; forestall &c.
(*be early*) 132.

come –, draw- on; draw near; approach, await, threaten; impend &c.
(*be destined*) 152.

Adj. future, to come; coming &c.
(*impending*) 152; next, near; near –,
close- at hand; eventual, ulterior; expectant, prospective, in prospect &c.
(*expectation*) 507.

Adv. prospectively, hereafter, on the
knees of the gods, in future; to-morrow,
the day after to-morrow; in -course, –
process, – the fulness- of time; eventually, ultimately, sooner or later;
proximo; *paulo post futurum*; in after
time; one of these days; after a -time,
– while.

from this time; hence-forth, -for-
wards; thence; thence-forth, -forward;
whereupon, upon which.

soon &c. (*early*) 132; on the -eve,
– point, – brink- of; about to; close
upon.

---

antiquity, antiqueness, *status quo*;
time immemorial; distance of time;
remote -age, – time; ancient history;
remote past; rust of antiquity; ancient-
ness.

pale-ontology, -ography, -ology; palætiology,* archæology; archaism, an-
tiquarianism, mediævalism, pre-Raph-
aelitism; retrospection, looking back,
memory &c._505.

laudator temporis acti; mediævalist,
pre-Raphaelite; antiqu-ary, -arian;
archæologist &c.; Oldbuck, Dryasdust.

ancestry &c. (*paternity*) 166.

V. be -past &c. *adj.*; have -expired
&c. *adj.*, – run its course, – had its
day; pass; pass –, go- -by, – away, –
off; lapse, blow over.

look –, trace –, cast the eyes- back;
exhume.

Adj. past, gone, gone by, over,
passed away, bygone, foregone;
elapsed, lapsed, preterlapsed, expired,
no more, run out, blown over, that
has been, whilom, extinct, never to
return, exploded, forgotten, irrecover-
able; obsolete &c. (*old*) 124; extinct as
the dodo.

former, pristine, *quondam*, *ci-devant*,
late; ancestral.

foregoing; last, latter; recent, over-
night; past, preterite, preter-perfect,
-pluperfect, past perfect.

looking back &c. *v.*; retro-spective,
-active; archæological &c. *n.*

Adv. formerly; of -old, – yore; erst, whilom, erewhile, time was,
ago, over; in -the olden time &c. *n.*; anciently, long -ago, – since;
a long -while, – time- ago; years –, ages- ago; some time -ago,
– since, – back.

yesterday, the day before yesterday; last -year, – season, –
month &c.; *ultimo*; lately &c. (*newly*) 123.

retrospectively; ere –, before –, till- now; hitherto, heretofore;
no longer; once, – upon a time; from time immemorial; in the
memory of man; time out of mind; already, yet, up to this time;
ex post facto.

Phr. time was; the time -has, – hath- been.

2. *Time with reference to a particular Period*

123. Newness.—**N.** newness &c.
adj.; neologism, neoterism; novelty,
recency; immaturity; youth &c. 127;
gloss of novelty.

124. Oldness.—**N.** oldness &c. *adj.*;
age, antiquity; cobwebs of antiquity.

maturity, ripeness; decline, decay;
senility &c. 128.

* Whewell.

innovation; renovation &c. (*restoration*) 660.

modernist, neologist, neoteric.

modernism, modernity; mushroom; latest fashion, *dernier cri*.

upstart, *parvenu, nouveau riche*.

V. renew &c. (*restore*) 660; modernize.

Adj. new, novel, recent, fresh, green; young &c. 127; evergreen; raw, immature; virgin; un-tried, -handseled, -used, -trodden, -beaten; fledgling.

late, modern, neoteric; new-born, -fashioned, -fangled, -fledged; of yesterday; just out, brand –, span-new, up to date, topical; vernal, renovated; innovatory.

fresh as -a rose, – a daisy, – paint; spick and span.

Adv. newly &c. *adj.*; afresh, anew, lately, just now, only yesterday, the other day; latterly, of late.

not long –, a short time- ago.

---

seniority, eldership, primogeniture.

archaism &c. (*the past*) 122; thing –, relic- of the past; megatherium.

tradition, prescription, custom, folklore, immemorial usage, common law.

V. be -old &c. *adj.*; have -had, – seen- its day; become -old &c. *adj.*; age, fade.

Adj. old, olden, ancient, antique; of long standing, time-honoured, venerable; eld-er, -est; first-born.

prime; prim-itive, -eval, -igenous; primordi-al, -nate; aboriginal &c. (*beginning*) 66; diluvian, antediluvian; pre-historic; patriarchal, preadamite; palæocrystic; fossil, paleozoic, preglacial, ante-mundane; archaic, classic, mediæval, pre-Raphaelite, ancestral, black-letter.

immemorial, traditional, prescriptive, customary, whereof the memory of man runneth not to the contrary; inveterate, rooted.

antiquated, of other times, rococo, of the old school, after-age, obsolete; fusty, moth-eaten; out of -date, – fashion; stale, old-fashioned, behind the -age, – times; exploded; gone out, – by; *passé*, outworn, run out; disused; senile &c. 128; time-worn; crumbling &c. (*deteriorated*) 659; second-hand.

old as -the hills, – Methuselah, – Adam, – history.

Adv. since the -world was made, – year one, – days of Methuselah.

---

125. Morning. [Noon.]—**N.** morning, morn, matins, forenoon, *a.m.*, prime, dawn, daybreak, daylight, sun-up, peep –, break- of day; aurora, Eos; first blush –, prime- of the morning; twilight, crepuscule, sunrise, cockcrow.

spring; vernal equinox.

noon; mid-, noon-day; noontide, meridian, prime.

summer, midsummer; summer solstice.

Adj. matin, matutinal; vernal, æstival.

Adv. at -sunrise &c. *n.*; with the lark, when the morning dawns.

127. Youth.—**N.** youth; juven- -ility, -escence; juniority; infancy; baby-, child-, boy-, girl-, youth-hood; *incunabula*; minority, immaturity, nonage, teens, tender age, bloom.

cradle, nursery, leading-strings, pupilage, puberty, *pucelage*.

126. Evening. [Midnight.]—**N.** evening, eve; decline –, fall –, close- of day; eventide, evensong, vespers; candlelight; nightfall, curfew, dusk, twilight, blind man's holiday; eleventh hour; sun-set, -down; going down of the sun, cock-shut, dewy eve, gloaming, bed-time.

afternoon, *post meridiem, p.m.*

autumn; fall, – of the leaf; autumnal equinox, Indian summer, harvest-time.

midnight; dead –, witching time- of night; winter, – solstice.

Adj. vesper-ine, autumnal, nocturnal, wintry, brumal, hiemal.

128. Age.—**N.** age; oldness &c. *adj.*; old –, advanced- age; sen-ility, -escence; years, anility, grey hairs, climacteric, grand climacteric, declining years, decrepitude, hoary age, caducity, superannuation; second childhood, -ishness; dotage; vale of years,

prime –, flower –, spring-tide –, seed-time –, golden season- of life; heyday of youth, school days; rising genera-tion, younger generation.

Adj. young, youthful, juvenile, green, callow, budding, sappy, *puisné*, beard-less, unfledged, unripe, under age, in one's teens; *in statu pupillari*; younger, junior.

decline of life, 'sear and yellow leaf'; three-score years and ten; green old age, ripe old age; longevity; time of life.

seniority, eldership; elders &c. (*vete-ran*) 130; firstling; *doyen*, dean, father; primogeniture; nostology.

V. be -aged &c. *adj.*; grow –, get-old &c. *adj.*; age; decline, wane.

Adj. aged; old &c. 124; elderly, senile; matronly, anile; in years; ripe, mellow, run to seed, declining, waning, past one's prime; grey, -headed; hoar, -y; venerable, time-worn, antiquated, *passé*, effete, doddering, decrepit, superannuated; advanced in -life, – years; stricken in years; wrinkled, marked with the crow's foot; having one foot in the grave; doting &c. (*imbecile*) 499.

old-, eld-er, -est; senior; first-born.

turned of, years old; of a certain age, no chicken, old as Me-thuselah; gerontic; ancestral; patriarchal &c. (*ancient*) 124.

129. Infant.—**N.** infant, babe, baby; nurse-, suck-, year-, wean-ling; *papoose, bambino*.

child, bairn, little- one, – tot, – mite, chick, brat, chit, pickaninny, kid, urchin; bant-, brat-ling; elf.

youth, boy, lad, slip, sprig, stripling, youngster, cub, unlicked cub, younker, callant, whipster, whipper-snapper, schoolboy, hobbledehoy, hopeful, ca-det, minor, master.

scion; sap-, seed-ling; tendril, olive-branch, nestling, chicken, duckling; larva, caterpillar, chrysalis, cocoon; tadpole, whelp, cub, pullet, fry, callow; codlin, -g; *fœtus*, calf, colt, pup, foal, kitten; lamb, -kin.

girl; lass, -ie; wench, miss, damsel, *demoiselle*, damozel; maid, -en; virgin; nymph; colleen; minx, baggage, school-girl; tomboy, flapper, hoyden.

Adj. infant-ine, -ile; puerile; boy-, girl-, child-, baby-, kitten-ish; baby; new-born, unfledged, new-fledged, callow.

in -the cradle, – swaddling clothes, – long clothes, – arms, – lead-ing strings; at the breast; in one's teens; young &c. 127.

130. Veteran.—**N.** veteran, old man, seer, patriarch, greybeard, dugout, grand-father, -sire; grandam, beldam; gaffer, gammer; hag, crone; pantaloon; sexage-, octoge-, nonage-, cente-narian; old stager; dotard &c. 501.

preadamite, Methuselah, Nestor, Rip van Winkle, old Parr; elders; fore-fathers &c. (*paternity*) 166.

131. Adolescence.—**N.** adolescence, pubescence, majority; adultness &c. *adj.*; manhood, virility, maturity; flower of age; prime –, meridian-of life.

man &c. 373; woman &c. 374; adult, no chicken.

V. come -of age, – to man's estate, – to years of discretion; attain majority, assume the *toga virilis*; have -cut one's eye-teeth, – sown one's wild oats, settle down.

Adj. adolescent, pubescent, of age; of -full, – ripe- age; out of one's teens, grown up, mature, full- blown, – grown, in one's prime, in full bloom, manly, virile, adult; womanly, matronly; marriageable, nubile.

3. *Time with reference to an Effect or Purpose*

132. Earliness.—N. earliness &c. *adj.*; morning &c. 125.

punctuality; promptitude &c. (*activity*) 682; haste &c. (*velocity*) 274; suddenness &c. (*instantaneity*) 113.

prematurity, precocity, precipitation, anticipation; prevenience, a stitch in time.

V. be -early &c. *adj.*, – beforehand &c. *adv.*; keep time, take time by the forelock, anticipate, forestall; have –, gain- the start; steal a march upon; gain time, draw on futurity; bespeak, secure, engage, pre-engage.

accelerate; expedite &c. (*quicken*) 274; make haste &c. (*hurry*) 684.

Adj. early, prime, timely, in time, punctual, forward; prompt &c. (*active*) 682; summary.

premature, precipitate, precocious; prevenient, anticipatory; rathe.

sudden &c. (*instantaneous*) 113; unexpected &c. 508; impending, imminent; near, – at hand; immediate.

Adv. early, soon, anon, betimes, rathe; eft, -soons; ere –, before- long; punctually &c. *adj.*; to the minute; in time; in -good, – military, – pudding, – due- time; time enough.

beforehand; prematurely &c. *adj.*; precipitately &c. (*hastily*) 684; too soon; before -its, – one's- time; in anticipation; unexpectedly &c. 508.

suddenly &c. (*instantaneously*) 113; before one can say 'Jack Robinson,' at short notice, extempore; on the spur of the -moment, – occasion; at once; on the -spot, – instant; at sight; off –, out of- hand; *à vue d'œil*; straight, -way, -forth; forthwith, incontinently, summarily, instanter, immediately, briefly, shortly, quickly, speedily, apace, before the ink is dry, almost immediately, presently, at the first opportunity, in no long time, by and by, in a while, directly.

Phr. touch and go, no sooner said than done.

134. Occasion.—N. occasion, opportunity, opening, room, scope, field; suitable –, proper- -time, – season; high time; opportuneness &c. *adj.*; tempestivity.

133. Lateness.—N. lateness &c. *adj.*; tardiness &c. (*slowness*) 275.

de-lay, -lation; cunctation, procrastination; detention; deferring &c. *v.*; filibuster, postponement, adjournment, prorogation, retardation, respite, reprieve, stay; protraction, prolongation, moratorium; contango; demurrage; remand; Fabian policy, *médecine expectante*, chancery suit; leeway; high time.

V. be -late &c. *adj.*; tarry, wait, stay, bide, take time; dawdle &c. (*be inactive*) 683; linger, loiter, saunter, lag behind; bide –, take- one's time; hang -about, – around, – back, – in the balance; gain time; hang fire; stand –, lie-over.

put off, defer, delay, lay over, suspend; shift –, stave- off; waive, retard, remand, postpone, adjourn; procrastinate; dally; prolong, protract; spin –, draw –, lengthen- out; prorogue; keep back; tide over; push –, drive- to the last; let the matter stand over; reserve &c. (*store*) 636; temporize; consult one's pillow, sleep upon it.

shelve, table, lay on the table.

lose an opportunity &c. 135; be kept waiting, dance attendance; kick –, cool- one's heels; *faire antichambre*; wait impatiently; await &c. (*expect*) 507; sit up, – at night.

Adj. late, tardy, slow, behindhand, belated, postliminious, posthumous, backward, unpunctual; dilatory &c. (*slow*), overdue 275; delayed &c. *v.*; in abeyance.

Adv. late; late-, back-ward; late in the day; at -sunset, – the eleventh hour, – length, – last, – long; ultimately; after –, behind- time; too late; too late for &c. 135.

slowly, leisurely, deliberately, at one's leisure; *ex post facto*; *sine die*.

Phr. *nonum prematur in annum.*

---

135. Intempestivity.—N. intempestivity; unseasonableness; unsuitable -, improper-time; unreasonableness &c. *adj.*; evil hour; *contretemps*; intrusion; anachronism &c. 115.

crisis, turn, juncture, emergency, conjuncture; turning point, given time.

nick of time; golden –, well-timed –, fine –, favourable- opportunity; clear stage, fair field; *mollia tempora*; *fata Morgana*; spare time &c. (*leisure*) 685.

V. seize &c. (*take*) 789 –, use &c. 677 –, give &c. 784- an -opportunity, – occasion; improve the occasion.

suit the occasion &c. (*be expedient*) 646.

strike the iron while it is hot, *battre le fer sur l'enclume*, make hay while the sun shines, take time by the forelock, *prendre la balle au bond*.

Adj. opportune, timely, well-timed, timeous, timeful, seasonable.

providential, lucky, fortunate, happy, favourable, propitious, auspicious, critical; suitable &c. 23; *obiter dicta*.

Adv. opportunely &c. *adj.*; in -proper, – due- -time, – course, – season; for the nonce; in the -nick, – fulness- of time; all in good time; just in time, at the eleventh hour, now or never.

by the -way, – by; *en passant, à propos*; *pro -re natâ, – hac vice*; *par parenthèse*, parenthetically, by way of parenthesis; while -speaking of, – on this subject; *ex tempore*; on the spur of the -moment, – occasion; on the spot &c. (*early*) 132.

Phr. *carpe diem*; *occasionem cognosce*; one's hour is come, the time is up; that reminds me.

V. be -ill timed &c. *adj.*; mistime, intrude, come amiss, break in upon; have other fish to fry; be -busy, – engaged, – tied up, – occupied.

lose –, throw away –, waste –, neglect &c. 460- an opportunity; allow –, suffer- the -opportunity, – occasion- to -pass, - slip, – go by, – escape, – lapse; waste time &c. (*be inactive*) 683; let slip through the fingers, lock the stable door when the steed is stolen.

Adj. ill-, mis-timed; untimely, intrusive, unseasonable; out of -date, – season; inopportune, timeless, untoward, *mal à propos*, unlucky, inauspicious, unpropitious, unfortunate, unfavourable; unsuited &c. 24; inexpedient &c. 647.

unpunctual &c. (*late*) 133; too late for; premature &c. (*early*) 132; too soon for; wise after the event.

Adv. inopportunely &c. *adj.*; as ill luck would have it, in an evil hour, the time having gone by, a day after the fair.

Phr. after meat mustard, after death the doctor.

3°. RECURRENT TIME

136. Frequency.—N. frequency, oftness; repetition, &c. 104.

V. recur &c. 104; do nothing but; keep, – on.

Adj. frequent, many times, not rare, thickcoming, incessant, perpetual, continual, constant, recurrent, repeated &c. 104; habitual &c. 613; hourly, &c. 138.

Adv. often, often to be met with, oft; oft-, often-times; frequently; repeatedly &c. 104; unseldom, not unfrequently; in -quick, – rapid- succession; many a time and oft; daily, hourly &c.; every -day, – hour, – moment &c.

perpetually, continually, constantly, incessantly, without ceasing, at all times, daily and hourly, night and day,

137. Infrequency.—N. infrequency, infrequence, rareness, rarity; fewness &c. 103; seldomness, uncommonness.

V. be -rare &c. *adj.*

Adj. un-, in-frequent; uncommon, sporadic, rare, – as a blue diamond; few &c. 103; scarce; almost unheard of, unprecedented, which has not occurred within the memory of the oldest inhabitant, not within one's previous experience.

Adv. seldom, rarely, scarcely, hardly; not often, unfrequently, infrequently, unoften; scarcely –, hardly- ever; once in a blue moon.

once; once -for all, – in a way; *pro hac vice*; like angels' visits, few and far between.

day and night, day after day, morning noon and night, ever and anon.

most often; commonly &c. (*habitually*) 613.

sometimes, occasionally, at times, now and then, from time to time, there being times when, *toties quoties*, often enough, again and again &c. 104.

138. Regularity of recurrence. **Periodicity.**—**N.** periodicity, intermittence; beat; oscillation &c. 314; pulse, pulsation; rhythm; alter-nation, -nateness, -nativeness, -nity.

bout, round, revolution, rotation, turn.

anniversary, birthday, jubilee, centenary, bi-, ter-centenary.

[Regularity of return] rota, cycle, period, stated time, routine; days of the week; Sunday, Monday &c.; months of the year; January &c.; feast, fast, saint's day &c.; Christmas, Easter, New Year's Day &c. 998; quarter-, Lady-, Midsummer-, Michaelmas-day; May Day, the King's Birthday; leap year; seasons.

punctuality, regularity, steadiness.

V. recur in regular -order, – succession; return, revolve, rotate; come -again, – in its turn; come round, – again; beat, pulsate; alternate; intermit.

Adj. periodic, -al; serial, recurrent, cyclic-, -al, rhythmic-, -al, even; recurring &c. *v.*; inter-, re-mittent; alternate, every other.

hourly; diurnal, daily; quotidian, tertian, weekly; hebdomad-al, -ary; bi-weekly, fortnightly; monthly, menstrual, catamenial; yearly, annual; biennial, triennial, &c.; bissextile; centennial, secular; paschal, lenten, &c.

regular, steady, punctual, constant, methodical, regular as clockwork.

Adv. periodically &c. *adj.*; at -regular intervals, – stated times; at -fixed, – established- periods; punctually &c. *adj.*; *de die in diem*; from day to day, day by day.

by turns; in -turn, – rotation; alternately, every other day, off and on, ride and tie, round and round.

139. Irregularity of recurrence.—**N.** irregularity, uncertainty, unpunctuality; fitfulness &c. *adj.*

Adj. irregular, uneven, uncertain, unpunctual, capricious, erratic, desultory, fitful, flickering; rambling, rhapsodical; spasmodic, unsystematic, unequal, variable, halting.

Adv. irregularly &c. *adj.*; by fits and starts &c. (*discontinuously*) 70.

Section VII. CHANGE

1°. Simple Change

140. [Difference at different times.] **Change.**—**N.** change, alteration, mutation, permutation, variation, modification, modulation, inflexion, mood, qualification, innovation, *metastasis*, deviation, shift, turn; diversion; break.

transformation, transfiguration; metamorphosis; metabolism; transmutation; transubstantiation; metagenesis, transanimation, transmigration, me-

141. [Absence of change.] **Permanence.**—**N.** stability &c. 150; quiescence &c. 265; obstinacy &c. 606.

permanence, -cy, persistence, fixity, fixity of purpose, endurance, durability; standing, *status quo*; maintenance, preservation, conservation; conservatism; *laissez-faire*; law of the Medes and Persians; standing dish.

V. let -alone, – be; persist, remain,

[45]

tempsychosis; version; metathesis; transmogrification; catalysis; *avatar*; alterative.

conversion &c. (*gradual change*) 144; revolution &c. (*sudden or radical change*) 146; inversion &c. (*reversal*) 218; displacement &c. 185; transference &c. 270.

changeableness &c. 149; tergiversation &c. (*change of mind*) 607.

V. change, alter, vary, wax and wane; modulate, diversify, qualify, tamper with; turn, shift, veer, jibe, tack, chop, shuffle, swerve, dodge, warp, deviate, turn aside, evert, intervert; pass to, take a turn, turn the corner, resume.

work a change, modify, vamp, revamp, superinduce; trans-form, -mute, -ume, -figure &c. *n.*; metamorphose, ring the changes; convert, resolve; revolutionize; chop and change; patch, re-shape.

innovate, introduce new blood, shuffle the cards, spin the wheel; give a -turn, – colour- to; influence, turn the scale; shift the scene, turn over a new leaf.

recast &c. 146; reverse &c. 218; disturb &c. 61; convert into &c. 144.

Adj. changed &c. *v.*; new-fangled; changeable &c. 149; transitional; modifiable; alterative.

Adv. *mutatis mutandis.*

Int. *quantum mutatus!*

Phr. 'a change came o'er the spirit of my dream'; *nous avons changé tout cela*; *tempora mutantur et nos mutamur in illis*; *non sum qualis eram.*

stay, tarry, rest; hold, – on; last, endure, bide, abide, aby, dwell, maintain, keep; stand, – still, – fast; subsist, live, outlive, survive; hold -, keepone's -ground, – footing; hold good.

Adj. stable &c. 150; persisting &c. *v.*; permanent; established, fixed; durable; unchanged &c. (change &c. 140); unrenewed; intact, inviolate; persistent; monotonous, uncheckered; unfailing.

un-destroyed, -repealed, -suppressed; conservative, *qualis ab incepto*; prescriptive &c. (*old*) 124; stationary &c. 265.

Adv. *in statu quo*; for good, finally; at a stand, -still; *uti possidetis*; without a shadow of turning.

Phr. as you were!; *j'y suis j'y reste*; *esto perpetua*; *nolumus leges Angliæ mutari*; let sleeping dogs lie.

---

142. [Change from action to rest.] **Cessation.—N.** cessation, discontinuance, desistance, desinence.

inter-, re-mission; sus-pense, -pension; interruption, hitch; hartal; stop; stopping &c. *v.*; closure, stoppage, halt; arrival &c. 292.

pause, rest, lull, respite, truce, armistice, drop; interregnum, abeyance.

closure &c. 261.

dead -stop, – stand, – lock; check-mate; comma, colon, semicolon, period, full stop; end &c. 67; death &c. 360; *cæsura.*

V. cease, discontinue, desist, stay; break -, leave- off; hold, stop, pull up, stall, stop short, check; stick, deadlock, hang fire; halt; pause, rest.

have done with, give over, surcease,

143. Continuance in action.—**N.** continu-ance, -ation; run; extension, prolongation; maintenance, perpetuation; persistence &c. (*perseverance*) 604a; repetition &c. 104.

V. continue, persist; go -, jog -, keep -, carry -, run – hold- on; abide, keep, pursue, stick to; endure; take -, maintain- its course; keep up.

sustain, uphold, hold up, keep on foot; follow up, perpetuate, prolong; maintain; preserve &c. 604a; harp upon &c. (*repeat*) 104.

keep -going, – alive, – at it, – the pot boiling, – the ball rolling, – up the ball; plod-, plug- along; slog on; die in harness; hold on -, pursue- the even tenor of one's way.

let be; *stare super antiquas vias*;

shut up shop; give up &c. (*relinquish*) 624.

hold –, stay- one's hand; rest on one's oars, repose on one's laurels.

come to a -stand, – standstill, – dead lock, – full stop; arrive &c. 292; go out, die away, peter out; wear -away, – off; pass away &c. (*be past*) 122; be at an end.

intromit, interrupt, suspend, interpel; inter-, re-mit; put -an end, – a stop, – a period- to; bring to a stand, -still; stop, cut out, cut short, arrest, avast; stem the -tide, – torrent; pull the check string; switch off.

Int. halt! hold! stop! enough! avast! have done! a truce to! soft! leave off! shut up! give over! chuck it!

quieta non movere; let things take their course.

Adj. continuing &c. *v.*; uninterrupted, unintermitting, unremitting, unvarying, unshifting; unreversed, unstopped, unrevoked, unvaried; sustained; undying &c. (*perpetual*) 112; inconvertible.

follow-up.

Int. carry on! right away!

Phr. *vestigia nulla retrorsum*; *labitur et labetur.*

---

144. [Gradual change to something different.] **Conversion.—N.** conversion, reduction, transmutation, transformation, development, resolution, assimilation; assumption; naturalization.

chemistry, alchemy; progress, growth, lapse, flux.

passage; transit, -ion; transmigration, shifting &c. *v.*; conjugation; convertibility.

crucible, alembic, caldron, retort, test tube &c.

convert, neophyte, proselyte, pervert, renegade, deserter, apostate, turncoat.

V. be converted into; become, get, wax; come –, turn- -to, – into; turn out, lapse, shift; run –, fall –, pass –, slide –, glide –, grow –, ripen –, open –, resolve itself –, settle –, merge- into; melt, grow, come round to, mature, mellow; assume the -form, – shape, – state, – nature, – character- of; illapse; assume a new phase, undergo a change.

convert –, resolve- into; make, render; mould, form &c. 240; remodel, new model, refound, reform, reorganize; assimilate –, bring –, reduce- to; transform.

Adj. converted into &c. *v.*; convertible, resolvable into; transitional; naturalized.

Adv. gradually &c. (*slowly*) 275; *in transitu* &c. (*transference*) 270.

145. Reversion.—N. reversion, return; revulsion; reaction.

turning point, turn of the tide; *status quo ante bellum*; calm before a storm.

alternation &c. (*periodicity*) 138; inversion &c. 219; recoil &c. 277; regression &c. 283; restoration &c. 660; relapse &c. 661; vicinism, atavism, throwback.

V. revert, turn back, return; relapse &c. 661; recoil &c. 277; retreat &c. 283; restore &c. 660; undo, unmake; turn the -tide, – scale; escheat.

Adj. reverting &c. *v.*; revulsive, reactionary.

Adv. *à rebours*, wrong side out.

146. [Sudden or violent change.] **Revolution.—N.** revolution, *bouleversement*, subversion, break up; destruction &c. 162; sudden –, radical –, sweeping –, organic- change; clean sweep, *coup d'état*, overthrow, *débâcle*; counter-revolution, rebellion &c. 742.

transilience, jump, leap, plunge, jerk, start; explosion; spasm, convulsion, throe, revulsion; storm, earthquake, eruption, upheaval, cataclysm.

legerdemain &c. (*trick*) 545.

V. revolutionize; new model, remodel, recast; strike out something new, break with the past; change the face of, unsex; revert &c. 742.

Adj. unrecognizable.

Revolutionary, Bolshevik &c. 742.

147. [Change of one thing for another.] **Substitution.—N.** substitution, subrogation, commutation; supplanting &c. *v.*, supersession, metonymy &c. (*figure of speech*) 521.

[Thing substituted] substitute, *succedaneum*, make-shift, temporary expedient, shift, *pis aller*, stop-gap, jury-mast, *locum tenens*, warming-pan, dummy, goat, scape-goat; double; changeling; *quid pro quo*, alternative; remount; representative &c. (*deputy*) 759; palimpsest.

price, purchase-money, consideration, equivalent.

V. substitute, put in the place of, change for; make way for, give place to; supply –, take- the place of; supplant, supersede, replace, cut out, serve as a substitute; step into –, stand in- the shoes of; make a shift –, put up- with; borrow of Peter to pay Paul; commute, redeem, compound for.

Adj. substituted &c. *v.*; vicarious, subdititious; substitutional.

Adv. instead; in -place, – lieu, – the stead, – the room- of; *faute de mieux.*

148. [Double or mutual change.] **Interchange.—N.** inter-, ex-change; com-, per-, inter-mutation; reciprocation, transposal, transposition, shuffling; reciprocity, castling [at chess]; hocus-pocus.

interchange-ableness, -ability.

barter &c. 794; tit for tat &c. (*retaliation*) 718; cross fire, battledore and shuttlecock; *quid pro quo.*

V. inter-, ex-, counter-change; bandy, transpose, shuffle, change hands, swap, trade, permute, reciprocate, commute; give and take, return the compliment; play at -puss in the corner, – battledore and shuttlecock; retaliate &c. 718; barter &c. 794.

Adj. interchanged &c. *v.*; reciprocal, mutual, commutative, interchanged &c. *v.*; interchangeable, intercurrent.

Adv. in exchange, *vice versâ, mutatis mutandis*, backwards and forwards, by turns, turn and turn about, turn about; each –, every one- in his turn.

2°. Complex Change

149. Changeableness.—N. changeableness &c. *adj.*; mutability, inconstancy; versatility, mobility; instability, unstable equilibrium; vacillation &c. (*irresolution*) 605; fluctuation, vicissitude; alternation &c. (*oscillation*) 314.

restlessness &c. *adj.*; fidgets, disquiet; dis-, in-quietude; unrest; agitation &c. 315.

moon, Proteus, chameleon, kaleidoscope, quicksilver, shifting sands, weathercock, harlequin, Cynthia of the minute, April showers; wheel of Fortune; transientness &c. 111.

V. fluctuate, vary, waver, flounder, flicker, flitter, flit, flutter, shift, shuffle, shake, totter, tremble, vacillate, wamble, turn and turn about, ring the changes; sway –, shift- to and fro; change and change about; oscillate

150. Stability.—N. stability; immutability &c. *adj.*; unchangeableness &c. *adj.*; constancy; stable equilibrium, immobility, soundness, vitality, stabiliment, stabilization, stiffness, ankylosis, solidity, *aplomb.*

establishment, fixture; rock, pillar, tower, foundation, leopard's spots, Ethiopian's skin, law of the Medes and Persians.

stabilimeter, stabilisator.

permanence &c. 141; obstinacy &c. 606.

V. be -firm &c. *adj.*; stick fast; stand –, keep –, remain- firm; weather the storm.

settle, establish, stablish, ascertain, fix, set, stabilitate, stabilize; retain, stet, keep hold; make -good, – sure; fasten &c. (*join*) 43; set on its legs, float; perpetuate.

&c. 314; vibrate –, oscillate- between two extremes; alternate; have as many phases as the moon.

Adj. change-able, -ful; changing &c. 140; mutable, variable, checkered, ever changing, kaleidoscopic, prote-an, -iform; versatile.

unstaid, inconstant; un-steady, -stable, -fixed, -settled; fluctuating &c. *v.*; restless; mercurial; agitated &c. 315; erratic, fickle; irresolute &c. 605; capricious &c. 608; touch-and-go; inconsonant, fitful, spasmodic; vibratory; vagrant, wayward, wavering; desultory; afloat; alternating; alterable, plastic, mobile; fleeting, transient &c. 111.

Adv. see-saw &c. (*oscillation*) 314; off and on.

settle down; strike –, take- root; take up one's abode &c. 184; build one's house on a rock.

Adj. unchangeable, immutable; un-alter-ed, -able; not to be changed, constant; permanent &c. 141; invariable, undeviating; stable, durable; perennial &c. (*diuturnal*) 110.

fixed, steadfast, firm, fast, steady, balanced; confirmed, valid, fiducial, immovable, irremovable, riveted, rooted; settled, established &c. *v.*; vested; incontrovertible, stereotyped, indeclinable.

tethered, anchored, moored, at anchor, on a rock, firm as a rock; firmly -seated, – established &c. *v.*; deep-rooted, ineradicable; inveterate; obstinate &c. 606.

transfixed, stuck fast, aground, high and dry, stranded.

indefeasible, irretrievable, intransmutable, incommutable, irresoluble, irrevocable, irreversible, reverseless, inextinguishable, irreducible; indissol-uble, -vable; indestructible, undying, imperishable, indelible, indeciduous; insusceptible, – of change.

Int. *stet.*

Present Events

151. Eventuality.—**N.** eventuality, event, occurrence, incident, affair, transaction, proceeding, fact; matter of –, naked- fact; phenomenon; advent.

business, concern; circumstance, particular, casualty, happening, accident, adventure, passage, crisis, pass, emergency, contingency, consequence &c. 154.

the world, life, things, doings, affairs, matters; things –, affairs- in general; the times, state of affairs, order of the day; course –, tide –, stream –, current –, run –, march- of -things, – events; ups and downs of life; chapter of accidents &c. (*chance*) 156; situation &c. (*circumstances*) 8.

V. happen, occur; take -place, – effect; come, become of; come -off, – about, – round, – into existence, – forth, – to pass, – on; pass, present itself; fall; fall –, turn- out; run, be on foot, fall in; be-fall, -tide, -chance; prove, eventuate, draw on; turn –, crop –, spring –, cast- up; super-, sur-vene; issue, emanate, arrive, ensue,

Future Events

152. Destiny.—**N.** destiny &c. (*necessity*) 601; hereafter, future –, post-existence; future state, next world, world to come, after life; futurity &c. 121; everlasting -life, – death; prospect &c. (*expectation*) 507.

V. impend; hang –, lie –, hover-over; threaten, loom, await, come on, approach, stare one in the face; fore-, pre-ordain; predestine, doom, fore-doom, foreshadow, have in store for.

Adj. impending &c. *v.*; destined; about to -be, – happen; coming, in store, to come, going to happen, instant, at hand, near; near –, close- at hand; overhanging, hanging over one's head, imminent; brewing, preparing, forthcoming; in the wind, on the cards, in reserve; that -will, – is to- be; in prospect &c. (*expected*) 507; looming in the -distance, – horizon, – future; unborn, in embryo; in the womb of -time; – futurity; on the knees of the gods; pregnant &c. (*producing*) 161.

Adv. in -time, – the long run; all in good time; eventually &c. 151; what-

arise, start, hold, take its course; pass off &c. (*be past*) 122.

meet with; experience; fall to the lot of; be one's -chance, – fortune, – lot; find; encounter, undergo; pass –, go-through; endure &c. (*feel*) 821.

Adj. happening &c. *v.*; going on, doing, current; in the wind, afloat; on -foot, – the *tapis*; at issue, in question; incidental.

eventful, momentous, signal; stirring, bustling, full of incident.

Adv. eventually, ultimately, in -the event of, – case; in the course of things; in the -natural, – ordinary- course of things; as -things, – times- go; as the world -goes, – wags; as the -tree falls, – cat jumps; as it may -turn out, – happen.

Phr. the plot thickens.

ever may happen &c. (*certainly*) 474; as -chance &c. 156- would have it.

Section VIII. CAUSATION

1°. Constancy of Sequence in Events

153. [Constant antecedent.] **Cause.** —**N.** cause, origin, source, principle, element; occasioner, prime mover, engine, turbine, motor, *primum mobile*; *vera causa*; author &c. (*producer*) 164; main-spring, agent; dynamo, generator, battery (electric); leaven; groundwork, foundation &c. (*support*) 215.

spring, fountain, well, font; fountain –, spring- head; *fons et origo*, genesis; descent &c. (*paternity*) 166; remote cause; influence.

pivot, hinge, turning-point, lever; key; kernel, core; proximate cause, *causa causans*; last straw that breaks the camel's back.

ground; reason, – why; why and wherefore, rationale, occasion, derivation; final cause &c. (*intention*) 620; *le dessous des cartes*; undercurrents.

rudiment, egg, germ, embryo, fœtus bud, root, *radix*, radical, etymon, nucleus, seed, stem, stalk, stock, *stirps*, trunk, tap-root; latent organism.

nest, cradle, nursery, womb, *nidus*, birth-, breeding-place, hot-bed.

caus-ality, -ation; origination; production &c. 161.

V. be the -cause &c. *n.*- of; originate; give -origin, – rise, – occasion- to; cause, occasion, sow the seeds of, kindle, suscitate; bring -on, – to pass, – about; produce; create &c. 161; set -up, – afloat, – on foot; found, broach,

154. [Constant sequent.] **Effect.**—**N.** effect, consequence, sequela; derivative, -tion; result; result-ant, -ance; upshot, issue, *dénouement*; outcome; termination, end &c. 67; development, outgrowth, fruit, crop, harvest, product, bud, blossom, florescence, ear.

production, produce, product, finished product, work, handiwork, fabric, performance; creature, creation; offspring, -shoot; first-fruits, -lings; *prémices*.

V. be the -effect &c. *n.*- of; be -due, – owing- to; originate -in, – from; rise –, arise –, take its rise –, spring –, proceed –, emanate –, come –, grow –, bud –, sprout –, germinate –, issue –, flow –, result –, follow –, derive its origin –, accrue- from; come -to, – of, – out of; depend –, hang –, hinge –, turn- upon.

take the consequences, sow the wind and reap the whirlwind.

Adj. owing to; resulting from &c. *v.*; resultant; derivable from; due to; caused &c. by, 153; dependent upon; derived –, evolved- from; derivative; hereditary.

Adv. of course, it follows that, naturally, consequently; as a –, in- consequence; through all, all along of, necessarily, eventually.

Phr. *cela va sans dire*, thereby hangs a tale.

institute, lay the foundation of, inaugurate; lie at the root of.

procure, induce, draw down, open the door to, superinduce, evoke, entail, operate; elicit, provoke.

conduce to &c. (*tend to*) 176; contribute; promote; have a -hand in, – finger in- the pie; determine, decide, turn the scale, give the casting vote; have a common origin; derive its origin &c. (*effect*) 154.

Adj. caused &c. *v.*; causal, original; prim-ary, -itive, -ordial; aboriginal; radical; inceptive, embry-onic, -otic; *in -embryo, – ovo*; seminal, germinal; formative, productive &c. 168; at the bottom of; connate, having a common origin.

Adv. because &c. 155; behind the scenes.

155. [Assignment of cause.] **Attribution.—N.** attribution, theory, etiology, ascription, reference to, rationale; accounting for &c. *v.*; palætiology,* imputation, derivation from.

fil-, affil-iation; pedigree &c. (*paternity*) 166.

explanation &c. (*interpretation*) 522; reason why &c. (*cause*) 153.

V. attribute –, ascribe –, impute –, refer –, lay –, point –, trace –, bring home- to; put –, set- down- to; charge –, ground- on; invest with, assign as cause, charge with, blame, lay at the door of, father upon; saddle with; affiliate; account for, derive from, point out the -reason &c. 153; theorize; tell how it comes; put the saddle on the right horse.

Adj. attributed &c. *v.*; attributable &c. *v.*; refer-able, -rible; due to, derivable from; owing to &c. (*effect*) 154; putative.

Adv. hence, thence, therefore, for, since, on account of, because, owing to; on that account; from -this, – that- cause; thanks to, forasmuch as; whence, *propter hoc.*

why? wherefore? whence? how -comes, – is, – happens- it? how does it happen?

in -some, – some such- way; some-how, – or other.

Phr. that is why; *hinc illæ lachrymæ; cherchez la femme.*

156. [Absence of assignable cause.] **Chance.†—N.** chance, indetermination, accident, fortune, hazard, hap, haphazard, chance-medley, random, luck, *raccroc*, casualty, fortuity, contingence, coincidence, adventure, hit; fate &c. (*necessity*) 601; equal chance; lottery, raffle, tombola, sweepstake; toss up &c. 621; turn of the -table, – cards; hazard of the die, chapter of accidents; cast –, throw- of the dice; heads or tails, wheel of Fortune, whirligig of chance; *sortes, – Virgilianæ.*

probability, possibility, contingency, odds, long odds, run of luck; main-chance.

theory of -probabilities, – chances; book-making; assurance; speculation, gamble, gaming &c. 621.

V. chance, hap, turn up; fall to one's lot; be one's -fate &c. 601; stumble on, light –, blunder –, hit- upon; take one's chance &c. 621.

Adj. casual, fortuitous, accidental, haphazard, random, stray, adventitious, adventive, causeless, incidental. contingent, uncaused, undetermined, indeterminate; possible &c. 470; unintentional &c. 621.

Adv. by -chance, – accident; casually; perchance &c. (*possibly*) 470; for aught one knows; as -good, – bad, – ill-luck &c. *n.*- would have it; as it may -be, – chance, – turn up, – happen; as the case may be.

2°. CONNECTION BETWEEN CAUSE AND EFFECT

157. Power.—N. power; poten-cy, -tiality; puissance, might, force; energy &c. 171; dint; right -hand, – arm;

158. Impotence.—N. impotence; in-, dis-ability; disablement, impuissance, imbecility, caducity; incapa-city,

* Whewell, 'History of the Inductive Sciences,' book xviii, vol. iii., p. 397 (3rd edit.).
† The word *Chance* has two distinct meanings: the first, the absence of assignable *cause*, as above; and the second, the absence of *design*—for the latter see 621.

ascendency, sway, control; pre-potency, -pollence; almightiness, omnipotence; authority &c. 737; strength &c. 159.

ability; ableness &c. *adj.*; competency; effi-ciency, -cacy; validity, cogency; enablement; vantage ground; influence &c. 175; horse power; dynamometer.

pressure; elasticity; gravity, electricity, magnetism, galvanism, voltaic electricity, voltaism, electro-magnetism, electrostatics, electrification, electric current &c.; attraction, repulsion; *vis -inertiæ, – mortua, – viva*; potential –, dynamic –, kinetic –, electrical –, chemical –, atomic- energy; friction, suction.

capability, capacity; *quid valeant humeri quid ferre recusent*; faculty, quality, attribute, endowment, virtue, gift, property, qualification, susceptibility.

V. be -powerful &c. *adj.*; gain -power &c. *n.*

belong –, pertain- to; lie –, be- in one's power; can.

give –, confer –, exercise- power &c. *n.*; empower, enable, invest; in-, en-due; endow, arm; strengthen &c. 159; compel &c. 744.

Adj. powerful, puissant; potent, -ial; capable, able; equal –, up- to; cogent, valid; effect-ive, -ual; efficient, efficacious, adequate, competent; multi-, pleni-, omni-, armi- potent; mighty, ascendent; almighty.

electric, electrical &c.

forcible &c. *adj.* (*energetic*) 171; influential &c. 175; productive &c. 168.

Adv. powerfully &c. *adj.*; by -virtue, – dint- of.

———

-bility; inapt-, inept-itude; indocility; invalidity, inefficiency, incompetence, disqualification.

telum imbelle, brutum fulmen, blank cartridge, flash in the pan, *vox et præterea nihil,* dead letter, bit of waste paper, dummy; scrap of paper.

inefficacy &c. (*inutility*) 645; failure &c. 732.

helplessness &c. *adj.*; prostration, paralysis, palsy, ataxia, apoplexy, syncope, sideration, *deliquium,* collapse, exhaustion, softening of the brain, emasculation, inanition, senility &c. 128; castrato, eunuch.

cripple, old woman, muff, mollycoddle, milksop.

V. be -impotent &c. *adj.*; not have a leg to stand on.

vouloir -rompre l'anguille au genou, – prendre la lune avec les dents.

collapse, faint, swoon, fall into a swoon, drop; go by the board; end in smoke &c. (*fail*) 732.

render -powerless &c. *adj.*; deprive of power; decontrol; dis-able, -enable; disarm, incapacitate, disqualify, unfit, invalidate, undermine, deaden, cramp, tie the hands; double up, prostrate, paralyze, muzzle, cripple, becripple, maim, lame, hamstring, draw the teeth of; throttle, strangle, *garrotte;* ratten, silence, sprain, clip the wings of, render *hors de combat,* spike the guns; take the wind out of one's sails, scotch the snake, put a spoke in one's wheel; break the -neck, – back; un-hinge, -fit; put out of gear.

unman, unnerve, devitalize, attenuate, enervate; emasculate, spay, caponize, castrate, geld; effeminize.

shatter, exhaust; weaken &c. 160.

Adj. powerless, impotent, unable, incapable, incompetent; ineff-icient, -ective; inept; un-fit, -fitted; un-, dis-qualified; unendowed; in-, un-apt; crippled, decrepit, disabled &c. *v.*; armless.

harmless, unarmed, weaponless, defenceless, *sine ictu,* unfortified, indefensible, vincible, pregnable, untenable.

para-lytic, -lyzed; palsied, imbecile; nerve-, sinew-, marrow-, pith-, lust-less; emasculate, disjointed; out of -joint, – gear; un--nerved, -hinged; water-logged, on one's beam ends, rudderless; laid on one's back; done up, dead beat, exhausted, shattered, demoralized; gravelled &c. (*in difficulty*) 704; helpless, unfriended, fatherless; without a leg to stand on, *hors de combat,* laid on the shelf.

null and void, nugatory, inoperative, good for nothing; dud; invertebrate; ineffectual &c. (*failing*) 732; inadequate &c. 640; inefficacious &c. (*useless*) 645.

159. [Degree of power.] **Strength.** —**N.** strength; power &c. 157; energy &c. 171; vigour, force; main –, physical –, brute- force; spring, elasticity, tone, tension, tonicity.

stoutness &c. *adj*; lustihood, stamina, nerve, muscle, sinew, thews and sinews, *physique*; pith, -iness; virility, vitality.

athlet-ics, -icism; gymnastics, feats of strength.

adamant, steel, iron, oak, heart of oak; iron grip; grit, bone.

athlete, gymnast, tumbler, acrobat; Atlas, Hercules, Antæus, Samson, Cyclops, Goliath, Titan; tower of strength; giant refreshed.

strengthening &c. *v.*; invigoration, refreshment, refocillation.

[Science of forces] dynamics, statics.

V. be -strong &c. *adj.*, – stronger; overmatch.

render -strong &c. *adj.*; give -strength &c. *n.*; strengthen, invigorate, brace, nerve, fortify, buttress, sustain, harden, case-harden, steel; gird; screw –, wind –, set- up; gird –, brace- up one's loins; recruit, set on one's legs; vivify; refresh &c. 689; refect; reinforce &c. (*restore*) 660.

Adj. strong, mighty, vigorous, forcible, hard, adamantine, stout, robust, sturdy, hardy, powerful, potent, puissant, valid.

resistless, irresistible, invincible, proof against, impregnable, unconquerable, indomitable, inextinguishable, unquenchable; incontestable; more than a match for; over-powering, -whelming; all-powerful; sovereign.

able-bodied; athletic, gymnastic; Herculean, Cyclopean, Atlantean; muscular, husky, brawny, wiry, well-knit, broad-shouldered, sinewy, strapping, stalwart, gigantic.

man-ly, -like, -ful; masculine, male, virile, in the prime of manhood.

un-weakened, -allayed, -withered, -shaken, -worn, -exhausted; in full -force, – swing; in the plenitude of power.

160. Weakness.—N. weakness &c. *adj.*; debility, atony, relaxation, languor, enervation; impotence &c. 158; infirmity; effeminancy, feminality; fragility, flaccidity; inactivity &c. 683.

declension –, loss –, failure- of strength; delicacy, invalidation, decrepitude, asthenia, adynamy, cachexy, *cachexia*, anæmia, bloodlessness, sprain, strain.

reed, thread, rope of sand, broken reed, house -of cards, – built on sand.

soft-, weak-ling; infant &c. 129; youth &c. 127.

V. be -weak &c. *adj.*; drop, crumble, give way, totter, tremble, shake, halt, limp, fade, languish, decline, flag, fail, have one foot in the grave.

render -weak &c. *adj.*; weaken, enfeeble, debilitate, shake, deprive of strength, relax, enervate; un-brace, -nerve; cripple, unman, &c. (*render powerless*) 158; cramp, reduce, sprain, strain, blunt the edge of; dilute, impoverish; decimate; extenuate; reduce -in strength, – the strength of; invalidate; *mettre de l'eau dans son vin.*

Adj. weak, feeble, debile; impotent &c. 158; relaxed, unnerved &c. *v.*; sap-, strength-, power-less; weakly, unstrung, flaccid, adynamic, asthenic; nervous.

soft, effeminate, feminate, womanish.

frail, fragile, shattery, frangible, brittle &c. 328; flimsy, unsubstantial, gimcrack, gingerbread; rickety, cranky; creachy; drooping, tottering &c. *v.*; broken, lame, halt, game, withered, shattered, shaken, crazy, shaky, tumble-down; palsied &c. 158; decrepit; C3.

languid, poor, poorly, infirm; faint, -ish; sickly &c. (*disease*) 655; dull, slack, evanid, spent, short-winded, effete; weatherbeaten; decayed, rotten, worn, seedy, languishing, wasted, washy, wishy-washy, laid low, pulled down, the worse for wear.

un-strengthened &c. 159, -supported, -aided, -assisted; aidless, defenceless &c. 158.

stubborn, thick-ribbed, made of iron, deep-rooted; strong as -a lion, – a horse, – brandy; sound as a roach; in -fine, – high- feather; in fine fettle; like a giant refreshed.

Adv. strongly &c. *adj.*; by -force &c. *n.*; by main force &c. (*by compulsion*) 744.

Phr. 'our withers are unwrung.'

on its last legs; weak as a -child, – baby, – chicken, – cat, – rat; weak as -water, – water gruel, – gingerbread, – milk and water; colourless &c. 429.

Phr. *non sum qualis eram.*

3°. Power in Operation

161. Production.—N. production, creation, construction, formation, fabrication, manufacture; building, architecture, erection, edification; coinage; organization; *nisus formativus*; putting together &c. *v.*; establishment; workmanship, performance; achievement &c. (*completion*) 729; effect &c. 154.

flowering, fructification, fruition.

bringing forth &c. *v.*; parturition, birth, birth-throe, child-birth, delivery, confinement, *accouchement*, travail, labour, midwifery, obstetrics; geniture; gestation &c. (*maturation*) 673; evolution, development, growth; genesis, fertilization, breeding, conception, germination, generation, *epigenesis*, pro-creation, -generation, -pagation; fecundation, impregnation; spontaneous generation; *arche-genesis, -biosis; bio-, abio-, homo-, xeno-genesis.**

authorship, publication; works, *œuvre, opus.*

edifice, building, structure, fabric, erection, pile, tower, flower, fruit.

V. produce, perform, operate, do, make, gar, form, construct, fabricate, frame, contrive, manufacture; weave, forge, coin, carve, chisel; build, raise, edify, rear, erect, put together; set –, run- up; establish, constitute, compose, organize, institute, get up; achieve, accomplish &c. (*complete*) 729.

flower, sprout, blossom, burgeon, bear fruit, fructify, spawn, teem, ean, yean, farrow, drop, calf, pup, whelp, kitten, kindle; bear, lay, bring forth, give birth to, lie in, be brought to bed of, evolve, pullulate, usher into the world.

make productive &c. 168; create; beget, conceive, get, generate, fecun-

162. [Non-production.] Destruction. —N. destruction; waste, dissolution, breaking up; di-, dis-ruption; consumption; disorganization.

fall, downfall, ruin, perdition, crash, smash, havoc, *délabrement, débâcle*; break -down, – up; prostration; desolation, *bouleversement*, wreck, crack-up, crash, wrack, shipwreck, cataclysm; Caudine Forks, Sedan.

extinction, annihilation; destruction of life &c. 361; knock-out, knock-down blow; doom, crack of doom.

destroying &c. *v.*; demo-lition, -lishment; biblioclasm; overthrow, subversion, suppression; abolition &c. (*abrogation*) 756; sacrifice; ravage, devastation, *sabotage, razzia*; incendiarism; revolution &c. 146; extirpation &c. (*extraction*) 301; *commencement de la fin*, road to ruin; dilapidation &c. (*deterioration*) 659.

V. be -destroyed &c.; perish; fall, – to the ground; tumble, topple; go –, fall- to pieces; break up; crumble, – to dust; go to -the dogs, – the wall, – smash, – shivers, – wreck, – pot, – wrack and ruin; go -by the board, – all to smash, – to pieces, – under; be all -over, – up- with; totter to its fall.

destroy; do –, make- away with; nullify; annul &c. 756; sacrifice, demolish; tear up; over-turn, -throw, -whelm; upset, subvert, put an end to; seal the doom of, do for, dish, undo; break -, cut- up; break –, cut –, pull –, mow –, blow –, beat- down; suppress, quash, put down; cut short, take off, blot out; dispel, dissipate, dissolve; consume.

smash, – to smithereens, quell, squash, squelch, crumple up, shatter,

* Huxley.

date, impregnate; pro-create, -generate, -pagate; engender; bring –, call- into -being, – existence; breed, hatch, develop, bring up.

induce, superinduce; suscitate; cause &c. 153; acquire &c. 775.

Adj. produc-ed, -ing &c. *v.*; productive of; prolific &c. 168; creative; formative; gen-etic, -ial, -ital; fertile, pregnant; *enceinte*, big –, fraught-with; with child, in the family way, teeming, parturient, in the straw, brought to bed of; puerper-al, -ous.

architectonic; constructive.

_____

shiver; batter; tear –, crush –, cut –, shake –, pull –, pick- to pieces; nip; tear to -rags, – tatters; crush –, knock-to atoms; pulverize; ruin; strike out; throw –, knock- -down, – over; lay by the heels; fell, sink, swamp, scuttle, wreck, crash, shipwreck, engulf, submerge; lay in -ashes, – ruins; sweep away, erase, expunge, strike out, delete, efface, raze; level, – with the -ground, – dust.

deal destruction, lay waste, ravage, gut; disorganize; dismantle &c. (*render useless*) 645; devour, swallow up, desolate, devastate, sap, mine, blast, confound; exterminate, extinguish, quench, annihilate; snuff –, put –, stamp –, trample- out; lay –, trample- in the dust; prostrate; tread –, crush –, trample- under foot; lay the axe to the root of; make -short work, – a clean sweep, – mince-meat- of; cut up root and branch; fling –, scatter- to the winds; throw overboard; strike at the root of, sap the foundations of, spring a mine, blow up; ravage with fire and sword; cast to the dogs; eradicate &c. 301.

Adj. destroyed &c. *v.*; perishing &c. *v.*; trembling –, nodding –, tottering- to its fall; in course of -destruction &c. *n.*; extinct.

destructive, subversive, ruinous, incendiary, deletory; destroying &c. *v.*; suicidal; deadly &c. (*killing*) 361.

Adv. with -crushing effect, – a sledge-hammer.

Phr. *delenda est Carthago.*

163. Reproduction.—**N.** reproduction, renovation; restoration &c. 660; renewal; new edition, reprint &c. 21; revival, regeneration, palingenesia, revivification; apotheosis; resuscitation, reanimation, resurrection, resurgence, reappearance, atavism; Phœnix; reincarnation.

generation &c. (*production*) 161; multiplication.

V. reproduce; restore &c. 660; revive, renovate, renew, regenerate, revivify, resuscitate, reanimate, refashion, stir the embers, put into the crucible; multiply, repeat, resurge.

crop up, spring up like mushrooms.

Adj. reproduced &c. *v.*; renascent, reappearing; reproductive; re-surgent; progenitive; Hydra-headed.

164. Producer.—**N.** producer, creator, deviser, designer, originator, inventor, author, founder, generator, mover, architect; grower, constructor, maker &c. (*agent*) 690.

166. Paternity.—**N.** paternity; parentage; fatherhood; consanguinity &c. 11.

parent, father, sire, dad, daddy, papa, governor, *pater*, *paterfamilias*, *abba*; genitor, progenitor, procreator, begetter; ancestor; grand-sire, -father; great-grandfather.

165. Destroyer.—**N.** destroyer &c. (destroy &c. 162); cankerworm &c. (*bane*) 663; iconoclast; assassin &c. (*killer*) 361; executioner &c. (*punish*) 975; Hun, Vandal, nihilist, anarchist.

167. Posterity.—**N.** posterity, progeny, breed, issue, offspring, brood, litter, seed, farrow, spawn, spat; family, children, grandchildren, heirs; great-grandchild.

child, son, daughter; kid; infant &c. 129; bantling, scion; shoot, sprout, olive branch, sprit, branch; off-shoot,

house, stem, trunk, tree, stock, *stirps*, pedigree, lineage, line, family, tribe, sept, race, clan; genealogy, descent, extraction, birth, ancestry; forefathers, forbears, patriarchs.

motherhood, maternity; mother, dam, mamma, *materfamilias*; grandmother; matriarch.

Adj. paternal, parental; maternal; matrilinear, patrilineal, patriarchal.

-set; ramification; descendant; heir, -ess; heir -apparent, – presumptive; chip of the old block; heredity; rising generation.

straight descent, sonship, line, lineage, filiation, primogeniture.

Adj. filial.

family, ancestral, linear,

168. Productiveness.—N. productiveness &c. *adj.*; fecundity, fertility, luxuriance, uberty.

pregnancy, pullulation, fructification, multiplication, propagation, procreation; superfetation.

milch cow, rabbit, hydra, warren, seed-plot, land flowing with milk and honey; second crop, after-crop, -growth, -math; fertilization.

V. make -productive &c. *adj.*; fructify; procreate, generate, fertilize, spermatize, impregnate; fecund-ate, -ify; teem, pullulate, multiply; produce &c. 161; conceive.

Adj. productive, prolific; teem-ing, -ful; fertile, fruitful, frugiferous, fruit-bearing; fructiferous; fecund, luxuriant; pregnant, uberous.

procre-ant, -ative; generative, life-giving, spermatic; originative; multiparous; omnific; propagable.

parturient &c. (*producing*) 161; profitable &c. (*useful*) 644.

169. Unproductiveness.—N. unproductiveness &c. *adj.*; infertility, steril; ity, infecundity; impotence &c. 158- unprofitableness &c. (*inutility*) 645.

waste, desert, Sahara, wild, wilderness, howling wilderness.

V. be -unproductive &c. *adj.*; hang fire, flash in the pan, come to nothing.

Adj. unproductive, inoperative, barren, addle, unfertile, unprolific, arid, sterile, unfruitful, acarpous, infecund; *sine prole*; fallow; teem-, issue-, fruitless; unprofitable &c. (*useless*) 645; null and void, of no effect.

170. Agency.—N. agency, operation, force, working, strain, function, office, maintenance, exercise, work, swing, play; inter-working, -action, procuration, procurement.

causation &c. 153; instrumentality &c. 631; influence &c. 175; action &c. (*voluntary*) 680; *modus operandi* &c. 627.

quickening –, maintaining- power; home stroke.

V. be -in action &c. *adj.*; operate, work; act, – upon; perform, play, support, sustain, strain, maintain, take effect, quicken, strike.

come –, bring- into -operation, – play; have -play, – free play; bring to bear upon.

Adj. operative, efficient, efficacious, practical, effectual.

at work, on foot; acting &c. (*doing*) 680; in -operation, – force, – action, – play, – exercise; acted –, wrought- upon.

Adv. by the -agency &c. *n.*- of; through &c. (*instrumentality*) 631; by means of &c. 632.

171. Physical Energy.—N. energy, physical energy, force; keenness &c. *adj.*; intensity, vigour, strength, elasticity; go; pep, live wire, high pressure; backbone, mettle, fire, vim.

acri-mony, -tude, -dity; causticity,

172. Physical Inertness.—N. inertness, dulness &c. *adj.*; inertia, *vis inertiæ*, inertion, inactivity, torpor, languor; dormancy, quiescence &c. 265; latency, inaction, passivity.

mental inertness; sloth &c. (*inac-*

virulence, poignancy; harshness &c. *adj.*; severity, edge, point; pungency &c. 392.

cantharides; Spanish fly; seasoning &c. (*condiment*) 393, stimulant, excitant.

activity, agitation, effervescence; ferment, -ation; ebullition, splutter, perturbation, stir, bustle; voluntary energy &c. 682; quicksilver.

resolution &c. (*mental energy*) 604; exertion &c. (*effort*) 686; excitation &c. (*mental*) 824.

V. give -energy &c. *n.*; energize, stimulate, kindle, excite, activate, exert; sharpen, pep up, intensify; inflame &c. (*render violent*) 173; wind up &c. (*strengthen*) 159.

strike, – into, – hard, – home; make an impression.

Adj. strong, energetic, forcible, active; strenuous, forceful, mettlesome, enterprising, go ahead; intense, deep-dyed, severe, keen, vivid, sharp, acute, incisive, trenchant, brisk, vigorous, live.

rousing, irritating; poignant; virulent, caustic, corrosive, mordant, harsh, stringent; double-edged, – shotted, – distilled; drastic, escharotic; racy &c. (*pungent*) 392; sarcastic &c. 932.

potent &c. (*powerful*) 157; radio-active.

Adv. strongly &c. *adj.*; *fortiter in re*; with telling effect.

Phr. the steam is up; *vires acquirit eundo*.

173. Violence.—N. violence, inclemency, vehemence, might, impetuosity; boisterousness &c. *adj.*; effervescence, ebullition; turbulence, bluster; uproar, riot, row, rumpus, *le diable à quatre*, devil to pay, all the fat in the fire.

severity &c. 739; ferocity, rage, berserk, fury; exacerbation, exasperation, malignity; fit, paroxysm, orgasm; force, brute force; outrage; *coup de main*; strain, shock, shog; spasm, convulsion, throe; hysterics, passion &c. (*state of excitability*) 825.

out-break, -burst; burst, bounce, dissilience, discharge, volley, explosion, blow up, blast, detonation, rush, eruption, displosion, torrent.

turmoil &c. (*disorder*) 59; ferment &c. (*agitation*) 315; storm, tempest, rough weather; squall &c. (*wind*) 349; earthquake, volcano, thunderstorm.

fury, dragon, demon, tiger, beldame, Tisiphone, Megæra, Alecto, madcap, wild beast; fire-eater &c. (*blusterer*) 887.

V. be -violent &c. *adj.*; run high; ferment, effervesce; romp, rampage; run -wild, – riot; break the peace;

tivity) 683; inexcitability &c. 826; irresolution &c. 605; obstinacy &c. 606; permanence &c. 141.

V. be -inert &c. *adj.*; hang fire, smoulder.

Adj. inert, inactive, passive, pacific; torpid &c. 683; sluggish, stagnant, dull, heavy, flat, slack, tame, slow, blunt; lifeless, dead, uninfluential.

latent, dormant, smouldering, unexerted.

Adv. inactively &c. *adj.*; in -suspense, -abeyance.

---

174. Moderation.—N. moderation; lenity &c. 740; temperance, temperateness, gentleness &c. *adj.*; sobriety; quiet; mental calmness &c. (*inexcitability*) 826.

moderating &c. *v.*; relaxation, remission, mitigation &c. 834; tranquillization, alleviation, assuagement, appeasement, contemporation, pacification.

measure, *juste milieu*, golden mean &c. 29.

moderator; lullaby, sedative, lenitive, demulcent, rose-water, balm, soothing syrup, poppy, opiate, anodyne, milk, opium, laudanum, 'poppy or mandragora'; wet blanket; palliative, calmative.

V. be -moderate &c. *adj.*; keep within -bounds, – compass; sober –, settle-down; keep the peace, remit, relent; take in sail.

moderate, soften, mitigate, temper, accoy; at-, con-temper; mollify, lenify, dull, take off the edge, blunt, obtund, sheathe, subdue, chasten; sober –, tone –, smooth- down; censor, blue-

rush, tear; rush head-long, -foremost; run amuck, raise a storm, make a riot; make –, kick up- a row, – a fuss; bluster, rage, roar, riot, storm; boil, – over; fume, foam, come in like a lion, wreak, bear down, ride rough-shod, out-Herod Herod; spread like wildfire.

break –, fly –, burst- out; bounce, shock, strain; break-, pry-, force-, prize- open.

render -violent &c. *adj.*; sharpen, stir up, quicken, excite, incite, urge, lash, stimulate; irritate, inflame, ex-acerbate, kindle, suscitate, foment; accelerate, aggravate, exasperate, con-vulse, infuriate, madden, lash into fury; fan –, add fuel to- the flame; *oleum addere camino.*

explode, go off, displode, fly, de-tonate, thunder, blow up, flash, flare, erupt, burst; let -off, – fly; discharge, detonize, fulminate.

Adj. violent, vehement, forcible; warm; acute, sharp; rough, rude, un-gentle, bluff, boisterous, wild, vicious; brusque, abrupt, waspish; impetuous; rampant.

turbulent; disorderly; blustering, raging &c. *v.*; troublous, riotous; tumultu-ary, -ous; obstreperous, up-roarious; extravagant, unmitigated; ravening, tameless; frenzied &c. (*insane*) 503; desperate &c. (*rash*) 863; infuriate, towering, furious, outrageous, frantic, hysteric, in hysterics.

fiery, flaming, scorching, hot, red-hot, ebullient.

savage, fierce, ferocious, fierce as a tiger.

excited &c. *v.*; un-quelled, -quenched, -extinguished, -repressed, -bridled, -ruly; headstrong; un-governable, -appeasable, -mitigable; un-, in-controllable; insup-, irre-pressible.

spasmodic, convulsive, explosive; detonating &c. *v.*; volcanic, meteoric; stormy &c. (*wind*) 349.

Adv. violently &c. *adj.*; amain; by -storm, – force, – main force; with might and main; tooth and nail, *vi et armis*, at the point of the -sword, – bayonet; at one fell swoop; with a high hand, through thick and thin; in desperation, with a vengeance; *à* –, *à toute-outrance*; head-long, -foremost, -first; like a bull at a gate.

pencil, weaken &c. 160; lessen &c; (*decrease*) 36; check; palliate.

tranquillize, assuage, appease, dul-cify, swage, lull, soothe, compose, still, calm, cool, quiet, hush, quell, sober, pacify, tame, damp, lay, allay, rebate, slacken, smooth, alleviate, rock to sleep, deaden, smother; throw -cold water on, – a wet blanket over; slake; curb &c. (*restrain*) 751; tame &c. (*subjugate*) 749; smooth over; pour oil on the -waves, – troubled waters; pour balm into, *mettre de l'eau dans son vin.*

go out like a lamb, 'roar you as gently as any sucking dove.'

Adj. moderate; lenient &c; 740; gentle, mild; cool, sober, temperate, reasonable, measured; tempered &c. *v.*; calm, unruffled, quiet, tranquil, still; slow, smooth, untroubled; tame; peace-ful, -able; pacific, halcyon.

un-exciting, -irritating; soft, bland, oily, demulcent, lenitive, anodyne; hyp-notic &c. 683; sedative; assuaging.

mild as mother's milk; milk and water; gentle as a lamb.

Adv. moderately &c. *adj.*; gingerly; *piano*; under easy sail, at half speed; within -bounds, – compass; in reason.

Phr. *est modus in rebus.*

4°. INDIRECT POWER

175. Influence.—N. influence; im-portance &c. 642; weight, pressure, preponderance, prevalence, sway, pull; predomi-nance, -nancy; ascendency; control, dominance, reign; authority

175a. Absence of Influence.—N. impotence &c. 158; inertness &c. 172; irrelevancy &c. 10.

V. have no -influence &c. 175.

Adj. uninfluential; unconduc-ing,

&c. 737; capability &c. (*power*) 157; interest; spell, magic, magnetism.

footing; purchase &c. (*support*) 215; play, leverage, vantage ground.

tower of strength, host in himself; protection, patronage, auspices.

V. have -influence &c. *n.*; be -influential &c. *adj.*; carry weight, actuate, sway, bias, weigh, tell; have a hold upon, magnetize, bear upon, gain a footing, work upon; take -root, – hold; strike root in.

run through, pervade; prevail, dominate, predominate, subject; out-, over-weigh; over-ride, -bear, – come; gain head; rage; be -rife &c. *adj.*; spread like wildfire; have –, get –, gain- -the upper hand, – full play.

be -recognized, – listened to; make one's voice heard, gain a hearing; play a -part, – leading part- in; lead, control, rule, master; get the mastery over; make one's influence felt, cut ice with; take the lead, pull the strings; turn –, throw one's weight into- the scale; set the fashion, lead the dance.

Adj. influential; important &c. 642; weighty; prevailing &c. *v.*; prevalent, rife, rampant, dominant, regnant, predominant, in the ascendant, hegemonical; authoritative, recognized, telling, with authority.

Adv. with telling effect.

-ive, -ting to; powerless &c. 158; irrelevant &c. 10.

———

176. Tendency.—**N.** tendency; apt-ness, -itude; proneness, proclivity, bent, turn, tone, bias, set, warp, leaning to, predisposition, inclination, conatus, propensity, susceptibility; liability &c. 177; quality, nature, temperament; characteristic, idio-crasy, -syncrasy; cast, vein, grain; humour, mood; drift &c. (*direction*) 278; con-duciveness, -ducement; applicability &c. (*utility*) 644; subservience &c. (*instrumentality*) 631.

V. tend, contribute, conduce, lead, dispose, incline, verge, bend to, warp, turn, trend, affect, carry, redound to, bid fair to, gravitate towards; prómote &c. (*aid*) 707.

Adj. tending &c. *v.*; conducive, working towards, in a fair way to, calculated to; liable &c. 177; subservient &c. (*instrumental*) 631; useful &c. 644; subsidiary &c. (*helping*) 707.

Adv. for, whither.

177. Liability.—**N.** lia-bility, -bleness; possibility, contingency; suscepti-vity, -bility.

V. be -liable &c. *adj.*; incur, lay oneself open to; run the –, stand a- chance; lie under, expose oneself to, open a door to.

Adj. liable, subject; in danger &c. 665; open –, exposed –, obnoxious- to; answerable, responsible, accountable, amenable; unexempt from; apt to; dependent on; incident to.

contingent, incidental, possible, on the cards, within range of, at the mercy of.

5°. COMBINATIONS OF CAUSES

178. Concurrence.—**N.** concurrence, cooperation, coagency; coincidence, consilience; union; agreement &c. 23; consent &c. (*assent*) 488; alliance; concert &c. 709; partnership &c. 712; collaboration, conformity.

V. con-cur, -duce, -spire, -tribute;

179. Counteraction.—**N.** counteraction, opposition; contrariety &c. 14; antagonism, polarity; clashing &c. *v.*; collision, interference, resistance, renitency, friction; reaction; retroaction; repercussion &c. (*recoil*) 277; counter-blast; neutralization &c. (*compensa-*

agree, unite, harmonize; hang –, pull-together &c. (*co-operate*) 709; help to &c. (*aid*) 707.

keep pace with, run parallel to; go –, go along –, go hand in hand- with.

Adj. concurring &c. *v.*; concurrent, conformable, joint, co-operative, concordant, coincident, concomitant, harmonious; in alliance with, banded together, of one mind, at one with; parallel.

Adv. with one consent.

———

tion) 30; *vis inertiæ*; check &c. (*hindrance*) 706.

voluntary -opposition &c. 708, – resistance &c. 719; repression &c. (*restraint*) 751.

V. counteract; run counter, clash, cross; interfere –, conflict- with; jostle; go –, run –, beat –, militate- against; stultify; antagonize, frustrate, oppose &c. 708; withstand &c. (*resist*) 719; hinder &c. 706; repress &c. (*restrain*) 751; react &c. (*recoil*) 277.

undo, neutralize, cancel; counterpoise &c. (*compensate*) 30; overpoise.

Adj. counteracting &c. *v.*; antagonistic, conflicting, retroactive, renitent, reactionary; contrary &c. 14.

Adv. although &c. 30; in spite of &c. 708; *malgré*; against.

CLASS II

WORDS RELATING TO SPACE

CLASS II

Words Relating to SPACE

Section I.　SPACE IN GENERAL

1°. Abstract Space

180. [Indefinite - space.] **Space.—N.** space, extension, extent, superficial extent, expanse, stretch; capacity, room, accommodation, scope, range, latitude, field, way, expansion, compass, sweep, play, swing, spread.

spare -, elbow -, house- room; stowage, roomage, margin; opening, sphere, arena; lee-, sea-, head-way.

open -, free- space; wide open spaces; void &c. (*absence*) 187; waste; wild-, wilder-ness; up-, bottom-, moor -land; *campagna, veldt*, prairie, steppe.

abyss &c. (*interval*) 198; unlimited space; infinity &c. 105; world, wide world; ubiquity &c. (*presence*) 186; length and breadth of the land.

proportions, acreage; acres, - roods and perches; square -inches, - yards &c.

Adj. spacious, roomy, extensive, expansive, capacious, ample; wide-spread, vast, world-wide, uncircumscribed; boundless &c. (*infinite*) 105; shore-, track-, path-less; large &c. 192.

Adv. extensively &c. *adj.*; wherever; everywhere; far and -near, - wide; right and left, all over, all the world over; throughout the -world, - length and breadth of the land; under the sun, in every quarter; in all -quarters, - lands; here, there and everywhere; from -pole to pole, - China to Peru, - Indus to the pole, - Dan to Beersheba, - end to end; on the face of the earth, in the wide world, from all points of the compass; to the -four winds, - uttermost parts of the earth.

180a. Inextension.—N. in-, non-extension; point; atom &c. (*smallness*) 32; pinprick; limitation &c. 229.

181. [Definite space.] **Region.—N.** region, sphere, sphere of influence, corridor, ground, soil, area, realm, hemisphere, quarter district, beat, orb, circuit, circle; pale &c. (*limit*) 233; com-, de-partment; domain, tract, territory, terrain, country, canton, county, shire, province, *arrondissement*, diocese, parish, township, borough, constituency, *commune*, ward, wapentake, hundred, riding, lathe, garth, soke, tithing, bailiwick; empire, kingdom, principality, duchy, grand -, arch- duchy, palatinate; republic, commonwealth, dominion, colony, state, island.

arena, precincts, *enceinte*, walk, march; patch, plot, enclosure, &c. 232; close, *enclave*, field, court; street &c. (*abode*) 189.

clime, climate, zone, meridian, latitude.

Adj. territorial, local, parochial, provincial, insular.

182. [Limited space.] **Place.—N.** place, lieu, spot, point, dot; niche, nook, &c. (*corner*) 244; hole; pigeonhole &c. (*receptacle*) 191; compartment; premises, precinct, station, confine; area, court, yard, quadrangle, square, compound; abode &c. 189; locality &c. (*situation*) 183.

ins and outs; every hole and corner.

Adv. somewhere, in some place, wherever it may be, here and there, in various places, *passim*.

2°. Relative Space

183. Situation.—**N.** situation, position, locality, *locale*, *status*, latitude and longitude; footing, standing, standpoint, post; stage; aspect, attitude, posture, *pose*.

place, site, base, station, seat, *venue*, whereabouts, environment, neighbourhood; bearings &c. (*direction*) 278; spot &c. (*limited space*) 182.

top-, ge-, chor-ography; map &c. 554.

V. be -situated, – situate; lie; have its seat in.

Adj. situ-ate, -ated; local, topical, topographical &c. *n.*

Adv. *in -situ*, – *loco*; here and there, *passim*; here-, there-, whereabouts; in place, here, there.

in –, amidst- such and such- -surroundings, – *environs*, – *entourage*.

184. Location.—**N.** loca-tion, -liza-tion; lodgment; de-, re-position; stow-, pack-age; collocation; packing, lading; establishment, settlement, installation; fixation; insertion &c. 300.

anchorage, roadstead, mooring, mooring mast, encampment, camp, bivouac.

plantation, colony, settlement, cantonment, encampment, reservation; colonization, domestication, situation; habitation &c. (*abode*) 189; cohabitation; 'a local habitation and a name'; indenization, naturalization.

V. place, situate, locate, localize, make a place for, put, lay, set, seat, station, lodge, quarter, post, install; storehouse, stow; establish, fix, pin, root; graft; plant &c. (*insert*) 300; shelve, pitch, camp, lay down, deposit, reposit; cradle; moor, tether, picket; pack, tuck in; embed; vest, invest in.

185. Displacement.—**N.** displacement, elocation, transposition.

ejectment &c. 297; exile &c. (*banishment*) 893; removal &c. (*transference*) 270; unshipment.

misplacement, dislocation &c. 61; fish out of water.

V. dis-place, -plant, -lodge, -nest, -establish; misplace, unseat, disturb; exile &c. (*seclude*) 893; ablegate, set aside, remove; take –, cart- away; take –, draft- off; lade &c. 184, unship.

unload, empty &c. (*eject*) 297; transfer &c. 270; dispel.

vacate; depart &c. 293.

Adj. displaced &c. *v.*; un-placed, -housed, -harboured, -established, -settled; house-, home-less; out of -place, – a situation.

misplaced, out of its element.

billet on, quarter upon, saddle with; load, lade, freight; pocket, put up, bag.

inhabit &c. (*be present*) 186; domesticate, colonize, populate, people; take –, strike- root; anchor; cast –, come to an- anchor; sit –, settle-down; settle; take up one's -abode, – quarters; plant –, establish –, locate- oneself; squat, perch, hive, *se nicher*, bivouac, burrow, get a footing; encamp, pitch one's tent; put up -at, – one's horses at; keep house.

indenizen, naturalize, adopt.

put back, replace &c. (*restore*) 660.

Adj. placed &c. *v.*; situate, posited, ensconced, embedded, embosomed, rooted; domesticated; vested in, unremoved.

moored &c. *v.*; at anchor.

3°. Existence in Space

186. Presence.—**N.** presence; occupancy, -ation; attendance; whereness.

permeation, pervasion; diffusion &c. (*dispersion*) 73.

187. [Nullibiety.*] **Absence.** — **N.** absence; inexistence &c. 2; non-residence, absenteeism; non-attendance, *alibi.*

* Bishop Wilkins.

ubi-ety, -quity, -quitariness; omni-presence.

bystander &c. (*spectator*) 444.

V. exist in space, be -present &c. *adj.*; assist at; make one -of, – at; look on, attend, remain; find –, present- oneself; show one's face; fall in the way of, occur in a place; lie, stand; occupy.

people; inhabit, dwell, reside, stay, sojourn, live, room, abide, bunk, lodge, nestle, roost, perch; take up one's abode &c. (*be located*) 184; tenant, occupy.

resort to, frequent, haunt; revisit.

fill, pervade, permeate; be -diffused, – disseminated- through; over-spread, -run; run through; meet one at every turn.

Adj. present; occupying, inhabiting &c. *v.*; moored &c. 184; residential, resi-ant, -dent, -dentiary; domiciled.

ubiquit-ous, -ary; omnipresent.

peopled, populous, full of people, inhabited.

Adv. here, there, where, everywhere, aboard, on board, at home, afield; on the spot; here, there and everywhere &c. (*space*) 180; in presence of, before; under the -eyes, – nose- of; in the face of; *in propriâ personâ*.

emptiness &c. *adj.*; void, *vacuum*; vac-uity, -ancy; *tabula rasa*; exemption; *hiatus* &c. (*interval*) 198; no man's land.

truant, absentee.

nobody; nobody -present, – on earth; no one; not a soul; *âme qui vive.*

V. be -absent &c. *adj.*; keep -away, – out of the way; play truant, absent oneself, stay away.

withdraw, make oneself scarce, vacate; go away, slip out, slip away, retreat &c. 293.

Adj. absent, not present, away, non-resident, gone, from home; missing; lost; wanted, wanting; omitted; nowhere to be found; inexistent &c. 2.

empty, void; blank, vac-ant, -uous; untenanted, -occupied, -inhabited; tenantless; desert, -ed; devoid; un-, uninhabitable.

exempt from, not having.

Adv. without, *minus*, nowhere; elsewhere; neither here nor there; in default of; *sans*; behind one's back.

Phr. the bird has flown, *non est inventus.*

---

188. Inhabitant. — N. inhabitant; habitant, resident, -iary; dweller, in-dweller; occup-ier, -ant, farmer, planter; householder, lodger, boarder, paying guest; inmate, tenant, renter, incumbent, sojourner, *locum tenens*, commorant; settler, squatter, backwoodsman, colonist; islander; denizen, citizen; burgher, oppidan, cockney, cit, townsman, burgess; villager; cot-tager, -tier, -ter; compatriot.

native, indigene, aboriginal, aborigines, autochthones; Briton, Englishman, John Bull; new comer &c. (*stranger*) 57.

garrison, crew; population; people &c. (*mankind*) 372; colony, settlement; household.

V. inhabit &c. (*be present*) 186; indenizen &c. (*locate oneself*) 184.

Adj. indigenous; enchorial; national, nat-ive, -al; autochthonous; British, English; colonial; domestic; domicil-

189. [Place of habitation, or resort.] **Abode.—N.** abode, dwelling, lodging, -s; diggings, domicile, residence, address, habitation, where one's lot is cast, local habitation, berth, seat, lap, sojourn, housing, quarters, headquarters, resiance, tabernacle, throne, ark.

home, fatherland, mother country, country &c. 181; home-stead, -stall; fireside, chimney corner; hearth, – stone; household gods, *lares et penates*, roof, household, housing, *dulce domum*, paternal domicile; native -soil, – land, blighty.

nest, *nidus*, snuggery; arbour, bower &c. 191; lair, den, cave, hole, hiding-place, cell, *sanctum sanctorum*, aerie, eyry, rookery, hive; *habitat*, haunt, covert, resort, retreat, perch, roost; nidification.

bivouac, camp, encampment, cantonment, castrametation; barrack, casemate, casern.

iated, -ed; naturalized, vernacular, domesticated; domiciliary.

in the occupation of; garrisoned -, occupied- by.

_____

tent &c. (*covering*) 223; building &c. (*construction*) 161; chamber &c. (*receptacle*) 191.

tenement, messuage, farm, farm-house, grange, *hacienda*.

cot, cabin, log cabin, shack, hut, *châlet*, croft, shed, booth, stall, hovel, bothy, shanty, igloo, tepee, wigwam; pen &c. (*inclosure*) 232; barn, bawn; kennel, sty, dog-hole, cote, coop, hutch, byre; cow-house, -shed; stable, dove-cote, shippen.

house, mansion, place, villa, cottage, box, lodge, hermitage, *rus in urbe*, folly, rotunda, tower, *château*, castle, pavilion, hotel, court, manor-house, capital messuage, hall, palace, alcazar; country seat; kiosk, bungalow; temple &c. 1000; home of rest, alms-, poor-, work-house, asylum; boarding-, lodging-house; flat, maisonette, duplex, penthouse, suite of rooms, apartments, rooms, room, building &c. 161; Mansion House, town hall, Capitol.

assembly-room, auditorium, coliseum, meeting-house, pump-room, spa, health resort, watering-place; club; theatre &c. 840; drill hall, gymnasium, church &c. 1000; Houses of Parliament &c. 696; school &c. 542; inn; hostel, -ry; hotel, tavern, caravansary, khan, hospice; public-, ale-, pot-, mug-house; gin-palace, gin mill; coffee-, eating-house; canteen, *restaurant*, *rôtisserie*, cafeteria, grill-room, *buffet*, *café*, *estaminet*, *posada*, *bodega*; bar; saloon, speakeasy, shebeen.

hamlet, village, thorp, dorp, ham, kraal; borough, burgh, town, county-seat, - town, city, capital, metropolis; suburb, quarter, parish &c. 181; ghetto; province, country.

street, place, terrace, parade, esplanade, promenade, pier, embankment, road, villas, row, walk, lane, alley, court, quadrangle, quad, wynd, close, yard, passage, rents, mansions, buildings, mews.

square, polygon, circus, crescent, mall, *piazza*, arcade, colonnade, peristyle, cloister; gardens, grove, residences; block of buildings, market-place, *place*.

anchorage, roadstead, roads; dock, basin, wharf, quay, port, harbour; dry-, graving-, floating-dock.

garden, park, pleasure-ground, pleasance, demesne.

V. take up one's abode &c. (*locate oneself*) 184; inhabit &c. (*be present*) 186.

Adj. urban, oppidan, metropolitan; suburban; provincial, rural, rustic; countrified; regional, parochial, domestic; cosmopolitan; palatial.

190. [Things contained.] **Contents.—N.** contents; cargo, lading, freight, shipment, load, bale, burden; cart-, ship-load; cup -, basket -, &c. (*receptacle*) 191- of; inside &c. 221; stuffing, ullage.

V. load, lade, ship, charge, fill, stuff.

191. Receptacle.—N. receptacle, container; inclosure &c. 232; recipient, receiver, reservatory.

compartment; cell, -ule; follicle; hole, corner, niche, recess, nook; crypt, stall, pigeon-hole, cove, oriel; cave &c. (*concavity*) 252.

capsule, vesicle, cyst, pod, calyx, *cancelli*, utricle, bladder, udder.

stomach, paunch, *venter*, abdomen, ventricle, crop, craw, ingluvies, maw, gizzard, bread-basket, belly, little Mary; mouth.

pocket, pouch, fob, sheath, scabbard, socket, bag, vanity bag, compact, sac, sack, saccule, despatch –, attaché-, tachy- case, wallet, scrip, card-, note- case, billfold, poke, knit, knap-, haver-, ruck-sack, sachel, satchel, reticule, budget, net; ditty-, -box, -bag, kitbag; portfolio; saddlebags, holster; quiver &c. (*magazine*) 636.

chest, box, coffer, caddy, case, casket, pyx, pix, *caisson*, desk, *bureau*, reliquary, shrine; trunk, portmanteau, band-box, *valise*, suitcase, hand-, traveling-, overnight-, Gladstone-, carpet-bag, brief case; boot, imperial; *vache*; cage, manger, rack.

vessel, vase, bushel, barrel; canister, jar; pottle, basket, punnet, pannier, buck-basket, hopper, maund, creel, cran, crate, cradle, bassinet, wisket, whisket, *jardinière, corbeille*, hamper, wastepaper basket, dosser, dorser, tray, hod, scuttle, utensil, spittoon, cuspidor.

[For liquids] cistern &c. (*store*) 636; vat, caldron, barrel, cask, puncheon, keg, rundlet, tun, butt, firkin, hogshead, kilderkin, carboy, amphora, ampulla, bottle, jar, leather bottle, decanter, ewer, cruse, carafe, crock, kit, canteen, flagon; demijohn; flask, -et; stoup, noggin, vial, phial, ampoulé, cruet, caster; gourd; urn, *épergne*, salver, *patella, tazza, patera*; pig-, big-gin; tea-, coffee-pot, percolator, *samovar*; tyg, nipperkin, pocket-pistol; tub, bucket, pail, skeel, pot, tankard, jug, pitcher, toby, mug, pipkin; gal-, gall-ipot, pannikin; matrass, receiver, retort, alembic, bolthead, can, kettle; bowl, basin, jorum, punch-bowl, cup, goblet, chalice, tumbler, glass, wineglass, rummer, beaker, tass, horn, saucepan, skillet, posnet, tureen, terrine, *casserole*, sauce-, gravy-boat.

plate, platter, paten, dish, vegetable –, *entrée*- dish, trencher, calabash, porringer, potager, saucer, pan, crucible.

shovel, trowel, spoon; table-, dessert-, tea-, egg-, salt-spoon; spatula, ladle; dipper; baler; watch-glass, thimble.

closet, commode, cupboard, cellaret, *chiffonnière*, locker, bin, bunker, *buffet*, press, safe, sideboard, drawer, chest of drawers, till, *scrutoire, secrétaire, écritoire*, davenport, book-case, cabinet, canterbury; corner cupboard, wardrobe.

chamber, apartment, room, cabin; office, court, hall, atrium; suite of rooms, flat, story; saloon, *salon*, parlour; presence-chamber; sitting-, drawing-, reception-, state-, living-, work-room; gallery, cabinet, closet, cubicle; pew, box; *boudoir; adytum, sanctum*; bed-room, dormitory, dressing-room; refectory, dining-room, *salle-à-manger*; nursery, school-room; library, study; *studio*; billiard-, bath-, smoking-room; den, canteen, mess, officers' mess; gun-, ward-, mess-room.

attic, loft, garret, cockloft, clerestory; cellar, vault, hold, cockpit; *entre-sol*; mezzanine floor; ground-floor, *rez-de-chaussée*; basement, kitchen, cook-house, galley, pantry, scullery, offices; store-room &c. (*depository*) 636; lumber-room; dust-hole, -bin; dairy, laundry, coach-house; *garage; hangar*; out-, pent-house; lean-to.

portico, porch, piazza, verandah, lobby, court, hall, vestibule, corridor, passage; ante-room, -chamber; lounge; *foyer, loggia*.

conservatory, green-house, glass-house, vinery, bower, arbour, summer-house, alcove, grotto, hermitage, pergola.

lodging &c. (*abode*) 189; bed &c. (*support*) 215; carriage &c. (*vehicle*) 272.

Adj. capsular; saccu-lar, -lated; recipient; ventricular, cystic, vascular, vesicular, cellular, camerated, locular, multilocular, poly-gastric; marsupial; siliqu-ose, -ous.

Section II. DIMENSIONS

1°. General Dimensions

192. Size.—N. size, magnitude, dimension, bulk, volume; largeness &c. *adj.*; greatness &c. (*of quantity*) 31; expanse &c. (*space*) 180; amplitude, mass; proportions.

capacity; ton-, tun-nage; calibre, scantling.

turgidity &c. (*expansion*) 194; corpulence, obesity; plumpness, &c. *adj.*; *embonpoint*, corporation, flesh and blood, lustihood.

hugeness &c. *adj.*; enormity, immensity, monstrosity.

giant, Brobdingnagian, Antæus, Goliath, Gog and Magog, Gargantua, monster, mammoth, Cyclops; whale, porpoise, behemoth, leviathan, elephant, hippopotamus; colossus; tun, lump, bulk, block, loaf, mass, clod, nugget, bushel, thumper, whopper, spanker, strapper; Triton among the minnows.

mountain, mound; heap &c. (*assemblage*) 72.

largest portion &c. 50; full-, life-size.

V. ve- large &c. *adj.*; become -large &c. (*expand*) 194.

Adj. large, big; great &c. (*in quantity*) 31; considerable, bulky, voluminous, ample, massive, massy; capacious, comprehensive; spacious &c. 180; mighty, towering, fine, magnificent.

corpulent, stout, fat, plump, squab, full, lusty, strapping, bouncing; portly, burly, well-fed, full-grown; stalwart, brawny, fleshy; goodly; in good -case, – condition; in condition; chopping, jolly; chub-, chubby-faced.

lubberly, hulky, unwieldy, lumpish, gaunt, spanking, whacking, whopping; thumping, thundering, hulking; overgrown; puffy &c. (*swollen*) 194.

huge, immense, enormous, mighty; vast, -y; amplitudinous, stupendous; monst-er, -rous; gigantic, elephantine;

193. Littleness.—N. littleness &c. *adj.*; smallness &c. (*of quantity*) 32; exiguity, inextension; parvi-tude, -ty; duodecimo; Elzevir edition, epitome, microcosm; rudiment; vanishing point; thinness &c. 203.

dwarf, pigmy, atomy, Liliputian, midget, chit, pigwidgeon, urchin, elf; doll, puppet; Tom Thumb, Hop-o'-my thumb, Humpty-dumpty; man-. mannikin; *homunculus*, dapperling, fingerling, dandiprat, cock-sparrow, scalawag.

animalcule, monad, mite, insect, emmet, fly, midge, gnat, shrimp, minnow, worm, maggot, entozoon; *bacillus*, microbe, micro-organism, *bacteria*; *infusoria*; microbe; grub; tit, tomtit, runt, mouse, small fry; millet-, mustard-seed; barley-corn; pebble, grain of sand; mole-hill, button, bubble.

point; atom &c. (*small quantity*) 32; fragment &c. (*small part*) 51; powder &c. 330; point of a pin, mathematical point; *minutiæ* &c. (*unimportance*) 643.

micro-graphy, -meter, -scope; vernier; scale.

V. be -little &c. *adj.*; lie in a nutshell; become small &c. (*decrease*) 36, (*contract*) 195.

Adj. little; small &c. (*in quantity*) 32; minute, diminutive, microscopic; inconsiderable &c. (*unimportant*) 643; exiguous, puny, tiny, wee, petty, minikin, miniature, pigmy, elfin; under sized; dwarf, -ed, -ish; spare, stunted, limited; cramp, -ed; pollard, Liliputian, dapper, pocket; port-ative, -able; duodecimo; dumpy, squat; compact, handy; short &c. 201.

impalpable, intangible, evanescent, imperceptible, invisible, inappreciable, infinitesimal, homœopathic; atomic, corpuscular, molecular; rudiment-ary, -al; embryonic.

weazen, scant, scraggy, scrubby;

giant, -like; colossal, Cyclopean, Brobdingnagian, Gargantuan, Titanic; infinite &c. 105.

large as life; plump as a -dumpling,
– partridge; fat as -a pig, – a quail,
– butter, – brawn, – bacon.

194. Expansion. — N. expansion;
increase &c. 35 -of size; enlargement,
extension, augmentation; ampli-fica-
tion, -ation; aggrandizement, spread,
increment, growth, development, pullulation, swell, dilation, dilatation, rarefaction; turg-escence, -idness, -idity;
obesity &c. (*size*) 192; dropsy, tume-
faction, intumescence, swelling, tumour, *diastole*, distension; puff-ing,
-iness; inflation; pandiculation.

dilatability, expansibility.

germination, growth, upgrowth; accretion &c. 35.

over-growth, -distension; hypertrophy, tympany.

bulb &c. (*convexity*) 250; plumper;
superiority of size.

V. become -larger &c. (large &c. 192);
expand, widen, enlarge, extend, grow,
increase, incrassate, swell, gather; fill
out; deploy, take open order, dilate,
stretch, spread; mantle, wax; grow –,
spring- up; bud, bourgeon, shoot,
sprout, germinate, put forth, vegetate,
pullulate, open, burst forth, flower,
blow &c. 734; gain –, gather- flesh;
outgrow; spread like wildfire, overrun.

be larger than; surpass &c. (*be superior*) 33.

render -larger &c. (large &c. 192);
expand, spread, extend, aggrandize,
distend, develop, amplify, spread out,
widen, magnify, rarefy, inflate, puff,
puff out, blow up, stuff, pad, cram;
exaggerate; fatten.

Adj. expanded &c. *v.*; larger &c.
(large &c. 192); swollen; expansive;
wide-open, -spread; fan-shaped; flabelliform; overgrown, exaggerated,
bloated, fat, turgid, tumid, hyper-
trophied, dropsical; pot-, swag-bellied;
œdematous, obese, puffy, pursy,
blowzy, distended; patulous; bulbous &c. (*convex*) 250; full-blown,
-grown, -formed; big &c. 192.

196. Distance.—N. distance; space
&c. 180; remoteness, farness; far- cry

thin &c. (*narrow*) 203; granular &c.
(*powdery*) 330; shrunk &c. 195.

Adv. in a -small compass, – nutshell;
on a small scale.

---

195. Contraction.—N. contraction,
reduction, diminution; decrease &c. 36-
of size; defalcation, decrement; lessening, shrinkage; collapse, emaciation,
attenuation, tabefaction, consumption,
marasmus, atrophy; systole, neck,
hour-glass.

condensation, compression, constraint, compactness; compendium &c.
596; squeezing &c. *v.*; strangulation;
corrugation; astringency, constrin-
gency; astringents, sclerotics; contractility, compressibility; coarctation.

inferiority in size.

V. become -small, – smaller; lessen,
decrease &c. 36; grow less, dwindle,
shrink, contract, narrow, shrivel, collapse, wither, lose flesh, wizen, fall
away, waste, wane, ebb; decay &c.
(*deteriorate*) 659.

be smaller than, fall short of; not
come up to &c. (*be inferior*) 34.

render smaller, lessen, diminish, contract, draw in, narrow, coarctate; constrict, constringe; condense, compress,
boil down, deflate, exhaust, empty;
squeeze, corrugate, crush, crumple up,
warp, purse up, pack, stow; pinch,
tighten, strangle; cramp; dwarf, be-
dwarf; shorten &c. 201; circumscribe
&c. 229; restrain &c. 751; fold &c. 258.

pare, reduce, attenuate, rub down,
scrape, file, grind, chip, shave, shear.

Adj. contracting &c. *v.*; astringent;
shrunk, contracted &c. *v.*; strangulated,
tabid, wizened, stunted; tabescent;
marasmic; waning &c. *v.*; neap; compact.

unexpanded &c. (expand &c. 194);
inswept; contractile; compressible;
smaller &c. (small &c. 193).

---

197. Nearness.—N. nearness &c.
adj.; proximity, propinquity; vicinity,

[67]

to; longinquity, elongation; offing, background; removedness; parallax; reach, span, stride; drift.

out-post, -skirt; horizon, sky-line; aphelion; foreign parts, *ultima Thule*, *ne plus ultra*, antipodes; long range, giant's stride.

dispersion &c. 73.

V. be -distant &c. *adj.*; extend –, stretch –, reach –, spread –, go –, get –, stretch away- to; range, outrange, outreach.

remain at a distance; keep –, stand- -away, – off, – aloof, – clear of.

Adj. distant; far -off, – away; remote, telescopic, distal, wide of; stretching to &c. *v.*; yon, -der; ulterior; trans-marine, -pontine, -atlantic, -alpine; tramontane; ultra-montane, -mundane; hyperborean, antipodean; inaccessible, out of the way; unapproach-ed, -able; incontiguous.

Adv. far -off, – away; afar, -off; off; away; a -long, – great, – good- way off; wide away, aloof; wide –, clear- of; out of -the way, – reach; abroad, yonder, farther, further, beyond; *outre mer*, over the border, far and wide, over the hills and far away; from pole to pole &c. (*over great space*) 180; to the -uttermost parts, – ends- of the earth; out of -hearing, – range, nobody knows where, *à perte de vue*, out of the sphere, wide of the mark; a far cry to.

apart, asunder; wide -apart, – asunder; *longo intervallo*; at arm's length.

-age; neighbourhood, adjacency; contiguity &c. 199.

short -distance, – step, – cut; earshot, close quarters, stone's throw; bow –, gun –, pistol- shot; hair's breadth, span; close-up.

purlieus, neighbourhood, vicinage, *environs*, *alentours*, suburbs, confines, *banlieue*, borderland; whereabouts.

bystander; neighbour, borderer.

approach &c. 286; convergence &c. 290; perihelion.

V. be -near &c. *adj.*; adjoin, hang about, trench on; border –, verge upon; stand by, approximate, tread on the heels of, cling to, clasp, hug; cuddle, huddle; hang upon the skirts of, hover over; burn; abut.

bring –, draw- -near &c. 286; converge &c. 290; crowd &c. 72; place -side by side &c. *adv.*

Adj. near, nigh; close –, near- at hand; close, neighbouring, propinquent, bordering upon; adjacent, adjoining, limitrophe; proxim-ate, -al; at hand, handy; near the mark, near run; home, intimate.

Adv. near, nigh; hard –, fast- by; close -to, – upon, – up; at the point of; next door to; within -reach, – call, – hearing, – earshot, – range; within an ace of; but a step, not far from, at no great distance; on the -verge, – brink, – skirts- of; in the -environs &c. *n.*; at one's -door, – feet, – elbow, – finger's end, – side; on the tip of one's tongue; under one's nose; within a -stone's throw &c. *n.*; in -sight, – presence- of; at close quarters; cheek by -jole, – jowl; beside, alongside, side by side, *tête-à-tête*; in juxtaposition &c. (*touching*) 199; yard-arm to yard-arm; at the heels of; on the confines of, at the threshold, bordering upon, verging to; in the way.

about; here-, there-abouts; roughly, in round numbers; approxim- -ately, -atively; as good as, well nigh.

---

198. Interval.—N. interval, interspace; separation &c. 44; break, gap, opening; hole &c. 260; chasm, *hiatus*, cæsura; inter-ruption, -regnum; interstice, *lacuna*, cleft, mesh, crevice, chink, rime, creek, cranny, crack, chap, slit, slot, fissure, scissure, rift, flaw, breach, fracture, rent, gash, cut, leak, dike, ha-ha.

199. Contiguity. — N. contiguity, contact, proximity, apposition, juxtaposition, touching &c. *v.*; abutment, osculation; meeting, appulse, appulsion, *rencontre*, rencounter, syzygy, coincidence, conjunction, coexistence; adhesion &c. 46.

border-land; frontier &c. (*limit*) 233; tangent.

gorge, defile, ravine, cañon, *crevasse*, abyss, abysm; gulf; inlet, frith, strait, gully, gulch, nullah; pass; notch; furrow &c. 259; yawning gulf; *hiatus -maxime, – valde- deflendus*; parenthesis &c. (*interjacence*) 228; void &c. (*absence*) 187; incompleteness &c. 530.

V. gape &c. (*open*) 260.

Adj. with an interval, far between.

Adv. at intervals &c. (*discontinuously*) 70; *longo intervallo.*

V. be -contiguous &c. *adj.*; join, adjoin, abut on, march with, border; tick, graze, touch, meet, osculate, kiss, come in contact, coincide; coexist; adhere &c. 46.

Adj. contiguous; touching &c. *v.*; in -contact &c. *n.*; conterminous, end to end, osculatory; pertingent; tangential.

hand to hand; close to &c. (*near*) 197; with no -interval &c. 198.

2°. LINEAR DIMENSIONS

200. Length.—N. length, longitude, span, extent, mileage.

line, bar, rule, stripe, streak, spoke, radius.

lengthening &c. *v.*; pro-longation, -duction, -traction; ten-sion, -sure; extension.

[Measures of length] line, nail, inch, hand, palm, foot, cubit, yard, ell, fathom, rod, pole, perch, furlong, mile, league; chain, metre, kilo-, centi-, milli- &c. -metre.

pedometer, perambulator, odometer, odograph, speedometer, cyclometer, log, telemeter, range finder; scale &c. (*measurement*) 466.

V. be -long &c. *adj.*; stretch out, sprawl; extend –, reach –, stretch- to; make a long arm, 'drag its slow length along.'

render -long &c. *adj.*; lengthen, extend, elongate; stretch; pro-long, -duce, -tract; let –, pay –, draw –, spin- out; drawl.

enfilade, look along, view in perspective.

Adj. long, -some; lengthy, lank, wiredrawn, outstretched; lengthened &c. *v.*; sesquipedalian &c. (*words*) 577; interminable, no end of.

line-ar, -al; longitudinal, oblong.

as long as -my arm, – to-day and to-morrow; unshortened &c. (shorten &c. 201).

Adv. lengthwise, at length, longitudinally, endlong, along; *tandem*; in a line &c. (*continuously*) 69; in perspective.

from -end to end, – stem to stern, – head to foot, – the crown of the head to the sole of the foot, – top to toe, – head to heels; fore and aft.

201. Shortness.—N. shortness &c. *adj.*; brevity; littleness &c. 193; a span.

shortening &c. *v.*; abbrevia-tion, -ture; abridgment, concision, retrenchment, curtailment, decurtation; reduction &c. (*contraction*) 195; epitome &c. (*compendium*) 596.

abridger, abstractor, epitomiser.

elision, ellipsis; conciseness &c. (*in style*) 572.

V. be -short &c. *adj.*; render -short &c. *adj.*; shorten, curtail, abridge, abbreviate, take in, reduce; compress &c. (*contract*) 195; epitomize &c. 596.

retrench, cut short, obtruncate; scrimp, cut, chop up, hack, hew; cut –, pare- down; clip, snip, dock, lop, prune; shear, shave, mow, reap, crop; snub; truncate, pollard, stunt, nip, nip in the bud, check the growth of; [in drawing] foreshorten.

Adj. short, brief, curt; compendious, compact; stubby, scrimp; shorn, stubbed; stumpy, thickset, podgy, stocky, pug; squab, -by; squat, dumpy; little &c. 193; curtailed of its fair proportions; short by; oblate; concise &c. 572; summary.

Adv. shortly &c. *adj.*; in short &c. (*concisely*) 572.

202. Breadth. Thickness.—N. breadth, width, latitude, amplitude; diameter, bore, calibre, radius; superficial extent &c. (*space*) 180.

thickness, crassitude; corpulence &c. (*size*) 192; dilatation &c. (*expansion*) 194.

V. be -broad &c. *adj.*; become -, render- -broad &c. *adj.*; expand &c. 194; thicken, widen.

Adj. broad, wide, ample, extended; discous; fan-like; out-spread, -stretched; wide as a church-door.

thick, dumpy, squab, squat, thickset, tubby; thick as a rope, stubby &c. 201.

203. Narrowness. Thinness. —N. narrowness &c. *adj.*; closeness, exility; exiguity &c. (*little*) 193.

line; hair's -, finger's -breadth; strip, streak, vein.

thinness &c. *adj.*; tenuity; emaciation, macilency, *marcór.*

shaving, slip &c. (*filament*) 205; threadpaper, skeleton, shadow, scrag, anatomy, spindle-shanks, barebones, lantern jaws, mere skin and bone.

middle constriction, stricture, neck, waist, isthmus, wasp, hour-glass; ridge, *ghaut*, pass; ravine &c. 198.

narrowing, coarctation, angustation, tapering; contraction &c. 195.

V. be -narrow &c. *adj.*; narrow, taper, contract &c. 195; render -narrow &c. *adj.*

Adj. narrow, close; slender, thin, fine; *svelte*; thread-like &c. (*filament*) 205; finespun, taper, slim, gracile, slight, slight-made; scant, -y; spare, delicate, incapacious; contracted &c. 195; unexpanded &c. (expand &c. 194); slender as a thread, capillary.

emaciated, lean, meagre, gaunt, macilent; lank, -y; weedy, skinny, scrawny, scraggy; starv-ed, -eling; attenuated, shrivelled, wizened, pinched, peaky, skeletal, spindling, spindle- -legged, -shanked; extenuated, tabid, marcid, bare-bone, raw-boned; herring-gutted; worn to a shadow, lean as a rake; thin as a -lath, - whipping post, - wafer; hatchet-faced; lantern-jawed.

204. Layer.—N. layer, stratum, course, bed, zone, *substratum*, floor, flag, stage, story, tier, slab, escarpment, table, tablet, panel, plaque; board, plank; trencher, platter.

plate; lam-ina, -ella; sheet, flake, foil, wafer, scale, coat, peel, pellicle, ply, thickness, membrane, film, leaf, slice, shive, cut, rasher, shaving, integument &c. (*covering*) 223.

stratification, lamination, scaliness, nest of boxes, coats of an onion.

V. slice, shave, pare, peel; plate, coat, veneer; cover &c. 223.

Adj. lamell-ar, -ated, -iform; laminated, -iferous; micaceous; schist-ose, -ous; scaly, filmy, membranous, flaky, squamous; folia-ted, -ceous; stratified, -form; tabular, discoid, spathic.

205. Filament.—N. filament, line; fibre, fibril; funicle, vein, hair, capillament, *cilium*, tendril, gossamer; hairstroke; harl.

wire, string, thread, packthread, cotton, sewing-silk, twine, twist, whipcord, cord, rope, cable, yarn, hemp, oakum, jute, wool, worsted.

strip, shred, slip, spill, list, band, fillet, *fascia*, ribbon, riband, tape, roll, lath, slat, strake, splinter, shiver, shaving.

beard &c. (*roughness*) 256; ramification; strand.

Adj. fil-amentous, -aceous, -iform; fibr-ous, -illous; thread-like, wiry, stringy, ropy; capill-ary, -iform; funicular, wire-drawn; anguilliform; flagelliform; hairy &c. (*rough*) 256; ligulate.

206. Height.—N. height, altitude, elevation, ceiling; eminence. pitch; loftiness &c. *adj.*; sublimity.

tallness &c. *adj.*; stature, procerity; prominence &c. 250.

207. Lowness.—N. lowness &c. *adj.*; debasement, depression; prostration &c. (*horizontal*) 213; depression &c. (*concave*) 252.

molehill; lowlands; bottomlands;

colossus &c. (*size*) 192; giant, grenadier, giraffe.

mount, -ain; hill, butte, monticle, fell, knap; cape; head-, fore-land; promontory; ridge, hog's back, dune; rising -, vantage- ground; down; moor, -land; Alp; up-, high-lands; heights &c. (*summit*) 210; knoll, hummock, hillock, barrow, mound, mole, *kopje*; steeps, bluff, cliff, craig, tor, peak, pike, clough; escarpment, edge, ledge, brae; dizzy height.

tower, pillar, column, pylon, obelisk, monument, steeple, spire, minaret, *campanile*, belfry, turret, roof, dome, cupola, pagoda, pyramid; sky scraper; Eiffel tower.

pole, pikestaff, maypole, flagstaff; mast, top -, topgallant- mast.

ceiling &c. (*covering*) 223.

high water; high -, flood -, spring- tide.

altimetry &c. (*angle*) 244; altimeter, height-finder, hypsometer, barograph.

V. be -high &c. *adj.*; tower, soar, command; hover; cap, culminate; overhang, hang over, impend, beetle; bestride, ride, mount; perch, surmount; cover &c. 233; overtop &c. (*be superior*) 33; stand on tiptoe.

become -high &c. *adj.*; grow, - higher, - taller; upgrow; rise &c. (*ascend*) 305.

render -high &c. *adj.*; heighten &c. (*elevate*) 307.

Adj. high, elevated, eminent, exalted, lofty, supernal; tall; gigantic &c. (*big*) 192; Patagonian; towering, beetling, soaring, hanging [gardens]; elevated &c. 307; upper; highest &c. (*topmost*) 210; monticolous, perching, hill-dwelling.

up-, moor-land; hilly, mountainous, alpine, sub-alpine, heaven-kissing; cloud-topt, -capt, -touching; aerial.

overhanging &c. *v.*; incumbent, overlying; super-incumbent, -natant, -imposed; prominent &c. 250.

tall as a -maypole, - poplar, - steeple; lanky &c. (*thin*) 203.

Adv. on high, high up, aloft, up, above, aloof, overhead; up -, above- stairs; in the clouds; on -tiptoe, - stilts, - the shoulders of; over head and ears; breast high.

over, upwards; from top to bottom &c. (*completely*) 52.

basement- ground-floor; *rez de chaussée* &c. 211; hold; feet, heels.

low water; low -, ebb -, neap -, spring- tide.

V. be -low &c. *adj.*; lie -low, - flat; underlie; crouch, slouch, wallow, grovel; lower &c. (*depress*) 308.

Adj. low, neap, debased; nether, -most; flat, level with the ground; lying low &c. *v.*; crouched, subjacent, squat, prostrate &c. (*horizontal*) 213.

Adv. under; be-, under-neath; below; down, -wards; adown, at the foot of; under-foot, -ground; down -, below-stairs; at a low ebb; below par.

---

208. Depth.—N. depth; deepness &c. *adj.*; profundity, depression &c. (*concavity*) 252.

hollow, pit, shaft, well, crater, abyss; gulf &c. 198; bowels of the earth, bottomless pit, hell.

soundings, depth of water, water, draught, submersion; plummet, sound, probe; sounding -rod, - line, - machine; lead; submarine, diving bell, bathysphere; diver.

V. be -deep &c. *adj.*; render -deep &c. *adj.*; deepen.

plunge &c. 310; sound, heave the lead, take soundings; dig &c. (*excavate*) 252.

209. Shallowness.—N. shallowness &c. *adj.*; shoals; mere scratch.

Adj. shallow, superficial; skin -, ankle -, knee- deep; just enough to wet one's feet; shoal, -y

---

Adj. deep, -seated; profound, sunk, buried; submerged &c. 310; sub-aqueous, -marine, -terranean, -terrene; underground.

bottom-, sound-, fathom-less; unfathom-ed, -able; abysmal; deep as a well, deep-sea.

knee-, ankle-deep.

Adv. beyond –, out of- one's depth; over head and ears, over one's head.

210. Summit.—N. summit, -y; top, vertex, apex, zenith, pinnacle, acme, acropolis, culmination, meridian, utmost height, *ne plus ultra*, height, pitch, maximum, climax, apogee; culminating –, crowning –, turning- point; turn of the tide, fountain head; water-shed, -parting; sky, pole.

tip, -top; crest, crow's nest, cap, truck, peak, nib; end &c. 67; crown, brow; head, nob, noddle, pate.

high places, heights.

top-, top-gallant mast, sky scraper; quarter –, hurricane- deck.

architrave, frieze, cornice, coping, coping-stone, zoophorus, capital, headpiece, capstone, epistyle, sconce, pediment, entablature; tympanum; ceiling &c. (*covering*) 223.

attic, loft, garret, house-top, upper story, roof.

V. culminate, cap, crown, top; overtop &c. (*be superior to*) 33.

Adj. highest &c. (high &c. 206); top; top-, upper-most; tip-top; culminating &c. *v.*; meridi-an, -onal; capital, head, polar, supreme, supernal, top-gallant.

Adv. a-top, at the top of – the tree, – the heap.

211. Base.—N. base, -ment; plinth, dado, wainscot, baseboard; foundation &c. (*support*) 215; substructure, sub·stratum, sump, ground, earth, pavement, floor, paving, flag, carpet, ground-floor, deck; footing, groundwork, basis; hold, bilge, orlop deck.

bottom, nadir, foot, sole, toe, hoof, keel, kelson, root.

Adj. bottom; under-, nether-most; fundamental; founded –, based –, grounded –, built- on.

212. Verticality. — N. verticality; erectness &c. *adj.*; perpendicularity; right angle, normal; azimuth circle.

wall, palisade, precipice, cliff, steep, bluff.

elevation, erection; square, plumb-line, plummet.

V. be -vertical &c. *adj.*; stand -up, – on end, – erect, – upright; stick –, cock-up.

render -vertical &c. *adj.*; set –, stick –, raise –, cock- up; erect, rear, raise, pitch, raise on its legs.

Adj. vertical, upright, erect, perpendicular, normal, plumb, straight, bolt upright; rampant; straight –, standing-up &c. *v.*; rectangular, orthogonal.

Adv. vertically &c. *adj.*; up, on end; up –, right- on end; *à plomb*, endwise; on one's legs; at right angles.

213. Horizontality.—N. horizontality; flatness; level, plane; stratum &c. 204; dead -level, – flat; level plane.

recumbency; lying down &c. *v.*; reclination, decumbence; de-, discumbency; proneness &c. *adj.*; accubation, supination, resupination, prostration; azimuth.

plain, floor, platform, bowling-green; cricket-ground; court; gridiron; baseball diamond; hockey rink; tennis-, croquet-ground, – lawn; billiard table; terrace, estrade, esplanade, *parterre*, table-land, *plateau*, ledge.

spirit-, level; T-square.

V. be -horizontal &c. *adj.*; lie, recline, couch; lie -down, – flat, – prostrate; sprawl, loll; sit down.

render -horizontal &c. *adj.*; lay, – down, – out; level, flatten, even, raze, equalize, smooth, align; prostrate, knock down, floor, fell, ground.

Adj. horizontal, level, even, plane;

flat &c. 251; flat as a -billiard table, – bowling green; alluvial; calm, – as a mill-pond; smooth, – as glass.

re-, de-, pro-, ac-cumbent; lying &c. *v.*; prone, supine, couchant, jacent, prostrate.

Adv. horizontally &c. *adj.*; on -one's back. – all fours, – its beam ends.

214. Pendency.—N. pend-, dependency; suspension, hanging &c. *v.*

pendant, drop, tippet, tassel, lobe, tail, train, flap, lappet, skirt, pig-tail, queue, pendulum.

peg, knob, button, hook, nail, stud, ring, staple, tenterhook; davit; fastening &c. 45; spar, horse.

chande-, gase-, electro-lier.

V. be -pendent &c. *adj.*; hang, depend, swing, dangle, droop, sag; swag; daggle, flap, trail, flow.

suspend, hang, sling, hook up, hitch, fasten to, append.

Adj. pend-ent, -ulous; pensile; hanging &c. *v.*; dependent; suspended &c. *v.*; lowering, overhanging, beetling, decumbent; loose, flowing.

having a -peduncle &c. *n.*; pedunculate, tailed, caudate.

215. Support.—N. support, ground, foundation, base, basis; *terra firma*; bearing, fulcrum, *point d'appui*, caudex, purchase, footing, hold, -*locus standi*; landing, – stage, – place; stage, platform; block; rest, resting-place; groundwork, *substratum*, sustentation, subvention; floor &c. (*basement*) 211.

supporter; aid &c. 707; prop, stand, anvil, fulciment; hod, stay, shore, skid, rib, sprag, truss, bandage; sleeper; stirrup, stilts, shoe, sole, heel, splint, lap; bar, rod, boom, sprit, outrigger.

staff, stick, crutch, alpenstock, bourdon; *bâton*, maulstick, colstaff, cowlstaff, staddle; stalk, ped-icel, -icle, – uncle.

post, pillar, shaft, column, pilaster; pediment, pedestal; plinth, shank, leg, socle, zocle; buttress, jamb, mullion, abutment; pile, baluster, banister, stanchion, king post; balustrade.

frame, -work, body, *chassis, fuselage*; scaffold, skeleton, beam, rafter, girder, lintel, joist, cantilever, travis, trave, corner-stone. summer, transom; rung, round, step, sill.

columella, back-bone; key-stone; axle, -tree; axis; arch, ogive, mainstay.

trunnion, pivot, rowlock; peg &c. (*pendency*) 214; tie-beam &c. (*fastening*) 45; thole pin.

board, ledge, shelf, hob, bracket, trevet, trivet, arbor, rack, hatrack; mantel, -piece, -shelf; slab, console; counter, dresser; flange, corbel; table, trestle, teapoy; shoulder; perch; horse; easel, desk; retable, predella.

seat, throne, dais; divan, musnud; chair, bench, form, stool, camp-stool, sofa, settee, davenport, stall, miserere, arm –, easy –, elbow –, rocking- chair; couch, day bed, *fauteuil*, woolsack, ottoman, settle, squab, bench, box, dicky; saddle, pannel, pillion; side –, pack- saddle; pommel.

bed, berth, pallet, tester, crib, cot, bassinet, hammock, shakedown, camp bed, bunk, truckle-bed, cradle, litter, stretcher, bedstead; four-poster, French bed; bedding, mattress, *paillasse*; pillow, bolster; mat, rug, cushion.

stool, footstool, hassock, faldstool, *prie-dieu*; tabouret; tripod. Atlas, Persides, Atlantes, Caryatides, Hercules.

V. be -supported &c.; lie –, sit –, recline –, lean –, loll –, rest –, stand –, step –, repose –, abut –, beat –, be based &c.- on; have at one's back; be-stride, -straddle.

support, bear, carry, hold, sustain, shoulder; hold –, back –, bolster –, shore- up; up-hold, -bear; prop; under-prop, -pin, -set; bandage, &c. 43; brace, truss; cradle, pillow.

give –, furnish –, afford –, supply –, lend- -support, – foundations; bottom, found, base, ground, embed.

maintain, keep on foot; aid &c. 707.

Adj. support-ing, -ed, &c. *v.*; atlantean, columellar; sustentative, fundamental, basal.

Adv. astride on, astraddle; pick-a-back.

216. Parallelism.—N. parallelism; coextension, concentricity, collimation.

V. be –, lie- parallel to; collimate.

Adj. parallel; coextensive, collateral, concentric, concurrent.

Adv. alongside, abreast &c. (*laterally*) 236.

---

217. Obliquity.—N. obliquity, inclination, skew, slope, slant; crookedness &c. *adj.*; slopeness; leaning &c. *v.*; bevel, bezel, ramp, tilt; bias, list, twist, swag, cant, lurch; distortion &c. 243; bend &c. (*curve*) 245; tower of Pisa.

acclivity, rise, ascent, grade, gradient, *glacis*, rising ground, hill, bank, declivity, downhill, dip, fall, devexity; gentle –, rapid- slope; easy -ascent, – descent; shelving beach; *talus*; *montagne Russe*; *facilis descensus Averni*.

steepness &c. *adj.*; cliff, precipice &c. (*vertical*) 212; escarpment, scarp.

[Measure of inclination] clinometer, theodolite, level, sextant, quadrant, protractor; angle, sine, cosine, tangent &c. hypothenuse.

diagonal; zigzag, chevron.

V. be -oblique &c. *adj.*; slope, slant, lean, incline, shelve, stoop, decline, descend, bend, heel, careen, sag, swag, seel, slouch, cant, sidle.

render -oblique &c. *adj.*; sway, bias; slope, slant; incline, bend, crook; cant, tilt; distort &c. 243.

Adj. oblique, inclined; sloping &c. *v.*; tilted &c. *v.*; recumbent, clinal, skew, askew, slant, aslant, bias, plagiedral, indirect, wry, awry, ajee, crooked; knock-kneed &c. (*distorted*) 243; bevel, out of the perpendicular.

uphill, rising, ascending, acclivous; downhill, falling, descending; declining, declivous, devex, anticlinal; steep, abrupt, precipitous, breakneck.

diagonal; trans-verse, -versal; athwart, antiparallel; curved &c. 245.

Adv. obliquely &c. *adj.*; on –, all on- one side; askew, askant, askance, aslope, asquint, edgewise, at an angle; side-long, -ways; slope-, slant-wise; by a side wind.

218. Inversion.—N. in-, e-, sub-, re-, retro-, intro-version; contraposition &c. 237; contrariety &c. 14; reversal; turn of the tide.

overturn; somer-sault, -set; summerset; *culbute*; revulsion; *pirouette*.

transposition, transposal, anastrophy, *metastasis, hyperbaton, anastrophe, hysteron-proteron*, hypallage, *synchysis, tmesis*, parenthesis; *metathesis*; palindrome; Spoonerism.

pronation and supination.

V. be -inverted &c.; turn –, go –, wheel- -round, – about, – to the right about; turn –, go –, tilt –, topple-over; capsize, turn turtle.

in-, sub-, retro-, intro-vert; reverse; up-, over-turn, -set; turn -topsy turvy &c. *adj.*; *culbuter*; transpose, put the cart before the horse, turn the tables.

Adj. inverted &c. *v.*; wrong side -out, – up; inside out, upside down; bottom –, keel- upwards; supine, on one's head, topsy turvy, *sens dessus sens dessous.*

inverse; reverse &c. (*contrary*) 14; opposite &c. 237.

topheavy, unstable.

Adv. inversely &c. *adj.*; hirdie-girdie; heels over head, head over heels.

219. Crossing.—N. crossing &c. *v.*; inter-section, – lacement, – twine-ment, -digitation; decussation, transversion; convolution &c. 248.

reticulation, meshwork, network; inosculation, anastomosis, inter-texture, mortise.

net, *plexus*, web, mesh, twill, skein, sleeve, felt, lace; wicker; mat, -ting; plait, trellis, wattle, lattice, grating, *grille*, gridiron, tracery, fretwork, filigree, reticle; tissue, netting, mokes.

cross, crucifix, rood, crisscross, crux; chain, wreath, braid, cat's cradle, knot; entanglement &c. (*disorder*) 59.

[woven fabrics] cloth, linen, muslin, cambric, drill, homespun, tweed, broadcloth &c.

V. cross, decussate; inter-sect, -lace, -twine, -twist, -weave, -digitate, -link.

twine, entwine, weave, inweave, twist, wreathe; anastomose, inoscu-late, dovetail, splice, link.

mat, plait, plat, braid, felt, twill; tangle, entangle, ravel; net, knot; dishevel, raddle.

Adj. crossing &c. *v.*; crossed, matted &c. *v.*; transverse.

cross, cruciform, crucial; reti-form, -cular, -culated; areolar, cancel-lated, mullioned, latticed, grated, barred, streaked; textile, secant, plexal; interfretted.

Adv. across, thwart, athwart, transversely, crosswise.

3°. Centrical Dimensions*

1. *General*

220. Exteriority. — N. exteriority; outside, exterior; surface, superficies; skin &c. (*covering*) 223; *superstratum*; disk, disc; face, facet.

excentricity; circumjacence &c. 227.

V. be -exterior &c. *adj.*; lie around &c. 227.

place -exteriorly, – outwardly, – out-side; put –, turn- out.

Adj. exter-ior, -nal; extraneous, outer, -most; out-ward, -lying, -side, -door; round about &c. 227; extra-mural.

superficial, skin-deep; frontal, dis-coid.

extraregarding; eccentric; outstand-ing; extrinsic &c. 6.

Adv. externally &c. *adj.*; out, with-out, over, outwards, *ab extra*, out of doors; *extra muros.*

221. Interiority.—N. interiority; in-side, interior, endocrine; interspace, subsoil, *substratum.*

contents &c. 190; substance, pith, marrow; backbone &c. (*centre*) 222; heart, bosom, breast, abdomen; vitals, viscera, entrails, bowels, belly, intes-tines, guts, chitterlings, womb, lap; gland, cell; internal organs, *penetralia*, recesses, innermost recesses; cave &c. (*concavity*) 252.

inhabitant &c. 188.

V. be -inside &c. *adj.*, – within &c. *adv.*

place –, keep- within; enclose &c. (*circumscribe*) 229; intern; embed &c. (*insert*) 300.

Adj. inter-ior, -nal; inner, inside, intimate, inward, intraregarding; in-, inner-most; deep-seated; visceral, intes-

* That is, Dimensions having reference to a centre.

in the open air; *sub -Jove, – dio*;
à la belle étoile, al fresco.

tine, -tinal; inland; subcutaneous; in-
terstitial &c. (*interjacent*) 228; in-
wrought &c. (*intrinsic*) 5; enclosed
&c. *v.*

home, domestic, indoor, intramural,
vernacular; endemic.

Adv. internally &c. *adj.*; inwards, within, in, inly; here-, there-,
where-in; *ab intra*, withinside; in –, within- doors; at home, in the
bosom of one's family.

222. Centrality.—N. centrality, centricalness, centre; middle &c. 68;
focus &c. 74.

core, kernel; nucleus, nucleolus; heart, pole, axis, pivot, fulcrum,
bull's eye; hub, nave, navel; *umbilicus*, spine, backbone, marrow, pith;
hot-bed; concentration &c. (*convergence*) 290; centralization; symmetry.

centre of -gravity, – pressure, – percussion, – oscillation, – buoyancy
&c. metacentre.

V. be -central &c. *adj.*; converge &c. 290.

render central, centralize, concentrate; bring to a focus.

Adj. centr-al, -ical; middle &c. 68; axial, pivotal, focal, umbilical,
concentric; middlemost, nuclear, centric, centraidal; spinal, vertebral.

Adv. middle; midst; centrally &c. *adj.*

223. Covering.—N. covering, cover;
canopy, tilt, awning, baldachin, tent,
marquee, *tente d'abri*, umbrella, parasol,
sunshade; veil (*shade*) 424; shield &c.
(*defence*) 717; hall.

roof, dome, cupola, mansard roof;
ceiling; thatch, tile; pan-, pen-tile;
tiling, shingles, slates, slating, leads;
shed &c. (*abode*) 189.

224. Lining.—N. lining, inner coating; coating &c. (*covering*) 223; stalactite, -agmite.

filling, stuffing, wadding, padding,
bushing.

wainscot, *parietes*, wall, brattice.

V. line, stuff, incrust, wad, pad, fill.

Adj. lined &c. *v.*

top, lid, covercle, door, *operculum*, eyelid, blind, curtain.

bandage, plaster, lint, wrapping, dossil, finger stall.

coverlet, counterpane, sheet, quilt, comforter, eiderdown; tarpaulin, blanket, rug, drugget, linoleum, oilcloth; housing.

in-, tegument; skin, pellicle, fleece, fell, fur, ermine, miniver,
sable, sealskin &c.; fabrikoid; leather, morocco, calf, pigskin, elk,
kid, cowhide &c.; shagreen, hide; pelt, -ry; cuticle, *dermis*, scarfskin, *epidermis*.

clothing &c. 225; mask &c. (*concealment*) 530.

peel, crust, bark, rind, *cortex*, husk, shell, coat.

capsule; ferrule; sheath, -ing; pod, cod; casing, case, theca;
elytron; involucrum; wrapp-ing, -er, cellophane; envelope, vesicle;
dermatology, conchology.

armour, -plate, armouring; veneer, facing; pavement; scale &c.
(*layer*) 204; coating, paint, stain; varnish &c. (*resin*) 356a; anointing
&c. *v.*; inunction; incrustation, superposition, obduction, ground,
enamel, whitewash, plaster, stucco, rough cast, pebble dash, compo;
rendering; cerement; ointment &c. (*grease*) 356.

V. cover; super-pose, -impose; over-lay, -spread; wrap &c. 225;
incase; face, case, veneer, pave, paper; tip, cap, bind, revet.

coat, paint, varnish, pay, incrust, stucco, cement, dab, plaster,
tar; wash; be-, smear; be-, daub; anoint, do over; gild, plate,

electroplate, japan, lacquer, lacker, enamel, whitewash; lay it on thick.

over-lie, -arch; conceal &c. 528.

Adj. covering &c. *v.*; cutaneous, dermal, cortical, cuticular, tegumentary, skinny, scaly, squamous; covered &c. *v.*; imbricated, loricated, armour-plated, iron-clad; under cover, hooded, cloaked, cowled.

225. Investment.—N. investment; covering &c. 223; dress, clothing, raiment, drapery, costume, attire, guise, toilet, *toilette*, trim; habiliment; vesture, -ment; garment, garb, palliament, apparel, wardrobe, wearing apparel, clothes, things.

array; tailoring, millinery; best bib and tucker; finery &c. (*ornament*) 847; full dress &c. (*show*) 882; garniture; theatrical properties.

outfit, equipment, *trousseau*; uniform, khaki, regimentals; academicals, canonicals &c. 999; livery, gear, harness, turn out, accoutrement, caparison, suit, rigging, trappings, traps, slops, togs, toggery; masquerade.

dishabille, morning dress, lounge suit, tea-gown, *kimono*, *négligé*, dressing-gown, *peignoir*, wrapper, undress; shooting-coat; smoking-jacket, mufti; rags, tatters, old clothes; mourning, weeds; duds; slippers.

robe, tunic, dolman, *paletot*, habit, gown, coat, coatee, frock, blouse, *pelisse*, middy, sagum, *toga*, smock-frock; frock-, dress-, morning-, tail-coat; dress-suit, – clothes, swallow-tail coat, dinner-, Eton-jacket.

cloak, pall; mantle, mantlet, mantua, shawl, *pelisse*, veil, yashmak; cape, tippet, kirtle, plaid, muffler, comforter, Balaclava helmet, haik, huke, chlamys, mantilla, tabard, housing, horse-cloth, burnous, *roquelaure*; *houppelande*; sur-, top, over-, great-coat; *surtout*, spencer, cardigan, sweater, blazer; mackintosh, waterproof, slicker, raincoat, oilskin, trench coat, ulster, monkey-, pea-, pilot-jacket, redingote; wraprascal, poncho, cardinal, pelerine, talma.

jacket, jumper, vest, jerkin, waistcoat, doublet, *camisole*, gabardine; stays, *corsage*, corset, corselet, bodice; stomacher; skirt, petticoat, slip, farthingale, kilt, jupe, crinoline, bustle, hobble skirt, *panier*, apron, pinafore; loin cloth.

trousers; breeches, trews, pantaloons, unmentionables, inexpressibles, overalls, pyjamas, smalls, small-clothes; tights, pants, shorts, drawers; knickerbockers, knickers, plus fours, bloomers, divided skirt; phil-, fill-ibeg.

226. Divestment.—N. divestment; taking off &c. *v.*

nudity; bareness &c. *adj.*; undress; dishabille &c. 225, altogether; nu-, denu-dation; decortication, depilation, excoriation, desquamation; moulting; exfoliation.

baldness, alopecia, acomia.

V. divest; uncover &c. (*cover* &c. 223); denude, bare, strip; undress, unclothe, disrobe &c. (dress, enrobe, &c. 225); uncoif; dismantle; uncase; put –, take –, cast- off; shed, doff; husk, peel, pare, decorticate, desquamate, excoriate, skin, scalp, flay, bark, expose, lay open; exfoliate, moult, mew; cast the skin.

Adj. divested &c. *v.*; bare, naked, nude; un-dressed, -draped, -clad, -clothed, -appareled; exposed; in dishabille; *décolleté*; bald, threadbare, ragged, callow, roofless.

in -a state of nature, – nature's garb, – buff, – native buff, – birthday suit; *in puris naturalibus*; with nothing on, stark naked; bald as a coot, bare as the back of one's hand; out at elbows; barefoot; bareback; leaf-, nap-, hairless, shaved, clean shaven, tonsured, beardless, bald-headed, acomous.

———

head-dress, -gear; cap, *béret*, tam o' shanter, glengarry, topee, sombrero; hat; cocked –, high –, tall –, top –, silk –, opera –, crush -hat, *gibus*, beaver, castor, bonnet, tile, wideawake, billy-cock; bowler; soft felt –, straw –, leghorn -hat, panama; toque; wimple; night-, mob-, skull-cap, biretta; hood, cowl, coif; capote, calach; scull-cap; kerchief, snood; head, *coiffure*; crown &c. (*circle*) 247; *chignon*, pelt, wig, front, peruke, periwig; caftan, turban, fez, *tarboosh*, taj, shako, csako, busby; *képi*, forage cap, bearskin; helmet &c. 717; mask, domino.

body clothes; linen; shirt, sark, smock, shift, *chemise*, *lingerie*; night-gown, -shirt; bed-gown, *sac de nuit*; jersey, guernsey; underclothing, -waistcoat.

neck-erchief, -cloth; tie, ruff, collar, cravat, stock, handkerchief, bandana, scarf; bib, tucker; dicky; boa; girdle &c. (*circle*) 247; cummerbund.

shoe, pump, brogue, boot, slipper, sandal, galoche, goloshes, arctics, rubber boots, overshoes, patten, clog, sabot; high-low; Blucher –, Wellington –, Hessian –, jack –, top- boot; Balmoral; legging, puttee, buskin, greave, galligaskin, moccasin, *gamache*, gambado, gaiter, spatter-dash, spat, antigropeles; stocking, hose, gaskins, trunk-hose, sock, hosiery.

glove, gauntlet, mitten, cuff, muffettee, wristband, sleeve.
swaddling cloth, baby-linen, *layette*; pocket-handkerchief.
shroud &c. 363.
clothier, tailor, milliner, *costumier*, sempstress, seamstress, snip; dress-, habit-, breeches-, shoe-maker; córdwainer, cobbler, Crispin, hosier, hatter; draper, linendraper, haberdasher, mercer.

V. invest; cover &c. 223; envelop, lap, involve; in-, en-wrap; wrap; fold –, wrap –, lap –, muffle- up; overlap; sheathe, swathe, swaddle, roll up in, shroud, circumvest.

vest, clothe, array, dress, dight, drape, robe, enrobe, attire, tire, garb, habilitate, apparel, accoutre, rig, fit out; bedizen, deck &c. (*ornament*) 847; perk; equip, harness, caparison; dress up.

wear; don; put –, huddle –, slip- on; mantle.

Adj. invested &c. *v.*; habited; dight, -ed; clad, *costumé*, shod, *chaussé*; *en grande tenue* &c. (*show*) 882.

sartorial.

---

227. Circumjacence.—N. circumjacence, -ambience; environment, encompassment; atmosphere, medium; surroundings, *entourage*.

outpost; border &c. (*edge*) 231; girdle &c. (*circumference*) 230; outskirts, *boulevards*, suburbs, purlieus, precincts, *faubourgs*, *environs*, *banlieue*, neighbourhood, vicinity.

V. lie -around &c. *adv.*; surround, beset, compass, encompass, environ, inclose, enclose, encircle, circle, embrace, circumvent, lap, gird; begird, girdle, engird; skirt, twine round; hem in &c. (*circumscribe*) 229; besiege, invest, blockade.

Adj. circum-jacent, -ambient, -fluent;

228. Interjacence.—N. inter-jacence, -currence, -venience, -location, -digitation, -penetration; permeation.

inter-jection, -polation, -lineation, -spersion, -calation; embolism.

inter-vention, -ference, -position; in-, ob-trusion; insinuation; insertion &c. 300; dovetailing; infiltration; intromission.

intermedi-um, -ary; go-between, agent, middleman, medium, bodkin, intruder, interloper; parenthesis, episode; fly-leaf.

partition, *septum*, diaphragm, midriff; party-wall, panel, vail, bulkhead, brattice, *cloison*; half-way house.

V. lie –, come –, get- between; inter-

ambient; surrounding &c. *v.*; circumferential, surburban.

Adv. around, about; without; on -every side, – all sides; right and left, all round, round about; in the neighbourhood.

—

vene, slide in, interpenetrate, permeate.

put between, introduce, intromit, import; throw –; wedge –, edge –, jam –, worm –, foist –, run –, plough –, work- in; inter-pose, -ject, -calate, -polate, -line, -leave, -sperse, -weave, -lard, -digitate; let in, dovetail, splice, mortise; insinuate, smuggle; infiltrate, ingrain.

interfere, put in an oar, thrust one's nose in; intrude, obtrude; have a finger in the pie; introduce the thin end of the wedge; thrust in &c. (*insert*) 300.

Adj. inter-jacent, -current, -venient, -vening &c. *v.*, -mediate, -mediary, -calary, -stitial, -costal, -mural, -planetary, -stellar; embolismal.

parenthetical, episodic; mediterranean; intrusive; embosomed; merged, mean, middle, medium, median.

Adv. between, betwixt; 'twixt; among, -st; amid, -st; 'mid, -st; in the thick of; betwixt and between; sandwich-wise; parenthetically, *obiter dictum.*

229. Circumscription.—N. circumscription, limitation, inclosure; confinement &c. (*restraint*) 751; circumvallation, encincture; envelope &c. 232.

V. circumscribe, limit, bound, confine, enclose; surround &c. 227; compass about; imprison &c. (*restrain*) 751; hedge –, wall –, rail- in; fence –, hedge- round; embar; picket, corral.

enfold, bury, incase, pack up, enshrine, inclasp; wrap up &c. (*invest*) 225; embosom.

Adj. circumscribed &c. *v.*; begirt, lapt; circumambient; buried –, immersed- in; embosomed, in the bosom of, imbedded, encysted, mewed up; imprisoned &c. 751; land-locked, in a ring fence.

230. Outline.—N. outline, circumference; peri-meter, -phery; ambit, circuit, lines, *tournure, contour,* profile, *silhouette,* lineaments; bounds, coastline.

zone, belt, girth, band, baldric, zodiac, girdle, tire, cingle, clasp, girt; *cordon* &c. (*inclosure*) 232; circlet &c. 247.

V. outline, delineate, *silhouette,* circumscribe &c. 229; profile, block out.

Adj. outlined &c. *v.*; circumferential, perimetric, peripheral.

231. Edge.—N. edge, verge, brink, brow, brim, margin, border, confines, skirt, rim, felloe, felly, flange, side, mouth; jaws, chops, chaps, *fauces;* lip, muzzle.

threshold, door, porch; portal &c. (*opening*) 260; coast, shore, strand, beach, bank, wharf, quay, dock.

frame, fringe, flounce, frill, list, trimming, edging, skirting, hem, selvedge, welt; furbelow, valance, exergue.

Adj. border, marginal, skirting; labial, labiated, marginated.

232. Inclosure.—N. inclosure, enclosure, envelope; case &c. (*receptacle*) 191; wrapper; girdle &c. 230.

pen, fold, croft, sty; pen-, in-, sheep-fold; paddock, pound, corral, kraal; yard, compound; net, seine net.

wall; hedge, -row; *espalier;* fence &c. (*defence*) 717; pale, paling, balustrade, rail, railing, gunwale; quickset hedge, park paling, circum-vallation, *enceinte*, ring fence.

barrier, barricade; gate, -way; door, hatch, *cordon*; prison &c. 752.

dike, dyke, ditch, fosse, moat, trench.

V. inclose; circumscribe &c. 229.

233. Limit.—N. limit, boundary, bounds, confine, *enclave*, term, bourn, verge, kerb-stone, curbstone, but, pale; termin-ation, -us; stint, frontier, precinct, marches.

boundary line, landmark; line of -demarcation, – circumvallation; pillars of Hercules; Rubicon, turning-point; *ne plus ultra*; sluice, flood-gate.

V. limit, bound, confine, define, circumscribe, demarcate, delimit, encompass.

Adj. definite; contermin-ate, -able, terminable, limitable; terminal, frontier, border, bordering, boundary.

Adv. thus far, – and no further.

2. *Special*

234. Front.—N. front; fore, – part; foreground; forefront, face, disk, disc, frontage, *façade*, *proscenium*, facia, frontispiece; priority, anteriority; obverse [of a medal].

fore –, front- rank, first line; van, -guard; advanced guard; outpost, scout.

brow, forehead, visage, physiognomy, phiz, features, countenance, map, mug; rostrum, beak, bow, stem, prow, prore, jib, bowsprit; forecastle.

pioneer &c. (*precursor*) 64; metoposcopy.

V. be –, stan'd- in front &c. *adj.*; front, face, confront, breast, brave; bend forwards; come to the -front, – fore.

Adj. fore, forward, anterior, front, frontal.

Adv. before; in -front, – the van, – advance; ahead, right ahead; fore-, head-most; in the foreground; before one's -face, – eyes; face to face, *vis-à-vis*.

236. Laterality.—N. laterality; side, flank, beam, quarter, lee; hand; cheek, jowl, jole, wing; profile; temple, *parietes*, loin, haunch, hip.

gable, -end; broadside; lee side.

points of the compass; East, Orient, Levant; West, occident; orientation.

V. be -on one side &c. *adv.*; flank, outflank; sidle; skirt, border.

Adj. lateral, sidelong; collateral;

235. Rear.—N. rear, back, posterior-ity; rear -rank, – guard; background, *hinterland*.

occiput, nape, scruff, chine; heels; tail, rump, croup, buttock, posteriors, bottom, seat, backside, scut, breech, *dorsum*, loin; dorsal –, lumbar- region; hind quarters.

stern, poop, after-part, counter; postern, heel-, tail-piece, crupper.

wake; train &c. (*sequence*) 281.

reverse; other side of the shield.

V. be -behind &c. *adv.*; fall astern; bend backwards; bring up the rear; follow &c. 622; tail, shadow.

Adj. back, rear; hind, -er, -most, -ermost; post-ern, -erior; dorsal, after; caudal, lumbar; mizzen.

Adv. behind; in the -rear, – ruck, – back-ground; behind one's back; at the -heels, – tail, – back- of; back to back.

after, -most, aft, abaft, astern, stern-most, aback, rear-, hind-, back-ward.

---

237. Contraposition.—N. contraposi-tion, opposition; polarity; inversion &c. 218; opposite side; antithesis; reverse, inverse; counterpart; antipodes; oppo-site poles, North and South.

V. be -opposite &c. *adj.*; subtend.

Adj. opposite; reverse, inverse; an-tipodal, subcontrary; fronting, facing, diametrically opposite.

Northern, Septentrional, Boreal, arc-

parietal, flanking, skirting; flanked; sideling.

many-sided; multi-, bi-, tri-, quadri-lateral.

East-ern, -ward, -erly; orient, -al, auroral, Levantine; West-ern, -ward, -erly; occidental, Hesperian; equa-torial.

Adv. side-ways, -long; broadside on; on one side, abreast, abeam, alongside, beside, aside; by, – the side of; side by side; cheek by jowl &c. (near) 197; to -windward, – leeward; laterally &c. adj.; right and left; on her beam ends.

tic; Southern, Austral, antarctic, polar.

Adv. over, – the way, – against; against; face to face, vis-à-vis; as poles asunder.

---

238. Dextrality. — N. dextrality; right, – hand; dexter, offside, star-board.

Adj. dextral, right-handed; ambi-dextral, dexterous, dextrorsal &c.

239. Sinistrality.—N. sinistrality; left, – hand; sinister, nearside, lar-board, port.

Adj. sinistral, sinister, sinistrorsal &c., left-handed, sinistromanual, sinis-trous.

Section III. FORM

1°. General Form

240. Form.—N. form, figure, shape; con-formation, -figuration; make, for-mation, frame, construction, design, cut, set, build, trim, cut of one's jib; stamp, type, cast, mould; fashion; contour &c. (outline) 230; structure &c. 329.

feature, lineament, outline, turn; phase &c. (aspect) 448; posture, atti-tude, pose.

[Science of form] morphology.

[Similarity of form] isomorphism.

forming &c. v.; form-, figur-, efform-ation; sculpture.

V. form, shape, figure, fashion, efform, carve, cut, chisel, hew, cast; rough-hew, -cast; sketch; block –, hammer- out; trim; lick –, put- into shape; model, knead, work up into, set, mould, sculpture; cast, stamp; built &c. (construct) 161.

Adj. formed &c. v.

[Receiving form] plastic, fictile, full-fashioned &c.

[Giving form] plasmic &c.

[Similar in form] isomorphous &c.

**241. [Absence of form.] Amorphism.
—N.** amorphism, informity, uncouth-ness; unlicked cub, rough diamond; rudis indigestaque moles; disorder &c. 59; deformity &c. 243.

disfigure-, deface-ment, deformation; mutilation.

V. [Destroy form] deface, disfigure, deform, mutilate, truncate; derange &c. 61.

Adj. shapeless, amorphous, mal-formed, formless; un-formed, -hewn, -fashioned, -shapen; rough, rude, Goth-ic, barbarous, rugged, in the rough; misshapen &c. 243.

**242. [Regularity of form.] Symmetry.
—N.** symmetry, shapeliness, finish; beauty &c. 845; proportion, eurythmy, eurythmic, uniformity, parallelism; bi-, tri-, multi-lateral symmetry; centrality &c. 222.

243. [Irregularity of form.] Distor-tion.—N. dis-, de-, con-tortion; knot, mop, warp, buckle, screw, twist; crookedness &c. (obliquity) 217; grim-ace; deformity; mal-, malcon-forma-tion; monstrosity, misproportion, want

arborescence, branching, ramification.

Adj. symmetrical, shapely, well set, finished; beautiful &c. 845; classic, chaste, severe.

regular, uniform, balanced; equal &c. 27; parallel, coextensive.

arbor-escent, -iform; dendr-iform, -oid; branching; ramous, ramose.

---

of symmetry, *anamorphosis*; ugliness &c. 846; teratology.

V. distort, contort, twist, warp &c. *n.*; wrest, writhe, make faces, deform, misshape.

Adj. distorted &c. *v.*; out of shape, irregular, unsymmetric, awry, wry, askew, crooked, sinuous; anamorphous; not -true, − straight; on one side, crump, deformed; mis-shapen, -begotten; mis-, ill-proportioned; ill-made; grotesque, crooked as a ram's horn; hump-, hunch-, bunch-, crook-backed; bandy; bandy-, bow-legged; bow-, knock-kneed; splay-, club-footed; taliped; round-shouldered; snub-nosed; curtailed of one's fair proportions; scalene, stumpy &c. (*short*) 201; gaunt &c. (*thin*) 203; bloated &c. 194.

Adv. all manner of ways.

2°. SPECIAL FORM

244. Angularity.—**N.** angular-ity, -ness; aduncity; angle, cusp, bend; fold &c. 258; notch &c. 257; fork, bifurcation.

elbow, knee, knuckle, ankle, groin, crotch, crutch, crane, fluke, scythe, sickle, zigzag, kimbo.

corner, nook, recess, niche, oriel.

right angle &c. (*perpendicular*) 212; obliquity &c. 217; angle of 45°, mitre; acute −, obtuse −, salient −, re-entrant −, spherical −, solid −, dihedral- angle.

angular -measurement, − elevation, − distance, − velocity; trigon-, goni-ometry; altimetry; clin-, graph-, goni-ometer; theodolite; transit circle; sextant, quadrant; dichotomy.

triangle, trigon, wedge; rectangle, square, lozenge, diamond; rhomb, -us; quadr-angle, -ilateral; parallelogram; quadrature; poly-, penta-, hexa-, hepta-, octa-, deca-gon.

Platonic bodies; cube, rhomboid; tetra-, penta-, hexa-, octa-, dodeca-, icosa-hedron; prism, pyramid; parallelopiped.

V. bend, fork, bifurcate, crinkle, divaricate, branch, ramify.

Adj. angular, bent, crooked, aduncous, uncinated, aquiline, jagged, serrated; falc-iform, -ated; furcular, furcated, forked, bifurcate, crotched; zigzag; dovetailed; knock-kneed, crinkled, akimbo, kimbo, geniculated; oblique &c. 217.

fusiform, wedge-shaped, cuneiform; tri-angular, -gonal, -lateral; quadr-angular, -ilateral; rectangular, square, foursquare, multilateral; polygonal &c. *n.*; cubical, rhomboidal, pyramidal.

245. Curvature.—**N.** curv-ature, -ity, -ation; incurv-ity, -ation; bend; flexure, -ion; conflexure; crook, hook, bought, bending; de-, inflexion; arcuation, devexity, turn; deviation, *détour*, sweep; curl, -ing; bough; recurv-ity, -ation; sinuosity &c. 248; aduncity.

curve, arc, arch, arcade, vault, dome, bow, crescent, *meniscus*, half-moon, lunule, horse-shoe, loop, crane-neck;

246. Straightness.—**N.** straightness, rectilinearity, directness; inflexibility &c. (*stiffness*) 323; straight −, right −, direct-, bee- line; short cut.

V. be -straight &c. *adj.*; have no turning; not -incline, − bend, − turn, − deviate- to either side; go straight; steer for &c. (*direction*) 278.

render straight, straighten, rectify; set −, put- straight; un-bend, -fold,

para-, hyper-bola; catenary, festoon; conch-, cardi-oid; caustic, instep; tracery.

V. be -curved &c. *adj.*; sweep, swag, sag; deviate &c. 279; turn; re-enter.

render -curved &c. *adj.*; bend, curve, incurvate; de-, in-flect; crook; turn, round, arch, arcuate, arch over, loop the loop, concamerate; bow, coil, curl, recurve, frizzle.

Adj. curved &c. *v.*; curvi-form, -lineal, -linear; devex, devious; recurv-ed, -ous; *retroussé*; crump; bowed &c. *v.*; vaulted; hooked; falc-iform, -ated; semicircular, crescentic; lun-iform, -ular; semi-lunar, meniscal; conchoidal; cord-iform, -ated; cardioid; heart-, bell-, pear-, fig-shaped; reniform; lenti-form, -cular; bow-legged &c. (*distorted*) 243; oblique &c. 217; circular &c. 247.

-curl &c. 248, -ravel &c. 219, -wrap.

Adj. straight; rectiline-ar, -al; direct, even, right, true, in a line; unbent &c. *v.*; un-deviating, -turned, -distorted, -swerving; straight as an arrow &c. (*direct*) 278; inflexible &c. 323.

----

247. [Simple circularity.] Circularity. —N. circularity, roundness; rotundity &c. 249.

circle, circlet, ring, washer, areola, hoop, roundlet, *annulus*, annulet, bracelet, armlet, armilla; ringlet; eye, loop, wheel; cycle, orb, orbit, rundle, zone, belt, *cordon*, band; sash, girdle, cestus, cincture, baldric, fillet, *fascia*, wreath, garland; crown, corona, coro-net, chaplet, snood, necklace, collar; noose, lasso, lariat.

ellipse, oval, ovule; ellipsoid, cycloid; epi-cycloid, -cycle; semi-circle; quadrant, sextant, sector.

V. make -round &c. *adj.*; round.

go round; encircle &c. 227; describe -a circle &c. 311.

Adj. round, rounded, circular, annular, orbicular; oval, ovate; elliptic, -al; ovoid, egg-shaped; pear-shaped &c. 245; cycloidal &c. *n.*; spherical &c. 249.

----

248. [Complex circularity.] Convolution. —N. winding &c. *v.*; con-, in-, circum-volution; wave, undulation, tortuosity, anfractuosity; sinu-osity, -ation, sinuousness; meandering, cir-cuit, circumbendibus, twist, twirl, windings and turnings, *ambages*; tor-sion; inosculation; reticulation &c. (*crossing*) 219.

coil, roll, curl, buckle, spire, spiral, helix, corkscrew, worm, volute, whorl, rundle; tendril; scollop, scallop, es-calop; kink.

serpent, snake, eel, maze, labyrinth.

V. be -convoluted &c. *adj.*; wind, twine, turn and twist, twirl; wave, undulate, meander; inosculate; en-twine, intwine; twist, coil, roll; wrinkle, curl, crisp, twill; frizz, -le; crimp, crape, indent, scollop, scallop; wring, intort; contort; wreathe &c. (*cross*) 219.

Adj. convoluted; winding, twisted &c. *v.*; tortile, tortive; wavy; und-ated, -ulatory; circling, snaky, snake-like, serpentine; serpent-, anguill-, verm-iform; vermicular; mazy, tortuous, anfractuous, sinuous, flexuous, wavy, sigmoidal.

involved, intricate, complicated, perplexed; labyrinth-ic, -ian, -ine; circuitous; peristaltic; dædalian, curly.

wreathy, frizzly, *crêpé*, buckled; ravelled &c. (*in disorder*) 59.

spiral, coiled, helical, turbinated.

Adv. in and out, round and round.

249. Rotundity.—N. rotundity; roundness &c. *adj.*; cylindricity; spher-icity, -oidity; globosity.

cylin-der, -droid; barrel, drum; roll, -er; *rouleau*, column, rolling-pin, rundle; chimney-pot, drain-pipe.

cone, conoid; pear-, egg-, bell-shape.

sphere, globe, ball, boulder, bowlder; spher-, ellips-, ge-, glob-oid, oblong –, oblate- spheroid; drop, spherule, globule, vesicle, bulb, bullet, pellet, *pelote*, clew, pill, marble, pea, knob, pommel, knot.

V. render -spherical &c. *adj.*; form into a sphere, sphere, roll into a ball; give -rotundity &c. *n.*; round.

Adj. rotund; round &c. (*circular*) 247; cylindr-ic, -ical, -oid; columnar, lumbriciform; conic, -al; spher-ical, -oidal; glob-ular, -ated, -ous, -ose; egg-, bell-, pear-shaped; ov-oid, -iform; gibbous; campaniform, -ulate, -iliform; fungiform, bead-like, moniliform, pyriform, bulbous; *teres atque rotundus*; round as -an orange, – an apple, – a ball, – a billiard ball, – a cannon ball.

3°. SUPERFICIAL FORM

250. Convexity. — N. convexity, prominence, projection, swelling, gibbosity, bilge, bulge, protuberance, protrusion; excrescency, camber.

intumescence; tumour, tumor; tubercle, -osity; excrescence; hump, hunch, bunch, gnarl.

tooth, knob, elbow, process, *apophysis*, condyle, bulb, node, nodule, nodosity, tongue, *dorsum*, boss, embossment, bump, clump; sugar-loaf &c. (*sharpness*) 253; bow; mamelon.

pimple, wen, wheal, *papula*, postule, pock, proud flesh, growth, goitre, *sarcoma*, caruncle, corn, bunion, wart, furuncle, polypus, adenoid, fungus, fungosity, *exostosis*, bleb, blister, blain; boil &c. (*disease*) 655; bubble, blob.

papilla, nipple, teat, pap, breast, dug, mammilla; proboscis, nose, neb, beak, snout, nozzle, snozzle; Adam's apple; belly, paunch, corporation; withers, back, shoulder, lip, flange.

peg, button, stud, ridge, rib, jutty, trunnion, snag.

cupola, dome, bee-hive; arch, balcony, eaves; pilaster.

relief, relievo, *cameo*; *basso-*, *mezzo-*, *alto-rilievo*; low-, bas-, high-relief.

hill &c. (*height*) 206; cape, promontory, mull; fore-, head-land; point of land, naze, ness, mole, jetty, hummock, ledge, spur.

V. be -prominent &c. *adj.*; project, bulge, protrude, bag, belly, pout, bouge, bunch; jut –, stand –, stick –, poke- out; stick –, bristle –, start –, cock –, shoot- up; swell –, hang –, bend- over; beetle.

render -prominent &c. *adj.*; raise 307; emboss, chase.

251. Flatness.—N. flatness &c. *adj.*; smoothness &c. 255.

plane; level &c. 213; plate, platter, table, tablet, slab.

V. render flat, flatten, squash; level &c. 213.

Adj. flat, plane, even, flush, scutiform, discoid; level &c. (*horizontal*) 213; smooth; flat as -a pancake, – a fluke, – a flounder, – a board, – my hand.

252. Concavity.—N. concavity, depression, dip; hollow, -ness; indentation, *intaglio*, cavity, antrum, dent, dint, dimple, follicle, pit, *sinus*, *alveolus*, *lacuna*; excavation, trench, sap, mine, tunnel, burrow; trough &c. (*furrow*) 259; honeycomb.

cup, basin, crater, punch-bowl; cell &c. (*receptacle*) 191; socket, faucet.

valley, vale, dale, dell, gap, dingle, combe, bottom, slade, strath, glade, grove, glen, cave, cavern, cove; grot, -to; alcove, *cul-de-sac*, blind alley; gully &c. 198; arch &c. (*curve*) 245; bay &c. (*of the sea*) 343.

excavator, sapper, miner.

V. be -concave &c. *adj.*; retire, cave in.

render -concave &c. *adj.*; depress, hollow; scoop, – out; gouge, dig, delve, excavate, dent, dint, mine, sap, undermine, burrow, tunnel, stave in.

Adj. depressed &c. *v.*; concave, hollow, stove in; dished; spoon-like; retiring; retreating; cavernous; porous &c. (*with holes*) 260; cellular, spongy, spongious; honeycombed, alveolar; infundibul-ar, -iform; funnel-, bell-shaped; campaniform, capsular; vaulted, arched.

Adj. convex, prominent, protuberant, underhung, undershot; projecting &c. *v.*; bossed, bossy, nodular, bunchy; clav-ate, -ated; hummocky, *moutonné*, mammiform; papul-ous, -ose; hemispheric, bulbous; bowed, arched; bold; bellied; tuber-ous, -culous; tumorous; cornute, knobby, odontoid; lenti-form, -cular; gibbous.

salient, in relief, raised, *repoussé*; bloated &c. (*expanded*) 194.

253. Sharpness.—N. sharpness &c. *adj.*; acuity, acumination; spinosity.

point, spike, spine, *spiculum*, tine; needle, pin; tack, nail; prick, -le; spur, rowel, barb; spit, cusp; horn, antler; snag; tag; thorn, bristle.

nib, tooth, incisor, tusk; spoke, cog, ratchet.

crag, crest, *arête*, cone, peak, sugar-loaf, pike, *aiguille*; spire, pyramid, steeple.

beard, *chevaux de frise*, porcupine, hedgehog, brier, bramble, thistle; comb, awn, bur.

wedge; knife-, cutting- edge; blade, edge-tool, cutlery, knife, penknife, whittle, razor; scalpel, bistoury, lancet; chisel; ploughshare, coulter; hatchet, axe, pick-axe, mattock, pick, adze, bill; bill-hook, cleaver, cutter; skiver; scythe, sickle, scissors, shears; sword &c. (*arms*) 727; bodkin &c. (*perforator*) 262.

sharpener, hone, strop; grind-, whet-stone; steel, emery.

V. be -sharp &c. *adj.*; taper to a point; bristle with.

render -sharp &c. *adj.*; sharpen, point, aculeate, acuminate, whet, barb, spiculate, set, strop, grind.

cut &c. (*sunder*) 44.

Adj. sharp, keen; acute; aci-cular, -form; acu-leated, -minated; pointed; tapering; conical, pyramidal; mucron-ate, -ated; spindle-, needle-shaped; spiked, spiky, ensiform, peaked, salient, cusp-ed; -idate, -idated; corn-ute, -uted, -iculate; prickly; spiny, spinous; thorny, bristling, muricated, pectinated, studded, thistly, briery; craggy &c. (*rough*) 256; snaggy; digitated, two-edged, fusiform; denti-form, -culated; toothed; odontoid; star-like; stell-ated, -iform; arrow-headed; arrowy, barbed, spurred, sagittal; spear-shaped, hastate; horned; conical.

cutting; sharp-, knife-edged; sharp -, keen- as a razor; sharp as a needle; sharpened &c. *v.*; set.

254. Bluntness.—N. bluntness &c. *adj.*

V. be -, render- blunt &c. *adj.*; obtund, dull; take off the -point, - edge; turn.

Adj. blunt, obtuse, dull, bluff.

---

255. Smoothness.—N. smoothness &c. *adj.*; polish, gloss; lubric-ity, -ation.

down, velvet, silk, satin; slide; bowling green &c. (*level*) 213; glass, ice; asphalt, pavement, flags.

roller, steam-roller; iron, flat-iron, tailor's goose; sand-, emery-paper; burnisher, turpentine and bees-wax.

V. smooth, -en; plane; file; mow, shave; level, roll; macadamize; polish, burnish, planish, levigate, calender, glaze; iron, hot-press, mangle; lubricate &c. (*oil*) 332.

256. Roughness.—N. roughness &c. *adj.*; tooth, grain, texture, ripple; asperity, rugosity, salebrosity, corrugation, nodosity; arborescence &c. 242.

brush, hair, beard, shag, mane, whisker, mutton-chops, *moustache*, *mustachio*, imperial, Van Dyke, tress, lock, curl, ringlet, *fimbriæ*, *cilia*, *villi*; eyelashes, eye-brows, love-lock.

plum-age, -osity; plume, *panache*, crest; feather, tuft, tussock, fringe, toupee.

wool, velvet, plush, nap, pile, floss,

Adj. smooth; polished &c. *v.*; even; level &c. 213; plane &c. (*flat*) 251; sleek, glossy; silken, silky; lanate, downy, velvety; glabrous, slippery, glassy, lubricous, oily, soft; unwrinkled; smooth as -glass, – ice, – velvet, – oil; slippery as an eel; woolly &c. (*feathery*) 256.

fluff, fur, down; byssus, moss, bur.

V. be -rough &c. *adj.*; go against the grain.

render -rough &c. *adj.*; roughen, rough cast, knurl; ruffle, crisp, crumple, crinkle, corrugate, engrail; set on edge, stroke –, rub- the wrong way, rumple.

Adj. rough, uneven; scabrous, knotted; nodular; rug-ged, -ose, -ous; asperous, crisp, salebrous, gnarled, unpolished, unsmooth, rough-hewn; knurled, cross-grained, crag-gy, -ged; crankling, scraggy, jagged, unkempt, prickly &c. (*sharp*) 253; arborescent &c. 242; leafy, well-wooded; feathery; plum-ose, -igerous; tufted, fimbriated, hairy, bristly, ciliated, filamentous, hirsute; crin-ose, -ite; bushy, hispid, villous, pappous, bearded, pilous, shaggy, shagged; fringed, befringed; set-ous, -ose, -aceous; 'like quills upon the fretful porcupine'; rough as a -nutmeg grater, – bear.

downy, velvety, flocculent, woolly; lan-ate, -ated; lanugin-ous, -ose; tomentous.

Adv. against the grain, in the rough, on edge.

257. Notch.—N. notch, dent, nick, cut; indent, -ation; serration; dimple.

embrasure, battlement, machicolation; saw, tooth, crenelle, scallop, scollop, vandyke.

V. notch, nick, cut, pink, mill, score, dent, indent, jag, scarify, scotch, crimp, scollop, crenulate, vandyke.

Adj. notched &c. *v.*; crenate, -d; dentate, -d; denticulate, -d; toothed, palmated, serrated.

258. Fold.—N. fold, plicature, pleat, plait, ply, crease; tuck, gather; flexion, flexure, joint, elbow, doubling, duplicature, wrinkle, rimple, crinkle, crankle, crumple, rumple, rivel, ruck, ruffle, dog's ear, corrugation, frounce, flounce, lapel; pucker, crow's feet.

V. fold, double, plicate, pleat, plait, crease, wrinkle, crinkle, crankle, curl, smock, cockle up, crocker, rimple, rumple, frizzle, frounce, rivel, twill, corrugate, ruffle, crimple, crumple, pucker; turn –, double- -down, – under; tuck, ruck, hem, gather.

Adj. folded &c. *v.*

259. Furrow.—N. furrow, groove, rut, *sulcus*, scratch, streak, *striæ*, crack, score, incision, slit; chamfer, fluting.

channel, gutter, trench, ditch, dike, dyke, moat, fosse, trough, kennel; ravine &c. (*interval*) 198.

V. furrow &c. *n.*; flute, groove, carve, corrugate, plough; incise, chase, enchase, grave, engrave, etch, bite in, cross-hatch.

Adj. furrowed &c. *v.*; ribbed, striated, sulcated, fluted, canaliculated; bisulc-ous, -ate; trisulcate; corduroy.

260. Opening.—N. hole, foramen; puncture, blow-out, perforation; pin-, key-, loop-, port-, peep-, mouse-, pigeon-hole; eye, – of a needle; eyelet; slot.

opening; apert-ure, -ness; hiation,

261. Closure.—N. closure, occlusion, blockade; shutting up &c. *v.*; obstruction &c. (*hindrance*) 706; gag; embolism; contraction &c. 195; infarction; con-, ob-stipation; blind -alley, – corner; *cul-de-sac*, *cæcum*; imper-foration,

yawning, oscitancy, dehiscence, pate-faction, pandiculation; gap, chasm &c. (*interval*) 198.

embrasure, window, casement, light; sky-, fan-light; lattice; bay-, bow-window; oriel; dormer, lantern.

out-, in-let; vent, vomitory; *embouchure*; orifice, mouth, sucker, muzzle, throat, gullet, placket, weasand, wizen, nozzle, *æsophagus*.

portal, porch, gate, ostiary, postern, wicket, trap-door, hatch, door; arcade; gate-, door-, hatch-, gang-way; lych-gate.

way, path &c. 627; thoroughfare; channel, passage, tube, pipe; water-pipe &c. 350; air-pipe &c. 351; vessel, tubule, canal, gut, fistula; adjutage, ajutage; chimney, smoke stack, flue, tap, funnel, gully, tunnel, main; mine, pit, adit, shaft; gallery.

alley, aisle, glade, lane, vista.

bore, calibre; pore; blind orifice.

por-ousness, -osity; sieve, cullender, colander; grater, shredder; cribble, riddle, screen; honeycomb.

apertion, perforation; piercing &c. *v.*; terebration, empalement, pertusion, puncture, acupuncture, penetration.

opener, key, master-key, *passe-partout*.

V. open, ope, gape, dehisce, yawn, bilge; fly open.

perforate, pierce, empierce, tap, bore, drill; mine &c. (*scoop out*) 252; tunnel; trans-pierce, -fix; enfilade, impale, spike, spear, gore, spit, stab, pink, puncture, lance, trepan, trephine, stick, prick, riddle, punch; stave in.

cut a passage through; make -way, – room- for.

un-cover, -close, -rip; lay –, cut –, rip –, throw- open.

Adj. open; perforated &c. *v.*; perforate; wide open, agape, **ajar**; un-closed, -stopped; oscitant, gaping, yawning; patent.

tubular, cannular, fistulous; per-vious, -meable; foraminous; vesi-, vas-cular; porous, follicular, cribriform, honeycombed, in-fundibular, riddled; tubul-ous, -ated, piped.

opening &c. *v.*; aperient.

Int. *open sesame!*

262. Perforator. — N. perforator, piercer, borer, auger, gimlet, stylet, drill, wimble, awl, bradawl, scoop, terrier, corkscrew, dibble, trocar, tre-pan, trephine, probe, bodkin, needle, stiletto, broach, reamer, rimer, warder, lancet; punch, -eon; spikebit, gouge; spear &c. (*weapon*) 727.

-viousness &c. *adj.*, -meability; stopper &c. 263; *operculum*.

V. close, occlude, plug; block –, stop –, fill –, bung –, cork –, button –, stuff –, shut –, dam- up, obturate; blockade; obstruct &c. (*hinder*) 706; bar, bolt, stop, seal, plumb; choke, throttle; ram down, tamp, dam, cram; trap, clinch; put to –, shut- the door; batten down the hatches.

Adj. closed &c. *v.*; shut, operculated; unopened.

unpierced, imporous, cæcal; imper-forate, -vious, -meable; impenetrable; un-, im-passable; invious; path-, way-less; untrodden.

unventilated; air-, water-tight; her-metically sealed; tight, snug.

————

263. Stopper.—N. stopper, stopple; plug, cork, bung, spike, spill, stop-cock, tap; rammer; ram, -rod; piston; stop-gap; wadding, stuffing, padding, stop-ping, dossil, pledget, tompion, tourni-quet, obturator; wad.

cover &c. 223; valve, slide valve; vent-peg, spigot.

janitor, door –, gate- keeper, porter, commissionaire, *concierge*, warder, beadle, Cerberus, usher, guard, sentry, sentinel; ostiary.

Section IV. MOTION

1°. Motion in General

264. [Successive change of place.*]
Motion.—N. motion, movement, move; motivity, motility, going &c. *v.*; unrest.

stream, current, flow, flux, run, course, stir; conduction, evolution; kinematics.

step, rate, pace, tread, stride, gait, clip, port, footfall, cadence, carriage, velocity, angular velocity; progress, locomotion; journey &c. 266; voyage &c. 267; transit &c. 270.

restlessness &c. (*changeableness*) 149; mobility; movableness, motive power; laws of motion; mobilization.

V. be -in motion &c. *adj.*; move, go, hie, gang, budge, stir, pass, flit; hover -round, – about; shift, slide, slither, glide; roll, – on; flow, stream, run, drift, sweep along; wander &c. (*deviate*) 279; walk &c. 266; change –, shift- one's -place, – quarters; dodge; keep -going, – moving.

put –, set- in motion; move; impel &c. 276; propel &c. 284; render mov- able, mobilize.

Adj. moving &c. *v.*; in motion; motile, transitional; motory, motive; shifting, movable, mobile, mercurial, unquiet; restless &c. (*changeable*) 149; nomadic &c. 266; erratic &c. 279.

Adv. under way; on the -move, – wing, – tramp, – march.

265. Quiescence.—N. rest; stillness &c. *adj.*; quiescence; stag-nation, -nancy; fixity, immobility, catalepsy; indisturbance; quietism.

quiet, tranquillity, calm; repose &c. 687; peace; dead calm, anticyclone; statue-like repose; silence &c. 403; not a -breath of air, – mouse stirring; sleep &c. (*inactivity*) 683.

pause, lull &c. (*cessation*) 142; stand, – still; standing still &c. *v.*; lock; dead -lock, – stop, – stand; full stop; fix; embargo.

resting-place; bivouac; home &c. (*abode*) 189; pillow &c. (*support*) 215; haven &c. (*refuge*) 666; goal &c. (*arrival*) 292.

V. be -quiescent &c. *adj.*; stand –, lie- still; keep quiet, repose, hold the breath.

remain, stay; stand, lie to, ride at anchor, remain *in situ*, mark time, tarry; bring –, heave –, lay- to; pull –, draw- up; hold, halt; stop, – short; rest, pause, anchor; cast –, come to an- anchor; rest on one's oars; repose on one's laurels, take breath; stop &c. (*discontinue*) 142.

stagnate, vegetate; *quieta non movere*; let -alone, – well alone; abide, rest and be thankful; keep within doors, stay at home, go to bed.

dwell &c. (*be present*) 186; settle &c. (*be located*) 184; alight &c. (*arrive*) 292.

stick, – fast; stand, – like a post; not stir a -peg, – step; be at a -stand &c. *n.*

quell, becalm, hush, stay, lull to sleep, lay an embargo on; put the brake on.

Adj. quiescent, still; motion-, move-less; fixed; stationary; at -rest, – a stand, – a stand-still, – anchor; stock-still; immotile; standing still &c. *v.*; sedentary, untravelled, stay-at-home; becalmed, stagnant, quiet; un-moved, -disturbed, -ruffled; calm, restful; cataleptic; immovable &c. (*stable*) 150; sleeping &c. (*inactive*) 683; silent &c. 403; still as -a statue, – a post, – a mouse, – death.

Adv. at a stand &c. *adj.*; *tout court*; at the halt.

Int. stop! stay! avast! halt! hold, – hard! whoa!

Phr. *requiescat in pace.*

* A thing cannot be said to *move* from one place to another, unless it passes in suc- cession through every intermediate place; hence motion is only such a change of place as is *successive*. 'Rapid, swift, &c., as thought' are therefore incorrect expressions.

266. [Locomotion by land.] **Journey.**
—**N.** travel; travelling &c. *v.*; wayfaring, campaigning.

journey, excursion, expedition, tour, trip, grand tour, circuit, peregrination, discursion, ramble, pilgrimage, *trek*, course, ambulation, march, walk, hike, promenade, constitutional, stroll, saunter, tramp, jog-trot, turn, stalk, perambulation; noctambulation; somnambulism, sleep walking; outing, ride, drive, airing, jaunt.

equitation, horsemanship, riding, *manège*, ride and tie.

roving, vagrancy, pererration; marching and countermarching; nomadism; vagabond-ism, -age; gadding; flit, -ting; migration; e-, im-, de-, inter-migration.

plan, itinerary, guide; hand-, road-book; Baedeker, Murray, Bradshaw, time table.

procession, parade, cavalcade, caravan, file, *cortège*, column.

[Organs and instruments of locomotion] vehicle &c. 272; locomotive &c. 271; legs, feet, pegs, pins, trotters.

traveller &c. 268.

V. travel, journey, course; tour; take –, go- a journey; take –, go out for- -a walk &c. *n.*; have a run; take the air.

flit, take wing; migrate, emigrate, *trek*; rove, prowl, roam, range, patrol, pace up and down, traverse; scour –, traverse- the country; peragrate; per-, circum-ambulate; nomadize, wander, ramble, stroll, saunter, hover, go one's rounds, straggle; gad, – about; expatiate.

walk, march, step, tread, pace, plod, wend; promenade; trudge, tramp; stalk, stride, straddle, strut, foot it, stump, bundle, bowl along, toddle; paddle; tread –, follow –, pursue- a path.

take horse, ride, drive, trot, amble, canter, prance, fisk, frisk, *caracoler*; gallop &c. (*move quickly*) 274; motor, cycle, taxi; go by -car, – train, – tram, – bus, – plane.

peg –, jog –, wag –, shuffle- on; stir one's stumps; bend one's -steps, – course; make –, find –, wend –, pick –, thread –, plough- one's way; coast, slide, glide, skim, skate, ski; march in procession, file off, defile.

go –, repair –, resort –, hie –, betake oneself- to.

Adj. travelling &c. *v.*; ambulatory, itinerant, peripatetic, peram-

267. [Locomotion by water, or air.] **Navigation.**—**N.** navigation; aquatics; boating, cruising, yachting; ship &c. 273; oar, scull, sweep, punt pole, paddle, – wheel, screw, propeller, stern wheel, sail, canvas.

natation, swimming; fin, flipper- fish's tail.

aerial navigation, air service, airways, airmanship, aero-donetics, -dynamics, -mechanics, -station, -statics, -nautics; ballooning, balloonry; balloon &c. 273; flying, flight, aviation, volitation; wing, pinion, *aileron*.

voyage, sail, cruise, passage, circumnavigation, *periplus*; head-, stern-, lee-way.

mariner, aeronaut &c. 269.

V. sail; put to sea &c. (*depart*) 293; take ship, get under way; spread -sail, – canvas; gather way, have way on; make –, carry- sail; plough the -waves, – deep, – main, – ocean; walk the waters.

navigate, warp, luff, scud, boom, kedge; drift, course, cruise, coast; hug the -shore, – land; circumnavigate.

ply the oar, row, paddle, pull, scull, punt, steam.

swim, float; buffet the waves, ride the storm, skim, *effleurer*, dive, wade.

fly, aviate, be wafted, hover, soar, drift, glide, plane, sideslip, *volplane*, pique, dive, spin, roll, loop, flutter; take -wing, – a flight; wing one's -flight, – way.

Adj. sailing &c. *v.*; seafaring, nautical, maritime, naval; sea-going, coasting; afloat; navigable, aquatic, natatory.

volitant, volant, aerostatic, aerial, aeronautic; alar, alate, pennate.

Adv. under -way, – sail, – canvas, – steam; on the wing.

bulatory, roving, rambling, gadding, discursive, vagrant, migratory, nomadic; circumforane-an, -ous; somnambular, nocti-, mundi-vagant; locomotive, automotive, self-moving.

way-faring, -worn; travel-stained.

Adv. on -foot, – horseback, – Shanks's mare; by the Marrowbone stage; *in transitu* &c. 270; *en route* &c. 282.

Int. come along!

268. Traveller.—N. traveller, wayfarer, voyager, itinerant, passenger.

tourist, excursionist, globe-trotter; explorer, adventurer, mountaineer, Alpine Club; peregrinator, wanderer, rover, straggler, rambler; bird of passage; gad-about, -ling; vagrant, scatterling, landloper, waifs and estrays, wastrel, stray; loafer; tramp, -er, hobo, beachcomber, vagabond, nomad, Bohemian, gipsy, Arab, Wandering Jew, Hadji, pilgrim, palmer; peripatetic; somnambulist, sleep walker, noctambulist; emigrant, fugitive, refugee, *émigré*.

runner, courier, King's messenger; Mercury, Iris, Ariel, comet.

pedestrian, walker, foot-passenger; cyclist; wheelman.

rider, horseman, equestrian, cavalier, jockey, rough rider, trainer, breaker, huntsman.

driver, coachman, whip, Jehu, charioteer, postilion, post-boy, carter, wagoner, drayman, truckman; cab-man, -driver; *voiturier, vetturino, condottiere*; engine-driver; stoker, fireman, guard, brakeman, conductor; chauffeur, automobilist, motorist, motor –, truck --, taxi- driver.

269. Mariner.—N. sailor, mariner, navigator, argonaut; sea-man, -farer, -faring man; yachtsman; tar, jack tar, salt, gob, sea-dog, shellback, able seaman, A.B.; man-of-war's man, bluejacket, marine, jolly; midshipman, middy, reefer; captain, commander, master mariner, skipper, mate; ship-, boat-, ferry-, water-, lighter-, barge-, longshore- man, hoveller; bargee, gondolier; oar-, -sman; rower; boat-, cock-swain; coxswain; steersman, helmsman, pilot; crew; lascar.

aerial navigator, aeronaut, balloonist, Icarus, aviator, pilot, observer, flyer, airman.

270. Transference.—N. transfer, -ence; trans-, e-location; displacement; *meta-stasis, -thesis*; removal; re-, a-motion; relegation; de-, as-portation; extradition, conveyance, draft; carrying, carriage; convection, -duction, -tagion, infection; transfusion; transfer &c. (*of property*) 783.

transit, transition; passage, ferry, gestation; portage, porterage, carting, cartage; shovelling &c. *v.*; vect-ion, -ure, -itation; shipment, freight, wafture; trans-mission, -port, -portation, -umption, -plantation, -lation; shift-, dodg-ing; dispersion &c. 73; transposition &c. (*interchange*) 148; traction &c. 285.

[Thing transferred] drift, alluvium, detritus, *moraine*; gift, legacy, bequest, lease; freight, mails, cargo, luggage, baggage, goods.

V. trans-fer, -mit, -port, -place, -plant; convey, assign, carry, bear, fetch and carry; carry –, ferry- over; hand, pass, forward; shift; conduct, convoy, bring, fetch, reach.

send, delegate, consign, mail, post, relegate, turn over to, pass the buck, deliver; ship, embark; waft; switch, shunt; transpose &c. (*interchange*) 148; displace &c. 185; throw &c. 284; drag &c. 285.

shovel, lade, dip, ladle, bale, decant, draft off, transfuse.

Adj. transferred &c. *v.*; drifted; movable; port-able, -ative; conductive; contagious, infectious.

transferable, assignable, conveyable, devisable, negotiable, transmissible.

Adv. from -hand to hand, – pillar to post.

on –, by- the way; on the -road, – wing; as one goes; *in transitu, en route, chemin faisant, en passant,* in mid-progress.

271. Carrier.—N. carrier, porter, red cap, bearer, messenger, postman, tranter, conveyer; stevedore; coolie; conductor, locomotive, tractor, caterpillar tractor, motor.

beast of burden, cattle, horse, steed, nag, palfrey, Arab, blood horse, thorough-bred, galloway, charger, courser, racer, hunter, jument, pony, filly, colt, foal, barb, roan, jade, hack, *bidet,* pad, cob, tit, punch, roadster, goer; race-, pack-, draft-, cart-, dray-, post-horse, mount; Shetland pony, sheltie; garran; jennet, genet, bayard, mare, stallion, gelding; stud.

Pegasus, Bucephalus, Rozinante.

ass, donkey, jackass, mule, hinny; sumpter -horse, – mule; reindeer; camel, dromedary, mehari, llama, elephant; carrier pigeon.

carriage &c. (*vehicle*) 272; ship &c. 273.

Adj. equine, asinine.

272. Vehicle.—N. vehicle, conveyance, carriage, car, caravan, van, furniture van, pantechnicon; wagon, wain, dray, cart, lorry.

carriole; sledge, sled, sleigh, bobsleigh, toboggan, *luge,* truck, tram; limber, tumbrel, pontoon; barrow; wheel-, hand- -barrow, – cart, trolley; perambulator; Bath –, wheel –, sedanchair, jinriksha, rickshaw; ekka; chaise; palan-keen, -quin; litter, horse-litter, brancard, crate, hurdle, stretcher, ambulance; velocipede, hobby-horse, coaster, scooter, go-cart; cycle; bi-, tri-, quadri-cycle; tandem, safety; skate, roller skate; ski, snow-shoe.

equipage, turn-out; coach, chariot, *quadriga,* chaise, phaëton, break, brake, mail-phaëton, wagonette, drag, curricle, tilbury, whisky, landau, *barouche,* victoria, brougham, clarence, calash, *calèche,* britzska, *araba,* kibitka; berlin; sulky, *désobligeant,* sociable, *vis-à-vis, dormeuse;* jaunting –, outside- car; *tarantass;* runabout; shay.

post-chaise; diligence, stage; stage –, mail –, hackney –, glass- coach; stage-wagon; car, omnibus, bus, fly, *cabriolet,* cab, hansom, shofle, fourwheeler, growler, *droshki,* drosky.

dog-cart, trap, gig, whitechapel, buggy, four-in-hand, unicorn, random, tandem; shandredhan, *char-à-banc.*

automobile, motor-, auto-, touring-, racing-, cycle-, side-, steam-, electric-

273. Ship.—N. ship, vessel, sail; craft, bottom.

navy, marine, fleet, flotilla, squadron; shipping.

man of war &c. (*combatant*) 726; transport, tender, store-ship; merchant ship, merchantman; packet, liner; whaler, slaver, collier, coaster, tanker, freighter, freight steamer, cargo boat, lighter; fishing-, pilot- boat; trawler, drifter; cable ship; hulk; yacht; floating palace, ocean greyhound.

ship, bark, barque, brig, snow, hermaphrodite brig; brigantine, barquentine; schooner; topsail –, fore and aft –, three masted- schooner; *chasse-marée;* sloop, cutter, corvette, clipper, foist, yawl, dandy, ketch, smack, lugger, barge, hoy, cat-, -boat, buss; sail-er, -ing vessel, wind jammer; steam-er, -boat, -ship; mail –, paddle –, screw –, sternwheel- steamer; tug; train-ferry; line of steamers &c.

boat, pinnace, launch, motor-boat, picket-boat; hydroplane; life-, long-, jolly-, bum-, fly-, cock-, ferry-, canalboat, dory, dugout, galliot; shallop, gig, funny, skiff, dingy, scow, cockleshell, wherry, coble, punt, cog, lerret; eight-, four-, pair- oar; randan; outrigger; float, raft, pontoon; prame, ice-yacht.

state barge, bucentaur.

catamaran, coracle, gondola, carvel, caravel; felucca, caique, canoe; trireme;

car; motor-, -omnibus, – bus, – cab, – cycle; limousine, landaulette, cabriolet, *coupé, voiturette*, runabout, electromobile, taxi, -cab.

train; passenger –, express –, freight –, subway –, special –, corridor –, parliamentary –, luggage –, goods-train, *train de luxe*; 1st-, 2nd-, 3rd-class- -train, – carriage, – compartment; Pullman –, sleeping-, club-, observation-, dining-, restaurant-car; mail-, luggage-, brake-van, coach, car, carriage; rolling stock; horse-box, cattle-truck.

tramcar, trolley-omnibus, trackless trolley.

shovel, spoon, spatula, ladle, hod, hoe; spade, spaddle, loy; spud; pitch-fork.

Adj. vehicular.

---

galley, – foist; bilander, dogger, hooker, howker; argosy, carack; galliass, galleon; galliot, polacca, polacre, corsair, tartane, junk, lorcha, praam, proa, prahu, saick, sampan, xebec, dhow; dahabeah; nuggar, cayak, piroque; trireme.

submarine, submersible.

aircraft (*combatant*) &c. 726; flying machine, air mail, aero-, air-, mono-, bi-, tri-, hydro aero-plane, plane, cabin plane, transport plane, *avion*, flying boat, glider, *aviette*, helicopter; balloon, air-, fire-, gas-, Mongolfier-, pilot-, captive-, free-, kite-, dirigible- balloon, air-ship, *Zeppelin*, blimp; kite, parachute.

nacelle, car, gondola, aileron; hangar, airport, landing field, airdrome; cat-walk, controls, rudder, tail.

Adj. marine, maritime, naval, nautical, seafaring, sea-, ocean-going, sea-worthy.

aerial, aeronautical, air-worthy, flying &c. *n.*

Adv. afloat, aboard; on -board, – ship board, – board ship.

2°. Degrees of Motion

274. Velocity.—N. velocity, speed, celerity; swiftness &c. *adj.*; rapidity, eagle speed; expedition &c. (*activity*) 682; pernicity; acceleration; haste &c. 684.

spurt, rush, dash, race, steeplechase; smart –, lively –, swift &c. *adj.* –, rattling –, spanking –, strapping- -rate, – pace; round pace; flying, flight.

gallop, canter, trot, round trot, run, scamper; hand -, full- gallop; swoop.

lightning, light, electricity, wind; cannon-ball, rocket, arrow, dart, quick-silver; telegraph, express train; torrent; swallow flight.

eagle, antelope, courser, race-horse, gazelle, greyhound, hare, doe, squirrel.

Mercury, Ariel, Camilla, Harlequin.

[Measurement of velocity] speed-ometer, log, -line, tachometer.

V. move quickly, trip, fisk; speed, hie, hasten, sprint, spurt, post, spank, scuttle; scud, -dle, scurry; scour, – the plain; scamper; run, – like mad; fly, race, run a race, cut away, cut and run, shoot, tear, whisk, whiz, sweep, skim, brush; cut -, bowl- along; rush

275. Slowness.—N. slowness &c. *adj.*; languor &c. (*inactivity*) 683; drawl; creeping &c. *v.*, lentor.

retardation; slackening &c. *v.*; delay &c. (*lateness*) 133; claudication.

jog-, dog-trot, walk; mincing steps; slow -march, – time.

slow -goer, – coach, – back; lingerer, loiterer, sluggard, tortoise, snail; dawdle &c. (*inactive*) 683.

V. move -slowly, &c. *adv.*; creep, crawl, lag, slug, walk, drawl, linger, loiter, saunter; plod, trudge, stump along, lumber; trail; drag; dawdle &c. (*be inactive*) 683; grovel, worm one's way, steal along; jog –, rub –, bundle-on; toddle, waddle, wabble, slug; traipse, slouch, shuffle, halt, hobble, limp, claudicate, shamble; flag, falter, totter, stagger; mince, step short; march in -slow time, – funeral procession; take one's time; hang fire &c. (*be late*) 133.

retard, relax; slacken, check, moderate, rein in, curb; reef; strike -, shorten -, take in- sail; put on the drag, apply the brake; clip the wings; reduce the

&c. (*be violent*) 173; dash -on, – off, – forward; bolt; trot, gallop, bound, flit, spring, dart, boom; march in -quick, – double-time; ride hard, get over the ground, scorch.

hurry &c. (*hasten*) 684; accelerate, put on; quicken; quicken –, mend- one's pace; clap spurs to one's horse; make -haste, – rapid strides, – forced marches, – the best of one's way; put one's best leg foremost, stir one's stumps, wing one's way, set off at a score; carry –, crowd- sail; go off like a shot, go ahead, gain ground; outstrip the wind, fly on the wings of the wind.

keep -up, – pace- with; outstrip &c. 303.

Adj. fast, speedy, swift, rapid, quick, fleet; nimble, agile, expeditious; express; active &c. 682; flying, galloping &c. *v.*; light-, nimble-footed; winged, eagle-winged, mercurial, electric, tele- graphic; light-legged, light of heel; swift as -an arrow &c. *n.*; quick as -lightning &c. *n.*, – thought.*

Adv. swiftly &c. *adj.*; with -speed &c. *n.*; apace; at -a great rate, – full speed, – railway speed; full -drive, – gallop; post-haste, in full sail, tantivy; trippingly; instantaneously &c. 113; like a shot.

under press of -sail, – canvas, – sail and steam; *velis et remis*, on eagle's wing, in double quick time; with -rapid, – giant- strides; *à pas de géant*; in seven league boots; whip and spur; *ventre à terre*; as fast as one's -legs, – heels- will carry one; as fast as one can lay feet to the ground, at the top of one's speed; by leaps and bounds; with haste &c. 684; in- high – gear, – speed.

Phr. *vires acquirit eundo.*

speed, decelerate; slacken -speed, – one's pace, lose ground; back -water, – pedal, put the engines astern, throttle down.

Adj. slow, slack; tardy; dilatory &c. (*inactive*) 683; gentle, easy; leisurely; deliberate, gradual; insensible, imper- ceptible; languid, sluggish, apathetic, phlegmatic, slow-paced, tardigrade, snail-like; creeping &c. *v.*

Adv. slowly &c. *adj.*; leisurely; *piano, adagio; largo, larghetto;* at half speed, under easy sail; at a -foot's, – snail's, – funeral- pace; slower than molasses in January; in slow time; with -mincing steps, – clipped wings; *haud passibus æquis;* in- low –, gear, – speed.

gradually &c. *adj.*; *gradatim*; by degrees, – slow degrees, – inches, – little and little; step by step; inch by inch, bit by bit, little by little, *seriatim*; consecutively.

3°. Motion Conjoined with Force

276. Impulse.—N. impulse, impul- sion, impetus; momentum; push, pulsion, thrust, shove, jog, jolt, brunt, booming, boost, throw; explosion &c. (*violence*) 173; propulsion &c. 284.

percussion, concussion, collision, oc- cursion, clash, encounter, cannon, *carambole*, appulse, shock, crash, bump; impact; *élan*; charge &c. (*attack*) 716; beating &c. (*punishment*) 972.

blow, dint, stroke, knock, tap, rap, slap, smack, pat, dab; fillip; slam, bang; hit, whack, thwack, clout; cuff &c. 972; squash, dowse, whap, swap, punch, thump, swipe, jab, pelt, kick, punce, calcitration; *ruade*; arietation; cut, thrust, lunge, yerk.

277. Recoil.—N. recoil; re-, retro- action; revulsion; rebound, *ricochet*; re-percussion, -calcitration; kick, *contre- coup;* springing back &c. *v.*; elasticity &c. 325; reflexion, reflex, reflux; rever- beration &c. (*resonance*) 408; rebuff, repulse; return.

ducks and drakes; boomerang; spring; reactionist, reactionary.

V. recoil, resile, react; spring –, fly –, bound- back; rebound, reverberate, repercuss, recalcitrate, echo, *ricochet*.

Adj. recoiling &c. *v.*; re-fluent, -percussive, -calcitrant, -actionary; retroactive.

Adv. on the -recoil &c. *n.*

* See note on 264.

hammer, sledge-hammer, mall, maul, mallet, flail; ram, -mer; battering-ram, monkey, pile-driver, punch, bat, tamper, tamping iron; cudgel &c. (*weapon*) 727; axe &c. (*sharp*) 253.

[Science of mechanical forces] mechanics, dynamics &c.

V. give an -impetus &c. *n.*; impel, push; start, give a start to, set going; drive, urge, boom; thrust, prod, foin; cant; elbow, shoulder, jostle, justle, hustle, hurtle, shove, jog, jolt, bean, encounter; run -, bump -, butt- against; knock -, run- one's head against; impinge.

strike, knock, hit, bash, tap, rap, bat, slap, flap, dab, pat, thump, beat, bang, slam, dash; punch, thwack, whack; hit -, strike- hard; swap, batter, dowse, baste; pelt, patter, skelter, buffet, belabour, tamp; fetch one a blow, swat; poke at, pink, lunge, yerk; kick, calcitrate; butt; strike at &c. (*attack*) 716; whip &c. (*punish*) 972; propel &c. 284.

come -, enter- into collision; collide; foul; fall -, run- foul of. throw &c. (*propel*) 284.

Adj. impelling &c. *v.*; im-pulsive, -pellent; booming; dynamic, -al; impelled &c. *v.*

4°. MOTION WITH REFERENCE TO DIRECTION

278. Direction.—**N.** direction, bearing, course, set, drift, tenor; tendency &c. 176; incidence; bending, trending &c. *v.*; dip, tack, aim, collimation; steer-ing, -age.

point of the compass, cardinal -, half -, quarter- points; North, East, South, West; N by E, ENE, NE by N, NE &c.; rhumb, azimuth, line of collimation.

line, path, road, range, quarter, line of march; a-, al-lignment; straight shot, bee-line.

V. tend -, bend -, point- towards; conduct -, go- to; point -to, - at; bend, trend, verge, incline, dip, determine.

steer -, make- -for, - towards; aim -, level- at; take aim; keep -, hold- a course; be bound for; bend one's steps towards; direct -, steer -, bend -, shape- one's course; align -, allignone's march; go straight, - to the point; march -on, - on a point.

ascertain one's -direction &c. *n.*; *s'orienter*, see which way the wind blows; box the compass.

Adj. directed &c. *v.*, - towards; pointing towards &c. *v.*; bound for; aligned -, alligned- with; direct, straight; un-deviating, -swerving; straightforward; North, -ern, -erly, &c. *n.*

directable· &c. *v.*

Adv. towards; on the -road, - high

279. Deviation. — **N.** deviation; swerving &c. *v.*; obliquation, warp, refraction; flection, flexion; sweep; de-flection, -flexure; declination.

diversion, digression, departure from, aberration, drift, sheer; divergence &c. 291; zigzag; *détour* &c. (*circuit*) 629.

[Desultory motion] wandering &c. *v.*; vagrancy, evagation; by-paths and crooked ways.

[Motion sideways, oblique motion] sidling &c. *v.*; *échelon*, leeway; knight's move (at chess).

V. alter one's course, deviate, depart from, turn, trend; bend, curve &c. 245; swerve, heel, bear off.

intervert; deflect; divert, - from its course; put on a new scent, shift, shunt, switch, wear, draw aside, crook, warp, short circuit.

stray, straggle; sidle, edge; diverge &c. 291; tralineate, digress, divagate, wander; wind, twist, meander, meander around Robin Hood's barn; veer, tack, sheer; turn -aside, - a corner, - away from; wheel, steer clear of; ramble, rove, drift; go -astray, - adrift; yaw, dodge; step aside, ease off, make way for, shy.

fly off at a tangent; glance off; turn, wheel -, face- about; turn -, face- to the right about; wabble &c. (*oscillate*) 314; go out of one's way &c. (*perform a circuit*) 629; lose one's way.

road- to; *versus*, to; hither, thither, whither; directly; straight, – forwards, – as an arrow; point blank; in a -direct, – straight- line -to, – for, – with; in a line with; full tilt at, as the crow flies.

before –, near –, close to –, against- the wind; windwards, in the wind's eye.

through, *via*, by way of; in all -directions, – manner of ways; *quaquaversum*, from the four winds.

280. [Going before.] **Precession.—N.** precession, leading, heading; precedence &c. 62; priority &c. 116; the lead, *le pas*; van &c. (*front*) 234; precursor &c. 64.

V. go -before, – ahead, – in the van, – in advance; precede, forerun; usher in, introduce, herald, head, take the lead; lead, – the way, – the dance; get –, have- the start; steal a march; get -before, – ahead, – in front of; outstrip &c. 303; take precedence &c. (*first in order*) 62.

Adj. foremost, first, leading &c. *v.*

Adv. in advance, before, ahead, in the van; fore-, head-most; in front.

Phr. *seniores priores.*

282. [Motion forwards; progressive motion.] **Progression.—N.** progress, -ion, -iveness; advancing &c. *v.*; advance, -ment; ongoing; flood-tide, headway; march &c. 266; rise; improvement &c. 658.

V. advance; proceed, progress; get -on, – along, – over the ground; gain ground; jog –, rub –, wag- on; go with the stream; keep –, hold on- one's course; go –, move –, come –, get –, pass –, push –, press- -on, – forward, – forwards, – ahead; press onwards, step forward; make –, work –, carve –, push –, force –, edge –, elbow- one's way; make -progress, – head, – way, – headway, – advances, – strides, – rapid strides &c. (*velocity*) 274; go –, shoot- ahead; distance; make up leeway.

Adj. advancing &c. *v.*; pro-gressive, -fluent; advanced.

Adj. deviating &c. *v.*; aberrant, errant; ex-, dis-cursive; devious, desultory, loose; rambling; stray, erratic, vagrant, undirected; circuitous, indirect, zigzag; crab-like.

Adv. astray from, round about, wide of the mark; to the right about; all manner of ways; circuitously &c. 629.

obliquely, sideling, like the move of the knight on a chessboard.

281. [Going after.] **Sequence.—N.** sequence, run; coming after &c. (*order*) 63; (*time*) 117; following; pursuit &c. 622.

follower, attendant, satellite, shadow, dangler, train.

V. follow; pursue &c. 622; go –, fly- after.

attend, beset, dance attendance on, dog, be-dog; tread -in the steps of, – close upon; be –, go –, follow- in the -wake, – trail, – rear- of; trail, follow as a shadow, hang on the skirts of; tread –, follow- on the heels of, tag after.

lag, get behind.

Adj. following &c. *v.*

Adv. behind; in the -rear &c. 235, – train of, wake of; after &c. (*order*) 63, (*time*) 117.

283. [Motion backwards.] **Regression.—N.** regress, -ion; retro-cession, -gression, -gradation, -action; *reculade*; retreat, withdrawal, retirement, re-migration; recession &c. (*motion from*) 287; recess; crab-like motion.

re-fluence, -flux; backwater, regurgitation, ebb, return; resilience; reflexion (*recoil*) 277; *volte-face*.

counter -motion, – movement, – march; veering, tergiversation, recidivation, backsliding, fall, relapse; deterioration &c. 659.

turning-point &c. (*reversion*) 145.

V. re-cede, -grade, -turn, -vert, -treat, -tire; retro-grade, -cede; back, – down, – out, crawl; withdraw; rebound &c. 277; go –, come –, turn –, hark –, draw –, fall –, get –, put –, run- back; lose ground; fall –, drop- astern; back water, put about; veer, – round; double,

Adv. forward, onward; forth, on ahead, under way, *en route* for, on -one's way, – the way, – the road, – the high road- to; in -progress, – mid progress; *in transitu* &c. 270.

Phr. *vestigia nulla retrorsum.*

---

wheel, counter-march; ebb, regurgitate; jib, shrink, shy.

turn -tail, – round, – upon one's heel, – one's back upon; retrace one's steps, dance the back step; sound –, beat- a retreat; go home.

Adj. receding &c. *v.*; retro-grade, -gressive; re-gressive, -fluent, -flex, -cidivous, -silient; crab-like; reactionary &c. 277; counter-clockwise.

Adv. back, -wards; reflexively, to the right about; *à reculons, à rebours.*

Phr. *revenons à nos moutons,* as you were.

284. [Motion given to an object situated in front.] **Propulsion.—N.** pro-pulsion, -jection; *vis a tergo*; push &c. (*impulse*) 276; e-, jaculation; ejection &c. 297; throw, fling, toss, shot, discharge, shy.

[Science of propulsion] gunnery, ballistics, archery.

missile, projectile, ball, *discus*, javelin, hammer, quoit, brickbat, shot, bullet; arrow, shaft, gun &c. (*arms*) 727.

shooter, shot; gunner, gun-layer; archer, toxophilite; bow-, rifle-, marksman; good –, crack- shot; sharpshooter &c. (*combatant*) 726.

V. propel, project, throw, fling, cast, pitch, chuck, toss, jerk, heave, shy, hurl; flirt, fillip.

dart, lance, tilt; e-, jaculate; fulminate, bolt, drive, sling, pitchfork.

send; send –, let –, fire- off; discharge, shoot; launch, send forth, let fly; dash.

put –, set- in motion; set agoing, start; give -a start, – an impulse- to; push, impel &c. 276; trundle &c. (*set in rotation*) 312; expel &c. 297.

carry one off one's legs; put to flight.

Adj. propelled &c. *v.*; propelling &c. *v.*; pro-pulsive, -jectile.

285. [Motion given to an object situated behind.] **Traction.—N.** traction; drawing &c. *v.*; draught, pull, haul; rake; 'a long pull, a strong pull and a pull all together'; towage, haulage.

V. draw, pull, haul, lug, rake, drag, draggle, tug, tow, trail, trawl, train; take in tow.

wrench, jerk, twitch.

Adj. drawing &c. *v.*; tractive, tractile; ductile.

---

286. [Motion towards.] **Approach.— N.** approach, approximation, appropinquation; access; appulse; afflux, -ion; advent &c. (*approach of time*) 121; pursuit &c. 622; convergence &c. 290.

V. approach, approximate; near; get –, go –, draw- near; come, – near, – to close quarters; move –, set in- towards; drift; make up to; gain upon; pursue &c. 622; tread on the heels of; bear up; make the land; hug the -shore, – land.

Adj. approaching &c. *v.*; approximative; convergent; affluent; impending, imminent &c. (*destined*) 152.

287. [Motion from.] **Recession.—N.** recession, retirement, withdrawal; retreat; retrocession &c. 283; departure &c. 293; recoil &c. 277; flight &c. (*avoidance*) 623.

V. recede, go, move from, retire, ebb, withdraw, shrink; come –, move –, go –, get –, drift- away; depart &c. 293; retreat &c. 283; move –, stand –, sheer- off; swerve from; fall back, stand aside; run away &c. (*avoid*) 623.

remove, shunt, side track, switch off.

Adj. receding &c. *v.*

Adv. on the road.

Int. come hither! approach! here! come! come near!

288. [Motion towards, actively.] **Attraction.**—**N.** attract-ion, -iveness; pull; drawing to, pulling towards, adduction, magnetism, gravity, attraction of gravitation; lure, bait, decoy.

lode-stone, -star; magnet, siderite, magnetite.

V. attract; draw -, pull -, drag-towards; adduce.

lure, bait, decoy.

Adj. attracting &c. *v.*; attrahent, attractive, adducent, adductive.

290. [Motion nearer to.] **Convergence.**—**N.** con-vergence, -fluence, -course, -flux, -gress, -currence, -centration; appulse, meeting; corradiation.

assemblage &c. 72; resort &c. (*focus*) 74; asymptote.

V. converge, concur; come together, unite, meet, fall in with; close -with, - in upon; centre -round, - in; enter in; pour in.

gather together, unite, concentrate, bring into a focus.

Adj. converging &c. *v.*; con-vergent, -fluent, -current; centripetal; asymptotical.

292. [Terminal motion at.] **Arrival.**—**N.** arrival, advent; landing; de-, disem-barkation; reception, welcome, *vin d'honneur.*

home, goal, bourn; landing-place, -stage; resting -, stopping -place; destination, harbour, haven, port; terminal, terminus, railway station, depot, airport; halt, halting -place, - ground; anchorage &c. (*refuge*) 666.

return, recursion, remigration; meeting; ren-, en-counter.

completion &c. 729.

V. arrive; get to, come to; come; reach, attain; come up, - with, - to; overtake; make, fetch; complete &c. 729; join, rejoin.

light, alight, dismount; land, go ashore; debark, disembark; put -in, - into; visit, cast anchor, pitch one's tent; sit down &c. (*be located*) 184; get to one's journey's end; make the

289. [Motion from, actively.] **Repulsion.**—**N.** repulsion; driving from &c. *v.*; repulse; abduction.

V. repel; push -, drive - &c. 276. from; chase, dispel; retrude; abduce, abduct; send away, repulse, dismiss.

keep at arm's length, turn one's back upon, give the cold shoulder; send packing; send -off, - away- with a flea in one's ear, - about one's business.

Adj. repelling &c. *v.*; repellant, repulsive; abducent, abductive.

291. [Motion further off.] **Divergence.**—**N.** diverg-ence, -ency; divarication, ramification, radiation; separation &c. (*disjunction*) 44; dispersion &c. 73; deviation &c. 279; aberration, declination.

V. diverge, divaricate, radiate; ramify; branch -, glance -, file- off; fly off, - at a tangent; spread, scatter, disperse &c. 73; deviate &c. 279; part &c. (*separate*) 44; splay apart.

Adj. diverging &c. *v.*; divergent, radiant, centrifugal; aberrant.

---

293. [Initial motion from.] **Departure.**—**N.** departure, decession, decampment; embarkation; take-off; outset, start; removal; exit &c. (*egress*) 295; exodus, Hejira, flight.

leave-taking, *congé*, valediction, valedictory, adieu, farewell, good-bye, stirrup-cup.

starting -point, - post; point -, place- of -departure, - embarkation; port of embarkation.

V. depart; go, - away; take one's departure, set out; set -, march -, put -, start -, be -, move -, get -, whip -, pack -, go -, take oneself- off; start, issue, march out, debouch; go -, sally-forth; sally, set forward; be gone.

leave a place, quit, vacate, evacuate, abandon; go off the stage, make ones' exit; retire, withdraw, remove; go -one's way, - along, - from home; take -flight, - wing; spring, fly, flit, wing

land; be in at the death; come –, get- -back, – home; return; come in &c. (*ingress*) 294; make one's appearance &c. (*appear*) 446; drop in; detrain; outspan.

come to hand; come -at, – across; hit; come –, light –, pop –, bounce –, plump –, burst –, pitch- upon; meet; en- ren-counter; come in contact.

Adj. arriving &c. *v.*; homeward-bound; terminal.

Adv. here, hither.

Int. welcome! hail! all hail! good-day, – morrow; greetings! hullo! well!

---

one's flight; fly –, whip- away; take off, hop off; embark; go -on board, – aboard; set sail; put –, go- to sea; sail, take ship; hoist blue Peter; get under way, weigh anchor; strike tents, break camp, decamp; walk one's chalks, make tracks, cut one's stick; cut and run; take leave; say –, bid- -good-bye &c. *n.*; disappear &c. 449; abscond &c. (*avoid*) 623; entrain, embus, emplane; saddle –, harness –, hitch- up; inspan.

Adj. departing &c. *v.*; valedictory; outward bound.

Adv. whence, hence, thence; with a foot in the stirrup; on the -wing, – move.

Int. begone! &c. (*ejection*) 297; to horse! all aboard! farewell! adieu! good-bye, – day! *au revoir! auf wiedersehen!* fare you well! so long! God -bless you, – speed! *bon voyage!*

---

294. [Motion into.] **Ingress.—N.** ingress; entrance, entry; introgression; influx; intrusion, inroad, incursion, invasion, irruption; pene-, interpenetration; illapse, import, importation, infiltration; immigration; admission &c. (*reception*) 296; insinuation &c. (*interjacence*) 228; insertion &c. 300.

inlet; way in; mouth, door &c. (*opening*) 260; path &c. (*way*) 627; conduit &c. 350; immigrant, visitor, incomer, newcomer, colonist.

V. have the *entrée*; enter; go –, come –, pour –, flow –, creep –, slip –, pop –, break –, burst- -into, – in; set foot on; burst –, break- in upon; invade, intrude, butt in, horn in, crash; insinuate itself; inter-, penetrate; infiltrate; find one's way –, wriggle –, worm oneself- into.

give entrance to &c. (*receive*) 296; insert &c. 300.

Adj. incoming, ingressive &c. *n.*; inward bound.

Adv. inward.

---

295. [Motion out of.] **Egress.—N.** egress, exit, issue; emer-sion, -gence; disemboguement; out-break, -burst; e-, pro-ruption; emanation; evacuation; ex-, trans-udation; extravasation, perspiration, sweating, leakage, percolation, distillation, oozing; gush &c. (*water in motion*) 348; outpour, -ing; effluence, effusion; efflux, -ion; drain; dribbling &c. *v.*; defluxion; drainage; out-come, -put; discharge &c. (*excretion*) 299.

export; expatriation; e-, re-migration; *débouche*; exodus &c. (*departure*) 293; emigrant, migrant, *émigré*, colonist.

outlet, vent, spout, tap, sluice, floodgate; pore; vomitory, out-gate, sallyport; way out; mouth, door &c. (*opening*) 260; path &c. (*way*) 627; conduit &c. 350; air-pipe &c. 351.

V. emerge, emanate, issue; go –, come –, move –, pass –, pour –, flow-out of; pass off, evacuate; migrate.

ex-, trans-ude; leak; run, – out, – through; per-, trans-colate; seep; strain, distil; perspire, sweat, drain, ooze; filter, filtrate; dribble, gush, spout, flow out; well, – out; pour, trickle &c. (*water in motion*) 348; effuse, extravasate, disembogue, discharge itself, debouch; come –, break- forth; burst- out, – through; find vent, escape &c. 671.

Adj. effused &c. *v.*; outgoing, outward bound.

Adv. outward.

296. [Motion into, actively.] **Reception.**—**N.** reception; admission, admittance, *entrée*, importation; initiation; intro-duction, -mission, -ception; im-mission, ingestion, imbibition, absorption, ingurgitation, inhalation; suction, sucking; eating, drinking &c. (*food*) 298; insertion &c. 300; interjection &c. 228.

V. give -entrance to, – admittance to, – the *entrée*; intro-duce, -mit; usher, admit, receive, import, initiate, bring in, open the door to, throw open, ingest, absorb, imbibe, inhale, infiltrate; let –, take –, suck- in; re-admit, -sorb, -absorb; snuff up; swallow, ingurgitate; engulf, engorge; gulp; eat, drink &c. (*food*) 298.

Adj. admit-ting &c. *v.*, -ted &c. *v.*; admissible; absorbent; introductory, introceptive, intromittent, initiatory.

---

297. [Motion out of, actively.] **Ejection.**—**N.** ejection, emission, effusion, rejection, expulsion, eviction, extrusion, trajection; discharge.

egestion, evacuation, vomition, disgorgement, voidance, eruption, eruptiveness; ruc-, eruc-tation, blood-letting, venesection, phlebotomy, paracentesis; tapping, drainage; clear-ance, -age, voidance; vomiting, excretion &c. 299.

deportation; banishment &c. (*punishment*) 972; rogue's march; relegation, extradition; dislodgment.

V. give -exit, – vent- to; let –, give –, pour –, send- out; des-, dis-patch; exhale, excern, excrete, disembogue, secrete, secern; extravasate, shed, void, evacuate, egest, emit; open the -sluices, – floodgates; turn on the tap; extrude, detrude; effuse, spend, expend; pour forth; squirt, spirt, spill, slop; perspire &c. (*exude*) 295; breathe, blow &c. (*wind*) 349.

tap, draw off; bale –, lade- out; let blood, broach.

eject, reject; expel, discard; cut, send to Coventry, boycott, ostracize; *chasser*; banish &c. (*punish*) 972; throw &c. 284 -out, – up, – off, – away, – aside; push &c. 276 -out, – off, – away, – aside; shovel –, sweep- -out, – away; brush –, whisk –, turn –, send- -off, – away; discharge; send –, turn –, cast- adrift; turn –, bundle- out; throw overboard; give the sack to; send -packing, – about one's business, – to the right about; strike off the roll &c. (*abrogate*) 756; turn out- neck and heels, – head and shoulders, – neck and crop; pack off; send away with a flea in the ear; send to Jericho; bow out, show the door to, dismiss, fire, sack.

turn out of -doors, – house and home; evict, oust; exorcise, un-house, -kennel; dislodge; un-, dis-people; depopulate; relegate, deport.

empty; drain, – to the dregs; sweep off; clear, – off, – out, – away; suck, draw off, extract; clean out, make a clean sweep of, clear decks, purge.

em-, dis-, disem-bowel; eviscerate, gut; unearth, root -out, – up; averruncate; weed –, get out; eliminate, get rid of, do away with, shake off; exenterate.

vomit, spew, puke, keck, retch; belch, – out, eruct, eructate; cast –, bring- up; disgorge; expectorate, salivate, clear the throat, hawk, spit, sputter, splutter, slobber, drool, drivel, slaver, slabber.

unpack, unlade, unload, unship; break bulk.

be let out; ooze &c. (*emerge*) 295.

Adj. emitt-ing, -ed &c. *v.*

begone! get you gone! get –, go- -away, – along, – along with you! go your way! away, – with! off with you! go, – about your business! be off! avaunt! aroynt! get out!

298. [Eating.] Food.—N. eating &c.
v.; deglutition, gulp, epulation, masti-
cation, manducation, rumination, gastronomy, gastrology; panto-, hippo-,
ichthyo-phagy &c.; gluttony &c. 957;
carnivorousness, vegetarianism.

mouth, jaws, mandible, mazard,
chops.

drinking &c. *v.*; potation, draught,
libation; carousal &c. (*amusement*) 840;
drunkenness &c. 959.

food, *pabulum*; aliment, nourishment, nutriment; susten-ance, -tation;
nurture, subsistence, provender, feed,
fodder, provision, ration, keep, commons, board; commissariat &c. (*provision*) 637; prey, forage, pasture,
pasturage; fare, cheer; diet, -ary;
regimen; belly timber, staff of life;
bread, -and cheese; proteins, carbohydrates, vitamines.

comestibles, eatables, victuals, edibles, *ingesta*; grub, prog, tack,
hard tack, meat; bread, -stuffs; cereals; viands, cates, delicacy,
dainty, creature comforts, contents of the larder, flesh-pots; festal
board; ambrosia; good -cheer, – living.

hors-d'œuvre; soup, pottage, *potage*, broth, *bouillon*, *consommé*,
purée, *borsch*, stock, skilly, gumbo; fish, – cakes, – pie; joint, *rôti*,
pièce de résistance, *relevé*, hash, *réchauffé*, stew, *ragoût*, fricassee,
mince, *salim*, *goulash*, *bouillabaisse*, remove, *entrée*, *croquette*, *rissole*,
sausage, curry, bubble and squeak; haggis, collops, giblets; poultry,
game &c.; biscuit, bun, scone, rusk, pancake, pie, pastry, pasty,
patty, *patisserie*, tart, turnover, *vol-au-vent*, *soufflé*, dumpling, pudding, duff, *compote*, fritters, cake, napoleon, *blancmange*, custard,
jelly, jam, sweets &c. 396; *entremet*; oatmeal, porridge, hasty pudding, gruel; eggs, omelet, cheese, matzoon, savoury; vegetable,
salad, *mayonnaise*, fruit; sauce, condiment &c. 393; kickshaws.

table, *cuisine*, bill of fare, *menu*, *table d'hôte*, ordinary, *à la carte*;
cover.

meal, repast, feed, spread; mess; dish, plate, course, side dish;
regale; regale-, refresh-, entertain-ment; refection, collation, picnic,
feast, banquet, junket; breakfast; lunch, -eon; *déjeuner*, bever,
tiffin, tea, dinner, supper, snack, whet, bait, dessert; pot-luck,
table d'hôte, *déjeuner à la fourchette*; hearty –, square –, substantial
–, full- -meal; blow out; light refreshment; pemmican.

mouthful, bolus, gobbet, tit-bit, morsel, sop, sippet.

drink, beverage, liquor, broth, soup; potion, dram, draught,
drench, swill; nip, peg, sip, sup, gulp.

wine, champagne, spirits, *liqueur*, beer, porter, stout, ale, malt
liquor, julep, Sir John Barleycorn, stingo, heavy wet, bitter, lager-
beer, cider; grog, toddy, flip, purl, punch, negus, cup, bishop,
posset, wassail; bitters, *apéritif*, high-ball, cocktail; whisky, rum,
absinthe; gin &c. (*intoxicating liquor*) 959; coffee, chocolate, cocoa,
tea, *maté*, the cup that cheers but not inebriates.

eating-house &c. 189.

299. Excretion.—N. excretion, discharge, emanation; ejection &c. 297;
exhalation, exudation, extrusion, secretion, effusion, extravasation, *ecchy-
mosis*, evacuation, cacation, defecation,
dysentery, dejection, *fæces*, excrement;
perspiration, sweat; sub-, exud-ation;
diaphoresis; sewage.

saliva, spittle, rheum; ptyalism,
salivation, catarrh, distemper; diar-
rhœa; *ejecta*, *egesta*, *sputum*, *sputa*;
excreta; lava; *exuviæ* &c. (*uncleanness*)
653.

hemorrhage, bleeding; catamenia,
menses; outpouring &c. (*egress*) 295;
leucorrhea.

V. excrete &c. (*eject*) 297; emanate
&c. (*come out*) 295.

Adj. excretory, fæcal, secretory;
ejective, eliminant.

V. eat, feed, fare, devour, swallow, take; gulp, bolt, snap; fall to; despatch, dispatch; discuss; take –, get –, gulp-down; lay –, tuck- in; lick, pick, peck; gormandize &c. 957; bite, champ, munch, cranch, craunch, crunch, chew, masticate, nibble, gnaw, mumble.

live on; feed –, batten –, fatten –, feast- upon; browse, graze, crop, regale; carouse &c. (*make merry*) 840; eat heartily, do justice to, play a good knife and fork, banquet.

break -bread, – one's fast; breakfast, lunch, dine, take tea, sup.

drink, – in, – up, – one's fill; quaff, sip, sup; suck, – up; lap; swig; swill, tipple &c. (*be drunken*) 959; empty one's glass, drain the cup; toss -off, – one's glass; wash down, crack a bottle, wet one's whistle.

cater, purvey &c. 637.

Adj. eatable, edible, esculent, comestible, alimentary; cereal, cibarious; dietetic; culinary; nutri-tive, -tious; succulent; drinkable, pot-able, -ulent; bibulous.

omn-, carn-, herb-, frug-, gran-, gramin-, phyt-ivorus; ichthyoph-agous.

prandial.

300. [Forcible ingress.] **Insertion.—** N. insertion, implantation, intercalation, embolism, introduction; interpolation, insinuation &c. (*intervention*) 228; planting &c. v.; injection, inoculation, importation, infusion; forcible -ingress &c. 294; immersion; submersion, -gence; dip, plunge; bath &c. (*water*) 337; interment &c. 363.

V. insert; intro-duce, -mit; put –, run- into; import; inject; interject &c. 228; infuse, instil, inoculate, impregnate, imbue, imbrue.

graft, ingraft, bud, plant, implant; dovetail.

obtrude; thrust –, stick –, ram –, stuff –, tuck –, press –, drive –, pop –, whip –, drop –, put- in; impact; empierce &c. (*make a hole*) 260.

embed; immerse, immerge, merge; bathe, soak &c. (*water*) 337; dip, plunge &c. 310.

bury &c. (*inter*) 363.

insert &c.- itself; plunge *in medias res.*

Adj. inserted &c. v.

301. [Forcible egress.] **Extraction.—** N. extraction; extracting &c. v.; removal, elimination, extrication, eradication, evolution.

evulsion, avulsion; wrench; expression, squeezing; extirpation, extermination; ejection &c. 297; export &c. (*egress*) 295; distillation.

extractor, corkscrew, forceps, pliers.

V. extract, draw, pit; take –, draw –, pull –, tear –, pluck –, pick –, get- out; wring from, wrench; extort; root –, weed –, grub –, rake- up, – out; eradicate; pull –, pluck- up by the roots; averruncate; unroot; uproot, pull up, extirpate, dredge.

remove; educe, elicit; evolve, extricate; eliminate &c. (*eject*) 297; eviscerate &c. 297.

express, squeeze –, press- out; distil.

Adj. extracted &c. v.

---

302. [Motion through.] **Passage.—N.** passage, transmission; permeation; pene-, interpene-tration; transudation, infiltration; *osmosis*, osmose, endos-, exos-mose; intercurrence; ingress &c. 294; egress &c. 295; path &c. 627; conduit &c. 350; opening &c. 260; journey &c. 266; voyage &c. 267.

V. pass, – through; perforate &c. (*hole*) 260; penetrate, permeate, thread, thrid, enfilade; go -through, – across; go –, pass- over; cut across; ford, cross; pass and repass, work; make –, thread –, worm –, force- one's way; make –, force- a passage; cut one's way through;

find its -way, – vent; transmit, make way, clear the course; traverse, go over the ground.

Adj. passing &c. *v.*; intercurrent; osmotic &c. *n.*

Adv. *en passant* &c. (*transit*) 270.

303. [Motion beyond.] **Overstep.—N.** trans-cursion, -ilience, -gression; infraction, intrusion; trespass; encroach-, infringe-ment; extravagation, transcendence; redundance &c. 641; ingress &c. 294.

V. transgress, surpass, pass; go- beyond, – by; show in –, come to the-front; shoot ahead of; steal a march –, gain- upon.

over-step, -pass, -reach, -go, -ride, -leap, -jump, -skip, -lap, -shoot the mark; out-strip, -leap, -jump, -go, -step, -run, -ride, -rival, -do; beat, – hollow; distance; leave in the -lurch, – rear; go one better, throw into the shade; exceed, transcend, surmount; soar &c. (*rise*) 305.

encroach, intrude, trespass, infringe, invade, trench upon, intrench on; strain; stretch –, strain- a point; pass the Rubicon.

Adj. surpassing &c. *v.*

Adv. beyond the mark, ahead.

304. [Motion short of.] **Shortcoming. —N.** shortcoming, failure; delinquency; falling short &c. *v.*; de-fault, -falcation; leeway; labour in vain, no go.

incompleteness &c. 53; imperfection &c. 651; insufficiency &c. 640; non-completion &c. 730; failure &c. 732.

V. come –, fall –, stop- -short, – short of; not reach; want; keep within -bounds, – the mark, – compass.

break down, stick in the mud, collapse, come to nothing; fall -through, – to the ground, – down; cave in, end in smoke, fizzle out, miss the mark, fail; lose ground; miss stays, slump.

Adj. unreached; deficient; short, – of; *minus*; out of depth; perfunctory &c. (*neglect*) 460.

Adv. within -the mark, – compass, – bounds; behindhand; *re infectâ*; to no purpose; far from it.

Phr. the bubble burst.

305. [Motion upwards.] **Ascent.—N.** ascent, ascension; rising &c. *v.*; rise, upgrowth; leap &c. 309; acclivity, hill &c. 217; stair, stairs, stair-case, -way, flight of -steps, – stairs; ladder, companion, – way; lift, elevator &c. 307.

rocket, lark; sky-rocket, -lark; Alpine Club.

V. ascend, rise, mount, arise, uprise; go –, get –, work one's way –, start –, spring –, shoot- up; zoom; aspire.

climb, clamber, ramp, scramble, swarm, *escalade*, surmount; scale, – the heights.

tower, soar, hover, spire, plane, swim, float, surge; leap &c. 309.

Adj. rising &c. *v.*; scandent, buoyant; super-natant, -fluitant; excelsior.

Adv. uphill.

306. [Motion downwards.] **Descent. —N.** descent, descension, declension, declination; fall; falling &c. *v.*; drop, cadence; subsidence, lapse; come-down, downfall, tumble, slip, tilt, trip, lurch, cropper, *culbute*; titubation, stumble; fate of Icarus; dive, nose-dive, *volplané*.

avalanche, *débâcle*, landslip, slide.

declivity, dip, hill; decline, drop.

V. descend; go –, drop –, come-down; fall, gravitate, drop, slip, slide, glissade, dive, plunge, settle; decline, slump, set, sink, droop, come down a peg.

dismount, alight, light, get down; swoop; stoop &c. 308; fall prostrate, precipitate oneself; let fall &c. 308.

tumble, trip, stumble, titubate, lurch, pitch, swag, topple; topple –, tumble- -down, – over; tilt, sprawl, plump down, come a cropper.

Adj. descending &c. *v.*; descendent, declivitous; downcast; decur-rent, sive; labent, deciduous; nodding to its fall.

Adv. down, -hill, -wards.

307. Elevation.—N. elevation; raising &c. *v.*; erection, lift; sublevation, upheaval; sublimation, exaltation; prominence &c. (*convexity*) 250.

lever &c. 633; crane, derrick, windlass, capstan, winch, dredger, lift, elevator, escalator, dumb waiter.

V. heighten, elevate, raise, lift, erect; set –, stick –, perch –, perk –, tilt- up; rear, hoist, heave; up-lift, -raise, -rear, -bear, -cast, -hoist, -heave; buoy, weigh, mount, give a lift; exalt, sublimate; place –, set- on a pedestal.

take –, drag –, fish- up; dredge.

stand –, rise –, get –, jump- up; spring to one's feet; hold -oneself, – one's head- up; draw oneself up to his full height.

Adj. elevated &c. *v.*; standing up; stilted, attollent, rampant.

Adv. on -stilts, – the shoulders of, – one's legs, – one's hind legs.

———

309. Leap.—N. leap, jump, hop, spring, bound, vault, saltation.

dance, caper, gambol; curvet, caracole; *gam-bade, -bado*; capriole, demivolt; buck, – jump; hop, skip and jump.

kangaroo, jerboa, chamois, goat, frog, grasshopper, flea.

V. leap; jump -up, – over the moon; hop, spring, bound, vault, ramp, cut capers, gambol, trip, skip, dance, caper; curvet, *caracole*; foot it, bob, bounce, flounce, start, frisk &c. (*amusement*) 840; jump about &c. (*agitation*) 315; trip it on the light fantastic toe, dance oneself off one's legs.

Adj. leaping &c. *v.*; saltatory, frisky.

Adv. on the light fantastic toe.

308. Depression.—N. lowering &c. *v.*; depression; dip &c. (*concavity*) 252; abasement; detrusion; reduction.

over-throw, -set, -turn; upset; prostration, subversion, precipitation.

bow; courtesy, curtsy; genuflexion, *kowtow*, obeisance, *salaam*.

V. depress, lower; let –, take- -down, – down a peg; cast; let -drop, – fall; sink, debase, bring low, abase, slash, reduce, detrude, pitch, precipitate.

over-throw, -turn, -set; upset, subvert, prostrate, level, fell; cast –, take –, throw –, fling –, dash –, pull –, cut –, knock –, hew- down; raze, – to the ground; humiliate, trample in the dust, pull about one's ears.

sit, – down; couch, squat, crouch, stoop, bend, bow, courtsey, curtsy; bob, duck, dip, genuflect, kneel; *kowtow, salaam*, make obeisance, prostrate oneself; bend, bow- the -head, – knee; incline the head; bow down; cower; recline &c. (*be horizontal*) 213.

Adj. depressed &c. *v.*; at a low ebb; prostrate &c. (*horizontal*) 213; detrusive.

310. Plunge.—N. plunge, dip, dive, header; ducking &c. *v.*; submergence, immersion, diver.

V. plunge, dip, souse, duck; dive, plump; take a -plunge, – header, make a plunge; bathe &c. (*water*) 337.

sub-merge, -merse; immerse, douse, sink, engulf, send to -the bottom, – Davy Jones' locker.

get out of one's depth; go -to the bottom, – down like a stone; founder, welter, wallow.

———

311. [Curvilinear motion.] **Circuition.—N.** circuition, circulation; turn, curvet; excursion; circum-vention, -navigation, -ambulation; north-west passage; ambit, gyre, lap, circuit &c. 629.

turning &c. *v.*; wrench; evolution; coil, helix, spiral; corkscrew.

V. turn, bend, wheel; go –, put- about; heel; go –, turn -round, – to the right about; turn on one's heel; make –, describe- a -circle, – complete circle; encircle; go –, pass- through -180°, – 360°.

circum-navigate, -aviate, -ambulate, -vent; put a girdle round the earth, go the round, make the round of.

turn –, round– a corner; double a point.

wind, circulate, meander; whisk, twirl; twist &c. (*convolution*) 248; make a *détour* &c. (*circuit*) 629.

Adj. turning &c. *v.*; circuitous; circum-foraneous, -fluent; devious, roundabout, circum-ambient, -flex, -navigable.

Adv. round about.

---

312. [Motion in a continued circle.] **Rotation.—N.** rotation, revolution, gyration, circulation, roll; circum-rotation, -volution, -gyration; volutation, circination, turbination, *pirouette*, convolution.

verticity; whir, whirl, swirl, eddy, vortex, whirlpool, gurge; cyclone, tornado; surge; *vertigo*, dizzy round; Maelstrom, Charybdis; Ixion; wheel of Fortune.

313. [Motion in a reverse circle.] **Evolution.—N.** evolution, unfolding, development; eversion &c. (*inversion*) 218.

V. evolve; un-fold, -roll, -wind, -coil, -twist, -furl, -twine, -ravel; disentangle; develop.

Adj. evolving &c. *v.*; evolved &c. *v.*

---

wheel, screw, propeller, whirligig, rolling stone, windmill; top, teetotum, merry-go-round; roller; cog-, fly-wheel, spit; jack; caster.

axis, axle, spindle, spool, pivot, pin, hinge, pole, swivel, gimbals, arbor, bobbin, mandrel, shaft.

[Science of rotatory motion] trochilics, gyrostatics.

V. rotate; roll, – along; revolve, spin; turn, – round; circumvolve; circulate, gyre, gyrate, wheel, whirl, swirl, twirl, trundle, troll, bowl; slew round.

roll up, furl; wallow, welter; box the compass; spin like a -top, – teetotum.

Adj. rotating &c. *v.*; rota-tory, -ry; circumrotatory, trochilic, vertiginous, gyratory; vortic-al, -ose.

Adv. head over heels, round and round, like a horse in a mill.

---

314. [Reciprocating motion, motion to and fro.] **Oscillation.—N.** oscillation; vibration, libration; motion of a pendulum; nutation; undulation; pulsation; pulse; throb; seismic disturbance.

alternation; coming and going &c. *v.*; ebb and flow, flux and reflux, ups and downs; wave, vibratiuncle, swing, beat, shake, wag, see-saw, dance, lurch, dodge; fluctuation; vacillation &c. (*irresolution*) 605.

seismometer, vibroscope, seismograph.

V. oscillate; vi-, li-brate; alternate, undulate, wave; sway, rock, swing; pulsate, beat; wag, -gle; nod, bob, courtesy, curtsy; tick; play; chatter, wamble, wabble; teeter, dangle, swag.

fluctuate, dance, curvet, reel, quake; quiver, quaver, shake, flicker; wriggle; roll, toss, pitch; flounder, stagger, totter, waddle; move –, bob- up and down &c. *adv.*; pass and repass, ebb and flow, come and go, shuttle; vacillate &c. 605.

brandish, shake, flourish.

Adj. oscillating &c. *v.*; oscill-, undul-, puls-, libr-atory; vibrat-ory, -ile; pendulous, shutterwise, seismic.

Adv. to and fro, up and down, backwards and forwards, see-saw, zigzag, wibble-wabble, in and out, from side to side, like buckets in a well.

---

315. [Irregular motion.] **Agitation.—N.** agitation, stir, tremor, shake, ripple, jog, jolt, jar, jerk, shock, succussion, trepidation, quiver, quaver, dance; jactit-ation, -ance; shuffling &c. *v.*; twitter, flicker, flutter.

disquiet, perturbation, commotion, turmoil, turbulence; tumult, -uation; hubbub, rout, bustle, fuss, racket, *subsultus*, staggers, megrims, epilepsy, fits, twitching, vellication, St. Vitus' dance.

spasm, throe, throb, palpitation, convulsion, paroxysm; tetanus.

disturbance &c. (*disorder*) 59; restlessness &c. (*changeableness*) 149.

ferment, -ation; ebullition, effervescence, hurly burly, *cahotage*; tempest, storm, ground swell, heavy sea, whirlpool, vortex &c. 312; whirlwind &c. (*wind*) 349.

V. be -agitated &c.; shake; tremble, – like an aspen leaf; quiver, quaver, quake, shiver, twitter, twire, dither, dodder; twitch, writhe, toss, shuffle, tumble, stagger, bob, reel, sway; wag, -gle, wiggle; wriggle, – like an eel; squirm; dance, stumble, shamble, flounder, totter, flounce, flop, curvet, prance.

throb, pulsate, beat, palpitate, go pit-a-pat; flutter, flitter, flicker, bicker; bustle.

ferment, effervesce, foam; boil, – over; bubble, – up; simmer.

toss –, jump- about; jump like a parched pea; shake like an aspen leaf; shake to its -centre, – foundations; be the sport of the winds and waves; reel to and fro like a drunken man; move –, drive- from post to pillar and from pillar to post; keep between hawk and buzzard.

agitate, shake, convulse, toss, tumble, bandy, wield, brandish, flap, flourish, whisk, jerk, hitch, jolt; jog, -gle; jostle, buffet, hustle, disturb, stir, shake up, churn, jounce, wallop, whip, vellicate.

Adj. shaking &c. *v.*; agitated, tremulous; de-, sub-sultory; shambling; giddy-paced, saltatory, convulsive, jerky, unquiet, restless, all of a twitter.

Adv. by fits and starts; subsultorily &c. *adj.*; *per saltum*; hop, skip and jump; in -convulsions, – fits, pit-a-pat.

CLASS III

WORDS RELATING TO MATTER

SECTION I. MATTER IN GENERAL

316. Materiality.—N. material-ity, -ness; materialization; corpor-eity, -ality; substantiality, material existence, incarnation, flesh and blood, *plenum*; physical condition.

matter, body, substance, brute matter, stuff, element, principle, protoplasm, plasma, *parenchyma*, material, *substratum*, hyle, *corpus*, *pabulum*; frame.

object, article, thing, something; still life; stocks and stones; materials &c. 635.

[Science of matter] physics; somatology, -ics; natural –, experimental-philosophy; physical science, *philosophie positive*, materialism, hylism; materialist, physicist.

V. materialize, incorporate, incarnate, substantiate, embody.

Adj. material, bodily; corpor-eal, -al; physical; somat-ic, -oscopic; sensible, tangible, ponderable, palpable, substantial; fleshly, incarnate.

objective, impersonal, neuter, unspiritual, materialistic.

317. Immateriality.—N. immateriality, -ness; incorporeity, dematerialization, unsubstantiality, spirituality; in-extension; astral plane.

personality; I, myself, me; *ego*, spirit &c. (*soul*) 450; astral body; immaterialism; spiritual-ism, -ist; subliminal –, subconscious- self.

V. disembody, spiritualize, dematerialize.

Adj. immateri-al, -ate; incorpor-eal, -al; asomatous, unextended; un-, disembodied; extramundane, supersensible, unearthly; pneumatoscopic; spiritual &c. (*psychical*) 450; aery.

personal, subjective.

---

318. World.—N. world, creation, nature, universe; earth, globe, wide world; *cosmos*; terraqueous globe, sphere; macro-, mega-cosm; music of the spheres.

heavens, sky, welkin, empyrean; starry -heaven, – host; firmament; vault –, canopy- of heaven; celestial spaces.

heavenly bodies, stars, luminaries, nebulæ; galaxy, milky way, galactic circle, *via lactea*.

sun, orb of day, Apollo, Phœbus; photo-, chromo-sphere; solar system; planet, -oid, asteroid; comet; satellite; moon, orb of night, Diana, Luna; aerolite, meteor; falling –, shooting- star; meteorite.

constellation, zodiac, signs of the zodiac, Charles's wain, Great Bear, Southern Cross, Orion's belt, Cassiopeia's chair, Pleiades &c.

colures, equator, ecliptic, orbit.

[Science of heavenly bodies] astronomy; urano-graphy, -logy; cosmo-logy, -graphy, -gony; *eidouranion*, orrery; geography; geodesy

&c. (*measurement*) 466; star-gazing, -gazer; astronomer; cosmogonist, geodesist, geographer; observatory.

Adj. cosmic, cosmical, mundane; terr-estrial, -estrious, -aqueous, -ene, -eous; telluric, earthly, geotic, geodetic, cosmogonal, under the sun; sub-lunary, -astral.

solar, heliacal; lunar; celestial, heavenly, empyreal, sphery; starry, stellar; sider-eal, -al; astral; nebular.

Adv. in all creation, on the face of the globe, here below, under the sun.

319. Gravity.—N. gravi-ty, -tation; weight; heaviness &c. *adj.*; specific gravity; ponderosity, pressure, load; bur-den, -then; ballast, counterpoise; lump –, mass –, weight- of.

lead, millstone, mountain, Ossa on Pelion.

weighing, ponderation, trutination; weights; avoirdupois –, troy –, apothecaries'- weight; grain, scruple, drachm, ounce, pound, lb., load, stone, hundredweight, cwt., ton, quintal, carat, pennyweight, tod, gramme, kilogramme &c.

[Weighing instrument] balance, scales, steelyard, beam, weighbridge, spring balance, weighing machine.

[Science of gravity] statics.

V. be -heavy &c. *adj.*; gravitate, weigh, press, cumber, load.

[Measure the weight of] weigh, poise.

Adj. weighty; weighing &c. *v.*; heavy, – as lead; ponder-ous, -able; lump-ish, -y; cumber-, burden-some; cumbrous, unwieldy, massive. in-, superin-cumbent.

320. Levity.—N. levity; lightness &c. *adj.*; imponderability, imponderables, buoyancy, volatility.

feather, dust, mote, down, thistle-down, flue, cobweb, gossamer, straw, cork, bubble; float, buoy; ether, air.

leaven, ferment, barm, yeast, enzyme.

V. be -light &c. *adj.*; float, swim, be buoyed up.

render -light &c. *adj.*; lighten, levitate; leaven.

Adj. light, subtile, subtle, airy; imponder-ous, -able; astatic, weightless, ethereal, sublimated; uncompressed, volatile; buoyant, floating &c. *v.*; barmy, frothy; portable.

light as -a feather, – thistle down, – air.

fermenting &c. *n.*

Section II. INORGANIC MATTER

1°. Solid Matter

321. Density.—N. density, solidity; solidness &c. *adj.*; impenetra-, impermea-bility; incompressibility; imporosity; cohesion &c. 46; constipation, consistence, spissitude.

specific gravity; hydro-, areo-meter.

condensation; solid-ation, -ification; consolidation; concretion, caseation, coagulation; petrifaction &c. (*hardening*) 323; crystallization, precipitation; deposit, precipitate, silt; inspissation; thickening &c. *v.*

indivisibility, indiscerptibility, indissolvableness.

solid body, mass, block, knot, lump; con-cretion, -crete, -glomerate; cake,

322. Rarity.—N. rarity; tenuity; absence of -solidity &c. 321; subtility; sponginess, compressibility.

rarefaction, expansion, dilatation, inflation, subtilization.

ether &c. (*gas*) 334.

V. rarefy, expand, dilate, subtilize, attenuate, thin.

Adj. rare, subtile, thin, fine, tenuous, compressible, flimsy, slight; light &c. 320; cavernous, spongy &c. (*hollow*) 252.

rarefied &c. *v.*; unsubstantial; uncom-pact, -pressed.

clot, stone, curd, coagulum, grume; bone, gristle, cartilage.

V. be -dense &c. *adj.*; become –, render- solid &c. *adj.*; solid-ify, -ate; concrete, set, take a set, consolidate, congeal, coagulate; curd, -le; fix, clot, cake, candy, precipitate, deposit, cohere, crystallize; petrify &c. (*harden*) 323.

condense, thicken, inspissate, incrassate; compress, squeeze, ram down, constipate.

Adj. dense, solid; solidified &c. *v.*; cohe-rent, -sive &c. 46; compact, close, serried, thickset; substantial, massive, lumpish; impenetrable, impermeable, imporous; incompressible; constipated; concrete &c. (*hard*) 323; knot-ted, -ty; gnarled; crystal-line, -lizable; thick, grumous, stuffy.

un-dissolved, -melted, -liquefied, -thawed.

in-divisible, -discerptible, -frangible, -dissolvable, -dissoluble, -soluble, -fusible.

323. Hardness.—N. hardness &c. *adj.*; rigidity, renitence, inflexibility, temper, callosity, durity.

induration, petrifaction; lapid-ifica-tion, -escence; vitri-, ossi-, corni-fica-tion; crystallization.

stone, pebble, flint, marble, rock, fossil, crag, crystal, quartz, granite, adamant; bone, cartilage; heart of oak, block, board, deal board; iron, steel; cast –, wrought- iron; nail; brick, con-crete; cement.

V. render -hard &c. *adj.*; harden, stiffen, indurate, petrify, temper, ossify, vitrify.

Adj. hard, rigid, stubborn, stiff, firm; starch, -ed; stark, unbending, unlim-ber, unyielding; inflexible, tense; in-durate, -d; gritty, proof.

adamant-ine, -ean; concrete, stony, rocky, lithic, granitic, vitreous; crys-talline; horny, corneous; bony; oss-eous, -ific; cartilaginous; hard as a -stone &c. *n.*; stiff as -buckram, – a poker.

324. Softness.—N. softness, pliable-ness &c. *adj.*; flexibility; pli-ancy, -ability; sequacity, malleability; flabbi-ness; duct-, tract-ility; extend-, extens-ibility; plasticity; inelasticity, flaccid-ity, laxity.

clay, wax, butter, dough, pudding; cushion, pillow, feather-bed, pad, down, padding, wadding.

mollification; softening &c. *v.*

V. render -soft &c. *adj.*; soften, mol-lify, mellow, relax, temper; mash, knead, squash, *massage*.

bend, yield, relent, relax, give.

Adj. soft, tender, supple; pli-ant, -able; flex-ible, -ile; lithe, -some; lis-som, limber, plastic; ductile; tract-ile, -able; malleable, extensile, sequacious, inelastic, mollient.

yielding &c. *v.*; flabby, limp, flimsy.

flaccid, flocculent, downy; spongy, œdematous, medullary, doughy, argil-laceous, mellow.

soft as -butter, – down, – silk; yield-ing as wax; tender as a chicken.

325. Elasticity. — N. elasticity, springiness, spring, resilience, reni-tency, buoyancy.

india-rubber, caoutchouc, gutta-percha, whalebone, gum elastic.

V. be -elastic &c. *adj.*; spring back &c. (*recoil*) 277.

Adj. elastic, tensile, springy, ductile, resilient, renitent, buoyant.

326. Inelasticity.—N. want of –, absence of- elasticity &c. 325; inelas-ticity &c. (*softness*) 324.

Adj. inelastic &c. (*soft*) 324.

---

327. Tenacity.—N. tenacity, tough-ness, strength; cohesion &c. 46; se-quacity; stubbornness &c. (*obstinacy*) 606; viscidity &c. 352.

leather; gristle, cartilage.

328. Brittleness.—N. brittleness &c. *adj.*; frag-, friab-, frangib-, fiss-ility; frailty; house of -cards, – glass.

V. be -brittle &c. *adj.*; live in a glass house.

V. be -tenacious &c. *adj.*; resist fracture.

Adj. tenacious, tough, cohesive, adhesive, strong, resisting, sequacious, stringy, gristly, cartilaginous, leathery, coriaceous, tough as whit-leather; stubborn &c. (*obstinate*) 606.

break, crack, snap, split, shiver, splinter, crumble, break short, burst, fly, give way; fall to pieces; crumble -to, – into- dust.

Adj. breakable, brittle, frangible, fragile, frail, friable, delicate, gimcrack, shivery, fissile; splitting &c. *v.*; lacerable, splintery, crisp, crimp, short, brittle as glass.

329. [Structure.] **Texture.—N.** structure, organization, anatomy, frame, mould, fabric, construction; frame-work, carcass, architecture; stratification, cleavage.

substance, stuff, *compages, parenchyma*; constitution, staple, organism.

[Science of structures] organ-, oste-, my-, splanchn-, neur-, angi-, aden-ology; angi-, aden-ography.

texture; inter-, con-texture; tissue, grain, web, surface; warp and -woof, – weft; tooth, nap &c. (*roughness*) 256; fineness –, coarseness- of grain.

[Science of textures] histology.

Adj. structural, organic; anatomic, -al.

text-ural, -ile; fine-, coarse-grained; fine, delicate, subtile, gossamery, filmy; coarse; home-spun; linsey-woolsey.

330. **Pulverulence.—N.** [State of powder.] pulverulence; sandiness &c. *adj.*; efflorescence; friability.

powder, dust, sand, shingle; sawdust; grit; attrition; meal, bran, flour, *farina*, spore, sporule; crumb, seed, grain; particle &c. (*smallness*) 32; thermion; limature, filings, *débris, detritus*, scobs, magistery, fine powder; *flocculi.*

smoke; cloud of -dust, – sand, – smoke; puff –, volume -of smoke; sand –, dust- storm.

[Reduction to powder] pulverization, comminution, attenuation, granulation, disintegration, subaction, contusion, trituration, levigation, abrasion, detrition, multure; limation; filing &c. *v.*

[Instruments for pulverization] mill, millstone, grater, rasp, file, pestle and mortar, nutmeg grater, teeth, molar, grinder, chopper, grindstone, kern, quern, muller.

V. come to dust; be -disintegrated, – reduced to powder &c.

reduce –, grind- to powder; pulverize, comminute, granulate, triturate, levigate; scrape, file, abrade, rub down, grind, grate, rasp, pound, bray, bruise; con-tuse, -tund; beat, crush, cranch, craunch, crunch, muller, scranch, crumble, disintegrate; attenuate &c. 195.

Adj. powdery, pulverulent, granular, mealy, floury, farinaceous, branny, furfuraceous, flocculent, dusty, sandy, sabulous; aren-ose, -arious, -aceous; gritty; efflorescent, impalpable.

pulverizable; friable, crumbly, shivery; pulverized &c. *v.*; attrite; in pieces.

331. Friction.—N. friction, attrition; rubbing &c. *v.*; erasure; con-frication, -trition; affriction, abrasion, arrosion, limature, frication, rub; elbow-grease; rosin; *massage.*

V. rub, scratch, abrade, scrape, scrub,

332. [Absence of friction. Prevention of friction.] **Lubrication.—N.** smoothness &c. 255; unctuousness &c. 355.

lubri-cation, -fication; anointment; oiling &c. *v.*

fray, rasp, graze, curry, scour, polish, rub out, erase, gnaw; file, grind &c. (*reduce to powder*) 330; *massage*.

set one's teeth on edge; rosin.

Adj. anatriptic, abrasive.

synovia; lubricant, graphite, glycerine, oil &c. 356; saliva; lather.

V. lubri-cate, -citate; oil, grease, lather, soap; wax.

Adj. lubricated &c. *v.*

2°. FLUID MATTER

1. *Fluids in General*

333. Fluidity.—**N.** fluidity, liquidity; liquidness &c. *adj.*; gaseity &c. 334; liquefaction &c. 334.

fluid, inelastic fluid; liquid, liquor; lymph, humour, juice, sap, serum, blood, serosity, gravy, rheum, ichor, sanies.

solu-bility, -bleness.

[Science of liquids] hydro-logy, -statics, -dynamics, hydraulics &c.

V. be -fluid &c. *adj.*; flow &c. (*water in motion*) 348; liquefy &c. 335.

Adj. liquid, fluid, serous, juicy, succulent, sappy; fluent &c. (*flowing*) 348.

liquefied &c. 335; uncongealed; soluble, hydrostatic &c. *n.*

334. Gaseity.—**N.** gaseity, gaseousness; vapourousness &c. *adj.*; flatulence, -lency; volatility, aeration, gasification.

elastic fluid, gas, air, vapour, ether, steam, fume, reek, *effluvium*, *flatus*; cloud &c. 353.

[Science of elastic fluids] pneumat-ics, -ostatics; aero-statics, -dynamics &c.

gas-, gaso-meter.

V. gassify, aerate, aerify; emit vapour &c. 336.

Adj. gaseous, aeriform, ethereal, aerial, airy, vaporous, volatile, evaporable; flatulent; aerostatic &c. *n.*

335. Liquefaction.—**N.** liquefaction; liquescen-ce, -cy, deliquescence; melting &c. (*heat*) 384; colliqu-ation, -efaction; thaw; de-, liquation; lixiviation, dissolution.

solution, apozem, lixivium, infusion, decoction, flux.

solvent, diluent, menstruum, alkahest, *aqua fortis*.

V. render -liquid &c. 333; liquefy, run, deliquesce; melt &c. (*heat*) 384; solve; dissolve, resolve; liquate; hold in solution; leach, lixiviate.

Adj. lique-fied &c. *v.*, -scent, -fiable; deliquescent, soluble, colliquative; solvent.

336. Vaporization. — **N.** vapor-, volatil-ization; gasification; e-, vaporation; distillation, cohobation, sublimation, exhalation; volatility.

vaporizer, still, retort, spray, atomizer; fumigation, steaming.

V. render -gaseous &c. 334; vaporize, volatilize; distil, sublime; evaporate, exhale, smoke, transpire, emit vapour, fume, reek, steam, fumigate.

Adj. volatilized &c. *v.*; reeking &c. *v.*; volatile; evaporable, vaporizable.

2. *Specific Fluids*

337. Water.—**N.** water; serum, serosity; lymph; rheum; diluent.

dilution, maceration, lotion; washing &c. *v.*; im-, mersion; humectation, infiltration, spargefaction, affusion, irrigation, *douche*, balneation, bath.

deluge &c. (*water in motion*) 348; high water, flood-, spring-tide.

338. Air.—**N.** air &c. (*gas*) 334; common -, atmospheric- air; atmosphere, stratosphere, isothermal layer, troposphere, Heaviside layer.

open, - air; sky, welkin; blue, - sky; cloud &c. 353.

weather, climate, rise and fall of the barometer, isobar.

V. be -watery &c. *adj.*; reek.

add water, water, wet; moisten &c.
339; dilute, dip, immerse; merge; im-,
sub-merge; plunge, souse, duck, drown;
soak, steep, macerate, pickle, wash,
sprinkle, sparge, lave, bathe, affuse,
splash, swash, douse, slosh, drench;
dabble, slop, slobber, irrigate, inundate,
deluge; syringe, inject, gargle; infiltrate, percolate.

Adj. watery, aqueous, aquatic, lymphatic; balneal, diluent; drenching &c.
v.; diluted &c. *v.*; weak; wet &c. (*moist*)
339.

Phr. the waters are out.

339. Moisture.—N. moisture; moist-
ness &c. *adj.*; hum-idity, -ectation;
madefaction, dew; *serein*; marsh &c.
345; Hygromet-ry, -er.

V. moisten, wet; humect, -ate;
sponge, damp, dampen, bedew; imbue,
imbrue, infiltrate, saturate; seethe,
sop; soak, drench &c. (*water*) 337.

be -moist &c. *adj.*; not have a dry
thread; perspire &c. (*exude*) 295.

Adj. moist, damp; watery &c. 337;
undried, humid, wet, dank, muggy,
dewy; roric; roscid; juicy.

wringing wet; wet -through, – to the
skin; saturated &c. *v.*

swashy, soggy, dabbled; reeking,
seething, dripping, soaking, soft, sodden, sloppy, muddy; swampy &c.
(*marshy*) 345; irriguous.

341. Ocean.—N. sea, ocean, main,
deep, brine, salt water, waters, waves,
billows, high seas, offing, great waters,
watery waste, 'vasty deep,' briny
ocean, herring pond, steamer track,
the seven seas; wave, tide &c. (*water
in motion*) 348.

hydrograph-y, -er, oceanography;
Neptune, Thetis, Triton, Naiad, Nereid; sea-nymph, Siren, mer-maid,
-man; trident, dolphin.

Adj. oceanic; mar-ine, -itime; pleagic,
-ian; sea-going, -worthy; hydrographic.

Adv. at –, on- sea; afloat, on the
high seas.

[Science of air] pneumatics, aero-logy,
-scopy, -graphy; meteorology, climatology; eudio-, baro-, aero-meter; aneroid,
baro-graph, -scope; weather-gauge,
-glass, -cock.

exposure to the -air, – weather; ventilation; aero-station, -nautics, -naut
&c. 265 and 269.

V. air, ventilate; fan &c. (*wind*) 349.

Adj. containing air, flatulent, effervescent; windy &c. 349.

atmospheric, airy; aeri-al, -form;
pneumatic; meteorological; weather-
wise.

Adv. in the open air, out of doors,
à la belle étoile, al fresco; sub -Jove, – dio.

340. Dryness.—N. dryness &c. *adj.*;
siccity, aridity, drought, ebb-, neap-
tide, low water.

drying, ex-, de-siccation; evapora-
tion; dehydration; arefaction, dephlegmation, drainage.

drier, desiccator.

V. be -dry &c. *adj.*; render -dry &c.
adj.; dry; dry –, soak- up; sponge,
swab, wipe; ex-, de-siccate, dehydrate,
anhydrate; drain, parch.

be fine, hold up.

Adj. dry, anhydrous, arid, waterless;
dried &c. *v.*; undamped; juice-, sap-
less; sear; husky; rainless, without
rain, fine; dry as -a bone, – dust, – a
stick, – a mummy, – a biscuit; desic-
cated; dehydrated; water-proof, -tight.

342. Land.—N. land, earth, ground,
dry land, *terra firma.*

continent, mainland, peninsula,
delta; tongue –, neck- of land; isthmus;
oasis; promontory &c. (*projection*) 250;
highland &c. (*height*) 206.

coast, shore, scar, strand, beach;
bank, lea; sea- board, -side, -shore,
-bank, -coast, -beach; rock-, iron-
bound coast; loom of the land; derelict;
innings; *alluvium*, alluvion.

soil, glebe, clay, loam, marl, cledge,
chalk, gravel, mould, subsoil, clod,
clot; rock, crag, cliff.

acres; real estate &c. (*property*) 780;
landsman, land-lubber, farmer.

geography &c. 318; agriculture &c.
371.

V. land, come to land; set foot on -the soil, – dry land; come –, go- ashore.

Adj. earthy; continental, midland; littoral, riparian, ripuarian; alluvial; terrene &c. (*world*) 318; landed, predial, territorial.

Adv. ashore; on -shore, – land.

343. Gulf. Lake.—N. land covered with water, gulf, gulph, bay, inlet, bight, estuary, arm of the sea, fiord, armlet; frith, firth, ostiary, mouth; lagune, lagoon; indraught; cove, creek; natural harbour; roads; strait, narrows; Euripus; sound, belt, gut, kyles.

lake, loch, lough, mere, tarn, plash, broad, pond, pool, lin, puddle, well, artesian well, tank, sump; standing –, dead –, sheet of- water; fish -, mill-pond; race; ditch, dike, dyke, dam; reservoir &c. (*store*) 636.

Adj. lacustrine; land locked.

344. Plain.—N. plain, table land, mesa, face of the country; open –, champaign-country; basin, downs, waste, weary waste, desert, tundra, wild, steppe, pampas, savanna, prairie, champaign, heath, common, wold, veld; moor, -land, uplands, fell; bush; *plateau* &c. (*level*) 213; *campagna*.

meadow, mead, haugh, pasturage, park, field, lawn, green, plat, plot, grass-plat, greensward, sward, grass, turf, sod, heather; lea, ley, lay; grounds.

Adj. campestrian, champaign, alluvial.

345. Marsh.—N. marsh, swamp, morass, marish, moss, fen, bog, quagmire, slough, sump, wash; mud, squash, slush.

Adj. marsh, -y; swampy, boggy, plashy, poachy, quaggy, soft; muddy, sloppy, squashy, spongy; paludal; moor-ish, -y; fenny.

346. Island.—N. island, isle, islet, eyot, ait, holm, reef, atoll, breaker; archipelago; islander.

Adj. insular, sea-girt.

3. *Fluids in Motion*

347. [Fluid in motion.] **Stream.—N.** stream &c. (*of water*) 348, (*of air*) 349.

V. flow &c. 348; blow &c. 349.

348. [Water in motion.] **River.—N.** running water.

jet, spirt, squirt, spout, splash, swash, rush, gush, *jet d'eau*; sluice, chute.

water-spout, -fall; fall, cascade, force, foss; lin, -n; ghyll, Niagara; cata-ract, -dupe, -clysm; *débâcle*, in-undation, deluge.

rain, -fall; *serein*; shower, scud; downpour, cloud burst; driving –, pouring –, drenching- rain; hyeto-logy, -graphy; rainy season, monsoon; predominance of Aquarius, reign of St. Swithin; mizzle, drizzle, *stillicidium*, plash; dropping &c. *v.*

stream, course, flux, flow, profluence; effluence &c. (*egress*) 295; defluxion; flowing &c. *v.*; current, tide, race.

spring; fount, -ain; rill, rivulet, gill,

349. [Air in motion.] **Wind.—N.** wind, draught, *flatus*, *afflatus*, air; breath, – of air; puff, whiff, zephyr; blow, drift; *aura*; stream, current; under-current.

gust, blast, breeze, squall, gale, half a gale, storm, tempest, hurricane, whirlwind, tornado, samiel, cyclone, typhoon; simoon; harmattan, monsoon, trade wind, sirocco, *mistral, bise, föhn*, tramontane, levanter; capful of wind; fresh –, stiff- breeze; keen blast; blizzard.

windiness &c. *adj.*; ventosity; rough –, dirty –, ugly –, stress of- weather; dirty-, windy-, mackerel- sky; mare's tail; thick –, black –, white- squall.

anemography, aerodynamics; wind-gauge, anemometer, weather-cock, vane.

gullet, rillet; stream-, brook-let; runnel, sike, burn, beck, brook, stream, river; reach; tributary.

body of water, torrent, rapids, flush, flood, swash, spate; spring -, high -, full-tide; bore; eagre, *hygre*; fresh, -et; undertow, indraught, reflux, under-current, eddy, vortex, gurge, whirlpool, Maelström, regurgitation, overflow; confluence, corrivation.

wave, billow, surge, swell, ripple; roller, ground swell, surf, breaker, white horses; comber, beach-comber; rough -, heavy -, cross -, long -, short -, chopping -, choppy- sea, choppiness; tidal wave.

[Science of fluids in motion] Hydro-dynamics; Hydraul-ics &c.; rain-gauge &c.

water-bearer, - carrier, Aquarius.

irrigation &c. (*water*) 337; pump; watering-pot, - cart; hydrant, stand-pipe, hose, sprinkler, drencher; fire-engine, squirt, syringe.

V. flow, run; meander; gush, pour, spout, roll, jet, well, issue; drop, drip, dribble, plash, squirt, spurt, spirtle, trill, trickle, distil, percolate; stream, overflow, inundate, deluge, flow over, splash, swash; guggle, murmur, babble, bubble, purl, gurgle, sputter, regurgitate; ooze, flow out &c. (*egress*) 295.

rain, - hard, - in torrents, - cats and dogs, - pitchforks; come down in sheets; pour with rain, drizzle, mizzle, spit, sprinkle, set in.

flow -, fall -, open -, drain- into; discharge itself, disembogue.

[Cause a flow] pour; pour out &c. (*discharge*) 297; shower down; irrigate, drench &c. (*wet*) 337; spill, splash.

[Stop a flow] stanch; dam, -up &c. (*close*) 261; obstruct &c. 706.

Adj. fluent; dif-, pro-, af-fluent; tidal; flowing &c. *v.*; meand-ering, -ry, -rous; fluvi-al, -atile; streamy, showery, rainy, drizzly, drizzling, pluvial, pluviose, stillicidous.

suf-, insuf-, per-, in-, af-flation; blowing, fanning &c. *v.*; ventilation.

sneezing &c. *v.*; sternutation; hic-cup, -cough; catching of the breath; breathing &c.

Eolus, Eurus, Boreas, Zephyr, cave of Eolus.

air-pump, lungs, bellows, blow-pipe, fan, blower; pulmotor, ventilator, punkah, aspirator, exhauster, ejector.

V. blow, waft; blow -hard, - great guns, - a hurricane &c. *n.*; whistle, roar, howl, ring in the shrouds; stream, issue.

respire, breathe, in-, ex-hale, puff; whif, -fle; gasp, wheeze; snuff, -le; sniff, -le; sneeze, cough, belch.

fan, ventilate; in-, per-flate; blow -, pump- up.

Adj. blowing &c. *v.*; windy, airy, æolian, flatulent; breezy, gusty, squally; stormy, tempestuous, blustering; bois-terous &c. (*violent*) 173.

pulmon-ic, -ary.

----

350. [Channel for the passage of water.] **Conduit.**—**N.** conduit, channel, duct, watercourse, race; head -, tail-race; adit, aqueduct, canal, trough, flume, gutter, pantile; dike, canyon, ravine, gorge, hollow, main, gully, moat, ditch, drain, sewer, culvert, *cloaca*, sough, kennel, siphon, *piscina*; pipe &c. (*tube*) 260; funnel; tunnel &c. (*passage*) 627; water -, waste- pipe; emunctory, gully-hole, artery, aorta, vein, blood vessel; lymphatic; throat, alimentary canal, intestine; pore, spout, scupper; ad-, a-jutage;

351. [Channel for the passage of air.] **Air-pipe.**—**N.** air-pipe, - shaft, - way, - passage, - tube; shaft, flue, chimney, funnel, vent, blow-hole, nostril, nozzle, throat, weasand, *trachea; bronch-us, -ia*; larynx, tonsils, wind-pipe, spiracle; venti-duct, -lator; louvre, Venetian blinds; blow-pipe &c. (*wind*) 349; pipe &c. (*tube*) 260.

----

hose; gar-, gur-goyle; penstock, weir; flood-, water-gate; sluice, lock, valve; rose; waterworks.

Adj. vascular &c. (*with holes*) 260.

3°. IMPERFECT FLUIDS

352. Semiliquidity.—N. semiliquidity; stickiness &c. *adj.*; visc-idity, -osity; gumm-, glutin-, muc-osity; spiss-, crass-itude; lentor; adhesiveness &c. (*cohesion*) 46.

inspiss-, incrass-ation; thickening, coagulation.

jelly, aspic, mucilage, gelatin, isinglass; colloid, mucus, phlegm; pituite, lava; glair, starch, gluten, albumen, milk, cream, protein; syrup, treacle; gum, size, glue, paste; wax, bee's-wax; emulsoid, emulsion, soup; squash, mud, slush, slime, ooze; moisture &c. 339; marsh &c. 345.

V. inspiss-, incrass-ate; coagulate, gelatinize, gelatinify, gel, jell, emulsify, thicken; mash, squash, churn, beat up.

Adj. semi-fluid, -liquid; half-melted, -frozen; milky, muddy &c. *n.*; lact-eal, -ean, -eous, -escent, -iferous; emulsive, curdled, thick, succulent, uliginous.

gelat-, album-, mucilag-, glut-inous; gelatine, mastic, amylaceous, ropy, clammy, clotted; vis-cid, -cous; sticky, tacky; slab, -by; lentous, pituitous; mu-cid, -culent, -cous.

353. [Mixture of air and water.] **Bubble.** [Cloud.]—**N.** bubble; foam, froth, head, fume, spume, lather, suds, spray, surf, yeast, barm, spindrift.

cloud, vapour, fog, mist, haze, steam; scud, rack, *nimbus*; *cumulus*, woolpack, *cirrus, stratus*; *cirro-, cumulostratus*; *cirro-cumulus*; mackerel sky, mare's tail, dirty sky.

[Science of clouds] nephelognosy, nephology.

effervescence, fermentation; bubbling &c. *v.*

nebula; cloudiness &c. (*opacity*) 426; nebulosity &c. (*dimness*) 422.

V. bubble, boil, foam, froth, spume, mantle, sparkle, guggle, gurgle; effervesce, ferment, fizzle; aerate; cloud, overcast, befog.

Adj. bubbling &c. *v.*; frothy, nappy, effervescent, sparkling, *mousseux*, up, fizzy, with a head on.

cloudy &c. *n.*; vaporous, nebulous, overcast; nubiferous, nephological; foggy, brumous.

354. Pulpiness.—N. pulpiness &c. *adj.*; pulp, paste, dough, sponge, curd, pap, rob, jam, pudding, mush, fool, poultice, grume.

Adj. pulpy &c. *n.*; pultaceous, grumous.

V. pulp, pulpify, mash.

355. Unctuousness.—N. unctuousness &c. *adj.*; unctuosity, lubricity; ointment &c. (*oil*) 356; anointment; lubrication &c. 332.

V. oil &c. (*lubricate*) 332.

Adj. unctuous, oily, oleaginous, adipose, sebaceous; fat, -ty; greasy; waxy, butyraceous, soapy, saponaceous, pinguid, lardaceous; slippery.

356. Oil.—N. oil, fat, butter, cream, grease, tallow, suet, lard, dripping, margarine, oleomargarine, exunge, blubber; glycerine, stearine, elaine, oleagine; soap; soft soap, wax, cerement; paraffin, spermaceti, adipocere; petroleum, mineral -, rock -, crystal- oil, kerosene, vegetable -, colza -, olive -, linseed -, cotton seed -, rape -, nut -, fusel- oil; animal -, neat's foot -, signal -, train- oil; ointment, unguent, liniment, salve, pomade, pomatum, brilliantine, spike -, nard.

356a. Resin.—N. resin, rosin, colophony; gum; lac, shellac, sealing-wax; amber, -gris; bitumen, pitch, tar, asphalt, -e, -um; varnish, copal, mastic, magilp, lacquer, japan.

V. varnish &c. (*overlay*) 223.

Adj. resinous, bituminous, pitchy, tarry.

Section III. ORGANIC MATTER

1°. Vitality

1. *Vitality in general*

357. Organization.—N. organized -world, – nature; living –, animated- nature; living beings; organic remains, organism; fossils; animal and vegetable kingdom, *fauna* and *flora*, biota.

prot-oplasm, -ein; albumen; structure &c. 329; organ-ization, -ism.

[Science of living beings] biology; natural history,* organic –, bio-chemistry, anatomy, physiology, embryology, morphology, evolution, Darwinism, Lamarkism, zoology &c. 368; botany &c. 369; naturalist, biologist &c.

Adj. organ-ic, -ized.

359. Life.—N. life; vi-tality, -ability; animation; vital -spark, – flame, – force.

respiration, wind; breath -of life, – of one's nostrils; life-blood; Archeus; existence &c. 1.

vivification, vitalization; revivification &c. 163; Prometheus; life to come &c. (*destiny*) 152.

[Science of life] physiology, etiology, embryology, biology; animal economy.

nourishment, staff of life &c. (*food*) 298.

V. be -alive &c. *adj.*; live, breathe, respire; subsist &c. (*exist*) 1; walk the earth; strut and fret one's hour upon a stage; be spared.

see the light, be born, come into the world; fetch –, draw- -breath, – the breath of life; quicken; revive; come to, – life.

give birth to &c. (*produce*) 161; bring to life, put into life, vitalize; vivi-fy, -ficate; reanimate &c. (*restore*) 660; keep -alive, – body and soul together, – the wolf from the door; support life.

have nine lives like a cat.

358. Inorganization. — N. mineral -world, – kingdom; unorganized –, inorganic –, brute –, inanimate- matter.

[Science of the mineral kingdom] mineralogy; geo-logy, -gnosy, -scopy; metall-urgy, -ography; lithology; orycto-logy, -graphy.

V. turn to dust, pulverize.

Adj. in-organic, -animate; unorganized; azoic; mineral.

---

360. Death.—N. death, dying &c. *v.*; de-cease, -mise; dissolution, departure, *obit*, release, rest, *quietus*, fall; loss, bereavement.

end &c. 67 –, cessation &c. 142 –, loss –, extinction –, ebb- of -life &c. 359.

death-warrant, -watch, -rattle, -bed; stroke –, agonies –, shades –, valley of the shadow –, jaws –, hand- of death; last -breath, – gasp, – agonies; dying -day, – breath, – agonies; swan song, *chant du cygne*; *rigor mortis*; Stygian shore; crossing the bar, the great adventure.

King -of terrors, – Death; Death, Angel of Death; mortality; doom &c. (*necessity*) 601.

euthanasia; happy release; break up of the system; natural -death, – decay; sudden –, violent- death; untimely end, watery grave; suffocation, *asphyxia*; heart failure; fatal disease &c. (*disease*) 655; death-blow &c. (*killing*) 361.

necrology, bills of mortality, obituary; death-song &c. (*lamentation*) 839.

V. die, expire, perish; meet one's -death, – end; pass away, be taken; yield –, resign- one's breath; resign

* The term *Natural History* is also used as relating to all the objects in Nature whether organic or inorganic, and including therefore *Mineralogy, Geology, Meteorology,* &c.

Adj. living, alive; in -life, – the flesh, – the land of the living; on this side of the grave, above ground, breathing, quick, animated, viable; lively &c. (*active*) 682; alive and kicking; tenacious of life.

vital; vivi-fying, -fied &c. *v.*; Promethean.

Adv. *vivendi causâ.*

---

one's -being, – life; end one's -days, – life, – earthly career; breathe one's last; cease to -live, – breathe; depart this life; be -no more &c. *adj.*; go –, drop –, pop -off; lose –, lay down –, relinquish –, surrender- one's life; drop –, sink- into the grave; close one's eyes; fall –, drop- dead, – down dead; break one's neck; give –, yield- up the ghost; be all over with one.

pay the debt to nature, shuffle off this mortal coil, take one's last sleep; go the way of all flesh; join the -greater number, – majority, – choir invisible, to life immortal awake; come –, turn- to dust; cross the Stygian ferry; go to -one's long account, – one's last home, – Davy Jones's locker, – the wall; receive one's death warrant, make one's will, die a natural death, go out like the snuff of a candle; come to an untimely end; catch one's death; go off the hooks, kick the bucket, peg out; go West; hop the twig, turn up one's toes; die a violent death &c. (*be killed*) 361; make the supreme sacrifice.

Adj. dead, lifeless; deceased, demised, departed, defunct; late, gone, no more; ex-, in-animate; out of the world, taken off, released; departed this life &c. *v.*; dead and gone; bereft of life, stone dead, dead as -a door nail, – a door post, – mutton, – a herring, – nits; launched into eternity, gathered to one's fathers, numbered with the dead, gone to a better land, behind the veil, beyond the grave, – mortal ken.

dying &c. *v.*; mori-bund, -ent, Acherontic; hippocratic; *in -articulo*, – *extremis*; in the -jaws, – agony- of death; going, – off; *aux abois*; on one's -last legs, – death bed; at -the point of death, – death's door, – the last gasp; near one's end, given over, booked, fey; with one foot in –, tottering on the brink of- the grave.

still-born; mortuary; deadly &c. (*killing*) 361.

Adv. *post -obit, – mortem.*

Phr. life -ebbs, – fails, – hangs by a thread; one's -days are numbered, – hour is come, – race is run, – doom is sealed; Death -knocks at the door, – stares one in the face; the breath is out of the body; the grave closes over one; *sic itur ad astra.*

---

361. [Destruction of life; violent death.] **Killing.—N.** killing &c. *v.*; homicide, manslaughter, murder, assassination, trucidation, occision; lynching, effusion of blood; blood, -shed; gore, slaughter, carnage, butchery; *battue*, gladiatorial combat.

massacre; *fusillade, noyade, pogrom*; thuggism; racketeering.

death blow, finishing stroke, *coup de grâce, quietus*; execution &c. (*capital punishment*) 972; judicial murder; martyrdom.

butcher, slayer, murderer, Cain, assassin, cut-throat, garrotter, *bravo*, thug, racketeer, gunman, mobster, gangster, Moloch, *matador, sabreur*; *guet-à-pens*; gallows, executioner &c. (*punishment*) 975; man-eater.

regicide, parricide, fratricide, infanticide, aborticide &c.

suicide, *felo de se, suttee, hara kiri*, Juggernaut; immolation, holocaust.

suffocation, strangulation, *garrotte*; hanging &c. *v.*

deadly weapon &c. (*arms*) 727; Aceldama; the potter's field, the field of blood.

fatal accident, violent death, casualty.

[Destruction of animals] slaughtering; phthiozoics;* sport, -ing; the chase, venery; hunting, coursing, shooting, fishing; pig-sticking; sports-, hunts-, fisher-man; hunter, Nimrod; slaughterer, knacker, slaughter-house, shambles, *abattoir*.

V. kill, put to death, slay, shed blood; murder, assassinate, butcher, slaughter; victimize, immolate; massacre; take away –, deprive of-life; make away with, put an end to; despatch, dispatch; burke settle, do, – to death, – for.

strangle, garrotte, hang, lynch, throttle, choke, stifle, suffocate, stop the breath, smother, asphyxiate, drown.

sabre; cut -down, – to pieces, – the throat; jugulate; stab, run through the body, bayonet; put to the -sword, – edge of the sword.

shoot, – dead; blow one's brains out; brain, knock on the head; stone, lapidate; give –, deal- a death blow; give a *-quietus*, – *coup de grâce*.

behead, bowstring &c. (*execute*) 972.

hunt, shoot &c. *n.*

cut off, nip in the bud, launch into eternity, send to one's last account, bump off, rub out, sign one's death warrant, strike the death knell of.

give no quarter, pour out blood like water; decimate; run amuck, wade knee-deep –, imbrue one's hands- in blood.

die a violent death, welter in one's blood; dash –, blow- out one's brains; commit suicide; kill –, -make away with –, put an end to- oneself.

Adj. killing &c. *v.*; murd-, slaught-erous; sanguin-ary, -olent; blood-stained, -thirsty; homicidal, red-handed; bloody, -minded; ensanguined, gory, sanguineous.

mortal, fatal, lethal; dead-, death-ly; mort-, leth-iferous; unhealthy &c. 657; internecine; suicidal.

sporting; piscator-ial, -y.

Adv. in at the death.

362. Corpse.—N. corpse, corse, carcass, bones, skeleton, dry-bones; defunct, relics, *relinquiæ*, remains, mortal remains, dust, ashes, earth, clay; mummy; carrion; food for- worms, – fishes; tenement of clay, this mortal coil.

shade, ghost, *manes*, apparition &c. 980.

organic remains, fossils.

Adj. cadaverous, corpse-like; unburied &c. 363.

363. Interment.—N. interment, burial, inhumation, sepulture, en-tombment; in-, humation; obs-, ex-equies; funeral, wake, pyre, funeral pile; cremation.

funeral -rite, – solemnity; knell, passing bell, tolling; dirge &c. (*lamentation*) 839; cypress; *obit*, dead march, muffled drum; coroner, mortician, undertaker, mute, mourner, professional mourner, pall-bearer; elegy; funeral -oration, – sermon; epitaph.

grave clothes, shroud, winding-sheet, cere-cloth; cerement.

coffin, shell, sarcophagus, urn, pall, bier, hearse, catafalque, cinerary urn.

grave, pit, sepulchre, tomb, vault, crypt, catacomb, mausoleum, *Golgotha*, house of death, narrow house, long home; cemetery, necropolis, boneyard; burial-place, -ground; grave-, church-yard; God's acre; mortuary, tope, cromlech, dolmen, menhir, barrow, tumulus, cairn;

* Bentham, 'Chrestomathia.'

ossuary; bone-, charnel-, dead-house; *Morgue*; lich-gate; crematorium.

sexton, grave-digger.

monument, memorial, cenotaph, shrine; grave-, head-, tomb-stone; *memento mori*; hatchment, stone, cross.

exhumation, disinterment; necropsy, autopsy, *post-mortem* examination.

V. inter, bury; lay in –, consign to- the -grave, – tomb; en-, in-tomb; inhume; lay out, prepare for burial, embalm, mummify; conduct a funeral, hold services; toll the knell; put to bed with a shovel.

exhume, disinter, unearth.

Adj. buried &c. *v.*; burial; fune-real, -brial; mortuary, sepulchral, cinerary; elegiac; necroscopic.

Adv. *in memoriam*; *post-obit, -mortem*; beneath –, under- the sod.

Phr. *hic jacet, ci-git, requiescat in pace.*

2. *Special Vitality*

364. Animality.—N. animal life; anima-tion, -lity, -lization; breath.

flesh, – and blood; corporeal nature; *physique*; strength &c. 159.

V. animalize, incorporate.

Adj. fleshly, incarnate, carnal, corporeal, human.

365. Vegetability.—N. vegetable life; vegeta-tion, -bility; herbage.

V. vegetate, germinate, sprout, shoot; cultivate.

Adj. vegetable &c. 367; rank, lush.

---

366. Animal.*—N. animal, – kingdom; *fauna*; brute creation.

beast, brute, creature, created being; creeping –, living- thing; dumb -animal, – creature.

flocks and herds, live stock; domes-tic –, wild- animals; game, *feræ naturæ*; beasts of the field, fowls of the air, denizens of the day.

vertebrate, bi-, quadru-ped, mammal, marsupial, bird, reptile, batrachian, amphibian, fish, crustacean, shell fish, articulate, mollusc, worm, insect, zoophyte; protozoon, animalcule &c. 193.

horse &c. (*beast of burden*) 271; cattle, kine, ox; bull, -ock; steer, stot; cow, milch-cow, calf, heifer, shorthorn; sheep; lamb, -kin; ewe –, pet- lamb; ewe, ram, tup; pig, swine, boar, hog, shoat, sow; tag, teg, wether.

dog, bitch, hound; pup, -py; whelp, cur, mutt, mongrel; house-, watch-, sheep-, shepherd's-, sporting-, fancy-, lap-, toy-, bull-, badger-dog; mastiff; blood-, grey-, stag-, deer-, fox-, otter-hound; harrier, beagle, spaniel, pointer,

367. Vegetable.*— N. vegetable – kingdom; *flora*, verdure.

plant; tree, shrub, bush; creeper; vine; herb, -age; grass.

annual; per-, bi-, tri-ennial; exotic.

timber; primeval –, virgin- forest; wood, -lands; hurst, frith, holt, weald, park, chase, greenwood, brake, grove, copse, coppice, *bocage, tope*, clump of trees, thicket, spinet, spinney; under-. brush-wood; boscage, scrub; the oak and the ash and the bonny ivy tree.

bush, jungle, prairie; heath, -er; fern, bracken; furze, gorse, whin broom; grass, turf, grassland, green-sward, green, lawn, meadow; pas-ture, -turage; turbary; sedge, rush, weed; fungus, mushroom, toadstool; lichen, moss, conferva, mould; seaweed &c.; growth, crop.

foliage, leafage, branch, bough, ram-age; spray &c. 51; leaf, frond, flag, petal, shoot, tendril.

flower, blossom, bud, bloom, bine; flowering plant; tree, sapling, pollard; timber-, fruit-tree; palm-, gum-tree; pulse, legume.

* Extended lists of names of specific varieties of animals, vegetables, &c., are beyond the scope of this work; see Introduction, p. xxv.

setter, retriever; Newfoundland; water
-dog, – spaniel; pug, poodle; dachshund;
Pinscher; turnspit; terrier; fox –, Skye-
terrier; Dandie Dinmont; colley.

cat; puss, -y; kitten; grimalkin; gib-,
tom-cat; mouser; fox, Reynard, vixen,
stag, deer, hart, buck, doe, roe, antelope.

bird; poultry, fowl, cock, hen,
chicken, chanticleer, partlet, rooster,
dunghill cock, barn-door fowl; feathered -tribes, – songster; sing-
ing –, dicky- bird; canary; finch; auk, dodo, moa, roc, phœnix.

snake, serpent, viper, adder; newt, eft; asp, vermin.

Adj. animal, zoological.

equine, bovine, vaccine, canine, feline; fishy; piscator-y, -ial;
molluscous, vermicular.

Adj. veget-able, -ous; herb-aceous,
-al; botanic; sylvan, silvan; arbor- ary,
-eous, -escent, -ical; dendritic, dendriform; woody, grassy; ver-dant,-durous;
floral, mossy; lign-ous, -eous; wooden,
leguminous; end-, ex-ogenous.

————

368. [The science of animals.] **Zoology.**—**N.** zoo-logy, -nomy, -graphy,
-tomy; anatomy; comparative anatomy; animal –, comparative- physiology; morphology.

anthrop-, ornith-, ichthy-, herpet-,
ophi-, malac-, helminth-, entom-,oryct-,
paleont-ology; ichthy- &c. -otomy;
taxidermy.

zo- &c. -ologist.

Adj. zoological &c. *n.*

370. [The economy or management
of animals.] **Cicuration.—N.** taming &c.
v.; cicuration, zoohygiantics; domestication, -ity; *manège*; veterinary art;
breeding, pisciculture, apiculture &c.

menagery, vivarium, zoological garden, zoo; bear-pit; aviary, apiary, hive;
aquarium, fishery, fish hatchery; duck-,
fish-pond; stud-farm; stock farm, dairy.
[Destruction of animals] phthisozo-
ics* &c. (*killing*) 361.

neat-, cow-, shep-herd, shepherdess;
grazier, drover, cowboy, cowkeeper;
trainer, breeder, groom, ostler &c. 746;
veterinary surgeon, vet, horse doctor;
farrier; keeper; game keeper.

cage &c. (*prison*) 752; hen-coop,
bird-cage, cauf; sheep-fold &c. (*inclosure*) 232.

V. tame, domesticate, acclimatize,
breed, tend, break in, train, corral,
round up; cage, bridle &c. (*restrain*)
751; ride &c. 266.

drive, yoke, harness, hitch; groom,

369. [The science of plants.] **Botany.**
—**N.** botany; phyto-graphy, -logy,
-tomy; vegetable physiology, herbori-
zation, dendr-, myc-, fung-, alg-ology;
flora, pomona; botanist &c.; botanic
garden &c. (*garden*) 371; *hortus siccus,
herbarium*, herbal.

herb-ist, -arist, -alist, -orist, -arian
&c.

V. botanize, herborize.

Adj. botanical &c. *n.*

371. [The economy or management
of plants.] **Agriculture.—N.** agriculture, cultivation, husbandry, farming;
georgics, geoponics; tillage, tilth, agronomy, gardening, spade husbandry,
vintage; hort-, arbor-, silv-, citr-, vit-,
flor-iculture; intensive culture; landscape gardening; forestry, afforestation.

husbandman, horticulturist, citri-
culturist, gardener, florist; agricult-or,
-urist; yeoman, farmer, cultivator,
tiller of the soil, ploughman, sower,
reaper; woodcutter, backwoodsman,
forester; vine grower, vintager; Boer;
Triptolemus.

field, meadow, garden; botanic –,
winter –, ornamental –, flower –, kitchen –, truck –, market –, hop- garden;
nursery; green-, hot-, glass-house;
conservatory, cucumber frame, *cloche*,
bed, border, seed-plot; grass-plat,
lawn; park &c. (*pleasure ground*) 840;
parterre, shrubbery, plantation, avenue,

* Bentham.

curry-comb; milk; shear; hatch; incubate.

Adj. pastoral, bucolic; tame, domestic, domesticated, broken in, gentle, docile.

———

arboretum, pinery, *pinetum*, orchard; vineyard, vinery; orangery; farm &c. (*abode*) 189.

V. cultivate; till, – the soil; farm, garden; sow, plant; reap, mow, cut; manure, dress the ground, dig, delve, dibble, hoe, plough, plow, harrow, rake, weed, lop and top, force, transplant, thin out, bed out, prune, graft.

Adj. agr-icultural, -arian, -estic.

arable; predial, rural, rustic, country, bucolic, Bœotian; horticultural.

372. Mankind.—N. man, -kind; human -race, – species, – nature; humanity, mortality, flesh, generation.

[Science of man] anthropo-logy, -graphy, -sophy; ethno-logy, -graphy; humanitarianism.

human being; person, -age; individual, creature, fellow creature, mortal, body, somebody, one; such a –, some- one; soul, living soul; earthling; party, head, hand; *dramatis personæ*.

people, persons, folk, public, society, world; community, – at large; general public; nation, -ality; state, realm; common-weal, -wealth; republic, body politic; million &c. (*commonalty*) 876; population &c. (*inhabitant*) 188.

cosmopolite; lords of the creation; ourselves.

Adj. human, mortal, personal, individual, national, civic, public, cosmopolitan; anthropoid.

373. Man.—N. man, male, he; man-hood &c. (*adolescence*) 131; gentleman, sir, master; yeoman, wight, swain, fellow, guy, blade, *beau*, chap, gaffer, good man; husband &c. (*married man*) 903; Mr., mister, *monsieur, sahib, Herr, señor, signor*; boy &c. (*youth*) 129; Adonis.

[Male animal] cock, drake, gander, dog, boar, stag, hart, buck, horse, entire horse, stallion; gib-, tom-cat; he-, Billy-goat; ram, tup; bull, -ock; capon, ox, gelding; steer, stot.

Adj. male, he, masculine; manly, virile; un-womanly, -feminine.

———

374. Woman.—N. woman, she, female, petticoat, skirt, moll, broad.

feminality, feminity, muliebrity; womanhood &c. (*adolescence*) 131; feminism; gynecology, gyniatrics, gynics.

womankind; the -sex, – fair; fair –, softer- sex; weaker vessel; the distaff side.

dame, madam, *madame*, mistress, Mrs., lady, *mem-sahib, Frau, señora, signora, donna, belle*, matron, dowager, goody, gammer; good -woman, – wife; squaw; wife &c. (*marriage*) 903; matron-age, -hood.

Venus, nymph, wench, *grisette*; little bit of fluff; girl &c. (*youth*) 129.

inamorata (love) &c. 897; courtesan &c. 962.

spinster, old maid, virgin, bachelor girl, new woman, amazon.

[Female animal] hen, slut, bitch, sow, doe, roe, mare; she-, Nanny-goat; ewe, cow; lioness, tigress; vixen.

gynecæum, harem, *seraglio, zenana, purdah*.

Adj. female, she; feminine, womanly, ladylike, matronly, maidenly; womanish, effeminate unmanly, gynecic.

2°. Sensation

(1.) *Sensation in general*

375. Physical Sensibility.—**N.** sensibility; sensitiveness &c. *adj.*; physical sensibility, feeling, perceptivity, anaphylaxis, susceptibility, æsthetics; moral sensibility &c. 822.

sensation, impression, effect; consciousness &c. (*knowledge*) 490.

external senses.

V. be -sensible &c. *adj.* -of; feel, perceive.

render, -sensible &c. *adj.*; excite, stir, sharpen, cultivate, tutor.

cause sensation, impress; excite –, produce- an impression.

Adj. sens-ible, -itive, -uous; æsthetic, perceptive, sentient; conscious &c. (*aware*) 490; impressionable, responsive, alive to.

acute, sharp, keen, vivid, lively, impressive, thin-skinned.

Adv. to the quick.

---

377. Physical Pleasure.—**N.** pleasure; physical –, sensual –, sensuous-pleasure; bodily enjoyment, animal gratification, sensuality; hedonism, luxuriousness &c. *adj.*; dissipation, round of pleasure; titillation, *gusto*, creature comforts, comfort, ease; pillow &c. (*support*) 215; luxury, lap of luxury; purple and fine linen; bed of -down, – roses; velvet, clover; cup of Circe &c. (*intemperance*) 954.

treat; diversion, divertisement, entertainment; refreshment, regale; feast; *délice*; dainty &c. 394; *bonne bouche.*

source of pleasure &c. 829; happiness &c. (*mental enjoyment*) 827.

V. feel –, experience –, receive-pleasure; enjoy, relish; luxuriate –, revel –, riot –, bask –, swim –, wallow-in; feast on; gloat -over, – on; smack the lips.

live -on the fat of the land, – in comfort &c. *adv.*; bask in the sunshine, *faire ses choux gras.*

give pleasure &c. 829.

376. Physical Insensibility.—**N.** insensibility, physical insensibility; obtuseness &c. *adj.*; palsy, paralysis, *anæsthesia, analgesia, narcosis, hypnosis,* twilight sleep, stupor, coma, trance, catalepsy; sleep &c. (*inactivity*) 683; moral insensibility &c. 823; numbness &c. 381.

anæsthetic agent, general –, local-anæsthetic, opium, ether, chloroform, cocaine, novocaine, chloral; nitrous oxide, laughing gas; refrigeration.

V. be -insensible &c. *adj.*; have a -thick skin, – rhinoceros hide.

render -insensible &c. *adj.*; blunt, pall, obtund, benumb, deaden, paralyze; anæsthetize, drug, dope; put under the influence of -chloroform &c. *n.*; hypnotize; stupefy, stun, narcotize.

Adj. insensible, unfeeling, senseless, comatose, dazed, impercipient, callous, thick-skinned, pachydermatous; hard, -ened; case-hardened; proof; obtuse, dull; anæsthetic; paralytic, palsied, numb, dead.

---

378. Physical Pain.—**N.** pain; suffering, -ance; bodily – physical- -pain, – suffering; mental suffering &c. 828; dolour, ache; aching &c. *v.*; smart; shoot, -ing; twinge, twitch, gripe, head-, ear-, tooth-ache; *migraine,* neuralgia, neuritis, lumbago, gout, sciatica; hurt, cut; sore, -ness; discomfort, *malaise; tic douloureux.*

spasm, cramp; nightmare, *ephialtes*; crick, stitch, kink; thrill, convulsion, throe; throb &c. (*agitation*) 315; pang.

sharp –, piercing –, throbbing –, shooting –, gnawing –, burning- pain; anguish, agony.

torment, torture; rack; cruci-ation, -fixion; martyrdom; martyr, toad under a harrow, vivisection.

V. feel –, experience –, suffer –, undergo- pain &c. *n.*; suffer, ache, smart, bleed; tingle, shoot; twinge, twitch, lancinate; writhe, wince, make a wry face; sit on -thorns, – pins and needles.

give –, inflict- pain; pain, hurt, chafe, sting, bite, gnaw, gripe, stab, grind;

Adj. enjoying &c. *v.*; luxurious, voluptuous, sensual, hedonistic, comfortable, cosy, snug, in comfort, at ease.

agreeable &c. 829; grateful, refreshing, comforting, cordial, genial; sensuous; palatable &c. 394; sweet &c. (*sugar*) 396; fragrant &c. 400; melodious &c. 413; lovely &c. (*beautiful*) 845.

Adv. in -comfort &c. *n.*; on -a bed of roses &c. *n.*; at one's ease.

pinch, tweak; grate, gall, fret, prick, pierce, wring, convulse; torment, torture; rack, agonize; crucify; ex-, cruciate; break on the wheel, put to the rack; flag &c. (*punish*) 972; grate on the ear &c. (*harsh sound*) 410.

Adj. in -pain &c. *n.*, – a state of pain; pained &c. *v.*

painful; aching &c. *v.*; biting, poignant; sore, raw, tender, with exposed nerve.

(2.) *Special Sensation*

1. *Touch*

379. [Sensation of pressure.] **Touch.—N.** touch; tact, -ion, -ility; feeling; palp-ation, -ability; manipulation; brush, tick, graze, contact &c. 199.

[Organ of touch] hand, finger, fore-finger, thumb, paw, feeler, *antenna*.

V. touch, feel, handle, finger, thumb, paw, fumble, grope, grabble; twiddle, tweedle; pass –, run- the fingers over, massage, rub, knead; palpate, stroke, manipulate, wield; throw out a feeler.

Adj. tact-ual, -ile; tangible, palpable; lambent.

380. Sensations of Touch.—N. itching &c. *v.*; titillation, formication, *aura*.

V. itch, tingle, creep, thrill, sting; prick, -le; tickle, titillate.

Adj. itching &c. *v.*

381. [Insensibility to touch.] **Numbness.—N.** numbness &c. (*physical insensibility*) 376; pins and needles.

local anæsthetic, cocaine, novocaine &c.; morphia.

V. benumb &c. 376; freeze, dull, deaden.

Adj. numb; benumbed &c. *v.*; intangible, impalpable.

2. *Heat*

382. Heat.—N. heat, caloric; temperature, warmth, fervour, calidity; incal-, incand-, recal-, decal-escence; glow, flush, blush; fever, hectic.

phlogiston; fire, spark, scintillation, flash, flame, blaze; arc; bonfire; firework, pyrotechny; wild-fire; sheet of fire, lambent flame; devouring element; conflagration.

summer, dog-days, canicule; baking &c. 384 –, white –, tropical –, Afric –, Bengal –, summer –, blood- heat; heat wave, sirocco, simoon; broiling sun; isolation; warming &c. 384.

sun &c. (*luminary*) 423; fire worshipper &c. 991; furnace &c. 386.

geyser, hot spring, volcano.

[Science of heat] pyrology; therm-

383. Cold.—N. cold, -ness &c. *adj.*; frigidity, gelidity, algidity, inclemency, *fresco*.

winter; depth of –, hard- winter; Siberia, Nova Zembla; Ant-, arctic, North –, South- Pole.

ice; snow, – flake, – crystal, – drift; sleet; hail, -stone; rime, frost; hoar –, white –, hard –, sharp- frost; icicle, thick-ribbed ice; fall of snow, snow storm, heavy fall, *avalanche*; ice-berg, -floe; floe, berg; *glacier*; *nevée*, *serac*.

[Sensation of cold] chilliness &c. *adj.*; chill; shivering &c. *v.*; gooseskin, -flesh; *rigor*, horripilation, chattering of teeth; frostbite, chilblain.

V. be -cold &c. *adj.*; shiver, starve, quake, shake, tremble, shudder, didder,

ology, -otics; thermometer &c. 389.

V. be -hot &c. *adj.*; glow, incandesce, flush, sweat, swelter, bask, smoke, reek, stew, simmer, seethe, boil, burn, singe, scorch, scald, grill, broil, blaze, flame; smoulder; parch, fume, pant.

heat &c. (*make hot*) 384; thaw, fuse, melt, give.

Adj. hot, heated, warm, mild, genial, tepid, lukewarm, unfrozen; therm-al, -ic; calorific; ferv-ent, -id; ardent; aglow.

sunny, torrid, tropical, estival, canicular; close, sultry, stifling, stuffy, suffocating, oppressive; reeking &c. *v.*; baking &c. 384.

red -, white -, smoking -, burning &c. *v.* -, piping- hot; like -a furnace, - an oven; hot as -fire, - pepper; hot enough to roast an ox.

fiery; incand-, incal-escent; candent, ebullient, glowing, smoking; on fire; blazing &c. *v.*; in -flames, - a blaze; alight, afire, ablaze; un-quenched, -extinguished; smouldering; in a -heat, - glow, - fever, - perspiration, - sweat; sudorific; swelter-ing, -ed; blood-hot, -warm; warm as -a toast, - wool; recalescent, thermogenic, pyrotechnic, feverish, febrile, inflamed.

volcanic, plutonic, igneous; isother-mal, -mic, -al.

Phr. Not a breath of air.

384. Calefaction.—N. increase of temperature; heating &c. *v.*; cale-, tepe-, torre-faction; melting, fusion; liquefaction &c. 335; burning &c. *v.*; kindling, combustion; in-, ac-cension; con-, cremation; scorification; cauter-y, -ization; ustulation, calcination; in-, cineration; cupellation; carbonization.

ignition, inflammation, adustion, flagration; de-, con-flagration; empyrosis, incendiarism; arson; *auto da fé*; suttee.

boiling &c. *v.*; coction, ebullition, estuation, elixation, decoction.

furnace &c. 386; blanket, flannel, fur, muffler, wrap; wadding &c. (*lining*) 224; clothing &c. 225.

match &c. (*fuel*) 388; incendiary, pyromaniac; *pétroleur*, *pétroleuse*; cauterant, caustic, lunar caustic, apozem, moxa.

sunstroke, *coup de soleil*; insolation, sunburn.

pottery, ceramics, crockery, porcelain, china; earthen-, stone-ware; pot,

quiver; perish with cold; chill &c. (*render cold*) 385.

Adj. cold, cool; chill, -y; gelid, frigid, algid; fresh, keen, bleak, raw, inclement, bitter, biting, niveous, cutting, nipping, piercing, pinching; clay-cold; starved &c. (*made cold*) 385; shivering &c. *v.*; aguish, *transi de froid*; frostbitten, -bound, -nipped.

cold as -a stone, - marble, - lead, - iron, - a frog, - charity, - Christmas; cool as -a cucumber, - custard.

icy, glacial, frosty, freezing, wintry, brumal, hibernal, boreal, arctic, antarctic, polar, Siberian, hyemal; hyperbore-an, -al; ice-bound; frozen out.

un-warmed, -thawed, -heated; isocheimal, -chimenal.

Adv. coldly, bitterly &c. *adj.*; *à pierre fendre.*

---

385. Refrigeration.—N. refrigeration, infrigidation, reduction of temperature; cooling &c. *v.*; con-gelation, -glaciation; ice &c. 383; solidification &c. (*density*) 321; refrigerator &c. 387.

extincteur; fire, - engine, - extinguisher, - annihilator, - brigade, - man; sprinkler, hose, hydrant, standpipe.

incombusti-bility, -bleness &c. *adj.*

V. cool, fan, refrigerate, refresh, ice; congeal, freeze, glaciate; benumb, starve, pinch, chill, petrify, chill to the marrow, nip, cut, pierce, bite, make one's teeth chatter; damp, slack; quench; put -, stamp- out; extinguish.

go -, burn- out.

Adj. cooled &c. *v.*; frozen out; cooling &c. *v.*; frigorific.

incombustible; un-, unin-flammable; fire-proof.

---

mug, *terra-cotta*, brick, clinker; cinder, ash, *scoriæ*; embers, dress, slag, products of combustion, coke, carbon, charcoal.

inflamma-, combusti-bility.

[Transmission of heat] diathermancy, transcalency.

V. heat, warm, chafe, stive, foment; make -hot &c. 382; sun oneself, bask in the sun.

fire; set -fire to, – on fire; kindle, enkindle, light, ignite, strike a light; apply the -match, – torch- to; re-kindle, -lume; fan –, add fuel to- the flame; poke –, stir –, blow- the fire; make a bonfire of; burn at the stake.

melt, thaw, fuse; liquefy &c. 335.

burn, inflame, roast, toast, fry, grill, singe, parch, bake, torrefy, scorch; brand, cauterize, sear, burn in; corrode, char, carbonize, calcine, incinerate; smelt, cupel, scorify; reduce to ashes; burn to a cinder; commit –, consign- to the flames.

boil, digest, stew, cook, seethe, scald, parboil, simmer; do to rags.

take –, catch- fire; blaze &c. (*flame*) 382.

Adj. heated &c. *v.*; molten, sodden; *réchauffé*; heating &c. *v.*

inflammable, burnable, inflammatory, combustible; diatherm-al -anous; burnt &c. *v.*; volcanic.

---

386. Furnace.—N. furnace, blast furnace, fire-box, stove, incinerator, destructor, crematorium, crematory, kiln, oven, oast-house; hot-, bake-, wash-house; laundry; conservatory; hearth, focus; athanor, hypocaust, reverberatory; volcano; forge, fiery furnace; *tuyère*, brasier, salamander, heater, warming-pan, foot-warmer, hot-water bottle; radiator; boiler, geyser, caldron, seething caldron, pot; urn, kettle; chafing-dish; retort, crucible, alembic, still; saggar.

fire-place, -dog, -irons; hearth, ingle, grate, range, kitchener; kitchen range; oil-, gas-, electric, -cooker, -stove; fireless cooker; fire; galley; ca-, cam-boose; poker, tongs, shovel, hob, trivet; and-, grid-iron; frying-, stew-pan &c.

hot –, Turkish –, Russian –, vapour –, shower –, warm- bath; *calidarium, tepidarium, sudatorium,* sudatory; *hammam.*

387. Refrigerator.—N. refrigerator, -y; *frigidarium*; cold storage; refriger-ating-plant, – machine; ice-house, -pail, -bag, -chest, -pack; cooler, damper; wine-cooler, freezing mixture.

---

388. Fuel.—N. fuel, firing, combustible, coal, wallsend, anthracite, bituminous coal, slack, culm, cannel coal, lignite, briquette, coke, carbon, charcoal; turf, peat, fire-wood, bobbing, faggot, log, yule log, ember, cinder &c. (*products of combustion*) 384; kindling wood, tinder, touch-wood; fumigator, sulphur, brimstone; incense; port-fire; fire-barrel, -ball, -brand.

fuel oil, gas, gasoline, electricity.

brand, torch, fuse; wick; spill, match, safety match, light, lucifer, congreve, vesuvian, vesta, fusee, locofoco; linstock; illuminant.

candle &c. (*luminary*) 423; oil &c. (*grease*), 356; petrol, gasoline, methylated –, spirit; gas, acetylene.

Adj. carbonaceous; combustible, inflammable.

V. stoke, fire, feed, add fuel to the flames.

389. Thermometer.—N. thermo-meter, -scope, -stat, -pile, differential thermometer; pyro-, calori-meter; radio micrometer &c.

3. *Taste*

390. Taste.—N. taste, flavour, gust, *gusto*, relish, savour; sapor, sapidity; twang, smack, smatch; after-taste, tang.

tasting; de-, gustation.

palate, tongue, tooth, stomach.

V. taste, savour, smatch, smack, flavour, twang; tickle the palate &c. (*savoury*) 394; smack the lips.

Adj. sapid, saporific; gusta-ble, -tory; strong; flavoured, spiced, savoury; palatable &c. 394.

391. Insipidity.—N. insipidity; taste-lessness &c. *adj.*

V. be -tasteless &c. *adj.*

Adj. void of -taste &c. 390; insipid; jejune; taste-, gust-, savour-less; in-gustible, mawkish, milk and water, weak, stale, flat, vapid, *fade*, wishy-washy, mild; untasted.

---

392. Pungency.—N. pungency, piquancy, poignancy, *haut-goût*, strong taste, twang, race, tang.

sharpness &c. *adj.*; acrimony, acridity; roughness &c. (*sour*) 397; unsavouriness &c. 395.

nitre, saltpetre; mustard, cayenne, caviare; seasoning &c. (*condiment*) 393; brine.

dram, cordial, nip, pick-me-up, bracer, potion.

nicotine, tobacco, snuff, quid; segar; cigar, -ette, gasper, fag; cheroot; weed; fragrant -, Indian- weed; pipe, clay pipe, churchwarden, brier, meerschaum, hookah, hubble-bubble.

V. be -pungent &c. *adj.*; bite the tongue.

render -pungent &c. *adj.*; season, spice, salt, pepper, pickle, brine, devil, curry.

smoke, chew, take snuff.

Adj. pungent, strong; high-, full-flavoured; high-tasted, -seasoned; gamy; sharp, stinging, rough, *piquant*, racy; biting, mordant; spicy; seasoned &c. *v.*; hot, – as pepper; peppery, vellicating, escharotic, meracious; acrid, acrimonious, bitter; rough &c. (*sour*) 397; unsavoury &c. 395.

salt, saline, brackish, briny; salt as -brine, – a herring, – Lot's wife.

393. Condiment.—N. condiment, flavouring, salt, mustard, pepper, cayenne, curry, seasoning, sauce, spice, cinnamon, chillies, relish, *sauce piquante*, caviare, pot-herbs, onion, garlic, pickle, chutney, nutmeg &c.

V. season &c. (*render pungent*) 392.

---

394. Savouriness.—N. savouriness &c. *adj.*; relish, zest.

tit-bit, dainty, delicacy, ambrosia, nectar, *bonne bouche*; game, turtle, venison.

V. taste good, be -savoury &c. *adj.*; tickle the -palate, – appetite; flatter the palate.

render -palatable &c. *adj.*

relish, like, smack the lips.

Adj. savoury, well-tasted, to one's taste, tasty, good, palatable, nice, dainty, delectable; tooth-ful, -some;

395. Unsavouriness.—N. unsavouri-ness &c. *adj.*; amaritude; acri-mony, -tude; roughness &c. (*sour*) 397; acerb-ity, austerity; gall and worm-wood, rue, quassia, aloes; sickener.

V. be -unpalatable &c. *adj.*; sicken, disgust, nauseate, pall, turn the stomach.

Adj. un-savoury, -palatable, -sweet; ill-flavoured, un-appetizing, -eatable, inedible; bitter, – as gall; acrid, acri-monious; rough.

offensive, repulsive, nasty; sickening

gustful, appetizing, lickerish, delicate, delicious, exquisite, rich, luscious, ambrosial.

Adv. *per amusare la bocca.*

Phr. *cela se laisse manger.*

396. Sweetness.—N. sweetness, dulcitude, saccharinity.

sugar, cane-, beet-sugar; saccharine, glucose, syrup, treacle, molasses, honey, manna; confection, -ary; sweets, grocery, conserve, preserve, *confiture*, jam, marmalade, julep; sugar-candy, -plum; licorice, liquorice, plum, lollipop, *bon bon, jujube*, comfit, sweetmeat, caramel, toffee, butterscotch.

nectar; hydromel, mead, metheglin, honeysuckle, *liqueur*, sweet wine.

pastry, pie, tart, puff, pudding, cake.

dulc-ification, -oration.

V. be -sweet &c. *adj.*

render -sweet &c. *adj.*; sugar, saccharize, sweeten; edulcorate; dulc-orate, -ify; candy; mull.

Adj. sweet, sugary; sacchar-ine, -iferous; dulcet, honied, candied, luscious, nectarious, melliferous; sweetened &c. *v.*

sweet as -a nut, – sugar, – honey.

&c. *v.*; nauseous; loath-, ful-some; unpleasant &c. 830.

---

397. Sourness.—N. sourness &c. *adj.*; acid, -ity; acetous fermentation; acerbity.

vinegar, verjuice, crab, alum.

V. be -, turn- -sour &c. *adj.*; set the teeth on edge.

render -sour &c. *adj.*; acid-ify, -ulate.

Adj. sour; acid, -ulous, -ulated; acerb; tart, crabbed; acet-ous, -ose; sour as vinegar, sourish, acescent, sub-acid; styptic, hard, rough; unripe, green.

---

4. *Odour*

398. Odour.—N. odour, smell, odorament, scent, effluvium; eman-, exhal-ation; fume, essence, trail, nidor, redolence.

sense of smell; scent; act of -smelling &c. *v.*

V. have an -odour &c. *n.*; smell, – of, – strong of; exhale; give out a -smell &c. *n.*; scent.

smell, scent; snuff, – up; sniff, nose, inhale.

Adj. odor-ous, -iferous; smelling, strong-scented; redolent, graveolent, nidorous, pungent.

[Relating to the sense of smell] olfactory, quick-scented.

399. Inodorousness.—N. inodorousness; absence –, want- of smell.

V. be -inodorous &c. *adj.*; not smell. deodorize.

Adj. inodor-ous, -ate; scentless; without –, wanting- smell &c. 398.

deodoriz-ed, -ing.

---

400. Fragrance. — N. fragrance, aroma, redolence, perfume, *bouquet*; sweet smell, aromatic perfume.

perfumery; incense; musk, frankincense; pastil, -le; myrrh, perfumes of Arabia, chypre; otto, ottar, attar; bergamot, balm, civet, *pot-pourri*, pulvil; nosegay, *boutonnière*; scent, -bag; *sachet*, scent-bottle, smelling bottle, *vinaigrette*; toilet water, *eau de Cologne*; thurible, censer, thurification.

perfumer; incense bearer.

401. Fetor.—N. fetor, fetidness; bad &c. *adj.*; -smell, – odour; stench, stink; mephitis, foul –, mal- odour; *empyreuma*; mustiness &c. *adj.*; rancidity; foulness &c. (*uncleanness*) 653.

stoat, polecat, skunk; assafœtida; fungus, garlic; stink-pot, -bomb.

V. have a -bad smell &c. *n.*; smell; stink, – in the nostrils, – like a polecat; smell -strong &c. *adj.*, – offensively.

Adj. fetid; strong-smelling; high, bad, strong, fulsome, offensive, noisome, rank, rancid, reasty, tainted, musty,

V. be -fragrant &c. *adj.*; have a -perfume &c. *n.*; smell sweet, scent, perfume, thurify, embalm.

Adj. fragrant, aromatic, redolent, spicy, balmy, scented; sweet-smelling, -scented; perfum-ed, -atory; thuriferous; fragrant as a rose, muscadine, ambrosial.

fusty, frouzy; olid, -ous; nidorous; smelling, stinking; putrid &c. 653; suffocating, mephitic; empyreumatic.

---

5. *Sound*

(i.) SOUND IN GENERAL

402. Sound.—N. sound, noise, strain; accent, twang, intonation, tone, tune; cadence; sonority, sonorousness &c. *adj.*; audibility; resonance &c. 408; voice &c. 580.

[Science of sound] acou-, acu-stics; catacoustics, cataphonics; phon-ics, -etics, -ology, -ography; dia-coustics, -phonics.

telephone, phonograph &c. 418.

V. produce sound; sound, make a noise; give out -, emit- sound; phonetize, phonate; resound &c. 408.

Adj. sounding; soniferous; sonorific; resonant, audible, acoustic, auditory, distinct; stertorous; phonic, sonant; phonetic.

---

403. Silence.—N. silence; stillness &c. (*quiet*) 265; peace, hush, lull, rest; muteness &c. 581; solemn -, awful -, dead -, deathlike- silence.

V. be -silent &c. *adj.*; hold one's tongue &c. (*not speak*) 585.

render -silent &c. *adj.*; silence, still, hush; stifle, muffle, gag, stop; muzzle, put to silence &c. (*render mute*) 581.

Adj. silent; still, -y; calm, quiet; noise-, sound-, speech-less; hushed &c. *v.*; mute &c. 581; aphonic.

soft, solemn, awful, deathlike, silent as the grave; inaudible &c. (*faint*) 405.

Adv. silently &c. *adj.*; *sub silentio*; in perfect silence.

Int. hush! 'sh! silence! soft! whist! tush! chut! tut! *pax!* mum's the word! hold your tongue! shut up! be silent! be quiet! stop that noise! hold your row! dry up! peace, be still!

Phr. one might hear a -feather, - pin- drop.

---

404. Loudness.—N. loudness, power; loud noise, din; clang, -or; clatter, noise, bombilation, roar, uproar, racket, static, grinders, hubbub, *fracas*, *charivari*, trumpet blast, blare, flourish of trumpets, fanfare, *tintamarre*, peal, swell, blast, alarum, boom; resonance &c. 408.

vociferation; pandemonium, hullaballoo &c. 411; lungs; Stentor; megaphone; siren.

artillery, cannon, gunfire, shellburst, bomb; thunder.

V. be -loud &c. *adj.*; peal, swell, clang, boom, thunder, fulminate, roar; resound &c. 408; speak up, shout &c. (*vociferate*) 411; bellow &c. (*cry as an animal*) 412; give tongue.

rend the -air, - skies; fill the air; din -, ring -, thunder- in the ear;

---

405. Faintness.—N. faintness &c. *adj.*; faint sound, whisper, breath; under-tone, -breath; murmur, hum, rustle, buzz, purr; plash; sough, moan, sigh, susurration; tinkle; 'still small voice.'

hoarseness &c. *adj.*; raucity.

silencer, soft pedal, damper, mute, *sourdine.*

V. whisper, breathe, murmur, purl, hum, gurgle, ripple, babble, flow; tinkle; mutter &c. (*speak imperfectly*) 583.

steal on the ear; melt in -, float on- the air.

muffle, mute, deaden, damp, stifle.

Adj. inaudible; scarcely -, just- audible; low, dull; stifled, muffled; hoarse, husky; gentle, soft, faint; floating; purling, flowing &c. *v.*;

pierce –, split –, rend- the -ears, – head; deafen, stun; *faire le diable à quatre*; make one's windows shake; awaken –, startle- the echoes; make the welkin ring.

Adj. loud, sonorous; high-, big-sounding; blatant; deep, full, powerful, noisy, clangorous, multisonous, *fortissimo*; thundering, deafening &c. *v.*; trumpet-tongued; ear-splitting, -rend-ing, -deafening; piercing; obstreperous, rackety, uproarious; enough to wake the -dead, – seven sleepers.

shrill &c. 410; clamorous &c. (*vociferous*) 411; stentor-ian, -ophonic.

Adv. loudly &c. *adj.*; aloud; at the top of one's voice, lustily, in full cry.

Phr. the air rings with.

whispered &c. *v.*; liquid; soothing; dulcet &c. (*melodious*) 413.

Adv. in a whisper, with bated breath, *sotto voce*, between the teeth, aside; *pian-o, -issimo; à la sourdine; con sordine*; out of earshot, inaudibly &c. *adj.*

(ii.) Specific Sounds*

406. [Sudden and violent sounds.] **Snap.—N.** snap &c. *v.*; rapping &c. *v.*; de-, crepitation; smack, clap, report; thud; burst, explosion, discharge, detonation, blow-out, back-fire, firing, salvo, volley, pistol-shot.

squib, cracker, gun, rifle, pop-gun.

V. rap, snap, tap, knock; click; clash; crack, -le; crash; pop; slam, bang, clap, thump, plump; toot; back-fire, explode, burst on the ear.

Adj. rapping &c. *v.*

Int. crash! bang!

407. [Repeated and protracted sounds.] **Roll.—N.** roll &c. *v.*; drumming &c. *v.*; tattoo; ding-dong; tantara; rataplan; whirr; rat-a-tat; rub-a-dub; pit-a-pat; quaver, clutter, *charivari*, racket; cuckoo; repetition &c. 104; peal of bells, devil's tattoo; reverberation &c. 408.

drumfire, barrage.

machine gun.

V. roll, drum, rumble, rattle, clatter, rustle, roar, drone, patter, clack.

hum, trill, shake; chime, peal, toll; tick, beat.

drum –, din- in the ear.

Adj. rolling &c. *v.*; monotonous &c. (*repeated*), 104; like a bee in a bottle.

---

408. Resonance.—N. resonance; ring &c. *v.*; ringing &c. *v.*; tintinnabulation; reflection, reverberation, clangor.

low –, base –, bass –, flat –, grave –, deep –, pedal- note; bass; *basso, – profondo*; bari-, bary-tone; *contralto*.

V. re-sound, -verberate, -echo; ring, ding, sing, jingle, gingle, chink, clink; tink, -le; chime; gurgle &c. 405; plash, guggle, echo, ring in the ear.

Adj. resounding &c. *v.*; resonant, tinnient, tintinnabulary; deep-toned, -sounding, -mouthed; hollow, sepulchral; gruff &c. (*harsh*) 410.

408a. Non-resonance. — N. thud, thump, dead sound; non-resonance; muffled drums, cracked bell; silencer, damper; mute, *sourdine*.

V. sound dead; stop –, damp- the -sound, – reverberations; deaden, muffle.

Adj. non-resonant, dead, muted. muffled.

---

409. [Hissing sounds.] **Sibilation.—N.** sibilation; hiss &c. *v.*; sternutation; high note &c. 410.

goose, serpent, snake.

* [The author's classification of sounds has been retained, though it does not entirely accord with the theories of modern science.—Ed.]

V. hiss, buzz, whiz, rustle; fizz, -le, sizzle, swish; wheeze, whistle, snuffle; squash; sneeze.

Adj. sibilant; hissing &c. *v.*; wheezy.

410. [Harsh sounds.] **Stridor.—N.** creak &c. *v.*; creaking &c. *v.*; discord &c. 414; stridor; harshness, roughness, sharpness &c. *adj.*; cacophony.

acute -, high- note; *soprano*, treble, tenor, *alto*, falsetto, *voce di testa*; shriek, cry &c. 411.

piccolo, fife, penny -whistle, - trumpet.

V. creak, grate, jar, burr, pipe, twang, jangle, clank, clink; scream &c. (*cry*) 411; yelp &c. (*animal sound*) 412; buzz &c. (*hiss*) 409.

set the teeth on edge, *écorcher les oreilles*; pierce -, split- the -ears, - head; offend -, grate upon -, jar upon- the ear.

Adj. creaking &c. *v.*; strident, stridulous, harsh, coarse, hoarse, horrisonous, raucous, metallic, rough, gruff, grum, sepulchral.

sharp, high, acute, shrill, high-pitched; trumpet-toned; piercing, ear-piercing; cracked; discordant &c. 414; cacophonous.

---

411. Cry.—N. cry &c. *v.*; voice &c. (*human*) 580; bark &c. (*animal*) 412.

vociferation, outcry, hullaballoo, chorus, clamour, hue and cry, plaint; lungs; stentor.

V. cry, roar, shout, bawl, brawl, halloo, halloa, hail, hoop, whoop, yell, bellow, howl, scream, screech, screak, shriek, shrill, squeak, squeal, squall, whine, whinny, pule, pipe, yaup.

cheer, hurrah; hoot; grumble, moan, groan.

snore, snort; grunt &c. (*animal sounds*) 412.

vociferate; raise -, lift up- the voice; call -, sing -, cry- out; exclaim; rend the air; thunder -, shout- at the -top of one's voice, - pitch of one's breath; *s'égosiller*; strain the -throat, - voice, - lungs; give a -cry &c.

Adj. crying &c. *v.*; clam-ant, -orous; vociferous; stentorian &c. (*loud*) 404; open-mouthed.

412. [Animal sounds.] **Ululation.—N.** cry &c. *v.*; crying &c. *v.*; ululation, latration, belling; reboation; call, note; bark, howl, yelp; twittering, woodnote; insect cry, fritinancy, drone; screech; cuckoo.

V. cry, ululate, howl, roar, bellow, blare, rebellow, bark, yelp; bay, - the moon; yap, growl, yarr, yawl, snarl, howl; grunt, -le; snort, squeak; neigh, bray; mew, mewl; purr, caterwaul, pule; bleat, low, moo; troat, croak, crow, screech, caw, coo, gobble, quack, cackle, gaggle, guggle; chuck, -le; cluck; clack; cheep, chirp, chirrup, twitter, sing, cuckoo; pout, wail, hum, buzz; hiss, blatter; hoot.

Adj. crying &c. *v.*; blatant, latrant; re-, mugient; deep-, full-mouthed.

Adv. in full cry.

(iii.) Musical Sounds

413. Melody. Concord.—N. melody, rhythm, measure; rhyme &c. (*poetry*) 597.

pitch, *timbre*, intonation, tone, overtone.

scale, gamut; diapason; diatonic -, chromatic -, enharmonic- scale; key, clef, chords,

modulation, temperament, syncope, syncopation, preparation, suspension, resolution.

414. Discord.—N. discord, -ance; dissonance, cacophony, caterwauling; harshness &c. 410; consecutive fifths.

[Confused sounds] Babel, pandemonium; Dutch -, cat's- concert; marrow-bones and cleavers.

V. be -discordant &c. *adj.*; jar &c. (*sound harshly*) 410.

Adj. discordant; dis-, ab-sonant; out of tune, tuneless; un-musical, -tunable; un-, im-melodious; un-, in-harmonious;

staff, stave, line, space, brace; bar, rest; *appogia-to*, *-tura*; *acciaccatura*, shake, *arpeggio*.

note, musical note, notes of a scale; sharp, flat, natural; high note &c. (*shrillness*) 410; low note &c. 408; interval; semitone; second, third, fourth &c.; diatessaron.

breve, semibreve, minim, crotchet, quaver; semi-, demisemiquaver; sustained note, drone, burden.

tonic; key-, leading-, fundamental- note; supertonic, mediant, dominant; sub-mediant, -dominant, organ-, pedal-point; octave, tetrachord; major –, minor- -mode, – scale, – key; Doric mode, passage, phrase.

concord, harmony; unison, -ance; chime, homophony; euphon-y, -ism; tonality; consonance; concent; part.

orchestration, harmonization, – phrasing.

[Science of harmony] harmon-y, -ics; thorough-, fundamental-bass; counterpoint; faburden.

piece of music &c. 415; composer, harmonist, contrapuntist.

V. be -harmonious &c. *adj.*; harmonize, chime, symphonize, transpose; put in tune, tune, accord, string; score, arrange, orchestrate.

Adj. harmoni-ous, -cal; in -concord &c. *n.*, – tune, – concert; unisonant, concentual, symphonizing, isotonic, homophonous, assonant, consonant.

measured, rhythmical, diatonic, chromatic, enharmonic.

melodious, musical; tuneful, tunable; sweet, dulcet, canorous; mell-ow, -ifluous; soft; clear, – as a bell; silvery; euphon-ious, -ic, -ical; symphonious; enchanting &c. (*pleasure-giving*) 829; fine-, full-, silver-toned.

Adv. harmoniously &c. *adj.*

sing-song; cacophonous; jarring, harsh &c. 410.

———

———

415. Music.—**N.** music, classical –, modern –, descriptive- music; concert, recital; strain, tune, air, *motif*; melody &c. 413; *aria, arietta*; piece of music, *sonata; rond-o, -eau; pastorale, cavatina*, roulade, *fantasia, toccata, concerto*, overture, symphony, symphonic poem, tone poem, prelude, voluntary, *intermezzo*, variations, *cadenza*; cadence; fugue, canon, serenade, *nocturne, notturno*, rhapsody, romance, *aubade*, dithyramb; opera, operetta; oratorio; composition, movement; stave.

instrumental music; full-, orchestral- score; minstrelsy, tweedledum and tweedledee, band, orchestra &c. 416; concerted piece, *potpourri*, medley, *capriccio*, incidental music; improvisation; peal.

vocal music, vocalism; chaunt, chant; psalm, -ody; hymn; song &c. (*poem*) 597; canticle, canzonet, *cantata, bravura, coloratura*; lay, ballad, ditty, carol, barcarolle, pastoral, recitative, *recitativo, solfeggio*, tonic sol-fa.

Lydian measures; slow -music, – movement; *adagio* &c. *adv.*; minuet; siren strains, soft music, lullaby; *berceuse*, cradle song, dump; dirge &c. (*lament*) 839; pibroch; martial music, march, funeral-, dead- march; dance music; waltz &c. (*dance*) 840; rag-time, syncopation, jazz.

solo, duet, *duo, trio*; quartet; quintet, sextet, septet; part song, descant, glee, madrigal, catch, round, chorus, *chorale*; antiphon, -y; accompaniment, second –, alto –, tenor –, bass- part; score, thorough bass; counterpoint.

composer &c. 413; musician &c. 416.

V. compose, perform &c. 416; attune.

Adj. musical; instrumental, orchestral, vocal, choral, lyric, operatic; harmonious &c. 413.

Adv. *adagio; largo, larghetto, andan-te, -tino; alla capella; maestoso, moderato; allegr-o, -etto; spiritoso, vivace, veloce; prest-o, -issimo; pian-o, -issimo, fort-e, -issimo, sforzando; con brio; capriccioso; scherz-o, -ando; legato, sostenuto, staccato, crescendo, diminuendo, rallentando, affettuoso, arioso; parlante, cantabile; obbligato; pizzicato, tremolo, vibrato.*

416. Musician. [Performance of Music.]—**N.** musician, *artiste, virtuoso,* performer, player, minstrel; bard &c. (*poet*) 597; instrumental-, organ-, accompan-, pian-, violin-, flaut-, harp-ist; harper, fiddler, fifer, trumpeter, piper, drummer; catgut scraper.

band, orchestra, waits.

vocal-, melod-ist; singer, warbler; songst-, chaunt-er, -ress; *diva, cantatrice,* coloratura, soprano, mezzo-soprano, alto, contralto, tenor, baritone, bass, *basso, -profondo.*

choir, quire, chorister; chorus, – singer; choral society, festival, *eisteddfod.*

nightingale, philomel, thrush; siren; Orpheus, Apollo, the Muses, Erato, Euterpe, Terpsichore; tuneful -nine, – quire.

composer &c. 413.

performance, virtuosity, execution, touch, expression, solmization.

V. play, pipe, strike –, tune- up, sweep the chords, tickle –, paw- the ivories, vamp, tweedle, fiddle; strike the lyre, beat the drum; blow –, sound –, wind- the horn; grind the organ; touch the -guitar &c. (*instruments*) 417; thrum, strum, twang, drum, beat –, keep- time, conduct.

execute, perform; accompany; sing –, play- a second; compose, write music, set to music, arrange, harmonize, orchestrate.

sing, chaunt, chant, hum, warble, carol, chirp, chirrup, lilt, purl, quaver, trill, shake, twitter, whistle; sol-fa; intone.

have -an ear for music, – a musical ear, – a correct ear, – absolute pitch.

Adj. playing &c. *v.*; musical, lyric.

Adv. *adagio, andante* &c. (*music*) 415.

417. Musical Instruments.—**N.** musical instruments; band; string-, brass-, drum and fife-, military-, bugle-, German-, dance-, jazz-band; orchestra, string quartet; orchestrion, orchestrelle.

[Stringed instruments] mono-, poly-chord; harp, lyre, lute, archlute, thearbo; mandol-a, -in, -ine; guitar; *ukulele;* psaltery, zither; bandore, cither, -n; gittern, rebeck, *bandurria,* banjo, zither banjo, *balalaika, samisen;* plectrum.

viol, -in, Cremona, Stradivarius; fiddle, kit; *vielle, viola, – d'amore, – di gamba;* tenor, *violoncello,* cello; bass, bass-, base-viol; double-bass, *contrabasso, violone,* hurdy-gurdy; strings, catgut; bow, fiddlestick.

piano, -forte; grand –, concert grand –, baby –, upright –, cottage- piano; pianino, pianette; harpsi-, clavi-, clari-, mani-chord; *clavier,* spinet, virginals; dulcimer, *cymbalo;* Eolian harp; piano-organ, -player, electric piano, player-piano, pianola.

[Wind instruments] organ, church –, pipe –, American- organ; har- moni-um, -phon; accordion, seraphina, concertina; melodeon; barrel- organ; humming top.

flute, fife, piccolo, flageolet, penny-whistle, reed instrument; clari-net, -onet; bass clarionet; saxophone; basset horn, *corno di bassetto*; musette, shawm, oboe, hautboy, *cor Anglais*, *corno Inglese*, bassoon, double bassoon, *contrafagotto*; bag-, union-pipes; ocarina, Pandean pipes; calliope; sirene, pipe, pitch-pipe; sourdet; whistle, catcall.

horn, bugle, key bugle, cornet, *cornet-à-pistons*, cornopean, clarion, trumpet, trombone, ophicleide, serpent; English-, French-, bugle-, sax-, flugel-, alt-, helicon-, post-horn; sackbut, euphonium, bombardon, tuba, bass tuba.

[Vibrating surfaces] cymbal, bell, gong, peal of bells, *carillon*; tambour, -ine; drum, tom-tom, tab-or, -ret, -ourine, -orin; *sistrum; grand caisse*, bass-, big-, side-, kettle-drum; *tympani*; war drums; tymbal, timbrel, castanet, bones; musical-glasses, -stones; harmonica, sounding-board, rattle; gramophone, phonograph.

[Vibrating bars] reed, tuning-fork, triangle, Jew's harp, musical box, harmonicon, xylophone, marimba, *celeste*.

sord-ine, -et; *sourd-ine, -et*; mute.

(iv.) PERCEPTION OF SOUND

418. [Sense of sound.] Hearing.—N. hearing &c. *v.*; audition, auscultation; eavesdropping; audibility; acoustics &c. 402.

acute –, nice –, delicate –, quick –, sharp –, correct –, musical -ear; ear for music.

ear, auricle, lug, acoustic organs, auditory apparatus, ear-drum, tympanum; ear-, speaking-trumpet, megaphone; telephone, radiophone, stethoscope, phonograph, gramophone, microphone.

hearer, auditor, listener, eavesdropper; audi-tory, -ence.

V. hear, overhear; hark, -en; list, -en; give –, lend –, bend- an ear; give attention; catch a sound, prick up one's ears; give -a hearing, – audience- to.

hang upon the lips of, be all ear, listen with both ears, monitor.

become audible; meet –, fall upon –, catch –, reach- the ear; be heard; ring in the ear &c. (*resound*) 408.

Adj. hearing &c. *v.*; auditory, auricular, aural, auditive, acoustic.

Adv. *arrectis auribus.*

Int. hark, – ye! hear! list, -en! *Oyez!* attention! lend me your ears!

419. Deafness.—N. deafness, hardness of hearing, surdity; inaudibility.

V. be -deaf &c. *adj.*; have no ear; shut –, stop –, close- one's ears; turn a deaf ear to.

render deaf, stun, deafen.

Adj. deaf, earless, surd; hard –, dull- of hearing; deaf-mute, stunned, deafened; stone deaf; deaf as -a post, – an adder, – a beetle, – a trunk-maker.

inaudible &c. 405; out of hearing.

6. *Light*

(i.) LIGHT IN GENERAL

420. Light.—N. light, ray, beam, stream, gleam, streak, pencil; sun-, moon-beam; dawn, aurora.

day; sunshine; light of -day, – heaven; sun &c. (*luminary*) 432, day-, broad day-, noontide- light; noon-tide, -day; glare.

421. Darkness.—N. darkness &c. *adj.*; blackness &c. (*dark colour*) 431; obscurity, gloom, murk; dusk &c. (*dimness*) 422; tenebrosity, umbrageousness.

Cimmerian –, Stygian –, Egyptian-darkness; night; midnight; dead of –,

glow &c. *v.*; afterglow, sunset; glimmering &c. *v.*; glint; play –, flood- of light; phosphorescence, lambent flame.

flush, halo, glory, nimbus, aureole, *aureola.*

spark, *scintilla*; *facula*; sparkling &c. *v.*; emication, scintillation, flash, blaze, coruscation, fulguration; flame &c. (*fire*) 382; lightning, *ignis fatuus*, &c. (*luminary*) 423, radio-activity.

lustre, sheen, shimmer, reflection; gloss, tinsel, spangle, brightness, brilliancy, splendour; ef-, re-fulgence; ful-gor, -gidity; dazzlement, resplendence, transplendency; luminousness &c. *adj.*; luminosity; lucidity; renitency; radi-ance, -ation; irradiation, illumination, phosphorescence, luminescence.

radiation, radiant heat, infra-red rays, visible radiation, ultra-violet –, actinic- rays, actinism; X –, Roentgen-rays; phot-, heli-ography; optical instruments &c. 445.

[Science of light] optics; photo-logy, -metry; di-, cat-optrics.

[Distribution of light] *chiaroscuro, clair-obscur*, clear obscure, breadth, light and shade, black and white, tonality, half-tone, mezzotint.

reflection, refraction, dispersion, double refraction, polarization, diffraction, interference.

illuminant &c. 423.

V. shine, glow, glitter, phosphoresce; glis-ter, -ten; twinkle, gleam; flare, – up; glare, beam, shimmer, glimmer, flicker, sparkle, scintillate, coruscate, flash, fulgurate, blaze; be -bright &c. *adj.*; reflect light, daze, dazzle, bedazzle, radiate, shoot out beams.

clear up, brighten.

lighten, enlighten; light, – up; irradiate, shine upon; give –, hang out- a light; cast –, throw –, shed- -lustre, – light- upon; illum-e, -ine, -inate; relume, strike a light; kindle &c. (*set fire to*) 384.

Adj. shining &c. *v.*; lumin-ous, -iferous; luc-id, -ent, -ulent, -ific, -iferous; illuminating, light, -some; bright, vivid, splendent, nitid, lustrous, shiny, brilliant, beamy, scintillant, radiant, lambent; sheen, -y; glossy,

witching time of- night; blind man's holiday; darkness -visible, – that can be felt; palpable, obscure; Erebus.

shade, shadow, umbra, penumbra; sciagraphy; *silhouette*; radiograph, skiagraph.

obscuration; ad-, ob-umbration; obtenebration, offuscation, caligation; extinction; eclipse, total eclipse; gathering of the clouds.

shading; distribution of shade; *chiaroscuro* &c. (*light*) 420.

noctivagation, noctograph, noctuary. obscurantist.

V. be -dark &c. *adj.*

darken, obscure, shade; dim; tone down, lower; over-cast, -shadow; cloud, eclipse; ob-, of-fuscate; ob-, ad-umbrate, cast into the shade; be-cloud, -dim, -darken; cast –, throw –, spread- a -shade, – shadow, – gloom.

extinguish; put –, blow –, snuff- out; doubt.

Adj. dark, -some, -ling; obscure, tenebrous, tenebrious, sombrous, pitch dark, pitchy; caliginous; black &c. (*in colour*) 431.

sunless, lightless &c. (*see* sun, light, &c. 423); sombre, dusky; unilluminated &c. (*see* illuminate &c. 420); nocturnal; dingy, lurid, gloomy; murk-y, -some; shady, umbrageous; overcast &c. (*dim*) 422; cloudy &c. (*opaque*) 426; darkened &c. *v.*

dark as -pitch, – a pit, – Erebus.

benighted; noctivag-ant, -ous.

Adv. in the -dark, – shade; at night.

422. Dimness.—N. dimness &c. *adj.*; darkness &c. 421; paleness &c. (*light colour*) 429.

half-light, *demi-jour*; partial -shadow, – eclipse; shadow of a shade; glimmer, -ing; nebulosity; cloud &c. 353; eclipse.

aurora, dusk, twilight, gloaming, blind man's holiday, shades of evening, crepuscule, cockshut time; break of day, daybreak, dawn.

moon-light, -beam, -shine; star-, owl's-, candle-, rush-, fire-light; farthing candle.

V. be –, grow- -dim &c. *adj.*; flicker, twinkle, glimmer; loom, lower; fade; darken; pale, – its ineffectual fire.

burnished, glassy, sunny, orient, meridian; noon-day, -tide; cloudless, clear; un-clouded, -obscured.

garish; re-, tran-splendent; re-, effulgent; ful-gid, -gent; relucent, splendid, blazing, in a blaze, ablaze, rutilant, meteoric, phosphorescent; aglow.

bright as silver; light -, bright- as -day, - noonday, - the sun at noonday.

optical, actinic; photo-genic, -graphic; heliographic, radioactive.

423. [Source of light &c.] **Luminary.** —N. luminary; light &c. 420; flame &c. (*fire*) 382.

spark, *scintilla*; phosphorescence.

sun, orb of day, day star, Phœbus, Apollo, Helios, Phaethon, Hyperion, Ra, Aurora; star, orb, meteor; falling -, shooting- star; blazing -, dog- star; Sirius, canicula, Aldebaran; morning star, Lucifer, Phosphor, evening star; Hesperus, Venus, planet, moon &c. 318; constellation, galaxy; northern light, aurora -borealis, - australis, zodiacal light; mock sun, parhelion.

lightning; fork -, sheet -, summer- lightning, St. Elmo's fire; phosphorus; *ignis fatuus*; Jack o' -, Friar's- lantern; Will o' the wisp, fire-drake, *Fata Morgana*.

glow-worm, fire-fly.

radium, luminous paint.

[Artificial light] gas; gas -, lime -, electric -, head -, search -, spot -, flash -, flood -, foot-light; lamp, oil -, gas -, arc -, incandescent- lamp; flare; lant-ern, -horn; dark lantern, bull's eye, projector; candle, *bougie*, tallow -, wax- candle; dip, farthing dip; taper, rush-light; oil &c. (*grease*) 356; wick, burner; Argand, moderator, duplex; torch, *flambeau*, link, brand; cresset; gase-, chande-, electro-lier; candelabrum, *girandole*, sconce, lustre, candle-stick.

firework, fizgig; pyrotechnics; Roman candle, Véry light, star shell, parachute light; rocket, lighthouse &c. (*signal*) 550.

V. illuminate &c. (*light*) 420.

Adj. self-luminous, incandescent; phosphor-ic, -escent; luminescent, fluorescent, radiant &c. (*light*) 420.

425. Transparency. — **N.** transparen-ce, -cy; translucen-ce, -cy; diaphaneity; luc-, pelluc-, limp-idity.

transparent medium, glass, crystal, mica; lymph, water.

V. be -transparent &c. *adj.*; transmit light.

Adj. transparent, pellucid, lucid, diaphanous; trans-, tra-lucent; limpid, clear, serene, crystalline, clear as crys-

render -dim &c. *adj.*; dim, bedim, obscure.

Adj. dim, dull, lack-lustre, dingy, darkish, shorn of its beams; dark 421.

faint, shadowed forth; glassy; bleary; cloudy; misty &c. (*opaque*) 426; muggy, fuliginous; nebul-ous, -ar; obnubilated, overcast, crepuscular, twilight, muddy, lurid, leaden, dun, dirty; looming &c. v.

pale &c. (*colourless*) 429; confused &c. (*invisible*) 447.

424. Shade.—**N.** shade; awning &c. (*cover*) 223; parasol, sunshade, umbrella; screen, curtain, shutter, blind, gauze, veil, mantle, mask; cloud, mist, gathering of clouds; smoke screen; smoked glasses, coloured spectacles; blinkers, blinders.

umbrage, glade; shadow &c. 421.

V. draw a curtain; put up -, close- a shutter; veil &c. v.; cast a shadow &c. (*darken*) 421; screen, obstruct the view.

Adj. shady, umbrageous, bowery.

426. Opacity.—**N.** opacity; opaqueness &c. *adj.*

film; cloud &c. 353.

V. be -opaque &c. *adj.*; obstruct the passage of light; ob-, of-fuscate.

Adj. opaque, impervious to light.

dim &c. 422; turbid, thick, muddy, opacous, obfuscated, fuliginous, cloudy, hazy, foggy, vaporous, nubiferous, muggy.

tal, vitreous, transpicuous, glassy, hyaline.

smoky, fumid, murky, dirty.

427. Semitransparency.—N. semitransparency, opalescence, milkiness, pearliness; gauze, muslin; film; mist &c. (*cloud*) 353; frosted glass.

Adj. semi-transparent, -pellucid, -diaphanous, -opacous, -opaque; opal-escent, -ine; pearly, milky, frosted, mat; misty.

(ii.) Specific Light

428. Colour.—N. colour, hue, tint, tinge, dye, complexion, shade, tincture, cast, livery, coloration, chromatism, glow, flush; tone, key.

pure –, positive –, primary –, primitive –, complementary- colour; three primaries; spectrum, chromatic dispersion; broken –, secondary –, tertiary-colour.

local colour, colouring, keeping, tone, value, aerial perspective.

[Science of colour] chromatics, spectrum analysis; prism, spectroscope.

pigment, colouring matter, paint, dye, wash, distemper, stain; medium; mordant; oil-paint &c. (*painting*) 556.

V. colour, dye, tinge, stain, tint, tinct, tone, paint, wash, ingrain, grain, illuminate, emblazon, imbue; paint &c. (*fine art*) 556; daub.

Adj. coloured &c. *v.*; colorific, tingent, tinctorial; chromatic, prismatic; full-, high-, deep-coloured; doubly-dyed; polychromatic.

bright, vivid, intense, deep; fresh, unfaded; rich, gorgeous; highly coloured; gay; variegated &c. 440.

gaudy, florid; garish; showy, flaunting, flashy; raw, crude; glaring, flaring; discordant, inharmonious.

mellow, harmonious, pearly, sweet, delicate, tender, refined.

429. [Absence of colour.] Achromatism.—N. achromatism; de-, discoloration; pall-or, -idity; paleness &c. *adj.*; etiolation; neutral tint, monochrome, black-and-white.

V. lose -colour &c. 428; fade, fly, go; become -colourless &c. *adj.*; turn pale, pale, whiten.

deprive of colour, decolorize, bleach, tarnish, achromatize, blanch, etiolate, wash out, tone down.

Adj. uncoloured &c. (*see* colour &c. 428); colourless, achromatic, hueless, pale, pallid; pale-, tallow-faced; faint, dull, cold, muddy, leaden, dun, wan, sallow, dead, dingy, ashy, ashen, ghastly, cadaverous, glassy, lack-lustre; discoloured &c. *v.*

light-coloured, fair, *blond*; white &c. 430.

pale as -death, – ashes, – a witch, – a ghost, – a corpse.

430. Whiteness.—N. whiteness &c. *adj.*; argent.

albification, albescence, albinism, etiolation.

snow, paper, chalk, milk, lily, ivory, silver, alabaster; white lead, chinese –, flake –, ivory –, zinc- white, white-wash, -ning, whiting.

V. be -white &c. *adj.*

render -white &c. *adj.*; whiten-bleach, blanch, etiolate, whitewash, silver, frost.

Adj. white; milky, milk-, snow-white; snowy, niveous, candid, chalky; hoar,

431. Blackness.—N. blackness &c. *adj.*; darkness &c. (*want of light*) 421; swarthness, lividity, dark colour, tone, colour; *chiaroscuro* &c. 420.

nigrification, infuscation, denigration.

jet, ink, ebony, coal, pitch, soot, smudge, charcoal, sloe, raven, crow; negro, blackamoor, man of colour, nigger, darky, Ethiopian, black.

[Pigments] lamp –, ivory –, blue-black; writing –, printing –, printer's –, Indian- ink.

V. be -black &c. *adj.*

-y; frosted, silvery; argent, -ine; canescent.

whitish, creamy, pearly, ivory, fair, *blond*, ash-blond, platinum blond; blanched &c. *v.*; high in tone, light.

white as -a sheet, – driven snow, – a lily, – silver; like -ivory &c. *n.*

render -black &c. *adj.*; blacken, infuscate, denigrate; blot, -ch; smutch; smirch; darken &c. 421.

Adj. black, sable, swarthy, sombre, dark, inky, ebon, atramentous, jetty; coal-, jet-black; fuliginous, pitchy, sooty, swart, dusky, dingy, murky, Ethiopic; low-toned, low in tone; of the deepest dye.

black as -jet &c. *n.*, – my hat, – a shoe, – a tinker's pot, – November, – thunder, – midnight; nocturnal &c. (*dark*) 421; nigrescent; gray &c. 432; obscure &c. 421.

Adv. in mourning.

432. Gray.—N. gray &c. *adj.*; neutral tint, silver, pepper and salt, *chiaroscuro*, *grisaille*, grayness.

[Pigments] Payne's gray; black &c. 431.

Adj. gray, grey; steel -, iron- gray, dun, drab, dingy, leaden, livid, sombre, sad, pearly; silver, -y, -ed; ash-en, -y; ciner-eous, -itious; grizzl-y, -ed; dove-, slate-, stone-, mouse-, ash-coloured; mole; cool.

433. Brown.—N. brown &c. *adj.*

[Pigments] bistre, ochre, sepia, Vandyke brown.

Adj. brown, adust, bay, dapple, auburn, chestnut, nutbrown, cinnamon, hazel, fawn, puce, *écru*, russet, tawny, fuscous, chocolate, maroon, foxy, tan, brunette, whitey-brown; snuff-, liver-coloured; brown as -a berry, – mahogany; reddish brown; copper-, rust- coloured; henna, bronze, khaki; russet, roan, sorrel.

sun-burnt; tanned &c. *v.*

V. render -brown &c. *adj.*; tan, embrown, bronze.

*Primitive Colours**

434. Redness.—N. red, scarlet, vermilion, cardinal, Post Office, red, carmine, crimson, pink, lake, *cerise*, cherry red, maroon, carnation, *couleur de rose*, *rose du Barry*; magenta, damask; flesh -colour; tint; colour; fresh -, high-colour; warmth; gules.

ruby, garnet, carbuncle; rose; rust, iron-mould.

[Dyes and pigments] cinnabar, cochineal; fuchsine; ruddle, madder, red-lead; Indian -, light -, Venetian- red; red ink, annotto.

redness &c. *adj.*; rub-escence, -icundity, -ification; erubescence, blush.

V. be -, become- -red &c. *adj.*; blush, flush, colour up, mantle, redden.

render -red &c. *adj.*; redden, rouge; rub-ify, -ricate; incarnadine; ruddle.

Adj. red &c. *n.*, -dish; rufous, ruddy, florid, incarnadine, sanguine, bloody, gory; ros-y, -eate; blowz-y, -ed; brunt; rubi-cund, -form;

Complementary Colours

435. Greenness.—N. green &c. *adj.*; blue and yellow; vert.

emerald, verd antique, verdigris, malachite, beryl, aquamarine, reseda.

[Pigments] *terre verte*, verditer, bice, chlorophyl.

greenness, verdure, verdancy; virid-ity, -escence.

Adj. green, verdant; glaucous, olive; porraceous; green as grass.

emerald -, pea -, grass -, apple -, sea -, olive -, bottle -, leaf- green.

greenish; vir-ent, -escent.

* The author's classification of colours has been retained, though it does not entirely accord with the theories of modern science: Complete lists of shades or pigments are beyond the scope of this work.

lurid, stammel, blood-red; russet, murrey, carroty, sorrel, lateritious.

rose-, ruby-, cherry-, claret-, wine-, plum-, flame-, flesh-, peach-, salmon-, brick-, brickdust-coloured, reddish brown &c. 433.

blushing &c. *v.*; erubescent; reddened &c. *v.*

red as -fire, – blood, – scarlet, – a turkeycock, – a lobster; warm, hot; foxy.

436. Yellowness.—N. yellow &c. *adj.*; or.

[Pigments] gamboge; cadmium –, chrome –, Indian –, lemon- yellow; orpiment, yellow ochre, Claude tint, aureolin.

crocus, saffron, topaz, gold.

jaundice; London fog; yellowness &c. *adj.*

Adj. yellow, aureate, gold, golden, gilt, gilded, flavous, citrine, fallow; fulv-ous, -id; sallow, luteous, fawny, creamy, sandy; xanth-ic, -ous; jaundiced.

gold-, citron-, saffron-, lemon-, sulphur-, amber-, straw-, primrose-, cream-coloured; flaxen, yellowish, buff.

yellow as a -quince, – guinea, – crow's foot.

437. Purple.—N. purple &c. *adj.*; blue and red, bishop's purple; aniline dyes, gridelin, amethyst; purpure.

livid-ness, -ity.

V. empurple.

Adj. purple, violet, plum-coloured, lavender, lilac, puce, *mauve*; livid.

438. Blueness.—N. blue &c. *adj.*; garter-blue; watchet.

[Pigments] ultramarine, smalt, cobalt, cyanogen; Prussian –, syenite-blue; bice, indigo, woad.

lapis lazuli, sapphire, turquoise.

blue-, bluish-ness; bloom.

Adj. blue, azure, cerulean; sky-blue, -coloured, -dyed; navy-blue, aquamarine, electric blue, royal blue, cyanic; bluish; atmospheric, retiring; cold.

439. Orange.—N. orange, red and yellow; gold; or; flame &c. colour, *adj.*

[Pigments] ochre, Mars orange, cadmium.

V. gild, warm.

Adj. orange; ochreous; orange-, gold-, flame-, copper-, brass-, apricot-coloured; warm, hot, glowing.

440. Variegation.—N. variegation; di-, tri-chroism; iridescence, irisation, play of colours, polychrome, maculation, spottiness, striæ.

spectrum, rainbow, iris, tulip, peacock, chameleon, butterfly, tortoise-shell; mackerel, – sky; zebra, leopard, mother-of-pearl, nacre, opal, marble, batik.

check, plaid, tartan, patchwork; mar-, par-quetry; mosaic, *tesseræ*, tesselation, chess-board, checkers, chequers; harlequin; Joseph's coat; tricolour; patches, bands, stripes, spots &c. of colour.

V. be -variegated &c. *adj.*; variegate, stripe, streak, checker, chequer; be-, speckle, fleck; be-, sprinkle; stipple, maculate, dot, bespot; tattoo, inlay, tesselate, damascene; embroider, braid, quilt.

Adj. variegated &c. *v.*; many-coloured, -hued; divers-, parti-coloured; di-, poly-chromatic; bi-, tri-, versi-colour; of all -the colours of the rainbow, – manner of colours; kaleidoscopic.

iridescent; opal-ine, -escent; prismatic, nacreous, pearly, shot, *gorge de pigeon, chatoyant*, irisated.

pied, piebald, skewbald; motley; mottled, marbled; pepper and salt, paned, dappled, clouded, cymophanous.

mosaic, tesselated, chequered, plaid; tortoiseshell &c. *n.*

spott-ed, -y; punctated, powdered; speckled &c. *v.*; freckled, flea-bitten, studded; fleck-ed, -ered; striated, barred, veined; brind-ed, -led; tabby; watered; grizzled; listed; embroidered &c. *v.*; dædal.

(iii.) PERCEPTIONS OF LIGHT

441. Vision.—N. vision, sight, optics, eye-sight.

view, look, espial, glance, ken, *coup d'œil*; glimpse, peep, glint; gaze, stare, leer; perlustration, contemplation; conspect-ion, -uity; regard, survey; in-, intro-spection; *reconnaissançe*, speculation, watch, espionage, *espionnage*, autopsy; ocular -inspection, – demonstration; sight-seeing.

macrography, micrography.

point of view; view-, stand-point; gazebo, loop-hole, *belvedere*, watch-tower.

field of view; theatre, amphitheatre, arena, vista, horizon; commanding –, bird's eye –, panoramic- view; periscope.

visual organ, organ of vision; eye; naked –, unassisted- eye; eye-ball, retina, pupil, iris, cornea, white; optics, orbs; saucer –, goggle –, gooseberry-eyes.

short sight &c. 443; clear –, sharp –, quick –, eagle –, piercing –, penetrating- -sight, – glance, – eye; perspicacity, discernment; catopsis.

eagle, hawk; cat, lynx; Argus.

evil eye; basilisk, cockatrice.

spectacles, telescope &c. 445.

V. see, behold, discern, perceive, have in sight, descry, sight, make out, discover, distinguish, recognize, spy, espy, ken; get –, have –, catch- a -sight, – glimpse- of; command a view of; witness, contemplate, speculate; cast –, set- the eyes on; be a -spectator &c. 444- of; look on &c. (*be present*) 186; see sights &c. (*curiosity*) 455; see at a glance &c. (*intelligence*) 498.

look, view, eye; lift up the eyes, open one's eye; look -at, – on, – upon, – over, – about one, – round; survey, scan, inspect; run the eye -over, – through; reconnoitre, glance -round, – on, – over; turn –, bend- one's looks upon; direct the eyes to, turn the eyes on, cast a glance, make eyes at.

observe &c. (*attend to*) 457; watch &c. (*care*) 459; see with one's own eyes; watch for &c. (*expect*) 507; peek, peep, peer, pry, take a peep; play at bo-peep.

look -full in the face, – hard at, – intently; strain one's eyes; fix –, rivet- the eyes upon; stare, gaze; pore over, gloat -over, – on; leer, ogle, glare; goggle; cock the eye, squint, gloat, look askance; give the glad eye.

Adj. seeing &c. *v.*; visual, ocular, -al; ophthalmic.

far-, clear-sighted &c. *n.*; eagle-, hawk-, lynx-, keen-, Argus-eyed.

visible &c. 446.

442. Blindness.—N. blindness, anopsia, cecity, excecation, *amaurosis*, cataract, ablepsy, prestriction; dim-sightedness &c. 443.

V. be -blind &c. *adj.*; not see; lose sight of; have the eyes bandaged; grope in the dark.

not look; close –, shut –, turn away –, avert- the eyes; look another way; wink &c. (*limited vision*) 443; shut the eyes –, be blind- to; wink –, blink- at.

render -blind &c. *adj.*; blind, -fold; hoodwink, dazzle; put one's eyes out; throw dust into one's eyes; *jeter de la poudre aux yeux*; screen from sight &c. (*hide*) 528.

Adj. blind; eye-, sight-, vision-less; dark; stone-, sand-, stark-blind; undiscerning; dim-sighted &c. 443.

blind as -a bat, – a buzzard, – a beetle, – a mole, – an owl; wall-eyed.

blinded &c. *v.*

Adv. blind-ly, -fold; darkly.

Adv. visibly &c. 446; in sight of, with one's eyes open.

at -sight, – first sight, – a glance, – the first blush; *primâ facie.*

Int. look! &c. (*attention*) 457.

Phr. the scales falling from one's eyes.

443. [Imperfect vision.] **Dim-sightedness.** [Fallacies of vision.]—**N.** dim –, dull –, half –, short –, near –, long –, double –, astigmatic –, failing- sight; dim &c. -sightedness; snow blindness; purblindness, lippitude; my-, presby-opia; confusion of vision; astigmatism, nystagmus; colour-blindness, dichromism, chromato-pseudo-blepsis, Daltonism; nyctalopy; *strabismus,* strabism, squint, cast in the eye, swivel eye, goggle eyes; obliquity of vision.

winking &c. *v.;* nictitation; blinkard, albino.

dizziness, swimming, scotomy; cataract; ophthalmia.

[Limitation of vision] eye shade, blinker, blinder; screen &c. (*hider*) 530.

[Fallacies of vision] *deceptio visûs*; refraction, distortion, illusion, false light, *anamorphosis,* virtual image, *spectrum, mirage,* looming, phasma; phant-asm, -asma, -om; vision; spectre, apparition, ghost; *ignis fatuus* &c. (*luminary*) 423; spectre of the Brocken; magic mirror; magic lantern &c. (*show*) 448; mirror, lens &c. (*instrument*) 445.

V. be -dim-sighted &c. *n.;* see double; have a -mote in the eye, – mist before the eyes, – film over the eyes; see through a -prism, – glass darkly; wink, blink, nictitate; squint; look ask-ant, -ance; screw up the eyes, glare, glower.

dazzle, glare, blur, swim, loom.

Adj. dim-sighted &c. *n.;* my-, presby-opic; astigmatic; moon-, mope-, blear-, goggle-, gooseberry-, one-eyed; blind of one eye, monoculous; half-, pur-, colour-blind; dichromatic.

blind as a bat &c. (*blind*) 442; winking &c. *v.*

444. Spectator.—**N.** spectator, beholder, observer, inspector, viewer, looker-on, onlooker, witness, eye-witness, bystander, passer by; sight-seer.

spy, scout; sentinel &c. (*warning*) 668.

V. witness, behold &c. (*see*) 441; look on &c. (*be present*) 186.

445. Optical Instruments.—**N.** optical instruments; lens, meniscus, magnifier, reading –, burning- glass; micro-, mega-, teino-scope; spectacles, glasses, barnacles, goggles, giglamps, eyeglass, *pince-nez,* monocle; periscopic lens; telescope, glass, lorgnette, binocular; spy-, opera-, field-glass, periscope, range finder.

mirror, reflector, speculum; looking-, pier-, cheval-, hand-glass.

prism; camera, *camera-lucida, -obscura*; projector, stereopticon, magic lantern &c. (*show*) 448; chro-, thau-matrope; stereo-, pseudo-, poly-, kaleido-scope.

photo-, opto-, erio-, actino-, luci-, radio-, spectro-meter; polari-, polemo-, spectro-scope, diffraction grating.

optics, optician, optometry, optometrist; microscop-y, -ist; photometry, photography; photographer.

446. Visibility.—**N.** visibility, perceptibility; conspicuousness, distinctness &c. *adj.;* conspicuity; appearance &c. 448; exposure; manifestation &c. 525; ocular -proof, – evidence, – demonstration; field of view &c. (*vision*) 441.

447. Invisibility.—**N.** invisibility, non-appearance, imperceptibility; indistinctness &c. *adj.;* mystery, delitescence.

concealment &c. 528; latency &c. 526.

V. be –, become- -visible &c. *adj.*; appear, emerge, open to the view; meet –, catch- the eye; present –, show –, manifest –, produce –, discover –, reveal –, expose –, betray-itself; stand -forth, – out; show; arise; peep –, peer –, crop- out; start –, spring –, show –, turn –, crop- up; glimmer, glitter, glow, loom; glare; burst forth, scintillate; burst upon the -view, – sight; heave in sight; come -in sight, – into view, – out, – forth, – forward; see the light of day; break through the clouds; make its appearance, show its face, materialize, appear to one's eyes, come upon the stage, enter; float before the eyes, speak for itself &c. (*manifest*) 525; attract the attention &c. 457; reappear; live in a glass house.

expose to view &c. 525.

Adj. visible, perceptible, perceivable, discernible, apparent; in -view, – full view, – sight; exposed to view, *en évidence*; unclouded.

obvious &c. (*manifest*) 525; plain, clear, distinct, definite; well-defined, -marked; in focus; recognizable, palpable, autoptical; glaring, staring, conspicuous; stereoscopic; in -bold, – strong, – high- relief.

periscopic, panoramic.

before –, under- one's eyes; before one, *à vue d'œil*, in one's eye, *oculis subjecta fidelibus.*

Adv. visibly &c. *adj.*; in sight of; before one's eyes &c. *adj.*; *veluti in speculum.*

V. be -invisible &c. *adj.*; be hidden &c. (*hide*) 528; lurk &c. (*lie hidden*) 526; escape notice.

render -invisible &c. *adj.*; conceal &c. 528; put out of sight.

not see &c. (*be blind*) 442; lose sight of.

Adj. invisible, imperceptible; un-, in-discernible; un-, non-apparent; out of –, not in- sight; *à perte de vue*; behind the -scenes, – curtain; view-, sight-less; in-, un-conspicuous; unseen &c. (*see* see &c. 441); covert &c. (*latent*) 526; eclipsed, under an eclipse.

dim &c. (*faint*) 422; mysterious, dark, obscure, confused; indistin-ct, -guishable; shadowy, indefinite, undefined; ill-defined, -marked; blurred, fuzzy, out of focus; misty &c. (*opaque*) 426; veiled &c. (*concealed*) 528; delitescent.

---

448. Appearance.—N. appearance, phenomenon, sight, spectacle, show, premonstration, scene, species, view, *coup d'œil*; look-out, out-look, prospect, vista, perspective, bird's-eye view, scenery, landscape, picture, *tableau*; display, exposure, *mise en scène*; scenery, *décor*; rising of the curtain.

phant-asm, -om &c. (*fallacy of vision*) 443.

pageant, *spectacle*; peep-, raree-, gallanty-show; *ombres chinoises*; projector, optical –, magic- lantern, phantasmagoria, dissolving views; cinema, -tograph; bio-scope, -graph; moving pictures, movies, film, screen &c.; pan-, di-, cosm-, ge-orama; *coup –, jeu- de théâtre*; pageantry &c. (*ostentation*) 882; insignia &c. (*indication*) 550.

aspect, phase, *phasis*, seeming; shape &c. (*form*) 240; guise, look,

449. Disappearance.—N. disappearance, evanescence, eclipse, occultation.

departure &c. 293; exit, vanishing point; dissolving views.

V. disappear, vanish, dissolve, fade, melt away, pass, go, avaunt; be -gone &c. *adj.*; leave -no trace, – 'not a rack behind'; go off the stage &c. (*depart*) 293; suffer –, undergo- an eclipse; be lost to –, retire from- -sight, – view.

lose sight of.

efface &c. 552.

Adj. disappearing &c. *v.*; evanescent; missing, lost; lost to -sight, – view; gone; *spurlos versenkt.*

Int. vanish! disappear! avaunt! &c. (*ejection*) 297.

---

complexion, colour, image, mien, air, cast, carriage, port, demeanour; presence, expression, first blush, face of the thing; point of view, light.

lineament, feature, trait, lines; out-line, -side; contour, *silhouette*, face, countenance, physiognomy, visage, phiz, mug, cast of countenance, profile, *tournure*, cut of one's jib, metoposcopy; outside &c. 220.

V. appear; be –, become- visible &c. 446; seem, look, show; present –, wear –, carry –, have –, bear –, exhibit –, take –, take on –, assume- the -appearance, – semblance- of; look like; cut a figure, figure; present to the view; show &c. (*make manifest*) 525.

Adj. apparent, seeming, ostensible; on view.

Adv. apparently; to all -seeming, – appearance; ostensibly, seemingly, as it seems, on the face of it, *primâ facie*; at the first blush, at first sight; in the eyes of; to the eye.

CLASS IV

Words relating to the INTELLECTUAL FACULTIES

CLASS IV

Words relating to the INTELLECTUAL FACULTIES

Division (I.) FORMATION OF IDEAS

Section I. Operations of Intellect in General

450. Intellect.—N. intellect, mind, understanding, reason, thinking principle; rationality; cogitative –, cognitive –, intellectual- faculties; faculties, senses, consciousness, observation, percipience, apperception, mentality, intelligence, intellection, intuition, association of ideas, instinct, flair, conception, judgment, wits, parts, capacity, intellectuality, reasoning power, brains, genius; wit &c. 498; ability &c. (*skill*) 698; wisdom &c. 498.

soul, spirit, ghost, inner man, heart, breast, bosom, *penetralia mentis, divina particula auræ,* heart's core; ego, psyche, pneuma, subconsciousness, subconscious, subliminal self; dual personality.

organ –, seat- of thought; *sensorium,* sensory, brain, gray matter; head, -piece; pate, noddle, skull, scull, *pericranium, cerebrum, cranium,* brain-pan, -box; sconce, upper story.

[Science of mind] metaphysics; psychics, psycho-logy, -metry, -genesis, -analysis, -physics, psychi-atry, -cal research, thought reading &c. 992; ideology; mental –, moral- philosophy; philosophy of the mind; pneumat-, phren-ology; no –, cranio-logy, -scopy.

ideal-ity, -ism; transcendental-, spiritual-ism; immateriality &c. 317.

metaphysician, psychologist &c.

V. note, notice, mark; take -notice, – cognizance- of; be -aware, – conscious- of; realize; appreciate; ruminate &c. (*think*) 451; fancy &c. (*imagine*) 515; conceive, reason, understand.

Adj. [Relating to intellect] intellectual, mental, rational, subjective, metaphysical, nooscopic, spiritual; ghostly; psych-ical, -ological; cerebral.

immaterial &c. 317; endowed with reason.

Adv. *in petto.*

450a. Absence or want of Intellect.— N. absence –, want- of -intellect &c. 450; imbecility &c. 499; brutality; brute -instinct, – force.

Adj. unendowed with reason.

---

451. Thought.—N. thought; excercitation –, exercise- of the intellect; reflection, cogitation, consideration, meditation, study, lucubration, speculation, deliberation, pondering; head-,

452. [Absence or want of thought.] **Incogitancy.—N.** incogitancy, vacancy, inunderstanding; inanity, fatuity &c. 499; thoughtlessness &c. (*inattention*) 458.

brain-work; cerebration; mentation, deep reflection; close study, application &c. (*attention*) 457.

abstract thought, abstraction, contemplation, musing; brown study &c. (*inattention*) 458; reverie, Platonism; depth of thought, workings of the mind, thoughts, inmost thoughts; self-counsel, -communing, -consultation.

association –, succession –, flow –, train –, current- of -thought, – ideas.

after –, mature- thought; reconsideration, second thoughts; retrospection &c. (*memory*) 505; excogitation; examination &c. (*inquiry*) 461; invention &c. (*imagination*) 515.

thoughtfulness &c. *adj.*

V. think, reflect, reason, cogitate, excogitate, consider, deliberate; bestow -thought, – consideration- upon; speculate, contemplate, meditate, ponder, muse, dream, ruminate; brood –, con- over; animadvert, study; bend –, apply- the mind &c. (*attend*) 457; digest, discuss, hammer at, weigh, perpend; realize, appreciate; fancy &c. (*imagine*) 515; trow.

take into consideration; take counsel &c. (*be advised*) 695; commune with –, bethink- oneself; collect one's thoughts; revolve –, turn over –, run over- in the mind; chew the cud –, sleep- upon; take counsel of –, advise with- one's pillow.

rack –, ransack –, crack –, beat –, cudgel- one's brains; set one's -brain, – wits- to work.

harbour –, entertain –, cherish –, nurture- an -idea &c. 453; take into one's head; bear in mind; reconsider.

occur; present –, suggest- itself; come –, get- into one's head; strike one, flit across the view, come uppermost, run in one's head; enter –, pass in –, cross –, flash on –, flash across –, float in –, fasten itself on –, be uppermost in –, occupy- the mind; have in one's mind.

make an impression; sink –, penetrate- into the mind; engross the thoughts.

Adj. thinking &c. *v.*; thoughtful, pensive, meditative, reflective, cogitative, museful, wistful, contemplative, speculative, deliberative, studious, sedate, introspective, Platonic, philosophical.

lost –, engrossed –, rapt –, absorbed- in thought &c. (*inattentive*) 458; deep musing &c. (*intent*) 457.

in the mind, under consideration, in contemplation.

Adv. all things considered; taking everything into account.

Phr. the mind being on the stretch; the -mind, – head- -turning, – running- upon.

V. not -think &c. 451; not think of; dismiss from the -mind, – thoughts &c. 451.

indulge in reverie &c. (*be inattentive*) 458.

put away thought; unbend –, relax –, divert- the mind.

Adj. vacant, unintellectual, unideal, unoccupied, unthinking, inconsiderate, thoughtless; absent &c. (*inattentive*) 458; diverted; irrational &c. 499; narrow-minded &c. 481.

un-thought of, -dreamt of, -considered; off one's mind; incogitable, not to be thought of, inconceivable.

---

453. [Object of thought.] **Idea.—N.** idea, notion, conception, thought, apprehension, impression, perception, image, sentiment, reflection, observation, consideration; abstract idea, principle; archetype.

view &c. (*opinion*) 484; theory &c.

454. [Subject of thought.] **Topic.—N.** subject of –, material for- thought; food for the mind, mental *pabulum*.

subject, -matter; matter, theme, topic, what it is about, *thesis*, text, business, affair, matter in hand, argument; motion, resolution; head, chap-

514; conceit, fancy; phantasy &c. (*imagination*) 515.

point of view &c. (*aspect*) 448; field of view.

_____

Adv. under -discussion, – consideration, – advisement; in -question, – the mind; on -foot, – the carpet, – the *tapis*; before the house, relative to &c. 9.

ter; case, point; proposition, theorem; field of inquiry; moot point, problem, &c. (*question*) 461.

V. float –, pass- in the mind &c. 451.

Adj. thought of; uppermost in the mind; *in petto*.

Section II. PRECURSORY CONDITIONS AND OPERATIONS

455. [The desire of knowledge.] **Curiosity. — N.** interest, thirst for knowledge; curi-osity, -ousness; inquiring mind; inquisitiveness.

sight-seer, quidnunc, newsmonger, Paul Pry, peeping Tom, eavesdropper; gossip &c. (*news*) 532; questioner, *enfant terrible*.

V. be -curious &c. *adj*.; take an interest in, stare, gape; prick up the ears, see sights, lionize; pry, speer; dig up.

Adj. curious, inquisitive, burning with curiosity, overcurious, nosey; inquiring &c. 461; prying; inquisitorial; agape &c. (*expectant*) 507; attentive &c. 457.

Phr. what's the matter? what next?

456. [Absence of curiosity.] **Incuriosity.—N.** incuriosity; incuriousness &c. *adj*.; *insouciance* &c. 866; indifference, apathy.

V. be -incurious &c. *adj*.; have no -curiosity &c. 455; take no interest in &c. 823; mind one's own business.

Adj. incurious, uninquisitive, uninterested, indifferent, bored; impassive &c. 823.

_____

457. Attention.—N. attention; mindfulness &c. *adj*.; intent-ness, -iveness; thought &c. 451; adverten-ce, -cy; observ-ance, -ation; consideration, reflection, perpension; heed; particularity; notice, regard &c. *v*.; circumspection &c. (*care*) 459; study, scrutiny, once-over; in-, intro-spection; revision, -al.

active –, diligent –, exclusive –, minute –, close –, intense –, deep –, profound –, abstract –, laboured –, deliberate- -thought, – attention, – application, – study.

minuteness, attention to detail &c. 459.

absorption of mind &c. (*abstraction*) 458.

indication, calling attention to &c. *v*.

V. be -attentive &c. *adj*.; attend, advert to, observe, look, see, view, remark, notice, regard, take notice, mark; give –, pay- -attention, – heed- to; listen in, incline –, lend- an ear to; trouble one's head about; give a

458. Inattention.—N. in-attention, -consideration; inconsiderateness &c. *adj*.; oversight; inadverten-ce, -cy; non-observance, disregard.

supineness &c. (*inactivity*) 683; *étourderie*; want of thought; heedlessness &c. (*neglect*) 460; *insouciance* &c. (*indifference*) 866.

abstraction; absence –, absorption-of mind; preoccupation, distraction, reverie, brown study, deep musing, fit of abstraction, woolgathering.

V. be -inattentive &c. *adj*.; overlook, disregard; pass by &c. (*neglect*) 460; not -observe &c. 457; think little of.

close –, shut- one's eyes to; wink at; pay no attention to; dismiss –, discard –, discharge- from one's -thoughts, – mind; drop the subject, think no more of; set –, turn –, put- aside; turn -away from, – one's attention from, – a deaf ear to, – one's back upon.

abstract oneself, dream, indulge in reverie.

escape -notice, – attention; come in

thought –, animadvert- to; occupy oneself with; contemplate &c. (*think of*) 451; look -at, – to, – after, – into, – over; see to; turn –, bend –, apply –, direct –, give- the -mind, – eye, – attention- to; have -an eye to, – in one's eye; bear in mind; take into -account, – consideration; keep in -sight, – view; have regard to, heed, mind, take cognizance of, be engaged in, entertain, recognize; make –, take-note of; note.

examine cursorily; glance -at, – upon, – over; cast –, pass- the eyes over; run over, turn over the leaves, dip into, perstringe; skim &c. (*neglect*) 460; take a cursory view of.

examine, – closely, – intently; scan, scrutinize, consider; give –, bend- one's mind to; overhaul, revise, pore over; inspect, review, pass under review; take stock of; fix –, rivet –, focus –, devote- the -eye, – mind, – thoughts, – attention- on *or* to; hear –, think- out; mind one's business.

revert –, hark back- to; watch &c. (*expect*) 507, (*take care of*) 459; hearken –, listen- to; prick up the ears; have –, keep- the eyes open; come to the point.

meet with attention; fall under one's -notice, – observation; be -under consideration &c. (*topic*) 454.

catch –, strike- the eye; attract notice; catch –, awaken –, wake –, invite –, solicit –, attract –, claim –, excite –, engage –, occupy –, strike –, arrest –, fix –, engross –, absorb –, rivet- the-attention, – mind, – thoughts; be -present to, – uppermost in- the mind.

bring under one's notice; point -out, – to, – at, – the finger at; lay the finger on, indigitate, indicate; direct –, call- attention to; show; put a -mark &c. (*sign*) 550- upon; call soldiers to 'attention'; bring forward &c. (*make manifest*) 525.

Adj. attentive, mindful, heedful, observant, regardful; alive –, awake- to, alert; observing &c. *v.*; taken up –, occupied- with; engaged –, engrossed –, interested –, wrapped- in; absorbed, rapt; breathless; pre-occupied &c. (*inattentive*) 458; watchful &c. (*careful*) 459; intent on, open-eyed, breathless, undistracted, upon the stretch; on the watch &c. (*expectant*) 507 steadfast.

Int. see! look, – here, – out, – alive, – you, – to it! mark! lo!

at one ear and go out at the other; forget &c. (*have no remembrance*) 506.

call off –, draw off –, call away –, divert –, distract- the -attention, – thoughts, – mind; put out of one's head; dis-concert, -compose; put out, confuse, perplex, bewilder, moider, fluster, muddle, dazzle; throw a sop to Cerberus.

Adj. inattentive; un-observant, -mindful, -heeding, -discerning; inadvertent; mind-, regard-, respect-less; listless &c. (*indifferent*) 866; blind, deaf; flighty, hand over head; cur-, percur-sory; giddy-, scatter-, hare-brained; unreflecting, écervelé, inconsiderate, off-hand, thoughtless, dizzy, muzzy, brainsick; giddy, – as a goose; wild, harum-scarum, rantipole, high-flying; heed-, care-less &c. (*neglectful*) 460.

absent, absent-minded, abstracted, *distrait*; lost; lost –, wrapped- in thought, woolgathering; rapt, in the clouds, bemused; dreaming –, musing-on other things; pre-occupied; engrossed &c. (*attentive*) 457; in a -reverie &c. *n.*; off one's guard &c. (*inexpectant*) 508; napping; dreamy.

disconcerted, put out &c. *v.*; rattled.

Adv. inattentively, inadvertently &c. *adj.*; *per incuriam, sub silentio.*

Int. stand -at ease, – easy!

Phr. the attention wanders; one's wits gone a -woolgathering, – bird's nesting; it never entered into one's head; the mind running on other things; one's thoughts being elsewhere; had it been a bear it would have bitten you.

———

behold! soho! hark, – ye! mind! halloo! observe! lo and behold! attention! *nota bene*; N.B.; *, †; I'd have you to know; notice! take notice! O yes! *Oyez!*

Phr. this is –, these are- to give notice.

459. Care. [Vigilance.]—**N.** care, solicitude, heed; heedfulness &c. *adj.*; scruple &c. (*conscientiousness*) 939.

watchfulness &c. *adj.*; vigilance, *surveillance*, eyes of Argus, watch, vigil, look out, watch and ward, *l'œil du maître.*

alertness &c. (*activity*) 682; attention &c. 457; prudence &c., circumspection &c. (*caution*) 864; forethought &c. 510; precaution &c. (*preparation*) 673; tidiness &c. (*order*) 58, (*cleanliness*) 652; accuracy &c. (*exactness*) 494; minuteness, attention to detail; meticulousness, nicety, circumstantiality.

V. be -careful &c. *adj.*; reck; take care &c. (*be cautious*) 864; pay attention to &c. 457; take care of; look –, see- -to, – after; keep -an eye, – a sharp eye- upon; keep -watch, – watch and ward; mount guard, set watch, watch; keep in -sight, – view; chaperon, play gooseberry; mind, – one's business.

look -sharp, – about one; look with one's own eyes; keep a -good, – sharp- look-out; have all one's -wits, – eyes- about one; watch for &c. (*expect*) 507; stand to; keep one's eyes –, have the eyes –, sleep with one eye- open.

take precautions &c. 673; protect &c. (*render safe*) 664.

do one's best &c. 682; mind one's Ps and Qs, speak by the card, pick one's steps.

Adj. care-, regard-, heed-ful; taking care &c. *v.*; particular; prudent &c. (*cautious*) 864; considerate; thoughtful &c. (*deliberative*) 451; provident &c. (*prepared*) 673; alert &c. (*active*) 682; sure-footed.

guarded, on one's guard; on the -*qui vive*, – alert, – watch, – look-out; awake, broad awake, vigilant; watch-, wake-, wist-ful; Argus-, lynx- eyed; wide awake &c. (*intelligent*) 498; on the watch for &c. (*expectant*) 507.

tidy &c. (*orderly*) 58, (*clean*) 652; accurate &c. (*exact*) 494; scrupulous

460. Neglect.—**N.** neglect; carelessness &c. *adj.*; trifling &c. *v.*; negligence; omission, laches, default; remissness, slackness, procrastination; supineness &c. (*inactivity*) 683; inattention &c. 458; nonchalance &c. (*insensibility*) 822; imprudence, recklessness &c. 863; slovenliness &c. (*disorder*) 59, (*dirt*) 653; improvidence &c. 674; non-completion &c. 730; inexactness &c. (*error*) 495.

paraleipsis [in rhetoric].

trifler, slacker, waster, waiter on Providence; Micawber.

V. be -negligent &c. *adj.*; take no care of &c. (take care of &c. 459); neglect; let -slip, – go; lay –, set –, cast –, put- aside; keep –, leave- out of sight; lose sight of.

overlook, disregard; pass -over, – by; let pass; blink; wink –, connive- at; gloss over; take no -note, – notice, – thought, – account- of; pay no regard to; *laisser aller*; allow to lie on the table.

scamp; trifle, fribble; do by halves; skimp; cut; slight &c. (*despise*) 930; play –, trifle- with; slur; skim, – the surface; *effleurer*; take a cursory view of &c. 457.

slur –, slip –, skip –, jump- over; pretermit, miss, skip, jump, omit, give the go-by to, push aside, throw into the background, shelve, sink; ignore, shut one's eyes to, refuse to hear, turn a deaf ear to; leave out of one's calculation; not -attend to &c. 457, – mind; not trouble -oneself, – one's head- -with, – about; forget &c. 506; be caught napping &c. (*not expect*) 508; leave a loose thread; let the grass grow under one's feet.

render -neglectful &c. *adj.*; put –, throw- off one's guard.

Adj. neglecting &c. *v.*; unmindful, negligent, neglectful; heedless, careless, thoughtless; perfunctory, remiss, slack.

inconsiderate; un-, in-circumspect;

&c. (*conscientious*) 939; *cavendo tutus* &c. (*safe*) 664.

Adv. carefully &c. *adj.*; with care, gingerly.

Phr. *quis custodiet ipsos custodes?*

---

off one's guard; un-wary, -watchful, -guarded; offhand.

supine &c. (*inactive*) 683; inattentive &c. 458; *insouciant* &c. (*indifferent*) 823; imprudent, reckless &c. 863; slovenly &c. (*disorderly*) 59, (*dirty*) 653; inexact &c. (*erroneous*) 495; improvident &c. 674.

neglected &c. *v.*; un-heeded, -cared for, -perceived, -seen, -observed, -noticed, -noted, -marked, -attended to, -thought of, -regarded, -remarked, -missed; shunted, shelved.

un-examined, -studied, -searched, -scanned, -weighed, -sifted, -explored.

abandoned; buried in a napkin, hid under a bushel.

Adv. negligently &c. *adj.*; hand over head, anyhow; in an unguarded moment &c. (*unexpectedly*) 508; *per incuriam.*

Int. never mind, no matter, let it pass; it will be all the same a hundred years hence.

---

461. Inquiry. [Subject of Inquiry. Question.]—**N.** inquiry; request &c. 765; search, research, quest; pursuit &c. 622.

examination, review, scrutiny, investigation, indagation; per-quisition, -scrutation, -vestigation; inqu-est, -isition; exploration; *exploitation,* ventilation.

sifting; calculation, analysis, dissection, resolution, induction; Baconian method.

strict -, close -, searching -, exhaustive- inquiry; narrow -, strict-search; study &c. (*consideration*) 451. *scire facias, ad referendum*; trial.

questioning &c. *v.*; interroga-tion, -tory; third degree; interpellation; chal lenge, examination, cross-examination, catechism; feeler, Socratic method, zetetic philosophy; leading question; discussion &c. (*reasoning*) 476; questionnaire, questionary.

reconnoitering, *reconnaissance*; prying &c. *v.*; espionage, *espionnage*; domiciliary visit, peep behind the curtain; lantern of Diogenes.

question, query, problem, *desideratum,* point to be solved, porism; subject -, field- of -inquiry, - controversy; point -, matter- in dispute; moot-point; issue, question at issue; bone of contention &c. (*discord*) 713; plain -, fair -, open- question; enigma &c. (*secret*) 533; knotty point &c. (*difficulty*) 704; *quod-libet*; threshold of an inquiry.

inquirer, investigator, experimenter, inquisitor, inspector, querist,

---

462. Answer.—**N.** answer, response, reply, replication, *riposte*, rejoinder, surrejoinder, rebutter, surrebutter, counter-evidence &c. 468, counter-charge, defence, plea; retort, repartee; contradiction &c. 536; rescript, -ion, antiphon, -y; acknowledgment; pass word; echo.

discovery &c. 480*a*; solution &c. (*explanation*) 522; rationale &c. (*cause*) 153; clue &c. (*indication*) 550.

Œdipus; oracle &c. 513; return &c. (*record*) 551.

V. answer, respond, reply, rebut, retort, rejoin; give -, return for- answer; acknowledge, echo.

explain &c. (*interpret*) 522; solve &c. (*unriddle*) 522; discover &c. 480*a*; fathom, hunt out &c. (*inquire*) 461; satisfy, set at rest, determine.

Adj. answering &c. *v.*; respon-sive, -dent; oracular; antiphonal; conclusive.

Adv. because &c. (*cause*) 153; on the -scent, - right scent.

Int. *eureka!*

---

examiner, catechist; scrut-ator, -ineer; analyst; quidnunc &c. (*curiosity*) 455.

V. make -inquiry &c. *n.*; inquire, seek, search, frisk, speer, look -for, – about for, – out for; scan, reconnoitre, explore, sound, rummage, ransack, pry, peer, look round; look –, go- -over, – through; spy, over-haul.

scratch the head, slap the forehead.

look –, peer –, pry- into every hole and corner; look behind the scenes; trace up; hunt –, fish –, dig –, ferret- out; unearth; leave no stone unturned.

seek a -clue, – clew; hunt, track, trail, shadow, mouse, dodge, trace; follow the -trail, – scent; pursue &c. 622; beat up one's quarters; fish for; feel for &c. (*experiment*) 463.

investigate; take up –, institute –, pursue –, follow up –, conduct –, carry on –, prosecute- -an inquiry &c. *n.*; look -at, – into; pre-examine; discuss, canvass, agitate.

examine, study, consider, calculate; dip –, dive –, delve –, go deep- into; make sure of, probe, sound, fathom; probe to the -bottom, – quick; scrutinize, analyze, anatomize, dissect, parse, resolve, sift, winnow; view –, try- in all its phases; thresh out.

bring in question, subject to examination; put to the proof &c. (*experiment*) 463; audit, tax, pass in review; take into consideration &c. (*think over*) 451; take counsel &c. 695.

ask, question, demand; put –, pop –, propose –, propound –, moot –, start –, raise –, stir –, suggest –, put forth –, ventilate –, grapple with –, go into- a question.

put to the question, interrogate, catechize, pump, grill; cross-question, -examine; dodge; require an answer; pick –, suck- the brains of; feel the pulse.

be -in question &c. *adj.*; undergo examination.

Adj. inquiry &c. *v.*; inquisitive &c. (*curious*) 455; requisit-ive, -ory; catechetical, inquisitorial, analytic; in -search, – quest- of; on the look-out for, interrogative, zetetic; all-searching.

un-determined, -tried, -decided; in -question, – dispute, – issue, – course of inquiry; under -discussion, – consideration, – investigation &c. *n.*, *sub judice*, moot, proposed; doubtful &c. (*uncertain*) 475.

Adv. what? why? wherefore? whence? whither? where? *quære?* how -comes, – happens, – is- it? what is the reason? what's -the matter, – up, – in the wind? what on earth? when? who?

463. Experiment.—N. experiment; essay &c. (*attempt*) 675; research &c. (*investigation*) 461; trial, tentative method, *tâtonnement*.

verification, probation, *experimentum crucis*, proof, criterion, diagnostic, test, tryout, crucial test, acid test.

crucible, reagent, check, touchstone, pix; assay, ordeal; ring.

empiricism, rule of thumb.

feeler; pilot -, messenger- balloon, *ballon d'essai*; pilot engine; scout; straw to show the wind.

speculation, random shot, leap in the dark.

analy-zer, -st; adventurer, explorer, sourdough, prospector; experiment-er, -ist, -alist; assayer.

V. experiment; essay &c. (*endeavour*) 675; try, assay, sample; make -an experiment, – trial of; give a trial to; put upon –, subject to- trial; experiment upon; rehearse; put –, bring –, submit- to the -test, – proof; prove, verify, test, touch, practise upon, try one's strength.

grope; feel –, grope- -for, – one's way; fumble; *tâttonner, aller à tâtons*; put –, throw- out a feeler; send up a pilot balloon; see how the -land lies, – wind blows; consult the barometer; feel the pulse; fish –, bob- for; cast –, beat- about for; angle, trawl, cast one's net, beat the bushes.

venture, try one's fortune &c. (*adventure*) 675; explore &c. (*inquire*) 461.

Adj. experimental; probat-ive, -ory, -ionary; analytic, docimastic; tentative; empirical; speculative, tentative.

under probation, on one's trial, on trial, on approval.

464. Comparison.—N. comparison, collation, contrast; identification. sim-ile, -ilitude; allegory &c. (*metaphor*) 521.

V. compare -to, – with; collate, confront; place side by side &c. (*near*) 197; set –, pit- against one another; contrast, balance.

identify, draw a parallel, parallel.

compare notes; institute a comparison; *parva componere magnis.*

Adj. comparative, relative; metaphorical &c. 521.

compared with &c. *v.*; comparable.

Adv. relatively &c. (*relation*) 9; as compared with &c. *v.*

465. Discrimination.—N. discrimination, distinction, differentiation, diagnosis, diorism; nice perception; perception –, appreciation- of difference; acuteness; estimation &c. 466; nicety, refinement; taste &c. 850; *critique*, judgement, tact; insight, discernment &c. (*intelligence*) 498; *nuances.*

V. discriminate, distinguish, differentiate, severalize; separate; draw the line, sift; separate –, winnow- the chaff from the wheat; split hairs.

estimate &c. (*measure*) 466; know -which is which, – one's stuff, – one's way about, – what is what, – 'a hawk from a handsaw.'

take into -account, – consideration; give –, allow- due weight to; weigh carefully.

Adj. discriminating &c. *v.*; dioristic, discriminative, critical, distinctive; nice.

Phr. *il y a fagots et fagots*; *rem acu tetigisti.*

465a. Indiscrimination.—N. indiscrimination; promiscuity; indistinctness, -ion; uncertainty &c. (*doubt*) 475; obtuseness.

V. not -indiscriminate &c. 465; overlook &c. (*neglect*) 460- a distinction; con-found, -fuse, jumble; swallow whole.

Adj. indiscriminate, undiscriminating, promiscuous; undistinguish-ed, -able, -ing; unmeasured.

466. Measurement.—N. measurement, admeasurement, mensuration, survey, valuation, appraisement, assessment, assize; estim-ate, -ation; dead reckoning; reckoning &c. (*numeration*) 85; gauging &c. *v.*

metrology, weights and measures, compound arithmetic.

measure, yard measure, standard, rule, foot-rule, chain, tape, staff, compass, callipers; dividers; gage, gauge, planimeter; meter, line, rod, check.

volt, kilowatt, ampere, candle power; horse power; axle load; foot pound.

flood –, high water- mark; Plimsoll mark; index &c. 550.

scale; gradu-ation, -ated scale; nonius; vernier &c. (*minuteness*) 193; pedo (*length*)- 200, sounding line &c. (*depth*) 208, thermo (*heat &c.* 389)-, baro (*air &c.* 338)-, dynamo (*power*)- 276, anemo (*wind* 349)-, gonio (*angle* 244)- meter; landmark &c. (*limit*) 233; balance &c. (*weight*) 310; optical instruments &c. 445.

co-ordinates, ordinate and abscissa, polar co-ordinates, latitude and longitude, declination and right ascension, altitude and azimuth.

geo-, stereo-, hypso-metry; metage; surveying, land surveying; geo-desy, -detics, -desia; ortho-, alti-metry; *cadastre*.

astrolabe, armillary sphere.

land, -surveyor; geometer, topographer, cartographer, hydrographer.

V. measure, meter, mete; value, assess, rate, appraise, estimate, form an estimate, set a value on; appreciate; standardize.

span, pace, step; apply the -compass &c. *n.*; gauge, plumb, probe, calliper, sound, fathom &c. 208; heave the -log, – lead; weigh &c. 319; survey.

take an average &c. 29; graduate.

Adj. measuring &c. *v.*; metric, -al; measurable; geodetical, cadastral, topographical.

Section III. Materials for Reasoning

467. Evidence [on one side.]—**N.** evidence; facts, premises, *data*, *præcognita*, grounds.

indication &c. 550; criterion &c. (*test*) 463.

testi-mony, -fication; attestation; deposition &c. (*affirmation*) 535; examination.

admission &c. (*assent*) 488; author-ity, warrant, credential, diploma, voucher, certificate, docket; record &c. 551; document, muniments; *pièce justificative*; deed, warranty &c. (*security*) 771; signature, seal &c. (*identification*) 550; exhibit, citation, reference.

witness, indicator; eye-, ear-witness; deponent; sponsor.

oral –, documentary –, hearsay –, external –, extrinsic –, internal –, intrinsic –, circumstantial –, cumula-tive –, *ex parte* –, presumptive –, collateral –, constructive- evidence; proof &c. (*demonstration*) 478; evidence in chief; finger prints, dactylogram.

secondary evidence; confirmation, corroboration, adminicle, support; rati-fication &c. (*assent*) 488; authentica-tion, verification; compurgation, wager of law, comprobation.

citation, reference.

V. be -evidence &c. *n.*; evince, show, betoken, tell of; indicate &c. (*denote*) 550; imply, involve, argue, bespeak, breathe.

have –, carry- weight; tell, speak

468. [Evidence on the other side, on the other hand.] **Counter-evidence.**— **N.** counter-evidence; evidence on the other -side, – hand; disproof; refuta-tion &c. 479; negation &c. 536; con-flicting evidence.

plea &c. 617; vindication &c. 937; counter-protest; *tu quoque* argument; other side –, reverse- of the shield.

V. countervail, oppose; run counter; rebut &c. (*refute*) 479; subvert &c. (*de-stroy*) 162; check, weaken; contravene; contradict &c. (*deny*) 536; tell another story, turn the -tables, – scale; alter the case; cut both ways; prove a negative.

audire alteram partem.

Adj. countervailing &c. *v.*; contra-dictory, in rebuttal.

un-attested, -authenticated, -sup-ported by evidence; supposititious, trumped up.

Adv. *per contra*, conversely, on the other hand.

469. Qualification.—N. qualification, limitation, modification, colouring.

allowance, grains of allowance, con-sideration, extenuating circumstances.

condition, proviso, exception; ex-emption; salvo, saving clause; discount &c. 813.

V. qualify, limit, modify, affect, temper, leaven, give a colour to, in-troduce new conditions.

allow –, make allowance- for; ad-

volumes; speak for itself &c. (*manifest*) 525.

rest –, depend- upon; repose on.

bear -witness &c. *n.*; give -evidence &c. *n.*; testify, depose, witness, vouch for; sign, seal, undersign, set one's hand and seal, sign and seal, deliver as one's act and deed, certify, attest; acknowledge &c. (*assent*) 488.

make absolute, confirm, ratify, corroborate, endorse, countersign, support, bear out, vindicate, uphold, warrant.

adduce, attest, cite, quote; refer –, appeal- to; call, – to witness; bring -forward, – into court; allege, plead; produce –, confront- witnesses; collect –, bring together –, rake up- evidence.

have –, make out- a case; establish, circumstantiate, authenticate, substantiate, verify, make good, quote chapter and verse; bring -home to, – to book.

Adj. showing &c. *v.*; evidential, indica-tive, -tory; deducible &c. 478; grounded –, founded –, based- on; first hand, authentic, verifiable; corroborative, confirmatory; significant, conclusive.

Adv. by inference; according to, witness, *a fortiori*; still -more, – less; *raison de plus*; in corroboration &c. *n.* of; *valeat quantum*; under -seal, – one's hand and seal.

mit exceptions, take into account. take exception, object.

Adj. qualifying &c. *v.*; conditional; extenuatory; exceptional &c. (*unconformable*) 83.

hypothetical &c. (*supposed*) 514; contingent &c. (*uncertain*) 475.

Adv. provided, – always; if, unless, but, yet; according as; conditionally, admitting, supposing; on the supposition of &c. (*theoretically*) 514; with the understanding, even, although, though, for all that, after all, at all events.

with grains of allowance, *cum grano salis*; *exceptis excipiendis*; wind and weather permitting; if possible &c. 470.

subject to; with this -proviso &c. *n.*

Degrees of Evidence

470. Possibility.—**N.** possibility, potentiality; what -may be, – is possible &c. *adj.*; compatibility &c. (*agreement*) 23.

practicability, feasibility; practicableness &c. *adj.*

contingency, chance &c. 156.

V. be -possible &c. *adj.*; stand a chance, have a leg to stand on; admit of, bear.

render -possible &c. *adj.*; put in the way of.

Adj. possible; on the -cards, – dice; *in posse*, within the bounds of possibility, conceivable, credible, imaginable; compatible &c. 23.

practicable, feasible, workable, performable, achievable; within -reach, – measurable distance; accessible, superable, surmountable; at-, ob-tainable; contingent &c. (*doubtful*) 475.

Adv. possibly, by possibility; perhaps, -chance, -adventure; may be, haply, mayhap.

471. Impossibility.—**N.** impossibility &c. *adj.*; what -cannot, – can never- be; sour grapes; infeasibility, impracticability, hopelessness &c. 859.

V. be -impossible &c. *adj.*; have no chance whatever.

attempt impossibilities; square the circle; discover the -philosopher's stone, – elixir of life, – secret of perpetual motion; wash a blackamoor white; skin a flint; make -a silk purse out of a sow's ear, – bricks without straw; have nothing to go upon; weave a rope of sand, build castles in the air, *prendre la lune avec les dents*, extract sunbeams from cucumbers, set the Thames on fire, milk a he-goat into a sieve, catch a weasel asleep, *rompre l'anguille au genou*, be in two places at once.

Adj. impossible; not -possible &c. 470; absurd, contrary to reason; unlikely, at variance with facts; unreasonable &c. 477; incredible &c. 485; beyond the bounds of -reason, – possi-

if possible, wind and weather permitting, God willing, *Deo volente*, D.V.

———————

impracticable, unachievable; un-, in-feasible; insuperable; un-, in-surmountable; unat-, unob-tainable; out of -reach, – the question; not to be -had, – thought of; beyond control; desperate &c. (*hopeless*) 859; incompatible &c. 24; inaccessible, uncomeatable, impassable impervious, innavigable, inextricable.

out of –, beyond- one's -power, – depth, – reach, – grasp; too much for; *ultra crepidam*.

Phr. the grapes are sour; *non possumus*; *non nostrum tantas componere lites.*

bility; from which reason recoils; visionary; inconceivable &c. (*improbable*) 473; prodigious &c. (*wonderful*) 870; un-, in-imaginable, unthinkable, not a Chinaman's chance.

472. Probability.—N. probability, likelihood; likeliness &c. *adj.*

vraisemblance, verisimilitude, plausibility; colour, semblance, show of; presumption; presumptive –, circumstantial- evidence; credibility.

reasonable –, fair –, good –, favourable- -chance, – prospect; prospect, well-grounded hope; chance &c. 156.

V. be -probable &c. *adj.*; give –, lend- colour to; point to; imply &c. (*evidence*) 467; bid fair &c. (*promise*) 511; stand fair for; stand –, run- a good chance.

presume, infer, suppose, take for granted.

think likely, dare say, flatter oneself; expect &c. 507; count upon &c. (*believe*) 484.

Adj. probable, likely, hopeful, to be expected, in a fair way.

plausible, specious, ostensible, colourable, *ben trovato*, well-founded, reasonable, credible, easy of belief, presumable, presumptive, apparent.

Adv. probably &c. *adj.*; belike; in all -probability, – likelihood; very –, most- likely; as likely as not; like enough; ten &c. to one; apparently, seemingly, according to every reasonable expectation; *primâ facie*; to all appearance &c. (*to the eye*) 448.

Phr. the -chances, – odds- are; appearances –, chances- are in favour of; there is reason to -believe, – think, – expect; I dare say; all Lombard Street to a China orange.

473. Improbability.—N. improbability, unlikelihood; unfavourable –, bad –, little –, small –, poor –, scarcely any –, no –, not a ghost of a- chance; bare possibility; long odds; incredibility &c. 485.

V. be -improbable &c. *adj.*; have a -small chance &c. *n.*

Adj. improbable, unlikely, contrary to all reasonable expectation, implausible.

rare &c. (*infrequent*) 137; unheard of, inconceivable; un-, in-imaginable; incredible &c. 485; more than doubtful.

Int. not likely! no fear!

Phr. the chances are against.

———————

474. Certainty.—N. certainty; necessity &c. 601; certitude, certainness, surety, assurance, sureness; dead –, moral- certainty; infallibleness &c. *adj.*; infallibility, reliability.

gospel, scripture, church, pope, court of final appeal; *res judicata*, *ultimatum*.

positiveness; dogmat-ism, -ist, -izer; *doctrinaire*, know-all, bigot, -ry; opin-

475. Uncertainty.—N. uncertainty, incertitude, doubt; doubtfulness &c. *adj.*; dubi-ety, -tation, -tancy, -ousness.

hesitation, suspense; perplexity, embarrassment, dilemma, quandary, Morton's fork, bewilderment; timidity &c. (*fear*) 860; indecision, vacillation &c. 605; *diaporesis*, indetermination.

vagueness &c. *adj.*; haze, fog; ob-

ionist, Sir Oracle; *ipse dixit*; zealot.

fact; positive –, matter of- fact; *fait accompli*.

V. be -certain &c. *adj.*; stand to reason.

render -certain &c. *adj.*; in-, en-, assure; clinch, make sure; determine, decide, set at rest, 'make assurance double sure'; know &c. (*believe*) 484; dismiss all doubt.

dogmatize, lay down the law.

Adj. certain, sure; assured &c. *v.*; solid, well-founded.

unqualified, absolute, positive, determinate, definite, clear, unequivocal, categorical, unmistakable, decisive, decided, ascertained.

inevitable, unavoidable, ineluctable, avoidless.

unerring, infallible; unchangeable &c. 150; to be depended on, trustworthy, reliable, bound.

un-impeachable, -deniable, -questionable; in-disputable, -contestable, -controvertible, -defeasible, -dubitable; irrefutable &c. (*proven*) 478; conclusive, without power of appeal, final.

indubious; without –, beyond a –, without a shade or shadow of- -doubt – question; past dispute; beyond all -question, – dispute; un-doubted, -contested, -questioned, -disputed; question-, doubt-less.

bigoted, fanatical, dogmatic, opinionat-ed, -ive, *doctrinaire*.

authoritative, authentic, official.

sure as -fate, – death and taxes, – a gun.

evident, self-evident, axiomatic; clear, – as day, – as the sun at noonday; obvious.

Adv. certainly &c. *adj.*; for certain, certes, sure, no doubt, doubtless, and no mistake, *flagrante delicto*, sure enough, to be sure, of course, as a matter of course, *à coup sur*, to a certainty, undoubtedly; in truth &c. (*truly*) 494; at -any rate, – all events; without fail; *coûte que coûte*; whatever may happen, if the worst come to the worst; come –, happen- what -may, – will; sink or swim; rain or shine.

Phr. *cela va sans dire*; there is -no question, – not a shadow of doubt;

scurity &c. (*darkness*) 421; ambiguity &c. (*double meaning*) 520; contingency, double contingency, possibility upon a possibility; conjecture; open question &c. (*question*) 461; *onus probandi*; blind bargain, pig in a poke, leap in the dark, something or other; needle in a bottle of hay; roving commission.

fallibility, unreliability, untrustworthiness, precariousness.

V. be -uncertain &c. *adj.*; wonder whether.

lose the -clue, – clew, – scent; miss one's way.

not know -what to make of &c. (*unintelligibility*) 519, – which way to turn, – whether one stands on one's head or one's heels; float in a sea of doubt, hesitate, flounder; lose -oneself, – one's head, – one's way, wander aimlessly; muddle one's brains.

render -uncertain &c. *adj.*; put out, pose, puzzle, perplex, embarrass; confuse, -found; bewilder, mystify, bother, moider, nonplus, addle the wits, throw off the scent; *ambiguas in vulgus spargere voces*; keep in suspense.

doubt &c. (*disbelieve*) 485; hang –, tremble- in the balance; depend.

Adj. uncertain; casual; random &c. (*aimless*) 621; changeable &c. 149.

doubtful, dubious; indecisive; un-settled, -decided, -determined; in suspense, open to discussion; controvertible; in question &c. (*inquiry*) 461; insecure, unstable.

vague; in-determinate, -definite; ambiguous, equivocal; undefin-ed, -able; confused &c. (*indistinct*) 447; mystic, mysterious, veiled, obscure, cryptic, oracular.

perplexing &c. *v.*; enigmatic, paradoxical, apocryphal, problematical, hypothetical; experimental &c. 463.

fallible, questionable, precarious, slippery, ticklish, debatable, disputable; un-reliable, -trustworthy.

contingent, – on, dependent on; subject to; dependent on circumstances; occasional; provisional.

unauth-entic, -enticated, -oritative; un-ascertained, -confirmed; undemonstrated; un-told, -counted.

in a -state of uncertainty, – cloud,

the die is cast &c. (*necessity*) 601.

———————

– fault, – a loss, – one's wit's end, – a *nonplus*; puzzled &c. *v.*; lost, abroad, *désorienté*; dis-tracted, -traught.

Adv. *pendente lite*; *sub spe rati*.

Phr. Heaven knows; who can tell? who shall decide when doctors disagree?

– maze; ignorant &c. 491; on the horns of a dilemma; afraid to say; out of one's reckoning, astray, adrift; at -sea,

Section IV. REASONING PROCESSES

476. Reasoning. — N. reasoning; ratio-cination, -nalism; dialectics, induction, generalization.

discussion, comment; ventilation; inquiry &c. 461.

argumentation, controversy, debate; polemics, wrangling; contention &c. 720; logomachy; dis-putation, -ceptation; paper war.

art of reasoning, logic.

process –, train –, chain- of reasoning; de-, in-duction; synthesis, analysis.

argument; case, plea, *plaidoyer*, opening; *lemma*, proposition, terms, premises, postulate, *data*, starting point, principle; inference &c. (*judgment*) 480.

pro-, syllogism; enthymeme, sorites, dilemma, *perilepsis*, *a priori* reasoning, *reductio ad absurdum*, horns of a dilemma, *argumentum ad hominem*, comprehensive argument.

reasoner, logician, dialectician; disputant; controver-sialist, -tist; wrangler, arguer, debater, polemic, casuist, rationalist; scientist.

logical sequence; good case; correct –, just –, sound –, valid –, cogent –, logical –, forcible –, persuasive –, persuasory –, consectary –, conclusive &c. 478 –, subtle- reasoning; force of argument; strong -point, – argument.

arguments, reasons, pros and cons.

V. reason, argue, discuss, debate, dispute, wrangle; bandy -words, – arguments; chop logic; hold –, carry on- an argument; controvert &c. (*deny*) 536; canvass; comment –, moralize-upon; consider &c. (*examine*) 461.

open a -discussion, – case; join –, be at- issue; moot; come to the point; stir –, agitate –, ventilate –, torture- a question; try conclusions; take up a -side, – case.

477. [The absence of reasoning.] **Intuition.** [False or vicious reasoning; show of reason.] **Sophistry.—N.** intuition, instinct, association; presentiment; rule of thumb.

sophistry, paralogy, perversion, casuistry, jesuitry, equivocation, evasion, mental reservation; chicane, -ry; quiddit, quiddity; mystification; special pleading; speciousness &c. *adj.*; nonsense &c. 497; word-, tongue-fence.

false –, vicious- reasoning; *petitio principii*, *ignoratio elenchi*; *post hoc ergo propter hoc*; *non sequitur*, *ignotum per ignotius*.

misjudgment &c. 481; false teaching &c. 538.

sophism, solecism, paralogism; quibble, quirk, *elenchus*, elench, fallacy, *quodlibet*, subterfuge, subtlety, quillet; inconsistency, antilogy; 'a mockery, a delusion and a snare'; claptrap, mere words; 'lame and impotent conclusion.'

meshes –, cobwebs- of sophistry; flaw in an argument; weak point, bad case.

over-refinement; hair-splitting &c. *v.*

sophist, casuist, paralogist.

V. judge -intuitively, – by intuition; hazard a proposition, talk at random.

reason -ill, – falsely &c. *adj.*; paralogize; misjudge &c. 481.

pervert, quibble; equivocate, mystify, evade, elude; gloss over, varnish; misteach &c. 538; mislead &c. (*error*) 495; cavil, refine, subtilize, split hairs; misrepresent &c. (*lie*) 544.

beg the question, reason in a circle, cut blocks with a razor, beat about the bush, play fast and loose, blow hot and cold, prove that black is white and white black, travel out of the record, *parler à tort et à travers*, put oneself out of court, not have a leg to stand on.

Adj. intuitive, instinctive, impulsive;

contend, take one's stand upon, insist, lay stress on; infer &c. 480.

follow from &c. (*demonstration*) 478.

Adj. rational; reasoning &c. *v.*; rationalistic; argumentative, controversial, dialectic, polemical; discursory, -ive; disputatious.

debatable, controvertible.

logical; in-, de-ductive; synthetic, analytic; relevant &c. 23.

Adv. for, because, hence, whence, seeing that, since, sith, then, thence, so; for -that, – this, – which- reason; for-, inasmuch as; whereas, *ex concesso*, considering, in consideration of; there-, where-fore; consequently, *ergo*, thus, accordingly; *a fortiori*.

in -conclusion, – fine; finally, after all, *au bout du compte*, on the whole, taking one thing with another.

rationally &c. *adj.*

---

478. Demonstration.—N. demonstration, proof; conclusiveness &c. *adj.*; *apodixis*, probation, comprobation.

logic of facts &c. (*evidence*) 467; *experimentum crucis* &c. (*test*) 463; argument &c. 476; irrefragability.

V. demonstrate, prove, establish, make good; show; evince &c. (*be evidence of*) 467; verify &c. 467; settle the question, reduce to demonstration, set the question at rest.

make out, – a case; prove one's point, have the best of the argument; draw a conclusion &c. (*judge*) 480.

follow, – of course; stand to reason; hold -good, – water.

Adj. demonstra-ting &c. *v.*, -tive, -ble; probative, unanswerable, conclusive; apodictic, -al; irre-sistible, -futable, -fragable, undeniable.

categorical, decisive, crucial.

demonstrated &c. *v.*; proven; un-confuted, -answered, -refuted; evident &c. 474.

deducible, consequential, consectary, inferential, following.

Adv. of course, in consequence, consequently, as a matter of course.

Phr. *probatum est*; there is nothing more to be said, Q.E.D., it must follow.

---

independent of –, anterior to- reason; gratuitous, hazarded; unconnected.

unreasonable, illogical, false, unsound, invalid; unwarranted, not following; inconsequent, -ial; inconsistent, incongruous; abson-ous, -ant; unscientific; untenable, inconclusive, incorrect; fall-acious, -ible; groundless, unproved.

deceptive, sophistical, sophisticated, casuistical, jesuitical; illus-ive, -ory; specious, hollow, plausible, *ad captandum*, evasive; irrelevant &c. 10.

weak, feeble, poor, flimsy, loose, vague, irrational; nonsensical &c. (*absurd*) 497; foolish &c. (*imbecile*) 499; frivolous, pettifogging, quibbling; fine-spun, over-refined.

at the end of one's tether, *au bout de son latin*.

Adv. intuitively &c. *adj.*; by intuition; illogically &c. *adj.*

Phr. *non constat*; that goes for nothing.

---

479. Confutation.—N. con-, re-futation; answer, complete answer; disproof, conviction, redargution, invalidation; expos-ure, -ition; clincher; retort; *reductio ad absurdum*; knock down –, *tu quoque-* argument.

V. con-, re-fute; parry, negative, disprove, redargue, expose, show the fallacy of, rebut, defeat; demolish &c. (*destroy*) 162; over-throw, -turn; scatter to the winds, explode, invalidate; silence; put –, reduce- to silence; clinch -an argument, – a question; give one a set down, stop the mouth, shut up; have, – on the hip; get the better of; confound, convince.

not leave a leg to stand on, cut the ground from under one's feet.

be confuted &c.; fail; expose –, show- one's weak point.

Adj. confut-ing, -ed &c. *v.*; capable of refutation; re-, con-futable.

condemned -on one's own showing, – out of one's own mouth.

Phr. the argument falls to the ground, *cadit quæstio*, it does not hold water, '*suo sibi gladio hunc jugulo.*'

Section V. Results of Reasoning

480. Judgment. [Conclusion.]—**N.** result, conclusion, upshot; deduction, inference, ergotism, illation; corollary, porism; moral.

estimation, valuation, appreciation, judication; di-, ad-judication; arbitrament, -ement, -ation; assessment, ponderation.

award, estimate; review, criticism, *critique*, notice, report.

decision, determination, judgment, finding, verdict, sentence, decree, − nisi, − absolute, − interlocutory; dictum; *res judicata.*

plébiscite, referendum, voice, casting vote; vote &c. (*choice*) 609; opinion &c. (*belief*) 484; good judgment &c. (*wisdom*) 498.

judge, jurist, umpire; arbi-ter, -trator; assessor, referee; censor, reviewer, critic; *connoisseur*; commentator &c. 524; inspector, inspecting officer.

V. judge, conclude; come to −, draw −, arrive at− a conclusion; ascertain, determine, make up one's mind.

deduce, derive, gather, collect, draw an inference, make a deduction, weet, ween.

form an estimate, estimate, size up, appreciate, value, count, assess, rate, rank, account; regard, consider, think of; look upon &c. (*believe*) 484.

settle; pass −, give− an opinion; decide, try, pronounce, rule; pass -judgment, − sentence; sentence, doom; find; give −, deliver− judgment; adjud-ge, -icate; arbitrate, award, report; bring in a verdict; make absolute, set a question at rest; confirm &c. (*assent*) 488.

comment, criticize; review, pass under review &c. (*examine*) 457; investigate &c. (*inquire*) 461.

hold the scales, sit in judgment; try −, hear− a cause.

Adj. judging &c. *v.*; judicious &c. (*wise*) 498; determinate, conclusive, censorious, critical &c. 932.

Adv. on the whole, all things considered.

481. Misjudgment. — N. misjudgment, obliquity of −, warped- judgment; mis-calculation, -computation, -conception &c. (*error*) 495; hasty conclusion.

prejud-gment, -ication, -ice; foregone conclusion; pre-notion, -vention, -conception, -dilection, -possession, -apprehension, -sumption, -sentiment; fixed −, preconceived- idea; *idée fixe; mentis gratissimus error;* fool's paradise.

esprit de corps, party spirit, race −, class- prejudice, partisanship, clannishness, *prestige.*

bias, warp, twist; hobby, fad, whim, craze, quirk, crotchet, partiality, infatuation, blind side, mote in the eye.

one-sided −, partial −, narrow −, confined −, superficial- -views, − ideas, − conceptions, − notions; narrow mind; bigotry &c. (*obstinacy*) 606; *odium theologicum*; pedantry; hypercriticism.

doctrinaire &c. (*positive*) 474.

V. mis-judge, -estimate, -think, -conjecture, -conceive &c. (*error*) 495; fly in the face of facts; mis-calculate, -reckon, -compute.

overestimate &c. 482; underestimate &c. 483.

pre-, fore-judge; pre-suppose, -sume, -judicate; dogmatize; have a -bias &c. *n.*; have only one idea; *jurare in verba magistri*, run away with the notion; jump −, rush- to a conclusion; look only at one side of the shield; view -with jaundiced eye, − through distorting spectacles; not see beyond one's nose; *dare pondus fumo*; get the wrong sow by the ear &c. (*blunder*) 699.

give a -bias, − twist; bias, warp, twist; pre-judice, -possess.

Adj. misjudging &c. *v.*; ill-judging, wrong-headed; prejudiced, prejudicial, &c. *v.*; jaundiced; short-sighted, purblind; partial, one-sided, superficial.

narrow-minded; confined, insular, provincial, parochial, illiberal, intolerant, narrow, besotted, infatuated, fanatical, cracked, warped, *entêté,* positive, dogmatic, dictatorial; conceited; opin-, opini-ative; opinion-ed, -ate, -ative, -ated; self-opinioned, wedded to an opinion, *opiniâtre*; bigoted &c. (*obstinate*) 606; crotchety, fussy, impracticable; unreason-able, -ing; stupid &c. 499; credulous &c. 486.

misjudged &c. *v.*

Adv. *ex parte.*

Phr. nothing like leather; the wish the father to the thought.

480a. [Result of search or inquiry.] **Discovery.—N.** discovery, invention, detection, disenchantment, disclosure, find, ascertainment, revelation.

trover &c. 775.

V. discover, find, determine, evolve; fix upon; find -, trace -, make -, hunt -, fish -, worm -, ferret -, root- out; fathom; bring -, draw- out; educe, elicit, bring to light, invent; dig -, grub -, fish- up; unearth, disinter.

solve, resolve; un-riddle, -ravel, -lock; pick -, open- the lock; find a -clue, - clew- to; interpret &c. 522; disclose &c. 529.

trace, get at; hit it, have it; lay one's -finger, - hands- upon; spot; get -, arrive- at the -truth &c. 494; put the saddle on the right horse, hit the right nail on the head.

be near the truth, burn; smoke, scent, sniff, smell a rat.

open the eyes to; see -through, - daylight, - in its true colours, - the cloven foot; detect; catch, - tripping.

pitch -, fall -, light -, hit -, stumble -, pop- upon; come across; meet -, fall in- with.

recognize, realize, verify, make certain of, identify.

Int. *eureka!*

482. Overestimation.—N. overestimation &c. *v.*; exaggeration &c. 549; vanity &c. 880; optim-, pessim-ism, -ist; megalomania.

much -cry and little wool, - ado about nothing; storm in a teacup; fine talking, rodomontade, gush, hot air, gas, bombast.

egotism &c. 880; boasting &c. 884.

V. over-estimate, -rate, -value, -prize, -weigh, -reckon, -strain, -praise; estimate too highly, attach too much importance to, make mountains of molehills, catch at straws; strain, magnify; exaggerate &c. 549; set too high a value upon; think -, make- -much, - too much- of; outreckon.

extol, - to the skies; make the -most, - best, - worst- of, eulogize, panegyrize, gush, puff, boost; make two bites of a cherry.

have too high an opinion of oneself &c. (*vanity*) 880.

Adj. overestimated &c. *v.*; oversensitive &c. (*sensibility*) 822; inflated, puffed up, exaggerated &c. 549.

Phr. all his geese are swans; *parturiunt montes.*

483. Underestimation.—N. underestimation; depreciation &c. (*detraction*) 934; pessim-ism, -ist; undervaluing &c. *v.*; modesty &c. 881.

V. under-rate, -estimate, -value, -reckon; depreciate; disparage &c. (*detract*) 934; not do justice to; mis-, dis-prize; ridicule &c. 856; slight &c. (*despise*) 930; neglect &c. 460; slur over, under-state.

make -light, - little, - nothing, - no account- of; minimize, belittle, run down, think nothing of; set -no store by, - at naught; shake off as dewdrops from the lion's mane.

Adj. depreciat-ing, -ed, -ive, -ory, &c. *v.*; un-appreciated, -valued, -prized; pejorative.

484. Belief.—N. belief; credence; credit; assurance; faith, trust, troth, confidence, presumption, sanguine expectation &c. (*hope*) 858; dependence on, reliance on.

persuasion, conviction, convincement, plerophory, self-conviction; certainty &c. 474; opinion, mind, view; conception, thinking; impression &c. (*idea*) 453; surmise &c. 514; conclusion &c. (*judgment*) 480.

tenet, dogma, principle, way of thinking; popular belief &c. (*assent*) 488.

firm -, implicit -, settled -, fixed -, rooted -, deep-rooted -, staunch -, unshaken -, steadfast -, inveterate -, calm -, sober -, dispassionate -, impartial -, well-founded- -belief, - opinion &c.; *uberrima fides*.

system of opinions, school, doctrine, articles, canons; declaration -, profession- of faith; tenets, *credenda*, creed; thirty-nine articles &c. (*orthodoxy*) 983a; catechism; assent &c. 488; *propaganda* &c. (*teaching*) 537.

credibility &c. (*probability*) 472.

V. believe, credit; give -faith, - credit, - credence- to; see, realize; assume, receive; set down -, take- for; have -, take- it; consider, esteem, presume.

count -, depend -, calculate -, pin one's faith -, reckon -, lean -, build -, rely -, rest- upon; lay one's account for; make sure of.

make oneself easy -about, - on that score; take on -trust, - credit; take for -granted, -gospel; allow -, attach- some weight to.

know, - for certain; have -, make- no doubt; doubt not; be - rest- -assured &c. *adj.*; persuade -, assure -, satisfy- oneself; make up one's mind.

give one credit for; confide -, believe -, put one's trust- in; place -, repose- implicit confidence in; take -one's word for, - at one's word; place reliance on, rely upon, swear by, regard to.

think, hold; take, - it; opine, be of opinion, conceive, trow, ween, fancy, apprehend; have -, hold -, possess -, entertain -, adopt -, imbibe -, embrace

485. Unbelief. Doubt.—N. un-, dis-, mis-belief; discredit, miscreance; infidelity &c. (*irreligion*) 989; dissent &c. 489; change of -opinion &c. 484; retraction &c. 607.

doubt &c. (*uncertainty*) 475; skepticism, misgiving, demur; dis-, mis-trust; misdoubt, suspicion, jealousy, scruple, qualm; *onus probandi*.

incredib-ility, -leness; incredulity; unbeliever &c. 487.

V. dis-believe, -credit; not -believe &c. 484; misbelieve; refuse to admit &c. (*dissent*) 489; refuse to believe &c. (*incredulity*) 487.

doubt; be -doubtful &c. (*uncertain*) 475; doubt the truth of; be -skeptical as to &c. *adj.*; diffide; dis-, mis-trust; suspect, smoke, scent, smell a rat; have -, harbour -, entertain- -doubts, - suspicions; have one's doubts.

demur, stick at, pause, hesitate, scruple, waver, stop and consider.

hang in -suspense, - doubt.

throw doubt upon, raise a question; bring -, call- in question; question, challenge, query; dispute; deny &c. 536; cavil; cause -, raise -, start -, suggest -, awake- a -doubt, - suspicion; ergotize.

startle, stagger; shake -, stagger- one's faith, - belief.

Adj. unbelieving; incredulous -, skeptical- as to; distrustful -, shy -, suspicious- of; doubting &c. *v.*

doubtful &c. (*uncertain*) 475; disputable; unworthy -, undeserving- of -belief &c. 484; questionable; sus-pect, -picious; open to -suspicion, - doubt; staggering, hard to believe, incredible, not to be believed, inconceivable.

fallible &c. (*uncertain*) 475; undemonstrable; controvertible &c. (*untrue*) 495.

Adv. *cum grano salis.*

Phr. *fronti nulla fides*; *nimium ne crede colori*; '*timeo Danaos et dona ferentes*'; *credat Judæus Apella*; let those believe who may.

–, get hold of –, hazard –, foster –, nurture –, cherish- -a belief, – an opinion &c. *n.*

view –, consider –, take –, hold –, conceive –, regard –, esteem –, deem –, look upon –, account –, set down- as; surmise &c. 514.

get –, take- it into one's head; come round to an opinion; swallow &c. (*credulity*) 486.

cause to -be believed &c. *v.*; satisfy, persuade, have the ear of, gain the confidence of, assure; con-vince, -vict, -vert; put across, sell; wean, bring round; bring –, put –, win- over; indoctrinate &c. (*teach*) 537; cram down the throat; produce –, carry- conviction; bring –, drive- home to.

go down, find credence, pass current; be -received &c. *v.*, – current &c. *adj.*; possess –, take hold of –, take possession of- the mind.

Adj. believing &c. *v.*; certain, sure, assured, positive, cocksure, satisfied, confident, unhesitating, convinced, secure.

under the impression; impressed –, imbued –, penetrated- with.

confiding, trustful, suspectless; unsusp-ecting, -icious; void of suspicion; credulous &c. 486; wedded to.

believed &c. *v.*; accredited, putative; unsuspected.

worthy of –, deserving of –, commanding- -belief, – confidence; credible, reliable, trusted, trustworthy, to be depended on, undoubted; satisfactory; probable &c. 472; fiduci-al, -ary; persuasive, impressive.

relating to belief, doctrinal.

Adv. in the -opinion, – eyes- of; *me judice*; me-seems, -thinks; to the best of one's belief; I -dare say, – doubt not, – have no doubt, – am sure; in my opinion; sure enough &c. (*certainty*) 474; depend –, rely- upon it; be –, rest- assured; I'll warrant you &c. (*affirmation*) 535.

---

486. Credulity.—N. credul-ity, -ousness &c. *adj.*; gull-, cull-ibility; gross credulity, infatuation; self-delusion, -deception; blind reasoning; superstition; one's blind side; bigotry &c. (*obstinacy*) 606; hyper-orthodoxy &c. 984; misjudgment &c. 481.

credulous person &c. (*dupe*) 547.

V. be -credulous &c. *adj.*; *jurare in verba magistri*; follow implicitly; swallow, – whole, gulp down; take on trust; take for -granted, – gospel; run away with -a notion, – an idea; jump –, rush- to a conclusion; think the moon is made of green cheese; take –, grasp- the shadow for the substance; catch at straws.

impose upon &c. (*deceive*) 545.

Adj. credulous, gullible; easily -deceived &c. 545; simple, green, soft, childish, silly, stupid; over-credulous, -confident; infatuated, superstitious; confiding &c. (*believing*) 484.

Phr. the wish the father to the thought; *credo quia impossibile.*

487. Incredulity.—N. incredul-ousness, -ity; skepticism, pyrrhonism; want of faith &c. (*irreligion*) 989.

suspiciousness &c. *adj.*; scrupulosity; suspicion &c. (*unbelief*) 485; dissent &c. 489.

unbeliever, skeptic, aporetic; atheist, agnostic, infidel, disbeliever, misbeliever, pyrrhonist &c. 989; heretic &c. (*heterodox*) 984.

V. be -incredulous &c. *adj.*; distrust &c. (*disbelieve*) 485; refuse to believe; shut one's -eyes, – ears- to; turn a deaf ear to; hold aloof; ignore; *nullis jurare in verba magistri.*

Adj. incredulous, skeptical, unbelieving, inconvincible; hard –, shy- of belief; suspicious, scrupulous, distrustful, heterodox &c. 984.

488. Assent.—N. assent, -ment; acquiescence, admission; nod; ac-, con-cord, -cordance; agreement &c. 23; affirm-ance, -ation; recognition, acknowledgment, avowal; confession, – of faith.

unanimity, common consent, *consensus*, acclamation, chorus, *vox populi*; popular –, current- -belief, – opinion; public opinion; concurrence &c. (*of causes*) 178; co-operation &c. (*voluntary*) 709.

ratification, confirmation, corroboration, approval, acceptance, *visa*; indorsement &c. (*record*) 551.

consent &c. (*compliance*) 762.

affirmant, consenter, covenantor, subscriber, endorser, upholder.

V. assent; give –, yield –, nod- assent; acquiesce; agree &c. 23; receive, accept, accede, accord, concur, lend oneself to, consent, coincide, reciprocate, go with; be -at one with &c. *adj.*; go along –, chime in –, strike in –, close- with; echo, enter into one's views, agree in opinion; vote –, give one's voice- for; recognize; subscribe –, conform –, defer- to; say -yes, – ditto, – amen, – aye- to.

acknowledge, own, admit, allow, avow, confess; concede &c. (*yield*) 762; come round to; abide by; permit &c. 760.

come to –, arrive at- -an understanding, – terms, – an agreement.

con-, af-firm; ratify, approve, endorse, countersign; visa; corroborate &c. 467.

go –, swim- with the stream, float with the current; be in the fashion, join in the chorus; be in every mouth.

Adj. assenting &c. *v.*; of one -accord, – mind; of the same mind, at one with, agreed, acquiescent, content; willing &c. 602.

un-contradicted, -challenged, -questioned, -controverted.

carried –, agreed- -*nem. con.* &c. *adv.*; unanimous; agreed on all hands, carried by acclamation.

affirmative &c. 535.

Adv. yes, yea, ay, aye, true; good; well; very -well, – true; well and good; just- so; to be sure, surely, 'thou hast said'; truly, exactly, precisely,

489. Dissent.—N. dissent; discordance &c. (*disagreement*) 24; difference –, diversity- of opinion.

non-conformity &c. (*heterodoxy*) 984; protestantism, recusancy, schism; disaffection; secession &c. 624; recantation &c. 607.

dissension &c. (*discord*) 713; discontent &c. 832; cavilling.

protest; contradiction &c. (*denial*) 536; non-compliance &c. (*rejection*) 764; disapprobation &c. 932; hartal.

dissent-ient, -er; non-juror, -content; recusant, sectary, schismatic, protestant, non-conformist, separatist, non-co-operator, conscientious objector, passive resister.

V. dissent, demur; call in question &c. (*doubt*) 485; differ in opinion, disagree; say -no &c. 536; refuse -assent, – to admit; cavil, protest, raise one's voice against, make bold to differ; repudiate; contradict &c. (*deny*) 536; agree to differ.

have no notion of, differ *toto cœlo*; revolt -at, – from the idea.

shake the head, shrug the shoulders; look -askance, – askant.

secede; recant &c. 607.

Adj. dissenting &c. *v.*; negative &c. 536; diss-ident, -entient; unconsenting &c. (*refusing*) 764; non-content, -juring; protestant, recusant; uncon-vinced, -verted.

unavowed, unacknowledged; out of the question.

discontented &c. 832; unwilling &c. 603; extorted.

sectarian, denominational, schismatic, heterodox, intolerant.

Adv. no &c. 536; at -variance, – issue- with; under protest; *non placet.*

Int. God forbid! not for the world; not on your life; I beg to differ; I'll be hanged if; never tell me; your humble servant, pardon me; tell that to the marines.

Phr. many men many minds; *quot homines tot sententiæ*; *tant s'en faut*; *il s'en faut bien.*

granted; *placet*; even –,

that's just it, indeed, certainly, certes, *ex concesso*; of course, unquestionably, assuredly, no doubt, doubtless, undoubtedly.

be it so; so -be it, – let it be, so mote it be; amen; with all my heart; willingly &c. 602.

affirmatively, in the affirmative.

with one -consent, – voice, – accord; unanimously, *und voce*, by common consent, in chorus, to a man, *nem. con.*; *nemine -contradicente, – dissentiente*; without a dissentient voice; as one man, one and all, on all hands.

---

490. Knowledge.—N. knowledge; cogn-izance, -ition, -oscence; acquaintance, experience, ken, privity, insight, familiarity; com-, ap-prehension; recognition; appreciation &c. (*judgment*) 480; intuition; consci-ence, -ousness; perception, precognition; acroamatics.

light, enlightenment; glimpse, inkling; side light; glimmer, -ing; dawn; scent, suspicion; impression &c. (*idea*) 453; discovery &c. 480a.

system –, body- of knowledge; science, philosophy, pansophy; theory, Etiology; circle of the sciences; pandect, doctrine, body of doctrine; cy-, ency-clopædia; school &c. (*system of opinions*) 484.

tree of knowledge; republic of letters &c. (*language*) 560.

erudition, learning, lore, scholarship, reading, letters; literature; book-learning, bookishness; biblio-mania, -latry; information, general information; store of -knowledge &c.; education &c. (*teaching*) 537; culture, attainments; acqui-rements, -sitions; accomplishments, proficiency; practical knowledge &c. (*skill*) 698; higher education, liberal education; dilettantism; rudiments &c. (*beginning*) 66.

deep –, profound –, solid –, accurate –, acroatic –, acroamatic –, vast –, extensive –, encyclopædical- -knowledge, – learning; omniscience, pantology.

march of intellect; progress –, advance- of -science, – learning; schoolmaster abroad.

V. know, ken, scan, wot; wot –, be aware &c. *adj.*- of; ween, weet, trow, have, possess.

conceive; ap-, com-prehend; take, realize, understand, appreciate; fathom, make out; recognize, discern, perceive, see, get a sight of, experience.

491. Ignorance. — N. ignorance, nescience, *tabula rasa*, crass ignorance, *ignorance crasse*; unacquaintance; unconsciousness &c. *adj.*; dark-, blindness; incomprehension, inexperience, simplicity.

unknown quantities, x, y, z.

sealed book, *terra incognita*, virgin soil, unexplored ground; dark ages.

[Imperfect knowledge] smattering, superficiality, half-learning, sciolism, glimmering; bewilderment &c. (*uncertainty*) 475; incapacity.

[Affectation of knowledge] pedantry; charlatan-ry, -ism.

V. be -ignorant &c. *adj.*; not -know &c. 490; know -not, – not what, – nothing of; have no -idea, – notion, – conception; not have the remotest idea; not know chalk from cheese.

ignore, be blind to; keep in ignorance &c. (*conceal*) 528.

see through a glass darkly; have a -film over the eyes, – glimmering &c. *n.*; wonder whether; not know what to make of &c. (*unintelligibility*) 519; not pretend –, not take upon oneself- to say.

Adj. ignorant, nescient; un-knowing, -aware, -acquainted, -apprized, -witting, -weeting, -conscious; wit-, weetless; a stranger to; unconversant.

un-informed, -cultivated, -versed, -instructed, -taught, -initiated, -tutored, -schooled, -guided, -enlightened; Philistine; behind the age.

shallow, superficial, green, rude, empty, half-learned, illiterate; un-read, -informed, -educated, -learned, -lettered, -bookish; empty-headed; lowbrow; pedantic.

in the dark; be-nighted, -lated; blind-ed, -fold; hoodwinked; misinformed; *au bout de son latin*, at the

know full well; have –, possess- some knowledge of; be -*au courant* &c. *adj.*; have -in one's head, – at one's fingers' ends; know by -heart, – rote; be master of; *connaître le dessous des cartes*, know what's what &c. 698.

see one's way; learn, discover &c. 480*a*.

come to one's knowledge &c. (*information*) 527.

Adj. knowing &c. *v.*; cognitive; acroamatic.

aware –, cognizant –, conscious- of; acquainted –, made acquainted- with; privy –, no stranger- to; *au -fait, – courant*; in the secret; up –, alive- ᵗo; sensible of; behind the -scenes, – curtain; let into; apprized –, informed- of; undeceived.

proficient –, versed –, read –, forward –, strong –, at home- in; conversant –, familiar- with.

erudite, instructed, learned, lettered, educated; high-brow; well-conned, -informed, -read, -grounded, -educated; enlightened, shrewd, insightful, *savant*, blue, bookish, scholastic, solid, profound, deep-read, book-learned; accomplished &c. (*skilful*) 698; omniscient; self-taught, -educated.

known &c. *v.*; ascertained, well-known, recognized, received, notorious, noted; proverbial; familiar, – as household words, to every schoolboy; hackneyed, trite, commonplace.

knowable, cogn-oscible, -izable.

Adv. to –, to the best of- one's knowledge.

Phr. one's eyes being opened &c. (*disclosure*) 529.

end of his tether; at fault; at sea &c. (*uncertain*) 475; caught tripping.

un-known, -apprehended, -explained, -ascertained, -investigated, -explored, -heard of, -perceived; concealed &c. 528; novel.

Adv. ignorantly &c. *adj.*; unawares; for -anything, – aught- one knows; not that one knows.

Int. God –, Heaven –, the Lord –, nobody- knows.

Phr. a little learning is a dangerous thing.

---

492. Scholar—N. scholar, *connoisseur*, *savant*, pundit, schoolman, professor, graduate, wrangler, moonshee; academ-ician, -ist; fellow, don, post graduate, advanced student; master –, bachelor- of arts; doctor, licentiate, gownsman; philo-sopher, -math; scientist, clerk; soph, -ist, -ister; linguist, classicist; glosso-, etymo-, philologist; philologer; lexico-, glosso-grapher; scholiast, commentator, annotator, grammarian; *littérateur, literati, dilettanti, illuminati*; Mezzofanti, admirable Crichton, Mæcenas.

book-worm, *helluo librorum*, biblio-phile, -maniac; blue-stocking, *bas-bleu*; big-wig, learned Theban.

learned –, literary- man; *homo multarum literarum*; man of -learning, – letters, – education; high-brow, intelligentsia.

antiquar-ian, -y; archæologist; sage &c. (*wise man*) 500.

pedant, *doctrinaire*; pedagogue, Dr. Pangloss; pantologist.

teacher &c. 540; schoolboy &c. (*learner*) 541.

Adj. learned &c. 490; brought up at the feet of Gamaliel.

493. Ignoramus.—N. ignoramus, illiterate, moron, dunce, numskull; wooden spoon; no scholar.

sciolist, smatterer, dabbler, half-scholar; *charlatan*; wiseacre.

novice, griffin; greenhorn &c. (*dupe*) 547; tyro &c. (*learner*) 541.

lubber &c. (*bungler*) 701; fool &c. 501; pedant &c. 492.

Adj. bookless, shallow, simple, dense, dumb, thick, dull, ignorant &c. 491.

---

494. [Object of knowledge.] **Truth.**
—**N.** fact, reality &c. (*existence*) 1;
plain matter of fact; nature &c. (*principle*) 5; truth, verity; gospel; orthodoxy &c. 983a; authenticity; veracity
&c. 543.

accuracy, exactitude; exact-, precise-ness &c. *adj.*; precision, delicacy;
rigour, mathematical precision, punctuality; clockwork precision &c. (*regularity*) 80.

orthology; *ipsissima verba*; letter of
the law, realism.

plain -, honest -, sober -, naked -,
unalloyed -, unqualified -, stern -,
exact -, intrinsic- truth; *nuda veritas*;
the very thing; not an -illusion &c.
495; real Simon Pure; unvarnished
tale; the truth, the whole truth and
nothing but the truth; just the thing.

V. be -true &c. *adj.*, – the case; stand
the test; have the true ring; hold
-good, – true, – water; conform to rule.

render -, prove- -true &c. *adj.*; substantiate &c. (*evidence*) 467.

get at the truth &c. (*discover*) 480a.

Adj. real, actual &c. (*existing*) 1;
veritable, true; certain &c. 474; substantially -, categorically- true &c.;
true -to the letter, – to life, – to scale,
– the facts, – as gospel; unimpeachable;
veracious &c. 543; unre-, uncon-futed;
un-ideal, -imagined; realistic.

exact, accurate, definite, precise, well
defined, just, right, correct, strict,
severe; close &c. (*similar*) 17; literal;
rigid, rigorous; scrupulous &c. (*conscientious*) 939; religiously exact, punctual, mathematical, scientific; faithful,
constant, unerring; curious, particular,
punctilious, meticulous, nice, delicate,
fine.

genuine, authentic, legitimate, pukka; orthodox &c. 983a; official, *ex
officio*.

pure, natural, sound, sterling; unsophisticated, -adulterated, -varnished,
-coloured; in its true colours.

well-grounded, -founded; solid, substantial, tangible, valid; undis-torted,
-guised; un-affected, -exaggerated, -romantic, -flattering.

Adv. truly &c. *adj.*; verily, indeed,
in reality; as a matter of fact; beyond

495. Error.—**N.** error, fallacy; misconception, -apprehension, -understanding; inexactness &c. *adj.*; laxity;
misconstruction &c. (*misinterpretation*)
523; miscomputation &c. (*misjudgment*) 481; *non-sequitur* &c. 477; misstatement, -report; anachronism; malapropism.

mistake; miss, fault, blunder, boner,
bloomer, howler, *quid pro quo*, cross
purposes, oversight, misprint, *erratum,
corrigendum*, slip, blot, flaw, loose
thread; trip, stumble &c. (*failure*) 732;
botchery &c. (*want of skill*) 699; slip
of the -tongue, – pen; *lapsus -linguæ,
– calami*, clerical error; bull &c. (*absurdity*) 497.

il-, de-lusion; false -impression, –
idea; bubble; self-deceit, -deception;
warped notion; mists of error; superstition, exploded notion.

heresy &c. (*heterodoxy*) 984; hallucination &c. (*insanity*) 503; false light
&c. (*fallacy of vision*) 443; dream &c.
(*fancy*) 515; fable &c. (*untruth*) 546;
bias &c. (*misjudgment*) 481; misleading
&c. *v.*

V. be -erroneous &c. *adj.*

cause error; mis-lead, -guide; lead
-astray, – into error; beguile, misinform &c. (*misteach*) 538; delude; give
a false -impression, – idea; falsify,
garble, misstate; deceive &c. 545; lie
&c. 544.

err; be -in error &c. *adj.*, – mistaken
&c. *v.*; be deceived &c. (*duped*) 547;
mistake, receive a false impression, deceive oneself; fall into -, lie under -,
labour under- -an error &c. *n.*; be in
the wrong, blunder; mis-apprehend,
-conceive, -understand, -reckon, -count,
-calculate &c. (*misjudge*) 481.

play -, be- at cross purposes &c.
(*misinterpret*) 523.

trip, stumble; lose oneself &c. (*uncertainty*) 475; go astray; fail &c. 732;
take the wrong sow by the ear &c.
(*mismanage*) 699; put the saddle on
the wrong horse; reckon without one's
host; take the shadow for the substance &c. (*credulity*) 486; dream &c.
(*imagine*) 515.

Adj. erroneous, untrue, false, devoid
of truth, fallacious, faulty, apocryphal,

-doubt, – question; with truth &c. (*veracity*) 543; certainly &c. (*certain*) 474; actually &c. (*existence*) 1; in effect &c. (*intrinsically*) 5.

exactly &c. *adj.*; *ad amussim*; *verbatim*, – *et literatim*; word for word, literally, *literatim, totidem verbis, sic*, to the letter, chapter and verse, *ipsissimis verbis*; *ad unguem*; to an inch; to a -nicety, – hair, – tittle, – turn, – T; *au pied de la lettre*; neither more nor less; in -every respect, – all respects; *sous tous les rapports*; at -any rate, – all events; strictly speaking.

Phr. the -truth, – fact- is; *rem acu tetigisti*.

---

scent; in the wrong box; at cross purposes, all in the wrong, all abroad, at sea.

Adv. more or less.

496. Maxim.—N. maxim, aphorism; apo-, apoph-thegm; *dictum*, saying, gnome, adage, saw, proverb, epigram; sentence, *mot*, motto, word, by-word, precept, moral, phylactery, *protasis*, brocard.

axiom, postulate, theorem, *scholium*, truism.

reflection &c. (*idea*) 453; conclusion &c. (*judgment*) 480; golden rule &c. (*precept*) 697; principle, *principia*; profession of faith &c. (*belief*) 484; formula.

wise –, sage –, received –, admitted –, recognized- maxim &c.; true –, common –, hackneyed –, trite –, commonplace- saying &c.

Adj. aphoristic, proverbial, phylacteric; axiomatic, gnomic.

Adv. as -the saying is, – they say.

---

unreal, ungrounded, groundless; unsubstantial &c. 4; heretical &c. (*heterodox*) 984; unsound; illogical &c. 477; wrong.

in-, un-exact; in-accurate, -correct; indefinite &c. (*uncertain*) 475.

illus-ive, -ory; delusive; mock; ideal &c. (*imaginary*) 515; spurious &c. 545; deceitful &c. 544; perverted.

controvertible, unsustain-able, -ed; unauthenticated, untrustworthy.

exploded, refuted, discarded.

in –, under an- error &c. *n.*; mistaken &c. *v.*; tripping &c. *v.*; out, – in one's reckoning; aberrant; beside –, wide of the- -mark, – truth; astray &c. (*at fault*) 475; on -a false, – the wrong- scent; in the wrong box; at cross purposes, all in the wrong, all abroad, at sea.

497. Absurdity.—N. absurd-ity, -ness &c. *adj.*; imbecility &c. 499; alogy, nonsense, paradox, inconsistency; stultiloqu-y, -ence, futility.

blunder, muddle, bull; Irish-, Hibernic-ism; slip-slop; anticlimax, bathos; sophism &c. 477.

farce, burlesque, *galimatias, amphigouri*, rhapsody; farrago &c. (*disorder*) 59; extravagance, romance; sciomachy.

joke, catch, sell, pun, verbal quibble, macaronic.

jargon, fustian, twaddle &c. (*no meaning*) 517; exaggeration &c. 549; moonshine, stuff; mare's nest.

vagary, tomfoolery, mummery, monkey- trick, practical joke, *boutade, escapade*.

V. play the fool &c. 499; stultify, blunder, muddle; joke; talk nonsense, *parler à tort et à travers*; *battre la campagne*; be -absurd &c. *adj.*

Adj. absurd, nonsensical, preposterous, egregious, senseless, farcical, inconsistent, ridiculous, extravagant, quibbling, futile; macaronic, punning, paradoxical.

foolish &c. 499; sophistical &c. 477; unmeaning &c. 517; without rhyme or reason; fantastic.

Int. fiddle-de-dee! pish! pish and tush! pho! stuff and nonsense! rubbish! rot! bosh! in the name of the Prophet—figs!

Phr. *credat Judæus Apella*; tell it to the marines.

Faculties

498. Intelligence. Wisdom.—N. intelligence, capacity, comprehension,

499. Imbecility. Folly.—N. want of -intelligence &c. 498, – intellect &c.

understanding; intellect &c. 450; nous, parts, sagacity, mother wit, wit, *esprit*, gumption, quick parts, grasp of intellect; acuteness &c. *adj.*; acumen, subtlety, penetration; perspica-cy, -city; discernment, long-headedness, due sense of, good judgment; discrimination &c. 465; craftiness, cunning &c. 702; refinement &c. (*taste*) 850.

head, brains, gray matter, head-piece, upper story, long head; eagle -eye, – glance; eye of a -lynx, – hawk.

wisdom, sapience, sense; good –, common –, plain –, horse- sense; clear thinking; rationality, reason; reasonableness &c. *adj.*; judgment; solidity, depth, profundity, calibre; enlarged views; reach –, compass- of thought; enlargement of mind.

genius, inspiration, *geist*, fire of genius, heaven-born genius, soul; talent &c. (*aptitude*) 698.

[Wisdom in action] prudence &c. 864; vigilance &c. 459; tact &c. 698; foresight &c. 510; sobriety, self-possession, *aplomb*, ballast, mental -poise, – balance.

a bright thought, inspiration, brain-wave, not a bad idea.

V. be -intelligent &c. *adj.*; have all one's wits about one; understand &c. (*intelligible*) 518; catch –, take in- an idea; take a -joke, – hint.

see -through, – at a glance, – with half an eye, – far into, – through a millstone; penetrate; discern &c. (*descry*) 441; foresee &c. 510.

discriminate &c. 465; know what's what &c. 698; listen to reason.

Adj. [Applied to persons] intelligent, quick of apprehension, keen, acute, alive, brainy, awake, bright, quick, sharp; quick-, keen-, clear-, sharp- -eyed, -sighted, -witted; wide awake; canny, shrewd, astute; clear-headed; far-sighted &c. 510; discerning, perspicacious, penetrating, piercing; argute; nimble-, needle-witted; sharp as a needle; alive to &c. (*cognizant*) 490; clever &c. (*apt*) 698; arch &c. (*cunning*) 702; *pas si bête*; acute &c. 682.

wise, sage, sapient, sagacious, reasonable, rational, sound, in one's right

450; shallow-, silli-, foolish-ness &c. *adj.*; imbecility, incapacity, vacancy of mind, poverty of intellect, clouded perception, poor head, apartments to let; stup-, stol-idity; hebetude, dull understanding, meanest capacity; short-sightedness; incompetence &c. (*unskilfulness*) 699.

one's weak side; bias &c. 481; infatuation &c. (*insanity*) 503.

simplicity, puerility, babyhood; dotage, anility, second childishness, senile dementia, fatuity; idio-cy, -tism; drivelling.

folly, frivolity, desipience, irrationality, trifling, ineptitude, nugacity, inconsistency, lip-wisdom, conceit; sophistry &c. 477; giddiness &c. (*inattention*) 458; eccentricity &c. 503; extravagance &c. (*absurdity*) 497; rashness &c. 863.

act of folly &c. 699.

V. be -imbecile &c. *adj.*; have no -brains, – sense &c. 498.

trifle, drivel, *radoter*, dote; ramble &c. (*madness*) 503; play the -fool, – monkey, – goat, take leave of one's senses; not see an inch beyond one's nose; stultify oneself &c. 699; talk nonsense &c. 497.

Adj. [Applied to persons] un-intelligent, -intellectual, -reasoning; mind-, wit-, reason-, brain-less; having no -head &c. 498; not -bright &c. 498; inapprehensible.

weak-, addle-, puzzle-, blunder-, muddle-, muddy-, pig-, beetle-, maggoty-, gross-headed; beef-, fat- -witted, -headed.

weak-, feeble-minded; dull-, shallow-, rattle-, lack-brained; half-, nit-, short-, dull-, blunt-witted; shallow-, clod-, addle-pated; dim-, short-sighted; thick-skulled; weak in the upper story.

shallow, *borné*, weak, wanting, soft, nutty, sappy, spoony; dull, – as a beetle; stupid, heavy, insulse, obtuse, blunt, stolid, doltish, asinine; inapt &c. 699; prosaic &c. 843.

child-ish, -like; infant-ine, -ile; baby-, bab-ish; puerile, anile; simple &c. (*credulous*) 486.

fatuous, idiotic, imbecile, moronic,

mind, sensible, *abnormis sapiens*, judicious, strong-minded.

un-prejudiced, -biassed, -bigoted, -prepossessed; un-dazzled, -perplexed; of unwarped judgment, impartial, equitable, fair, broad-minded.

cool; cool-, long-, hard-, strong-headed; long-sighted, calculating, thoughtful, reflecting; solid, deep, profound.

oracular; heaven-directed, -born.

prudent &c. (*cautious*) 864; sober, staid, solid; considerate, politic, wise in one's generation; watchful &c. 459; provident &c. (*prepared*) 673; in advance of one's age; wise as -a serpent, – Solomon, – Solon.

[Applied to actions] wise, sensible, reasonable, judicious; well-judged, -advised; prudent, politic; expedient &c. 646.

---

500. Sage.—N. sage, wise man; pundit; master -mind, – spirit of the age; longhead, thinker, philosopher.

authority, oracle, mentor, luminary, shining light, *esprit fort*, *magnus Apollo*, Solon, Solomon, Nestor, Magi, 'second Daniel.'

man of learning &c. 492; expert &c. 700; wizard &c. 994.

[Ironically] wiseacre, bigwig.

Adj. wise, learned; authoritative, oracular; erudite &c. 490; venerable, reverenced, revered, *emeritus*.

---

502. Sanity.—N. sanity; soundness &c. *adj.*; rationality, normality, sobriety, lucidity, lucid interval; senses, sober senses, sound mind, *mens sana*.

drivelling; blatant, babbling; vacant; sottish; bewildered &c. 475.

blockish, unteachable; Bœot-ian, -ic; bovine; un-gifted, -discerning, -enlightened, -wise, -philosophical; apish.

foolish, silly, senseless, irrational, insensate, nonsensical, inept; maudlin.

narrow-minded &c. 481; bigoted &c. (*obstinate*) 606; giddy &c. (*thoughtless*) 458; rash &c. 863; eccentric &c. (*crazed*) 503.

[Applied to actions] foolish, unwise, indiscreet, injudicious, improper, unreasonable, without reason, ridiculous, silly, stupid, asinine; ill-imagined, -advised, -judged, -devised; inconsistent, irrational, unphilosophical; extravagant &c. (*nonsensical*) 497; sleeveless, idle; useless &c. 645; inexpedient &c. 647; frivolous &c. (*trivial*) 643; absurd &c. 497.

Phr. *Davis sum non Œdipus.*

501. Fool.—N. fool, idiot, tomfool, wiseacre, simpleton, Simple Simon, nit-wit, witling, dizzard, donkey, ass; ninny, -hammer; moron, dolt, booby, Tom Noddy, looby, hoddy-doddy, noddy, nonny, noodle, nizy, owl; goose, -cap; *imbécile*; gaby, *radoteur*, nincompoop, *badaud*, zany; trifler, babbler; pretty fellow; natural, *niais*.

child, baby, infant, innocent, milksop, sop.

oaf, lout, loon, lown, dullard, doodle, calf, colt, buzzard, block, put, stick, stock, numps, tony.

bull-, dunder-, addle-, block-, dull-, logger-, jolt-, jolter-, beetle-, gross-, thick-, giddy-head; num-, thickskull; lack-, shallow-brain; half-, lack-wit; dunder-pate; fat-head, poor stick.

sawney, gowk; clod, -hopper; clod-, clot-poll, -pate; bull-calf; men of Bœotia, wise men of Gotham.

un sot à triple étage, sot; jobbernowl, changeling, mooncalf, *gobemouche*.

dotard, driveller; old -fogey, – woman; crone, grandmother.

greenhorn &c. (*dupe*) 547; dunce &c. (*ignoramus*) 493; lubber &c. (*bungler*) 701; madman &c. 504.

one who -will not set the Thames on fire, – did not invent gunpowder; *qui n'a pas inventé la poudre*; no conjuror.

503. Insanity.—N. disordered -reason, – intellect; diseased –, unsound –, abnormal- mind; derangement, unsoundness.

V. be -sane &c. *adj.*; retain one's senses, – reason.

become -sane &c. *adj.*; come to one's senses, sober down.

render -sane &c. *adj.*; bring to one's senses, sober.

Adj. sane, rational, reasonable, *compos mentis*, of sound mind; sound, -minded.

self-possessed; sober, -minded.

in one's -sober senses, – right mind; in possession of one's faculties.

Adv. sanely &c. *adj.*

---

insanity, lunacy; madness &c. *adj.*; mania, *rabies, furor*, mental alienation, paranoia, aberration; *amentia*, dementation, -tia, -cy; *dementia præcox; morosis*, idiocy, phrenitis, frenzy, raving, incoherence, wandering, delirium, calenture of the brain, delusion, hallucination; lycanthropy, brain storm, *delirium tremens*, D.T.'s.

vertigo, dizziness, swimming; sunstroke, *coup de soleil*, siriasis.

fanaticism, infatuation, craze; oddity, eccentricity, twist, monomania; klepto-, dipso-mania; hypochondriasis &c. (*low spirits*) 837; *melancholia*, hysteria.

screw –, tile –, slate- loose; bee in one's bonnet, rats in the upper story. dotage &c. (*imbecility*) 499.

V. be –, become- -insane &c. *adj.*; lose one's senses, – reason, – faculties, – wits; go –, run- mad, run amuck; rave, dote, ramble, wander; drivel &c. (*be imbecile*) 499; have a -screw loose &c. *n.*, – devil; *avoir le diable au corps*; lose one's head &c. (*be uncertain*) 475.

derange, render –, drive- -mad &c. *adj.*; madden, dementate, addle the wits, derange the head, infatuate, befool; turn -the brain, – one's head.

Adj. insane, mad, lunatic; crazy, crazed, *aliéné, non compos mentis*; not right, cracked, touched; bereft of reason; unhinged, deranged, unsettled in one's mind; insensate, reasonless, beside oneself, demented, daft; phren-, fren-zied, -etic; possessed, – with a devil; far gone, maddened, moonstruck; shatterpated; barmy; mad-, scatter-, shatter-, crack-brained; off one's head; bug-house, *loco*.

maniacal; manic, manic-depressive; delirious, light-headed, incoherent, rambling, doting, wandering; frantic, raving, stark staring mad, amok, amuck.

corybantic, dithyrambic; rabid, giddy, vertiginous, dizzy, wild, haggard, mazed; flighty; distr-acted, -aught; bewildered &c. (*uncertain*) 475.

mad as a -March hare, – hatter; of -unsound mind &c. *n.*; touched –, wrong –, not right- in one's -head, – mind, – wits, – upper story; out of one's -mind, – senses, – wits; not in one's right mind.

fanatical, infatuated, odd, eccentric; hypp-ed, -ish.

imbecile, silly &c. 499.

Adv. like one possessed.

Phr. the mind having lost its balance; the reason under a cloud; *tête -exaltée, -montée.*

---

504. Madman.—**N.** madman, lunatic, maniac, bedlamite, candidate for Bedlam, raver, madcap; energumen; paranoiac; auto-, mono-, pyro-, megalo-, dipso-, klepto-maniac; hypochondriac &c. (*low spirits*) 837.

dreamer &c. 515; rhapsodist, seer, high-flier, enthusiast, crank, eccentric, nut, fanatic, *fanatico; exalté*; knight errant, Don Quixote. idiot &c. 501.

Section VI. Extension of Thought

1°. *To the Past*

505. Memory.—N. memory, remembrance; reten-tion, -tiveness; tenacity; *veteris vestigia flammæ*; tablets of the memory; readiness.

reminiscence, recognition, recurrence, recollection, rememoration; retrospect, -ion; after-thought.

suggestion &c. (*information*) 527; prompting &c. *v.*; hint, reminder, token of remembrance, *memento, souvenir*, keepsake, relic, *memorandum*; remembrancer, flapper; memorial &c. (*record*) 551; commemoration &c. (*celebration*) 883.

things to be remembered, *memorabilia*.

art of –, artificial- memory; *memoria technica*; mnemo-nics, -technics; phrenotypics; Mnemosyne; memorandum-, note-, engagement-, prompt-book.

retentive –, tenacious –, green –, trustworthy –, capacious –, faithful –, correct –, exact –, ready –, prompt-memory.

V. remember, mind; retain the -memory, – remembrance- of; keep in view.

have –, hold –, bear –, carry –, keep –, retain- in *or* in the -thoughts, – mind, – memory, – remembrance; be in –, live in –, remain in –, dwell in –, haunt –, impress- one's -memory, – thoughts, – mind.

sink in the mind; run in the head; not be able to get it out of one's head; be deeply impressed with; rankle &c. (*revenge*) 919.

recur to the mind; flash -on the mind, – across the memory.

recognize, recollect, bethink oneself, recall, call up, conjure up, retrace; look –, trace- -back, – backwards; think –, look back- upon; review; call –, recall –, bring- to mind; remembrance; carry one's thoughts back; rake up the past.

suggest &c. (*inform*) 527; prompt; put –, keep- in mind; remind; fan the embers; call –, summon –, rip- up; renew; *infandum renovare dolorem*; task –, tax –, jog –, flap –, refresh –, rub up –, awaken-the memory; pull by the sleeve; bring back to the memory, put in remembrance, memorialize.

get –, have –, learn –, know –, say –, repeat- by -heart – rote; drive –, get- into -one's head; say one's lesson; repeat, – as a parrot; have at one's fingers' ends.

506. Oblivion.—N. oblivion; forgetfulness &c. *adj.*; obliteration &c. 552, of –, insensibility &c. 823 to- the past.

short –, treacherous –, loose –, slippery –, failing- memory; decay –, failure –, lapse- of memory; memory like a sieve; waters of -Lethe, – oblivion, *amnesia*.

pardon, acquittal, amnesty, oblivion; absolution.

V. forget; be -forgetful &c. *adj.*; fall –, sink- into oblivion; have -a short memory &c. *n.*, – no head.

forget one's own name, have on the tip of one's tongue, come in at one ear and go out at the other.

slip –, escape –, fade from –, die away from- the memory; lose, – sight of.

unlearn; efface &c. 552 –, discharge-from the memory; consign to -oblivion, – the tomb of the Capulets; think no more of &c. (*turn the attention from*) 458; cast behind one's back, wean one's thoughts from; let bygones be bygones &c. (*forgive*) 918.

Adj. forgotten &c. *v.*; unremembered, past recollection, bygone, out of mind; buried –, sunk- in oblivion; clean forgotten; gone out of one's -head, – recollection.

forgetful, oblivious, mindless, heedless, Lethean; insensible &c. 823- to the past.

Phr. *non mi ricordo*; the memory -failing, – deserting one, – being at (*or* in) fault.

---

commit to memory; memorize; con, – over; fix –, rivet –, imprint –, impress –, stamp –, grave –, engrave –, store –, treasure up –, bottle up –, embalm –, enshrine- in the memory; load –, store –, stuff –, burden- the memory with.

redeem from oblivion; keep the memory -alive, – green; *tangere ulcus*; keep up the memory of; commemorate &c. (*celebrate*) 883.

make a note of &c. (*record*) 551.

Adj. remember-ing, -ed &c. *v.*; mindful, reminiscential; retained in the memory &c. *v.*; pent up in one's memory; fresh; green, – in remembrance, still vivid; unforgotten, present to the mind; within one's -memory &c. *n.*; indelible; not to be forgotten, unforgettable, enduring; uppermost in one's thoughts; memorable &c. (*important*) 642.

Adv. by -heart, – rote; without book, *memoriter*.

in memory of; *in memoriam*; suggestive.

Phr. *manet altâ mente repostum*; *forsan et hæc olim meminisse juvabit.*

2°. To the Future

507. Expectation.—N. expect-ation, -ance, -ancy; anticipation, reckoning, calculation; contingency; foresight &c. 510.

contemplation, prospection, look out; prospect, perspective, horizon, vista; destiny &c. 152.

suspense, waiting, abeyance: curiosity &c. 455; anxious –, ardent –, eager –, breathless –, sanguine- expectation; torment of Tantalus.

presumption, hope &c. 858; trust &c. (*belief*) 484; prognostication, auspices &c. (*prediction*) 511.

V. expect; look -for, – out for, – forward to; hope for, anticipate; have in -prospect, – contemplation; keep in view; contemplate, promise oneself; not -wonder &c. 870 -at, – if.

wait –, tarry –, lie in wait –, watch –, bargain- for; keep a -good, – sharp-look-out for; await; stand at 'attention,' abide, bide one's –, mark- time, watch.

foresee &c. 510; prepare for &c. 673; forestall &c. (*be early*) 132; count upon &c. (*believe in*) 484; think likely &c. (*probability*) 472; make one's mouth water.

lead one to expect &c. (*predict*) 511; have in store for &c. (*destiny*) 152.

prick up one's ears, hold one's breath.

Adj. expectant; expecting &c. *v.*; in -expectation &c. *n.*; on the watch &c. (*vigilant*) 459; open -eyed, -mouthed;

508. Inexpectation.—N. in-, non-expectation; false expectation &c. (*disappointment*) 509; miscalculation &c. 481; unforeseen contingency, the unforeseen, the unexpected.

surprise, sudden burst, thunderclap, blow, shock; bolt out of the blue; eye-opener; wonder &c. 870.

V. not -expect &c. 507; be taken by surprise; start; miscalculate &c. 481; not bargain for; come –, fall- upon.

be -unexpected &c. *adj.*; come -unawares &c. *adv.*; turn up, pop, drop from the clouds; come –, burst –, flash –, bounce –, steal –, creep- upon one; come –, burst- like a thunderclap, -bolt; take –, catch- -by surprise, – unawares, – napping.

pounce –, spring a mine- upon.

surprise, startle, take aback, electrify, stun, stagger, take away one's breath, throw off one's guard; astonish &c. (*strike with wonder*) 870.

Adj. non-expectant; surprised &c. *v.*; un-warned, -aware; off one's guard; inattentive &c. 458.

un-expected, -anticipated, -prepared for, -looked for, -foreseen, -hoped for; dropped from the clouds; beyond –, contrary to –, against- expectation; out of one's reckoning; unheard of &c. (*exceptional*) 83; startling; sudden &c. (*instantaneous*) 113.

Adv. abruptly, unexpectedly, plump, pop, *à l'improviste*, unawares; without

agape, gaping, all agog; on -tenter-hooks, – tiptoe, – the tiptoe of expectation; *aux aguets*; ready; curious &c. 455; looking forward to; prepared for; on the rack.

expected &c. *v.*; long expected, foreseen; in prospect &c. *n.*; prospective; in -one's eye, – view, – the horizon; impending &c. (*destiny*) 152.

Adv. expectantly; in the event of; on the watch &c. *adj.*; with -breathless expectation &c. *n.*, – bated breath, – eyes, – ears strained; *arrectis auribus*; on edge.

Phr. we shall see; *nous verrons.*

-notice, – warning, – saying 'by your leave'; like a -thief in the night, – thunderbolt; in an unguarded moment; suddenly &c. (*instantaneously*) 113.

Int. heyday! &c. (*wonder*) 870.

Phr. little did one -think, – expect; nobody would ever -suppose, – think, – expect; who would have thought?

---

509. [Failure of expectation.] **Disappointment.—N.** disappointment, disillusionment; blighted hope, balk; blow; slip 'twixt cup and lip; non-fulfilment of one's hopes; sad –, bitter- disappointment; trick of fortune; afterclap; false –, vain- expectation; miscalculation &c. 481; fool's paradise; much cry and little wool.

V. be disappointed; look -blank, – blue; look –, stand- -aghast &c. (*wonder*) 870; find to one's cost; laugh on the wrong side of one's mouth; find one a false prophet.

disappoint; crush –, dash –, balk –, disappoint –, blight –, falsify –, defeat –, not realize- one's -hope, – expectation; balk, jilt, bilk; play one -false, – a trick; dash the cup from the lips; tantalize; dumb-found, -founder; disillusion, -ize; dissatisfy, disgruntle.

Adj. disappointed &c. *v.*; disconcerted, aghast; out of one's reckoning; disgruntled.

Phr. the mountain brought forth a mouse; *nascitur ridiculus mus; parturiunt montes; diis aliter visum,* the bubble burst; one's countenance falling.

510. Foresight.—N. foresight, prospicience, prevision, longsightedness; anticipation; providence &c. (*preparation*) 673.

fore-thought, -cast; pre-deliberation, -surmise; foregone conclusion &c. (*prejudgment*) 481; prudence &c. (*caution*) 864.

foreknowledge; *prognosis*; pre-cognition, -science, -notion, -sentiment; second sight; sagacity &c. (*intelligence*) 498.

prospect &c. (*expectation*) 507; foretaste; prospectus &c. (*plan*) 626.

V. foresee; look -forwards to, – ahead, – beyond; scent from afar; feel in one's bones; look –, pry –, peep- into the future.

see one's way; see how the -land lies, – wind blows, – cat jumps.

anticipate; expect &c. 507; be beforehand &c. (*early*) 132; predict &c. 511; fore-know, -judge, -cast; surmise; have an eye to the -future, – main chance; *respicere finem*; keep a sharp look-out &c. (*vigilance*) 459; forewarn &c. 668.

Adj. foreseeing &c. *v.*; prescient; anticipatory; far-seeing, -sighted; sagacious &c. (*intelligent*) 498; weather-wise; provident &c. (*prepared*) 673; prospective &c. 507.

Adv. against the time when.

511. Prediction.—N. prediction, announcement; program, programme &c. (*plan*) 626; premonition &c. (*warning*) 668; *prognosis*, prophecy, vaticination, Mantology, prognostication, premonstration, augur-y, -ation; a-, ha-riolation; fore-, a-boding; bode-, abode-ment; omin-ation,

-ousness; auspices, forecast; sign, presage, prognostic; omen &c. 512; horoscope, nativity; sooth, -saying; fortune-telling; divination; crystal gazing, necromancy &c. 992; prophet &c. 512.

[Divination by the stars] astrology, horoscopy, astromancy, judicial astrology.*

[Place of prediction] *adytum.*

prefigur-ation, -ement; prototype, type.

V. predict, prognosticate, prophesy, vaticinate, divine, foretell, sooth-say, augurate, tell fortunes; cast a -horoscope, − nativity; advise; forewarn &c. 668.

presage, augur, bode; a-, fore-bode, -cast; fore-, be-token; pre-figure, -show; portend; fore-show, -shadow, shadow forth, typify, ominate, signify, point to, precurse.

usher in, herald, premise, announce; lower.

hold out −, raise −, excite- -expectation, − hope; bid fair, promise, lead one to expect; be the -precursor &c. 64.

Adj. predicting &c. *v.*; predictive, prophetic, fatidical, vaticinal, oracular, Sibylline, haruspical, weatherwise.

ominous, presageful, portentous; augur-ous, -al, -ial; auspici-al, -ous; prescious, monitory, extispicious, premonitory, precusory, significant of, pregnant with, big with the fate of.

Phr. 'coming events cast their shadows before.'

512. Omen.—N. omen, portent, presage, prognostic, augury, auspice; sign &c. (*indication*) 550; herald, forerunner, harbinger &c. (*precursor*) 64.

bird of ill omen; signs of the times; gathering clouds; warning &c. 668.

prefigurement &c. 511.

513. Oracle.—N. oracle; prophet, -ess; seer, soothsayer, augur, fortune-teller, palmist, medium, clairvoyant, crystal gazer, witch, geomancer, *aruspex*; a-, ha-ruspice; Sibyl; Python, -ess; Pythia; Pythian −, Delphian- oracle; Monitor, Sphinx, Tiresias, Cassandra, Sibylline leaves; Zadkiel, Old Moore; sorcerer &c. 994; interpreter &c. 524.

Section VII. Creative Thought

514. Supposition.—N. supposition, assumption, postulation, condi-tion, pre-supposition, hypothesis, postulate, *postulatum*, theory, *data*; pro-, position; *thesis*, theorem; proposal &c. (*plan*) 626.

* The following terms, expressive of different forms of divination, have been col-lected from various sources, and are here given as a curious illustration of bygone superstitions:

Divination *by oracles*, Theomancy; *by the Bible*, Bibliomancy; *by ghosts*, Psycho-mancy; *by spirits seen in a magic lens*, Cristallomantia; *by shadows or manes*, Scio-mancy; *by appearances in the air*, Aeromancy, Chaomancy; *by the stars at birth*, Genethliacs; *by meteors*, Meteoromancy; *by winds*, Austromancy; *by sacrificial ap-pearances*, Aruspicy (*or* Haruspicy), Hieromancy, Hieroscopy; *by the entrails of animals sacrificed*, Hieromancy; *by the entrails of a human sacrifice*, Anthropomancy; *by the entrails of fishes*, Ichthyomancy; *by sacrificial fire*, Pyromancy; *by red-hot iron*, Sidero-mancy; *by smoke from the altar*, Capnomancy; *by mice*, Myomancy; *by birds*, Orniscopy, Ornithomancy; *by a cock picking up grains*, Alectryomancy (*or* Alectoromancy); *by fishes*, Ophiomancy; *by herbs*, Botanomancy; *by water*, Hydromancy; *by fountains*,

bare –, vague –, loose- -supposition, – suggestion; conceit; conjecture; guess, – work; rough guess, shot; conjecturality; surmise, suspicion, inkling, suggestion, suggestiveness, association of ideas, hint; presumption &c. (*belief*) 484; divination, speculation.

theorist, speculator, doctrinarian, hypothesist.

V. suppose, conjecture, surmise, suspect, guess, divine; theorize; pre-sume, -surmise, -suppose; assume, fancy, wis, take it; give a guess, speculate, believe, dare say, take it into one's head, take for granted.

put forth; pro-pound, -pose; moot; hypothesize; start, put a case, submit, move, make a motion; hazard –, throw out –, put forward- a - suggestion, – conjecture.

allude to, suggest, hint, put it into one's head.

suggest itself &c. (*thought*) 451; run in the head &c. (*memory*) 505; marvel –, wonder- -if, – whether.

Adj. supposing &c. *v.*; given, mooted, postulatory; assumed &c. *v.* supposit-ive, -itious; gratuitous, speculative, conjectural, hypothetical, suppositional, theoretical, academic, supposable, presumptive, putative.

suggestive, allusive, stimulating.

Adv. if, – so be; an; on the -supposition &c. *n.*; *ex hypothesi*; in -case, – the event of; *quasi*, as if, provided; perhaps &c. (*by possibility*) 470; for aught one knows.

515. Imagination.—N. imagination; originality; invention; fancy; inspiration; *verve*; empathy.

warm –, heated –, excited –, sanguine –, ardent –, fiery –, boiling –, wild –, bold –, daring –, playful –, lively –, fertile- -imagination, – fancy.

'mind's eye'; 'such stuff as dreams are made of.'

ideal-ity, -ism; romanticism, utopianism, castle-building; dreaming; frenzy; ecs-, ex-tasy; calenture &c. (*delirium*) 503; reverie, brown study, trance; somnambulism.

conception, *vorstellung*, excogitation, 'a fine frenzy,' poetic frenzy, divine afflatus; cloud-, dream-land; flight –, fumes- of fancy; 'thick-coming fancies'; creation –, coinage- of the brain; imagery, word painting.

conceit, maggot, figment, myth, dream, vision, shadow, chimera; phan-tasm, -tasy; fantasy, fancy; whim, -sey; vagary, rhapsody, romance, *extravaganza*; air-drawn dagger, bugbear, nightmare; flying Dutchman, great sea-serpent, man in the moon, castle in the air, *château en Espagne*; Utopia, Atlantis, happy valley, millennium, fairy land; land of Prester John, kingdom of Micomicon; work of fiction &c. (*novel*) 594; poetry &c. 597; drama &c. 599; Arabian nights; *le pot au lait*; dream of Alnaschar &c. (*hope*) 858; day –, golden- dream.

illusion &c. (*error*) 495; phantom &c. (*fallacy of vision*) 443; *Fata*

Pegomancy; *by a wand*, Rhabdomancy; *by dough of cakes*, Crithomancy; *by meal*, Aleuromancy, Alphitomancy; *by salt*, Halomancy; *by dice*, Cleromancy; *by arrows*, Belomancy; *by a balanced hatchet*, Axinomancy; *by a balanced sieve*, Coscinomancy; *by a suspended ring*, Dactyliomancy; *by dots made at random on paper*, Geomancy; *by precious stones*, Lithomancy; *by pebbles*, Pessomancy; *by pebbles drawn from a heap*, Psephomancy; *by mirrors*, Catoptromancy; *by writings in ashes*, Tephramancy; *by dreams*, Oneiromancy; *by the hand*, Palmistry, Chiromancy; *by nails reflecting the sun's rays*, Onychomancy; *by finger rings*, Dactylomancy; *by numbers*, Arithmancy; *by drawing lots*, Sortilege; *by passages in books*, Stichomancy; *by the letters forming the name of the person*, Onomancy, Nomancy; *by the features*, Anthroposcopy; *by the mode of laughing*, Geloscopy; *by ventriloquism*, Gastromancy; *by walking in a circle*, Gyromancy; *by dropping melted wax into water*, Ceromancy; *by currents*, Bletonism.

Morgana &c. (*ignis fatuus*) 423; vapour &c. (*cloud*) 353; stretch of the imagination &c. (*exaggeration*) 549.

idealist, romanticist, visionary; mopus; romancer, dreamer; somnambulist; rhapsodist &c. (*fanatic*) 504.

V. imagine, fancy, conceive; ideal-, real-ize; dream, – of; 'give to airy nothing a local habitation and a name.'

create, originate, devise, invent, coin, fabricate; improvise, strike out something new.

set one's wits to work; strain –, crack- one's invention; rack –, ransack –, cudgel- one's brains; excogitate.

give -play, – the reins, – a loose- to the -imagination, – fancy; empathize; indulge in reverie.

conjure up a vision; fancy –, represent –, picture –, figure- to oneself; envisage.

float in the mind; suggest itself &c. (*thought*) 451.

Adj. imagined &c. *v.*; *ben trovato*; air-drawn, -built.

imagin-ing &c. *v.*, -ative; original, inventive, creative, fertile, productive; ingenious.

romantic, high-flown, flighty, extravagant, fanatic, enthusiastic, Utopian, Quixotic; preposterous, rhapsodical.

ideal, unreal; in the clouds, *in nubibus*; unsubstantial &c. 4; illusory &c. (*fallacious*) 495; fictitious, theoretical, hypothetical.

fabulous, legendary; myth-ic, -ological; chimerical; imagin-, visionary; notional; fan-cy, -ciful, -tastic, -tastical; whimsical; fairy, -like.

dreamy, entranced, vaporous.

Division (II.) COMMUNICATION OF IDEAS
Section I. Nature of Ideas Communicated

516. [Idea to be conveyed.] **Meaning.** [Thing signified.]—**N.** meaning; signific-ation, -ance; sense, expression; im-, pur-port; drift, tenor, implication, connotation, essence, force, spirit bearing, colouring; scope.

matter; subject, -matter; argument, text, sum and substance; gist &c. 5.

general –, broad –, substantial –, colloquial –, literal –, plain –, simple –, accepted –, natural –, unstrained –, true &c. (*exact*) 494 –, honest &c. 543 –, *primâ facie* &c. (*manifest*) 525- meaning.

literality; literal interpretation; after acceptation; allusion &c. (*latency*) 526; suggestion &c. (*information*) 527; synonym; figure of speech &c. 521; acceptation &c. (*interpretation*) 522.

V. mean, signify, express, connote, denote; im-, pur-port; convey, imply, breathe, indicate, bespeak, bear a sense; tell –, speak- of; touch on; point –, allude- to; drive at; involve &c. (*latency*) 526; declare &c. (*affirm*) 535.

517. [Absence of meaning.] **Unmeaningness.**—**N.** unmeaningness &c. *adj.*; scrabble, scribble, scrawl, daub, (*painting*), strumming (*music*).

empty sound, dead letter, *vox et præterea nihil*; 'a tale told by an idiot, full of sound and fury, signifying nothing'; 'sounding brass and a tinkling cymbal.'

nonsense, jargon, gibberish, jabber, mere words, hocus-pocus, fustian, rant, bombast, balderdash, palaver, patter, flummery, *verbiage*, babble, *bavardage*, *baragouin*, platitude, *niaiserie*; inanity; rigmarole, rodomontade; truism; *nugæ canoræ*; twaddle, twattle, fudge, trash; stuff, – and nonsense; bosh, rubbish, rot, drivel, moonshine, wish-wash, fiddle-faddle, flapdoodle; absurdity &c. 497; vagueness &c. (*unintelligibility*) 519.

V. mean nothing; be -unmeaning &c. *adj.*; twaddle, quibble, rant, gabble, scrabble &c. *n.*

Adj. unmeaning; meaning-, sense-less;

understand by &c. (*interpret*) 522.

Adj. meaning &c. *v.*; expressive, suggestive, meaningful, allusive; signific-ant, -ative, -atory; pithy; full of –, pregnant with- meaning.

declaratory &c. 535; intelligible &c. 518; literal, metaphrastic; synonymous; tantamount &c. (*equivalent*) 27; implied &c. (*latent*) 526; explicit &c. 525; literal &c. 562.

Adv. to that effect; that is to say &c. (*being interpreted*) 522.

literally; evidently, from the context.

518. Intelligibility.—N. intelligibility, clearness, clarity, explicitness &c. *adj.*; lucidity, perspicuity; legibility, plain speaking &c. (*manifestation*) 525; precision &c. 494; a word to the wise.

V. be -intelligible &c. *adj.*; speak -for itself, – volumes; tell its own tale, lie on the surface.

render -intelligible &c. *adj.*; popularize, simplify, clear up; elucidate &c. (*explain*) 522.

understand, comprehend; take, – in; catch, grasp, recognize, follow, collect, master, make out; see -with half an eye, – daylight, – one's way; enter into the ideas of; come to an understanding.

Adj. intelligible; clear, – as -day, – crystal, – noonday; lucid; per-, transpicuous; luminous, transparent; comprehensible.

easily understood, easy to understand, for the million, intelligible to the meanest capacity, popularized.

plain, distinct, explicit, clear-cut; positive; definite &c. (*precise*) 494.

graphic, vivid, telling; expressive &c. (*meaning*) 516; illustrative &c. (*explanatory*) 522.

un-ambiguous, -equivocal, -mistakable &c. (*manifest*) 525, -confused; legible, recognizable; obvious &c. 525.

Adv. in plain -terms, – words, – English.

Phr. he that runs may read &c. (*manifest*) 525.

nonsensical; void of -sense &c. 516. in-, un-expressive; vacant, fatuous; not significant; insignificant.

trashy, washy, inane, vague, trumpery, trivial, fiddle-faddle, twaddling, quibbling.

unmeant, not expressed; tacit &c. (*latent*) 526.

inexpressible, undefinable, incommunicable.

Int. rubbish! &c. 497.

519. Unintelligibility.—N. unintelligibility, incomprehensibility, imperspicuity; inconceivableness, vagueness &c. *adj.*; obscurity; ambiguity &c. 520; doubtful meaning; uncertainty &c. 475; perplexity &c. (*confusion*) 59; spinosity; *obscurum per obscurius*; mystification &c. (*concealment*) 528; latency &c. 526; transcendentalism.

paradox; enigma, riddle &c. (*secret*) 533; *dignus vindice nodus*; sealed book; steganography, freemasonry.

pons asinorum, asses' bridge; double –, high- Dutch, Greek, Hebrew; jargon &c. (*unmeaning*) 517.

obscurantist.

V. be -unintelligible &c. *adj.*; require -explanation &c. 522; have a doubtful meaning, pass comprehension.

render -unintelligible &c. *adj.*; conceal &c. 528; darken &c. 421; confuse &c. (*derange*) 61; perplex &c. (*bewilder*) 475.

not -understand &c. 518; lose, – the clue; miss; not know what to make of, be able to make nothing of, give it up; not be able to -account for, – make either head or tail of; be at sea &c. (*uncertain*) 475; wonder &c. 870; see through a glass darkly &c. (*ignorance*) 491.

not understand one another; play at cross purposes &c. (*misinterpret*) 523.

Adj. un-intelligible, -accountable, -decipherable, -discoverable, -knowable, -fathomable; in-cognizable, -explicable, -scrutable; inap-, incomprehensible; insol-vable, -uble; impenetrable.

illegible, indecipherable, as Greek to one, unexplained, paradoxical; enigmatic, -al; puzzling, baffling.

obscure, dark, muddy, clear as mud, seen through a mist, dim, nebulous, shrouded in mystery; undiscernible &c. (*invisible*) 447; misty &c. (*opaque*) 426; hidden &c. 528; latent &c. 526.

indefinite &c. (*indistinct*) 447; perplexed &c. (*confused*) 59; undetermined, vague, loose, ambiguous; mysterious; mystic, -al; transcendental; occult, recondite, esoteric, abstruse, crabbed.

incon-ceivable, -ceptible; searchless; above –, beyond –, past-comprehension; beyond one's depth; unconceived.

inexpressible, undefinable, incommunicable, unutterable, ineffable, unpronounceable.

520. [Having a double sense.] **Equivocalness.**—**N.** equivocalness &c. *adj.*; double -meaning &c. 516; ambiguity, *double entendre*, pun, para-gram, *calembour*, quibble, *équivoque*, anagram; conundrum &c. (*riddle*) 533; word-play &c. (*wit*) 842; homonym, -y; amphibo-ly, -logy; ambiloquy.

Sphinx, Delphic oracle.

equivocation &c. (*duplicity*) 544; white lie, mental reservation &c. (*concealment*) 528.

V. be -equivocal &c. *adj.*; have two -meanings &c. 516; equivocate &c. (*palter*) 544.

Adj. equivocal, ambiguous, amphibolous, homonymous; double-tongued &c. (*lying*) 544.

521. Metaphor.—**N.** figure of speech; *façon de parler*, way of speaking, colloquialism.

phrase &c. 566; figure, trope, metaphor, tralatition, metonymy, enallage, *catachresis, synecdoche, autonomasia*; irony, satire, figurative-ness &c. *adj.*; image, -ry; *metalepsis*, type, anagoge, simile, personifica-tion, *prosopopæia*, allegory, apologue, parable, fable; allusion, adum-bration; application; euphemism; euphuism.

V. employ -metaphor &c. *n.*; personify, allegorize, adumbrate, shadow forth, apply, allude –, refer- to.

Adj. metaphorical &c. *n.*; figurative, catachrestical, typical, tralati-tious, parabolic, allegorical, allusive, anagogical; ironical; colloquial.

Adv. so to -speak, – say, – express oneself; as it were.

Phr. *mutato nomine de te fabula narratur.*

522. Interpretation.—**N.** interpreta-tion, definition; explan-, explic-ation; solution, answer; rationale; plain –, simple –, strict- interpretation; mean-ing &c. 516.

translation; rend-ering, -ition; red-dition; literal –, free- translation; key, crib; secret; clew &c. (*indication*) 550; Rosetta stone.

exegesis; ex-pounding, -position; Hermeneutics; comment, -ary; infer-ence &c. (*deduction*) 480; illustration, exemplification; gloss, annotation, *scholium*, note; e-, di-lucidation, enucle-ation; *éclaircissement, mot de l'énigme*.

symptomat-, semei-ology; metopo-scopy, physiognomy; diagnosis, prog-

523. Misinterpretation. — **N.** mis-interpretation, -apprehension, -under-standing, -acceptation, -construction, -application; *catachresis*; cross -read-ing, – purposes; mistake &c. 495.

misrepresentation, perversion, exag-geration &c. 549; false -colouring, – construction; abuse of terms; parody, travesty; falsification &c. (*lying*) 544.

V. mis-interpret, -apprehend, -under-stand, -conceive, -judge, -doubt, -spell, -translate, -construe, -apply; mistake &c. 495.

misrepresent, pervert; garble &c. (*falsify*) 544; distort, detort; travesty, play upon words; stretch –, strain –, wrest- the -sense, – meaning; explain

nosis; paleography &c. (*philology*) 560.

accept-ion, -ation, -ance; light, reading, lection, construction, version.

equivalent, – meaning &c. 516; synonym; para-, meta-phrase; convertible terms, apposition; dictionary &c. 562; polyglot.

V. interpret, explain, define, construe, translate, render; do –, turn-into; transfuse the sense of.

find out &c. 480*a*- -the meaning &c. 516- of; read; spell –, figure –, make- out; decipher, decode, unravel, disentangle, puzzle out; find the key of, enucleate, resolve, solve; read between the lines.

account for; find –, tell- the cause &c. 153- of; throw –, shed--light, – new light, – a fresh light- upon; clear up, elucidate.

illustrate, exemplify; unfold, expound, comment upon, annotate; popularize &c. (*render intelligible*) 518.

take –, understand –, receive –, accept- in a particular sense; understand by, put a construction on, be given to understand.

Adj. explanatory, expository; explica-tive, -tory; exegetical; hermeneutic, interpretive, illustrative, elucidative, annotative, scholiastic.

polyglot; literal; para-, meta-phrastic; cosignificative, synonymous; equivalent &c. 27.

Adv. in -explanation &c. *n.*; that is to say, *id est, videlicet*, to wit, namely, in other words.

literally, strictly speaking; in -plain, – plainer- -terms, – words, – English; more simply.

away; put a -bad, – false- construction on; give a false colouring, look through -rose coloured –, – dark – spectacles.

be –, play- at cross purposes.

Adj. misinterpreted &c. *v.*; untranslat-ed, -able.

Adv. at cross purposes.

---

524. Interpreter.—N. interpreter, translator, ex-positor, -pounder, -ponent, -plainer; demonstrator.

scholiast, commentator, annotator; meta-, para-phrast.

spokesman, speaker, mouthpiece, prolocutor; diplomat &c. 758.

guide, courier, dragoman, *valet de place, cicerone*, showman; oneiro-critic; Œdipus; oracle &c. 513.

Section II. Modes of Communication

525. Manifestation.—N. manifestation; unfolding; plainness &c. *adj.*; plain speaking; expression; showing &c. *v.*; exposition, demonstration, *séance*; exhibition, production; display, showing off &c. 882, premonstration. [Thing shown] exhibit, show.

indication &c. (*calling attention to*) 457; publicity &c. 531; disclosure &c. 529; openness &c. (*honesty*) 543, (*artlessness*) 703; *épanchement*, prominence.

V. make –, render- -manifest &c. *adj.*; bring -forth, – forward, – to the front, – into view; give notice; express; represent, set forth, exhibit; show, – up; expose; produce; hold up –, expose- to view; set –, place –, lay-

526. Latency.—N. latency, inexpression; hidden –, occult- meaning; occultness, occultism, mysticism, mystery, cabala, symbolism, anagoge; silence &c. (*taciturnity*) 585; concealment &c. 528; more than meets the -eye, – ear; Delphic oracle; *le dessous des cartes*, undercurrent.

allusion, insinuation, implication; innuendo &c. 527; adumbration; 'something rotten in the state of Denmark.'

snake in the grass &c. (*pitfall*) 667; secret &c. 533.

darkness, invisibility, imperceptibility.

latent influence, power behind the throne; friend at court, wire puller.

before -one, – one's eyes; tell to one's face; trot out, put through one's paces, unfold, show off, show forth, unveil, bring to light, display, demonstrate, unroll; lay open; draw –, bring- out; bring out in strong relief; call –, bring- into notice; hold up the mirror; wear one's heart upon his sleeve; show one's -face, – colours; manifest oneself; speak out; make no -mystery, – secret- of; unfurl the flag; proclaim &c. (*publish*) 531.

indicate &c. (*direct attention to*) 457; disclose &c. 529; elicit &c. 480a; interpret &c. 522.

be -manifest &c. *adj.*; appear &c. (*be visible*) 446; transpire &c. (*be disclosed*) 529; speak for itself, stand to reason; stare one in the face; loom large, appear on the horizon, rear its head; give -token, – sign, – indication of; tell its own tale &c. (*intelligible*) 518; go without saying.

Adj. manifest, apparent; salient, striking, demonstrative, prominent, in the foreground, notable, pronounced.

flagrant; notorious &c. (*public*) 531; arrant; stark staring; unshaded, glaring.

defin-ed, -ite; distinct, conspicuous &c. (*visible*) 446; obvious, evident, incontestable, unmistakable, not to be mistaken, plain, clear, palpable, self-evident, autoptical; intelligible &c. 518; clear as -day, – daylight, – noonday; plain as -a pikestaff, – the sun at noonday, – the nose on one's face, – the way to the parish church.

ostensible; open, – as day; overt, patent, express, explicit; naked, bare, literal, downright, undisguised, exoteric.

V. be -latent &c. *adj.*; lurk, smoulder, underlie. make no sign; escape -observation, – detection, – recognition; lie hid &c. 528.

laugh in one's sleeve; keep back &c. (*conceal*) 528.

involve, imply, implicate, connote, import, understand, allude to, infer, leave an inference; symbolize; whisper &c. (*conceal*) 528.

Adj. latent; lurking &c. *v.*; secret &c. 528; occult, symbolic, mystic; implied &c. *v.*; dormant.

un-apparent, -known, -seen &c. 441; in the background; invisible &c. 447; indiscoverable, dark; impenetrable &c. (*unintelligible*) 519; un-spied, -suspected.

un - said, - written, - published, -breathed, -talked of, -told &c. 527, -sung, -exposed, -proclaimed, -disclosed &c. 529, -pronounced, -mentioned, -expressed; not expressed, tacit.

un-developed, -solved, -explained, -traced, -discovered &c. 480a, -tracked, -explored, -invented.

indirect, crooked, inferential; by -inference, – implication; implicit; constructive; allusive, covert, muffled; steganographic; under-stood, -hand, -ground; concealed &c. 528; delitescent.

Adv. by a side wind; *sub silentio*; in the background; behind -the scenes, – one's back, – the veil; below the surface; on the tip of one's tongue; secretly &c. 528; between the lines; by a mutual understanding.

Phr. 'thereby hangs a tale.' 'that is another story.'

unreserved; frank, plain spoken &c. (*artless*) 703; barefaced, brazen, bold, shameless, daring, flaunting, loud.

manifested &c. *v.*; disclosed &c. 529; expressible, capable of being shown, producible; in-, un-concealable.

Adv. manifestly, openly &c. *adj.*; before one's eyes, under one's nose, to one's face, face to face, above board, *cartes sur table*, on the stage, in plain sight, in open court, in the open, – streets; at the cross roads; in market overt; in the face of -day, – heaven; in -broad –, open- daylight; without reserve; at first blush, *primâ facie*, on the face of; in set terms.

Phr. *cela saute aux yeux*; he that runs may read; you can see it with half an eye; it needs no ghost to tell us; the meaning lies on the surface; *cela va sans dire*; *res ipsa loquitur*.

527. Information.—N. information, enlightenment, acquaintance, knowledge &c. 490; publicity &c. 531.

communication, intimation; not-ice, -ification; e-, an-nunciation; announcement; representation, round robin, presentment.

case, estimate, specification, report, advice, monition; news &c. 532; return &c. (*record*) 551; account &c. (*description*) 594; statement &c. (*affirmation*) 535.

mention; acquainting &c. *v.*; instruction &c. (*teaching*) 537; outpouring; intercommunication, communicativeness.

informant, authority, teller, announcer, annunciator, harbinger, herald, intelligencer, commentator, columnist, reporter, exponent, mouthpiece; informer, keek, eavesdropper, delator, detective, sleuth; *mouchard*, spy, stool pigeon, newsmonger; messenger &c. 534; *amicus curiæ.*

valet de place, cicerone, pilot, guide; guide-, hand-book; *vade mecum*; manual; map, plan, chart, gazetteer; itinerary &c. (*journey*) 266.

hint, suggestion, wrinkle, innuendo, inkling, whisper, passing word, word in the ear, subaudition, cue, by-play; gesture &c. (*indication*) 550; gentle – broad- hint; *verbum sapienti*; word to the wise; insinuation &c. (*latency*) 526.

V. tell; inform, – of; acquaint, – with; impart, – to; make acquainted with, bring to the ears of, apprise, advise, enlighten, awaken.

let fall, mention, express, intimate, represent, communicate, make known; publish &c. 531; notify, signify, specify, convey the knowledge of.

let one –, have one to- know; serve notice, give one to understand; give notice; set –, lay –, put- before; point out, put into one's head; put one in possession of; instruct &c. (*teach*) 537; direct the attention to &c. 457.

an-nounce, -nunciate; report, – progress; bring –, send –, leave –, writeword; tele-graph, -phone; ring –, call-up; wire; retail, render an account; give an account &c. (*describe*) 594; state &c. (*affirm*) 535.

528. Concealment.—N. concealment; hiding &c. *v.*; occultation, mystification.

seal of secrecy; screen &c. 530; disguise &c. 530; masquerade; masked battery; hiding place &c. 530; cipher, code, crypt-, stegan-ography; invisible –, sympathetic- ink; palimpsest; freemasonry.

stealth, -iness; obreption; slyness &c. (*cunning*) 702.

latit-ancy, -ation; seclusion &c. 893; privacy, secrecy, secretness; *incognita.*

reticence; reserve; mental –, reservation, aside; *arrière pensée*, suppression, evasion, white lie, misprision; silence &c. (*taciturnity*) 585; suppression of truth &c. 544; underhand dealing; close-, secretive-ness &c. *adj.*; mystery.

latency &c. 526; snake in the grass; secret &c. 533.

V. conceal, hide, secrete, stow away, put out of sight; lock –, seal –, bottle-up.

cover, screen, cloak, veil, shroud; screen from -sight, – observation; draw the veil; draw –, close- the curtain; curtain, shade, eclipse, throw a veil over; be-cloud, -fog, -mask; mask, disguise; ensconce, muffle, smother; whisper.

keep -from, – back, – to oneself; keep -snug, – close, – secret, – dark; bury; sink, suppress; keep -from, – out of- -view, – sight; keep in –, throw into- the -shade, – background; cover up one's tracks; stifle, hush up, withhold, reserve; fence with a question; ignore &c. 460.

code, codify, use a cipher.

keep -a secret, – one's own counsel; hold one's tongue &c. (*silence*) 585; make no sign, not let it go further; not breathe a -word, – syllable- about; not let the right hand know what the left is doing; hide one's light under a bushel, bury one's talent in a napkin.

keep –, leave- in -the dark, – ignorance; blind, – the eyes; blindfold, hoodwink, mystify; puzzle &c. (*render uncertain*) 475; bamboozle &c. (*deceive*) 545.

be -concealed &c. *v.*; suffer an eclipse;

disclose &c. 529; show cause; explain &c. (*interpret*) 522.

hint; give an inkling of; give -, drop -, throw out- a hint; insinuate; allude -, make allusion- to; glance at; tip off, tip the wink &c. (*indicate*) 550; suggest, prompt, give the cue, breathe; whisper, - in the ear.

give a bit of one's mind; tell one plainly, - once for all; speak volumes.

un-deceive, -beguile; set right, correct, open the eyes of, disabuse.

be -informed of &c.; know &c. 490; learn &c. 539; get scent of, gather from; awaken -, open one's eyes- to; become -alive, - awake- to; keep posted; hear, overhear, understand.

come to one's -ears, - knowledge; reach one's ears.

Adj. informed &c. *v.*; *communiqué*; reported &c. *v.*; published &c. 531; advisory.

expressive &c. 516; explicit &c. (*open*) 525, (*clear*) 518; plain-spoken &c. (*artless*) 703.

declara-, nuncupa-, exposi-tory; declarative, enunciative, communicat-ive, -ory; oral.

Adv. from information received; according to -rumour, - report; in the air; from what one can gather.

Phr. a little bird told me.

---

retire from sight, couch; hide oneself; lie -hid, - in ambush, - low, - *perdu*, - snug, - close; seclude oneself &c. 893; lurk, sneak, skulk, slink, pussy-foot, prowl; steal -into, - out of, - by, - along; play at -bopeep, - hide and seek; hide in holes and corners.

Adj. concealed &c. *v.*; hidden; veiled, secret, recondite, mystic, cabalistic, occult, dark; cryptic, -al; private, privy, *in petto*, auricular, clandestine, close, inviolate.

behind a -screen &c. 530; under -cover, - an eclipse; in -ambush, - hiding, - disguise; in a -cloud, - fog, - mist, - haze, - dark corner; in the -shade, - dark; clouded, wrapt in clouds; invisible &c. 447; buried, underground, *perdu*; incommunicado; secluded &c. 893.

un-disclosed &c. 529, -told &c. 527; covert &c. (*latent*) 526; mysterious &c. (*unintelligible*) 519.

irrevealable, inviolable; confidential; esoteric; not to be spoken of.

obreptitious, furtive, stealthy, feline; skulking &c. *v.*; surreptitious, underhand, hole and corner; sly &c. (*cunning*) 702; secretive, evasive, noncommittal, reserved, reticent, uncommunicative, buttoned up; close, - as wax; taciturn &c. 585.

Adv. secretly &c. *adj.*; in -secret, - private, - one's sleeve, - holes and corners; in the dark &c. *adj.*

januis clausis, with closed doors, *à huis clos*; hugger-mugger, *à la dérobée*; under the -cloak of, - rose, - table; *sub rosâ, en tapinois*, in the background, aside, on the sly, with bated breath, *sotto voce*, in a whisper, without beat of drum, *à la sourdine*.

in -, strict- confidence; confidentially &c. *adj.*; between -ourselves, - you and me; *entre nous, inter nos*, under the seal of secrecy; in -code, - cipher.

underhand, by stealth, like a thief in the night; stealthily &c. *adj.*; behind -the scenes, - the curtain, - one's back, - a screen &c. 530; *incognito*; *in camerâ*.

Phr. it -must, - will- go no further; 'tell it not in Gath,' nobody the wiser.

529. Disclosure.—N. disclosure; retection; unveiling &c. *v.*; deterration, revealment, revelation; divulgence, expos-ition, -ure; *exposé*; whole truth; tell-tale &c. (*news*) 532.

acknowledgment, avowal; confession, -al; shrift.

530. Ambush. [Means of concealment.]—**N.** hiding-place; secret -place, - drawer; recess, hole, funk hole, holes and corners; closet, crypt, *adytum*, ab-ditory, *oubliette*, safe, - deposit.

am-bush, -buscade; stalking horse; lurking-hole, -place; secret path,

bursting of a bubble; *dénouement.*

V. dis-close, -cover, -mask; draw –, draw aside –, lift –, raise –, lift up –, remove –, tear- the -veil, – curtain; un-mask, -veil, -fold, -cover, -seal, -kennel; take off –, break- the seal; lay -open, – bare; expose; open, – up; bare, bring to light; evidence; make - clear, – evident, – manifest; evince.

divulge, reveal, break; let into the secret; reveal the secrets of the prison-house; tell &c. (*inform*) 527; breathe, utter, blab, peach; let -out, – fall, – drop, – the cat out of the bag; betray; tell tales, – out of school; come out with; give -vent, – utterance- to; open the lips, blurt out, vent, whisper about; speak out &c. (*make manifest*) 525; make public &c. 531; unriddle &c. (*find out*) 480a; split; blow the gaff; break the news.

acknowledge, allow, concede, grant, admit, own, confess, avow, throw off all disguise, turn inside out, make a clean breast; show one's -hand, – cards; unburden –, disburden- one's -mind, – conscience, – heart; open –, lay bare –, tell a piece of- one's mind; unbosom oneself, own to the soft impeachment; say –, speak- the truth; turn -King's, –Queen's, –State's- evidence.

raise –, drop –, lift –, remove –, throw off- the mask; expose; debunk; lay open; un-deceive, -beguile; disabuse, set right, correct, open the eyes of; *désillusionner.*

be -disclosed &c.; transpire, come to light; come in sight &c. (*be visible*) 446; become known, escape the lips; come –, ooze –, creep –, leak –, peep –, crop- out; show its -face, – colours; discover &c. itself; break through the clouds, flash on the mind.

Adj. disclosed &c. *v.*

Int. out with it!

Phr. the murder is out; a light breaks in upon one; the scales fall from one's eyes; the eyes are opened.

backstairs; retreat &c. (*refuge*) 666.

screen, cover, shade, blinker; veil, curtain, blind, *purdah,* cloak, cloud.

mask, vizor, visor, disguise, masquerade dress, domino; *camouflage.*

pitfall &c. (*source of danger*) 667; trap &c. (*snare*) 545.

V. ambush, ambuscade, lie in ambush &c. (*hide oneself*) 528; lie in wait for; set a trap for &c. (*deceive*) 545.

Adv. *aux aguets.*

---

531. Publication.—**N.** publication; public -announcement &c. 527; promulgation, propagation, proclamation, pronouncement, encyclical, *pronunciamento*; circulation, indiction, edition, imprint, impression, printing; hue and cry.

publicity, notoriety, currency, flagrancy, cry, *bruit*; *vox populi*; report &c. (*news*) 532.

the Press, fourth estate, public press, newspaper, periodical, journal, gazette; house organ, trade publication, tabloid; daily, weekly, monthly, quarterly, annual, magazine, monograph, book; review; news sheet, special edition, supplement, feature, rotogravure, comic strips; leaflet, pamphlet; telegraphy; publisher &c. *v.*

circular, – letter; manifesto, advertisement, puff, placard, bill, *affiche,* broadside, poster; notice &c. 527; programme.

V. publish; make -public, – known &c. (*information*) 527; speak –, talk- of; broach, utter; put forward; circulate, propagate, promulgate; spread –, abroad; rumour, diffuse, disseminate, evulgate; put –, give –, send- forth; emit, edit, get out; issue; cover, report; bring –, lay –, drag- before the public; give -out, – to the world; put –, bandy –, hawk –, buzz –, whisper –, bruit –, blaze- about; drag into the -open day, – limelight; voice.

proclaim, herald, blazon; blaze -, noise- abroad; sound a trumpet; trumpet -, thunder- forth; give tongue; announce with -beat of drum, - flourish of trumpets; proclaim -from the housetops, - at Charing Cross, at the cross roads; declare, declaim.

advertise, placard; post, - up; *afficher*, publish in the Gazette, send round the crier.

raise a -cry, - hue and cry, - report; set news afloat.

telegraph, cable, wireless, broadcast.

be -published &c.; be -, become- public &c. *adj.*; come out; go -, fly -, buzz -, blow- about; get -about, - abroad, - afloat, - wind; find vent; see the light; go forth, take air, acquire currency, pass current; go -the rounds, - the round of the newspapers, - through the length and breadth of the land; *virum volitare per ora*; pass from mouth to mouth; spread; run -, spread- like wildfire.

Adj. published &c. *v.*; current &c. (*news*) 532; in circulation, public; notorious; flagrant, arrant; open &c. 525; trumpet-tongued; encyclical, promulgatory; exoteric.

Adv. publicly &c. *adj.*; in open court, with open doors; in the limelight.

Int. *Oyez!* O yes! notice!

Phr. notice is hereby given; this is -, these are- to give notice.

---

532. News.—N. news; information &c. 527; piece -, budget- of -news, - information; report, story, yarn, copy, filler, intelligence, tidings; stop press news.

word, advice, *aviso*, message; dis-, des-patch; radio, telegram, cable, wireless telegram, radio-gram, marconi-gram, communication, errand, embassy; *bulletin*.

rumour, hearsay, *on dit*, flying rumour, news stirring, cry, buzz, *bruit*, fame; talk, *oui-dire*, scandal, eavesdropping; town -, table- talk; tittle-tattle; *canard*, topic of the day, idea afloat.

fresh -, stirring -, old -, stale- news; glad tidings; old -, stale- story.

narrator &c. (*describe*) 594; news-, scandal-monger; tale-bearer; tell-tale, gossip, tattler, busy-body, chatterer; informer.

V. transpire &c. (*be disclosed*) 529; rumour &c. (*publish*) 531.

Adj. many-tongued; rumoured; publicly -, currently- -rumoured, - reported; rife, current, floating, afloat, going about, in circulation, in everyone's mouth, all over the town.

Adv. as the story -goes, - runs; as they say, it is said.

533. Secret.—N. secret; dead -, profound- secret; *arcanum*, mystery; latency &c. 526; Asian mystery; sealed book, secrets of the prison-house; *le dessous des cartes.*

enigma, riddle, puzzle, nut to crack, conundrum, charade, rebus, logogriph; mono-, ana-gram; acrostic, cross-word puzzle; Sphinx; *crux criticorum.*

maze, labyrinth, Hyrcynian wood.

problem &c. (*question*) 461; paradox &c. (*difficulty*) 704; unintelligibility &c. 519; *terra incognita* &c. (*ignorance*) 491.

Adj. secret &c. (*concealed*) 528.

---

534. Messenger.—N. messenger, envoy, emissary, legate; nuncio, internuncio; intermediary; ambassador &c. (*diplomatist*) 758.

marshal, flag-bearer, herald, crier, trumpeter, bellman, pursuivant, *parlementaire, apparitor.*

courier, runner, dawk, *estafette*; Hermes, Mercury, Iris, Ariel.

postman, letter carrier, telegraph boy, messenger boy, district messenger; despatch rider, commissionaire, errand-boy.

mail; post, -office; letter-bag; mail -boat, - train, - coach, - van, aerial mail; tele-graph, -phone; cable, wire; carrier-pigeon; wireless tele-graph, -phone; radiotele-graph, -phone.

journalist, newspaperman, reporter; gentleman –, representative- of the press; sob sister; penny-a-liner; special –, war –, own- correspond-ent; spy, scout; informer &c. 527.

535. Affirmation.—N.

affirm-ance, -ation; statement, allegation, assertion, predication, declaration, word, aver-ment.

asseveration, adjuration, swearing, oath, affidavit; deposition &c. (record) 551; avouchment, assurance; protest, -ation; profession; acknowledgment &c. (assent) 488; pledge.

vote, voice, suffrage, ballot.

remark, observation; position &c. (proposition) 514; saying, dictum, sen-tence, ipse dixit.

emphasis, positiveness, peremptori-ness; dogmatism &c. (certainty) 474; dogmatist &c. 887.

V. assert; make -an assertion &c. n.; have one's say; say, affirm, predicate, declare, state, represent; protest, pro-fess.

put -forth, – forward; advance, allege, propose, propound, enunciate, enounce, broach, set forth, hold out, maintain, contend, pronounce, pretend.

depose, depone, aver, avow, avouch, asseverate, swear; make –, take one's-oath; make –, swear –, put in- an affidavit; take one's Bible oath, kiss the book, vow, vitam impendere vero; swear till -one is black in the face, – all's blue; be sworn, call Heaven to witness; vouch, warrant, certify, assure, swear by bell, book and candle.

swear by &c. (believe) 484; insist –, take one's stand- upon; emphasize, lay stress on; assert -roundly, – positively; lay down, – the law; raise one's voice, dogmatize, have the last word; rap out; repeat; re-assert, -affirm.

announce &c. (information) 527; ac-knowledge &c. (assent) 488; attest &c. (evidence) 467; adjure &c. (put to one's oath) 768.

Adj. asserting &c. v.; declaratory, predicatory, pronunciative, affirmative, soi-disant; positive; certain &c. 474; express, explicit &c. (patent) 525; absolute, emphatic, flat, broad, round, pointed, marked, distinct, decided, confident, assertive, insistent, trenchant, dogmatic, definitive, formal, solemn, categorical, peremptory; un-retracted; predicable, affirmable.

536. Negation.—N.

ne-, abne-gation; denial; dis-avowal, -claimer; abjura-tion; contra-diction, -vention; recu-sation, protest; rebuttal; recusancy &c. (dissent) 489; flat –, emphatic- -con-tradiction, – denial; démenti.

qualification &c. 469; repudiation &c. 610; retractation &c. 607; confuta-tion &c. 479; refusal &c. 764; prohibi-tion &c. 761.

V. deny; contra-dict, -vene; contro-vert, give denial to, gainsay, negative, shake the head.

dis-own, -affirm, -claim, -avow; re-cant &c. 607; revoke &c. (abrogate) 756.

dispute, impugn, traverse, rebut, join issue upon; bring –, call- in question &c. (doubt) 485.

deny -flatly, – peremptorily, – em-phatically, – absolutely, – wholly, – en-tirely; give the lie to, belie.

repudiate &c. 610; set aside, ignore &c. 460; rebut &c. (confute) 479; qualify &c. 469; refuse &c. 764.

Adj. denying &c. v.; denied &c. v.; contradictory; negat-ive, -ory; revoca-tory; recusant &c. (dissenting) 489; at issue upon.

Adv. no, nay, not, nowise; not a -bit, – whit, – jot; not -at all, – in the least, – so; no such thing; nothing of the -kind, – sort; quite the contrary, tout au contraire, far from it; tant s'en faut; on no account, in no respect; by -no, – no manner of- means; negatively.

Phr. there never was a greater mis-take; I know better; non hæc in fœdera.

Adv. affirmatively &c. *adj.*; in the affirmative.

with emphasis, *ex cathedrâ*, without fear of contradiction.

I must say, indeed, i' faith, let me tell you, why, give me leave to say, marry, you may be sure, I'd have you to know; upon my -word, – honour; by my troth, egad, I assure you; by -jingo, – Jove, – George, – &c.; troth, seriously, sadly; in –, in sober- -sadness, – truth, – earnest; of a truth, truly, pardi, perdy; in all conscience, upon oath; be assured &c. (*belief*) 484; yes &c. (*assent*) 488; I'll -warrant, – warrant you, – engage, – answer for it, – be bound, – venture to say, – take my oath; in fact, as a matter of fact, forsooth, joking apart; so help me God; not to mince the matter.

Phr. quoth he; *dixi.*

537. Teaching.—N. teaching &c. *v.*; instruction; edification; education; pedagogy; tuition; tutor-, tutel-age; direction, guidance.

qualification, preparation; train-, school-ing &c. *v.*; discipline; exer-cise, -citation; drill, practice.

persuasion, proselytism, propagand-ism, *propaganda*; in-doctrination, -culcation, -oculation.

explanation &c. (*interpretation*) 522; lesson, lecture, sermon, homily; apologue, parable; discourse, prelection, preachment, disquisition.

exercise, task; *curriculum*; course, – of study; grammar, three R's, initi-ation, A. B. C. &c. (*beginning*) 66.

elementary –, primary –, secondary –, grammar school –, high school –, college –, university –, technical –, liberal –, classical –, religious –, de-nominational –, moral –, secular- edu-cation; technical –, vocational- train-ing; university extension lectures; propædeutics, moral tuition; evening classes, correspondence course.

physical education, gymnastics, calis-thenics, eurythmics; *sloyd*.

V. teach, instruct, edify, school, tutor; cram, prime, coach; enlighten &c. (*inform*) 527.

in-culcate, -doctrinate, -oculate, -fuse, -stil, -fix, -graft, -filtrate; im-bue, -pregnate, -plant; graft, sow the seeds of, disseminate, propagandize.

give an idea of; put -up to, – in the way of; set right.

sharpen the wits, enlarge the mind; give new ideas, open the eyes, bring forward, 'teach the young idea how to shoot'; improve &c. 658.

538. Misteaching.—N. mis-teaching, -information, -intelligence, -guidance, -direction, -persuasion, -instruction, -leading &c. *v.*; perversion, false teach-ing; sophistry &c. 477; college of Laputa; the blind leading the blind.

V. mis-inform, -teach, -direct, -guide, -instruct, -correct; pervert; put on a false –, throw off the- scent; deceive &c. 545; mislead &c. (*error*) 495; mis-represent; lie &c. 544; *ambiguas in vulgum spargere voces*, preach to the wise, teach one's grandmother to suck eggs.

render unintelligible &c. 519; bewil-der &c. (*uncertainty*) 475; mystify &c. (*conceal*) 528; unteach.

Adj. misteaching &c. *v.*; unedifying.

Phr. *piscem natare doces.*

539. Learning.—N. learning; acqui-sition of -knowledge &c. 490, – skill &c. 698; acquirement, attainment; edification, scholarship, erudition; lore; information; self-instruction; study, reading, perusal; inquiry &c. 461.

ap-, prenticeship; pupil-age, -arity; tutelage, novitiate, matriculation.

docility &c. (*willingness*) 602; apti-tude &c. 698.

V. learn; acquire –, gain –, receive –, take in –, drink in –, imbibe –, pick up –, gather –, get –, obtain –, collect –, glean- -knowledge, – information, – learning.

acquaint oneself with, master; make oneself -master of, – acquainted with; grind, cram; get –, coach- up; learn by -heart, – rote.

read, spell, peruse; con –, pore –; thumb- over; wade through; dip into;

expound &c. (*interpret*) 522; lecture; prelect; read –, give- a -lesson, – lecture, – sermon, – discourse; hold forth, preach; sermon-, moral-ize; point a moral.

train, discipline; bring up, – to; educate, form, ground, prepare, qualify, drill, exercise, practice, habituate, familiarize with, nurture, dry-nurse, breed, rear, take in hand; break, – in; tame; pre-instruct; initiate; inure &c. (*habituate*) 613.

put to nurse, send to school.

direct, guide; direct attention to &c. (*attention*) 457; impress upon the -mind, – memory; beat into, – the head; convince &c. (*belief*) 484.

Adj. teaching &c. *v.*; taught &c. *v.*; educational; scholastic, academic, doctrinal; disciplinal; instructive, didactic, hortative, pedagogic, tutorial.

Phr. the schoolmaster abroad.

540. Teacher.—N. teacher, trainer, instructor, institutor, master, tutor, don, director, Corypheus, dry nurse, coach, grinder, crammer; governor, bear-leader; governess, duenna; disciplinarian.

professor, lecturer, reader, prelector, prolocutor, preacher; Boanerges; pastor &c. (*clergy*) 996; schoolmaster, dominie, ˄usher, pedagogue, abecedarian; schoolmistress, dame, monitor, proctor, pupil-teacher.

expositor &c. 524; preceptor, guide; mentor &c. (*adviser*) 695; pioneer, apostle, missionary, propagandist, moonshee; example &c. (*model for imitation*) 22.

professorship &c. (*school*) 542.

tutelage &c. (*teaching*) 537.

Adj. professorial, tutorial &c. 537.

run the eye -over, – through; turn over the leaves.

study; be -studious &c. *adj.*; consume the midnight oil, mind cne's book.

go to -school, – college, – the university; serve -an (*or* one's) apprenticeship, – one's time; learn one's trade; be -informed &c. 527; be -taught &c. 537.

Adj. studious; schol-astic, -arly; teachable; docile &c. (*willing*) 602; apt &c. 698, industrious &c. 682; learned, erudite.

Adv. at one's books; *in statu pupillari* &c. (*learner*) 541.

541. Learner.—N. learner, scholar, student, *alumnus*, *élève*, pupil; ap-, prentice; articled clerk; school-boy, -girl, beginner, tyro, abecedarian, alphabetarian.

recruit, novice, neophyte, tenderfoot, inceptor, *débutant*, catechumen, probationer; undergraduate; freshman, frosh; sophomore, junior, senior; junior –, senior- soph; sophister, questionist, fellow-, commoner, pensioner, exhibitioner, sizar, scholar, fellow, advanced –, post graduate –, research- student.

class, form, grade, standard, remove; pupilage &c. (*learning*) 539.

disciple, follower, apostle, proselyte; fellow student, school-mate, -fellow, class mate, condisciple.

Adj. *in statu pupillari*, in leading strings, sophomoric.

542. School.—N. school, academy, university, *alma mater*, college, seminary, Lyceum; instit-ute, -ution, *conservatoire*; *palæstra, gymnasium*.

day -. boarding –, public –, preparatory –, elementary –, primary –, infant –, dame's –, grammar –, middle class –, Board –, County –, Council –, parochial –, denominational –, Sunday –, National –, British and Foreign –, collegiate –, secondary –, continuation –, night –, correspondence –, secretarial –, military –, law –, medical –, business –, technical- school; technical –, training- college; Polytechnic; training ship; *Kindergarten*, nursery, *crèche*, reformatory.

pulpit, desk, reading desk, ambo, class-, lecture-room, theatre, amphitheatre, forum, stage, rostrum, platform, hustings, tribune.

school –, horn –, text- book; grammar, primer, abecedary, rudiments, manual, *vade mecum*, Lindley Murray, Cocker.

professor-, lecture-, reader-ship; chair; schoolmaster &c. 540.
School Board, Council of Education; *propaganda*.
Adj. scholastic, academic, collegiate; educational.
Adv. *ex cathedrâ.*

---

543. Veracity.—N. veracity; truth-fulness, frankness &c. *adj.*; truth, sooth, sincerity, candour, honesty, fidelity; plain dealing, *bona fides*; love of truth; probity &c. 939; ingenuous-ness &c. (*artlessness*) 703.

the truth the whole truth and noth-ing but the truth; honest –, sober-truth &c. (*fact*) 494; unvarnished tale; light of truth.

V. speak –, tell- the truth; speak by the card; paint in its –, show oneself in one's-true colours; make a clean breast &c. (*disclose*) 529; speak one's mind &c. (*be blunt*) 703; not -lie &c. 544, – deceive &c. 545.

Adj. truthful, true; ver-acious, -edi-cal; scrupulous &c. (*honourable*) 939; sincere, candid, frank, open, straight-forward, unreserved; open-, true-, simple- hearted; honest, trustworthy; undissembling &c. (dissemble &c. 544); guileless, pure; unperjured, true blue, as good as one's word; unaffected, un-feigned, *bonâ fide*; outspoken, ingenu-ous &c. (*artless*) 703; undisguised &c. (*real*) 494.

Adv. truly &c. (*really*) 494; on oath; in plain words &c. 703; in –, with –, of a –, in good –, very- truth; as the -dial to the sun, – needle to the pole; honour bright; troth; in good -sooth, – earnest; unfeignedly, with no non-sense, in sooth, sooth to say, *bonâ fide*, *in foro conscientiæ*; without equivoca-tion; *cartes sur table*, from the bottom of one's heart; by my troth &c. (*affirmation*) 535.

544. Falsehood. — N. false-hood, -ness; fals-ity, -ification; misrepresen-tation; deception &c. 545; untruth &c. 546; guile; bad faith; lying &c. *v.*; mis-representation; mendacity, perjury, false swearing; forgery, invention, fabrication; subreption; covin.

perversion –, suppression- of truth; *suppressio veri*; perversion, distortion, false colouring; exaggeration &c. 549; prevarication, equivocation, shuffling, fencing, evasion, fraud; *suggestio falsi* &c. (*lie*) 546; mystification &c. (*con-cealment*) 528; simulation &c. (*imita-tion*) 19; dis-simulation, -sembling; deceit.

sham; pretence, pretending, malin-gering.

lip-homage, – service; mouth honour; hollowness; mere -show, – outside, eye-wash, window dressing; duplicity, double dealing, insincerity, hypocrisy, cant, humbug, casuistry; jesuit-ism, -ry; pharisaism; Machiavelism, 'organ-ized hypocrisy'; crocodile tears, mealy-mouthedness, quackery; charlatan-ism, -ry; gammon; bun-kum, -come; flam, bam, flim-flam, cajolery, flattery; Judas kiss; perfidy &c. (*bad faith*) 940; *il volto sciolto i pensieri stretti.*

unfairness &c. (*dishonesty*) 940; art-fulness &c. (*cunning*) 702; misstate-ment &c. (*error*) 495.

V. be -false &c. *adj.*, – a liar &c. 548; speak -falsely &c. *adv.*; tell -a lie &c. 546; lie, fib; lie like a trooper; swear falsely, forswear, perjure oneself, bear false witness.

mis-state, -quote, -cite, -report, -represent; belie, falsify, pervert, distort; put a false construction upon &c. (*misinterpret*) 523.

prevaricate, equivocate, quibble; palter, – to the understanding; *répondre en Normand*; trim, shuffle, fence, mince the truth, beat about the bush, blow hot and cold, play fast and loose.

garble, gloss over, disguise, give a colour to; give –, put- a -gloss, – false colouring- upon; colour, varnish, cook, dress up, embroider: varnish right and puzzle wrong, exaggerate &c. 549.

invent, fabricate; trump -, get- up; forge, hatch, concoct; romance &c. (*imagine*) 515; cry 'wolf!'

dis-semble, -simulate; feign, assume, put on, pretend, make believe; play -false, - a double game; coquet; act -, play- a part; affect &c. 855; simulate, pass off for; counterfeit, fake, sham, make a show of; malinger; swing the lead; say the grapes are sour.

cant, play the hypocrite, sham Abraham, *faire pattes de velours*, put on the mask, clean the outside of the platter, lie like a conjuror; hang out -, hold out -, sail under- false colours; 'commend the poisoned chalice to the lips'; *ambiguas in vulgus spargere voces*; deceive &c. 545.

Adj. false, deceitful, mendacious, unveracious, fraudulent, untruthful, dishonest; faith-, truth-, troth-less; un-fair, -candid; evasive; un-, dis-ingenuous; hollow, insincere, *Parthis mendacior*; forsworn.

canting; hypocrit-, jesuit-, pharisa-ical; tartuffish; Machiavelian; double-tongued, -faced, -handed, -minded, -hearted, -dealing; two-faced, bare-faced; Janus-faced; smooth-faced, -spoken, -tongued; plausible; mealy-mouthed; affected &c. 855.

collus-ive, -ory; artful &c. (*cunning*) 702; perfidious &c. 940, spurious &c. (*deceptive*) 545; untrue &c. 546; falsified &c. *v.*; covinous.

Adv. falsely &c. *adj.*; *à la Tartufe*, with a double tongue; out of whole cloth; slily &c. (*cunning*) 702.

545. Deception.—N. deception; falseness &c. 544; untruth &c. 546; impos-ition, -ture; fraud, deceit, guile; fraudulen-ce, -cy; covin; knavery &c. (*cunning*) 702; misrepresentation &c. (*falsehood*) 544.

delusion, gullery, bluff, spoof, *blague*; juggl-ing, -ery; sleight of hand, legerdemain; presti-giation, -digitation; magic &c. 992; conjur-ing, -ation; hocus pocus, jockeyship; trickery, coggery, hanky-panky, chicanery, pettifogging, sharp practice; *supercherie*, cozenage, circumvention, ingannation, collusion; treachery &c. 940; practical joke.

trick, cheat, wile, ruse, blind, feint, plant, bubble, fetch, catch, chicane, juggle, reach, hocus, bite; thimble-rig, card-sharping, artful dodge, machination, swindle, hoax; tricks upon travellers; confidence trick; stratagem &c. (*artifice*) 702; theft &c. 791.

snare, trap, pitfall, decoy, gin; sprin-ge, -gle; noose, hook; bait, decoy-duck, tub to the whale, baited trap, *guet-à-pens*; cobweb, net, meshes, toils, mouse-trap, bird-lime; ambush &c. 530; trap-door, sliding panel, false bottom; spring-net. -gun; mask, -ed battery; mine; booby trap.

Cornish hug; wolf in sheep's clothing &c. (*deceiver*) 548; disguise, -ment; false colours, masquerade, mummery, borrowed plumes; *pattes de velours*.

mockery &c. (*imitation*) 19; copy &c. 21; counterfeit, sham, brummagem, make-believe, forgery, fraud, fake; lie &c. 546; 'a mockery, a delusion, and a snare,' hollow mockery.

whited -, painted- sepulchre; tinsel, paste, false jewellery, scagliola, ormolu, German silver, Britannia metal, paint; jerry building; man of straw.

illusion &c. (*error*) 495; *ignis fatuus* &c. 423; *mirage* &c. 443.

V. deceive, take in; defraud, cheat, jockey, do, cozen, diddle, nab, gyp, chouse, double cross, play one false, bilk, cully, jilt, bite, pluck, swindle, victimize; abuse; mystify; blind one's eyes; blindfold, hoodwink, spoof, bluff; throw dust into the eyes, 'keep the word of promise to the ear and break it to the hope,' 'draw a herring across the trail.'

impose –, practise –, play –, put –, palm –, foist- upon; snatch a verdict.

circumvent, overreach; out-reach, -wit, -manœuvre; steal a march upon, give the go-by to, leave in the lurch.

set –, lay- a -trap, – snare- for; bait the hook, forelay, spread the toils, lime; decoy, waylay, lure, beguile, delude, inveigle; tra-, tre-pan; kidnap; let-, hook-in; trick; en-, in-trap, -snare, entoil, benet; nick, springe; catch, – in a trap; sniggle, entangle, illaqueate, hocus, practise on one's credulity, dupe, gull, hoax, fool, befool, bamboozle; hum, -bug; gammon, stuff up, dope, sell; play a -trick, – practical joke- upon one; balk, trip up, throw a tub to a whale; fool to the top of one's bent, send on -a wild goose chase, – a fool's errand; make -game, – a fool, – an April fool, – an ass- of; trifle with, cajole, flatter; come over &c. (*influence*) 615; gild the pill, make things pleasant, divert, put a good face upon; dissemble &c. 544.

cog, – the dice, play with marked cards; live by one's wits, play at hide and seek; obtain money under false pretences &c. (*steal*) 791; conjure, juggle, practise chicanery; gerrymander.

play –, palm –, foist –, fob- off.

lie &c. 544; misinform &c. 538; mislead &c. (*error*) 495; betray &c. 940; be -deceived &c. 547.

Adj. deceived &c. *v.*; deceiving &c. *v.*; cunning &c. 702; prestigi-ous, -atory; decept-ive, -ious; deceitful, covinous; delus-ive, -ory; illus-ive, -ory; elusive, insidious, *ad captandum vulgus.*

untrue &c. 546; mock, sham, make-believe, counterfeit, faked, pseudo, spurious, so-called, pretended, feigned, trumped up, bogus, scamped, fraudulent, tricky, factitious, artificial, bastard; surreptitious, illegitimate, contraband, adulterated, sophisticated; unsound, rotten at the core; colourable; disguised; meretricious; tinsel, pinchbeck, plated; catch-penny; Brummagem; simulated &c. 544.

Adv. under -false colours, – the garb of, – cover of; over the left.

Phr. *fronti nulla fides.*

546. Untruth.—N. untruth, falsehood, lie, story, thing that is not, fib, bounce, crammer, taradiddle, whopper.

forgery, fabrication, invention; mis-statement, -representation; per-version, falsification, gloss, *suggestio falsi*; exaggeration &c. 549.

fiction; fable, nursery tale; romance &c. (*imagination*) 515; untrue –, false –, trumped up- -story, – statement; thing devised by the enemy; *canard*; shave, sell, hum, yarn, traveller's tale, Canterbury tale, cock and bull story, fairy tale, clap-trap.

myth, moonshine, bosh, all my eye, -and Betty Martin, mare's nest, farce.

irony; half truth, white lie, pious fraud; mental reservation &c. (*concealment*) 528.

pretence, pretext; false -plea &c. 617; subterfuge, evasion, shift, shuffle, make-believe; sham &c. (*deception*) 545.

profession, empty words; Judas kiss &c. (*hypocrisy*) 544; disguise &c. (*mask*) 530.

V. have a false meaning; not ring true.

pretend, sham, feign, counterfeit, make believe.

Adj. untrue, false, trumped up; void of -, without- foundation; far from the truth, false as dicer's oaths; unfounded, *ben trovato*, invented, fabulous, fabricated, forged; fict-, fact-, supposit-, surrept-itious; e-, il-lusory; ironical; satirical; evasive; *soi-disant* &c. (*misnamed*) 565.

Phr. *se non e vero e ben trovato.*

547. Dupe.—N. dupe, gull, gudgeon, *gobemouche*, cull, cully, victim, sucker, pigeon, April fool; laughing stock &c. 857; Cyclops, simple Simon, flat, mug, greenhorn; fool &c. 501; puppet, cat's paw.

V. be -deceived &c. 545, – the dupe of; fall into a trap; swallow –, nibble at- the bait; bite; catch a Tartar.

Adj. credulous &c. 486; mistaken &c. (*error*) 495.

548. Deceiver.—N. deceiver &c. (deceive &c. 545); dissembler, hypocrite; sophist, Pharisee, Jesuit, Mawworm, Pecksniff, Joseph Surface, Tartufe, Janus; serpent, snake in the grass, cockatrice, Judas, wolf in sheep's clothing; Molly Maguire; jilt; shuffler.

liar &c. (lie &c. 544); story-teller, perjurer, false-witness, *menteur à triple étage*, Scapin.

impostor, pretender, capper, decoy, fraud, *soi-disant*, humbug; adventurer; Cagliostro, Fernam Mendez Pinto; ass in lion's skin &c. (*bungler*) 701; actor &c. (*stage player*) 599.

quack, *charlatan*, mountebank, saltimbanco, *saltimbanque*, empiric, quacksalver, medicaster.

conjuror, juggler, magician, necromancer, trickster, prestidigitator, medium, jockey; crimp; decoy-duck, stool pigeon; rogue, knave, cheat; swindler &c. (*thief*) 792; jobber.

549. Exaggeration.—N. exaggeration; expansion &c. 194; hyperbole, stretch, strain, colouring; high colouring, caricature, *caricatura*; extravagance &c. (*nonsense*) 497; Baron Munchausen; men in buckram, yarn, fringe, embroidery, traveller's tale; Pelion upon Ossa.

storm in a teacup; much ado about nothing &c. (*over-estimation*) 482; puffery &c. (*boasting*) 884; rant &c. (*turgescence*) 577.

figure of speech, *façon de parler*; stretch of -fancy, – the imagination; flight of fancy &c. (*imagination*) 515.

false colouring &c. (*falsehood*) 544; aggravation &c. 835.

V. exaggerate, magnify, pile up, aggravate; amplify &c. (*expand*) 194; overestimate &c. 482; hyperbolize; over-charge, -state, -draw, -lay, -shoot the mark, -praise; make -much, – the most- of; strain, – a point; stretch, – a point; go great lengths; spin a long yarn; draw –, shoot with- a long-bow; deal in the marvellous.

out-Herod Herod, run riot, talk at random.

heighten, overcolour; colour -highly, – too highly; embroider, *broder*; flourish; colour &c. (*misrepresent*) 544; puff &c. (*boast*) 884.

Adj. exaggerated &c. *v.*; overwrought; bombastic &c. (*magniloquent*) 577; hyperbolical, on stilts; fabulous, extravagant, preposterous, egregious, *outré*, high-flying.

Adv. hyperbolically &c. *adj.*

Section III. MEANS OF COMMUNICATING IDEAS
1.° *Natural Means*

550. Indication.—N. indication; symbol-ism, -ization; semeio-logy, -tics; sign of the times.

lineament, feature, *trait*, characteristic, trick, diagnostic; divining-rod; cloven hoof; footfall; means of recognition; earmark.

sign, symbol; ind-ex, -ice, -icator; point, -er; marker; exponent, note, token, symptom.

type, figure, emblem, cipher, device; representation &c. 554; epigraph, motto, posy.

gest-ure, -iculation; pantomime; wink, glance, leer; nod, shrug, beck; touch, nudge; grip; dactylo-logy, -nomy; freemasonry, telegraphy, chirology, by-play, dumb-show; cue; hint &c. 527; clue, clew, key, scent, track &c. 551.

signal, -post; rocket, blue light; watch-fire, -tower; telegraph, sema-phore, flag-staff; cresset, fiery cross; calumet; heliograph, signal-, flash-lamp.

mark, line, stroke, dash, score, stripe, streak, scratch, tick, dot, point, notch, nick, blaze; asterisk, red letter, Italics, heavy type, inverted commas, quotation marks, sublineation, underlining, jotting; print; impr-int, -ess, -ession; note, annotation, mark of exclamation.

[For identification] badge, criterion; counter-check, -mark, -sign, -foil; duplicate, tally; label, tab, ticket, stub, billet, letter, counter, *tessera*, card, bill, check; witness, voucher; stamp; *cachet*; trade -, Hall- mark; broad arrow; signature; address -, visiting- card; *carte de visite*; credentials &c. (*evidence*) 467; passport, identity book; attesta-tion; hand, - writing, sign-manual; cipher; monogram, - mark, seal, sigil, signet; autograph, -y; paraph, brand; superscription; in-, en-dorsement; title, heading, rubric, docket; *mot -de passe, - du guet*; *passe-parole*; shibboleth; watch-, catch-, pass-word; open *sesame*.

insignia; banner, -et, -ol; bandrol; flag, colours, streamer, standard, eagle, labarum, oriflamb, *oriflamme*; figure-head; ensign; pen-non, -nant, -dant; burgee, blue Peter, jack, ancient, gonfalon, union-jack; tricolour, stars and stripes; bunting.

heraldry, crest; coat of -, arms; armorial bearings, hatchment; e-, scutcheon; shield, supporters; livery, uniform; cockade, *epaulette*, brassard, chevron; garland, chaplet, love-knot, fillet, favour.

[Of locality] beacon, cairn, post, staff, flagstaff, hand, pointer, vane, cock, weathercock; guide-, hand-, finger-, directing-, sign-post; pillars of Hercules, pharos, signal fire; land-, sea-mark; lighthouse, balize; pole-, load-, lode-star; cynosure, guide; address, direction, name; sign, -board.

[Of the future] warning &c. 668; omen &c. 512; prefigurement &c. 511. [Of the past] trace record &c. 551. [Of danger] warning &c. 668; alarm &c. 669. [Of authority] sceptre &c. 747. [Of triumph] trophy &c. 733. [Of quantity] gauge &c. 466. [Of distance] mile-stone, -post. [Of disgrace] brand, fool's cap, stigma, mark of Cain. [For detection] check, tell-tale; test &c. (*experiment*) 463.

notification &c. (*information*) 527; advertisement &c. (*publication*) 531.

word of command, call; bugle-, trumpet-call; reveille, taps; bell, alarum, cry; battle -, rallying- cry.

church, bell, angelus, sacring bell; muezzin.

exposition &c. (*explanation*) 522; proof &c. (*evidence*) 463; pattern &c. (*prototype*) 22.

V. indicate; be the -sign &c. *n.*- of; denote, betoken; argue, testify &c. (*evidence*) 467; bear the -impress &c. *n.*- of; con-note, -notate.

represent, stand for; typify &c. (*prefigure*) 511; symbolize.

put -an indication, - a mark, - &c. *n.*; note, mark, tick, blaze, stamp, earmark; set one's seal upon; label, ticket, docket; dot, spot, score, dash, trace, chalk; print; im-print, -press, surprint; engrave, stereotype, electrotype.

make a -sign &c. *n.*; signalize; give –, hang out- a signal; beck, -on; gesture; nod; wink, glance, leer, nudge, shrug, tip the wink; gesticulate; raise –, hold up- the -finger, – hand; saw the air, suit the action to the word.

wave –, unfurl –, hoist –, hang out- a banner &c. *n.*; wave -the hand, – a kerchief; give the cue &c. (*inform*) 527; show one's colours; give –, sound- an alarm; beat the drum, sound the trumpets, raise a cry.

sign, seal, attest &c. (*evidence*) 467; underline &c. (*give importance to*) 642; call attention to &c. (*attention*) 457; give notice &c. (*inform*) 527.

Adj. indicat-ing &c. *v.*, -ive, -ory; de-, con-notative; diacritical, representative, typical, symbolic, pantomimic, pathognomonic, symptomatic, ominous, characteristic, demonstrative, diagnostic, exponential, emblematic, armorial; individual &c. (*special*) 79.

known –, recognizable- by; indicated &c. *v.*; pointed, marked. [Capable of being denoted] denotable; indelible.

Adv. in token of; symbolically &c. *adj.*; in dumb show.

Phr. *ecce signum*; *ex ungue leonem, ex pede Herculem.*

---

551. Record.—N. trace, vestige, relic, remains; scar, *cicatrix*; foot-step, -mark, -print; track, mark, wake, trail, spoor, scent, *piste.*

monument, hatchment, escutcheon, slab, tablet, trophy, achievement; obelisk, pillar, column, monolith, cromlech, dolmen; memorial; *memento* &c. (*memory*) 505; testimonial, medal, ribbon, order; commemoration &c. (*celebration*) 883.

record, note, minute; *dossier*; register, -try; census, roll &c. (*list*) 86; cartulary, diptych, Domesday book; entry, memorandum, indorsement, inscription, copy, duplicate, docket; notch &c. (*mark*) 550; muniment, deed &c. (*security*) 771; document; deposition, *procès-verbal*; affidavit; certificate &c. (*evidence*) 467.

552. [Suppression of sign.] Obliteration.—N. obliteration; erasure, rasure; effacement; cancel, -lation; cassation; circumduction; deletion, blot; *tabula rasa.*

V. efface, obliterate, erase, rase, expunge, cancel; blot –, take –, rub –, scratch –, strike –, wipe –, wash –, sponge- out; wipe –, rub- off; wipe away; deface, render illegible; draw the pen through, apply the sponge.

be -effaced &c.; leave no -trace &c. 449; 'leave not a rack behind.'

Adj. obliterated &c. *v.*; out of print; printless; leaving no trace; intestate; un-recorded, -registered, -written.

Int. *dele*; out with it!

---

note-, memorandum-, pocket-, commonplace-book; portfolio; scoring-board, -sheet; bulletin board; card index, file; pigeon-holes, *excerpta, adversaria,* jottings, dottings.

gazette, -er; newspaper, magazine &c. 531; alman-ac, -ack; calendar, ephemeris, noctuary, diary, log, journal, account-, cash-, day-book, ledger.

archive, scroll, state-paper, Congressional Record, return, blue-book; statistics &c. 86; *compte rendu*; Acts –, Transactions –, Proceedings- of; Hansard's Debates; chronicle, annals; legend; history, biography &c. 594.

registration; en-, in-rolment; tabulation; entry, booking; signature &c. (*identification*) 550; recorder &c. 553; journalism.

drawing, photograph &c. 554; phonograph –, gramophone-record; music roll.

V. record; put –, place- upon record; go on record; chronicle, calendar, hand down to posterity; keep up the memory of &c. (*remember*) 505; commemorate &c. (*celebrate*) 883; report &c. (*inform*) 527; commit to –, reduce to- writing; put –, set down- -in writing, – in black and white; put –, jot –, take –, write –, note –, set- down; note, minute, put on paper; take –, make- a -note, – minute, – memorandum; make a return.

mark &c. (*indicate*) 550; sign &c. (*attest*) 467.

enter, book; post, – up; insert, make an entry of; mark –, tick-off; register, list, docket, enroll, inscroll; file &c. (*store*) 636.

Adv. on record.

553. Recorder.—N. recorder, notary, clerk; regis-trar, -trary, -ter; prothonotary; amanuensis, secretary, scribe, stenographer, remem-brancer, book-keeper, *custos rotulorum*, Master of the Rolls.

annalist; histori-an, -ographer; chronicler, journalist, reporter, col-umnist; biographer &c. (*narrator*) 594; antiquary &c. (*antiquity*) 122; memorialist.

draughtsman &c. 559; engraver 558; photographer, cinematographer, camera man.

Recording instrument, recorder, camera, phonograph, gramophone, dictaphone, telegraphone, telautograph, printing telegraph, tape ma-chine, ticker, time recorder, cash register, turnstile, speedometer, voting machine, seismograph, photostat.

554. Representation.—N. represent--ation, -ment; imitation &c. 19; illus-tration, delineation, depictment, por-trayal; imagery, portraiture, iconog-raphy; design, -ing; art, fine arts; painting &c. 556; sculpture &c. 557; engraving &c. 558; photography, radi-ography, skiagraphy.

person-ation, -ification; impersona-tion; drama &c. 599.

555. Misrepresentation.—N. mis-representation, distortion, exaggera-tion; daubing &c. *v.*; bad likeness, daub, sign-painting; scratch, carica-ture; *anamorphosis*.

V. misrepresent, distort, overdraw, travesty, parody, burlesque, exagger-ate, caricature, daub.

Adj. misrepresented &c. *v.*

———

picture, drawing, sketch, draught, draft; tracing; copy &c. 21; photo-, helio-graph; daguerreo-, talbo-, calo-, helio-type; cabinet, *carte-de-visite*, snapshot; X-ray photo-graph; radio-gram, -graph, skia-graph, -gram.

image, likeness, icon, portrait; striking –, speaking- likeness; very image; effigy, fac-simile.

figure, – head; puppet, doll, *figurine*, aglet, manikin, lay-figure, model, *marionnette*, *fantoccini*, bust; waxwork, statue, -tte, auto-maton, Robot.

hieroglyphic, anaglyph; dia-, mono-gram, -graph.

map, plan, chart; ground plan, projection, elevation; ichno-, carto-graphy; atlas; outline, scheme; view &c. (*painting*) 556.

artist, draughtsman &c. 559.

V. represent, delineate; depict, -ure; portray; picture; take –, catch- a likeness &c. *n.*; hit off, photograph, daguerreotype; figure; shadow -forth, – out; adumbrate; body forth; describe &c. 594; trace, copy; mould.

dress up; illustrate, symbolize.

paint &c. 556; carve &c. 557; engrave &c. 558.

person-ate, -ify; impersonate; assume a character; pose as; act;

play &c. (*drama*) 599; mimic &c. (*imitate*) 19; hold the mirror up to nature.

Adj. represent-ing &c. *v.*, -ative; illustrative; represented &c. *v.*; imitative, figurative.

like &c. 17; graphic &c. (*descriptive*) 594.

556. Painting.—N. painting; depicting; drawing &c. *v.*; design; perspective, skiagraphy; *chiaroscuro* &c. (*light*) 420; composition; treatment, values, atmosphere, tone, technique.

historical –, portrait –, miniature –, landscape –, marine –, flower –, scene- painting; scenography.

school, style; the grand style, high art, *genre*, portraiture; ornamental art &c. 847.

mono-, poly-chrome; *grisaille*.

pallet, palette; easel; brush, pencil, stump; blacklead, charcoal, crayons, chalk, pastel; paint &c. (*colouring matter*) 428; water-, body-, oil-colour; oils, oil-paint; varnish &c. 356*a*; *gouache*, tempera, distemper, fresco, water-glass; enamel; encaustic painting; *graffito, gesso*; mosaic; tapestry.

picture, painting, piece, *tableau*, canvas; oil &c.- painting; fresco, cartoon; easel –, cabinet- picture; drawing, draught, draft; pencil &c. –, watercolour- drawing; sketch, outline; study.

portrait &c. (*representation*) 554; whole –, full –, half- length; kitcat, head; miniature; shade, *silhouette*; profile.

landscape, sea-piece, -scape; view, scene, prospect; interior; bird's-eye view; pan-, di-orama; still life.

picture –, art- gallery; *studio, atelier.*

V. paint, design, limn, draw, sketch, pencil, scratch, shade, stipple, hatch, dash off, chalk out, square up; colour, dead-colour, wash, varnish; draw in -pencil &c. *n.*; paint in -oils &c. *n.*; stencil; depict &c. (*represent*) 554.

Adj. painted &c. *v.*; pictorial, graphic, picturesque, decorative; classical, romantic, pre-Raphaelite, modern, cubist, futurist, vorticist.

pencil, oil &c. *n.*

Adv. in -pencil &c. *n.*

Phr. *fecit, delineavit.*

557. Sculpture.—N. sculpture, insculpture; carving &c. *v.*; statuary ceramics, plastic arts.

high –, low –, bas- relief; relievo; *basso-, alto-, mezzo-relievo; intaglio* anaglyph; medal, -lion; *cameo.*

marble, bronze, *terra cotta*; ceramic ware, pottery, porcelain, china, earthenware, faïence, enamel, *cloisonné.*

statue &c. (*image*) 554; cast &c. (*copy*) 21; glyptotheca.

V. sculpture, carve, cut, chisel, model, mould; cast.

Adj. sculptured &c. *v.*; in relief, anaglyptic, ceroplastic, ceramic; parian; marble &c. *n.*

558. Engraving.—N. engraving, chalcography; line –, mezzotint –, stipple –, chalk- engraving; dry-point, bur; etching, aquatinta; plate –, copper-plate –, steel –, wood-, process-, photo-engraving; xylo-, ligno-, glypto-, cero-, litho-, chromolitho-, photolitho-, zinco-, glypho- -graphy, -graph.

impression, print, engraving, plate; steel-, copper-plate; etching; mezzo-, aqua-, litho-tint; cut, woodcut, block; stereo-, grapho-, auto-, helio-type; half-tone; *photogravure, rotogravure.*

graver, *burin*, etching-point, style; plate, stone, wood-block, negative; die, punch, stamp.

printing; plate –, copper-plate –, intaglio –, anastatic –, lithographic –, colour –, three colour- printing; type-printing &c. 591.

illustr-, illumin-ation; *vignette*, initial letter, *cul de lampe*, tail-piece.

V. engrave, grave, stipple, scrape, etch; bite, – in; lithograph &c. *n.*; print.

Adj. insculptured; engraved &c. *v.*

Phr. *sculpsit, imprimit.*

559. Artist.—N. artist; painter, limner, drawer, sketcher, delineator; cartoon-, caricatur-ist, designer, engraver; draughtsman; copyist; enamel-ler, -list.

historical –, landscape –, genre –, marine –, flower –, portrait –, miniature –, scene –, sign- painter; engraver; Apelles; sculptor, carver, chaser, modeller, lapidary, *figuriste*, statuary; Phidias, Praxiteles; Royal Academician.

photographer, retoucher.

2°. *Conventional Means*

1. *Language generally*

560. Language.—N. language; phraseology &c. 569; speech &c. 582; tongue, lingo, vernacular, slang; mother –, vulgar –, native- tongue; household words; King's *or* Queen's English; idiom; dialect &c. 563.

volapuk, esperanto, ido, occidental, Ro.

confusion of tongues, Babel, *pasigraphie*; pantomime &c. (*signs*) 550; *onomatopœia.*

phil-, gloss-, glott-ology; linguistics, chrestomathy; paleo-logy; -graphy; comparative grammar.

literature, letters, polite literature, *belles lettres*, muses, humanities, *literæ humaniores*, republic of letters, dead languages, classics; genius of a language; scholarship &c. (*knowledge*) 490.

linguist &c. (*scholar*) 492.

V. speak, say, express by words &c. 566.

Adj. lingu-al, -istic; dialectic; vernacular, current, colloquial, slangy; bilingual, polyglot; literary.

561. Letter.—N. letter; character; hieroglyphic &c. (*writing*) 590; type &c. (*printing*) 591; capitals; majus-, minus-cule; alphabet, ABC, abecedary, Christ-cross-row.

consonant, vowel, diphthong; mute, surd; sonant, liquid, labial, dental, palatal, guttural.

syllable; mono-, dis-, poly-syllable; affix, prefix, suffix.

spelling, orthography; phon-ography, -etic spelling; ana-, meta-grammatism.

cipher, monogram, anagram; double –, acrostic.

V. spell.

Adj. literal; alphabetical, abecedarian; syllabic; uncial &c. (*writing*) 590; phonetic, voiced, mute &c. *n.*

562. Word.—N. word, term, vocable; name &c. 564; phrase &c. 566; root, etymon; derivative; part of speech &c. (*grammar*) 567.

dictionary, vocabulary, word book,

563. Neology.—N. neolo-gy, -gism; new-fangled expression; barbarism; caconym; archaism, black letter, monkish Latin; corruption; missaying, antiphrasis.

lexicon, index, glossary, thesaurus, *gradus*, *delectus*, concordance.

etymology, lexicology, derivation; phonology, orthoepy; gloss-, termin-, orism-ology; paleology &c. (*philology*) 560; comparative philology.

lexicograph-er, -y; glossographer &c. (*scholar*) 492; etymologist; logolept.

verbosity, verbiage, loquacity &c. 584.

Adj. verbal, literal; titular, nominal. [Similarly derived] conjugate, parony-mous; derivative.

Adv. verbally &c. *adj.*; *verbatim* &c. (*exactly*) 494.

---

paronomasia, play upon words; word-play &c. (*wit*) 842; *double-entente* &c. (*ambiguity*) 520; palindrome, paragram, clinch; abuse of -language, – terms.

dialect, brogue, *patois*, provincialism, broken English, *lingua franca*; Brit-, Gall-, Scott-, Hibern-icism; American-ism; Gipsy lingo, Romany, pidgin English.

dog Latin, macaronics, gibberish, confusion of tongues, Babel; jargon.

colloquialism &c. (*figure of speech*) 521; by-word; technicality, lingo, slang, cant, *argot*, St. Giles's Greek, thieves' Latin, peddler's French, flash tongue, Billingsgate, Wall Street slang.

pseudonym &c. (*misnomer*) 565; Mr. So-and-so; what d'ye call 'em, what's his name; thingum-my, -bob; *je ne sais quoi*.

neologist, coiner of words.

V. coin words.

Adj. neologic, -al; rare; archaic; obsolete &c. (*old*) 124; colloquial, dialectic, slang, cant.

---

564. Nomenclature. — N. nomen-clature; naming &c. *v.*; nuncupation, nomination, baptism; orismology; *onomatopœia*; antonomasia.

name; appella-tion, -tive; designa-tion; title; head, -ing, caption; denomi-nation; by-name, epithet.

style, proper name; præ-, ag-, cog-nomen; patronymic, surname; cog-nomination; compellation, description; empty -title, – name; handle to one's name; namesake, eponym.

synonym, antonym.

term, expression, noun; by-word; convertible terms &c. 522; technical term; cant &c. 563.

V. name, call, term, denominate, designate, style, entitle, intitule, clepe, dub, christen, baptize, nickname, char-acterize, specify, define, distinguish by the name of; label &c. (*mark*) 550.

be -called &c. *v.*; take –, bear –, go (*or* be known) by –, go (*or* pass) under –, rejoice in- the name of.

Adj. named &c. *v.*; hight, yclept, known as; what one may -well, – fairly, – properly, – fitly- call.

nuncupa-tory, -tive; cognominal, titular, nominal; orismological.

---

565. Misnomer.—N. misnomer; *lucus a non lucendo*; Mrs. Malaprop; what d'ye call 'em &c. (*neologism*) 563.

nickname, *sobriquet*, by-name, han-dle, moniker; assumed -name, – title; *alias*; *nom de -guerre, – plume, – théâtre*; pseudonym, pen name, stage name.

V. mis-name, -call, -term; nick-name; assume -a name, – an alias.

Adj. misnamed &c. *v.*; pseudony-mous; *soi-disant*; self-called, -styled, -christened; so-called.

nameless, anonymous; without a –, having no- name; innominate, un-named.

Adv. in no sense.

---

566. Phrase.—N. phrase, expression, set phrase; sentence, paragraph; figure of speech &c. 521; idi-om, -otism; turn of expression.

paraphrase &c. (*synonym*) 522; periphrase &c. (*circumlocution*) 573; motto &c. (*proverb*) 496.

phraseology &c. 569.

V. express, phrase; word, – it; give -words, – expression- to; voice; arrange in –, clothe in –, put into –, express by- words; couch in terms; find words to express; speak by the card.

Adj. expressed &c. *v.*; idiomatic.

Adv. in -round, – set, – good, set- terms; in set phrases.

567. Grammar.—N. grammar, accidence, syntax, *praxis*, analysis, paradigm, punctuation; parts of speech; inflexion, case, declension, conjugation; *jus et norma loquendi*; Lindley Murray &c. (*school-book*) 542; correct style; philology &c. (*language*) 560.

V. parse, analyze; decline, conjugate; punctuate.

Adj. grammatical; syntactic; inflexional.

568. Solecism.—N. solecism; bad -, false -, faulty- grammar; slip, error; slip of the -pen, – tongue; *lapsus calami-, – linguæ; faux pas*; slip-slop; bull.

V. use -bad, – faulty- grammar; solecize, commit a solecism; murder the -King's, – Queen's- English; break Priscian's head.

Adj. ungrammatical; in-correct, -accurate; faulty, improper, incongruous, abnormal.

---

569. Style.—N. style, diction, phraseology, wording; manner, strain; composition; mode of expression, choice of words, literary power, ready pen, pen of a ready writer; command of language &c. (*eloquence*) 582; authorship; *la morgue littéraire*.

V. express by words &c. 566; write.

Various Qualities of Style

570. Perspicuity.—N. perspicuity &c. (*intelligibility*) 518; plain speaking &c. (*manifestation*) 525; defin-iteness, -ition; exactness &c. 494; perspicuousness, logical acuteness.

Adj. lucid &c. (*intelligible*) 518; explicit &c. (*manifest*) 525; exact &c. 494.

571. Obscurity.—N. obscurity &c. (*unintelligibility*) 519; involution; hard words; ambiguity &c. 520; vagueness &c. 475, inexactness &c. 495; what d'ye call 'em &c. (*neologism*) 563; cloudiness, confusion.

Adj. obscure &c. *n.*; crabbed, involved, confused.

572. Conciseness.—N. conciseness &c. *adj.*; brevity, 'the soul of wit,' laconism; Tacitus; ellipsis; syncope; abridgment &c. (*shortening*) 201; compression &c. 195; epitome &c. 596; monostitch; portmanteau word, telescope word, protogram.

V. be -concise &c. *adj.*; condense &c. 195; abridge &c. 201; abstract &c. 596; come to the point.

Adj. concise, brief, short, terse, close; to the point, exact; neat, compact, condensed, pointed; laconic, curt, pithy, trenchant, summary; pregnant; compendious &c. (*compendium*) 596; succinct; elliptical, epigrammatic, crisp, sententious.

Adv. concisely &c. *adj.*; briefly,

573. Diffuseness.—N. diffuseness &c. *adj.*; amplification &c. *v.*; dilating &c. *v.*; verbosity, *verbiage*, wordiness, cloud of words, *copia verborum*; flow of words &c. (*loquacity*) 584.

poly-, tauto-, batto-, perisso-logy; pleonasm, exuberance, redundance; thrice-told tale; prolixity; circumlocution, *ambages*; periphra-se, -sis; roundabout phrases; episode; expletive; penny-a-lining; padding, drivel, twaddle, rigmarole; richness &c. 577.

V. be -diffuse &c. *adj.*; run out on, descant, expatiate, enlarge, dilate, amplify, expand, inflate, pad; launch –, branch- out; rant.

maunder, prose; harp upon &c. (*repeat*) 104; dwell on, insist upon.

summarily; in -brief, – short, – a word, – few words, – a nutshell; for shortness sake; to -come to the point, – make a long story short, – cut the matter short, – be brief; it comes to this, the long and the short of it is.

-winded, -spun, -drawn out; prosing, maundering; roundabout; digressive; dis-, ex-cursive; rambling, episodic; flatulent, frothy.

digress, ramble, *battre la campagne*, beat about the bush, perorate, spin a long yarn, protract; spin –, swell –, draw- out, drivel.

Adj. dif-, pro-fuse; wordy, verbose, largiloquent, copious, exuberant, effusive, pleonastic, lengthy; long, -some, diffusive, spun out, protracted, prolix, circumlocutory, periphrastic, ambagious,

Adv. diffusely &c. *adj.*; at large, *in extenso*; about it and about it.

574. Vigour.—N. vigour, power, force; boldness, raciness &c. *adj.*; spirit, point, antithesis, piquancy; *verve*, glow, fire, warmth, ardour, enthusiasm; 'thoughts that breathe and words that burn'; strong language; punch; gravity, sententiousness; elevation, loftiness, sublimity.

eloquence; command of -words, – language.

Adj. vigorous, nervous, powerful, forcible, trenchant, mordant, biting, incisive, impressive; sensational.

spirited, lively, glowing, sparkling, racy, bold, slashing; pungent, *piquant*, full of point, pointed, pithy, antithetical; sententious.

lofty, elevated, sublime, grand, weighty, ponderous; eloquent; vehement, petulant, impassioned; poetic.

Adv. in -glowing, – good set, – no measured- terms.

575. Feebleness.—N. feebleness &c. *adj.*

Adj. feeble, bald, tame, meagre, insipid, nerveless, jejune, vapid, trashy, cold, frigid, poor, dull, dry, languid; pros-ing, -y, -aic; unvaried, monotonous, weak, frail, washy, wishy-washy, sloppy; sketchy, slight; careless, slovenly, loose, lax; slip-shod, -slop; inexact; dis-jointed, -connected; puerile, childish; flatulent; rambling &c. (*diffuse*) 573.

576. Plainness.—N. plainness &c. *adj.*; simplicity, severity; plain -terms, – English; Saxon English; household words.

V. speak plainly; call a spade 'a spade'; plunge *in medias res*; come to the point.

Adj. plain, simple; un-ornamented, -adorned, -varnished; home-ly, -spun; neat; severe, chaste, pure, Saxon; commonplace, matter of fact, natural, prosaic, sober, unimaginative.

dry, unvaried, monotonous &c. 575.

Adv. in plain -terms, – words, – English, – common parlance; point blank.

577. Ornament. — N. ornament; floridness &c. *adj.*; turg-idity, -escence; altiloquence &c. *adj.*; orotundity; declamation, teratology; well-rounded periods; elegance &c. 578.

inversion, antithesis, alliteration, *paronomasia*; figurativeness &c. (*metaphor*) 521.

flourish; flowers of -speech, – rhetoric; euph-uism, -emism.

big-, high-sounding words; macrology, *sesquipedalia verba*, sesquipedalianism; Alexandrine; inflation, pretension; rant, bombast, fustian, bunkum, balderdash, prose run mad; fine writing; Minerva press.

phrasemonger; euph-uist, -emist.

V. ornament, overlay with ornament, overcharge; smell of the lamp.

Adj. ornamented &c. *v.*; beautified &c. 847; ornate, florid, rich, flowery; euph-uistic, -emistic; sonorous; high-, big-sounding; inflated, swelling, tumid; turg-id, -escent; pedantic, pompous, stilted;

high-flown, -flowing; sententious, rhetorical, declamatory; grandiose; grand-, magn-, alt-iloquent; sesquipedal, -ian; Johnsonian, mouthy; bombastic; fustian; frothy, flashy, flaming, flamboyant.

antithetical, alliterative; figurative &c. 521; artificial &c. (*inelegant*) 579.

Adv. *ore rotundo*; with rounded phrase.

578. Elegance.—N. elegance, purity, grace, ease, felicity, distinction, gracefulness, refinement, readiness &c. *adj.*; concinnity, euphony, numerosity, balance, rhythm, symmetry, proportion; restraint; good taste, propriety.

well rounded -, well turned -, flowing- periods; the right word in the right place; antithesis &c. 577.

purist, stylist.

V. point an antithesis, round a period.

Adj. elegant, polished, classical, Attic, correct, Ciceronian, artistic; chaste, pure, Saxon, academical.

graceful, easy, readable, fluent, flowing, tripping; unaffected, natural, unlaboured; mellifluous; euph-onious, -emistic; rhythmical, balanced, symmetrical.

felicitous, happy, neat; well -, neatly- -put, - expressed.

579. Inelegance. — N. inelegance; vulgarity, bad taste; stiffness &c. *adj.*; unlettered Muse; barbarism; slang &c. 563; solecism &c. 568; mannerism &c. (*affectation*) 855; euphuism; fustian &c. 577; cacophony; want of balance; words that -break the teeth, - dislocate the jaw.

V. be -inelegant &c. *adj.*

Adj. inelegant, graceless, ungraceful, unpolished; harsh, abrupt; dry, stiff, cramped, formal, *guindé*; forced, laboured, awkward; artificial, mannered, ponderous; turgid &c. 577; affected, euphuistic; barbarous, uncouth, grotesque, rude, crude, halting; vulgar, offensive to ears polite.

2. *Spoken Language*

580. Voice.—N. voice; vocality; organ, lungs, bellows; good -, fine -, powerful &c. (*loud*) 404 -, musical &c. 413- voice; intonation; tone &c. (*sound*) 402- of voice.

vocalization; cry &c. 411; strain, utterance, prolation; exclam-, ejacul-, vocifer-ation; enunci-, articul-ation; articulate sound, distinctness; clearness, - of articulation; stage whisper; delivery; attack.

accent, -uation; emphasis, stress; broad -, strong -, pure -, native -, foreign- accent; pronunciation.

[Word similarly pronounced] homonym.

orthoepy; euphony &c. (*melody*) 413.

gastri-, ventri-loquism; ventriloquist; polyphon-ism, -ist.

[Science of voice] phonology &c. (*sound*) 402.

V. sing, speak, utter, breathe, voice; give -utterance, - tongue; cry &c.

581. Aphony.—N. aphony, *aphonia*; dumbness &c. *adj.*; obmutescence; absence -, want- of voice; dysphony; silence &c. (*taciturnity*) 585; raucity; harsh &c. 410 -, unmusical &c. 414- voice; *falsetto*, 'childish treble'; mute, dummy, deaf mute.

V. keep silence &c. 585; speak -low, - softly; whisper &c. (*faintness*) 405.

silence; render -mute, - silent &c. 403; muzzle, muffle, suppress, smother, gag, strike dumb, dumb-found, -founder; drown the voice, put to silence, stop one's mouth, cut one short. stick in the throat.

Adj. aphon-ous, -ic, dumb, mute; deaf-mute, - and dumb; mum; tongue-tied; breath-, tongue-, voice-, speech-, word-less; mute as a -fish, - stockfish, - mackerel; silent &c. (*taciturn*) 585; muzzled; in-articulate, -audible.

croaking, raucous, hoarse, husky,

(*shout*) 411; ejaculate, rap out; vocalize, prolate, articulate, enunciate, enounce, pronounce, accentuate, aspirate, deliver, mouth; emit, murmur, whisper, – in the ear, croon, yodel.

Adj. vocal, phonetic, oral; ejaculatory, articulate, distinct, stertorous; cnunciative; accentuated, aspirated; euphonious &c. (*melodious*) 413.

582. Speech.—N. speech, faculty of speech; locution, talk, parlance, verbal intercourse, prolation, oral communication, word of mouth, *parole*, palaver, prattle; effusion.

oration, recitation, delivery, say, address, speech, lecture, harangue, sermon, *tirade*, screed, formal speech, salutatory, peroration; prelection; speechifying; soliloquy &c. 589; allocution &c. 586; interlocution &c. 588.

oratory; elo-cution, -quence; rhetoric, declamation; grandi-, multiloquence; burst of eloquence; facundity; talkativeness; flow –, commandof -words, – language; *copia verborum*; power of speech, gift of the gab; *usus loquendi*.

speaker &c. *v.*; spokesman; pro-, inter-locutor; mouthpiece, Hermes; ora-tor, -trix, -tress; Demosthenes, Cicero; rhetorician; stump –, platform-orator, tub-thumper; elocutionist; speech-maker, patterer, *improvisatore*.

V. speak, – of; say, utter, pronounce, deliver, give utterance to; utter –, pour- forth; breathe, let fall, come out with; rap –, blurt- out; have on one's lips; have at the -end, – tip- of one's tongue.

break silence; open one's -lips, – mouth; lift –, raise- one's voice; give –, wag the- tongue; talk, outspeak; put in a word or two.

hold forth; make –, deliver- -a speech &c. *n.*; speechify, harangue, declaim, stump, flourish, spout, rant, recite, lecture, preach, sermonize, discourse, be on one's legs; have –, say- one's say; expatiate &c. (*speak at length*) 573; speak one's mind.

soliloquize &c. 589; tell &c. (*inform*) 527; speak to &c. 586; talk together &c. 588.

be -eloquent &c. *adj.*; have -a tongue in one's head, – the gift of the gab &c. *n.*

pass –, escape- one's lips; fall from the -lips, – mouth.

Adj. speaking &c., spoken &c. *v.*; oral, lingual, phonetic, not written, unwritten, outspoken; elo-quent, -cutionary; orat-, rhetorical; declamatory; grandiloquent &c. 577; talkative &c. 584.

dry, hollow, sepulchral, hoarse as a raven.

Adv. with -bated breath, – the finger on the lips; *sotto voce*; in a -low tone, – cracked voice, – broken voice; in an aside.

Phr. *vox faucibus hæsit.*

---

583. [Imperfect Speech.] Stammering.—N. inarticulateness; stammering &c. *v.*; hesitation &c. *v.*; impediment in one's speech; aphasia, titubancy, traulism; whisper &c. (*faint sound*) 405; lisp, drawl, tardiloquence; nasal -tone, – accent; twang; *falsetto* &c. (*want of voice*) 581; broken -voice, – accents, – sentences.

brogue &c. 563; slip of the tongue, *lapsus linguæ.*

V. stammer, stutter, hesitate, falter, hammer; balbu-tiate, -cinate; haw, hum and haw, be unable to put two words together.

mumble, mutter; maund, -er; whisper &c. 405; mince, lisp; jabber, gabble, gibber; sp-, spl-utter; muffle, mump; drawl, mouth; croak; speak -thick, – through the nose; snuffle, clip one's words; murder the -language, – King's (*or* Queen's) English; mis-pronounce, -say.

Adj. stammering &c. *v.*; inarticulate, guttural, nasal; tremulous.

Adv. *sotto voce* &c. (*faintly*) 405.

Adv. orally &c. *adj.*; by word of mouth, *vivâ voce*, from the lips of.
Phr. quoth –, said- he &c.

584. Loquacity. — N. loquac-ity, -iousness; talkativeness &c. *adj.*; garrulity; multiloquence, much speaking, effusion, wordiness.

jaw; gab, -ble; jabber, chatter; prate, prattle, cackle, clack; twaddle, twattle, rattle; *caquet, -terie*; blabber, *bavardage*, bibble-babble, gibble-gabble; small talk &c. (*converse*) 588.

fluency, flippancy, volubility, flowing tongue; flow, – of words; *flux de -bouche, – mots, – paroles*; *copia verborum, cacoëthes loquendi*; verbosity &c. (*diffuseness*) 573; gift of the gab &c. (*eloquence*) 582.

talker; chatter-er, -box; babbler &c. *v.*; rattle; ranter; sermonizer, proser, driveller; wind bag; gossip &c. (*converse*) 588; magpie, jay, parrot, poll, Babel; *moulin à paroles*.

V. be -loquacious &c. *adj.*; talk glibly, pour forth, patter; prate, palaver, prose, chatter, prattle, clack, jabber, jaw; rattle, – on; twaddle, twattle; babble, gabble; out-talk; talk oneself -out of breath, – hoarse; maunder, gush, blatter; talk a donkey's hind leg off; expatiate &c. (*speak at length*) 573; gossip &c. (*converse*) 588; din in the ears &c. (*repeat*) 104; talk -at random, – nonsense &c. 497; be hoarse with talking.

Adj. loquacious, talkative, conversational, garrulous, linguacious, multiloquous; chattering &c. *v.*; chatty &c. (*sociable*) 892; declamatory &c. 582; open-mouthed.

fluent, voluble, glib, flippant; long-tongued, -winded &c. (*diffuse*) 573.

Adv. trippingly on the tongue; glibly &c. *adj.*
Phr. the tongue running -fast, – loose, – on wheels.

585. Taciturnity.—N. silence, muteness, obmutescence; taciturnity, pauciloquy, costiveness, curtness; reserve, reticence &c. (*concealment*) 528; *aposiopesis.*

man of few words.

V. be -silent &c. *adj.*; keep silence; hold one's -tongue, – peace, – jaw; not speak &c. 582; say nothing; seal –, close –, put a padlock on- the -lips, – mouth; put a bridle on one's tongue; keep one's tongue between one's teeth; make no sign, not let a word escape one; keep a secret &c. 528; not have a word to say; lay –, place- the finger on the lips; render mute &c. 581.

stick in one's throat.

Adj. silent, mute, mum; silent as -a post, – a stone, – the grave &c. (*still*) 403; dumb &c. 581.

taciturn, sparing of words; close, – mouthed, – tongued; laconic, costive, inconversable, curt; reserved; reticent &c. (*concealing*) 528.

Int. tush! silence! mum! hush! *chut!* hist! tut! &c. 403.

---

586. Allocution. — N. allocution, alloquy, address; speech &c. 582; apostrophe, interpellation, appeal, invocation, salutation; word in the ear.

[Feigned dialogue] dialogism.

platform &c. 542; audience &c. (*interview*) 588.

V. speak to, address, accost, make up to, apostrophize, appeal to, invoke; hail, salute; call to, halloo.

take -aside, – by the button, button-hole; talk to in private.

lecture &c. (*make a speech*) 582.

Int. soho! halloo! hey! hist! hi!

587. Response &c., *see* Answer 462.

---

588. Interlocution.—N. interlocution; collocution, colloquy, converse, conversation, confabulation, talk, discourse, verbal intercourse; communion, oral communication, commerce; dia-, duo-, tria-logue.

causerie, chat, chit-chat; small –, table –, teatable –, town –, village –, idle- talk; tattle, gossip, tittle-tattle; babble, -ment; *tripotage*, cackle, prittle-prattle, *on dit*; talk of the -town, – village.

conference, parley, interview, audience, *pourparler*; *tête-à-tête*; reception, *conversazione*; congress &c. (*council*) 696; pow-wow.

hall of audience, *durbar*, coliseum, assembly hall, auditorium.

palaver, debate, logomachy, war of words, controversy.

talker, gossip, tattler; Paul Pry; tabby; chatterer &c. (*loquacity*) 584; interlocutor &c. (*spokesman*) 582; conversation-ist, -alist; dialogist.

'the feast of reason and the flow of soul'; *mollia tempora fandi*.

V. talk together, converse, confabulate; hold –, carry on –, join in –, engage in- a conversation; put in a word; shine in conversation; bandy words; parley; palaver; chat, gossip, tattle; prate &c. (*loquacity*) 584.

discourse –, confer –, commune –, commerce- with; hold -converse, – conference, – intercourse; talk it over; be closeted with; talk with one -in private, – *tête-à-tête*.

Adj. conversing &c. *v.*; interlocutory; convers-ational, -able; discursive, -çoursive; chatty &c. (*sociable*) 892; colloquial, *tête-à-tête*, confabulatory.

589. Soliloquy.—N. soliloquy, monologue, apostrophe.

solilo-quist, -quizer, monologist.

V. soliloquize; say –, talk- to oneself; say aside, think aloud, apostrophize.

Adj. soliloquizing &c. *v.*

Adv. aside.

---

3. *Written Language*

590. Writing.—N. writing &c. *v.*; chiro-, stelo-, cero-graphy, graphology; stylography; pen-craft, -script, -manship; quill-driving; typewriting.

writing, manuscript, MS., *literæ scriptæ*; these presents.

stroke –, dash- of the pen; *coup de plume*; line; pen and ink.

letter &c. 561; uncial writing, cuneiform character, arrow-head, Ogham, Runes, futhorc; hieroglyphic, hieratic, demotic; script; contraction.

short-hand; steno-, brachy-, tachy-graphy; secret writing, writing in cipher; crypt-, stegan-ography; phono-, pasi-, poly-, logo-graphy.

copy; tran-, re-script; draft, rough –, fair- copy; handwriting; signature, sign-manual; auto-, mono-, holo-graph; hand, fist; mark.

calligraphy; good –, running –,

591. Printing.—N. printing; block –, type- printing, lino-, mono-type; plate printing &c. (*engraving*) 558; the press &c. (*publication*) 531; composition.

print, letterpress, text, matter, standing type; context, note, page, column; over-running; head-, foot-line, title.

typography; stereo-, electro-, apro-type; type, black letter, heavy type, font, fount; pi, pie; capitals &c. (*letters*) 561; diamond, pearl, nonpareil, minion, brevier, bourgeois, long primer, small pica, pica, english, great primer.

folio &c. (*book*) 593; copy, impression, pull, proof, galley –, author's –, page- proof, revise.

printer, compositor, reader; printer's devil.

V. print; compose; put –, go- to press; pass –, see- through the press;

flowing –, cursive –, legible –, copper-plate –, round –, bold- hand.

cacography, *griffonage, barbouillage*; bad –, cramped –, crabbed –, illegible-hand; scribble &c. *v.*; *pattes de mouche*; ill-formed letters; pot-hooks and hangers.

stationery; pen, quill, goose-quill, reed; stylographic-, fountain-pen; pencil, style, stylus; paper, foolscap, parchment, vellum, papyrus, pad, tablet, block, note book, slate, marble, pillar, table, black board.

ink-bottle, -pot, -stand, -well, -horn; typewriter.

transcription &c. (*copy*) 21; inscription &c. (*record*) 551; super-scription &c. (*indication*) 550.

composition, authorship; *cacoethes scribendi*.

writer, scribe, amanuensis, scrivener, secretary, clerk, penman, copyist, transcriber, quill-driver; writer for the press &c. (*author*) 593.

shorthand writer, stenographer; typewriter, typist.

V. write, pen; copy, engross; write out, – fair; transcribe; scribble, scrawl, scrabble, scratch; interline; stain paper; write down &c. (*record*) 551; sign &c. (*attest*) 467; take down, – in shorthand; typewrite, type.

compose, indite, draw up, redact, draft, formulate; dictate; in-scribe, throw on paper, dash off; concoct.

take -up the pen, – pen in hand; shed –, spill –, dip one's pen in- ink.

Adj. writing &c. *v.*; written &c. *v.*; in -writing, – black and white; under one's hand.

uncial, Runic, cuneiform, hieroglyphical &c. *n.*

Adv. *currente calamo*; pen in hand.

592. Correspondence. — N. corre-spondence, letter, epistle, note, *billet,* post-, letter-card, missive, circular, form letter; favour, *billet-doux*; des-, dis-patch; *bulletin,* communication &c. 532; these presents; rescript, -ion; post &c. (*messenger*) 534; letter writer, correspondent.

V. correspond, – with; write –, send a letter- to; keep up a correspondence; drop a line to; despatch; communicate with; circularize.

Adj. epistolary.

593. Book.—N. book, -let; writing, work, volume, tome, opuscule; tract, -ate; *livret; brochure, libretto,* hand-book, treatise, text-book, codex, man-ual, pamphlet, monograph, enchiridion, circular, publication; book of poems; novel; chap-book.

part, issue, number, *livraison*; album, portfolio; periodical, serial, magazine, *ephemeris,* annual, journal.

paper, bill, sheet, broadsheet, screed; leaf, -let; fly-leaf, page; quire, ream.

chapter, section, head, article, para-graph, passage, clause, supplement, appendix; *feuilleton.*

folio, quarto, octavo; duo-, sexto-, octo-decimo.

en-, cyclopædia, dictionary, lexicon, thesaurus, concordance, anthology, bibliography; compilation, compendium, catalogue &c. 86; library, bibliotheca; the press &c. (*publication*) 531.

writer, author, *littérateur,* essayist, journalist, publicist; scribe, penman, war –, special –, correspondent; pen, scribbler, the scrib-bling race; ghost, hack, literary hack, Grub-street writer; writer for –, gentleman of –, representative of- the press; reporter, penny-a-liner; editor, sub-editor; playwright &c. 599; poet &c. 597.

bookseller, publisher; biblio-pole, -polist, -grapher; librarian; book -collector, – worm.

book -shop, – club, circulating –, lending –, public- library; publishing house.

knowledge of books, bibliography; book-learning &c. (*knowledge*) 490.

594. Description.—N. description, account, statement, report; *exposé* &c. (*disclosure*) 529; specification, particulars, scenario, plot; state –, summary- of facts; brief &c. (*abstract*) 596; return &c. (*record*) 551; *catalogue raisonné* &c. (*list*) 86; guide-book &c. (*information*) 527.

delineation &c. (*representation*) 554; sketch, vignette; monograph; minute –, detailed –, particular –, circumstantial –, graphic- account; narration, recital, rehearsal, relation.

histori-, chron-ography; historic Muse, Clio; history; bi-, autobi-ography; necrology, obituary.

narrative, history; memoir, memorials; annals &c. (*chronicle*) 551; tradition, legend, saga, epic, epos, story, tale, historiette; personal narrative, journal, letters, life, adventures, fortunes, experiences, confessions; anecdote, ana, *trait*.

work of fiction, short story, novelette, novel, romance, penny dreadful, shilling shocker, Minerva press; fairy –, nursery- tale; fable, allegory, parable, apologue.

relator &c. *v.*; *raconteur*; historian &c. (*recorder*) 553; biographer, fabulist, novelist, story teller, romancer, teller of tales, spinner of yarns, anecdotist.

V. describe; set forth &c. (*state*) 535; draw a picture, picture; portray &c. (*represent*) 554; characterize, particularize; narrate, relate, recite, recount, sum up, run over, recapitulate, rehearse, fight one's battles over again.

unfold &c. (*disclose*) 529- a tale; tell; give –, render- an account of; report, make a report, draw up a statement.

detail; enter into –, descend to- -particulars, – details.

Adj. descriptive, graphic, narrative, epic, suggestive, well-drawn; historic; auto-, biographical, realistic, expository, tradition-al, -ary; legendary; fabulous, mythical; anecdotic, storied; described &c. *v.*

595. Dissertation.—N. dissertation, treatise, essay; *thesis*, theme; tract, -ate, -ation, excursus; discourse, memoir, disquisition, lecture, sermon, homily, pandect.

commentary, review, *critique*, criticism, article; lead-er, -ing article, editorial; argument, running commentary.

investigation &c. (*inquiry*) 461; study &c. (*consideration*) 451; discussion &c. (*reasoning*) 476; exposition &c. (*explanation*) 522.

commentator, critic, essayist, pamphleteer; publicist, reviewer, leader writer, editor, annotator.

V. dissert –, descant –, write –, touch- upon a subject; dissertate; treat of –, take up –, ventilate –, discuss –, deal with –, go into –, canvass –, handle –, do justice to- a subject; comment, criticize, interpret &c. 522.

Adj. dis-cursive, -coursive; disquisitional, disquisitionary; expository, critical.

596. Compendium.—N. compend, -ium; abstract, *précis*, epitome, *multum in parvo*, analysis, pandect, digest, sum and substance, brief, abridgment, summary, *aperçu*, draft, minute, note; synopsis, text-book, *conspectus*, outlines, syllabus, contents, heads, prospectus.

album; scrap –, note –, memorandum –, commonplace- book; extracts, *excerpta*, cuttings; fugitive -pieces, – writings; *spicilegium*, flowers, anthology, miscellany, *collectanea, analecta*; compilation.

recapitulation, *résumé*, review.

abbrevia-tion, -ture; contraction; shortening &c. 201; compression &c. 195.

V. abridge, abstract, epitomize, summarize; make –, prepare –, draw –, compile- an abstract &c. *n.*

recapitulate, review, skim, run over, sum up.

abbreviate &c. (*shorten*) 201; condense &c. (*compress*) 195; compile &c. (*collect*) 72; edit, blue pencil.

Adj. compendious, synoptic, analectic, analytical; abridged &c. *v.*

Adv. in -short, – epitome, – substance, – few words.

Phr. it lies in a nutshell.

---

597. Poetry.—N. poetry, poetics, poesy, Muse, Calliope, tuneful Nine, Parnassus, Helicon, Pierides, Pierian spring, afflatus, inspiration.

versification, rhyming, making verses; prosody, scansion, orthometry.

poem; epic, – poem; epopee, *epopæa*, ode, epode, idyl, lyric, eclogue, pastoral, bucolic, georgic, dithyramb, anacreontic, sonnet, roundelay, *rondel, rondoletto, rondeau, rondo*, triolet; madrigal, canzonet, *cento*, monody, elegy, palinode; rhapsody.

dramatic –, lyric- poetry; opera; posy, anthology.

song, ballad, lay; love –, drinking –, war –, folk –, sea- song; lullaby; music &c. 415; nursery rhymes.

[Bad poetry] doggerel, Hudibrastic verse, prose run mad; macaronics; macaronic –, leonine- verse; runes.

canto, stanza, distich, verse, line, couplet, triplet, quatrain, sestet; *strophe, antistrophe*, refrain, chorus, burden.

verse, rhyme, assonance, crambo, metre, measure, foot, numbers, strain, rhythm; accentuation &c. (*voice*) 580; iambus, dactyl, spondee, trochee, anapæst &c.; hex-, pent-ameter; Alexandrine; blank verse, alliteration.

elegiacs &c. *adj.*; elegiac &c. *adj.* -verse, – metre, – poetry.

poet, – laureate; laureate; minor poet, bard, lyrist, scald, troubadour, *trouvère*; minstrel; minne-, meister-singer; *improvisatore*; versifier, sonneteer; ballad monger; rhym-er, -ist, -ester; poetaster.

V. poetize, sing, versify, make verses, rhyme, scan.

Adj. poetic, -al; lyric, -al; tuneful; epic; dithyrambic &c. *n.*; metrical; a-, catalectic; elegiac, iambic, trochaic, spondaic, anapæstic; Ionic, Sapphic, Alcaic, Pindaric.

598. Prose.—N. prose, – writer, pros-aism, -aist, -er.

V. prose, write prose.

write -prose, – in prose.

Adj. pros-y, -aic; unpoetical.

rhymeless, unrhymed, in prose, not in verse.

---

599. The Drama.—N. the -drama, – stage, – theatre, – play; theatricals, dramaturgy, histrionic art, buskin, sock, *cothurnus*, Melpomene and Thalia, Thespis.

play, drama, stage-play, piece, five-act play, tragedy, comedy, opera, comic opera, *vaudeville, comedietta, lever de rideau*, curtain raiser, interlude, afterpiece, exode, farce, *divertissement, extravaganza*, burletta, harlequinade, pantomime, mimodrama, burlesque, *opéra bouffe*, musical comedy, review, revue, intimate revue, variety, cabaret entertainment, *ballet, spectacle*, masque, *drame, comédie drame*; melo-drama, -drame; *comédie larmoyante*, emotional drama, sensation drama, tragi-, farcical-comedy; mono-drame, -logue; duologue; trilogy; charade, *proverbe*; mystery, miracle –, morality- play.

act, scene, *tableau*; in-, intro-duction; pro-, epi-logue, curtain; *libretto*, book, script.

performance, representation, show, *mise en scène*, stagery, *jeu de théâtre*, stage-craft; acting; gesture &c. 550; impersonation &c. 554; stage business, gag, patter, buffoonery.

theatre; play-, opera-house; house; music hall; *cabaret*; amphitheatre, circus, hippodrome; puppet-show, *fantoccini*; *marionnettes*, Punch and Judy.

cinema, -tograph-, picture –, theatre, the pictures, the movies, the talkies.

auditory, *auditorium*, front of the house, stalls, boxes, balcony, dress –, upper- -circle, – boxes, amphitheatre, pit, gallery; *foyer*; green-room; dressing rooms, *coulisses*.

flat; drop, – scene; wing, screen, side-scene; transformation scene, curtain, act-drop, safety –, fire- curtain; *proscenium*, forestage.

stage, revolving stage, scene, the boards; star –, grave –, trap, mezzanine floor; flies; gridiron, floats, battens, footlights; lime –, spot –, flood –, bunch-lights; scenery, set, *décor*; orchestra;

theatrical -costume, – properties, props.

part, *rôle*, character, cast, *dramatis personæ*; *répertoire*.

actor, player; stage –, strolling- player; old –, stager, performer; mime, -r; *artiste*; com-, trag-edian, straight man; *tragédienne*, Thespian, Roscius, star.

pantomimist, clown, harlequin, *buffo*, buffoon, *farceur, grimacier*, pantaloon, columbine; *Pierrot, Pierrette*; punch, -inello; *pulcinell-o, -a*; mute, *figurante*, general utility; super, -numerary, extra.

mummer, guiser, guisard, gysart, masque.

mountebank, Jack Pudding; tumbler, posture-master, acrobat, equilibrist, juggler, contortionist; *danseuse, ballerina*, ballet -dancer, – girl, *coryphée; bayadère, geisha*; chorus -singer, – girl.

company; first tragedian, *prima donna*, lead, leading lady, protagonist; *jeune premier*; juvenile lead, *débutant, -e*; light –, genteel –, low- -comedy, – comedian; *soubrette*, walking gentleman, *amoroso*, heavy, heavy father, *ingénue, jeune veuve, commère, compère*.

property man, *costumier*, machinist, stage hand, electrician, prompter, call-boy; director, manager; stage –, acting –, business- manager; *entrepreneur, impresario*, producer, press agent.

dramatic -author, – writer; play-writer, -wright; dramatist, mimographer; dramatic critic.

V. act, play, perform; stage, produce, put on the stage; personate &c. 554; mimic &c. (*imitate*) 19; enact; play –, act –, go through –, perform- a part; rehearse, spout, gag, rant; 'strut and fret one's hour upon a stage'; tread the -stage, – boards; come out; star.

Adj. dramatic; theatric, -al; scenic, histrionic, anctorial, comic, tragic, buskined, farcical, tragi-comic, melodramatic, operatic; stagey spectacular; stagestruck.

Adv. on the -stage, – boards; before -the floats, – an audience; in the limelight, behind the footlights; behind the scenes.

CLASS V

Words relating to THE VOLUNTARY POWERS*

CLASS V

WORDS RELATING TO THE VOLUNTARY POWERS*

DIVISION (I.) INDIVIDUAL VOLITION

Section I. VOLITION IN GENERAL

1°. *Acts of Volition*

600. Will.—N. will, volition, conation†, velleity; will and pleasure, free-will; freedom &c. 748; discretion; choice, inclination, intent, purpose, option &c. (*choice*) 609; voluntariness; spontane-ity, -ousness; originality.

pleasure, wish, desire, mind; frame of mind &c. (*inclination*) 602; intention &c. 620; predetermination &c. 611; self-control &c. determination &c. (*resolution*) 604; will-power.

V. will, list; see –, think- fit; determine &c. (*resolve*) 604; settle &c. (*choose*) 609; volunteer.

have a will of one's own; do what one chooses &c. (*freedom*) 748; have it all one's own way; have one's -will, – own way.

use –, exercise- one's discretion; take -upon oneself, – one's own course, – the law into one's own hands; do -of one's own accord, – upon one's own -responsibility, – authority; take the bit between one's teeth; take responsibility; originate &c. (*cause*) 153.

Adj. voluntary, volitive, volitional, wilful; free &c. 748; optional; discretion-al, -ary; volitient; dictatorial.

minded &c. (*willing*) 602; prepense &c. (*predetermined*) 611; intended &c. 620; autocratic; unbidden &c. (bid &c. 741); spontaneous; original &c. (*causal*) 153.

Adv. voluntarily &c. *adj.*; at -will, – pleasure; *à -volonté, – discrétion; al piacere; ad -libitum, – arbitrium;* as -one thinks proper, – it seems good to.

601. Necessity.—N. involuntariness; instinct, blind –, natural- impulse; inborn –, innate- proclivity; the force of circumstances.

necessi-ty, -tation, necessarianism; obligation; compulsion &c. 744; subjection &c. 749; stern –, hard –, dire –, imperious –, inexorable –, iron –, adverse- -necessity, – fate; what must be.

desti-ny, -nation; fatality, fate, *kismet*, doom, foredoom, election, predestination; pre-, fore-ordination; lot, fortune; fatalism, determinism; inevitableness &c. *adj.*; spell &c. 993.

star, -s; planet, -s; astral influence; sky, Fates, Norns, *Parcæ*, Sisters three, Clotho, Lachesis, Atropos; book of fate; God's will, will of Heaven; wheel of Fortune, Ides of March, Hobson's choice.

last -shift, – resort; *dernier ressort; pis aller* &c. (*substitute*) 147; necessaries &c. (*requirement*) 630.

necess-arian, -itarian; fatalist, determinist; automaton.

V. lie under a necessity; be -fated, – doomed, – destined &c., – in for, – under the necessity of; have no -choice, – alternative; be- obliged –, forced –, driven –, one's -fate &c. *n.*-to; be -pushed to the wall, – driven into a corner, – unable to help, – drawn irresistibly.

destine, doom, foredoom, devote; pre-destine, -ordain; cast a spell &c. 992; necessitate; compel &c. 744.

---

* Conative powers or faculties (Hamilton).   †Hamilton.

of one's own -accord, – free will; *proprio* –, *suo* –, *ex mero- motu*; out of one's own head; by choice &c. 609; purposely &c. (*intentionally*) 620; deliberately &c. 611.

Phr. *stet pro ratione voluntas; sic volo sic jubeo.*

Adj. necessary; needful &c. (*requisite*) 630.

fated; destined &c. *v.*; fateful; elect; spell-bound.

compulsory &c. (*compel*) 744; uncontrollable, inevitable, unavoidable, irresistible, irrevocable, inexorable, binding; avoid-, resist-less; written in the book of fate.

involuntary, instinctive, automatic, blind, mechanical; un-conscious, -witting, -thinking; unintentional &c. (*undesigned*) 621; impulsive &c. 612.

Adv. necessarily &c. *adv.*; of -necessity, – course; *ex necessitate rei*; needs must; perforce &c. 744; *nolens volens*; will he nil he, willy nilly, *bon gré mal gré*, willing or unwilling, *coûte que coûte*, forcefully. *faute de mieux*; by stress of; if need be.

Phr. it cannot be helped; there is no- help for, – helping- it; it -will, – must, – must needs- be, – be so, – have its way; the die is cast; *jacta est alea*; *che sarà sarà*; 'it is written'; one's- days are numbered, – fate is sealed; *Fata obstant*; *diis aliter visum.*

602. Willingness.—N. willingness, voluntariness &c. *adj.*; willing mind, heart.

disposition, inclination, leaning, *animus*; frame of mind, humour, mood, vein; bent &c. (*turn of mind*) 820; *penchant* &c. (*desire*) 865; aptitude &c. 698.

doc-ility, -ibleness, tractability; persuasi-bleness, -bility; pliability &c. (*softness*) 324.

geniality, cordiality; goodwill; alacrity, readiness, earnestness, forwardness, enthusiasm; zeal, eagerness &c. (*desire*) 865.

assent &c. 488; compliance &c. 762; pleasure &c. (*will*) 600.

labour of love, self-appointed task; volunteer, -ing, gratuitous service; unpaid worker, amateur.

V. be -willing &c. *adj.*; incline, lean to, mind, propend; had as lief; lend –, give –, turn- a willing ear; have -a, – half a, – a great- mind to; hold –, cling- to; desire &c. 865.

see –, think- -good, – fit, – proper; acquiescence &c. (*assent*) 488; comply with &c. 762.

swallow –, nibble at- the bait; gorge the hook; swallow hook, line and sinker; have –, make- no scruple of; make no bones of; jump –, catch- at; meet half way; volunteer, offer oneself &c. 763.

603. Unwillingness.—N. unwillingness &c. *adj.*; indispos-ition, -edness; disinclination, aversation, aversion; nolleity, nolition; renitence; reluctance; indifference &c. 866; backwardness &c. *adj.*; slowness &c. 275; want of -alacrity, – readiness; indocility &c. (*obstinacy*) 606.

scrupul-ousness, -osity; qualms of conscience, delicacy, demur, scruple, qualm, shrinking, recoil; hesitation &c. (*irresolution*) 605; fastidiousness &c. 868.

averseness &c. (*dislike*) 867; dissent &c. 489; refusal &c. 764.

slacker, scrimshanker, *embusqué*, unwilling worker, forced labor.

V. be -unwilling &c. *adj.*; nill; dislike &c. 867; grudge, begrudge; not be able to find it in one's heart to, not have the stomach to.

demur, stick at, scruple, stickle; hang fire, run rusty, slack, shirk, scamp, give up, fight shy of, not pull fair; recoil, shrink, swerve; hesitate &c. 605; avoid &c. 623.

oppose &c. 708; dissent &c. 489; refuse &c. 764.

Adj. unwilling; not in the vein, loth, shy of, disinclined, indisposed, averse, reluctant, not content; adverse &c. (*opposed*) 708; laggard, backward, remiss, slack, slow to; renitent; indifferent &c. 866; scrupulous; squeamish

Adj. willing, minded, fain, disposed, inclined, favourable; favourably-minded, -inclined, -disposed; nothing loth; in the -vein, – mood, – humour, – mind.

ready, forward, enthusiastic, earnest, eager; bent upon &c. (*desirous*) 865; predisposed, propense.

docile; persua-dable, -sible; suasible, easily persuaded, facile, easy-going; amenable; tractable &c. (*pliant*) 324; genial, gracious, cordial, hearty; content &c. (*assenting*) 488.

voluntary, gratuitous, spontaneous; unasked &c. (ask &c. 765); unforced &c. (*free*) 748.

Adv. willingly &c. *adj.*; fain, freely, as lief, heart and soul; with -pleasure, – all one's heart, – open arms; with -good, – right good- will; *de bonne volonté, ex animo*; *con amore*, heart in hand, nothing loth, without reluctance, of one's own accord, graciously, with a good grace, without demur.

à la bonne heure; by all -means, – manner of means; to one's heart's content; yes &c. (*assent*) 488.

Int. sure, -ly! of course!

&c. (*fastidious*) 868; repugnant &c. (*dislike*) 867; rest-iff, -ive; demurring &c. *v.*; unconsenting &c. (*refusing*) 764; involuntary &c. 601; grudging, irreconcilable.

Adv. unwillingly &c. *adj.*; grudgingly, with a heavy heart; with -a bad, – an ill- grace; against –, sore against- -one's wishes, – one's will, – the grain; *invitâ Minervâ*; *à contre cœur*; *malgré soi*; in spite of -one's teeth, – oneself; *nolens volens* &c. (*necessity*) 601; perforce &c. 744; under protest; no &c. 536; not for the world, far be it from me; not if I can help it; if I must I must.

---

604. Resolution.—N. determination, will; iron –, unconquerable- will; will of one's own, decision, resolution, backbone, grit; strength of -mind, – will; resolve &c. (*intent*) 620; *intransigeance*; firmness &c. (*stability*) 150; energy, manliness, vigour; game, pluck; resoluteness &c. (*courage*) 861; zeal &c. 682; *aplomb*; desperation; devot-ion, -edness.

mastery over self; self-control, -command, -mastery, -possession, -reliance, -government, -restraint, -conquest, -denial; moral -courage, – strength, – fibre; perseverance &c. 604a; tenacity; obstinacy &c. 606; bull-dog; British lion.

V. have -determination &c. *n.*; know one's own mind; be -resolved &c. *adj.*; make up one's mind, will, resolve, determine; decide &c. (*judgment*) 480; form –, come to- a -determination, – resolution, – resolve; conclude, fix, seal, determine once for all, bring to a crisis, drive matters to an extremity; take a decisive step &c. (*choice*) 609; take upon oneself &c. (*undertake*) 676.

devote oneself –, give oneself up- to; throw away the scabbard, kick down

605. Irresolution.—N. irresolution, infirmity of purpose, indecision; in-, un-determination, loss of will power; unsettlement; uncertainty &c. 475; demur, suspense; hesi-tating &c. *v.*, -tation, -tancy; vacillation; ambivalence; changeableness &c. 149; fluctuation; alternation &c. (*oscillation*) 314; caprice &c. 608; lukewarmness.

fickleness, levity, *légèreté*; pliancy &c. (*softness*) 324; weakness; timidity &c. 860; cowardice &c. 862; half measures.

waverer, ass between two bundles of hay; shuttlecock, butterfly; time-server, opportunist, turn coat.

V. be -irresolute &c. *adj.*; hang –, keep- in suspense; leave '*ad referendum*'; think twice about, pause; dawdle &c. (*inactivity*) 683; remain neuter; dilly dally, hesitate, boggle, hover, wobble, shilly-shally, hum and haw, demur, not know one's own mind; debate, balance; dally –, coquet- with; will and will not, *chasser-balancer*; go half-way, compromise, make a compromise; be thrown off one's balance, stagger like a drunken man; be afraid &c. 860; let 'I dare not' wait upon 'I would'; falter, waver.

the ladder, nail one's colours to the mast, set one's back against the wall, set one's teeth, put one's foot down, burn one's bridges, take one's stand; stand firm &c. (*stability*) 150; steel oneself; stand no nonsense, not listen to the voice of the charmer.

buckle to; put –, lay –, set- one's shoulder to the wheel; put one's heart into; run the gantlet, make a dash at, take the bull by the horns; beard the lion in his den; rush –, plunge– *in medias res*; go in for; insist upon, make a point of; set one's heart, – mind-upon.

stick at nothing; make short work of &c. (*activity*) 682; not stick at trifles; go -all lengths, – the whole hog; persist &c. (*persevere*) 604a; go down with colours flying, die game; go through fire and water, ride in the whirlwind and direct the storm.

Adj. resolved &c. *v.*; determined; strong-willed, -minded; resolute &c. (*brave*) 861; self-possessed, plucky, tenacious; decided, definitive, peremptory; un-hesitating, -flinching, -shrinking; firm, cast iron, indomitable, game to the backbone; inexorable, relentless, not to be -shaken, – put down; *tenax propositi*; inflexible &c. (*hard*) 323; obstinate &c. 606; steady &c. (*persevering*) 604a; unbending, un-yielding, irrevocable; firm as a rock; grim.

earnest, serious; set –, bent –, intent- upon.

steeled –, proof- against; *in utrumque paratus*.

Adv. resolutely &c. *adj.*; in –, in good- earnest; seriously, joking apart, earnestly, heart and soul; on one's metal; manfully, like a man, with a high hand; with a strong hand &c. (*exertion*) 686.

at any -rate, – risk, – hazard, – price, – cost, – sacrifice; at all -hazards, – risks, – events; cost what it may; *coûte que coûte*; *à tort et à travers*; once for all; neck or nothing; rain or shine; with colours nailed to the mast.

Phr. *spes sibi quisque.*

vacillate &c. 149; change &c. 140; retract &c. 607; fluctuate; alternate &c. (*oscillate*) 314; keep off and on, play fast and loose; blow hot and cold &c. (*caprice*) 608.

shuffle, palter, blink; trim.

Adj. irresolute, infirm of purpose, double-minded, half-hearted; un-decided, -resolved, -determined; drifting; shilly-shally; fidgety, tremulous; wobbly; hesitating &c. *v.*; off one's balance; at a loss &c. (*uncertain*) 475.

vacillating &c. *v.*; unsteady &c. (*changeable*) 149; unsteadfast, fickle, unreliable, irresponsible, unstable, without ballast; capricious &c. 608; volatile, frothy; light, -some, -minded; giddy; fast and loose.

weak, feeble-minded, frail; timid &c. 860; cowardly &c. 862; facile; pliant &c. (*soft*) 324; unable to say 'no,' easy-going.

revocable, reversible.

Adv. irresolutely &c. *adj.*; irresolved-ly; in faltering accents; off and on; from pillar to post; see-saw &c. 314.

Int. 'how happy could I be with either!'

604a. Perseverance.—N. perseverance; continuance &c. (*inaction*) 143; permanence &c. (*absence of change*) 141; firmness &c. (*stability*) 150.

constancy, steadiness; singleness –, tenacity- of purpose; persistence, plodding, patience; sedulity &c. (*industry*) 682; pertina-cy, -city, -ciousness; iteration &c. 104.

bottom, game, pluck, stamina, backbone, grit; indefatiga-bility, bleness; bulldog courage.

V. persevere, persist; hold -on, – out; die in the last ditch, be in at the death; stick –, cling –, adhere- to; stick to one's text, keep on; keep to –, maintain- one's -course, – ground; bear –, keep –, hold-up; plod; stick to work &c. (*work*) 686; continue &c. 143; follow up; die -in harness, – at one's post.

Adj. persevering, constant; stead-y, -fast; un-deviating, -wavering, -faltering, -swerving, -flinching, -sleeping, -flagging, -drooping; steady as time; uninter-, un-remitting; plodding; industrious &c. 682; strenuous &c. 686; pertinacious; persist-ing, -ent.

solid, sturdy, staunch, stanch, true to oneself; unchangeable &c. 150; unconquerable &c. (*strong*) 159; indomitable, game to the last, indefatigable, untiring, unwearied, never tiring.

Adv. through -evil report and good report, – thick and thin, – fire and water; *per fas et nefas*; without fail, sink or swim, at any price, *vogue la galère*; in sickness and in health.

Phr. never say die; *vestigia nulla retrorsum.*

606. Obstinacy.—N. obstinateness &c. *adj.*; obstinacy, tenacity; perseverance &c. 604a; immovability; old school; inflexibility &c. (*hardness*) 323; obdur-acy, -ation; dogged resolution; resolution &c. 604; ruling passion; blind side.

self-will, contumacy, perversity; pervica-cy, -city; indocility.

bigotry, intolerance, dogmatism; opinia-try, -tiveness; fixed idea &c.; intractability, incorrigibility; (*prejudgment*) 481; fanaticism, zealotry, infatuation, monomania, opinionativeness.

mule; opin-ionist, -ionatist, -iator, -ator; stickler, dogmatist, die-hard, bitter-ender; bigot; zealot, enthusiast, fanatic.

V. be -obstinate &c. *adj.*; stickle, take no denial, fly in the face of facts; opinionate, be wedded to an opinion, hug a belief; have one's own way &c. (*will*) 600; persist &c. (*persevere*) 604a; have –, insist on having- the last word.

die -hard, – fighting, fight -against destiny, – to the last ditch; not yield an inch, stand out.

Adj. obstinate, tenacious, stubborn, obdurate, case-hardened; inflexible &c. (*hard*) 323; immovable, not to be moved; inert &c. 172; unchangeable &c. 150; inexorable &c. (*determined*) 604; mulish, obstinate as a mule, pig-headed.

dogged; sullen, sulky; un-moved, -influenced, -affected.

wilful, self-willed, perverse; res-ty, -tive, -tiff; pervicacious, wayward, refractory, unruly; head-y, -strong; *entêté*; contumacious; cross-grained.

607. Tergiversation.—N. change of -mind, – intention, – purpose; after-thought.

tergiversation, recantation; palin-ode, -ody; renunciation; abjur-ation, -ement; defection &c. (*relinquishment*) 624; going over &c. *v.*; apostasy; retract-ion, -ation; withdrawal, dis-avowal &c. (*negation*) 536; revo-cation, -kement; reversal; repentance &c. 950; *redintegratio amoris.*

coquetry, flirtation; vacillation &c. 605; back-sliding, recidivation.

turn-coat, -tippet; rat, apostate, renegade, mugwump; con-, per-vert; proselyte, deserter; backslider, recidiv-ist; black leg.

time-server, -pleaser; timist, Vicar of Bray, trimmer, ambidexter; weather-cock &c. (*changeable*) 149; Janus.

V. change one's -mind, – intention, – purpose, – note; abjure, renounce; withdraw from &c. (*relinquish*) 624; wheel –, turn –, veer- round; turn a *pirouette*; go over –, pass –, change –, skip- from one side to another; go to the right about; box the compass, shift one's ground, go upon another tack; back down, crawl, crawfish.

apostatize, change sides, go over, rat; recant, retract; revoke; rescind &c. (*abrogate*) 756; recall, forswear, abjure, unsay; come -over, – round- to an opinion.

draw in one's horns, eat one's words; eat –, swallow- the leek; swerve, flinch, back out of, retrace one's steps, think better of it; come back –, return- to one's first love; turn over a new leaf &c. (*repent*) 950.

arbitrary, dogmatic, opinionated, positive, bigoted; prejudiced &c. 481; prepossessed, infatuated; stiff-backed, -necked, -hearted; hard-mouthed, hidebound; unyielding; im-pervious, -practicable, -persuasible; unpersuadable; in-, un-tractable; incorrigible, deaf to advice, impervious to reason; crotchety &c. 608.

Adv. obstinately &c. *adj.*

Phr. *non possumus*; no surrender.

trim, shuffle, play fast and loose, blow hot and cold, coquet, flirt, hold with the hare but run with the hounds; straddle; *nager entre deux eaux*; wait to see how the -cat jumps, – wind blows.

Adj. changeful &c. 149; irresolute &c. 605; ductile, slippery as an eel, trimming, ambidextrous, timeserving; coquetting &c. *v.*

revocatory, reactionary.

Phr. 'a change came o'er the spirit of my dream.'

---

608. Caprice.—N. caprice, fancy, humour; whim, -sey, -wham; crotchet, *capriccio*, quirk, freak, maggot, fad, vagary, prank, fit, flimflam, *escapade*, *boutade*, wild-goose chase; capriciousness &c. *adj.*; kink.

V. be -capricious &c. *adj.*; have a maggot in the brain; take it into one's head, strain at a gnat and swallow a camel; blow hot and cold; play -fast and loose, – fantastic tricks.

Adj. capricious; erratic, eccentric, fitful, hysterical; full of -whims &c. *n.*; maggoty; inconsistent, fanciful, fantastic, whimsical, crotchety, particular, humoursome, freakish, skittish, wanton, wayward; contrary; captious; arbitrary; unrestrained, undisciplined; not amenable to reason; uncomfortable &c. 83; penny wise and pound foolish; fickle &c. (*irresolute*) 605; frivolous, sleeveless, giddy, volatile.

Adv. by fits and starts, without rhyme or reason, at one's own sweet will.

Phr. *nil fuit unquam sic impar sibi*; the deuce is in him.

---

609. Choice.—N. choice, option; discretion &c. (*volition*) 600; preoption; alternative; dilemma; *embarras de choix*; adoption, co-optation; novation; decision &c. (*judgment*) 480.

election, poll, ballot, vote, voice, suffrage, plumper, cumulative vote; *plebiscitum*, *plébiscite*, *vox populi*; referendum, electioneering; voting &c. *v.*; franchise; ballot box; slate, ticket.

selection, excerption, gleaning, eclecticism; *excerpta*, gleanings, cuttings, scissors and paste; pick &c. (*best*) 650.

preference, prelation; predilection &c. (*desire*) 865.

V. offer for one's choice, set before; hold out -, present -, offer- the alternative; put to the vote.

use -, exercise -, one's- -discretion, - option; adopt, take up, embrace, espouse; choose, elect, co-opt; take -, make- one's choice; make choice of, fix upon.

vote, poll, hold up one's hand; divide.

settle; decide &c. (*adjudge*) 480; list

609a. Absence of Choice.—N. no -, Hobson's- choice; first come, first served; necessity &c. 601; not a pin to choose &c. (*equality*) 27; any, the first that comes.

neutrality, indifference; indecision &c. (*irresolution*) 605.

V. be -neutral &c. *adj.*; have no choice; waive, not vote; abstain -, refrain- from voting; leave undecided; make a virtue of necessity.

Adj. neu-tral, -ter; indifferent; undecided &c. (*irresolute*) 605.

Adv. either &c. (*choice*) 609.

---

610. Rejection.—N. rejection, repudiation, exclusion; declination; refusal &c. 764.

V. reject; set -, lay- aside; give up; decline &c. (*refuse*) 764; exclude, except, eliminate; pluck, spin; cast.

repudiate, scout, set at naught; fling -, cast -, thrown -, toss- -to the winds, - to the dogs, - overboard, - away; send to the right about; dis-

&c. (*will*) 600; make up one's mind &c. (*resolve*) 604.

select; pick, – and choose; pick –, single- out, excerpt; cull, glean, winnow; sift –, separate –, winnow- the chaff from the wheat; pick up, pitch upon; pick one's way; indulge one's fancy.

set apart, reserve, mark out for; mark &c. 550.

prefer; have -rather, – as lief; fancy &c. (desire) 865; be persuaded &c. 615.

take a -decided, – decisive- step; commit oneself to a course; pass –, cross- the Rubicon; cast in one's lot with; take for better or for worse.

Adj. optional; co-optative; discretional &c. (*voluntary*) 600; on approval.

eclectic; choosing &c. *v.*; preferential; chosen &c. *v.*; choice &c. (*good*) 648.

Adv. optionally &c. *adj.*; at pleasure &c. (*will*) 600; either, – the one or the other; or; at the option of; whether or not; once for all; for one's money.

by -choice, – preference; in preference; rather, before.

claim &c. (*deny*) 536; discard &c. (*eject*) 297, (*have done with*) 678.

Adj. rejected &c. *v.*; reject-aneous, -itious; not -chosen &c. 609, – to be thought of; out of the question.

Adv. neither, – the one nor the other; no &c. 536.

Phr. *non hæc in fœdera.*

---

611. Predetermination. — N. premeditation, -deliberation, -determination, -destination; foreordination; foregone conclusion; *parti pris*; resolve, propendency; intention &c. 620; project &c. 626.

V. pre-determine, -destine, -meditate, -resolve, -concert; foreordain; resolve beforehand.

Adj. pre-pense, -meditated &c. *v.*, -designed; advised, studied, designed, calculated; aforethought; intended &c. 620; foregone.

well-laid, -devised, -weighed; maturely considered; cut and dried; cunning.

Adv. advisedly &c. *adj.*; with premeditation, deliberately, all things considered, with eyes open, in cold blood; intentionally &c. 620.

612. Impulse.—N. impulse, sudden thought; *impromptu*, improvisation; inspiration, hunch, flash, spurt.

improvisatore, improvisatrice, improviser, extemporizer; creature of impulse.

V. flash on the mind.

say what comes uppermost; improvise, extemporize; rise to the occasion; spurt.

Adj. extemporaneous, impulsive, indeliberate; improvis-ed, -ate, -atory; un-, unpre-meditated; *improvisé*; unprompted, -guided; natural, unguarded; spontaneous &c. (*voluntary*) 600; instinctive &c. 601.

Adv. extem-pore, -poraneously; offhand, *impromptu*, *à l'improviste*; improviso; on the spur of the -moment, – occasion.

613. Habit.—N. habit, -ude; assuetude, -faction; wont; run, way.

common –, general –, natural –, ordinary –, habitual- -course, – run, – state- of things; matter of course; beaten -path, – track, – ground.

prescription, custom, use, usage, immemorial usage, practice; tradition; prevalence, observance; conventional-

614. Desuetude.—N. desuetude, disusage; disuse &c. 678; want of -habit, – practice; inusitation; newness to; new brooms.

infraction of usage &c. (*unconformity*) 83; non-prevalence; 'a custom more honoured in the breach than the observance.'

V. be -unaccustomed &c. *adj.*; leave

ism, -ity; mode, fashion, vogue; *etiquette* &c. (*gentility*) 852; order of the day, cry; conformity &c. 82.

habitué, addict.

one's old way, old school, consuetude, *veteris vestigia flammæ*; *laudator temporis acti*.

rule, standing order, precedent, routine; red-tape, -tapism; pipe-clay; rut, groove.

cacoëthes; bad –, confirmed –, inveterate –, intrinsic &c. 5- habit; addiction, trick.

training &c. (*education*) 537; seasoning, hardening, inurement; radication; second nature, acclimatization; knack &c. (*skill*) 698.

V. be -wont &c. *adj.*

fall into a custom &c. (*conform to*) 82; tread –, follow- the beaten -track, – path; *stare super antiquas vias*; move in a rut, run on in a groove, go round like a horse in a mill, go on in the old jog-trot way.

habituate, inure, harden, season, caseharden; accustom, familiarize; naturalize, acclimatize; keep one's hand in; train &c. (*educate*) 537.

get into the -way, – knack- of; learn &c. 539; cling –, adhere- to; repeat &c. 104; acquire –, contract –, fall into- a -habit, – trick; addict oneself –, take- to; accustom oneself to.

be -habitual &c. *adj.*; prevail; come into use, become a habit, take root; gain –, grow- upon one.

Adj. habitual; ac-, customary; prescriptive; accustomed &c. *v.*; traditional; of -daily, – every-day- occurrence; wonted, usual, general, ordinary, common, frequent, every-day, household, jog-trot; well-trodden, -known; familiar, vernacular, trite, commonplace, banal, bromidic, conventional, regular, set, stock, officinal, established, stereotyped; pre-vailing, -valent; current, received, acknowledged, recognized, accredited; of course, admitted, understood.

conformable &c. 82; according to -use, – custom, – routine; in -vogue, – fashion; fashionable &c. (*genteel*) 852.

wont; used – given – addicted –, attuned –, habituated &c. *v.*- to; in the habit of; *habitué*; at home in &c. (*skilful*) 698; seasoned; permeated –, imbued- with; devoted –, wedded- to; never free from.

hackneyed, fixed, rooted, deep-rooted, ingrafted, permanent, inveterate, besetting; naturalized; ingrained &c. (*intrinsic*) 5.

Adv. habitually &c. *adj.*; always &c. (*uniformly*) 16.

as -usual, – is one's wont, – things go, – the world goes, – the sparks fly upwards; *more -suo, – solito*.

as a rule, for the most part; generally &c. *adj.*; most often, – frequently.

Phr. *cela s'entend*.

off –, cast off –, break off –, wean oneself of –, violate –, break through –, infringe- -a habit, – a custom, – a usage; break one's fetters; disuse &c. 678; wear off.

Adj. un-accustomed, -used, -wonted, -seasoned, -inured, -habituated, -trained; new; green &c. (*unskilled*) 699; fresh, original, unhackneyed.

unusual &c. (*unconformable*) 83; unconventional, non-observant; disused &c. 678.

Adv. just for once.

2°. *Causes of Volition*

615. Motive.—N. motive, springs of action.

reason, ground, call, principle; main-

615a. Absence of Motive.—N. absence of motive; caprice &c. 608; chance &c. (*absence of design*) 621.

spring, *primum mobile*, key-stone; the why and the wherefore; *pro* and *con*, reason why; secret –, ulterior- motive, *arrière-pensée*; intention &c. 620.

inducement, consideration; attraction &c. 288; loadstone; magnet, -ism, -ic force; allect-ation, -ive; temptation, enticement, *agacerie*, allurement, witchery; bewitch-ment, -ery; charm; spell &c. 993; fascination, blandishment, cajolery; seduc-tion, -ement; honeyed words, voice of the tempter, son of the Sirens; forbidden fruit, golden apple.

persuasi-bility, -bleness; attractability; impress-, suscept-ibility; softness; persuas-, attract-iveness; tantalization.

influence, prompting, dictate, instance; impuls-e, -ion; incit-ement, -ation; press, instigation; provocation &c. (*excitation of feeling*) 824; inspiration; per-, suasion; encouragement, advocacy; exhortation, advice &c. 695; solicitation &c. (*request*) 765; lobbying.

incentive, stimulus, spur, fillip, whip, goad, rowel, provocative, whet, dram.

bribe, lure; decoy, – duck; bait, trail of a red herring; bribery and corruption; sop, – for Cerberus.

prompter, tempter; seduc-er, -tor; suggester, coaxer, wheedler; instigator, firebrand, incendiary; Siren, Circe; *agent provocateur*; lobbyist.

V. induce, move; draw, – on; bring in its train, give an -impulse &c. *n.*-to; inspire; put up to, prompt, call up; attract, beckon.

V. have no motive; scruple &c. (*be unwilling*) 603.

Adj. without rhyme or reason; aimless &c. (*chance*) 621.

Adv. capriciously; out of mere caprice.

616. Dissuasion.—**N.** dissuasion, dehortation, expostulation, remonstrance; deprecation &c. 766.

discouragement, damper, wet blanket; warning.

cohibition &c. (*restraint*) 751; curb &c. (*means of restraint*) 752; check &c. (*hindrance*) 706.

reluctance &c. (*unwillingness*) 603; contraindication.

V. dissuade, dehort, cry out against, remonstrate, expostulate, warn, contraindicate.

disincline, indispose, shake, stagger; dispirit; dis-courage, -hearten, -enchant; deter; hold –, keep- back &c. (*restrain*) 751; render -averse &c. 603; repel; turn aside &c. (*deviation*) 279; wean from; act as a drag &c. (*hinder*) 706; throw cold water on, damp, cool, chill, blunt, calm, quiet, quench; deprecate &c. 766.

Adj. dissuading &c. *v.*; dissuasive; dehortatory, expostulatory; monit-ive, -ory.

dissuaded &c. *v.*; uninduced &c. (induce &c. 615); unpersuadable &c. (*obstinate*) 606; averse &c. (*unwilling*) 603; repugnant &c. (*dislike*) 867.

stimulate &c. (*excite*) 824; spirit up, inspirit; a-, rouse; ecphorize; animate, incite, provoke, instigate. set on, actuate; act –, work –, operate- upon; encourage; pat –, clap- on the -back, – shoulder.

influence, weigh with, bias, sway, incline, dispose, predispose, turn the scale, inoculate; lead, – by the nose; have –, exercise-influence- -with, – over, – upon; go –, come- round one; turn the head, magnetize.

persuade; prevail -with, – upon; overcome, carry; bring -round, – to one's senses; draw –, win –, gain –, come –, talk- over; procure, enlist, engage; invite, court.

tempt, seduce, overpersuade, entice, allure, captivate, fascinate, intrigue, bewitch, carry away, charm, conciliate, wheedle, coax, lure, suggest; inveigle; tantalize; cajole &c. (*deceive*) 545.

tamper with, bribe, suborn, grease the palm, bait with a silver hook, gild the pill, make things pleasant, put a sop into the pan, throw a sop to, bait the hook.

enforce, force; impel &c. (*push*) 276; propel &c. 284; whip, lash, goad, spur, prick, urge; egg –, hound –, hurry- on; drag &c. 285; exhort; advise &c. 695; call upon &c., press &c. (*request*) 765; advocate.

set -an example, – the fashion; keep in countenance; back up.

be -persuaded &c.; yield to temptation, come round; concede &c. (*consent*) 762; obey a call; follow -advice, – the bent, – the dictates of; act on principle.

Adj. impulsive, motive; suas-, persuas-, hortat-ive, -ory; protreptical; inviting, tempting &c. *v.*; seductive, attractive, irresistible; fascinating &c. (*pleasing*) 829; provocative &c. (*exciting*) 824.

induced &c. *v.*; disposed; persuadable &c. (*docile*) 602; spellbound; instinct –, smitten- with; inspired &c. *v.*- by.

Adv. because, therefore &c. (*cause*) 155; from -this, – that- motive; for -this, – that- reason; for; by reason –, for the sake –, on the score –, on account- of; out of, from, as, forasmuch as.

for all the world; on principle.

617. [Ostensible motive, ground, or reason assigned.] **Plea.—N.** plea, pretext; allegation, advocation; ostensible -motive, – ground, – reason; excuse &c. (*vindication*) 937; colour; gloss, guise.

loop-, starting-hole; how to creep out of, salvo, come off.

handle, peg to hang on, room, *locus standi*; stalking-horse, *cheval de bataille*, cue.

pretence &c. (*untruth*) 546; put off, subterfuge, dust thrown in the eyes; blind; moonshine; mere –, shallow- pretext; lame -excuse, – apology; tub to a whale; false plea, sour grapes; makeshift, shift, white lie; special pleading &c. (*sophistry*) 477; soft sawder &c. (*flattery*) 933.

V. plead, allege; shelter oneself under the plea of; excuse &c. (*vindicate*) 937; gloss over; lend a colour to; furnish a -handle &c. *n.*; make a -pretext, – handle- of; use as a plea &c. *n.*; take one's stand upon, make capital out of; pretend &c. (*lie*) 544.

Adj. ostensible &c. (*manifest*) 525; excusing; alleged, apologetic; pretended &c. 545.

Adv. ostensibly; under -colour, – the plea, – the pretence- of.

3°. *Objects of Volition*

618. Good.—N. good, benefit, advantage; improvement &c. 658; interest, service, behoof, behalf; weal; main chance, *summum bonum*, common weal; 'consummation devoutly to be wished'; gain, boot; profit, harvest.

boon &c. (*gift*) 784; good turn; blessing, benison; world of good; piece of good -luck, – fortune; nuts, prize, windfall, godsend, waif, treasure trove.

good fortune &c. (*prosperity*) 734; happiness &c. 827.

[Source of good] goodness &c. 648; utility &c. 644; remedy &c. 662; pleasure-giving &c. 829.

Adj. commendable &c. 931; useful &c. 644; good &c., beneficial &c. 648.

619. Evil.—N. evil, ill, harm, hurt, mischief, nuisance; machinations of the devil, Pandora's box, ills that flesh is heir to.

blow, buffet, stroke, scratch, bruise, wound, gash, mutilation; mortal -blow, – wound; *immedicabile vulnus*; damage, loss &c. (*deterioration*) 659.

disadvantage, prejudice, drawback.

disaster, accident, casualty; mishap &c. (*misfortune*) 735; bad job, devil to pay; calamity, bale, woe, catastrophe, tragedy; ruin &c. (*destruction*) 162; adversity &c. 735.

mental suffering &c. 828. [Evil spirit] demon &c. 980. [Cause of evil] bane &c. 663. [Production of evil]

V. benefit, profit, advantage, serve, help, avail; do good to, gain, prosper, flourish.

Adv. well, aright, satisfactorily, favourably, not amiss; all for the best; to one's -advantage &c. *n.*; in one's -favour, – interest &c. *n.*

Phr. so far so good.

---

badness &c. 649; painfulness &c. 830; evil doer &c. 913.

outrage, wrong, injury, foul play; bad –, ill- turn; disservice; spoliation &c. 791; grievance, crying evil.

V. be in trouble &c. (*adversity*) 735; harm, injure, hurt, do disservice to.

Adj. disastrous, bad &c. 649; awry, out of joint; disadvantageous, injurious, harmful.

Adv. amiss, wrong, ill, to one's cost.

Section II. PROSPECTIVE VOLITION*
1°. *Conceptional Volition*

620. Intention.—N. intent, -ion, -ionality; purpose; *quo animo*; project &c. 626; undertaking &c. 676; predetermination &c. 611; design, ambition.

contemplation, mind, *animus*, view, purview, proposal; study; look out.

final cause; *raison d'être*; *cui bono*; object, aim, end; 'the be all and the end all'; drift &c. (*meaning*) 516; tendency &c. 176; destination, mark, point, butt, goal, target, bull's-eye, quintain; prey, quarry, game.

decision, determination, resolve; set –, settled- purpose; *ultimatum*; resolution &c. 604; wish &c. 865; *arrière-pensée*; motive &c. 615.

[Study of final causes] teleology.

V. intend, purpose, design, mean; have to; propose to oneself; harbour a design; have in -view, – contemplation, – one's eye, – *petto*; have an eye to.

bid –, labour- for; be –, aspire –, endeavour- after; be –, aim –, drive –, point-, level - at; take aim; set before oneself; study to.

take upon oneself &c (*undertake*) 676; take into one's head; meditate, contemplate; think – dream –, talk-of; premeditate &c. 611; compass, calculate; dest-ine, -inate; propose.

project &c. (*plan*) 626; have a mind to &c. (*be willing*) 602; desire &c. 865; pursue &c. 622.

Adj. intended &c. *v.*; intentional, advised, express, determinate; prepense &c. 611; bound for; intending &c. *v.*; minded, disposed, inclined;

621. [Absence of purpose in the succession of events.] **Chance.†—N.** chance &c. 156; lot, fate &c. (*necessity*) 601; luck; good luck &c. (*good*) 618; bad luck &c. 735; wheel of fortune; mascot; swastika.

speculation, venture, stake, flutter, flier, gamble, game of chance; mere –, random- shot; blind bargain, leap in the dark; pig in a poke &c. (*uncertainty*) 475; fluke, pot-luck.

drawing lots; sorti-legy, -tion; *sortes*, – *Virgilianæ*; *rouge et noir*, hazard, *roulette*, pitch and toss, chuck-farthing, cup-tossing, heads or tails, cross and pile, wager; bet, -ting; risk, stake, plunge; gambling; the turf.

stock exchange, bourse, board of trade, curb exchange.

gaming-, gambling-, betting-house; hell; betting ring, totalisator; dice, – box; dicer; gam-bler, -ester, plunger, stock operator, manipulator, punter; man of the turf; adventurer, speculator; bookmaker, layer, backer.

V. chance &c. (*hap*) 156; stand a chance &c. (*be possible*) 470.

toss up; cast –, draw- lots; leave –, trust- -to chance, – to the chapter of accidents; tempt fortune; chance it, take one's chance; run –, incur –, encounter- the -risk, – chance; stand the hazard of the die.

speculate, try one's luck, set on a cast, raffle, put into a lottery, buy a pig in a poke, shuffle the cards.

risk, venture, hazard, stake; lay, – a wager; make a bet, wager, bet, gamble,

---

* That is, volition having reference to a future object.   † See note on 156.

bent upon &c. (*earnest*) 604; at stake, on the -anvil, – *tapis*; in -view; – prospect, – the breast of; *in petto*; teleological.

Adv. intentionally &c. *adj.*; advisedly, wittingly, knowingly, designedly, purposely, on purpose, by design, studiously, pointedly; with -intent &c. *n.*; deliberately &c. (*with premeditation*) 611; with one's eyes open, in cold blood.

for; with -a view, – an eye- to; in order -to, – that; to the end –, with the intent- that; for the purpose –, with the view –, in contemplation –, on account- of.

in pursuance of, pursuant to; *quo animo*; to all intents and purposes.

---

622. [Purpose in action.] **Pursuit.**— **N.** pursuit; pursuing &c. *v.*; prosecution; pursuance; enterprise &c. (*undertaking*) 676; business &c. 625; adventure &c. (*essay*) 675; quest &c. (*search*) 461; scramble, hue and cry, game; hobby.

chase, hunt, *battue*, race, steeplechase, hunting, coursing; ven-ation, -ery; fox-chase; sport, -ing; shooting, angling, fishing, hawking.

pursuer; hunt-er, -sman; sportsman, Nimrod, the field; hound &c. 366.

V. pursue, prosecute, follow; run –, make –, be –, hunt –, prowl- after; shadow; carry on &c. (*do*) 680; engage in &c. (*undertake*) 676; set about &c. (*begin*) 66; endeavour &c. 675; court &c. (*request*) 765; seek &c. (*search*) 461; aim at &c. (*intention*) 620; follow the trail &c. (*trace*) 461; fish for &c. (*experiment*) 463; press on &c. (*haste*) 684; run a race &c. (*velocity*) 274.

chase, give chase, course, dog, hunt, hound, stalk; tread –, follow- on the heels of &c. (*sequence*) 281.

rush upon; rush headlong &c. (*violence*) 173; ride –, run- full tilt at; make a leap –, jump –, snatch- at; run down; start game.

tread a path; take –, hold- a course; shape –, direct –, bend- one's -steps, – course; play a game; fight –, elbow- one's way; follow up; take -to, – up; go in for; ride one's hobby.

Adj. pursuing &c. *v.*; in quest of &c.

game, play for; play at chuck-**farthing**.

Adj. fortuitous &c. 156; unintentional, -ded; accidental; not meant; un-designed, -purposed; unpremeditated &c. 612; never thought of.

indiscriminate, promiscuous; undirected, random; aim-, drift-, design-, purpose-, cause-less; without purpose. possible &c. 470.

Adv. casually &c. 156; unintentionally &c. *adj.*; unwittingly.

en passant, by the way, incidentally; as it may happen; at -random, – a venture, – haphazard; as luck would have it, by -chance, – good fortune; un-, -luckily.

---

623. [Absence of pursuit.] **Avoidance.** —**N.** abst-ention, -inence; forbearance; refraining &c. *v.*; inaction &c. 681; neutrality.

avoidance, evasion, elusion; seclusion &c. 893.

avolation, flight; escape &c. 671; retreat &c. 287; recoil &c. 277; departure &c. 293; rejection &c. 610.

shirker &c. *v.*; slacker; truant; fugitive, refugee; runa-way, -gate; renegade; deserter.

V. abstain, refrain, spare, not attempt; not do &c. 681; maintain the even tenor of one's way.

eschew, keep from, let alone, have nothing to do with; keep –, stand –, hold- -aloof, – off; take no part in, have no hand in.

avoid, shun; steer –, keep- clear of; fight shy of; keep -one's, – at a respectful- distance; keep –, get- out of the way; evade, elude, turn away from; set one's face against &c. (*oppose*) 708; deny oneself.

shrink; hang –, hold –, draw- back; recoil &c. 277; retire &c. (*recede*) 287; flinch, blink, blench, shy, shirk, dodge, parry, make way for, give place to.

beat a retreat; turn -tail, – one's back; take to one's heels; run, -away, – for one's life; cut and run; be off, – like a shot; fly, flee; fly –, flee –, run away- from; take –, take to- flight; desert, elope; make –, scamper –, sneak –, shuffle –, sheer- off; break –,

(*inquiry*) 461; in -pursuit, – full cry, – hot pursuit; on the scent.

Adv. in pursuance of &c. (*intention*) 620; after.

Int. tally-ho! yoicks! so-ho!

————

burst –, tear oneself –, slip –, slink –, steal- -away, – away from; slip cable, part company, turn on one's heel; sneak out of, play truant, give one the go by, give leg bail, take French leave, slope, decamp, flit, bolt, abscond, levant, skedaddle, absquatulate, cut one's stick, walk one's chalks, show a light pair of heels, make oneself scarce; escape &c. 671; go away &c. (*depart*) 293; abandon &c. 624; reject &c. 610.

lead one a -dance, – a merry chase, – pretty dance; throw off the scent, play at hide and seek.

Adj. unsought, unattempted; avoiding &c. *v.*; neutral; shy of &c. (*unwilling*) 603; elusive, evasive, distant; fugitive, runaway; shy, wild.

Adj. lest, in order to avoid.

Int. forbear! keep –, hands- off! *sauve qui peut!* devil take the hindmost!

624. Relinquishment.—N. relinquish-, abandon-ment; desertion, defection, secession, withdrawal; cave of Adullam; *nolle prosequi.*

discontinuance &c. (*cessation*) 142; renunciation &c. (*recantation*) 607; abrogation &c. 756; resignation &c. (*retirement*) 757; desuetude &c. 614; cession &c. (*of property*) 782.

V. relinquish, give up, abandon, desert, forsake, leave in the lurch; depart –, secede –, withdraw- from; back – out of, – down from, leave, go back on one's word, quit, take leave of, bid a long farewell; vacate &c. (*resign*) 757.

renounce &c. (*abjure*) 607; forego, have done with, drop; write off; disuse &c. 678; discard &c. 782; wash one's hands of; drop all idea of; *nolle-pros.*; lose interest in.

break –, leave- off; desist; stop &c. (*cease*) 142; hold –, stay- one's hand; quit one's hold; give over, shut up shop.

throw up the -game, – cards; give up the -point, – argument; pass to the order of the day, move the previous question, table the motion.

Adj. unpursued; relinquished &c. *v.*; relinquishing &c. *v.*

Int. avast &c.! (*stop*) 142.

625. Business.—N. business, occupation, employment; pursuit &c. 622; what one is doing-, – about; affair, concern, matter, case, undertaking.

matter in hand, irons in the fire; thing to do, *agendum*, task, work, job, chore, errand, transaction, commission, mission, charge, care; duty &c. 926.

part, *rôle*, cue; province, function, look-out, department, capacity, sphere, orb, field, line; walk, – of life; beat, round, routine; race, career.

office, place, post, incumbency, living; situation, appointment, billet, berth, employ; service &c. (*servitude*) 749; engagement; undertaking &c. 676.

vocation, calling, profession, *métier*, cloth, faculty; industry, art; industrial arts; craft, mystery, handicraft; trade &c. (*commerce*) 794.

exercise; work &c. (*action*) 680; avocation; press of business &c. (*activity*) 682.

V. pass –, employ –, spend- one's time in; employ oneself -in, – upon;

occupy –, concern- oneself with; make it one's -business &c. *n.*; undertake &c. 676; enter a profession; betake oneself to, turn one's hand to; have to do with &c. (*do*) 680.

drive a trade; carry on –, do –, transact- -business, – a trade &c. *n.*; keep a shop; ply one's task, – trade; labour in one's vocation; pursue the even tenor of one's way; attend to -business, – one's work.

officiate, serve, act; act –, play- one's part; do duty; serve –, discharge –, perform- the -office, – duties, – functions- of; hold –, fill- -an office, – a place, – a situation; hold a portfolio.

be -about, – doing, – engaged in, – employed in, – occupied with, – at work on; have one's hands in, have in hand; have on one's -hands, – shoulders; bear the burden; have one's hands full &c. (*activity*) 682.

be -in the hands of, – on the stocks, – on the anvil; pass through one's hands.

Adj. business-like; work-a-day; professional; official, functional; busy &c. (*actively employed*) 682; on –, in- -hand, – one's hands; afoot; on -foot, – the anvil; going on; acting.

Adv. in the course of business, all in a day's work; professionally &c. *adj.*

626. Plan.—**N.** plan, scheme, design, project; propos-al, -ition; suggestion; resolution, motion; precaution &c. (*provision*) 673; deep-laid &c. (*premeditated*) 611- plan &c.; racket.

system &c. (order) 58; organization &c. (*arrangement*) 60; germ &c. (*cause*) 153; Five Year Plan.

sketch, skeleton, outline, draught, draft, *ébauche*, *brouillon*; rough -cast, – draft, – draught, – copy; copy; proof, revise.

forecast, *programme*, prospectus, scenario; *carte du pays*; card; bill, protocol; order of the day, list of agenda, *memorandum*; bill of fare &c. (*food*) 298; base of operations; platform, plank.

rôle; policy &c. (*line of conduct*) 692.

contrivance, invention, expedient, receipt, nostrum, artifice, device, gadget; stratagem &c. (*cunning*) 702; trick &c. (*deception*) 545; alternative, loophole, shift &c. (*substitute*) 147; last shift &c. (*necessity*) 601.

measure, step; stroke, – of policy; master stroke; trump-, court-card; *cheval de bataille*, great gun; *coup*, – *d'état*; clever –, bold –, good- -move, – hit, – stroke; bright -thought, – idea, great idea.

intrigue, cabal, plot, frame-up, conspiracy, complot, machination; under-, counter-plot.

schem-ist, -atist; strategist, machinator, schemer; projector, author, builder, artist, promoter, designer &c. *v.*; conspirator; *intrigant* &c. (*cunning*) 702.

V. plan, scheme, design, frame, contrive, project, forecast, sketch; conceive, devise, invent &c. (*imagine*) 515; set one's wits to work &c. 515; spring a project; fall –, hit- upon; strike –, chalk –, cut –, lay –, map-out; lay down a plan; shape –, mark- out a course; predetermine &c. 611; concert, preconcert, preestablish; prepare &c. 673; hatch, – a plot; concoct; take -steps, – measures.

cast, recast, systematize, organize; arrange &c. 60; digest, mature.

plot; counter-plot, -mine; dig a mine; lay a train; intrigue &c. (*cunning*) 702.

Adj. planned &c. *v.*; strategic, -al; planning &c. *v.*; in course of preparation &c. 673; under consideration; on the -*tapis*, – carpet, – table.

627. Method. [Path.]—**N.** method, way, manner, wise, gait, form, mole, fashion, tone, guise; *modus operandi*; procedure &c. (*line of conduct*) 692.

path, road, route, course; line of -way, – road; trajectory, orbit, track, beat, tack.

steps; stair, -case; flight of stairs, ladder, stile.

bridge, viaduct, gauntry, pontoon, stepping stone, plank, gangway, catwalk, drawbridge; pass, ford, ferry, tunnel, subway, elevated; pipe &c. 260.

door; gateway &c. (*opening*) 260; channel, passage, avenue, means of access, approach, perron, adit, entrance; artery, lane, alley, aisle, lobby, corridor, cloister; back- door, -stairs; secret passage; covert-way.

road-, path-, stair-way; thoroughfare; highway, pike, turnpike, trail, parkway, *boulevard*; turnpike –, royal –, coach- road; broad –, King's –, Queen's- highway; beaten -track, – path; horse –, bridle- road, – track, – path; pathway; walk, *trottoir*, foot-path, pavement, flags, side-walk; by –, cross- -road, – path, – way; cut; short -cut &c. (*mid-course*) 628; *carrefour*; private –, occupation- road; highways and byways; rail-, tram-road, -way; funicular, ropeway, causeway; defile, cutting; canal &c. (*conduit*) 350; street &c. (*abode*) 189.

Adv. how; in what -way, – manner; by what mode; so, in this way, after this fashion, on these lines.

one way or another, anyhow; somehow or other &c. (*instrumentality*) 631; by way of; *viâ*; *in transitu* &c. 270; on the high road to.

Phr. *hæ tibi erunt artes.*

628. Mid-course.—N. middle-, mid-course; moderation, mean &c. 29; middle &c. 68; *juste milieu*, *mezzo termine*, golden mean, *aurea mediocritas*.

straight &c. (*direct*) 278 -course, – path; short –, cross- cut; short-circuit; great circle sailing.

neutrality; half –, half and half-measures; compromise.

V. keep in –, steer –, preserve- -a middle, – an even- course; go straight &c. (*direct*) 278.

go half way, compromise, make a compromise.

Adj. neutral, average, even, impartial, moderate, straight &c. (*direct*) 278.

629. Circuit.—N. circuit, round-about way, digression, divagation, *détour*, circum-ambience, -ambulation, bendibus, *ambages*, loop; winding &c. (*circuition*) 311; zigzag &c. (*deviation*) 279.

V. perform –, make- a circuit; go -round about, – out of one's way; make a *détour*; meander &c. (*deviate*) 27; circumambulate.

lead a pretty dance; beat about, – the bush; make two bites of a cherry.

Adj. circuitous, indirect, round-about; zig-zag &c. (*deviating*) 279; circum-ambient, -ambulatory.

Adv. by -a side wind, – an indirect course; in a roundabout way; from pillar to post.

630. Requirement.—N. requirement, need, wants, necessities; necessaries, – of life; stress, exigency, pinch, *sine quâ non*, matter of necessity; case of -need, – life or death.

needfulness, essentiality, necessity, indispensability, urgency, prerequisite.

requisition &c. (*request*) 765, (*exaction*) 741; run upon; demand –, call- for.

desideratum &c. (*desire*) 865; want &c. (*deficiency*) 640.

charge, claim, command, injunction, requisition, mandate, order, *ultimatum.*

V. require, need, want, have occasion for, entail; not be able to -do without, – dispense with; prerequire.

render necessary, necessitate, create a necessity for, call for, put in requisition; make a requisition &c. (*ask for*) 765, (*demand*) 741.

stand in need of; lack &c. 640; desiderate; desire &c. 865; be -necessary &c. *adj.*

Adj. required &c. *v.*; requisite, needful, necessary, imperative, essential, indispensable, prerequisite; called for; in -demand, – request.

urgent, exigent, pressing, instant, crying, absorbing.

in want of; destitute of &c. 640.

Adv. *ex necessitate rei* &c. (*necessarily*) 601; of –, out of stern- necessity; at a pinch.

Phr. there is no time to lose; it cannot be -spared, – dispensed with.

2° *Subservience to Ends*

1. *Actual Subservience*

631. Instrumentality.—N. instrumentality; aid &c. 707; subservien-ce, -cy; mediation, inter-vention, -mediacy, medium, inter-medium, -mediary, vehicle, hand; agency &c. 170.

minister, handmaid, servant, slave, maid, valet; midwife, *accoucheur*, obstetrician; go-between; cat's paw; stepping-stone.

key; master –, pass –, latch- key; 'open sesame'; passport, *passe partout*, safe-conduct; influence.

instrument &c. 633; expedient &c. (*plan*) 626; means &c. 632.

V. subserve, minister, tend, mediate, intervene; come –, go- between, interpose; pull the strings; be -instrumental &c. *adj.*; pander to.

Adj. instrumental; useful &c. 644; ministerial, subservient, mediatorial; inter-mediate, -vening; conducive.

Adv. through, by, *per*; where-, there-, here-by; by the -agency &c. 170- of; by dint of; by –, in- virtue of; through the -medium &c. *n.*- of; along with; on the shoulders of; by means of &c. 632; by –, with- -the aid &c. (*assistance*) 707- of.

per fas et nefas, by fair means or foul; somehow, – or other; by hook or by crook.

632. Means.—N. means, resources, revenue, wherewithal, ways and means, income; capital &c. (*money*) 800; stock in trade &c. 636; provision &c. 637; a shot in the locker; appliances &c. (*machinery*) 633; means and appliances; conveniences; cards to play; expedients &c. (*measures*) 626; two strings to one's bow; sheet anchor &c. (*safety*) 666; aid &c. 707; medium &c. 631.

V. find –, have –, possess- means &c. *n.*; provide the wherewithal.

Adj. instrumental &c. 631; mechanical &c. 633.

Adv. by means of, with; by -what, – all, – any, – some- means; where-, here-, there-with; wherewithal.

how &c. (*in what manner*) 627; through &c. (*by the instrumentality of*) 631; with –, by- the aid &c. (*assistance*) 707- of; by the -agency &c. 170- of.

633. Instrument.—N. machinery, mechanism, engineering.

instrument, organ, tool, implement, utensil, contrivance, machine, motor, engine, lathe, gin, mill, pump.

gear; tack-le, -ling, trice, rigging, gear, apparatus, appliances; plant, *matériel*; harness, trappings, fittings, accoutrements; equip-ment, -age;

appointments, furniture, upholstery; chattels; paraphernalia &c. (*belongings*) 780; *impedimenta*.

mechanical powers; lever, -age; mechanical advantage; crow, -bar; handspike, gavelock, jemmy, arm, limb, wing; oar, paddle; pulley, sheave; parbuckle; wheel and axle; wheel-, clock-work; wheels within wheels; pinion, gear wheel, spur –, bevel- gearing, chains, belting, crank, winch, capstan, windlass, crane, derrick, hoist, lift &c. 307; cam; pedal; wheel &c. (*rotation*) 312; inclined plane; wedge; screw; jack; spring, mainspring.

handle, hilt, haft, shaft, heft, shank, blade, trigger, tiller, helm, treadle, key; turnscrew, screwdriver, spanner, wrench.

hammer &c. (*impulse*) 276; edge tool &c. (*cut*) 253; borer &c. 262; vice, teeth &c. (*hold*) 781; nail, rope &c. (*join*) 45; peg &c. (*hang*) 214; support &c. 215; spoon &c. (*vehicle*) 272; arms &c. 727; oar &c. (*navigation*) 267.

Adj. instrumental &c. 631; mechanical, machinal, automatic, self-acting; brachial.

634. Substitute.—N. substitute &c. 147; deputy &c. 759; proxy, alternative, understudy.

635. Materials.—N. material, raw material, stuff, stock, staple; building materials, bricks and mortar; metal; stone; clay, brick; crockery &c. 384; compo, -sition; reinforced –, ferro-, concrete; cement; wood, ore, timber; gravel, cobbles, macadam, asphalt, tarmac.

materials; supplies, munition, fuel, grist, household stuff; *pabulum* &c. (*food*) 298; ammunition &c. (*arms*) 727; contingents; relay, rein-forcement; baggage &c. (*personal property*) 780; means &c. 632.

Adj. raw &c. (*unprepared*) 674; wooden &c. *n*.

636. Store.—N. stock, fund, mine, vein, lode, quarry; spring; fount, -ain; well, -spring; milch-cow.

stock in trade, supply; heap &c. (*collection*) 72; treasure; reserve, *corps de réserve*, reserve fund, nest-egg, savings, *bonne bouche*.

crop, harvest, mow, vintage; yield, product, gleanings.

store, accumulation, hoard, rick, stack; lumber; relay &c. (*provision*) 637.

store-house, -room, -closet; depository, *dépôt*, *cache*, safe deposit, vault, pantechnicon, re-pository, -servatory, -pertory; *repertorium*; promptuary, warehouse, *entrepôt*, magazine, dump, buttery, larder, pantry, panary, lanary, still-room, spence; crib, garner, granary, silo, barn; bunker; thesaurus; bank &c. (*treasury*) 802; armoury; arsenal; dock; gallery, museum, library, conservatory, hot-house; menag-ery, -erie, aquarium, zoological gardens.

reservoir, cistern, tank, sump, pond, mill-pond; gasometer.

budget, quiver, bandolier, portfolio; coffer &c. (*receptacle*) 191.

conservation; storing &c. *v.*; storage.

dictionary &c. 562; list &c. 86.

V. store; put –, lay –, set- by; stow away; set –, lay- apart; store –, hoard –, treasure –, lay –, heap –, put –, garner –, save- up; *cache*; accumulate, amass, hoard, fund, garner, save, bank.

conserve, reserve; keep –, hold- back; husband, – one's resources.

deposit; stow, stack, load, dump; harvest; heap, collect &c. 72; lay -in, – down, – by, store &c. *adj.*; keep, file [papers]; lay in &c. (*provide*) 637; preserve &c. 670; put by for a rainy day.

Adj. stored &c. *v.*; in -store, – reserve, – ordinary; spare, super-numerary.

637. Provision.—N. provision, sup-ply; grist, – to the mill; subvention &c. (*aid*) 707; resources &c. (*means*) 632.

providing &c. *v.*; purveyance; rein-forcement; commissary, commissariat.

rations; iron –, emergency- rations; provender &c. (*food*) 298; *viaticum*; ensilage.

caterer, purveyor, commissary, quar-termaster, steward, housekeeper, man-ciple, feeder, batman, victualler, store-keeper, grocer, provision merchant, green-, grocer, *comprador, restaurateur*; sutler &c. (*merchant*) 797; innkeeper, publican, confectioner, baker, butcher, wine merchant, vintner.

V. provide; make -provision, – due provision for; lay in, – a stock, – a store.

sup-ply, -peditate; furnish; find, – one in; arm.

cater, victual, provision, purvey, for-age; beat up for; stock, – with; make good, replenish; fill, – up; recruit, feed, ration.

have in -store, – reserve; keep, – by one, – on foot; have to fall back upon; store &c. 636; provide against a rainy day &c. (*economy*) 817.

639. Sufficiency.—N. sufficiency, adequacy, enough, withal, *quantum sufficit*, satisfaction, competence; no less.

mediocrity &c. (*average*) 29.

fill; fulness &c. (*completeness*) 52; plen-itude, -ty; abundance; copiousness &c. *adj.*; amplitude, galore, lots, pro-fusion; full measure; 'good measure pressed down, shaken together and running over.'

luxuriance &c. (*fertility*) 168; afflu-ence &c. (*wealth*) 803; fat of the land; 'a land flowing with milk and honey'; cornucopia; horn of -plenty, – Amal-thæa; mine &c. (*stock*) 636.

outpouring; flood &c. (*great quantity*) 31; tide &c. (*river*) 348; repletion &c. (*redundance*) 641; satiety &c. 869; rich man &c. 803.

638. Waste.—N. consumption, ex-penditure, exhaustion; dispersion &c. 73; ebb; leakage &c. (*exudation*) 295; loss &c. 776; wear and tear; waste; prodigality &c. 818; misuse &c. 679; wasting &c. *v.*; rubbish &c. (*useless*) 645.

mountain in labour.

V. spend, expend, use, consume, swallow up, exhaust, deplete; impov-erish; spill, drain, empty; disperse &c. 73.

cast –, throw –, fling –, fritter- away; burn the candle at both ends, waste; squander &c. 818.

'waste its sweetness on the desert air'; cast -one's bread upon the waters, – pearls before swine; employ a steam engine to crack a nut, waste powder and shot, break a butterfly on a wheel; labour in vain &c. (*useless*) 645; cut a whetstone with a razor, pour water into a sieve; tilt at windmills.

leak &c. (*run out*) 295; run to waste; ebb; melt away, run dry, dry up.

Adj. wasted &c. *v.*; at a low ebb.

wasteful &c. (*prodigal*) 818; penny wise and pound foolish.

Phr. *magno conatu magnas nugas; le jeu n'en vaut pas la chandelle.*

640. Insufficiency.—N. insufficiency; inadequa-cy, -teness; incompetence &c. (*impotence*) 158; deficiency &c. (*incom-pleteness*) 53; imperfection &c. 651; shortcoming &c. 304; paucity; stint; scantiness &c. (*smallness*) 32; none to spare; bare subsistence.

scarcity, dearth; want, need, lack, poverty, exigency; inanition, starva-tion, famine, drought.

dole, pittance, mite; short -allow-ance, – commons; half-rations; ban-yan –, fast- day, Lent.

emptiness, poorness &c. *adj.*; deple-tion, vacancy, flaccidity; ebb-tide; low water; 'a beggarly account of empty boxes'; indigence &c. (*poverty*) 804; insolvency &c. (*non-payment*) 808; poor man &c. 804; bankrupt &c. 808.

V. be -insufficient &c. *adj.*; not -suf-

V. be -sufficient &c. *adj.*; suffice, do, just do, satisfy, pass muster; have -enough &c. *n.*; eat –, drink –, have-one's fill; roll –, swim- in; wallow in &c. (*superabundance*) 641.

abound, exuberate, teem, flow, stream, rain, shower down; pour, – in; swarm; bristle with.

render -sufficient &c. *adj.*; replenish &c. (*fill*) 52.

Adj. sufficient, enough, adequate, up to the mark, commensurate, compe-tent, satisfactory, valid, tangible.

measured; moderate &c. (*temperate*) 953.

full &c. (*complete*) 52; ample; plen-ty, -tiful, -teous; plenty as blackberries; copious, abundant; abounding &c. *v.*; replete, enough and to spare, flush; choke-full; well-stocked, -provided; lib-eral; unstint-ed, -ing; stintless; without stint; un-sparing, -measured; lavish &c. 641; wholesale.

rich; luxuriant &c. (*fertile*) 168; afflu-ent &c. (*wealthy*) 803; wantless; big with &c. (*pregnant*) 161.

un-exhausted, -wasted; exhaustless, inexhaustible.

Adv. sufficiently, amply &c. *adj.*; full; in -abundance &c. *n.*; with no sparing hand; to one's heart's content, *ad libitum*, without stint.

Phr. cut and come again.

fice &c. 639; come short of &c. 304; run dry.

want, lack, need, require; *caret*; be in want &c. (*poor*) 804; live from hand to mouth.

render- insufficient &c. *adj.*; drain of resources; impoverish &c. (*waste*) 638; stint &c. (*begrudge*) 819; put on short -commons, – allowance.

do -insufficiently &c. *adv.*; scotch the snake.

Adj. insufficient, inadequate; too -little &c. 32; not -enough &c. 639; unequal to; incompetent &c. (*impotent*) 158; 'weighed in the balance and found wanting'; perfunctory &c. (*neglect*) 460; deficient &c. (*incomplete*) 53; wanting &c. *v.*; imperfect &c. 651; ill-furnished, -provided, -stored, -off.

slack, at a low ebb; empty, vacant, bare; short –, out –, destitute –, de-void –, bereft &c. 789 –, denuded- of; dry, drained.

un -provided, -supplied, -furnished; un-replenished, -fed; un-stored, -treas-ured; empty-handed.

meagre, poor, thin, scrimp, sparing, spare, stinted, stunted; skimpy; starv-ed, -eling; half-starved, emaci-ated, famine-stricken, famished, under-fed, undernourished; jejune.

scant &c. (*small*) 32; scarce; not to be had, – for love or money, – at any price; scurvy; stingy &c. 819; at the end of one's tether; without -resources &c. 632; in want &c. (*poor*) 804; in debt &c. 806.

Adv. insufficiently &c. *adj.*; in default –, for want- of; failing.

641. Redundance.—N. redundance; too -much, – many; super-abundance, -fluity, -fluence, -saturation; nimiety, transcendency, ex-uberance, profuseness; profusion &c. (*plenty*) 639; repletion, enough in all conscience, *satis superque*, lion's share; more than -enough &c. 639; plethora, engorgement, congestion, load, surfeit, sickener; turges-cence &c. (*expansion*) 194; over-dose, -measure, -supply, -flow; inun-dation &c. (*water*) 348; avalanche.

accumulation &c. (*store*) 636; heap &c. 72; drug, – in the market; glut; crowd; burden.

excess; sur-, over-plus, epact; margin; remainder &c. 40; duplicate; surplusage, expletive; work of –, supererogation; *bonus, bonanza*.

luxury; intemperance &c. 954; extravagance &c. (*prodigality*) 818; exorbitance, lavishment.

pleonasm &c. (*diffuseness*) 573; too many irons in the fire; embar-rassment of riches; money to burn.

V. super-, over-abound; know no bounds, swarm; meet one at every turn; creep –, bristle- with; overflow; run –, flow –, well –, brim-over; run riot; over-run, -stock, -lay, -charge, -dose, -feed, -burden, -load, -do, -whelm, -shoot the mark &c. (*go beyond*) 303; surcharge, supersaturate, gorge, glut, load, drench, whelm, inundate, deluge, flood; drug, – the market.

choke, cloy, accloy, suffocate; pile up, lay it on, – with a trowel, lay on thick; impregnate with; lavish &c. (*squander*) 818.

send –, carry- coals to Newcastle, – owls to Athens; teach one's grandmother to suck eggs; *pisces natare docere*; kill the slain, 'gild refined gold,' 'paint the lily'; butter one's bread on both sides, put butter upon bacon; employ a steam-engine to crack a nut &c. (*waste*) 638.

exaggerate &c. 549; wallow in; roll in &c. (*plenty*) 639; remain on one's hands, hang heavy on hand, go a begging.

Adj. redundant; too -much, – many; exuberant, inordinate, super-abundant, excessive, overmuch, replete, profuse, lavish; prodigal &c. 818; exorbitant; overweening; extravagant; overcharged &c. *v.*; super-saturated, drenched, overflowing; running -over, – to waste, – down.

crammed –, filled- to overflowing; gorged, stuffed, ready to burst; dropsical, turgid, plethoric, full-blooded; obese &c. 194; voluminous.

superfluous, unnecessary, needless, supervacaneous, uncalled for, to spare, in excess; over and above &c. (*remainder*) 40; *de trop*; adscititious &c. (*additional*) 37; supernumerary &c. (*reserve*) 636; on one's hands, spare, duplicate, supererogatory, expletive; *un peu fort*.

Adv. over, too, over and above; over –, too- much; too far; without –, beyond –, out of- measure; with . . . to spare; over head and ears; up to one's -eyes, – ears; *extra*; beyond the mark &c. (*transcursion*) 303; over one's head.

Phr. it never rains but it pours.

2. *Degree of Subservience*

642. Importance.—N. importance, consequence, moment, prominence, consideration, mark, materialness.

import, significance, concern; emphasis, interest.

greatness &c. 31; superiority &c. 33; notability &c. (*repute*) 873; weight &c. (*influence*) 175; value &c. (*goodness*) 648; usefulness &c. 644.

gravity, seriousness, solemnity; no -joke, – laughing matter; pressure, urgency, stress; matter of life and death.

memorabilia, notabilia, great doings; red-letter day.

great -thing, – point; main chance, 'the be all and end all,' cardinal point, outstanding feature; substance, gist &c. (*essence*) 5; sum and substance, *gravamen*, head and front; important -, principal -, prominent -, essential-part; half the battle; *sinè quâ non*; breath of one's nostrils &c. (*life*) 359; cream, salt, core, kernel, heart, nucleus;

643. Unimportance.—N. unimportance, insignificance, nothingness, immateriality.

triviality, trivia, fribble, levity, frivolity; paltriness &c. *adj.*; poverty; smallness &c. 32; vanity &c. (*uselessness*) 645; matter of -indifference &c. 866; no object; side issue.

nothing, – to signify, – worth speaking of, – particular, – to boast of, – to speak of; small -, no great -, trifling &c. *adj.* -matter; mere -joke, – nothing; hardly -, scarcely- anything; nonentity, cipher, figurehead; no great shakes, *peu de chose*; child's play; small beer.

toy, plaything, popgun, paper pellet, gimcrack, gewgaw, bauble, trinket, *bagatelle*, kickshaw, knicknack, whimwham, trifle, 'trifles light as air.'

trumpery, trash, rubbish, stuff, *fatras*, frippery; 'leather or prunello'; chaff, drug, froth, bubble, smoke, cob-

key, -note, -stone; corner stone; trump-card &c. (*device*) 626; salient points.

top-sawyer, first fiddle, *prima donna*, chief, big-wig; triton among the minnows.

V. be -important &c. *adj.*, – somebody, – something; import, signify, matter, be an object; carry weight &c. (*influence*) 175; make a figure &c. (*repute*) 873; be in the ascendant, come to the front, lead the way, take the lead, play first fiddle, throw all else into the shade; lie at the root of; deserve –, merit –, be worthy- -of notice, – regard, – consideration.

attach –, ascribe –, give- importance &c. *n.*- to; value, care for; set store -upon, – by; mark &c. 550; mark with a white stone, underline; write –, put –, print- in -italics, – capitals, – large letters, – large type, – letters of gold; accentuate, emphasize, lay stress on.

make -a fuss, – a stir, – a piece of work, – much ado- about; make -of, – much of.

Adj. important; of -importance &c. *n.*; momentous, material; to the point; not to be -overlooked, – despised, – sneezed at; egregious; weighty &c. (*influential*) 175; of note &c. (*repute*) 873; notable, prominent, salient, signal; memorable, remarkable; worthy of -remark, – notice; never to be forgotten; stirring, eventful.

grave, serious, earnest, noble, grand, solemn, impressive, commanding, imposing.

urgent, pressing, critical, instant.

paramount, essential, vital, all-absorbing, radical, cardinal, chief, main, prime, primary, principal, leading, capital, foremost, overruling; of vital &c. importance.

in the front rank, first-rate, A1; superior &c. 33; considerable &c. (*great*) 31; marked &c. *v.*; rare &c. 137.

significant, telling, trenchant, emphatic, pregnant; *tanti*.

Adv. materially &c. *adj.*; in the main; above all, *par excellence*, to crown all.

———

web; weed; refuse &c. (*inutility*) 645; scum &c. (*dirt*) 653.

joke, jest, snap of the fingers; fudge &c. (*unmeaning*) 517; fiddlestick, – end; pack of nonsense, mere farce.

straw, pin, fig, continental, button, rush; bulrush, feather, halfpenny, farthing, brass farthing, doit, peppercorn, jot, rap, pinch of snuff, old song.

minutiæ, details, minor details, small fry; dust in the balance, feather in the scale, drop in the ocean, flea-bite, molehill; fingle-fangle.

nine days' wonder, *ridiculus mus*; flash in the pan &c. (*impotence*) 158; much ado about nothing &c. (*overestimation*) 482; storm in a teacup.

V. be -unimportant &c. *adj.*; not -matter &c. 642; go for –, matter –, signify- -little, – nothing, – little or nothing; not matter a -straw &c. *n.*

make light of &c. (*underestimate*) 483; catch at straws &c. (*overestimate*) 482.

Adj. unimportant; of -little, – small, – no- -account, – importance &c. 642; immaterial; un-, non-essential; not vital; irrelevant, incidental, indifferent.

subordinate &c. (*inferior*) 34; *médiocre* &c. (*average*) 29; passable, fair, respectable, tolerable, commonplace; uneventful, mere, common; ordinary &c. (*habitual*) 613; inconsiderable, so-so, insignificant, inappreciable, nugatory.

trifling, trivial; slight, slender, light, flimsy, frothy, idle; puerile &c. (*foolish*) 499; airy, shallow; weak &c. 160; powerless &c. 158; frivolous, petty, niggling; pid-, ped-dling; fribble, inane, ridiculous, farcical; fini-cal, -kin; fiddle-faddle, namby-pamby, wishy-washy, milk and water.

poor, paltry, pitiful; contemptible &c. (*contempt*) 930; sorry, mean, meagre, shabby, miserable, wretched, vile, scrubby, scrannel, weedy, niggardly, scurvy, putid, beggarly, worthless, twopenny-halfpenny, cheap, trashy, catchpenny, gimcrack, trumpery, one-horse; toy.

not worth -the pains, – while, – mentioning, – speaking of, – a thought, – a curse, – a straw, – rap &c. *n.*; beneath –, unworthy of- -notice, – regard, – consideration, – contempt; *de lanâ caprinâ*; vain &c. (*useless*) 645.

Adv. slightly &c. *adj.*; rather, somewhat, pretty well, fairly well, tolerably.

for aught one cares.

Int. no matter! pish! tush! tut! pshaw! pugh! pooh, -pooh! fudge! bosh! humbug! fiddle-stick, – end! fiddlededee! never mind! *n'importe!* what -signifies, – matter, – boots it, – of that, –'s the odds! a fig for! stuff! nonsense! stuff and nonsense!

Phr. *magno conatu magnas nugas; le jeu n'en vaut pas la chandelle;* it -matters not, – does not signify; it is of no -consequence, – importance.

644. Utility.—N. utility; usefulness &c. *adj.*; efficacy, efficiency, adequacy; service, use, stead, avail; help &c. (*aid*) 707; applicability &c. *adj.*; subservience &c. (*instrumentality*) 631; function &c. (*business*) 625; value; worth &c. (*goodness*) 648; money's worth; productiveness &c. 168; *cui bono* &c. (*intention*) 620; utilization &c. (*use*) 677; step in the right direction.

common weal, public good; utilitarianism &c. (*philanthropy*) 910.

V. be -useful &c. *adj.*; avail, serve; subserve &c. (*be instrumental to*) 631; conduce &c. (*tend*) 176; answer –, serve- -one's turn, – a purpose.

act a part &c. (*action*) 680; perform –, discharge- -a function &c. 625; do –, render- -a service, – good service, – yeoman's service; bestead, stand one in good stead; be the making of; help &c. 707.

bear fruit &c. (*produce*) 161; bring grist to the mill; profit, remunerate; benefit &c. (*do good*) 648.

find one's -account, – advantage- in; reap the benefit of &c. (*be better for*) 658.

render useful &c. (*use*) 677.

Adj. useful; of -use &c. *n.*; serviceable, usable, proficuous, good for; subservient &c. (*instrumental*) 631; conducive &c. (*tending*) 176; subsidiary &c. (*helping*) 707.

advantageous &c. (*beneficial*) 648; profitable, gainful, remunerative, worth one's salt; in-, valuable; prolific &c. (*productive*) 168.

adequate; ef-ficient, -ficacious; effect-ive, -ual; practicable, expedient &c. 646.

645. Inutility.—N. inutility; uselessness &c. *adj.*; inefficacy, futility; inep-, inap-titude; unsubservience; inadequacy &c. (*insufficiency*) 640; inefficiency &c. (*incompetence*) 158; unskilfulness &c. 699; disservice; unfruitfulness &c. (*unproductiveness*) 169; labour -in vain, – lost, – of Sisyphus; lost -trouble, – labour; work of Penelope; sleeveless errand, wild goose chase, mere farce.

tautology &c. (*repetition*) 104; supererogation &c. (*redundance*) 641.

vanitas vanitatum, vanity, inanity, worthlessness, nugacity; triviality &c. (*unimportance*) 643.

caput mortuum, waste paper, dead letter; blunt tool.

litter, rubbish, lumber, odds and ends, cast-off clothes; button-top; shoddy; rags, orts, trash, refuse, sweepings, scourings, off-scourings, dross, slag, waste, rubble, dottle, drast, *débris*; stubble, leavings; broken meat; dregs &c. (*dirt*) 653; weeds, tares; rubbish heap, dust hole; *rudera*, deads.

fruges consumere natus &c. (*drone*) 683.

V. be -useless &c. *adj.*; go a begging &c. (*redundant*) 641; fail &c. 732.

seek –, strive- after impossibilities; use vain efforts, labour in vain, roll the stone of Sisyphus, beat the air, lash the waves, *battre l'eau avec un bâton, donner un coup d'épée dans l'eau*, fish in the air, milk the ram, drop a bucket into an empty well, sow the sand; bay the moon; preach –, speak- to the winds; whistle jigs to a milestone; kick against the pricks, *se battre contre des moulins*; lock the stable door

applicable, available, ready, handy, at hand, tangible; commodious, adaptable; of all work.

Adv. usefully &c. *adj.*; *pro bono publico.*

render -useless &c. *adj.*; dis-mantle, -mast, -mount, -qualify, -able; unrig; cripple, lame &c. (*injure*) 659; spike guns, clip the wings; put out of gear.

Adj. useless, inutile, inefficacious, futile, unavailing, bootless; inoperative &c. 158; inadequate &c. (*insufficient*) 640; in-, un-sub-servient; inept, inefficient &c. (*impotent*) 158; of no -avail &c. (*use*) 644; ineffectual &c. (*failure*) 732; incompetent &c. (*unskilful*) 699; 'stale, flat and unprofitable'; superfluous &c. (*redundant*) 641; dispensable; thrown away &c. (*wasted*) 638; abortive &c. (*immature*) 674.

worth-, value-less; unsaleable; not worth a straw &c. (*trifling*) 643; dear at any price.

vain, empty, inane; gain-, profit-, fruit-less; un-serviceable, -profitable; ill-spent; unproductive &c. 169; *hors de combat*; barren, sterile, impotent, unproductive; effete, past work &c. (*impaired*) 659; obsolete &c. (*old*) 124; fit for the -dust-hole, — wastepaper basket; good for nothing; of no earthly use; not worth -having, — powder and shot; leading to no end, uncalled for; un-necessary, -needed, superfluous.

Adv. uselessly &c. *adj.*; to -little, — no, — little or no- purpose.

Int. *cui bono?* what's the good!

when the steed is stolen &c. (*too late*) 135; hold a farthing candle to the sun; cast pearls before swine &c. (*waste*) 638; carry coals to Newcastle &c. (*redundance*) 641; wash a blackamoor white &c. (*impossible*) 471.

---

646. [Specific subservience.] **Expedience.—N.** expedien-ce, -cy; desirableness, -bility &c. *adj.*; fitness &c. (*agreement*) 23; utility &c. 644; propriety; advantage; opportunism, pragmatism.

high time &c. (*occasion*) 134.

V. be -expedient &c. *adj.*; suit &c. (*agree*) 23; befit; suit -, befit- the -time, — season, — occasion.

conform &c. 82.

Adj. expedient; desir-, advis-, acceptable; convenient; worth while, meet; fit, -ting; due, proper, eligible, seemly, becoming; befitting &c. *v.*; opportune &c. (*in season*) 134; *in loco*; suitable &c. (*accordant*) 23; applicable &c. (*useful*) 644; practical, effective, pragmatical; suitable, handy.

Adv. in the right place; conveniently &c. *adj.*; in the nick of time.

Phr. *operæ pretium est.*

647. Inexpedience.—N. inexpedien-ce, -cy; undesira-bleness, -bility &c. *adj.*; discommodity, impropriety; unfitness &c. (*disagreement*) 24; inutility &c. 645; inconvenience, inadvisability; disadvantage.

V. be -inexpedient &c. *adj.*; come amiss &c. (*disagree*) 24; embarrass &c. (*hinder*) 706; put to inconvenience; pay too dear for one's whistle.

Adj. inexpedient, undesirable; un-, in-advisable; objectionable; troublesome, in-apt, -eligible, -admissible, -convenient; in-, dis-commodious; disadvantageous; inappropriate, unsuitable, unfit &c. (*inconsonant*) 24.

ill-contrived, -advised; unsatisfactory; unprofitable &c., unsubservient &c. (*useless*) 645; inopportune &c. (*unseasonable*) 135; out of -, in the wrong-place; improper, unseemly.

clumsy, awkward; cum-brous, -bersome; lumbering, unwieldy, hulky; unmanageable &c. (*impracticable*) 704; impedient &c. (*in the way*) 706; unnecessary &c. (*redundant*) 641.

Phr. it will never do.

648. [Capability of producing good. Good qualities.] **Goodness.**—N. goodness &c. *adj.*; excellence, merit; virtue &c. 944; value, worth, price.

super-excellence, -eminence; superiority &c. 33; perfection &c. 650; *coup de maître*; master-piece, *chef d'œuvre*, prime, flower, cream, *élite*, pick, A1, none such, *nonpareil*, *crême de la crême*, flower of the flock, cock of the roost, salt of the earth; champion.

tid-bit; gem, – of the first water; *bijou*, precious stone, jewel, pearl, diamond, ruby, brilliant, treasure; good thing; *rara avis*, one in a thousand.

beneficence &c. 906; good man &c. 948.

V. be -beneficial &c. *adj.*; produce –, do- -good &c. 618; profit &c. (*be of use*) 644; benefit; confer a -benefit &c. 618.

be the making of, do a world of good, make a man of.

produce a good effect; do a good turn, confer an obligation; improve &c. 658.

do no harm, break no bones.

be -good &c. *adj.*; excel, transcend &c. (*be superior*) 33; bear away the bell.

stand the -proof, – test; pass -muster, – an examination.

challenge comparison, vie, emulate, rival.

Adj. harm-, hurt-less; unobnoxious; in-nocuous, -nocent, -offensive.

beneficial, valuable, of value; serviceable &c. (*useful*) 644; advantageous, profitable, edifying; salutary &c. (*healthful*) 656.

favourable; propitious &c. (*hopegiving*) 858; fair.

good, – as gold; excellent; better; superior &c. 33; above par; nice, fine; genuine &c. (*true*) 494.

best, choice, select, picked, elect, eximious, *recherché*, rare, priceless; unpara-goned, -lleled &c. (*supreme*) 33; superlatively &c. 33- good; superfine, -excellent; bonzer; of the first water; first-rate, -class; high-wrought; exquisite, very best, crack, prime, tip-top, gilt-edged, capital, cardinal; standard &c. (*perfect*) 650; inimitable.

admirable, estimable; praiseworthy &c. (*approve*) 931; pleasing &c. 829; *couleur de rose*, precious, of great price;

649. [Capability of producing evil. Bad qualities.] **Badness.**—N. hurtfulness &c. *adj.*; virulence.

evil doer &c. 913; bane &c. 663; plague-spot &c. (*insalubrity*) 657; evil star, ill wind; snake in the grass, skeleton in the closet; *amari aliquid*, thorn in the side; Jonah, jinx, hoodoo.

malignity; malevolence &c. 907; tender mercies [ironically].

ill-treatment, annoyance, molestation, abuse, oppression, persecution, outrage; misusage &c. 679; injury &c. (*damage*) 659.

badness &c. *adj.*; peccancy, abomination; painfulness &c. 830; pestilence &c. (*disease*) 655; guilt &c. 947; depravity &c. 945.

V. be -hurtful &c. *adj.*; cause –, produce –, inflict –, work –, do- evil &c. 619; damnify, endamage, hurt, harm, scathe; injure &c. (*damage*) 659; pain &c. 830.

wrong, aggrieve, oppress, persecute; trample –, tread –, bear hard –, put-upon; overburden; weigh -down, – heavy on; victimize; run down; molest &c. 830.

maltreat, abuse; ill-use, -treat; thwart, buffet, bruise, scratch, maul; smite &c. (*scourge*) 972; do -violence, – harm, – a mischief; stab, pierce, outrage.

do –, make- mischief; bring –, get-into trouble.

destroy &c. 162.

Adj. hurt-, harm-, scath-, bane-, baleful; injurious, deleterious, detrimental, noxious, pernicious, mischievous, full of mischief, mischief-making, malefic, malignant, nocuous, noisome; prejudicial; dis-serviceable, -advantageous; wide-wasting.

unlucky, sinister; obnoxious, untoward, disastrous.

oppressive, burdensome, onerous; malign &c. (*malevolent*) 907.

corrupting &c. (corrupt &c. 659); virulent, venomous, envenomed, corrosive; poisonous &c. (*morbific*) 657; deadly &c. (*killing*) 361; destructive &c. (*destroying*) 162; inauspicious &c. 859.

bad, ill, arrant, as bad as bad can be, dreadful; hor-rid, -rible; dire; rank,

costly &c. (*dear*) 814; worth -its weight in gold, -a king's ransom; matchless, peerless, invaluable, inestimable, precious as the apple of the eye.

tolerable &c. (*not very good*) 651; up to the mark, un-exceptionable, -objectionable; satisfactory, tidy.

in -good, – fair- condition; fresh; unspoiled; sound &c. (*perfect*) 650.

Adv. beneficially &c. *adj.*; well &c. 618.

---

peccant, foul, fulsome; rotten, – at the core.

vile, base, villainous; mean &c. (*paltry*) 643; injured &c., deteriorated &c. 659; unsatisfactory, exception, -able, indifferent; below par &c. (*imperfect*) 651; ill-contrived, -conditioned; wretched, sad, grievous, deplorable, lamentable; piti-ful, -able, woeful &c. (*painful*) 830.

evil, wrong; depraved &c. 945; shocking; reprehensible &c. (*disapprove*) 932.

hateful, – as a toad; abominable, detestable, execrable, cursed, accursed, confounded; damn-ed, -able; infernal; diabolic &c. (*malevolent*) 907.

inadvisable &c. (*inexpedient*) 647; unprofitable &c. (*useless*) 645; incompetent &c. (*unskilful*) 699; irremediable &c. (*hopeless*) 859.

Adv. badly &c. *adj.*; wrong, ill; to one's cost; where the shoe pinches.

Phr. bad is the best; the worst come to the worst.

650. Perfection. — **N.** perfection; perfectness &c. *adj.*; indefectibility; impecc-ancy, -ability.

pink, *beau idéal*, phœnix, paragon; pink –, acme- of perfection; *ne plus ultra*; summit &c. 210.

cygne noir; philosopher's stone; chrysolite, Koh-i-noor, black tulip.

model, standard, pattern, mirror, admirable Crichton; trump; very prince of.

master-piece, -stroke, super-excellence &c. (*goodness*) 648; transcendence &c. (*superiority*) 33.

V. be -perfect &c. *adj.*; transcend &c. (*be supreme*) 33.

bring to perfection, perfect, ripen, mature; consummate, complete &c. 729; put in trim &c. (*prepare*) 673; put the finishing touch to.

Adj. perfect, faultless, ideal; indefective, -ficient, -fectible; immaculate, spotless, impeccable; free from -imperfection &c. 651; un-blemished, -injured &c. 659; sound, – as a roach; in perfect condition; scathless, intact, harmless; seaworthy &c. (*safe*) 644; right as a trivet; *in seipso totus teres atque rotundus*; consummate &c. (*complete*) 52; finished &c. 729; complete in itself.

best &c. (*good*) 648; model, standard; inimitable, unparagoned, unparalleled &c. (*supreme*) 33; superhuman, divine;

651. Imperfection.—**N.** imperfection; imperfectness &c. *adj.*; deficiency; inadequacy &c. (*insufficiency*) 640; peccancy &c. (*badness*) 649; immaturity &c. 674.

fault, defect, weak point; screw loose; rift within the lute; fly in the ointment; flaw &c. (*break*) 70; gap &c. 198; twist &c. 243; taint, attainder; bar sinister, hole in one's coat; blemish &c. 848; weakness &c. 160; half-blood, touch of the tar brush; shortcoming &c. 304; drawback; seamy side.

mediocrity; no great -shakes, – catch; not much to boast of.

V. be -imperfect &c. *adj.*; have a -defect &c. *n.*; lie under a disadvantage; spring a leak.

not –, barely- pass muster; fall short &c. 304.

Adj. imperfect; not -perfect &c. 650; de-ficient, -fective; faulty, unsound, mutilated, tainted; out of -order, – tune; cracked, leaky; sprung; warped &c. (*distort*) 243; lame; injured &c. (*deteriorated*) 659; peccant &c. (*bad*) 649; frail &c. (*weak*) 160; inadequate &c. (*insufficient*) 640; crude &c. (*unprepared*) 674; incomplete &c. 53; found wanting; below par; short-handed; below –, under- its full -strength, – complement.

indifferent, middling, ordinary, medi-

beyond all praise &c. (*approbation*) 931; *sans peur et sans reproche.*

Adv. to perfection, to the limit; perfectly &c. *adj.*; *ad unguem*; clean, – as a whistle.

---

ocre; average &c. 29; so-so; *così-così*, milk and water; tolerable, fair, passable; pretty -well, – good; rather –, moderately- good; good –, well- enough; decent; not -bad, – amiss; inobjectionable, admissible, bearable, only better than nothing.

secondary, inferior; second-rate, -best, one-horse.

Adv. almost &c.; to a limited extent, rather &c. 32; pretty, moderately; only; considering, all things considered, enough.

Phr. *surgit amari aliquid.*

652. Cleanness.—N. cleanness &c. *adj.*; purity; cleaning &c. *v.*; purification, defecation &c. *v.*; purgation, lustration; de-, abs-tersion; epuration, mundation, ablution, lavation, colature; disinfection &c. *v.*; drain-, sewerage.

lavatory, bath, -room; swimming pool, natatorium; public baths; hot –, cold –, Turkish –, Swedish –, Russian –, vapour- bath; *hammam*, laundry, washhouse; washerwoman, laundress, laundryman; scavenger, cleaner, sweeper, goodie; crossing sweeper, white wings, dustman, sweep.

brush; broom, besom, carpet-sweeper, vacuum-cleaner, mop, squilgee, rake, shovel, sieve, riddle, screen, filter; scraper, strigil.

napkin, *serviette*, cloth, table-, carving-cloth, table-linen, napery, maukin, handkerchief, towel, sudary; doyley, doily, duster, sponge, mop, swab.

cover, drugget, mat, doormat.

soap, wash, lotion, detergent, cathartic, purgative; purifier &c. *v.*; dentifrice, tooth-powder, -paste; mouth wash; disinfectant.

V. be –, render- clean &c. *adj.*

clean, -se; mundify, rinse, wring, flush, full, wipe, mop, sponge, scour, swab, scrub, holystone, brush up.

wash, shampoo, lave, launder, buck; abs-, de-terge; clear, purify; de-purate, -spumate, -fecate; purge, expurgate; Bowdlerize; elutriate, lixiviate, edulcorate, clarify, refine, rack; fil-ter, -trate; drain, strain.

disinfect, sterilize, pasteurize, fumigate, ventilate, deodorize; whitewash.

sift, winnow, screen, riddle, pick, weed, comb, rake, brush, sweep.

653. Uncleanness.—N. uncleanness &c. *adj.*; impurity; immundi-ty, -city; impurity &c. [of mind] 961.

defilement, contamination &c. *v.*; defœdation; soil-ure, -iness; abomination; leaven; taint, -ure; fetor &c. 401.

decay; putre-scence, -faction; corruption; mould, must, mildew, dry-rot, *mucor*, rubigo, caries.

slovenry; slovenliness &c. *adj.*; squalor.

dowdy, drab, slut, malkin, slattern, sloven, slammerkin, scrub, draggletail, mudlark, dustman, sweep; beast.

dirt, filth, soil, slop; dust, cobweb, flue; smoke, soot, smudge, smut, grime, raff.

sordes, dregs, grounds, lees; sedi-, settle-ment; heel-tap; dross, -iness; mother, precipitate, *scoriæ*, ashes, cinders, recrement, slag; scum, froth.

hog-wash, swill, ditch-, dish-, bilge-water; rinsings, cheese-parings; sweepings &c. (*useless refuse*) 645; off-, out-scourings; off-scum; *caput mortuum*, *residuum*, sprue, feculence, clinker, draff; scurf, -iness; *exuviæ*, morphew; fur, -fur; dandruff; tartar.

riffraff; vermin, louse, cootie, flea, bug.

mud, mire, quagmire, *alluvium*, silt, sludge, slime, slush, slosh.

spawn, offal, garbage, carrion; *excreta* &c. 299; slough, peccant humour, pus, matter, suppuration, *lienteria*; *fæces*, excrement, ordure, dung; sew-, sewer-age; muck, coprolite; guano, manure, compost.

dunghill, *coluvies*, mixen, midden, bog, laystall, sink, w.c., water-, earth-closet, latrine, privy, jakes, John's; cess, -pool; sump, sough, *cloaca*, drain,

rout –, clear –, sweep &c.- out; make a clean sweep of.

Adj. clean, -ly; pure; immaculate; spot-, stain-, taint-less; without a stain, un-stained, -spotted, -soiled, -sullied, -tainted, -infected, -adulterated; aseptic; sweet, – as a nut.

neat, spruce, tidy, trim, gimp, clean as a new penny, like a cat in pattens; cleaned &c. *v.*; kempt.

Adv. neatly &c. *adj.*; clean as a whistle.

———

sewer, common sewer; Cloacina; dust-hole.

sty, pig-sty, lair, den, Augean stable, sink of corruption; slum, rookery.

V. be –, become- unclean &c. *adj.*; rot, putrefy, fester, rankle, reek; stink &c. 401; mould, -er; go -bad &c. *adj.*

render -unclean &c. *adj.*; dirt, -y; soil, smoke, tarnish, slaver, spot, smear, daub, blot, blur, smudge, smutch, smirch; d-, dr-abble, -aggle; spatter, slubber; be-smear &c., -mire, -slime, -grime, -foul; splash, stain, distain, maculate, sully, pollute, defile, debase, contaminate, taint, leaven; corrupt &c. (*injure*) 659; cover with -dust &c. *n.*; drabble in the mud.

wallow in the mire; slob-, slab-ber.

Adj. unclean, dirty, filthy, grimy; soiled &c. *v.*; not to be handled with kid gloves; dusty, snuffy, smutty, sooty, smoky; thick, turbid, dreggy; slimy.

uncleanly, slovenly, untidy, sluttish, dowdy, slatternly, draggle-tailed; un-combed, -kempt, -scoured, -swept, -wiped, -washed, -strained, -purified; squalid.

nasty, coarse, foul, impure, offensive, abominable, beastly, reeky, reechy; fetid &c. 401.

mouldy, lentiginous, musty, mildewed, rusty, moth-eaten, mucid, rancid, bad, gone bad, touched, fusty, reasty, rotten, corrupt, tainted, high, fly-blown, maggoty; putr-id, -escent, -efied; purulent, carious, peccant, fec-al, -ulent; stercoraceous, excrementitious; scurfy, impetiginous; gory, bloody, rotting &c. *v.*; rotten as -a pear, – cheese.

crapulous &c. (*intemperate*) 954; gross &c. (*impure in mind*) 961.

654. Health.—N. health, sanity; soundness &c. *adj.*; vigour; good –, perfect –, excellent –, rude –, robust-health; bloom, *mens sana in corpore sano*; Hygeia; incorrupti-on, -bility; good state –, clean bill- of health, eupepsia.

V. be in health &c. *adj.*; bloom, flourish.

keep -body and soul together, – on one's legs; enjoy -good, – a good state of- health; have a clean bill of health.

return to health; recover &c. 660; get better &c. (*improve*) 658; take a -new, – fresh- lease of life; convalesce, be convalescent, recruit; restore to health; cure &c. (*restore*) 660.

Adj. health-y, -ful; in -health &c. *n.*; well, sound, strong, fit, hearty, hale, fresh, blooming, green, whole; florid, flush, hardy, stanch, staunch,

655. Disease.*—N. disease; illness, sickness &c. *adj.*; ailing &c. *v.*; 'the ills that flesh is heir to'; morb-idity, -osity; infirmity, ailment, indisposition; complaint, disorder, malady; distemper, -ature.

visitation, attack, seizure, stroke, fit, epilepsy, apoplexy, shock, shell-shock.

delicacy, loss of health, valetudinarianism, invalidism, cachexy; *cachexia*, atrophy, *marasmus*; indigestion, *dyspepsia*; decay &c. (*deterioration*) 659; malnutrition, decline, consumption, palsy, paralysis, prostration; occupational diseases.

taint, pollution, infection, contagion, septicity, septicæmia, blood poisoning, pyæmia, epi-, en-demic; murrain, plague, pestilence, virus, pox.

sore, ulcer, abscess, fester, boil; pimple &c. (*swelling*) 250; carbuncle,

* Extended lists of different diseases are beyond the scope of this work.

brave, robust, vigorous, weather-proof; convalescent.

un-scathed, -injured, -maimed, -marred, -tainted; sound of wind and limb, safe and sound; without a scratch.

on one's legs; sound as a -roach, – bell; fresh as -a daisy, – a rose, – April; picture of health; bursting with health; fit as a fiddle; hearty as a buck; in -fine, – high- feather; in -good case, – full bloom; in fine fettle; pretty bobbish, tolerably well, as well as can be expected.

sanitary &c. (*health-giving*) 656; sanatory &c. (*remedial*) 662.

gathering, whitlow, imposthume, peccant humour, issue; rot, canker, cancer, *carcinoma, caries,* mortification, corruption, gangrene, *sphacelus,* leprosy, eruption, rash, breaking out, venereal disease.

fever, calenture; inflammation.

fatal &c. (*hopeless*) 859- -disease &c.; dangerous illness, galloping consumption, churchyard cough; general breaking up, break up of the system.

[Disease of mind] neurasthenia; idiocy &c. 499; insanity &c. 503.

martyr to disease; cripple; 'the halt, the lame and the blind'; valetudinar-y, -ian; invalid, patient, case; sick-room, -chamber, hospital &c. 662.

[Science of disease] path-, eti-, nos-ology, therapeutics, diagnosis, prognosis.

V. be -ill &c. *adj.*; ail, suffer, labour under, be affected with, complain of; droop, flag, languish, halt; sicken, peak, pine, waste away, fail, lose strength; gasp.

keep one's bed; feign sickness &c. (*falsehood*) 544, malinger.

lay -by, – up; take –, catch- -a disease &c. *n.,* – an infection; be stricken by; break out.

Adj. diseased; ailing &c. *v.*; ill, – of; taken ill, seized with; indisposed, unwell, sick, squeamish, poorly, seedy; affected –, afflicted- with illness; laid up, confined, bed-ridden, invalided, in hospital, on the sick list; out of -health, – sorts; valetudinary.

un-sound, -healthy; sickly, morbose, healthless, infirm, chlorotic, unbraced, drooping, flagging, lame, halt, crippled, halting.

morbid, tainted, vitiated, peccant, contaminated, poisoned, septic, tabid, mangy, leprous, cankered; rotten, – to, – at- the core; withered, palsied, paralytic, tuberculous; dyspeptic.

touched in the wind, broken-winded, spavined, gasping; *hors de combat* &c. (*useless*) 645.

weak-ly, -ened &c. (*weak*) 160; decrepit; decayed &c. (*deteriorated*) 659; incurable &c. (*hopeless*) 859; in declining health; cranky; in a bad way, in danger, prostrate; moribund &c. (*death*) 360.

morbific, epidemic &c. 657.

---

656. Salubrity.—N. salubrity, salubriousness; healthiness &c. *adj.*

fine -air, – climate; eudiometer.

[Preservation of health] *hygiène*; valetudinarian, -ism, preventorium, sanitarian; *sanitarium, sanitorium,* immunity.

V. be -salubrious &c. *adj.*; agree with, be good for; assimilate &c. 23.

Adj. salu-brious, -tary, -tiferous, wholesome; health-y, -ful; sanitary, prophylactic, benign, bracing, tonic,

657. Insalubrity.—N. insalubrity; unhealthiness &c. *adj.*; non-naturals; plague spot; malaria &c. (*poison*) 663; death in the pot, contagion.

Adj. insalubrious; un-healthy, -wholesome; noxious, noisome, foul; morbi-fic, -ferous; mephitic, septic, azotic, deleterious; pesti-lent, -ferous, -lential; virulent, venomous, envenomed, poisonous, toxic, narcotic.

contagious, infectious, catching, taking, communicable, epidemic, zymotic;

invigorating, good for, nutritious, hyg-eian, -ienic.

in-noxious, -nocuous, -nocent; harmless, uninjurious, uninfectious; immune.

sanative &c. (*remedial*) 662; restorative &c. (*reinstate*) 660; useful &c. 644.

658. Improvement.—N. improvement; a-, melioration; betterment; mend, amendment, emendation; mending &c. *v.*; advancement; advance &c. (*progress*) 282; ascent &c. 305; promotion, preferment; elevation &c. 307; increase &c. 35.

cultiv-, civiliz-ation; menticulture, culture, march of intellect; eugenics, euthenics, meliorism, telesis.

reform, -ation; revision, radical reform; second thoughts, correction, *limæ labor*, refinement, elaboration; purification &c. 652; repair &c. (*restoration*) 660; recovery &c. 660.

revise; revised -, new- edition.

reformer, radical, progressive.

V. improve; be -, become -, getbetter; mend, amend.

advance &c. (*progress*) 282; ascend &c. 305; increase &c. 35; fructify, ripen, mature; pick up, come about, rally, take a favourable turn; turn -over a new leaf, – the corner; raise one's head, sow one's wild oats; recover &c. 660.

be -better &c. *adj.*, – improved by; turn to -right, – good, – best- account; profit by, reap the benefit of; make -good use of, – capital out of; place to good account; take advantage of.

render better, improve, emend, make over, better; a-, meliorate; correct.

improve -, refine- upon; rectify; enrich, mellow, elaborate, fatten.

promote, cultivate, advance, forward, enhance; bring -forward, – on; foster &c. 707; invigorate &c. (*strengthen*) 159.

touch -, rub -, brush -, furbish -, bolster -, vamp -, brighten -, warmup; polish, cook, make the most of, set off to advantage; prune; repair &c. (*restore*) 660; put in order &c. (*arrange*) 60.

review, revise, edit, redact; make -corrections, – improvements &c. *n.*; doctor &c. (*remedy*) 662; purify &c. 652.

sporadic, endemic, pandemic, epizoötic.

innutritious, indigestible, ungenial; uncongenial &c. (*disagreeing*) 24.

deadly &c. (*killing*) 361.

---

659. Deterioration.—N. deterioration, debasement; want, ebb; recession &c. 287; retrogradation &c. 283; decrease &c. 36.

degenera-cy, -tion, -teness; degradation; deprav-ation, -ement; depravity &c. 945; demoralization, retrogression.

impairment, inquination, injury, damage, loss, detriment, delaceration, outrage, havoc, inroad, ravage, scath; perversion, prostitution, vitiation, discoloration, oxidation, pollution, defœdation, poisoning, venenation, leaven, contamination, canker, corruption, adulteration, alloy.

decl-ine, -ension, -ination; decadence, -cy; falling off &c. *v.*; caducity, decreptitude, senility.

decay, dilapidation, ravages of time, wear and tear; cor-, e-rosion; mouldi-, rotten-ness; moth and rust, dry-rot, blight, marasmus, atrophy, collapse; disorganization; *délabrement* &c. (*destruction*) 162.

wreck, mere wreck, honeycomb, *magni nominis umbra*.

V. be -, become--worse,--deteriorated &c. *adj.*; have seen better days, deteriorate, degenerate, fall off; wane &c. (*decrease*) 36; ebb; retrograde &c. 283; decline, droop; go down &c. (*sink*) 306; go -downhill, – on from bad to worse, – farther and fare worse; jump out of the frying pan into the fire.

run to -seed, – waste; swale, sweal; lapse, be the worse for; break, – down; spring a leak, crack, start; shrivel &c. (*contract*) 195; fade, go off, wither, moulder, rot, rankle, decay, go bad; go to -, fall into- decay; 'fall into the sear and yellow leaf,' rust, crumble, shake; totter, – to its fall; perish &c. 162; die &c. 360.

[Render less good] deteriorate; weaken &c. 160; put back; taint, infect, contaminate, poison, empoison,

relieve, refresh, revive, infuse new blood into, recruit, re-invigorate, re-new, revivify, freshen, build -afresh, – anew; uplift, inspire.

re-form, -model, -organise; new model, civilize.

view in a new light, think better of, appeal from Philip drunk to Philip sober.

palliate, mitigate; lessen &c. 36- an evil.

Adj. improving &c. *v.*; progressive, improved &c. *v.*; better, – off, – for; all the better for; better advised.

reform-, emend-atory; reparatory &c. (*restorative*) 660; remedial &c. 662.

corrigible, improvable, curable, ac-cultural.

Adv. on -consideration, – reconsider-ation, – second thoughts, – better advice; *ad melius inquirendum*; on the -mend, – up grade.

---

envenom, canker, corrupt, exulcerate, pollute, vitiate, inquinate; de-, em-base; denaturalize, leaven; de-flower, -bauch, -file, -prave, -grade; stain &c. (*dirt*) 653; discolour; alloy, adulterate, sophisticate, tamper with, prejudice.

pervert, prostitute, demoralize, bru-talize; render vicious &c. 945; compro-mise.

embitter, ex-, acerbate, aggravate.

injure, impair, labefy, damage, harm, hurt, shend, scathe, spoil, mar, despoil, dilapidate, waste; overrun; ravage; pillage &c. 791.

wound, stab, pierce, maim, lame, surbate, cripple, hough, hamstring, hit between wind and water, scotch, mangle, mutilate, disfigure, blemish, deface, warp.

blight, rot; cor-, e-rode, eat away; wear -away, – out; gnaw, – at the root of; sap, mine, undermine, shake, sap the foundations of, break up; dis-organ-ize, -mantle, -mast; destroy &c. 162.

damnify &c. (*aggrieve*) 649; do one's worst; knock down; deal a blow to; play -havoc, – sad havoc, – the mischief, – the deuce, – the very devil- -with, – among; decimate.

Adj. unimproved &c. (improve &c. 658); deteriorated &c. *v.*; altered, – for the worse; injured &c. *v.*; sprung; withering, spoiling, &c. *v.*; on the -wane, – decline; tabid; degenerate; worse; the –, all the- worse for; out of -repair, – tune; imperfect &c. 651; the worse for wear; battered; weather-ed, -beaten; stale, *passé*, shaken, dilapidated, frayed, faded, wilted, shabby, second-hand, second-rate, threadbare; worn, – to- -a thread, – a shadow, – the stump, rags; reduced, – to a skeleton, skeletonized; far gone.

decayed &c. *v.*; moth-, worm-eaten; mildewed, rusty, mouldy, spotted, seedy, time-worn, moss-grown; discoloured; effete, wasted, crumbling, mouldering, rotten, cankered, blighted, tainted; depraved &c. (*vicious*) 945; decrep-id, -it; broken down; done, – for, – up; worn out, used up; fit for the -dust-hole, – wastepaper basket; past work &c. (*useless*) 645.

at a low ebb, in a bad way, on one's last legs, washed -up, – out; undermined, deciduous; nodding to its fall &c. (*destruction*) 162; tottering &c. (*dangerous*) 665; past cure &c. (*hopeless*) 859; fatigued &c. 688; backward, retrograde &c. (*retrogressive*) 283; deleterious &c. 649; behind the times.

Adv. on the down grade; beyond hope.

Phr. out of the frying pan into the fire; *ægrescit medendo*.

---

660. Restoration.—**N.** restor-ation, -al; re-instatement, -placement, -habi-litation, -establishment, -construction; reproduction &c. 163; re-novation, -newal; reviv-al, -escence; refreshment

661. Relapse.—**N.** relapse, lapse; falling back &c. *v.*; retrogradation &c. (*retrogression*) 283; deterioration &c. 659.

[Return to, or recurrence of a bad

&c. 689; re-suscitation, -animation, -vivification, -viction; Phœnix; reorganization.

renaissance, renascence, rebirth, second youth, rejuvenation, rejuvenescence, new birth; regenera-tion, -cy, -teness; palingenesis, reconversion, resurgence, resurrection.

redress, retrieval, reclamation, recovery; convalescence; resumption, *résumption*.

recurrence &c. (*repetition*) 104; *réchauffé*, *rifacimento*.

cure, recure, sanation; healing &c. *v.*; redintegration; rectification, instauration.

repair, reparation, mending; recruiting &c. *v.*; cicatrization; disinfection; tinkering.

reaction; redemption &c. (*deliverance*) 672; restitution &c. 790; relief &c. 834.

mender, repairer, renewer; tinker, cobbler; doctor &c. 662; *vis medicatrix* &c. (*remedy*) 662.

curableness.

V. return to the original state; recover, rally, revive; come -to, – round, – to oneself; pull through, weather the storm, be oneself again; get -well, – round, – the better of, – over, – about; rise from -one's ashes, – the grave; resurge, resurrect; survive &c. (*outlive*) 110; resume, reappear; come to, – life again; live –, rise- again; relive.

heal, skin over, cicatrize; right itself.

restore, put back, place *in statu quo*; re-instate, -place, -seat, -habilitate, -establish, -estate, -install.

re-construct, -build, -organize, -constitute; reconvert; re-new, -novate; recondition; regenerate; rejuvenate.

re-deem, -claim, -cover, -trieve; rescue &c. (*deliver*) 672.

redress, recure; cure, heal, remedy, doctor, physic, medicate; break of; bring round, set on one's legs.

re-suscitate, -vive, -animate, -vivify, -call to life; reproduce &c. 163; warm up; reinvigorate, refresh &c. 689.

redintegrate, make whole; recoup &c. 790; make -good, – all square; rectify; put –, set- -right, – to rights, – straight; set up, correct; put in order &c. (*arrange*) 60; refit, recruit; fill up, – the ranks; reinforce.

repair, mend; put in -repair, – thorough repair, – complete repair; retouch, botch, vamp, tinker, doctor, cobble; do –, patch –, plaster –, vamp- up; darn, fine-draw, heel-piece; stop a gap, stanch, staunch, caulk, calk, careen, splice, bind up wounds.

Adj. restored &c. *v.*; *redivivus*, convalescent; in a fair way; none the worse; rejuvenated, renascent.

restoring &c. *v.*; restorative, recuperative; sana-, repara-tive, -tory; curative, remedial.

restor-, recover-, san-, remedi-, retriev-, cur-able.

Adv. *in statu quo*; as you were.

Phr. *revenons à nos moutons*.

state] backsliding, recidivation, recrudescence.

V. relapse, lapse; fall –, slide –, sinkback; have a relapse; return; retrograde &c. 283; recidivate; fall off &c. 659-again.

———

662. Remedy.—N. remedy, help, redress; antidote, anti-toxin, anti-,

663. Bane.—N. bane, curse, thorn in the -side, -flesh, bugbear, *bête noire*;

counter-poison, prophylactic, antiseptic, germicide, bactericide, corrective, restorative, stimulant, pick-me-up, tonic; sedative &c. 174; palliative; febrifuge; alter-ant, -ative; specific; emetic, carminative; narcotic &c. *adj.*; Nepenthe, Mithridate.

cure; radical –, perfect –, certain-cure; sovereign remedy.

physic, medicine, patent medicine, Galenicals, simples, drug, potion, draught, dose, pill, bolus, lozenge, tablet, tabloid, capsule; electuary; linct-us, -ure; medicament.

nostrum, receipt, recipe, prescription; catholicon, panacea, elixir, *elixir vitæ*, philosopher's stone; balm, balsam, cordial, theriac, ptisan.

salve, ointment, cerate, oil, lenitive, lotion, cosmetic; plaster; epithem, embrocation, liniment, cataplasm, sinapism, arquebusade, traumatic, vulnerary, pepastic, poultice, collyrium, depilatory.

compress, pledget; bandage &c. (*support*) 215.

treatment, medical treatment, regimen; diet-ary, -etics; *vis medicatrix, – naturæ; médecine expectante*; seton, blood-letting, bleeding, venesection, phlebotomy, cupping, leeches; operation, surgical operation; tonsillectomy, appendectomy; injection, electrolysis, massage.

pharma-cy, -cology, -ceutics; acology; materia medica, pharmacopœia, therapeutics, therapy, posology, pathology &c. 655; homœ-, hetero-, all-, hydr-opathy; cold water –, open air- cure; dietetics; sur-, chirur-gery, osteopathy; healing art, leechcraft, practice of medicine; ortho-pædy, -praxy; dentistry, midwifery, obstetrics, gynæcology.

faith -cure, – healing, Christian science; psycho-therapy, -analysis, psychiatry.

hospital, infirmary, clinic; pest-, lazar-house; lazaretto, lazaret; lock hospital; *maison de santé; ambulance*; dispensary; *sanatorium, sanitarium*, spa, baths, pump-room, well; *hospice*; Red Cross; nursing home; asylum.

doctor, physician, surgeon; medical –, general- practitioner, consultant, specialist; medical attendant; medical student, medico; chemist, apothecary, pharmacopolist, druggist; leech; Æsculapius, Hippocrates, Galen; *accoucheur*, gynæcologist, midwife, oculist, aurist, dentist; operator; osteopath, bonesetter; nurse, monthly nurse, sister; dresser; *masseur, masseuse*.

V. apply a -remedy &c. *n.*; doctor, dose, physic, nurse, minister to, attend, dress the wounds, plaster, bandage, poultice; heal, cure, work a cure, kill or cure, remedy, stay (disease), snatch from the jaws of death; prevent &c. 706; relieve &c. 834; palliate &c. 658;

evil &c. 619; hurtfulness &c. (*badness*) 649; painfulness &c. (*cause of pain*) 830; scourge &c. (*punishment*) 975; *damnosa hereditas*; white elephant.

sting, fang, thorn, tang, bramble, briar, nettle.

poison, leaven, virus, venom; intoxicant; arsenic, Prussic acid, antimony, tartar emetic, strychnine, nicotine, cyanide of potassium, corrosive sublimate; curare; hyoscine &c.; poison-, mustard-, tear-gas; carbon di-, monoxide; ptomaine poisoning, botulism; miasm, mephitis, malaria, azote, sewer gas; pest, stench &c. 401.

rust, worm, moth, moth and rust, fungus, mildew; dry-rot; canker, -worm; cancer; torpedo; viper &c. (*evil-doer*) 913; demon &c. 980.

hemlock, hellebore, nightshade, *belladonna*, henbane, aconite; Upas tree.

drugs, dope, opium, morphia, morphine, cocaine, heroin, hashish, bhang. [Science of poisons] Toxicology.

Adj. baneful &c. (*bad*) 649; poisonous &c. (*unwholesome*) 657.

---

restore &c. 660; drench with physic; consult, operate, extract, deliver; bleed, cup, let blood, transfuse; electrolyse; psycho-analyse.

Adj. remedial; restorative &c. 660; corrective, palliative, healing; sana-tory, -tive; prophylactic; salutiferous &c. (*salutary*) 656; medic-al, -inal; therapeutic, surgical, chirurgical, orthopedic, epulotic, paregoric, tonic, corroborant, analeptic, balsamic, anodyne, hypnotic, neurotic, narcotic, sedative, lenitive, demulcent, emollient; depuratory; deter-sive, -gent; abstersive, disinfectant, febrifugal, alternative; traumatic, vulnerary.

dietetic, alimentary; nutrit-ious, -ive; peptic; alexi-pharmic, -teric; remedi-, cur-able.

3. *Contingent Subservience*

664. Safety.—N. safety, security, impregnability; invulnera-bility, -bleness &c. *adj.*; danger -past, – over; storm blown over; coast clear; escape &c. 671; means of escape, safety-valve; safeguard, palladium, sheet anchor, rock, tower of strength.

guardian-, ward-, warden-ship; tutelage, custody, safe keeping; preservation &c. 670; protection, auspices.

safe-conduct, escort, convoy; guard, shield &c. (*defence*) 717; guardian angel, tutelary -god, – deity, – saint; *genius loci.*

protector, guardian; ward-en, -er; preserver, custodian, *duenna, chaperon,* third person.

watch-, ban-dog; Cerberus; watch-, patrol-, police-man, constable, peeler, bobby, copper, cop, bull, flat-foot, detective, armed guard; sentinel, sentry, scout &c. (*warning*) 668; garrison; guard-ship.

[Means of safety] refuge &c., anchor &c. 666; precaution &c. (*preparation*) 673; quarantine, *cordon sanitaire.* [Sense of security] confidence &c. 858.

V. be -safe &c. *adj.*; keep one's head above water, tide over, save one's bacon; ride out –, weather- the storm; light upon one's feet; bear a charmed life; escape &c. 671; possess nine lives.

make –, render- -safe &c. *adj.*; protect, watch over; take care of &c. (*care*) 459; preserve &c. 670; cover, screen, shelter, shroud, flank, ward; guard &c. (*defend*) 717; secure &c. (*restrain*) 751; intrench, fence round &c. (*circumscribe*) 229; house, nestle, ensconce; take charge of.

665. Danger.—N. danger, peril, insecurity, jeopardy, risk, hazard, venture, precariousness, slipperiness; instability &c. 149; defencelessness &c. *adj.*

exposure &c. (*liability*) 177; vulnerability; vulnerable point, heel of Achilles; forlorn hope &c. (*hopelessness*) 859.

[Dangerous course] leap in the dark &c. (*rashness*) 863; road to ruin, *facilis descensus Averni,* hair-breadth escape.

cause for alarm; source of danger &c. 667. [Approach of danger] rock –, breakers- ahead; storm brewing; clouds -in the horizon, – gathering; warning &c. 668; alarm &c. 669. [Sense of danger] apprehension &c. 860.

V. be -in danger &c. *adj.*; be exposed to –, run into –, incur –, encounter- -danger &c. *n.*; run a risk; lay oneself open to &c. (*liability*) 177; lean on –, trust to- a broken reed; feel the ground sliding from under one, have to run for it; have the -chances, – odds- against one.

hang by a thread, totter; tremble on the -verge, – brink; sleep –, stand -on a volcano; sit on a barrel of gunpowder, live in a glass house.

bring –, place –, put- in -danger &c. *n.*; endanger, expose to danger, imperil; jeopard, -ize, compromise; sail too near the wind &c. (*rash*) 863; put one's head in the lion's mouth.

adventure, risk, hazard, venture, stake, set at hazard; run the gauntlet &c. (*dare*) 861; engage in a forlorn hope.

threaten &c. 909- danger; run one

escort, convoy; garrison; watch, mount guard, patrol, scout, spy.

make assurance double sure &c. (*caution*) 864; take up a loose thread; take precautions &c. (*prepare for*) 673; take in a reef; double reef topsails.

seek safety; take –, find- shelter &c. 666; run into port.

Adj. safe, secure, sure; in -safety, – security; have an anchor to windward; on the safe side; under the -shield of, – shade of, – wing of, – shadow of one's wing; under -cover, – lock and key; out of -danger, – the meshes, – harm's way; in -harbour, – port; on sure ground, at anchor, high and dry, above water, on *terra firma*; un-threatened, -molested; protected &c. *v.*; *cavendo tutus*; panoplied &c. (*defended*) 717.

snug, sea-, air-worthy; weather-, water-, fire-, bomb-proof.

defensible, tenable, proof against, invulnerable; un-assailable, -attackable; im-pregnable, -perdible; founded on a rock; inexpugnable.

safe and sound &c. (*preserved*) 670; harmless; scathless &c. (*perfect*) 650; unhazarded; not -dangerous &c. 665.

protecting &c. *v.*; guardian, tutelary; preservative &c. 670; trustworthy &c. 939.

Adv. *ex abundanti cautelâ*; with impunity.

Phr. all's well; all clear; *salva res est*; *suave mari magno*; safety first.

---

hard; lay a trap for &c. (*deceive*) 545.

Adj. in -danger &c. *n.*; endangered &c. *v.*; fraught with danger; danger-, hazard-, peril-, parl-, pericul-ous; unsafe, unprotected &c. (safe, protect &c. 664); insecure, untrustworthy, unreliable; built upon sand, on a sandy basis.

defence-, fence-, guard-, harbour-less; unshielded; vulnerable, expugnable, unsheltered, exposed; open to &c. (*liable*) 177.

aux abois, at bay; on -the wrong side of the wall, – a lee shore, – the rocks.

at stake, in question; precarious, aleatory, critical, ticklish; slip-pery, -py; hanging by a thread &c. *v.*; with a halter round one's neck; between -the hammer and the anvil, – Scylla and Charybdis, – two fires; on the -edge, – brink, – verge of a- -precipice, – volcano; in the lion's den, on slippery ground, under fire; not out of the wood.

un-warned, -admonished, -advised; unprepared &c. 674; off one's guard &c. (*inexpectant*) 508.

tottering; un-stable, -steady; shaky, top-heavy, tumble-down, ramshackle, crumbling, waterlogged; help-, guide-less; in a bad way; reduced to –, at the last extremity; trembling in the balance; nodding to its fall &c. (*destruction*) 162.

threatening &c. 909; ominous, ill-omened; alarming &c. (*fear*) 860; explosive; poisonous &c. 657.

adventurous &c. (*rash*) 863, (*bold*) 861.

Int. stop! look out! beware! take care!

Phr. *incidit in Scyllam qui vult vitare Charybdim*; *nam tua res agitur paries dum proximus ardet.*

---

666. [Means of safety.] **Refuge.—N.** refuge, sanctuary, retreat, fastness; stronghold, keep, last resort; ward; prison &c. 752; asylum, ark, home, almshouse, refuge for the destitute; hiding-place &c. (*ambush*) 530; *sanctum sanctorum* &c. (*privacy*) 893.

roadstead, anchorage; breakwater, mole, port, haven; harbour, – of refuge; sea-port; pier, jetty, embankment, quay.

667. [Source of danger.] **Pitfall.—N.** rocks, reefs, coral reef, sunken rocks, snags; sands, quicksands, Goodwin sands, sandy foundation; slippery ground; breakers, shoals, shallows, bank, shelf, flat, lee shore, iron-bound coast; rock –, breakers- ahead; derelict.

precipice; abyss, chasm, pit, crevasse; maelstrom, whirlpool, eddy, vortex, rapids, current, bore, tidal wave; storm, squall, hurricane, whirl-

covert, shelter, abri, screen, lee-wall, wing, shield, umbrella; splash-, dash-board, mudguard.

wall &c. (*inclosure*) 232; fort &c. (*defence*) 717.

anchor, kedge; grap-nel, -pling iron; sheet-, mushroom-anchor, main-stay; support &c. 215; check &c. 706; ballast.

jury-mast; vent-peg; safety -valve, – lamp; lightning conductor.

means of escape &c. (*escape*) 671; life-boat, swimming belt, cork jacket; life preserver, breeches buoy; parachute, plank, stepping-stone. safeguard &c. (*protection*) 664.

V. seek –, take –, find- refuge &c. *n.*; seek –, find- safety &c. 664; throw oneself into the arms of; claim sanctuary; take to the -hills, – woods; make port, reach shelter, bar –, bolt –, lock -the door, – gate; let the portcullis down; raise the drawbridge.

wind; volcano; ambush &c. 530; pit-fall, trap-door; trap &c. (*snare*) 545.

sword of Damocles; wolf at the door, snake in the grass, viper in one's bosom, death in the pot; latency &c. 526.

ugly customer, dangerous person, *le chat qui dort*; firebrand, hornet's nest.

Phr. *latet anguis in herbâ*; *proximus ardet Ucalegon.*

---

668. Warning.—N. warning, caution, *caveat*; notice &c. (*information*) 527; premoni-tion, -shment; prediction &c. 511; contraindication; symptom; lesson, dehortation; admonition, monition; alarm &c. 669.

handwriting on the wall, *tekel upharsin*, yellow flag; fog-signal, -horn; siren; monitor, warning voice, Cassandra, signs of the times, Mother Carey's chickens, stormy petrel, bird of ill omen, gathering clouds, clouds in the horizon, cloud no bigger than a man's hand, death-watch.

watch-tower, beacon, signal-post; light-house &c. (*indication of locality*) 550.

sent-inel, -ry; watch, -man; watch and ward; watch-, ban-, house-dog; patrol, vedette, picket, bivouac, scout, spy, spial; advanced –, rear-guard, lookout, flagman.

cautiousness &c. 864.

V. warn, caution; fore-, pre-warn; ad-, pre-monish; give -notice, – warning; menace &c. (*threaten*) 909; put on one's guard; sound the alarm &c. 669; croak.

beware, ware; take -warning, – heed at one's peril; watch out for; keep watch and ward &c. (*care*) 459.

Adj. warning &c. *v.*; premonitory, monitory, cautionary; admonitory, -tive; ominous, threatening, lowering, minatory, symptomatic.

warned &c. *v.*; on one's guard &c. (*careful*) 459, (*cautious*) 864.

Adv. *in terrorem* &c. (*threat*) 909.

Int. beware! ware! take care! mind –, take care-what you are about; mind! look out!

Phr. *ne reveillez pas le chat qui dort*; *fœnum habet in cornu.*

669. [Indication of danger.] Alarm.—N. alarm; alarum, larum, alarm bell, tocsin, *alerte*, beat of drum, sound of trumpet, note of alarm, hue and cry, signal of distress, S.O.S.; blue-lights; war-cry, -whoop; warning &c. 668; fog-signal, -horn; siren; yellow flag; danger signal; red -light, – flag; fire -bell, – alarm; burglar alarm, police whistle, watchman's rattle.

false alarm, cry of wolf; bug-bear, -aboo.

V. give –, raise –, sound –, beat- the *or* an -alarm &c. *n.*; alarm; warn &c. 668; ring the tocsin; *battre la générale*; cry wolf.

Adj. alarming &c. *v.*

Int. *sauve qui peut! qui vive?* who goes there?

670. Preservation.—N. preservation; safe keeping; conservation &c. (*storage*) 636; maintenance, upkeep, support, sustentation, conservatism; *vis conservatrix*; salvation &c. (*deliverance*) 672; drying &c. *v.*

[Means of preservation] prophylaxis; preserv-er, -ative; canned goods; cold pack; hygi-astics, -antics; cover, drugget; *cordon sanitaire.*

[Superstitious remedies] charm &c. 993.

V. preserve, maintain, keep, sustain, support; keep -up, – alive; not willingly let die; shore –, bank- up; nurse; save, rescue; be –, make-safe &c. 664; take care of &c. (*care*) 459; guard &c. (*defend*) 717.

stare super antiquas vias; hold one's own; hold –, stand- -one's ground &c. (*resist*) 719.

embalm, dry, cure, smoke, salt, pickle, season, kyanize, bottle, pot, tin, can; husband &c. (*store*) 636.

Adj. preserving &c. *v.*; conservative; prophylactic; preserva-tory, -tive; hygienic.

preserved &c. *v.*; un-impaired, -broken, -injured, -hurt, -singed, -marred; safe, – and sound; intact, with a whole skin, without a scratch.

Phr. *nolumus leges Angliæ mutari.*

671. Escape.—N. escape, scape; avolation, elopement, flight, get-away; evasion &c. (*avoidance*) 623; retreat; narrow –, hairbreadth-escape; close –, near- shave; come off, impunity.

[Means of escape] loophole &c. (*opening*) 260; path &c. 627; secret -door, – passage; refuge &c. 666; vent, – peg; safety-valve; draw-bridge, fire-escape.

reprieve &c. (*deliverance*) 672; liberation &c. 750.

refugee &c. (*fugitive*) 623.

V. escape, scape; make –, effect –, make good- one's escape, make a get-away; get -off, – clear off, – well out of; *échapper belle*, save one's bacon; weather the storm &c. (*safe*) 664; escape scot-free.

elude &c., make off &c. (*avoid*) 623; march off &c. (*go away*) 293; give one the slip; slip through the -hands, – fingers; slip the collar, wriggle out of; break -loose, – from prison; break –, slip –, get- away; find -vent, – a hole to creep out of.

Adj. escap-ing, -ed &c. *v.*; stolen away, fled.

Phr. the bird has flown.

672. Deliverance.—N. deliverance, extrication, rescue; repriev-e, -al; respite; ransom; liberation &c. 750; truce, armistice; redemption, salvation; riddance; gaol delivery; exemption, day of grace; redeem-ableness.

V. deliver, extricate, rescue, save, redeem, ransom, free, liberate, release, set free, redeem, emancipate; bring -off, – through; *tirer d'affaire*, get the wheel out of the rut; snatch from the jaws of death, come to the rescue; rid; retrieve &c. (*restore*) 660; be –, get- rid of.

Adj. saved &c. *v.*; extric-, redeem-, rescu-able.

Phr. to the rescue!

3°. *Precursory Measures*

673. Preparation.—N. preparation; providing &c. *v.*; provi-sion, -dence; anticipation &c. (*foresight*) 510; pre-caution, -concertation, -disposition;

674. Non-Preparation. — N. non-, absence of –, want of- preparation; un-preparedness; inculture, inconcoction, improvidence.

forecast &c. (*plan*) 626; rehearsal, note of preparation.

[Putting in order] arrangement &c. 60; clearance; adjustment &c. 23; tuning; equipment, outfit, accoutrement, armament, array.

ripening &c. *v.*; maturation, evolution; elaboration, concoction, digestion; gestation, hatching, incubation, sitting.

groundwork, datum, first stone, cradle, stepping-stone; foundation, scaffold &c. (*support*) 215; scaffolding, *échafaudage.*

[Preparation -of men] training &c. (*education*) 537; inurement &c. (*habit*) 613; novitiate; [– of food] cook-ing, -ery; brewing, culinary art; [– of the soil] till-, plough-, sow-ing; semination, cultivation.

[State of being prepared] prepared-, readi-, ripe-, mellow-ness; maturity; *un impromptu fait à loisir.*

[Preparer] preparer, teacher, coach, trainer, pioneer; *avant-courrier, ·coureur*; sappers and miners, paviour, navvy; packer, stevedore; warming-pan; precursor &c. 64.

V. prepare; get -, make- ready; make preparations, settle preliminaries, get up, sound the note of preparation; address oneself to.

set -, put- in order &c. (*arrange*) 60; forecast &c. (*plan*) 626; prepare -, plough -, dress- the ground; till -, cultivate- the soil; predispose, sow the seed, lay a train, dig a mine; lay -, fix- the -foundations, – basis, -groundwork; dig the foundations, erect the scaffolding; lay the first stone &c. (*begin*) 66.

rough-hew; cut out work; block -, hammer- out; lick into shape &c. (*form*) 240.

elaborate, mature, ripen, mellow, season, bring to maturity; nurture &c.

(*aid*) 707; hatch, cook, brew; temper; anneal, smelt; dry, cure &c. 670.

equip, arm, man; fit-out, -up; furnish, rig, dress, garnish, betrim, accoutre, array, fettle, fledge; dress -, furbish -, brush -, vamp- up; refurbish; sharpen one's tools, trim one's foils, set, prime, attune; whet the -knife, – sword; wind -, screw- up; adjust &c. (*fit*) 27; put in -trim, – train, – gear, – working order, – tune, – a groove for, – harness; pack, stow away, store.

immaturity, crudity; rawness &c. *adj.*; abortion; disqualification.

[Absence of art] nature, state of nature; virgin soil, unweeded garden; rough diamond, neglect &c. 460.

rough copy &c. (*plan*) 626; germ &c. 153; raw material &c. 635.

improvisation &c. (*impulse*) 612.

V. be -unprepared &c. *adj.*; want -, lack- preparation; lie fallow; *s'embarquer sans biscuits*; live from hand to mouth.

[Render unprepared] dismantle &c. (*render useless*) 645; undress &c. 226.

extemporize, improvise.

surprise, pay a surprise visit, take by surprise, drop in upon, take unawares; take pot-luck.

Adj. un-prepared &c. [prepare &c. 673]; without -preparation &c. 673; incomplete &c. 53; rudimental, embryonic, abortive; immature, unripe, raw, green, crude; coarse; rough, -cast, -hewn; in the rough; un-hewn, -formed, -fashioned, -wrought, -laboured, -blown, -cooked, -boiled, -concocted, -cut, -polished.

callow, un-hatched, -fledged, -nurtured, -licked, -taught, -educated, -cultivated, -trained, -tutored, -drilled, -exercised; precocious, premature; un-, in-digested; un-mellowed, -seasoned, -leavened.

fallow; un-sown, -tilled; natural, in a state of nature; undressed; in dishabille, *en déshabille, en négligé.*

un-, dis-qualified; unfitted; ill-digested; un-begun, -ready, -arranged, -organized, -furnished, -provided, -equipped, -trimmed; out of -gear, – order; dismantled &c. *v.*

shiftless, improvident, unthrifty, thoughtless, unguarded; happy-go-lucky; caught napping &c. (*inexpectant*) 508; unpremeditated &c. 612.

Adv. extempore &c. 612.

———

train &c. *(teach)* 537; inure &c. *(habituate)* 613; breed; prepare &c.- for; rehearse; make provision for; take -steps, – measures, – precautions; provide, – against; beat up for recruits; open the door to &c. *(facilitate)* 705.

set one's house in order, make all snug; clear -decks, – for action; close one's ranks; shuffle the cards.

prepare oneself; serve an apprenticeship &c. *(learn)* 539; lay oneself out for, get into harness, gird up one's loins, buckle on one's armour, *reculer pour mieux sauter*, prime and load, shoulder arms, get the steam up, put the horses to.

guard –, make sure- against; forearm, make sure, prepare for the evil day, have a rod in pickle, provide against a rainy day, feather one's nest; lay in provisions &c. 637; make investments; keep on foot.

be -prepared, – ready &c. *adj.*; hold oneself in readiness, watch and pray, keep one's powder dry; lie in wait for &c. *(expect)* 507; anticipate &c. *(foresee)* 510; *principiis obstare*; *veniente occurrere morbo.*

Adj. preparing &c. *v.*; in -preparation, – course of preparation, – agitation, – embryo, – hand, – train; afoot, afloat; on -foot, – the stocks, – the anvil; under consideration &c. *(plan)* 626; brewing, hatching, forthcoming, brooding; in -store for, – reserve.

precautionary, provident; prepara-tive, -tory; provisional, in-choate, under revision; preliminary &c. *(precedent)* 62.

prepared &c. *v.*; in readiness; ready, – to one's hand, – made, cut and dried; ready for use, reach me down; made to one's hand, handy, on the table, made to order; in gear; in working -order, – gear; snug; in practice.

ripe, mature, mellow; practised &c. *(skilled)* 698; laboured, elab-orate, highly-wrought, smelling of the lamp, worked up.

in -full feather, – best bib and tucker; in –, at- harness; in – the saddle, – arms, – battle array, – war paint; up in arms; armed -at all points, – to the teeth, – *cap-à-pie*; sword in hand; booted and spurred.

in utrumque –, semper- paratus; on the alert &c. *(vigilant)* 459; at one's post.

Adv. in -preparation, – anticipation of; afoot, astir, abroad; abroach.

675. Essay.—N. essay, trial, endeavour, aim, attempt; venture, ad-venture, speculation, *coup d'essai, début*; probation &c. *(experiment)* 463.

V. try, essay; experiment &c. 463; endeavour, strive; tempt, tackle, take on, attempt, make an attempt; venture, adventure, speculate, take one's chance, tempt fortune; try one's -fortune, – luck, – hand; use one's endeavour; feel –, grope –, pick- one's way.

try hard, push, make a bold push, use one's best endeavour; do one's best &c. *(exertion)* 686.

Adj. essaying &c. *v.*; experimental &c. 463; tentative, empirical, probationary.

Adv. experimentally &c. *adj.*; on trial, at a venture; by rule of thumb. if one may be so bold.

676. Undertaking.—N. undertaking; compact &c. 769; engagement &c. *(promise)* 768; enter-, em-prise; venture &c. 675; pilgrimage; mat-ter in hand &c. *(business)* 625; move; first move &c. *(beginning)* 66.

V. undertake; engage –, embark- in; launch –, plunge- into; volunteer; apprentice oneself to; engage &c. (*promise*) 768; contract &c. 769; take upon -oneself, – one's shoulders; devote oneself to &c. (*determination*) 604.

take -up, – in hand; tackle; set –, go- about; set –, fall- -to, – to work; launch forth; set up shop; put in -hand, – execution; set forward; break the neck of a business, be in for; put one's hand to; betake oneself to, turn one's hand to, go to do; begin &c. 66; broach, institute, &c. (*originate*) 153; put –, lay- one's -hand to the plough, – shoulder to the wheel.

have in hand &c. (*business*) 625; have many irons in the fire &c. (*activity*) 682.

Adj. undertaking &c. *v.*; on the anvil &c. 625; adventurous, venturesome.

Int. here goes!

677. Use.—N. use; employ, -ment; exer-cise, -citation; appli-cation, -ance; adhibition, disposal; consumption; agency &c. (*physical*) 170; usufruct; usefulness &c. 644; recourse, resort, avail, pragmatism.

[Conversion to use] utilization, service, wear.

[Way of using] usage.

V. use, make use of, employ, put to use; apply, put in -action, – operation, – practice; set -in motion, – to work.

ply, work, wield, handle, manipulate; play, – off; exert, exercise, practise, avail oneself of, profit by; resort –, have recourse –, recur –, take –, betake oneself- to; take -up with, – advantage of; lay one's hands on, try.

render useful &c. 644; mould; turn to -account, – use; convert to use, utilize, administer; work up; call –, bring- into play; put into requisition; call –, draw- forth; press –, enlist- into the service; bring to bear upon, devote, dedicate, consecrate, apply, adhibit, dispose of; make a -handle, – cat's paw- of.

fall back upon, make a shift with; make the -most, – best- of.

use –, swallow- up; consume, absorb, expend; tax, task, wear, put to task.

Adj. in use; used &c. *v.*; well-worn, -trodden.

useful &c. 644; subservient &c. (*instrumental*) 631; utilitarian; pragmatical.

678. Disuse.—N. forbearance, abstinence; disuse; relinquishment &c. 782; desuetude &c. (*want of habit*) 614.

V. not use; do without, dispense with, let alone, not touch, forbear, abstain, spare, waive, neglect; keep back, reserve.

lay -up, – by, – on the shelf, – up in a napkin; shelve; set –, put –, lay- aside; disuse, leave off, have done with; supersede; discard &c. (*eject*) 297; dismiss, give warning.

throw aside &c. (*relinquish*) 782; make away with &c. (*destroy*) 162; cast –, heave –, throw- overboard; cast to the -dogs, – winds; dismantle &c. (*render useless*) 645.

lie –, remain- unemployed &c. *adj.*

Adj. not used &c. *v.*; un-employed, -applied, -disposed of, -spent, -exercised, -touched, -trodden, -essayed, -gathered, -culled; uncalled for, not required.

disused &c. *v.*; done with; run down, used up, cast off.

679. Misuse.—N. mis-use, -usage, -employment, -application, -appropriation.

abuse, profanation, prostitution, desecration; waste &c. 638.

V. mis-use, -employ, -apply, -appropriate.

desecrate, abuse, profane, prostitute; waste &c. 638; over-task, -tax, -work; squander &c. 818.

cut a whetstone with a razor, employ a steam-engine to crack a nut; catch at a straw.

Adj. misused &c. *v.*

Section III. Voluntary Action

1°. *Simple Voluntary Action*

680. Action.—N. action, performance; doing &c. *v.*; perpetration; exercise, -citation; movement, operation, evolution, work; labour &c. (*exertion*) 686; *praxis*, execution; procedure &c. (*conduct*) 692; handicraft; business &c. 625; agency &c. (*power at work*) 170.

deed, act, overt act, stitch, touch, gest; transaction, job, doings, dealings, proceeding, measure, step, manœuvre, bout, passage, move, stroke, blow; *coup, – de main, – d'état; tour de force* &c. (*display*) 882; feat, exploit, stunt; achievement &c. (*completion*) 729; handiwork, workmanship, craftsmanship; manufacture; stroke of policy &c. (*plan*) 626.

actor &c. (*doer*) 690.

V. do, perform, execute; achieve &c. (*complete*) 729; transact, enact; commit, perpetrate, inflict; exercise, prosecute, carry on, work, practise, play.

employ oneself, ply one's task; officiate, have in hand &c. (*business*) 625; labour &c. 686; be at work; pursue a course; shape one's course &c. (*conduct*) 692.

act, operate; take -action, – steps; strike a blow, lift a finger, stretch forth one's hand; take in hand &c. (*undertake*) 676; put oneself in motion; put in practice; carry into execution &c. (*complete*) 729; act upon.

be -an actor &c. 690; take –, act –, play –, perform- a part in; participate in; have a -hand in, – finger in the pie; have to do with; be a -party to, – participator in; bear –, lend- a hand; pull an oar, run in a race; mix oneself up with &c. (*meddle*) 682.

be in action; come into operation &c. (*power at work*) 170.

Adj. doing &c. *v.*; acting; in action; in harness; on duty; at work; in operation &c. 170; up to one's ears in work, in the midst of things.

Adv. in the -act, – midst of, – thick of; red-handed, *in flagrante delicto*; while one's hand is in.

681. Inaction.—N. inaction, passiveness, abstinence from action; non-interference; Fabian –, conservative-policy; neglect &c. 460; stagnation, vegetation; loafing.

inactivity &c. 683; rest &c. (*repose*) 687; quiescence &c. 265; want of –, in- occupation; unemployment; idle hours, time hanging on one's hands, *dolce far niente*; sinecure.

V. not -do, – act, – attempt; be -inactive &c. 683; abstain from doing, do nothing, hold, spare; not -stir, – move, – lift- a -finger, – foot, – peg; fold one's -arms, – hands; leave –, let- alone; let -be, – pass, – things take their course, – it have its way, – well alone; *quieta non movere; stare super antiquas vias;* rest and be thankful, live and let live; lie –, rest- upon one's oars; *laisser -aller, – faire;* stand aloof; refrain &c. (*avoid*) 623; keep oneself from doing; remit –, relax- one's efforts; desist &c. (*relinquish*) 624; stop &c. (*cease*) 142; pause &c. (*be quiet*) 265.

wait, lie in wait, bide one's time, take time, tide it over.

cool –, kick- one's heels; loaf, while away the -time, – tedious hours; pass –, fill up –, beguile- the time; talk against time; waste time &c. (*inactive*) 683.

lie -by, – on the shelf, – in ordinary, – idle, – to, – fallow; keep quiet, slug; have nothing to do, whistle for want of thought; twiddle one's thumbs.

undo, do away with; take -down, – to pieces; destroy &c. 162.

Adj. not doing &c. *v.*; not done &c. *v.*; undone; passive; un-occupied, -employed; out of -employ, – work, – a job; fallow; *désœuvré*.

Adv. *re infectâ*, at a stand, *les bras croisés*, with folded arms; with the hands -in the pockets, – behind one's back; *pour passer le temps*.

Int. so let it be! stop! &c. 142; hands off!

Phr. nothing doing; *cunctando restituit rem*.

682. Activity.—N. activity; briskness, liveliness &c. *adj.*; animation, life, vivacity, spirit, verve, dash, energy, go.

nimbleness, agility; smartness, quickness &c. *adj.*; velocity &c. 274; alacrity, promptitude; des-, dis-patch; expedition; haste &c. 684; punctuality &c. (*early*) 132.

eagerness, zeal, ardour, *perfervidum ingenium, empressement,* earnestness, intentness; *abandon*; vigour &c. (*physical energy*) 171; devotion &c. (*resolution*) 604; exertion &c. 686.

industry, assiduity; assiduousness &c. *adj.*; sedulity; laboriousness; drudgery &c. (*labour*) 686; painstaking, diligence; perseverance &c. 604a; indefatigation; habits of business.

vigilance &c. 459; wakefulness; sleep-, rest-lessness; *pervigilium, insomnia*; racketing.

movement, bustle, hustle, stir, fuss, ado, bother, pottering; fidget, -iness; flurry &c. (*haste*) 684.

officiousness; dabbling, meddling; inter-ference, -position, -meddling, butting in, intrusiveness; tampering with, intrigue.

press of business, no sinecure, plenty to do, many irons in the fire, great doings, busy hum of men, battle of life, thick of -things, – the action; the madding crowd.

housewife, busy bee; new brooms; sharp fellow, blade; hustler, devotee, enthusiast, fan, zealot, fanatic; meddler, intermeddler, intriguer, busybody, kibitzer, pickthank.

V. be -active &c. *adj.*; busy oneself in; stir, -about, – one's stumps; bestir -, rouse- oneself; speed, hasten, peg away, lay about one, bustle, fuss; raise -, kick up- a dust; push; make a -push, – fuss, – stir; go ahead, push forward; flight -, elbow- one's way; make progress &c. 282; toil &c. (*labour*) 686; drudge, plod, persist &c. (*persevere*) 604a; keep -up the ball, – the pot boiling.

look sharp; have all one's eyes about one &c. (*vigilance*) 459; rise, arouse oneself, get up early, hustle, push; be about, keep moving, steal a march, kill two birds with one stone; seize the opportunity &c. 134; lose no time, not

683. Inactivity.—N. inactivity; inaction &c. 681; inertness &c. 172; obstinacy &c. 606.

lull &c. (*cessation*) 142; quiescence &c. 265; rust, -iness.

idle-, remiss-ness &c. *adj.*; sloth, indolence, indiligence; otiosity, dawdling &c. *v.*

dullness &c. *adj.*; languor; segni-ty, -tude; lentor; sluggishness &c. (*slowness*) 275; procrastination &c. (*delay*) 133; torp-or, -idity, -escence; stupor &c. (*insensibility*) 823; somnolence; drowsiness &c. *adj.*; nodding &c. *v.*; oscit-ation, -ancy; pandiculation, hypnotism, lethargy; heaviness, heavy eye-lids, sand in the eyes.

sleep, slumber; sound -, heavy -, balmy- sleep; Morpheus, dreamland; coma, trance, catalepsy, hypnosis, ecstasis, dream, hibernation, nap, doze, snooze, *siesta*, wink of sleep, forty winks, snore; Hypnology.

dull work; pottering; relaxation &c. (*loosening*) 47; Castle of Indolence.

[Cause of inactivity] lullaby, *berceuse*; anæsthetic, sedative &c. 174; torpedo.

idler, drone, droil, dawdle, mopus; do-little, *fainéant*, dummy, sleeping partner; afternoon farmer; truant &c. (*runaway*) 623; lounger, *lazzarone*, floater, loafer, tramp, beggar, cadger; lub-ber, -bard; slow-coach &c. (*slow*) 275; opium -, lotus- eater; slug; lag-, slug-gard, lie-abed; slumberer, dormouse, marmot; waiter on Providence, *fruges consumere natus.*

V. be -inactive &c. *adj.*; do nothing &c. 681; move slowly &c. 275; let the grass grow under one's feet; take one's time, dawdle, poke, drawl, droil, lag, hang back, slouch; loll, -op; lounge, loaf, loiter; go to sleep over; sleep at one's post, *ne battre que d'une aile.*

take -it easy, - things as they come; lead an easy life, vegetate, swim with the stream, eat the bread of idleness; loll in the lap of -luxury, – indolence; waste -, consume -, kill -, lose- time; burn daylight, waste the precious hours.

idle -, trifle -, fritter -, fool- away time; spend -, take- time in; ped-, pid-dle; potter, putter, dabble, faddle,

lose a moment, make the most of one's time, not suffer the grass to grow under one's feet, improve the shining hour, make short work of; dash off; make haste &c. 684; do one's best, take pains &c. (*exert oneself*) 686; do –, work- wonders.

have -many irons in the fire, – one's hands full, – much on one's hands; have other -things to do, – fish to fry; be busy; not have a moment -to spare, – that one can call one's own.

have one's fling, run the round of; go all lengths, stick at nothing, run riot.

outdo; over-do, -act, -lay, -shoot the mark; make a toil of a pleasure.

have a hand in &c. (*act in*) 680; take an active part, put in one's oar, have a finger in the pie, mix oneself up with, trouble one's head about, intrigue; agitate.

tamper with, meddle, moil; inter-meddle, -fere, -pose; obtrude; poke –, thrust- one's nose in, butt in.

Adj. active; brisk, – as a lark, – as a bee; lively, animated, vivacious; alive, – and kicking; frisky, spirited, stirring.

nimble, – as a squirrel; agile; light-, nimble-footed; featly, tripping.

quick, prompt, yare, instant, ready, alert, spry, sharp, smart, slick, go-ahead; fast &c. (*swift*) 274; quick as a lamplighter, expeditious; awake, broad awake; wide awake &c. (*intelligent*) 498.

forward, eager, ardent, strenuous, zealous, enterprising, pushing, in earnest; resolute &c. 604.

industrious, assiduous, diligent, sedulous, notable, painstaking; intent &c. (*attention*) 457; indefatigable &c. (*persevering*) 604a; unwearied; unsleeping, sleepless, never tired; plodding, hard-working &c. 686; business-like, workaday.

bustling; restless, – as a hyæna; fussy, fidgety, pottering; busy, – as a hen with one chicken.

working, labouring, at work, on duty, in harness; up in arms; on one's legs, at call; up and -doing, – stirring.

busy, occupied; hard at -work, – it; up to one's ears in, full of business, busy as a bee.

meddling &c. *v.*; meddlesome, pushing, officious, overofficious, *intrigant*.

astir, stirring; a-going, -foot; on foot; in full swing; eventful; on the alert &c. (*vigilant*) 459.

fribble, fiddle-faddle; dally, dilly-dally.

sleep, slumber, be asleep; hibernate; oversleep; sleep like a -top, – log, – dormouse; sleep -soundly, – heavily; doze, drowze, snooze, nap; take a -nap &c. *n.*; dream; snore; settle –, go –, go off- to sleep; drop off; fall –, drop-asleep; close –, seal up- -the -eyes, – eyelids; weigh down the eyelids; get sleepy, nod, yawn; go to bed, turn in.

languish, expend itself, flag, hang fire; relax.

render -idle &c. *adj.*; sluggardize; mitigate &c. 174.

Adj. inactive; motionless &c. 265; unoccupied &c. (*doing nothing*) 681.

indolent, lazy, slothful, idle, otiose, lusk, remiss, slack, inert, torpid, sluggish, languid, supine, heavy, dull, leaden, lumpish; exanimate, soulless; listless; dron-y, -ish; lazy as Ludlam's dog.

dilatory, laggard; lagging &c. *v.*; slow &c. 275; rusty, flagging; lackadaisical, maudlin, fiddle-faddle; pottering &c. *v.*; shilly-shally &c. (*irresolute*) 605.

sleeping &c. *v.*; asleep; fast –, dead –, sound- asleep; in a sound sleep; sound as a top, dormant, comatose; in the -arms, – lap- of Morpheus.

sleep-y, -ful; dozy, drowsy, somnolent, torpescent; lethargic, -al; heavy, – with sleep; napping; somni-fic, -ferous; sopor-ous, -ific, -iferous; hypnotic; balmy, dreamy; un-, una-wakened.

sedative &c. 174.

Adv. inactively &c. *adj.*; at leisure &c. 685.

Phr. the eyes begin to draw straws.

Adv. actively &c. *adj.*; with -life and spirit, – might and main &c. 686, – haste &c. 684, – wings; full tilt, *in mediis rebus*.

Int. be –, look- -alive, – sharp! move –, push- on! keep moving! go ahead! stir your stumps! *age quod agis!*

Phr. *carpe diem* &c. (*opportunity*) 134; *nulla dies sine lineâ*; *nec mora nec requies*; no sooner said than done &c. (*early*) 132; catch a weasel asleep.

---

684. Haste.—N. haste, urgency; des-, dis-patch; acceleration, spurt, spirt, forced march, rush, dash; velocity &c. 274; precipit-ancy, -ation, -ousness &c. *adj.*; impetuosity; *brusquerie*; hurry, scurry, scuttle, drive, scramble, push, hustle, bustle, fuss, fidget, flurry, flutter, splutter.

V. haste, hasten; make -haste, – a dash &c. *n.*; hurry –, dash –, whip –, push –, press- -on, – forward; hurry, skurry, scuttle along, bundle on, dart to and fro, bustle, flutter, scramble; plunge, – headlong; run, race, speed; dash off; rush &c. (*violence*) 173.

bestir oneself &c. (*be active*) 682; lose -no time, – not a moment, – not an instant; make short work of; make the best of one's -time, – way.

be -precipitate &c. *adj.*; jump at; be in -haste, – a hurry &c. *n.*; have -no time, – not a moment- -to lose, – to spare; work -under pressure, – against time.

quicken &c. 274; accelerate, expedite, put on, precipitate, urge, whip, spur, flog, goad.

Adj. hasty, hurried, *brusque*; scrambling, cursory, precipitate, headlong, furious, boisterous, impetuous, hot-headed; feverish, fussy; pushing.

in -haste, – a hurry &c. *n.*; in -hot, – all- haste; breathless, pressed for time, hard pressed, urgent.

Adv. with -haste, – all haste, – breathless speed; in haste &c. *adj.*; apace &c. (*swiftly*) 274; amain; all at once &c. (*instantaneously*) 113; at short notice &c., immediately &c. (*early*) 132; posthaste; by -express, – telegraph, – wire, – wireless, – air mail.

hastily, precipitately &c. *adj.*; helter-skelter, hurry-skurry, holus-bolus; slap-dash, -bang; full-tilt, -drive; heels over head, head and shoulders, headlong, *à corps perdu*.

by -fits and starts, – spurts; hop, skip and jump.

Phr. *sauve qui peut*, devil take the hindmost, no time to be lost; no sooner said than done &c. (*early*) 132; a word and a blow.

Int. hurry up! look alive! get a move on! buck up! double march! rush! urgent!

685. Leisure.—N. leisure; spare -time, – hours, – moments; vacant hour; time, – to spare, – on one's hands; holiday &c. (*rest*) 687; *otium cum dignitate*, ease.

V. have -leisure &c. *n.*; take one's -time, – leisure, – ease; repose &c. 687; move slowly &c. 275; while away the time &c. (*inaction*) 681; be -master of one's time, – an idle man; *desipere in loco*.

Adj. leisurely; slow &c. 275; deliberate, quiet, calm, undisturbed; at -leisure, – one's ease, – a loose end.

Phr. time hanging heavy on one's hands.

---

686. Exertion.—N. exertion, effort, strain, tug, pull, stress, force, pressure, throw, stretch, struggle, spell, spurt, spirt; stroke –, stitch- of work.

687. Repose.—N. repose, rest, silken repose; sleep &c. 683.

relaxation, breathing time; halt, pause &c. (*cessation*) 142; respite.

'a strong pull, a long pull and a pull all together'; dead lift; heft; gymnastics, sports; exer-cise, -citation; wear and tear; ado; toil and trouble; uphill -, hard -, warm- work; harvest time.

labour, work, toil, travail, manual labour, sweat of one's brow, swink, operoseness, drudgery, slavery, fagging, hammering; *limæ labor*.

trouble, pains, duty; resolution &c. 604; energy &c. (*physical*) 171.

V. exert oneself; exert -, tax- one's energies; use exertion.

labour, work, toil, moil, sweat, fag, drudge, slave, drag a lengthened chain, wade through, strive, strain; make -, stretch- a long arm; pull, tug, ply; ply -, tug at- the oar; do the work; take the labouring oar.

bestir oneself (*be active*) 682; take trouble, trouble oneself.

work hard; rough it; put forth -one's strength, - a strong arm; fall to work, bend the bow; buckle to, set one's shoulder to the wheel &c. (*resolution*) 604; work like a -Briton, - horse, - carthorse, - galley-slave, - coalheaver; labour -, work- day and night; redouble one's efforts; do double duty; work double -hours, - tides; sit up, burn the -midnight oil, - candle at both ends; stick to &c. (*persevere*) 604a; work -, fight- one's way; lay about one, hammer at.

take pains; do one's -best, - level best, - utmost; do -the best one can, - all one can, - all in one's power, - as much as in one lies, - what lies in one's power; use one's -best, - utmost- endeavour; try one's -best, - utmost; play one's best card; put one's -best, - right- leg foremost; have one's whole soul in one's work, put all one's strength into, strain every nerve; spare no -efforts, - pains; go all lengths; go through fire and water &c. (*resolution*) 604; move heaven and earth, leave no stone unturned.

Adj. labouring &c. *v.*

laborious, operose, elaborate; strained; toil-, trouble-, burden-, weari-some; uphill; herculean, gymnastic, athletic, palestric.

hardworking, painstaking, strenuous, energetic.

hard at work, on the stretch.

Adv. laboriously &c. *adj.*; lustily; with -might and main, - all one's might, - a strong hand, - sledge-hammer, - much ado; to the best of one's abilities, *totis viribus, vi et armis, manibus pedibusque*, tooth and nail, *unguibus et rostro*, hammer and tongs, heart and soul; through thick and thin &c. (*perseverance*) 604a.

by the sweat of one's brow, *suo Marte*.

day of rest, *dies non*, Sabbath, Lord's day, holiday, red-letter day, vacation, recess.

V. repose; rest, - and be thankful; take -rest, - one's ease.

relax, unbend, slacken; take breath &c. (*refresh*) 689; rest upon one's oars; pause &c. (*cease*) 142; stay one's hand.

lie down; recline, - on a bed of down, - on an easy chair; go to -rest, - bed, - sleep &c. 683.

take a holiday, shut up shop; lie fallow &c. (*inaction*) 681.

Adj. reposing &c. *v.*; unstrained.

Adv. at rest.

---

688. Fatigue.—**N.** fatigue; weariness &c. 841; yawning, drowsiness &c. 683; lassitude, tiredness, fatigation, exhaustion; sweat.

anhelation, shortness of breath, panting; faintness; collapse, prostration,

689. Refreshment.—**N.** bracing &c. *v.*; recovery of -strength &c. 159; restoration, revival &c. 660; repair, refection, refocillation, refreshment, regalement, bait; relief &c. 834.

V. brace &c. (*strengthen*) 159; rein-

swoon, fainting, *deliquium*, syncope, lipothymy.

V. be -fatigued &c. *adj.*; yawn &c. (*get sleepy*) 683; droop, sink, flag; lose -breath, – wind; gasp, pant, puff, blow, drop, swoon, faint, succumb.

fatigue, tire, weary, bore, irk, fag, jade, harass, exhaust, knock up, wear out, prostrate.

tax, task, strain; over-task, -work, -burden, -tax, -strain.

Adj. fatigued &c. *v.*; weary &c. 841; drowsy &c. 683; drooping &c. *v.*; haggard; toil-, way-worn; footsore, surbated, weatherbeaten; faint; done -, used -, knocked- up; exhausted, prostrate, spent; over-tired, -spent, -fatigued; forspent; unre-freshed, -stored.

worn, – out; battered, shattered, pulled down, seedy, altered.

breath-, wind-less; short of –, out of -breath, – wind; blown, puffing and blowing; short-breathed; anhelous; broken-, short-winded.

ready to drop, more dead than alive, dog -tired, – weary, walked off one's legs, tired to death, on one's last legs, played out, *hors de combat.*

fatiguing &c. *v.*; tire-, irk-, weari-some; weary; trying.

vigorate; air, freshen up, refresh, recruit; repair &c. (*restore*) 660; fan, refocillate.

breathe, respire; draw –, take –, gather –, take a long –, regain –, recover- breath; get better, raise one's head; recover –, regain –, renew- one's strength &c. 159; perk up.

come to oneself &c. (*revive*) 660; feel like a giant refreshed.

Adj. refreshing &c. *v.*; recuperative &c. 660.

refreshed &c. *v.*; un-tired, -wearied.

---

690. Agent.—N. doer, actor, agent, performer, perpetrator, operator; execu-tor, -trix; practitioner, worker, stager.

bee, ant, working bee, labouring oar, shaft horse, servant –, maid-of all work, general servant, factotum.

workman, artisan; crafts-, handicrafts-man; mechanic, operative; working –, labouring- man; hewers of wood and drawers of water, labourer, navvy; hand, man, day labourer, journeyman, hack; mere -tool &c. 633; porter, docker, stevedore, beast of burden, drudge, fag.

maker, artificer, artist, wright, manufacturer, architect, contractor, builder, mason, bricklayer, smith, forger, Vulcan; black-, tin-smith; carpenter; ganger, platelayer.

machinist, mechanician, engineer, electrician, plumber, gasfitter &c.

semp-, sem-, seam-stress; needle-, char-, work-woman; tailor, cord-wainer.

minister &c. (*instrument*) 631; servant &c. 746; representative &c. (*commissioner*) 758, (*deputy*) 759.

co-worker, fellow-worker, party to, participator in, co-operator, colleague, associate, collaborator, *particeps criminis*, *dramatis personæ*; *personnel.*

Phr. '*quorum pars magna fui.*'

---

691. Workshop.—N. work-shop, -house; laboratory; manufactory, mill, factory, armoury, arsenal, mint, forge, loom; cabinet, *studio*, *bureau, atelier*; hive, – of industry; nursery; hot-house, -bed; kitchen, kitchenette; dock, -yard; slip, yard, wharf; found-ry, -ery; furnace; vineyard, orchard, farm, kitchen garden.

melting pot, crucible, alembic, caldron, mortar, *matrix.*

2°. *Complex Voluntary Action*

692. Conduct.—N. dealing, transaction &c. (*action*) 680; business &c. 625.

tactics, game, policy, polity; general-, statesman-, seaman-ship; strate-gy, -gics; plan &c. 626.

husbandry; house-keeping, -wifery; stewardship; *ménage*; regimen, *régime*; econom-y, -ics; political economy; management; government &c. (*direction*) 693.

execution, manipulation, treatment, campaign, career, life, course, walk, race.

conduct; behaviour; de-, com-portment; carriage, *maintien*, demeanour, guise, bearing, manner, mien, air, observance.

course -, line- of -conduct, - action, - proceeding; *rôle*; process, ways, practice, procedure, *modus operandi*; method &c., path &c. 627.

V. transact, execute; des-, dis-patch; proceed with, discharge; carry -on, - through, - out, - into effect; work out; go -, get- through; enact; put into practice; officiate &c. 625.

behave -, comport -, demean -, carry -, bear -, conduct -, acquit-oneself.

run a race, lead a life, play a game; take -, adopt- a course; steer -, shape- one's course; play one's- -part, - cards; shift for oneself; paddle one's own canoe.

conduct; manage &c. (*direct*) 693.

deal -, have to do- with; treat, handle a case; take -steps, - measures.
Adj. conducting &c. *v.*; strategical, business-like, practical, economic, executive.

693. Direction.—N. direction; manage-ment, -ry; government, gubernation, conduct, legislation, regulation, guidance; steer-, pilot-age; reins, - of government; helm, rudder, controls, joy stick, needle, compass, binnacle; guiding -, load -, lode -, pole- star; cynosure.

super-vision, -intendence; *surveillance*, oversight; eye of the master; control, charge, auspices; board of control &c. (*council*) 696; command &c. (*authority*) 737.

premier-, senator-ship; director &c. 694; chair, seat, portfolio.
statesmanship; state-, king-craft.

minis-try, -tration; administration; steward-, proctor-ship; agency.
V. direct, manage, govern, conduct; order, prescribe, cut out work for; head, lead; lead -, show- the way; take the lead, lead on; regulate, guide, steer, pilot; take -, be at- the helm; have -, handle -, hold -, take- the reins, handle the ribbons; drive, tool; tackle.

super-intend, -vise; overlook, control, keep in order, look after, see to, oversee, legislate for; administer, ministrate; patronize; have the -care, - charge- of; have -, take- the direction; pull the -strings, - wires; rule &c. (*command*) 737; have -, hold- -office, - the portfolio; preside, - at the board; take -, occupy -, be in- the chair; pull the stroke oar.
Adj. directing &c. *v.*; executive, supervisory, hegemonic.
Adv. at the -helm, - head of, in charge of; under the auspices of.

694. Director.—N. director, manager, governor, rector, comptroller; super-intendent, -visor; intendant; over-seer, -looker; foreman, boss, straw boss; supercargo, husband, inspector, visitor, ranger, surveyor, ædile, moderator, monitor, taskmaster; master &c. 745; leader, ring-leader, demagogue, corypheus, conductor, fugleman, precentor, bell-wether, agitator.

[250]

guiding star &c. (*guidance*) 693; adviser &c. 695; guide &c. (*information*) 527; pilot; helmsman; steers-man, -mate; man at the wheel; wire-puller.

driver, whip, Jehu, charioteer; coach-, car-, cab-man, jarvey; postilion, *vetturino*, muleteer, teamster; whipper in; engineer, engine driver, motorman, *chauffeur*.

head, – man; principal, president, speaker; chair, -man; captain &c. (*master*) 745; superior; dean; mayor &c. (*civil authority*) 745; vice-president, prime minister, premier, vizier, grand vizier; dictator.

officer, functionary, minister, official, red-tapist, bureaucrat; man –, Jack- in office; office-bearer; person in authority &c. 745.

statesman, strategist, legislator, lawgiver, politician, administrator, statist, statemonger; Minos, Draco; arbiter &c. (*judge*) 967; king maker, power behind the throne.

board &c. (*council*) 696.

secretary, – of state; Reis Effendi; vicar &c. (*deputy*) 759; steward, factor; agent &c. 758; bailiff, middleman; ganger, clerk of works; landreeve; factotum, major-domo, seneschal, housekeeper, shepherd, *croupier*; proctor, procurator, curator, librarian.

Adv. *ex officio.*

695. Advice.—N. advice, counsel, adhortation; word to the wise; suggestion, submonition, recommendation, advocacy, consultation.

exhortation &c. (*persuasion*) 615; expostulation &c. (*dissuasion*) 616; admonition &c. (*warning*) 668; guidance &c. (*direction*) 693.

instruction, charge, injunction.

adviser, prompter; counsel, -lor; monitor, mentor, Nestor, *magnus Apollo*, senator; teacher &c. 540.

guide, manual, chart &c. (*information*) 527.

physician, leech, archiater; arbiter &c. (*judge*) 967.

refer-ence, -ment; consultation, conference, parley, *pourparler* &c. 696.

V. advise, counsel; give -advice, – counsel, – a piece of advice; suggest, prompt, submonish, recommend, prescribe, advocate; exhort &c. (*persuade*) 615.

enjoin, enforce, charge, instruct, call; call upon &c. (*request*) 765; dictate.

expostulate &c. (*dissuade*) 616; admonish &c. (*warn*) 668.

advise with; lay heads –, consult- together; compare notes; hold a council, deliberate, be closeted with.

confer, consult, refer to, call in; take –, follow- advice; follow implicitly; be advised by, have at one's elbow, take one's cue from.

Adj. recommendatory; hortative &c. (*persuasive*) 615; dehortatory &c. (*dissuasive*) 616; admonitory &c. (*warning*) 668; consultative.

Int. go to!

696. Council.—N. council, committee, subcommittee, *comitia*, court, chamber, cabinet, board, bench, staff; consultation.

senate, *senatus*, parliament, house, – of Lords, – Peers, – Commons, legislature, legislative assembly, federal council, chamber of deputies, directory, *reichsrath*, *rigsdag*, *cortes*, storthing, witenagemote, *junta*, divan, *musnud*, *sanhedrim*, Amphictyonic council; *duma*, *zemstvo*, *soviet*, *cheka*, *ogpu*; *Dail Eireann*; caput, consistory, chapter, syndicate; court of appeal &c. (*tribunal*) 966; board of -control, – works; vestry; county –, borough –, district –, parish –, town- council, local board.

cabinet –, privy- council, royal commission; cockpit, convocation, synod, congress, congregation, convention, diet, states-general, aulic council.

League of Nations, assembly, *caucus*, conclave, *clique*, conventicle; meeting, sitting, *séance*, conference, session, hearing, palaver, *pourparler*, *durbar*, pow-wow, house; *quorum*.

senator; member, – of parliament; councillor, M.P., representative of the people.

Adj. senatorial, curule, parliamentary.

697. Precept.—N. precept, direction, instruction, charge; prescript, -ion; *recipe*, receipt; golden rule; maxim &c. 496.

commandment, rule, ruling, canon, law, code, *corpus juris*, *lex scripta*, common –, unwritten –, canon-law; the Ten Commandments; act, statute, convention, rubric, stage direction, regulation; form, -ula, -ulary; technicality; nice point.

order &c. (*command*) 741.

698. Skill.—N. skill, skilfulness, address; dexter-ity, -ousness; adroitness, expertness &c. *adj.*; proficiency, competence, craft, callidity, facility, knack, trick, sleight; master-y, -ship; excellence, panurgy; ambidext-erity, -rousness; sleight of hand &c. (*deception*) 545.

sea-, air-, marks-, horse-manship; tight-, rope-dancing.

accomplish-, acquire-, attain-ment; art, science; techn-icality, -ology, -ique; practical –, technical- knowledge; technocracy; finish, technic.

knowledge of the world, world wisdom, *savoir-faire*; tact; mother wit &c. (*sagacity*) 498; discretion &c. (*caution*) 864; *finesse*; craftiness &c. (*cunning*) 702; management &c. (*conduct*) 692; *ars celare artem*; self-help.

cleverness, talent, ability, ingenuity, capacity, parts, talents, faculty, endowment, *forte*, turn, gift, genius, flair, feeling; intelligence &c. 498; sharpness, readiness &c. (*activity*) 682; invention &c. 515; apt-ness, -itude; turn –, capacity –, genius- for; felicity, capability, *curiosa felicitas*, qualification, habilitation.

proficient &c. 700.

masterpiece, *coup de maître*, *chef-d'œuvre*, *tour de force*; good stroke &c. (*plan*) 626.

V. be -skilful &c. *adj.*; excel in, be master of; have -a turn for &c. *n.*

know -what's what, – a hawk from a handsaw, – what one is about, – on

699. Unskilfulness.—N. unskilfulness &c. *adj.*; want of -skill &c. 698; incompeten-ce, -cy; in-ability, -felicity, -dexterity, -experience; clumsiness; disqualification, unproficiency; quackery.

folly, stupidity &c. 499; indiscretion &c. (*rashness*) 863; thoughtlessness &c. (*inattention*) 458, (*neglect*) 460.

mis-management, -conduct; impolicy; maladministration; mis-rule, -government, -application, -direction, -feasance.

absence of rule, rule of thumb; bungling &c. *v.*; failure &c. 732; screw loose; too many cooks.

blunder &c. (*mistake*) 495; *étourderie*, *gaucherie*, act of folly, *balourdise*; botch, -ery; bad job, sad work.

sprat sent out to catch a whale, much ado about nothing, wildgoose chase.

bungler &c. 701; fool &c. 501.

layman, amateur.

V. be -unskilful &c. *adj.*; not see an inch beyond one's nose; blunder, bungle, boggle, fumble, muff, botch, bitch, flounder, loppet, stumble, trip; hobble &c. 275; put one's foot in it; make a -mess, – hash, – sad work- of; overshoot the mark.

play -tricks with, – Puck; mis-manage, -conduct, -direct, -apply, -send.

stultify –, make a fool of –, commit-oneself; act foolishly; play the fool; put oneself out of court; lose one's -head, – cunning.

begin at the wrong end; do things

which side one's bread is buttered, – what's o'clock, – a thing or two; have cut one's -eye, – wisdom- teeth.

see -one's way, – where the wind lies, – which way the wind blows; have -all one's wits about one, – one's hand in; *savoir vivre*; *scire quid valeant humeri quid ferre recusent*.

look after the main chance; cut one's coat according to one's cloth; live by one's wits; exercise one's discretion, feather the oar, sail near the wind; stoop to conquer &c. (*cunning*) 702; play one's -cards well, – best card; hit the right nail on the head, put the saddle on the right horse.

take advantage of, make the most of; profit by &c. (*use*) 677; make a hit &c. (*succeed*) 731; make a virtue of necessity; make hay while the sun shines &c. (*occasion*) 134.

Adj. skilful, dexterous, adroit, expert, apt, slick, handy, quick, deft, ready, resourceful, gain; smart &c. (*active*) 682; proficient, good at, up to, at home in, master of, a good hand at, *au fait*, thoroughbred, masterly, crack, accomplished; conversant &c. (*knowing*) 490.

experienced, practised, skilled; up –, well up- in; in -practice, – proper cue; competent, efficient, qualified, capable, fitted, fit for, up to the mark, trained, initiated, prepared, primed, finished.

clever, able, ingenious, felicitous, gifted, talented, endowed, cute, inventive &c. 515; shrewd, sharp &c. (*intelligent*) 498; cunning &c. 702; alive to, up to snuff, not to be caught with chaff; discreet.

neat-handed, fine-fingered, ambidextrous, sure-footed; cut out –, fitted- for.

technical, artistic, scientific, dædalian, shipshape; workman-, business-, statesman-like.

Adv. skillfully &c. *adj.*; well &c. 618; artistically; with -skill, – consummate skill; *secundum artem, suo Marte*; to the best of one's abilities &c. (*exertion*) 686; like a machine.

---

by halves &c. (*not complete*) 730; make two bites of a cherry; play at cross purposes; strain at a gnat and swallow a camel &c. (*caprice*) 608; put the cart before the horse; lock the stable door when the horse is stolen &c. (*too late*) 135.

not know -what one is about, – one's own interest, – on which side one's bread is buttered; stand in one's own light, quarrel with one's bread and butter, throw a stone in one's own garden, kill the goose which lays the golden eggs, pay dear for one's whistle, cut one's own throat, burn one's fingers; knock –, run- one's head against a stone wall; fall into a trap, catch a Tartar, bring the house about one's ears; have too many -eggs in one basket (*imprudent*) 863, – irons in the fire.

mistake &c. 495; take the shadow for the substance &c. (*credulity*) 486; be in the wrong box, aim at a pigeon and kill a crow; take –, get- the wrong sow by the ear, – the dirty end of the stick; put -the saddle on the wrong horse, – a square peg into a round hole, – new wine into old bottles.

cut a whetstone with a razor; hold a farthing candle to the sun &c. (*useless*) 645; fight with –, grasp at- a shadow; catch at straws, lean on a broken reed, reckon without one's host, pursue a wildgoose chase; go on a fool's –, sleeveless- errand; go further and fare worse; loose –, miss- one's way; fail &c. 732.

Adj. un-skilful &c. 698; unskilled, inexpert; bungling &c. *v.*; awkward, clumsy, unhandy, lubberly, *gauche*, *maladroit*; left-, heavy-handed; slovenly, slatternly; gawky.

adrift, at fault.

in-, un-apt; inhabile; un-tractable, -teachable; giddy &c. (*inattentive*) 458; inconsiderate &c. (*neglectful*) 460; stupid &c. 499; inactive &c. 683; incompetent; un-, dis-, ill-qualified; unfit; quackish; raw, green, inexperienced, rusty, out of practice.

un-accustomed, -used, -trained &c. 537, -initiated, -conversant &c. (*ignorant*) 491; shiftless; unbusinesslike, unpractical; unstatesmanlike.

un-, ill-, mis-advised; ill-devised, -imagined, -judged, -contrived, -conducted; un-, mis-guided; misconducted, foolish, wild; infelicitous; penny wise and pound foolish &c. (*inconsistent*) 608.

Phr. one's fingers being all thumbs; the right hand forgets its cunning.

il se noyerait dans une goutte d'eau.

incidit in Scyllam qui vult vitare Charybdim; out of the frying pan into the fire.

---

700. Proficient.—N. proficient, expert, adept, dab; *connoisseur* &c. (*scholar*) 492; master, -hand; topsawyer, *prima donna*, first fiddle, *chef de cuisine*; protagonist; past master; profess-or, -ional, specialist.

picked man; medallist, prizeman.

veteran; old -stager, – campaigner, – soldier, – file, – hand; man of -business, – the world.

nice –, good –, clean- hand; practised –, experienced- -eye, – hand; marksman; good –, dead –, crack- shot; rope-dancer, funambulist, acrobat, contortionist; cunning man; conjuror &c. (*deceiver*) 548; wizard &c. 994.

genius; master-mind, – head, – spirit;

cunning –, sharp -blade, – fellow; jobber; cracksman &c. (*thief*) 792; politician, tactician, diplomat, -ist, strategist.

pantologist, admirable Crichton, Jack of all trades; prodigy of learning; walking encyclopædia; mine of information.

701. Bungler.—N. bungler; blunderer, -head; marplot, fumbler, lubber, lout, oaf, duffer, stick, clown; bad -, poor- -hand, – shot; butter-fingers.

no conjuror, flat, muff, slow coach, looby, lubber, swab; clod, yokel, hick, awkward squad, novice, greenhorn, jaywalker, *blanc-bec.*

land lubber; fresh water –, fair weather- sailor; horse-marine; fish out of water, ass in lion's skin, jackdaw in peacock's feathers; quack &c. (*deceiver*) 548; Lord of Misrule.

sloven, slattern, trapes.

Phr. *il n'a pas inventé la poudre*; h' will never set the Thames on fire.

---

702. Cunning.—N. cunning, craft; cunningness, craftiness &c. *adj.*; subtlety, artificiality; manœuvring &c. *v.*; temporization; circumvention.

chicane, -ry; sharp practice, knavery, jugglery; concealment &c. 528; guile, duplicity &c. (*falsehood*) 544; foul play.

diplomacy, politics; Machiavellism; jobbery, back-stairs influence, gerrymandering.

art, -ifice; device, machination; plot &c. (*plan*) 626; manœuvre, stratagem, dodge, artful dodge, wile; trick, -ery &c. (*deception*) 545; *ruse, – de guerre*; *finesse*, side-blow, thin end of the wedge, shift, go by, subterfuge, evasion; white lie &c. (*untruth*) 546; juggle, *tour de force*; tricks -of the trade, – upon travellers; imposture, deception; *espièglerie*; net, trap &c. 545.

Ulysses, Machiavel, sly boots, fox,

703. Artlessness.—N. artlessness &c. *adj.*; nature, simplicity; innocence &c. 946; *bonhomie, naïveté, abandon*, candour, sincerity; singleness of -purpose, – heart; honesty &c. 939; plain speaking; *épanchement.*

rough diamond, matter of fact man; *le palais de vérité; enfant terrible.*

V. be -artless &c. *adj.*; look one in the face; wear one's heart upon his sleeves for daws to peck at; think aloud; speak -out, – one's mind; be free with one, call a spade a spade.

Adj. artless, natural, pure, native, simple, plain, inartificial, untutored, unsophisticated, *ingénu*, unaffected, *naïve*; sincere, frank; open, – as day; candid, ingenuous, guileless, unsuspicious, childlike; honest &c. 939; innocent &c. 946; Arcadian; undesigning, straightforward, unreserved, unvarnished, above-board; simple-, single-

reynard; Scotch-, Yorkshire-man; Yankee; intriguer, *intrigant*, schemer, trickster.

V. be -cunning &c. *adj.*; have cut one's eye-teeth; contrive &c. (*plan*) 626; live by one's wits; manœuvre; intrigue, gerrymander, *finesse*, double, temporize, stoop to conquer, *reculer pour mieux sauter*, circumvent, steal a march upon; overreach &c. 545; throw off one's guard; surprise &c. 508; outdo, get the better of, snatch from under one's nose; snatch a verdict; waylay, undermine, introduce the thin end of the wedge; play -a deep game, - tricks with; have an axe to grind; *ambiguas in vulgum spargere voces*; flatter, make things pleasant.

Adj. cunning, crafty, artful; skilful &c. 698; subtle, feline, vulpine; cunning as a -fox, - serpent; deep, - laid; profound; designing, contriving; intriguing &c. *v.*; strategic, diplomatic, politic, Machiavellian, time-serving; artificial; trick-y, -sy; wily, sly, slim, insidious, stealthy, foxy; underhand &c. (*hidden*) 528; subdolous; deceitful &c. 545; double-tongued, -faced; shifty; crooked; arch, pawky, shrewd, acute; sharp, - as a needle; canny, astute, leery, knowing, up to snuff, too clever by half, not to be caught with chaff.

Adv. cunningly &c. *adj.*; slily, on the sly, by a side wind.

Phr. diamond cut diamond.

minded; frank-, open-, single-, simple-hearted; open and above-board.

free-, plain-, out-spoken; blunt, downright, direct, matter of fact, unpoetical; unflattering.

Adv. in plain -words, - English; without mincing the matter; not to mince the matter &c. (*affirmation*) 535.

Phr. *Davus sum non Œdipus; liberavi animam meam.*

Section IV. ANTAGONISM

1°. *Conditional Antagonism*

704. Difficulty.—N. difficulty; hardness &c. *adj.*; impracticability &c. (*impossibility*) 471; tough -, hard -, uphill- work; hard -, Herculean -, Augean- task; task of Sisyphus, Sisyphean labour, tough job, teaser, rasper, dead lift.

dilemma, embarrassment; perplexity &c. (*uncertainty*) 475; involvement; intricacy; entanglement &c. 59; cross fire; awkwardness, delicacy, ticklish card to play, deadlock, knot, Gordian knot, *dignus vindice nodus*, net, meshes, maze; coil &c. (*convolution*) 248; crooked path.

nice -, delicate -, subtle -, knotty-point; vexed question, *vexata quæstio*, poser; puzzle &c. (*riddle*) 533; paradox; hard -, nut to crack; bone to pick, *crux, pons asinorum*, where the shoe pinches.

nonplus, quandary, strait, pass, pinch, pretty pass, stress, brunt; criti-

705. Facility. — N. facility, ease; easiness &c. *adj.*; capability; feasibility &c. (*practicability*) 470; flexibility, pliancy &c. 324; smoothness &c. 255; convenience.

plain -, smooth -, straight- sailing; mere child's play, holiday task.

smooth water, fair wind; smooth - royal- road; clear -coast, - stage; *tabula rasa; full play* &c. (*freedom*) 748.

disen-cumbrance, -tanglement; de-oppilation; permission &c. 760.

V. be -easy &c. *adj.*; go on -, run-smoothly; have -full play &c. *n.*; go -, run- on all fours; obey the helm, work well.

flow -, swim -, drift -, go- with the--stream, - tide; see one's way; have -it all one's own way, - the game in one's own hands; walk over the course, win -at a canter, - hands down; make -light of, - nothing of; be at home in &c. (*skilful*) 698.

cal situation, crisis; trial, rub, emergency, exigency, scramble.

scrape, hobble, slough, quagmire, hot water, hornet's nest; sea -, peck- of troubles; pretty kettle of fish; pickle, stew, *imbroglio*, mess, muddle, botch, fuss, bustle, ado; false position; set fast, stand; dead -lock, - set; fix, horns of a dilemma, *cul de sac*; hitch; stumbling block &c. (*hindrance*) 706.

V. be -difficult &c. *adj.*; run one hard, go against the grain, try one's patience, put one out; put to one's -shifts, - wit's end; go hard with -, try- one; pose, perplex &c. (*uncertain*) 475; bother, nonplus, gravel, bring to a dead lock; be -impossible &c. 471; be in the way of &c. (*hinder*) 706.

meet with -, labour under -, get into -, plunge into -, struggle with -, contend with -, grapple with- difficulties; labour under a disadvantage; be -in difficulty &c. *adj.*

fish in troubled waters, buffet the waves, swim against the stream, scud under bare poles.

have -much ado with, - a hard time of it; come to the -push, - pinch; bear the brunt.

grope in the dark, lose one's way, weave a tangled web, walk among eggs.

get into a -scrape &c. *n.*; bring a hornet's nest about one's ears; be put to one's shifts; flounder, boggle, struggle; not know which way to turn &c. (*uncertain*) 475; get -tangled up, - wound up; *perdre son latin*; stick - at, - in the mud, - fast; come to a -stand, - dead lock; hold the wolf by the ears.

render -difficult &c. *adj.*; encumber, embarrass, ravel, entangle; put a spoke in the wheel &c. (*hinder*) 706; lead a pretty dance.

Adj. difficult, not easy, hard, tough; trouble-, toil-, irk-some; operose, laborious, onerous, arduous, Herculean, formidable; sooner -, more easily- said than done; difficult -, hard- to deal with; ill-conditioned, crabbed; not -to be handled with kid gloves, - made with rosewater.

awkward, unwieldy, unmanageable; intractable, stubborn &c. (*obstinate*) 606; perverse, refractory, plaguy, trying, thorny, rugged; knot-ted, -ty; invious; path-, track-less; labyrinthine &c. (*convoluted*) 248; intricate, complicated &c. (*tangled*) 59; impracticable &c. (*impossible*) 471; not -feasible &c. 470; desperate &c. (*hopeless*) 859.

embarrassing, perplexing &c. (*uncertain*) 475; delicate, ticklish,

render -easy &c. *adj.*; facilitate, smooth, ease; popularize; lighten, - the labour; free, clear; dis-encumber, -embarrass, -entangle, -engage; deobstruct, unclog, extricate, unravel; untie -, cut- the knot; disburden, unload, exonerate, emancipate, free from, deoppilate; humour &c. (*aid*) 707; lubricate &c. 332; relieve &c. 834.

leave -a hole to creep out of, - a loophole, - the matter open; give -the reins to, - full play, - full swing; make way for; open the -door to, - way; prepare -, smooth -, clear- the -ground, - way, - path, - road; pave the way, bridge over; permit &c. 760.

Adj. easy, facile; feasible &c. (*practicable*) 470; easily -managed, - accomplished; within reach, accessible, easy of access, for the million, open to.

manageable, wieldy; towardly, tractable; submissive; yielding, ductile; pliant &c. (*soft*) 324; glib, slippery; smooth &c. 255; on -friction wheels, - velvet; convenient.

un-, dis-burdened, -encumbered, -embarrassed; exonerated; un-loaded, -obstructed, -trammelled, - impeded, -restrained &c. (*free*) 748; at ease, light.

at -, quite at- home; in -one's element, - smooth water.

Adv. easily &c. *adj.*; readily, smoothly, swimmingly, *ad lib.*, on easy terms, single-handed.

Phr. touch and go.

Int. all clear!

critical; beset with –, full of –, surrounded by –, entangled by –, encompassed with- difficulties.

under a difficulty; in -difficulty, – hot water, – the suds, – a cleft stick, – a fix, – the wrong box, – a scrape &c. *n.*, – deep water, – a fine pickle; *in extremis*; between -two stools, – Scylla and Charybdis; surrounded by -shoals, – breakers, – quicksands; at cross purposes; not out of the wood.

reduced to straits; hard –, sorely- pressed; run hard; pinched, put to it, straitened; hard -up, – put to it, – set; put to one's shifts; puzzled, at a loss &c. (*uncertain*) 475; at -the end of one's tether, – one's wit's end, – a nonplus, – a standstill; gravelled, nonplussed, stranded, aground; stuck –, set- fast; up a tree, at bay, *aux abois*, driven -into a corner, – from post to pillar, – to extremity, – to one's wit's end, – to the wall; *au bout de son latin*; out of one's -depth, – reckoning; put –, thrown -out.

accomplished with difficulty; hard-fought, -earned.

Adv. with -difficulty, – much ado; hardly &c. *adj.*; uphill; against the -stream, – grain; *à rebours*; *invitâ Minervâ*; in the teeth of; at –, upon- a pinch; at long odds.

Phr. ay there's the rub; *hic labor hoc opus*; things are come to a pretty pass.

2°. *Active Antagonism*

706. Hindrance. — N. prevention, preclusion, obstruction, stoppage; prohibition; inter-ruption, -ception, -clusion; hindrance, impedition; retardment, -ation; constriction; embarrassment, oppilation; coarctation, stricture, restriction; anchor &c. 666; restraint &c. 751 & 752; inhibition &c. 761; blockade &c. (*closure*) 261; picketing.

inter-ference, -position; obtrusion; dis-couragement, -countenance, -approval, -approbation; opposition &c. 708.

impediment, let, obstacle, obstruction, knot, knag; check, hitch, *contretemps*, *impasse*, screw loose, grit in the oil.

bar, stile, barrier; turn-stile, -pike; gate, portcullis; bulwark, parapet, barricade &c. (*defence*) 717; wall, dead wall, breakwater, groyne; bulkhead, block, buffer; stopper &c. 263; boom, dam, weir, burrock.

drawback, objection; stumbling-block, -stone; lion in the path; snag; snags and sawyers.

en-, in-cumbrance; clog, skid, shoe, spoke; brake, drag, – chain, – weight; stay, stop; preventive, prophylactic; contraception; load, burden, fardel,

707. Aid.—N. aid, -ance; assistance, help, opitulation, succour; support, lift, advance, furtherance, promotion; coadjuvancy &c. (*co-operation*) 709.

patronage, championship, countenance, favour, interest, advocacy, auspices.

sustentation, subvention, subsidy, bounty, alimentation, nutrition, nourishment, maintenance; manna in the wilderness; food &c. 298; means &c. 632.

ministr-y, -ation; subministration; accommodation.

relief, rescue; help at a dead lift; supernatural aid; *deus ex machinâ*.

supplies, reinforcements, succours, contingents, recruits; support &c. (*physical*) 215; adjunct, ally &c. (*helper*) 711.

V. aid, assist, help, succour, lend one's aid; come to the aid &c. *n.*- of; contribute, subscribe to; bring –, give –, furnish –, afford –, supply- -aid &c. *n.*; render assistance; give –, stretch –, lend –, bear –, hold out- a -hand, – helping hand; give one a -lift, – cast, – turn; take -by the hand, – in tow; help a lame dog over a stile, lend wings to.

onus, millstone round one's neck, *im-pedimenta*; dead weight; lumber, pack; nightmare, Ephialtes, incubus, old man of the sea; remora.

difficulty &c. 704; insuperable &c. 471- obstacle; estoppel; ill wind; head wind &c. (*opposition*) 708; trammel, tether &c. (*means of restraint*) 752; hold back, counterpoise; damper, wet blanket, hinderer, marplot, kill-joy, dog in the manger, interloper; trail of a red herring; opponent &c. 710.

V. hinder, impede, impedite, embarrass.

keep -, stave -, ward- off; picket; obviate; a-, ante-vert; turn aside, draw off, prevent, forefend, nip in the bud; retard, slacken, check, let; counter-act, -check; preclude, debar, foreclose, estop; inhibit &c. 761; shackle &c. (*restrain*) 751; restrict, restrain, cohibit.

obstruct, filibuster, stop, stay, bar, bolt, lock; block, - up; belay, barricade; block -, stop- the way; dam up &c. (*close*) 261; put on the -brake &c. *n.*; scotch -, lock -, put a spoke in- the wheel; put a stop to &c. 142; traverse, contravene; inter-rupt, -cept; oppose &c. 708; hedge -in, - round; cut off; interclude.

inter-pose, -fere, -meddle &c. 682.

cramp, hamper; clog, - the wheels; cumber; en-, in-cumber; handicap; choke; saddle -, load- with; overload, lay; lumber, trammel, tie one's hands, put to inconvenience; in-, discommode; discompose; hustle, drive into a corner; choke off.

run -, fall- foul of; cross the path of, break in upon.

thwart, frustrate, disconcert, balk, foil, baffle, snub, override, circumvent; defeat &c. 731; spike guns &c. (*render useless*) 645; spoil, mar, clip the wings of; cripple &c. (*injure*) 659; put an extinguisher on; damp; dishearten &c. (*dissuade*) 616; discountenance, throw cold water on, spoil sport; lay -, throw-a wet blanket on; cut the ground from under one, take the wind out of one's sails, undermine; be -, stand- in the way of; act as a drag; hang like a millstone round one's neck.

relieve, rescue; set -up, - agoing, - on one's legs; bear -, pull- through; give new life to, be the making of; reinforce, recruit; set -, put -, push-forward; give -a lift, - a shove, - an impulse- to; promote, further, forward, advance; speed, expedite, quicken, hasten.

support, sustain, uphold, prop, hold up, bolster.

cradle, nourish; nurture, nurse, dry nurse, suckle, put out to nurse; manure, cultivate, force; foster, cherish, foment; feed -, fan- the flame.

serve; do service to, tender to, pander to; ad-, sub-, minister to; tend, attend, wait on; take care of &c. 459; entertain; smooth the bed of death.

oblige, accommodate, consult the wishes of; humour, cheer, encourage.

second, stand by; back, - up; pay the piper, abet; work -, make interest -, stick up -, take up the cudgels- for; take up -, espouse -, adopt- the cause of; advocate, beat up for recruits, press into the service; squire, give moral support to, keep in countenance, countenance, patronize; lend -oneself, - one's countenance- to; smile -, shine-upon; favour, befriend, take up, take in hand, enlist under the banners of; side with &c. (*co-operate*) 709.

be of use to; subserve &c. (*instrument*) 631; benefit &c. 648; render a service &c. (*utility*) 644; conduce &c. (*tend*) 176.

Adj. aiding &c. *v.*; auxiliary, adjuvant, helpful; coadjuvant &c. 709; subservient, ministrant, ancillary, accessory, subsidiary.

at one's beck; friendly, amicable, favourable, propitious, well-disposed; neighbourly; obliging &c. (*benevolent*) 906.

Adv. with -, by- -the aid &c. *n.*- of; on -, in- behalf of; in -aid, - the service, - the name, - favour, - furtherance-of; on account of; for the sake of, on the part of; *non obstante*.

Int. help! save us! to the rescue! S.O.S.!

Adj. hindering &c. *v.*; obstr-uctive, -uent; impedi-tive, -ent; intercipient; prophylactic &c. (*remedial*) 662.

in the way of, unfavourable; onerous, burdensome; cumb-rous, -ersome; obtrusive.

hindered &c. *v.*; wind-bound, water-logged, heavy laden; hard pressed.

unassisted &c. (*see* assist &c. 707); single-handed, alone; deserted &c. 624.

708. Opposition.—N. opposition, antagonism; oppug-nancy, -nation; impugnation; contravention; counteraction &c. 179; counterplot.

cross-fire, under-current, head-wind.

clashing, collision, conflict, lack of harmony, contest.

competition, two of a trade, rivalry, emulation, race; war to the knife.

absence of -aid &c. 707; resistance &c. 719; restraint &c. 751; hindrance &c. 706.

V. oppose, counteract, run counter to; withstand &c. (*resist*) 719; control &c. (*restrain*) 751; hinder &c. 706; antagonize, oppugn, fly in the face of, go dead against, kick against, fall foul of; set -, pit- against; face, confront, cope with; make a -stand, - dead set-against; set -oneself, one's face- against; protest -, vote -, raise one's voice-against; disfavour, turn one's back upon; set at naught, slap in the face, slam the door in one's face.

be -, play- at cross purposes; counter-work, -mine; thwart, overthwart.

stem, breast, encounter; stem -, breast- the -tide, - current, - flood; buffet the waves; beat up -, make head- against; grapple with; kick against the pricks &c. (*resist*) 719; contend &c. 720 -, do battle &c. (*warfare*) 722- -with, - against.

contra-dict, -vene; belie; go -, run -, beat -, militate- against; come in conflict with.

emulate &c. (*compete*) 720; rival, spoil one's trade.

Adj. oppos-ing, -ed &c. *v.*; adverse, antagonistic; ambivalent; contrary &c. 14; at variance &c. 24; at issue, at war with; in opposition; 'agin the Government.'

un-favourable, -friendly; hostile, inimical, cross, unpropitious.

709. Co-operation.—N. co-operation; coadju-vancy, -tancy; coagency, co-efficiency; concert, concurrence, complicity, participation; union &c. 43; amalgamation, combination &c. 48; collusion.

association, alliance, colleagueship, jointstock, copartnership, trust, cartel, pool, ring, combine, interlocking directorate; confederation &c. (*party*) 712; federation, coalition, fusion; a long pull, a strong pull and a pull all together; log-rolling, freemasonry.

unanimity &c. (*assent*) 488; *esprit de corps*, party spirit; clan-, partisan-ship; reciprocity, concord &c. 714.

V. co-operate, co-adjute, concur; conduce &c. 178; combine, cartelize, unite one's efforts; keep -, draw -, pull -, club -, hang -, hold -, league -, band -, be banded- together; stand -, put-shoulder to shoulder; act in concert, join forces, fraternize, cling to one another, conspire, concert, lay one's heads together; confederate, be in league with; collude, understand one another, play into the hands of, hunt in couples.

side -, take side -, go along -, go hand in hand -, join hands -, make common cause -, strike in -, unite -, join -, mix oneself up -, take part -, play along -, cast in one's lot- with; join -, enter into- partnership with; rally round, follow the lead of; come to, pass over to, come into the views of; be -, row -, sail- in the same boat; sail on the same tack.

be a party to, lend oneself to; participate; have a -hand in, - finger in the pie; take -, bear- part in; second &c. (*aid*) 707; take the part of, play the game of; espouse a -cause, - quarrel.

Adj. co-operating &c. *v.*; in -co-operation &c. *n.*, - league &c. (*party*) 712;

in hostile array, front to front, with crossed bayonets, at daggers drawn; up in arms; resistant &c. 719.

competitive, emulous.

Adv. against, *versus*, counter to, in conflict with, at cross purposes.

against the -grain, – current, – stream, – wind, – tide; with a head-wind; with the wind -ahead, – in one's teeth.

in spite, in despite, in defiance; in the -way, – teeth, – face- of; across; a-, over-thwart; where the shoe pinches.

though &c. 30; even; *quand même*; *per contra*.

Phr. *nitor in adversum*.

coadju-vant, -tant; hand and glove with.

favourable &c. 707- to; un-opposed &c. 708.

Adv. as one man &c. (*unanimously*) 488; shoulder to shoulder; in co-operation with.

_____

710. Opponent.—N. opponent, antagonist, adversary; adverse party, opposition; enemy &c. 891; assailant.

oppositionist, obstructive; obscurantist; brawler, wrangler, brangler, disputant, extremist, irreconcilable, diehard, bitter-ender.

malcontent; Jacobin, Fenian &c. 742; demagogue, reactionist.

passive resister, conscientious objector.

rival, competitor, contestant.

_____

711. Auxiliary.—N. auxiliary; recruit; assistant; adju-vant, -tant; adjunct; help, -er, -mate, -ing hand; midwife; colleague, partner, mate, *confrère*, co-operator; coadju-tor, -trix; collaborator.

ally; friend &c. 890, confidant, *fidus Achates*, pal, chum, buddy, *alter ego*.

confederate; ac-, complice; accessory, – after the fact; *particeps criminis*.

aide-de-camp, secretary, clerk, associate, marshal; right-hand; candle-, bottle-holder; hand-maid; servant &c. 746; puppet, cat's-paw, stooge, dependent, creature, jackal; tool, *âme damnée*; satellite, adherent, parasite.

votary, disciple; secta-rian, -ry; seconder, backer, upholder, supporter, abettor, advocate, partisan, champion, patron, friend at court, mediator.

friend in need, Jack at a pinch, *deus ex machinâ*, guardian angel, fairy godmother; special providence, tutelary genius.

712. Party.—N. party, faction, side, denomination, class, communion, set, crowd, crew, band, horde, posse, phalanx; regiment &c. 726; family, clan &c. 166.

Tories, Conservatives, Unionists, Whigs, Liberals, Radicals, Labour party, Socialists, Communists &c.; Republicans, Democrats, Farmer-Labor; *Fascisti*, Revolutionaries &c. 742.

community, body, fellowship, sodality, solidarity; con-, fraternity; sorority; brother-, sister-hood.

Freemasons, Knights Templars, Odd Fellows, Ku Klux Klan &c.

knot, gang, *clique*, ring, circle; *coterie*, club, *casino*.

corporation, corporate body, guild; establishment, company; co-partnership; firm, house; joint concern, joint-stock company, trust, investment trust, combine &c. 709.

society, association; instit-ute, -ution; union; trade-union; league, syndicate, alliance, *Verein, Bund, Zollverein*, combination; league –, alliance- offensive and defensive; coalition; federation; confedera -tion, -cy; junto, cabal, *camarilla, camorra, brigue*; freemasonry; party spirit &c. (*co-operation*) 709.

staff; cast, *dramatis personæ*.

V. unite, join; club together &c. (*co-operate*) 709; cement –, form- a party &c. *n.*; associate &c. (*assemble*) 72.

Adj. in -league, – partnership, – alliance &c. *n.*

bonded –, banded –, linked &c. (*joined*) 43- together; embattled; confederated, federative, joint, corporate, leagued, fraternal, masonic, cliquish.

Adv. hand in hand, side by side, shoulder to shoulder, *en masse*, in the same boat.

---

713. Discord.—N. disagreement &c. 24; dis-cord, -accord, -sidence, -sonance; jar, clash, shock; jarring, jostling &c. *v.*; screw loose.

variance, difference, dissension, misunderstanding, cross purposes, odds, *brouillerie*; division, split, rupture, disruption, division in the camp, house divided against itself, rift within the lute; disunion, breach; schism &c. (*dissent*) 489; feud, faction.

quarrel, dispute, rippet, spat, tiff, *tracasserie*, squabble, altercation, words, high words; wrangling &c. *v.*; jangle, brabble, cross questions and crooked answers, snip-snap; family jars.

polemics; litigation; strife &c. (*contention*) 720; warfare &c. 722; outbreak, open rupture; breaking off of negotiations, recall of ambassadors; declaration of war.

broil, brawl, row, racket, hubbub, rixation; embroilment, embranglement, *imbroglio*, *fracas*, breach of the peace, piece of work, scrimmage, rumpus; breeze, squall; riot, disturbance &c. (*disorder*) 59; commotion &c. (*agitation*) 315; bear garden, Donnybrook Fair.

subject of dispute, ground of quarrel, battle ground, disputed point; bone -of contention, – to pick; apple of discord, *casus belli*; question at issue &c. (*subject of inquiry*) 461; vexed question, *vexata quæstio*, brand of discord.

troublous times; cat-and-dog life; contentiousness &c. *adj.*; enmity &c. 889; hate &c. 898; Kilkenny cats; disputant &c. 710; strange bedfellows.

V. be -discordant &c. *adj.*; disagree, come amiss &c. 24; clash, jar, jostle, pull different ways, conflict, have no measures with, misunderstand one another; differ; dissent &c. 489; have a -bone to pick, – crow to pluck- with.

fall out, quarrel, dispute; litigate; controvert &c. (*deny*) 536;

714. Concord.—N. concord, accord, harmony, symphony, homology; agreement &c. 23; sympathy &c. (*love*) 897; response; union, unison, unity; bonds of harmony; peace &c. 721; unanimity &c. (*assent*) 488; league &c. 712; happy family.

rapprochement; *réunion*; amity &c. (*friendship*) 888; reciprocity; alliance, *entente cordiale*, good understanding, conciliation, arbitration, peacemaker &c. 724.

V. agree &c. 23; accord, harmonize with; fraternize; be -concordant &c. *adj.*; go hand in hand; blend –, tone in- with; run parallel &c. (*concur*) 178; understand one another; pull together &c. (*co-operate*) 709; put up one's horses together, sing in chorus.

side –, sympathize –, go –, chime in –, fall in- with; come round; be pacified &c. 723; assent &c. 488; enter into the -ideas, – feelings- of; reciprocate.

hurler avec les loups; go –, swim- with the stream.

pour oil on troubled waters, keep in good humour, render accordant, put in tune; come to an understanding, meet half-way; keep the –, remain at- peace.

Adj. concordant, congenial; agreeing &c. *v.*; in- accord &c. *n.*; harmonious, united, cemented; banded together &c. 712; allied; friendly &c. 888; fraternal; conciliatory; at one with; of one mind &c. (*assent*) 488.

at peace, in still water; tranquil &c. (*pacific*) 721.

Adv. with one voice &c. (*assent*) 488; in concert with, hand in hand; on one's side, unanimously.

squabble, wrangle, jangle, brangle, bicker, nag; spar &c. (*contend*) 720; have -words &c. *n.* with; fall foul of.

split; break –, break squares –, part company- with; declare war, try conclusions; join –, put in- issue; pick a quarrel, fasten a quarrel on; sow –, stir up- -dissension &c. *n.*; embroil, estrange, entangle, disunite, widen the breach; set -at odds, – together by the ears; set –, pit- against; rub up the wrong way.

get into hot water, fish in troubled waters, brawl; kick up a -row, – dust; turn the house out of window.

Adj. discordant; disagreeing &c. *v.*; out of tune, dissonant, inharmonious, harsh, grating, jangling, ajar, on bad terms; dissentient &c. 489; inconsistent, contradictory, incongruous, discrepant; un--reconciled, -pacified.

quarrelsome, unpacific; gladiatorial, controversial, polemic, disputatious; factious; liti-gious, -gant; pettifogging.

at odds, at loggerheads, at daggers drawn, at variance, at issue, at cross purposes, at sixes and sevens, at feud, at high words; up in arms, together by the ears, in hot water, embroiled.

torn, disunited.

Phr. *quot homines tot sententiæ*; no love lost between them, *non nostrum tantas componere lites.*

715. Defiance.—N. defiance; daring &c. *v.*; dare, challenge, *cartel*; threat &c. 909; war-cry, -whoop.

V. defy, dare, beard; brave &c. (*courage*) 861; bid defiance to; set at -defiance, – naught; hurl defiance at; dance the war dance; snap the fingers at, laugh to scorn; disobey &c. 742.

show -fight, – one's teeth, – a bold front; bluster, look big, stand akimbo; double –, shake- the fist; threaten &c. 909.

challenge, call out; throw –, fling- down the -gauntlet, – gage, – glove.

Adj. defiant; defying &c. *v.*; with arms akimbo; rebellious, insolent; reckless, greatly daring.

Adv. in -defiance, – the teeth- of; under one's very nose.

Int. do your worst! come if you dare! come on! marry come up! hoity toity!

Phr. *noli me tangere; nemo me impune lacessit.*

716. Attack.—N. attack; assault, – and battery; onset, onslaught, charge.

aggression, drive, offence; incursion, inroad, invasion; irruption; outbreak; *estrapade, ruade; coup de main,* sally, *sortie, camisade,* raid, foray; run -at, – against; dead set at.

storm, -ing; boarding, *escalade*; siege, investment, obsession, bombardment, cannonade; air raid.

fire, volley; platoon –, file –, rapid-fire; *fusillade*; sharp-shooting, sniping; broadside; raking –, cross –, machine gun- fire; volley of grapeshot, *feu d'enfer*; salvo.

cut, thrust, lunge, pass, *passado, carte* and *tierce,* home thrust; *coup de pied*; kick, punch &c. (*impulse*) 276.

717. Defence.—N. defence, protection, guard, ward; shielding &c. *v.*; propugnation; preservation &c. 670; guardianship.

self-defence, -preservation; resistance &c. 719.

safeguard &c. (*safety*) 664; screen &c. (*shelter*) 666, (*concealment*) 530; barrage; fortification; muni-tion, -ment; bulwark, fosse, moat, ditch, intrenchment, trench, dugout, gas mask; dike, dyke; parapet, parados, sunk fence, embankment, mound, mole, bank; earth- field-work, gabions; fence, wall, dead wall, contravallation; paling &c. (*inclosure*) 232; palisade, haha, stockade, *stoccado, laager, sangar*; barri-er, -cade; boom; portcullis, *chevaux de*

battue, razzia, Jacquerie, dragonnade; devastation &c. 162.

assailant, aggressor, invader.

base of operations, point of attack.

V. attack, assault, assail; set –, fall- upon; charge, impugn, break a lance with, enter the lists.

assume –, take- the offensive; be –, become- the aggressor; strike the first blow, fire the first shot, throw the first stone at; lift a hand –, draw the sword- against; take up the cudgels; advance –, march- against; march upon, invade, harry; come on, show fight.

strike at, poke at, thrust at; aim –, deal- a blow at; give –, fetch- one a -blow, – kick; have a -cut, – shot, – fling, – shy- at; be down –, pounce- upon; fall foul of, pitch into, launch out against; bait, slap on the face; make a -thrust, – pass, – set, – dead set- at; dunt; bear down upon.

close with, come to close quarters, bring to bay.

ride full tilt against; let fly at, dash at, run a tilt at, rush at, tilt at, run at, fly at, hawk at, have at, let out at; make a -dash, – rush at; attack tooth and nail; strike home; drive –, press- one hard; be hard upon, run down, strike at the root of.

lay about one, run amuck.

fire -upon, – at, – a shot at; shoot at, pop at, level at, let off a gun at; open fire, pepper, bombard, shell, pour a broadside into; fire -a volley, – red- hot shot; spring a mine.

throw -a stone, – stones- at; stone, lapidate, pelt; hurl -at, – against, – at the head of.

beset, besiege, beleaguer; lay siege to, invest, open the trenches, plant a battery, sap, mine; storm, board, scale the walls.

cut and thrust, bayonet, butt; kick, strike &c. (*impulse*) 276; whip &c. (*punish*) 972.

Adj. attacking &c. *v.*; aggressive, offensive, obsidional.

up in arms; on the warpath; over the top.

Adv. on the offensive.

Int. 'up and at them!'

---

frise; aba-, abat-, abba-tis; *vallum,* circumvallation, battlement, rampart, scarp; e-, counter-scarp; glacis, case- mate.

mine, countermine.

buttress, abutment; shore &c. (*sup- port*) 215.

breastwork, *banquette*, curtain, mant- let, bastion, demilune, redan, ravelin; advanced –, horn –, out- work, lunette; barb-acan, -ican; redoubt; fort-elage, -alice; lines; coast defence.

loop-hole, machicolation; sally-port, postern gate.

hold, stronghold, fastness; asylum &c. (*refuge*) 666; keep, donjon, fort- ress, citadel; capitol, castle; tower, – of strength; fort, barracoon, pah, sconce, martello tower, peel-house, block-house, rath; wooden walls; turret, barbette.

buffer, corner-stone, fender, apron, mask, gauntlet, thimble, carapace, armour, shield, buckler; target, targe, ægis, breastplate, cuirass, plastron, habergeon, mail, coat of mail, brigan- dine, hauberk, lorication, helmet, helm, basinet, sallet, salade, heaume, morion, murrion, armet, cabaset, vizor, cas- quetel, siege-cap, head-piece, casque, steel helmet, tin hat; *pickelhaube,* csako; shako &c. (*dress*) 225; bearskin; panoply; truncheon &c. (*weapon*) 727.

garrison, picket, piquet; defender, protector; guardian &c. (*safety*) 664; trabant, body guard, champion; knight- errant, Paladin; propugner.

V. defend, forfend, fend; shield, screen, shroud; fence round &c. (*cir- cumscribe*) 229; fence, intrench; guard &c. (*keep safe*) 664; guard against; take care of &c. (*vigilance*) 459; bear harm- less; keep –, ward –, beat- off; hinder &c. 706.

parry, repel, propugn, put to flight; give a warm reception to [*ironical*]; hold –, keep- at -bay, – arm's length.

stand –, act- on the defensive; show fight; maintain –, stand- one's ground; stand by; hold one's own; bear –, stand- the brunt; fall back upon, hold, stand in the gap.

Adj. defending &c. *v.*; defensive; mural; armed, – at all points, – *cap-à- pie,* – to the teeth; panoplied, accoutred, harnessed; iron-plated, -clad; loop-holed, castellated, machicolated, casemated; defended &c. *v.*; proof against, bomb-, bulletproof; protective.

Adv. defensively; on the -defence, – defensive; in defence; at bay, *pro aris et focis.*

Int. no surrender! *il ne passeront pas!*

Phr. defence not defiance.

718. Retaliation. — N. retaliation, reprisal, retort; counter-stroke, -blast, -plot, -project; retribution, *lex talionis*; reciprocation &c. (*reciprocity*) 12.

requital, desert, tit for tat, give and take, blow for blow, *quid pro quo*, a Roland for an Oliver, measure for measure, an eye for an eye, diamond cut diamond, the biter bit, a game at which two can play; boomerang.

recrimination &c. (*accusation*) 938; revenge &c. 919; compensation &c. 30; reaction &c. (*recoil*) 277.

V. retaliate, retort, turn upon; pay -off, – back; pay in -one's own, – the same- coin; cap; reciprocate &c. 148; turn the tables upon, return the compliment; give -a *quid pro quo* &c. *n.*, – as much as one takes; give and take, exchange -blows; – fisticuffs; be -quits, – even- with; pay off old scores.

serve one right, be hoist on one's own petard, throw a stone in one's own garden, catch a Tartar.

Adj. retaliating &c. *v.*; retalia-tory, -tive; retributive, recriminatory, reciprocal.

Adv. in retaliation; *en revanche.*

Phr. *mutato nomine de te fabula narratur; par pari refero; tu quoque;* you're another; *suo sibi gladio hunc jugulo.*

719. Resistance. — N. resistance, stand, front, oppugnation; opposition &c. 708; renitence, reluctation, recalcitration, recalcitrance; repugnance; kicking &c. *v.*

repulse, rebuff.

insurrection &c. (*disobedience*) 742; strike; turn –, lock –, barring- out; *levée en masse, Jacquerie;* riot &c. (*disorder*) 59.

V. resist; not -submit &c. 725; repugn, reluctate, withstand; stand up –, strive –, bear up –, be proof –, make head- against; stand, – firm, – one's ground, – the brunt of, – out; hold -one's ground, – one's own, – out.

breast the -wave, – current; stem the -tide, – torrent; face, confront, grapple with; show a bold front &c. (*courage*) 861; present a front; make a –, take one's- stand.

kick, – against; recalcitrate, kick against the pricks; oppose &c. 708; fly in the face of; lift the hand against &c. (*attack*) 716; rise up in arms &c. (*war*) 722; strike, turn out; draw up a round robin &c. (*remonstrate*) 932; revolt &c. (*disobey*) 742; make a riot.

prendre le mors aux dents; take the bit between the teeth; sell one's life dearly, die hard, keep at bay; repel, repulse.

Adj. resisting &c. *v.*; resist-ive, -ant; refractory &c. (*disobedient*) 742; recalcitrant, re-nitent, -pulsive, -pellant; up in arms.

proof against; unconquerable &c. (*strong*) 159; stubborn, unconquered; indomitable &c. (*persevering*) 604a; unyielding &c. (*obstinate*) 606.

Int. hands off! keep off!

720. Contention. — N. contention, strife; contest, -ation; struggle; belligerency; opposition &c. 708.

controversy, polemics; debate &c. (*discussion*) 476; war of words, logomachy, litigation; paper war, ink slinging; high words &c. (*quarrel*) 713; sparring &c. *v.*

721. Peace.—N. peace; amity &c. (*friendship*) 888; harmony &c. (*concord*) 714; tranquillity &c. (*quiescence*) 265; truce &c. (*pacification*) 723; pacificism; pipe –, calumet- of peace.

piping time of peace, quiet life; neutrality.

V. be at peace; keep the peace &c.

competition, rivalry; corrival-ry, -ship; agonism, *concours*, match, race, horse-racing, heat, steeple chase, point-to-point race, handicap; boat race, regatta; field-day; sham fight, Derby day; turf, sporting, bull-fight, tauro-machy, *gymkhana*, rodeo, Olympiad.

wrestling, *ju-jitsu*, pugilism, boxing, fisticuffs, spar, mill, set-to, scrap, round, bout, event; prize-fighting; quarter-staff, single stick; gladiatorship, gymnastics; athletic-s, – sports; games of skill &c. 840.

shindy; *fracas* &c. (*discord*) 713; clash of arms; tussle, scuffle, broil, fray; affray, -ment; velitation; col-, luctation; brabble, *brigue*, scramble, *mêlée*, scrimmage, stramash, bush-fighting.

free –, stand up –, hand to hand –, running- fight.

conflict, skirmish; ren-, en-counter; *rencontre*, collision, affair, brush, fight; battle, – royal; combat, action, engagement, joust, tournament; tilt, -ing; tourney, list; pitched battle, guerilla warfare.

death-struggle, struggle for life or death, Armageddon; hard knocks, sharp contest, tug of war.

naval -engagement, – battle; *naumachia*, sea-fight.

duel, -lo; single combat, monomachy, satisfaction, *passage d'armes*, passage of arms, affair of honour; triangular duel; hostile meeting, digladiation; appeal to arms &c. (*warfare*) 722.

deeds –, feats- of arms; pugnacity; combativeness &c. *adj.*; bone of contention &c. 713.

V. contend; contest, strive, struggle, scramble, wrestle; spar, square; exchange -blows, – fisticuffs; scrap, mix with, fib, justle, tussle, tilt, box, stave, fence; skirmish; fight &c. (*war*) 722; wrangle &c. (*quarrel*) 713.

contend &c. –, grapple –, engage –, close –, buckle –, bandy –, try conclusions –, have a brush &c. *n.* –, tilt- with; encounter, fall foul of, pitch into, clapperclaw, run a tilt at; oppose &c. 708; reluct.

join issue, come to blows, be at loggerheads, set-to, come to the scratch, exchange shots, measure swords, meet hand to hand; take up the -cudgels, – glove, – gauntlet; enter the lists; couch one's lance; give satisfaction; appeal to arms &c. (*warfare*) 722.

lay about one; break the peace.

compete –, cope –, vie –, race- with; outvie, emulate, rival; run a race; contend &c. –, stipulate –, stickle- for; insist upon, make a point of.

Adj. contending &c. *v.*; together by the ears, at loggerheads, at war, at issue.

competitive, rival; belligerent; contentious, combative, bellicose, unpeaceful; warlike &c. 722; quarrelsome &c. 901; pugnacious; pugilistic, gladiatorial; palestric, -al.

Phr. *a verbis ad verbera*; a word and a blow.

(*concord*) 714; make peace &c. 723.

Adj. pacific; peace-able, -ful; calm, tranquil, untroubled, halcyon; blood-less; neutral.

Phr. the storm blown over; the lion lies down with the lamb.

---

722. Warfare.—N. warfare; fighting &c. *v.*; hostilities; war, arms, the sword; Mars, Bellona, grim visaged war, *horrida bella*, Armageddon.

appeal to -arms, – the sword; ordeal

723. Pacification.—N. pacification, conciliation; reconcil-iation, -ement; shaking of hands, accommodation, ar-rangement, adjustment; terms, com-promise; amnesty, deed of release.

–, wager- of battle; *ultima ratio regum,* arbitrament of the sword.

battle array, campaign, crusade, expedition; mobilization; state of siege; battle-field &c. (*arena*) 728; warpath.

art of war, tactics, strategy, castrametation; general-, soldier-ship; aerial –, submarine –, naval –, chemical- warfare; military evolutions, ballistics, gunnery; chivalry; poison gas; gunpowder, shot, – and shell.

battle, tug of war &c. (*contention*) 720; service, campaigning, active service, tented field; fiery cross, trumpet, clarion, bugle, pibroch, slogan; war-cry, -whoop; battle cry, beat of drum, rappel, tom-tom; word of command; pass-, watch-word.

war to the -death, – knife; *guerre à -mort, – outrance*; open –, internecine –, civil- war.

V. arm; raise –, mobilize- troops; raise up in arms; take up the cudgels &c. 720; take up –, fly to –, appeal to- -arms, – the sword; draw –, unsheathe- the sword; dig up the hatchet; go to –, declare –, wage –, let slip the dogs of- war; cry havoc; kindle –, light- the torch of war; raise one's banner, send round the fiery cross; hoist the black flag; throw –, fling- away the scabbard; enrol, enlist, join up; take the field; take the law into one's own hands; do –, give –, join –, engage in –, go to- battle; flesh one's sword; set to, fall to, engage, measure swords with, draw the trigger, cross swords; come to -blows, – close quarters; fight; combat; contend &c. 720; battle –, break a lance- with.

serve; see –, be on- -service, – active service; campaign; wield the sword, shoulder a musket, smell powder, be under the fire; spill –, imbrue the hands in- blood; be on the warpath.

carry on -war, – hostilities; keep the field; fight the good fight; go over the top; cut one's way through; fight -it out, – like devils, – one's way, – hand to hand; sell one's life dearly.

Adj. conten-ding, -tious &c. 720; armed, – to the teeth, – cap-à-pie; sword in hand; in –, under –, up in- arms; at war with; bristling with arms; in -battle array, – open arms, – the field; embattled.

unpacific, unpeaceful; belligerent, combative, armigerous, bellicose, martial, warlike; mili-tary, -tant; soldier-like, -ly; chivalrous; strategical, internecine.

Adv. *flagrante bello,* in the -thick of the fray, – cannon's mouth; at the -sword's point, – point of the bayonet.

Int. *væ victis!* to arms! to your tents O Israel!

Phr. the battle rages.

peace-offering; olive-branch; overtures; pipe –, calumet –, preliminaries- of peace.

truce, armistice; suspension of -arms, – hostilities; breathing-time; convention; *modus vivendi*; flag of truce, white flag, *parlementaire, cartel.*

hollow truce, *pax in bello*; drawn battle.

V. pacify, tranquillize, compose; allay &c. (*moderate*) 174; reconcile, propitiate, placate, conciliate, meet half-way, hold out the olive-branch, heal the breach, make peace, restore harmony, bring to terms.

settle –, arrange –, accommodate- -matters, – differences; set straight; make up a quarrel, *tantas componere lites*; come to -an understanding, – terms; bridge over, hush up; make -it, – matters- up; shake hands.

raise a siege; put up –, sheathe- the sword; bury the hatchet, lay down one's arms, turn swords into ploughshares; smoke the calumet of peace, close the temple of Janus; keep the peace &c. (*concord*) 714; be -pacified &c.; come round.

Adj. conciliatory, pacificatory; composing &c. *v.*; pacified &c. *v.*

Phr. *requiescat in pace.*

———

724. Mediation.—N. media-tion, -torship, -tization; inter-vention, -position, -ference, -meddling, -cession; parley, negotiation, arbitration; flag of truce &c. 723; good offices, peace-offering; diploma-tics, -cy; compromise &c. 774.

mediator, intercessor, peacemaker, make-peace, negotiator, go-between; diplomatist &c. (*consignee*) 758; moderator, propitiator, umpire, arbitrator.

V. media-te, -tize; inter-cede, -pose, -fere, -vene; step in, negotiate; meet half-way; arbitrate; *magnas componere lites.*

Adj. mediatory, propitiatory, diplomatic.

725. Submission.—N. submission, yielding, acquiescence, compliance; non-resistance; obedience &c. 743; submissiveness, deference.

surrender, cession, capitulation, resignation.

obeisance, homage, kneeling, genuflexion, courtesy, curtsy, *salaam, kowtow*, prostration.

V. succumb, submit, yield, bend, resign, defer to, accede.

lay down –, deliver up- one's arms; hand over one's sword; lower –, haul down –, strike- one's flag, – colours; deliver the keys of the city.

surrender, – at discretion; cede, capitulate, come to terms, retreat, beat a retreat; draw in one's horns &c. (*humility*) 879; give -way, – ground, – in, – up; cave in; suffer judgment by default; bend, – to one's yoke, – before the storm; reel back; bend –, knuckle- -down, – to, – under; knock under.

humble oneself; eat -dirt, – the leek, – humble pie; bite –, lick- the dust; be –, fall- at one's feet; craven; crouch before, throw oneself at the feet of; swallow the -leek, – pill; kiss the rod; turn the other cheek; *avaler des couleuvres*, gulp down.

obey &c. 743; kneel to, bow to, pay homage to, cringe to, truckle to; bend the -neck, – knee; kneel, fall on one's knees, bow submission, courtesy, curtsy, *kowtow*; make obeisance.

pocket the affront; make -the best of, – a virtue of necessity; grin and abide, shrug the shoulders, resign oneself; submit with a good grace &c. (*bear with*) 826.

Adj. surrendering &c. *v.*; submissive, resigned, crouching; down-trodden; down on one's marrow bones; on one's bended knee; weak-kneed, un-, non-resisting; pliant &c. (*soft*) 324; undefended.

untenable, indefensible; humble &c. 879.

Phr. have it your own way; it can't be helped; amen &c. (*assent*) 488.

726. Combatant.—N. combatant; disputant, controversialist, polemic, litigant, belligerent; competitor, rival, corrival; fighter, assailant, aggressor; champion, Paladin; moss-trooper, swashbuckler, fire-eater, duellist, bully, bludgeon-man, rough, fighter, fighting-man, prize-fighter, pugilist, pug, boxer, bruiser, the fancy, gladiator, athlete, wrestler; fighting-, game-cock; swordsman, *sabreur.*

warrior, soldier, Amazon, man-at-arms, armigerent; campaigner, veteran; red-coat, military man, *rajpoot*, brave.

armed force, troops, soldiery, military, forces, sabaoth, the army, standing army, regulars, the line, troops of the line, militia, territorials, yeomanry, volunteers, trainband, fencible; auxiliary –, reserve- forces; reserves, *posse comitatus*, national guard, *gendarme*, beefeater; guards, -man; yeoman of the guard, life guards, household troops.

janissary; myrmidon; Mama-, Mame-luke; spahee, *spahi*, Cossack,

Croat, Pandour; irregular, free lance, *franc-tireur*, *bashi-bazouk*, *guerilla*, *condottiere*; mercenary.

levy, draught, commando; *Land-wehr*, *-sturm*; conscript, recruit, rookie, cadet, raw levies.

private, – soldier; Tommy Atkins, rank and file, peon, trooper, doughboy, sepoy, *askari*, *légionnaire*, legionary, food for powder, cannon fodder; officer &c. (*commander*) 745; subaltern, ensign, shave-tail, standard bearer, non-com; spear-, pike-man; halberdier, lancer; musketeer, carabineer, rifleman, sharpshooter, yager, skirmisher; grenadier, fusileer; archer, bowman.

horse and foot; horse –, foot- soldier; cavalry, horse, artillery, horse –, field –, heavy –, mountain- artillery, infantry, light horse, *voltigeur*, *Uhlan*, mounted rifles, dragoon, hussar, trooper; light –, heavy-dragoon; heavy; *cuirassier*; gunner, cannoneer, bombardier, artilleryman, matross; sapper, – and miner; engineer; light infantry, rifles, *chasseur*, *zouave*; military train, supply and transport, coolie.

army, – corps, *corps d'armée*, host, division, column, wing, detachment, *escadrille*, garrison, flying column, brigade, regiment, *corps*, battalion, squadron, company, platoon, battery, subdivision, section, squad; piquet, picket, guard, rank, file; legion, phalanx, cohort; cloud of skirmishers; impi.

war-horse, charger, *destrier*.

armoured -train, – car; tank.

marine, man of war's man &c. (*sailor*) 269; navy, first line of defence, wooden walls; naval forces, fleet, flotilla, armada, squadron.

man-of-war, warship; H.M.S., U.S.S.; capital ship; line-of-battle ship, battle ship; super-, dreadnought, battle –, armoured –, protected – light- cruiser; scout, flotilla leader; destroyer, torpedo boat; submarine, submersible, U-boat; submarine chaser, eagle boat, mystery ship, Q-boat; mine-layer, -sweeper; ship of the line, iron-clad, turret-ship, ram, Monitor, floating battery; first-rate, frigate, sloop of war, corvette, gunboat, bomb-vessel, fire-boat; flag ship, guard ship, cruiser; airplane carrier; privateer; tender; depôt –, parent- ship; store –, troop- ship; transport, catamaran.

aircraft &c. 273, air force, scout, fighter, bomber, troop carrier, aerial patrol, seaplane, flying boat, torpedo plane; airship, Zeppelin; rigid –, semi-rigid –, non-rigid- airship; dirigible –, free –, captive –, kite –, observation- balloon.

anti-aircraft guns, searchlights, sound locators; catapult.

727. Arms.—N. arm, -s; weapon, deadly weapon; arma-ment, -ture; panoply, stand of arms; armour &c. (*defence*) 717; armoury &c. (*store*) 636.

ammunition; powder, – and shot; explosive; propellant; gun-powder, -cotton; dynam-, melin-, cord-, lydd-ite; trinitrotoluene, T.N.T., ammonal; cartridge; ball cartridge, *cartouche*, fire-ball; dud, black Maria; 'villainous saltpetre'; poison –, mustard –, lachrymatory –, tear- gas.

sword, sabre, broadsword, cutlass, falchion, scimitar, cimeter, brand, whinyard, bilbo, glaive, glave, rapier, skean, Toledo, Ferrara, tuck, claymore, creese, kris, *kukri*, dagger, dirk, hanger, poniard, stiletto, stylet, dudgeon, bayonet; sword-bayonet, -stick; side arms, foil, blade, steel; axe, bill; pole-, battle-axe; gisarm, halberd, partisan, tomahawk, bowie-knife; at-, att-, yat-aghan; yatachan; good –, trusty –, naked-sword; cold –, naked- steel.

club, mace, truncheon, staff, bludgeon, cudgel, life-preserver, shillelagh, sprig; hand-, quarter-staff; bat, cane, stick, knuckle-duster, sand bag.

gun, piece; fire-arms; artillery, ordnance; siege –, battering-train; park, battery; cannon, gun of position, heavy –, siege –, field –, mountain –, anti-aircraft –, breech loading –, quick firing- gun; field piece, mortar, trench mortar, mine thrower, howitzer, carronade, culverin, basilisk; falconet, jingal, swivel, *pederero*, *bouche à feu*; smooth bore, rifled cannon; Armstrong –, Lancaster –, Paixhan –, Whitworth –, Parrott –, Krupp –, Gatling –, Maxim –, Vickers –, Hotchkiss –, Lewis –, machine- gun; tommy gun, Thompson's submachine gun; *mitrailleu-r*, *-se*; pompom; blow pipe.

small arms; musket, -ry, firelock, flintlock, fowling-piece, shot gun, rifle, *fusil*, caliver, carbine, blunderbuss, musketoon, Brown Bess, matchlock, harquebuss, *arquebuse*, haguebut; petronel; smallbore; breech-, muzzle-loader; Miniè –, Enfield –, Westley Richards –, Snider –, Springfield –, Martini-Henry –, Lee-Metford –, Lee-Enfield –, Mauser –, Männlicher –, magazine –, repeating- rifle; needle-gun, *chassepot*; pistol, -et; revolver, automatic pistol, automatic; wind-, air-gun; flame –, gas-projector.

bow, cross-bow, arbalest, balister, catapult, sling; battering-ram &c. (*impulse*) 276; gunnery; ballistics &c. (*propulsion*) 284.

missile, bolt, projectile, shot, pellet, ball; grape; grape –, canister –, bar –, cannon –, langrel –, langrage –, round –, chain- shot; explosive; incendiary –, expanding –, soft-nosed –, dum-dum- bullet; slug, stone, brickbat; hand –, rifle- grenade; high explosive –, incendiary –, star –, gas- shell; depth –, gas –, incendiary –, stink- bomb; petard, torpedo, carcass, rocket; congreve, – rocket; shrapnel, *mitraille*; thunderbolt; mine, land mine, infernal machine.

pike, lance, spear, spontoon, javelin, assagai, throwing stick, dart, djerrid, arrow, reed, shaft, bolt, boomerang, harpoon, gaff.

728. Arena.—N. arena, field, platform; scene of action, theatre; walk, course; hustings; stage, boards &c. (*playhouse*) 599; amphitheatre; Coli-, Colos-seum; Flavian amphitheatre, hippodrome, circus, race-course, track, *stadium*, *corso*, turf, cockpit, bear-garden, playground, playing fields, *gymnasium*, *palæstra*, ring, lists; tilt-yard, -ing ground; *Campus Martius*, *Champ de Mars*; aerodrome, airport, air base, flying field.

theatre –, seat- of war; battle-field, -ground; field of -battle, – slaughter; no man's land; Aceldama, camp; the enemy's camp; trysting-place &c. (*place of meeting*) 74.

Section V. Results of Voluntary Action

729. Completion.—N. completion; accomplish-, achieve-, fulfil-ment; performance, execution; des-, dis-patch; consummation, culmination, climax; finish, conclusion, effectuation; close &c. (*end*) 67; terminus &c. (*arrival*) 292; winding up; *finale*, *dénouement*, catastrophe, issue, upshot, result; final –, last –, crowning –, finishing- -touch, – stroke; last finish, *coup de grâce*;

730. Non-Completion.—N. non-completion, -fulfilment; shortcoming &c. 304; incompleteness &c. 53; drawn -battle, – game; work of Penelope, task of Sisyphus.

non-performance, inexecution; neglect &c. 460.

V. not -complete &c. 729; leave -unfinished &c. *adj.*, – undone; neglect &c. 460; let -alone, – slip; lose sight of.

crowning of the edifice; coping-, keystone; missing link &c. 53; superstructure, *ne plus ultra*, work done, *fait accompli*.

elaboration; finality; completeness &c. 52.

V. effect, -uate; accomplish, achieve, compass, consummate, hammer out; bring to -maturity, – perfection; perfect, complete; elaborate.

do, execute, make; go –, get- through; work out, enact; bring -about, – to bear, – to pass, – through, – to a head.

des-, dis-patch; knock –, finish –, polish- off; make short work of; dispose of, set at rest; perform, discharge, fulfil, realize; put in -practice, – force; carry -out, – into effect, – into execution; make good; be as good as one's word.

do thoroughly, not do by halves, go the whole hog; drive home; be in at the death &c. (*persevere*) 604*a*; carry through, play out, exhaust, deliver the goods, fill the bill.

finish, bring to a close &c. (*end*) 67; wind up, stamp, clinch, seal, set the seal on, put the seal to; give the -final touch &c. *n.* to; put the -last, – finishing- hand to; crown, – all; cap.

ripen, culminate; come to a -head, – crisis; come to its end; die -a natural death, – of old age; run -its course, – one's race; touch –, reach –, attain- the goal; reach &c. (*arrive*) 292; get in the harvest.

Adj. completing, final; conclu-ding, -sive; crowning &c. *v.*; exhaustive, complete, mature, perfect, consummate.

done, completed &c. *v.*; done for, sped, wrought out; highly wrought &c. (*preparation*) 673; thorough &c. 52; ripe &c. (*ready*) 673.

Adv. completely &c. (*thoroughly*) 52; to crown all, out of hand.

Phr. the race is run; *actum est*; *finis coronat opus*; *consummatum est*; *c'en est fait*; it is all over; the game is played out, the bubble has burst.

fall short of &c. 304; do things by halves; scotch the snake, not kill it; hang fire; be slow to; collapse &c. 304.

Adj. not completed &c. *v.*; incomplete &c. 53; uncompleted, unfinished, unaccomplished, unperformed, unexecuted; sketchy, addle.

in progress, in hand; going on, proceeding; on one's hands; on the fire; on the stocks; in preparation; lacking the finishing touch.

Adv. *re infectâ*.

————

731. Success.—**N.** success, -fulness; speed; advance &c. (*progress*) 282.

trump card; hit, stroke; lucky –, fortunate –, good- -hit, – stroke; bold –, master- stroke; *coup de maître*, checkmate; half the battle, prize; profit &c. (*acquisition*) 775; best seller.

continued success; good fortune &c. (*prosperity*) 734; time well spent.

advantage over; edge; upper-, whiphand; ascendancy, mastery; expugnation, conquest, victory, subdual; subjugation &c. (*subjection*) 749.

triumph &c. (*exultation*) 884; proficiency &c. (*skill*) 698; conqueror, victor, winner, champion; master of the -situation, – position.

V. succeed; be -successful &c. *adj.*;

732. Failure. — **N.** failure; nonsuccess, -fulfilment; dead failure, successlessness; abortion, miscarriage; *brutum fulmen* &c. 158; labour in vain &c. (*inutility*) 645; no go; inefficacy; inefficaciousness &c. *adj.*; vain –, ineffectual –, abortive- -attempt, – efforts; flash in the pan, 'lame and impotent conclusion'; frustration; slip 'twixt cup and lip &c. (*disappointment*) 509.

blunder &c. (*mistake*) 495; fault, omission, miss, oversight, slip, trip, stumble, claudication, footfall; false –, wrong- step; *faux pas*, titubation, *bévue*, *faute*, lurch; botchery &c. (*want of skill*) 699; scrape, jam, mess, muddle, foozle, *fiasco*, breakdown.

mishap &c. (*misfortune*) 735; split,

gain one's -end, – ends; crown with success.

gain –, attain –, carry –, secure –, win- -a point, – an object; put over; make a go of; manage to, contrive to; accomplish &c. (*effect, complete*) 729; do –, work- wonders.

come off -well, – successfully, – with flying colours; make short work of; take –, carry- by storm; bear away the bell; win -one's spurs, – the battle; win –, carry –, gain- the -day, – prize, – palm; climb on the bandwagon; have -the best of it, – it all one's own way, – the game in one's own hands, – the ball at one's feet, – one on the hip; walk over the course; carry all before one, remain in possession of the field; score a success, win hands down.

speed; make progress &c. (*advance*) 282; win –, make –, work –, find- one's way; strive to some purpose; prosper &c. 734; drive a roaring trade; make profit &c. (*acquire*) 775; reap –, gather- the -fruits, – benefit of, – harvest; make one's fortune, get in the harvest, turn to good account; turn to account &c. (*use*) 677.

triumph, be triumphant; gain –, obtain- -a victory, – an advantage; chain victory to one's car.

surmount –, overcome –, get over- -a difficulty, – an obstacle &c. 706; *se tirer d'affaire*; make head against; stem the -torrent, – tide, – current; weather -the storm, – a point; turn a corner, keep one's head above water, tide over; master; get –, have –, gain- the -better of, – best of, – upper hand, – ascendancy, – whip hand, – start of; distance; surpass &c. (*superiority*) 33.

defeat, conquer, vanquish, discomfit; over-come, throw, -power, -master, -match, -set, -ride, -reach; out-wit, -do, -flank, -manœuvre, -general, -vote; take the wind out of one's adversary's sails; beat, – hollow; rout, lick, drub, floor, worst; put -down, – to flight, – to the rout, – *hors de combat*, – out of court.

silence, quell, nonsuit, checkmate, upset, confound, nonplus, trump; baffle &c. (*hinder*) 706; circumvent, elude; trip up, – the heels of; drive

collapse, smash, blow, explosion. repulse, rebuff, defeat, rout, over-throw, discomfiture; beating, drubbing; *quietus*, nonsuit, subjugation; check-, fool's-mate.

fall, downfall, ruin, perdition; wreck &c. (*destruction*) 162; death-blow; bankruptcy &c. (*non-payment*) 808.

losing game, *affaire flambée*.

victim, prey; bankrupt.

V. fail; be -unsuccessful &c. *adj.*; not -succeed &c. 731; make -vain efforts &c. *n.*; do –, labour –, toil- in vain; lose one's labour, take nothing by one's motion; bring to naught, make nothing of; wash a blackamoor white &c. (*impossible*) 471; roll the stone of Sisyphus &c. (*useless*) 645; do by halves &c. (*not complete*) 730; lose ground &c. (*recede*) 283; flunk; fall short of &c. 304.

miss, – one's aim, – the mark, – one's footing, – stays; slip, trip, stumble; make a -slip &c. *n.*, – blunder &c. 495, – mess of, – botch of; bitch it, mis-carry, abort, go up like a rocket and come down like the stick, reckon with-out one's host; get the wrong sow by the ear &c. (*blunder, mismanage*) 699.

limp, halt, hobble, titubate; fall, tumble; lose one's balance; fall -to the ground, – between two stools; flounder, falter, stick in the mud, run aground, split upon a rock; run –, knock –, dash- one's head against a stone wall; break one's back; break down, sink, drown, founder, have the ground cut from under one; get into -trouble, – a mess, – a scrape; come to grief &c. (*adversity*) 735; go to -the wall, – the dogs, – pot; lick –, bite- the dust; be -defeated &c. 731; have the worst of it, lose the day, come off second best, lose; fall a prey to; succumb &c. (*submit*) 725; not have a leg to stand on.

come to nothing, end in smoke; fall -to the ground, – through, – dead, – still-born, – flat; slip through one's fingers; hang –, miss- fire; flash in the pan, collapse; topple down &c. (*descent*) 305; go to wrack and ruin &c. (*destruction*) 162.

go amiss, go wrong, go cross, go hard with, go on a wrong tack; go on –,

-into a corner, – to the wall; run hard, put one's nose out of joint.

settle, do for; break the -neck of, – back of; capsize, sink, shipwreck, drown, swamp; subdue; subjugate &c. (*subject*) 749; reduce; make the enemy bite the dust; victimize, roll in the dust, trample under foot, put an extinguisher upon.

answer, – the purpose; avail, prevail, take effect, do, turn out well, work well, take, tell, bear fruit; hit -it, – the mark, – the right nail on the head; nick it; turn up trumps, make a hit; find one's account in.

Adj. succeeding &c. *v.*; successful; prosperous &c. 734; triumphant; flushed –, crowned- with success; victorious; set up; in the ascendant; unbeaten &c. (*see* beat &c. *v.*); well-spent; felicitous, effective, in full swing.

Adv. successfully &c. *adj.*; with flying colours, in triumph, swimmingly; *à merveille*, beyond all hope; to some –, good- purpose; to one's heart's content.

Phr. *veni vidi vici*, the day being one's own, one's star in the ascendant; *omne tulit punctum*.

come off –, turn out –, work- ill; take -a wrong, – an ugly- turn; gang agley.

be all -over with, – up with; explode; dash one's hopes &c. (*disappoint*) 509; defeat the purpose; upset the apple cart; sow the wind and reap the whirlwind, jump out of the frying pan into the fire.

Adj. unsuccessful, successless; failing, tripping &c. *v.*; at fault; unfortunate &c. 735.

abortive, addle, still-born; fruitless, sterile, bootless; ineffect-ual, -ive; inefficient &c. (*impotent*) 158; inefficacious; lame, hobbling, *décousu*; insufficient &c. 640; unavailing &c. (*useless*) 645; of no effect.

aground, grounded, swamped, stranded, cast away, wrecked, foundered, capsized, shipwrecked, non-suited; foiled; defeated &c. 731; struck –, borne –, broken- down; down-trodden; over-borne, -whelmed; all up with; beaten to a frazzle.

lost, undone, ruined, broken; bankrupt &c. (*not paying*) 808; played out; done -up, – for; dead beat, ruined root and branch, *flambé*, knocked on the head; destroyed &c. 162.

frustrated, thwarted, crossed, unhinged, disconcerted, dashed; thrown -off one's balance, – on one's back, – on one's beam ends; unhorsed, in a sorry plight; hard hit.

stultified, befooled, dished, hoist on one's own.petard; victimized, sacrificed.

wide of the mark &c. (*error*) 495; out of one's reckoning &c. (*inexpectation*) 508; left in the lurch; thrown away &c. (*wasted*) 638; unattained; uncompleted &c. 730.

Adv. unsuccessfully &c. *adj.*; to little or no purpose, in vain, *re infectâ*.

Phr. the bubble has burst, the game is up, all is lost; the devil to pay; *parturiunt montes* &c. (*disappointment*) 509.

733. Trophy.—N. trophy; medal, prize, palm; ribbon, blue ribbon, *cordon bleu*; citation; cup; laurel, -s; bays, crown, chaplet, wreath, civic crown; Victoria Cross, V.C., *Croix de Guerre*, Iron Cross; Distinguished Service Cross, Medal of Honor, Congressional Medal; insignia &c. 550; feather in one's cap &c. (*honour*) 873; decoration &c. 877; garland, triumphal arch.

triumph &c. (*celebration*) 883; flying colours &c. (*show*) 882.
monumentum ære perennius.

734. Prosperity.—N. prosperity, welfare, well-being; affluence &c. (*wealth*) 803; success &c. 731; thrift, roaring

735. Adversity.—N. adversity, evil &c. 619; failure &c. 732; bad –, ill –, evil –, adverse –, hard- -fortune, – hap,

trade; chicken in every pot, the full dinner pail; good –, smiles of- fortune; blessings, godsend.

luck; good –, run of- luck; sunshine; fair -weather, – wind; palmy –, bright –, halcyon- days; piping times, tide, flood, high tide.

Saturnia regna, Saturnian age; golden -time, – age; bed of roses; fat of the land, milk and honey, loaves and fishes, fleshpots of Egypt.

made man, lucky dog, *enfant gâté*, spoiled child of fortune.

upstart, *parvenu*, *nouveau riche*, profiteer, skipjack, mushroom.

V. prosper, thrive, flourish; be -prosperous &c. *adj.*; drive a roaring trade; go on -well, – smoothly, – swimmingly; sail before the wind, swim with the tide; run -smooth, – smoothly, – on all fours.

rise –, get on- in the world; work –, make- one's way; look up; lift –, raise- one's head, make one's -fortune, – pile, feather one's nest.

flower, blow, blossom, bloom, fructify, bear fruit, fatten, batten.

keep oneself afloat; keep –, hold- one's head above water; light –, fall- on one's -legs, – feet; drop into a good thing; bear a charmed life; bask in the sunshine; have a -good, – fine- time of it; have a run, – of luck; have the -good fortune &c. *n.* to; take a favour- able turn; live -on the fat of the land, – in clover.

Adj. prosperous; thriving &c. *v.*; in a fair way, buoyant; well -off, – to do, – to do in the world; set up, at one's -ease; rich &c. 803; in good case; in -full, – high- feather; fortunate, lucky, in luck; born -with a silver spoon in one's mouth, – under a lucky star; on the sunny side of the hedge.

auspicious, propitious, providential.

palmy, halcyon; agreeable &c. 829; *couleur de rose.*

Adv. prosperously &c. *adj.*; swim- mingly; as good luck would have it; beyond all -expectation, – hope, – one's wildest dreams.

Phr. one's star in the ascendant, all for the best, one's course runs smooth.

– luck, – lot; frowns of fortune; evil -dispensation, – star, – genius; ups and downs of life, broken fortunes; hard -case, – lines, – life; sea -, peck- of troubles; hell upon earth; slough of despond; jinx.

trouble, humiliation, hardship, curse, blight, blast, load, pressure.

pressure of the times, iron age, evil day, time out of joint; hard -, bad -, sad- times; rainy day, cloud, dark cloud, gathering clouds, ill wind; visitation, infliction; affliction &c. (*painfulness*) 830; bitter -pill, – cup; care, trial; the sport of fortune.

mis-hap, -chance, -adventure, -fortune; disaster, calamity, catastrophe; accident, casualty, cross, reverse, check, *contretemps*, rub, pinch, setback.

losing game; falling &c. *v.*; fall, down-fall, come-down; ruin-ation, -ousness; undoing; extremity; ruin &c. (*destruction*) 162.

V. be -ill off &c. *adj.*; go hard with; fall on evil, – days; go on ill; not -prosper &c. 734.

go -downhill, – to rack and ruin &c. (*destruction*) 162, – to the dogs; fall, – from one's high estate; decay, sink, decline, go down in the world; have seen better days; bring down one's grey hairs with sorrow to the grave; come to grief; be all -over, – up- with; bring a -wasp's, – hornet's- nest about one's ears.

Adj. unfortunate, unblest, unhappy, unlucky; im-, un-prosperous; luck-, hap-less; out of luck; in trouble, in a bad way, in an evil plight; under a cloud; clouded; ill -, badly- off; in adverse circumstances; poor &c. 804; behindhand, down in the world, decayed, undone; on the road to ruin, on its last legs, on the wane; in one's utmost need.

planet-struck, devoted; born -under an evil star, – with a wooden ladle in one's mouth; ill-fated, -starred, -omened; inconspicuous, ominous, doomed, unpropitious.

adverse, untoward; disastrous, calamitous, ruinous, dire, deplorable.

Adv. if the worst come to the worst, as ill luck would have it, from bad to worse, out of the frying pan into the fire.

Phr. one's star is on the wane; one's luck -turns, – fails; the game is up, one's doom is sealed, the ground crumbles under one's feet, *sic transit gloria mundi, tant va la cruche à l'eau qu'à la fin elle se casse.*

736. Mediocrity.—N. moderate –, average- circumstances; respectability; middle classes, *bourgeoisie*; mediocrity; golden mean &c. (*midcourse*) 628, (*moderation*) 174.

V. jog on; go –, get on- -fairly, – quietly, – peaceably, – tolerably, – respectably; steer a middle course &c. 628.

Adj. middling, so-so, fair, medium, moderate, mediocre, second-, third- &c. -rate.

Division (II). INTERSOCIAL VOLITION*

Section I. General Intersocial Volition

737. Authority.—N. authority; influence, patronage, power, preponderance, credit, *prestige*, prerogative, jurisdiction; right &c. (*title*) 924.

divine right, dynastic rights, authoritativeness; absolut-eness, -ism; despotism, tyranny; *jus nocendi.*

command, empire, sway, rule; domin-ion, -ation; sovereignty, supremacy, suzerainty; lord-, head-ship; chiefdom; seignior-y, -ity, hegemony, patriarchate, patriarchy; master-y, -ship, -dom; government &c. (*direction*) 693; dictation, control.

hold, grasp; grip, -e; reach; iron sway &c. (*severity*) 739; fangs, clutches, talons; rod of empire &c. (*sceptre*) 747.

reign, regnancy, *régime*, dynasty; director-, dictator-ship; protector-ate, -ship; caliphate, pashalic, electorate; presiden-cy, -tship; administration; pro-, consulship; prefecture; seneschalship; magistra-ture, -cy; raj.

empire; monarchy; king-hood, -ship; royalty, regality, autocracy, monocracy, arist-archy, -ocracy; oligarchy, democracy, demogogy; republic, -anism, federalism; socialism, collectivism; communism, bolshevism, syndicalism; mob law, mobocracy, ochlocracy, ergatocracy; *vox populi, imperium in imperio*; bureaucracy; beadle-, bumble-dom; stratocracy; martial law, military -power, – government; feodality, feudal system, feudalism.

Thearchy, diarchy; du-, tri-, heter-archy; du-, tri-umvirate; auto-cracy, -nomy; limited monarchy; constitutional -government, – monarchy; home rule, autonomy; self-government, -determination; representative government; Soviet government.

738. [Absence of authority.] Laxity. —N. laxity; lax-, loose-, slack-ness; toleration &c. (*lenity*) 740; freedom &c. 748.

anarchy, interregnum; relaxation; loosening &c. *v.*; remission; dead letter, *brutum fulmen*, misrule; licence, licentiousness; insubordination &c. (*disobedience*) 742; lynch law &c. (*illegality*) 964; nihilism.

[Deprivation of power] dethronement, deposition, usurpation, abdication.

V. be -lax &c. *adj.*; *laisser -faire, – aller*; hold a loose rein; give -the reins to, – rope enough, – a loose to; tolerate; relax; misrule.

go beyond the length of one's tether; have one's -swing, – fling; act without -instructions, – authority; act on one's own responsibility, usurp authority.

dethrone, depose; abdicate.

Adj. lax, loose; slack; remiss &c. (*careless*) 460; weak.

relaxed; licensed; reinless, unbridled; anarchical; unauthorized &c. (*unwarranted*) 925.

* Implying the action of the will of one mind over the will of another.

gyn-archy, -ocracy, -æocracy; petticoat government, matri-archate, matriarchy.

[Vicarious authority] commission &c. 755; deputy &c. 759; permission &c. 760.

country, state, realm, commonwealth, canton, constituency, toparchy, municipality, polity, body politic, *posse comitatus.*

person in authority &c. (*master*) 745; judicature &c. 965; cabinet &c. (*council*) 696; usurper; seat of -government, – authority; head-quarters.

[Acquisition of authority] accession; installation &c. 755; usurpation.

V. authorize &c. (*permit*) 760; warrant &c. (*right*) 924; dictate &c. (*order*) 741; have –, hold –, possess –, exercise –, exert –, wield--authority &c. *n.*

be -at the head of &c. *adj.*; hold –, be in –, fill an- office; hold –, occupy- a post; be -master &c. 745.

rule, sway, command, control, administer; govern &c. (*direct*) 693; lead, preside over, reign; possess –, be seated on –, occupy-the throne; sway –, wield- the sceptre; wear the crown.

have –, get- the -upper, – whip- hand; gain a hold upon, pre-ponderate, dominate, boss, rule the roost; over-ride, -rule, -awe; lord it over, hold in hand, keep under, make a puppet of, lead by the nose, hold in the hollow of one's hand, turn round one's little finger, bend to one's will, hold one's own, wear the breeches; have -the ball at one's feet, – it all one's own way, – the game in one's own hand, – on the hip, – under one's thumb; be master of the situation; take the lead, play first fiddle, set the fashion; give the law to; carry with a high hand; lay down the law; 'ride in the whirl-wind and direct the storm'; rule with a rod of iron &c. (*severity*) 739.

ascend –, mount- the throne, take the reins, – into one's hand; assume -authority &c. *n.*, – the reins of government; take –, assume the- command.

be -governed by, – in the power of; be under -the rule of, – the domination of.

Adj. ruling &c. *v.*; regnant, at the head, dominant, paramount, supreme, predominant, preponderant, in the ascendant, influential; gubernatorial; imperious; authoritative, executive, administrative, clothed with authority, official, *ex officio*, ministerial, bureaucratic, departmental, imperative, peremptory, overruling, absolute; hege-monic, -al; arbitrary; compulsory &c. 744; stringent.

regal, sovereign; royal, -ist; monarchical, kingly; imperial, -istic; princely; feudal; aristo-, auto-cratic; oligarchic &c. *n.*; democratic, republican, dynastic.

at one's command; in one's -power, – grasp; under control; authorized &c. (*due*) 924.

Adv. in the name of, by the authority of, *de par le Roi*, in virtue of; under the auspices of, in the hands of.

at one's pleasure; by a -dash, – stroke- of the pen; *ex mero motu*; *ex cathedrâ.*

Phr. the grey mare the better horse; 'every inch a king.'

---

739. Severity.—N. severity; strict-ness, formalism, harshness &c. *adj.*; rigour, stringency, austerity; inclem-

740. Lenity. — N. leni-ty, -ence, -ency; moderation &c. 174; toler-ance, -ation; mildness, gentleness; favour;

ency &c. (*pitilessness*) 914a; arrogance &c. 885.

arbitrary power; absolut-, despotism; dictatorship, autocracy, tyranny, domineering, oppression; assumption, usurpation; inquisition, reign of terror, martial law; iron -heel, – rule, – hand, – sway; tight grasp; brute -force, – strength; coercion &c. 744; strong –, tight- hand.

hard -lines, – measure; tender mercies [ironical]; sharp practice; bureaucracy, red tape; pipe-clay, officialism.

tyrant, disciplinarian, martinet, stickler, formalist, bashaw, despot, hard master, Draco, oppressor, inquisitor, extortioner, harpy, vulture, bird of prey.

V. be -severe &c. *adj.*

assume, usurp, arrogate, take liberties; domineer, bully &c. 885; tyrannize, inflict, wreak, stretch a point, put on the screw; be hard upon; bear –, lay- a heavy hand on; be –, come- down upon; illtreat; deal -hardly with, – hard measure to; rule with a rod of iron, chastise with scorpions; dye with blood; oppress, override; trample –, tread- -down, – upon, – under foot; crush under an iron heel, ride roughshod over; rivet the yoke; hold –, keep- a tight hand; force down the throat; coerce &c. 744; give no quarter &c. (*pitiless*) 914a.

Adj. severe; strict, hard, harsh, dour, rigid, stiff, stern, rigorous, uncompromising, exacting, exigent, *exigeant*, inexorable, inflexible, obdurate, austere, relentless, Spartan, Draconian, stringent, straitlaced, puritanical, prudish, searching, unsparing, ironhanded, hardheaded, peremptory, absolute, positive, arbitrary, imperative; coercive &c. 744; tyrannical, despotic, masterful, extortionate, grinding, withering, oppressive, inquisitorial; inclement &c. (*ruthless*) 914a; cruel &c. (*malevolent*) 907; haughty, arrogant &c. 885.

Adv. severely &c. *adj.*; with a -high, – strong, – tight, – heavy-hand.

at the point of the -sword, – bayonet.

Phr. *Delirant reges plectuntur Achivi.*

indulgen-ce, -cy; clemency, mercy, forbearance, quarter; compassion &c. 914.

V. be -lenient &c. *adj.*; tolerate, bear with; *parcere subjectis*, give quarter.

indulge, allow one to have his own way, spoil.

Adj. lenient; mild, – as milk; gentle, soft; tolerant, indulgent, easy-going; clement &c. (*compassionate*) 914; forbearing; complaisant, long-suffering.

---

741. Command.—N. command, order, ordinance, act, *fiat*, bidding, *dictum*, hest, behest, call, beck, nod.

des-, dis-patch; message, direction, injunction, charge, instructions; appointment, fixture.

demand, exaction, imposition, requisition, claim, reclamation, revendication; *ultimatum* &c. (*terms*) 770; request &c. 765; requirement.

dictation; dict-, mand-ate; *caveat*, decree, decree -nisi, – absolute, *senatus consultum*; precept; pre-, re-script; writ, ordination, bull, edict, decretal, dispensation, prescription, brevet, placet, ukase, *firman*, hattisheriff, warrant, passport, *mittimus*, *mandamus*, summons, subpœna, *nisi prius*, interpellation, citation; word, – of command; *mot d'ordre*; bugle –, trumpet- call; beat of drum, tattoo; order of the day; enactment &c. (*law*) 963; *plébiscite* &c. (*choice*) 609.

V. command, order, decree, enact, ordain, dictate, direct, give orders.

prescribe, set, appoint, mark out; set –, prescribe –, impose- a task; set to work, put in requisition &c. 926.

bid, enjoin, charge, call upon, instruct; require, – at the hands of; exact, impose, tax, task; demand; insist on &c. (*compel*) 744.

claim, lay claim to, revendicate, reclaim.

cite, summon; call –, send- for; subpœna; beckon.

issue a command; make –, issue –, promulgate- -a requisition, – a decree, – an order &c. *n.*; give the -word of command, – word, – signal; call to order; give –, lay down- the law; assume the command &c. (*authority*) 737; remand.

be -ordered &c.; receive an order &c. *n.*

Adj. commanding &c. *v.*; authoritative &c. 737; decret-ory, -ive, -al; imperative, jussive, decisive, final.

Adv. in a commanding tone; by a -stroke, – dash- of the pen; by order, at beat of drum, on the first summons; at the word of command.

Phr. the decree is gone forth; *sic volo sic jubeo*; *le Roi le veut.*

---

742. Disobedience.—N. disobedience, insubordination, contumacy; infraction, -fringement; violation, non-compliance; non-observance &c. 773.

revolt, rebellion, mutiny, outbreak, rising, uprising, putsch, insurrection, *émeute*; riot, tumult &c. (*disorder*) 59; strike &c. (*resistance*) 719; barring out; defiance &c. 715.

mutinousness &c. *adj.*; mutineering; sedition, treason; high –, petty –, misprision of- treason; *premunire*; *lèse-majesté*; violation of law &c. 964; defection, secession, revolution, *sabotage*, bolshevism, *Sinn Fein*.

insurgent, mutineer, rebel, revolter, rioter, traitor, *carbonaro*, *sansculottes*, red republican, communist, Fenian, chartist, *frondeur*; seceder, runagate, brawler, anarchist, demagogue; suffragette; Spartacus, Masaniello, Wat Tyler, Jack Cade; bolshevist, bolshevik, maximalist, ringleader.

V. disobey, violate, infringe; shirk; set at defiance &c. (*defy*) 715; set authority at naught, run riot, fly in the face of, bolt, take the law into one's own hands; kick over the traces.

turn –, run- restive; champ the bit; strike &c. (*resist*) 719; rise, – in arms; secede; mutiny, rebel.

Adj. disobedient; uncompl-ying, -iant; unsubmissive, unruly, ungovernable; insubordinate, impatient of control; rest-iff, -ive; refractory, contumacious; recusant &c. (*refuse*) 764; recalcitrant; resisting &c. 719; lawless, mutinous, seditious, insurgent, riotous, revolutionary.

disobeyed, unobeyed; unbidden.

743. Obedience.—N. obedience; observance &c. 772; compliance; submission &c. 725; subjection &c. 749; non-resistance; passiveness, passivity, resignation.

allegiance, loyalty, fealty, homage, deference, devotion, fidelity, constancy.

submiss-ness, -iveness; ductility &c. (*softness*) 324; obsequiousness &c. (*servility*) 886.

V. be -obedient &c. *adj.*; obey, bear obedience to; submit &c. 725; comply, answer the helm, come at one's call; do -one's bidding, – what one is told, – suit and service; attend to orders, serve -devotedly, – loyally, – faithfully.

follow, – the lead of, – to the world's end; serve &c. 746; play second fiddle.

Adj. obedient; compl-ying, -iant; law-abiding, loyal, faithful, leal, devoted; at one's -call, – command, – orders, – beck and call; under -beck and call, – control.

restrainable; resigned, passive; submissive &c. 725; henpecked; pliant &c. (*soft*) 324.

unresist-ed, -ing.

Adv. obediently &c. *adj.*; in compliance with, in obedience to.

Phr. to hear is to obey; as –, if- you please; at your service.

---

744. Compulsion.—N. compulsion, coercion, coaction, constraint, eminent domain, duress, enforcement, press, conscription.

force; brute –, main –, physical- force; the sword, *ultima ratio*; club –, mob –, lynch- law; *argumentum baculinum, le droit du plus fort*, martial law.

restraint &c. 751; necessity &c. 601; *force majeure*; Hobson's choice; the spur of necessity.

V. compel, force, make, drive, coerce, constrain, enforce, necessitate, oblige.

force upon, press; cram –, thrust –, force- down the throat; say it must be done, make a point of, insist upon, take no denial; put down, dragoon.

extort, wring from; put –, turn- on the screw; drag into; bind, – over; pin –, tie- down; require, tax, put in force; commandeer; restrain &c. 751.

Adj. compelling &c. *v.*; coercive, coactive; inexorable &c. 739; compuls-ory, -atory; obligatory, stringent, peremptory, binding.

forcible, not to be trifled with; irresistible &c. 601; compelled &c. *v.*; fain to.

Adv. by -force &c. *n.*, – force of arms; on compulsion, perforce; *vi et armis*, under the lash; at the point of the -sword, – bayonet; forcibly; by a strong arm.

under protest, in spite of one's teeth; against one's will &c. 603; *nolens volens* &c. (*of necessity*) 601; by stress of -circumstances, – weather; under press of; *de rigueur*.

745. Master.—N. master, *padrone*; lord, – paramount; command-er, -ant; captain; chief, -tain; *sahib*, sirdar, sachem, sheik, head, senior, governor, *duce*, ruler, dictator; leader &c. (*director*) 694.

lord of the ascendant; cock of the -walk, – roost; grey mare; mistress.

potentate; liege, – lord; suzerain, sovereign, monarch, autocrat, despot, tyrant, oligarch, overlord.

crowned head, emperor, king, anointed king, majesty, *imperator*, protector, president, stadtholder, judge.

cæsar, kaiser, czar, sultan, grand Turk, caliph, imaum, shah, padishah, sophi, mogul, great mogul, khan, cham; lama, tycoon, mikado, inca, cazique; domn; vaivode; wai-, way-wode; landamman; seyyid, cacique.

prince, duke &c. (*nobility*) 875; archduke, doge, elector; seignior; mar-, land-grave; rajah, emir, nizam, nawab, negus.

empress, queen, sultana, czarina, princess, infanta, duchess, margravine, begum, maharani.

regent, viceroy, exarch, palatine,

746. Servant.—N. subject, liegeman; servant, retainer, follower, henchman, servitor, domestic, menial, help, lady help, *employé, attaché*; official.

retinue, suite, *cortège*, staff, court.

attendant, squire, usher, page, buttons, donzel, footboy; dog robber; train-, cup-bearer; waiter, busboy, tapster, butler, livery servant, lackey, footman, flunkey, valet, *valet de chambre*; boots; scout, gyp; equerry, groom; jockey, hostler, ostler, tiger, orderly, messenger, cad, gillie, caddie; *wallah*; journeyman, herdsman, swineherd.

bailiff, castellan, seneschal, chamberlain, *major-domo*, groom of the chambers.

secretary; under –, assistant- secretary; clerk; clerical staff, stenographer, subsidiary; agent &c. 758; subaltern; under-ling, -strapper; man.

maid, -servant, waitress; handmaid; *confidente*, lady's maid, abigail, *soubrette*; nurse, *bonne, ayah*; nurse-, nursery-, house-, parlour-, waiting-, chamber-, kitchen-, scullery-, between –, laundry –, dairy-maid; *femme –, fille-de chambre; camarista; chef de cuisine*,

khedive, hospodar, beglerbeg, three-tailed bashaw, pasha, pashaw, bashaw, bey, beg, dey, scherif, tetrarch, satrap, mandarin, subhadar, nabob, maharajah; burgrave; laird &c. (*proprietor*) 779; High Commissioner.

the -authorities, – powers that be, – government; staff, *état major*, aga, official, man in office, person in authority.

[Naval authorities] admiral, -ty, – of the fleet; rear-, vice-, port-admiral; senior-, naval officer, S.N.O., commodore, captain, commander, lieutenant-commander, lieutenant, sub-lieutenant, midshipman, warrant –, petty- officer, leading seaman; skipper, mate, master.

[Military authorities] marshal, field-marshal, *maréchal*; general, -issimo; commander-in-chief, *seraskier*, *hetman*; lieutenant-, major-general; commandant; colonel, lieutenant-colonel, major, captain, centurion, skipper, lieutenant, second-lieutenant, officer, staff-officer, *aide de camp*, brigadier, brigade-major, adjutant, *jemidar*, ensign, cornet, cadet, subaltern, warrant officer, quartermaster, noncommissioned officer, N.C.O.; sergeant, -major; top-sergeant, colour sergeant; corporal, -major; lance-, acting-corporal; drum major; shavetail.

[Air authorities] air -marshal, – commodore; group captain, squadron leader, wing commander, flight lieutenant, flying –, pilot-officer.

[Civil authorities] judge &c. 967; mayor, -alty; prefect, chancellor, archon, provost, magistrate, syndic; alcalde, alcaid; burgomaster, *corregidor*, seneschal, alderman, warden, constable, portreeve; lord mayor, sheriff; officer &c. (*executive*) 965.

cordon bleu, cook, scullion, Cinderella; maid –, servant- of all work, tweeny, general servant, girl, slavey; laundress, bed-maker, goodie, char-woman &c. (*worker*) 690.

serf, vassal, slave, negro, helot; bondsman, -woman; bondslave; *âme damnée*, *odalisque*, ryot, *adscriptus glebæ*; vill-ain, -ein; bead-, bede-sman; sizar; pension-er, -ary; client; dependant, -ent; hanger on, stooge, satellite; parasite &c. (*servility*) 886; led captain; *protégé*, ward, hireling, mercenary, puppet, creature.

badge of slavery; bonds &c. 752.

V. serve; minister to, wait –, attend –, dance attendance –, pin oneself-upon; squire, tend, hang on the sleeve of, char, do for; fag; valet.

Adj. in the train of; in one's -pay, – employ; at one's call &c. (*obedient*) 743; in bonds.

---

747. [Insignia of authority.] **Sceptre.—N.** sceptre, regalia, rod of empire, sword of state, mace, *fasces*, wand; staff, – of office; *bâton*, truncheon; flag &c. (*insignia*) 550; ensign –, emblem –, badge –, insignia- of authority, rank marks, brassard, badge, sash; cocked –, brass- hat.

epaulette, aiguilette, crown, star, eagle, bar, double bar, pip, stripe, chevron, curl, ring, anchor, shoulder-strap, tab.

throne, chair, musnud, divan, dais, woolsack.

toga, pall, mantle, robes of state, ermine, purple.

crown, coronet, diadem, tiara, triple crown, mitre, crozier, cardinal's hat &c.; cap of maintenance; decoration; title &c. 877; portfolio.

key, signet, seals, talisman; helm; reins &c. (*means of restraint*) 752.

748. Freedom.—N. freedom, liberty, independence; licence &c. (*permission*) 760; facility &c. 705.

scope, range, latitude, play; free –, full- -play, – scope; free stage and no

749. Subjection. — N. subjection; depend-ence, -ance, -ency; subordination; thrall, thraldom, enthralment, subjugation, bondage, serfdom; feudal-ism, -ity; vassalage, villenage; slavery,

favour; swing, full swing, elbow-room, margin, rope, wide berth; Liberty Hall.

franchise, denization; free –, freed-, livery- man; denizen.

autonomy, self-government, home-rule, self-determination, liberalism, free trade; non-interference &c. 706.

immunity, exemption; emancipation &c. (*liberation*) 750; en-, af-franchise-ment; rights, privileges.

free land, freehold; allodium; frank-almoigne, mortmain.

independent, free-lance, -thinker, -trader.

V. be -free &c. *adj.*; have -scope &c. *n.*, – the run of, – one's own way, – a will of one's own, – one's fling; do what one -likes, – wishes, – pleases, – chooses; go at large, feel at home, paddle one's own canoe; stand on one's -legs, – rights; shift for oneself.

take a liberty; make -free with, – oneself quite at home; use a freedom; take -leave, – French leave.

set free &c. (*liberate*) 750; give the reins to &c. (*permit*) 760; allow –, give-scope &c. *n.* to; give a horse his head.

make free of; give the -freedom of, – franchise; en-, af-franchise.

laisser -faire, – aller; live and let live; leave to oneself; leave –, let- alone; mind one's own business.

Adj. free, – as air; out of harness, independent, at large, loose, scot free; left -alone, – to oneself.

in full swing; uncaught, uncon-strained, unbuttoned, unconfined, un-restrained, unchecked, unprevented, unhindered, unobstructed, unbound, uncontrolled, untrammelled.

unsubject, ungoverned, unenslaved, unenthralled, unchained, unshackled, unfettered, unreined, unbridled, un-curbed, unmuzzled, unimpeded.

unrestricted, unlimited, unconditional; absolute; discretionary &c. (*optional*) 600.

unassailed, unforced, uncompelled.

unbiassed, unprejudiced, uninfluenced, spontaneous.

free and easy; at –, at one's- ease; *dégagé*, quite at home; wanton, rampant, irrepressible, unvanquished.

exempt; freed &c. 750; freeborn; autonomous, freehold, allodial; *gratis* &c. 815.

unclaimed, going a begging.

Adv. freely &c. *adj.*; *ad libitum* &c. (*at will*) 600.

enslavement, involuntary servitude.

service; servi-tude, -torship; ten-dence, employ, tutelage, clientship; liability &c. 177; constraint &c. 751; oppression &c. (*severity*) 739; yoke &c. (*means of restraint*) 752; submission &c. 725; obedience &c. 743.

V. be -subject &c. *adj.*; be –, lie- at the mercy of; depend –, lean –, hang-upon; fall -a prey to, – under; play second fiddle.

be a -mere machine, – puppet, – foot-ball; not dare to say one's soul is his own; drag a chain.

serve &c. 746; obey &c. 743; submit &c. 725.

break in, tame; subject, subjugate; master &c. 731; tread -down, – under foot; weigh down; drag at one's chariot wheels; reduce to -subjection, – slavery; en-, in-, be-thral; enslave, lead captive; take into custody &c. (*restrain*) 751; rule &c. 737; drive into a corner, hold at the sword's point; keep under; hold in -bondage, – leading strings, – swad-dling clothes.

Adj. subject, dependent, subordi-nate; feud-al, -atory; in subjection to, under control; in -leading strings, – harness; subjected, enslaved &c. *v.*; constrained &c. 751; subservient, ser-vile, fawning, slavish, obsequious, cringing; down-trodden; over-borne, -whelmed; under the lash, on the hip, led by the nose, henpecked; the -pup-pet, – sport, – plaything- of; under one's -orders, – command, – thumb; like dirt under one's feet; a slave to; at the mercy of; in the -power, – hands, – clutches- of; at the feet of; at one's beck and call &c. (*obedient*) 743; liable &c. 177; parasitical; stipendiary.

Adv. under.

_____

750. Liberation.—**N.** liberation, disengagement, release, disenthrallment, enlargement, emancipation; af-, enfranchisement; manumission; discharge, dismissal.

deliverance &c. 672; redemption, extrication, acquittance, absolution; acquittal &c. 970; escape &c. 671.

V. liberate, free; set -free, – clear, – at liberty; render free, emancipate, release; en-, af-franchise; manumit; enlarge; dis-band, -charge, -miss, -enthral; let -go, – loose, – out, – slip; cast -, turn- adrift; deliver &c. 672; absolve &c. (*acquit*) 970; reprieve.

unfetter &c. 751; untie &c. 44; loose &c. (*disjoin*) 44; loosen, relax; un-bolt, -bar, -close, -cork, -clog, -hand, -bind, -latch, -chain, -harness; dis-engage, -entangle; clear, extricate, unloose.

gain -, obtain -, acquire- one's -liberty &c. 748; get -rid, – clear- of; deliver oneself from; shake off the yoke, slip the collar; break -loose, – prison; tear asunder one's bonds, cast off trammels; escape &c. 671.

Adj. at -liberty, – large, free, liberated &c. *v.*; out of harness &c. 748; adrift.

Int. unhand me! let me go!

---

751. Restraint.—**N.** restraint; hindrance &c. 706; coercion &c. (*compulsion*) 744; cohibition, constraint, repression; discipline, control, self-restraint &c. 604.

confinement; durance, duress; im-, prisonment; incarceration, coarctation, entombment, mancipation, durance vile, thrall, -dom, limbo, captivity; blockade; quarantine; detention.

arrest, -ation; custody, keep, care, charge, ward, restringency.

curb &c. (*means of restraint*) 752; *lettres de cachet.*

limitation, restriction, protection, monopoly; prohibition &c. 761; economic pressure.

prisoner &c. 754.

V. restrain, check; put -, lay- under restraint; en-, in-, be-thral; restrict; debar &c. (*hinder*) 706; constrain; coerce &c. (*compel*) 744; curb, control; hold -, keep- -back, – from, – in, – in check, – within bounds; hold in -leash, – leading strings; withhold.

keep under; repress, suppress; smother; pull in, rein in; hold, – fast; keep a tight hand on; prohibit &c. 761; in-, co-hibit.

enchain; fasten &c. (*join*) 43; fetter, shackle; en-, trammel; bridle, muzzle, gag, pinion, manacle, handcuff, tie one's hands, hobble, bind hand and foot; swathe, swaddle; pin -, peg- down; tether, picket; tie, – up, – down; secure; forge fetters.

confine; shut -, clap -, lock -, box -, mew -, bottle -, cork -, seal -, button- up; shut -, hem -, bolt -, wall -, rail- in; impound, pen, coop; enclose &c. (*circumscribe*) 229; cage; in-, en-cage; close the door upon, cloister; imprison, immure; incarcerate, entomb; clap -, lay- under hatches; put in -irons, – a strait waistcoat; throw -, cast- into prison; put into bilboes.

arrest; take -up, – charge of, – into custody; take -, make- -prisoner, – captive; captivate; lead -captive, – into captivity; send -, commit- to prison; commit; give in -charge, – custody; subjugate &c. 749.

Adj. re-, con-strained; imprisoned &c. *v.*; pent up; jammed in, wedged in; under -restraint, – lock and key, – hatches; serving -, doing- time; in swaddling clothes; on *parole*; in custody &c. (*prisoner*) 754; cohibitive; coactive &c. (*compulsory*) 744.

stiff, restringent, straitlaced, hide-bound.

ice-, wind-, weather-bound; 'cabined, cribbed, confined'; in Lob's pound, laid by the heels.

Adv. in captivity, under arrest, behind the bars, in -prison, – jail, – durance vile.

752. [Means of restraint.] Prison.—N. prison, -house; jail, gaol, cage, coop, den, death house, condemned -, cell; stronghold, fortress, keep, donjon, dungeon, *Bastille, oubliette,* bridewell, house of correction, hulks, toll-booth, panopticon, penitentiary, guard-room, clink, can, stir, tronk, jug, lock-up, hold; round -, watch -, station -, sponging-house; station; house of detention, black hole, pen, fold, pound; enclosure &c. 232; penal settlement; chain gang; debtors' prison; reformatory; federal penitentiary, state prison; criminal lunatic asylum; bilboes, stocks, limbo, quod.

Dartmoor, Newgate, Fleet, Marshalsea; King's (*or* Queen's) Bench; Sing Sing, Dannemora.

bond; strap, bandage, splint, tourniquet; irons, pinion, gyve, fetter, shackle, trammel, manacle, handcuff, bracelets, darbies, strait waistcoat, strait-jacket.

yoke, collar, halter, harness; muzzle, gag, bit, brake, curb, snaffle, bridle; rein, -s; ribbons, lines, bearing-rein; martingale, leading string; tether, picket, band, guy, chain; cord &c. (*fastening*) 45.

bolt, bar, lock, padlock, rail, wall; paling, palisade; fence; barrier, barricade.

brake, drag &c. (*hindrance*) 706.

753. Keeper.—N. keeper, custodian, *custos,* ranger, warder, jailer, gaoler, turnkey, castellan, guard; watch, -dog, -man; Charley; sen-try, -tinel; watch and ward; *concierge,* coast-guard, *guarda costa,* gamekeeper.

escort, body guard, convoy.

protector, governor, duenna; guardian; governess &c. (*teacher*) 540; nurse, *bonne, ayah, amah.*

754. Prisoner.—N. prisoner, captive, *détenu,* close prisoner.

jail-bird, ticket-of-leave man.

V. stand committed; be -imprisoned &c. 751.

Adj. imprisoned &c. 751; in -prison, - quod, - durance vile, - limbo, - custody, - charge, - chains; under -lock and key, - hatches; on *parole*; detained at his Majesty's pleasure.

755. [Vicarious authority.] Commission.—N. commission, delegation; con-, as-signment; procuration; deputation, legation, mission, embassy; agency, agentship; power of attorney, proxy; clerkship.

errand, charge, *brevet,* diploma, *exequatur,* permit &c. (*permission*) 760.

appointment, nomination, return; charter; ordination; installation, inauguration, investiture; accession, coronation, enthronement.

vicegerency; regency, regentship.

viceroy &c. 745; consignee &c. 758; deputy &c. 759.

V. commission, delegate, depute; consign, assign; charge; in-, en-trust; turn over to; commit, - to the hands of; authorize &c. (*permit*) 760.

put in commission, accredit, engage, hire, bespeak, appoint, name, nominate, return, ordain; install, induct,

756. Abrogation.—N. abrogation, annulment, nullification; cancelling &c. *v.*; cancel; revo-cation, -kement; repeal, rescission, defeasance.

dismissal, *congé,* demission; depos-al, -ition; sack, dethronement; disestablish-, disendow-ment; deconsecration.

aboli-tion, -shment; dissolution.

counter-order, -mand; repudiation, retractation; recantation &c. (*tergiversation*) 607.

V. abrogate, annul, cancel; destroy &c. 162; abolish; revoke, repeal, rescind, reverse, retract, recall; over-rule, -ride; set aside; disannul, dissolve, quash, nullify, declare null and void; dis-establish, -endow; deconsecrate.

disclaim &c. (*deny*) 536; ignore, repudiate; recant &c. 607; divest oneself, break off.

counter-mand, -order; do away with; sweep -, brush- away; throw -over-

inaugurate, invest, crown; en-roll, -list.

employ, empower; give power of attorney to; set -, place- over; send out.

be commissioned, be accredited; represent, stand for; stand in the -stead, - place, - shoes- of.

Adj. commissioned &c. *v.*

Adv. *per procuratione.*

board, - to the dogs; scatter to the winds, cast behind.

dismiss, discard; cast -, turn- -off, - out, - adrift, - out of doors, - aside, - away; send -off, - away, - about one's business; discharge, get rid of, fire out, fire &c. (*eject*) 297; jilt.

cashier; break; oust; set down, unseat, -saddle; un-, de-, disen-throne; depose, uncrown; unfrock, strike off the roll; dis-bar, -bench.

be -abrogated &c.; receive its quietus.

Adj. abrogated &c. *v.; functus officio.*

Int. get along with you! begone! go about your business! away with!

757. Resignation.—N. resignation, retirement, abdication, renunciation, abjuration, disclaimer, abandonment, relinquishment.

V. resign; give -, throw- up; lay down, throw up the cards, wash one's hands of, abjure, renounce, forego, disclaim, abandon, relinquish, retract, demit; deny &c. 536.

abrogate &c. 756; desert &c. (*relinquish*) 624; get rid of &c. 782.

abdicate; vacate, - one's seat; accept the stewardship of the Chiltern Hundreds; retire; tender -, send in -, hand in- one's resignation.

Adj. abdicant, renunciatory &c. *v.*

Phr. 'Othello's occupation's gone.'

758. Consignee.—N. consignee, trustee, nominee, committee.

delegate; commiss-ary, -ioner; emissary, envoy, commissionaire; messenger &c. 534.

diplomatist, diplomat, *corps diplomatique,* embassy; am-, em-bassador; representative, resident, consul, legate, nuncio, internuncio, *chargé d'affaires, attaché.*

vicegerent &c. (*deputy*) 759; plenipotentiary.

functionary, placeman, curator; treasurer &c. 801; agent, factor, bailiff, steward, clerk, secretary, attorney, solicitor, proctor, broker, underwriter, commission agent, auctioneer, one's man of business; factotum &c. (*director*) 694; caretaker.

negotiator, go between; middleman; under agent, *employé;* servant &c. 746.

salesman; commercial, - traveller; bagman, *commis-voyageur,* touter.

newspaper -, own -, war -, special- correspondent; reporter.

759. Deputy.—N. deputy, substitute, vice, proxy, *locum tenens,* delegate, representative, next friend, surrogate, secondary.

regent, vicegerent, vizier, minister, vicar; premier &c. (*director*) 694; chancellor, prefect, provost, warden, lieutenant, archon, consul, proconsul; viceroy &c. (*governor*) 745; commissioner &c. 758; plenipotentiary, *alter ego.*

team, eight, eleven; champion.

V. be -deputy &c. *n.*; stand -, appear -, hold a brief -, answer- for; represent; stand -, walk- in the shoes of; stand in the stead of.

substitute, ablegate, accredit; commission, empower, delegate &c. 755.

Adj. acting; vice, -regal; accredited to.

Adv. in behalf of, by proxy.

Section II. Special Intersocial Volition

760. Permission.—N. permission, leave; allow-, suffer-ance; toler-ance, -ation; liberty, law, licence, concession, grace; indulgence &c. (*lenity*) 740; favour, dispensation, exemption, release; connivance; vouchsafement.

authorization, warranty, accordance, admission.

permit, warrant, *brevet*, precept, sanction, authority, *firman*; pass, -port; furlough, licence, *carte blanche*, ticket of leave; grant, charter, patent.

V. permit; give -permission &c. *n.*, – power; let, allow, admit; suffer, bear with, tolerate, recognize; concede &c. 762; accord, vouchsafe, favour, humour, gratify, indulge, stretch a point; wink at, connive at; shut one's eyes to.

grant, empower, charter, enfranchise, privilege, confer a privilege, license, authorize, warrant; sanction; entrust &c. (*commission*) 755.

give -*carte blanche*, – the reins to, – scope to &c. (*freedom*) 748; leave -alone, – it to one, – the door open; open the -door to, – floodgates; give a loose to.

let off; absolve &c. (*acquit*) 970; release, exonerate, dispense with.

ask –, beg –, request- -leave, – permission.

761. Prohibition.—N. pro-, in-hibition; *veto*, disallowance; interdict, -ion; injunction; embargo, ban, *verboten*, taboo, proscription; *index expurgatorius*; restriction &c. (*restraint*) 751; hindrance &c. 706; forbidden fruit.

V. pro-, in-hibit; forbid, put one's *veto* upon, disallow; bar; debar &c. (*hinder*) 706, forefend.

keep -in, – within bounds; restrain &c. 751; cohibit, withhold, limit, circumscribe, clip the wings of, restrict, narrow; interdict, taboo; put –, place- under -an interdiction, – the ban; proscribe, censor; exclude, shut out; shut –, bolt –, show- the door; warn off; dash the cup from one's lips; forbid the banns.

Adj. prohibit-ive, -ory; interdictive; proscriptive; restrictive, exclusive; forbidding &c. *v.*

prohibited &c. *v.*; not -permitted &c. 760; unlicensed, contraband, under the ban of; illegal &c. 964; unauthorized, not to be thought of.

Adv. on no account &c. (*no*) 536.

Int. forbid it heaven! &c. (*deprecation*) 766.

hands –, keep- off! hold! stop! avast!
Phr. that will never do.

Adj. permitting &c. *v.*; permissive, indulgent; permitted &c. *v.*; patent, chartered, permissible, allowable, lawful, legitimate, legal; legalized &c. (*law*) 963; licit; unforbid, -den; unconditional.

Adv. permissibly; by –, with –, on- -leave &c. *n.*; *speciali gratiâ*; under favour of; *pace*; *ad libitum* &c. (*freely*) 748, (*at will*) 600; by all means &c. (*willingly*) 602; yes &c. (*assent*) 488.

---

762. Consent.—N. consent; assent &c. 488; acquiescence; approval &c. 931; compliance, agreement, concession; yield-ance, -ingness; accession, acknowledgment, acceptance, agnition.

settlement, ratification, confirmation, adjustment.

permit &c. (*permission*) 760; promise &c. 768.

V. consent; assent &c. 488; yield assent, admit, allow, concede, grant, yield; come -over, – round; give in to, acknowledge, agnize, give consent, comply with, acquiesce, agree to, fall in with, accede, accept, embrace an offer, close with, take at one's word, have no objection.

satisfy, meet one's wishes, settle, come to terms &c. 488; not -refuse &c. 764; turn a willing ear &c. (*willingness*) 602; jump at; deign, vouchsafe; promise &c. 768.

Adj. consenting &c. *v.*; agreeable, compliant; agreed &c. (*assent*) 488; unconditional.

Adv. yes &c. (*assent*) 488; by all means &c. (*willingly*) 602; if –, as-you please; be it so, so be it, well and good, of course.

763. Offer.—**N.** offer, proffer, presentation, tender, bid, overture; pro-pos-al, -ition; motion, invitation; candidature; offering &c. (*gift*) 784.

V. offer, proffer, present, tender; bid; propose, move; make -a motion, – advances; start; invite, hold out, place- at one's disposal, – in one's way, put forward.

hawk about; offer for sale &c. 796; press &c. (*request*) 765; lay at one's feet.

offer –, present- oneself; volunteer, come forward, be a candidate; stand –, bid- for; seek; be at one's service; go a begging; bribe &c. (*give*) 784.

Adj. offer-ing, -ed &c. *v.*; in the market, for sale, to let, disengaged, on hire.

---

764. Refusal.—**N.** refusal, rejection; non-, in-compliance; denial; declining &c. *v.*; declension; peremptory –, flat –, point blank- refusal; repulse, rebuff; discountenance.

recusancy, renunciation, abnegation, negation, protest, disclaimer; dissent &c. 489; revocation &c. 756.

V. refuse, reject, deny, decline; nill, negative; refuse –, withhold- one's assent; shake the head; close the -hand, – purse; grudge, begrudge, be slow to, hang fire.

be deaf to; turn -a deaf ear to, – one's back upon; set one's face against, discountenance, not hear of, have nothing to do with, wash one's hands of, stand aloof, forswear, set aside, cast behind one; not yield an inch &c. (*obstinacy*) 606.

resist, cross; not -grant &c. 762; repel, repulse; shut –, slam- the door in one's face; rebuff; send -back, – to the right about, – away with a flea in the ear; deny oneself, not be at home to; discard &c. (*repudiate*) 610; rescind &c. (*revoke*) 756; disclaim, protest; dissent &c. 489.

Adj. refusing &c. *v.*; rest-ive, -iff; recusant; uncomplying, non-compliant, unconsenting, uncomplaisant, protestant; not willing to hear of, deaf to.

refused &c. *v.*; ungranted, out of the question, not to be thought of, impossible.

Adv. no &c. 536; on no account, not for the world; no thank you.

Phr. *non possumus*; [ironically] your humble servant; *bien obligé*.

765. Request.—**N.** requ-est, -isition; claim &c. (*demand*) 741; petition, suit, prayer; begging letter, round-robin.

motion, overture, application, canvass, address, appeal, apostrophe; imprecation; rogation; proposal, proposition.

orison &c. (*worship*) 990; incantation &c. (*spell*) 993.

mendicancy; asking, panhandling, begging &c. *v.*; postulation, solicitation, invitation, entreaty, importunity, supplication, instance, impetration, imploration, obsecration, obtestation, invocation, interpellation.

V. request, ask; beg, crave, sue, pray, petition, solicit, invite, pop the question, make bold to ask; beg -leave, – a boon; apply to, call to, put to; call -upon, – for; make –, address –, prefer –, put up- a -request, – prayer, – petition;

766. [Negative request.] Deprecation.—**N.** deprecation, expostulation; remonstrance; intercession, mediation.

V. deprecate, protest, expostulate, enter a protest, intercede for.

Adj. deprecatory, expostulatory, intercessory, mediatorial.

deprecated, protested.

un-, unbe-sought; unasked &c. (*see* ask &c. 765).

Int. cry you mercy! God forbid! forbid it Heaven! Heaven -forefend, – forbid! far be it from! hands off! &c. (*prohibition*) 761.

---

make -application, – a requisition; ask –, trouble- one for; claim &c. (*demand*) 741; offer up prayers &c. (*worship*) 990; whistle for.

beg hard, entreat, beseech, plead, supplicate, implore, apostrophize; conjure, adjure; obtest; cry to, kneel to, appeal to; invoke, evoke; impetrate, imprecate, ply, press, urge, beset, importune, dun, tax, clamour for; cry -aloud, – for help; fall on one's knees; throw oneself at the feet of; come down on one's marrow-bones.

beg from door to door, send the hat round, go a begging; mendicate, mump, cadge, panhandle, beg one's bread.

dance attendance on, besiege, knock at the door.

bespeak, canvass, tout, make interest, court; seek, bid for &c. (*offer*) 763; publish the banns.

Adj. requesting &c. *v.*; precatory; suppli-ant, -cant, -catory; invoc-, imprec-, rog-atory; postulant, mendicant.

importunate, clamorous, urgent; solicitous; cap in hand; on one's -knees, – bended knees, – marrow-bones.

Adv. prithee, do, please, pray; be so good as, be good enough; have the goodness, vouchsafe, will you, I pray thee, if you please.

Int. for -God's, – heaven's, – goodness', – mercy's- sake.

767. Petitioner.—N. petitioner, solicitor, applicant; suppli-ant, -cant; suitor, candidate, claimant, postulant, aspirant, competitor, bidder; place –, pot- hunter; prizer.

beggar, mendicant, mumper, sturdy beggar, cadger, panhandler.

canvasser, barker, touter &c. 768.

sycophant, parasite &c. 886.

Section III. Conditional Intersocial Volition

768. Promise.—N. promise, undertaking, word, troth, plight, pledge, *parole*, word of honour, vow; oath &c. (*affirmation*) 535; profession, assurance, warranty, guarantee, insurance, obligation; contract &c. 769.

engagement, pre-engagement: affiance; betroth, -al, -ment; marriage -compact, – vow.

V. promise; give a -promise &c. *n.*; undertake, engage; make –, form- an engagement; enter -into, – on- an engagement; bind –, tie –, pledge –, commit –, take upon- oneself; vow; swear &c. (*affirm*) 535, give –, pass –, pledge –, plight- one's -word, – honour, – credit, – troth; betroth, plight faith; take the vows.

assure, warrant, guarantee, vouch for, avouch, covenant &c. 769; attest &c. (*bear witness*) 467.

hold out an expectation; contract an obligation; become -bound to, – sponsor for; answer –, be answerable- for; secure; give security &c. 771; underwrite.

adjure, administer an oath, put to one's oath, swear a witness.

Adj. promising &c. *v.*; promissory; votive; under hand and seal; upon -oath, – affirmation.

promised &c. *v.*; affianced, pledged, bound; committed, compromised; in for it.

Adv. as one's head shall answer for; upon my honour.

Phr. in for a penny, in for a pound.

768a. Release from engagement.— N. release &c. (*liberation*) 750.

Adj. absolute; unconditional &c. (*free*) 748.

769. Compact.—N. compact, contract, agreement, bargain, deal, transaction; affidation; pact, -ion; bond, covenant, indenture.

stipulation, settlement, convention; compromise, *cartel*.

protocol, treaty, *concordat*, *Zollverein*, *Sonderbund*, charter, *Magna Charta*, Pragmatic Sanction.

negotiation &c. (*bargaining*) 794; diplomacy &c. (*mediation*) 724; negotiator &c. (*agent*) 758.

ratification, completion, signature, seal, sigil, signet.

V. contract, covenant, agree for, engage &c. (*promise*) 768.

treat, negotiate, stipulate, make terms; bargain &c. (*barter*) 794.

make –, strike- a bargain; come to -terms, – an understanding; compromise &c. 774; set at rest; close, – with; conclude, complete, settle; confirm, ratify, clench, subscribe, underwrite; en-, in-dorse; put the seal to; sign, seal &c. (*attest*) 467; indent.

take one at one's word, bargain by inch of candle.

Adj. contractual, agreed &c. *v.*; conventional; under hand and seal; signed, sealed and delivered.

Phr. *caveat emptor*.

770. Conditions.—N. conditions, terms; articles, – of agreement.

clauses, provisions; proviso &c. (*qualification*) 469; covenant, stipulation, obligation, *ultimatum*, *sine quâ non*; *casus fœderis*.

V. make –, come to- -terms &c. (*contract*) 769; make it a condition, stipulate, insist upon, make a point of; bind, tie up.

Adj. conditional, provisional, guarded, fenced, hedged in.

Adv. conditionally &c. (*with qualification*) 469; provisionally, *pro re natâ*; on condition; with a reservation.

771. Security.—N. security; guaran-ty, -tee; gage, warranty, bond, tie, pledge, plight, mortgage, debenture, hypothecation, bill of sale, lien, pignus, pawn, pignoration; real security; bottomry; collateral, vadium.

stake, deposit, earnest, handsel, caution.

promissory note; bill, – of exchange; I.O.U.; personal security, covenant, specialty; *parole* &c. (*promise*) 768.

acceptance, indorsement, signature, execution, stamp, seal.

spon-sor, -sion, -sorship; surety, bail; mainpernor, hostage.

recognizance; deed –, covenant- of indemnity.

authentication, verification, warrant, certificate, voucher, docket, doquet; record &c. 551; probate, attested copy.

receipt; ac-, quittance; discharge, release.

muniment, title-deed, instrument; deed, – poll; assurance, insurance, indenture; charter &c. (*compact*) 769; charter-poll; paper, parchment, settlement, will, testament, last will and testament, codicil.

V. give -security, – bail, – substantial bail; go bail; pawn, impawn, hock, spout, mortgage, hypothecate, impignorate.

guarantee, warrant, assure; accept, indorse, underwrite, insure.

execute, stamp; sign, seal &c. (*evidence*) 467.

let, sett; grant –, take –, hold- a lease; hold in pledge; lend on security &c. 787.

Adj. secure, -ed; pledged &c. *v.*; in pawn, on deposit.

772. Observance.—N. observance, performance, compliance; obedience

773. Non-observance. — N. non-observance &c. 772; evasion, inob-

&c. 743; fulfilment, satisfaction, discharge; acquit-tance, -tal.

adhesion, acknowledgment; fidelity &c. (*probity*) 939; exact &c. 494- observance.

V. observe, comply with, respect, acknowledge, abide by; cling to, adhere to, be faithful to, act up to; meet, fulfil; carry -out, – into execution; execute, perform, keep, satisfy, discharge; do one's office.

perform –, fulfill –, discharge –, acquit oneself of- an obligation; make good; make good –, keep- one's -word, – promise; redeem one's pledge; keep faith with, stand to one's engagement.

Adj. observant, faithful, true, loyal; honourable &c. 939; true as the -dial to the sun, – needle to the pole; punct-ual, -ilious; meticulous; literal &c. (*exact*) 494; as good as one's word.

Adv. faithfully &c. *adj.*

---

servance, failure, omission, neglect, laches, laxity, informality.

infringement, infraction; violation, transgression.

retractation, repudiation, nullification; protest; forfeiture.

lawlessness; disobedience &c. 742; bad faith &c. 940.

V. fail, neglect, omit, elude, evade, give the go by to, cut, set aside, ignore; shut –, close- one's eyes to, avoid.

infringe, transgress, pirate, violate, break, trample under foot, do violence to, drive a coach and six through.

discard, protest, repudiate, fling to the winds, set at naught, nullify, declare null and void; cancel &c. (*wipe off*) 552.

retract, go back from, be off, forfeit, go from one's word, palter; stretch –, strain- a point.

Adj. violating &c. *v.*; lawless, transgressive; elusive, evasive; lax, casual; non-observant.

unfulfilled &c. (*see* fulfil &c. 772).

774. Compromise.—N. com-promise, -mutation, -position; middle term, *mezzo termine*; compensation &c. 30; adjustment, mutual concession.

V. com-promise, -mute, -pound; take the mean; split the difference, meet one half way, give and take; come to terms &c. (*contract*) 769; submit to –, abide by- arbitration; patch up, bridge over, fix up, arrange; adjust, – differences; agree; make -the best of, – a virtue of necessity; take the will for the deed.

Section IV. POSSESSIVE RELATIONS*

1°. *Property in general*

775. Acquisition.—N. acquisition; gaining &c. *v.*; obtainment; procuration, -ement; purchase, descent, inheritance; gift &c. 784.

recovery, retrieval, revendication, replevin; redemption, salvage, trover; find, *trouvaille*, foundling.

gain, thrift; money-making, -grubbing; lucre, filthy lucre, loaves and fishes, the main chance, pelf; emolument &c. 973; wealth &c. 803.

profit, earnings, winnings, innings, clean-up, pickings, perquisite, net profit; income &c. (*receipt*) 810; proceeds, -duce, -duct; out-come, -put;

776. Loss.—N. loss; de-, perdition; forfeiture, lapse.

privation, bereavement; deprivation &c. (*dispossession*) 789; riddance.

V. lose; incur –, experience –, meet with- a loss; miss; mislay, let slip, allow to slip through the fingers, squander; be without &c. (*exempt*) 777a; forfeit.

get rid of &c. 782; waste &c. 638.

be lost, lapse.

Adj. losing &c. *v.*; not having &c. 777a.

shorn of, deprived of; denuded, bereaved, bereft, *minus*, cut off; dispos-

* That is, relations which concern property.

return, fruit, crop, harvest, tilth; second crop, aftermath; benefit &c. (*good*) 618.

sweepstakes, trick, prize, pool.

[Fraudulent acquisition] subreption; theft, stealing &c. 791.

V. acquire, get, gain, win, earn, obtain, procure, gather, annex; collect &c. 72; pick, – up; glean, take &c. 789.

find; come –, pitch –, light- upon; scrape -up, – together; get in, reap and carry, net, bag, sack, bring home, secure, come across, derive, draw, get in the harvest.

profit; make –, draw- profit; turn to -profit, – account; make -capital out of, – money by; obtain a return, reap the fruits of; reap –, gain- an advantage; turn -a penny, – an honest penny; make the pot boil, bring grist to the mill; make –, coin –, raise- money; raise -funds, – the wind; fill one's pocket &c. (*wealth*) 803.

treasure up &c. (*store*) 636; realize, clear; produce &c. 161; take &c. 789.

get back, recover, regain, retrieve, revendicate, replevy, redeem, come by one's own.

come -by, – in for; receive &c. 785; inherit; step into, – a fortune, – the shoes of; succeed to.

get -hold of, – between one's finger and thumb, – into one's hand, – at; take –, come into –, enter into- possession.

be -profitable &c. *adj.*; pay, answer.

accrue &c. (*be received*) 785.

Adj. acquir-ing, -ed &c. *v.*; acquisitive; productive, profitable, advantageous, gainful, remunerative, paying, lucrative.

sessed &c. 789; rid of, quit of; out of pocket.

lost &c. *v.*; long lost; irretrievable &c. (*hopeless*) 859; irredentist; off one's hands.

Int. farewell to! adieu to! good riddance!

---

777. Possession.—**N.** possession, seisin; ownership &c. 780; occupancy; hold, -ing; tenure, tenancy, feodality, dependency; villenage; socage, chivalry, knight service.

exclusive possession, impropriation, monopoly, corner; retention &c. 781; pre-possession, -occupancy; nine points of the law.

future possession, heritage, inheritance, heirship, reversion, fee, seigniority, feud, fief.

bird in hand, *uti possidetis, chose* in possession.

V. possess, have, hold, occupy, enjoy; be -possessed of &c. *adj.*; have -in hand &c. *adj.*; own &c. 780; command.

inherit; come -to, – in for.

engross, monopolize, forestall, regrate, impropriate, have all to oneself, corner; have a firm hold of &c. (*retain*) 781; get into one's hand &c. (*acquire*) 775.

belong to, appertain to, pertain to; be -in one's possession &c. *adj.*; vest in.

Adj. possessing &c. *v.*; worth; possessed of, seized of, master of, in possession of; endowed –, blest –, instinct –, fraught –, laden –, charged –, instilled –, with.

possessed &c. *v.*; on hand, by one; in hand, in store, in stock; in one's -hands, – grasp, – possession; at one's -command, – disposal; one's own &c. (*property*) 780.

unsold; unshared.

777a. Exemption.—N. exemption; exception, immunity, privilege, release &c. 927*a*; absence &c. 187.

V. not -have &c. 777; be -without &c. *adj.*

Adj. exempt from, devoid of, without, unpossessed of, unblest with, immune from.

not -having &c. 777; unpossessed; untenanted &c. (*vacant*) 187; without an owner.

unobtained, unacquired.

778. [Joint possession.] **Participation.—N.** participation; co-, joint-tenancy; possession -, tenancy- in common; joint -, common- stock; co-, partnership; communion; community of -possessions, - goods; communalism, communism, socialism, collectivism; co-operation &c. 709; profit sharing.

snacks, co-portion, picnic, hotchpotch; co-heirship, -parceny, -parcenary; gavelkind.

participator, sharer; co-, partner; shareholder; co-, joint-tenant; tenants in common; co-heir, -parcener.

communist, socialist.

V. par-ticipate, -take; share, - in; come in for a share; go -shares, - snacks, - halves; share and share alike.

have -, possess -, be seized- -in common, - as joint tenants &c. *n.* join in; have a hand in &c. (*co-operate*) 709.

Adj. partaking &c. *v.*; communistic, socialistic, co-operative, profit sharing.

Adv. share and share alike.

779. Possessor.—N. possessor, holder; occup-ant, -ier; tenant; person -, man- -in possession &c. 777; renter, lodger, lessee, under-lessee; zemindar, ryot; tenant -on sufferance, - at will, - from year to year, - for years, - for life.

owner; propriet-or, -ress, -ary; impropriator, master, mistress, lord.

land-holder, -owner, -lord, -lady; lord -of the manor, - paramount; heritor, laird, vavasour, landed gentry, mesne lord.

cestui-que-trust, beneficiary, mortgagor.

grantee, feoffee, relessee, devisee; legat-ee, -ary.

trustee; holder &c.- of the legal estate; mortgagee.

right -, rightful- owner.

[Future possessor] heir, - apparent; - presumptive; heiress; inherit-or, -ress, -rix; reversioner, remainder-man.

780. Property.—N. property, possession, *suum cuique, meum et tuum.*

owner-, proprietor-, lord-ship; seignority; empire &c. (*dominion*) 737.

interest, stake, estate, right, title, claim, demand, holding; tenure &c. (*possession*) 777; vested -, contingent -, beneficial -, equitable-interest; use, trust, benefit; legal -, equitable- estate; seisin.

absolute interest, paramount estate, freehold; fee, - simple, - tail; estate -in fee, - in tail, - tail; estate in tail -male, - female, - general.

limitation, term, lease, settlement, strict settlement, particular estate; estate -for life, - for years, - *pur autre vie*; remainder, reversion, expectancy, possibility.

dower, dowry, *dot*, jointure, marriage portion, appanage, inheritance, heritage, patrimony, alimony; legacy &c. (*gift*) 784.

assets, belongings, means, resources, circumstances; wealth &c. 803; money &c. 800; what one -is worth, - will cut up for; estate and effects.

landed -, real- -estate, - property; realty; land, -s; subdivision; plot, site; tenements; hereditaments; corporeal -, incorporeal- hereditaments; acres; ground &c. (*earth*) 342; acquest; messuage.

territory, state, kingdom, principality, realm, empire, protectorate, margravate, dependancy, colony, sphere of influence, mandate.

manor, honour, domain, demesne; farm, ranch, plantation, *hacienda*; allodium &c. (*free*) 748; fieff, feoff, feud, zemindary, dependency.

free-, copy-, lease-holds; chattels real; fixtures, plant, heirloom easement; folkland; right of -common, - user.

personal -property, - estate, - effects; personalty, chattels, goods, effects, movables; stock, - in trade; things, traps, rattle-traps, paraphernalia; equipage &c. 633.

parcels, appurtenances.

impedimenta; lug-, bag-gage; bag and baggage; pelf; cargo, lading.

rent-roll; income &c. (*receipts*) 810.

patent, copyright; *chose* in action; credit &c. 805; debt &c. 806.

V. possess &c. 777; be the -possessor &c. 779- of own; have for one's own, - very own; come in for, inherit; enfeoff.

savour of the realty.

be one's -property &c. *n.*; belong to; ap-, pertain to.

Adj. one's own; landed, predial, manorial, allodial, seigniorial; free-, copy-, lease-hold; feu-, feo-dal; hereditary, entailed, personal.

Adv. to one's -credit, - account; to the good.

to one and -his heirs for ever, - the heirs of his body, - his heirs and assigns, - his executors, administrators and assigns.

---

781. Retention.—N. retention; retaining &c. *v.*; keep, detention, custody; tenacity, firm hold, grasp, gripe, grip, iron grip.

fangs, teeth, claws, talons, nail, hook, tentacle, *tenaculum*; bond &c. (*vinculum*) 45.

clutches, tongs, forceps, pincers, nippers, pliers, tweezers, vise.

paw, hand, finger, wrist, fist, neaf, neif.

bird in hand; captive &c. 754.

V. retain, keep; hold, - fast, - tight, - one's own, - one's ground; clinch, clench, clutch, grasp, gripe, hug, have a firm hold of.

secure, withold, detain; hold -, keepback; keep close; husband &c. (*store*) 636; reserve; have -, keep- in stock &c. (*possess*) 777; entail, tie up, settle.

Adj. retaining &c. *v.*; retentive, tenacious.

unforfeited, undeprived, undisposed, uncommunicated.

incommunicable, inalienable; in mortmain; in strict settlement.

Phr. *uti possidetis.*

---

782. Relinquishment. — N. relinquishment, abandonment &c. (*of a course*) 624; renunciation, expropriation, dereliction; cession, surrender, dispensation; resignation &c. 757; riddance.

derelict &c. *adj.*; jetsam; waif, foundling, orphan.

V. relinquish, give up, surrender, yield, cede; let -go, - slip; spare, drop, resign, forego, renounce, abjure, abandon, expropriate, give away, dispose of, part with; lay -aside, - apart, - down, - on the shelf &c. (*disuse*) 678; set -, put- aside; make away with, cast behind; discard, cast off, dismiss; maroon.

give -notice to quit, - warning; supersede; be -, get- -rid of, - quit of; eject &c. 297.

rid -, disburden -, divest -, dispossess- oneself of; wash one's hands of; divorce, desert; disinherit, cut off.

cast -, throw -, pitch -, fling- -away, - aside, - overboard, - to the dogs; cast -, throw -, sweep- to the winds; put -, turn -, sweep- away; jettison; quit one's hold.

Adj. relinquished &c. *v.*; cast off, derelict; unowned, unappropriated, un-

culled; left &c. (*residuary*) 40; divorced; disinherited.
Int. away with!

2°. *Transfer of Property*

783. Transfer.—N. transfer, conveyance, assignment, alienation, abalienation; demise, limitation; conveyancing; transmission &c. (*transference*) 270; enfeoffment, bargain and sale, lease and release; exchange &c. (*interchange*) 148; barter &c. 794; substitution &c. 147.

succession, reversion; shifting -use, – trust; devolution.

V. transfer, convey; alien, -ate; assign; grant &c. (*confer*) 784; consign; make –, hand- over; pass, hand, transmit, negotiate; hand down; exchange &c. (*interchange*) 148.

change -hands, – from one to another; devolve, succeed; come into possession &c. (*acquire*) 775; take over.

abalienate; disinherit; dispossess &c. 789; substitute &c. 147.

Adj. alienable, negotiable, transferable, reversional.

Phr. estate coming into possession.

784. Giving.—N. giving &c. *v.*; bestowal, donation; present-ation, -ment; accordance; con-, cession; delivery, consignment, dispensation, communication, endowment; invest-ment, -iture; award.

almsgiving, charity, liberality, generosity; philanthropy &c. 910.

[Thing given] gift, donation, present, *cadeau*; fairing; free gift, boon, favour, benefaction, grant, offering, oblation, sacrifice, immolation.

grace, act of grace, *bonus, bonanza*.

allowance, contribution, subscription, subsidy, tribute, subvention.

bequest, legacy, devise, will, dotation, appanage; dowry; voluntary -settlement, – conveyance &c. 783; amortization.

alms, largess, bounty, dole, sportule, donative, help, oblation, offertory, Peter's pence, *honorarium*, gratuity, Maundy money, Christmas box, Easter offering, vail, tip, *douceur*, drink money, *pourboire, trinkgeld, backsheesh*; fee &c. (*recompense*) 973; consideration.

bribe, bait, ground-bait; peace-offering, handsel.

785. Receiving.—N. receiving &c. *v.*; acquisition &c. 775; reception &c. (*introduction*) 296; suscipiency, acceptance, admission.

re-, ac-cipient; assignee, devisee; lega-tee, -tary; grantee, feoffee, donee, relessee, lessee.

sportulary, stipendiary; beneficiary; pension-er, -ary; almsman.

income &c. (*receipt*) 810.

V. receive; take &c. 789; acquire &c. 775; admit.

take in, catch, touch; pocket; put into one's -pocket, – purse; accept; take off one's hands.

be received; come -in, – to hand; pass –, fall- into one's hand; go into one's pocket; fall to one's -lot, – share; come –, fall- to one; accrue; have -given &c. 784 to one.

Adj. receiving &c. *v.*; re-, suscipient.

received &c. *v.*; given &c. 784; second-hand.

not given, unbestowed &c. (*see* give, bestow &c. 784).

giver, grantor &c. *v.*; donor, feoffer, settlor; almoner; testator; investor, subscriber, contributor; fairy godmother; Santa Claus, benefactor &c. 816.

V. deliver, hand, pass, put into the hands of; hand –, make –, deliver –, pass –, turn- over.

present, give away, dispense, dispose of; give –, deal –, dole –, mete –, fork –, shell –, squeeze- out.

pay &c. 807; render, impart, communicate.

concede, cede, yield, part with, shed cast; spend &c. 809.

give, bestow, confer, grant, accord, award, assign.

entrust, consign, vest in.

make a present; allow, contribute, subscribe, donate, furnish its quota.

invest, endow, settle upon; bequeath, leave, devise.

furnish, supply, help; ad-, minister to; afford, spare; accommodate -, indulge -, favour- with; shower down upon; lavish, pour on, thrust upon; tip, bribe; tickle -, grease- the palm; offer &c. 763; sacrifice, immolate.

Adj. giving &c. *v.*; given &c. *v.*; allow-ed, -able; concessional; communicable; charitable, eleemosynary, sportulary, tributary; *gratis* &c. 815.

786. Apportionment.—N. apportion-, allot-, consign-, assign-, appointment; appropriation; dis-pensation, -tribution; allocation, division, deal; repartition; administration.

dividend, portion, contingent, share, allotment, lot, cut, split, measure, dose; dole, meed, pittance; *quantum*, ration; ratio, proportion, quota, *modicum*, mess, allowance.

V. apportion., divide; cut, split, divvy; distribute, administer, dispense; billet, allot, detail, cast, share, mete; portion -, parcel -, doleout; deal, carve.

partition, assign, appropriate, appoint.

come in for one's share &c. (*participate*) 778.

Adj. apportioning &c. *v.*; respective.

Adv. respectively, each to each.

787. Lending.—N. lending &c. *v.*; loan, advance, accommodation, feneration; mortgage &c. (*security*) 771; investment.

mont de piété, pawnshop, hock shop, spout, my uncle's.

lender, pawnbroker, money lender, usurer.

V. lend, advance, loan, accommodate with; lend on security; pawn &c. (*security*) 771.

intrust, invest; place -, put- out to interest; sink, risk.

let, demise, lease, sett, under-, sub-let.

Adj. lending &c. *v.*; lent &c. *v.*; unborrowed &c. (*see* borrowed &c. 788).

Adv. in advance; on -loan, - security.

788. Borrowing. — N. borrowing pledging, pawning.

borrowed plumes; plagiarism &c. (*thieving*) 791.

replevin.

V. borrow, desume; pawn.

hire, rent, farm; take a -lease, - demise; take -, hire- by the -hour, - mile, - year &c.

raise -, take up- money; float bonds; raise the wind; fly a kite, borrow of Peter to pay Paul; run into debt &c. (*debt*) 806.

make use of, plagiarize, pirate.

replevy.

789. Taking.—N. taking &c. *v.*; reception &c. (*taking in*) 296; deglutition &c. (*taking food*) 298; appropriation, prehension, prensation; capture, caption; ap-, de-prehension; abreption, seizure; ab-duction, -lation; subtraction &c. (*subduction*) 38; abstraction, ademption.

790. Restitution.—N. restitution, return; ren-, red-dition; reinstatement, restoration; reinvestment, recuperation; repatriation; rehabilitation &c. (*reconstruction*) 660; reparation, atonement, indemnity, compensation, recompense.

release, replevin, redemption; recov-

dispossession; depriv-ation, -ement; bereavement; divestment; disherison; distraint, distress; sequestration, confiscation, attachment, execution; eviction &c. 297.

rapacity, extortion, vampirism, predacity, blood-sucking; theft &c. 791.

resumption; repris-e, -al; recovery &c. 775.

clutch, swoop, wrench; grip &c. (retention) 781; haul, take, catch; scramble.

taker, captor, capturer; vampire; extortioner.

V. take, catch, hook, nab, bag, sack, pocket, put into one's pocket, scrounge; receive; accept.

reap, crop, cull, pluck; gather &c. (get) 775; draw.

ap-, im-propriate; assume, possess oneself of; take possession of; commandeer; lay –, clap- one's hands on; help oneself to; make free with, dip one's hands into, lay under contribution; intercept; scramble for; deprive of.

take –, carry –, bear- -away, – off; abstract; hurry off –, run away- with; abduct; steal &c. 791; ravish; seize; pounce –, spring- upon; swoop -to, – down upon; take by -storm, – assault; snatch, reave.

snap up, nip up, whip up, catch up; kidnap, crimp, capture, lay violent hands on.

get –, lay –, take –, catch –, lay fast –, take firm- hold of; lay by the heels, take prisoner; fasten upon, grip, grapple, embrace, gripe, clasp, grab, clutch, collar, throttle, take by the throat, claw, clinch, clench, make sure of.

catch at, jump at, make a grab at, snap at, snatch at; reach, make a long arm, stretch forth one's hand.

take -from, – away from; deduct &c. 38; retrench &c. (curtail) 201; dispossess, ease one of, snatch from one's grasp; tear –, tear away –, wrench –, wrest –, wring- from; extort; deprive of, bereave; disinherit, cut off with a shilling.

oust &c. (eject) 297; divest; levy, distrain, confiscate; sequest-er, -rate, accroach; usurp; despoil, strip, fleece, shear, displume, impoverish, eat out of house and home; drain, – to the dregs; gut, dry, exhaust, swallow up; absorb &c. (suck in) 296; draw off; suck, – like a leech, – the blood of.

retake, resume; recover &c. 775.

Adj. taking &c. v.; privative, prehensile; pred-aceous, -al, -atory, -atorial; rap-acious, -torial; ravenous: parasitic; all-devouring, -engulfing.

bereft &c. 776.

Adv. at one fell swoop.

Phr. give an inch and take an ell.

ery &c. (getting back) 775; remitter, reversion.

V. return, restore; recondition; give –, carry –, bring- back; render, – up; give up; let go, unclutch; dis-, re-gorge; regurgitate; recoup, reimburse, repay, indemnify, reinvest, remit, rehabilitate; repair &c. (make good) 660.

redeem, recover &c. (get back) 775; take back again; revest, revert.

Adj. restoring &c. v.; recuperative &c. 660; in full restitution, to compensate for.

Phr. suum cuique.

---

791. Stealing.—N. stealing &c. v.; theft, thievery, robbery, latrociny, direption; abstraction, appropriation; plagiar-y, -ism; rape, kidnapping, depredation; raid, hold up.

spoliation, plunder, pillage; sack, -age; rapine, *brigandage*, highway robbery, foray, *razzia*; black-mail; piracy, privateering, buccaneering; filibuster-ing, -ism; burglary; house-breaking; cattle-stealing, -rustling, -lifting.

peculation, embezzlement; fraud &c. 545; larceny, petty larceny, pilfering, shop-lifting.

thievishness, rapacity, kleptomania, Alsatia; den of -Cacus, – thieves.

licence to plunder, letters of marque.

V. steal, thieve, rob, purloin, pilfer, filch, lift, prig, bag, nim, crib, cabbage, palm; abstract; appropriate, plagiarize.

convey away, carry off, abduct, kidnap, shanghai, impress, crimp; make –, walk –, run- off with; run away with; spirit away; seize &c. (*lay violent hands on*) 789.

plunder, pillage, rifle, sack, loot, ransack, spoil, spoliate, despoil, strip, sweep, gut, forage, levy black-mail, pirate, pickeer, maraud, lift cattle, rustle, poach, smuggle, run.

stick –, hold- up.

swindle, peculate, embezzle; sponge, mulct, rook, bilk, pluck, pigeon, skin, fleece, diddle; defraud &c. 545; obtain under false pretences; live by one's wits.

rob –, borrow of- Peter to pay Paul; set a thief to catch a thief.

disregard the distinction between *meum* and *tuum*.

Adj. thieving &c. *v.*; thievish, light-fingered; fur-acious, -tive; piratical; pred-aceous, -al, -atory, -atorial; raptorial &c. (*rapacious*) 789.

stolen &c. *v.*

Phr. *sic vos non vobis.*

792. Thief.—N. thief, robber, *homo trium literarum*, pilferer, rifler, filcher, plagiarist.

spoiler, depredator, pillager, marauder; harpy, shark, land-shark, falcon, moss-trooper, bushranger, Bedouin, brigand, freebooter, bandit, thug, dacoit, pirate, corsair, viking, Paul Jones; buccan-eer, -ier; piqu-, pick-eerer; rover, ranger, privateer, filibuster; rapparee, wrecker, picaroon; smuggler, poacher, plunderer; racketeer.

highwayman, Dick Turpin, Claude Duval, Macheath, knight of the road, footpad, sturdy beggar; abductor, kidnapper.

cut-, pick-purse; pick-pocket, light-fingered gentry; sharper; card-, skittle-sharper; crook; thimble-rigger; rook, Greek, blackleg, leg, welsher, defaulter; Autolycus, Cacus, Barabbas, Jeremy Diddler, Robert Macaire, artful dodger, trickster; swell mob, *chevalier d'industrie*; shop-lifter.

swindler, peculator; forger, coiner, counterfeiter, shoful; fence, receiver of stolen goods, duffer; smasher.

burglar, housebreaker; cracks-, mags-man; Bill Sikes, Jack Sheppard, Jonathan Wild, Raffles, cat burglar.

793. Booty.—N. booty, spoil, plunder, prize, loot, graft, swag, pickings, boodle; *spolia opima*, prey; blackmail; stolen goods.

Adj. looting &c. *n.*; manubial, spoliative.

3°. *Interchange of Property*

794. Barter.—N. barter, exchange, scorse, truck system; interchange &c. 148.

a Roland for an Oliver; *quid pro quo*; com-mutation, -position.

trade, commerce, mercature, buying and selling, bargain and sale; traffic, business, nundination, custom, shopping; commercial enterprise, speculation, jobbing, stock-jobbing, *agiotage*, brokery, arbitrage.

dealing, transaction, negotiation, bargain.

free trade.

V. barter, exchange, truck, scorse, swop; interchange &c. 148; commutate &c. (*substitute*) 147; compound for.

trade, traffic, buy and sell, give and take, nundinate; carry on –, ply –, drive- a trade; be in -business, – the city; keep a shop, deal in, employ one's capital in.

trade –, deal –, have dealings- with; transact –, do- business with; open –, keep- an account with.

bargain; drive –, make- a bargain; negotiate, bid for; dicker, haggle, higgle; chaffer, huckster, cheapen, beat down; stickle, – for; out-, under-bid; ask, charge; strike a bargain &c. (*contract*) 769.

speculate, give a sprat to catch a herring; buy in the cheapest and sell in the dearest market; rig the market.

Adj. commercial, mercantile, trading; interchangeable, marketable, staple, in the market, for sale.

wholesale, retail.

Adv. across the counter; on 'change.

---

795. Purchase.—N. purchase, emption; buying, purchasing, shopping; pre-emption, refusal.

coemption, bribery; slave trade.

buyer, purchaser, *emptor*, vendee; patron, employer, client, customer, *clientèle*.

V. buy, purchase, invest in, procure; rent &c. (*hire*) 788; repurchase, buy in.

keep in one's pay, bribe, suborn; pay &c. 807; spend &c. 809.

make –, complete- a purchase; buy over the counter; pay cash for.

shop, market, go a shopping.

Adj. purchased &c. *v.*

Phr. *caveat emptor.*

---

796. Sale.—N. sale, vent, disposal; auction, roup, Dutch auction; custom &c. (*traffic*) 794.

vendi-bility, -bleness.

seller, salesman; peddler, smous; vender, vendor, consignor; merchant &c. 797; auctioneer.

V. sell, vend, dispose of, effect a sale; sell -over the counter, – by auction &c. *n.*; dispense, retail; deal in &c. 794; sell -off, – out; turn into money; realize; bring -to, – under- the hammer; put up to auction; auction, offer –, put up- for sale; hawk, peddle, bring to market; offer &c. 763; undersell; dump, unload.

let; mortgage &c. (*security*) 771.

Adj. under the hammer, in the market, for sale.

saleable, marketable, vendible, in demand, having a ready sale; unsaleable &c., unpurchased, unbought; on one's hands.

---

97. Merchant.—N. merchant, trader, dealer, monger, chandler, salesman; changer; regrater; shop-keeper, -man; trades-man, -people, -folk.

retailer; chapman, hawker, huckster, higgler; peddler, smous, pedlar, *colporteur*, cadger, Autolycus; sutler, *vivandière*; coster-man, -monger; market woman; cheap jack; caterer &c. 637; tallyman.

money-broker, -changer, -lender; stock-broker, -jobber; cambist, usurer, moneyer, banker.

jobber; broker &c. (*agent*) 758; buyer &c. 795; seller &c. 796.

concern; firm &c. (*partnership*) 712.

798. Merchandise. — N. merchandise, ware, commodity, effects, goods, article, stock, produce, staple commodity; stock in trade &c. (*store*) 636; cargo &c. (*contents*) 190.

799. Mart.—N. mart; market, -place, *forum*; fair, bazaar, staple; stock –, exchange; 'change, *bourse*, Wall Street, Rialto, hall, guildhall; toll-booth, custom-house; Tattersalls.

shop, stall, booth; wharf; office, chambers, counting-house, *bureau*; coun-, comp-ter.

ware-house, -room; *dépôt*, interposit, *entrepôt*, *emporium*, establishment; store &c. 636.

open market, market-overt.

4°. *Monetary Relations*

800. Money.—N. money -matters, – market; finance; accounts &c. 811; funds, treasure; capital, stock; assets &c. (*property*) 780; wealth &c. 803; supplies, ways and means, wherewithal, sinews of war, almighty dollar, needful, cash.

sum, amount; balance, -sheet; sum total; proceeds &c. (*receipts*) 810.

currency, circulating medium, specie; coin, – of the realm; piece, hard cash, dollar, sterling coin; pounds shillings and pence; £ s. d., guineas; pocket, breeches pocket, purse; money in hand; the best, ready, – money; filthy lucre, shekels, roll, jack, rhino, blunt, dust, bawbees, brass, dibs, dough, mopus, tin, salt, chink, oof, spondulics, pile, wads.

precious metals, gold, silver, copper, nickel; bullion, bar, ingot, nugget.

petty cash; pocket-, pin-money; small –, change; small coin, loose cash; doit, stiver, rap, mite, farthing, *sou*, penny, shilling, bob, tanner, tester, groat, guinea, ducat; *rouleau*; *wampum*; good –, round –, lump-sum; power –, mint –, tons- of money; plum, lac of rupees, millions, money-bags, miser's hoard, stocking, mine of wealth &c. 803.

[Science of coins] numismatics, chrysology.

paper-money; money –, postal –, Post Office- order; note, – of hand; bank –, treasury- note; Bradbury; promissory note; I O U., bond; bill, – of exchange; draft, check, order, warrant, *coupon*, debenture, exchequer bill, *assignat*, greenback, gold –, silver- certificate.

copper, nickel, dime, quarter, two bits, half a dollar, dollar, buck, simoleon, fiver, tenner, a twenty, a sawbuck, a century, a grand; eagle, double eagle.

gold standard, bimetallism, fiat money; rate of –, exchange; in-, de-flation.

remittance &c. (*payment*) 807; credit &c. 805; liability &c. 806; solvency &c. 803.

draw-er, -ee; oblig-or, -ee; moneyer, coiner, counterfeiter, forger.

false –, bad- money; base –, counterfeit- coin, flash note, slip, kite; Bank of Elegance.

argumentum ad crumenam.

V. amount to, come to, mount up to; touch the pocket; draw, – upon; endorse &c. (*security*) 771; issue, utter, circulate; discount &c. 813.

forge, counterfeit, coin, circulate –, pass- bad money.

Adj. monetary, pecuniary, crumenal, fiscal, financial, sumptuary, numismatical; sterling; solvent &c. 803.

801. Treasurer.—N. treasurer; bursar, -y; purser, purse-bearer; cash-keeper, banker; depositary; questor, receiver, steward, trustee, chartered -, accountant; Accountant-General, almoner, liquidator, paymaster, cashier, teller; cambist; money-changer &c. (*merchant*) 797.

financier, Chancellor of the Exchequer, minister of finance; Secretary of the Treasury, Director of the Budget, Controller of Currency.

802. Treasury.—N. treasury, bank, exchequer, almonry, fisc, hanaper, bursary; safe; strong-box, -hold, -room; coffer; chest &c. (*receptacle*) 191; depository &c. 636; till, -er; cash-box, -register, purse, pocket-book, wallet; money-bag, -belt, -box; *porte-monnaie*.

purse-strings; pocket, breeches pocket.

sinking fund; stocks; government -, public -, parliamentary- -stocks, - funds, - securities, bonds; gilt-edged securities; Consols, Liberty bonds, government bonds, *crédit mobilier*.

803. Wealth.—N. wealth, riches, fortune, handsome fortune, opulence, affluence; good -, easy- circumstances; independence; competence &c. (*sufficiency*) 639; solvency, soundness, solidity.

provision, livelihood, maintenance; alimony, dowry; means, resources, substance; property &c. 780; command of money.

income &c. 810; capital, money; round sum &c. (*treasure*) 800; mint of money, mine of wealth, *El Dorado*, Pactolus, Golconda, Potosi, *bonanza*; philosopher's stone.

long -, full -, well lined -, heavy-purse; purse of Fortunatus.

pelf, Mammon, lucre, filthy lucre; loaves and fishes; fleshpots of Egypt.

rich -, moneyed -, warm- man; man of substance; capitalist, millionaire, Nabob, Crœsus, Midas, Plutus, Dives, Timon of Athens; Timo-, Pluto-cracy; Danaë.

V. be -rich &c. *adj.*; roll -, wallow-in -wealth, - riches; have money to burn.

afford, well afford; command -money, - a sum; make both ends meet, hold one's head above water.

become -rich &c. *adj.*; fill one's -pocket &c. (*treasury*) 802; feather one's nest, clean up -, make- a fortune; make money &c. (*acquire*) 775.

enrich, imburse.

worship -Mammon, - the golden calf.

Adj. wealthy, rich, affluent, opulent, moneyed, monied, worth -a great deal,

804. Poverty.—N. poverty, indigence, penury, pauperism, destitution, want; need, -iness; lack, necessity, privation, distress, difficulties, wolf at the door.

bad -, poor -, needy -, embarrassed -, reduced -, straitened- circumstances; slender -, narrow- means; straits; hand to mouth existence, *res angusta domi*, low water, impecuniosity.

beggary; mendi-cancy, -city; broken -, loss of- fortune; insolvency &c. (*non-payment*) 808.

empty -purse, - pocket; light purse; beggarly account of empty boxes.

poor man, pauper, mendicant, mumper, beggar, starveling; *pauvre diable*.

V. be -poor &c. *adj.*; want, lack, starve, live from hand to mouth, have seen better days, go down in the world, be on one's uppers, come upon the parish; go to -the dogs, - wrack and ruin; not have a -penny &c. (*money*) 800, - shot in one's locker; beg one's bread; *tirer le diable par la queue*; run into debt &c. (*debt*) 806.

render -poor &c. *adj.*; impoverish; reduce, - to poverty; pauperize, fleece, ruin, bring to the parish.

Adj. poor, indigent; poverty -stricken; badly -, poorly -, ill- off; poor as -a rat, - a church mouse, - Job's turkey, - Job; fortune-, dower-, money-, penni-less; unportioned, unmoneyed; impecunious; broke, flat; out -, short- of -money, - cash; without -, not worth- a rap &c. (*money*) 800; *qui n'a pas le sou*, out of pocket, hard up; out at

– much; well -to do, – off; warm; well –, provided for.

made of money; rich as Crœsus; rolling in -riches, – wealth.

flush, – of -cash, – money, – tin; in -funds, – cash, – full feather; solvent, solid, sound, pecunious, out of debt, all straight; able to pay 20s in the £.

Phr. one's ship coming in.

———

-elbows, – heels; seedy, bare-footed; beggar-ly, -ed; destitute; fleeced, strapped, stripped; bereft, bereaved; reduced.

in -want &c. *n.*; needy, necessitous, distressed, pinched, straitened; put to one's -shifts, – last shifts; unable to -keep the wolf from the door, – make both ends meet; embarrassed, under hatches; involved &c. (*in debt*) 806; insolvent &c. (*not paying*) 808.

Adv. *in formâ pauperis.*

Phr. *zonam perdidit.*

805. Credit.—N. credit, trust, tick, score, tally, account.

letter of credit, circular note; duplicate; mortgage, lien, debenture, paper credit, floating capital; draft; securities.

creditor, lender, lessor, mortgagee; dun; usurer.

V. keep –, run up- an account with; entrust, credit, accredit.

place to one's -credit, – account; give –, take- credit; fly a kite.

Adj. credit-ing, -ed; accredited.

Adv. on -credit &c. *n.*; to the -account, – credit- of.

———

806. Debt.—N. debt, obligation, liability, indebtment, debit, score.

arrears, deferred payment, deficit, default; insolvency &c. (*non-payment*) 808; bad debt.

interest; usance, usury; premium; floating -debt, – capital.

debtor, debitor; mortgagor; defaulter &c. 808; borrower.

V. be -in debt &c. *adj.*; owe; incur –, contract- a debt &c. *n.*; run up -a bill, – a score, – an account; go on tick, put on the cuff; borrow &c. 788; run –, get- into debt; outrun the constable.

answer –, go bail- for; back one's note.

Adj. indebted; liable, chargeable, answerable for.

in -debt, – embarrassed circumstances, – difficulties; incumbered, involved; involved –, plunged –, deep –, over head and ears- in debt; deeply involved; fast tied up; insolvent &c. (*not paying*) 808; *minus*, out of pocket.

unpaid; unrequited, unrewarded; owing, due, in arrear, outstanding.

807. Payment.—N. pay-, defrayment; discharge; ac-, quittance; settlement, clearance, liquidation, satisfaction, reckoning, arrangement.

acknowledgment, release; receipt, – in full, – in full of all demands; voucher.

repayment, reimbursement, retribution; pay &c. (*reward*) 973; money paid &c. (*expenditure*) 809.

ready money &c. (*cash*) 800; stake, remittance, instalment.

payer, liquidator &c. 801.

V. pay, defray, make payment; pay -down, – on the nail, – ready money, – at sight, – in advance; cash, honour a bill, acknowledge; redeem; pay in kind.

808. Non-payment.—N. non-payment; default, defalcation; protest, repudiation; application of the sponge; whitewashing.

insolvency, bankruptcy, failure; overdraft, overdrawn account; insufficiency &c. 640; run upon a bank.

waste paper bonds; dishonoured –, protested- bills; bogus cheque.

bankrupt, insolvent debtor, lame duck, man of straw, welsher, stag, defaulter, absconder, levanter.

V. not -pay &c. 807; fail, break, stop payment; become -insolvent, – bankrupt; be gazetted.

protest, dishonour, repudiate, nullify.

pay under protest; button up one's

pay one's -way, – shot, – footing; pay -the piper, – sauce for all, – costs; do the needful; come across; shell –, fork- out; come down with, – the dust; tickle –, grease- the palm; expend &c. 809; put –, lay- down.

discharge, settle, quit, acquit oneself of; account –, reckon –, settle –, be even –, be quits- with; strike a balance; settle –, balance –, square-accounts with; quit scores; foot the bill; wipe –, clear- off old scores; satisfy; pay in full; satisfy –, pay in full of- all demands; clear, liquidate; pay -up, – old debts.

disgorge, make repayment; repay, refund, reimburse, retribute; make compensation &c. 30.

Adj. paying &c., paid &c. *v.*; owing nothing, out of debt, all straight, clear of -debt, – encumbrance; unowed, never indebted.

Adv. to the tune of; on the nail; money –, cash- down; cash on delivery.

pockets, draw the purse strings; apply the sponge; pay over the left shoulder, get whitewashed; swindle &c. 791; run up bills, fly kites.

Adj. not paying; in debt &c. 806; behindhand, in arrear; beggared &c. (*poor*) 804; unable to make both ends meet; *minus*; worse than nothing.

insolvent, bankrupt, in the gazette, gazetted, ruined.

unpaid &c. (*outstanding*) 806; *gratis* &c. 815; unremunerated.

---

809. Expenditure.—N. expenditure, money going out; out-goings, -lay; expenses, disbursement; prime cost &c. (*price*) 812; circulation; run upon a bank.

[Money paid] payment &c. 807; pay &c. (*remuneration*) 973; bribe &c. 973; fee, footing, garnish; subsidy; tribute, Peter's pence; contingent, quota; donation &c. 784.

pay in advance, earnest, handsel, deposit, instalment.

investment; purchase &c. 795.

V. expend, spend; run –, get-through; pay, disburse; open –, loose –, untie- the purse strings; lay –, shell –, fork- out; bleed; make up a sum, invest, sink money.

fee &c. (*reward*) 973; pay one's way &c. (*pay*) 807; subscribe &c. (*give*) 784; subsidize, bribe.

Adj. expend-ing, -ed &c. *v.*; sumptuary, liberal &c. 816; open-handed, lavish &c. 818; extensive &c. 814.

810. Receipt.—N. receipt, accountable –, conditional –, binding –, return-receipt; value received, money coming in; income, incomings, innings, revenue, return, proceeds; gross receipts, net profit; earnings &c. (*gain*) 775.

rent, – roll; rent-al, -age; rack-rent.

premium, *bonus*; sweepstakes, tontine, 'prize, drawing.

pension, annuity; jointure &c. (*property*) 780; alimony, pittance; emolument &c. (*remuneration*) 973.

V. receive &c. 785; take money; draw –, derive- from; get, be in receipt of, acquire &c. 775; take &c. 789.

bring in, yield, afford, pay, return; accrue &c. (*be received from*) 785.

Adj. receiv-ing, -ed &c. *v.*; profitable &c. (*gainful*) 775.

---

811. Accounts.—N. accounts, accompts; commercial –, monetary-arithmetic; statistics &c. (*numeration*) 85; money matters, finance, budget, bill, score, reckoning, account.

books, account book, ledger; day –, cash –, pass- book; journal; debtor and creditor –, cash –, petty cash –, running- account; account-current; balance, – sheet; *compte rendu*, account settled.

book-keeping, audit; double –, single- entry; reckoning &c. 85.

chartered –, certified public –, accountant; auditor, actuary, book-keeper; financier &c. 801; accounting party.

V. keep accounts, enter, post, book, credit, debit, carry over; take stock; balance –, make up –, square –, settle –, wind up –, cast up –, add up –, tot up- accounts; make accounts square.

bring to book, audit, tax, surcharge and falsify.

falsify –, garble –, cook –, doctor- an account.

Adj. monetary &c. 800; account-able, -ing; statistical.

812. Price.—N. price, amount, cost, expense, prime cost, charge, figure, demand, damage, fare, hire; wages &c. (*remuneration*) 973.

dues, duty, toll, tax, impost, cess, sess, tallage, levy, capitation-, poll-, income-, sur-, sales-, super-tax; gabel, *gabelle*; gavel, *octroi*, custom, tariff, excise, assessment, taxation, benevolence, tithe, tenths, exactment, ransom, salvage; broker-, wharf-, lighter-, ton-, freight-age.

worth, rate, value, valuation, appraisement, money's worth, par value; penny &c. -worth; price current, market price, quotation; what it will -fetch &c. *v.*

bill &c. (*account*) 811; shot.

V. bear –, set –, fix- a price; appraise, assess, price, charge, demand, ask, require, exact, run up; distrain; run up a bill &c. (*debt*) 806; have one's price; liquidate.

amount to, come to, mount up to; stand one in.

fetch, sell for, cost, bring in, yield, afford.

Adj. priced &c. *v.*; to the tune of, *ad valorem*; mercenary, venal.

Phr. no penny. no paternoster; *point d'argent, point de Suisse*, no longer pipe, no longer dance, no song, no supper.

one may have it for.

814. Dearness. — N. dearness &c. *adj.*; high –, famine –, fancy- price; overcharge; extravagance; exorbitance; extortion; heavy pull upon the purse; Pyrrhic victory.

V. be -dear &c. *adj.*; cost -much, – a pretty penny; rise in price, look up.

overcharge, bleed, fleece, skin, extort.

pay -too much, – through the nose, – too dear for one's whistle.

Adj. dear; high, -priced; of great price, expensive, costly, precious, dear bought; unreasonable, **extravagant**, exorbitant, extortionate.

at a premium; not to be had, – for love or money; beyond –, above- price; priceless, of priceless value.

Adv. dear, -ly; at great –, heavy- cost; *à grands frais*.

Phr. prices looking up; *le jeu ne vaut pas la chandelle*.

813. Discount.—N. discount, abatement, concession, reduction, depreciation, allowance, qualification, set off, drawback, poundage, *agio*, percentage; rebate, -ment; backwardation, contango; salvage; tare and tret.

V. discount, bate; a-, re-bate; deduct, reduce, mark down, take off, allow, give, make allowance; tax, depreciate.

Adj. discounting &c. *v.*

Adv. at a discount, below par.

815. Cheapness.—N. cheapness, low price; depreciation; bargain; good penny &c.- worth, *bon marché*.

[Absence of charge] gratuity; free -quarters, – seats, – admission, – warren; pass, Annie Oakley; run of one's teeth; nominal price, peppercorn rent; labour of love.

drug in the market.

V. be -cheap &c. *adj.*; cost little; come down –, fall- in price.

buy for -a mere nothing, – an old song; have one's money's worth; cheapen, beat down.

Adj. cheap; low, – priced; moderate, reasonable; in-, un-expensive; well –, worth the money; *magnifique et pas cher*; good –, cheap- at the price; dirt –, dog- cheap; cheap, -as dirt, – and nasty; catchpenny.

reduced, marked down, half-price, depreciated, unsaleable.

gratuitous, *gratis*, free, for love,

– nothing; cost-, expense-less; without charge, not charged, untaxed; scot –, shot –, rent- free; free of -cost, – expense; honorary, unbought, unpaid, complimentary.

Adv. for a mere song; at -cost price, – prime cost, – a reduction, – a bargain; on the cheap.

816. Liberality.—N. liberality, generosity, munificence; bount-y, -eousness, -ifulness; hospitality; charity &c. (*beneficence*) 906.

benefactor, free giver, Lady Bountiful.

V. be -liberal &c. *adj.*; spend –, bleed- freely; shower down upon; open one's purse strings &c. (*disburse*) 809; spare no expense, give -with both hands, – *carte blanche.*

Adj. liberal, free, generous; charitable &c. (*beneficent*) 906; hospitable; bount-iful, -eous; handsome; unsparing, ungrudging; open-, free-, full-handed; open-, large-, free-hearted; munificent, princely, unstinting.

overpaid.

Adv. liberally, ungrudgingly, with open hand.

---

818. Prodigality.—N. prodi-gality, -gence; unthriftiness, waste, -fulness; profus-ion, -eness; extravagance; squandering &c. *v.*; lavishness; malversation.

prodigal; spend-, waste-thrift; losel, play-boy, spender, squanderer, locust.

V. be -prodigal &c. *adj.*; squander, lavish, sow broadcast; pour forth like water; pay through the nose &c. (*dear*) 814; spill, waste, dissipate, exhaust, drain, eat out of house and home, overdraw, outrun the constable; run -out, – through; misspend; throw -good money after bad, – the helve after the hatchet; burn the candle at both ends; make ducks and drakes of one's money; squander one's substance, spend money like water; fool –, potter –, muddle –, fritter –, throw- away one's money; pour water into a sieve, kill the goose that lays the golden eggs; *manger son blé en herbe.*

Adj. prodigal, profuse, thriftless, unthrifty, improvident, wasteful, losel,

817. Economy.—N. economy, frugality; thrift, -iness; prudence, care, husbandry, good housewifery, savingness, retrenchment.

savings; prevention of waste, save-all; cheese parings and candle ends; parsimony &c. 819.

V. be -economical &c. *adj.*; economize, save; retrench; cut- down expenses, – one's coat according to one's cloth, make both ends meet, keep within compass, meet one's expenses, pay one's way; keep one's head above water; husband &c. (*lay by*) 636; save –, invest- money; put out to interest; provide –, save- -for, – against- a rainy day; feather one's nest; look after the main chance.

Adj. economical, frugal, careful, thrifty, saving, chary, spare, sparing; parsimonious &c. 819.

underpaid.

Adv. sparingly &c. *adj.*; *ne quid nimis.*

819. Parsimony. — N. parsimony, parcity; parsimoniousness, stinginess &c. *adj.*; stint; illiberality, avarice, tenacity, avidity, rapacity, extortion, venality, cupidity; selfishness &c. 943; *auri sacra fames.*

miser, niggard, churl, screw, tightwad, skinflint, crib, codger, muckworm, money-grubber, pinchfist, scrimp, lickpenny, hunks, curmudgeon, *Harpagon*, Silas Marner, harpy, extortioner, usurer.

V. be -parsimonious &c. *adj.*; grudge, begrudge, stint, skimp, pinch, gripe, screw, dole out, hold back, withhold, starve, famish, live upon nothing, skin a flint.

drive a -bargain, – hard bargain; cheapen, beat down; stop one hole in a sieve; have an itching palm, grasp, grab.

Adj. parsimonious, penurious, stingy, miserly, mean, shabby, peddling, scrubby, pennywise, near, niggardly,

extravagant, lavish, dissipated, over liberal; full-handed &c. (*liberal*) 816.

penny wise and pound foolish.

Adv. with an unsparing hand; money burning one's pocket; recklessly profuse.

Int. hang the expense!

---

frugal to excess; close; fast-, close-, strait-handed; close-, hard-, tight-fisted; tight, sparing; chary; grudging, griping &c. *v.*; illiberal, ungenerous, churlish, hidebound, sordid, mercenary, venal, covetous, usurious, avaricious, greedy, extortionate, rapacious.

Adv. with a sparing hand.

CLASS VI

Words relating to the SENTIENT and MORAL POWERS.

CLASS VI

Words relating to the SENTIENT and MORAL POWERS.

～～～～～

Section I. AFFECTIONS IN GENERAL

820. Affections.—N. affections, character, qualities, disposition, nature, spirit, tone; temper, -ament; *diathesis*, idiosyncrasy; cast -, habit -, frame- of -mind, - soul; predilection, turn; natural -, turn of mind; bent, bias, predisposition, proneness, proclivity; propen-sity, -sedness, -sion, -dency; vein, humour, mood, grain, mettle; sympathy &c. (*love*) 897.

soul, heart, breast, bosom, inner man; heart's -core, - strings, - blood; heart of hearts, *penetralia mentis*; secret and inmost recesses of the -, cockles of one's- heart; inmost -heart, - soul; back-bone.

passion, pervading spirit; ruling -, master- passion; *furore*; fulness of the heart, heyday of the blood, flesh and blood, flow of soul, force of character.

V. have -, possess- -affections &c. *n.*; be of a -character &c. *n.*; be -affected &c. *adj.*; breathe.

Adj. affected, characterized, formed, moulded, cast; at-, tempered; framed; pre-, disposed; prone, inclined; having a -bias &c. *n.*; tinctured -, imbued -, penetrated -, eaten up- with.

inborn, inbred, ingrained, in the grain, congenital, inherent, bred in the bone; deep-rooted, ineffaceable, inveterate; pathoscopic.

Adv. in one's -heart &c. *n.*; at heart; heart and soul &c. 821; in the -vein, - mood.

821. Feeling.—N. feeling; suffering &c. *v.*; endurance, tolerance, sufferance, supportance, experience, response; sympathy &c. (*love*) 897; impression, inspiration, affection, sensation, emotion, pathos, deep sense.

fire, warmth, glow, unction, *gusto*, vehemence; ferv-our, -ency; heartiness, cordiality; earnestness, eagerness; *empressement*, ardour, zeal, passion, enthusiasm, *verve*, *furore*, fanaticism; excitation of feeling &c. 824; fulness of the heart &c. (*disposition*) 820; passion &c. (*state of excitability*) 825; ecstasy &c. (*pleasure*) 827.

blush, suffusion, flush; hectic; tingling, thrill, kick, turn, shock; agitation &c. (*irregular motion*) 315; quiver, heaving, flutter, flurry, fluster, twitter, tremor; throb, -bing; pulsation, palpitation, painting; trepid-, perturb-ation; ruffle, hurry of spirits, pother, stew, ferment.

V. feel; receive an -impression &c. *n.*; be -impressed with &c. *adj.*; entertain -, harbour -, cherish- -feeling &c. *n.*

respond; catch the -flame, - infection; enter the spirit of.

bear, suffer, support, sustain, endure, brook, thole, aby; abide &c.

(*be composed*) 826; experience &c. (*meet with*) 151; taste, prove; labour –, smart- under; bear the brunt of, brave, stand.

swell, glow, warm, flush, blush, change colour, mantle; turn -colour, – pale, – red, – black in the face; blench, crimson, whiten, pale, tingle, thrill, heave, pant, throb, palpitate, go pit-a-pat, tremble, quiver, flutter, twitter; stagger, reel; shake &c. 315; be -agitated, – excited &c. 824; look -blue, – black; wince, draw a deep breath.

impress &c. (*excite the feelings*) 824.

Adj. feeling &c. *v.*; sentient; sensuous; sensor-ial, -y; emo-tive, -tional; of –, with- feeling &c. *n.*

warm, quick, lively, smart, strong, sharp, acute, cutting, piercing, incisive; keen, – as a razor; trenchant, pungent, racy, *piquant*, poignant, caustic.

impressive, deep, profound, indelible; deep-, home-, heart-felt; swelling, soul-stirring, deep-mouthed, heart-expanding, electric, thrilling, rapturous, ecstatic.

earnest, wistful, eager, breathless; fer-vent, -vid; gushing, passionate, warmhearted, hearty, cordial, sincere, zealous, enthusiastic, glowing, ardent, burning, red-hot, fiery, flaming; boiling, – over.

pervading, penetrating, absorbing; rabid, raving, feverish, fanatical, hysterical; impetuous &c. (*excitable*) 825; overmastering.

impressed –, moved –, touched –, affected –, penetrated –, seized –, imbued &c. 820- with; devoured by; wrought up &c. (*excited*) 824; struck all of a heap; rapt; in a -quiver &c. *n.*; enraptured &c. 829.

Adv. heart and soul, from the bottom of one's heart, *ab imo pectore*, *de profundis*, at heart, *con amore*, heartily, devoutly, over head and ears.

Phr. the heart -big, – full, – swelling, – beating, – pulsating, – throbbing, – thumping, – beating high, – melting, – overflowing, – bursting, – breaking.

---

822. Sensibility. — N. sensi-bility, -bleness, -tiveness; moral sensibility; impress-, affect-ibility; suscepti-ble-ness, -bility, -vity; mobility; viva-city, -ciousness; tender-, soft-ness; sentimental-ity, -ism.

excitability &c. 825; fastidiousness &c. 868; physical sensibility &c. 375.

sore -point, – place; where the shoe pinches.

V. be -sensible &c. *adj.*; have a -tender, – warm, – sensitive- heart.

take to –, treasure up in the- heart; shrink.

'die of a rose in aromatic pain'; touch to the quick.

Adj. sensi-ble, -tive; impressi-ble, -onable; suscepti-ve, -ble; alive to, impassion-able, -ed; gushing; warm-, tender-, soft-hearted; tender –, as a chicken; soft, sentimental, romantic; enthusiastic, highflying, spirited, mettlesome, vivacious, lively, expressive, mobile, tremblingly alive; excitable

823. Insensibility.—N. insensi-bility, -bleness; moral insensibility; inertness, *inertia*, *vis inertiæ*; impassi-bility, -bleness; inappetency, apathy, phlegm, dulness, hebetude, supineness, luke-warmness, insusceptibility, unimpress-ibility.

cold -fit, – blood, – heart; cold-, cool-ness; frigidity, *sang-froid*; stoicism, imperturbation &c. (*inexcitability*) 826; *nonchalance*, unconcern, dry eyes; *insouciance* &c. (*indifference*) 866; recklessness &c. 863; callousness; heart of stone, stock and stone, marble, deadness.

torp-or, -idity; obstupefaction, leth-argy, coma, trance; sleep &c. 683; suspended animation; stup-or, -efac-tion; paralysis, palsy; numbness &c. (*physical insensibility*) 376.

neutrality; quietism, vegetation.

V. be -insensible &c. *adj.*; have a rhinoceros hide; show -insensibility &c. *n.*; not -mind, – care, – be affected

&c. 825; over-sensitive, without skin, thin-skinned; fastidious &c. 868.

Adv. sensibly &c. *adj.*; to the -quick, – inmost core.

by; have no desire for &c. 866; have –, feel –, take- no interest in; *nil admirari*; not care a -straw &c. (*unimportance*) 643 for; disregard &c. (*neglect*) 460; set at naught &c. (*make light of*) 483; turn a deaf ear to &c. (*inattention*) 458; vegetate.

render -insensible, – callous; blunt, obtund, numb, benumb, paralyze, chloroform, deaden, hebetate, stun, stupefy; brut-ify, -alize.

inure; harden, – the heart; steel, case-harden, sear.

Adj. insensible, unconscious; impassi-ve, -ble; blind to, deaf to, dead to; un-, in-susceptible; unimpress-ionable, -ible; passion-, spirit-, heart-, soul-less; unfeeling, unmoral.

apathetic; leuco-, phlegmatic; dull, frigid; cold, -blooded, -hearted; unemotional; cold as charity; flat, obtuse, inert, supine, sluggish, torpid; sleepy &c. (*inactive*) 683; languid, half-hearted, tame; numb, -ed; comatose; anæsthetic &c. 376; stupefied, chloroformed, palsy-stricken.

indifferent, lukewarm; Laodicean; careless, mindless, regardless; inattentive &c. 458; neglectful &c. 460; disregarding.

unconcerned, *nonchalant, pococurante, insouciant, sans souci*; un-ambitious &c. 866.

un-affected, -ruffled, -impressed, -inspired, -excited, -moved, -stirred, -touched, -shocked, -struck; unblushing &c. (*shameless*) 885; unanimated; vegetative.

callous, thick-skinned, pachydermatous, impervious; hard, -ened; inured, case-hardened; steeled –, proof- against; imperturbable &c. (*inexcitable*) 826; unfelt.

Adv. insensibly &c. *adj.*; *æquo animo*; without being -moved, – touched, – impressed; in cold blood; with -dry eyes, – withers unwrung.

Phr. never mind; it is of no consequence &c. (*unimportant*) 643; it cannot be helped; nothing coming amiss; it is all -the same, – one- to.

824. Excitation.—N. excitation of feeling; mental –, excitement; suscitation, galvanism, stimulation, piquancy, provocation, inspiration, calling forth, infection; interest, animation, agitation, perturbation; subjugation, fascination, intoxication; en-, ravishment; entrancement, high pressure.

unction, impressiveness &c. *adj.*; emotional appeal; melodrama; psychological moment, crisis; sensationalism.

trial of temper, *casus belli*; irritation &c. (*anger*) 900; passion &c. (*state of excitability*) 825; thrill &c. (*feeling*) 821; repression of feeling &c. 826.

V. excite, affect, touch, move, impress, strike, interest, intrigue, animate, inspire, impassion, smite, infect; stir –, fire –, warm- the blood; set astir; a-, wake; a-, waken; call forth; e-, pro-voke; raise up, summon up, call up, wake up, blow up, get up, light up; raise; get up steam, rouse, arouse, stir, fire, kindle, enkindle, apply the torch, set on fire, inflame, illuminate.

stimulate; ex-, suscitate; inspirit; spirit up, stir up, work up; infuse life into, give new life to; bring –, introduce- new blood; quicken;

sharpen, whet; work upon &c. (*incite*) 615; hurry on, give a fillip, put on one's mettle.

fan the -fire, – flame; blow the coals, stir the embers; fan, – into a flame; foster, heat, warm, foment, raise to a fever heat; keep -up, – the pot boiling; revive, rekindle; rake up, rip up.

stir –, play on –, come home to- the feelings; touch -a string, – a chord, – the soul, – the heart; go to one's heart, penetrate, pierce, go through one, touch to the quick, open the wound; possess –, pervade –, penetrate –, imbrue –, absorb –, affect –, disturb- the soul.

absorb, rivet the attention; sink into the -mind, – heart; prey on the mind; intoxicate; over-whelm, -power; *bouleverser*, upset, turn one's head.

fascinate; enrapture &c. (*give pleasure*) 829.

agitate, perturb, ruffle, fluster, flutter, shake, disturb, faze, startle, shock, stagger; give one a -shock, – turn; strike -dumb, – all of a heap; stun, astound, electrify, galvanize, petrify.

irritate, sting; cut, – to the -heart, – quick; try one's temper; fool to the top of one's bent, pique; infuriate, madden, make one's blood boil; lash into fury &c. (*wrath*) 900.

be -excited &c. *adj.*; flash up, flare up; catch the infection; thrill &c. (*feel*) 821; mantle; work oneself up; seethe, boil, simmer, foam, fume, flame, rage, rave; run mad &c. (*passion*) 825.

Adj. excited &c. *v.*; wrought up, on the *qui vive*, astir, sparkling; in a -quiver &c. 821, – fever, – ferment, – blaze, – state of excitement; in hysterics; black in the face, over-wrought; hot, red-hot, flushed, feverish; all -of a twitter, – of a flutter, – of a dither, – in a pucker; with -quivering lips, – tears in one's eyes.

flaming; boiling, – over; ebullient, seething; foaming, – at the mouth; fuming, raging, carried away by passion, wild, raving, frantic, mad, distracted, distraught, beside oneself, out of one's wits, amuck, ready to burst, *bouleversé*, demoniacal.

lost, *éperdu*, tempest-tossed; haggard; ready to sink.

stung to the quick, up, on one's high ropes.

exciting &c. *v.*; impressive, warm, glowing, fervid, swelling, impos-ing, spirit-stirring, thrilling; high-wrought; soul-stirring, -subduing; heart-swelling, -thrilling; agonizing &c. (*painful*) 830; telling, sensa-tional, melodramatic, hysterical; over-powering, -whelming; more than flesh and blood can bear.

piquant &c. (*pungent*) 392; spicy, appetizing, provocative, *provoquant*, tantalizing.

Adv. till one is black in the face.

Phr. the heart -beating high, – going pit-a-pat, – leaping into one's mouth; the blood -being up, – boiling in one's veins; the eye -glisten-ing, – 'in a fine frenzy rolling'; the head turned.

---

825. [Excess of sensitiveness.] **Excit-ability.**—**N.** excitability, impetuosity, vehemence; boisterousness &c. *adj.*; turbulence; impatience, intolerance, non-endurance; irritability &c. (*irasci-bility*) 901; itching &c. (*desire*) 865; wincing; disquiet, -ude; restlessness; fidge-ts, -tiness; agitation &c. (*irregular motion*) 315.

826. [Absence of excitability, or of excitement.] **Inexcitability.**—**N.** inex-cit-, imperturb-, inirrit-ability; even temper, tranquil mind, dispassion; tol-erance, toleration, patience.

passiveness &c. (*physical inertness*) 172; hebet-ude, -ation; impassibility &c. (*insensibility*) 823; stupefaction.

coolness, calmness &c. *adj.*; compo-

trepidation, perturbation, ruffle, hurry, -skurry, fuss, flurry; fluster, flutter; pother, stew, ferment; whirl; thrill &c. (*feeling*) 821; state -, fever- of excitement; transport.

passion, excitement, flush, heat; fever, -heat; fire, flame, fume, blood boiling; tumult; effervescence, ebullition; boiling, – over; whiff, gust, storm, tempest; scene, breaking out, burst, fit, paroxysm, explosion; out-break, -burst; agony.

violence &c. 173; fierceness &c. *adj.*; rage, fury, *furor, furore*, desperation, madness, distraction, raving, delirium, brain storm; frenzy, hysterics; intoxication; tearing -, raging- passion, towering rage; anger &c. 900.

fascination, infatuation, fanaticism; Quixot-ism, -ry; *tête montée*.

V. be -impatient &c. *adj.*; not be able to -bear &c. 826; bear ill, wince, chafe, champ the bit; be in a -stew &c. *n.*; be out of all patience, fidget, fuss, not have a wink of sleep; toss, – on one's pillow.

lose one's temper &c. 900; break -, burst -, fly- out; go -, fly- -off, – off the handle, – off at a tangent; explode; flare up, flame up, fire up, burst into a flame, take fire, fire, burn; boil, – over; foam, fume, rage, rave, rant, tear; go -, run- -wild, – mad; go into hysterics; run -riot, – amuck; *battre la campagne, faire le diable à quatre*, play the deuce; raise -Cain, – the devil.

Adj. excitable, easily excited, in an excitable state; highly strung; irritable &c. (*irascible*) 901; impatient, intolerant.

feverish, febrile, hysterical; delirious, mad, moody, maggoty-headed.

unquiet, mercurial, electric, galvanic, hasty, hurried, restless, fidgety, fussy; chafing &c. *v.*

startlish, mettlesome, high mettled, skittish.

vehement, demonstrative, violent, wild, furious, fierce, fiery, hot-headed, mad-cap.

over-zealous, enthusiastic, impassioned, fanatical; rabid &c. (*eager*) 865.

rampant, clamorous, uproarious, tur-

sure, placidity, indisturbance, imperturbation, *sang-froid*, tranquillity, serenity; quiet, -ude; peace of mind, mental calmness.

staidness &c. *adj.*; gravity, sobriety, Quakerism; philosophy, equanimity, stoicism, command of temper; self-possession, -control, -command, -restraint; presence of mind.

submission &c. 725; resignation; suffer-, support-, endur-, long-suffer-, forbear-ance; longanimity; fortitude; patience -of Job, – 'on a monument,' – 'sovereign o'er transmuted ill'; moderation; repression -, subjugation- of feeling; restraint &c. 751.

tranquillization &c. (*moderation*) 174.

V. be -composed &c. *adj.*

laisser -faire, – aller; take things -easily, – as they come; take it easy, run on, live and let live; take -easily, – coolly, – in good part; *æquam serva e mentem*.

bear, – well, – the brunt; go through, support, endure, brave, disregard.

tolerate, suffer, stand, bide; abide, aby; bear -, put up -, abide- with; acquiesce; submit &c. (*yield*) 725; submit with a good grace; resign -, reconcile- oneself to; brook, digest, eat, swallow, pocket, stomach; make -light of, – the best of, – a virtue of necessity; put a good face on, keep one's countenance; carry -on, – through; check &c. 751- oneself.

compose, appease &c. (*moderate*) 174; propitiate; repress &c. (*restrain*) 751; render insensible &c. 823; overcome -, allay -, repress- one's -excitability &c. 825; master one's feelings.

make -oneself, – one's mind- easy; set one's mind at -ease, – rest.

calm -, cool- down; thaw, grow cool.

be -borne, – endured; go down.

Adj. in-, un-excitable; imperturbable; unsusceptible &c. (*insensible*) 823; un-, dis-passionate; cold-blooded, inirritable; enduring &c. *v.*; stoical, Platonic, philosophic, staid, stayed; sober, – minded; grave; sober -, grave- as a judge; sedate, demure, cool-, level-headed; steady.

easy-going, peaceful, placid, calm; quiet, – as a mouse; tranquil, serene;

bulent, tempestuous, tumultuary, boisterous.

impulsive, impetuous, passionate; uncontroll-ed, -able; ungovernable, irrepressible, stanchless, inextinguishable, burning, simmering, volcanic, ready to burst forth.

excit-ed, -ing &c. 824.

Int. pish! pshaw!

Phr. *noli me tangere.*

---

cool, - as -a cucumber, - custard; undemonstrative.

temperate &c. (*moderate*) 174; composed, collected; un-excited, -stirred, -ruffled, -disturbed, -perturbed, -impassioned; unoffended; unresisting.

meek, tolerant; patient, - as Job; submissive &c. 725; tame; content, resigned, chastened, subdued, lamblike; gentle, - as a lamb; *suaviter in modo*; mild, - as mother's milk; soft as peppermint; armed with patience, bearing with, clement, forbearant, long-suffering.

Adv. 'like patience on a monument smiling at grief'; *æquo animo*, in cold blood &c. 823; more in sorrow than in anger.

Int. patience! and shuffle the cards.

Section II. PERSONAL AFFECTIONS*

1°. Passive Affections

827. Pleasure.—N. pleasure, gratification, enjoyment, fruition; ob-, delectation; relish, zest; *gusto* &c. (*physical pleasure*) 377; satisfaction &c. (*content*) 831; complacency.

well-being; good &c. 618; snugness, comfort, ease; cushion &c. 215; *sans souci*, mind at ease.

joy, gladness, delight, glee, cheer, sunshine; cheerfulness &c. 836.

treat, refreshment; frolic, fun, lark, gambol, merry-making; amusement &c. 840; luxury &c. 377; hedonism.

mens sana in corpore sano.

happiness, felicity, bliss; beati-tude, -fication; enchantment, transport, rapture, ravishment, ecstasy; *summum bonum*; paradise, elysium &c. (*heaven*) 981; third -, seventh- heaven; unalloyed -happiness &c.

honeymoon; palmy -, halcyon- days; golden -age, - time; *Saturnia regna*, Eden, Arcadia, happy valley, Agapemone; Cockaigne.

V. be pleased &c. 829; feel -, experience- pleasure &c. *n.*; joy; enjoy -, hug- oneself; be in -clover &c. 377, - elysium &c. 981; tread on enchanted ground; fall -, go- into raptures.

feel at home, breathe freely, bask in the sunshine.

be -pleased &c. 829- with; receive -, derive- pleasure &c. *n.*- from; take -pleasure &c. *n.*- in; delight in, rejoice

828. Pain. — N. mental suffering, pain, dolour; suffer-ing, -ance; ache, smart &c. (*physical pain*) 378; passion.

displeasure, dissatisfaction, discomfort, discomposure, disquiet; *malaise*; inquietude, uneasiness, vexation of spirit; taking; discontent &c. 832.

dejection &c. 837; weariness &c. 841.

annoyance, irritation, worry, infliction, visitation; plague, bore; bother, -ation; stew, vexation, mortification, chagrin, *esclandre*; *mauvais quart d'heure.*

care, anxiety, solicitude, trouble, trial, ordeal, fiery ordeal, shock, blow, cark, dole, fret, burden, load.

concern, grief, sorrow, distress, affliction, woe, bitterness, gloom, heartache; heavy -, aching -, bleeding -, brokenheart; heavy affliction, gnawing grief.

unhappiness, infelicity, misery, tribulation, wretchedness, desolation; despair &c. 859; extremity, prostration, depth of misery.

nightmare, *ephialtes*, incubus.

anguish, agony; throe, tor-ture, -ment; crucifixion, martyrdom; pang, twinge, stab; the rack, the stake; purgatory &c. (*hell*) 982.

hell upon earth; iron age, reign of terror; slough of despond &c. (*adversity*) 735; peck -, sea- of troubles; ills that flesh is heir to &c. (*evil*) 619;

---

* Or those which concern one's own state of feeling.

in, indulge in, luxuriate in; gloat over &c. (*physical pleasure*) 377; enjoy, relish, like; love &c. 897; take -to, – a fancy to; have a liking for; enter into the spirit of.

take in good part.

treat oneself to, solace oneself with.

Adj. pleased &c. 829; not sorry; glad, -some; pleased as Punch.

happy, blest, blessed, blissful, beati-fied; happy as -a king, – the day is long; thrice happy, *ter quaterque beatus*; enjoying &c. *v.*; joyful &c. (*in spirits*) 836; hedonic.

in -a blissful state, – paradise &c. 981, – raptures, – ecstasies, – a trans-port of delight.

comfortable &c. (*physical pleasure*) 377; at ease; content &c. 831; *sans souci*, in clover.

overjoyed, entranced, enchanted; enraptured; en-, ravished; transported; fascinated, captivated.

with -a joyful face, – sparkling eyes.

pleasing &c. 829; ecstatic, beat-ic, -ific; painless, unalloyed, without alloy, cloudless.

Adv. happily &c. *adj.*; with pleasure &c. (*willingly*) 60; with -glee &c. *n.*

Phr. one's heart leaping with joy.

miseries of human life; unkindest cut of all.

sufferer, victim, prey, martyr, object of compassion, wretch, shorn lamb.

V. feel –, suffer –, experience –, un-dergo –, bear –, endure- pain &c. *n.*; smart, ache &c. (*physical pain*) 378; suffer, bleed, ail; be the victim of; bear –, take up- the cross.

labour under afflictions; quaff the bitter cup, have a bad time of it; fall on evil days &c. (*adversity*) 735; go hard with, come to grief, fall a sacrifice to, drain the cup of misery to the dregs, sup full of horrors.

sit on thorns, be on pins and needles, wince, fret, chafe, worry oneself, be in a taking, fret and fume, take -on, – to heart.

grieve; mourn &c. (*lament*) 839; yearn, repine, pine, droop, languish, sink; give way; despair &c. 859; break one's heart; weigh upon the heart &c. (*inflict pain*) 830.

Adj. in –, in a state of –, full of- pain &c. *n.*; suffering &c. *v.*; pained, afflicted, worried, displeased &c. 830; aching, griped, sore &c. (*physical pain*) 378; on the rack, in limbo; between hawk and buzzard.

un-comfortable, -easy; ill at ease; in a -taking, – way; disturbed; dis-contented &c. 832; out of humour &c. 901*a*; weary &c. 841.

heavy laden, stricken, crushed, a prey to, victimized, ill-used.

unfortunate &c. (*hapless*) 735; to be pitied, doomed, devoted, accursed, undone, lost, stranded.

unhappy, infelicitous, poor, wretched, miserable, woe-begone; cheerless &c. (*dejected*) 837; careworn.

concerned, sorry; sorrow-ing, -ful; cut up, chagrined, horrified, horror-stricken; in –, plunged in –, a prey to- grief &c. *n.*; in tears &c. (*lamenting*) 839; steeped to the lips in misery; heart-stricken, -broken, -scalded; broken-hearted; in despair &c. 859.

Phr. 'the iron entered into our soul'; '*hæret lateri lethalis arundo*'; one's heart bleeding.

---

829. [Capability of giving pleasure; cause or source of pleasure.] **Pleasur-ableness.**—**N.** pleasurable-, pleasant-, agreeable-ness &c. *adj.*; pleasure giv-ing, jocundity, delectability; amuse-ment &c. 840.

attraction &c. (*motive*) 615; attract-iveness, -ability; invitingness &c. *adj.*; charm, fascination, captivation, en-

830. [Capability of giving pain; cause or source of pain.] **Painfulness.** —**N.** painfulness &c. *adj.*; trouble, care &c. (*pain*) 828; trial; af-, in-fliction; cross, blow, stroke, burden, load, curse; bitter -pill, – draught, – cup; waters of bitterness.

annoyance, grievance, nuisance, vex-ation, mortification, sickener; bore,

chantment, witchery, seduction, winsomeness, winning ways, amenity, amiability, sweetness.

loveliness &c. (*beauty*) 845; sunny –, bright- side; sweets &c. (*sugar*) 396; goodness &c. 648; manna in the wilderness, land flowing with milk and honey.

treat; regale &c. (*physical pleasure*) 377; dainty; tit-, tid-bit; nuts, *sauce piquante*.

V. cause –, produce –, create –, give –, afford –, procure –, offer –, present –, yield- pleasure &c. 827.

please, charm, delight; gladden &c. (*make cheerful*) 836; take, captivate, fascinate; enchant, entrance, enrapture, transport, bewitch; en-, ravish.

bless, beatify; satisfy; gratify, – desire &c. 865; slake, satiate, quench; indulge, humour, flatter, tickle; tickle the palate &c. (*savoury*) 394; regale, refresh; enliven; treat; amuse &c. 840; take –, tickle –, hit- one's fancy; meet one's wishes; win –, gladden –, rejoice –, warm the cockles of- the heart; do one's heart good.

attract, allure &c. (*move*) 615; stimulate &c. (*excite*) 824; interest, intrigue.

make things pleasant, popularize, gild the pill, sweeten.

Adj. causing pleasure &c. *v.*; pleasure-giving; pleas-ing, -ant, -urable; agreeable, cushy; grat-eful, -ifying; leef, lief, acceptable; welcome, – as the roses in May; welcomed; favourite; to one's -taste, – mind, – liking, – heart's content; satisfactory &c. (*good*) 648.

refreshing; comfortable; cordial; genial; glad, -some; sweet, delectable, nice, dainty; delic-ate, -ious; dulcet; luscious &c. 396; palatable &c. 394; luxurious, voluptuous; sensual &c. 377.

attractive &c. 615; inviting, prepossessing, engaging; win-ning, -some; taking, fascinating, captivating, killing; seduc-ing, -tive; alluring, enticing; appetizing &c. (*exciting*) 824; cheering &c. 836; bewitching; interesting, absorbing, enchanting, entrancing, enravishing.

charming; delightful, felicitous, exquisite; lovely &c. (*beautiful*) 845;

bother, pother, hot water, sea of troubles, hornet's nest, plague, pest.

cancer, ulcer, sting, thorn; canker &c. (*bane*) 663; scorpion &c. (*evil-doer*) 913; dagger &c. (*arms*) 727; scourge &c. (*instrument of punishment*) 975; carking –, canker worm of- care.

mishap, misfortune &c. (*adversity*) 735; *désagrément*, *esclandre*, rub.

source of -irritation, – annoyance; wound, sore subject, skeleton in the closet; thorn in -the flesh, – one's side; where the shoe pinches, gall and wormwood.

sorry sight, heavy news, provocation; affront &c. 929; head and front of one's offending.

infestation, molestation; malignity &c. (*malevolence*) 907.

V. cause –, occasion –, give –, bring –, induce –, produce –, create –, inflict- pain &c. 828; pain, hurt, wound.

pinch, prick, gripe &c. (*physical pain*) 378; pierce, lancinate, cut.

hurt –, wound –, grate upon –, jar upon- the feelings; wring –, pierce –, lacerate –, break –, rend- the heart; make the heart bleed; tear –, rend- the heart-strings; draw tears from the eyes.

sadden; make -unhappy &c. 828; plunge into sorrow, grieve, fash, afflict, distress; cut -up, – to the heart.

displease, annoy, incommode, discommode, discompose, trouble, disquiet, disturb, thwart, cross, perplex, molest, tease, rag, tire, irk, vex, mortify, wherret, worry, plague, bother, pester, bore, pother, harass, harry, badger, heckle, bait, beset, infest, persecute, importune, be troublesome.

wring, harrow, torment, torture; put to the -rack, – question; break on the wheel, rack, scarify; cruci-ate, -fy; convulse, agonize; barb the dart; plant a -dagger in the breast, – thorn in one's side.

irritate, provoke, sting, nettle, try the patience, pique, fret, rile, tweak the nose, chafe, gall; sting –, wound –, cut- to the quick; aggrieve, affront, enchafe, enrage, ruffle, sour the temper; give offence &c. (*resentment*) 900.

ravishing, rapturous; heartfelt, thrill-ing, ecstatic; beat-ic, -ific; seraphic; empyrean; elysian &c. (*heavenly*) 981.
palmy, halcyon, Saturnian.

Phr. *decies repetita placebit.*

———

maltreat, bite, snap at, assail, bully; smite &c. (*punish*) 972.

sicken, disgust, revolt, nauseate, dis-enchant, repel, offend, shock, stink in the nostrils; go against –, turn- the stomach; make one sick, set the teeth on edge, go against the grain, grate on the ear; stick in one's -throat, – gizzard; rankle, gnaw, corrode, horrify, appal, freeze the blood; chill the spine; make the -flesh creep, – hair stand on end; make the blood -curdle, – run cold; make one shudder.

haunt, – the memory; weigh –, prey- on the -heart, – mind, – spirits; bring one's grey hairs with sorrow to the grave; add a nail to one's coffin.

Adj. causing pain, hurting &c. *v.*; hurtful &c. (*bad*) 649; painful; dolor-ific, -ous; unpleasant; un-, dis-pleasing; disagreeable, unpalat-able, bitter, distasteful; uninviting; unwelcome; undesir-able, -ed; obnoxious; unacceptable, unpopular, thankless.

unsatisfactory, untoward, unlucky, uncomfortable.

distressing; afflict-ing, -ive; joy-, cheer-, comfort-less; dismal, disheartening; depress-ing, -ive; dreary, melancholy, grievous, piteous; woeful, rueful, mournful, deplorable, pitiable, lamentable; sad, affecting, touching, pathetic.

irritating, provoking, stinging, annoying, aggravating, mortify-ing, galling; unaccommodating, invidious, vexatious; trouble-, tire-, irk-, weari-some; plagu-ing, -y; awkward.

importunate; teas-, pester-, bother-, harass-, worry-, torment-, cark-ing.

in-toler-, -suffer-, -support-able; un-bear-, -endur-able; past bear-ing; not to be -borne, – endured; more than flesh and blood can bear; enough to -drive one mad, – provoke a saint, – make a parson swear, – try the patience of Job.

shocking, terrific, grim, appalling, crushing; dreadful, fearful, frightful; thrilling, tremendous, dire; heart-breaking, -rending, -wounding, -corroding, -sickening; harrowing, rending.

odious, hateful, execrable, repulsive, repellent, abhorrent; horri-d, -ble, -fic, -fying; offensive; nause-ous, -ating; disgust-, sicken-, revolt-ing; nasty; loath-some, -ful; fulsome; vile &c. (*bad*) 649; hideous &c. 846.

sharp, acute, sore, severe, grave, hard, harsh, cruel, biting, acri-monious, caustic; cutting, corroding, consuming, racking, excruciat-ing, searching, searing, grinding, grating, agonizing; envenomed.

ruinous, disastrous, calamitous, tragical; desolating, withering; burdensome, onerous, oppressive; cumb-rous, -ersome.

Adv. painfully &c. *adj.*; with -pain &c. 828; deuced.

Int. *hinc illæ lachrymæ!* woe is me!

Phr. *surgit amari aliquid*; the place being too hot to hold one; the iron entering into the soul.

———

831. Content.—N. content, -ment, -edness; complacency, satisfaction, en-tire satisfaction, ease, heart's ease, peace of mind; serenity &c. 826; cheer-

832. Discontent. — N. discontent, -ment; dissatisfaction; dissent &c. 489; labour unrest.

disappointment, mortification; cold

fulness &c. 836; ray of comfort; comfort &c. (*well-being*) 827.

re-, conciliation; resignation &c. (*patience*) 826.

waiter on Providence.

V. be -content &c. *adj.*; rest -satisfied, – and be thankful; take the good the gods provide, let well alone, feel oneself at home, hug oneself, lay the flattering unction to one's soul.

take -up with, – in good part; assent &c. 488; be reconciled to, make one's peace with; get over it; take -heart, – comfort; put up with &c. (*bear*) 826.

render -content &c. *adj.*; set at ease, comfort; set one's -heart, – mind- at -ease, – rest; speak peace; conciliate, reconcile, win over, propitiate, disarm, beguile; content, satisfy; gratify &c. 829.

be -tolerated &c. 826; go down, – with; do.

Adj. content, -ed; satisfied &c. *v.*; at -ease, – one's ease, – home; with the mind at ease, *sans souci, sine curâ*, easy-going, not particular; conciliatory; unrepining, of good comfort; resigned &c. (*patient*) 826; cheerful &c. 836.

un-afflicted, -vexed, -molested, -plagued; serene &c. 826; at rest; snug, comfortable; in one's element.

satisfactory, satisfying, ample, sufficient, adequate, tolerable.

Adv. to one's heart's content; *à la bonne heure*; all for the best.

Int. amen &c. (*assent*) 488; very well, so much the better, well and good; it –, that- will do; it cannot be helped.

Phr. nothing comes amiss.

comfort; regret &c. 833; repining, taking on &c. *v.*; inquietude, vexation of spirit, soreness; heart-burning, -grief; querulousness &c. (*lamentation*) 839; hypercriticism.

malcontent, grumbler, growler, croaker, *laudator temporis acti*; censurer, complainer, faultfinder, murmurer, Adullamite, Diehard, Bitterender.

the Opposition, cave of Adullam, indignation meeting, 'winter of our discontent.'

V. be -discontented &c. *adj.*; quarrel with one's bread and butter; repine; regret &c. 833; wish one at the bottom of the Red Sea; take -on, – to heart; shrug the shoulders; make a wry –, pull a long- face; knit one's brows; look -blue, – black, – black as thunder, – blank, – glum.

take -in bad part, – ill; fret, chafe, make a piece of work; grumble, croak, grouse; lament &c. 839.

cause -discontent &c. *n.*; dissatisfy, disappoint, mortify, put out, disconcert; cut up; dishearten.

Adj. discontented; dissatisfied &c. *v.*; unsatisfied, ungratified; dissident; dissentient &c. 489; malcontent, exigent, exacting, hypercritical.

repining &c. *v.*; regretful &c. 833; down in the mouth &c. (*dejected*) 837.

in -high dudgeon, – a fume, – the sulks, – the dumps, – bad humour; glum, sulky; sour, – as a crab; soured, sore; out of -humour, – temper.

disappointing &c. *v.*; unsatisfactory.

Int. so much the worse!

Phr. that –, it- will never do.

---

833. Regret.—**N.** regret, repining; home sickness, nostalgia; *mal –, maladie-du pays*; lamentation &c. 839, contrition, compunction, penitence &c. 950.

bitterness, heart-burning.

laudator temporis acti &c. (*discontent*) 832.

V. regret, deplore; bewail &c. (*lament*) 839; repine, cast a longing lingering look behind; rue, – the day; repent &c. 950; *infandum renovare dolorem*.

prey –, weigh –, have a weight- on the mind; leave an aching void.

Adj. regretting &c. *v.*; regretful; home-sick.

regretted &c. *v.*; much to be regretted, regrettable; lamentable &c. (*bad*) 649.

Int. what a pity! hang it!

Phr. 'tis -pity, – too true.

834. Relief.—N. relief; deliverance; refreshment &c. 689; easement, softening, alleviation, mitigation, palliation &c. 174; soothing, lullaby; cradle song, *berceuse.*

solace, consolation, comfort, encouragement.

lenitive, restorative &c. (*remedy*) 662; poultice &c. *v.*; cushion &c. 215; crumb of comfort, balm in Gilead; aspirin.

V. relieve, ease, alleviate, mitigate, palliate, soothe, addulce; salve; soften, – down; foment, stupe, poultice; assuage, allay.

cheer, comfort, console; encourage, bear up, pat on the back, give comfort, set at ease; enliven, gladden –, cheer- the heart.

remedy; cure &c. (*restore*) 660; refresh; pour -balm into, – oil on.

smooth the ruffled brow of care, temper the wind to the shorn lamb, lay the flattering unction to one's soul.

disburden &c. (*free*) 705; take off a load of care.

be relieved; breathe more freely, draw a long breath; take comfort; dry –, wipe- the -tears, – eyes.

Adj. relieving &c. *v.*; consolatory, soothing; assua-ging, -sive; bal-my, -samic; lenitive, palliative; anodyne &c. (*remedial*) 662; curative &c. 660.

835. Aggravation.—N. aggravation, heightening; exacerbation; exasperation; overestimation &c. 482; exaggeration &c. 549.

V. aggravate, render worse, heighten, embitter, sour; ex-, acerbate; exasperate, envenom; tease, provoke, enrage.

add fuel to the -fire, – flame; fan the flame &c. (*excite*) 824; go from bad to worse &c. (*deteriorate*) 659.

Adj. aggravated &c. *v.*; worse, unrelieved; aggravable; aggravating &c. *v.*

Adv. out of the frying pan into the fire, from bad to worse, worse and worse.

Int. so much the worse!

---

836. Cheerfulness.—N. cheerfulness &c. *adj.*; geniality, gaiety, *l'allegro*, cheer, good humour, spirits; high –, animal –, flow of- spirits; glee, high glee, light heart; sunshine of the -mind, – breast; *gaieté de cœur, bon naturel.*

liveliness &c. *adj.*; life, alacrity, vivacity, animation, *allégresse*; jocundity, joviality, jollity; levity; jocularity &c. (*wit*) 842.

mirth, merriment, hilarity, exhilaration; laughter &c. 838; merry-making &c. (*amusement*) 840; heyday, rejoicing &c. 838; marriage bells.

nepenthe, Euphrosyne.

optimism &c. (*hopefulness*) 858; self-complacency.

V. be -cheerful &c. *adj.*; have the mind at ease, smile, put a good face upon, keep up one's spirits; view -the bright side of the picture, – things *en couleur de rose*; *ridentem dicere verum,*

837. Dejection.—N. dejection; dejectedness &c. *adj.*; depression, prosternation; lowness –, depression- of spirits; weight –, oppression –, damp- on the spirits; low –, bad –, drooping –, depressed- spirits; heart sinking; heaviness –, failure- of heart.

heaviness &c. *adj.*; infestivity, gloom; weariness &c. 841; *tædium vitæ*, disgust of life; *mal du pays* &c. (*regret*) 833.

melancholy; sadness &c. *adj.*; *il penseroso, melancholia*, dismals, mumps, mopes, lachrymals, dumps, blues, blue devils, doldrums, vapours, megrims, spleen, horrors, hypochondriasis, pessimism; despondency, slough of Despond; disconsolateness &c. *adj.*; hope deferred, blank despondency.

prostration, – of soul; broken heart; despair &c. 859; cave of -despair, – Trophonius.

cheer up, brighten up, light up, bear up; chirp, take heart, cast away care, drive dull care away, perk up.

rejoice &c. 838; carol, chirrup, lilt; frisk, rollick, give a loose to mirth.

cheer, enliven, elate, exhilarate, gladden, inspirit, animate, raise the spirits, inspire; put in good humour; cheer –, rejoice- the heart; delight &c. (*give pleasure*) 829.

Adj. cheerful; happy &c. 827; cheery, -ly; of good cheer, smiling; blithe; in –, in good- spirits; in high -spirits, – feather; happy as -the day is long, – a king; gay, – as a lark; *allegro*; light, -some, -hearted; buoyant, *débonnaire*, bright, free and easy, airy; janty, jaunty, canty; spright-ly, -ful; spry; spirit-ed, -ful; lively; animated, breezy, vivacious; brisk, – as a bee; sparkling; sportive; full of -play, – spirit; all alive.

sunny, palmy; hopeful &c. 858.

merry, – as a -cricket, – grig, – marriage bell; joyful, joyous, jocund, jovial; jolly, – as a thrush, – as a sandboy; blithesome; glee-ful, -some; hilarious, rattling.

winsome, bonny, hearty, buxom.

play-ful, -some; *folâtre*, playful as a kitten, tricksy, frisky, frolicsome; gamesome; jocose, jocular, waggish; mirth-, laughter-loving; mirthful, rollicking.

elate, -d; exulting, jubilant, flushed; rejoicing &c. 838; cock-a-hoop.

cheering, inspiriting, exhilarating; cardiac, -al; pleasing &c. 829; flourishing, halcyon.

Adv. cheerfully &c. *adj.*

Int. never say die! come! cheer up! hurrah! &c. 838; 'hence loathed melancholy!' begone dull care! away with melancholy!

---

demureness &c. *adj.*; gravity, solemnity; long –, grave- face.

hypochondriac, seek-sorrow, self-tormentor, *heautontimorumenos*, *malade imaginaire*, *médecin tant pis*; croaker, pessimist; mope, mopus.

[Cause of dejection] affliction &c. 830; sorry sight; *memento mori*; damper, wet blanket, Job's comforter; death's head, skeleton at the feast.

V. be -dejected &c. *adj.*; grieve; mourn &c. (*lament*) 839; take on, give way, lose heart, despond, droop, sink.

lower, look downcast, frown, pout; hang down the head; pull –, make- a long face; laugh on the wrong side of the mouth; grin a ghastly smile; look -blue, – like a drowned man; lay –, take- to heart.

mope, brood over; fret; sulk; pine, – away; yearn; repine &c. (*regret*) 833; despair &c. 859.

refrain from laughter, keep one's countenance; be –, look- grave &c. *adj.*; repress a smile, keep a straight face.

depress; dis-courage, -hearten; dispirit; damp, dull, deject, lower, sink, dash, knock down, unman, prostrate, break one's heart; frown upon; cast a -gloom, – shade- on; sadden; damp –, dash –, wither- one's hopes; weigh –, lie heavy –, prey- on the -mind, – spirits; damp –, depress- the spirits.

Adj. cheer-, joy-, spirit-less; uncheerful, -y; unlively; unhappy &c. 828; melancholy, dismal, sombre, dark, gloomy, adust, *triste*, clouded, murky, lowering, frowning, lugubrious, Acherontic, funereal, mournful, lamentable, dreadful.

dreary, flat; dull, – as -a beetle, – ditchwater; depressing &c. *v.*

'melancholy as a gib cat'; oppressed with –, a prey to- melancholy; downcast, -hearted; down -in the mouth, – on one's luck; heavy-hearted; in the -dumps, – suds, – sulks, – doldrums; in doleful dumps, in bad humour; sullen; mumpish, dumpish; mopish, moping; moody, glum; sulky &c. (*discontented*) 832; out of -sorts, – humour, – heart, – spirits; ill at ease, low-spirited, in low spirits, a cup too low; weary &c. 841; dis-couraged, -heartened; desponding; chop-, jaw-, crest-fallen.

sad, pensive, *penseroso*, tristful; dole-some, -ful; woebegone, lachrymose, in tears, melancholic, hypped, hypochondriacal, bilious, jaundiced, atrabilious, saturnine, splenetic; lackadaisical.

serious, sedate, staid, stayed; grave, – as -a judge, – an under-taker, – a mustard pot; sober, solemn, demure; grim; grim-faced, -visaged; rueful, wan, long-faced.

disconsolate; un-, in-consolable; forlorn, comfortless, desolate, *désolé*, sick at heart; soul-, heart-sick; *au désespoir*; in despair &c. 859; lost.

overcome; broken-, borne-, bowed-down; heart-stricken &c. (*mental suffering*) 828; cut up, dashed, sunk; unnerved, unmanned; down-fallen, -trodden; broken-hearted; care-worn.

Adv. with -a long face, – tears in one's eyes; sadly &c. *adj.*

Phr. the countenance falling; the heart -failing, – sinking within-one.

838. [Expression of pleasure.] **Rejoicing.—N.** rejoicing, exultation, triumph, jubilation, heyday, flush, revelling; merry-making &c. (*amusement*) 840; jubilee &c. (*celebration*) 883; pæan, *Te Deum* &c. (*thanksgiving*) 990; congratulation &c. 896; applause &c. 971.

smile, simper, smirk, grin; broad -, sardonic- grin.

laughter, giggle, titter, crow, cheer, chuckle, snicker, snigger, shout; Homeric laughter, horse -, hearty- laugh; guffaw; burst -, fit -, shout -, roar -, peal- of laughter; cachinnation.

risibility; derision &c. 856.

Momus; Democritus the Abderite; rollicker; Laughter holding both his sides.

V. rejoice; thank -, bless- one's stars; congratulate -, hug- oneself; rub -, clap- one's hands; smack the lips, fling up one's cap; dance, skip, caleer; sing, carol, chirrup, chirp; hurrah; cry for -, leap with- joy; exult &c. (*boast*) 884; triumph; hold jubilee &c. (*celebrate*) 883; make merry &c. (*sport*) 840; sing a pæan of joy.

smile, simper, smirk; grin, – like a Cheshire cat; mock, laugh in one's sleeve; laugh, – outright; giggle, titter, snigger, crow, smicker, chuckle, snicker, cackle; burst -out, – into a fit of laughter; shout, split, roar.

shake -, split -, hold both- one's sides; roar -, die- with laughter.

raise laughter &c. (*amuse*) 840.

Adj. rejoicing &c. *v.*; jubilant, exultant, triumphant; flushed, elated; laughing &c. *v.*; risible; ready to -burst, – split, – die with laughter; convulsed with laughter.

839. [Expression of pain.] **Lamentation.—N.** lament, -ation; wail, complaint, plaint, murmur, mutter, grumble, groan, moan, whine, whimper, sob, sigh, suspiration, heaving, deep sigh.

cry &c. (*vociferation*) 411; scream, howl; outcry, wail of woe, frown, scowl.

tear; weeping &c. *v.*; flood of tears, fit of crying, lachrymation, melting mood, weeping and gnashing of teeth.

plaintiveness &c. *adj.*; languishment; condolence &c. 915.

mourning, weeds, willow, cypress, crêpe, crape, deep mourning; sackcloth and ashes; knell &c. 363; dump, death-song, dirge, coronach, keen, *nenia*, requiem, elegy, *epicedium*; threne; mon-, thren-ody; jeremiad; ululation.

mourner, professional mourner, keener; grumbler &c. (*discontent*) 832; Niobe; Heraclitus.

V. lament, mourn, deplore, grieve, weep over; be-wail, -moan; keen; condole with &c. 915; fret &c. (*suffer*) 828; wear -, go into -, put on- mourning; wear -the willow, – sackcloth and ashes; *infandum renovare dolorem* &c. (*regret*) 833; give sorrow words.

sigh; give -, heave -, fetch- a sigh; 'waft a sigh from Indus to the pole'; sigh 'like furnace'; wail.

cry, weep, sob, greet, blubber, pipe, snivel, bibber, whimper, pule; pipe one's eye; drop -, shed- -tears, – a tear; melt -, burst- into tears; *fondre en larmes*; cry -oneself blind, – one's eyes out.

scream &c. (*cry out*) 411; mew &c. (*animal sounds*) 412; groan, moan,

laughable &c. (*ludicrous*) 853.

Int. hip, hip, -hurrah! huzza! aha! hail! tolderolloll! tra-la la! Heaven be praised! *io triumphe! tant mieux!* so much the better.

Phr. the heart leaping with joy.

———

whine, yammer; roar; roar –, bellow-like a bull; cry out lustily, rend the air, yell.

frown, scowl, make a wry face, grimace, gnash one's teeth, wring one's hands, tear one's hair, beat one's breast, roll on the ground, burst with grief.

complain, murmur, mutter, grumble, growl, clamour, make a fuss about, croak, grunt, maunder; deprecate &c. (*disapprove*) 932.

cry out before one is hurt, complain without cause.

Adj. lamenting &c. *v.*; in mourning, in sackcloth and ashes; crying, sorrowing, -ful &c. (*unhappy*) 828; mourn-, tear-ful; lachrymose; plaint-ive, -ful, quer-ulous, -imonious; in the melting mood.

in tears, with tears in one's eyes; with -moistened, – watery-eyes; bathed –, dissolved- in tears; 'like Niobe all tears.'

elagiac, epicedial, threnetic.

Adv. *de profundis; les larmes aux yeux.*

Int. heigh-ho! alas! alack! O dear! ah –, woe is- me! lackadaisy! well –, lack –, alack- a day! well-a-way! alas the day! *O tempora! O mores!* what a pity! *miserabile dictu!* O lud lud! too true!

Phr. tears -standing in, – starting from- the eyes; eyes -suffused, – swimming, – brimming –, overflowing- with tears.

840. Amusement.—N. amuse-, entertain-ment; diver-sion, -tissement; reaction, relaxation, solace; pastime, *passetemps*, sport; labour of love; pleasure &c. 827.

fun, frolic, merriment, whoopee, jollity; jovial-ity, -ness; heyday; laughter &c. 838; jocos-ity, -eness; droll-, buffoon-, tomfool-ery; mummery, masquing, pleasantry; wit &c. 842; quip, quirk.

play; game, – at romps; gambol, romp, prank, antic, rig, lark, spree, skylarking, vagary, trick, monkey trick, *gambade, fredaine, escapade, échappée,* bout, *espièglerie*; practical joke &c. (*ridicule*) 856.

dance; round –, square –, solo –, step –, tap –, clog –, skirt –, sand –, folk –, morris- dance, *pas seul,* step, turn, *chassé,* cut, shuffle, double shuffle; hop, reel, rigadoon, saraband, hornpipe, bolero, fandango, pavan, tarantella, minuet, waltz, polka; galop, -ade; Schottische, *pas de quatre,* Boston, one-, two-step, rumba, tango, maxixe, fox-, turkey-trot, shimmy, ragtime, cakewalk, jazz, blues, Charleston; jig, breakdown, fling, strathspey; *alle-*

841. Weariness.—N. weariness, defatigation, boredom, *ennui*; lassitude &c. (*fatigue*) 688; drowsiness &c. 683.

disgust, nausea, loathing, sickness; satiety &c. 869; *tædium vitæ* &c. (*dejection*) 837.

wearisome-, tedious-ness &c. *adj.*; dull work, tedium, monotony, twice told tale.

bore, button-hole, proser, wet blanket; heavy hours, 'the enemy' [time].

V. weary; tire &c. (*fatigue*) 688; bore; bore –, weary –, tire- -to death, – out of one's life, – out of all patience; set –, send- to sleep.

pall, sicken, nauseate, disgust.

harp on the same string; drag its -slow, – weary- length along.

never hear the last of; be -tired &c. *adj.* -of, – with; yawn; die with *ennui.*

Adj. wearying &c. *v.*; wearing; weari-, tire-, irk-some; uninteresting, stupid, bald, devoid of interest, dry, monotonous, dull, arid, tedious, humdrum, mortal, flat; pros-y, -ing; slow; soporific, somniferous, dormitive.

disgusting &c. *v.*; unenjoyed.

weary; tired &c. *v.*; drowsy &c. (*sleepy*) 683; uninterested, flagging,

mande; gavot, -te; mazurka, morisco; quadrille, lancers, country dance, *cotillon*, polonaise, Sir Roger de Coverley, Swedish dance; *ballet* &c. (*drama*) 599; ball; *bal, – masqué, – costumé*; masquerade, fancy dress ball; *thé dansant*; Terpsichore, choreography, Russian ballet, classical dancing; eurythmics; nautch dance, *danse du ventre*, cancan.

festivity, merry-making; party &c. (*social gathering*) 892; *fête*, festival, gala, *ridotto*; revel-s, -ry, -ling; carnival, brawl, saturnalia, high jinks; feast, banquet &c. (*food*) 298; regale, *symposium*, wassail; carous-e, -al; jollification, junket, wake, pic-nic, *fête champêtre*, garden party, gymkhana, regatta, track meet, field-day, jamboree, treat.

round of pleasures, dissipation, a short life and a merry one, racketing, holiday making, high jinks.

rejoicing &c. 838; jubilee &c. (*celebration*) 883.

bonfire, fireworks, *feu-de-joie*, rocket, catherine wheel, roman candle &c.

holiday; gala –, red letter –, play- day; high days and holidays; high –, Bank- holiday; May –, Derby- day; Saint –, Easter –, Whit- Monday; King's birthday, Empire Day; *mi-carême*; *Bairam*; wayzgoose, bean feast, beano.

place of amusement, theatre &c. 599; concert-, ball-, assembly-room; music-hall, cinema, movies, talkies, vaudeville; hippodrome, circus, rodeo; *casino, kursaal*; winter garden; park, pleasance, arbour; garden &c. 371; pleasure-, play-, cricket-, football-, polo-, croquet-, archery-, hunting-ground; golf links, race course, stadium, gridiron, bowl, speedway, racing track, ring; gymnasium, swimming pool; shooting gallery; tennis-, racket-court; bowling-green, -alley; croquet-lawn, rink, skating rink; roller-coaster, roundabout, carousel, merry-go-round; swing; *montagne russe*; switchback, scenic railway &c.

game, – of -chance, – skill; athletic sports, gymnastics; fencing; archery, rifle-shooting; tournament, pugilism &c. (*contention*) 720; sporting &c. 622; horse-racing, the turf; aquatics &c. 267; skating, roller skating; ski-running, -joring, -jumping, bobsleighing, luging, tobogganing, winter sports; sliding; cricket, tennis, lawn –, table –, deck- tennis, rackets, fives, squash, ping pong, trap bat and ball, battledore and shuttlecock, badminton, *la grâce*; pall mall, tip-cat, croquet, golf, curling, hockey, basketball, soccer, football, Rugby, Association, *pallone*, polo; tent-pegging, tilting at the ring, quintain, greasy pole; quoits, *discus*; throwing the hammer, putting the -weight, – shot, tossing the caber; knurr and spell; leap-frog, hop, skip and jump; French and English, tug of war; blind man's buff, hunt the slipper, hide-and-seek, kiss in the ring; snapdragon; cross questions and crooked answers; jig-saw puzzle; rounders, base-ball, *la crosse* &c.; angling; swimming, diving, water-polo.

billiards, pool, pyramids, snooker, bagatelle; bowls, skittles, ninepins, kail, American bowls.

cards; bridge, auction, contract, whist, rubber; round game, coon-can, loo, cribbage, *bésique*, pinocle, euchre, drole, *écarté*, skat, picquet, all-fours, quadrille, ombre, reverse, Pope Joan, commit;

used up, worn out, *blasé*, life-weary, weary of life; sick of.

Adv. wearily &c. *adj.*; *usque ad nauseam.*

Phr. time hanging heavily on one's hands; *toujours perdrix; crambe repetita.*

———

bo-, boa-ston; *vingt-et-un*; *quinze*, thirty-one, put-and-take, speculation, connections, brag, cassino, lottery, commerce, snip-snap-snorem,
lift smoke, blind hookey, Polish bank, poker, banker; faro; Earl of
Coventry, Napoleon, nap, patience, pairs; old maid, fright, beggar-
my-neighbour; *baccarat, chemin de fer, monté, roulette.*

chess, draughts, backgammon, dominoes, checkers, mah jong,
merelles, nine men's morris, go-bang, solitaire; game of –, fox and-
goose; loto; &c.*

morra; gambling &c. (*chance*) 621.

toy, plaything, bauble; doll &c. (*puppet*) 554; teetotum; knick-
knack &c. (*trifle*) 643; magic lantern &c. (*show*) 448; peep-, puppet-,
raree-, gallanty-show; marionettes, Punch and Judy; toy-shop;
'quips and cranks and wanton wiles, nods and becks and wreathed
smiles.'

sportsman, gamester, gambler &c. 621; reveller, master of the
-ceremonies, – revels; *arbiter elegantiarum.*

V. amuse, entertain, divert, enliven; tickle, – the fancy; titillate,
raise a smile, put in good humour; cause –, create –, occasion –,
raise –, excite –, produce –, convulse with- laughter; set the table
in a roar, be the death of one.

recreate, solace, cheer, rejoice; please &c. 829; interest; treat,
regale.

amuse oneself; game; play, – a game, – pranks, – tricks; sport,
disport, toy, wanton, revel, junket, feast, carouse, banquet, make
merry; drown care; drive dull care away; frolic, gambol, frisk,
romp; caper; dance &c. (*leap*) 309; keep up the ball; run a rig,
sow one's wild oats, have one's fling, paint the town red, take
one's pleasure; see life; *desipere in loco*, play the fool.

make –, keep- holiday; go a Maying.

while away –, beguile- the time; kill time, dally.

Adj. amusing, entertaining, diverting &c. *v.*; recreative, lusory;
pleasant &c. (*pleasing*) 829; laughable &c. (*ludicrous*) 853; witty
&c. 842; fest-ive, -al; jovial, jolly, jocund, roguish, rompish; sporting; playful, – as a kitten; sportive, ludibrious.

amused &c. *v.*; 'pleased with a feather, tickled with a straw.'

Adv. 'on the light fantastic toe,' at play, in sport.

Int. *vive la bagatelle! vogue la galère!*

Phr. *Deus nobis hæc otia fecit; dum vivimus vivamus.*

842. Wit.—N. wit, -tiness; attic
-wit, – salt; atticism; salt, *esprit*, point,
fancy, whim, humour, drollery, pleasantry.

farce, buffoonery, fooling, tomfoolery; harlequinade &c. 599; broad
-farce, – humour; fun, *espièglerie*; *vis
comica.*

jocularity; jocos-ity, -eness; face-
tiousness; wagg-ery, -ishness; whim-
sicality; comicality &c. 853.

smartness, ready wit, banter, *badi-*

843. Dulness.—N. dulness, heaviness, flatness; infestivity &c. 837;
stupidity &c. 499; want of originality,
dearth of ideas.

prose, matter of fact; heavy book,
conte à dormir debout; platitude.

V. be -dull &c. *adj.*; prose, plati-
tudinize, take *au sérieux*, be caught
napping.

render -dull &c. *adj.*; damp, depress,
throw cold water on, lay a wet blanket
on; fall flat upon the ear; hang fire.

* A curious list of games is given in Sir Thomas Urquhart's translation of Rabelais'
Life of Gargantua, book i. chapter 22.

nage, *persiflage*, retort, repartee, *quid pro quo*; ridicule &c. 856.

facetiæ, quips and cranks; jest, joke, capital joke; standing -jest, – joke; conceit, quip, quirk, crank, quiddity, *concetto*, *plaisanterie*, brilliant idea; merry –, bright –, happy- thought; sally; flash, – of wit, – of merriment; scintillation; *mot*, – *pour rire*; witticism, smart saying, *bon mot*, *jeu d'esprit*, epigram; jest book; dry joke, *quodlibet*, cream of the jest.

word-play, *jeu de mots*; play -of, – upon- words; pun, -ning; *double entente* &c. (*ambiguity*) 520; quibble, verbal quibble; conundrum &c. (*riddle*) 533; anagram, acrostic, double acrostic, *nugæ canoræ*, trifling, idle conceit, *turlupinade*.

old joke, Joe Miller, chestnut, hoary-headed jest.

V. joke, jest, cut jokes; crack a joke; perpetrate a -joke, – pun; make -fun of, – merry with; set the table in a roar &c. (*amuse*) 840; scintillate.

retort, flash back; banter &c. (*ridicule*) 856; *ridentem dicere verum*; joke at one's expense.

Adj. witty, attic, salty; quick-, nimble-witted; keen, clever, smart, brilliant, pungent, jocular, jocose, funny, waggish, facetious, whimsical, humorous, gilbertian; playful &c. 840; merry and wise; pleasant, sprightly, *spirituel*, sparkling, epigrammatic, full of point, *ben trovato*; comic &c. 853.

Adv. in joke, in jest, in sport, in play.

Adj. dull, – as ditch water; dry, insipid, jejune; unentertaining, uninteresting, unlively, unimaginative; heavisome, heavy-gaited; insulse; dry as dust; pros-y, -ing, -aic; matter of fact, commonplace, banal, pointless; 'weary, flat, stale and unprofitable.'

stupid, slow, flat, sluggish, ponderous, humdrum, monotonous; melancholic &c. 837; stolid &c. 499; plodding.

Phr. *Davus sum non Œdipus.*

---

844. Humorist.—N. humorist, wag, wit, reparteeist, epigrammatist, gag man, punster; *bel esprit*, life of the party; wit-snapper, -cracker, -worm; joker, jester, jokesmith, Joe Miller, *drôle de corps*, *gaillard*, spark, *persiffleur*, banterer.

buffoon, *farceur*, merry-andrew, mime, tumbler, acrobat, mountebank, charlatan, posturemaster, harlequin, punch, *pulcinella*, scaramouch, clown; wearer of the -cap and bells, – motley; motley fool; pantaloon, gipsy; jack -pudding, – in the green, – a dandy; zany; mad-cap, pickle-herring, witling, caricaturist, *grimacier*.

2°. Discriminate Affections

845. Beauty.—N. beauty, the beautiful, *le beau ideal*, loveliness.

[Science of the perception of beauty] Callæsthetics.*

form, elegance, grace, beauty unadorned; symmetry &c. 242; comeliness, fairness &c. *adj.*; pulchritude, polish, gloss; good -effect, – looks; *belle tournure*; bloom, brilliancy, radiance, splendour, gorgeousness, magnificence; sublimi-ty, -fication.

846. Ugliness.—N. ugliness &c. *adj.*; deformity, inelegance; disfigurement &c. (*blemish*) 848; want of symmetry, inconcinnity; distortion &c. 243; squalor &c. (*uncleanness*) 653.

forbidding countenance, vinegar aspect, hanging look, wry face, '*spretæ injuria formæ.*'

eyesore, object, figure, sight, fright, spectre, scarecrow, hag, harridan, satyr, witch, toad, baboon, monster,

---

* Whewell, 'Philosophy of the Inductive Sciences.'

concinnity, delicacy, . refinement; charm, *je ne sais quoi*, style, *chic*, swank.

Venus, – of Milo; Aphrodite, Hebe, the Graces, Peri, Houri, Cupid, Apollo, Hyperion, Adonis, Antinous, Narcissus; Helen of Troy.

peacock, butterfly; flower, flow'ret gay, rose, lily, asphodel; garden; flower of, pink of; *bijou*; jewel &c. (*ornament*) 847; work of art.

pleasurableness &c. 829.

beautifying; landscape gardening; decoration &c. 847; calisthenics.

V. be -beautiful &c. *adj.*; shine, beam, bloom; become one &c. (*accord*) 23; set off, grace, flatter one.

render -beautiful &c. *adj.*; beautify; polish, burnish; gild &c. (*decorate*) 847; set out.

'snatch a grace beyond the reach of art.'

Adj. beaut-iful, -eous; handsome; pretty; lovely, graceful, elegant; delicate, dainty, refined, exquisite; fair, personable, comely, seemly; bonny; good-looking; well-favoured, -made, -formed, -proportioned; proper, shapely; symmetrical &c. (*regular*) 242; harmonious &c. (*colour*) 428; sightly.

fit to be seen, passable, not amiss.

goodly, dapper, tight, jimp; gimp; janty, jaunty; natty, quaint, trim, tidy, neat, spruce, smart, tricksy.

bright, -eyed; rosy-, cherry-cheeked; rosy, ruddy; blooming, in full bloom.

brilliant, shining; beam-y, -ing; sparkling, swanky, splendid, resplendent, dazzling, glowing; glossy, sleek.

showy, specious; rich, gorgeous, superb, magnificent, grand, fine, sublime, imposing; majestic 873.

artistic, -al; æsthetic; pict-uresque, -orial; *fait à peindre*, paintable; well-composed, -grouped, -varied; curious.

enchanting &c. (*pleasure-giving*) 829; attractive &c. (*inviting*) 615; becoming &c. (*accordant*) 23; ornamental &c. 847.

undeformed, undefaced, unspotted; spotless &c. (*perfect*) 650.

Caliban, Æsop, '*monstrum horrendum informe ingens cui lumen ademptum.*'

V. be -ugly &c. *adj.*; look ill, grin horribly a ghastly smile, make faces.

render -ugly &c. *adj.*; deface; dis-, de-figure; deform, spoil, distort &c. 243; blemish &c. (*injure*) 659; soil &c. (*render unclean*) 653.

Adj. ugly, – as -sin, – a toad, – a scarecrow, – a dead monkey; plain, bald &c. 226; homely &c. (*unadorned*) 849; ordinary, unornamental, inartistic; unsightly, unseemly, uncomely, unshapely, unlovely; sightless, seemless; not fit to be seen; unbeaut-eous, -iful; beautiless; shapeless &c. (*amorphous*) 241; course; garish, over-decorated &c. 882.

mis-shapen, -proportioned; monstrous; gaunt &c. (*thin*) 203; dumpy &c. (*short*) 201; curtailed of its fair proportions; ill-made, -shaped, -proportioned; crooked &c. (*distorted*) 243; hard-featured, -visaged; ill-, hard-, evil-favoured; ill-looking; unprepossessing.

graceless, inelegant; ungraceful, ungainly, uncouth; stiff; rugged, rough, gross, rude, awkward, clumsy, slouching, rickety; gawky; lump-ing, -ish; lumbering; hulk-y, -ing; unwieldy.

squalid, haggard; grim, -faced, -visaged; grisly, ghastly; ghost-, death-like; cadaverous, gruesome.

frightful, hideous, odious, uncanny, forbidding, repellant, repulsive; horri-d, -ble; shocking &c. (*painful*) 830.

foul &c. (*dirty*) 653; dingy &c. (*colourless*) 429; gaudy &c. (*colour*) 428; disfigured &c. *v.*; discoloured (*blemished*) &c. 848.

---

847. Ornament. — N. ornament, -ation, -al art; ornat-ure, -eness; adorn-ment, decoration, embellishment; architecture.

garnish, polish, varnish, French pol-

848. Blemish.—N. blemish, disfigurement, deformity; defect &c. (*imperfection*) 651; flaw; injury &c. (*deterioration*) 659; spots on the sun; eyesore.

ish, gilding, japanning, lacquer, ormolu, enamel.

cosmetics, rouge, powder, lipstick, lip salve, mascara; manicure, nail polish; permanent –, Marcel –, finger-wave.

pattern, diaper, powdering, panelling, graining, pargeting, inlay, detail; texture &c. 329; richness; tracery, moulding, beading, reeding, fillet, listel, strapwork, *coquillage*, flourish, *fleur-de-lis*, arabesque, fret, *anthemion*; egg and -tongue, – dart; *astragal*, zigzag, *acanthus*, *cartouche*; pilaster &c. (*projection*) 250; cyma, ogee.

em-, broidery, needlework; knitting, crochet, tatting, brocade, *brocatelle*, beads, bugles; galloon, lace, gimp, *guipure*, fringe, trapping, border, edging, insertion, *motif*, trimming; *passementerie*; drapery, hanging, tapestry, arras; millinery, ermine.

wreath, festoon, garland, lei, chaplet, flower, nosegay, *bouquet*, posy, 'daisies pied and violets blue.'

tassel, knot; shoulder-knot, *épaulette*, epaulet, aigulet, *aiguillette*, frog; star, rosette, bow; feather, plume, *panache*, *aigrette*.

jewel, -ry, -lery; bijoutry; *bijou*, -*terie*; diadem, tiara; pendant, trinket, locket, necklace, armilla, bracelet, bangle, armlet, anklet, ear-, nose- ring, carcanet, chain, *châtelaine*, albert, brooch, torque.

gem, precious stone; diamond, brilliant, beryl, aquamarine, alexandrite, cat's eye, emerald, calcedony, chrysoprase, cornelian, jasper, bloodstone, agate, heliotrope; girasol, -e; onyx, plasma; sard, -onyx; garnet, lapis-lazuli, opal, peridot, chrysolite, sapphire, ruby; spinel, -le; balais; oriental –, topaz; turquois, -e; zircon, jacinth, hyacinth, carbuncle, amethyst; moonstone; pearl, coral.

finery, frippery, gewgaw, gimcrack, knick-knack, tinsel, spangle, sequin, *clinquant*, pinch-beck, paste; excess of ornament &c. (*vulgarity*) 851; gaud, pride, ostentation; frills and furbelows.

illustration, illumination, *vignette*; *fleuron*; head-, tail-piece; *cul-de-lampe*; flowers of rhetoric &c. 577; work of art, article of vertu, *bric-à-brac*, curio, *bibelot*.

V. ornament, embellish, enrich, decorate, adorn, beautify, adonize.

smarten, furbish, polish, gild, varnish, whitewash, enamel, japan, lacquer, paint, grain.

garnish, trim, dizen, bedizen, prink, prank; trick –, fig- out; deck, bedeck, dight, bedight, array; dress, – up, preen, spruce up,

stain, blot, slur; spot, -tiness; speck, -le; blur, freckle, mole, *macula*, patch, blotch, birthmark, blain, maculation, tarnish, smudge, smear; dirt &c. 653; bruise, black eye, scar, wem; pustule; excrescence, pimple &c. (*protuberance*) 250.

V. disfigure &c. (*injure*) 659; speckle; render ugly &c. 846.

Adj. pitted, freckled, discoloured, bloodshot, bruised, disfigured; stained &c. *n.*; imperfect &c. 651; injured &c. (*deteriorated*) 659.

849. Simplicity. — N. simplicity; plain-, homeli-ness; undress, nudity, nakedness, beauty unadorned, chastity, chasteness.

V. be -simple &c. *adj.*

render -simple &c. *adj.*; simplify, chasten, strip of ornament.

Adj. simple, plain; home-ly, -spun; ordinary, household.

natural, unaffected; free from -affectation, – ornament; *simplex munditiis*; *sans façon*, *en déshabillé*, nude, naked.

chaste, inornate, severe.

un-adorned, -ornamented, -decked, -garnished, -arranged, -trimmed, -varnished.

bald, flat, dull, blank.

titivate; spangle, bespangle, powder; embroider, work; chase, tool, emboss, fret; emblazon, blazon, illuminate; illustrate.

become &c. (*accord with*) 23.

Adj. ornamented, beautified &c. *v.*; ornate, rich, gilt, begilt, tesse-lated, enamelled, inlaid; festooned; topiary.

smart, gay, tricksy, flowery, glittering; new-gilt, -spangled; fine, – as -a Mayday queen, – fivepence, – a carrot fresh scraped; pranked out, bedight, well-groomed.

in full dress &c. (*fashion*) 852; *en grande -tenue*, – *toilette*; in best bib and tucker, in Sunday best, *endimanché*; dressed to ad-vantage.

showy, flashy; gaudy &c. (*vulgar*) 851; garish; gorgeous.

ornamental, decorative; becoming &c. (*accordant*) 23.

850. [Good taste.] **Taste.—N.** taste; good -, refined -, cultivated- taste; delicacy, refinement, fine feeling, gust, *gusto*, tact, *finesse*; nicety &c. (*discrimination*) 465; polish, elegance, grace.

virtu; dilettanteism, virtuosity; fine art; cul-ture, -ivation.

[Science of taste] æsthetics.

man of -taste &c.; *connoisseur*, judge, critic, *conoscente*, *virtuoso*, *amateur*, *dilettante*, Aristarchus, Corinthian, *arbiter elegantiarum*, stagirite, euphemist.

'caviare to the general.'

V. appreciate, judge, criticize, dis-criminate &c. 465.

Adj. in good taste; tasteful, tasty; unaffected, pure, chaste, classical, attic; cultivated, refined; dainty; æsthetic, artistic; elegant &c. 578; euphemistic.

to one's -taste, – mind; after one's fancy; *comme il faut*; *tiré à quatre épingles*.

Adv. elegantly &c. *adj.*

Phr. *nihil tetigit quod non ornavit.*

852. Fashion.—N. fashion, style, *ton*, *bon ton*, society; good -, polite-society; drawing room, civilized life, civilization, town, *beau monde*, high life, court; world; fashionable -, gay-world; Vanity Fair; show &c. (*ostentation*) 822.

manners, breeding &c. (*politeness*) 894; air, demeanour &c. (*appearance*) 448; *savoir faire*; gentlemanliness, gentility, decorum, propriety, *bienséance*; conventions -, dictates- of society; Mrs. Grundy; convention, -ality; punctilio; form, -ality; etiquette, point of

851. [Bad taste.] **Vulgarity.—N.** vulgar-ity, -ism; barbar-, Vandal-, Gothic-ism; *mauvais goût*, bad taste; Babbittry; *gaucherie*, awkwardness, want of tact; ill-breeding &c. (*discourtesy*) 895; ungentlemanly be-haviour.

coarseness &c. *adj.*; indecorum, misbehaviour.

low-, homeli-ness; low life, *mauvais ton*, rusticity; boorishness &c. *adj.*; brutality; rowdy-, ruffian-, blackguard-ism; ribaldry; slang &c. (*neology*) 563.

bad joke, *mauvaise plaisanterie*.

[Excess of ornament] gaudi-, tawdri-ness; false ornament; finery, frippery, trickery, tinsel, gewgaw, *clinquant*.

rough diamond, tomboy, hoyden, cub, unlicked cub; clown &c. (*commonalty*) 876; Hun, Goth, Vandal, Bœotian; vulgarian; snob, cad, bound-er, gent; *parvenu* &c. 876; frump, dowdy; slattern &c. 653.

V. be -vulgar &c. *adj.*; misbehave; talk -, smell of the- shop.

Adj. in bad taste, vulgar, unrefined. gutter.

coarse, indecorus, ribald, gross; un-seemly, unbeseeming, unpresentable; *contra bonos mores*; ungraceful &c. (*ugly*) 846.

dowdy; slovenly &c. (*dirty*) 653; ungenteel, shabby genteel; low &c. (*plebeian*) 876; uncourtly; uncivil &c. (*discourteous*) 895; ill-bred, -mannered; underbred; ungentleman-ly, -like; un-ladylike, unfeminine; wild, – as an unbacked colt.

unkempt, uncombed, untamed, un-licked, unpolished, uncouth, plebeian;

etiquette; custom &c. 613; mode, vogue, style, go; rage &c. (*desire*) 865; prevailing taste, *dernier cri*, dress &c. 225.

man -, woman- of -fashion, - the world; height -, pink -, star -, glass -, leader- of fashion; *arbiter elegantiarum* &c. (*taste*) 850; upper ten thousand &c. (*nobility*) 875; *élite* &c. (*distinction*) 873.

V. be -fashionable &c. *adj.*, - the rage &c. *n.*; have a run, pass current.

follow -, conform to -, fall in with-the fashion &c. *n.*; go with the stream &c. (*conform*) 82; *savoir -vivre*, - *faire*; keep up appearances, behave oneself.

set the -, bring into- fashion; give a tone to -, cut a figure in- society, rub shoulders with nobility, keep one's carriage.

Adj. fashionable; in -fashion &c. *n.*; *à la mode, comme il faut*; admitted -, admissible- in -society &c. *n.*; presentable, decorous, punctilious, conventional &c. (*customary*) 613; genteel; well-bred, -mannered, -behaved, -spoken; gentleman-like, -ly; ladylike; civil, polite &c. (*courteous*) 894.

polished, refined, thoroughbred, courtly; *distingué*, aristocratic, unembarrassed, poised, *dégagé*; ja-, jau-nty; dashing, fast, showy, high toned, toney.

modish, stylish, in the latest style, *recherché*; new-fangled &c. (*unfamiliar*) 83.

in -court, - full, - evening- dress; *en grande tenue* &c. (*ornament*) 847.

Adv. fashionably &c. *adj.*; for fashion's sake.

incondite; heavy, rude, awkward; home-ly, -spun, -bred; provincial, hick, countrified, rustic, uncultivated, freshwater; boorish, clownish; savage, brutish, blackguard, rowdy, snobbish; barbar-ous, -ic; Gothic, unclassical doggerel, heathenish, tramontane, outlandish; Bohemian.

obsolete &c. (*antiquated*) 124; unfashionable, old-fashioned, out of date; new-fangled &c. (*unfamiliar*) 83; fantastic, odd &c. (*ridiculous*) 853.

particular; affected &c. 855; meretricious; extravagant, monstrous, horrid; shocking &c. (*painful*) 830.

gaudy, tawdry, bedizened, tricked out, gingerbread; obtrusive, flaunting, loud, flashy, garish, showy.

---

853. Ridiculousness.—**N.** ridiculousness &c. *adj.*; comical-, odd-ity &c. *adj.*; extravagance, drollery.

farce, comedy; burlesque &c. (*ridicule*) 856; buffoonery &c. (*fun*) 840; frippery; doggerel verses; Irish bull, Hibernianism, Hibernicism; Spoonerism; absurdity &c. 497; bombast &c. (*unmeaning*) 517; anti-climax, bathos; monstrosity &c. (*unconformity*) 83; laughing stock &c. 857.

V. be -ridiculous &c. *adj.*; pass from the sublime to the ridiculous; make one laugh; play the fool, make a fool of oneself, commit an absurdity.

play a joke on, make a -fool of, - sucker of, - monkey of.

Adj. ridiculous, ludicrous; comic, -al; droll, funny, laughable, *pour rire*, grotesque, farcical, odd; whimsical, - as a dancing bear; fanciful, fantastic, queer, rum, quizzical, waggish, quaint, *bizarre*; eccentric &c. (*unconformable*) 83; strange, outlandish, out of the way, *baroque*, *rocaille*, rococo; awkward &c. (*ugly*) 846.

absurd, extravagant, *outré*, monstrous, preposterous, bombastic, inflated, stilted, burlesque, mock heroic.

drollish; serio-, tragic-comic; gimcrack, contemptible &c. (*unimportant*) 643; doggerel; ironical &c. (*derisive*) 856; risible.

Phr. *'risum teneatis amici?'* *rideret Heraclitus.*

854. Fop.—**N.** fop, fine gentleman; swell; dand-y, -iprat; exquisite, coxcomb, toff, beau, macaroni, blade, blood, buck, man about town, fast man; fribble, jemmy, spark, popinjay, puppy, prig, *petit maître*; jacka-napes, -dandy; man milliner; Jemmy Jessamy, carpet-knight, masher, Dundreary, Johnnie, dude.

belle, fine lady, *coquette*, flirt.

855. Affectation.—**N.** affectation; affectedness &c. *adj.*; acting a part &c. *v.*; pretence &c. (*falsehood*) 544, (*ostentation*) 882; boasting &c. 884.

charlatanism, quakery, shallow profundity, humbug, pretension, airs, pedantry, purism, precisianism, euphuism, prunes and prisms; tera-tology &c. (*altiloquence*) 577.

mannerism, *simagrée*, grimace.

conceit, foppery, dandyism, man millinery, coxcombry, puppyism.

stiffness, formality, buckram; prudery, demureness, coquetry, mock modesty, *minauderie*, sentimentalism; *mauvaise honte*, false shame.

affector, performer, actor; pedant, pedagogue, *doctrinaire*, purist, euphuist, mannerist; shoneen; *grimacier*; lump of affectation, *précieuse ridicule*, *bas bleu*, blue stocking, poetaster; prig, hypocrite; charlatan &c. (*deceiver*) 548; *petit maître* &c. (*fop*) 854; flatterer &c. 935; *coquette*, prude, puritan; precisian, formalist.

V. affect, act a part, put on; give oneself airs &c. (*arrogance*) 885; boast &c. 884; coquet; simper, mince, attitudinize, strike a pose, pose; flirt a fan; over-act, -play, -do.

Adj. affected, full of affectation, pretentious, pedantic, stilted, stagey, theatrical, big-sounding, *ad captandum*, canting, insincere.

not natural, unnatural; self-conscious; *maniéré*; artificial; over-wrought, -done, -acted; euphuistic &c. 577.

stiff, starch, formal, prim, smug, demure, *tiré à quatre épingles*, quakerish, puritanical, prudish, pragmatical, priggish, conceited, cox-comical, foppish, dandified; fini-cal, -kin, -cky; mincing, simpering, namby-pamby, sentimental, languishing.

856. Ridicule.—**N.** ridicule, derision; sardonic -smile, – grin; irrision; snigger; scoffing &c. (*disrespect*) 929; mockery, quiz, banter, irony, *persiflage*, raillery, chaff, *badinage*; quizzing &c. *v.*

squib, satire, skit, quip, quib, grin.

parody, burlesque, travesty; farce &c. (*drama*) 599; caricature, take-off.

buffoonery &c. (*fun*) 840; practical joke, horseplay.

V. ridicule, deride; laugh at, grin at, smile at; snigger; laugh in one's sleeve; banter, rally, chaff, joke, twit, quiz, poke fun at, jolly, roast, rag; fleer; play –, play tricks- upon; fool, – to the top of one's bent; show up.

satirize, parody, caricature, burlesque, travesty.

turn into ridicule; make merry with; make -fun, – game, – a fool, – an April fool- of; rally; scoff &c. (*disrespect*) 929.

raise a laugh &c. (*amuse*) 840; play the fool, make a fool of oneself.

be ridiculous &c. 853.

Adj. deris-ory, -ive; mock; sarcastic, ironical, quizzical, burlesque, Hudibrastic; scurrilous &c. (*disrespectful*) 929.

Adv. in -ridicule &c. *n.*

857. [Object and cause of ridicule.] **Laughing-stock.—N.** laughing-, jesting-, gazing-stock; butt, game, fair game; April fool &c. (*dupe*) 547.

original, oddity; queer -, odd- fish; quiz, square toes; old -, fogey *or* fogy.

monkey; buffoon &c. (*jester*) 844; pantomimist &c. (*actor*) 599.

jest &c. (*wit*) 842.

3°. Prospective Affections

858. Hope.—N. hope, -s; desire &c. 865; fervent hope, sanguine expectation, trust, confidence, reliance; faith &c. (*belief*) 484; affiance, assurance; secur-eness, -ity; reassurance.

good -omen, - auspices; promise, well-grounded hopes; good -, bright-prospect; clear sky.

as-, pre-sumption; anticipation &c. (*expectation*) 507.

hopefulness, buoyancy, optimism, enthusiasm, heart of grace, aspiration; optimist, utop-ian, -ist; Pollyanna.

castles in the air, *châteaux en Espagne*, hope chest, *le pot au lait*, Utopia, millennium; day -, golden-dream; dream of Alnaschar; airy hopes, fool's paradise; *mirage* &c. (*fallacies of vision*) 443; fond hope.

beam -, ray -, gleam -, glimmer -, dawn -, flash -, star- of hope; cheer; bit of blue sky, silver lining of the cloud, bottom of Pandora's box, balm in Gilead.

anchor, sheet-anchor, main-stay; staff &c. (*support*) 215; heaven &c. 981.

V. hope, trust, confide, rely on, put one's trust in, lean upon; pin one's -hope, - faith- upon &c. (*believe*) 484.

feel -, entertain -, harbour -, indulge -, cherish -, feed -, foster -, nourish -, encourage -, cling to -, live in- hope &c. *n.*; see land; feel -, rest- -assured, - confident &c. *adj.*

presume; promise oneself; expect &c. (*look forward to*) 507.

hope for &c. (*desire*) 865; anticipate.

be -hopeful &c. *adj.*; look on the bright side of, view on the sunny side, make the best of it, hope for the best; put -a good, - a bold, - the best- face upon; keep one's spirits up; take heart, - of grace; be of good -heart, - cheer; flatter oneself, lay the flattering unction to one's soul.

859. [Absence, want, or loss of hope.] **Hopelessness.—N.** hopelessness &c. *adj.*; despair, desperation; despondency &c. (*dejection*) 837; pessimism.

hope deferred, dashed hopes; vain expectation &c. (*disappointment*) 509.

airy hopes &c. 858; forlorn hope; bad -job, - business; *enfant perdu*; gloomy -, black spots in the- horizon; slough of Despond, cave of Despair.

Job's comforter; bird of -bad, - ill-omen.

V. despair; lose -, give up -, abandon -, relinquish- -all hope, - the hope of; give -up, - over; yield to despair; falter; despond &c. (*be dejected*) 837; *jeter le manche après la cognée.*

inspire -, drive to- despair &c. *n.*; disconcert; dash -, crush -, shatter -, destroy- one's hopes; hope against hope.

Adj. hopeless, desperate, despairing, in despair, *au désespoir*, forlorn; inconsolable &c. (*dejected*) 837; broken-hearted.

out of the question, not to be thought of; impracticable &c. 471; past -hope, - cure, - mending, - recall; at one's last gasp &c. (*death*) 360; given -up, - over.

incurable, cureless, immedicable, remediless, beyond remedy; incorrigible; irre-parable, -mediable, -coverable, -versible, -trievable, -claimable, -deemable, -vocable; ruined, undone; immitigable.

unpromising, unpropitious; inauspicious, ill-omened, threatening, clouded over, lowering, ominous.

Phr. '*lasciate ogni speranza voi ch' entrate*'; its days are numbered; the worst come to the worst.

860. Fear.—N. fear, timidity, diffidence, want of confidence; apprehensive-, fearful-ness &c. *adj.*; solicitude,

catch at a straw, hope against hope, count one's chickens before they are hatched.

give –, inspire –, raise –, hold out- hope &c. *n.*; raise expectations; en- courage, hearten, cheer, assure, re- assure, buoy up, embolden; promise, bid fair, augur well, be in a fair way, look up, flatter, tell a flattering tale.

Adj. hoping &c. *v.*; in -hopes &c. *n.*; hopeful, confident; secure &c. (*certain*) 484; sanguine, in good heart, buoyed up, buoyant, elated, flushed, exultant, enthusiastic; utopian.

unsus-pecting, -picious; fearless, free –, exempt from- -fear, – suspicion, – distrust, – despair; undespairing, self- reliant.

probable, on the high road to; within sight of -shore, – land; promising, propitious; of –, full of- promise; of good omen, *de bon augure*; reassuring; encouraging, cheering, in- spiriting, looking up, bright, roseate, *couleur de rose*, rose-coloured.

Adv. hopefully &c. *adj.*

Int. God speed! good luck!

Phr. *nil desperandum*; never say die, *dum spiro spero*, *latet scintillula forsan*, all is for the best, *spero meliora*; the wish being father to the thought; 'hope told a flattering tale'; *rusticus expectat dum defluat amnis*.

anxiety, care, apprehension, misgiving; mistrust &c. (*doubt*) 485; suspicion, qualm; hesitation &c. (*irresolution*) 605.

nervous-, restless-ness &c. *adj.*; in-, dis-quietude; flutter, trepidation, fear and trembling, perturbation, tremor, quivering, shaking, trembling, throb- bing heart, palpitation, ague fit, cold sweat; abject fear &c. (*cowardice*) 862; mortal funk, heart-sinking, despond- ency; despair &c. 859.

fright; affright, -ment; alarm, pavor, dread, awe, terror, horror, dismay, consternation, panic, scare, stampede [of horses].

intimidation, terrorism, reign of terror.

[Object of fear] bug-bear, -aboo; scarecrow; hobgoblin &c. (*demon*) 980; daymare, nightmare, Gorgon, Medusa, mormo, ogre, Hurlothrumbo, raw head and bloody bones, fee faw fum, *bête noire*, *enfant terrible*.

alarmist &c. (*coward*) 862.

V. fear, stand in awe of; be -afraid &c. *adj.*; have -qualms &c. *n.*; appre- hend, sit upon thorns, eye askance; distrust &c. (*disbelieve*) 485.

hesitate &c. (*be irresolute*) 605; falter, funk, cower, crouch; skulk &c. (*coward- ice*) 862; let 'I dare not' wait upon 'I would'; take -fright, – alarm; start, wince, flinch, shy, shrink; fly &c. (*avoid*) 623.

tremble, shake; shiver, – in one's shoes; shudder, flutter; shake –, tremble- -like an aspen leaf, – all over; quake, quaver, quiver, quail; get the wind up.

grow –, turn- pale; blench, stand aghast; not dare to say one's soul is one's own.

inspire –, excite- -fear, – awe; raise apprehensions; give –, raise –, sound- an alarm; alarm, startle, scare, cry 'wolf,' disquiet, dismay; fright, -en; affright, terrify; astound; frighten from one's propriety; frighten out of one's -wits, – senses, – seven senses; awe; strike -all of a heap, – an awe into, – terror; harrow up the soul, appal, unman, petrify, horrify.

make one's -flesh creep, – hair stand on end, – blood run cold, – teeth chatter; chill one's spine; take away –, stop- one's breath; make one -tremble &c.

haunt, obsess, beset; prey –, weigh- on the mind.

put in -fear, – bodily fear; terrorize, intimidate, cow, daunt, over- awe, abash, deter, discourage; browbeat, bully; threaten &c. 909.

Adj. fearing &c. *v.*; frightened &c. *v.*; in -fear, – a fright &c. *n.*; haunted with the -fear &c. *n.*- of.

afraid, fearful; tim-id, -orous; nervous, diffident, coy, faint-hearted, tremulous, shaky, afraid of one's shadow, apprehensive, restless, fidgety; more frightened than hurt.

aghast; awe-, horror-, terror-, panic- -struck, -stricken; frightened to death, white as a sheet; pale, – as -death, – ashes, – a ghost; breathless, in hysterics.

inspiring fear &c. *v.*; alarming; formidable, redoubtable; perilous &c. (*danger*) 665; portentous; fear-ful, -some; dread, -ful; fell; dire, -ful; shocking; terri-ble, -fic; tremendous; horri-d, -ble, -fic; ghastly; awful, awe-inspiring, eerie, weird; revolting &c. (*painful*) 830.

Adv. *in terrorem.*

Int. 'angels and ministers of grace defend us!'

Phr. *ante tubam trepidat*; *horresco referens*, one's heart failing one, *obstupui steteruntque comæ et vox faucibus hæsit.*

---

861. [Absence of fear.] **Courage.**—**N.** courage, bravery, valour; resolute-, bold-ness &c. *adj.*; spirit, daring, gallantry, intrepidity; contempt –, defiance- of danger; derring-do; audacity; rashness &c. 863; dash; defiance &c. 715; confidence, self-reliance.

man-liness, -hood; nerve, pluck, mettle, game; heart, – of grace; spunk, gameness, grit, face, virtue, hardihood, fortitude; firmness &c. (*stability*) 150; heart of oak; bottom, backbone &c. (*perseverance*) 604a.

resolution &c. (*determination*) 604; tenacity, bull-dog courage.

prowess, heroism, chivalry.

exploit, feat, achievement; heroic -deed, – act; bold stroke.

man, – of mettle; hero, demigod, paladin, heroine, Amazon, Hector, Joan of Arc; lion, tiger, panther, bull-dog; game-, fighting-cock; bully, fire-eater &c. 863; dare-devil.

V. be -courageous &c. *adj.*; dare, venture, make bold; face –, front –, affront –, confront –, brave –, defy –, despise –, mock- danger; look in the face; look -full, – boldly, – danger- in the face; meet, – in front; brave, beard; defy &c. 715.

take –, muster –, summon up –, pluck up- courage; nerve oneself, take heart; take –, pluck up- heart of grace; hold up one's head, screw one's courage to the sticking place; come -to, – up to- the scratch; stand, – to one's guns, – fire, – against; bear up, – against; hold out &c. (*persevere*) 604a.

put a bold face upon; show –,

862. [Excess of fear.] **Cowardice.**—**N.** cowardice, pusillanimity; cowardliness &c. *adj.*; timidity, effeminacy.

poltroonery, baseness; dastard-ness, -y; abject fear, funk; Dutch courage; fear &c. 860; white feather, faint heart.

coward, poltroon, dastard, sneak, recreant; shy –, dunghill- cock; coistril, milksop, white-liver, nidget, cur, craven, one that cannot say 'Boo' to a goose; Bob Acres, Jerry Sneak.

alarm-, terror-, pessim-ist; runagate &c. (*fugitive*) 623; shirker.

V. quail &c. (*fear*) 860; be -cowardly &c. *adj.*, – a coward &c. *n.*; funk; cower, skulk, sneak; flinch, shy, fight shy, slink, turn tail; run away &c. (*avoid*) 623; show the white feather, have cold feet, show a yellow streak.

Adj. coward, -ly; fearful, shy; tim-id, -orous; skittish; poor-spirited, spiritless, soft, effeminate.

weak-minded; infirm of purpose &c. 605; weak-, faint-, chicken-, lily-, pigeon-hearted; yellow; white-, lily-, milk-livered; milksop, smock-faced; unable to say 'Boo' to a goose.

dastard, -ly; base, craven, sneaking, dunghill, recreant; unwar-, unsoldier-like.

'in face a lion but in heart a deer.' unmanned; frightened &c. 860.

Int. *sauve qui peut!* devil take the hindmost!

Adv. in fear and trembling, in fear of one's life, in a blue funk.

Phr. *ante tubam trepidat*, one's courage oozing out.

present- a bold front, face the music; envisage; show fight.

bell the cat, take the bull by the horns, beard the lion in his den, march up to the cannon's mouth, go through fire and water, run the gauntlet, go over the top.

give -, infuse -, inspire- courage; reassure, encourage, embolden, inspirit, cheer, hearten, nerve, put upon one's mettle, rally, raise a rallying cry; pat on the back, make a man of, keep in countenance.

Adj. courageous, brave; val-iant, -orous; gallant, intrepid; spirit-ed, -ful; high-spirited, -mettled; mettlesome, game, plucky; man-ly, -ful; resolute; stout, -hearted; iron-, lion-hearted; heart of oak; Penthesilean.

bold, - spirited; daring, audacious; fear-, daunt-, dread-, awe-less; un-daunted, -appalled, -dismayed, -awed, -blenched, -abashed, -alarmed, -flinching, -shrinking, -blenching; apprehensive; confident, self-reliant; bold as -a lion, - brass.

enterprising, adventurous; ventur-ous, -esome; dashing, chival-rous; soldierly &c. (*warlike*) 722; heroic.

fierce, savage; pugnacious &c. (*bellicose*) 720.

strong-minded, hardy, doughty; firm &c. (*stable*) 150; determined &c. (*resolved*) 604; dogged, indomitable &c. (*persevering*) 604*a*.

up to, - the scratch; upon one's mettle; reassured &c. *v.*; un-feared, undreaded.

Phr. one's blood being up.

---

863. Rashness.—N. rashness &c. *adj.*; temerity, want of caution, imprudence, indiscretion; over-confidence, presumption, audacity.

precipit-ancy, -ation; impetuosity; levity; foolhardi-hood, -ness; heed-, thought-lessness &c. (*inattention*) 458; carelessness &c. (*neglect*) 460; desperation; Quixotism, knight-errantry; fire-eating.

gam-ing, -bling; blind bargain, leap in the dark, fool's paradise; too many eggs in one basket.

desperado, rashling, mad-cap, dare-devil, Hotspur, fire-eater, bully, *bravo*, Hector, scapegrace, *enfant perdu*; Don Quixote, knight-errant, Icarus; adventurer; gam-bler, -ester; dynamitard.

V. be -rash &c. *adj.*; stick at nothing, play a desperate game; run into danger &c. 665; play with -fire, - edge tools.

carry too much sail, sail too near the wind, ride at single anchor, go out of one's depth.

take a leap in the dark, buy a pig in a poke.

donner tête baissée; knock one's head against a wall &c. (*be unskilful*) 699; rush on destruction; kick against the

864. Caution.—N. caution; cautious-ness &c. *adj.*; discretion, prudence, cautel, heed, circumspection, calcula-tion, deliberation; safety first.

foresight &c. 510; vigilance &c. 459; warning &c. 668.

coolness &c. *adj.*; self-possession, -command; presence of mind, *sang froid*; well-regulated mind; worldly wisdom, Fabian policy.

V. be -cautious &c. *adj.*; take -care, - heed, - good care; have a care; mind, - what one is about; be on one's guard &c. (*keep watch*) 459; make assurance double sure; ca' canny.

bespeak &c. (*be early*) 132.

think twice, look before one leaps, keep one's weather eye open, count the cost, look to the main chance, cut one's coat according to one's cloth; feel one's -ground, - way; see how the land lies &c. (*foresight*) 510; wait to see how the cat jumps; bridle one's tongue; *reculer pour mieux sauter* &c. (*prepare*) 673; let well alone, let sleeping dogs lie, *ne pas réveiller le chat qui dort*.

keep out of -harm's way, - troubled waters; keep at a respectful distance, stand aloof; keep -, be- on the safe side.

pricks, tempt Providence, go on a for-lorn hope.

count one's chickens before they are hatched; reckon without one's host; catch at straws; trust to –, lean on- a broken reed.

Adj. rash, incautious, indiscreet, in-judicious; imprudent, improvident, temerarious; uncalculating; heedless; careless &c. (*neglectful*) 460; without ballast, heels over head; giddy &c. (*inattentive*) 458; wanton, reckless, wild, madcap; desperate, devil-may-care.

hot-blooded, -headed, -brained; head-long, -strong; break-neck; fool-hardy; harebrained; precipitate, im-pulsive.

over-confident, -weening; ventur-esome, -ous; adventurous, Quixotic; fire-eating, cavalier; free-and-easy.

off one's guard &c. (*inexpectant*) 508.

Adv. post haste, *à corps perdu*, hand over head, *tête baissée*, head-foremost; happen what may.

Phr. neck or nothing, the devil being in one.

husband one's resources &c. 636.

caution &c. (*warn*) 668.

Adj. cautious, wary, guarded; on one's guard &c. (*watchful*) 459; *cavendo tutus; in medio tutissimus.*

care-, heed-ful; cautelous, stealthy, chary, shy of, circumspect, prudent, canny, safe, non-committal, discreet, politic; sure-footed &c. (*skilful*) 698.

unenterprising, unadventurous, cool, steady, self-possessed; over-cautious.

suspicious, leery, vigilant.

Adv. cautiously, gingerly &c. *adj.*

Int. have a care! look out! *cave canem!*

Phr. *timeo Danaos; festina lente.*

---

865. Desire.—N. desire, wish, fancy, fantasy; want, need, exigency.

mind, inclination, leaning, bent, *ani-mus*, partiality, *penchant*, predilection; propensity &c. 820; willingness &c. 602; liking, love, fondness, relish.

longing, hankering; solicitude, anx-iety; yearning, coveting; aspiration, ambition, vaulting ambition; eagerness, zeal, ardour, *empressement*, breathless impatience, over-anxiety; solicitude, impetuosity &c. 825.

appet-ite, -ition, -ence, -ency; sharp appetite, keenness, hunger, stomach, twist; thirst, -iness; drouth, mouth-watering; itch, -ing; prurience, *caco-ëthes*, cupidity, lust, concupiscence.

edge of -appetite, – hunger; torment of Tantalus; sweet –, lickerish- tooth; itching palm; longing –, wistful –, sheep's- eye.

avidity; greed, -iness; covetous-, ravenous-ness &c. *adj.*; grasping, crav-ing, canine appetite, rapacity; voracity &c. (*gluttony*) 957.

passion, rage, *furore*, mania, *manie*; inextinguishable desire; dips-, klept-, mon-omania.

[Person desiring] desirer, lover, *ama-*

866. Indifference.—N. indifference, neutrality; coldness &c. *adj.*; uncon-cern, *insouciance, nonchalance*; want of -interest, – earnestness; anorexy, in-appetency; apathy &c. (*insensibility*) 823; supineness &c. (*inactivity*) 683; disdain &c. 930; recklessness &c. 863; inattention &c. 458.

V. be -indifferent &c. *adj.*; stand neuter; take no interest in &c. (*insensi-bility*) 823; have no -desire &c. 865, – taste, – relish- for; not care for; care nothing -for, – about; not care a -straw &c. (*unimportance*) 643 -about, – for; not mind.

set at naught &c. (*make light of*) 483; spurn &c. (*disdain*) 930.

Adj. indifferent, cold, frigid, luke-warm; cool, – as a cucumber; uncon-cerned, *insouciant*, phlegmatic, *pococu-rante*, easy-going, devil-may-care, care-less, listless, lackadaisical, feckless; half-hearted; un-ambitious, -aspiring, -desirous, -solicitous, -attracted.

un-attractive, -alluring, -desired, -de-sirable, -cared for, -wished, -valued, all one to.

insipid &c. 391; vain.

Adv. for aught one cares.

teur, votary, devotee, aspirant, solicitant, candidate; cormorant &c. 957; sycophant.

[Object of desire] *desideratum*; want &c. (*requirement*) 630; 'consummation devoutly to be wished'; attraction, magnet, allurement, fancy, temptation, seduction, lure, fascination, *prestige*, height of one's ambition, idol; whim, -sey; maggot; hobby, -horse.

Fortunatus's cap, wishing cap, love potion.

V. desire; wish, – for; be -desirous &c. *adj.*; have a -longing &c. *n.*; hope &c. 858.

care for, affect, like, list; take to, cling to, take a fancy to; fancy; prefer &c. (*choose*) 609.

have -an eye, – a mind- to; find it in one's heart &c. (*be willing*) 602; have a fancy for, set one's eyes upon; cast a sheep's eye –, look sweet- upon; take into one's head, have at heart, be bent upon; set one's -cap at, – heart upon, – mind upon; covet.

want, miss, need, lack, desiderate, feel the want of; would fain -have, – do; would be glad of.

be -hungry &c. *adj.*; have a good appetite, play a good knife and fork; hunger –, thirst –, crave –, lust –, itch –, hanker –, run mad- after; raven –, die- for; burn to.

desiderate; sigh –, cry –, gape –, gasp –, pine –, pant –, languish –, yearn –, long –, be on thorns –, hope- for; aspire after; catch at, grasp at, jump at.

woo, court, solicit; fish –, spell –, whistle –, put up- for; ogle.

cause –, create –, raise –, excite –, provoke- desire; whet the appetite; appetize, titillate, allure, attract, take one's fancy, tempt; hold out -temptation, – allurement; tantalize, make one's mouth water, *faire venir l'eau à la bouche*.

gratify desire &c. (*give pleasure*) 829.

Adj. desirous; desiring &c. *v.*; orectic, appetitive; inclined &c. (*willing*) 602; partial to; fain, wishful, optative; anxious, wistful, curious; at a loss for, sedulous, solicitous.

craving, hungry, sharp-set, peckish,

Int. never mind.

867. Dislike.—N. dis-like, -taste, -relish, -inclination, -placency.

reluctance; backwardness &c. (*unwillingness*) 603.

repugnance, disgust, queasiness, turn, nausea, loathing; avers-eness, -ation, -ion; abomination, antipathy, abhorrence, horror; mortal –, rooted--antipathy, – horror; hatred, detestation; hate &c. 898; animosity &c. 900; hydrophobia.

sickener; gall and wormwood &c. (*unsavoury*) 395; shuddering, cold sweat.

V. dis-, mis-like, -relish; mind, object to; have rather not, not care for; have –, conceive –, entertain –, take--a dislike, – an aversion- to; have no -taste, – stomach- for.

shun, avoid &c. 623; eschew; withdraw –, shrink –, recoil- from; not be able to -bear, – abide, – endure; shrug the shoulders at, shudder at, turn up the nose at, look askance at; make a -mouth, – wry face, – grimace; make faces.

loathe, nauseate, abominate, detest, abhor; hate &c. 898; take amiss &c. 900; have enough of &c. (*be satiated*) 869.

cause –, excite- dislike; disincline, repel, sicken; make –, render- sick; turn one's stomach, nauseate, wamble, disgust, shock, stink in the nostrils; go against the -grain, – stomach; stick in the throat; make one's blood run cold &c. (*give pain*) 830; pall.

Adj. disliking &c. *v.*; averse to, loth, adverse; shy of, sick of, out of conceit with; disinclined; heart-, dog-sick; queasy.

disliked &c. *v.*; uncared for, unpopular; out of favour; repulsive, repugnant, repellent; abhorrent, insufferable, fulsome, nauseous; loath-some, -ful; offensive; disgusting &c. *v.*; disagreeable &c. (*painful*) 830; unsavoury &c. 395.

Adv. *usque ad nauseam.*

Int. faugh! foh! ugh!

868. Fastidiousness.—N. fastidiousness &c. *adj.*; nicety, meticulosity,

ravening, with an empty stomach, esurient, lickerish, thirsty, athirst, parched with thirst, pinched with hunger, famished, dry, drouthy; hungry as a -hunter, – hawk, – horse, – church mouse.

greedy, – as a hog; over-eager, voracious; ravenous, – as a wolf; open-mouthed, covetous, rapacious, grasping, extortionate, exacting, sordid, *alieni appetens*; insati-able, -ate; unquenchable, quenchless; omnivorous.

unsatisfied, unsated, unslaked.

eager, avid, keen; burning, fervent, ardent; agog; all agog; breathless; impatient &c. (*impetuous*) 825; bent –, intent –, set- -on, – upon; mad after, *enragé*, rabid, dying for, devoured by desire.

aspiring, ambitious, vaulting, sky-aspiring.

desirable; popular; desired &c. *v.*; in demand; pleasing &c. (*giving pleasure*) 829; appeti-zing, -ble; tantalizing.

Adv. wistfully &c. *adj.*; fain.

Int. would -that, – it were! O for! *esto perpetua!* if only!

Phr. the wish being father to the thought; *sua cuique voluptas*; *hoc erat in votis*, the mouth watering, the fingers itching; *aut Cæsar aut nullus*.

---

have -enough of, – quite enough of, – one's fill, – too much of; be -satiated &c. *adj.*

Adj. satiated &c. *v.*; overgorged; *blasé*, used up, sick of, heart-sick.

Int. enough! hold! *eheu jam satis!*

hypercriticism, difficulty in being pleased, *friandise*, epicurism, *omnia suspendens naso*.

discrimination, discernment, good taste, perspicacity.

epicure, gourmet.

[Excess of delicacy] prudery, prudishness, primness.

V. be -fastidious &c. *adj.*; split hairs, discriminate, have a sweet tooth.

mince the matter; turn up one's nose at &c. (*disdain*) 930; look a gift horse in the mouth, see spots on the sun.

Adj. fastidious, meticulous, exacting, nice, delicate, *délicat*, finical, finicky, difficult, dainty, lickerish, squeamish, thin-skinned; s-, queasy; hard –, difficult- to please; querulous, particular, over-particular, straitlaced, prudish, prim, scrupulous; censorious &c. 932; hypercritical, discriminating, discerning, perspicacious.

Phr. *noli me tangere.*

869. Satiety.—N. satiety, satisfaction, saturation, repletion, glut, surfeit; weariness &c. 841.

spoiled child; *enfant gâté*; too much of a good thing, *toujours perdrix*; *crambe repetita*.

V. sate, satiate, satisfy, saturate; cloy, quench, slake, pall, glut, gorge, surfeit; bore &c. (*weary*) 841; tire &c. (*fatigue*) 688; spoil.

4°. Contemplative Affections

870. Wonder.—N. wonder, marvel; astonish-, amaze-, wonder-, bewilderment; amazedness &c. *adj.*; admiration, awe; stup-or, -efaction; stound, fascination; sensation; surprise &c. (*inexpectation*) 508; cynosure.

note of admiration; thaumaturgy &c. (*sorcery*) 992.

V. wonder, marvel, admire; be -surprised &c. *adj.*; start; stare; open –, rub –, turn up- one's eyes; gloar; gape, open one's mouth, hold one's breath;

871. [Absence of wonder.] **Expectance.—N.** expectan-ce, -cy &c. (*expectation*) 507; calmness, composure, tranquillity, serenity, coolness, imperturbability &c. 826.

nine days' wonder.

V. expect &c. 507; not -be surprised, – wonder &c. 870; *nil admirari*, make nothing of.

Adj. expecting &c. *v.*; unamazed, astonished at nothing; *blasé* &c. (*weary*) 841; unimaginative, calm, serene, im-

look –, stand- -aghast, – agog; look blank &c. (*disappointment*) 509; *tomber des nues*; not believe one's -eyes, – ears, – senses.

not be able to account for &c. (*un-intelligible*) 519; not know whether one stands on one's head or one's heels.

surprise, astonish, amaze, astound; dumbfound, -er; startle, dazzle; strike, – with -wonder, – awe; electrify; stun, stupefy, petrify, confound, bewilder, flabbergast; stagger, throw on one's beam ends, fascinate, turn the head, take away one's breath, strike dumb; make one's -hair stand on end, – tongue cleave to the roof of one's mouth; make one stare.

take by surprise &c. (*be unexpected*) 508.

be -wonderful &c. *adj.*; beggar –, baffle- description; stagger belief.

Adj. surprised &c. *v.*; aghast, all agog, breathless, agape; open-mouthed; awe-, thunder-, moon-, planet-struck; spell-bound; lost in -amazement, – wonder, – astonishment; struck all of a heap, unable to believe one's senses, like a duck in thunder.

wonderful, wondrous; surprising &c. *v.*; unexpected &c. 508; un-heard of; mysterious &c. (*inexplicable*) 519; miraculous; *foudroyant*.

in-describable, -expressible, -effable; un-utterable, -speakable.

monstrous, prodigious, stupendous, marvellous; in-conceivable, -credible; in-, un-imaginable; strange &c. (*uncommon*) 83; passing strange.

striking &c. *v.*; over-whelming; wonder-working.

Adv. wonderfully &c. *adj.*; fearfully; for a –, in the name of-wonder; strange to say; *mirabile -dictu, – visu*; to one's great surprise.

with -wonder &c. *n.*, – gaping mouth, – open eyes, – upturned eyes; eyes starting out of one's head.

Int. lo, – and behold! O! hey-day! halloo! what! indeed! really! surely! humph! hem! good -lack, – heavens, – gracious! – lord! by jove! gad so! well a day! dear me! only think! lack-a-daisy! my -stars, – goodness! gracious goodness! goodness gracious! mercy on us! heavens and earth! God bless me! bless -us, – my heart! odzookens! *O gemini!* adzooks! hoity-toity! strong! Heaven save –, bless- the mark! can such things be! zounds! 'sdeath! what -on earth, – in the world! who would have thought it! &c. (*inexpectation*) 508; fancy! did you ever? you don't say so! what do you say to that! how now! where am I? well I'm blowed! &c.

Phr. *vox faucibus hæsit*; one's hair standing on end.

perturbable &c. 826; expected &c. *v.*; foreseen.

common, ordinary &c. (*habitual*) 613.

Int. no wonder; of course; why not?

---

872. Prodigy.—**N.** prodigy, phenomenon; wonder, -ment; genius, marvel, miracle; freak, monster &c. (*unconformity*) 83; curiosity, lion, infant prodigy, sight, spectacle; *jeu* –, *coup- de théâtre*; gazing-stock; sign; portent &c. 512.

bursting of a -shell, – bomb; volcanic eruption, peal of thunder; thunder-clap, -bolt.

what no words can paint; wonders of the world; *annus mirabilis*; *dignus vindice nodus*.

5°. Intrinsic Affections*

873. Repute.—**N.** distinction, mark, name, figure; repute, reputation, char-

874. Disrepute.—**N.** disrepute, dis-credit; ill-, bad- -repute, -name, -odour,

* Or personal affections derived from the opinions or feelings of others.

acter; good –, high- repute; note, notability, notoriety, *éclat*, 'the bubble
reputation,' vogue, celebrity; fame,
famousness; renown; popularity, *aura
popularis*; esteem, approval, approbation &c. 931; credit, *succès d'estime*,
prestige, talk of the town; name to
conjure with.

glory, honour; lustre &c. (*light*) 420;
illustriousness &c. *adj.*

account, regard, respect; reputable-
ness &c. *adj.*; respectability &c. (*probity*) 939; good -name, – report; fair
name.

dignity; stateliness &c. *adj.*; solemnity, grandeur, splendour, nobility,
majesty, sublimity.

rank, standing, brevet rank, precedence, *pas*, station, place, *status*; position, – in society; order, degree, *locus
standi*, caste, condition.

greatness &c. *adj.*; eminence; height
&c. 206; importance &c. 642; pre-,
super-eminence; high mightiness, primacy; top of the -ladder, – tree.

elevation; ascent &c. 305; super-,
ex-altation; dignification, aggrandizement.

dedication, consecration, enthronement, canonization, apotheosis, deification, celebration, enshrinement, glorification.

hero, man of mark, great card, celebrity, worthy, lion, *rara avis*, notability, somebody; man of rank &c.
(*nobleman*) 875; pillar of the -state,
– society, – church.

chief &c. (*master*) 745; first fiddle
&c. (*proficient*) 700; scholar &c. 492;
cynosure, mirror; flower, pink, pearl;
paragon &c. (*perfection*) 650; choice
and master spirits of the age; *élite*;
star, sun, constellation, galaxy.

ornament, honour, feather in one's
cap, halo, aureole, nimbus; halo –,
blaze- of glory; blushing honours;
laurels &c. (*trophy*) 733.

memory, posthumous fame, niche in
the temple of fame; immor-tality, -tal
name; *magni nominis umbra*.

V. be conscious of glory; be proud
of &c. (*pride*) 878; exult &c. (*boast*)
884; be vain of &c. (*vanity*) 880.

be -distinguished &c. *adj.*; shine &c.

-favour; disapprobation &c. 932; in-
gloriousness, derogation; a-, de-base-
ment; abjectness &c. *adj.*; degradation,
dedecoration; 'a long farewell to all
one's greatness'; odium, obloquy, op-
probrium, ignominy.

dishonour, disgrace; shame, humiliation; scandal, baseness, vileness;
perfidy, turpitude &c. (*improbity*) 940;
infamy.

tarnish, taint, defilement, pollution.

stain, blot, spot, blur, stigma, brand,
reproach, imputation, slur.

crying –, burning- shame; *scandalum
magnatum*, badge of infamy, blot in
one's escutcheon; bend –, bar- sinister;
champain, point champain; by-word
of reproach; Ichabod.

argumentum ad verecundiam; sense
of shame &c. 879.

V. be -inglorious &c. *adj.*; incur
-disgrace &c. *n.*; have –, earn- a bad
name; put –, wear- a halter round one's
neck; disgrace –, expose- oneself.

play second fiddle; lose caste; pale
one's ineffectual fire; recede into the
shade; fall from one's high estate; keep
in the background &c. (*modesty*) 881;
be conscious of disgrace &c. (*humility*)
879; look -blue, – foolish, – like a fool;
cut a -poor, – sorry- figure; laugh on
the wrong side of the mouth; make a
sorry face, go away with a flea in one's
ear, slink away.

cause -shame &c. *n.*; shame, disgrace,
put to shame, dishonour; throw –,
cast –, fling –, reflect- dishonour &c.
n. upon; be a -reproach &c. *n.* to; derogate from.

tarnish, stain, blot, sully, taint; dis-
credit; degrade, debase, defile; beggar;
expel &c. (*punish*) 972.

impute shame to, brand, post, stigmatize, vilify, defame, slur, cast a slur
upon, hold up to shame, send to Coventry; tread –, trample- under foot;
show up, drag through the mire, heap
dirt upon; reprehend &c. 932.

bring low, put down, snub; take
down a peg, – lower, – or two.

obscure, eclipse, outshine, take the
shine out of; throw –, cast- into the
shade; overshadow; leave –, put- in
the background; push into a corner,

(*light*) 420; shine forth, figure; make –, cut- a -figure, – dash, – splash.

rival, surpass; out-shine, -rival, -vie, -jump; emulate, vie with, eclipse; throw –, cast- into the shade; overshadow.

live, flourish, glitter, scintillate, flaunt; gain –, acquire- honour &c. *n.*; play first fiddle &c. (*be of importance*) 642; bear the -palm, – bell; lead the way; take -precedence, – the wall of; gain –, win- -laurels, – spurs, – golden opinions &c. (*approbation*) 931; graduate, take one's degree, pass one's examination, win a -scholarship, – fellowship.

make -a, – some- -noise, – noise in the world; leave one's mark, exalt one's horn, star, have a run, be run after; enjoy popularity, come -into vogue, – to the front; raise one's head.

enthrone, signalize, immortalize, deify, exalt to the skies; hand one's name down to posterity.

consecrate; dedicate to, devote to; enshrine, inscribe, blazon, lionize, blow the trumpet, crown with laurel.

confer –, reflect- honour &c. *n.* on; shed a lustre on; redound to one's honour, ennoble.

give –, do –, pay –, render- honour to; honour, accredit, pay regard to, dignify, glorify; sing praises to &c. (*approve*) 931; look up to; exalt, aggrandize, elevate, nobilitate.

Adj. distinguished, *distingué*, noted; of -note &c. *n.*; honoured &c. *v.*; popular; fashionable &c. 852.

in good odour; in –, in high- favour; reput-, respect-, credit-able.

remarkable &c. (*important*) 642; notable, notorious; celebrated, renowned, in every one's mouth, talked of; fam-ous, -ed; far-famed; conspicuous, to the front; foremost; in the -front rank, – ascendant.

imperishable, deathless, immortal, never fading, *ære perennius*; time-honoured.

illustrious, glorious, splendid, brilliant, radiant; bright &c. 420; full-blown; honorific.

eminent, prominent; high &c. 206; in the zenith; at the -head of, – top of the tree; peerless, of the first water; superior &c. 33; super-, pre-eminent.

great, dignified, proud, noble, honourable, worshipful, lordly, grand, stately, august, princely, imposing, solemn, transcendent, majestic, sacred, sublime, heaven-born, heroic, *sans peur et sans reproche*; sacrosanct.

Int. hail! all hail! *ave! viva! vive!* long life to! glory –, honour- be to!

put one's nose out of joint; put out, – of countenance.

upset, throw off one's centre; discompose, disconcert; put to the blush &c. (*humble*) 879.

Adj. disgraced &c. *v.*; blown upon; shorn of -its beams, – one's glory; overcome, down-trodden; loaded with -shame &c. *n.*; in -bad repute &c. *n.*; out of -repute, – favour, – fashion, – countenance; at a discount; under -a cloud, – an eclipse; unable to show one's face; in the -shade, – background; out at elbows, down in the world, down and out.

inglorious; nameless, renownless, obscure, unknown to fame; un-noticed, -noted, -honoured, -glorified.

shameful; dis-graceful, -creditable, -reputable; despicable; questionable; unbecoming, unworthy; derogatory; degrading, humiliating, *infra dignitatem*, dedecorous; scandalous, infamous, too bad, unmentionable; ribald, opprobrious; arrant, shocking, outrageous, notorious, shady.

ignominious, scrubby, dirty, abject, vile, beggarly, pitiful, low, mean, shabby; base &c. (*dishonourable*) 940.

Adv. to one's shame be it spoken.

Int. fie! shame! for shame! *proh pudor! O tempora! O mores!* ough! *sic transit gloria mundi!*

Phr. one's name -being in every mouth, – living for ever; *sic itur ad astra, fama volat, aut Cæsar aut nullus*; not to know him argues oneself unknown; none but himself could be his parallel, *palmam qui meruit ferat.*

875. Nobility.—N. nobility, rank, condition, distinction, optimacy, blood, *pur sang*, birth, high descent, order; quality, gentility; blue blood of Castile; *ancien régime.*

high life, *haut monde*; upper -classes, – ten thousand; *élite*, aristocracy, great folks; fashionable world &c. (*fashion*) 852; salariat.

peer, -age; house of -lords, – peers; lords, – temporal and spiritual; *noblesse*; baronage, knightage; noble, -man; lord, -ling; grandee, *magnifico, hidalgo*; don, -ship; aristocrat, swell, three-tailed bashaw; gentleman, squire, squireen, patrician, laureate.

gentry, gentlefolk; squirarchy, better sort, *magnates, primates, optimates.*

king &c. (*master*) 745; prince, crown prince, *Dauphin*; duke; marquis, -ate; earl, viscount, baron, thane, banneret; baronet, -cy; knight, -hood; count, armiger, laird; sig-, seig-nior; esquire, boyar, margrave, vavasour, sheik, emir, ameer, scherif, *pasha*, effendi, sahib.

queen &c. 745; princess, begum, duchess, marchioness; countess &c.; lady, dame.

personage –, man- of -distinction, – mark, – rank; nota-bles, -bilities; celebrity, big-wig, magnate, great man, star; *magni nominis umbra*; 'every inch a king'; grand Panjandrum.

V. be -noble &c. *adj.*

Adj. noble, exalted; of -rank &c. *n.*; princely, titled, patrician, aristocratic; high-, well-born; of gentle blood; gen-teel, *comme il faut*, gentlemanlike, courtly &c. (*fashionable*) 852; highly respectable.

Adv. in high quarters.

877. Title.—N. title, honour; knight-hood &c. (*nobility*) 875.

royal –, serene- highness, excellency, grace; lordship, worship, Rt. Hon., rever-ence, -end; esquire, sir; madam, *madame*; master, mistress, Mr., Mrs., *signor, señor, Mein Herr, mynheer*;

876. Commonalty.—N. commonalty, democracy; obscurity; low -condition, – life, – society, – company; *bourgeoisie*; mass of -the people, – society; Brown, Jones, and Robinson; Tom, Dick, and Harry; lower –, humbler- -classes, – orders; vulgar –, common- herd; rank and file, *hoc genus omne*; the -many, – general, – crowd, – people, – popu-lace, – multitude, – million, – masses, – mobility, – peasantry; king Mob; proletariat, *fruges consumere nati*, great unwashed; man in the street.

mob; rabble, – rout; chaff, rout, horde, *canaille*; scum –, *residuum* –, dregs- of -the people, – society; swinish multitude, *fæx populi*; *profanum* –, *ignobile- vulgus*; vermin, riff-raff, tag-rag and bobtail; small fry.

commoner, one of the people, demo-crat, plebeian, republican, proletary, *prolétaire, roturier*, Mr. Snooks, *bour-geois, épicier*, Philistine, cockney; *grisette, demi-monde.*

peasant, countryman, boor, carle, churl; vill-ain, -ein; serf, kern, tyke, tike, chuff, ryot, fellah; long-shore-man; swain, clown, hind; clod, -hopper; hobnail, yokel, hick, rube, cider squeezer, bog-trotter, bumpkin; plough-man, -boy; rustic, chawbacon, tiller of the soil; hewers of wood and drawers of water, groundling; gaffer, loon, put, cub, Tony Lumpkin, looby, lout, under-ling; *gamin*, guttersnipe, street arab, mudlark; rough, rowdy, ruffian, roughneck; pot-wallopper, slubberde-gullion; vulgar –, low- fellow; cad, curmudgeon.

upstart, *parvenu, nouveau-riche*, skip-jack; nobody, – one knows; *hesterni quirites, pessoribus orti*; *bourgeois gentil-homme, novus homo*, snob, gent, mush-room, no one knows who, adventurer; man of straw.

beggar, panhandler, gaberlunzie, muckworm, mudlark, *sans-culotte*, raff, tatterdemalion, caitiff, ragamuffin, Pariah, outcast of society, tramp, weary Willie, bum, vagabond, *chiffon-*

your -, his- honour; handle to one's name.

decoration, laurel, palm, wreath, garland, bays, medal, ribbon, riband, blue ribbon, *cordon*, cross, crown, coronet, star, garter; feather, – in one's cap; chevron, epaulet, *épaulette*, colours, cockade; livery; order, arms, armorial bearings, shield, scutcheon, crest, reward &c. 973.

---

nier, rag-picker, Cinderella, cinder-wench, scrub, jade; boots, gossoon.

Goth, Vandal, Hottentot, savage, barbarian, Yahoo; unlicked cub, rough diamond.

barbar-ousness, -ism; Bœotia.

V. be -ignoble &c. *adj.*, – nobody &c. *n.*

Adj. ignoble, common, mean, low, base, vile, sorry, scrubby, beggarly, below par; no great shakes &c. (*unimportant*) 643; home-ly, -spun; vulgar, low-minded; snobbish, *parvenu*.

plebeian, proletarian; of -low, – mean- -parentage, – origin, extraction; low-, base-, earth-born, low bred; mushroom, dunghill, risen from the ranks; unknown to fame, obscure, untitled.

rustic, uncivilized; lout-, boor-, clown-, churl-, brut-, raff-ish; rude, unlicked, unpolished.

barbar-ous, -ian, -ic, -esque; cockney, born within sound of Bow bells.

underling, menial, servile, subaltern.

Adv. below the salt.

---

878. Pride.—N. dignity, self-respect, *mens sibi conscia recti*.

pride; haughtiness &c. *adj.*; high notions, *hauteur*; vainglory, crest; arrogance &c. (*assumption*) 885; pomposity &c. 882.

proud man, highflier; fine -gentleman, – lady; *grande dame*.

V. be -proud &c. *adj.*; put a good face on; look one in the face; stalk abroad, perk oneself up; presume, swagger, strut; rear -, lift up -, hold up- one's head; hold one's head high, look big, take the wall, 'bear like the Turk no rival near the throne,' carry with a high hand; ride the -, mount on one's- high horse; set one's back up, bridle, toss the head; give oneself airs &c. (*assume*) 885; boast &c. 884.

pride oneself on; glory in, take a pride in; pique -, plume -, hug- oneself; stand upon, be proud of; put a good face on; not -hide one's light under a bushel, – put one's talent in a napkin; not think small beer of oneself &c. (*vanity*) 880.

Adj. dignified; stately; proud, -crested; lordly, baronial; lofty-minded; high-souled, -minded, -mettled, -handed, -plumed, -flown, -toned.

---

879. Humility.—N. hum-ility, -bleness; meek-, low-ness; lowli-ness, -hood; abasement, self-abasement, -effacement; submission &c. 725; resignation.

condescension; affability &c. (*courtesy*) 894.

modesty &c. 881; verecundity, blush, suffusion, confusion; sense of -shame, – disgrace; humiliation, mortification; let -, set- down.

V. be -humble &c. *adj.*; deign, vouchsafe, condescend; humble -, demean- oneself; stoop, – to conquer; carry coals; submit &c. 725; submit with a good grace &c. (*brook*) 826; yield the palm.

lower one's -tone, – note; sing small, draw in one's horns, sober down; hide one's -face, – diminished head; not dare to show one's face, take shame to oneself, not have a word to say for oneself; feel -, be conscious of- -shame, – disgrace; drink the cup of humiliation to the dregs; eat -humble pie, – one's words, – dirt; be humiliated, receive a snub.

blush -for, – up to the eyes; redden, change colour; colour up; hang one's head, look foolish, feel small.

render humble; humble, humiliate;

haughty, paughty, insolent, lofty, high, mighty, swollen, puffed up, flushed, blown; vain-glorious; purse-proud, fine; proud as -a peacock, Lucifer; bloated with pride.

supercilious, disdainful, bumptious, magisterial, imperious; high -handed, - and mighty; overweening, consequential; arrogant &c. 885; unblushing &c. 880.

stiff, -necked; starch; perked -, stuck- up; in buckram, straitlaced; prim &c. (*affected*) 855.

on one's -high horses, - tight ropes, -high ropes; on stilts; *en grand seigneur*.

Adv. with head erect, with one's nose in the air.

Phr. *odi profanum vulgus et arceo.*

---

let -, set -, take -, tread -, frown-down; snub, abash, abase, make one sing small, strike dumb; teach one -his distance, - his place; take down a peg, - lower; throw -, cast- into the shade &c. 874; stare -, put- out of countenance; put to the blush; confuse, ashame, mortify, disgrace, crush; send away with a flea in one's ear.

get a set down.

Adj. humble, lowly, meek; modest &c. 881; humble-, sober-minded; un-offended; submissive &c. 725; servile &c. 886.

condescending; affable &c. (*courteous*) 894.

humbled &c. *v.*; bowed down, resigned; abashed, ashamed, dashed; out of countenance; down in the mouth; down on one's -knees, - marrow-bones; humbled in the dust, brow-beaten; chap-, crest-fallen; dumbfoundered, flabbergasted, struck all of a heap.

shorn of one's glory &c. (*disrepute*) 874.

Adv. with -downcast eyes, - bated breath, - bended knee; on all fours, on one's feet.

under correction, with due deference.

Phr. I am your -obedient, - very humble- servant; my service to you.

880. Vanity.—N. vanity; conceit, -edness; self-conceit, -complacency, -confidence, -sufficiency, -esteem, -love, -approbation, -praise, -glorification, -laudation, -gratulation, -applause, -admiration; *amour-propre*; selfishness &c. 943.

airs, pretensions, mannerism; egotism; prigg-ism, -ishness; coxcombery, gaudery, vainglory, elation; pride &c. 878; ostentation &c. 882; assurance &c. 885.

vox et præterea nihil; *cheval de bataille.*

ego-ist, -tist; peacock, coxcomb &c. 854; Sir Oracle &c. 887.

V. be -vain &c. *adj.*, - vain of; pique oneself &c. (*pride*) 878; lay the flattering unction to one's soul.

have -too high, - an overweening-opinion of -oneself, - one's talents; blind oneself as to one's own merit; not think -small beer, - *vin ordinaire*-of oneself; put oneself forward; fish

881. Modesty.—N. modesty; humility &c. 879; diffidence, timidity; retiring disposition, unobtrusiveness, bashfulness &c. *adj.*; *mauvaise honte*; blush, -ing; verecundity; self-knowledge.

reserve, constraint; demureness &c. *adj.*; blushing honours.

V. be -modest &c. *adj.*; retire, reserve oneself; give way to; draw in one's horns &c. 879; hide one's face.

keep -private, - in the background, - one's distance; pursue the noiseless tenor of one's way, 'do good by stealth and blush to find it fame,' hide one's light under a bushel, cast a sheep's eye.

Adj. modest, diffident; humble &c. 879; timid, timorous, bashful; shy, nervous, skittish, coy, sheepish, shame-faced, blushing, over-modest.

unpreten-ding, -tious; un-obtrusive, -assuming, -ostentatious, -boastful, -aspiring; poor in spirit.

for compliments; give oneself airs &c.
(*assume*) 885; boast &c. 884.

render -vain &c. *adj.*; inspire with
-vanity &c. *n.*; inflate, puff up, turn
up, turn one's head.

Adj. vain, – as a peacock; conceited,
assured, overweening, pert, forward,
perky; vain-glorious, high-flown; ostentatious &c. 882; puffed up, inflated,
flushed.

self-satisfied, -confident, -sufficient, -flattering, -admiring, -ap-
plauding, -glorious, -opinionated; *entêté* &c. (*wrong-headed*) 481;
wise in one's own conceit, pragmatical, overwise, pretentious, priggish; egotistic, -al; *soi-disant* &c. (*boastful*) 884; arrogant &c. 885.

un-abashed, -blushing; un-constrained, -ceremonious; free and
easy.

Adv. vainly &c. *adj.*

Phr. how we apples swim!

out of countenance &c. (*humbled*)
879.

reserved, constrained, demure.

Adv. humbly &c. *adj.*; quietly, privately; without -ceremony, – beat of
drum; *sans façon*.

---

882. Ostentation.—N. ostentation, display, show, flourish, parade,
étalage, pomp, array, state, solemnity; dash, splash, glitter, strut,
swank, side, swagger, pomposity; preten-se, -sions; showing off; fuss.

magnificence, splendour; *coup d'œil*; grand doings.

coup de théâtre; stage -effect, – trick; clap-trap; *mise en scène*; *tour
de force*; *chic*.

demonstration, flying colours; tomfoolery; flourish of trumpets &c.
(*celebration*) 883; pageant, -ry; spectacle, exhibition, procession; turn –,
set- out; grand function; *fête*, gala, field-day, review, march past,
promenade, insubstantial pageant.

dress; court -, full -, evening -, ball -, fancy- dress; tailoring, millinery, man-millinery, frippery; foppery, equipage.

ceremon-y, -ial; ritual; form, -ality; etiquette; punct-o, -ilio, -ilious-
ness; starched-, stateli-ness.

mummery, solemn mockery, mouth honour.

attitudinarian; fop &c. 854.

V. be -ostentatious &c. *adj.*; come –, put oneself- forward; attract
attention, star it.

make -, cut- a -figure, – dash, – splash; strut, blow one's own trumpet;
figure, – away; make a show, – display; glitter.

show -off, – one's paces; parade, march past; display, exhibit, put
forward, hold up; trot –, hang- out; sport, brandish, blazon forth;
dangle, – before the eyes.

cry up &c. (*praise*) 931; *prôner*, flaunt, emblazon, prink, set off,
mount, have framed and glazed.

put a good, – smiling- face upon; clean the outside of the platter &c.
(*disguise*) 544.

Adj. ostentatious, showy, dashing, pretentious; ja-, jau-nty; grand,
pompous, palatial; high-sounding; turgid &c. (*big-sounding*) 577;
garish, gorgeous; gaudy, – as a -peacock, – butterfly, – tulip; flaunting,
flashing, flaming, glittering; gay &c. (*ornate*) 847; colourful.

splendid, magnificent, sumptuous.

theatrical, dramatic, spectacular, scenic, ceremonial, ritual, -istic.

solemn, stately, majestic, formal, stiff, ceremonious, punctilious,
starch-ed, -y.

en grande tenue, in best bib and tucker, in Sunday best, *endimanché*.

Adv. with -flourish of trumpet, – beat of drum, – flying colours, – a brass band.

ad captandum vulgus.

883. Celebration.—N. celebration, solemnization, jubilee, diamond jubilee, commemoration, ovation, pæan, triumph, jubilation.

triumphal arch, bonfire, salute; salvo, – of artillery; *feu de joie*, flourish of trumpets, *fanfare*, colours flying, illuminations, fireworks.

inauguration, installation, presentation; *début*, coming out, birth-day anniversary, bi-, ter-, centenary; silver –, golden –, diamond-wedding, -day; coronation; Lord Mayor's show; harvest home, red letter day, festival; trophy &c. 733; *Te Deum* &c. (*thanksgiving*) 990; fête &c. 882; holiday &c. 840.

V. celebrate, keep, signalize, do honour to, commemorate, solemnize, hallow, mark with a red letter, hold high festival, maffick.

pledge, drink to, toast, hob and nob.

inaugurate, install, instate, induct, chair.

rejoice &c. 838; kill the fatted calf, hold jubilee, roast an ox, fire a salute.

Adj. celebrating &c. *v.*; commemorative, celebrated, immortal.

Adv. in -honour, – commemoration, – celebration of.

Int. hail! all hail! *io -pæan, – triumphe!* 'see the conquering hero comes!'

884. Boasting.—N. boasting &c. *v.*; boast, vaunt, crake; preten-ce, -sions; puff, -ery; flourish, *fanfaronnade*; gasconade; bluff, swank, brag, -gardism; bravado, bunkum, Buncombe; highfalutin; jact-itation, -ancy; bounce, rant, bluster; venditation, vapouring, rodomontade, bombast, fine talking, tall talk, magniloquence, teratology, heroics; jingoism, Chauvinism; exaggeration &c. 549; gas, hot air.

vanity &c. 880; *vox et præterea nihil*; much cry and little wool, *brutum fulmen*.

exultation; glorification; flourish of trumpets; triumph &c. 883.

boaster; bragg-art, -adocio; hot air merchant; Gascon, *fanfaron*, pretender, fourflusher, *soi-disant*; windbag, blowhard, bluffer; chau-vinist; blusterer &c. 887; charlatan, jack-pudding, trumpeter; puppy &c. (*fop*) 854.

V. boast, make a boast of, brag, vaunt, puff, show off, flourish, crake, crack, trumpet, strut, swagger, vapour, bluff; draw the long bow.

exult, crow over, neigh, chuckle, triumph; glory, gloat, jubilate; throw up one's cap; talk big, *se faire valoir, faire claquer son fouet*, take merit to oneself, make a merit of, sing *Io triumphe*, holloa before one is out of the wood.

Adj. boasting &c. *v.*; magniloquent, flaming, Thrasonic, stilted, gas-conading, braggart, boastful, pretentious, *soi-disant*; vain-glorious &c. (*conceited*) 880.

elate, -d; jubilant, triumphant, exultant; in high feather; flushed, – with victory; cock-a-hoop; on stilts.

vaunted &c. *v.*

Adv. vauntingly &c. *adj.*; with a brass band.

Phr. 'let the galled jade wince.'

885. [Undue assumption of superiority.] **Insolence.**—**N.** insolence; haughtiness &c. *adj.*; arrogance, airs; overbearance, brashness, bumptiousness, contumely, disdain; domineering &c. *v.*; tyranny &c. 739.

impertinence; cheek, nerve, sauce; sauciness &c. *adj.*; flippancy, dicacity, petulance, procacity, bluster; swagger, -ing &c. *v.*; bounce; terrorism; jingoism, chauvinism.

as-, pre-sumption; beggar on horseback; usurpation.

impudence, assurance, audacity, self-assertion, hardihood, front, face, brass; shamelessness &c. *adj.*; effrontery, hardened front, face of brass.

assumption of infallibility.

malapert, saucebox &c. (*blusterer*) 887.

V. be -insolent &c. *adj.*; bluster, vapour, swagger, swell, give oneself airs, snap one's fingers, kick up a dust; swear &c. (*affirm*) 535; rap out oaths; roister.

arrogate; as-, pre-sume; make -bold, – free; take a liberty, give an inch and take an ell.

domineer, bully, dictate, hector; lord it over, bulldoze; *traiter de haut, regarder de haut en bas*; exact; snub, huff, beard, fly in the face of; put to the blush; bear –, beat- down; browbeat, intimidate; trample –, tread- -down, – under foot; dragoon, ride roughshod over, terrorize.

out-face, -look, -stare, -brazen, -brave; stare out of countenance; brazen out; lay down the law; teach one's grandmother to suck eggs; assume a lofty bearing; talk –, look- big; put on big looks, act the *grand seigneur*; mount –, ride- the high horse; toss the head, carry with a high hand.

tempt Providence, want snuffing.

Adj. insolent, haughty, arrogant, imperious, magisterial, dictatorial, arbitrary; high-handed, high and mighty; contumelious, supercilious, overbearing, intolerant, domineering; overweening, high-flown.

flippant, pert, cavalier, saucy, forward, impertinent, fresh, malapert.

precocious, assuming, would-be, bumptious.

bluff; brazen-, browed-faced, shameless, aweless, unblushing, unabashed; bold-, bare-faced; dead –, lost- to shame.

886. Servility.—**N.** servility; slavery &c. (*subjection*) 749; obsequiousness &c. *adj.*; subserviency; abasement; pros-tration, -ternation; genuflexion &c. (*worship*) 990; fawning &c. *v.*; tuft-hunting, time-serving, flunkeyism; sycophancy &c. (*flattery*) 933; humility &c. 879.

sycophant, parasite, yes-man; toad, -y, -eater; tuft-hunter; snob, flunkey, lap-dog, spaniel, lick-spittle, smell-feast, *Græculus esuriens*, hanger on, stooge, *cavaliere servente*, led captain, carpet knight; time-server, fortune-hunter, Vicar of Bray, Sir Pertinax Mac Sycophant, pick-thank; flatterer &c. 935; doer of dirty work; *âme damnée*, tool; reptile; slave &c. (*servant*) 746; courtier; sponge, jackal; truckler.

V. cringe, bow, stoop, kneel, bend the knee; fall on one's knees, prostrate oneself; worship &c. 990.

sneak, crawl, crouch, cower, truckle to, grovel, fawn, toady, lick the feet of, kiss the hem of one's garment.

pay court to; feed –, fatten –, batten- on; dance attendance on, pin oneself upon, hang on the sleeve of, *avaler des couleuvres*, keep time to, fetch and carry, do the dirty work of.

go with the stream, follow the crowd, worship the rising sun, hold with the hare and run with the hounds.

Adj. servile, obsequious; supple, – as a glove; soapy, oily, pliant, cringing, fawning, slavish, grovelling, snivelling, mealy-mouthed; beggarly, sycophantic, parasitical; abject, prostrate, down on one's marrow-bones; base, mean, sneaking; crouching &c. *v.*

Adv. hat –, cap- in hand.

impudent, audacious, presumptuous, free and easy, devil-may-care, rollicking; janty, jaunty; roistering, blustering, hectoring, swaggering, vapouring; thrasonic, fire-eating, 'full of sound and fury.'

Adv. insolently, with a high hand; *ex cathedrâ*.

Phr. one's bark being worse than his bite.

887. Blusterer.—N. bluster-, swagger-, vapour-, roister-, brawl-er; brazen-face; *fanfaron*; braggart &c. (*boaster*) 884; bully, terrorist, rough, rough-neck; hooligan, hoodlum, larrikin, ruffian; Mo-hock, -hawk; drawcansir, swashbuckler, Captain Boabdil, Sir Lucius O'Trigger, Thraso, Pistol, Parolles, Bombastes Furioso, Hector, Chrononhotonthologos; jingo; desperado, dare-devil, fire-eater; fury &c. (*violent person*) 173; rowdy.

puppy &c. (*fop*) 854; prig; Sir Oracle, dogmatist, *doctrinaire*, stump orator, jack-in-office; saucebox, malapert, jackanapes, minx; bantam-cock.

Section III. SYMPATHETIC AFFECTIONS

1°. Social Affections

888. Friendship. — N. friendship, amity; friendliness &c. *adj.*; brother-hood, fraternity, sodality, confraternity, sorosis, sisterhood; harmony &c. (*concord*) 714; peace &c. 721.

firm -, staunch -, intimate -, familiar -, bosom -, cordial -, tried -, devoted -, lasting -, fast -, sincere -, warm -, ardent- friendship.

cordiality, fraternization, *entente cordiale*, good understanding, *rapprochement*, sympathy, fellow-feeling, response, welcomeness; *camaraderie*.

affection &c. (*love*) 897; favouritism; goodwill &c. (*benevolence*) 906; partiality.

acquaintance, familiarity, intimacy, intercourse, fellowship, knowledge of; introduction.

V. be -friendly &c. *adj.*, – friends &c. 890, – acquainted with &c. *adj.*; know; have the ear of; keep company with &c. (*sociality*) 892; hold communication -, have dealings -, sympathize- with; have a leaning to; bear good will &c. (*benevolence*) 906; love &c. 897; make much of; befriend &c. (*aid*) 707; introduce to.

set one's horses together; hold out -, extend- the right hand of -friendship, – fellowship; become -friendly &c. *adj.*; make -friends &c. 890 with; break the ice, be introduced to; make -, pick -, scrape- acquaintance with; get into favour, gain the friendship of.

shake hands with, fraternize, embrace; receive with open arms, throw oneself into the arms of; meet half way, take in good part.

Adj. friendly; amic-able, -al; well affected, unhostile, neighbourly, brotherly, fraternal, sisterly, sympathetic, harmonious, hearty, cordial, warm-hearted, devoted.

889. Enmity.—N. enmity, hostility; unfriendliness &c. *adj.*; discord &c. 713.

alienation, estrangement; dislike &c. 867; hate &c. 898; antagonism.

heartburning; animosity &c. 900; malevolence &c. 907.

V. be -inimical &c. *adj.*; keep -, hold-at arm's length; be at loggerheads; bear malice &c. 907; fall out; take umbrage &c. 900; harden the heart, alienate, estrange.

Adj. inimical, unfriendly, hostile; at -enmity, – variance, – swords points, – daggers drawn, – open war with; up in arms against; in bad odour with.

on bad -, not on speaking- terms; cool; cold, -hearted; estranged, alienated, disaffected, irreconcilable.

friends -, well -, at home -, hand in hand- with; on -good, - friendly, - amicable, - cordial, - familiar, - intimate- -terms, - footing; on -speaking, - visiting- terms; in one's good -graces, - books.

acquainted, familiar, intimate, thick, hand and glove, hail fellow well met, free and easy; welcome.

Adv. amicably &c. *adj.*; with open arms; *sans cérémonie*; arm in arm.

890. Friend.—N. friend, - of one's bosom, intimate acquaintance, neighbour, well-wisher; *alter ego*; best -, bosom -, fast- friend; *amicus usque ad aras*; *fidus Achates*; *persona grata*.

favourer, *fautor*, patron, backer, Mæcenas; tutelary saint, good genius, advocate, partisan, sympathiser; ally; friend in need &c. (*auxiliary*) 711.

associate, compeer, comrade, mate, companion, *confrère*, *camarade*, *confidante*, colleague; old -, crony; side-kick; chum, buddy, bunkie, roommate, pal; play-fellow, -mate; classmate, schoolfellow; bedfellow, -mate; maid of honour.

compatriot; fellow -, countryman, - townsman.

shop-, ship-, mess-mate; fellow -, boon -, pot- companion; copartner.

Arcades ambo, Pylades and Orestes, Castor and Pollux, Nisus and Euryalus, Damon and Pythias, *par nobile fratrum*.

host, Amphitryon, Boniface; guest, visitor, frequenter, *habitué*; *protégé*.

891. Enemy.—N. enemy; antagonist, foeman; open -, bitter- enemy; opponent &c. 710; back friend.

public enemy, enemy to society, traitor, anarchist &c. 743.

Phr. every hand being against one:

---

892. Sociality.—N. soci-ality, -ability, -ableness &c. *adj.*; social intercourse; consociation; inter-course, -community; consort-, companion-, fellow-, comrade-ship; clubbism; *esprit de corps*.

conviviality; good -fellowship, - company, *camaraderie*; joviality, jollity, *savoir-vivre*, festivity, festive board, merry-making; loving cup; hospitality, heartiness; cheer.

welcome, -ness; greeting; hearty -, warm -, welcome- reception; urbanity &c. (*courtesy*) 894; intimacy, familiarity.

good -, jolly- fellow, good mixer, Rotarian; *bon enfant*.

social -, family- circle; circle of acquaintance, *coterie*, society, company.

social -gathering, - *réunion*; assembly &c. (*assemblage*) 72; party, entertainment, reception, *levée*, at home, *conversazione*, *soirée*, *matinée*, evening -, morning -, afternoon -, garden -, dinner -, tea -, cocktail- party; symposium, sing-song; kettle-, drum; *partie carrée*, dish of tea, *ridotto*, rout, house-

893. Seclusion. Exclusion.—N. seclusion, privacy; retirement; concealment; reclusion, recess; snugness &c. *adj.*; delitescence; rustication, *rus in urbe*; solitude, solitariness &c. (*singleness*) 87; isolation; loneliness &c. *adj.*; estrangement from the world, anchoritism, voluntary exile; aloofness.

cell, hermitage; convent &c. 1000; *sanctum sanctorum*; study, library, den; hide-out.

depopulation, desertion, desolation; wilderness &c. (*unproductive*) 169; howling wilderness; rotten borough, Old Sarum.

exclusion, excommunication, banishment, exile, ostracism, proscription; cut, - direct; dead cut.

inhospit-ality, -ableness &c. *adj.*; un-, dis-sociability; domesticity, Darby and Joan.

recluse, hermit, eremite, cenobite; anchor-et, -ite; Simon Stylites; Troglodyte, Timon of Athens, Santon, *solitaire*, ruralist, disciple of Zimmermann, closet cynic, Diogenes; outcast, Pariah,

warming; ball, prom, hop, dance, *thé dansant*; festival &c. (*amusement*) 840; wedding breakfast; 'the feast of reason and the flow of soul.'

visit, -ing; round of visits; call, morning call; interview &c. (*interlocution*) 588; assignation; tryst, -ing place; appointment.

club &c. (*association*) 712.

V. be -sociable &c. *adj*.; know; be -acquainted &c. *adj*.; associate -, sort -, keep company -, walk hand in hand -with; eat off the same trencher, club together, consort, bear one company, join; make acquaintance with &c. (*friendship*) 888; make advances, fraternize, embrace; intercommunicate.

be -, feel -, make oneself- at home with; make free with; crack a bottle with; take pot luck with, receive hospitality, live at free quarters.

visit, pay a visit; interchange -visits, - cards; call -at, - upon; leave a card; drop in, look in; look one up, beat up one's quarters.

entertain; give a -party &c. *n*.; be at home, see one's friends, hang out, keep open house, do the honours; receive, - with open arms; welcome; give a warm reception &c. *n*. to; kill the fatted calf.

Adj. sociable, companionable, clubbable, clubby, conversable, cosy, cosey, chatty, conversational; homiletical.

convivial; fest-ive, -al; jovial, jolly, hospitable.

welcome, - as the roses in May; *fêté*, entertained.

free and easy, hail fellow well met, familiar, on visiting terms, acquainted.

social, neighbourly; international, cosmopolitan, gregarious.

Adv. *en famille*, in the family circle; *sans -façon*, - *cérémonie*, arm in arm.

castaway, outsider, pilgarlic; wastrel, foundling, orphan.

V. be -, live- secluded &c. *adj*.; keep -, stand -, hold oneself- -aloof, - in the background; keep snug; shut oneself up; deny -, seclude- oneself; creep into a corner, rusticate, *aller planter ses choux*; retire, - from the world; hermetize, take the veil; abandon &c. 624.

cut, - dead; refuse to -associate with, - acknowledge; look cool -, turn one's back -, shut the door- upon; repel, blackball, excommunicate, exclude, exile, expatriate; banish, outlaw, maroon, ostracize, proscribe, cut off from, send to Coventry, keep at arm's length, draw a cordon round; boycott, blockade, lay an embargo on, isolate.

depopulate; dis-, un-people.

Adj. secluded, sequestered, retired, delitescent, private, bye; out of the -world, -way; in a backwater; 'the world forgetting by the world forgot.'

snug, domestic, stay-at-home.

unsociable; un-, dis-social; inhospitable, cynical, inconversable, unclubbable, *sauvage*, eremetic.

solitary; lone-ly, -some; isolated, single.

excluded, estranged; unfrequented; uninhabit-able, -ed; tenantless; un-tenanted, -occupied; abandoned; deserted, - in one's utmost need; unfriended; kith-, friend-, home-less; lorn, forlorn, desolate.

un-visited, -introduced, -invited, -welcome; under a cloud, left to shift for oneself, derelict, outcast, outside the gates.

banished &c. *v*.; under an embargo.

Phr. *noli me tangere*.

---

894. Courtesy.—N. courtesy; respect &c. 928; good -manners, - behaviour, - breeding; manners; politeness &c. *adj*.; *bienséance*, urbanity, comity, gentility; gentle -, breeding; polish, presence, cultivation, culture; civili-ty, -zation; amenity, suavity; good -temper, - humour; amiability, easy temper, complacency, soft tongue,

895. Discourtesy.—N. discourtesy; ill-breeding; ill -, bad -, ungainly-manners; insuavity; grouchiness; uncourteousness &c. *adj*., tactlessness; rusticity, inurbanity; illiberality, incivility, displacency.

disrespect &c. 929; procacity, impudence; barbar-ism, -ity; misbehaviour, brutality, blackguardism, conduct un-

mansuetude; condescension &c. (*humility*) 879; affability, complaisance, *prévenance*, amiability, gallantry, chivalry; pink of -politeness, – courtesy.

compliment; fair –, soft –, sweet-words; honeyed phrases, flattering remarks, ceremonial; salutation, reception, presentation, introduction, *accueil*, greeting, recognition; welcome, *abord*, respects, *devoir*, regards, remembrances; kind -regards, – remembrances; love, best love, duty; deference.

obeisance &c. (*reverence*) 928; bow, courtesy, curtsy, scrape, *salaam*, *kowtow*, bowing and scraping; kneeling; genuflexion &c. (*worship*) 990; obsequiousness &c. 886; capping, shaking hands &c. *v.*; grip of the hand, embrace, hug, squeeze, *accolade*, loving cup, *vin d'honneur*, pledge; love token &c. (*endearment*) 902; kiss, buss, salute.

mark of recognition, nod; 'nods and becks and wreathed smiles'; valediction &c. 293; condolence &c. 915.

V. be -courteous &c. *adj.*; show -courtesy &c. *n.*

mind one's P's and Q's, behave oneself, be all things to all men, conciliate, speak one fair, take in good part; make –, do- the amiable; look as if butter would not melt in one's mouth; mend one's manners.

receive, do the honours, usher, greet, hail, bid welcome; welcome, – with open arms; shake hands; hold out –, press –, squeeze- the hand; bid God speed; speed the parting guest; cheer, serenade.

salute; embrace &c. (*endearment*) 902; kiss, – hands; drink to, pledge, hob and nob; move to, nod to; smile upon.

uncover, cap; touch –, take off- the hat; doff the cap; pull the forelock; present arms; make way for; bow; make one's bow; scrape, curtsy, courtesy; bob a -curtsy, – courtesy; kneel; bow –, bend- the knee; salaam, *kowtow*.

visit, wait upon, present oneself, pay one's respects, pay a visit &c. (*sociability*) 892; dance attendance on &c. (*servility*) 886; pay attentions to; do homage to &c. (*respect*) 928.

becoming a gentleman, *grossièreté*, *brusquerie*; vulgarity &c. 851.

churlishness &c. *adj.*; spinosity, perversity; moroseness &c. (*sullenness*) 901*a*.

bad-, ill-temper; sternness &c. *adj.*; austerity; moodishness, captiousness &c. 901; cynicism; tartness &c. *adj.*; acrimony, acerbity, virulence, asperity.

scowl, black looks, frown; short answer, rebuff; hard words, contumely; unparliamentary language, personality.

bear, bruin, brute, grouch, blackguard, beast; unlicked cub; frump, cross-patch; saucebox &c. 887.

V. be -rude &c. *adj.*; insult &c. 929; treat with discourtesy; take a name in vain; make -bold, – free- with; take a liberty; stare out of countenance, ogle, point at, put to the blush.

cut; turn -one's back upon, – on one's heel; give the cold shoulder; keep at -a distance, – arm's length; look -cool, – coldly, – black- upon; show the door to, send away with a flea in the ear.

lose one's temper &c. (*resentment*) 900; sulk &c. 901*a*; frown, scowl, glower, pout; snap, snarl, growl.

render -rude &c. *adj.*; brut-alize, -ify.

Adj. dis-, un-courteous; uncourtly; ill-bred, -mannered, -behaved, -conditioned; unbred; unmanner-ly, ed; im-, un-polite; un-polished, -civilized, -genteel; ungentleman-like, -ly; unladylike; blackguard; vulgar &c. 851; dedecorous; foul-mouthed, -spoken; abusive.

un-civil, -gracious, -ceremonious; cool; pert, forward, obtrusive, impudent, rude, saucy, precocious; insolent &c. 885.

repulsive; un-complaisant, -accommodating, -neighbourly, -gallant; inaffable; un-gentle, -gainly; rough, rugged, bluff, blunt, gruff; churl-, boor-, bear-ish; brutal, *brusque*; stern, harsh, austere; cavalier.

tart, sour, crabbed, sharp, short, trenchant, sarcastic, crusty, biting, caustic, virulent, bitter, acrimonious, venomous, contumelious; snarling &c, *v.*; surly, – as a bear; perverse; grim.

prostrate oneself &c. (*worship*) 990. give -, send- one's duty &c. *n.* to.

render -polite &c. *adj.*; polish, civilize, humanize.

Adj. courteous, polite, civil, mannerly, urbane; well-behaved, -mannered, -bred, -brought up, gently bred, of gentle -breeding, – manners, good-mannered, polished, civilized, cultivated; refined &c. (*taste*) 850; gentlemanlike &c. (*fashion*) 852; gallant, chivalrous, on one's good behaviour.

fine -, fair -, soft- spoken; honey-mouthed, -tongued; oily, unctuous, bland, suave; obliging, conciliatory, complaisant, complacent; obsequious &c. 886.

ingratiating, winning; gentle, mild; good-humoured, cordial, gracious, amiable, tactful, addressful, affable, genial, friendly, familiar; neighbourly.

Adv. courteously &c. *adj.*; with a good grace; with -open, – outstretched- arms; *à bras ouverts*; *suaviter in modo*, in good humour.

Int. hail! welcome! well met! *ave!* all hail! good -day, – morning &c., – morrow! God speed! *pax vobiscum!* may your shadow never be less! *chin-chin!*

sullen &c. 901*a*; peevish &c. (*irascible*) 901.

Adv. discourteously &c. *adj.*; with -discourtesy &c. *n.*, – a bad grace.

---

896. Congratulations.—N. con-, gratulation; felicitation; salute &c. 894; condolence &c. 915; compliments of the season; good -, best- wishes.

V. con-, gratulate; felicitate, compliment; give -, wish one- joy; tender -, offer- one's congratulations; wish -many happy returns of the day, – a merry Christmas and a happy new year.

congratulate oneself &c. (*rejoice*) 838.

Adj. con-, gratulatory.

---

897. Love.—N. love; fondness &c. *adj.*; liking; inclination &c. (*desire*) 865; regard, dilection, admiration, fancy.

affection, sympathy, fellow-feeling; tenderness &c. *adj.*; heart, brotherly love; benevolence &c. 906; attachment.

yearning, tender passion, *affaire de coeur*, *amour*, gallantry, passion, flame, devotion, fervour, enthusiasm, transport of love, rapture, enchantment, infatuation, adoration, idolatry.

narcissism, Œdipus complex, Electra complex.

Cupid, Venus, Eros; myrtle; true lover's knot; love -token, – suit, – affair, – tale, – story; the old story, plighted love; courtship &c. 902; *amourette*.

maternal love.

attractiveness, charm; popularity; favourite &c. 899.

lover, suitor, follower, admirer, adorer, wooer, amoret, beau, sweet-

898. Hate.—N. hate, hatred, vials of hate; Hymn of Hate.

dis-affection, -favour; alienation, estrangement, coolness; enmity &c. 889; animosity &c. 900.

umbrage, pique, grudge; dudgeon, spleen; bitterness, – of feeling; ill -, bad- blood; acrimony; malice &c. 907; implacability &c. (*revenge*) 919.

repugnance &c. (*dislike*) 867; odium, unpopularity; loathing, detestation, antipathy; object of -hatred, – execration; abomination, aversion, *bête noire*; enemy &c. 891; bitter pill; source of annoyance &c. 830.

V. hate, detest, abominate, abhor, loathe; recoil -, shudder- at; shrink from, view with horror, hold in abomination, revolt against, execrate; scowl &c. 895; disrelish &c. (*dislike*) 867.

owe a grudge; bear -spleen, – a grudge, – malice &c. (*malevolence*) 907; conceive an aversion to.

heart, inamorato, swain, young man, flame, love, truelove; leman, Lothario, gallant, paramour, *amoroso, cavaliere servente,* captive, *cicisbeo; caro sposo,* Don Juan, sheik, ladies' man, squire of dames, Knave of Hearts.

inamorata, lady-love, idol, darling, duck, Dulcinea, angel, goddess, *cara sposa;* mistress.

betrothed, affianced, *fiancée.*

flirt, *coquette;* amorette; pair of turtle doves; abode of love, *agapemone.*

V. love, like, affect, fancy, care for, take an interest in, be partial to, sympathize with; be -in love &c. *adj.*-with; have –, entertain –, harbour –, cherish- a -love &c. *n.* for; regard, revere; take to, bear love to, be wedded to; set one's affections on; make much of, feast one's eyes on; hold dear, prize, treasure; hug, cling to, cherish, pet, caress &c. 902.

burn; adore, idolize, love to distraction, *aimer eperdument;* dote -on, – upon.

take a fancy to, fall for, be stuck on, look sweet upon; become -enamoured &c. *adj.*; fall in love with, lose one's heart; desire &c. 865.

excite love; win –, gain –, secure –, engage- the -love, – affections, – heart; take the fancy of; have a place in –, wind round- the heart; attract, attach, endear, charm, fascinate, captivate, bewitch, seduce, enamour, enrapture, turn the head.

get into favour; ingratiate –, insinuate –, worm- oneself; propitiate, curry favour with, pay one's court to, make a date with, *faire l'aimable,* set one's cap at, flirt, coquet.

Adv. loving &c. *v.*; fond of; taken –, struck- with; smitten, bitten; attached to, wedded to; enamoured; charmed &c. *v.*; in love; love-sick; over head and ears in love.

affectionate, tender, sweet upon, sympathetic, loving, fond, amorous, amatory; erotic, uxurious, ardent, passionate, rapturous, devoted, motherly.

loved &c. *v.*; beloved; well –, dearly- beloved; dear, precious, darling, pet, little; favourite, popular.

congenial; to –, after- one's -mind, – taste, – fancy, – own heart.

in one's good -graces &c. (*friendly*) 888; dear as the apple of one's eye, nearest to one's heart.

lovable, adorable; lovely, sweet; attractive, seductive, winning; charming, engaging, interesting, enchanting, captivating, fascinating, intriguing, bewitching; amiable, like an angel, angelic, seraphic.

excite –, provoke- hatred &c. *n.*; be -hateful &c. *adj.*; stink in the nostrils; estrange, alienate, repel, set against, sow dissension, set by the ears, envenom, incense, irritate, rile, ruffle, vex; horrify &c. 830.

Adj. hating &c. *v.*; abhorrent; averse from &c. (*disliking*) 867; set against.

bitter &c. (*acrimonious*) 895; implacable &c. (*revengeful*) 919.

un-loved, -beloved, -lamented, -deplored, -mourned, -cared for, -endured, -valued; disliked &c. 867.

crossed in love, forsaken, rejected, love-lorn, jilted.

obnoxious, hateful, odious, abominable, repulsive, offensive, shocking; disgusting &c. (*disagreeable*) 830.

invidious, spiteful; malicious &c. 907.

insulting, irritating, provoking.

[Mutual hate] at -daggers drawn, – swords points; not on speaking terms &c. (*enmity*) 889.

Phr. no love lost between.

---

899. Favourite.—N. favourite, pet, cosset, minion, idol, jewel, spoiled child, *enfant gâté;* led captain; crony; fondling; apple of one's eye, man after one's own heart; *persona grata.*

love, dear, darling, duck, honey, jewel; mopsey, moppet; sweetheart &c. (*love*) 897.

general –, universal- favourite; idol of the people; matinée idol, movie –, radio- star.

900. Resentment.—N. resentment, displeasure, animosity, anger, wrath, indignation; vexation, exasperation, bitter resentment, wrathful indignation.

pique, umbrage, huff, miff, soreness, dudgeon, acerbity, virulence, bitterness, acrimony, asperity, spleen, gall; heart-burning, -swelling; rankling.

ill –, bad- -humour, – temper; irascibility &c. 901; ill blood &c. (*hate*) 898; revenge &c. 919.

excitement, irritation; warmth, bile, choler, ire, fume, pucker, dander, ferment, ebullition; towering -passion, – rage, *acharnement*, angry mood, taking, pet, tiff, passion, fit, tantrums.

burst, explosion, paroxysm, storm, rage, fury, desperation; violence &c. 173; fire and fury; vials of wrath; gnashing of teeth, hot blood, high words.

scowl &c. 895; sulks &c. 901a.

[Cause of umbrage] affront, provocation, offence; indignity &c. (*insult*) 929; grudge, crow to pluck, sore subject; red rag to a bull; *casus belli.*

Furies, Erinys, Eumenides, Alecto, Megæra, Tisiphone.

buffet, slap in the face, box on the ear, rap on the knuckles.

V. resent; take -amiss, – ill, – to heart, – offence, – umbrage, – huff, – exception; take in -ill part, – bad part, – dudgeon; *ne pas entendre raillerie*; breathe revenge, cut up rough.

fly –, fall –, get- into a -rage, – passion; bridle –, bristle –, froth –, fire –, flare- up; open –, pour out- the vials of one's wrath.

pout, knit the brow, frown, scowl, lower, snarl, growl, gnarl, gnash, snap; redden, colour; look -black, – black as thunder, – daggers; bite one's thumb; show –, grind- one's teeth; champ the bit.

chafe, mantle, fume, kindle, fly out, take fire; boil, – over; boil with -indignation, – rage; rage, storm, foam; vent one's -rage, – spleen; lose one's temper, stand on one's hind legs, stamp the foot, kick up a row, fly off the handle, cut up rough; stamp –, quiver –, swell –, foam- with rage; burst with anger; raise Cain, breathe fire and fury.

have a fling at; bear malice &c. (*revenge*) 919.

cause –, raise- anger; affront, offend; give -offence, – umbrage; anger; hurt the feelings; insult, discompose, fret, ruffle, nettle, heckle, huff, pique; excite &c. 824; irritate, stir the blood, stir up bile; sting, – to the quick; rile, provoke, chafe, wound, incense, inflame, enrage, aggravate, add fuel to the flame, fan into a flame, widen the breach, envenom, embitter, exasperate, infuriate, kindle wrath; stick in one's gizzard; rankle &c. 919.

put out of humour; put one's -monkey, – back- up; set –, get- one's back up; raise one's -gorge, – dander, – choler; work up into a passion; make -one's blood boil, – the ears tingle; throw into a ferment, madden, drive one mad; lash into -fury, – madness; fool to the top of one's bent; set by the ears.

bring a hornet's nest about one's ears.

Adj. angry, wrath, irate; ire-, wrath-ful; cross &c. (*irascible*) 901; sulky &c. 901a; bitter, virulent; acrimonious &c. (*discourteous*) &c. 895; violent &c. 173.

warm, burning; boiling, – over; fuming, raging; foaming, – at the mouth; convulsed with rage.

offended &c. *v.*; waxy, *acharné*; wrought, worked up; indignant, hurt, sore, peeved; set against.

fierce, wild, rageful, furious, mad with rage, fiery, infuriate, rabid, savage; relentless &c. 919.

flushed with -anger, – rage; in a -huff, – stew, – fume, – pucker, – passion, – rage, – fury; on one's high ropes, up in arms; in high dudgeon.

Adv. angrily &c. *adj.*; in the height of passion; in the heat of -passion, – the moment.

Int. *tantæne animis cælestibus iræ!* marry come up! zounds! 'sdeath!

Phr. one's -blood, – back, – monkey- being up; *fervens difficili bile jecur*; the gorge rising, eyes flashing fire; the blood -rising, – boiling; *hæret lateri lethalis arundo.*

901. Irascibility.—N. irascibility, temper; crossness &c. *adj.*; susceptibility, procacity, petulance, irritability, tartness, acerbity, protervity; pugnacity &c. (*contentiousness*) 720.

excitability &c. 825; bad –, fiery –, crooked –, irritable &c. *adj.*-temper; *genus irritabile*, hot blood.

ill humour &c. (*sullenness*) 901a; asperity &c., churlishness &c. (*discourtesy*) 895.

huff &c. (resentment) 900; a word and a blow.

Sir Fretful Plagiary; brabbler, Tartar; shrew, vixen, virago, termagant, dragon, scold, Xanthippe; porcupine; spit-fire; fire-eater &c. (*blusterer*) 887; fury &c. (*violent person*) 173.

V. be -irascible &c. *adj.*; have a -temper &c. *n.*, – devil in one; fire up &c. (*be angry*) 900.

Adj. irascible; bad-, ill-tempered; irritable, susceptible; excitable &c. 825; thin-skinned &c. (*sensitive*) 822; fretful, fidgety; on the fret.

hasty, over-hasty, quick, warm, hot, testy, touchy, techy, tetchy; like -touchwood, – tinder; huffy; pet-tish, -ulant; waspish, snapp-y, -ish, peppery, fiery, passionate, choleric, shrewish, 'sudden and quick in quarrel.'

querulous, captious, mood-y, -ish; quarrelsome, contentious, disputatious; pugnacious &c. (*bellicose*) 720; cantankerous, exceptious; restive &c. (*perverse*) 901a; churlish &c. (*discourteous*) 895.

cross, – as -crabs, – two sticks, – a cat, – a dog, – the tongs; like a bear with a sore head; fractious, peevish, *acariâtre.*

in a bad temper; sulky &c. 901a; angry &c. 900.

resent-ful, -ive; vindictive &c. 919.

Int. pish!

901a. Sullenness.—N. sullenness &c. *adj.*; morosity, spleen; churlishness &c. (*discourtesy*) 895; irascibility &c. 901.

moodiness &c. *adj.*; perversity; obstinacy &c. 606; torvity, spinosity; crabbedness &c. *adj.*

ill –, bad- -temper, – humour; sulks, dudgeon, mumps, doleful dumps, doldrums, fit of the sulks, *bouderie*, black looks, scowl; huff &c. (*resentment*) 900.

V. be -sullen &c. *adj.*; sulk; frown, scowl, lower, glower, grouse, grouch, crab, gloam, pout, have a hang-dog look, glout.

Adj. sullen, sulky; ill-tempered, -humoured, -affected, -disposed; in -an ill, – a bad, ·· a shocking- -temper, – humour; out of -temper, –

humour; knaggy, **torvous,** crusty, **crabbed; sore as a** boil; surly &c:
(*discourteous*) 895.

moody; spleen-ish, -ly; splenetic, cankered.

cross, -grained; perverse, wayward, humoursome; restive; cantankerous, refractory, intractable, exceptious, sinistrous, deaf to reason,
unaccommodating, rusty, crust, froward.

dogged &c. (*stubborn*) 606.

grumpy, glum, grim, grum, morose, frumpish; in the -sulks &c. *n.*;
out of sorts; scowl-, glower-, growl-ing.

peevish &c. (*irascible*) 901.

902. [Expression of affection or love.] **Endearment.—N.** endearment, caress; blandish-, blandi-ment; *épanchement,* fondling, billing
and cooing, dalliance.

embrace, salute, kiss, buss, smack, osculation, deosculation; amorous
glances; ogle, side glance, sheep's eyes.

courtship, wooing, suit, addresses, the soft impeachment; lovemaking; an affair; serenading; caterwauling.

flirting &c. *v.*; flirtation, gallantry; coquetry, spooning.

true lover's knot, plighted love, engagement, bethrothal; love -tale,
– token, – letter; *billet-doux,* valentine.

honeymoon; Strephon and Chloe, 'Arry and 'Arriet.

V. caress, fondle, pet, dandle, nurse; pat, – on the -head, – cheek;
chuck under the chin, smile upon, coax, wheedle, cosset, coddle, cocker;
make -of, – much of, pamper; cherish, foster, kill with kindness.

clasp, hug, cuddle; fold –, strain- in one's arms; nestle, nuzzle, neck,
embrace, kiss, buss, smack, blow a kiss; salute &c. (*courtesy*) 894.

bill and coo, spoon, toy, dally, flirt, coquet; galli-, gala-vant; philander; make love; pay one's -court, – addresses, – attentions- to;
serenade; court, woo; set one's cap at; be –, look- sweet upon; ogle,
cast sheep's eyes upon; *faire les yeux doux.*

fall in love with, win the affections &c. (*love*) 897; die for.

propose; make –, have- an offer; pop the question; plight one's
-troth, – faith; become -engaged, – betrothed.

Adj. caressing &c. *v.*; 'sighing like furnace'; love-sick, spoony.

caressed &c. *v.*

903. Marriage.—N. marriage, matrimony, wedlock, union, intermarriage,
vinculum matrimonii, nuptial tie, knot.

married state, coverture, bed, cohabitation.

match; betrothment &c. (*promise*)
768; wedding, nuptials, Hymen, bridal;
e-, spousals; leading to the altar &c.
v.; nuptial benediction, *epithalamium.*

torch –, temple- of Hymen; hymeneal altar; honeymoon.

bride, bridegroom; brides-maid,
-man.

best –, grooms-man, page, usher.

married -man, – woman, – couple;
neogamist, Benedick, partner, spouse,
mate, yokemate; husband, man, con-

904. Celibacy.—N. celibacy, singleness, single blessedness; bachelor-hood,
-ship; miso-gamy, -gyny.

virginity, *pucelage*; maiden-hood,
-head.

unmarried man, bachelor, Cœlebs,
agamist, old bachelor; miso-gamist,
-gynist; celibate.

unmarried woman, spinster; maid,
-en; virgin, *feme sole,* old maid; bachelor girl; nun &c.

V. live single; keep bachelor hall.

Adj. un-married, -wedded; wife-,
spouse-less; single, virgin, celibate.

905. Divorce.—N. divorce, -ment;
separation; judicial separation, separ-

sort, baron; old –, good- man; wife of one's bosom; help-meet, -mate, rib, better half, grey mare, old woman, good wife; feme, – coverte; squaw, lady; matron, -age, -hood; man and wife; wedded pair, Darby and Joan.

affinity, soul-mate.

mono-, bi-, di-, deutero-, tri-, poly-gamy; mormonism; poly-andry; Turk, Bluebeard.

unlawful –, left-handed –, companionate –, morganatic –, ill-assorted- marriage; *mésalliance*; *mariage de convenance*; an affair.

match-maker, marriage broker, matrimonial agent.

V. marry, wive, take to oneself a wife; be -married, – spliced; go –, pair- off; wed, espouse, lead to the hymeneal altar, take 'for better, for worse,' give one's hand to, bestow one's hand upon; remarry; intermarry.

marry, join, handfast; couple &c. (*unite*) 43; tie the nuptial knot; give -away, – in marriage; affy, affiance; betroth &c. (*promise*) 768; publish –, bid- the banns; be asked in church.

Adj. married &c. *v.*; one, – bone and one flesh.

marriageable, nubile.

engaged, betrothed, affianced.

matrimonial, marital, conjugal, connubial, wedded; nuptial, hymeneal, spousal, bridal.

Phr. the grey mare the better horse.

ate maintenance; *separatio a -mensâ et thoro, – vinculo matrimonii.*

widowhood, viduage, viduity, weeds.

widow, -er; relict; dowager; *divorcée*; cuckold.

V. live -separately, – apart; separate, divorce, disespouse, put away; wear the horns.

2°. DIFFUSIVE SYMPATHETIC AFFECTIONS

906. Benevolence.—N. benevolence, Christian charity; God's -love, – grace; good-will; philanthropy &c. 910; un-selfishness &c. 942.

good -nature, – feeling, – wishes; kind-, kindli-ness &c. *adj.*; lovingkind-ness, benignity, brotherly love, charity, humanity, fellow-feeling, sympathy; goodness –, warmth- of heart; *bon-homie*; kind-heartedness; amiability, milk of human kindness, tenderness; love &c. 897; friendship &c. 888.

toleration, consideration, generosity; mercy &c. (*pity*) 914.

charitableness &c. *adj.*; bounty, alms-giving; good works, beneficence, the luxury of doing good.

acts of kindness, a good turn; good –, kind- -offices, – treatment.

good Samaritan, sympathizer, well-wisher, philanthropist, *bon enfant*; altruist.

V. be -benevolent &c. *adj.*; have one's heart in the right place, bear good will; wish -well, – God speed;

907. Malevolence.—N. malevolence; bad intent, -ion; un-, dis-kindness; ill -nature, – will, – blood; bad blood; enmity &c. 889; hate &c. 898; malig-nity; malice, – aforethought, – pre-pense; maliciousness &c. *adj.*; spite, despite; resentment &c. 900.

uncharitableness &c. *adj.*; incom-passionateness &c. 914a; gall, venom, rancour, rankling, virulence, mordac-ity, acerbity; churlishness &c. (*dis-courtesy*) 895.

hardness of heart, heart of stone, obduracy; cruelty; cruelness &c. *adj.*; brutality, savagery; fer-ity, -ocity; barbarity, inhumanity, immanity, truc-ulence, ruffianism; evil eye, cloven -foot, – hoof; Inquisition; torture.

ill –, bad- turn; affront &c. (*disre-spect*) 929; outrage, atrocity; ill usage; intolerance, bigotry, persecution; ten-der mercies [ironical]; 'unkindest cut of all.'

V. be -malevolent &c. *adj.*; bear –, harbour- -spleen, – a grudge, – mal-

view –, regard- with an eye of favour; take in good part; take –, feel- an interest in; be –, feel- interested- in; sympathize with, feel for; fraternize &c. (*be friendly*) 888.

enter into the feelings of others, do as you would be done by, meet half-way.

treat well; give comfort, smooth the bed of death; do -good, – a good turn; benefit &c. (*goodness*) 648; render a service, be of use; aid &c. 707.

Adj. benevolent; kind, -ly; well-meaning; amiable; obliging, accommodating, indulgent, considerate, gracious, complacent, good-humoured.

warm-, soft-, kind-, tender-, large-, broad-hearted; merciful &c. 914; philanthropic &c. 910; charitable, beneficent, humane, benign, benignant; bount-eous, -iful &c. 816.

good-, well-natured; spleenless; sympath-izing, -etic; complaisant &c. (*courteous*) 894; kindly, well-meant, -intentioned.

fatherly, motherly, brotherly, sisterly; pat-, mat-, frat-ernal; friendly &c. 888.

Adv. with -a good intention, – the best intentions.

Int. God speed! much good may it do!

ice; betray –, show- the cloven foot.

hurt &c. (*physical pain*) 378; annoy &c. 830; injure, harm, wrong; do -harm, – an ill office- to; outrage; disoblige, malign, plant a thorn in the breast.

molest, worry, harass, haunt, harry, bait, tease, throw stones at; play the devil with; hunt down, dragoon, hound; persecute, oppress, grind; maltreat; ill-treat, -use.

wreak one's malice on, do one's worst, break a butterfly on the wheel; dip –, imbrue- one's hands in blood; have no mercy &c. 914a.

Adj. male-, unbene-volent; unbenign; ill-disposed, -intentioned, -natured, -conditioned, -contrived; evil-minded, -disposed.

malicious; malign, -ant; rancorous; de-, spiteful; mordacious, caustic, bitter, envenomed, acrimonious, virulent; un-amiable, -charitable; maleficent, venomous, grinding, galling.

harsh, disobliging; un-kind, -friend-ly, -gracious; treacherous; inofficious; invidious; uncandid; churlish &c. (*uncourteous*) 895; surly, sullen &c. 901a.

cold, -blooded, -hearted; hard-, flint-, marble-, stony-hearted; hard of heart, unnatural; ruthless &c. (*unmerciful*) 914a; relentless &c. (*revengeful*) 919.

cruel; brut-al, -ish; savage, – as a -bear, – tiger; ferine, feral, ferocious; inhuman; barbarous, fell, untamed, tameless, truculent, incendiary; bloodthirsty &c. (*murderous*) 361; atrocious.

fiend-ish, -like; demoniacal; diabolic, -al; devilish, infernal, hellish, Satanic.

Adv. malevolently &c. *adj.*; with -bad intent &c. *n.*

---

908. Malediction.—N. malediction, malison, curse, imprecation, denunciation, execration, anathema, ban, proscription, excommunication, commination, thunders of the Vatican, fulmination, *maranatha*, aspersion, vilification, vituperation, scurrility.

abuse; foul –, bad –, strong –, unparliamentary- language, Lime-house; Billingsgate, sauce, evil speaking; cursing &c. *v.*; profane swearing, oath.

threat &c. 909; more bark than bite; invective &c. (*disapprobation*) 932.

V. curse, accurse, imprecate, damn, swear at; slang; curse with bell, book and candle; invoke –, call down- curses on the head of; devote to destruction.

execrate, beshrew, scold; anathematize &c. (*censure*) 932; hold up to execration, denounce, proscribe, excommunicate, fulminate, thunder against; threaten &c. 909; curse up hill and down dale.

curse and swear; swear, – like a trooper; fall a cursing, rap out an oath, damn, cuss.

Adj. curs-ing, -ed &c. *v.*; maledictory.

Int. woe to! beshrew! *ruat cælum!* ill –, woe- betide! confusion seize! damn! confound! blast! curse! devil take! hang! out with! a plague –, out- upon! aroynt! *honi soit!*

Phr. *delenda est Carthago.*

909. Threat.—N. threat, menace; defiance &c. 715; abuse, minacity, intimidation; fulmination; commination &c. (*curse*) 908; gathering clouds &c. (*warning*) 668.

V. threat, -en; menace; snarl, growl, gnarl, mutter, bark, bully. defy &c. 715; intimidate &c. 860; keep –, hold up –, hold out- *in terrorem*; shake –, double –, clinch- the fist at; thunder, talk big, fulminate, use big words, bluster, look daggers.

Adj. threatening, menacing; mina-tory, -cious; comminatory, abusive; *in terrorem*; ominous &c. (*predicting*) 511; defiant &c. 715; under the ban.

Int. *væ victis!* at your peril! do your worst!

910. Philanthropy. — N. philan-thropy; altruism, humanit-y, -arian-ism; universal benevolence; *deliciæ humani generis*; cosmopolitanism, utilitarianism, the greatest happiness of the greatest number, social science, sociology.

common weal, public welfare, social-ism, communism.

patriotism, civism, nationality, love of country, *amor patriæ*, public spirit.

chivalry, knight errantry; generosity &c. 942.

philanthropist, altruist &c. 906; utilitarian, Benthamite, socialist, communist, cosmopolite, citizen of the world, *amicus humani generis*; knight errant; patriot.

Adj. philanthropic, altruistic, humanitarian, utilitarian, cosmopolitan; public-spirited, patriotic; humane, large-hearted &c. (*benevolent*) 906; chival-ric, -rous, generous &c. 942.

Adv. *pro -bono publico, – aris et focis.*

Phr. '*humani nihil a me alienum puto.*'

911. Misanthropy.—N. misanthropy, incivism; egotism &c. (*selfishness*) 943; moroseness &c. 901a; cynicism; defeatism.

misanthrope, misanthropist, egotist, cynic, man-hater, Timon, Diogenes.

woman-hater, misogynist.

Adj. misanthropic, antisocial, unpatriotic; egotistical &c. (*selfish*) 943; morose &c. 901a.

————

912. Benefactor. — N. benefactor, saviour, good genius, tutelary saint, patron, guardian angel, fairy god-mother, good Samaritan; *pater patriæ*; salt of the earth &c. (*good man*) 948; auxiliary &c. 711.

————

913. [Maleficent being.] Evil-doer. —N. evil- -doer, – worker; wrong doer &c. 949; mischief maker, marplot; oppressor, tyrant; firebrand, incendiary, pyromaniac, anarchist, destroyer, Hun, *Boche*, Vandal, iconoclast; communist; terrorist, *apache*, gunman, gangster, racketeer.

savage, brute, ruffian, barbarian, semi-barbarian, caitiff, desper-ado; Mo-hock, -hawk; bludgeon man, bully, rough, hooligan, larrikin, dangerous classes, ugly customer; thief &c. 792.

cockatrice, scorpion, hornet; viper, adder; snake, – in the grass;

serpent, cobra, asp, rattlesnake, anaconda; canker-, wire-worm; locust, Colorado beetle; torpedo; bane &c. 663.

cannibal; Anthropophag-us, -ist; bloodsucker, vampire, ogre, ghoul, gorilla; vulture; gyr-, ger-falcon.

wild beast, tiger, hyæna, butcher, hangman; cut-throat &c. (*killer*) 361; blood-, sleuth-, hell-hound.

hag, hellhag, beldam, Jezebel.

monster; fiend &c. (*demon*) 980; homicidal maniac, devil incarnate, demon in human shape; Frankenstein's monster.

harpy, siren, vampire; Furies, Eumenides &c. 900.

Attila, scourge of the human race.

Phr. *fœnum habet in cornu.*

3°. Special Sympathetic Affections

914. Pity.—N. pity, compassion, commiseration; bowels, – of compassion; condolence &c. 915; sympathy, fellow-feeling, tenderness, yearning, forbearance, humanity, mercy, clemency, exorability; leniency &c. (*lenity*) 740; charity, ruth, long-suffering.

melting mood; *argumentum ad misericordiam*; quarter, grace, *locus pœnitentiæ.*

sympathizer, champion, partisan.

V. pity; have –, show –, take- pity &c. *n.*; commiserate, compassionate; condole &c. 915; sympathize; feel –, be sorry –, yearn- for; weep, melt, thaw, enter into the feelings of.

forbear, relent, relax, give quarter, wipe the tears, *parcere subjectis*, give a *coup de grâce*, put out of one's misery; be cruel to be kind.

raise –, excite- pity &c. *n.*; touch, soften; melt, – the heart; appeal to one's better feelings; propitiate, disarm.

ask for -mercy &c. *n.*; supplicate &c. (*request*) 765; cry for quarter, beg one's life, kneel; deprecate.

Adj. pitying &c. *v.*; pitiful, compassionate, sympathetic, touched.

merciful, clement, ruthful; humane; humanitarian &c. (*philanthropic*) 910; tender, – hearted, – as a chicken; soft, – hearted; unhardened; lenient &c. 740; exorable, forbearing; melting &c. *v.*; weak.

Int. for pity's sake! mercy! have –, cry you- mercy! God help you! poor -thing, – dear, – fellow! woe betide! *quis talia fando temperet a lachrymis!*

Phr. one's heart bleeding for; *haud ignara mali miseris succurrere disco.*

914a. Pitilessness.—N. pitilessness &c. *adj.*; inclemency; inexorability, hardness of heart; inflexibility; severity &c. 739; malevolence &c. 907.

V. have no –, shut the gates of-mercy &c. 914; give no quarter.

Adj. piti-, merci-, ruth-, bowel-less; unpitying, unmerciful, inclement; in-, un-compassionate; inexorable, inflexible; harsh &c. 739; cruel &c. 907; unrelenting &c. 919.

---

915. Condolence.—N. condolence; lamentation &c. 839; sympathy, consolation.

V. condole with, console, sympathize &c. 914, share one's misery; feel for; express –, testify- pity; afford –, supply- consolation; lament &c. 839- with; send one's condolences.

4°. Retrospective Sympathetic Affections

916. Gratitude. — N. gratitude, thankfulness, gratefulness, feeling of obligation.

acknowledgment, recognition thanksgiving, giving thanks.

thanks, praise, benediction; pæan; *Te Deum* &c. (*worship*) 990; grace, – before, – after- meat; thank-offering. requital.

V. be -grateful &c. *adj.*; thank; give –, render –, return –, offer –, tender-thanks &c. *n.*; acknowledge, requite.

feel –, be –, lie- under an obligation; *savoir gré*; not look a gift horse in the mouth; never forget, overflow with gratitude; thank –, bless- one's stars; fall on one's knees.

Adj. grateful, thankful, obliged, beholden, indebted to, under obligation.

Int. thanks! many thanks! gramercy! much obliged! thank you! thank Heaven! Heaven be praised!

917. Ingratitude.—N. ingratitude, thanklessness, oblivion of benefits; unthankfulness.

'benefits forgot'; thankless -task, – office.

V. be -ungrateful &c. *adj.*; forget benefits; look a gift horse in the mouth.

Adj. un-grateful, -mindful, -thankful; thankless, ingrate, wanting in grati-tude, insensible of benefits.

forgotten; un-acknowledged, -thank-ed, -requited, -rewarded; ill-requited.

Int. thank you for nothing! '*et tu Brute !*'

---

918. Forgiveness.—N. forgiveness, pardon, condonation, grace, remission, absolution, amnesty, oblivion; indul-gence; reprieve.

conciliation; reconciliation &c. (*paci-fication*) 723; propitiation.

excuse, exoneration, quittance, re-lease, indemnity; bill –, act –, cove-nant –, deed- of indemnity; exculpa-tion &c. (*acquittal*) 970.

longanimity, placability, forbear-ance; *amantium iræ*; *locus pœni-tentiæ*.

V. forgive, – and forget; pardon, condone, think no more of, let bygones be bygones, shake hands; forget an injury, bury the hatchet; clean the slate.

excuse, pass over, overlook; wink at &c. (*neglect*) 460; bear with; allow –, make allowances- for; let one down easily, not be too hard upon, pocket the affront; blot out one's transgres-sion.

let off, remit, absolve, give absolu-tion, reprieve; acquit &c. 970.

beg –, ask –, implore- pardon &c. *n.*; conciliate, propitiate, placate; make up a quarrel &c. (*pacify*) 723; let the wound heal.

919. Revenge.—N. revenge, -ment; vengeance; avenge-ment, -ance; sweet revenge, *vendetta*, death-feud, eye for an eye, blood for blood, a Roland for an Oliver; retaliation &c. 718; day of reckoning.

rancour, vindictiveness, implacabil-ity; malevolence &c. 907; ruthlessness &c. 914a.

avenger, vindicator, Nemesis, Eume-nides.

V. re-, a-venge; take –, have one's-revenge; breathe -revenge, – vengeance; wreak one's -vengeance, – anger; give no quarter.

have -accounts to settle, – a crow to pluck, – a rod in pickle; pay off old scores.

keep the wound green; harbour -revenge, – vindictive feeling; bear malice; rankle, – in the breast; have at one's mercy.

Adj. revenge-, venge-ful; vindictive, rancorous; pitiless &c. 914a; ruthless, rigorous, avenging, retaliative.

unforgiving, unrelenting; inexorable, stony-hearted, implacable; relent-, re-morse-less.

æternum servans sub pectore vulnus; rankling, immitigable.

Adj. forgiving, placable, conciliatory. forgiven &c. *v.*; un-resented, -avenged, -revenged.

Adv. cry you mercy.

Phr. *veniam petimusque damusque vicissim*; more in sorrow than in anger.

Phr. *manet -cicatrix, – altâ mente repostum.*
revenge is sweet.

———

920. Jealousy.—N. jealous-y, -ness; jaundiced eye, heartburning; green-eyed monster; yellows; Juno.

V. be -jealous &c. *adj.*; view with -jealousy, – a jealous eye.

Adj. jealous, – as a Barbary pigeon; jaundiced, yellow-eyed, horn-mad.

921. Envy.—N. envy; enviousness &c. *adj.*; rivalry; *jalousie de métier.*

V. envy, covet, lust after, crave, burst with envy, regard with envious eyes.

Adj. envious, invidious, covetous; *alieni appetens.*

Section IV. MORAL AFFECTIONS
1°. Moral Obligations

922. Right.—N. right; what -ought to, – should- be; fitness &c. *adj.*; *summum jus.*

justice, equity; equitableness &c. *adj.*; propriety; fair play, impartiality, measure for measure, give and take, *lex talionis*, square deal.

Astræa, Nemesis, Themis.

scales of justice, even-handed justice, retributive justice, *suum cuique*; clear stage –, fair field- and no favour; Queensberry rules.

morals &c. (*duty*) 926; law &c. 963; honour &c. (*probity*) 939; virtue &c. 944.

V. be -right &c. *adj.*; stand to reason.

see -justice done, – one righted, – fair play; do justice to; recompense &c. (*reward*) 973; hold the scales even, give and take; serve one right, put the saddle on the right horse; give -every one, – the devil- his due; *audire alteram partem.*

deserve &c. (*be entitled to*) 924.

Adj. right, good; just, reasonable; fit &c. 924; equ-al, -able, -itable; even-handed, fair, – and square.

legitimate, justifiable, rightful; as it -should, – ought to- be; lawful &c. (*permitted*) 760, (*legal*) 963.

deserved &c. 924.

Adv. rightly &c. *adj.*; in -justice, – equity, – reason.

without -distinction of, – regard to, – respect to- persons; upon even terms.

Int. all right!

923. Wrong. — N. wrong; what -ought not to, – should not- be; *malum in se*; unreasonableness, grievance; shame.

injustice; unfairness &c. *adj.*; iniquity, foul play, partiality, leaning; favour, -itism; nepotism, party spirit, partisanship; undueness &c. 925; unlawfulness &c. 964.

robbing Peter to pay Paul &c. *v.*; the wolf and the lamb; vice &c. 945.

a custom more honoured in the breach than the observance.

V. be -wrong &c. *adj.*; cry to heaven for vengeance.

do -wrong &c. *n.*; be -inequitable &c. *adj.*; favour, lean towards; encroach; impose upon; reap where one has not sown; give an inch and take an ell; rob Peter to pay Paul.

Adj. wrong, -ful; bad, too bad; unjust, -fair; in-, un-equitable; unequal, partial, one-sided.

objectionable; un-reasonable, -allowable, -warrantable, -justifiable; not cricket, not playing the game; improper, unfit; unjustified &c. 925; illegal &c. 964; iniquitous, criminal; immoral &c. 945; injurious &c. 649.

in the wrong, – box.

Adv. wrongly &c. *adj.*

Phr. it will not do; this is too bad.

———

924. Dueness.—N. due, -ness; right, privilege, prerogative, prescription, title, claim, pretension, demand, birthright.

immunity, licence, liberty, franchise; vested -interest, – right; licitness.

sanction, authority, warranty, charter; warrant &c. (*permission*) 760; constitution &c. (*law*) 963; tenure; bond &c. (*security*) 771.

deserts, merits, dues.

claimant, appellant; plaintiff &c. 938.

V. be -due &c. *adj.* to, – the due &c. *n.* of; have -right, – title, – claim- to; be entitled to; have a claim upon; belong to &c. (*property*) 780.

deserve, merit, be worthy of, richly deserve.

demand, claim; call upon –, come upon –, appeal to- for; re-vendicate, -claim; exact; insist -on, – upon; challenge; take one's stand, make a point of, require, lay claim to, assert, assume, arrogate, make good; substantiate; vindicate a -claim, – right; make out a case.

give –, confer- a right; sanction, entitle; authorize &c. 760; sanctify, legalize, ordain, prescribe, allot.

give every one his due &c. 922; pay one's dues; have one's -due, – rights; stand upon one's rights.

use a right, assert, enforce, put in force, lay under contribution.

Adj. having a right to &c. *v.*; entitled to; claiming; deserving, meriting, worthy of.

privileged, allowed, sanctioned, warranted, authorized; ordained, prescribed, constitutional, chartered, enfranchised.

prescriptive, presumptive; absolute, indefeasible; un-, in-alienable; imprescriptible, inviolable, unimpeachable, unchallenged; sacrosanct.

due to, merited, deserved, condign, richly deserved, *emeritus*.

allowable &c. (*permitted*) 760; lawful, licit, legitimate, legal; legalized &c. (*law*) 963.

square, unexceptionable, right; equitable &c. 922; due, *en règle*; fit, -ting; correct, proper, meet, befitting, becoming, seemly; decorous; creditable, up to the mark, right as a trivet; just –, quite- the thing; *selon les règles*.

Adv. duly, *ex officio*, *de jure*; by -right, – divine right; as is -fitting, – proper, – fitting and proper; *jure divino*, *Dei gratiâ*, in the name of.

Phr. *civis Romanus sum.*

925. [Absence of right.] **Undueness —N.** undueness &c. *adj.*; *malum prohibitum*; impropriety; illegality &c. 964.

falseness &c. *adj.*; emptiness –, invalidity- of title; illegitimacy.

loss of right, disfranchisement, forfeiture.

usurpation, assumption, tort, violation, breach, encroachment, presumption, seizure, stretch, exaction, imposition, lion's share.

usurper, pretender, Carlist; impostor.

V. be -undue &c. *adj.*; not be -due &c. 924.

infringe, encroach, trench on, exact; arrogate, – to oneself; give an inch and take an ell; stretch –, strain- a point; usurp, violate, do violence to; sail under false colours.

dis-franchise, -entitle, -qualify; invalidate.

relax &c. (*be lax*) 738; misbehave &c. (*vice*) 945; misbecome.

Adj. undue; unlawful &c. (*illegal*) 964; unconstitutional, *ultra vires*; illicit; un-authorized, -warranted, -allowed, -sanctioned, -justified; un-, dis-entitled, -qualified; un-privileged, -chartered.

illegitimate, bastard, spurious, false; usurped, tortious.

un-deserved, -merited, -earned; unfulfilled.

forfeited, disfranchised.

improper; un-meet, -fit, -befitting, -seemly; un-, mis-becoming; seemless; *contra bonos mores*; not the thing, out of the question, not to be thought of; preposterous, pretentious, would- be.

926. Duty.—**N.** duty, what ought to be done, moral obligation, accountableness, liability, *onus*, responsibility; bounden –, imperative- duty; call, – of duty.

allegiance, fealty, tie; engagement &c. (*promise*) 768; part; function, calling &c. (*business*) 625.

morality, morals, decalogue; case of conscience; conscientiousness &c. (*probity*) 939; conscience, inward monitor, still small voice within, sense of duty, tender conscience.

dueness &c. 924; propriety, fitness, seemliness, amenableness, decorum; the -thing, – proper thing; the -right, – proper- thing to do.

[Science of morals] eth-ics, -ology; deon-, are-tology; moral –, ethical-philosophy; casuistry, polity.

observance, fulfilment, discharge, performance, acquittal, satisfaction, redemption; good behaviour.

V. be -the duty of, – incumbent &c. *adj.* on, – responsible &c. *adj.*; behoove, become, befit, beseem; belong –, pertain- to; fall to one's lot; devolve on; lie -upon, – on one's head, – at one's door; rest -with, – on the shoulders of.

take upon oneself &c. (*promise*) 768; be –, become- -bound to, – sponsor for; be responsible for; incur a -responsibility &c. *n.*; be –, stand –, lie- under an obligation; have to answer for, owe it to oneself.

impose a -duty &c. *n.*; enjoin, require, exact; bind, – over; saddle with, prescribe, assign, call upon, look to, oblige.

927. Dereliction of Duty.—**N.** dere; liction of duty; fault &c. (*guilt*) 947- sin &c. (*vice*) 945; non-observance, -performance, -co-operation; neglect, carelessness, laziness, incompetence, eye-service, relaxation, infraction, violation, transgression, failure, evasion, indolence; dead letter.

slacker, loafer, striker, non-co-operator.

V. violate; break, – through; infringe; set -aside, – at naught; trample -on, – under foot; slight, neglect, evade, renounce, forswear, repudiate; wash one's hands of; escape, transgress, fail.

call to account &c. (*disapprobation*) 932.

927a. Exemption.—**N.** exemption, freedom, irresponsibility, immunity, liberty, licence, release, exoneration, excuse, dispensation, absolution, franchise, renunciation, discharge; exculpation &c. 970; *ægrotat*.

V. be -exempt &c. *adj.*

exempt, release, acquit, discharge, quit-claim, remise, remit; free, set at liberty, let off, pass over, spare, excuse, dispense with, give dispensation, license; stretch a point; absolve &c. (*forgive*) 918; exonerate &c. (*exculpate*) 970; save the necessity.

Adj. exempt, free, immune, at liberty, scot free; released &c. *v.*; unbound, unencumbered; irresponsible, unaccountable, not answerable; excusable.

---

enter upon –, perform –, observe –, fulfil –, discharge –, adhere to –, acquit oneself of –, satisfy- -a duty, – an obligation; act one's part, redeem one's pledge, do justice to, be at one's post; do duty; do one's duty &c. (*be virtuous*) 944.

be on one's good behaviour, mind one's P's and Q's.

Adj. obligatory, binding; imperative, peremptory; stringent &c. (*severe*) 739; behooving &c. *v.*; incumbent –, chargeable- on; under obligation; obliged –, bound –, tied- by; saddled with.

due –, beholden –, bound –, indebted- to; tied down; compromised &c. (*promised*) 768; in duty bound.

amenable, liable, accountable, responsible, answerable.

right, meet &c. (*due*) 924; moral, ethical, casuistical, conscientious, ethological.

Adv. with a safe conscience, as in duty bound, on one's own responsibility, at one's own risk, *suo periculo*; *in foro conscientiæ*; *quamdiu se bene gesserit*; at one's post, on duty.

Phr. *dura lex sed lex.*

2°. MORAL SENTIMENTS

928. Respect.—**N.** respect, regard, consideration; courtesy &c. 894; attention, deference, reverence, honour, esteem, estimation, veneration, admiration; approbation &c. 931.

homage, fealty, obeisance, genuflexion, kneeling, prostration; obsequiousness &c. 886; salaam, *kowtow*, bow, presenting arms, salute.

respects, regards, duty, *devoirs*, *égards*.

devotion &c. (*piety*) 987.

V. respect, regard; revere, -nce; hold in reverence, honour, venerate, hallow; esteem &c. (*approve of*) 931; think much of; entertain –, bear- respect for; have a high opinion of; look up to, defer to; pay -attention, – respect &c. *n.*- to; do –, render- honour to; do the honours, hail; show courtesy &c. 894; salute, present arms; do –, pay- homage to; pay tribute to, kneel to, bow to, bend the knee to; fall down before, prostrate oneself, kiss the hem of one's garment; worship &c. 990.

keep one's distance, make room, observe due decorum, stand upon ceremony.

command –, inspire- respect; awe, impose, overawe, dazzle.

Adj. respecting &c. *v.*; respectful, deferential, decorous, reverential, obsequious, ceremonious, bare-headed, cap in hand, on one's knees; prostrate &c. (*servile*) 886.

respected &c. *v.*; in high -esteem, – estimation; time-honoured, venerable, *emeritus*.

Adv. in deference to; with -all, – due, – the highest- respect; with submission.

saving your -grace, – presence; *salva sit reverentia*; *pace tanti nominis*.

Int. hail! all hail! *esto perpetua!* may your shadow never be less!

---

929. Disrespect. — **N.** dis-respect, -esteem, -estimation, -favour, -repute; low estimation; disparagement &c. (*dispraise*) 932, (*detraction*) 934.

irreverence; slight, neglect; *spretæ injuria formæ*; superciliousness &c. (*contempt*) 930.

vilipendency, contumely, affront, dishonour, insult, indignity, outrage, discourtesy &c. 895; practical joking; scurrility, scoffing, sibilation; ir-, derision; mockery; irony &c. (*ridicule*) 856; sarcasm.

hiss, hoot, gibe, flout, jeer, scoff, gleek, taunt, sneer, quip, fling, wipe, slap in the face.

V. hold in disrespect &c. (*despise*) 930; misprize, disregard, slight, undervalue, depreciate, trifle with, set at naught, pass by, push aside, overlook, turn one's back upon, laugh in one's sleeve; be -disrespectful &c. *adj.*, – discourteous &c. 895; treat with -disrespect &c. *n.*; set down, browbeat.

dishonour, desecrate; insult, affront, outrage.

speak slightingly of; disparage &c. (*dispraise*) 932; vilipend, call names; throw –, fling- dirt; drag through the mud, point at, indulge in personalities; make -mouths, – faces; bite the thumb; take –, pluck- by the beard; toss in a blanket, tar and feather.

have –, hold- in derision; deride, scoff, sneer, laugh at, snigger, ridicule, gibe, mock, jeer, taunt, twit, niggle, gleek, gird, flout, fleer; roast, turn into ridicule; guy, burlesque &c. 856; laugh to scorn &c. (*contempt*) 930; smoke; fool; make -game, – a fool, – an April fool- of; play a practical joke; rag; lead one a dance, run the rig upon, have a fling at, scout, hiss, hoot, mob.

Adj. disrespectful; aweless, irreverent; disparaging &c. 934; insulting &c. *v.*; supercilious &c. (*scornful*) 930; rude, derisive, contemptuous, sarcastic; scurri-le, -lous; contumelious.

un-respected, -worshipped, -envied, -saluted; un-, dis-regarded.

Adv. disrespectfully &c. *adj.*

930. Contempt.—N. contempt, disdain, scorn, sovereign contempt; despi-sal, -ciency; vilipendency, contumely; slight, sneer, spurn, by-word.

contemptuousness &c. *adj.*; scornful eye; smile of contempt; derision &c. (*disrespect*) 929.

[State of being despised] despisedness.

V. despise, contemn, scorn, disdain, feel contempt for, view with a scornful eye, disregard, slight, not mind; pass by &c. (*neglect*) 460.

look down upon; hold -cheap, – in contempt, – in disrespect; think -nothing, – small beer- of; make light of; underestimate &c. 483; esteem -slightly, – of small or no account; take no account of, care nothing for; set no store by; not care a -straw &c. (*unimportance*) 643; set at naught, laugh in one's sleeve, snap one's fingers at, shrug one's shoulders, turn up one's nose at, pooh-pooh, damn with faint praise; sneeze –, whistle –, sneer- at; curl up one's lip, toss the head, *traiter de haut*; laugh at &c. (*be disrespectful*) 929.

point the finger of –, hold up to –, laugh to- scorn; scout, hoot, flout, hiss, scoff at.

turn -one's back, – a cold shoulder- upon; tread –, trample- -upon, – under foot; spurn, kick; fling to the winds &c. (*repudiate*) 610; send away with a flea in the ear.

Adj. contemptuous; disdain-, scorn-ful; withering, contumelious, supercilious, cynical, haughty, bumptious, cavalier; derisive.

contemptible, despicable; pitiable; pitiful &c. (*unimportant*) 643; despised &c. *v.*; down-trodden; unenvied.

Adv. contemptuously &c. *adj.*

Int. a fig for &c. (*unimportant*) 643; bah! never mind! away with! hang it! fiddle-de-dee!

931. Approbation.—N. approbation; approv-al, -ement; sanction, advocacy; nod of approbation; esteem, estimation, good opinion, golden opinions, admiration; love &c. 897; appreciation, regard, account, popularity, *kudos*, credit; repute &c. 873.

commendation, praise; laud, -ation; good word; meed –, tribute- of praise; encomium; eulog-y, -ium; *éloge*, panegyric; homage, hero worship; benediction, blessing, benison.

applause, plaudit, clap; clapping, – of hands; accl-aim, -amation; cheer; pæan, hosannah; shout –, peal –, chorus –, thunders- of -applause &c.; Kentish fire; Prytaneum; blurb.

V. approve; think -good, – much of, well of, – highly of; esteem, value, prize; set great store -by, – on.

do justice to, appreciate; honour, hold in esteem, look up to, admire; like &c. 897; be in favour of, wish God speed; hail, – with satisfaction.

stand –, stick- up for; uphold, hold

932. Disapprobation.—N. disapprobation, -val; improbation; dis-esteem, -valuation, -placency; odium; dislike &c. 867; dissent &c. 489.

dis-praise, -commendation; blame, censure, obloquy; detraction &c. 934; disparagement, depreciation; denunciation; condemnation &c. 971; ostracism; boycott; black-list, -ball; *index -expurgatorius, – librorum prohibitorum.*

animadversion, reflection, stricture, objection, exception, criticism; sardonic -grin, – laugh; sarcasm, insinuation, innuendo; bad –, poor –, left-handed- compliment.

satire; sneer &c. (*contempt*) 930; taunt &c. (*disrespect*) 929; cavil, carping, censoriousness; hypercriticism &c. (*fastidiousness*) 868.

reprehension, remonstrance, expostulation, reproof, reprobation, admonition, increpation, reproach; rebuke, reprimand, castigation, jobation, lecture, curtain lecture, blow up, wigging, dressing, – down; rating, scolding, trim-

up, countenance, sanction; clap –, pat-
on the back; keep in countenance, endorse, give credit, recommend; mark
with a white -mark, – stone.

commend, praise; be-, laud; compliment, pay a tribute, bepraise; clap,
– the hands; applaud, cheer, acclaim,
acclamate, encore; panegyrize, eulogize, cry up, *prôner*, puff; extol, – to
the skies; magnify, glorify, exalt, boost,
swell, make much of; flatter &c. 933;
bless, give a blessing to; have –, say- a
good word for; speak -well, – highly,
– in high terms- of; sing –, sound –,
chaunt –, resound- the praises of; sing
praises to; cheer –, applaud- to the
-echo, – very echo.

redound to the -honour, – praise, –
credit- of; do credit to; deserve -praise
&c. *n.*; recommend itself; pass muster.

be -praised &c.; receive honourable
mention; be in -favour, – high favour-
with; ring with the praises of, win
golden opinions, gain credit, find favour
with, stand well in the opinion of;
laudari a laudato viro.

Adj. approving &c. *v.*; in favour of;
lost in admiration.

commendatory, complimentary, ben-
edictory, laudatory, panegyrical, eulo-
gistic, encomiastic, acclamatory, lavish
of praise, uncritical.

approved, praised &c. *v.*; un-cen-
sured, -impeached; popular, in good
odour; in high esteem &c. (*respected*)
928; in –, in high- favour.

deserving –, worthy of- praise &c. *n.*;
praiseworthy, commendable, of estimation; good &c. 648; meritorious, estimable, creditable, plausible, unimpeachable; beyond all praise.

Adv. commendably, with credit, to
admiration; well &c. 681; with three
times three.

Int. hear, hear! well done! *brav-o! -a!
-i! bravissimo! euge! macte virtute!* so far
so good, that's right, quite right; *op-
time!* one cheer more; may your shadow never be less! *esto perpetua!* long
life to! *viva! evviva!* God speed! *valete
et plaudite! encore! bis!*

Phr. *probatum est.*

---

ming; correction, set down, rap on the
knuckles, *coup de bec*, rebuff; slap, – on
the face; home thrust, hit; frown, scowl,
black look.

diatribe; jeremiad; *tirade*, philippic.

clamour, outcry, hue and cry; hiss,
-ing; sibilation, cat-call; execration &c.
908.

chiding, upbraiding &c. *v.*; exprobration, abuse, vituperation, invective,
objurgation, contumely, personal remarks; hard –, cutting –, bitter- words.

evil-speaking; bad language &c. 908;
personality.

V. disapprove; dislike &c. 867; lament &c. 839; object to, take exception to; be scandalized at, think ill
of; view with -disfavour, – dark eyes,
– jaundiced eyes; *nil admirari*, dis-
value, improbate.

frown upon, look grave; bend –,
knit- the brows; shake the head at,
shrug the shoulders; turn up the nose
&c. (*contempt*) 930; look -askance, –
black upon; look with an evil eye;
make a wry -face, – mouth- at; set
one's face against.

dis-praise, -commend, -parage; deprecate, speak ill of, not speak well of,
slate, condemn &c. (*find guilty*) 971.

blame; lay –, cast- blame upon;
censure, *fronder*, reproach, pass censure
on, reprobate, impugn.

remonstrate, expostulate, recriminate.

reprehend, chide, admonish; bring –,
call- -to account, – over the coals, – to
order; take to task, reprove, lecture,
bring to book; read a -lesson, – lecture-
to; rebuke, correct.

reprimand, chastise, castigate, lash,
blow up, trounce, trim, *laver la tête*,
overhaul; give it one, – finely; gibbet.

accuse &c. 938; impeach, denounce;
hold up to -reprobation, – execration;
expose, brand, gibbet, stigmatize;
show –, pull –, take- up; cry 'shame'
upon; be outspoken; raise a hue and
cry against.

execrate &c. 908; exprobrate, speak
daggers, vituperate; abuse, – like a
pickpocket; scold, rate, objurate, upbraid, fall foul of; jaw; rail, – at, – in
good set terms; bark at; anathematize,

call names; call by -hard, – ugly- names; a-, re-vile; vili-fy, -pend; bespatter; backbite; clapperclaw; rave –, thunder –, fulminate- against; load with reproaches; lash with the tongue.

exclaim –, protest –, inveigh –, declaim –, cry out –, raise one's voice- against.

decry; cry –, run –, frown- down; clamour, hiss, hoot, mob, ostracize; draw up –, sign- a round robin; black-ball, -list.

animadvert –, reflect- upon; glance at; cast -reflection, – re- proach, – a slur- upon; insinuate, damn with faint praise; 'hint a fault and hesitate dislike'; not to be able to say much for.

scoff at, point at; twit, taunt &c. (*disrespect*) 929; sneer at &c. (*despise*) 230; satirize, lampoon; defame &c. (*detract*) 934; depre- ciate, find fault with, criticize, cut up; pull –, pick- to pieces; take exception; cavil; peck –, nibble –, carp- at; be -censorious &c. *adj.*; pick -holes, – a hole, – a hole in one's coat; make a fuss about.

take –, set- down; snub, snap one up, give a rap on the knuckles; throw a stone -at, – in one's garden; have a -fling, – snap- at; have words with, pluck a crow with; give one a -wipe, – lick with the rough side of the tongue.

incur blame, excite disapprobation, scandalize, shock, revolt; get a bad name, forfeit one's good opinion, be under a cloud, come under the ferule, bring a hornet's nest about one's ears.

take blame, stand corrected; have to answer for.

Adj. disapproving &c. *v.*; scandalized.

disparaging, condemnatory, damnatory, denunciatory, reproach- ful, abusive, objurgatory, clamorous, vituperative; defamatory &c. 934.

satirical, sarcastic, sardonic, cynical, dry, sharp, cutting, biting, severe, virulent, withering, trenchant, hard upon; censorious, criti- cal, captious, carping, hypercritical; fastidious &c. 868; sparing of –, grudging- praise.

disapproved, chid &c. *v.*; in bad odour, blown upon, unapproved; unblest; at a discount, exploded; weighed in the balance and found wanting.

blameworthy, reprehensible &c. (*guilt*) 947; to –, worthy of- blame, answerable, uncommendable, exceptionable, not to be thought of, bad &c. 649; vicious &c. 945.

un-lamented, -bewailed, -pitied.

Adv. with a wry face; reproachfully &c. *adj.*

Int. it is too bad! it -won't, – will never- do! marry come up! Oh! come! 'sdeath!

forbid it Heaven! God –, Heaven- forbid! out –, fie- upon it! away with! tut! *O tempora! O mores!* shame! fie, – for shame! out on you!

tell it not in Gath!

933. Flattery.—N. flattery, adula- tion, gloze; bland-ishment, -iloquence; cajolery; fawning, wheedling &c. *v.*; captation, coquetry, sycophancy, ob- sequiousness, flunkeyism, toad-eating, tuft-hunting; snobbishness.

incense, honeyed words, flummery; bun-kum, -combe; blarney, *placebo*, but-

934. Detraction.—N. detraction, dis- paragement, depreciation, vilification, obloquy, scurrility, scandal, defama- tion, aspersion, traducement, slander, calumny, obtrectation, evil-speaking, backbiting, *scandalum magnatum.*

personality, libel, squib, lampoon, skit, pasquinade; *chronique scandaleuse.*

ter; soft -soap, – sawder; rose water.

voice of the charmer, mouth honour; lip-homage; euphemism; unctuousness &c. *adj.*

V. flatter, praise to the skies, puff; wheedle, cajole, glaver, coax; fawn, – upon; humour, gloze, soothe, pet, coquet, slaver, butter; be-spatter, -slubber, -plaster, -slaver; lay it on thick, overpraise; earwig, cog, col-logue; truckle –, pander *or* pandar –, pay court- to; court; creep into the good graces of; curry favour with, hang on the sleeve of; fool to the top of one's bent; lick the dust.

lay the flattering unction to one's soul, gild the pill, make things pleasant.

overestimate &c. 482; exaggerate &c. 549.

Adj. flattering &c. *v.*; adulatory; mealy-, honey-mouthed; honeyed; smooth, – tongued; soapy, oily, unc-tuous, blandiloquent, specious; fine-, fair-spoken; plausible, servile, syco-phantic, fulsome; courtier-ly, -like.

Adv. *ad captandum.*

---

935. Flatterer.—N. flatterer, adula-tor; eu-logist, -phemist; optimist, en-comiast, *laudator*, whitewasher, booster.

toad-y, -eater; sycophant, courtier, pickthank, Sir Pertinax MacSycophant; *flâneur*, *prôneur*; puffer, touter, *cla-queur*; claw-back, ear-wig, doer of dirty work; parasite, hanger on &c. (*servility*) 886.

---

937. Vindication.—N. vindication, justification, warrant; exoneration, ex-culpation; acquittal &c. 970; white-washing.

extenuation; pallia-tion, -tive; soft-ening, mitigation.

reply, defence; recrimination &c. 938.

apology, gloss, varnish; plea &c. 617; salvo; excuse, extenuating circum-stances; allowance, – to be made; *locus pœnitentiæ.*

apologist, vindicator, justifier; de-fendant &c. 938.

justifiable charge, true bill.

sarcasm, cynicism; criticism (*disap-probation*) 932; invective &c. 932; en-venomed tongue; *spretæ injuria formæ.*

detractor &c. 936.

V. detract, derogate, decry, depre-ciate, disparage; run –, cry- down; minimize, make light of; belittle, sneer at &c. (*contemn*) 930; criticize, pull to pieces, pick a hole in one's coat, asperse, cast aspersions, blow upon, bespatter, blacken; vili-fy, -pend; avile; give a dog a bad name, brand, malign, back-bite, libel, lampoon, traduce, slander, defame, calumniate, bear false witness against; speak ill of behind one's back.

'damn with faint praise, assent with civil leer; and without sneering, others teach to sneer.'

fling dirt &c. (*disrespect*) 929; ana-thematize &c. 932; dip the pen in gall, view in a bad light.

Adj. detracting &c. *v.*; defamatory, detractory, derogatory; disparaging, libellous; scurril-e, -ous; abusive; foul-spoken, -tongued, -mouthed; slander-ous; calumni-ous, -atory; sar-castic, -donic; satirical, cynical.

---

936. Detractor.—N. detractor, re-prover; cens-or, -urer; cynic, critic, caviller, carper, wordcatcher.

defamer, backbiter, slanderer, knock-er, Sir Benjamin Backbite, lampooner, satirist, traducer, libeller, calumniator, dearest foe, dawplucker, Thersites; Zoilus; good-natured –, candid- friend [satirically]; reviler, vituperator, casti-gator; shrew &c. 901.

disapprover, *laudator temporis acti.*

---

938. Accusation. — N. accusation, charge, imputation, slur, inculpation, exprobration, delation; crimination; in-, ac-, re-crimination; *tu quoque* argu-ment; invective &c. 932.

de-nunciation, -nouncement; libel, challenge, citation, arraignment; im-, ap-peachment; indictment, bill of in-dictment, true bill; lawsuit &c. 969; condemnation &c. 971.

gravamen of a charge, head and front of one's offending, *argumentum ad hominem*; scandal &c. (*detraction*) 934; *scandalum magnatum.*

V. justify, warrant; be an -excuse &c. *n.*- for; lend a colour, furnish a handle; vindicate; ex-, dis-culpate; acquit &c. 970; clear, set right, exonerate, whitewash.

extenuate, palliate, excuse, soften, apologize, varnish, slur, gloze; put a -gloss, – good face- upon; mince; gloss over, bolster up, help a lame dog over a stile.

advocate, defend, plead one's cause; stand –, stick –, speak- up for; contend –, speak- for; bear out, keep in countenance, support; plead &c. 617; say in defence; plead ignorance; confess and avoid, propugn, put in a good word for.

take the will for the deed, make allowance for, do justice to; give -one, – the Devil- his due.

make good; prove -the truth of, – one's case; be justified by the event.

Adj. vindicat-ed, -ing &c. *v.*; vindicat-ive, -ory; palliative; exculpatory; apologetic.

excusable, defensible, pardonable; veni-al, -able; specious, plausible, justifiable.

Phr. '*honi soit qui mal y pense.*'

accuser, prosecutor, plaintiff, complainant, petitioner; relator, informer; appellant.

accused, defendant, prisoner, panel, co-, respondent; litigant.

V. accuse, charge, tax, impute, twit, taunt with, reproach.

brand with reproach; stigmatize, slur; cast a -stone at, – slur on; incriminate; inculpate, implicate; call to account &c. (*censure*) 932; take to -blame, – task; put in the black book.

inform against, indict, denounce, arraign; im-, ap-peach; have up, show up, pull up; challenge, cite, lodge a complaint; prosecute, bring an action against &c. 969.

charge –, saddle- with; lay to one's -door, – charge; lay the blame on, bring home to; cast –, throw- in one's teeth; cast the first stone at.

have –, keep- a rod in pickle for; have a crow to pluck with.

trump up a charge.

Adj. accusing &c. *v.*; accusat-ory, -ive; imputative, denunciatory; re-, criminatory.

accused &c. *v.*; suspected; under -suspicion, – a cloud, – *surveillance*; in -custody, – detention; in the -lock up, – watch house, – house of detention.

accusable, imputable; in-defensible, -excusable; un-pardonable, -justifiable; vicious &c. 945.

Int. look at home; *tu quoque* &c. (*retaliation*) 718.

3°. Moral Conditions

939. Probity.—**N.** probity, integrity, rectitude; uprightness &c. *adj.*; honesty, faith; honour; good faith, *bona fides*; purity, clean hands.

fairness &c. *adj.*; fair play, justice, equity, impartiality, principle; grace.

constancy; faithfulness &c. *adj.*; fidelity, loyalty; incorrupt-ion, -ibility.

trustworthiness &c. *adj.*; truth, candour, singleness of heart; veracity &c. 543; tender conscience &c. (*sense of duty*) 926.

punctil-iousness, -io; delicacy, nicety; scrupul-osity, -ousness &c. *adj.*; scruple; point, – of honour; punctuality.

dignity &c. (*repute*) 873; respectability, -bleness &c. *adj.*; gentleman; man of -honour, – his word; *fidus*

940. Improbity. N. improbity; dishon-esty, -our; deviation from rectitude; disgrace &c. (*disrepute*) 874; fraud &c. (*deception*) 545; lying &c. 544; bad –, Punic- faith; *mala –, Punica- fides*; infidelity; faithlessness &c. *adj.*; Judas kiss, betrayal; scrap of paper.

breach of -promise, – trust, – faith; prodition, disloyalty, divided allegiance, treason, high treason; apostacy &c. (*tergiversation*) 607; non-observance &c. 773.

shabbiness &c. *adj.*; villainy; baseness &c. *adj.*; abjection, debasement, turpitude, moral turpitude, laxity, trimming, shuffling.

perfidy; perfidiousness &c. *adj.*;

Achates, preux chevalier, galantuomo; truepenny, trump, brick; true Briton, white man, sportsman.

court of honour, a fair field and no favour; *argumentum ad verecundiam.*

V. be -honourable &c. *adj.*; deal -honourably, – squarely, – impartially, – fairly; speak the truth &c. (*veracity*) 543; tell the truth and shame the devil, *vitam impendere vero*; show a proper spirit, make a point of; do one's duty &c. 944; play the game.

redeem one's pledge &c. 926; keep –, be as good as- one's -promise, – word; keep faith with, not fail.

give and take, *audire alteram partem*, give the devil his due, put the saddle on the right horse.

redound to one's honour.

Adj. upright; honest, – as daylight; veracious &c. 543; virtuous &c. 944; honourable; fair, right, just, equitable, impartial, even-handed, square; fair –, open- and aboveboard.

constant, – as the northern star; faithful, loyal, staunch; true, – blue, – to one's colours, – to the core, – as the needle to the pole; true-hearted, trust-y, -worthy; as good as one's word, to be depended on, incorruptible.

manly, straightforward &c. (*ingenuous*) 703; frank, candid, open-hearted.

conscientious, tender - conscienced, right-minded; high-principled, -minded; scrupulous, religious, strict; nice, punctilious, correct, punctual; respect-, reput-able; gentlemanlike.

inviol - able, - ate; un - violated, -broken, -betrayed; un-bought, -bribed.

innocent &c. 946; pure; stainless; un-stained, -tarnished, -sullied, -tainted, -perjured; uncorrupt, -ed; unde-filed, -praved, -bauched; *integer vitæ scelerisque purus; justus et tenax propositi.*

chivalrous, jealous of honour, *sans peur et sans reproche*; high-spirited.

supra-mundane, unworldly, over-scrupulous.

Adv. honourably &c. *adj.*; *bona fide*; on the square, in good faith, honour bright, *foro conscientiæ*, with clean hands; by fair means.

treachery, double-dealing; unfairness &c. *adj.*; knavery, roguery, rascality, foul-play; jobb-ing, -ery; Tammany, graft; venality, nepotism; corruption, job, shuffle, fishy transaction, barratry; sharp practice, heads I win, tails you lose; mouth-honour &c. (*flattery*) 933.

V. be -dishonest &c. *adj.*; play false; break one's -word, – faith, – promise; jilt, betray, forswear; shuffle &c. (*lie*) 544; live by one's wits, sail near the wind; play with marked cards.

disgrace –, dishonour –, demean –, degrade- oneself; derogate, stoop, grovel, sneak, lose caste; sell oneself, go over to the enemy; seal one's infamy.

Adj. dishon-est, -ourable; un-conscientious, -scrupulous; fraudulent &c. 545; knavish; disgraceful &c. (*disreputable*) 874; wicked &c. 945.

false-hearted, disingenuous; unfair, one-sided; double, -tongued, -faced; time-serving, crooked, tortuous, insidious, Machiavellian, dark, slippery; questionable; fishy; perfidious, treacherous, perjured.

infamous, arrant, foul, base, vile, low, ignominious, blackguard.

contemptible, abject, mean, shabby, little, paltry, dirty, scurvy, scabby, sneaking, grovelling, scrubby, rascally, pettifogging; beneath one; not cricket.

low-minded, -thoughted; base-minded.

undignified, indign; unbe-coming, -seeming, -fitting; de-rogatory, -grading; *infra dignitatem*; ungentleman-ly, -like; un-knightly, -chivalric, -manly, -handsome; recreant, inglorious.

corrupt, venal; debased, mongrel.

faithless, of bad faith, false, unfaithful, disloyal; untrustworthy; trust-, troth-less; lost to shame, dead to honour.

Adv. dishonestly &c. *adj.*; *malâ fide*, like a thief in the night, by crooked paths; by foul means.

Int. *O tempora! O mores!*

---

941. Knave.—N. knave, rogue, villain; Scapin, rascal; Lazarillo de Tormes; bad man &c. 949; blackguard &c. 949.

traitor, betrayer, arch-traitor, conspirator, stool pigeon, Judas, Catiline; reptile, serpent, snake in the grass, wolf in sheep's clothing, sneak, Jerry Sneak, tell-tale, squealer, mischief-maker, trimmer; renegade &c. (*tergiversation*) 607; truant, recreant; sycophant &c. (*servility*) 886.

942. Disinterestedness.—N. disinterestedness &c. *adj.*; generosity; liberal-ity, -ism; altruism; benevolence &c. 906; elevation, loftiness of purpose, exaltation, magnanimity; chival-ry, -rous spirit; heroism, sublimity.

self-denial, -abnegation, -effacement, -sacrifice, -immolation, -control &c. (*resolution*) 604; stoicism, devotion, martyrdom, *suttee*.

labour of love.

V. be -disinterested &c. *adj.*; make a sacrifice, lay one's head on the block; put oneself in the place of others, do as one would be done by, do unto others as we would men should do unto us.

Adj. disinterested; unselfish; self-denying, -sacrificing, -devoted; generous.

handsome, liberal, noble; noble-, high-minded; princely, great, high, elevated, lofty, exalted, spirited, stoical, magnanimous; great-, large-hearted, chivalrous, heroic, sublime.

un-bought, -bribed; uncorrupted &c. (*upright*) 939.

943. Selfishness.—N. selfishness &c. *adj.*; self-love, -indulgence, -worship, -interest; ego-tism, -ism; egocentrism, narcissism; *amour propre* &c. (*vanity*) 880; nepotism.

worldliness &c. *adj.*; world wisdom. illiberality; meanness &c. *adj.*

time-server; tuft-, fortune-hunter; self-seeker; jobber, worldling; egotist, egoist, monopolist, nepotist, profiteer; temporizer, trimmer; dog in the manger, charity that begins at home.

V. be -selfish &c. *adj.*; please -, indulge -, coddle- oneself; consult one's own -wishes, - pleasure; look after one's own interest; feather one's nest; take care of number one, have an eye to the main chance, know on which side one's bread is buttered; give an inch and take an ell; wangle.

Adj. selfish; self-seeking, -indulgent, -interested; wrapt up -, centred- in self; egotistic, -al; egoistical; egocentric.

illiberal, mean, ungenerous, narrow-minded; mercenary, venal; covetous &c. 819.

unspiritual; earthly, -minded; mundane; worldly, -minded, -wise; time-serving.

interested; *alieni appetens sui profusus.*

Adv. ungenerously &c. *adj.*; to gain some private ends; from selfish -, interested- motives.

Phr. *après nous le déluge.*

944. Virtue.—N. virtue; virtuousness &c. *adj.*; morality; moral rectitude; integrity &c. (*probity*) 939; nobleness &c. 873.

morals; ethics &c. (*duty*) 926; cardinal virtues.

merit, worth, desert, excellence, credit; self-control &c. (*resolution*) 604; self-denial &c. (*temperance*) 953.

well-doing; good -actions, - behaviour; discharge -, fulfilment -, performance- of duty; well-spent life; innocence &c. 946.

V. be -virtuous &c. *adj.*; practise virtue &c. *n.*; do -, fulfil -, perform -,

945. Vice.— N. vice; evil -doing, - courses; wrong doing; wickedness, viciousness &c. *adj.*; iniquity, peccability, demerit; sin, Adam; old -, offending- Adam.

immorality, impropriety, indecorum, scandal, laxity, looseness of morals; want of -principle, - ballast; obliquity, backsliding, infamy, demoralization, pravity, depravity, pollution; hardness of heart; brutality &c. (*malevolence*) 907; corruption &c. (*debasement*) 659; knavery &c. (*improbity*) 940; profligacy; lust &c. 961; flagrancy, atrocity; cannibalism.

discharge- one's duty; redeem one's pledge &c. 926; act well, – one's part; fight the good fight; acquit oneself well; command –, master- one's passions; keep -straight, – in the right path.

set -an, – a good- example; be on one's -good, – best- behaviour.

Adj. virtuous, good; innocent &c. 946; meritorious, deserving, worthy, desertful, correct; dut-iful, -eous; moral; right, -eous, -minded; well-intentioned, creditable, laudable, commendable, praiseworthy; above –, beyond- all praise; excellent, admirable; sterling, pure, noble.

exemplary; match-, peer-less; saintly, -like; heaven-born, angelic, seraphic, godlike.

Adv. virtuously &c. *adj.*; *e merito.*

---

infirmity; weakness &c. *adj.*; weakness of the flesh, frailty, imperfection; error; weak side; foible; fail-ing, -ure; crying –, besetting- sin; defect, deficiency, shortcoming; cloven foot.

lowest dregs of vice, sink of iniquity, Alsatian den; *gusto picaresco.*

fault, crime; criminality &c. (*guilt*) 947.

sinner &c. 949.

V. be -vicious &c. *adj.*; sin, commit sin, do amiss, err, transgress; misdemean –, forget –, misconduct- oneself; mis-do, -behave; fall, lapse, slip, trip, offend, trespass; deviate from the -line of duty, – path of virtue &c. 944; take a wrong course, go astray; hug a -sin, – fault; sow one's wild oats.

render -vicious &c. *adj.*; demoralize, brutalize; corrupt &c. (*degrade*) 659.

Adj.* vicious; sinful; sinning &c. *v.*; wicked, iniquitous, bad, immoral, unrighteous, wrong, criminal; naughty, incorrect; undut-eous, -iful.

unprincipled, lawless, disorderly, *contra bonos mores*, indecorous, unseemly, improper; dissolute, profligate, scampish; unworthy; worth-, desert-less; disgraceful, recreant; reprehensible, blameworthy, uncommendable; dis-creditable, -reputable.

base, sinister, scurvy, foul, gross, vile, black, grave, facinorous, felonious, nefarious, shameful, scandalous, infamous, villainous, of a deep dye, heinous; flag-rant, -itious; atrocious, incarnate, accursed.

Mephistophelian, satanic, diabolic, hellish, infernal, stygian, fiend-ish, -like, hell-born, demoniacal, devilish.

mis-created, -begotten; demoralized, corrupt, depraved.

evil-minded, -disposed; ill-conditioned; malevolent &c. 907; heart-, grace-, shame-, virtue-less; abandoned, lost to virtue; unconscionable; sunk –, lost –, deep –, steeped- in iniquity.

incorrigible, irreclaimable, obdurate, reprobate, past praying for; culpable, reprehensible &c. (*guilty*) 947.

unjustifiable; in-defensible, -excusable; inexpiable, unpardonable, irremissible.

weak, frail, lax, infirm, imperfect, indiscreet; demoralizing, degrading.

Adv. wrong; sinfully &c. *adj.*; without excuse.

Int. *O tempora! O mores!*

---

946. Innocence. — N. innocence; guiltlessness &c. *adj.*; incorruption, impeccability.

clean hands, clear conscience, *mens sibi conscia recti.*

innocent, new born babe, lamb, dove.

V. be -innocent &c. *adj.*; *nil conscire sibi nullâ pallescere culpâ.*

---

947. Guilt.—N. guilt, -iness; culpability; crimin-ality, -ousness; deviation from rectitude &c. (*improbity*) 940; sinfulness &c. (*vice*) 945; peccability.

mis-conduct, -behaviour, -doing, -deed; malpractice, fault, sin, error, transgression; dereliction, delinquency; indiscretion, lapse, slip, trip, *faux pas,*

---

* Most of these adjectives are applicable both to the act and to the agent.

acquit &c. 970; exculpate &c. (*vindicate*) 937.

Adj. innocent, not guilty; unguilty; guilt-, fault-, sin-, stain-, blood-, spotless; clear, immaculate; *rectus in curiâ*; un-spotted, -blemished, -erring; undefiled &c. 939; unhardened, Saturnian; Arcadian &c. (*artless*) 703.

in-, un-culpable; unblam-ed, -able; blameless, inerrable, above suspicion; irrepr-oachable, -ovable, -ehensible; un-exceptionable, -objectionable, -impeachable; salvable; venial &c. 937.

harmless; in-offensive, -noxious, -nocuous; dove-, lamb-like; pure, harmless as doves; innocent as -a lamb, – the babe unborn; more sinned against than sinning.

virtuous &c. 944; un-reproved, -impeached, -reproached.

Adv. innocently &c. *adj.*; with clean hands; with a -clear, – safe- conscience.

948. Good Man. — N. good man, worthy.

good woman, goddess, *madonna*, virgin.

model, paragon &c. (*perfection*) 650; good example; hero, demigod, seraph, angel; innocent &c. 946; saint &c. (*piety*) 987; benefactor &c. 912; philanthropist &c. 910; Aristides.

brick, trump, rough diamond, ugly duckling.

salt of the earth; one in ten thousand; one of the best.

Phr. *si sic omnes!*

peccadillo; flaw, blot, omission; fail-ing, -ure.

offence, trespass; mis-demeanour, -feasance, -prision; tort; mal-efaction, -feasance, -versation; crime, felony.

enormity, atrocity, outrage; deadly –, mortal –, unpardonable- sin; died without a name.

corpus delicti.

Adj. guilty, to blame, culpable, pec-cable, in fault, censurable, reprehensible, blameworthy, uncommendable, illaudable; weighed in the balance and found wanting; exceptionable, objectionable.

Adv. *in flagrante delicto*; red-handed, in the very act.

949. Bad Man.—N. bad man, wrongdoer, worker of iniquity; evil-doer &c. 913; sinner; the -wicked &c. 945; bad example.

rascal, scoundrel, villain, miscreant, caitiff; wretch, reptile, viper, serpent, cockatrice, basilisk, urchin; tiger, monster; devil &c. (*demon*) 980; devil incarnate; demon in human shape, Nana Sahib; hell-hound, -cat; rake-hell.

bad woman, jade, Jezebel, adultress, &c. 962.

scamp, scapegrace, rip, runagate, ne'er-do-well, reprobate, *roué*, rake; limb; one who has sold himself to the devil, fallen angel, *âme damnée, vaurien,* *mauvais sujet,* loose fish, sad dog; lost –, black- sheep; castaway, recreant, defaulter; prodigal &c. 818; libertine &c. 962.

rough, rowdy, ugly customer, ruffian, hoodlum, bully; Jonathan Wild; hangman; incendiary; thief &c. 792; murderer &c. 361.

culprit, delinquent, criminal, malefactor, misdemeanant; felon; convict, jail-bird, ticket-of-leave man; outlaw.

blackguard, *polisson,* loafer, sneak; raps-, ras-callion; cullion, mean wretch, varlet, kern, *âme-de-boue, drôle*; cur, dog, hound, whelp, mongrel; lown, loon, runnion, outcast, vagabond; rogue &c. (*knave*) 941; scum of the earth, riff-raff; *Arcades ambo.*

Int. sirrah!

950. Penitence.—N. penitence, contrition, compunction, repentance, remorse; regret &c. 833.

self-reproach, -reproof, -accusation,

951. Impenitence.—N. impenitence, irrepentance, recusance.

hardness of heart, seared conscience, induration, obduracy.

-condemnation, -humiliation; stings –, pangs –, qualms –, prickings –, twinge –, twitch –, touch –, voice- of conscience; compunctious visitings of nature.

acknowledgment, confession &c. (*disclosure*) 529; apology &c. 952; recantation &c. 607; penance &c. 952; resipiscence.

awakened conscience, deathbed repentance, *locus pœnitentiæ*, stool of repentance, cutty stool.

penitent, Magdalen, prodigal son, returned prodigal, a sadder and a wiser man.

V. repent, be sorry for; be -penitent &c. *adj.*; rue; regret &c. 833; think better of; recant &c. 607; knock under &c. (*submit*) 725; plead guilty; sing -*miserere*, – *de profundis*; cry *peccavi*; own oneself in the wrong; acknowledge, confess &c. (*disclose*) 529; humble oneself; beg pardon &c. (*apologize*) 952; turn over a new leaf, put on the new man, turn from sin; reclaim; repent in sackcloth and ashes &c. (*do penance*) 952; learn by experience.

Adj. penitent; repenting &c. *v.*; repentant, contrite; conscience-smitten, -stricken; self-accusing, -convicted.

penitenti-al, -ary; chastened, reclaimed; not hardened; unhardened.

Adv. *meâ culpâ*.

Phr. *peccavi*; *erubuit*; *salva res est*; *vous l'avez voulu, Georges Dandin*.

V. be -impenitent &c. *adj.*; steel –, harden- the heart; die -game, – and make no sign.

Adj. impenitent, uncontrite, obdurate; hard, -ened; seared, recusant; unrepentant; relent-, remorse-, grace-, shrift-less.

lost, incorrigible, irreclaimable.

unre-claimed, -formed; unrepented, unatoned.

---

952. Atonement.—N. atonement, reparation; compromise, composition; compensation &c. 30; quittance, quits; indemni-ty, -fication; expiation, redemption, reclamation, conciliation, propitiation.

amends, apology, *amende honorable*, satisfaction; peace –, sin –, burnt- offering; scapegoat, sacrifice.

penance, fasting, maceration, sackcloth and ashes, white sheet, shrift, flagellation, lustration; purga-tion, -tory.

V. atone, – for; expiate; propitiate; make -amends, – good; reclaim, redeem, repair, ransom, absolve, purge, shrive, do penance, stand in a white sheet, repent in sackcloth and ashes.

set one's house in order, wipe off old scores, make matters up; pay the -forfeit, – penalty.

apologize, beg pardon, express regret, *faire amende honorable*, give satisfaction; come –, fall- down on one's -knees, – marrow bones.

Adj. propitiatory, expiatory; sacrific, -ial, -atory; piacul-ar, -ous.

4°. Moral Practice

953. Temperance.—N. temperance moderation, sobriety, soberness.

forbearance, abnegation; self-denial, -restraint, -control &c. (*resolution*) 604.

frugality; vegetarianism, teetotalism, total abstinence, prohibition; abst-inence, -emiousness, asceticism &c. 955; system of -Pythagoras, – Cornaro; Pythagorism, Stoicism.

954. Intemperance.—N. intemperance; sensuality, animalism, carnality; pleasure; effeminacy, silkiness; luxur-y, -iousness; lap of -pleasure, – luxury.

indulgence; high-, free- living, inabstinence, self-indulgence; voluptuousness &c. *adj.*; epicur-ism, -eanism; sybaritism.

vegetarian; Pythagorean, gymnoso-phist; teetotaler &c. 958; abstainer.

V. be -temperate &c. *adj.*; abstain, forbear, refrain, deny oneself, spare; know when one has had enough; take the pledge; look not upon the wine when it is red.

Adj. temperate, moderate, sober, frugal, sparing; abst-emious, -inent; within compass; measured &c. (*sufficient*) 639.

Pythagorean; vegetarian; teetotal, pussy-foot.

———

dissipation; licentiousness &c. *adj.*; debauchery; crapulence.

revel-s, -ry; debauch, carousal, jollification, drinking bout, wassail, Saturnalia, orgies; excess, too much; intoxication &c. 959.

Circean cup; drug habit &c. 663.

V. be -intemperate &c. *adj.*; indulge, exceed; live -well, – high, – on the fat of the land; give a loose to -indulgence &c. *n.*; dine not wisely but too well; wallow in -voluptuousness &c. *n.*; plunge into dissipation.

revel, rake, live hard, run riot, sow one's wild oats; slake one's -appetite, – thirst; swill; pamper.

Adj. intemperate, inabstinent, intoxicated &c. 958; sensual, self-indulgent; voluptuous, luxurious, licentious, wild, dissolute, rakish, fast, debauched.

brutish, crapulous, swinish, piggish, hoggish, bestial.

Paphian, Epicurean, Sybaritical; bred –, nursed- in the lap of luxury; indulged, pampered, full-fed.

954a. Sensualist.—N. Sybarite, voluptuary, Sardanapalus, man of pleasure, carpet knight; epicure, -an; *gourm-et, -and*; gormandizer, gutling, glutton, pig, hog; votary –, swine- of Epicurus; sensualist; Heliogabalus; free –, hard- liver; libertine &c. 962; hedonist.

955. Asceticism.—N. asceticism, puritanism, sabbatarianism; cynicism, austerity; total abstinence.

mortification, maceration, sackcloth and ashes, flagellation; penance &c. 952; fasting &c. 956; martyrdom.

ascetic; anchor-et, -ite; martyr; *Heautontimorumenos*; hermit &c. (*recluse*) 893; puritan, sabbatarian, cynic.

Adj. ascetic, austere, puritanical; cynical; over-religious.

956. Fasting. — N. fasting; exrophagy; famishment, starvation; banting.

fast, *jour maigre*; fast –, banyan-day; Lent, quadragesima; Rama-dan, -zan; spare –, meagre- diet; lenten -diet, – entertainment; *soupe maigre*, short -rations, – commons; Barmecide feast; hunger strike.

V. fast, starve, clem, famish, perish with hunger; dine with Duke Humphrey; make two bites of a cherry.

Adj. lenten, quadragesimal; unfed; starved &c. *v.*; half-starved; fasting &c. *v.*; hungry &c. 865.

———

play a good knife and fork &c. (*appetite*) 865. pamper, indulge.

957. Gluttony.—N. gluttony; greed; greediness &c. *adj.*; voracity.

epicurism; good –, high- living; edacity, gulosity, crapulence; gutt-, guzz-ling; over-indulgence.

good cheer, blow out; feast &c. (*food*) 298; gastronomy.

epicure, *bon vivant, gourmand*; glutton, cormorant, hog, belly-god, Apicius, gastronome, gormandizer.

V. gormandize, gorge; over-gorge, -eat- oneself; engorge, eat one's fill, cram, stuff, stodge, glut, satiate; gutt-le, guzz-le; bolt, devour, gobble up; gulp &c. (*swallow food*) 298; raven, eat out of house and home.

have the stomach of an ostrich;

Adj. gluttonous, greedy; gormandizing &c. *v.*; edacious, omnivorous, crapulent, swinish, voracious, devouring.

pampered; over-fed, -gorged.

958. Sobriety.—**N.** sobriety; teetotalism, temperance &c. 953.

water-drinker; teetotal-er, -ist; abstainer, Good Templar, Rechabite, band of hope; prohibitionist, pussyfoot.

V. take the pledge.

Adj. sober, – as a judge; dry, on the water wagon.

---

959. Drunkenness.—**N.** drunkenness &c. *adj.*; intemperance; drinking &c. *v.*; inebri-ety, -ation; ebri-ety, -osity; befuddlement; insobriety; intoxication; temulency, bibacity, wine-bibbing; com-, potation; deep potations, bacchanals, *bacchanalia*, libations.

oino-, dipso-mania; *delirium tremens*, d.t.; alcohol, -ism.

drink; alcoholic drinks, alcohol, booze; gin, blue ruin, grog, brandy, port wine; punch, -bowl; cup, rosy wine, flowing bowl; drop, – too much; dram; beer, wine, spirits &c. (*beverage*) 298; cocktail, nip, peg; stirrup cup.

drunkard, sot, toper, tippler, bibber, wine-bibber; hard –, gin –, dram- drinker; soak, soaker, sponge, tun; love-, toss-pot; thirsty soul, reveller, carouser; Bacchanal, -ian; Bacch-al, -ante; devotee to Bacchus, dipsomaniac.

V. get –, be- drunk &c. *adj.*; see double; take a -drop, – glass- too much; drink, tipple, tope, booze, bouse, guzzle, swill, soak, sot, lush, bib, swig, carouse; sacrifice at the shrine of Bacchus; take to drinking; drink -hard, – deep, – like a fish; have one's swill, drain the cup, splice the main brace, take a hair of the dog that bit you.

liquor, – up; wet one's whistle, take a whet; lift one's elbow; crack a –, pass the- bottle; toss off &c. (*drink up*) 298; go to the -ale, – public-house.

make one -drunk &c. *adj.*; inebriate, fuddle, fuzzle, get into one's head.

Adj. drunk, tipsy; intoxicated; inebri-ous, -ate, -ated; in one's cups; in a state of -intoxication &c. *n.*; temulent, -ive; fuddled, mellow, cut, boosy, fou, fresh, merry, elevated, squiffy; plastered, befuddled, sozzled; flush, -ed; flustered, disguised, groggy, beery; topheavy; potvaliant, glorious; potulent; over-come, -taken; whittled, screwed, tight, primed, oiled, corned, raddled, sewed up, lushy, nappy, muddled, muzzy, bosky, obfuscated, maudlin; crapulous, dead –, blind- drunk.

inter pocula; in –, the worse for- liquor, having had a drop too much, half seas over, three sheets in the wind; under the table, blind to the world, one over the eight.

drunk as -a piper, – a fiddler, – a lord, – Chloe, – an owl, – David's sow, – a wheelbarrow.

drunken, bibacious, bibulous, sottish; given –, addicted- to -drink, – the bottle; toping &c. *v.*; wet.

Phr. *nunc est bibendum.*

960. Purity.—**N.** purity; decency, decorum, delicacy; continence, chastity, honesty, virtue, modesty, shame; pudicity, *pucelage*, virginity.

vestal, virgin, Joseph, Hippolytus; Lucretia, Diana; prude.

961. Impurity.—**N.** impurity; uncleanness &c. (*filth*) 653; immodesty; grossness &c. *adj.*; indelicacy, indecency; impudicity; obscenity, ribaldry, smut, bawdry, *double entendre*, *équivoque*; Aretinism; pornography.

Adj. pure, undefiled, modest, delicate, decent, decorous; *virginibus puerisque*; chaste, continent, virtuous, honest, Platonic.

———

concupiscence, lust, carnality, flesh, salacity; pruriency, lechery, lasciviency, lubricity, lewdness.

incontinence, intrigue, *faux pas*; *amour, -ette*; gallantry; debauchery, libertinism, *libertinage*, fornication; *liaison*; wenching, venery, dissipation.

seduction; defloration, defilement, abuse, violation, rape; incest.

social evil, harlotry, stupration, whoredom, concubinage, cuckoldom, adultery, advoutry, *crim. con.*; free love.

seraglio, harem, zenana; brothel, bagnio, stew, bawdy-house, *lupanar*, house of ill fame, *bordel*, kip.

V. be -impure &c. *adj.*; intrigue; debauch, defile, assault, attack, seduce; prostitute; abuse, violate, deflower; commit -adultery &c. *n.*

Adj. impure; unclean &c. (*dirty*) 653; not to be mentioned to ears polite; immodest, shameless; in-decorous, -delicate, -decent; loose, suggestive, *risqué*, coarse, gross, broad, free, equivocal, smutty, fulsome, ribald, obscene, bawdy, pornographic.

concupiscent, prurient, lickerish, rampant, lustful; carnal, -minded; lewd, lascivious, lecherous, libidinous, erotic, ruttish, salacious; Paphian; voluptuous; incestuous.

unchaste, light, wanton, licentious, adulterous, debauched, dissolute; of -loose character, – easy virtue; frail, gay, riggish, incontinent, meretricious, rakish, gallant, dissipated; no better than she should be; on the -town, – streets, – *pavé*, – loose.

adulterous, incestuous, bestial.

962. Libertine.—N. libertine; voluptuary &c. 954*a*; rake, debauchee, loose fish, rip, rake-hell, fast man; *intrigant*, gallant, seducer, fornicator, lecher, satyr, goat, whoremonger, *paillard*, adulterer, gay deceiver, Lothario, Don Juan, Blue-beard.

adulteress, advoutress, courtesan, prostitute, strumpet, tart, hustler, chippy, broad, harlot, whore, punk, *fille de joie*; woman, – of the town; street-walker, Cyprian, miss, piece; frail sisterhood, fallen woman; demirep, wench, trollop, trull, baggage, hussy, drab, bitch, jade, skit, rig, quean, mopsy, slut, minx, harridan; woman -of easy virtue &c. (*unchaste*) 961; wanton, fornicatress; Jezebel, Messalina, Delilah, Thaïs, Phryne, Aspasia, Lais, *lorette, cocotte, petite dame, grisette; demi-monde*; white slave.

concubine, mistress, fancy woman, kept woman, doxy, *chère amie, bona roba.*

pimp; pand-er, -ar; bawd, *conciliatrix*, procuress, mackerel; wittol.

5°. Institutions

963. Legality.—N. legality; legitima-cy, -teness, legitimization.

legislature; law, code, *corpus juris*, constitution, pandect, charter, act, enactment, statute, rule; canon &c. (*precept*) 697; ordinance, institution; regulation; by-, bye-law, rescript; decree &c. (*order*) 741; *ordonnance*;

964. ⌊Absence or violation of law.⌋
Illegality.—N. lawlessness; breach –, violation- of law; disobedience &c. 742; unconformity &c. 83.

arbitrariness &c. *adj.*; antinomy, violence, brute force, despotism, out-lawry.

mob –, lynch –, club –, Lydford –,

standing order; *plébiscite* &c. (*choice*) 609.

legal process; form, -ula, -ality; rite; arm of the law; *habeas corpus*.

[Science of law] jurisprudence, nomology; legislation, codification.

equity, common law; *lex -, lex non-scripta*, unwritten law; law of nations, international law, *jus gentium*; *jus civile*; civil -, criminal -, canon -, statute -, ecclesiastical- law; *lex mercatoria*.

constitutional-ism, -ity; justice &c. 922.

V. legalize, legitimize; enact, ordain; decree &c. (*order*) 741; pass a law; legislate; codify, formulate; authorize.

Adj. legal, legitimate; according to law; vested, constitutional, chartered, legalized; lawful &c. (*permitted*) 760; statut-able, -ory; legislat-orial, -ive.

Adv. legally &c. *adj.*; in the eye of the law; *de jure*.

———

martial -, drumhead- law; *coup d'état*; *le droit du plus fort*; *argumentum baculinum*.

illegality, informality, unlawfulness, illegitimacy, bar sinister.

trover and conversion; smuggling, boot-legging, rum-running, poaching; simony.

speakeasy, speakie, blind pig.

V. offend against -, violate- the law; set the law at defiance, ride rough-shod over, drive a coach and six through a statute; make the law a dead letter, take the law into one's own hands.

smuggle, run, poach.

Adj. illegal; prohibited &c. 761; not allowed, unlawful, illegitimate, illicit, contraband, actionable.

unchartered, unconstitutional; un-warrant-ed, -able; unauthorized; informal, unofficial; in-, extra-judicial.

lawless, arbitrary; despotic, -al; summary, irresponsible; un-answer-able, -accountable.

null and void; a dead letter.

Adv. illegally &c. *adj.*; with a high hand, in violation of law.

965. Jurisdiction. [Executive.]—**N.** jurisdiction, judicature, administration of justice, soc; executive, commission of the peace; magistracy &c. (*authority*) 737.

judge &c. 967; tribunal &c. 966; municipality, corporation, bailiwick, shrievalty; lord lieutenant; lord -, mayor, city manager, alderman &c. 745; sheriff, bailie, shrieve, chief -, constable; police, - force; constabulary, bumbledom.

officer; proctor, high -, commissioner; bailiff, tipstaff, bum-bailiff, catchpoll, beadle; police-man, -constable, -sergeant; *sbirro, alguazil, gendarme*, kavass, *lictor*, macebearer, *huissier*, bedel.

press-gang; exciseman, gauger, custom-house officer, *douanier*.

coroner, edile, ædile, portreeve, paritor; *posse comitatus*.

V. judge, sit in judgment.

Adj. executive, administrative, municipal; inquisitorial, causidical; judic-atory, -iary, -ial; juridical.

Adv. *coram judice*.

966. Tribunal.—**N.** tribunal, court, board, bench, judicatory, curia; court of -justice, - law, - arbitration; inquisition; guild.

justice -, judgment -, mercy- seat; woolsack; bar, - of justice; dock; forum, hustings, *bureau*, drum-head; jury-, witness-box.

senate-house, town-hall, theatre; House of -Lords, - Commons.

assize, eyre; ward-, burgh-mote; superior courts of Westminster; court of -record, - oyer and terminer, - assize, - appeal, - error; High court of -Judicature, - Appeal; Judicial Committee of the Privy Council; Star-Chamber; Court of -Chancery, - King's *or* Queen's Bench, - Exchequer, - Common Pleas, - Probate, - Arches, - Admiralty, - Criminal Appeal; Lords Justices' -, Rolls -, Vice Chancellor's -,

Stannary –, Divorce –, Palatine –, ecclesiastical –, county –, police-court; sessions; quarter –, petty- sessions; court -leet, – baron, – of pie poudre, – of common council; board of green cloth.

court-martial; drum-head court-martial; *durbar*, divan; Areopagus; *rota*.

Adj. judicial &c. 965; appellate; curial.

967. Judge.—**N.** judge; justi-ce, -ciar, -ciary; chancellor; justice –, judge- of assize; recorder, common serjeant; puisne –, assistant –, county court- judge; conservator –, justice- of the peace, J.P.; court &c. (*tribunal*) 966; grand –, petty –, coroner's- jury; panel, juror, juryman; twelve men in a box; magistrate, police magistrate, stipendiary, the great unpaid, beak; his -worship, – honour, – lordship; deemster, moderator.

Lord -Chancellor, – Justice; Master of the Rolls, Vice-Chancellor; Lord Chief -Justice, – Baron; Mr. Justice; Baron, – of the Exchequer.

jurat, assessor; arbi-ter, -trator; umpire; refer-ee, -endary; revising barrister; domesman; censor &c. (*critic*) 480; official –, receiver.

archon, tribune, prætor, *ephor*, syndic, *podestà*, mullah, ulema, mufti, cadi, kadi; Rhadamanthus.

litigant &c. (*accusation*) 938.

V. adjudge &c. (*determine*) 480; try a -case, – prisoner.

Adj. judicial &c. 965.

Phr. 'a Daniel come to judgment.'

968. Lawyer.—**N.** lawyer, jurist, legist, civilian, pundit, publicist, jurisconsult, legal adviser, advocate; barrister, – at law; counsel, -lor; King's *or* Queen's counsel; K.C.; Q.C.; silk gown, leader; junior, – counsel; stuff gown, serjeant-at-law, bencher; tubman; judge &c. 967.

bar, legal profession, gentleman of the long robe; junior –, outer –, inner- bar; Inns of Court; equity draftsman, conveyancer, pleader, special pleader.

solicitor, attorney, proctor; notary, – public; scrivener, cursitor; writer, – to the signet; S.S.C.; limb of the law; pettifogger.

V. practise -at, – within- the bar; plead; call –, be called- -to, – within- the bar; take silk.

Adj. learned in the law; at the bar; forensic.

969. Lawsuit.—**N.** lawsuit, suit, action, cause, petition; litigation; dispute &c. 713.

citation, arraignment, prosecution, impeachment; accusation &c. 938; presentment, true bill, indictment.

apprehension, arrest; committal; imprisonment &c. (*restraint*) 751.

writ, summons, subpœna, *latitat, nisi prius*; *habeas corpus*.

pleadings; declaration, bill, claim; *procès-verbal*, bill of right, information, *corpus delicti*; affidavit, state of facts; answer, replication, plea, demurrer, rebutter, rejoinder; surre-butter, -joinder.

suitor, party to a suit; litigant &c. 938; libellant.

hearing, trial; verdict &c. (*judgment*) 480; appeal, – motion; writ of error; *certiorari*.

case, decision, precedent, ruling; decided case, reports.

V. go to –, appeal to the- law; bring to -justice, – trial, – the bar; put on trial, pull up; accuse &c. 938; prefer –, file- a claim &c. *n.*; take the law of, inform against.

serve with a writ, cite, apprehend, arraign, sue, prosecute, bring an action against, indict, impeach, attach, distrain, commit; arrest; summon, -s; give in charge &c. (*restrain*) 751.

empanel a jury, implead, join issue; close the pleadings; set down for hearing.

try, hear a cause; sit in judgment; adjudicate &c. 480.

Adj. litigious &c. (*quarrelsome*) 713; *qui tam*; *coram –, sub- judice.*

Adv. *pendente lite.*

Phr. *adhuc sub judice lis est.*

---

970. Acquittal. — N. acquit-tal, -ment; clearance, exculpation, exoneration; discharge &c. (*release*) 750; *quietus,* absolution, compurgation, reprieve, respite; pardon &c. (*forgiveness*) 918.

[Exemption from punishment] impunity, immunity.

V. acquit, exculpate, exonerate, clear; absolve, whitewash, assoil, discharge, release; liberate &c. 750.

reprieve, respite; pardon &c. (*forgive*) 918; let off, – scot free.

Adj. acquitted &c. *v.*; un-condemned, -punished, -chastised; recommended to mercy.

971. Condemnation.—N. condemnation, conviction, proscription, damnation; death warrant; penalty &c. 974.

attain-der, -ture, -tment.

V. condemn, convict, cast, bring home to, find guilty, damn, doom, sign the death warrant, sentence, pass sentence on, attaint, confiscate, proscribe, sequestrate; non-suit.

disapprove &c. 932; accuse &c. 938. stand condemned.

Adj. condem-, dam-natory; condemned &c. *v.*; non-suited &c. (*failure*) 732; self-convicted.

Phr. *mutato nomine de te fabula narratur.*

---

972. Punishment.—N. punishment, punition; chast-isement, -ening; correction, castigation.

discipline, infliction, trial; judgment; penalty &c. 974; retribution; thunderbolt, Nemesis; requital &c. (*reward*) 973; penology; retributive justice.

lash, scaffold &c. (*instrument of punishment*) 975; imprisonment &c. (*restraint*) 751; chain gang; transportation, banishment, expulsion, deportation, exile, involuntary exile, ostracism; penal servitude, hard labour; galleys &c. 975; beating &c. *v.*; flagellation, fustigation, gantlet, *strappado, estrapade, bastinado, argumentum baculinum,* stick law, rap on the knuckles, box on the ear; blow &c. (*impulse*) 276; stripe, cuff, kick, buffet, pummel; slap, – in the face; wipe, douse; *coup de grâce;* torture, rack; picket, -ing; *dragonnade;* capital punishment, extreme penalty; execution; hanging &c. *v.*; de-capitation, -collation; *garrot-te, -to;* electrocution, lethal chamber; crucifixion, impalement; martyrdom, *auto-da-fé; noyade; hara-kiri,* happy despatch.

V. punish; chast-ise, -en; castigate, correct, inflict punishment, administer correction, deal retributive justice.

visit upon, pay; pay –, serve- out; settle with, get even with, get one's own back; do for; make short work of, give a lesson to, strafe, serve one right, make an example of; have a rod in pickle for; give it one.

strike &c. 276; deal a blow to, administer the lash, smite; slap, – the face; smack, cuff, box the ears, spank, thwack, thump, beat, lay on, swinge, buffet; thresh, thrash, pummel, drub, leather, trounce, baste, belabour; lace, – one's jacket; dress, give a -dressing, – down; trim, warm, wipe, tund, cob, bang, strap, comb, lash, lick, larrup, whallop, whop, flog, scourge, whip, birch, cane, give the stick, switch, flagellate, horsewhip, *bastinado*, towel, rub down with an oaken towel, rib roast, dust one's jacket, fustigate, pitch into, lay about one, beat black and blue; beat to a -mummy, – jelly; give a black eye; hit on the head; sandbag.

tar and feather; pelt, stone, lapidate; mast-head, keelhaul.

execute; bring to the -block, – gallows; behead; de-capitate, -collate; guillotine; hang, turn off, gibbet, bowstring, hang, draw and quarter; shoot; decimate; burn; electrocute; break on the wheel, crucify; em-, im-pale; flay; lynch; put to death.

torture; put -on, – to- the rack; picket.

banish, exile; trans-, de-port; expel, ostracize; rusticate; drum out; dismiss, -bar, -bench; strike off the roll, unfrock; post.

suffer, – for, – punishment; be -flogged, – hanged &c.; come to the gallows, dance upon nothing, die in one's shoes; be rightly served.

Adj. punishing &c. *v.*; penal; puni-tory, -tive; inflictive, castigatory; punished &c. *v.*

Int. *à la lanterne!*

973. Reward.—**N.** reward, recompense, remuneration, prize, meed, guerdon, reguerdon; indemni-ty, -fication, price; quittance; compensation; reparation, *ersatz*, assythment, redress; retribution, reckoning, acknowledgment, requital, amends, sop; atonement; consideration, return, *quid pro quo*; salvage, perquisite; vail &c. (*donation*) 784; *douceur*, bribe, bait, baksheesh, tip; hush-, smart-money; blackmail; carcelage; *solatium*.

allowance, salary, stipend, wages; pay, -ment; emolument; tribute; batta, shot, scot; premium, fee, *honorarium*; hire.

crown &c. (*decoration of honour*) 877.

V. re-ward, -compense, -pay, -quite; re-, munerate; compensate; fee, tip, bribe; pay one's footing &c. (*pay*) 807; make amends, indemnify, atone; satisfy, acknowledge.

get for one's pains, reap the fruits of.

Adj. remunerat-ive, -ory; munerary, compensatory, retributive, reparatory.

974. Penalty.—**N.** penalty; retribution &c. (*punishment*) 972; pain, pains and penalties; *peine forte et dure*; penance &c. (*atonement*) 952; the devil to pay.

fine, mulct, amercement; forfeit, -ure; escheat, damages, deodand, sequestration, confiscation, *premunire*.

V. penalize, fine, mulct, amerce, sconce, confiscate; sequest-rate, -er; escheat; estreat, forfeit.

975. [Instrument of punishment.] **Scourge.**—**N.** scourge, rod, cane, stick; ra-, rat-tan; birch, – rod; rod in pickle; switch, ferule, cudgel, truncheon; rubber hose.

whip, lash, strap, thong, cowhide, knout; cat, – o'-nine-tails, *sjambok*, quirt; rope's end.

pillory, stocks, whipping-post; cuck-, duck-ing stool; brank; triangle, wooden horse, maiden, thumbscrew, boot, rack, wheel, iron heel; treadmill, crank, galleys.

scaffold; block, axe, *guillotine*; stake; cross; gallows, gibbet, Tyburn tree; drop, noose, rope, halter, bowstring; electric chair, lethal chamber.

house of correction &c. (*prison*) 752.

gaol-, jail-er; executioner; hang-, heads-man; Jack Ketch; lyncher.

Section V. RELIGIOUS AFFECTIONS

1°. Superhuman Beings and Regions

976. Deity.—N. Deity, Divinity; God-head, -ship; Omnipotence, Providence.

[Quality of being divine] divin-eness, -ity.

God, Lord, Jehovah, *Deus*; The -Almighty, – Supreme Being, – First Cause; *Ens Entium*; Author –, Creator- of all things; Author of our being; The -Infinite, – Eternal; The All-powerful, -wise, -merciful, -holy; The Omni-potent, -scient.

[Attributes and perfections] infinite -power, – wisdom, – goodness, – justice, – truth, – love, – mercy; omni-potence, -science, -presence; unity, immutability, holiness, glory, majesty, sovereignty, infinity, eternity.

The -Trinity, – Holy Trinity, – Trinity in Unity, – Triune God; Three in One and One in Three.

God the Father; The -Maker, – Creator, – Preserver.

[Functions] creation, preservation, divine government; The-ocracy, -archy; providence; ways –, dealings –, dispensations –, visitations- of Providence.

God the Son, Jesus, Christ; The -Messiah, – Anointed, – Saviour, – Redeemer, – Mediator, – Intercessor, – Advocate, – Judge; The Son of -God, – Man, – David; The Only Begotten; The Lamb of God, The Word; Em-, Im-manuel; The -King of Kings and Lord of Lords, – King of Glory, – Prince of Peace, – Good Shepherd, – Way, – Truth, – Life, – Bread of Life, – Light of the World; The -Lord our, – Sun of- Righteousness.

The -Incarnation, – Hypostatic Union, – Word made Flesh.

[Functions] salvation, redemption, atonement, propitiation, mediation, intercession, judgment.

God the Holy Ghost, The Holy Spirit, Paraclete; The -Comforter, – Consoler, – Spirit of Truth, – Dove.

[Functions] inspiration, unction, regeneration, sanctification, consolation.

eon, æon, special providence, *Deus ex machinâ*; *Avatar*.

V. create, uphold, preserve, govern &c.

atone, redeem, save, propitiate, mediate &c.

predestinate, elect, call, ordain, bless, justify, sanctify, glorify &c.

Adj. almighty, holy, hallowed, sacred, divine, heavenly, celestial; messianic; sacrosanct; all-powerful, -wise, -seeing, -knowing; omnipotent, omniscient; supreme.

super-human, -natural; ghostly, spiritual, hyperphysical, unearthly; the-istic, -ocratic, deistic; anointed.

Adv. *jure divino*, by divine right; *Deo volente*, D.V.

977. [Beneficent spirits.] **Angel.—N.** angel, archangel; heavenly host, choir invisible, host of heaven, sons of God; Michael, Gabriel &c.; seraph, -im; cherub, -im; ministering spirit, morn-

978. [Maleficent spirits.] **Satan.—N.** Satan, the Devil, Lucifer, Ahrimanes, Belial; Sammael, Zamiel, Beelzebub, the Prince of the Devils; Mephistopheles, his satanic majesty.*

* The slang expressions 'the -deuce, – dickens, – old Gentleman; old -Nick, – Scratch, – Horny, – Harry, – Gooseberry,' have not been inserted in the text.

ing star; saint, *Madonna*; Our Lady, the Blessed Virgin, the Virgin Mary.

Adj. angelic, seraphic, cherubic.

---

the tempter; the evil -one, – spirit; the -author of evil, – wicked one, – old Serpent; the Prince of -darkness, – this world, – the power of the air; the -foul, – arch- fiend; the devil incarnate; the -common enemy, – angel of the bottomless pit; Abaddon, Apollyon, Mammon.

fallen angels, unclean spirits, devils; the -rulers, – powers- of darkness; inhabitants of Pandemonium; demon &c. 980.

diabolism; devil-ism, -ship, -dom, -ry, -worship; *diablerie*; satanism, manicheism; the cloven foot; black magic &c. 992.

Adj. satanic, diabolic, devilish, infernal, hell-born.

*Heathen, Mythological and other fabulous Deities and Powers**

979. Jupiter.—N. god, -dess; heathen gods and goddesses; Pantheon; Jupiter, Jove, Zeus, Apollo, Mars, Mercury, Neptune, Vulcan, Bacchus, Pluto, Saturn, Cupid, Eros, Pan; Juno, Ceres, Proserpina, Dina, Minerva, Pallas, Athenae, Venus, Aphrodite, Vesta; The Fates &c. 601.

Allah, Brahma, Vishnu, Siva, Shiva, Krishna, Juggernaut, Buddha; Ra, Isis, Osiris; Belus, Bel, Baal, Asteroth &c.; Thor, Odin; Mumbo Jumbo; good –, tutelary- genius; demiurge, familiar, – spirit; Sibyl; fairy, fay; sylph, -id; Ariel, peri, nymph, nereid, dryad, oread, sea-maid, Banshee, Benshie, Ormuzd; Oberon, Titania, Mab, hamadryad, naiad, mermaid, kelpie, Ondine, nix, nixie, sprite; denizens of the air; pixy &c. (*bad spirit*) 980.

mythology; heathen –, fairy- mythology; Lemprière, folklore.

Adj. fairy-, sylph-like; sylphic.

---

980. Demon.—N. demon, -ry, -ism, -ology; evil genius, fiend, familiar, – spirit, devil; bad –, unclean- spirit; cacodemon, incubus, Frankenstein's monster, succubus and succuba, Titan, Shedim, Mephistopheles, Asmodeus, Moloch, Belial, Ahriman, fury, The Furies &c. 900; harpy; Friar Rush.

vampire, ghoul; af-, ef-freet; afrite; ogre, -ss; gnome, gin, djinn, imp, deev, *lamia*; bo-gie, -gle; nis, kobold, flibbertigibbet, fairy, brownie, pixy, elf, dwarf, urchin, Puck, Robin Goodfellow; lepre-, cluri-chaune; troll, dwerger, sprite, oaf, changeling, bad fairy, nixe, pigwidgeon, Will-o'-the-wisp; Erl King.

[Supernatural appearance] ghost, spectre, apparition, genie, spirit, shade, shadow, vision, phantom &c. 443; materialization (*spiritualism*) 992; hob-, goblin; wraith, spook, werwolf, boggart, banshee, *loup-garou*, *lemures*; evil eye.

nisse, necks; mer-man, -maid, -folk; siren, Lorelei; satyr, faun.

Adj. supernatural, weird, uncanny, unearthly, spectral; ghost-ly, -like; elf-in, -like; fiend-ish, -like; impish, demoniacal; haunted.

981. Heaven.—N. heaven; kingdom of -heaven, – God; heavenly kingdom; throne –, presence- of God; inheritance of the saints in light.

Paradise, Eden, abode of the blessed; Holy City, New Jerusalem; celestial bliss, glory.

[Mythological -heaven] Olympus; [– paradise] Elysium, Elysian fields, Arcadia, bowers of bliss, garden of the Hesperides, Islands of the Blessed;

982. Hell.—N. hell, bottomless pit, place of torment; habitation of fallen angels; Pandemonium, Abaddon, Domdaniel.

hell fire; everlasting -fire, – torment; lake of fire and brimstone; fire that is never quenched, worm that never dies.

purgatory, limbo, gehenna, abyss.

[Mythological hell] Tartarus, Hades, Avernus, Styx, Stygian creek, pit of Acheron, Cocytus, Phlegethon, Lethe;

* Only a selection of those best known to literature is included.

happy hunting-ground; third –, seventh- heaven; Valhalla (Scandinavian); Nirvana (Buddhist).

future state, eternity, eternal life, life after death, eternal home, resurrection, translation; resuscitation &c. 660; apotheosis, deification.

Adj. heavenly, celestial, supernal, unearthly, from on high, paradisiacal, beatific, elysian, Olympian, Arcadian.

infernal regions, *inferno*, shades below, realms of Pluto.

Pluto, Rhadamanthus, Erebus, Charon, Cerberus; Tophet.

Adj. hellish, infernal, stygian.

2°. Religious Doctrines

983. [Religious Knowledge.] **Theology.—N.** Theology (natural and revealed); Theo-gony, -sophy; Divinity; Hagio-logy, -graphy; Caucasian mystery; monotheism; religion; religious -persuasion, – sect, – denomination; cult; creed &c. (*belief*) 484; articles –, declaration –, profession –, confession- of faith.

theolog-ue, -ian; divine, schoolman, canonist, monotheist.

Adj. theological, religious; canonical; denominational; sectarian &c. 984.

983a. Orthodoxy.—N. orthodoxy; strictness, soundness, religious truth, true faith; truth &c. 494.

Christian-ity, -ism; Catholic-ism, -ity; 'the faith once delivered to the saints'; hyperorthodoxy &c. 984; iconoclasm.

the Holy –, the Orthodox- Church; Catholic –, Universal –, Apostolic –, Established- Church; temple of the Holy Ghost; Church –, body –, members –, disciples –, followers- of Christ; Christian, – community; true believer; canonist &c. (*theologian*) 983; Christendom, collective body of Christians, the Church Militant.

canons &c. (*belief*) 484; thirty-nine articles; Apostles' –, Nicene –, Athanasian- Creed; Church Catechism; textuary.

Adj. orthodox, sound, literal, strict, faithful, catholic, schismless, Christian, evangelical, scriptural, divine, monotheistic; true &c. 494.

984. Heterodoxy. [Sectarianism.]— **N.** heterodoxy; error &c. 495; false doctrine, heresy, schism; schismantic-ism, -alness; recusancy, backsliding, apostasy; atheism &c. (*irreligion*) 989.

bigotry &c. (*obstinacy*) 606; fanaticism, iconoclasm; hyperorthodoxy, precisianism, bibliolatry, hagiolatry, sabbatarianism, puritanism; idolatry &c. 991; superstition &c. (*credulity*) 486; dissent &c. 489.

sectar-ism, -ianism; nonconformity; secularism; syncretism, religious sects; the clash of creeds.

protestant-, advent-, Arian-, Erastian-, Calvin-, quaker-, method-, anabapt-, Pusey-, tractarian-, ritual-, Origen-, Sabellian-, Socinian-, De-, The-, mon-, material-, positiv-, latitudinarian-ism &c.

High –, Low –, Broad –, Free-Church; ultramontanism; monasticism; pap-ism, -istry; papacy; Anglican-, Catholic-, Roman-ism; popery, Scarlet Lady, Church of Rome, Greek Church; Christian Science, The Church of Christ Scientist.

pagan-, heathen-, ethic-ism; mythology; animism; poly-, di-, tri-, pan-theism; dualism; heathendom.

Juda-, Gentil-, Mahometan-, Islam-, Turc-, Brahmin-, Hindoo-, Buddh-, Lama-, Confucian-, Shinto-, Sabian-, Gnostic-, Soofee-, Hylothe-, Mormon-ism.

Theosophy; Spiritualism, Occultism.

heretic, antichrist; pagan, heathen; pai-, pay-nim; *giaour*; gentile; pan-, poly-theist; idolator; misbeliever, apostate, backslider.

bigot &c. (*obstinacy*) 606; fanatic, dervish, abdal, iconoclast.

latitudinarian, limitarian, Deist, Theist, Unitarian; positivist, materialist; agnostic, sceptic &c. 989.

schismatic; sectar-y, -ian, -ist; seceder, separatist, recusant, dissenter; non-conformist, -juror; Huguenot, Protestant; orthodox dissenter, Congregationalist, Independent; Episcopalian, Presbyterian; Lutheran, Calvinist, Quaker, Methodist, Wesleyan; Ana-, Baptist; Dunker; Mormon, Latter-day Saint, Irvingite, Sandemanian, Glassite, Erastian; Sub-, Supra-lapsarian; Gentoo, Antinomian, Swedenborgian, Adventist, Plymouth Brother; Theosophist &c.

Catholic, Roman Catholic, Romanist, papist, ultramontane; Old Catholic, tractarian, Anglican, Puseyite, ritualist; Puritan.

Jew, Hebrew, Rabbist; Mahometan, Mohammedan, Mussulman, Moslem, Islamite, Osmanli; Brahm-in, -an; Parsee, Sofi, Soofee; Buddhist; Zoroastrian, Magi, Gymnosophist, fire-worshipper, Sabian, Gnostic, Sadducee, Rosicrucian &c.

Adj. heterodox, heretical; un-orthodox, -scriptural, -canonical; antiscriptural, apocryphal; un-, anti-christian; schismatic, recusant, iconoclastic; sectarian; dis-senting, -sident; secular &c. (*lay*) 997.

pagan; heathen, -ish; ethnic, -al; gentile, painim; pan-, polytheistic; agnostic, sceptic.

Judaical, Mohammedan, Moslem, Brahminical, Buddhist &c. *n.* Romish, Protestant &c. *n.*

bigoted &c. (*prejudiced*) 481, (*obstinate*) 606; superstitious &c. (*credulous*) 486; fanatical; idolatrous &c. 991; visionary &c. (*imaginative*) 515.

985. Revelation.—N. revelation, inspiration, *afflatus.*

Word, – of God; Scripture; the -Scriptures, – Bible, – Book of Books; Holy -Writ, – Scriptures; inspired writings, Gospel.

Old Testament, Septuagint, Vulgate, Pentateuch; Octateuch; the -Law, – Jewish Law, – Prophets; major –, minor- Prophets; Hagio-grapha, -logy; Hierographa; Apocrypha.

New Testament; Gospels, Evangelists, Acts, Epistles, Apocalypse, Revelations.

Talmud; Mishna, Masorah.

prophet &c. (*seer*) 513; evangelist, apostle, disciple, saint; the –, the Apostolical- fathers; Holy Men of old, inspired -writers, – penmen.

Adj. scriptural, biblical, sacred, prophetic; evangel-ical, -istic; apostolic, -al; inspired, theopneustic, apocalyptic, ecclesiastical, canonical, textuary.

986. Pseudo-Revelation.*—N. the -Koran, – Alcoran; Ly-king, Shaster, Vedas, Zendavesta, Vedidad, Purana, Edda; Go-, Gau-tama; Book of Mormon.

[False prophets and religious founders] Buddha, Zoroaster, Zerdhusht, Confucius, Mahomet.

[Idols] golden calf &c. 991; Baal, Moloch, Dagon.

* See note on page 378.

3°. Religious Sentiments

987. Piety.—N. piety, religion, the-ism, faith; religiousness, holiness &c. *adj.*; saintship; religionism; sanctimony &c. (*assumed piety*) 988; reverence &c. (*respect*) 928; humility, veneration, de-votion; prostration &c. (*worship*) 990; grace, unction, edification; sancti-ty, -tude; consecration.

spiritual existence, odour of sanctity, beauty of holiness.

theopathy, beatification, adoption, regeneration, conversion, justification, sanctification, salvation, inspiration, bread of life; Body and Blood of Christ.

believer, convert, theist, Christian, devotee, pietist; the -good, – righteous, – just, – believing, – elect; Saint, *Madonna*.

the children of -God, – the kingdom, – light.

V. be -pious &c. *adj.*; have -faith &c. *n.*; believe, receive Christ; revere &c. 928; worship &c. 950; be -converted &c.

convert, edify, sanctify, hallow, keep holy, beatify, regenerate, inspire, con-secrate, enshrine.

Adj. pious, religious, devout, de-voted, reverent, godly, heavenly minded, humble; pure, – in heart; holy, spiritual, pietistic; saint-ly, -like; seraphic, sacred, solemn.

believing, faithful, Christian, Catho-lic.

elected, adopted, justified, sanctified, regenerated, inspired, consecrated, con-verted, unearthly, not of the earth.

---

988. Impiety.—N. impiety; sin &c. 945; irreverence; profan-eness &c. *adj.*, -ity, -ation; blasphemy, desecration, sacrilege; scoffing &c. *v.*

[Assumed piety] hypocrisy &c. (*false-hood*) 544; pietism, cant, pious fraud; lip-devotion, -service, -reverence; mis-devotion, formalism, austerity; sancti-mon-y, -iousness &c. *adj.*; pharisaism, precisianism; sabbat-ism, -arianism; *odium theologicum*, sacerdotalism; bigo-try &c. (*obstinacy*) 606, (*prejudice*) 481.

hardening, backsliding, declension, perversion, reprobation apostacy, re-cusancy.

sinner &c. 949; scoffer, blasphemer; sacrilegist; worldling; hypocrite &c. (*dissembler*) 548; Scribes and Pharisees; Tartufe, Maw-worm.

bigot; saint [ironically]; Pharisee, sabbatarian, formalist, methodist, puri-tan, pietist, precisian, religionist, de-votee, ranter, fanatic, wowser.

the -wicked, – evil, – unjust, – repro-bate; son of -men, – Belial, – the wicked one; children of darkness.

V. be -impious &c. *adj.*; profane, desecrate, blaspheme, revile, scoff; swear &c. (*malediction*) 908; commit sacrilege.

snuffle; turn up the whites of the eyes; idolize.

Adj. impious; irreligious &c. 989; desecrating &c. *v.*; profane, irreverent, sacrilegious, blasphemous.

un-hallowed, -sanctified, -regenerate; hardened, perverted, reprobate.

hypocritical &c. (*false*) 544; canting, pietistical, sanctimonious, unctuous, pharisaical, over-righteous, righteous over much.

bigoted, fanatical &c. 481 & 606; priest-ridden.

Adv. under the -mask, cloak, – pretence, – form, – guise- of religion.

989. Irreligion.—N. irreligion, indevotion; ungodliness &c. *adj.*; laxity, quietism, apathy, indifference, passivity.

scepticism, doubt; un-, dis-belief; incredul-ity, -ousness &c. *adj.*; want of -faith, – belief; pyrrhonism; doubt &c. 485; agnosticism. atheism, deism; hylotheism; materialism; positivism; nihilism. infidelity, freethinking, antichristianity, rationalism.

atheist, anti-christian, sceptic, unbeliever, deist, infidel, pyr-rhonist; *giaour*, heathen, alien, gentile, Nazarene; *esprit fort*, free-thinker, latitudinarian, rationalist; materialist, positivist, nihilist, agnostic.

V. be -irreligious &c. *adj*.; disbelieve, lack faith; doubt, question &c. 485.

dechristianize; serve Mammon, love darkness better than light.

Adj. irreligious; in-, un-devout; devout-, god-, grace-less; un-godly, -holy, -sanctified, -hallowed; atheistic, without God.

sceptical, free-thinking; un-believing, -converted; incredulous, faithless, lacking faith; deistical; un-, anti-christian.

worldly, mundane, earthly, carnal, unspiritual; worldly &c.-minded.

Adv. irreligiously &c. *adj*.

4°. Acts of Religion

990. Worship.—N. worship, adoration, devotion, aspiration, latria, homage, service, humiliation; kneeling, genuflexion, prostration.

prayer, invocation, supplication, rogation, intercession, orison, holy breathing; petition &c. (*request*) 765; collect, litany, Lord's prayer, paternoster, *Ave Maria*, rosary; bead-roll; latria, dulia, hyperdulia, vigils; revival; cult.

thanksgiving; giving -, returning- thanks; grace, praise, glorifica-tion, benediction, doxology, hosanna; h-, allelujah; *Te Deum, non nobis Domine, nunc dimittis*; pæan.

psalm, -ody; hymn, plainsong, chant, chaunt, response, anthem, motet; antiphon, -y.

oblation, sacrifice, incense, libation; burnt -, votive -, thank-offering; offertory, collection.

discipline; self-discipline, -examination, -denial; fasting.

divine service, office, duty; morning prayer; mass, matins, evensong, vespers, compline; holy day &c. (*rites*) 998.

worshipper, congregation, communicant, celebrant.

V. worship, lift up the heart, aspire; revere &c. 928; adore, do serv-ice, pay homage; humble oneself, kneel; bow -, bend- the knee; fall -down, - on one's knees; prostrate oneself, bow down and worship, recite the rosary.

pray, invoke, supplicate; put -, offer- up -prayers, - petitions; beseech &c. (*ask*) 765; say one's prayers, tell one's beads.

return -, give- thanks; say grace, bless, praise, laud, glorify, magnify, sing praises; give benediction, lead the choir, intone, chant, sing.

propitiate, offer sacrifice, fast, deny oneself; vow, offer vows, give alms.

work out one's salvation; go to church; attend -service, - mass; communicate &c. (*rite*) 998.

Adj. worshipping &c. *v*.; devout, devotional, reverent, pure, solemn; fervid &c. (*heartfelt*) 821.

Int. h-, allelujah! hosanna! glory be to God! O Lord! pray God that! God -grant, - bless, - save, - forbid! *sursum corda*.

991. Idolatry.—N. idol-atry, -ism; demon-ism, -olatry; idol -, demon -, devil -, fire- worship; zoolatry, fetishism, Mari-, Bibli-, ecclesi-, heli-olatry.

deification, apotheosis, canonization; hero worship.

sacrifices, hecatomb, holocaust; human sacrifices, immolation, mactation, infanticide, self-immolation, *suttee*.

idol, golden calf, graven image, fetish, *avatar*, Juggernaut, joss, *lares et penates*; Baal &c. 986.

idolater &c. *n.*

V. worship -idols, - pictures, - relics; put on a pedestal, bow down to, prostrate oneself before, make sacrifice to; deify, canonize, idolize.

Adj. idolatrous.

992. Sorcery.—N. sorcery; superstition; occult -art, - sciences; black -, magic; the black art, necromancy, theurgy, thaumaturgy; demon-ology, -omy, -ship; *diablerie*, bedevilment; witch-craft, -ery; glamour; fetis-hism, -ism; ghost dance; hoodoo, voodoo; Shamanism [Esquimaux], vampirism; conjuration; bewitchery, exorcism, enchantment, incantation, obsession, possession, mysticism, second sight, mesmerism, animal magnetism; od -, odylic- force; electro-biology, *clairvoyance*; spiritualism, spirit-rapping, table-turning; thought reading, telepathy, thought transference, automatic writing, *planchette*, ouija board; crystal gazing; spirit manifestation, materialization, astral body, ectoplasm &c.

divination &c. (*prediction*) 511; sortilege, ordeal, *sortes Virgilianæ*; hocus-pocus &c. (*deception*) 545; oracle &c. 513.

V. practice -sorcery &c. *n.*; cast a -horoscope, - nativity; conjure, exorcise, charm, enchant; be-witch, -devil; overlook, look on with the evil eye; entrance, mesmerize, magnetize; fascinate &c. (*influence*) 615; taboo; wave a wand; rub the -ring, - lamp; cast a spell; call up spirits, - from the vasty deep; raise spirits from the dead; raise -, lay- ghosts; command genii.

Adj. magic, -al; mystic, weird, cabalistic, talismanic, phylacteric, incantatory; charmed &c. *v.*

993. Spell.—N. spell, charm, incantation, exorcism, weird, cabala, exsufflation, cantrap, runes, abracadabra, hocus-pocus, open *sesame*, counter-charm, Ephesian letters, bell, book and candle, Mumbo-jumbo, evil-eye, fee-faw-fum.

talisman, amulet, periapt, telesm, phylactery, philtre, wish-bone, merry-thought, mascot, scarab, swastika; fetish; *agnus Dei*.

wand, caduceus, rod, divining rod, lamp of Aladdin, magic carpet, seven-league boots; magic ring; wishing -, Fortunatus's- cap.

994. Sorcerer.—N. sorcerer, magician; thaumat-, the-urgist; conjuror, necromancer, seer, wizard, witch; fairy &c. 980; *lamia*, hag, warlock, charmer, exorcist, voodoo, mage, diviner, dowser; cunning -, medicine- man, witch doctor; Shaman, figure-flinger, ecstatica, medium, *clairvoyant*, mesmerist, hypnotist; *deus ex machinâ*; astrologer; soothsayer &c. 513.

Katerfelto, Cagliostro, Merlin, Comus, Mesmer, Rosicrucian; Hecate, Circe, Lilith, siren, weird sisters; witch of Endor.

5°. RELIGIOUS INSTITUTIONS

995. Churchdom.—N. church, -dom; ministry, apostleship, priesthood, prelacy, hierarchy, church government, christendom, pale of the church.

clerical-, sacerdotal-, episcopalian-, ultramontan-ism; Theocracy; ecclesiolog-y, -ist; priestcraft, *odium theologicum.*

monach-ism, -y; monasticism, monkhood.

[Ecclesiastical offices and dignities] pontificate, primacy, arch-bishopric, archiepiscopacy; prelacy; bishop-ric, -dom; episcop-ate, -acy; see, diocese, deanery, stall; canon-ry, -icate; prebend, -aryship; benefice, incumbency, glebe, advowson, living, cure, – of souls; rector-ship; vicar-iate, -ship; pastor-ate, -ship; deacon-ry, -ship; -curacy; chaplain, -cy, -ship; cardinal-ate, -ship; abbacy, presbytery.

holy orders, ordination, institution, consecration, induction, reading in, preferment, translation, presentation.

popedom, papacy; the -Vatican, – apostolic see, – see of Rome; re-ligious sects &c. 984.

council &c. 696; conclave, college of cardinals, convocation, synod, consistory, chapter, vestry, presbytery; sanhedrim, *congé d'élire*; ecclesiastical courts, consistorial court, court of Arches.

V. call, ordain, induct, prefer, translate, consecrate, present, elect, bestow.

take -orders, – the veil, – vows.

Adj. ecclesi-astical, -ological; clerical, sacerdotal, priestly, prelatical, pastoral, ministerial, capitular, theocratic; hierarchical, archiepiscopal; episcopal, -ian; canonical; mon-astic, -achal; monkish; abbati-al, -cal; pontifical, papal, apostolic; ultramontane, priest-ridden.

---

996. Clergy.—N. clergy, clericals, ministry, priesthood, presbytery, the cloth, the pulpit.

clergyman, divine, ecclesiastic, churchman, priest, presbyter, hiero-phant, pastor, shepherd, minister, clerk in holy orders; father, – in Christ; *padre, abbé, curé*; patriarch; reverend; black coat; confessor; sky pilot.

dignitaries of the church; ecclesi-, hier-arch; eminence, reverence, elder, primate, metropolitan, archimandrite, archbishop, bishop, prelate, diocesan, suffragan, dean, subdean, archdeacon, prebendary, canon, rural dean, rector, parson, vicar, perpetual curate, residentiary, beneficiary, incumbent, chaplain, curate, – in charge; deacon, -ess; preacher; lay reader, lecturer; capitular; missionary, propagan-dist, Jesuit, revivalist, field preacher.

churchwarden, sidesman; clerk, precentor, choir; almoner, *suisse*, verger, beadle, sexton, sacristan; acol-yth, -othyst, -yte; thurifer; chorister, choir boy.

[Roman Catholic priesthood] Pope, *Papa*, Holy Father, pontiff, high priest, cardinal; ancient –, flamen; confessor, penitentiary; spiritual director.

cenobite, conventual, abbot, prior, monk, friar, lay brother, beadsman, mendicant, pilgrim, palmer; canon-regular, -secular; Jesuit, Franciscan, Friars minor, Minorites; Observant, Capuchin, Dominican, Carmelite; Augustinian; Gilbertine; Austin-, Black-, White-, Grey-, Crossed-, Crutched-Friars; Bonhomme, Carthusian, Benedictine, Cistercian, Trappist, Cluniac, Premonstratensian, Maturine; Templar. Hospitaller.

997. Laity.—N. laity, flock, fold, congregation, assembly, brethren, people.

temporality, secularization.

layman, civilian; parishioner, cate-chumen; secularist.

V. secularize.

Adj. secular, lay, laical, civil, tem-poral, profane.

---

abb-, prior-, canon-ess; mother superior; *religieuse*, nun, sister, *beguine*, novice, postulant.

[Under the Jewish dispensation] prophet, priest, high priest, Levite; Rabbi, -n; scribe.

[Mohammedan &c.] mullah, ulema, imauam, sheik; so-fi, -phi; mufti, hadji, muezzin, dervish; fa-kir, -quir; brahmin, gooroo, druid, bonze, santon, abdal, Lama, talapoin, caloyer &c.

V. take orders &c. 995.

Adj. the –, the very –, the Right- Reverend; ordained, in orders, called to the ministry.

998. Rite.—N. rite; ceremon-y, -ial; ordinance, observance, function, duty; form, -ulary; solemnity, sacrament; incantation &c. (*spell*) 993; service, psalmody &c. (*worship*) 990; liturgies.

ministration; preach-ing, -ment; predication, sermon, homily, exhortation, lecture, discourse, pastoral.

baptism, christening, chrism, immersion; baptismal regeneration; font; circumcision.

confirmation; imposition –, laying on- of hands; churching, purification, ordination &c. (*churchdom*) 995; excommunication.

Eucharist, Lord's supper, communion; the –, the holy- sacrament; celebration, high celebration; *missa cantata*; offertory; introit; consecration; con-, tran-substantiation; real presence; elements, bread and wine; mass; high –, low –, dry- mass.

matrimony &c. 903; burial &c. 363; visitation of the sick.

seven sacraments, impanation, extreme unction, last rites, *viaticum*, invocation of saints, canonization, transfiguration, auricular confession; fasting; maceration, flagellation, sackcloth and ashes; penance &c. (*atonement*) 952; absolution; telling of beads, reciting the rosary, processional; thurification, incense, holy water, aspersion.

relics, rosary, beads, reliquary, host, cross, rood, crucifix, pax, pix, pyx, *agnus Dei*, censer, thurible, patera, urceole; chalice, patten, Holy Grail, sangrail; seven-branch candle stick, monstrance, sacring bell.

ritual, rubric, canon, ordinal; liturgy, prayer-book, book of common prayer, pietas, euchology, litany, lectionary; missal, breviary, mass-book, bead-roll.

psalter; psalm –, hymn- book; hymn-al, -ology; psalmody.

ritual-, ceremonial-ism; sabbat-ism, -arianism; ritualist, sabbatarian.

holyday, feast, fast; Sabbath, Passover, Pentecost; Advent, Christmas, Noel, Epiphany, Lent, Shrove Tuesday, Ash Wednesday, Maundy Thursday; Passion –, Holy- week; Good Friday, Easter, Ascension Day, Whitsuntide; Trinity Sunday, Corpus Christi; All-Saints' –, – Souls'- Day; Candle-, Lam-, Martin-, Michael-mas; hogmanay; Rama-dan, -zan; Bairam &c. &c.

V. perform service, do duty, minister, officiate, baptize, dip, sprinkle; confirm. lay hands on; give –, administer –, take –, receive –. attend –, partake of- the -sacrament, – communion; communicate; celebrate mass; administer –, receive- extreme unction; anele, shrive, absolve, confess; do penance; genuflect; cross oneself, make the sign of the cross.

excommunicate, ban with bell, book and candle.

preach, sermonize, predicate, lecture.

Adj. ritual, -istic; ceremonial, liturgic; baptismal, eucharistical; paschal.

999. Canonicals.—N. canonicals, vestments; robe, gown, Geneva gown, frock, pallium, surplice, cassock, dalmatic, scapulary, cope. scarf, tunicle, chasuble, alb, *alba*, stole; fan-on, -nel; tonsure, cowl, hood; calo-te, -tte; bands; capouch, amice, orarium, ephod; apron, lawn sleeves, pontificals, pall; mitre, tiara, triple crown; shovel –, cardinal's- hat; biretta; crosier; pastoral staff; costume &c. 225.

1000. Temple.—N. place of worship; house of -God, – prayer.

temple, cathedral, minister, church, kirk, chapel, meeting-house, bethel, tabernacle, conventicle, *basilica*, fane, holy place, chantry, oratory.

synagogue; mosque; marabout; pantheon; pagoda; joss-house; dagobah, tope; kiosk.

parsonage, rectory, vicarage, manse, deanery, glebe, church house; Vatican; bishop's palace; Lambeth.

altar, shrine, sanctuary, Holy of Holies, *sanctum sanctorum*, sacr-arium, -isty; communion –, holy –, Lord's- table; table of the Lord; pyx; baptistery, font; piscina, stoup; aumbry; sedile; reredos; rood -loft, – screen; jube.

chancel, quire, choir, nave, aisle, transept, lady chapel, vestry, crypt, cloisters, porch; triforum, clerestory, churchyard, *golgotha*, calvary, Easter sepulchre; stall, pew, sitting; pulpit, ambo, lectern, reading-desk, confessional, prothesis, credence, baldachin, *baldacchino*; jesse, apse, belfry; chapter-house; presbytery.

monastery, priory, abbey, friary, convent, nunnery, cloister.

Adj. claustral, cloistered; monast-ic, -erial; conventual.

INDEX

INDEX

N.B.: The numbers refer to the headings under which the words or phrases occur. When the same word or phrase may be used in various senses, the several headings under which it, or its synonyms, will be found, according to those meanings, are indicated by the words printed in Italics. These words in Italics are not intended to explain the meaning of the word or phrase to which they are annexed, but only to assist in the required reference.

When the word given in the Index is itself the title or heading of a category, the number of reference is printed in blacker type, thus: **abode 189.**

---

come – 658
get – *public* 531
  recover 660
  go – *turn* 311
  going – *news* 532
  not know what
    one is – 699
  put –
    turn round 283
  round – 311
  send – one's busi-
    ness 756
  set – 676
  turn – *invert* 218
  what it is – 454
  what one is – 625
  – it and about it
    573
  – to 121
  – to be 152
above 206
  – all 33, 642
  – board
    manifest 525
    artless 703
    fair 939
  – comprehension
    519
  – ground 359
  – the mark 33
  – par 31, 648
  – praise 944
  – price 814
  – stairs 206
  – suspicion 946
  – water *safe* 664
above-mentioned
  preceding 62
  repeated 104
  prior 116
abracadabra 993
Abraham,
  sham – 544
abrasion
  paring 38
  filing 330, 331
abreast 216, 236
abreption 789
abri 666
  – tente d' – 233
abridge *lessen* 36
  shorten 201
  - *in writing* 572,
    596
abridgment
  compendium 596
abroach 673
abroad
  extraneous 57
  distant 196
  uncertain 475

get – *public* 531
abrogation 756
abrupt *sudden* 113
  violent 173
  steep 217
  unexpected 508
  style 579
abruption 44
abscess 655
abscissa 466
abscission
  retrenchment 38
  division 44
abscond
  escape 623
  not pay 808
absence 187
  – of choice 609a
  – of influence
    175a
  – of intellect 450a
  – of mind 458
  – of motive 615a
absentee 187
absinthe 298
absolute
  not relative 1
  great 31
  complete 52
  certain 474
  affirmative 535
  authoritative 737
  severe 739
  free 748
  unalienable 924
  make – 467, 480
  – interest 980
absolution 978
absolutism 506, 739
absolve
  liberate 750
  forgive 918
  exempt 927a
  shrive 952
  acquit 970
absonant 414, 477
absorb *combine* 48
  take in 296
  consume 677
  – the mind 457,
    458
  – the soul 824
  – ed in thought
    451
absorbing 630, 821,
  829
absquatulate 623
abstain 623
  disuse 678
  temperance 953
  – from action 681

– from voting 609a
abstainer 953, 958
abstemious 953
absterge 652
abstersive 662
abstinence [*see*
  abstain]
  total – 953, 955
abstract
  separate 44
  abridge 596
  take 789
  steal 791
  in the – *apart* 44
  alone 87
  – idea 453
  – oneself
    inattention 458
  – thought 451
  attention 457
abstracted
  inattentive 458
abstruse 519
absurdity
  impossible 471
  nonsense **497**
  ridiculous 853
abundant *great* 31,
  63
  enough 639
abundanti cautelâ,
  ex – 664
abuse *deceive* 545
  ill-treat 649
  misuse 679
  malediction 908
  threat 909
  upbraid 932
  violate 961
  – of language 563
  – of terms 523
abusive 895, 934
abut *near* 197 *touch*
  199, 215
abutment 717
aby *remain* 141
  endure 821, 826
abysmal *deep* 208
abyss *space* 180
  depth 208
  interval 198
  danger 667
  hell 982
A.C. 106
academic
  teaching 537, 542
  theory 514
academical
  style 578
academicals
  225 *robes*

academician 492
  Royal – 559
academy 542
acanthus 847
a capite ad calcem
  52
acariâtre 901
acarpous 169
acatalectic 597
acaudal 38
accede 488, 725, 762
accelerate
  early 132
  stimulate 173
  velocity 274
  hasten 684
accension 384
accent *sound* 402
  tone of voice 580
  rhythm 597
accentuate 642
accentuated 580
accept *assent* 488
  consent 762
  receive 785
  take 789
acceptable 646, 829
acceptance 771
acceptation 522
acception 522
access 286
  easy of – 705
  means of – 627
accessible 470, 705
accession
  adjunct 39
  increase 35
  addition 37
  - *to office* 737, 755
  consent 762
accessory
  extrinsic 6
  additive 37
  adjunct 39
  accompanying 88
  aid 707
  auxiliary 711
acciaccatura 413
accidence 567
accident *event* 151
  chance 156
  disaster 619
  misfortune 735
  fatal – 361
accidental
  extrinsic 6
  fortuitous 156
  undesigned 621
accidents,
  trust to the chap-
    ter of – 621

aery 317
Æsculapius 662
Æsop 846
æsthetic
  sensibility 375
  beauty 845
  taste 850
æstival 125
æternum servans
  sub pectore vul-
  nus 919
ætiology [see etiol-
  ogy]
afar 196
affable 879, 894
affair event 151
  topic 454
  business 625
  battle 720
  love 902, 903
  - of honour 720
affaires, charge d' –
  758
affaire de coeur 897
affect relate to 9
  tend to 176
  qualify 469
  feign 544
  touch 824
  desire 865
  love 897
affectation **855**
affected with
  feeling 821
  disease 655
affectibility 822
affecting 830
affection 821, 897
affections **820**
affettuoso 415
affiance 768, 858
affianced 897, 903
affiche 531
affidation 769
affidavit
  affirmation 535
  record 551
  lawsuit 969
affiliation
  relation 9
  kindred 11
  attribution 155
affine 11
affinitive 9
affinity 9, 17
  mate 905
affirmation **535**, 488
affix add 37
  sequel 39
  fasten 43
  letter 561

afflation 349
afflatus 349, 597,
  985
afflict 830
  - with illness 655
affliction pain 828
  infliction 830
  adversity 735
affluence
  sufficiency 639
  prosperity 734
  wealth 803
affluent river 348
afflux 286
afford supply 784
  wealth 803
  yield 810
  sell for 812
  - aid &c. 707
afforestation 371
affranchise
  make free of 748
  liberate 750
affray 720
affreet 980
affriction 331
affright 860
affront molest 830
  provocation 900
  insult 929
  - danger 861
affuse 337
afield 186
afire 382
afloat extant 1
  unstable 149
  going on 151
  ship 273
  navigation 267
  ocean 341
  news 532
  preparing 673
keep oneself – 734
set – publish 531
afoot on hand 625
  preparing 673
  astir 682
afore 116
aforementioned 116
aforesaid
  preceding 62
  repeated 104
  prior 116
aforethought 611
aforetime 116
afraid 860
  be – irresolute 605
  - to say uncertain
  475
afresh 104, 123
Afric heat 382

Afrikander 57
afrite 980
aft 235
after in order 63
  in time 117
  too late 135
  rear 235
  pursuit 622
  be – intention 620
  pursuit 622
  go – follow 281
  - all for all that 30
  qualification 469
  on the whole 476
  - time 133
after acceptance
  516
after-age 124
after-clap 509
after-crop 65, 168
after-dinner 117
after-glow 40, 65,
  420
after-growth 65
after-life 152
aftermath
  sequel 65
  fertile 168
  profit 775
aftermost 235
afternoon 126
  - farmer 683
after-part 65, 235
after-piece 599
after-taste 65, 390
after-thought
  thought 451
  memory 505
  change of mind
  607
after-time 121
afterwards 117
age 745
agacerie 615
again 90, 104
  - and again 136
  come – periodic 138
  fall off – 661
  live – 660
against
  counteraction 179
  anteposition 237
  provision 673
  voluntary opposi-
  tion 708
  chances – 473
  declaim – 932
  false witness – 934
  go – 708
  set – actively 898
  set one's face –

764, 932
stand up – resist
  719
raise &c. one's
  voice – 489
  - one's will 744
  - one's expecta-
  tion 508
  - the grain difficult
  704
  painful 830
  dislike 867
  - the stream 704
  - the time when
  510
  - one's will 744
  - one's wishes 603
agamist 904
agape open 260
  curious 455
  expectant 507
  wonder 870
Agapemone 827,
  897
agate 847
age time 106
  period 108
  long time 110
  era 114
  present time 118
  oldness 124
  advanced life **128**
  of – 131
from age to – 112
age quod agis! 682
agency
  physical **170**
  instrumentality
  631
  means 632
  employment 677
  voluntary action
  680
  direction 693
  commission 755
agenda 625, 626
agent physical 153
  intermediary 228
  voluntary **690**
  consignee 759
  - provocateur 615
agentship 755
ages: for – 110
  - ago 122
agglomerate 46, 72
agglutinate 46
aggrandize
  in degree 35
  in bulk 194
  honour 873
aggravate

increase 35
vehemence 173
exaggerate 549
render worse 659
distress 835
exasperate 900
aggravating 830
aggravation 835
aggregate 50, 72, 84
aggregation 46
aggression 716
aggressor 726
aggrieve 649, 830
aggroup 72
aghast
   disappointed 509
   fear 860
   wonder 870
agile 274, 682
agio 813
agiotage 794
agitate *move* 315
   inquire 461
   activity 682
   excite the feelings
   824
 – *a question* 476
agitation [*see* agitate]
   changeableness
   149
   energy 171
   motion **315**
   in – *preparing* 673
agitator *leader* 694
aglet 554
agley, gang – 732
aglow 382, 420
agnate 11
agnition 762
agnomen 564
agnostic 487
agnosticism 984,
   989
agnus Dei 993, 998
ago 122
   not long – 123
agog *expectant* 507
   desire 865
   wonder 870
agoing 682
   set – 707
agonism 720
agonizing 824, 830
agony 378, 828
 – *of death* 360
 – *of excitement*
   825
agrarian 371
agree *accord* 23
   concur 178

assent 488
concord 714
consent 762
compact 769
compromise 774
 – in opinion 488
 – with *salubrity*
   656
agreeable
   comfortable 82
   physically 377
   mentally 829
agreeably to 82
agreement 23 [*see*
   agree]
   compact 769
agrestic 371
agriculture 371
agronomy 371
aground *fixed* 150
   in difficulty 704
   failure 732
ague-fit 860
aguets, aux –
   expectation 507
   ambush 530
aguish *cold* 383
ah me! 839
aha! *rejoicing* 838
ahead 234, 280
   go – *progression*
   282
   shoot – *transcur-
   sion* 303
   activity 682
   rock – 665, 667
Ahrimanes 987, 980
aid 707, 906
   by the – of 631,
   632
aide-de-camp 711,
   745
aidless 160
aigrette 847
aiguille 253
aiguillette 747, 847
aigulet 847
ail 655, 828
aileron 267, 273
ailment 655
aim 278, 620, 675
 – a blow at 716
aimable 894
   faire l' – 897
aimer éperdument
   897
aimless *without
   motive* 615a
   chance 621
air *unsubstantial* 4
   broach 66

lightness 320
gas 334
atmospheric **338**
wind 349
tune 415
appearance 448
refresh 689
demeanour 692
fashionable 852
beat the – 645
fill the – 404
fine – *salubrity* 656
fish in the – 645
fowls of the – 366
in the – 527
rend the – 404
take – 531
air-balloon 273
air base 728
air-commodore 745
aircraft 273, 726
air-drawn 515
airdrome 273
air-force 726
air-gun 727
airing 266
air-mail 273
airman 269
airmanship 698
air-marshal 745
air-passage 351
air-pipe 351
airport 273, 292,
   728
air-pump 349
air-raid 716
airs *affectation* 855
   pride 878
   vanity 880
   arrogance 885
air-shaft 351
air service 267
airship 273, 726
air-tight 261
airways 267
airworthy 273, 664
airy [*see* air]
   windy 349
   unimportant 643
   gay 836
 – *hopes* 858, 859
   give to – nothing
   a local habita-
   tion &c. 515
aisle *passage* 260
   way 627
   in a church 1000
ait 346
ajar *open* 260
   discordant 713
ajee 217

ajutage 260, **350**
akimbo *angular* 244
   stand – 715
akin *related* 9
   consanguineous 11
   similar 17
al fresco 220
alabaster *white* 430
alack! 839
alacrity *willing* 602
   active 682
   cheerful 836
Aladdin's lamp 993
alar 267
alarm *warning* 668
   notice of danger
   669
   fear 860
   cause for – 665
   give an – *indicate*
   550
alarmist 862
alarum 114, 550, 669
alas! 839
alate 267
alb 999
albeit 30
albert
   chain 847
albification 430
albinescence 430
albinism 430
albino 443
album 593, 596
albumen
   semi-liquid 352
   protein 357
Alcaic 597
alcaid 745
alcalde 745
alcazar 189
alchemy 144
alcohol 995
Alcoran 986
alcove 191, 252
Aldebaran 423
alderman 745
ale 298
alea, jacta est – 601
aleatory 665
Alecto 173
alectromancy 511
alehouse 189
   go to the – 959
alembic
   conversion 144
   vessel 191
   furnace 386
   laboratory 691
alentours 197
alert *watchful* 457,

459
active 682
alerte 669
aleuromancy 511
Alexandrine
  ornate style 577
  verse 597
alexandrite 848
alexipharmic 662
alexiteric 662
algebra 85
algid 383
algology 369
algorithm 85
alguazil 965
alias
  otherwise 18
  pseudonym 565
alibi 187
alien *irrelevant* 10
  foreign 57
  transfer 783
  gentile 989
alienable 783
alienate
  transfer 783
  estrange 44, 889
  set against 898
alienation
  mental - 503
alieni appetens
  grasping 865
  envious 921
  selfish 943
alienism 54
align 278
alight *stop* 265
  arrive 292
  descend 306
  on fire 382
alike 17
  share and share -
  778
aliment *food* 298
alimentary 662
  - canal 350
alimentation
  aid 707
alimony
  property 780
  provision 803
  income 810
aliquot 51, 84
aliter visum, diis -
  601
alive
  living 359
  intelligent 498
  active 682
  cheerful 836
  be - with 102

keep - *continue*
143
keep the memory
  - 505
look - 684
- to *attention* 457
  cognizant 490
  informed 527
  able 698
  sensible 822
alkahest 335
all *whole* 50
  complete 52
  generality 78
  - absorbing 642
in - ages 112
- aboard 495
- agog 865
- in all 50
- along 106
- along of 154
- but 32
- colours 440
- considered 451,
  480
- day long 110
- devouring 190
in - directions 278
- engrossing 190
at - events *compensation* 30
  qualification 469
  true 494
  resolve 604
- fours *easy* 705
  cards 840
- in good time 152
- hail! *welcome* 292
  honour to 873
  celebration 883
  courtesy 894
- hands *everybody*
  78
on - hands 488
- of a dither 824
- of a heap 72
- knowing 976
- manner of *difference* 15
  multiform 81
with - one's might
  686
- at once 113
- one 27, 866
- out 52
- over *end* 67
  universal 78
  destruction 162
  space 180
at - points 52
- in one's power

686
- powerful
  mighty 159
  God 976
in - quarters 180
with - respect 928
in - respects 52,
  494
- right! 922
- Saints' day 998
- searching 461
- seeing 976
on - sides 227
- sorts *diverse* 16a
  mixed 41
  multiform 81
- talk 4
- things to all
  men 894
- the time 106
at - times 136
- together 50
- ways 243, 279
- wise 976
- the world and
  his wife 78
of - work
  useful 644
  maid - 746
Allah 979
allay
  moderate 174
  pacify 723
  relieve 834
- excitability 826
allective 615
allege *evidence* 467
  assert 535
  plea 617
allegiance 743, 926
allegory 464, 521,
  594
allegro *music* 415
  cheerful 836
allelujah 990
allemande 840
all-embracing 76
alleviate 174, 834
alley *court* 189
  passage 26
  way 627
alliance *relation* 9
  kindred 11
  physical co-operation 178
  voluntary co-operation 709
  party 712
  union 714
allied to *like* 17
alligation 43

allign 278
alliteration
  similarity 17
  style in writing
  577
  poetry 597
allocation 60, 786
allocution **586**
allodium *free* 748
  property 780
allopathy 662
alloquy 586
allot *arrange* 60
  distribute 786
  due 924
allow *assent* 488
  admit 529
  permit 760
  consent 762
  give 784
- to have one's
  own way 740
allowable 760, 924
allowance
  qualification 469
  gift 784
  allotment 786
  discount 813
  salary 973
  with grains of -
  485
  make - for *forgive*
  918
  vindicate 937
alloy *mixture* 41
  combination 48
  debase 659
allude *hint* 514
  mean 516
  refer to 521
  latent 526
  inform 527
allure *move* 615
  create desire 865
alluring 829
allusive
  relative 9
alluvial *level* 213
  land 342
  plain 344
alluvium
  deposit 40
  land 342
  soil 653
ally *combine* 48
  auxiliary 711
  friend 891
alma mater 542
almanac
  list 86
  chronometry 114

moral 828
angular 244
– velocity 264
angularity **244**
angusta domi, res
– 804
angustation 203
anhelation 688
anhydrate 340
anhydrous 340
aniline dyes 437
anility 128, 499
animadvert
consider 451
attend to 457
reprehend 932
animal **366**
female – 374
– cries 412
– economy 359
– gratification 377
– life 364
– physiology 368
– spirits 836
– and vegetable
kingdom 357
animalcule 193, 366
animalism
sensuality 954
animality **364**
animate
induce 615
excite 824
enliven 836
animation
life 359
animality 364
activity 682
vivacity 836
suspended – 823
animism 984
animo, ex – 602
quo – 620
animosity
dislike 867
enmity 889
hatred 898
anger 900
animus
willingness 602
intention 620
desire 865
ankle 244
– deep 208, 209
anklet 847
ankylosis 150
annalist 114, 553
annals
chronology 114
record 551
account 594

anneal 673
annex
addition 37
adjunct 39
junction 43
acquire 775
Annie Oakley 815
annihilate 2, 162
anniversary 138
anno 106
Anno Domini
era 106
old age 124
annotation 522, 550
annotator 524
scholar 492
interpreter 524
editor 595
annotto 434
announce
predict 511
inform 527
publish 531
assert 535
announcer 527
annoy
molest 649, 907
disquiet 830
annoyance 828
source of – 830
annual *periodic* 138
plant 367
book 593
annuity 810
annul 162, 750
annular 247
annunciate 527
annus magnus 108
anodyne
lenitive 174
remedial 662
relief 834
anoint *coat* 223
lubricate 332
oil 355
anointed
deity 976
king 745
anomaly 59, 83
disorder 59
irregularity 83
anon 132
anonymous 565
anopsia 442
anorexy 866
another
different 15
repetition 104
– story 468, 526
go upon – tack 607
– time 119

answer
to an inquiry **462**
confute 479
solution 522
succeed 731
pecuniary profit
775
pleadings 969
require an – 461
– for *deputy* 759
promise 768
go bail 806
I'll – for it 535
– the helm 745
– the purpose 731
– to *correspond* 9
– one's turn 644
answerable
agreement 23
liable 177
bail 806
duty 926
censurable 932
ant 690
Antæus 159, 192
antagonism
difference 14
physical 179
voluntary 708
enmity 889
antagonist 710, 891
antagonistic 24
antarctic 237
antecedence 62, 116
antecedent 64
antechamber 191
ante Christum 106
antedate 115
antediluvian 124
antelope 274
antemundane 124
antenna 379
anteposition 62
anterior
in order 62
in time 116
in place 234
– to reason 477
anteroom 191
antevert 706
anthem 990
anthemion 847
anthology
book 533
collection 596
poem 597
anthracite 388
anthropoid 372
anthropology
zoology 368
mankind 372

anthropomancy 511
anthropophagi 913
anthroposcopy 511
anthroposophy 372
antic 840
anti-aircraft gun
564, 727
antichambre,
faire – 133
antichristian 984,
989
antichronism 115
anticipate
anachronism 115
priority 116
future 121
early 132
expect 507
foresee 510
prepare 673
hope 858
in – 116
anticlimax
decrease 36
bathos 497, 853
anticlinal 217
anticyclone 265
antidote 662
antigropelos 225
antilogarithm 84
antilogy 477
antimony 663
Antinomian 984
antinomy 964
Antinous 845
antiparallel 217
antipathy 867, 898
antiphon *music* 415
answer 462
worship 990
antiphrasis 563
antipodes
difference 14
distance 196
contraposition
237
antipoison 660
antiquary
past times 122
scholar 492
historian 553
antiquas vias,
stare super –
613, 670
antiquated 128
antique 124
antiquity 122
antiscriptural 984
antiseptic 652, 662
antisocial 911
antistrophe 597

antithesis
  contrast 14
  difference 15
  opposite 237
  style 574, 577
antitoxin 662
antitype 22
antler 253
antonomasia
  metaphor 521
  nomenclature 564
antonym 14
antrum 252
anvil *support* 215
  on the –
  intended 620
  in hand 625
  preparing 673
anxiety *pain* 828
  fear 860
  desire 865
anxious expectation
  507
any *some* 25
  part 51
  no choice 609a
  at – *price* 604a
  at – *rate*
  certain 474
  true 494
  at all hazards 604
anybody 78
anyhow 460, 627
anything one
  knows, for – 491
aorist 109, 119
aorta 350
apace *early* 132
  swift 274
apache 913
apart 44, 87
  set – 636
  wide – 196
apartment 191
  –s 189
  –s to let
  imbecile 499
apathetic 275
apathy
  indifference 465
  insensibility 823
  irreligion 989
ape *imitate* 19
Apelles 559
aperçu 596
aperture 260
apex 210
aphasia 583
aphelion 196
aphonic 403
aphony 581

aphorism 496
aphrodite 845, 979
apiary 370
apiculture 370
Apicius 957
apiece 79
apish 19, 499
aplanatic 429
aplomb
  stability 150
  self-possession
  498
  resolution 604
Apocalypse 985
Apocrypha 985
apocryphal
  uncertain 475
  erroneous 495
  heterodox 984
apodictic 478
apodosis 67
apogee 210
apograph 21
Apollo *sun* 318
  music 416
  luminary 423
  beauty 845
  god 979
  magnus – 500, 695
Apollyon 978
apologue
  metaphor 521
  teaching 537
  description 594
apology *excuse* 617
  vindication 937
  penitence 950
  atonement 952
apophthegm 496
apophysis 250
apoplexy 158, 655
aporetic 487
aposiopesis 585
apostasy
  recantation 607
  dishonour 940
  heterodoxy 984
apostate
  convert 144
  turncoat 607
  impiety 988
apostle *teacher* 540
  disciple 541
  inspired 985
  –'s creed 983a
apostolic 985
  – church 983a
  – see 995
apostrophe
  address 586
  soliloquy 589

  appeal 765
apothecary 662
  –'s weight 319
apothegm 496
apotheosis
  resuscitation 163
  canonization 873
  heaven 981
  hero worship 991
apozem 335, 384
appal 830, 860
appanage
  property 780
  gift 784
apparatus 633
apparel 225
apparent
  visible 446
  appearing 448
  probable 472
  manifest 525
  heir – 779
apparition
  fallacy of vision
  443
  spirit 980
apparitor 534
appeach 938
appeal 586, 765
  court of – 966
  – to arms 722
  – motion 969
  – from Philip
  drunk to Philip
  sober 658
  – to *call to witness*
  467
  – to for (*claim*) 924
appear 446, 525
  – for 759
  – in print 591
appearance 448
  make one's – 292
  to all – 448
  probable 472
appearances
  keep up – 852
appease 174
appellant 924, 938
appellate 966
appellation 564
append *add* 37
  sequence 63
  hang 214
appendage 39
appendectomy 662
appendix
  adjunct 39
  sequel 65
  end 67
  book 593

appertain
  related to 9
  component 56
  belong 777
  property 780
appetite 865
  tickle the –
  savoury 394
appetizing 865
  exciting 824
applaud 931
apple – of discord
  713
  golden –
  allurement 615
  – of one's eye *good*
  648
  love 897
  favorite 899
  – off another tree
  15
  how we –s swim!
  880
apple-green 435
apple-pie order 58
appliance *use* 677
  –s *means* 632
  machinery 633
applicable *relevant*
  23
  useful 644
  expedient 646
applicability 9
applicant 767
application *study*
  457
  metaphor 521
  use 677
  request 765
apply, *use* 677
  – a match 384
  – the match to **a**
  train 66
  – the mind 457
  – a remedy 662
appoggiatura 413
appointment
  employment 625
  order 741
  charge 755
  assignment 786
  interview 892
appointments
  gear 633
apportion *arrange*
  60
  disperse 73
  allot 786
apportionment **786**
appositeness 9
apposition

chapter 593
review 595
goods 798
articled clerk 541
articles
 thirty-nine – 983*a*
 – of agreement
  770
 – of faith 484, 983
articulate 366
articulation
 junction 43
 speech 580
articulo, in –
 transient 111
 dying 360
artifice 626, 702
artificer 690
artificial
 fictitious 545
 cunning 702
 affected 855
 – *language* 579
artillery
 explosion 404
 arms 727
artilleryman 726
artisan 690
artist *painter* &c.
 559
 contriver 626
 agent 690
artiste *music* 416
 drama 599
artistic *skilful* 698
 beautiful 845
 taste 850
 – *language* 578
artlessness **703**
aruspex 513
aruspicy 511
arundo, hæret
 lateri lethalis –
  828
as *motive* 615
 – broad as long 27
 – can be 52
 – good as 27
 – if *similar* 17
 suppose 514
 – little as may be
  32
 – it may be
 circumstance 8
 event 151
 chance 156
 – much again 90
 – soon as 120
 – they say 496, 532
 – things are 7
 – things go 151,

613
– to 9
– usual 82
– it were 17, 521
– you were 141,
 283
– well as 37
– the world wags
 151
ascend *be great* 31
 increase 35
 rise 305
 improve 658
ascendancy
 power 157
 influence 175
 success 731
ascendant
 lord of the – 745
 in the –
 influence 175
 important 642
 success 731
 authority 737
 repute 873
 one's star in the –
 prosperity 734
ascension
 [see ascend]
 calefaction 384
 – Day 998
ascent
 [see ascend]
 gradient 217
 rise **305**
 glory 873
ascertain *fix* 150
 determine 480
ascertained 474,
 490
ascertainment 480*a*
asceticism **955**
ascititious
 intrinsic 6
 additional 37
 supplementary 52
ascribe 155
aseptic 652
ash 384
 – coloured 432
 – blond 430
ashen 429
Ash Wednesday
 998
ashamed 879
ashes *corpse* 362
 dirt 653
 lay in – 162
 pale as – 429, 860
 rise from one's –
  660

ashore 342
 go – *arrive* 292
ashy 429
Asian mystery 533
aside *laterally* 236
 whisper 405
 private 528
 say – 589
 set &c. – *displace*
  185
 neglect 460
 negative 536
 reject 610
 disuse 678
 abrogate 756
 discard 782
 step – 279
asinine *ass* 271
 fool 499
ask *inquire* 461
 request 765
 for sale 794
 price 812
 – *leave* 760
askance 217
 eye – *fear* 860
 look – *vision* 441,
  443
 dissent 489
 dislike 867
 disapproval 932
askari 726
asked in church 903
askew 217, 243
aslant 217
asleep 683
aslope 217
Asmodeus 980
asomatous 317
asp *animal* 366
 evil-doer 913
Aspasia 962
aspect *feature* 5
 state 7
 situation 183
 appearance 448
aspen leaf
 shake like an –
  315, 860
asperity
 roughness 256
 discourtesy 895
 anger 900
 irascibility 901
asperse 934
aspersion
 malediction 908
 rite 998
asphalte
 smooth 255
 resin 356*a*

 material 635
asphodel 845
aspic 352
asphyxia 360
asphyxiate 361
aspirant 767, 865
aspirate 580
aspirator 349
aspire *rise* 305
 hope 858
 desire 865
 worship 990
aspirin 834
asportation 270
asquint 217
ass *beast of burden*
  271
 fool 501
 make an – of
 delude 545
 – between two
  bundles of
  hay 605
 –'s bridge 519
 – in lion's skin
 cheat 548
 bungler 701
assafœtida 401
assagai 727
assail 716, 830
assailant 710, 726
assassin, –ate 361
assault 716, 961
 take by – 789
assay 463
asseguay 727
assemblage **72**
assembly
 council 696
 society 892
 religious 997
assembly hall 588
assembly room 189
assent *belief* 484
 agree **488**
 willing 602
 consent 762
 content 831
assert 535, 924
assess *measure* 466
 determine 480
 tax 812
assessor
 judge 967
assets 780, 800
asseverate 535
assiduity 110
assiduous 682
assign
 commission 755
 transfer 270, 783

autoptical 446, 535
autotype 558
autumn 126
auxiliary **711**
   additional 34
   helpful 707
   – forces 726
avail *benefit* 618
   useful 644
   succeed 731
   of no – 645
   – oneself of 677
avalanche *fall* 306
   snow 383
   redundance 641
avaler les couleu-
   vres 725, 886
avant-courier 64,
   673
avant-propos 64
avarice 819
avast! *stop* 142, 265
   desist 624
   forbid 761
avatar *change* 140
   deity 976
   idol 991
avaunt! 297, 449
ave! *honour* 873
   courtesy 894
Ave maria 990
avenge 919
avenue
   plantation 371
   way 627
aver 535
average *mean* 29,
   628
   médiocre 651
   – circumstances
   736
   take an – 466
Averni, facilis de-
   scensus – 217,
   665
Avernus 982
averruncate 297,
   301
aversion *unwilling-*
   ness 603
   dislike 867
   hate 898
avert 706
   – the eyes 442
aviary 370
aviation 267
aviator 269
avidity *avarice* 819
   desire 865
airette 273
avile 932, 934

avion 273
aviso 532
avocation 625
avoidance **623**
avoidless 474, 601
avoirdupois 319
avolation 623, 671
avouch 535, 768
avow *assent* 488
   disclose 529
   assert 535
avulsion 44, 301
avuncular 11
await *future* 121
   be kept waiting
   133
   impend 152
   expect 507
awake *attentive* 457
   careful 459
   intelligent 498
   active 682
   – to life immortal
   360
awaken *inform* 527
   excite 824
   – the attention 457
   – the memory 505
award *adjudge* 480
   give 784
aware 490
away 187, 196
   break – 623
   fly – 293
   move – 287
   take – from 789
   get &c. – 671
   throw &c. –
   eject 297
   reject 610
   waste 638
   relinquish 782
   – from *unrelated* 10
   – with! 930, 932
   do – with *undo* 681
   abrogate 756
awe *fear* 860
   wonder 870
   respect 928
aweless *fearless* 861
   insolent 885
   disrespectful 329
awful 31, 860
   – silence 403
awhile 111
awkward
   inelegant 579
   inexpedient 647
   unskilful 699
   difficult 704
   painful 830

   ugly 846
   vulgar 851
   ridiculous 853
   – squad 701
awl 262
awn 253
awning 223, 424
awry *oblique* 217
   distorted 243
   evil 619
axe *edge tool* 253
   impulse 276
   weapon 727
   for beheading 975
   have an – to grind
   702
Axinomancy 511
axiom 496
axiomatic 474
axis *support* 215
   centre 222
   rotation 312
axle 312
   wheel and – 633
axle load 466
axletree 215
ay 488
ayah 746, 753
aye *ever* 112
   yes 488
azimuth
   horizontal 213
   direction 278
   measurement 466
   – circle 212
azoic 358
azote 663
azotic 657
azure 438
azygous *single* 87

B

Baal 979, 986
Babbittry 851
babble *rivulet* 348
   faint sound 405
   unmeaning 517
   talk 584, 588
babbler 501
babbling
   foolish 499
babe 129
   innocent as the –
   unborn 946
Babel *confusion* 59
   discord 414
   tongues 560
   jargon 563
   loquacity 584

baboon 846
baby *infant* 129
   fool 501
   – linen 225
babyhood 127
babyish 499
baccarat 840
bacchanals 959
Bacchus 979
   drink 959
bachelor 904
   – of arts 492
   – girl 374
bacillus 193
back *rear* 235
   shoulder 250
   aid 707
   behind one's –
   latent 526
   hidden 528
   come – 292
   give – 790
   fall – *relapse* 661
   go – 283
   go – from *retract*
   773
   have at one's – 215
   hold – *avoid* 623
   keep – *reserve* 636
   look – 505
   on one's – *impo-*
   tent 158
   horizontal 213
   failure 732
   pat on the –
   incite 615
   encourage 861
   approve 931
   pay – *retaliate* 718
   put – *deteriorate*
   659
   restore 660
   send – 764
   take – again 790
   carry one's
   thoughts – 505
   some time – 122
   spring – 277
   trace – 505
   turn – 283
   turn one's – 283
   turn one's – upon
   repel 289
   inattention 458
   avoid 623
   oppose 508
   seclusion 893
   discourtesy 895
   disrespect 929
   contempt 930
   set one's – against

the wall 604
– to back 235
– down 283
– one's note 806
– out *retire* 283
change sides 607
relinquish 624
– pedal 273
– up *support* 215
influence 615
aid 707
put one's – up
anger 900
set one's – up
pride 878
backbite 932, 934
backbiter 936
backbone
intrinsic 5
energy 171
frame 215
centre 222
resolution 604
persevere 604*a*
soul 820
game to the – 604
back door 627
back down 607
backer 711
back-fire 406
back friend 891
backgammon 840
background
distance 196
rear 235
in the –
latent 526
ignoble 874
keep in the –
hide 528
modest 881
seclusion 893
put one in the –
874
throw into the –
460
backsheesh 784,
973
backside 235
backslider 607
backsliding
regression 283
tergiversation 607
relapse 661
vice 945
heterodox 984
impiety 988
backstairs
ambush 530
way 627
– *influence* 702

backward
tardy 133
regression 283
unwilling 603
deteriorate 659
backwardation 813
backwards 283
bend – 325
– and forwards
interchange 148
oscillation 314
backwater 275, 283
in a – 893
backwoodsman
inhabitant 188
agriculture 371
bacon
butter upon – 641
save one's – 664,
671
Baconian method
461
bacteria 193
bactericide 660
**baculinum, argu-
mentum –**
compel 744
lawless 964
punish 972
bad 649
unclean 653
wrong 923
– blood 898, 907
go – 653, 659
– business 859
– case 477
– chance 473
put a – construc-
tion on 523
– debt 806
– fairy 980
– faith 940
– grace 895
– habit 613
– hand 701
– humour
discontent 832
dejection 837
anger 900
sullen 901*a*
not a – idea 498
– intent 907
– job *evil* 619
botch 699
hopeless 859
– joke 851
– language 908
view in a – light
934
– luck &c. 735

– man **949**
– money 800
– name 932, 934
in – odour 889
take in – part 832,
900
– repute 874
– smell 401
– spirit 980
– spirits 837
– taste 579, 851
– temper 900, 901,
901*a*
on – terms 713,
889
– time of it 828
– turn 619, 907
in a – way
disease 655
worse 659
danger 665
adversity 735
– woman 949
from – to worse
aggravation 835
badaud 501
badge 550
– of authority 747
– of infamy 874
– of slavery 746
badger 830
– dog 366
badinage 842, 856
badly off
adversity 735
poor 804
badminton 840
badness **649**
Baedeker 266
baffle *hinder* 706
defeat 731
– description
unconformable 83
wonder 870
baffling
puzzling 519
bag *put up* 184
receptacle 191
protrude 250
acquire 775
take 789
steal 791
– and baggage 780
bagatelle
trivial 643
pastime 840
baggage 270
minx 129
materials 635
property 780

hussy 962
baggy 47
bagman 758
bagnio 961
bagpipes 417
bah! 930
bail 771
go – 806
leg – 623
bailie 965
bailiff
director 694
servant 746
factor 758
officer 965
bailiwick
region 181
jurisdiction 965
Bairam
holiday 840
rite 998
bairn 129
bait *attraction* 288
food 298
trap 545
lure 615
refresh 689
attack 716
bribe 784
harass 830
swallow the – 547
bake 384
bakehouse 386
baker 637
baker's dozen 98
baking heat 382
bal 840
balais 847
balaclava helmet
225
balance *equal* 27
mean 29
compensate 30
remainder 40
numeration 85
weigh 319
compare 464
style 578
hesitate 605
money 800
accounts 811
in the – 475
the mind losing its
– 503
off one's –
irresolute 605
fail 732
want of – 579
– accounts with
pay 807

worse than bite 885
barker 767
barleycorn
little 193
Barleycorn, Sir
John - 298
barm *leaven* 320
bubbles 353
Barmecide feast
956
barmy 320, 503
barn 189
barnacles 445
barndoor fowl 366
barograph 206, 338
barometer *air* 338
measure 466
consult the - 463
baron *peer* 875
husband 903
court - 966
- of the Exchequer
967
baronet 875
baronial 878
baroque 853
baroscope 338
barouche 272
barque 273
barrack 189
barracoon 717
barrage 407, 717
barratry 940
barred 219, 440
barrel 191, 249
- organ 417
barren 169, 645
barricade *fence* 232
obstacle 706
defence 717
prison 752
barrier [*see* barri-
cade]
barring *save* 38
excluding 55
except 83
- out *resist* 719
disobey 742
barrister 968
revising - 967
barrow
mound 206
vehicle 272
grave 363
barter
reciprocate 12
interchange 148
commerce **794**
barytone 408
basal 215

bas-bleu
scholar 492
affectation 855
base
site 183
lowest part **211**
support 215
bad 649
cowardly 862
shameful 874
servile 886
dishonourable 940
vicious 945
- ball 840
- born 876
- coin 800
- note 408
- of operations
plan 626
attack 716
- viol 417
baseball diamond
213
baseboard 211
based on *ground of*
belief 467
baseless 2, 4
basement *cellar* 191
lowest part 207,
211
bash 276
bashaw 739, 745
bashful 881
bashi bazouk 726
basilica 1000
basilisk *sight* 441
cannon 737
serpent 949
basin *dock* 189
vessel 191
hollow 252
plain 344
basinet 717
basis
lowest part 211
support 215
preparation 673
bask *physical enjoy-*
ment 377
warmth 382
prosperity 734
moral enjoyment
827
basket 191
- of 190
bas-relief 250, 557
bass *music* 415
- note 408
- viol 417
basset horn 417
bassinet 191, 215

bassoon 417
basso-profondo 408
basso-rilievo 250,
557
bastard 545, 925
baste *beat* 276
punish 972
Bastille 752
bastinado 972
bastion 717
bat 276, 727
batch 25, 72
bate *diminish* 36
subtract 38
reduce price 813
bated breath
with - *faint sound*
405
expecting 507
hiding 528
whisper 581
humble 879
bath 337, 652
public -s 652
warm - 386
- room 191, 652
Bath chair 272
bathe *immerse* 300
plunge 310
water 337
bathos 497
bathysphere 208
batik 440
batman 637
bâton *support* 215
sceptre 747
batrachian 366
betta 973
battalion 726
batten
feed 298
stage lighting 599
- down the
hatches 261
- on 886
batter *destroy* 162
beat 276
battered 659, 688
battering-ram 276
battering-train 727
battery *electric* 153
artillery 726
guns 727
floating - 726
plant a - 716
battle 720, 722
half the - 642
win the - 731
- array *order* 60
prepare 673
war 722

- axe 727
- cruiser 726
- cry 550, 722
- field *arena* 728
- ground *discord*
713
- ship 726
- with *oppose* 708
battledore and
shuttlecock
interchange 148
game 840
battlement 257, 717
battre
- la campagne
nonsense 497
diffuse style 573
excitable 825
- l'eau avec un
bâton 645
- le fer sur l'en-
clume 134
- la générale 669
se - contre des
moulins 645
ne - que d'une aile
683
battology
repeat 104
diffuse style 373
battue *pursuit* 622
attack 716
kill 361
bauble 643, 840
bavardage 517, 584
bawd 962
bawdy, - house 961
bawl 411
bawn 189
bay *concave* 252
gulf 343
cry 412
brown 433
at - *danger* 665
difficulty 704
defence 717, 719
bring to - 716
- the moon 645
- window 260
bayadére 599
bayard 271
bayonet *kill* 361
attack 716
weapon 727
crossed -s 708
at the point of the
- *war* 722
severity 739
coercion 744
bays *trophy* 733
crown 877

belike 472
belittle
decrease 36
underestimate 482
disparage 934
bell 417, 550
alarm – 669
bear away the –
goodness 648
success 731
repute 873
church – 350
cracked – 408a
passing – 363
– book and candle
swear 535
curse 908
spell 993
rite 998
– the cat 861
– shape 249, 252
belladonna 663
belle 374, 854
a la – étoile 220, 845
belles-lettres 560
belli, casus – 824
bellicose 720, 722
bellied 250
belligerent
contentious 720
warlike 722
combatant 726
belling 412
bellman 354
bello, flagrante – 722
Bellona 722
bellow *loud* 404
cry 411
animal cry 412
wail 839
bellows 349, 580
bells, peal of – 407
bellwether 64, 694
belly *receptacle* 191
inside 221
convex 250
–ful 52, 639
– god 957
– timber 298
belomancy 511
belong to *related* 9
component 56
included 76
attribute 157
property 777, 780
duty 926
beloved 897
below 207
here – 318

– the mark 32
– par 34, 207
bad 649
indifferent 651
discount 813
ignoble 876
– its full strength 651
– stairs 207
belt *outline* 230
ring 247
strait 343
swimming – 666
belting 633
Belus 979
belvedere 441
bemask 528
bemingle 41
bemire 653
bemoan 839
bemused 458
bench *support* 215
council 696
tribunal 966
Bench, King's – 752
bencher 968
bend *oblique* 217
angle 244
curve 245
incline 278
deviate 279
depression 308
circuit 311
give 324
submit 725
– backwards 235
– the bow 686
– the brows 932
– one's course 27
– the knee
bow down 308
submit 725
humble 879
servile 886
courtesy 894
respect 928
worship 990
– one's looks upon 441
– the mind 457
– over 250
– to rules &c. 82
– sinister 874
– one's steps 622
– to *tend* 176
– towards 278
– to one's will 737
beneath 207
– one 940
– notice 643

Benedick 903
Benedictine 996
benediction
gratitude 916
approval 931
worship 990
nuptial – 903
benefaction 784
benefactor 816, **912**
benefice 995
beneficent 906
beneficial 648
– interest 780
beneficiary
possessor 779
receive 785
clergy 996
benefit *good* 618
use 644
do good 648
aid 707
acquisition 775
property 780
benevolence 906
reap the – of 131
benefits forgot 917
bene gesserit, quamdiu se – 926
benet 545
benevolence
tax 812
love 897
kindness **906**
universal – 910
Bengal heat 382
benighted
dark 421
ignorant 491
benign 656, 906
benignant 906
benison 618, 931
Benjamin's mess 33, 50
Benshie 979
bent *tendency* 176
angle 244
turn of mind 820
desire 865
fool to the top of one's – 856
– on *willing* 602
resolved 604
intention 620
desirous 865
Benthamite 910
ben trovato
likely 472
imagination 515
untruth 546
wit 842

benumb
insensible 376
cold 385
deaden affections 823
beplaster 933
bepraise 931
bequest 270
gift 784
bereavement
death 360
loss 776
take away 789
bereft *poor* 804
– of life 360
– of reason 503
béret 225
berg, ice – 383
bergamot 400
berlin 272
berth *lodging* 189
bed 215
office 625
beryl *green* 435
jewel 847
beseech 765, 990
beseem 926
berserk 173, 503
beset *surround* 227
follow 281
attack 716
entreat 765
annoy 830
haunt 860
– with difficulties 704
besetting 78, 613
– sin 945
beshrew 908
beside *except* 83
near 197
alongside 236
– the mark 10, 495
– oneself 503, 824
besides 37
besiege
surround 227
attack 716
solicit 765
bésique 840
beslaver 933
beslime 653
beslubber 933
besmear 233, 653
besom 652
besotted 481
bespangle 847
bespatter *dirt* 653
disapprove 932
flatter 933
detract 934

bigamy 903
biggin 191
bight 343
bigot *positive* 474
 prejudice 481
 obstinate 606
 heterodox 984
 impious 988
bigotry 907
bigwig *scholar* 492
 sage 500
 nobility 875
bijou *goodness* 648
 beauty 845
 ornament 847
bilander 273
bilateral 90, 236
bilbao 727
bilboes 752
 put into – 751
bile 900
bilge *base* 211
 convex 250
 yawn 260
 – water 653
bilious 837
bilingual 560
bilk
 disappoint 509
 cheat 545
 steal 791
bill *list* 86
 hatchet 253
 placard 531
 ticket 550
 paper 593
 plan 626
 weapon 727
 money order 800
 money account 811
 charge 812
 in law 969
 true – 969
 – and coo 902
 – of exchange 771
 – of fare *food* 298
 plan 626
 – of indictment 938
 –s of mortality 360
 – of sale 771
billet *locate* 184
 ticket 550
 apportion 786
billet *epistle* 592
 – doux 902
billfold 191
billhook 253
billiard – ball 249
 – room 191

– table *flat* 213
billiards 840
Billingsgate 563, 908
billion 98
billow *sea* 348
 river 341
billy-cock 225
billy-goat 373
bimetallism 800
bin 191
binary 89
bind *connect* 43
 cover 223
 compel 744
 condition 770
 obligation 926
 – hand and foot 751
 – oneself 768
 – over 744
 – up wounds 660
binding 681, 744
bine 367
binnacle 693
binocular 445
binomial 89
biogenesis 161
biograph 448
biography 594
biology 357, 359
bioscope 448
biota 357
biparous 89
bipartite 44, 91
biplane 273
biplicity 89
biquadrate 96
birch *flog* 972
 – rod 975
bird 366
 kill two –s with one stone 682
 –'s eye view 441, 448
 –s of a feather 17
 the – has flown 187, 671
 – in hand 777, 781
 – of ill omen
 omen 512
 warning 668
 hopeless 859
 – of passage 268
 – of prey 739
 a little – told me 527
birdcage 370
birdlime *glue* 45
 trap 545
biretta 999

birth *beginning* 66
 production 161
 paternity 166
 nobility 875
 – place 153
 – right 924
birthday 138, 883
 – suit 226
birthmark 848
bis *repeat* 104
 approval 931
biscuits, s'embar-quer sans – 674
bise 349
bisection 68, **91**
bishop *punch* 298
 clergy 996
 –'s palace 1000
 –'s purple 437
bishopric 995
bisque 33
bissextile 138
bistoury 253
bistre 433
bisulcate 259
bit
 small quantity 32
 part 51
 interval 106
 curb 752
 just a – 26
 – by bit
 by degrees 26
 by instalments 51
 in detail 79
 slowly 275
 – between the teeth 600, 719
bitch *animal* 366
 female 374
 clumsy 699
 fail 732
 impure 962
bite *eat* 298
 physical pain 378
 cold 385
 cheat 545
 dupe 547
 etch 558
 mental pain 830
 – the dust 725
 – in 259
 – the thumb 900, 929
 – the tongue 392
biter bit 718
biting *pain* 378
 cold 383
 pungent 392
 painful 830
 discourteous 895

censorious 932
bitten 897
bitter *beer* 298
 cold 383
 taste 392, 395
 painful 830
 acrimonious 895
 hate 898
 angry 900
 malevolent 907
 – end 67
 – ender 606, 710, 832
 – pill 735
 – words 932
bitterly *greatly* 31
bitterness
 [see bitter]
 pain 828
 regret 833
bitumen 356*a*
bituminous coal 388
bivouac
 encamp 184
 camp 189
 repose 265
 watch 668
bi-weekly 138
bizarre 83, 853
blab 529
blabber 584
black *colour* 431
 crime 945
 look – *feeling* 821
 discontent 832
 angry 900
 – art 992
 – and blue
 beat 972
 – board 590
 – book 938
 – eye 848, 972
 – in the face
 swear 535
 excitement 821, 824
 – flag 722
 – hole *crowd* 72
 prison 752
 – lead 556
 – letter *old* 124
 barbarism 563
 print 591
 – list 932
 – looks
 discourteous 895
 sullen 901*a*
 disapprove 932
 magic 998
 – mail *theft* 791

[415]

breach *crack* 44
  gap 198
  quarrel 713
  violation 925
  custom honoured
    in the – 614
  – of faith 940
  – of law 83, 964
  – of the peace 713
bread 298
  beg – 765
  selfish 943
  quarrel with –
    and butter 699
  – of idleness 683
  – of life *Christ* 976
  piety 987
  – upon the waters
    638
  – and wine 998
breadbasket 191
breadth 202
  chiaroscuro 420
break
  fracture 44
  discontinuity 70
  change 140
  gap 198
  carriage 272
  crumble 328
  disclose 529
  cashier 756
  violate 773, 927
  bankrupt 808
  – away 623
  – bread 298
  – bulk 297
  – camp 293
  – of day *morning*
    125
  twilight 422
  – down *destroy*
    162
  fall short 304
  decay 659
  fail 732
  dance 840
  – one's fetters 614
  – forth 295
  – ground 66
  – a habit 614
  – the heart *pain*
    828, 830
  dejection 837
  – the ice 888
  – in *ingress* 294
  domesticate 370
  teach 537
  tame 749
  – in upon *derange*
    61

inopportune 135
  hinder 706
  – a lance 716, 722
  – a law 83
  – loose 671, 750
  – one's neck
  powerless 158
  die 360
  – the neck of
  task 676
  success 731
  – the news 529
  – no bones 648
  – of 660
  – off *cease* 142
  relinquish 624
  abrogate 756
  – out *begin* 66
  violent 173
  disease 655
  excited 825
  – the peace 173,
    720
  – Priscian's head
    568
  – prison 750
  – the ranks 61
  – short 328
  – silence 582
  – the teeth 579
  – the thread 70
  – through the
    clouds *visible*
    446
  disclose 529
  – through a cus-
    tom 614
  – up *disjoin* 44
  decompose 49
  end 67
  revolution 146
  destroy 162
  – up of the system,
    360, 665
  – on the wheel
  physical pain 378
  mental pain 830
  punishment 972
  – with 713
  – with the past
    146
  – word *deceive* 525
  improbity 940
breaker
  of horses 268
  reef 346
  wave 348
breakers 348, 667
  surrounded by –
    704
  – ahead 665

breakfast 298
breakneck
  precipice 217
  rash 863
breakwater
  refuge 666
  obstruction 706
breast *interior* 221
  confront 234
  convex 250
  mind 450
  oppose 708
  soul 820
  at the – 129
  in the – of 620
  – the current 719
  – high 206
breastplate 717
breastwork 717
breath *instant* 113
  breeze 349
  life 359
  animality 364
  faint sound 405
  with bated – 581
  hold – *quiet* 265
  expect 507
  wonder 870
  not a – of air 265,
    382
  out of – 688
  in the same – 120
  shortness of – 688
  take – 265, 689
  take away one's –
  unexpected 508
  fear 860
  wonder 870
breathe *exist* 1
  blow 349
  live 359
  faint sound 405
  evince 467
  mean 516
  inform 527
  disclose 529
  utter 580
  speak 582
  refresh 689
  – freely 827, 834
  – one's last 360
  not – a word 528
breathing time 687,
  723
breathless
  voiceless 581
  out of breath 688
  feeling 821
  fear 860
  eager 865
  wonder 870

  – attention 457
  – expectation 507
  – impatience 865
  – speed 684
bred in the bone 820
breech 235
  – loader 727
breeches 225
  wear the – 737
  – buoy 666
  – maker 225
  – pocket
    money 800, 802
breed *kind* 75
  multiply 161
  progeny 167
  animals 370
  rear 537
breeding 161, 852,
  894
breeze *wind* 349
  discord 713
breezy 836
brethren 997
breve 413
brevet
  warrant 741
  commission 755
  permit 760
  – rank 873
breviary 998
brevier 591
brevity 201, 572
brew 41, 673
brewing
  impending 152
  storm – 665
bribe *equivalent* 30
  tempt 615
  offer 763
  gift 784
  buy 795
  expenditure 809
  reward 973
bric-à-brac 847
brick *hard* 323
  pottery 384
  material 635
  trump 939, 948
  make -s without
    straw 471
  – colour 434
brickbat 727
bricklayer 690
bride 903
bridewell 752
bridge 45, 627
  – over *join* 43
  facilitate 705
  make peace 723
  compromise 774

brouillerie 713
brouillon 626
brow *top* 210
  edge 231
  front 234
browbeat
  intimidate 860
  swagger 885
  disrespect 929
  —en *humbled* 879
brown **433**
  — Bess 727
  — study 451, 458
Brown, Jones and
  Robinson 876
brownie 980
browse 298
bruin 895
bruise *powder* 330
  hurt 619
  injure 649
  blemish 848
bruiser 726
bruit
  report 531, 532
brumal 126, 383
brumous 353
Brummagem 545
brunette 433
brunt *beginning* 66
  impulse 276
  bear the —
    difficulty 704
    defence 717
    endure 821, 826
brush *rough* 256
  rapid motion 274
  graze 379
  clean 652
  fight 720
  paint — 556
  — away *reject* 297
  abrogate 756
  — up *clean* 652
  furbish 658
  prepare 673
brushwood 367
brusque *violent* 173
  haste 684
  discourtesy 895
brutal *vulgar* 851
  rude 895
  savage 907
brutalize
  [*see* brutal]
  corrupt 659
  deaden 823
  vice 945
brute *animal* 366
  rude 895
  maleficent 913

— force
  strength 159
  violence 173
  animal 450a
  severe 739
  compulsion 744
  lawless 964
  — *matter* 316, 358
Brute, et tu 917
brutish [*see* brute]
  vulgar 851
  ignoble 876
  intemperate 954
brutum fulmen
  impotent 158
  failure 732
  lax 738
  boast 884
bubble
  unsubstantial 4
  transient 111
  little 193
  convexity 250
  light 320
  water 348
  air **353**
  error 495
  deceit 545
  trifle 643
  — burst
  fall short 304
  disappoint 509
  fail 732
  — *reputation* 873
  — and squeak 298
  — up *agitation* 315
buccaneer 791, 792
bucentaur 273
Bucephalus 271
buck *stag* 366
  male 373
  wash 652
  money 800
  fop 854
  — *basket* 191
  — jump 309
  — up 684
bucket 191
  kick the — 360
  drop — in empty
    well 645
  like —s in well 314
buckle *tie* 43
  fastening 45
  distort 243
  curl 248
  — on one's armour
    673
  — to 604, 686
  — with *grapple* 720
buckler 717

buckram 855, 878
  men in — 549
bucolic
  pastoral 370
  poem 597
bud 367
  beginning 66
  germ 153
  expand 194
  graft 300
  — from 154
Buddha 979, 986
Buddhism 984
budding *young* 127
buddy 711, 890
budge 264
budget *heap* 72
  bag 191
  store 636
  finance 811
  — of news 532
buff 436
  blind man's — 840
  native — 226
buffer
  hindrance 706
  defence 717
buffet 191
  strike 276
  agitate 315
  evil 619
  bad 649
  affront 900
  smite 972
  — the waves 704,
    708
  bar 189
buffo 599
buffoon *actor* 599
  humorist 844
  butt 857
buffoonery 840, 842
bug 653
bugaboo 669, 860
bugbear
  imaginary 155
  bane 663
  alarm 669
  fear 860
buggy 272
bugle
  instrument 417
  war-cry 722
  ornament 847
  — call 550, 741
build *construct* 161
  form 240
  — anew 658
  — upon a rock 150
  — up *compose* 54
  — upon *belief* 484

builder 626, 690
building material
  635
buildings 189
built on *basis* 211
bulb 249, 250
bulge 250
bulk 50, 192
  — large 31
bulkhead 228, 706
bull *animal* 366
  male 373
  error 495
  absurdity 497
  solecism 568
  police 664
  ordinance 741
  — in a china shop
    59
  like a — at a gate
    173
  take the — by the
    horns 604, 861
Bull, John — 188
bullcalf 501
bulldog *animal* 366
  pluck 604, 604a
  courage 861
bulldoze 885
bullet *ball* 249
  arms 727
  missile 284
bulletin 532, 592
  — board 551
bullfight 720
bullhead 501
bullion 800
bullseye *centre* 222
  lantern 423
  aim 620
bully *fighter* 726
  maltreat 830
  frighten 860
  courage 861
  rashness 863
  bluster 885
  blusterer 887
  threaten 909
  evil doer 913
  bad man 949
bulrush
  worthless 643
bulwark 706, 717
bum 876
bumbailiff 965
bumbledom 737,
  965
bumboat 273
bump 250, 276
  — off 361
bumper 52

bumpkin 876
bumptious
  proud 878
  insolent 885
  contemptuous 930
bun 298
bunch *collection* 72
  protuberance 250
  – *light* 599
bunchbacked 243
Buncombe
  [*see* bunkum]
Bund 712
bundle *packet* 72
  go 266
  – *on* 275, 684
  – *out* 297
bung 263
  – *up* 261
bungalow 189
bungle 59, 699
bungler 701
bunion 259
bunk 186, 215
bunker 181
bunkie 890
bunkum *lie* 544
  style 577
  boast 884
  flattery 933
bunting 550
buoy *raise* 307
  float 320
  hope 858
buoyant
  floating 305
  light 320
  elastic 325
  prosperous 734
  cheerful 836
  hopeful 858
bur *clinging* 46
  sharp 253
  rough 256
  in engraving 558
burden *lading* 190
  weight 319
  melody 413
  poetry 597
  too much 641
  clog 706
  oppress 828
  care 830
  – *the memory* 505
  – *of a song*
  repetition 104
burdensome
  [*see* burden]
  hurtful 649
  labouring 686
bureau *chest* 191

office 691
shop 799
tribunal 960
bureaucracy 737
bureaucrat 694
burgee 550
burgeon
  [*see* bourgeon]
burgess 188
burgh 189
burgher 188
burghmote 966
burglar 792
  – *alarm* 669
burglary 791
burgomaster 745
burgrave 745
burial 363
buried *deep* 208
  imbedded 229
  hidden 528
  – *in a napkin* 460
  – *in oblivion* 506
burin 558
burke 361
burlesque
  imitation 19
  travesty 21
  absurdity 497
  misrepresent 555
  drama 599
  comic 853
  ridicule 856
burletta 599
burly 192
burn *near* 197
  rivulet 348
  hot 382
  consume 384
  near the truth
    480a
  excited 825
  love 897
  punish 972
  – *the candle at*
    both ends
  waste 638
  exertion 686
  prodigal 818
  – *daylight* 683
  – *one's bridges* 604
  – *one's fingers* 699
  – *in* 384
  – *out* 385
  – *to* 865
burner 423
burning [*see* burn]
  passion 821
  angry 900
  – *glass* 445
  – *with curiosity*

455
  – *pain* 378
  – *shame* 874
burnish *polish* 255
  shine 420
  beautify 845
burnous 225
burnt [*see* burn]
  red 434
  – *offering* 952, 990
burr 410
burrock 706
burrow *lodge* 184
  excavate 252
bursar 801
bursary 802
burst *disjoin* 44
  instantaneous 113
  explosion 173
  brittle 328
  sound 406
  paroxysm 825
bubble –
  disclosure 529
  all over 729
  ready to –
  replete 641
  excited 824
  – *of anger* 900
  – *away* 623
  – *of eloquence* 582
  – *of envy* 921
  – *into a flame* 825
  – *forth begin* 66
  expand 194
  be seen 446
  –*ing with health*
    654
  – *with grief* 839
  – *in* 294
  – *of laughter* 838
  – *out* 295
  – *upon arrive* 292
  unexpected 508
  – *into tears* 839
burthen
  [*see* burden]
bury *enclose* 229
  inter 363
  conceal 528
  – *the hatchet* 918
  – *one's talent* 528
busboy 746
busby 225
bush *branch* 51
  jungle 344
  shrub 367
  beat about the –
    629
bushel *much* 31
  multitude 102

receptacle 191
size 192
hid under a – 460
not hide light un-
  der a – 878
bush-fighting 720
bushing 224
bushranger 792
bushy 256
business *event* 151
  topic 454
  occupation **625**
  commerce 794
  full of – 682
  man of –
  proficient 700
  consignee 758
  mind one's –
  incurious 456
  attentive 457
  careful 459
  let alone 748
  send about one's –
    297
  stage – 599
business-like
  orderly 58
  business 625
  active 682
  practical 692
  skilful 698
buskin *dress* 225
  drama 599
buss *boat* 273
  courtesy 894
  endearment 902
bust 554
bustle *energy* 171
  dress 225
  agitation 315
  activity 682
  haste 684
  difficulty 704
bustling
  [*see* bustle]
  eventful 151
busy 682
busybody 532, 682
but
  on the other hand
    30
  except 83
  limit 233
  qualifying 469
  – *now* 118
butcher *kill* 361
  provisions 637
  evil-doer 913
butler 746
butt *cask* 191
  push 276

calcine 384
calcitrate 276
calculate
　reckon 85
　investigate 461
　expect 507
　intend 620
　– upon 484
calculated
　tending 176
　premeditated 611
calculation
　[see calculate]
　caution 864
calculating [ditto]
　prudent 498
　– machine 85
calculus 85
caldron
　convert 144
　vessel 191
　heat 386
　laboratory 691
calèche 272
caleer 838
calefaction 384
calembour 520
calendar list 86
　chronicle 114
　record 551
calender 255
calenture 503, 655
calf young 129
　give birth 161
　leather 223
　animals 366
　fool 501
　golden – 986, 991
Caliban 846
calibrate 26
calibre degree 26
　size 192
　breadth 202
　opening 260
　intellectual
　　capacity 498
calidarium 356
calidity 382
caliginous 421
caliph 745
caliphate 737
calisthenics
　training 537
　beauty 845
caliver 727
calk 660
call cry 412
　signal 550
　name 564
　motive 615
　visit 892

sanctify 976
ordain 995
at one's – 682, 743
within – 197
– to account 932
– attention to 457
– to the bar 968
– into being 161
– of duty 926
– for require 630
　order 741
　ask 765
– forth
　resort to 677
　excite 824
– in advice 695
– to mind 505
– to the ministry
　996
– names 929, 932
– into notice 525
– off the attention
　458
– to order 741
– out cry 411
　challenge 715
– over number 85
– into play 677
– in question 485
– the roll 85
– up 527
– up spirits 992
– to 586
– up recollect 505
　motive 615
　excite 824
– upon
　demand 741
　request 765
　visit 892
　duty 924, 926
– to witness 467
callæsthetics 845
callant 129
call-boy
　theatre 599
called, so – 545
callidity 698
calligraphy 590
calling
　business 625
Calliope 417, 597
callipers 466
callosity 323
callous 376, 823
callow young 127
　infant 129
　bare 226
　unprepared 674
calm physical 174
　quiet 265

dissuade 616
leisure 685
peace 721
moral 826
unamazed 871
– belief &c. 484
– before a storm
　145
calmative 174
caloric 382
calorimeter 389
calote 999
calotype 556
caloyer 996
calumet token 550
– of peace 721, 723
calumniator 936
calumny 934
calvary 1000
Calvinism 984
calyx 191
cam 633
camarade 890
camaraderie 888,
　892
camarilla 712
camarista 746
camber 250
cambist 797, 801
camboose 386
camel 271
　swallow a – 608,
　694
cameo convex 250
　sculpture 557
camera 445, 553
　in – 528
　– lucida 445
　– obscura 445
camerated 191
camilla 274
camisade 716
camisole 225
camorra 712
camouflage 530
camp locate 184
　abode 189
　military 728
　– bed 215
　– stool 215
campagna 180, 344
campaign 692, 722
campaigner 726
campaigning 266
campaniform 249,
　252
campanile 206
campestrian 344
Campus Martius
　728
can power 157

mug 191
preserve 670
jail 752
best one – 686
– it be! 870
canaille 876
canal opening 260
　conduit 350
　way 627
　– boat 273
canard 532, 546
canary 366
cancan
　dance 840
cancel
　compensate 30
　neutralize 179
　obliterate 552
　abrogate 756
　repudiate 773
cancellated 219
cancelli 191
cancer disease 655
　bane 663
　painful 830
candelabrum 423
candent 382
candid white 430
　sincere 543
　ingenuous 703
　honourable 939
candidate 767, 865
candidature 763
candle 423
　bargain by inch of
　　– 769
　burn – at both
　　ends 686
　not fit to hold a –
　　to 34
　– ends 40, 817
　– holder 711
　– light 126, 422
　– power 466
　– stick 423, 998
　hold – to sun 645
Candlemas 998
candour
　veracity 543
　artlessness 705
　honour 939
candy dense 321
　sweet 396
cane weapon 727
　punish 972
　scourge 975
canescent 430
Canicula 423
canicular 382
caniculated 259
canine 366

caravan 266, 272
caravansary 189
caravel 273
carbine 727
carbohydrates 298
carbon 388
– dioxide 663
– monoxide 663
carbonaro 742
carbonization 384
carboy 191
carbuncle *red* 434
abscess 655
jewel 847
carcanet 847
carcass
structure 329
corpse 362
bomb 727
carcelage 973
carcinoma 655
card *unravel* 60
ticket 550
plan 626
address – 550
by the – 82
great – 873
house of –s 328
leave a – 892
on the –s 152, 177, 470
play one's – 692
play one's best – 686
play one's –s well 698
playing –s 840
shuffle the –s
begin again 66
change 140
chance 621
prepare 673
speak by the –
care 459
veracity 543
phrase 566
throw up the –s 757
ticklish – 704
trump – 626
– index 60, 86, 551
–s to play 632
cardcase 191
cardiac 836
cardigan 225
cardinal *intrinsic* 5
dress 225
red 434
important 642
excellent 648
priest 995, 996

–'s hat 747
– points 278
– virtues 944
cardioid 245
card-sharper 792
card-sharping 545
care *attention* **459**
business 625
adversity 735
custody 751
economy 817
pain 828
fear 860
for aught one –s 643, 866
begone dull – 836
drive – away 840
have the – of 693
take – 665, 864
take – of 459
– for *important* 642
desire 865
love 897
careen *slope* 217
repair 660
career 625, 692
careless
inattentive 458
neglectful 460, 927
feeble 575
insensible 823
indifferent 866
caress 897, 902
caret *incomplete* 53
want 640
careworn 828, 837
cargo 270
large quantity 31
contents 190
property 780
goods 798
– boat 273
caricature
likeness 19
copy 21
exaggerate 549
misrepresent 555
ridicule 856
caricaturist 844
caries 49, 653, 655
carillon 417
cariole 272
carious 563
carking 828
– care 830
carle 876
Carlist 925
car-load 31
carman 694

Carmelite 996
carminative 662
carmine 434
carnage 361
carnal 364
intemperate 954
impure 961
irreligious 989
carnation 434
carnival 840
carnivorous 298
carol
music 415, 416
cheerful 836
rejoice 838
caro sposo 897
carouse *feast* 298
festivity 840
intemperance 954
drinking 959
carousel 840
carp at 932
carpe diem 134
carpenter 690
carper 936
carpet 211
on the –
topic 454
project 626
– bag 191
– knight *fop* 854
servile 886
sybarite 954a
– sweeper 652
carrefour 627
carriage *gait* 264
transference 270
vehicle 272
aspect 448
conduct 692
keep one's – 852
carried
– by acclamation &c. 488
– away by passion 824
carrier **271**
– pigeon 534
carrion 362, 653
carronade 727
carroty 434
carry
conduce to 176
support 215
transfer 270
induce 615
reap and – 775
– all before one 731
– coals 879
– conviction 484

– into execution 729, 772
– with a high hand
authority 737
pride 878
insolence 885
– in the mind 505
– off *take* 789
steal 791
– on [see below]
– oneself 692
– out *conduct* 692
complete 729
– over
transfer 270
accounts 811
– a point 731
– by storm 731
– through 692, 729
– weight
influence 175
evidence 467
importance 642
carry on
continue 143
pursue 622
do 680
conduct 692
undertake 326
– an argument 476
– business 625
– an enquiry 461
– a trade 794
– war 722
cart 272
– away 185
– before the horse
disorder 59
inversion 218
bungling 699
– horse 271
work like a –
horse 686
– load 31, 190
cartage 270
carte *list* 86
à la – 298
– blanche 760, 816
– du pays 626
– and tierce 716
– de visite 550
photograph 554
cartel
combination 709
defiance 715
truce 723
compact 769
cartelize 709
carter 268

cry 411
aid 707
pleasure 827
relief 834
mirth 836
rejoicing 838
amusement 840
courage 861
sociality 892
welcome 894
applaud 931
good – *hope* 858
high living 957
cheerfulness 836
cheerless 830, 837
cheeseparings
remains 40
dirt 653
economy 817
chef de cuisine
proficient 700
servant 746
chef-d'œuvre 648,
698
cheka 696
chemin
– de fer
game 840
– faisant 270
chemise 225
chemist 662
Chemistry 144
organic – 357
cheque 800
chequer 440
– roll 86
cherchez la femme
155
chère amie 962
cherish *aid* 707
love 897
endearment 902
– a belief 484
– feelings &c. 821
– an idea &c. 451
cherry
– red 434
two bites of a –
overrate 482
roundabout 629
clumsy 699
cherry-cheeked 845
cherry-coloured
434
cheroot 392
cherub 977
Cheshire cat 838
chess 840
chessboard 440
chest 191, 802
chestnut-colour 433

cheval-de-bataille
plea 617
plan 626
vanity 880
cheval-glass 445
chevalier 875
– d'industrie 792
chevaux de frise
253, 717
chevron
angle 217
indication 550
badge 747
decoration 877
chew 298
– the cud 451
– tobacco 392
chiaroscuro
light 420
grey 432
painting 556
chiasma 43
chic 845, 882
chicane
sophistry 477
deceit 545 .
cunning 702
chicken 129, 366
– in every pot 733
count –s before
hatched 858,
863
tender as a – *soft*
324
sensitive 822
compassionate
914
chickenhearted 862
chide 932
chief *principal* 642
master 745
evidence in – 467
– constable 765
– part 31
Chief Justice 967
chiefdom 737
chieftain 745
chiffonnier 876
chiffonnière 191
chignon 225
chilblain 383
child
infant 129
offspring 167
fool 501
– of God 987
–'s play 643, 705
with – 161
childbirth 161
childhood 127
childish

credulous 486
foolish 499
feeble 575
– treble 581
childlike 703
chiliad 98
chill *cold* 383
render cold 385
indispose 616
– the spine 830,
860
chillies 393
Chiltern Hundreds
757
chime
repetition 104
roll 407
resonance 408
melody 413
– in with *agree* 23
conform 82
assent 488
concord 714
chimera 83, 515
chimney 260, 351
– corner 189
– pot 249
china 384, 557
China to Peru 180
chine 235
chinese white 430
chink *gap* 198
sound 408
money 800
chip *small* 32
detach 44
bit 51
reduce 195
– of the old block
similar 17
copy 21
offspring 167
chippy 962
Chirography 590
Chirology 550
Chiromancy 511
chirp
bird-note 412
sing 416
cheerful 836
rejoice 838
chirrup [*see* chirp]
chirurgery 662
chisel
fabricate 161
form 240
sharp 253
sculpture 557
chit 129, 193
chit-chat 588
chitterlings 221

chivalry *war* 722
tenure 777
courage 861
courtesy 894
philanthropy 910
honour 939
generosity 942
chlamys 225
chloroform 376, 823
chlorophyl 435
chlorotic 655
chock full 52
chocolate
food 298
colour 433
choice *will* 600
election 609
excellent 648
absence of – **609a**
by – 600
– spirits 873
– of words 569
choir *sing* 416
church music 996
church 1000
– boy 996
– invisible 360,
977
choke *close* 261
stifle 361
redundant 641
hinder 706
–full *complete* 52
replete 639
–off 706
choler 900
choleric 901
choose 609
do what one –s 748
chop *disjoin* 44
change 140
– logic 476
– up 201
chopfallen 837
chopper 330
chopping
large 192
– sea 348
chops *mouth* 66
jaws 231
food 298
choral 415
chord 413
chore 625
choreography 840
chorister 416, 996
chorography 183
chorus
shout 411
song 415
singers 416

unanimity 488
poetry 597
opera 599
concord 714
– girl 599
chose
– in action 780
– in possession
 777
chouse 545
choux gras, faire
 ses – 377
chrestomathy 560
chrism 998
Christ 976
 Church of – 893*a*
 receive – 987
Christ-cross-row
 561
christen 564, 998
Christendom 983*a*,
 995
Christian 983*a*, 987
– charity 906
– science 662, 984
Christmas 138, 998
Christmas-box 784
chromatic
 colour 428
– scale *music* 413
chromato-pseudo-
 blepsis 443
chromatrope 445
chrome 436
chromolithograph
 558
chromosphere 318
chronic 110
chronicle
 measure time 114
 annals 551
chronicler 553
chronography
 measure time 114
 description 594
chronology 114
chronometry 114
Chrononhotontho-
 logos 887
chrysalis 129
chrysoprase 847
chrysolite 847
 perfection 650
chrysology 800
chubby 192
chuck *throw* 284
 animal cry 412
– it 142
– under chin 902
chuck-farthing 621
chuckle

animal cry 412
laugh 838
exult 884
chuff 876
chum 711, 890
chunk 51
Church
 infallible 474
 orthodox 983*a*
 Christendom 995
 temple 1000
 dignitaries of –
 996
 go to – 990
 High –, Low – &c.
 984
– of Christ 983*a*
– bell 550
– house 1000
churchdom **995**
churching 998
churchman 996
churchwarden 996
 pipe 392
churchyard 363,
 1000
– cough 655
churl *boor* 876
churlish
 niggard 819
 rude 895
 sulky 901*a*
 malevolent 907
churn 315, 352
chut! *silent* 403
 taciturn 585
chute 348
chutney 393
chypre 400
cibarious 298
cicatrix 551
 manet – 919
cicatrize 660
Cicero 582
cicerone 524, 527
ciceronian 578
cicisbeo 897
cicuration **370**
cider 298
cider squeezer 876
ci-devant 122
cigar 392
ci-git 363
cilia 205, 256
cimeter 727
Cimmerian 421
cinch 45
cincture 247
cinder
 combustion 384
 dirt 653

Cinderella
 servant 746
 commonalty 876
cinema 448, 599,
 840
cinematograph 448
cinematographer
 553
cinerary 363
cineration 384
cinereous 432
cingle 230
cinnabar 434
cinnamon 393, 433
cinque 98
cipher
 unsubstantial 4
 number 84
 compute 85
 zero 101
 concealment 528
 mark 550
 letter 561
 unimportant 643
 writing in – 590
Circe 615, 994
 –an cup 377, 954
circination 312
circle *region* 181
 embrace 227
 form 247
 party 712
 describe a – 311
 great – sailing 628
– of acquaintance
 892
– of the sciences
 490
circlet 247
circling 248
circuit *region* 181
 outline 230
 winding 248
 tour 266
 indirect path 311
 indirect course
 629
circuition **311**
circuitous 279, 311
– method 629
circular *round* 247
 publication 531
 letter 592
 pamphlet 593
– note 805
circularity **247**
circularize 592
circulate
 circuit 311
 rotate 312
 publish 531

circulating medium
 800
circulation
 [*see* circulate]
 in – *news* 532
– of money 809
circumambient 227,
 229, 311, 629
circumambulate
 travel 266
 go round 311, 629
circumaviate 311
circumbendibus
 248, 629
circumcision 44,
 998
circumduction 552
circumference 230
circumferential 227
circumflex 311
circumfluent
 lie round 227
 move round 311
circumforaneous
 travelling 266
 circuition 311
circumfuse 73
circumgyration 312
circumjacence **227**
circumjacence **312**
circumlocution 573
circumnavigate
 navigation 267
 circuition 311
circumrotation 312
circumscribe
 surround 229
 limit 233, 761
circumscription **229**
circumspection
 attention 457
 care 459
 caution 459
circumstance
 phase 8
 event 151
circumstances
 property 780
 bad – 804
 depend on – 475
 good – 803
 under the – 8
circumstantial 8
– account 594
– evidence 467
 probability 472
circumstantiality
 459
circumstantiate 467
circumvallation
 enclosure 229,
 232

clear-obscure 420
cleat 45
cleavage
  cutting 44
  structure 329
cleave *sunder* 44
  adhere 46
  bisect 91
cleaver 253
cledge 342
clef 413
cleft *divided* 44
  bisected 91
  chink 198
  in a – stick
  difficulty 704
clem 956
clement
  lenient 740
  long-suffering
   826
  compassionate
   914
clench *compact* 769
  retain 781
  take 789
clepe 564
clepsydra 114
clerestory 191, 1000
clergy 996
clerical 995, 996
  – error 495
  – staff 746
clerk *scholar* 492
  recorder 553
  writer 590
  helper 711
  servant 746
  agent 758
  clergy 996
  articled – 541
  – in holy orders
   995
  – of works 694
clerkship
  commission 755
cleromancy 511
clever
  intelligent 498
  skilful 698
  smart 842
  too – by half 702
clew *ball* 249
  interpretation 522
  indication 550
  seek a – 461
click 406
client
  dependant 746
  customer 795
clientship

subjection 749
cliff *height* 206
  vertical 212
  steep 217
  land 342
climacteric 128
climate *region* 181
  weather 338
  fine – 656
climatology 338
climax
  supremacy 33
  summit 210
  culmination 729
climb 305
  – on the band-
   wagon 731
clime 181
clinal 217
clinch *fasten* 43
  close 261
  certify 474
  pun 563
  complete 729
  clutch 781
  snatch 789
  – an argument 47
  – the fist at 909
clincher 479
cling *adhere* 46
  – to *near* 197
  willing 602
  persevere 604a
  habit 613
  observe 772
  desire 865
  love 897
  – to hope 858
  – to one another
   709
clinic 662
clink
  resonance 408
  stridor 410
  prison 752
clinker *brick* 384
  dirt 653
clinometer
  oblique 217
  angle 244
clinquant
  ornament 847
  vulgar 851
Clio 594
clip *shorten* 201
  – the wings
  powerless 158
  speed 264
  slow 275
  useless 645
  hinder 706

prohibit 761
  – one's words 583
clipper 273
clipping
  small piece 51
clique *conclave* 696
  party 712
cloaca *conduit* 350
  foul 653
Cloacina 653
cloak *dress* 225
  conceal 528
  disguise 530
cloaked 223
cloche 371
clock 114
clockwork 633
  by – *uniform* 16
  order 58
  regular 80
clod *lump* 192
  earth 342
  fool 501
  bungler 701
clodhopper 876
clodpated
  stupid 499
clog *shoe* 225
  hinder 706
  – dance 840
cloison 228
cloisonné 557
cloister *arcade* 189
  way 627
  restraint 751
  convent 1000
close *similar* 17
  tight 43
  end 67
  field 181
  court 189
  near 197
  narrow 203
  shut 261
  dense 321
  warm 382
  hidden 528
  concise 572
  taciturn 585
  complete 729
  stingy 819
  examine –ly 457
  keep – *hide* 528
  retain 781
  tread – upon 281
  – the door upon
  restrain 751
  – the ears 419
  – the eyes
  die 360
  not see 442

  – one's eyes to
  not attend 458
  set at naught 773
  – at hand
  to-morrow 121
  imminent 152
  near 197
  – the hand
  refuse 764
  – in upon 290
  – inquiry 461
  –ly packed 72
  – prisoner 754
  – quarters 197
  approach 286
  attack 716
  battle 722
  – one's ranks 673
  – study
  thought 451
  attention 457
  – up 197, 290
  – with *cohere* 46
  assent 488
  attack 716
  contend 720
  consent 762
  compact 769
close-mouthed 585
closet
  receptacle 191
  ambush 530
closeted with
  conference 588
  advice 695
close-up 197
closure 142, **261**
clot *solidify* 321
  earth 342
cloth *vocation* 625
  napkin 652
  clergy 996
clothes 225
  grave – 363
  – basket 191
clothier 225
Clotho 601
clotpoll 501
clotted 352
cloud
  assemblage 72
  multitude 102
  mist 353
  shade 424
  screen 520
  break through the
   –s 446
  drop from the –s
   508
  in a – 475, 528
  in the –s

CLO

lofty 206
inattentive 458
dreaming 515
under a –
  insane 503
  adversity 735
  disrepute 874
  secluded 893
  censured 932
  accused 938
– burst 348
–capt 206
– of dust 330, 353
–s gathering
  dark 421
  danger 665
  warning 668
– no bigger than a
  man's hand 668
– of skirmishers
  726
– of smoke 353
– of words 573
clouded
  variegated 440
  dejected 837
  hopeless 859
– perception 499
cloudiness 571
cloudland 515
cloudless
  light 420
  happy 827
cloudy dim 422,
  426
clough 206
clout 276
cloven 91
cloven foot
  mark 550
  malevolence 907
  vice 945
  Satan 978
see the – 480a
show the – 907
clover
  luxury 377
  prosperity 734
  comfort 827
clown
  pantomime 599
  bungler 702
  buffoon 844
  vulgar 851
  rustic 876
cloy 641, 869
club
  place of meeting
   74
  house 189
  association 712

COA

weapon 727
sociality 892
– law
  compulsion 744
  lawless 964
– together
  co-operate 709
clubby 892
club car 272
clubfooted 243
cluck 412
clue 550
seek a – 461
clump
  assemblage 72
  projecting mass
   250
– of trees 367
clumsy
  unfit 647
  awkward 699
  ugly 846
Cluniac 996
clurichaune 980
cluster 72
clutch retain 781
  seize 789
clutches 737
in the – of 749
clutter 407
coacervation 72
coach
  carriage 272
  teach 537
  tutor 540, 673
– painter 540
– road 627
drive a – and six
  through 964
– up 539
coachhouse 191
coachman 268, 694
coaction 744
coadjutant 709
coadjutor 711
coadjuvancy 709
coagency 178, 709
coagmentation 72
coagulate
  cohere 46
  density 321
  semi-liquid 352
coal 388
call over the –s
  932
carry –s 879
– black 431
carry –s to New-
  castle 641
coalesce
  identity 13

COC

combine 48
coalheaver
  work like a – 686
coalition 43, 709,
  712
coaming 232
coaptation 23
coarctation
  decrease 36
  contraction 195
  narrow 203
  impede 706
  restraint 751
coarse harsh 410
  dirty 653
  unpolished 674
  garish 846
  vulgar 851
  impure 961
– grain 329
coast border 231
  slide 266
  navigate 267
  land 342
– defence 717
– line 230
coaster 273
coastguard 753
coat layer 204
  paint 223
  habit 225
cut – according to
  cloth 698
– of arms 550
– of mail 717
coating, inner –
  224
coax persuade 615
  endearment 902
  flatter 933
cob horse 271
  punish 972
cobalt 438
cobble mend 660
cobbler 225
cobbles 635
coble 273
cobra 913
cobweb light 320
  fiction 545
  flimsy 643
  dirt 653
–s of antiquity
  124
–s of sophistry
  477
cocaine 376, 381,
  663
cochineal 434
cock bird 366
  male 373

COD

game – 861
– boat 273
– and bull story
  546
– the eye 441
– of the roost
  best 648
  master 745
– up vertical 212
  convex 250
cockade badge 550
  title 877
cock-a-hoop
  gay 836
  exulting 884
Cockaigne 827
cockatrice
  monster 83
  piercing eye 548
  evil-doer 913
  miscreant 949
cockcrow 125
cocked hat 225, 745
cocker fold 258
  caress 902
Cocker
  school book 542
according to – 82
cockle fold 258
– of one's heart
  820
cockleshell 273
cockloft 191
cockney
  Londoner 188
  plebeian 876
cockpit hold 191
  council 696
  arena 728
cockshut
  morning 125
  evening 126
  dusk 422
cock-sparrow 193
cocksure 484
cockswain 269
cocktail 298, 959
– party 892
cocoa 298
cocotte 962
coction 384
Cocytus 982
cod shell 223
coddle 902
– oneself 943
code conceal 528
  precept 697
  law 963
codex 593
codger 819
codicil sequel 65

comfit 396
comfort
　pleasure 377
　delight 827
　content 831
　relief 834
　give – 906
comfortable
　pleasing 829
comforter
　covering 223
Comforter 976
comfortless
　painful 830
　dejected 837
comic. *wit* 842
　ridiculous 853
　– opera 599
　– strips 531
coming [*see* come]
　impending 152
　– events
　prediction 511
　– out 883
　– time 121
comitia 696
comity 894
comma 142
　inverted –s 550
command *high* 206
　requisition 630
　authority 737
　order **741**
　possess 777
　at one's –
　obedient 743
　– belief 484
　– of language
　writing 574
　speaking 582
　– of money 803
　– one's passions
　944
　– respect 928
　– one's temper
　826
　– a view of 441
commandant 745
commander 269
commandeer 744,
　789
commanding
　[*see* command]
　important 642
commando 726
commandment 697
comme deux
　gouttes d'eau 17
comme il faut
　taste 850
　fashion 852

genteel 875
commemorate 883
commence 66
commencement de
　la fin *end* 67
　destruction 162
commend 931
　– the poisoned
　chalice 544
commendable 944
commensurate
　accordant 23
　numeral 85
　adequate 639
comment
　reason 476
　judgment 480
　interpretation 522
　criticize 595
commentary 595
commentator 492,
　524, 527
commerce
　conversation 588
　barter 794
　cards 840
commercial 811
　– arithmetic 811
　– traveller 758
commère 599
commination 908,
　909
commingle 41
comminute 330
commiserate 914
commissariat 637
commissary
　provisions 637
　consignee 758
commission
　task 625
　delegate **755**, 759
　Royal – 696
　– of the peace 965
commissioner 758
commissionaire
　doorkeeper 263
　messenger 534
　consignee 758
commissure 43
commis-voyageur
　758
commit *do* 680
　delegate 755
　cards 840
　arrest 969
　– an absurdity 853
　– oneself to a
　course 609
　– to the flames
　384

– to memory 505
– oneself
　clumsy 699
　promise 768
　– to prison 751
　– sin 945
　– to writing 551
committee
　council 696
　consignee 758
　(*director* 694)
commix 41
commode 191
commodious 644
commodity 798
commodore 745
common
　general 78
　ordinary 82
　plain 344
　habitual 613
　trifling 643
　base 876
　in – *related* 9
　participate 778
　right of – 780
　short –s 640
　tenant in – 778
　make – cause 709
　– consent 488
　– council 966
　– course 613
　– herd 876
　– law *old* 124
　law 697, 963
　– measure 84
　– origin 153
　– parlance 576
　– place 82
　– place book
　record 551
　compendium 596
　– saying 496
　– sense 498
　– sewer 653
　– stock 778
　– weal
　mankind 372
　good 681
　utility 644
　philanthropy 910
Common Pleas
　Court of – 966
commonalty **876**
commoner 876
commonplace
　usual 82
　known 490
　plain 576
　habit 613
　unimportant 643

dull 843
commons 298
commonwealth
　territory 181
　community 372
　authority 737
commorant 188
commotion 315
communalism 778
commune
　township 181
commune with 588
　– oneself 451
communibus annis
　29
communicant 990
communicate
　join 43
　tell 527
　correspond 592
　give 784
　sacrament 998
communication
　news 532
　of disease 657
　oral – 582, 588
communion
　discourse 588
　society 712
　participation 778
　sacrament 998
　hold – with 888
　– table 1000
communiqué 527
communism 737
communist
　party 712
　rebel 742
　participation 778
　philanthropy 910
　evil doer 913
community
　party 712
　– at large 372
　– of goods 778
commutation
　compensation 30
　substitution 147
　interchange 148
　compromise 774
　barter 794
commutual 12
compact
　joined 43
　united 87
　receptacle 191
　small 193
　compressed 195
　compendious 201
　dense 321
　bargain **769**

compages
whole 50
structure 329
compagination 43
companion *match*
17
accompaniment
88
ladder 305
friend 890
companionable 892
companionship 892
companionway 305
company
assembly 72
actors 599
party, partner-
ship 712
troop 726
sociality 892
bear – 88
in – *with* 88
comparable 9
comparative 464
degree 26
– *anatomy* 368
comparatively 32
compare 464
– *notes* 695
comparison 464
compartition 44
compartment
part 51
region 181
place 182
cell 191
carriage 272
compass
degree 26
space 180
surround 227
measure 466
intend 620
guidance 693
achieve 729
box the –
azimuth 278
rotation 312
keep within –
moderation 174
fall short 304
economy 817
points of the – 236
in a small – 193
– *about* 229
– *of thought* 498
compassion 914
object of – 828
compatible
consentaneous 23
possible 470

compatriot
inhabitant 188
friend 890
compeer *equal* 27
friend 890
compel 744
compellation 564
compendency 43
compendious 201
compendium 596
book 593
compensate
make up for 30
requite 973
compensation 30
compère 599
competence
power 157
sufficiency 639
skill 698
wealth 803
competition
opposition 708
contention 720
competitor
opponent 710
combatant 726
candidate 767
compilation
collect 72
book 593
compendium 596
compile 54
complacent
pleased 827
content 831
courteous 894
kind 906
complain 839
complainant 938
complaint
illness 655
murmur 839
lodge a – 938
– *without cause*
839
complaisant
lenient 740
courteous 894
kind 906
complement
adjunct 39
remainder 40
part 52
arithmetic 84
complementary
correlation 12
colour 428
complete
entire 52
accomplish 729

compact 769
– *answer* 479
– *circle* 311
in a – *degree* 31
completeness 52
completion 729
complex 59
complexion
state 7
colour 428
appearance 448
compliance
conformity 82
obedience 743
consent 762
observance 772
complicate
derange 61
complicated
disorder 59
convolution 248
complice 711
complicity 709
compliment
courtesy 894, 896
praise 931
poor – 932
–s *of season* 896
complimentary
free 815
complot 626
comply [*see* compli-
ance]
compo *coating* 223
material 635
component 56
componere lites
723, 724
comport
– *oneself* 692
– *with* 23
compos mentis 502
compose
make up 54, 56
produce 161
moderate 174
music 416
write 590
printing 591
pacify 723
assuage 826
composed
self-possessed 826
composer
music 413
composite 41
composition 54
[*see* compose]
combination 48
piece of music 415
picture 556

style 569
writing 590
building material
635
compromise 774
barter 794
atonement 952
compositor
printer 591
compost 653
composure 826, 871
compotation 959
compote 298
compound
mix 41
combination 48
limited space 182
enclosure 232
compromise 774
– *arithmetic* 466
– *for substitute* 147
barter 794
comprador 637
comprehend
compose 54
include 76
know 490
understand 518
comprehension [*see*
comprehend]
intelligence 498
comprehensive 76
complete 50
general 78
wide 192
– *argument* 476
compress
contract 195
curtail 201
condense 321
remedy 662
compressible 322
comprise 76
comprobation
evidence 467
demonstration 478
compromise
dally with 605
mid-course 628
taint 659
danger 665
pacify 723
compact 769
compound 774
atone 952
compromised
promised 768
compter 799
compte rendu
record 551
accounts 811

conquer 731
conquered
  (*failure* 732)
conquering hero
  comes 883
conqueror 731
consanguinity **11**
consciarecti, mens—
  pride 878
  innocence 946
conscience
  knowledge 490
  moral sense 926
  in all – *great* 31
  affirmation 535
  awakened – 950
  qualms of – 603
  clear – 946
  stricken – 950
  tender – 926
  honour 939
conscientious 926
  scrupulous 939
  – objector 489
conscious
  intuitive 450
  knowledge 490
  – of disgrace 874
  – of glory 873
conscript 726
conscription 744
consecrate *use* 677
  dedicate 873
  sanctify 987
  holy orders 995
consecration
  rite 998
consectory 478
  – reasoning 476
consecution 63
consecutive
  following 63
  continuous 69
  – fifth 414
consecutively
  slowly 275
consensus 488
  – of opinion 23
consent *assent* 488
  compliance **762**
  with one – 178
consentaneous
  agreeing 23
  (*expedient* 646)
consequence
  event 151
  effect 154
  importance 642
  in – 478
  of no – 643
  take the –s 154

consequent 63
consequential
  deducible 478
  arrogant 878
consequently
  reasoning 476
  effect 154
conservation
  permanence 141
  storage 636
  preservation 670
conservatism 141,
  670
conservative 141,
  712
  – policy 681
conservatoire 542
conservator
  of the peace 967
conservatory
  receptacle 191
  floriculture 371
  furnace 386
  store 636
conserve 396, 636
consider *think* 451
  attend to 457
  examine 461
  adjudge 480
  believe 484
considerable
  in degree 31
  in size 192
  important 642
considerate
  careful 459
  judicious 498
  benevolent 906
consideration
  purchase money
    147
  thought 451
  idea 453
  attention 457
  qualification 469
  inducement 615
  importance 642
  gift 784
  benevolence 906
  respect 928
  requital 973
  deserve – 642
  in – of
    compensation 30
    reasoning 476
  on – 658
  take into –
    thought 451
    attention 457
  under –
    topic 454

inquiry 461
plan 626
considered, all
  things –
  collectively 50
  judgment 480
  premeditation 611
  imperfection 651
consign
  transfer 270
  commission 755
  property 783
  give 784
  – to the flames 384
  – to oblivion 506
  – to the tomb 363
consignee **758**
consignor 796
consignment
  commission 755
  gift 784
  apportionment
    786
consilience 178
consist
  – in 1
  – of 54
consistence
  density 321
consistency
  uniformity 16
  agreement 23
consistently with
  82
consistory
  council 696
  church 995
consolation
  relief 834
  condole 915
  religious 976
console
  table 215
Consoler
  the – 976
consolidate
  unite 46, 48
  condense 321
consols 802
consommé 298
consonant
  agreeing 23
  musical 413
  letter 561
consort
  accompany 88
  associate 892
  spouse 903
  – with 23
consortium 23
consortship 892

conspection 441
conspectus 596
conspicuous
  visible 446
  famous 873
conspiracy 626
conspirator 626
  traitor 941
conspire
  concur 178
  co-operate 709
constable
  policeman 664
  governor 745
  officer 965
constant
  fixed 5
  uniform 16
  continuous 69
  regular 80
  continual 112
  frequent 136
  regular 138
  immutable 150
  exact 494
  persevering 604a
  obey 743
  faithful 939
  – flow 69
constellation
  stars 318
  luminary 423
  glory 873
consternation 860
constipation
  closure 261
  density 321
constituency 181,
  737
constituent 51, 56
constitute
  compose 54, 56
  produce 161
constitution
  nature 5
  state 7
  composition 54
  structure 329
  charter 924
  law 963
constitutional
  walk 226
  – government 737
constrain
  compel 744
  restrain 751
  abash 881
constraint 195
constrict 195, 706
constringe 195
construct 161

construction 161
  form 240
  structure 329
  meaning 522
  put a false – upon 523
constructive
  latent 526
  – evidence 467
constructor 164
construe 522
consubstantiation 998
consuetude 618
consul 758, 759
consulship 737
consult 695
  – one's pillow 133
  – one's own wishes 943
  – the wishes of 707
consultant 662
consultation 695, 696
consume
  destroy 162
  waste 638
  use 677
  – away 36
  – time
  time 106
  inactivity 683
consumere natus, fruges – 683
consuming 830
consummate
  great 31
  complete 52
  completed 729
  – skill 698
consummation
  end 67
  completion 729
  – devoutly to be wished
  good 618
  desire 865
consumption [*see* consume]
  decrease 36
  shrinking 195
  disease 655
contact 199
  come in –
  arrive 292
contagion
  transfer 270
  disease 655
  unhealthy 657
contain
  be composed of 54

include 76
container 191
contaminate
  soil 653
  spoil 659
contaminated
  diseased 655
contango 133, 813
contemn 930
contemper 174
contemplate
  view 441
  think 451
  expect 507
  purpose 620
contemporary 120
contemporation 174
contempt 930
  – of danger 861
contemptible
  unimportant 643
  dishonourable 940
contend
  reason 476
  assert 535
  fight 720
  – with difficulties 704
  – for
  vindicate 937
content
  assenting 488
  willing 602
  calm 826
  satisfied **831**
  to one's heart's –
  sufficient 639
  success 731
contention 720
contentious 901
contents
  ingredients 56
  list 86
  components **190**
  synopsis 596
conterminate
  end 67
  limit 233
conterminous 199
contesseration 72
contest 709, 720
contestant 710
context 591
  from the – 516
contexture 329
contiguity 199
continence 960
continent
  land 342
continental 643
contingency

event 151
  uncertainty 475
  expectation 507
contingent
  conditional 8
  casual 156
  liable 177
  possible 470
  uncertain 475
  supply 635
  aid 707
  allotted 786
  donation 809
  unforeseen 508
  – duration **108a**
  – interest 780
continual
  perpetual 112
  frequent 136
continuance 143
continuation
  adjunct 39
  sequence 63
  sequel 65
  – school 542
continue
  endure 106, 110
  persist 143
continued 69
  – success 731
continuity 69
  uniformity 16
contortion
  distortion 243
  convolution 248
contortionist 599, 700
contour
  outline 230
  appearance 448
contra 14
  per – 708
  – bonos mores
  vulgar 851
  improper 925
  vice 945
contraband
  deceitful 545
  prohibited 761
  illicit 964
contrabasso 417
contraception 706
contract
  shrink 195
  narrow 203
  promise 768
  bargain 769
  bridge 840
  – a debt 806
  – a habit 613
  – an obligation

768
contractility 195
contraction 195
  short-hand 590
  compendium 596
contractor 690
contradict
  contrary 14
  answer 462
  dissent 489
  deny 536
  oppose 708
contradictory
  disagreement 24
  evidence 468
  discord 713
contradistinction 15
contraindicate
  dissuade 616
  warning 668
contraire, tout au – 536
contralto 408, 416
contraposition
  inversion 218
  reversion **237**
contrapuntist 413
contrariety 14
contrary
  opposite 14
  antagonistic 179
  captious 608
  opposing 708
  quite the – 536
  – to expectation
  improbable 473
  unexpected 508
  – to reason 471
contrast
  contrariety 14
  difference 15
  comparison 464
contravallation 717
contravene
  contrary 14
  counterevidence 468
  deny 536
  hinder 706
  oppose 708
contre cœur, à – 603
contre-coup 277
contretemps
  ill-timed 135
  hindrance 706
  misfortune 735
contribute
  cause 153
  tend 176
  concus 178

coportion 778
copper *money* 800
  policeman 664
copper-coloured
  433, 439
copper-plate
  engraving 558
  writing 590
coppice 367
coprolite 653
copse 367
copula 45
copulation 43
copy
  imitate 19
  facsimile **21**
  prototype 22
  news 532
  record 551
  represent 554
  write 590
  for the press 591
  plan 626
– book 22
copyhold 780
copyist
  imitator 19
  artist 559
  writer 590
copyright 780
coquet *lie* 544
  change the mind
  607
  affected 855
  endearment 902
  flattery 933
– with
  irresolute 605
coquette
  affected 854, 855
  flirt 897
coquillage 847
coracle 273
coral 847
– reef 667
coram judice
  jurisdiction 965
  lawsuit 969
cor Anglais 417
corbeille 191
corbel 215
cord *tie* 45
  filament 205
cordage 45
cordated 245
cordial
  pleasure 377
  dram 392
  willing 602
  remedy 662
  feeling 821

grateful 829
friendly 888
courteous 894
cordiform 245
cordite 727
cordon
  inclosure 232
  circularity 247
  decoration 877
  – bleu 733, 746
  – sanitaire
  safety 664
  preservation 670
corduroy 259
cordwainer
  shoemaker 225
  artificer 690
core *gist* 5
  source 153
  centre 222
  gist 642
  true to the – 939
coriaceous 327
Corinthian 850
co-rival
  [see corrival]
cork *plug* 263
  lightness 320
  – jacket 666
  – up *close* 261
  restrain 751
corking pin 45
corkscrew
  spiral 248
  perforator 262
  circuition 311
cormorant
  desire 865
  gluttony 957
corn
  projection 250
Cornaro 953
cornea 441
corned 959
cornelian 847
corneous 323
corner *place* 182
  receptacle 191
  angle 244
  monopoly 777
  – creep into a –
  893
  in a dark – 528
  drive into a – 706
  push into a – 874
  rub off –s 82
  – turn a – 311
  turn the – 658
  – stone
  support 215
  importance 642

defence 717
cornet *music* 417
  officer 745
cornice 210
corniculate 253
cornification 323
Cornish hug 545
corno 417
cornopean 417
cornucopia 639
cornute
  projecting 250
  sharp 253
corollary
  adjunct 39
  deduction 480
corona 247
coronach 839
coronation
  enthronement 755
  celebration 883
coroner 363, 965
  –'s jury 967
coronet *hoop* 247
  insignia 747
  title 877
corporal
  corporeal 316
  officer 745
corporate 43
  – body 712
corporation
  bulk 192
  convex 250
  association 712
  jurisdiction 965
corporeal 3, 316,
  364
  – hereditaments
  780
corporeity 316
corps *assemblage* 72
  troops 726
à – perdu
  haste 684
  rash 863
  – de reserve 636
corpse **362**
corpulence 192
corpus 316
  – Christi 998
  – delicti
  guilt 947
  lawsuit 969
  – juris
  precept 697
  law 963
corpuscle
  small 32
  little 193
corradiation

focus 74
convergence 290
corral 232, 370
correct
  orderly 58
  true 494
  inform 527
  disclose 529
  improve 658
  repair 660
  due 924
  censure 932
  honourable 939
  virtuous 944
  punish 972
  – ear 416, 418
  – memory 505
  – reasoning 476
  – style
  grammatical 567
  elegant 578
correction
  [see correct]
  house of – 752
  under – 879
corrective 662
corregidor 745
correlation
  relation 9
  reciprocity **12**
correspondence
  correlation 12
  similarity 17
  agreement 23
  writing **592**
  – course 537
correspondent
  messenger 534
  journalist 593
  consignee 758
corresponding
  similar 17
  agreeing 23
corridor *region* 181
  place 191
  passage 627
  – train 272
corrigendum 495
corrigible 658
corrival 726
corrivalry 720
corrivation 348
corroborant 662
corroboration
  evidence 467
  assent 488
corrode *burn* 384
  erode 659
  afflict 830
corrosive
  [see corrode]

acrid 171
destructive 649
– *sublimate* 663
corrugate
  derange 61
  constrict 195
  roughen 256
  rumple 258
  furrow 259
corruption
  decomposition 49
  neology 563
  foulness 653
  disease 655
  deterioration 659
  improbity 940
  vice 945
corrupting
  noxious 649
corsage 225
corsair 273, 792
corse 362
corselet 225
corset 225
corso 728
cortège
  adjunct 39
  continuity 69
  accompaniment 88
  journey 266
  suite 746
cortes 696
cortex
  cortical 223
coruscate 420
corvette 273, 726
corybantic 503
coryphée 599
Corypheus
  teacher 540
  director 694
coscinomancy 511
cosey 892
cosignificative 522
cosine 217
cosmetic
  remedy 662
  ornament 847
cosmic 318
cosmogony &c. 318
cosmopolitan
  abode 189
  mankind 372
  philanthropic 910
  sociality 892
cosmorama 448
cosmos 60, 318
Cossack 726
cosset
  darling 899

caress 902
cost 812
  pay –s 807
  to one's –
   evil 619
   badness 649
  – *what it may* 604
  – *price* 815
costermonger 797
costless 815
costly 814
costive
  taciturn 585
costume 225
  theatrical – 599
costumé 225
  bal – 840
costumier 225
  theatrical 599
cosy *snug* 377
  sociable 892
cot *abode* 189
  bed 215
cote 189
cotenancy 778
coterie *class* 75
  junto 712
  society 892
coterminous 120
cothurnus 599
cotillon 840
cottage 189
  – *piano* 417
cottager 188
cotter 188
cotton 205
  – *seed oil* 356
couch *lie* 213
  bed 215
  stoop 308
  lurk 528
  – *one's lance* 720
  – *in terms* 566
couchant 213
couci-couci 651
cough 349
  churchyard – 655
couleur de rose
  good 648
  prosperity 734
  view en – 836
coulisses 599
coulter 253
council
  senate **696**
  church 995
  hold a – 695
  – of education 542
  – school 542
councillor 696
counsel

advice 695
lawyer 968
keep one's own –
  528
take – *think* 451
  inquire 461
  be advised 695
count *clause* 51
  item 79
  compute 85
  estimate 480
  lord 875
  – *one's chickens*
   before they are
   hatched 858,
   863
  – *the cost* 864
  – *upon*
   believe 484
   expect 507
  to be –ed on one's
   fingers 103
countenance
  face 234
  appearance 448
  favour 707
  approve 931
  keep in –
   conform 82
   induce 615
   encourage 861
   vindicate 937
  keep one's –
   brook 826
   not laugh 837
  out of –
   abashed 879
  put out of – 874
  stare out of – 885
  – *falling*
   disappointment
   509
   dejection 837
counter *contrary* 14
  number 84
  table 215
  stern 235
  token 550
  shop-board 799
  over the –
   barter 794
   buy 795
   sell 796
  run – 179
  – *to* 708
counteract
  compensate 30
  physically 179
  hinder 706
  voluntarily 708
counteraction 14,

179
counterbalance 30
counterblast
  counteract 179
  retaliate 718
countercharge 462
counterchange
  correlation 12
  interchange 148
countercharm 993
countercheck
  mark 550
  hindrance 706
counterclaim 30
counter-evidence
  468
counterfeit
  imitate 19
  copy 21
  simulate 544
  sham 545
  coinage 792
counterfoil 550
countermand 756
countermarch 266,
  283
countermark 550
countermine
  plan 626
  oppose 708
countermotion 283
counterorder 756
counterpane 223
counterpart
  match 17
  copy 21
  reverse 237
counterplot
  plan 626
  oppose 708
  retaliate 718
counterpoint 415
counterpoise
  compensate 30
  weight 319
  hinder 706
counter-poison 662
counterpole 14
counter-project 718
counter-protest 468
counter-revolution
  146
counterscarp 717
countersign
  evidence 467
  assent 488
  mark 550
counterstroke 718
countervail
  outweigh 28
  compensate 30

rotation 312
wind 349
cyclopædia
  knowledge 490
  book 593
Cyclopean
  strong 159
  huge 192
Cyclops
  monster 83
  mighty 159
  huge 192
  dupe 547
cygne
  chant du – 360
  – noir 650
cylindric 249
cyma 847
cymbal 417
cymbalo 417
cymophanous 440
cynic
  misanthrope 911
  detractor 936
  ascetic 955
  closet – 893
cynical
  contemptuous 930
  censorious 932
  detracting 934
cynicism
  discourtesy 895
  contempt 930
cynosure sign 550
  direction 693
  wonder 870
  repute 873
Cynthia of the
  minute 149
cypher [see cipher]
cypress
  interment 363
  mourning 839
Cyprian 962
cyst 191
czar 745

D

da capo 104
dab small 32
  paint 223
  slap 276
  clever 700
dabble water 337
  dirty 653
  meddle 682
  fribble 683
dabbled wet 339
dabbler 493

dachshund 366
dacoit 792
dactyl 597
dactylogram 467
dactyliomancy 511
dactylonomy
  numeration 85
  symbol 550
dad 166
daddy 166
dado 211
dædal
  variegated 440
dædalion
  convoluted 248
  artistic 698
daft 503
dagger 727
  look –s anger 900
  threat 909
  air drawn – 515
  plant – in breast
  give pain 830
  speak –s 932
  at –s drawn
  opposed 708
  discord 713
  enmity 889
  hate 898
daggle hang 214
  dirty 653
dagobah 1000
Dagon 986
daguerreotype
  represent 554
  paint 556
dahabeah 273
Dail Eireann 696
daily
  frequent 136
  periodic 138
  – occurrence
  normal 82
  habitual 613
  – paper 531
dainty food 298
  savoury 394
  pleasing 829
  delicate 845
  tasty 850
  fastidious 868
dairy 191, 370
  – maid 946
dais support 215
  throne 747
daisy
  fresh as a – 654
  – pied 847
dale 252
dally delay 133
  irresolute 605

inactive 683
amuse 840
fondle 902
dalmatic 999
Daltonism 443
dam parent 166
  close 261
  pond 343
  obstruct 706
damage evil 619
  injure, spoil 659
  price 812
damages 974
damascene 440
damask 434
dame
  woman 374
  teacher 540
  lady 875
damn
  malediction 908
  condemn 971
  – with faint
    praise 932, 934
damnable 649
damnatory
  disapprove 932
  condemn 971
damnify
  damage 649
  spoil 659
damnosa hereditas
  663
Damocles
  sword of – 667
Damon and
  Pythias 890
damozel 129
damp
  moderate 174
  moist 339
  cold 385
  sound 405
  dissuade 616
  hinder 706
  depress 837
  dull 843
  – the sound 408a
damper 387
damsel
  youth 129
  female 374
Dan to Beersheba
  52, 180
Danaë 803
Danaos, timeo –
  doubt 485
  caution 864
dance
  jump 309
  oscillate 314

agitate 315
rejoice 838
sport 840
sociality 892
lead the – 175
lead one a –
  run away 623
  circuit 629
  difficult 704
  practical joke 929
St. Vitus' – 315
– attendance
  waiting 133
  follow 281
  servant 746
  petition 765
  servility 886
– the back step
  283
– upon nothing
  972
– the war dance
  715
dance-band 417
dance-music 415
dander 900
Dandie Dinmont
  366
dandiprat 193
dandle 902
dandruff 653
dandy
  ship 273
  fop 854
dandyism 855
danger 665
  in – liable 177
  source of – 667
  – past 664
  – signal 669
dangerous
  [see danger]
  – classes 913
  – illness 655
  – person 667
dangle hang 214
  swing 314
  display 882
dangler 281
Daniel sage 500
  judge 967
dank 339
Dannemora 752
danseuse 599
dapper
  little 193
  elegant 845
dapple 433
dappled 440
darbies
  handcuffs 752

Darby and Joan
  secluded 893
  married 903
dare *defy* 715
  face danger 861
  – not 860
  – say *probable* 472
  believe 484
  suppose 514
dare-devil
  courage 861
  rash 863
  bluster 887
daring 861
  unreserved 525
  – imagination 515
dark
  obscure 421
  dim 422
  black 431
  blind 442
  invisible 447
  unintelligible 519
  latent 526
  joyless 837
  insidious 940
  in the –
  ignorant 491
  leap in the –
  experiment 463
  chance 621
  rash 863
  keep – *hide* 528
  – ages 491
  – cloud 735
  view with – eyes
  932
  – lantern 423
darkly
  see through a
  glass – 443
darkness [*see* dark]
  421
  children of – 988
  love – better than
  light 989
  powers of – 978
darky 431
darling *beloved* 897
  favourite 899
darn 660
dart *swift* 274
  propel 284
  missile 727
  – to and fro 684
Dartmoor 752
Darwinism 357
dash
  small quantity 32
  mix 41
  swift 276

fling 284
  mark 550
  courage 861
  cut a – *repute* 873
  display 882
  – at *resolution* 604
  attack 716
  – board 666
  – cup from lips 761
  – down 308
  – hopes
  disappoint 509
  fail 732
  dejected 837
  despair 859
  – on 274
  – off *paint* 556
  write 590
  active 682
  haste 684
  – of the pen 590
dashed [*see* dash]
  humbled 879
dashing
  fashionable 852
  brave 861
  ostentatious 882
dastard 862
data *evidence* 467
  reasoning 476
  supposition 514
date *time* 106
  chronology 114
datum 673
daub *cover* 223
  paint 428
  misrepresent 555
  dirt 653
daughter 167
daunt 860
dauntless 861
Dauphin 875
davenport 191, 215
davit 214
Davus sum non
  Œdipus
  unintelligent 499
  artless 703
  dull 843
Davy Jones' locker
  310
dawdle *tardy* 133
  slow 275
  inactive 683
dawk 534
dawn
  precursor 64
  begin 66
  priority 116
  morning 125
  light 420

dim 422
  glimpse 490
dawplucker 936
day
  period 108
  present time 118
  light 410
  all – 110
  clear as –
  certain 474
  intelligible 518
  manifest 525
  close of – 126
  decline of – 126
  denizens of the –
  366
  good old –'s 122
  have had its – 124
  one fine – 119
  open as – 703
  order of the – 613
  red letter – 642
  see the light of –
  446
  – after day
  diuturnal 110
  frequent 136
  – by day
  repeatedly 104
  time 106
  periodic 138
  – after the fair
  135
  –s gone by 122
  – of judgment 121
  happy as the – is
  long 827, 836
  – and night
  frequent 136
  labour – and night
  686
  –s numbered
  transient 111
  death 360
  – one's own 731
  – of rest 686
  – star 423
  – after to-morrow
  121
  – before yesterday
  122
  –s of week 138
  all in –'s work 625
daybed 215
daybook *record* 551
  accounts 811
daybreak
  morning 125
  dim 422
day-dream
  fancy 515

hope 858
day-labourer 690
daylight 125, 420
  see – *intelligible*
  518
  – saving 114
daymare 859
daze 420
dazed 376
dazzle
  light 420
  blind 422, 443
  put out 458
  astonish 870
  awe 928
dazzling
  [*see* dazzle]
  beautiful 845
de: – die in diem
  time 106
  periodic 138
  – facto 1
  – fond en comble
  52
  – novo 104
  – omnibus rebus
  81
  – profundis 821
deacon 996
deaconry 995
dead *complete* 52
  inert 172
  colourless 429
  lifeless 360
  insensible 376
  – against
  contrary 14
  oppose 708
  more – than alive
  688
  – asleep 683
  – beat
  powerless 158
  – certainty 474
  – colour 556
  – cut 893
  – drunk 959
  – failure 732
  – flat 213
  – heat 27
  – languages 560
  – letter
  impotent 158
  unmeaning 517
  useless 645
  laxity 738
  exempt 927
  illegal 964
  – level 16
  – lift *exertion* 686
  difficulty 704, 706

kill 361
play *havoc* 659
punish 972
decipher 522
decision
judgment 480
resolution 604
intention 620
law case 969
decisive
certain 474
proof 478
commanding 741
take a – step 609
deck *floor* 211
beautify 847
declaim 531, 582
– against 932
declamatory
style 577
speech 582
declaration
affirmation 535
law pleadings 969
– of faith
belief 484
theology 983
– of war 713
declaratory
meaning 516
inform 527
declare
publish 531
declension
[see decline]
grammar 567
backsliding 988
declensions 5
declination
[see decline]
deviation 279
measurement 466
rejection 610
decline *decrease* 36
old 124
weaken 160
descent 306
grammar 567
be unwilling 603
reject 610
disease 655
become worse 659
adversity 735
refuse 764
– of day 126
– of life 128
declivity *slope* 217
descent 306
decoction 335, 384
decode 522
decollate 972

décolleté 226
decoloration 429
decomposition 49
deconsecrate 756
decontrol 158
décor 448, 599
decoration
insignia 747
ornament 847
title 877
decorative 556
decorous
[see decorum]
fashionable 862
proper 924
respectful 928
decorticate 226
decorum
fashion 852
duty 926
purity 960
décousu
discontinuous 70
failure 732
decoy *attract* 288
deceive 545
deceiver 548
entice 615
decrease 36, 195
decree
judgment 480
order 741
law 963, 969
decrement
decrease 36
thing deducted **40a**
contraction 195
decrepit *old* 128
weak 158, 160
disease 655
decayed 659
decrepitate 406
decrescendo 36
decretal 741
decry *underrate* 483
censure 932
detract 934
decumbent 213
decuple 98
decursive 306
decurtation 201
decussation 219
dedecorous
disreputable 874
discourteous 895
dedicate *use* 677
inscribe 873
deduce *deduct* 38
infer 480
deducible
evidence 467

proof 478
deduct *retrench* 38
deprive 789
subtract 813
deduction
[see deduce]
decrement 40a
reasoning 476
deed *evidence* 467
record 551
act 680
security 771
–s of arms 720
– without a name 947
deem 484
deemster 967
deep *great* 31
profound 208
sea 341
sonorous 404
cunning 702
plough the – 267
– colour 428
– in debt 806
– game 702
– knowledge 490
– mourning 839
– note 408
– potations 959
– reflection 451
– sense 821
– sigh 839
– study 457
in – water 704
deepen 35
deep-dyed
intense 171
black 431
vicious 945
deep-felt 821
deep-laid *plan* 626
deep-mouthed
resonant 408
bark 412
thrilling 821
deep-musing 458
deep-read 490
deep-rooted
stable 150
strong 159
belief 484
habit 613
affections 820
deep-sea 208
deep-seated 208, 221
deer 366
in heart a – 862
deev 980
deface

destroy form 241
obliterate 552
injure 659
render ugly 846
defalcation
incomplete 53
contraction 195
shortcoming 304
non-payment 808
defame *shame* 874
censure 932
detract 934
defamer 936
defatigation 841
default
incomplete 53
shortcoming 304
neglect 460
insufficiency 640
debt 806
non-payment 808
in – of 187
judgment by – 725
defaulter *thief* 792
non-payer 808
rogue 949
defeasance 756
defeat
confute 479
succeed 731
failure 732
– one's hope 509
defeatism 911
defecate 652
defecation 299
defect
decrement 40a
incomplete 53
imperfect 651
failing 945
defection
relinquishment 624
disobedience 742
defective
incomplete 53
insufficient 640
imperfect 651
defence
plea 462
resist **717**
vindication 937
first line of – 726
defenceless
impotent 158
weak 160
exposed 665
defendant 938
defensible *safe* 664
excusable 937
defensive alliance

712
defer 133
  – to *assent* 488
  submit 725
  respect 928
deference
  obedience 743
  humility 879
  courtesy 894
  respect 928
defiance 715, 909
  threat 909
  in – *opposition* 708
  set at – *disobey* 742
  – of *danger* 861
deficiency
  [*see* deficient]
  vice 945
deficient
  inferior 34
  incomplete 53
  shortcoming 304
  insufficient 640
  imperfect 651
deficit
  incompleteness 53
  debt 806
defigure 846
defile
  interval 198
  march 266
  dirt 653
  spoil 659
  shame 874
  impure 961
define
  specify 79
  limit 233
  explain 522
  name 564
definite
  [*see* define]
  visible 446
  certain 474
  exact 494
  intelligible 518
  manifest 525
  perspicuous 570
definition
  interpretation 521
definitive *final* 67
  affirmative 535
  decided 604
deflagration 384
deflate 195
deflation
  currency 800
deflect
  curve 245
  deviate 279
deflower

spoil 659
violate 961
defluxion
  egress 295
  flowing 348
defœdation 653,
  659
deform 241
deformity
  distortion 243
  ugliness 846
  blemish 848
defraud *cheat* 545
  swindle 791
defray 807
deft *suitable* 23
  clever 698
defunct 360, 362
defy 715
  disobey 742
  threaten 909
  – *danger* 861
dégagé *free* 748
  fashion 852
degenerate 659
deglutition 298
degradation
  deterioration 659
  shame 874
  dishonour 940
degree 26
  term 71
  honour 873
  by –s 26
  by slow –s 275
degustation 390
dehiscence 260
dehort
  dissuade 616
  advise 695
dehydrate 340
Dei gratiâ 924
deification 873, 981
deify
  honour 873
  idolatry 991
deign
  condescend 762
  consent 879
Deism
  heterodoxy 984
  irreligion 989
Deity 976
  tutelary – 664
dejection
  excretion 299
  melancholy **837**
déjeûner 298
délabrement 162
delaceration 659
delation 938

delator 527
delay 133
dele 552
delectable
  savoury 394
  agreeable 829
delectation 827
delectus 562
delegate
  transfer 270
  commission 755
  consignee 758
  deputy 759
delenda est
  Carthago
  destroy 162
  curse 908
delete 162
deleterious
  pernicious 649
  unwholesome 657
deletion 552
deletory
  destructive 162
deliberate
  slow 275
  think 451
  attentive 457
  leisure 685
  advise 695
  cautious 864
deliberately
  [*see* deliberate]
  late 133
  with premedi-
  tation 611
delicacy *weak* 160
  slender 203
  dainty 298
  brittleness 328
  texture 329
  savoury 394
  colour 428
  exact 494
  scruple 603
  ill health 655
  difficult 704
  pleasing 829
  beauty 845
  taste 850
  fastidious 868
  honour 939
  pure 960
  delicate ear 418
délice 377
delicious *taste* 394
  pleasing 829
delicti, corpus –
  guilt 947
  lawsuit 969
delicto, in

flagrante – 947
delight
  pleasure 827
  pleasing 829
Delilah 962
delimit 233
delineate
  outline 230
  represent 554
  describe 594
delineator 559
delineavit 556
delinquency 304,
  947
delinquent 949
deliquation 335
deliquesce 36
deliquescence 335
deliquium
  paralysis 158
  fatigue 688
delirant reges
  plectuntur
  Achivi 739
delirium
  raving 503
  passion 825
  – *tremens* 503,
  959
delitescence
  invisible 447
  latency 526
  seclusion 893
deliver
  transfer 270
  utter 580, 582
  birth 662
  rescue 672
  liberate 750
  give 784
  relieve 834
  – as one's *act and*
  deed 467
  – the *goods* 729
  – *judgment* 480
  – a *speech* 582
deliverance 672
delivery
  [*see* deliver]
  bring forth 161
  cash on – 807
dell 252
Delphic oracle
  prophetic 513
  equivocal 520
  latent 526
delta 342
delude *error* 495
  deceive 545
deluge *crowd* 72
  water 337

flood 348
redundance 641
delusion
[*see* delude]
insane 503
self − *credulous*
486
delve *dig* 252
till 371
− into *inquire* 461
demagogue
director 694
malcontent 710
rebel 742
demagogy 737
demand
inquire 461
order 741
ask 765
price 812
claim 924
in − *require* 630
desire 865
saleable 796
demarcation 233
dematerialize 317
demean oneself
conduct 692
humble 879
dishonour 940
demeanour
aid 448
conduct 692
fashion 852
demency 503
dementia 503
demerit 945
demesne
abode 189
property 780
demi- 91
demigod *hero* 861
angel 948
demigration 266
demijohn 191
demi-jour 422
demi-lune 717
demi-monde
plebeian 876
licentious 962
démenti 536
demirep 962
demise *death* 360
transfer 783
lease 787
demisemiquaver
413
demission 756
demit 757
demiurge
deity 979

demivolt 309
demobilize 73
democracy *rule* 737
commonalty 876
Democrats
party 712
Democritus 838
demoiselle 129
demolish 479
demon *violent* 173
bane 663
devil **980**
− in human shape
913, 949
− worship 991
demoniacal
malevolent 907
furious 824
wicked 945
demonology
demons 980
sorcery 992
demonstration
number 85
proof **478**
manifest 525
ostentation 882
ocular − 441, 446
demonstrative
manifest 525
indicative 550
vehement 825
demonstrator 524
demoralize
unnerve 158
spoil 659
vicious 945
Demosthenes 582
demotic 590
demulcent
mild 174
soothing 662
demur
disbelieve 485
dissent 489
unwilling 603
hesitate 605
without − 602
demure
grave 826
sad 837
affected 855
modest 881
demurrage 132
demurrer 969
den *abode* 189
study 191, 893
sty 653
prison 752
− of thieves 791

denary 98
denaturalize
corrupt 659
denaturalized
abnormal 83
dendriform 242, 367
dendrology 369
denial
negation 536
refusal 764
self− 953
denigrate 431
denization 748
denizen
inhabitant 188
freeman 748
−s of the air 979
−s of the day 366
**Denmark, rotten in
the state of −**
526
denomination
class 75
name 564
sect 712
religious − 983
denominational
dissent 489
theological 983
− education 537
denominator 84
denote
specify 79
mean 516
indicate 550
dénouement
end 67
result 154
disclosure 529
completion 729
denounce
curse 908
disapprove 932
accuse 938
dense
crowded 72
ignorant 493
density **321**
dent 252, 257
dental 561
denticulated 253,
257
dentifrice 652
dentistry 662
denude 226
denuded *loss* 776
− of
insufficient 640
denunciation
[*see* denounce]
deny *dissent* 489

negative 556
refuse 764
− oneself
avoid 623
seclude 893
temperate 953
ascetic 990
Deo volente 470,
976
deobstruct 705
deodand 974
deodorize 399
clean 652
deontology 926
deoppilation 705
deorganization 61
deosculation 902
depart 293
− from
deviate 15, 279
relinquish 624
− this life 360
departed
non-existent 2
department
class 75
region 181
business 625
departure 293
new − 66
point of − 293
depend *hang* 214
contingent 475
− upon
be the effect of 154
evidence 467
trust 484
− on circumstan-
ces 475
**depended on, to
be −**
certain 474
reliable 484
honourable 939
dependency 777,
780
dependent
effect 154
liable 177
hanging 214
puppet 711
servant 746
subject 749
deperdition 776
dephlegmation 340
depict 554, 556
describe 594
depilation 226
depilatory 662
depletion 638, 640
deplorable *bad* 649

disastrous 735
painful 830
deplore *regret* 833
complain 839
remorse 950
deploy 194
depone 535
deponent 467
depopulate
eject 297
desert 893
deportation
removal 270
emigration 297
expulsion 972
deportment 692
depose
evidence 467
declare 535
dethrone 738, 756
deposit *place* 184
precipitate 321
store 636
security 771
payment 809
depositary 801
deposition
[*see* depose,
deposit]
record 551
depository 636
depôt *terminal* 292
store 636
shop 799
– ship 726
deprave *spoil* 659
depraved *bad* 649
vicious 945
deprecation 766
pity 914
disapprove 932
depreciation
decrease 36
underestimate 483
discount 813
cheap 815
disrespect 929
censure 932
detraction 934
accusation 938
depredation 791
depredator 792
deprehension 789
depression
lowness 207
depth 208
concavity 252
lowering **308**
dejection 837
dulness 843
depressing

[458]

painful 830
deprive *subduct* 38
take 798
– of life 361
– of power 158
– of property 789
– of strength 160
deprived of 776
depth *physical* **208**
mental 498
out of one's – 304,
310
– bomb 727
– of misery 828
– of thought 451
– of winter 383
depurate *clean* 652
improve 658
depuratory 662
deputation 755
depute 755
deputies, chamber
of – 696
deputy **759**
dequantitate 36
derangement **61**
mental – 503
Derby-day 720
derelict *land* 342
danger 667
relinquish 782
outcast 893
dereliction
relinquishment
624, 782
guilt 947
– of duty **927**
deride
ridicule 856
disrespect 929
contempt 930
derivation
origin 153, 154,
155
verbal 562
derive
attribute 155
deduce 480
acquire 775
income 810
dermal 223
dermatology 223
dernier
– cri 850
– ressort 601
dérobée, à la – 528
derogate
underrate 483
disparage 934
dishonour 940
– from 874

derogatory
shame 874
dishonour 940
derrick 307, 633
derring-do 861
dervish 996
désagrément 830
descant *music* 415
diffuseness 573
loquacity 584
dissert 595
descend *slope* 217
go down 306
– to particulars
special 79
describe 594
descendant 167
descensus Averni,
facilis – 665
descent *lineage* 166
fall **306**
inheritance 775
description
kind 75
name 564
narration **594**
descriptive music
415
descry 441
desecrate
misuse 679
disrespect 929
profane 988
desert
unproductive 169
empty 187
plain 344
run away 623
relinquish 624,
782
merit 944
waste sweetness
on – air 638
deserted
outcast 893
deserter 144, 607,
623
desertless 945
deserts 924
deserve
be entitled to 924
merit 944
– notice 642
– belief 484
désespoir, au –
dejected 837
hopeless 859
déshabillé, en –
not dressed 226
unprepared 674
homely 849

desiccate 340
desiccator 340
desiderate *need* 630
desire 865
desideratum
inquiry 461
requirement 630
desire 865
design
prototype 22
form 240
delineation 554
painting 556
intention 620
plan 626
designate
specify 79
call 564
designation 75
designed
aforethought 611
designer 164, 559
designing
cunning 702
designless 621
désillusioner 529
desinence *end* 67
discontinuance
142
desipience 499
desipere in loco 840
desirable 646
desire **865**
will 600
have no – for 866
desist
discontinue 142
relinquish 624
inaction 681
desk *box* 191
support 215
school 542
pulpit 1000
désobligeant 272
désœuvré 681
desolate *alone* 87
ravage 162
afflicted 828
dejected 837
secluded 893
desolating
painful 830
désorienté 475
despair *grief* 828,
859
despatch *eject* 297
kill 361
news 532
epistle 592
expedition 682
haste 684

conduct 692
complete 729
command 741
happy – 972
– case 191
– food 298
– rider 534
desperado
rash 863
blusterer 887
evil-doer 913
desperate great 31
violent 173
impossible 471
resolved 604
difficult 704
excitable 825
hopeless 859
rash 863
anger 900
despicable
trifling 643
shameful 874
contemptible 930
despise 930
– danger 861
despite 30, 907
in – 708
despoil injure 659
take 789
rob 791
despond 837, 860
despot 745
despotism
authority 737
severity 739
arbitrary 964
despumate 652
desquamation 226
dessert 298
dessous des cartes
cause 153
latent 526
secret 533
connaître le – 490
dessus dessous
sens – 218
destination end 67
arrival 292
intention 620
destiny chance **152**
fate 601
fight against – 606
destitute
insufficient 640
poor 804
refuge for – 666
destrier 726
destroy
demolish 162
injure 659

– hopes 859
– life 361
destroyed
[see destroy]
inexistent 2
failure 732
destroyer 165
warship 726
evil-doer 913
destructive
bad 649
destructor 383
desuetude 614
disuse 678
desultory
disordered 59
fitful 70
multiform 81
irregular in time
139
changeable 149
deviating 279
agitated 315
desume 788
detach 44
detached
irrelated 10
loose 47
detachment
part 51
army 726
detail describe 594
special portions
79
allot 786
ornament 847
attention to –
457, 459
in – 51
details
minutiæ 32
unimportant 643
detain 781
detect 480a
detective 527, 664
detention 133, 751,
781
house of – 752
in house of – 938
détenu 754
deter dissuade 616
alarm 860
deterge clean 652
detergent
remedy 662
deterioration 659
determinate
special 79
exact 474
conclusive 480
intended 620

determine end 67
define 79
cause 153
direction 278
satisfy 462
make sure 474
judge 480
discover 480a
resolve 604
determined
resolute 604
determinism 601
deterration 529
detersion 652
detersive 662
detest dislike 867
hate 898
detestable 649
dethronement
anarchy 738
abrogation 756
detonate
explode 173
sound 406
detortion form 243
meaning 523
détour curve 245
circuit 629
detract subduct 38
underrate 483
defame 934
slander 938
detraction 934
detractor 936
detrain 292
detriment
evil 619
deterioration 659
detrimental 649
detrition 330
detritus
fragments 51
deposit 270
powder 330
detrude
cast out 297
cut down 308
detruncate 38
deuce two 89
devil 978
play the – 825
– is in him 608
deuced great 31
painful 830
deus 976
– ex machinâ
aid 707
auxiliary 711
deity 976
sorcerer 994
deuterogamy 903

devastate
destroy 162
havoc 659
develop
increase 35
produce 161
expand 194
evolve 313
development 144,
154
devexity
bending 217
curvature 245
deviate vary 20a
change 140
turn 279
diverge 291
circuit 629
– from 15
– from rectitude
940
– from virtue 945
deviation 279
device motto 550
expedient 626
artifice 702
devil
seasoned food 392
evil-doer 913
bad man 949
Satan 978
demon 980
fight like –s 722
have a – 503
machinations of
the – 619
play the – with
injure 659
malevolent 907
printer's – 591
raise the – 828
– may care
rash 863
indifferent 866
insolent 885
give the – his due
right 922
vindicate 937
fair 939
– in one
headstrong 863
temper 901
– to pay
disorder 59
violence 173
evil 619
failure 732
penalty 974
– take 908
– take the hind-
most

discous 202
discover
  perceive 441
  solve 462
  find 480a
  disclose 529
  – *itself*
  be seen 446
discovery 480a
discredit
  disbelief 485
  dishonour 874
discreditable
  vicious 945
discreet *careful* 459
  cautious 864
discrepancy 15
discrepant 24, 713
discrete
  separate 44, 70
  single 87
discretion *will* 600
  choice 609
  skill 698
  caution 864
  surrender at – 725
  use – 609
  years of – 131
discrétion à – 600
discrimination
  difference 15
  nice perception
  465
  wisdom 498
  taste 850
  fastidiousness 868
disculpate 937
discumbency 213
discursion 266
discursive
  moving 264
  migratory 266
  wandering 279
  argumentative 476
  diffuse style 573
  conversable 588
  disserting 595
discus 840
discuss *eat* 298
  reflect 451
  inquire 461
  reason 476
  dissert 595
discussion
  [*see* discuss]
  open to – 475
  under – 461
disdain
  indifference 866
  fastidious 868
  arrogance 885

  pride 878
  contempt 930
disease 655
  occupational – 655
  –d mind 503
disembark 292
disembarrass 705
disembody
  decompose 49
  disperse 73
  spiritualize 317
disembogue
  emit 295
  eject 297
  flow out 348
disembowel 297,
  301
disembroil 60
disenable 158
disenchant
  discover 480a
  dissuade 616
  displease 830
disencumber 705
disendow 756
disengage
  detach 44
  facilitate 705
  liberate 750
disengaged
  to let 763
disentangle
  separate 44
  arrange 60
  unroll 313
  decipher 522
  facilitate 705
  liberate 750
disenthral 750
disenthrone 756
disentitle 925
disespouse 905
disestablish
  displace 185
  abrogate 756
disesteem 929, 932
disfavour
  oppose 708
  hate 898
  disrespect 929
  view with – 932
disfigure
  deface 241
  injure 659
  deform 846
  blemish 848
disfranchise 925
disgorge *emit* 297
  flow out 348
  restore 790
  pay 807

disgrace
  shame 874
  dishonour 940
  sense of – 879
disgraceful
  vice 945
disgruntle 509
disguise
  unlikeness 18
  conceal 528
  mask 530
  falsify 544
  untruth 546
disguised in drink
  959
disgust *taste* 395
  offensive 830
  weary 841
  dislike 867
  hatred 898
  – of life 837
dish *destroy* 162
  plate 191
  food 298
  – of tea 892
dishabille
  undress 225
  unprepared 674
dishearten
  dissuade 616
  pain 830
  discontent 832
  deject 837
dished 252, 732
disherison 789
dishevel
  loose 47
  untidy 59
  disorder 61
  disperse 73
  intermix 219
dishonest *false* 544
  base 940
dishonour
  disrepute 874
  disrespect 929
  baseness 940
  – bills 808
dish-water 653
disillusion 509
disincline
  dissuade 616
  dislike 867
disinclined 603
disinfect
  purify 652
  restore 660
disinfectant 662
disingenuous
  false 544
  dishonourable 940

disinherit
  relinquish 782
  transfer 783
  deprive 789
disintegrate
  separate 44
  decompose 49
  pulverize 330
disinter *exhume* 363
  discover 480a
disinterested 942
disjecta membra
  separate 44
  disorder 59
  dispersed 73
  – poetæ 597
disjoin 44
disjointed
  disorder 59
  powerless 158
  style 575
disjunction 44
disjunctive 70
diskindness 907
dislike 867
  reluctance 603
  hate 898
dislocate
  separate 44
  put out of joint 61
dislocated
  disorder 59
dislodge
  displace 185
  eject 297
disloyal 940
dismal
  depressing 830
  dejected 837
dismantle
  destroy 162
  divest 226
  render useless 645
  injure 659
  disuse 678
dismask 529
dismast
  render useless 645
  injure 659
  disuse 678
dismay 860
dismember
  separate 44
  disperse 73
dismiss
  send away 289
  discharge 297
  discard 678
  liberate 750
  abrogate 756
  relinquish 782

punish 972
– from the mind
452, 458
dismount
arrive 292
descend 306
render useless 645
disnest 185
disobedience 742
non-observance
773
disoblige 907
disorder
confusion **59**
derange 61
turbulent 173
disease 655
–ed intellect 503
disorderly
unprincipled 945
disorganize
derange 61
destroy 162
spoil 659
disorganized 59
disown 536
dispair 44
disparage
underrate 483
disrespect 929
dispraise 932
detract 934
disparity
different 15
dissimilar 18
disagreeing 24
unequal 28
isolated 44
dispart 44
dispassionate 826
– opinion 484
dispatch
[see despatch]
dispel scatter 73
destroy 162
displace 185
repel 289
dispensable
useless 645
dispensary 662
dispensation
[see dispense]
command 741
licence 760
relinquishment
782
exemption 927a
–s of Providence
976
dispense
disperse 73

give 784
apportion 786
retail 796
– with
disuse 678
permit 760
exempt 927a
cannot be –d with
630
dispeople
eject 297
expatriate 893
disperse
separate 44
scatter 73
diverge 291
waste 638
dispersion 73
– of light 420
chromatic – 428
dispirit
discourage 616
sadden 837
displacement
derange 61
remove **185**
transfer 270
displacency
dislike 867
incivility 895
disapprobation
932
displant 185
display appear 448
show 525
parade 882
displease 830
displeasure 828
anger 900
displosion 173
displume 789
disport 840
disposal
[see dispose]
at one's – 763, 777
dispose
arrange 60
tend 176
induce 615
– of use 677
complete 729
relinquish 782
give 784
sell 796
disposed 620
disposition
nature 5
order 58
arrangement 60
inclination 602
mind 820

dispossess
transfer 783
take away 789
– oneself of 782
dispraise 932
dispread 73
disprize 483
disproof
counter-evidence
468
confutation 479
disproportion
irrelation 10
disagreement 24
disprove 479
disputable 475, 485
disputant 710, 726
disputatious 901
dispute
discuss 476
doubt 485
deny 536
discord 713
in – 461
disqualification
incapacitate 158
useless 645
unprepared 674
unskilful 699
disentitle 925
disquiet
changeable 149
agitation 315
excitement 825
uneasiness 828
give pain 830
disquietude
apprehension 860
disquisition 539,
595
disregard
overlook 458
neglect 460
make light of 483
insensible to 823,
826
disrespect **929**
contempt 930
– of time 115
disrelish 867, 898
disreputable 874
vicious 945
disrepute 874, 929
disrespect 929
despise 930
disrobe 226
disruption
disjunction 44
destruction 162
discord 713
dissatisfaction

disappointment
509
sorrow 828
discontent 832
dissect
anatomize 44, 49
investigate 461
dissemblance 18
dissemble 544
dissembler 548
disseminate
scatter 73
pervade 186
publish 531
teach 537
dissension 713
sow – 898
dissent
disagree **489**
refuse 764
heterodoxy 984
dissentient 15
dissentious 24
dissertation 595
disservice
disadvantage 619
useless 645
disserviceable 649
dissever 44
dissidence
disagreement 24
dissent 489
discord 713
discontent 832
heterodoxy 984
dissilience 173
dissimilarity 18
dissimulate 544
dissipate scatter 73
destroy 162
pleasure 377
prodigality 818
amusement 840
intemperance **954**
dissolute 961
dissocial 893
dissociate 44
dissociation
irrelation 10
separation 44
dissolute 961
profligate 945
intemperate 954
dissolution
[see dissolve]
decomposition 49
destruction 162
death 360
dissolve vanish 2, 4
liquefy 335
disappear 449

division
[see divide]
part 51
class 75
arithmetic 85
discord 713
military 726
divisor 84
divorce
separation 44
relinquish 782
matrimonial **905**
Divorce Court 966
divulge 529
divulsion 44
divvy 786
dixi 535
dizen 847
dizzard 501
dizzy
dimsighted 443
confused 458
vertigo 503
– height 206
– round 312
djerrid 727
djinn 980
do fare 7
suit 23
produce 161
cheat 545
act 680
complete 729
succeed 731
I beg 765
all one can – 686
plenty to – 682
thing to – 625
– away with
destroy 162
eject 297
abrogate 756
– battle 722
– one's bidding
743
– business 625
– to death 361
– as done by 906,
942
– for destroy 162
kill 361
conquer 731
serve 746
punish 972
– good 906
– harm 907
– honour 873
– into
translate 522
– justice to 595
– like 19

– little 683
– no harm 648
– nothing 681
– nothing but 136
– one's office 772
– as others do 82
– over 223
– as one pleases
748
– a service
useful 644
aid 707
– up 660
have to – with
680, 692
– without 678
– the work 686
– wrong 923
docere, pisces na-
tare – 641
docile domesticated
370
learning 539
willing 602
docimastic 463
dock diminish 36
cut off 38
port 189
shorten 201
edge 231
store 636
tribunal 966
docked
incomplete 53
docker 690
docket
list 86
evidence 467
note 550
record 551
security 771
dockyard 691
doctor
learned man 492
restore 660
remedy 662
after death the –
135
– accounts 811
when –s disagree
475
doctrinaire
positive 474
pedant 492
affectation 855
blusterer 887
doctrinal 537
doctrinarian 514
doctrine tenet 484
knowledge 490
document 551

documentary
evidence 467
dodder 315
doddering 128
dodecahedron 244
dodge change 140
shift 264
deviate 279
oscillate 314
pursue 461
avoid 623
stratagem 702
dodger, artful – 792
dodo 366
extinct as the –
122
doe swift 274
deer 366
female 374
doer
originator 164
agent 690
doff 226
– the cap 894
dog follow 281
animal 366
male 373
pursue 622
wretch 949
cast to the –s
destroy 162
reject 610
disuse 678
abrogate 756
relinquish 782
fire – 386
go, to the –s
destruction 162
fail 732
adversity 735
poverty 804
sea – 269
watch –
safety 664
warning 668
keeper 753
hair of – that bit
you 959
let sleeping –s lie
141
– in manger 706,
943
–tired 686
–s of war 722
dog-cart 272
dog-cheap 815
dog-days 382
doge 745
dogged
obstinate 606
valour 861

sullen 901a
dogger 273
doggerel
verse 597
ridiculous 851,
853
dog-hole 189
dog-Latin 563
dogma tenet 484
theology 983
dogmatic
certain 474
positive 481
assertion 535
obstinate 606
dogmatist 887
dog's ear 258
dog robber 746
dog-sick 867
dog-star 423
dog-trot 275
dog-weary 688
doily 852
doing
up and – 682
what one is – 625
doings
events 151
actions 680
conduct 692
doit trifle 643
coin 800
dolce far niente 681
doldrums
dejection 837
sulks 901a
dole
small quantity 32
scant 640
give 784
allot 786
parsimony 819
grief 828
doleful 837
– dumps 901a
doll small 193
image 554
dollar 800
dolman 225
dolmen 363, 551
dolorem, infandum
renovare – 833
dolorous 830
dolour
physical 378
moral 828
dolphin 341
dolt 501
doltish 499
domain
class 75

write 590
- up a statement 594
- upon *money* 800
- the veil 528
drawback *evil* 619
  imperfection 651
  hindrance 706
  discount 813
drawbar 45
drawbridge
  way 627
  escape 671
  raise the - 666
drawcansir 887
drawee 800
drawer
  receptacle 191
  artist 559
  - of water 690
drawers
  dress 225
drawhead 45
drawing
  delineation 554, 556
  prize 810
drawing-room
  assembly 72
  room 191
  fashion 852
drawl *prolong* 200
  creep 275
  in speech 583
  sluggish 683
drawn *equated* 27
  - battle
  - irresistibly 601
  pacification 723
  incomplete 730
dray 272
  - horse 271
drayman 268
dread 860
dreadful *great* 31
  bad 649
  dire 830
  depressing 837
  fearful 860
dreadless 861
dreadnought
  warship 726
dream
  unsubstantial 4
  error 495
  fancy 515
  sleep 683
  golden - 858
  - of *think* 451
  intend 620
  - on other things

458
dreamer
  madman 504
  imaginative 515
dreamy
  unsubstantial 4
  inattentive 458
  sleepy 683
dreary
  monotonous 16
  solitary 87
  melancholy 830, 837
dredge *collect* 72
  extract 301
  raise 307
dregs
  remainder 40
  refuse 645
  dirt 653
  - of the people 876
  - of vice 945
drench *drink* 298
  water 337
  redundance 641
  - with physic 662
drencher 248
drenching rain 348
dress
  uniformity 16
  agree 23
  equalize 27
  clothes 225
  prepare 673
  ornament 847
  ostentation 882
  full - 852
  - circle 599
  - the ground 371
  - up *falsehood* 544
  represent 554
  - wounds 662
  - to advantage 847
dress-coat 225
dresser
  sideboard 215
  surgeon 662
dressing 932, 972
  - room 191, 599
dressing-gown 225
dressmaker 225
dribble 295, 348
driblet 25, 32
drift
  accumulate 72
  distance 196
  motion 264
  flying 267
  float 267
  transfer 270

direction 278
deviation 279
approach 286
wind 349
meaning 516
intention 620
snow - 383
drifter 273
drifting 605
driftless 621
drill *fabric* 219
  bore 260
  auger 262
  teach 537
  prepare 673
  - hall 191
drink
  swallow 296
  liquor 298
  tipple 959
  - one's fill
  enough 639
  - in *imbibe* 296, 298
  - in learning 539
  - to *celebrate* 883
  courtesy 894
drinking-bout 954
drink-money 784
drip 295, 348
dripping *wet* 330
  fat 356
drive *airing* 266
  impel 276
  propel 284
  break in 370
  urge 615
  haste 684
  direct 693
  attack 716
  compel 744
  - at *mean* 516
  intend 620
  - a bargain
  barter 794
  parsimony 819
  - care away 836
  - a coach and six through 83
  - into a corner
  difficult 704
  hinder 706
  defeat 731
  subjection 749
  - to despair 859
  - matters to an extremity 604
  - from *repel* 289
  - one hard 716
  - home 729
  - in 300

- to the last 133
- out 297
- trade
  business 625
  barter 794
drivel *slobber* 297
  imbecile 499
  mad 503
  rubbish 517
driveller 501, 584
driver 268
  director 694
driving rain 348
drizzle 348
droil 683
droit du plus fort 744
drôle *cards* 840
drole 949
  - de corps 844
drollery
  amusement 840
  wit 842
  ridiculous 853
dromedary 271
drone *slow* 275
  sound 407, 412, 413
  inactive 683
drool 297
droop
  weak 160
  hang 214
  sink 306
  disease 655
  decline 659
  flag 688
  sorrow 828
  dejection 837
drop *small quantity* 32
  discontinue 142
  powerless 158
  bring forth 161
  spherule 249
  emerge 295
  fall 306
  trickle 348
  relinquish 624
  discard 782
  gallows 975
  let - 308
  ready to -
  fatigue 688
  - asleep 683
  - astern 283
  - from the couds 508
  - dead 360
  - by drop
  by degrees 26

in parts 51
– in the bucket 32
– in upon 674
– into a good
   thing 734
– into the grave
   360
– a hint 527
– all idea of 624
– in *arrive* 292
immerse 300
sociality 892
– the mask 529
– off *decrease* 36
die 360
sleep 683
– in the ocean
trifling 643
– the subject 458
– too much 959
dropping fire 70
drop-scene 599
dropsical 194, 641
droshki 272
dross
remainder 40
slag 384
trash 643, 645
dirt 653
drought
dryness 340
insufficiency 640
drouth *desire* 865
drove
assemblage 72
multitude 102
drover 370
drown
affusion 337
kill 361
ruin 731, 732
– *care* 840
– the voice 581
drowsy *slow* 275
sleepy 683
weary 841
drub
defeat 731, 732
punish 972
drudge *labour* 686
worker 682, 690
drug
render insensible
   376
superfluity 641
trash 643
remedy 662
bane 663
– in the market
   815
drugget

cover 223
clean 652
preserve 670
druggist 662
druid 996
drum
repeat 104
cylinder 249
sound 407
music 417
party 892
beat of –
signal 550
alarm 669
war 722
command 741
parade 882
ear – 418
muffled –
funeral 363
non-resonance
   408a
– and fife band 417
– fire 407
– out 972
drum-head 964,
   966
drum-major 745
drummer 416
drunken 959
reel like a – man
   315
drunkenness 959
dry *arid* 340
style 575, 576, 579
hoarse 581
scanty 640
preserve 670
exhaust 789
tedious 841
dull 842
thirsty 865
cynical 932
teetotal 958
run – 640
with – eyes 823
– dock 189
– joke 842
– land 342
– the tears 834
– up 340, 638
dryad 979
dry-as-dust
antiquarian 122
dull 843
dryness 340
dry-nurse
teach 537
teacher 540
aid 707
dry-point 558

dry-rot
dirt 653
decay 659
bane 663
dualism 984
duality 89
duarchy 737
dub 564
dubious 475
ducat 800
duce 745
duchess 745, 875
duchy 181
duck *stoop* 308
plunge 310
water 337
darling 897, 899
play –s and
   drakes
recoil 277
prodigality 818
–'s egg
zero 101
– in thunder 870
ducking-stool 975
duckling 127
duck-pond 370
duct 350
ductile
elastic 323
flexible 324
trimming 607
easy 705
docile 743
dud 158, 727
dude 854
duds 225
dudgeon
dagger 727
discontent 832
churlishness 895
hate 898
anger 900
sullenness 901a
due
expedient 646
owing 806
proper 924, 926
give his – to
right 922
vindication 937
fair 939
in – course 109
occasion 134
– respect 928
– sense of 498
– time
soon 132
– to
cause and effect
   154, 155

give – weight 465
duel 720
duellist 726
dueness 924
duenna
teacher 540
guardian 664
keeper 753
dues 812
duet 415
duff 298
duffer
bungler 701
smuggler 792
dug 250
dug-out
old man 130
boat 273
defence 717
duke *ruler* 745
noble 875
dulce domum 189
dulcet
sweet 396
sound 405
melodious 413
agreeable 829
dulcify 174, 396
dulcimer 417
Dulcinea 897
dulcorate 396
dulia 990
dull *weak* 160
inert 172
moderate 174
blunt 254
insensible 376,
   381
sound 405
dim 422
colourless 429
ignorant 493
stolid 499
style 575
inactive 683
unapt 699
callous 823
dejected 837
weary 841
prosing 843
simple 849
– of hearing 419
– sight 443
dullard 501
dullness 843
duly 924
duma 696
dumb 581
– animal 366
– show 550
– waiter 307

strike –
  ignorant 493
  astonish 870
  humble 879
dumbfounder
  disappoint 509
  silence 581
  astonish 870
  humble 879
dummy
  substitute 147
  impotent 158
  speechless 581
  inactive 683
dump *music* 415
  store 636
  lament 839
  undersell 796
dumpling 298
dumps
  discontent 832
  dejection 837
  sulk 901a
dumpy *little* 193
  short 201
  thick 202
dun *dim* 422
  colourless 429
  grey 432
  importune 765
  creditor 805
dunce
  ignoramus 493
  fool 501
dunderhead 501
dune 206
dung 653
dungeon 752
dunghill
  dirt 653
  cowardly 862
  baseborn 876
  – *cock* 366
Dunker 984
dunt 716
duo 415
duodecimal 99
duodecimo
  little 193
  book 593
duodenary 98
duologue
  interlocution 588
  drama 599
dupe
  credulous 486
  deceive 545
  deceived **547**
duplex 90, 189
duplicate
  imitate 19

copy 21
double 90
tally 550
record 551
redundant 641
pawn 805
duplication
  imitation 19
  doubling **90**
  repetition 104
duplicature
  fold 258
duplicity
  duality 89
  falsehood 544
dura lex sed lex 926
durable
  long time 110
  stable 150
durance 141, 751
  in – 754
duration 106
  contingent – **108a**
  infinite – 112
durbar
  conference 588
  council 696
  tribunal 966
duress
  compulsion 744
  restraint 751
during 106
  – *pleasure &c.*
  108a
durity 323
dusk
  evening 126
  half-light 422
dusky
  dark 421
  black 431
dust *levity* 320
  powder 330
  corpse 362
  trash 643
  dirt 653
  money 800
  come to –
  die 360
  come down with
    the – 807
  humbled in the –
    879
  kick up a – 885
  level with the –
    162
  lick the –
    submit 725
    fail 732
  make to bite the –
    731

turn to –
  deorganized 358
  die 360
  – in the balance
    643
  throw – in the
    eyes
    blind 442
    deceive 545
    plead 617
  – one's jacket 972
duster 652
dust-bin, dust-hole
  191, 645
  fit for the –
    useless 645
    dirty 653
    spoilt 659
dustman
  cleaner 652
dust-storm 330
dusty
  powder 330
  dirt 653
Dutch
  double – 519
  high – 519
  – auction 796
  – courage 862
Dutchman, flying
  515
dutiful 944
duty
  business 625
  work 686
  tax 812
  courtesy 894
  obligation **926**
  respect 928
  worship 990
  rite 998
  do one's –
    virtue 944
  on – 680, 682
duumvirate 737
Duval, Claude –
  792
D.V. 470, 976
dwarf
  lessen 36
  small 193
  elf 980
dwell
  reside 186
  abide 265
  – upon
    descant 573
dweller 188
dwelling 184, 189
dwindle *lessen* 36
  shrink 195

dyad 89
dye 428
dying 360
dyke [*see* dike]
dynamic energy
  157
dynamics 276
dynamitard 863
dynamite 727
dynamo 153
dynasty 737
dysentery 299
dyspepsia 655
dysphony 581

E

each 79
  – to each 786
  – other 12
  – in his turn 148
eager
  willing 602
  active 682
  ardent 821
  desirous 865
  – *expectation* 507
eagle
  standard 550
  money 800
  – *boat* 726
  – *eye* *sight* 441
  intelligence 498
  – *winged* *swift* 274
  insignia 747
eagre 348
ean 161
ear 418
  corn 154
  come to one's –s
    527
  din in the –
    loud 404
    drum 407
  all – 418
  have the – of
    belief 484
    friendship 888
  lend an –
    hear 418
    attend 457
  meet the – 418
  nice – 418
  no – 419
  offend the – 410
  pick up the –s
    attention 457
    expectation 507
  put about one's –s
    308

economic pressure
  751
economy
  order 58
  conduct 692
  frugality **817**
  animal – 359
écorcher les oreilles
  410
ecphorize 615
écru 433
ecstasis 683
ecstasy
  frenzy 515
  transport 821
  rapture 827
ecstatic 829
ecstatica 994
ectoplasm 992
ectype 21
ecumenical 78
edacity 957
Edda 986
eddy
  whirlpool 348
  current 312
  danger 667
Eden 827
edge *energy* 171
  height 206
  brink **231**
  sidle 279
  advantage 731
  cutting – 253
  on – 256, 507
  take the – off 174
  – of hunger 865
  – in 228
  – one's way 282
edge-tools 253
  play with – 863
edgewise 217
edging
  obliquity 217
  border 231
  ornament 847
edible 298
edict 741
edification
  building 161
  teaching 537
  learning 539
  piety 987
edifice 161
edifying *good* 648
edile 965
edit
  publication 531
  condense 596
  revise 658
edition, new – 658

editor 593
educate 537
educated 490
  self – 490
education
  teaching 537
  knowledge 490
  man of – 492
  higher – 490
educational 537,
  542
educe *extract* 301
  discover 480a
educt 40
eduction 40a
edulcorate 396, 652
eel 248
  wriggle like an –
  315
eerie 860
efface
  delete 162
  disappear 449
  obliterate 552
  – from the
   memory 506
effect
  consequence **154**
  product 161
  impression 375
  complete 729
  carry into – 692
  with crushing –
  162
  in – 5
  take – 731
  to that – 516
effective
  capable 157
  useful 644
effectuation 729
expedient 646
effects 780, 798
effectual 731
effectually 52
effectuate 729
effeminate
  weak 160
  womenlike 374
  timorous 862
  sensual 954
effeminize 158
effendi 875
effervesce
  energy 171
  violence 173
  agitate 315
  bubble 353
  excited 825
effervescent 338
effete *old* 128

  weak 160
  useless 645
  spoiled 659
efficacious
  [*see* efficient]
efficient
  power 157
  agency 170
  utility 644
  skill 698
effigy 21, 554
effleurer *skim* 267,
  460
efflorescence 330
effluxion of time
  109
effluence *egress* 295
  flow 348
effluvium 334, 398
efflux 295
efformation 240
effort 686
effreet 980
effrontery 885
effulgence 420
effuse
  pour out 295, 297
  excrete 299
  speech 582
  loquacity 584
effusion of blood
  361
effusive 573
eft 366
eftsoons 117
egad 535
égards 928
egesta 299
egestion 297
egg *beginning* 66
  cause 153
  food 298
  walk among –s
  704
  too many –s in
   one basket
  unskilful 699
  (*imprudent* 863)
  – and dart
   ornament 847
  – on 615
egg-shaped 247,
  249
ego *intrinsic* 5
  speciality 79
  immaterial 317
  non – 6
egocentrism 943
egotism
  vanity 880
  cynicism 911

  selfishness 943
egregious
  exceptional 83
  absurd 497
  exaggerated 549
  important 642
egregiously 31, 33
egress **295**
Egyptian darkness
  421
eheu! fugaces
  labuntur anni
  111
eiderdown 223
eidouranion 318
Eiffel tower 206
eight *number* 98
  boat 273
  representative 759
eisteddfod 72, 416
eighty 98
either *choice* 609
  happy with – 605
ejaculate
  propel 284
  utter 580
ejection 185, **297**
ejecta 299
ejector 349
eke *also* 37
  – out *complete* 52
  spin out 110
ekka 272
El Dorado 803
elaborate
  improve 658
  prepare 673
  laborious 686
  work out 729
elaine 356
élan 276
elapse 109, 122
elastic fluid 334
elasticity
  power 157
  strength 159
  energy 171
  spring **325**
elate *cheer* 836
  rejoice 838
  hope 858
  vain 880
  boast 884
elbow *angle* 244
  projection 250
  push 276
  at one's –
  near 197
  advice 695
  lift one's –

infringe 925
encumber 704, 706
encumbrance
  clear of − 807
encyclical 531
encyclopædia 490,
  593
  walking − 700
encyclopædical
  general 78
  − knowledge 490
encysted 229
end
  termination **67**
  effect 154
  object 620
  at an − 142
  come to its − 729
  one's journey's −
    292
  on − 212
  put an − to
    destroy 162
    kill 361
  begin at the
    wrong − 699
  − one's days 360
  −s of the earth 196
  − to end *space* 180
  touching 199
  length 200
  − of life 360
  − in smoke 732
  − of one's tether
    sophistry 477
    ignorant 491
    insufficient 640
    difficult 704
endamage 649
endanger 665
endear 897
endearment **902**
endeavour
  pursue 622
  attempt 675
  use one's best −
    686
  − after 620
endemic
  special 79
  interior 221
  disease 657
endimanché 847,
  882
endless
  multitudinous
    102
  infinite 105
  perpetual 112
endlessly 16
endlong 200

endocrine 221
endogenous 367
endorse
  evidence 467
  assent 488
  compact 769
  − *a bill* 800
  approve 931
endorsement 550
endosmose 302
endow
  confer power 157
endowed with
  possessed of 777
endowment
  intrinsic 5
  power 157
  talent 698
  gift 784
endrogynous 83
endue 157
endure *time* 106
  last 110
  persist 143
  continue 141
  undergo 151
  feel 821
  submit to 826
  unable to − 867
  − for ever 112
  − pain 828
enduring
  indelible 505
endwise 212
enemy *time* 841
  foe 891
  the common − 978
  thing devised by
    the − 546
  − to society 891
energumen 504
energy *power* 157
  strength 159
  physical **171**
  resolution 604
  activity 682
enervate 158, 160
enfant, bon − 906
  − gâté
  prosperity 734
  satiety 869
  favorite 899
  − perdu
  hopeless 859
  reckless 863
  − terrible
  curiosity 455
  artless 703
  object of fear 860
enfeeble 160
enfeoff 780, 783

Enfield rifle 727
enfilade
  lengthwise 200
  pierce 260
  pass through 302
enfold 229
enforce *urge* 615
  advise 695
  compel 744
  require 924
enfranchise
  free 748
  liberate 750
  permit 760
enfranchised 924
engage
  bespeak 132
  induce 615
  undertake 676
  do battle 722
  commission 755
  promise 768
  compact 769
  I'll −
  affirmation 535
  − the attention
    457
  − with 720
engaged
  marriage 903
  be − 135
  − in *attention* 457
engagement
  business 625
  battle 720
  betrothal 902
engaging
  pleasing 829
  amiable 897
engender 161
engine 153, 633
engine-driver 268
engineer 690, 694,
  726
engineering 633
engird 227
English 188
  broken − 563
  king's − 560
  murder the king's
    − 568
  plain −
  intelligible 518
  interpreted 522
  style 576
  − horn 417
engorge
  swallow 296
  gluttony 957
engorgement
  too much 641

engrail 256
engrave
  furrow 259
  mark 550
  − in the memory
    505
engraver 559
engraving 21, 22,
  558
engross *write* 590
  possess 777
  − the thoughts
  thought 451
  attention 457
engrossed in
  thought 451
engulf
  destroy 162
  plunge 310
  swallow up 296
enhance
  increase 35
  improve 658
enharmonic 413
enigma
  question 461
  secret 533
enigmatic
  uncertain 475
  unintelligible 517
  obscure 519
enigme, mot d' −
  522
enjoin *advise* 695
  command 741
  prescribe 926
enjoy
  physically 377
  possess 777
  morally 827
  − health 654
  − popularity 873
  − a state 7
enkindle *heat* 384
  excite 824
enlarge
  increase 35
  swell 194
  in writing 573
  liberate 750
  − the mind 537
enlarged views 498
enlighten
  illumine 420
  inform 527
  teach 537
enlightened
  knowledge 490
enlist *engage* 615
  war 722
  commission 755

under the ban-
  ners of 707
– into the service
  677
enliven
  delight 829
  cheer 836
  amuse 840
enmity **889**
ennoble 873
ennui 841
enormity
  crime 947
enormous *great* 31
  big 192
– number 102
enough *much* 31
  no more! 142
  sufficient 639
  moderately 651
  satiety 869
know when one
  has had – 953
– in all conscience
  641
– to drive one
  mad 830
– and to spare 639
enounce 535, 580
enrage 830, 900
enragé 865
enrapture
  excite 824
  beatify 829
  love 897
enraptured 827
enravish 829
enravished 827
enravishment 824
enrich
  improve 658
  wealth 803
  ornament 847
enrobe 225
enroll *list* 86
  record 551
– troops 722
  commission 755
ens *essence* 1
Ens Entium 976
ensample 22
ensanguined 361
ensconce
  conceal 528
  safety 664
ensconced
  located 184
ensemble 50
enshrine
  circumscribe 229
  repute 873

sanctify 987
– in the memory
  505
ensiform 253
ensign
  standard 550
  officer 726
  master 745
– of authority 747
ensilage 637
enslave 749
ensnare 545
ensue *follow* 63, 117
  happen 151
ensure 474
entablature 210
entail *cause* 153
  tie up property
  781
entangle
  interlink 43
  derange 61
  ravel 219
  entrap 545
  embroil 713
entangled
  disorder 59
– by difficulties
  704
entend, cela s' – 613
entente
  agreement 23
  alliance 714
  friendship 888
enter *go in* 294
  appear 446
  note 551
  accounts 811
– into the compo-
  sition of 56
– into details
  special 79
  describe 594
– into an engage-
  ment 768
– into the feelings
  of 914
– into the ideas of
  understand 518
  concord 714
– in *converge* 290
– the lists
  attack 716
  contention 720
– the mind 451
– a profession 625
– into the spirit of
  feel 821
  delight 827
– upon 66
– into one's views

488
enterprise
  pursuit 622
  undertaking 676
  commercial – 794
enterprising
  active 171, 682
  courageous 861
entertain
  bear in mind 457
  support 707
  amuse 840
  sociality 892
– doubts 485
– feeling 821
– an idea 451
– an opinion 484
entertainment 840
  pleasure 377
  repast 298
entêté 481, 606
enthral
  subjection 749
  restraint 751
enthrone 873
enthronement 755
enthusiasm
  language 574
  willingness 602
  feeling 821
  hope 858
  love 897
enthusiast
  madman 504
  obstinate 606
  active 682
enthusiastic
  imaginative 515
  sensitive 822
  excitable 825
  sanguine 858
enthymeme 476
entice 615
enticing 829
entire *whole* 50
  complete 52
  continuous 69
– horse 373
entirely *much* 31
entitle *name* 564
  give a right 924
entity 1
entoil 545
entomb *inter* 363
  imprison 751
Entomology 368
entourage 88, 183,
  227
entozoon 193
entrails 221
entrammel 751

entrance
  beginning 66
  ingress 294
  way 627
  enrapture 827,
  829
  magic 992
  give – to 296
entranced 515
entrancement 824
entrap 545
entrain 293
entre nous 528
entreat 765
entrée
  reception 296
  dish 298
  give the – 296
  have the – 294
– dish 191
entremet 298
entrepôt 636, 799
entrepreneur 599
entre-sol 191
entrust
  commission 755
  give 784
  credit 805
entry *beginning* 66
  ingress 294
  record 551
entwine *join* 43
  intersect 219
  convolve 248
enucleate 522
enumerate 85
– among 76
enumeration 86
enunciate
  inform 527
  affirm 535
  voice 580
envelop 225
envelope 223, 232
envenom
  deprave 659
  exasperate 835
  hate 898
  anger 900
envenomed
  bad 649
  insalubrious 657
  painful 830
  malevolent 907
– tongue 934
environ 227
environment 183
environs 197
  in such and such –
  183
envisage 515, 861

envoy
  messenger 534
  consignee 758
envy **921**
enwrap 225
enzyme 320
Eolian harp 417
Eolus 349
eon 976
épanchement
  manifest 525
  artless 703
  endearment 902
epact 641
épaulette
  badge 550, 747
  ornament 847
  decoration 877
éperdu 824
épergne 191
ephemeral 111
ephemeris
  calendar 114
  record 551
  book 593
Ephesian letters
  993
ephialtes
  physical pain 378
  hindrance 706
  mental pain 828
ephod 999
ephor 967
epic 594, 597
epicedium 839
epicene 81, 83
épicier 876
epicure
  fastidious 868
  sybarite 954a
  glutton 957
epicurean 954
Epicurus, system
  of − 954
epicy-cle, -cloid
  247
epidemic
  general 78
  disease 655
  insalubrity 657
epidermis 223
epigenesis 161
epigram 496, 842
epigrammatic 572
epigrammatist 844
epigraph 550
epilepsy 315, 655
epilogue
  sequel 65
  end 67
  drama 599

èpingles, tiré à
  quatre − 855
Epiphany 998
episcopal 995
Episcopalian 984
episcopate 995
episode
  adjunct 39
  discontinuity 70
  interjacence 228
episodic
  irrelative 10
  style 573
epistle 592
Epistles 985
epistrophe 104
epistyle 210
epitaph 363
epithalamium 903
epithem 662
epithet 564
epitome
  miniature 193
  short 201
  concise 572
epizoötic 657
epoch *time* 106
  instant 113
  date 114
  present time 118
epode 597
eponym 564
epopœa 597
epos 594
epulation 298
epulotic 662
epuration 652
equable 16, 922
equal *even* 27
  equitable 922
  − *chance* 156
  − *times* 120
  − *to power* 157
equality 13, **27**
equalize 213
equanimity 826
equate 27, 30
equations 85
equator 68, 318
equatorial 68, 236
equerry 746
equestrian 268
equibalanced 27
equidistant 68
equilibration 27
equilibrist 599
equilibrium 27
equine *carrier* 271
  horse 366
equinox 125, 126
equip 225, 673

equipage
  vehicle 272
  instruments 633
  display 882
equiparent 27
equipment 633
equipoise &c. 27, 30
equiponderate 30
equitable *wise* 498
  just 922
  due 924
  honourable 939
  − *interest* 780
equitation 266
equity *right* 922
  honour 939
  law 963
  in − 922
  − *draftsman* 968
equivalent
  identical 13
  equal 27
  compensation 30
  substitute 147
  translation 522
equivocalness
  dubious 475
  double meaning
  520
  impure 961
equivocate
  sophistry 477
  palter 520
  lie 544
equivocation
  [see equivocate]
  without − 543
équivoque
  double meaning
  520
  impure 961
era *time* 106, 108
  date 114
eradicate
  destroy 162
  extract 301
erase *destroy* 162
  obliterate 331, 552
Erastian 984
erasure 552
Erato 416
ere 116
  − long 132
  − now 116
  past 122
Erebus *dark* 421
  hell 982
erect *build* 161
  vertical 212
  raise 307
  with head − 878

− the scaffolding
  673
erewhile 116, 122
ergatocracy 737
ergo 476
ergotism 480
ergotize 485
eriometer 445
Erinys 900
Erl King 980
ermine
  badge of authority
  747
  ornament 847
erode 36, 659
Eros 897, 979
erosion 36
erotic 897, 961
err − *in opinion* 495
  − *morally* 945
errand
  message 532
  business 625
  commission 755
errand-boy 534
errant 279
erratic
  irregular 139
  changeable 149
  wandering 279
  capricious 608
erratum 495
erroneous 495
error *fallacy* **495**
  vice 945
  guilt 947
  court of − 966
  writ of − 969
ersatz 973
erst 122
erubescence 434
erubuit salva res
  est 95
eruct 297
eructate 297
erudition 490, 539
eruption
  upheaval 146
  violence 173
  egress 295, 297
  disease 655
  volcanic − 872
escadrille 726
escalade
  mounting 305
  attack 716
escalator 307
escalop 248
escapade
  absurdity 497
  freak 608

prank 840
escape
  flight **671**
  liberate 750
  evade 927
  means of − 664,
    666
  − the lips
    disclosure 529
    speech 582
  − the memory 506
  − notice &c.
    invisible 447
    inattention 458
    latent 526
escarp 717
escarpment
  stratum 204
  height 206
  oblique 217
escharotic
  caustic 171
  pungent 392
eschatology 67
escheat 144, 974
eschew
  avoid 623
  dislike 867
esclandre 828, 830
escort
  accompany 88
  safeguard 664
  keeper 753
escritoire 191
esculent 298
escutcheon 550
esoteric
  private 79
  concealed 528
Espagne, château
  en − *fancy* 515
  hope 858
espalier 232
especial 79
especially 33
espial 441
espiéglerie
  cunning 702
  fun 840
  wit 842
espionnage 441,
  461
esplanade
  houses 189
  flat 213
espouse
  choose 609
  marriage 903
  − a cause *aid* 707
  co-operate 709
esprit

shrewdness 498
  wit 842
bel − 844
− de corps
  bias 481
  co-operation 709
  sociality 892
  (*party* 712)
− fort
  thinker 500
  irreligious 989
espy 441
esquire 875, 877
essay
  experiment 463
  dissertation 595
  endeavour **675**
essayist 593, 595
esse 1
essence
  nature 5
  scent 398
essential
  intrinsic 5
  great 31
  required 630
  important 642
essentially
  intrinsically 5
  substantially 3
essential stuff 5
establish
  settle 150
  create 161
  place 184
  evidence 467
  demonstrate 478
  − equilibrium 27
established
  permanent 141
  habit 613
  − church 983*a*
establishment
  party 712
  shop 799
estafette 534
estaminet 189
estate *condition* 7
  property 780
  come to man's −
    131
esteem
  believe 484
  repute 873
  approve 931
  in high − 928
estimable 648
estimate
  measure 466
  adjudge 480
  information 527

− too highly 482
estimation
  [*see* esteem,
    estimate]
estime
  succès d' − 873
estival 382
esto perpetua!
  perpetuity 112
  permanence 141
  desire 865
estop 706
estrade 213
estrange
  alienate 44, 889
  discord 713
  hate 898
estranged
  secluded 893
estrapade
  attack 716
  punishment 972
estreat 974
estuary 343
estuation 384
esurient 865
et − cætera
  add 37
  include 76
  plural 100
  − hoc genus omne
    similar 17
    include 76
    multiform 81
étalage 882
état major 745
etch *furrow* 259
  engraving 558
eternal 112
− home 981
Eternal, the − 976
eterne 112
eternify 112
eternity 112
  an − 110
  launch into − 360,
    361
ether
  lightness 320
  rarity 322
  vapour 334
  anæsthetic 376
ethereal 4
ethicism 984
ethics 926
Ethiopian 431
−'s skin 150
Ethiopian's skin
  unchangeable 150
ethnology 372
ethnic 984

ethology 926
ethos 5
etiolate 429, 430
etiology *causes* 155,
  359
  knowledge 490
  disease 655
etiquette
  custom 613
  fashion 832
  ceremony 882
étoile, à la belle −
  out of doors 220
  in the air 338
Eton jacket 225
étourderie
  inattention 458
  unskilfulness 699
etymological 560
etymology 562
etymon *origin* 153
  verbal 562
Eucharist 998
euchology 998
euchre 840
eudiometer
  air 338
  salubrity 656
euge! 931
eugenics 658
eulogist 935
eulogize 482
eulogy 931
Eumenides *fury*
  900
  evil-doers 913
  revenge 919
eunuch 158
eupepsia 654
euphemism
  metaphor 521
  style 577, 578
  flattery 933
euphemist
  man of taste 850
  flatterer 935
euphony 413, 578
Euphrosyne 836
euphuism
  metaphor 521
  elegant style 577
  affected style 579
  affectation 855
Eurasian 41
eureka! 462, 480*a*
Euripus 343
Eurus 349
eurythmics 537,
  840
eurythmy 242
Euterpe 416

exacting
severe 739
discontented 832
grasping 865
fastidious 868
exaction
[*see* exact]
undue 925
exactly
just so 488
exaggeration
increase 35
expand 194
overestimate 482
magnify **549**
misrepresent 555
exalt
increase 35
elevate 307
extol 931
– one's horn 873
exalté 504
tête –e 503
exalted *high* 206
repute 873
noble 875
magnanimous
942
examination
[*see* examine]
evidence 467
undergo – 461
examine 457, 461
example
pattern 22
instance 82
bad – 949
good – 948
make an – of 974
set a good – 944
exanimate
dead 360
supine 360
exarch 745
exasperate
exacerbate 173
aggravate 835
enrage 900
excavate 252
excecation 442
exceed *surpass* 33
remain 40
transgress 303
intemperance 954
excel *surpass* 33
– in *skilful* 698
excellence 648, 944
excellence, par –
642
excellency 877
excelsior 305

except *subduct* 38
exclude 55
reject 610
exception
unconformity 83
qualification 469
exemption 777a
disapproval 932
take –
qualify 469
resent 900
exceptionable
bad 649
guilty 947
exceptional
original 20
extraneous 57
unconformable 83
in an – degree 31
exceptious 901,
901a
exceptis
excipiendis 469
excern 297
excerpt 609
excerpta *parts* 51
compendium 596
selections 609
excerption 609
excess
remainder 40
redundance 641
intemperance 954
excessive 31
exchange
reciprocity 12
interchange 148
transfer 783
barter 794
mart 799
bill of – 771
rate of – 800
– blows &c.
retaliation 718
battle 720
Exchequer 802
Baron of – 967
Court of – 966
– bill 800
excise 812
exciseman 965
excision 38
excitability **825,**
901
excitation **824**
excite *energy* 171
violence 173
- *morally* 824
– attention 457
– desire 865
– hope 811

– an impression
375
– love 897
excited fancy 515
excitement 824, 825
anger 900
exclaim 411
– against 932
exclamation 580
mark of – 550
exclude
leave out 42, 55
reject 610
prohibit 761
banish 893
exclusion **55, 57**
exclusive
simple 42
omitting 55
special 79
irregular 83
forbidding 761
– of 38
– possession **777**
– thought 457
excogitate 451, 515
excommunicate
banish 893
curse 908
rite 998
excoriate 226
excrement
excretion 299
dirt 653
excrescence
projection 250
blemish 848
excreta
excretion 299
dirt 653
excretion 297, **299**
excruciating 378,
830
exculpate
forgive 918
vindicate 937
acquit 970
excursion 266, 311
excursionist 268
excursive
deviating 279
- *style* 573
excursus 595
excuse *plea* 617
forgive 918
exempt 927a
vindicate 793
execrable 649, 830
execrate 898, 908
execution
music 416

action 680
conduct 692
signing 771
observance 772
punishment 972
carry into –
complete 729
put in –
undertaking 676
executioner 975
executive
conduct 692
direction 693
authority 737
judicature 965
executor 690
to one and his –s
&c., *property*
780
exegetical 522
exemplar 22
exemplary 944
exemplify
quote 82
illustrate 522
exempt *free* 748
dispensation 927a
– from *absent* 187
unpossessed 777a
exemption
exception 83
qualification 469
deliverance 692
permission 760
non-possession
777a
non-liability **927a**
exenterate 297
exequatur 755
exequies 363
exercise
operation 170
teach 537
task 625
use 677
act 680
exert 686
– authority 737
– discretion 600
– the intellect 451
– power 157
exergue 231
exert *use* 677
– authority 737
– oneself 686
exertion 171, **686**
exfoliate 226
exhalation
ejection 297
excretion 299
vapour 336

– plea *untruth* 546
plea 617
– position 704
– pretences 791
– prophet
disappoint 509
pseudo-revelation
986
– reasoning 477
– scent 495, 538
– shame 855
– statement 546
– step 732
– teaching 538
– witness
deceiver 548
detraction 934
falsehood 544, 546
falsetto *squeak* 410
want of voice 581
falsify *error* 495
falsehood 544,
546
– accounts 811
– one's hope 509
falter *slow* 275
stammer 583
hesitate 605
slip 732
hopeless 859
fear 860
faltering accents
605
fame *greatness* 31
news 532
renown 873
familiar
known 490
habitual 613
sociable 892
affable 894
– *spirit* 979, 980
on – terms 888
familiarize
teach 537
habit 613
famille, en – 892
family
kin 11
class 75
ancestors 166
posterity 167
party 712
in the bosom of
one's – 221
happy – 714
– circle 892
– jars 713
– likeness 17
– tie 11
in the – way 161

famine 640
– price 814
famine-stricken
640
famish
stingy 819
fasting 956
famished
insufficient 640
hungry 865
famous 873
famously 31
fan *blow* 349
cool 385
refresh 689
stimulate 824
flirt a – 855
– the embers 505
– the flame
violence 173
heat 384
aid 707
excite 824
– into a flame
anger 900
–shaped 194
fanatic
madman 504
imaginative 515
zealot 682
religious – 988
fanatical
misjudging 481
insane 503
emotional 821
excitable 825
heterodox 984
over-righteous 988
fanaticism 606
fanciful
imaginative 515
capricious 608
ridiculous 853
fancy *think* 451
idea 453
believe 484
suppose 514
imagine 515
caprice 608
choice 609
pugilism 726
wit 842
desire 865
wonder 870
love 897
after one's – 850
indulge one's –
609
take a – to
delight in 827
desire 865

take one's –
please 829
– dog 366
– dress 840
– price 814
– woman 962
fandango 840
**fandi, mollia tem-
pora** – 588
fane 1000
fanfare *loudness*
404
celebration 883
fanfaron 887
fanfaronnade 884
fangs *venom* 663
rule 737
retention 781
fan-light 260
fan-like 202
fannel 999
fanon 999
fantasia 415
fantastic *odd* 83
absurd 497
imaginative 515
capricious 608
unfashionable 851
ridiculous 853
fantasy
imagination 515
desire 865
fantoccini 554, 599
faquir 996
far – away 196
– be it from
unwilling 603
deprecation 766
– between
disjunction 44
few 103
interval 198
– from it
unlike 18
shortcoming 304
no 536
– from the truth
546
– and near 180
– off 196
– and wide 31,
180, 196
farce
absurdity 497
untruth 546
drama 599
wit 842
ridiculous 853
mere –
unimportant 643
useless 645

farceur
actor 599
humorist 844
fardel
bundle 72
hindrance 706
fare *state* 7
food 298
price 812
bill of –
list 86
farewell
departure 293
relinquishment
624
loss 776
– to greatness 874
far-famed 873
far-fetched 10
far-flung 73
far-gone
much 31
insane 503
spoiled 654
farinaceous 330
farm *till* 371
property 780
rent 788
farmer 188, 342,
371
afternoon – 683
farm-house 189
Farmer-Labor 712
faro 840
farrago 59
farrier 370
farrow
produce 161
litter 167
multitude 102
far-sighted 442, 510
farther 196
[*and see* further]
farthing
quarter 97
worthless 643
coin 800
– candle 422
farthingale 225
fasces 747
fascia 205, 247
fascicule 51
fasciculated 72
fascinate
influence 615
excite 824
please 829
astonish 870
love 897
conjure 992
fascinated

ornament 847
decoration 877
in full —
  prepared 673
  prosperous 734
  rich 803
hear a — drop 403
in high —
  health 654
  cheerful 884
pleased with a —
  840
— in one's cap
  honour 873
  decoration 877
— one's nest
  prepare 673
  prosperity 734
  wealth 803
  economy 817
  selfish 943
— the oar 698
— in the scale 643
feather-bed 324
feathered tribes
  366
feathery 256
featly 682
feature
  character 5
  component 56
  form 240
  appearance 448
  press 531
  lineament 550
  — in 56
features
  face 234
febrifuge 662
febrile 382, 825
fecal 653
fecit 556
feckless 866
feculence 653
fecund 168
fecundate 161
federal council 696
  — penitenciary 752
federalism 737
federation 48, 709,
  712
fee *possession* 777
  property 780
  pay 809
  reward 973
feeble *weak* 160
  illogical 477
feeble-minded 497,
  605
feebleness
  style **575**

feed *eat* 298
  supply 637
  — the flame 707
fee-faw-fum
  bugbear 860
  spell 993
feel *sense* 375
  touch 379
  emotion 821
  — for *try* 463
  benevolence 906
  pity 914
  condole with 915
  — the pulse 461
  — the want of 865
  — one's way
  essay 675
  caution 864
feeler 379
  inquiry 461
  experiment 463
feeling 698, **821**
feet *low* 207
  walkers 266
at one's —
  near 197
  subjection 749
  humility 879
fall at one's —
  submit 725
fall on one's —
  prosper 734
lick the — of
  servile 886
light upon one's —
  safe 664
spring to one's —
  307
throw oneself at
  the — of
  entreat 765
feign 544, 546
feigned 545
feint 545
felicitas, curiosa —
  698
felicitate 896
felicitous
  agreeing 23
  — *style* 578
  skilful 698
  successful 731
  pleasant 829
felicity 827
feline *cat* 366
  stealthy 528
  cunning 702
fell *destroy* 162
  mountain 206
  lay flat 21
  skin 223

lay low 308
  moor 344
  dire 860
  malevolent 907
fellah 876
felloe 231
fellow *similar* 17
  equal 27
  companion 88
  dual 89
  man 373
  scholar 492, 541
fellow-commoner
  541
fellow-companion
  890
fellow-countryman
  890
fellow-creature 372
fellow-feeling
  friendship 888
  love 897
  benevolence 906
  pity 914
fellowship
  partnership 712
  distinction 873
  friendship 888
  companionship
  890
  good — 892
fellow-student 541
fellow-worker 690
felly 231
felo-de-se 361
felon 949
felonious 945
felony 947
felt *texture* 219
  heart— 821
felucca 273
female 374
feme coverte 903
feme sole 904
feminality
  weakness 160
  woman 374
feminine 374
feminism 374
femme de chambre
  746
fen 345
fence *enclose* 232
  evade 544
  defence 717
  fight 720
  prison 752
  thief 792
  — round 229
  — with a question
  528

fenced 770
fenceless 665
fencible 726
fencing 840
feneration 787
fend 717
fender 717
Fenian 710, 742
fenum habet in
  cornu 668, 913
feodal 780
feodality 737, 777
feoff *property* 780
feoffee 779, 785
feoffer 784
feræ naturæ 366
feral 907
ferine 907
ferment
  disorder 59
  energy 171
  violence 173
  agitation 315
  lightness 320
  effervesce 353
  emotion 821
  excitement 824,
  825
  anger 900
fermentation,
  acetous — 397
fern 367
ferocity 173, 907
Ferrara
  sword 727
ferret out 461, 480*a*
ferro-concrete 635
ferrule 223
ferry 270, 627
ferry-boat 273
ferry-man 269
fertile 161, 168
  — *imagination* 515
ferule 975
  come under the —
  932
fervent *hot* 382
  desirous 865
  — *hope* 858
fervid *hot* 382
  heartfelt 821
  excited 824
fervour *heat* 382
  animation 821
  love 897
festal *eating* 298
  social 892
fester 653, 655
festina lente 864
festival
  music 416

fire-ball *fuel* 388
  arms 727
fire-balloon 273
fire-barrel 388
fire-bell 669
fire-boat 726
fire-brand
  fuel 388
  instigator 615
  dangerous man
    667
  incendiary 913
fire-brigade 385
fire-curtain 599
fire-drake 423
fire-eater
  fighter 726
  blusterer 887
fire-eating
  rashness 863
  insolence 885
fire-engine 348
fire-escape 671
fire-extinguisher
  385
fire-fly 423
fireless cooker 386
fire-light 422
firelock 727
fireman *stoker* 268
  extinguisher 385
fire-place 386
fire-proof 385, 644
fireside 189
firewood 388
firework
  fire 382
  luminary 423
  celebration 883
  amusement 840
fire-worship 991
fire-worshipper 984
firing *fuel* 388
  explosion 406
firkin 191
firm
  junction 43
  stable 150
  hard 323
  resolute 604
  partnership 712
  merchant 797
  brave 861
  stand – 719
  – as a rock 604
  – belief 484
  – hold 781
firmament 318
firman 741, 760
first 66
  – blush

  morning 125
  leading 280
  vision 441
  appearance 448
  manifest 525
  – blow 716
  – cause 976
  – that comes 609a
  – fiddle
  importance 642
  proficient 700
  authority 737
  – come first
    served 609a
  – and foremost 66
  – impression 66
  – and last 87
  – line 234
  come back to –
    love 607
  – move 66
  – opportunity 132
  at – sight 448
  – stage 66
  – stone
  preparation 673
  attack 716
  on the – summons
    741
  of the – water
  best 648
  repute 873
first-born 124, 128
first-fruits 154
first-hand 20, 467
firstlings 128, 154
first-rate
  important 642
  excellent 648
  man-of-war 726
firth 343
fisc 802
fiscal 800
fish *food* 298
  sport 361, 622
  animal 366
  food for –es 362
  other – to fry
    ill-timed 135
    busy 682
  queer – 857
  – in the air 645
  – for compliments
    880
  – for *seek* 4
  experiment 463
  desire 865
  – hatchery 370
  – out *inquire* 461
  discover 480a
  – in troubled

  waters
  difficult 704
  discord 713
  – up *raise* 307
  find 480a
  – out of water
  disagree 24
  unconformable 83
  displaced 185
  bungler 701
fisherman 361
fishery 370
fishing *kill* 361
  pursue 622
fishing-boat 273
fishpond 343, 370
fish-trail 267
fishy transaction
  940
fisk 266, 274
fissile 328
fission 44
fissure 44
  chink 198
fist
  handwriting 590
  grip 781
  shake the –
  defy 515
  threat 909
fisticuffs 720
fistula 260
fit *state* 7
  agreeing 23
  equal 27
  paroxysm 173
  agitation 315
  caprice 608
  expedient 646
  healthy 654
  disease 655
  excitement 825
  anger 900
  right 922
  due 924
  duty 926
  in –s 315
  think – 600
  – of abstraction
    458
  – of crying 839
  – for 698
  – out *dress* 225
  prepare 673
  – to be seen 845
  by –s and starts
  irregular 59
  discontinuous 70
  agitated 315
  capricious 608
  haste 684

fitful
  irregular 139
  changeable 149
  capricious 608
fittings 633
five 98
  division by – 99
  – act play 599
  – and twenty 98
Five Year Plan 626
fiver 800
fives *game* 840
fix *join* 43
  arrange 60
  establish 150
  place 184
  immovable 265
  solidify 321
  resolve 604
  difficulty 704
  – the eyes upon
    441
  – the foundations
    673
  – the memory 505
  – the time 114
  – the thoughts
    457
  – up 774
  – upon *discover*
    480a
  choose 609
fixed *intrinsic* 5
  permanent 141
  stable 150
  quiescent 265
  habitual 613
  – idea 481
  – opinion 484
  – periods 138
fixity 141
fixity of purpose
  141
fixture
  appointment 741
  property 780
fizgig 423
fizz 409
fizzle 353
  – out 304
flabelliform 194
flabbergast 870,
  879
flabby 324
flabbiness 324
flaccid *weak* 160
  soft 324
  empty 640
flag *weak* 160
  flat stone 204
  floor 211

- of words 582,
584
flower *essence* 5
produce 161
vegetable 367
prosper 734
beauty 845
ornament 847
repute 873
- of age 131
- of flock 648
- of life 127
- painting 556,
559
flowering plant 367
flowers
anthology 596
- of rhetoric 577
flowing
[*see* flow]
- periods 578
fluctuate
change 149
oscillate 314
irresolute 605
flue *opening* 260
air-pipe 351
down 320
dust 653
fluent
differential 84
fluid 333
stream 348
- *language* 578
speech 584
fluff 256
little bit of - 374
fluid 333
- in motion 347
fluidity 333
fluke *hook* 244
chance 621
flummery
unmeaning 517
flattery 933
flunk 732
flunkey
servant 746
servile 886
flunkeyism 933
flurry *hurry* 684
agitation 821
excitability 825
flush *flat* 251
flood 348
heat 382
light 420
colour 428
red 434
abundant 639
wash 652

health 654
feeling 821
passion 825
rejoicing 838
in liquor 959
- of cash 803
flushed
[*see* flush]
excited 824
cheerful 836
hopeful 858
proud 878
vain 880
- with rage 900
- with success 731
- with victory 884
fluster
distract 458
move 821
excite 824, 825
flustered *tipsy* 959
flute
furrow 259
music 417
flutter
variable 149
agitation 315
gamble 621
hurry 684
emotion 821
excite 824, 825
fear 860
fluvial 348
flux
conversion 144
motion 264
liquefaction 335
flow 348
- and reflux 314
- of time 109
flux de paroles 584
fluxion 84
fluxions 85
fly *vanish* 4
time 109
transient 111
burst 173
minute 193
wings 267
vehicle 272
swift 274
depart 293
break 328
lose colour 429
shun 623
- to arms 722
- at 716
- back 277
- in the face of
oppose 708
resist 719

disobey 742
insolence 885
- in the face of
facts 481, 606
- from 623
- kites
borrow 788
credit 805
not pay 808
- off 291
- in the ointment
651
- open 260
- out *violent* 173
excitable 825
angry 900
fly-blown 653
fly-boat 273
flyer 269
flying [*see* fly]
- colours
success 731
display 882
celebrate 883
- boat 273, 726
- column 726
- field 728
- fish 83
- machine 273
- officer 745
- rumour 532
fly-leaf
interjacent 228
book 593
fly-wheel 312
foal 129, 271
foam *violent* 173
boil 315
spray 353
excitement 824,
825
- with rage 900
fob 191
- off 545
focal 222
focis, pro aris et -
717
focus 74
centre 222
furnace 386
bring into a -
collect 72
convergence 290
in - *visible* 446
out of - *dim* 447
- the thoughts 457
fodder 298
foe 891
fœderis, casus - 770
foehn 349
fœnum habet in

cornu 668, 913
fœtor 401
fœtus 129, 153
fog 353, 475
in a - 528
London - 436
fogey 500, 857
foggy
opaque 426
fog-signal 668, 669
foh! 867
foible 945
foil *contrast* 14
lamina 204
baffle 706
weapon 727
defeat 731
foiled 732
foin 276
foist *ship* 273
- in 228
- upon 545
folâtre 836
fold *fold* 39
bisect 91
inclosure 232
plait **258**
prison 752
congregation 997
- one's arms 681
- in one's arms
902
- up 225
foliaceous 204
foliage 367
foliate 85
foliated 204
folio 593
folk 372
folk-dance 840
folk-lore 124, 979
folk-song 597
follicle *cyst* 191
hollow 252
follicular 260
follow
- *in order* 63
conform to 82
- *in time* 117
- *in motion* 281
understand 518
pursue 622
obey 743
- advice 695
- the dictates of
615
- the example of
19
- from
result from 154
be proved by 478

the decree has
gone – 741
forthcoming 152,
673
forthwith 132
fortification 717
fortify 159
fortiori, a – 467, 476
fortissimo 404
fortiter in re 171
fortitude 826, 861
fortnightly 138
fortress 717, 752
fortuitous
extrinsic 6
chance 156
undersigned 621
– concourse of
atoms 59
fortunate
opportune 134
successful 731
prosperous 734
Fortunatus's – cap
wish 865
spell 993
– purse 803
fortune *chance* 156
fate 601
wealth 803
be one's – 151
clean up a – 803
evil – 621, 735
good – 734
make one's –
succeed 731
wealth 803
tempt –
hazard 621
essay 675
trick of – 509
try one's – 675
wheel of – 601, 621
fortune-hunter 886,
943
fortuneless 804
fortune-teller 513
fortune-telling 511
fortunes of
narrative 594
forty 98
– winks 683
forum 799
school 542
tribunal 966
forward *early* 132
transmit 270
advance 282
willing 602
improve 658
active 682

help 707
vain 880
insolent 885
uncourteous 895
bend – 234
come –
in sight 446
offer 763
display 882
look – to 507
move – 282
press – *haste* 684
put – *aid* 507
offer 763
put oneself – 880
set – 676
– in *knowledge* 490
foss 348
fosse
inclosure 232
ditch 259
defence 717
fossil
ancient 124
hard 323
organic 357
dry bones 362
foster *aid* 707
excite 824
caress 902
– a belief 484
fou 959
foudroyant 870
foul
collide 276
bad 649
dirty 653
unhealthy 657
ugly 846
base 940
vicious 945
fall – of
oppose 708
quarrel 713
attack 716
fight 720
censure 932
run – of
impede 706
– fiend 978
– means 940
– language
malediction 908
– odour 401
– play *evil* 619
cunning 702
wrong 923
improbity 940
foul-mouthed 895
foul-spoken 934
found 153, 215

foundation
beginning 66
stability 150
base 211
support 215
lay the –s 673
sandy – 667
shake to its –s 315
founded
well – 472
– on *base* 211
evidence 467
founder
originator 164
sink 310
fail 732
religious –s 986
foundery 691
founding 22
foundling
trover 775
derelict 782
outcast 893
fount *type* 591
fountain
source 153
river 348
store 636
– head 210
– pen 590
four 95
on all –s 13, 23
horizontal 213
easy 705
prosperous 734
humble 879 ·
– in hand 272
– score &c. 98
– square 244
– times 96
from the – winds
278
fourflusher 884
fourfold 96
four-oar 273
four-poster 215
fourth 96, 97
musical 413
– estate 531
four-wheeler 272
fowl 366
fowling-piece 727
fox *animal* 366
cunning 702
– chase 622
fox-trot 840
foxy *colour* 433, 434
cunning 720
foyer 191, 599
fracas
disorder 59

noise 404
discord 713
contention 720
fraction *part* 51
numerical 84
less than one **100a**
fractious 901
fracture
disjunction 44
discontinuity 70
fissure 198
fragile 160, 328
fragment
small 32, 193
part 51, 100a
fragrance **400**
fragrant weed 392
frail *weak* 160
brittle 328
feeble 575
irresolute 605
imperfect 651
failing 945
impure 961
– sisterhood 962
frais, à grands –
481
frame
condition 7
make 161
support 215
border 231
form 240
substance 316
structure 329
contrive 626
cucumber – 371
have –d and
glazed 822
– of mind
inclination 602
disposition 820
frame-up 626
framework
support 215
structure 329
franchise
voting 609
freedom 748
right 924
exemption 927a
Franciscan 996
franc-tireur 726
frangible 160, 328
frank *open* 525
sincere 543
artless 703
honourable 939
frankalmoigne 748
Frankenstein 913,
980

frankincense 400
frantic
  violent 173
  delirious 503
  excited 824
fraternal
  brother 11
  concord 714
  friendly 888
fraternity
  [see fraternal]
  party 712
fraternize
  co-operate 48, 709
  agree 714
  sympathize 888
  associate 892
fratricide 361
Frau 374
fraud
  falsehood 544
  deception 545
  pretender 548
  dishonour 940
  pious – 988
fraught *full* 52
  pregnant 161
  possessing 777
  – with danger 665
fray *rub* 331
  battle 720
  in the thick of
    the – 722
frayed 659
frazzle
  beaten to a – 732
freak 608, 872
  – of Nature 83
freckle 848
freckled 440
fredaine 840
free
  detached 44, 47
  unconditional 52
  liberate 672
  unobstructed 705
  at liberty 748, 750
  gratis 815
  liberal 816
  insolent 885
  exempt 927a
  impure 961
  – balloon 273
  – and easy
  cheerful 836
  adventurous 863
  vain 880
  insolent 885
  friendly 888
  sociable 892
  – fight 720

– from
  simple 42
  never – from 613
  – gift 784
  – from imperfec-
    tion 650
  – lance 726
  – land 748
  – liver 954a
  – love 961
  make – of 748
  – play 170, 748
  – quarters
  cheap 815
  hospitality 892
  – space 180
  – stage 748
  – trade
  commerce 794
  – translation 522
  – will 600
  make – with
  frank 703
  take 789
  sociable 892
  uncourteous 895
freebooter 792
freeborn 748
freedman 748
freedom 748
free-handed 816
freehold 780
freely
  willingly 602
freeman 748
freemasonry
  unintelligible 519
  secret 528
  sign 550
  co-operation 709
  party 712
free-spoken 703
freethinker 989
freeze
  benumb 381
  cold 385
  – the blood 830
freezing 383
  – mixture 387
freight *lade* 184
  cargo 190
  transfer 270
freightage 812
freighter 273
freight train 272
French
  peddler's – 563
  – and English 840
  – horn 417
  – leave *avoid* 623
  freedom 748

– polish 847
frenetic 503
frenzy
  madness 503
  imagination 515
  excitement 825
frequency 136
frequent
  in number 104
  in time 136
  in space 186
  habitual 613
  visit 892
fresco *cold* 383
  painting 556
al –
  out of doors 220
  in the air 338
fresh *additional* 37
  new 123
  flood 348
  cold 383
  colour 428
  remembered 505
  unaccustomed 614
  good 648
  healthy 654
  impertinent 885
  tipsy 959
  – breeze 349
  – colour 434
  – news 532
freshen 658, 689
freshet 348
freshman 541
freshwater 851
freshwater sailor
  701
fret *suffer* 378
  grieve 828
  gall 830
  discontent 832
  sad 837
  ornament 847
  irritate 900
  – and fume 828
fretful 901
fret-work 219
friable 328, 330
friandise 868
friar 996
  –'s lantern 423
  – Rush 980
  Black –s 996
friary 1000
fribble
  slur over 460
  trifle 643
  dawdle 683
  fop 854
fricassee 298

frication 331
friction *force* 157
  obstacle 179
  rubbing **331**
  on – wheels 705
friend 711, **890**
  candid – 936
  next – 759
friendless 893
friendly 714, **894**
friends, be – 888
  see one's – 892
friendship 9, **888**
frieze 210
frigate 726
fright
  cards 840
  alarm 860
frightful 31, 830,
  846
frightfully 31
frightfulness 860
frigid
  cold 383
  – *style* 575
  callous 823
  indifferent 866
frigidarium 387
frigorific 385
frill 231, 248
  frills and furbe-
  lows 847
fringe
  border 231
  lace 256
  exaggeration 549
  ornament 847
frippery
  trifle 643
  ornament 847
  finery 851
  ridiculous 853
  ostentation 882
frisk *prance* 266
  leap 309
  search 461
  gay 836
  amusement 840
frisky 682, 836
frith *chasm* 198
  strait 343
  forest 367
fritinancy 412
fritter *small* 32
  – away *lessen* 36
  waste 638
  – away time 683
fritters 298
frivolous
  unreasonable 477
  foolish 499

tendency 176
little 193
rough 256
weight 319
texture 329
powder 330
paint 428
temper 820
ornament 847
against the –
rough 256
unwilling 603
opposing 708
in the – 820
–s of allowance
qualification 469
doubt 485
like –s of sand
incoherent 47
gramercy 916
graminivorous 298
grammar
beginning 66
teaching 537
school 542
language 567
bad – 568
comparative – 560
grammarian 492
gramme 319
gramophone 417,
418, 553
granary 636
grand
great 31
style 574
important 642
money 800
handsome 845
glorious 873
ostentatious 882
– climacteric 128
– doings 882
– duchy 181
– jury 967
en – seigneur
proud 878
insolent 885
en –e tenue
ornament 847
show 882
– piano 417
– style 556
– tour 266
– Turk 745
– vizier 694
grandam 130
grandchildren 167
grandee 875
grande dame 878
grandeur 873

grandfather 130,
166
grandiloquent 577
grandiose 577
grandmother 166
simple 501
teach – 538
grandsire 130, 166
grange 189
granite 323
granivorous 298
grano salis, cum
469, 485
grant admit 529
permit 760
consent 762
confer 784
God – 990
– a lease 771
granted 488
take for –
believe 484
suppose 514
grantee
possessor 779
receiver 785
granular 330
granulate 330
granule 32
grapes, sour –
unattainable 471
falsehood 544
excuse 617
grape-shot
attack 716
arms 727
graph 554
graphic
intelligible 518
painting 556
descriptive 594
graphite 332
graphito 556
graphology 590
graphometer 244
graphotype 558
grapnel 666
grapple
fasten 43
clutch 789
– with
- a question 461
- difficulties 704
oppose 708
resist 719
contention 720
grappling-iron
fastening 45
safety 666
grasp
comprehend 518

power 737
retain 781
seize 789
in one's – 737
possess 777
tight – severe 739
– at 865
– of intellect 498
grasping
miserly 819
covetous 865
grass 344, 367
let the – grow
under one's feet
neglect 460
inactive 683
not let the – &c.
active 682
grasshopper 309
grass-plat 371
grate rub 330
physical pain 378
stove 386
– on the ear
harsh sound 410
– on the feelings
830
grated
barred 219
grateful
physically pleas-
ant 377
agreeable 829
thankful 916
grater 260, 330
gratification
animal – 377
moral – 827
gratify 829
permit 760
please 829
grating [see grate]
lattice 219
harsh 713
gratis 815
gratitude 916
gratuitous
inconsequent 477
supposititious
514
voluntary 602
payless 815
gratuity
gift 784
gratis 815
gratulate 896
gravaman 642
– of a charge 938
grave great 31
engrave 259, 558
tomb 363

important 642
composed 826
distressing 830
sad 837
heinous 945
beyond the – 360
look –
disapprove 932
rise from the – 660
silent as the – 403
sink into the – 360
on this side of the
– 359
– in the memory
505
– note 408
– trap 599
gravel
earth 342
material 635
puzzle 704
graveolent 398
graven image 991
graver 558
graving dock 189
gravitate
descend 306
weigh 319
– towards 176
gravity force 157
weight 319
vigour 574
importance 642
sedateness 826
seriousness 827
centre of – 222
specific –
weight 319
density 321
gravy 333
– boat 191
gray 432 [and see
grey]
graze touch 199
browse 298
rub 331
brush 379
grazier 370
gré, savoir – 916
grease
lubricate 332
oil 356
– the palm
tempt 615
give 784
pay 807
greasy 355
great much 31
big 192
glorious 873
magnanimous

942
(*important* 642)
− bear 318
− circle sailing 628
− coat 225
− doings
  importance 642
  bustle 682
− folks 875
− gun 626
− hearted 942
− Mogul 745
− number 102
− primer 591
− quantity 31
greater 33
− number 102
− part 31
  nearly all 50
greatest 33
greatness 31
greave 225
greed
  desire 865
  gluttony 957
greedy
  avaricious 819
green
  new 123
  young 127
  lawn 344
  grass 367
  unripe 397
  colour 435
  credulous 486
  novice 491
  unused 614
  healthy 654
  immature 674
  unskilled 699
  board of − cloth
  966
− memory 505
− old age 128
greenback 800
green-eyed mon-
  ster 920
greenhorn
  novice 493
  dupe 547
  bungler 701
greenhouse
  receptacle 191
  horticulture 371
greenness 435
green-room 599
greensward 344
Greenwich time
  114
greenwood 367
Greek

unintelligible 519
sharper 792
St. Giles's − 563
− Church 984
− Kalends 107
greet *weep* 839
  hail 894
greeting
  sociality 892
  −'s! 292
gregarious 892
grenade 727
grenadier
  tall 206
  soldier 726
grey 432
− beard 130
− friar 996
− hairs 128
bring − hairs to
  the grave
  adversity 735
  harass 830
− mare
  ruler 737
  master 745
  wife 903
− matter
  brain 498
−hound
  swift 274
  animal 366
  ocean −hound 273
gridelin 437
gridiron
  flatness 213
  crossing 219
  stove 386
  stage 599
  stadium 840
grief 828
  come to − 735
grievance
  evil 619
  painful 830
  wrong 923
grieve *mourn* 828
  pain 830
  dejected 837
  complain 839
grievous 649, 830
grievously 31
griffin 83, 366, 493
griffo 41
griffonage 590
grig *merry* 836
grill 382, 384, 461
− room 189
grille 219
grim
  resolved 604

painful 830
doleful 837
ugly 846
discourteous 895
sullen 901a
−visaged war 722
grimace 243, 839,
  855
grimacier
  actor 599
  humorist 844
  affected 855
grimalkin 366
grimy 652
grin *laugh* 838
  ridicule 856
− and abide 725
− a ghastly smile
  dejected 837
  ugly 846
grind
  reduce 195
  sharpen 253
  pulverize 330
  pain 378
  learn 539
  oppress 907
− the organ 416
− one's teeth 900
grinder
  teacher 330
  noise 404
grinding 739, 830
grindstone 253, 330
grip
  indication 550
  power 737
  retention 781
  clutch 789
− of the hand 894
gripe [*see* grip]
  pain 378
  parsimony 819
grisaille
  grey 432
  painting 556
grisette
  woman 374
  commonalty 876
  libertine 962
grisly 846
grist
  materials 635
  provision 637
− to the mill
  useful 644
  acquire 775
gristle 321, 327
grit
  strength 159
  powder 330

stamina 604a
courage 861
− in the oil
  hindrance 706
gritty 323
grizzled
  grey 432
  variegated 440
groan 411, 839
groat 800
grocer 637
grocery 396
grog 298, 959
groin 244
groom 370, 746
− well
− of the chambers
  746
−'s man 903
groove
  furrow 259
  habit 613
in a − 16
move in a − 82
put in a − for 673
grope
  feel 379
  experiment 463
  try 675
in the dark 442,
  704
gross
  great 31
  whole 50
  number 98
  ugly 846
  vulgar 851
  vicious 945
  impure 961
− credulity 486
− receipts 810
grosshead 501
grossheaded 499
grossièreté 895
grot [*see* grotto]
grotesque
  odd 83
  distorted 243
− *style* 579
  ridiculous 853
grotto
  alcove 191
  hollow 252
grouch 895, 901a
ground
  cause 153
  region 181
  base 211
  lay down 213
  support 215
  coating 223

land 342
plain 344
evidence 467
teach 537
motive 615
plea 617
above − 359
down to the − 52
dress the − 371
fall to the − 732
get over the − 274
go over the − 302
level with the −
162
maintain one's −
persevere 604a
play− 840
prepare the − 673
stand one's −
defend 717
resist 719
− bait 784
− cut from under
one 732
− floor
chamber 191
low 207
base 211
− on
attribute 155
− plan 554
− of quarrel 713
− sliding from
under one 665
− swell
agitation 315
waves 348
grounded
stranded 732
well− 490
− on basis 211
evidence 467
groundless
unsubstantial 4
illogical 477
erroneous 495
groundling 876
grounds
dregs 653
groundwork
precursor 64
cause 153
basis 211
support 215
preparation 673
group
marshal 60
cluster 72
− captain 745
grouping 60
grouse 852, 901a

grout 45
grove
street 189
glade 252
wood 367
grovel
below 207
move slowly 275
cringe 886
base 940
grow
increase 35
become 144
expand 194
− from
effect 154
− into 144
− less 195
− taller 206
− together 46
− up 194
− upon one 613
grower 164
growl cry 412
complain 839
discourtesy 895
anger 900
threat 909
growler cab 272
discontented 832
sulky 901a
grown up 131
growth [see grow]
development 161
- in size 194
tumour 250
vegetation 367
groyne 706
grub
small animal 193
food 298
− up
eradicate 301
discover 480a
Grub-street writer
593
grudge
unwilling 603
refuse 764
stingy 819
hate 898
anger 900
bear a − 907
owe a − 898
grudging 603
− praise 932
gruel 298
gruesome 846
gruff
harsh sound 410
discourteous 895

grum
harsh sound 410
morose 901a
grumble
cry 411
complain 832,
839
grume 321, 354
grumous 321, 354
grumpy 901a
Grundy, Mrs. 852
grunt 412
complain 839
guano 653
guarantee 768, 771
guard
travelling 268
safety 664
defence 717
soldier 726
sentry 753
advanced − 668
mount −
care 459
safety 664
off one's −
inexpectant 508
throw off one's −
cunning 702
on one's −
careful 459
cautious 864
rear − 668
− against
prepare 673
defence 717
− ship 664, 726
guarda costa 753
guarded
conditions 770
guardian
safety 664
defence 717
keeper 753
− angel
helper 711
benefactor 912
guardless 665
guard-room 752
gubernation 693
gubernatorial 737
gudgeon 547
guerdon 973
guernsey 225
guerre:
nom de − 565
− à outrance &c.
722
guerilla 726
− warfare 720
guess 514

guesswork 514
guest 890
paying − 188
guet:
mot de − 550
−à-pens 545
guffaw 838
guggle
gush 348
bubble 353
resound 408
cry 412
guide
pattern 22
courier 524
teach 537
teacher 540
indicate 550
direct 693
director 694
advise 695
guide-book 527
guided by, be − 82
guideless 665
guide-post 550
guiding star 693
guild 712, 966
guildhall 799
guile
deceit 544, 545
cunning 702
guileless 543, 703
guillotine 972, 975
guilt 947
guiltless 946
guilty:
find − 971
plead − 950
guindé 579
guinea 800
guipure 847
guisard 599
guise
state 7
dress 225
appearance 448
plea 617
mode 627
conduct 692
guiser 599
guitar 417
gulch 198
gules 434
gulf
interval 198
deep 208
lake 343
gull 545, 547
gullible 486
gullet throat 260
rivulet 348

gully *gorge* 198
  hollow 252
  opening 260
  conduit 350
gulosity 957
gulp *swallow* 296
  take food 298
  – down
  credulity 486
  submit 725
gum *fastening* 45
  fasten 46
  resin 356a
  – elastic 325
  – tree 367
gumbo 298
gummy 352
gumption 498
gun *report* 406
  weapon 727
  great – 626
  blow great –s 349
  sure as a – 474
gunboat 726
gunfire 404
gunman 361
gunner 776
gunnery
  warfare 722
  cannon 727
gunlayer 284
gunpowder
  warfare 722
  ammunition 727
  not invent – 665
  sit on barrel of –
    501
gunroom 193
gun-shot 197
gunwale 232
gurge 312, 348
gurgle
  flow 348
  bubble 353
  faint sound 405
  resonance 408
gurgoyle 350
gush
  flow out 295
  flood 348
  exaggeration 482
  talk 584
gushing
  emotional 821
  impressible 822
gusset 43
gust *wind* 349
  physical taste 390
  passion 825
  moral taste 850
gustation 390

gustful 394
gustless 391
gusto [*see* gust]
  physical pleasure
    377
  emotion 821
gut *destroy* 162
  opening 260
  strait 343
  eviscerate 297
  sack 789
  steal 791
gutling 954a
guts *inside* 221
guttapercha 325
gutter *groove* 259
  conduit 350
  vulgarity 851
guttersnipe 876
guttle 957
guttural
  letter 561
  inarticulate 583
guy
  fastening 45, 752
  fellow 373
  disrespect 929
  grotesque 853
guzzle
  gluttony 957
  drunkenness 959
gybe [*see* jibe]
gymkhana 720, 840
gymnasium 191
  school 542
  arena 728, 840
gymnast 159
gymnastics
  training 537
  exercise 686
  contention 720
  sport 840
gymnosophist
  abstainer 953
  sectarian 984
gynander 83
gynarchy 727
gynecæum 374
gynecology 662
gyniatrics 374
gynics 374
gyp 545, 746
gyre 311
gyrate 312
gyrfalcon 913
gyromancy 511
gyrostat 312
gysart 599
gyve 752

H

habeas corpus 963,
  969
haberdasher 225
habergeon 717
habiliment 225
habilitation 698
habit
  essence 5
  coat 225
  custom 613
  want of – 614
  –s of business 682
  – of mind 820
habitant 188
habitat 189
habitation 189
habit-maker 225
habitual
  unvariable 16
  orderly 58
  ordinary 82
  customary 613
habituate 537, 613
habitude
  state 7
  habit 613
habitué 613
hacienda 189, 780
hack *cut* 44
  shorten 201
  horse 271
  writer 594
  worker 690
  literary – 593
hackle 44
hackney-coach 272
hackneyed
  known 490
  trite 496
  habitual 613
Hades 982
Hadji
  traveller 268
  priest 996
hæ tibi erunt artes
  627
hæret lateri lethalis
  arundo
  displeasure 828
  anger 900
haft 633
hag *age* 128
  ugly 846
  wretch 913
  witch 994
haggard
  insane 503
  tired 688
  wild 824

  ugly 846
haggis 298
haggle *cut* 44
  chaffer 794
Hagiographa 985
Hagiolatry 984
Hagiology 983, 985
haguebut 727
ha-ha *trench* 198,
  719
haik 225
hail *welcome* 292
  ice 383
  call 586
  rejoicing 838
  honour to 873
  celebration 883
  courtesy 894
  salute 928
  approve 931
  –fellow well met
  friendship 888
  sociality 892
hailstone 383
hair *small* 32
  filament 205
  roughness 256
  to a – 494
  –'s breadth
  near 197
  narrow 203
  –breadth escape
  danger 665
  escape 671
  –s on the head
  multitude 102
  make one's –
    stand on end
  distressing 830
  fear 860
  wonder 870
hairless 226
hairy *rough* 256
halberd 727
halberdier 726
halcyon *calm* 174
  peace 721
  prosperous 734
  joyful 827, 829
hale 654
half 91
  – the battle
  important 642
  success 731
  – distance 68
  – a dozen *six* 98
  several 102
  see with – an **eye**
  intelligent 498
  intelligible 518
  manifest 525

height 206
projection 250
headlong
hurry 684
rush 863
rush –
violence 173
headman 694
headmost
front 234
precession 280
head-piece
summit 210
intellect 450
helmet 717
ornament 847
head-quarters
focus 74
abode 189
authority 737
head-race 350
head-stone 363
heads
compendium 596
– or tails 156, 621
lay – together
advice 695
co-operate 709
– I win tails you
lose
unfair 940
headship 737
headsman 975
headstrong
violent 173
obstinate 606
rash 863
headway *space* 180
navigation 267
progression 282
headwind 708
headwork 451
heady 606
heal *restore* 660
remedy 662
let the wound –
forgive 918
– the breach
pacify 723
healing art 662
health 654
picture of – 654
healthiness 655
health resort 189
healthy 656
heap *quantity* 31
collection 72
store 636
too many 641
heaps 102
rubbish – 645

hear
audition 418
be informed 527
not – of (refuse)
764
– a cause
adjudge 480
lawsuit 969
– hear! 931
– and obey 743
– out 457
hearer 418
hearing 418, 696
[*see* hear]
gain a – 175
give a – 418
hard of – 419
out of – 196
within – 197
hearken 457
hearsay 532
– evidence 467
hearse 363
heart
intrinsicality 5
interior 221
centre 222
mind 450
willingness 602
essential 642
affections 820
courage 861
love 897
man after one's
own – 899
with all one's –
438, 602
at – 820, 821
from bottom of –
543
beating – 821, 824
break the – 830
by –
memory 505
go to one's – 824
in good – 858
with a heavy –
603
know by – 490
lay to – 837
learn by – 539
lift up the – 990
lose – 837
lose one's – 897
nearest to one's –
897
not find it in one's
– 603
have a place in
the – 897
put one's – into

604
set one's – upon
604
take –
content 831
hope 858
courage 861
take to –
sensibility 822
discontent 832
dejection 837
anger 900
warm – 822
wind round the –
897
– bleeding for 914
to one's –'s con-
tent
willing 602
enough 639
success 731
pleasure 829
–'s core
mind 450
affections 820
– expanding 821
– failing one 837,
860
do one's – good
829
– of grace 858
– in hand 602
– leaping with joy
827, 838
– leaping into
one's mouth 824
– of oak
strong 159
hard 323
– in right place
906
– sinking *fear* 860
– and soul
completely 52
willing 602
resolute 604
exertion 686
feeling 821
– of stone 823, 907
– swelling 824
heartache 828
heart-breaking 821,
830
heart-broken 828
heartburning
discontent 832
regret 833
enmity 889
anger 900
jealousy 920
hearten 858, 861

heartfelt 821, 829
hearth
home 189
fireplace 386
heartless 823, 945
heart-rending 830
heartsease 831
heart-shaped 245
heart-sick
dejection 837
dislike 867
satiety 869
heart-stricken 828
**heart-strings, tear
the** – 830
hearty
willing 602
healthy 654
feeling 821
cheerful 836
friendly 888
social 892
– laugh 838
– meal 298
– reception 892
heat *warmth* **382**
make hot 384
contest 720
excitement 824,
825
dead – 27
– of passion 900
– wave 382
heated imagination
515
heater 386
heath *moor* 344
plant 367
heathen 984, 989
– mythology 979
heathenish 851
heather *moor* 344
plant 367
heaume 717
**heautontimoru-
menos** 837, 955
heave *raise* 307
emotion 821
– the lead 208,
466
– a sigh 839
– in sight 446
– to 265
heaven 827, **981**
call – to witness
535
in the face of –
525
light of – 420
move – and earth
686

will of – 601
– forfend! 766
– knows 475, 491
– be praised 838, 916
for –'s sake 765
heaven-born
  wise 498
  repute 873
  virtue 944
heaven-directed 498
heaven-kissing 206
heavenly
  celestial 318
  rapturous 829
  divine 976
  of heaven 981
  – bodies 318
  – host 977
  – kingdom 981
heavenly-minded 987
heavens 318
  – and earth! 870
Heaviside layer 338
heavisome 843
heavy *great* 31
  inert 172
  weighty 319
  stupid 499
  actor 599
  sleepy 683
  dull 843
  brutish 851
  – affliction 828
  – artillery 726
  – cost 814
  – dragoon 726
  – father 599
  – gaited 843
  – gun 727
  – hand
  clumsy 699
  severe 739
  – on hand 641
  – heart *loth* 603
  pain 828
  dejection 837
  – hours 841
  – on the mind 837
  – news 830
  – sea
  agitation 515
  waves 348
  – sleep 683
  – type 591
  – wet 298
heavy-laden 706, 828

hebdomadal 138
Hebe 845
hebetate 823, 826
hebetude
  imbecile 499
  insensible 823
  inexcitable 826
Hebrew
  unintelligible 519
  Jew 984
Hecate 994
hecatomb
  number 98
  sacrifice 991
heckle 830, 900
hectic 382, 821
Hector *brave* 861
  rash 863
  bully 885, 887
hedge
  compensate 30
  inclosure 232
  – in
  circumscribe 229
  hinder 706
  conditions 770
hedgehog 253
hedonism 377, 827
hedonist 954a
heed *attend* 457
  care 459
  beware 668
  caution 864
heedful 457
heedless
  inattentive 458
  neglectful 460
  oblivious 506
  rash 863
heel *support* 215
  lean 217
  deviate 279
  go round 311
  iron – 975
  lay by the –s 162
  turn on one's –
  go back 283
  go round 311
  avoid 623
  – of Achilles 665
heel-piece
  sequel 65
  back 235
  repair 660
heel-tap
  remainder 40
  dress 653
heels *lowness* 207
  at the – of
  near 197
  behind 235

cool one's – 681
follow on the – of 281
laid by the – 751
lay by the – 789
show a light pair of – 623
take to one's – 623
tread on the – of
  near 197
  follow 281
  approach 286
  – over head
  inverted 218
  hasty 684
  rash 863
heft *handle* 633
  exertion 686
hegemony
  influence 175
  direction 693
  authority 737
heifer 366
heigho! 839
height *degree* 26
  altitude **206**
  summit 210
  at its –
  great 31
  supreme 33
  draw oneself up to his full – 307
  – finder 206
heighten
  increase 35
  elevate 307
  exaggerate 549
  aggravate 835
hegira [*see* hejira]
heinous 945
heir *futurity* 121
  posterity 167
  inheritor 779
heirloom 780
heirship 777
hejira 293
Helen of Troy 845
heliacal 318
helical 248
Helicon 597
helicon-horn 417
helicopter 273
Heliogabalus 954a
heliograph
  signal 550
  picture 556
heliography 550
  light 420
  painting 556
Helios 423

heliotrope 847
heliotype 558
helix 248
hell *abyss* 208
  gaming-house 62
  gehenna **982**
  – upon earth
  misfortune 735
  pain 828
  – broke loose 59
hell-born 945, 978
hellebore 663
hell-hound 913, 949
hellish
  malevolent 907
  vicious 945
  hell 982
helluo librorum 492
helm *handle* 633
  sceptre 747
  (*authority* 737)
  answer the – 743
  at the – 693
  obey the – 705
  take the – 693
helmet 225, 717
helminthology 368
helmsman 269, 694
helot 746
help *benefit* 618
  utility 644
  remedy 662
  aid 707
  servant 746
  give 784
  it can't be –ed
  submission 725
  never mind 823
  content 831
  God – you 914
  so – me God 535
  – oneself to 789
helper 711
helpless 158, 665
helpmate
  auxiliary 711
  wife 903
helter-skelter 59, 684
helve
  throw the – after the hatchet 818
hem *edge* 231
  fold 258
  indeed! 870
  kiss the – of one's garment 886
  – in *enclose* 220
  restrain 751
hemi- 91
hemisphere 181

hemispheric 250
hemlock 663
hemorrhage 299
hemp 205
hen 366, 374
female 374
– with one chicken
busy 682
henbane 663
hence
arising from 155
departure 293
deduction 476
– loathed mel-
ancholy 836
henceforth 121
henchman 746
hencoop 370
hendiadis 91
henna 433
henpecked 743, 749
heptagon 244
heptarchy 98
Heraclitus 839
rideret – 853
herald
precursor 64
precession 280
predict 511
forerunner 512
proclaim 531
messenger 534
heraldry 550
herb 367
herbage 365
herbal 369
herbivorous 298
herborize 369
herculean
strong 159
exertion 686
difficult 704
Herculem, ex pede
– 550
Hercules 159, 215
pillars of – 233,
550
herd 72, 102
herdsman 746
here
situation 183
presence 186
arrival 292
come –! 286
– below 318
– goes 676
– and there
dispersed 73
few 103
place 182, 183
– there and

everywhere
diversity 16a
space 180
omnipresence 186
– to-day and gone
to-morrow 111
hereabouts 183,
197
hereafter 121, 152
hereby 631
hereditament 780
hereditary
intrinsic 5
derivative 154,
167
heredity 167
herein 221
heresy 495, 984
heretic 984
heretofore 122
hereupon 106
herewith 88, 632
heritage
futurity 121
possession 777
property 780
heritor 779
hermaphrodite 83
– brig 273
hermeneutics 522
Hermes 534, 582
hermetically 261
hermit 893, 955
hermitage
house 189
cell 191
seclusion 893
hero *brave* 861
glory 873
good man 948
– worship 931, 991
Herod, out-Herod
– 549
heroic [*see* hero]
magnanimous
942
mock – 853
heroics 884
heroin 663
heroine 861
herpetology 368
Herr 373
herring
pungent 392
– pond 341
draw a – across
the trail 545
trail of a red –
615, 706
herring-gutted 203
hesitate

uncertain 475
sceptical 485
stammer 583
reluctant 603
irresolute 605
fearful 860
Hesperian 236
Hesperides, garden
of the – 981
Hesperus 423
Hessian boot 225
hest 741
hesterni quirites
876
heterarchy 737
heteroclite 83
heterodoxy 489,
984
heterogeneous
unrelated 10
different 15
mixed 41
multiform 81
exceptional 83
heterogeneity 15,
16a
heteromorphism
16a
hetman 745
hew *cut* 44
shorten 201
fashion 240
– down 308
hewers of wood
workers 690
commonalty 876
hexagon 98, 244
hexahedron 244
hexameter 98, 597
hey! 586
heyday
exultation 838
festivity 840
wonder 870
– of the blood 820
– of youth 127
hiation 260
hiatus 198
hibernal 383
hibernate 683
Hibernicism 497,
563
hic:
– jacet 363
– labor hoc opus
704
hick 701, 851, 876
hiccup 349
hid under a bushel
460

hidalgo 875
hidden 528
– meaning 526
hide *skin* 223
conceal 528
– diminished **head**
inferior 34
decrease 36
humility 879
– one's face
modesty 881
– and seek
deception 545
avoid 623
game 840
hide-bound 751,
819
hideous 846
hide-out 893
hiding-place
abode 189
ambush 530
refuge 666
hie 264, 274
– to 266
hiemal 126
hierarch 996
hierarchy 995
hieratic 590
hieroglyphic
representation
554
letter 561
writing 590
hierographa 985
hieromancy 511
hierophant 996
hieroscopy 511
higgle 794
higgledy piggledy
59
higgler 797
high *much* 31
lofty 206
fetid 401
treble 410
foul 653
noted 873
proud 878
from on – 981
on – 206
think –ly of 931
– art 556
– celebration 998
– colour
colour 428
red 434
exaggerate 549
– commissioner
745
– days and holi-

H.M.S. 726
hoar *aged* 128
  white 430
  – frost 383
hoard 636
hoarse
  husky 405
  harsh 410
  voiceless 581
  talk oneself – 584
hoary [*see* hoar]
hoax 545
hob *support* 215
  stove 386
  – and nob
  celebration 883
  courtesy 894
hobble
  limp 275
  awkward 699
  difficulty 704
  fail 732
  shackle 751
  – skirt 225
hobbledehoy 129
hobby
  crotchet 481
  pursuit 622
  desire 865
hobby-horse 272
hobgoblin
  fearful 860
  demon 980
hobo 268
hobnail 876
Hobson's choice
  necessity 601
  no choice 609a
  compulsion 744
hoc genus omne
  876
hock 771
hock shop 787
hockey 840
hockey rink 213
hocus 545
hocus-pocus
  interchange 148
  unmeaning 517
  cheat 545
  conjuration 992
  spell 993
hod
  receptacle 191
  support 215
  vehicle 272
hoddy-doddy 501
hodge-podge 41, 59
hoe 272, 371
hog *animal* 366
  sensualist 954a

glutton 957
(greedy as a – 865
  go the whole – 604
hog's back 206
hogmanay 998
hogshead 191
hog-wash 653
hoist 307
  – the black flag
   722
  – a flag 550
  – on one's own
   petard
   retaliation 718
   failure 732
hoity-toity! 815,
  870
hold *cohere* 46
  contain 54
  remain 141
  cease 142
  go on 143
  happen 151
  receptacle 191
  cellar 207
  base 211
  support 215
  halt 265
  believe 484
  be passive 681
  defend 717
  power 737
  restrain 751
  prison 752
  prohibit 761
  possess 777
  retain 781
  enough! 869
  have a firm – 781
  have a – upon 175
  gain a – upon 737
  get – of 789
  quit one's – 782
  take – 175
  – aloof
  stay away 187
  distrust 487
  avoid 623
  – an argument
   476
  – authority 737
  – back *avoid* 623
  store 636
  hinder 706
  restrain 751
  retain 781
  miserly 819
  – one's breath
  wonder 870
  – converse 588
  – a council 695

– fast 751, 781
– forth *teach* 537
  speak 582
– good 478, 494
– one's ground
  141
– in hand 737
– one's hand
  cease 142
  relinquish 624
– hard 265
– up one's head
  861
– a lease 771
– a meeting 72
– off 623
– office 693
– on
  continue 141, 143
  persevere 604a
  – out [*see below*]
– one's own
  preserve 670
  defend 717
  resist 719
– oneself in readi-
  ness 673
– in remembrance
  505
– both one's sides
  838
– a situation 625
– in solution 335
– to 602
– together 43, 709
– one's tongue
  403, 585
– up [*see below*]
– oneself up 307
hold out
  endure 106
  affirm 535
  persevere 604a
  resist 719
  offer 763
  brave 861
  – expectation
  predict 511
  promise 768
  – temptation 865
hold up
  continue 143
  support 215
  not rain 340
  aid 707
  rob 791
  display 882
  extol 931
  – one's hand
  sign 550
  threat 609

– to execration
  cures 908
  censure 932
– the mirror 525
– to scorn 930
– to shame 874
– to view 525
holder 779
holdfast 45
holding
  tenancy 777
  property 780
hole *place* 182
  hovel 189
  receptacle 191
  opening 260
  ambush 530
  – in one's coat 651
  – and corner
  place 182
  peer into – 461
  hiding 528, 530
  – to creep out of
  plea 617
  escape 671
  facility 705
holiday *leisure* 685
  repose 687
  amusement 840
  – task *easy* 705
holiness *God* 976
  piety 987
holloa 411
  – before one is out
  of the wood 884
hollow
  unsubstantial 4
  completely 52
  incomplete 53
  depth 208
  concavity 252
  channel 350
  - *sound* 408
  specious 477
  false 544
  voiceless 581
  beat – 731
  – truce 723
holm 346
holocaust
  kill 361
  sacrifice 991
  (*destruction* 162)
holograph 590
holster 191
holt 367
holus bolus 684
Holy *of God* 976
  pious 987
  keep – 987
  – breathing 990

hopper 191
horary 108
horde
  assemblage 72
  party 712
  commonalty 876
horizon
  distance 196
  view 441
  expectation 507
  appear on the –
  525
  gloomy – 859
horizontality 213
horn
  receptacle 191
  sharp 253
  music 417
  draw in one's –s
  recant 607
  submit 725
  humility 879
  exalt one's – 873
  wear the –s 905
  –s of a dilemma
  reasoning 476
  difficulty 704
  – in 294
  – mad 920
  – of plenty 639
hornbook 542
hornet
  evil-doer 913
  –'s nest
  pitfall 667
  difficulty 704
  adversity 735
  painful 830
  resentment 900
  censure 932
hornpipe 840
hornwork 717
horny 323
Horny, old – 978
horology 114
horoscope 511, 992
horresco referens
  860
horrible *great* 31
  noxious 649
  dire 830
  ugly 846
  fearful 860
horrid [*see* horrible]
  vulgar 851
horrida bella 722
horrific [*see*
  horrible]
horrified 828, 860
horrify 830, 860
horripilation 383

horrisonous 410
horror 860, 867
  view with – 898
horrors 837
  sup full of – 828
horror-stricken 828
hors de combat
  impotent 158
  useless 645
  tired out 688
  put – 731
hors-d'œuvre 298
horse *hang on* 214
  stand 215
  carrier 271
  animal 366
  male 373
  cavalry 726
  ride the high –
  885
  put the –s to 673
  put up one's –s at
  184
  put up one's –s
  together
  concord 714
  friendship 888
  take – 266
  to – 293
  war – 726
  work like a – 686
  – artillery 726
  – of another colour
  15
  – doctor 370
  – and foot 726
  – laugh 838
  – marine 701
  like a – in a mill
  613
  – racing
  pastime 840
  contention 720
  – soldier 726
  – track 627
horseback 266
horse-cloth 225
horseman 268
horsemanship
  riding 266
  skill 698
horseplay 856
horse power 466
horse-shoe 245
horse-whip 972
hortation 615, 695
hortative 537
horticulture 371
hortus siccus 369
hosanna 931, 990
hose

  stockings 225
  pipe 348, 350
  extinguisher 385
hosier 225
hospice 189, 662
hospitable 816, 892
hospital 189, 662
  in – 655
hospitality
  [*see* hospitable]
hospodar 745
host *collection* 72
  multitude 102
  army 726
  friend 890
  rite 998
  reckon without
  one's –
  error 495
  unskilful 699
  rash 863
  – of heaven 977
  – in himself 175
hostage 771
hostel 189
hostelry 189
hostile
  disagreeing 24
  opposed 708
  enmity 889
  in – array 708
  – meeting 720
hostilities 722
hostility 889
hostler 746
hot *violent* 173
  warm 382
  pungent 392
  red 434
  orange 439
  excited 824
  irascible 901
  make – 384
  – air 482, 884
  – bath 386
  – blood *rash* 863
  angry 900
  irascible 901
  blow – and cold
  inconsistent 477
  falsehood 544
  tergiversation 607
  caprice 608
  in – haste 684
  in – pursuit 622
  – water
  difficulty 704
  quarrel 713
  painful 830
  – water bottle 386
hot air merchant

  884
hot-bed *cause* 153
  centre 222
  workshop 691
Hotchkiss gun 727
hotchpotch
  mixture 41
  confusion 59
  participation 778
hotel 189
hot-headed 684,
  825
hothouse
  conservatory 371,
  636
  furnace 386
  workshop 691
hot-press 255
Hotspur 863
Hottentot 876
hough 659
hound *animal* 366
  hunt 622
  persecute 907
  wretch 949
  hold with the hare
  but run with the
  –s 607
  – on 615
houppelande 225
hour *period* 108
  point of time 113
  present time 118
  improve the shin-
  ing – 682
  one's – is come
  occasion 134
  death 360
  – after hour 110
hour-glass
  chronometer 114
  contraction 195
  narrow 203
Houri 845
hourly *time* 106
  frequent 136
  periodical 138
house *family* 166
  locate 184
  abode 189
  theatre 599
  make safe 664
  council 696
  firm 712
  before the – 454
  keep – 184
  eat out of – and
  home
  prodigal 818
  gluttony 957
  turn out of – and

home 297
- of cards 160
- of correction
   prison 752
   punishment 975
- of death 363
- of detention 752
- divided against
   itself 713
bring the – about
   one's ears 699
- of Commons
   696, 966
- of God 1000
- of Lords 696,
   875, 966
set one's – in
   order 952
- of peers 696, 875
- of prayer 1000
- built on sand
   160
turn – out of win-
   dow 713
housebreaker 792
housebreaking 791
house-dog 366
household
   inhabitants 188
   abode 189
   – gods 189
   – stuff 635
   – troops 726
   – words
   known 490
   language 560
   plain 576, 849
householder 188
housekeeper 637,
   694
housekeeping 692
houseless 185
housemaid 746
house-organ 531
Houses of Parlia-
   ment 191, 696
house-top 210
   proclaim from –
   531
house-room 180
house-warming 892
housewife 682
housewifery 692,
   817
housing
   lodging 189
   covering 223
   horse-cloth 225
hovel 189
hoveller 269
hover *high* 206

rove 266
soar 267
ascend 305
irresolute 605
– about
move 264
– over
near 197
how *way* 627
   means 632
– comes it?
   attribution 155
   inquiry 461
   – now 870
howbeit 30
however
   degree 26
   notwithstanding
   30
   except 83
howitzer 727
howker 273
howl
   wind 349
   human cry 411
   animal cry 412
   lamentation 839
howler 495
howling wilderness
   169, 893
hoy 273
hoyden *girl* 129
   rude 851
hub 222
hubble-bubble 392
hubbub *stir* 315
   noise 404
   discord 713
huckster 794, 797
huddle
   disorder 59
   derange 61
   collect 72
   hug 197
   – on 225
Hudibrastic 856
   – verse 597
hue 428
   – and cry *cry* 411
   proclaim 531
   pursuit 622
   alarm 669
   raise a – and cry
   932
hueless 429
huff 885, 900
huffy 901
hug *cohere* 46
   border on 197
   retain 781
   courtesy 894

love 897
   endearment 902
   – a belief 606
   – oneself
   pleasure 827
   content 831
   rejoicing 838
   pride 878
   – the shore
   navigation 267
   approach 286
   – a sin 945
huge 31, 192
hugger-mugger 528
Huguenot 984
huis clos, à – 528
huissier 965
huke 225
hulk *body* 50
   ship 273
hulks 752
hulky *big* 192
   unwieldy 647
   ugly 846
hull 50
hullabaloo 404, 411
hullo! 292
hum
   faint sound 405
   continued sound
   407
   animal sound 412
   sing 416
   deceive 545, 546
   – and haw
   stammer 583
   irresolute 605
busy – of men 682
human 372
   – race 372
   – sacrifices 991
humane
   benevolent 906
   philanthropic 910
   merciful 914
humanitarian 372,
   910
humanities 560
humanize 894
humano capiti cer-
   vicem jungere
   equinam 24
humation 363
humble *meek* 879
   modest 881
   pious 987
   –r classes 876
   – oneself
   submit 725
   meek 879
   penitent 950

worship 990
eat – pie 725, 879
your – servant
   dissent 489
   refusal 764
humbug
   falsehood 544
   deception 545
   deceiver 548
   trifle 643
   affectation 855
humdrum 841, 843
humectate 337, 339
humid 339
humiliate 308
humiliation
   adversity 735
   disrepute 874
   sense of shame
   879
   worship 990
   self – 950
humility **879**, 987
humming-top 417
hummock 206, 250
humorist **844**
humorous 842
humour *essence* 5
   tendency 176
   liquid 333
   disposition 602
   caprice 608
   aid 707
   indulge 760
   affections 820
   please 829
   wit 842
   flatter 933
   (*fun* 840)
   in the – 602
   out of – 901a
   peccant –
   unclean 853
   disease 655
humoursome
   capricious 608
   sulky 901a
hump 250
hump-backed 243
humph! 870
Humphrey, dine
   with Duke – 956
Humpty-dumpty
   193
Hun 165, 851, 913
hunch 250, 612
hunch-backed 243
hundred
   number 98
   many 102
   region 181

the same a – years
hence 460
hundredth 99
hundredweight 319
hunger 865
hunger-strike 956
hunks 819
hunt *inquiry* 461
pursuit 622
– after 622
– in couples 709
– down 907
– out *inquiry* 461
discover 480a
– slipper 840
hunter *horse* 271
killer 361
pursuer 622
place &c. – 767
hunting 361, 622
hunting-ground 840
happy – 981
hurdle 272
hurdy-gurdy 417
hurl 284
– against 716
– defiance 715
hurler avec les
loups 82, 714
Hurlothrumbo 860
hurly-burly 315
hurrah 411, 836,
838
hurricane 349, 667
– deck 210
hurry *haste* 684
excite 825
– forward 684
– off with 789
– on 615
– of spirits 821
– up 684
hurst 367
hurt
physical pain 378
evil 619
maltreat 649
injure 659
more frightened
than – 860
– the feelings
pain 830
anger 900
hurtful 649
hurtle 276
hurtless 648
husband
store 636
director 694
spouse 903
husbandman 371

husbandry
agriculture 371
conduct 692
economy 817
hush *moderate* 174
stop 265
silence 403
taciturn 585
– up
conceal 528
pacify 723
hush-money 30,
973
husk 223, 226
husky *strong* 159
dry 340
faint sound 405
hoarse 581
hussar 726
hussy 962
hustings
school 542
arena 728
tribunal 966
hustle
perturb 61
push 276
agitate 315
activity 682
hinder 706
hustler 682, 962
hut 189
hutch 189
huzza 838
hyacinth
jewel 847
hyæna 913
hyaline 425
hybrid
mixture 41
exception 83
hydra
monster 83, 366
productive 168
– headed 163
hydrant 348, 385
hydraulics 333, 348
hydro-aeroplane
273
hydrodynamics
333, 348
hydrography 341
hydrology 333
hydrolysis 49
hydromancy 511
hydromel 396
hydropathy 662
hydrophobia 867
hydroplane 273
hydrostatics 333
hyemal 383

hyetology 348
hygeian 656
hygiantics 670
hygienic 656, 670
hygre 348
hygrometry 339
hyle 316
hylism 316
hylotheism 984,
989
Hymen 903
hymeneal 903
hymn *song* 415
worship 990
– of hate 898
hymn-book 998
hyoscine 663
hypallage 218
hyperbation 218
hyperbola 245
hyperbole 549
hyperborean
far 196
cold 383
hypercriticism
misjudgment 481
discontent 832
fastidiousness 868
censure 932
hyperdulia 990
Hyperion 423, 845
– to a satyr 14
hyperorthodoxy 984
hyperphysical 976
hypertrophy 194
hyphen 45
hypnology 683
hypnotic
remedy 662
sleep 683
hypnotize 376
hypocaust 386
hypochondriac
madman 504
low spirits 837
hypochondriasis
837
hypocrisy
falsehood 544
religious – 988
hypocrite 548, 855
play the – 544
hypostasis 1, 3
Hypostatic union
976
hypothecate 771
hypothenuse 217
hypothesis 514
hypothesize 514
hypothetical 475,
514

hypped *insane* 503
dejected 837
hypsometer 206
Hyrcynian wood
533
hysteria
insanity 503
hysteric *violent* 173
hysterical
spasmodic 608
emotional 821
excitable 825
hysterics 173
in – *excited* 824
frightened 860
hysteron proteron
218

I

I 79
iambic 597
ibidem 13
Icarus
navigator 269
rash 863
fate of – 306
ice *cold* 383
refrigerate 385
iceberg 383
ice-bound 383
restraint 751
ice-chest 385
ice-house 387
ice-yacht 273
Ichabod 874
ichnography 554
ichor 333
ichthyology 368
ichthyomancy 511
ichthyophagous 298
icicle 383
icon 554
iconoclasm 983a,
984
iconoclast 165, 913
iconography 554
icosahedron 244
id est 522
idea
small quantity 32
notion 453
give an – of 537
ideal *unreal* 2
completeness 52
erroneous 495
imaginary 515
perfect 650
ideality 450, 515
idée fixe 481

imaum 745, 996
imbecile 158, 499
imbécile 501
imbecility 499
imbed [see embed]
imbedded 229
imbibe 296
  – learning 539
imbrangle 61
imbricated 223
imbroglio
  disorder 59
  difficulty 704
  discord 713
imbrue
  impregnate 300
  moisten 339
  – one's hands in
    blood
  killing 361
  war 722
  – the soul 824
imbue mix 41
  impregnate 300
  moisten 339
  tinge 428
  teach 537
imbued
  affections 820
  – with
  belief 484
  habit 613
  feeling 821
imburse 803
imitation
  copying 19
  copy 21
  representation
    554
immaculate
  perfect 650
  clean 652
  innocent 946
immanent 5, 132
immanity 907
Immanuel 976
immaterial
  unsubstantial 4
immateriality
  spiritual 317
  trifling 643
immature 123, 674
immeasurable 31,
  105
immediate
  continuous 69
immediately 113,
  132
immedicabile
  vulnus 619
immedicable 859

immelodious 414
immemorial 124
  from time – 122
  – usage 613
immense great 31
  infinite 105
  – size 192
immerge}
immerse}
  introduce 300
  dip 337
immersed in 229
immethodical 59
immigrant
  alien 57
  entering 294
immigration 266,
  294
imminent 152, 286
immiscible 47
immission 296
immitigable
  hopeless 859
  revenge 919
immix 41
immobility 150, 265
immoderately 31
immodest 961
immolation
  killing 361
  giving 784
  sacrifice 991
immoral 923, 945
immortal
  perpetual 112
  glorious 873
  celebrated 883
immotile 265
immovable
  stable 150
  quiescent 265
  obstinate 606
immundicity 653
immunity
  health 656
  freedom 748
  right 924
  exemption 777a,
    927a
immure 751
immutable
  stable 150
  deity 976
imo pectore, ab –
  821
imp 980
impact contact 43
  impulse 276
  insertion 300
impair 659
impale transfix 260

execute 972
impalpable
  small 193
  powder 330
  intangible 381
impanation 998
impar sibi 608
imparity 28
impart inform 527
  give 784
impartial
  judicious 498
  neutral 628
  just 922
  honourable 939
  – opinion 484
impassable
  closed 261
  impossible 471
impasse 706
impassible 823
impassion 824
impassionable 822
impassioned
  – language 574
  excited 825
impassive 823
impatient 825
  – of control 742
impawn 771
impeach
  censure 932
  accuse 938
  go to law 969
impeachment,
  soft – 902
impeccability 650,
  946
impecunious 804
impede 706
impediment 706
  – in speech 583
impedimenta 633,
  780
impel push 276
  induce 615
impend
  future 121
  imminent 132
  destiny 152
  overhang 206
impenetrable
  closed 261
  solid 321
  unintelligible 519
  latent 526
impenitence 951
imperative
  require 630
  command 737,
    741

severe 739
  duty 926
imperator 745
imperceptible
  small 32
  minute 193
  slow 275
  invisible 447
  latent 526
impercipient 376
imperdible 664
imperfect
  incomplete 53
  failing 651
  vicious 945
imperfection 651
  inferiority 34
  vice 945
imperfectly 32
imperforate 261
imperial
  trunk 191
  beard 256
  authority 737
imperil 665
imperious
  command 737
  proud 878
  arrogant 885
  – necessity 601
imperishable 112
  stable 150
  glorious 873
imperium in
  imperio 737
impermanent 111
impermeable
  closed 261
  dense 321
impersonal
  general 78
  neuter 316
impersonate 19,
  554
impersonator 19
imperspicuity 519
impersuasible 606
impertinent
  irrelevant 10
  insolent 885
imperturbable 823,
  826
impervious
  closed 261
  impossible 471
  insensible 823
  – to light 426
  – to reason 606
impetiginous 653
impetrate 765
impetuous

boisterous 173
hasty 684
excitable 825
rash 863
eager 865
impetus 276
impi 726
impiety **988**
impignorate 787
impinge 276
implacable 848, 919
implant *insert* 300
teach 537
implanted
adventitious 6
implausible 473
implead 969
implement 633
impletion 52
implex 41
implicate *involve* 54,
526
accuse 938
implicated *related* 9
component 56
implication
disorder 59
meaning 516
latency 526
implicit 526
- belief 484
implore 765
imply *evidence* 467
mean 516
involve 526
impolicy 699
impolite 895
imponderable 4,
320
imporous 261, 321
import
put between 228
ingress 294
take in 296
insert 300
mean 516
imply 526
be of consequence
642
importance **642**
greatness 30
attach - to 642
attach too much
- to 482
of no - 643
importune 765, 830
impose *order* 741
awe 928
- upon
credulity 486
deceive 545

be *unjust* 923
imposing
important 642
exciting 824
glorious 873
imposition [*see*
impose]
undue 925
- of hands 998
impossibile, credo
quia - 486
impossibilities,
seek after - 645
impossibility **471**
impossible 471
refusal 764
- quantity
algebra 84
impost 812
imposthume 655
impostor 548, 925
imposture 545
impotence **158**
impotent conclu-
sion 732
impound 791
impoverish
weaken 160
waste 638
despoil 789
render poor 804
impracticable
impossible 471
misjudging 481
obstinate 606
difficult 704
imprecation
prayer 765
curse 908
impregnable 159,
664
impregnate *mix* 41
combine 48
fecundate 161,
168
insert 300
teach 537
- with 641
impresario 599
imprescriptible 924
impress *cause*
sensation 375
mark 550
compel 791
excite feeling 824
- upon the mind
memory 505
teach 537
impressed with
belief 484
feeling 821

impressible
motive 615
sensibility 822
impression
sensation 375
idea 453
belief 484
printing 531
mark 550
engraving 558
print 591
emotion 821
make an -
act 171
thought 451
impressionable
375, 822
impressive
language 574
important 642
feeling 821, 824
imprimis 66
imprimit 558
imprint
publisher 531
indication 550
- in the memory
505
imprison
circumscribe 229
restrain 751
punish 972
improbability **473**
improbate 932
improbity **940**
impromptu 612
- fait à loisir 673
improper
incongruous 24
foolish 499
solecism 568
inexpedient 647
wrong 923
unmeet 925
vicious 945
- time 135
impropriate 777,
789
impropriator 779
improve 658
- the occasion 134
- the shining
hour 682
- upon 658
improvement **658**
improvident
careless 460
not preparing 674
prodigal 818
rash 863
improvisation

music 415
improvisatore
speech 582
poetry 597
impulse 612
improvise
imagination 515
impulse 612
unprepared 674
improviste, à l'-
508, 612
improvisatrice
612
imprudent 460, 863
impudent 885, 895
impudicity 961
impugn *deny* 536
attack 716
blame 932
impugnation 708
impuissance 158
impulse *push* **276**
sudden thought
612
motive 615
blind - 601
creature of - 612
give an - to
propel 284
aid 707
impulsive [*see*
impulse]
intuitive 477
excitable 825
rash 863
impunity *escape* 671
acquittal 970
with - *safely* 664
impurity 653, **961**
imputation
ascribe 155
slur 874
accuse 938
in 221
go - 294
- as much as
relation 9
degree 26
- the circum-
stances 8
- doors 221
- durancevile 751
- for
- force 1
undertake 676
promise 768
- re 9
- and out 314
-s and outs 182
in: - articulo 111
- extenso *whole* 50

disorder 59
impossible 471
infallibility 474
 assumption of –
  885
infamy *shame* 874
 dishonour 940
 vice 945
infancy 66, 127
infandum renovare
  dolorem 505,
  833
infant 129
 fool 501
 – *prodigy* 872
Infanta 745
infanticide 361, 991
infantine 129
 foolish 499
infantry 726
infarction 261
infatuation
 misjudgment 481
 credulity 486
 folly 499
 insanity 503
 obstinacy 606
 passion 825
 love 897
infeasible 471
infect *mix with* 41
 contaminate 659
 excite 824
infectâ, re –
 shortcoming 304
 non-completion
  730
 failure 732
infection
 transference 270
 disease 655
infectious 270, 657
infecund 169
infelicity
 inexpertness 699
 misery 828
infelicitous 24
infer 472
inference 476, 480
 by – 467
inferential
 demonstrative 478
 latent 526
inferiority
 in degree **34**
 in size 195
 imperfection 651
 personal – 34
infernal *bad* 649
 malevolent 907
 wicked 945

satanic 978
 – *machine* 727
 – *regions* 982
infertility 169
infest 830
infestivity 837, 843
infibulation 43
infidel 487, 989
infidelity
 dishonour 940
 irreligion 989
infiltrate *mix* 41
 intervene 228
 interpenetrate 294
 moisten 337, 339
 teach 537
infiltration
 passage 302
Infinite, the – 976
infinite 105
 – *goodness* 976
infinitely *great* 31
infinitesimal
 small 32
 little 193
 – *calculus* 85
infinity 105
infirm *weak* 160
 disease 655
 vicious 945
 – *of purpose* 605
infirmary 662
infirmity
 [*see* infirm]
infix 537
inflame
 render violent 173
 burn 384
 excite 824
 anger 900
inflamed 382
inflammable 384,
  388
inflammation
 heating 384
 disease 655
inflate *increase* 35
 expand 194
 blow 349
inflated
 overestimation
  482
 style 573, 577
 ridiculous 853
 vain 880
inflation
 [*see* inflate]
 rarefaction 322
 currency 800
inflect 245
inflexible *hard* 323

resolved 604
 obstinate 606
 stern 739
 inexorable 914a
inflexion
 change 140
 curvature 245
 grammar 567
inflict *act upon* 680
 severity 739
 – *evil* 649
 – *pain*
 bodily pain 378
 mental pain 830
 – *punishment* 972
infliction
 adversity 735
 mental pain 828,
  830
 punishment 972
influence 153
 change 140
 physical – **175**
 inducement 615
 instrumentality
  631
 authority 737
 absence of – **175a**
 sphere of – 780
 make one's – *felt*
  631
influx 294
infold 232
inform 527
 – *against*
 accuse 938
 go to law 969
informal 83, 964
informality 773
informant 527
information
 knowledge 490
 communication
  527
 learning 539
 lawsuit 969
 pick up – 539
informer 532
informity 241
infra dignitatem
  874, 940
infraction
 trespass 303
 disobedience 742
 non-observance
  773
 exemption 927
 – *of usage &c.*
 unconformity 83
 desuetude 614
infrangible

combined 46
 dense 321
infra-red rays 420
infrequency 137
infrigidation 385
infringe
 transgress 303
 disobey 742
 not observe 773
 undueness 925
 dereliction 927
 – *a law &c.* 83
infundibular 252,
  269
infuriate
 violent 173
 excite 824
 anger 900
infuscate 431
infuse *mix* 41
 insert 300
 teach 537
 – *courage* 861
 – *life into* 824
 – *new blood* 658
infusible 321
infusion [*see* infuse]
 liquefaction 335
infusoria 193
ingannation 545
ingathering 72
ingemination 90
ingenerate 5
ingenious 515, 698
ingenite 5
ingenium, per-
  fervidum – 682
ingénu *artless* 703
ingénue *actress* 599
ingenuity 698
ingenuous 703
ingesta 298
ingestion 296
ingle 388
inglorious 874, 940
ingluvies 191
ingot 800
ingraft *add* 37
 join 43
 insert 300
 teach 537
ingrafted
 extrinsic 6
 habit 613
ingrain
 insinuate 228
 colour 428
ingrained
 intrinsic 5
 combined 48
 habit 613

character 820
ingrate 917
ingratiate 897
ingratiating 894
ingratitude 917
ingredient 51, 56
ingress 294
  forcible – 300
ingurgitate 296
ingustible 391
inhabile 699
inhabit 186
inhabitant 188
inhale *receive* 296
  breathe 349
  smell 398
inharmonious
  discord 713
  – colour 428
  – sound 414
inhere 1
inherent 5, 820
inherit 775, 777
inheritance 780
  – of the saints 981
inherited
  intrinsic 5
inheritor 779
inhesion 5
inhibit *hinder* 706
  restrain 751
  prohibit 761
inhospitable 893
inhuman 907
inhume 363
inimaginable
  impossible 471
  improbable 473
  wonderful 870
inimical 708, 889
inimitable
  non-imitation 20
  supreme 33
  very good 648
  perfect 650
iniquity 923, 945
  worker of – 949
inirritability 826
initial 66
  – letter 558
initiate *begin* 66
  admit 296
  teach 537
initiated *skilful* 698
initiative 66
inject 300, 337
injection 662
injudicial 964
injudicious 499,
  863
injunction

acquirement 630
  advice 695
  command 741
  prohibition 761
injure *evil* 619
  damage 659
  spite 907
injuria formæ,
  spretæ – 846,
  930
injury *evil* 619
  badness 649
  damage 659
injustice 923
ink 431
  pen and – 590
  before the – is dry
  132
  – slinging 720
inkle 45
inkling
  knowledge 490
  supposition 514
  information 527
inkstand 590
inland 221
inlay 440, 847
inlet *beginning* 66
  interval 198
  opening 260
  ingress 294
  - *of the sea* 343
inly 221
inmate 188
inmost 221
  to the – core 822
  – soul 820
  – thoughts 451
inn 189
  – s of Court 968
innate 5, 601
innavigable 471
inner 221
  – coating 224
  – man *intellect* 450
  affections 820
innermost recesses
  221
innings *land* 342
  acquisition 775
  receipt 810
innkeeper 601
innocence 946
innocent *fool* 501
  good 648
  healthy 656
  artless 703
  guiltless 946
innocuous *good* 648
  healthy 656
  innocent 946

innominate 565
innovation
  variation 20a
  new 123
  change 140
innoxious
  salubrious 656
  innocent 946
innuendo *hint* 527
  censure 932
innumerable 105
innutritious 657
inobservance 773
inoccupation 681
inoculate
  insert 300
  teach 537
  influence 615
inodorous 399
inoffensive 648, 946
inofficious 907
inoperative
  powerless 158
  unproductive 169
  useless 645
inopportune
  untimely 135
  inexpedient 647
inordinate 31, 641
inorganization 358
inornate 849
inosculate *join* 43
  intersect 219
  convoluted 248
inquest 461
inquietude
  changeable 149
  uneasy 828
  discontent 832
  apprehension 860
inquinate 659
inquire 461
  – into 595
inquirer 461
inquiring mind 455
inquiry 461
inquisition
  inquiry 461
  severity 739
  torture 907
  tribunal 966
inquisitive 455
inquisitorial
  prying 455
  inquiry 461
  severe 739
  jurisdiction 965
inroad *ingress* 294
  devastation 659
  invasion 716
inrolment 551

insalubrity 657
insanity 503
insatiable 865
inscribe 590, 873
inscription 551
inscroll 551
inscrutable 519
insculpture 557
insculptured 558
insecable 43, 87
insect *minute* 193
  animal 366
  – cry 412
insecure
  uncertain 475
  danger 665
insensate
  foolish 499
  insane 503
insensibility
  slow 275
  physical 376
  moral 823
  – of benefits 917
  – to the past 506
inseparable 43, 46
insert *locate* 184
  interpose 228
  enter 294
  put in 300
  record 551
  – itself 300
insertion 300
  adjunct 39
  ornament 847
inservient 645
inseverable 43, 87
inside 221
  – out 218
  turn – out 529
insidious
  deceitful 545
  cunning 702
  dishonourable 940
insight 465, 490
insignia 550
  – of authority 747
insignificant
  unmeaning 517
  unimportant 643
insincere 544, 855
insinuate
  intervene 228
  ingress 294
  insert 300
  latency 526
  hint 527
  ingratiate 897
  blame 932
insipid
  style 575

dull 840
insipidity
  tasteless **391**
  indifferent 866
insist *argue* 476
  command 741
  – upon *affirm* 535
  dwell on 573
  be determined 604
  contend 720
  compel 744
  conditions **770**
  due 924
insnare 545
insobriety 959
insolation 382, 384
insolence 878, 885
insoluble *dense* 321
  unintelligible 519
insolvable 519
insolvent
  poverty 804
  debt 806
  non-payment 808
insomnia 682
insouciance
  thoughtlessness
    458
  supineness 823
  indifference 866
inspan 293
inspect 441, 457
inspector 444
  inquisitor 461
  judge 480
  director 694
inspiration
  wisdom 498
  imagination 515
  poetry 577
  impulse 612
  motive 615
  feeling 821
  Deity 976
  revelation 985
  religious - 987
inspire *improve* 658
  prompt 615
  animate 824
  cheer 836
  – *courage* 861
  – *hope* 858
  – *respect* 928
inspirit *incite* 615
  animate 824
  encourage 861
inspiriting
  hopeful 858
inspissate 321, 352
instability 149
install *locate* 184

commission 755
  celebrate 883
instalment
  portion 51
  payment 807, 809
instance
  example 82
  motive 615
  solicitation 765
instant *moment* 113
  present 118
  destiny 152
  required 630
  importance 642
  active 682
  lose not an – 684
  on the – 132
instantaneity **113**
instanter 113, 132
instar omnium 17,
  82
instate 883
instauration 660
instead 147
instep 245
instigate 615
instil *extrinsic* 6
  mix 41
  insert 300
  teach 537
instinct
  intellect 450
  intuition 477
  impulse 601
  – with *motive* 615
  possession 777
  brute – *450a*
instinctive
  inborn 5
institute *begin* 66
  cause 153
  produce 161
  academy 542
  society 712
  – an *inquiry* 461
institution
  academy 542
  society 712
  political - 963
  church 995
institutor 540
instruct *teach* 537
  advise 695
  precept 697
  order 741
instructed 490
instructor 540
instrument
  implement **633**
  security 771
  musical – 417

optical – 445
  recording – 553
instrumental 631
  – *music* 415
instrumentalist 416
instrumentality **631**
insuavity 895
insubordinate 742
insubstantial 4
  – *pageant* 882
insufferable
  painful 830
  dislike 867
insufficiency **640**
insufflation 349
insular *unrelated* 10
  detached 44
  single 87
  local 181
  island 346
  prejudice 481
insulate 44
insulse 499, 843
insult *rudeness* 895
  offence 900
  disrespect 929
insulting 898
insuperable 471
  – *obstacle* 706
insupportable 830
insuppressible 173
insurance 768, 771
insure
  make sure 474
  obtain security
    771
insurgent 742
insurmountable
  471
insurrection 719,
  742
insusceptible 823
  – of *change* 150
inswept 195
intact
  permanent 141
  perfect 650
  preserved 670
intaglio *mould* 22
  concave 252
  sculpture 557
  engraving 558
intangible *little* 193
  numb 381
integer 50, 84
integer vitæ scele-
  risque purus 939
integral 50
  – *calculus* 85
  – *part* 56
integrate 50

integrity *whole* 50
  probity 939
  virtue 944
integument 223
intellect **450**
  absence of – **450a**
  exercise of the –
    451
intellectual 450
intelligence
  mind 450
  capacity **498**
  news 532
intelligencer 527
intelligentsia 492
intelligibility **518**
intemperance **954**
  drunkenness 959
intempestivity **135**
intend 620
intendant 694
intended *will* 600
  predetermined
    611
intense *great* 31
  energetic 171
  – *colour* 428
  – *thought* 457
intensification 35
intensify
  increase 35
  stimulate 171
intensity *degree* 26
  greatness 31
  energy 171
intensive culture
  371
intent *attention* 457
  will 600
  design 620
  active 682
  – upon *desire* 8C5
  resolved 604
intention **620**
  bad – 607
  good – 906
intently, look – 441
intents and pur-
  poses, to all –
  27, 52
inter 363
interact 12
inter: – *alia* 82
  – *nos* 528
interaction 170
interbreeding 41
intercalate 228
intercalation 300
intercede
  mediate 724
  deprecate 766

itinerary 266, 527
itur ad astra, sic –
  360
ivory 430
Ixion 312

J

jab 276
jabber
  unmeaning 517
  stammer 583
  chatter 584
jacent 213
jacet, hic – 363
jacinth 847
jack
  rotation 312
  ensign 550
  instrument 633
  money 800
Jack – Cade 742
  – Ketch 975
  – o' lantern 423
  – in office
  director 694
  bully 887
  – at a pinch 711
  – Pudding
  actor 599
  humorist 844
  boaster 884
  before one can say
  ' – Robinson'
  132
  – tar 269
  – of all trades 700
jack-a-dandy 844,
  854
jackal
  auxiliary 711
  servility 886
jackanapes 854,
  887
Jackass 271
jack-boot 225
jackdaw in pea-
  cock's feathers
  701
jacket 225
  cork – 666
Jacobin 710
Jacquerie 716, 719

jacta est alea 601
jactitation
  tossing 315
  boasting 884
jaculation 284
jade *horse* 271
  fatigue 688
  low woman 876
  scamp 949
  drab 962
jag 257
jagged 244
jail 752
  – bird
  prisoner 754
  bad man 949
jailer 753, 975
jakes 653
jalousie de métier
  921
jam *squeeze* 43
  crowd 72
  food 298
  pulp 354
  sweet 396
  scrape 732
  – in *interpose* 228
jamb 215
jamboree 840
jammed in 751
jangle
  harsh sound 410
  quarrel 713
janissary 726
janitor 263
janty *gay* 836
  pretty 845
  stylish 852
  showy 882
  insolent 885
January 138
januis clausis 528
Janus *deceiver* 607
  tergiversation 607
  close the temple
  of – 723
Janus-faced 544
japan *coat* 223
  resin 356a
  ornament 847
jar *clash* 24
  vessel 191
  agitation 315
  stridor 410
  discord 713
  – upon the feel-
  ings 830
jardinière 191
jargon
  absurdity 497
  no meaning 517

  unintelligible 519
  neology 563
jarvey 694
jasper 847
jaundiced
  yellow 436
  prejudiced 481
  dejected 837
  jealous 920
  view with – eyes
  disapprove 932
jaunt 266
jaunting car 272
jaunty [*see* janty]
javelin 727
jaw *chatter* 584
  scold 932
jaw-fallen 837
jaws *mouth* 231
  eating 298
  – of death 360
jay 584
jaywalker 701
jazz 415, 840
  – band 417
jealous of honour
  939
jealousy 920
  suspicion 485
jecur, difficili bile –
  900
jeer 929
Jehovah 976
Jehu 268, 694
jejune *insipid* 391
  style 575
  scanty 640
  dull 843
jell 352
jelly 298, 352
  beat to a – 972
jemidar 745
jemmy *lever* 633
  dandy 854
je ne sais quoi
  exceptional 83
  what d'ye call 'em
  563
  beauty 845
jennet 271
jeopardy 665
jerboa 309
jeremiad
  lament 839
  invective 932
Jericho, send to –
  297
jerk *start* 146
  throw 284
  pull 285
  agitate 315

jerkin 225
jerks, by – 70
Jerry Sneak 862,
  941
jersey 225
Jerusalem
  the new – 981
Jessamy, Jemmy –
  854
jesse 1000
jest *trifle* 643
  wit 842
jest-book 842
jester 844
jesting-stock 857
Jesuit *deceiver* 548
  priest 996
jesuitical 477, 544
Jesus 976
jet *stream* 348
  – black 431
jetsam 73, 782
jettison 782
jetty *protection* 250
  harbour 666
jeu
  le – n'en vaut pas
  la chandelle
  waste 638
  unimportant 643
  dear 814
  – d'esprit 842
  – de mots 842
  – de théâtre 599
jeune
  – premier 599
  – veuve 599
Jew's harp 417
jewel *gem* 648
  ornament 847
  favourite 899
jewellery, false –
  545
Jezebel *wicked* 913
  wretch 949
  courtesan 962
jib *front* 234
  regression 283
  cut of one's –
  form 240
  appearance 448
jibe 140
jiffy 113
jig 840
jig-saw puzzle 840
jilt *disappoint* 509
  deceive 545
  deceiver 548
  cast off 756
  dishonour 940
jilted 898

jimp 845
jingal 727
jingle 408
jingo 887
jingoism 884
jinks, high – 840
jinriksha 272
jinx 649, 735
Joan of Arc 861
job *business* 625
  action 680
  unfair 940
  tough – 704
Job:
  patience of – 826,
    830
  poor as – 804
  –'s comforter
  dejection 837
  hopeless 859
jobation 932
jobber
  deceiver 548
  tactician 700
  merchant 797
  trickster 943
jobbernowl 501
jobbery 702, 940
jobbing *barter* 794
jockey *rider* 268
  deceive 545
  deceiver 548
  servant 746
jocose 836, 842
jocoseness *fun* 840
jocular 836, 842
jocund 836, 840
jocundity 829
Joe Miller 842, 844
jog *push* 276
  shake 315
  – the memory 505
  – on *continue* 143
  trudge 266
  slow 275
  advance 282
  mediocrity 736
joggle 315
jog-trot
  trudge 266
  slow 275
  habit 613
John Doe and
    Richard Roe 4
Johnny 894
John's 653
Johnsonian 577
joie, feu de – 883
join *connect* 43
  assemble 72
  contiguous 199

arrive 292
party 712
sociality 892
marry 903
– battle 722
– in the chorus 488
– forces, hands,
    709
– in 778
– issue *discuss* 476
  deny 536
  quarrel 713
  contend 720
  lawsuit 969
– the majority 360
– up
  enlist 723
– with 709
joint *junction* 43
  part 51
  accompanying 88
  concurrent 178
  meat 298
– concern 721
joint-stock 709, 778
joint-tenancy 778
jointure 780
joist 215
joke *absurdity* 497
  trifle 643
  wit 842
  ridicule 856
  in – 842
  mere – 643
  no – *existing* 1
  important 642
  practical –
    deception 545
    ridicule 856
    disrespect 929
  take a – 498
joker 844
jokesmith 844
joking apart 535,
    604
jole 236
jollification
  amusement 840
  intemperance 954
jollity 840, 892
jolly *plump* 192
  marine 269
  gay 836
  ridicule 856
– boat 273
– fellow 892
jolt 276, 315
jolthead 501
Jonah 649
Jones
  Davy –' locker 360

Paul – 792
jorum 191
Joseph 960
  –'s coat 440
joss 991
– house 1000
jostle *rush* 276
  jog 315
  clash 713
jot 32, 643
jotting 550, 551
jounce 315
journal *annals* 114
  newspaper 531
  record 551
  magazine 593
  narrative 594
  accounts 811
journalist
  messenger 534
  recorder 553
  author 593
journey 266
journeyman
  artisan 690
  servant 746
joust 720
Jove 979
  by – 870
  sub –
    out of doors 220
    air 338
jovial *gay* 836
  amusement 840
  social 892
jowl 236
joy 827
  give one – 896
joyful 836
joyless *painful* 830
  sad 837
joy stick 693
J.P. 967
Juan, Don – 962
jube 1000
jubeo, sic volo sic –
    741
jubilant *gay* 836
  rejoicing 838
  boastful 884
jubilee 138, 883
jubilitate 884
Judæus Apella,
    credat –
  disbelief 485
  absurdity 497
Judaism 984
Judas *deceiver* 548
  knave 941
– kiss
  hypocrisy 544

base 940
judge *decide* 480
  master 745
  taste 850
  magistrate **967**
Judge *deity* 976
Judgment
  Day of – 67
judgment
  intellect 450
  discrimination
    465
  decision **480**
  wisdom 498
  sentence 972
judgment-seat 966
judicata, res –
  certain 574
  judgment 480
judication 480
judicatory 965, 966
judicature 965
Judicature, High
    Court of – 966
judice: coram –
  jurisdiction 965
  lawsuit 969
  me – 481
  sub – *inquiry* 461
    lawsuit 969
judicial 965
– Astrology 511
– murder 361
– separation 905
judicious 498
jug 191, 752
juggernaut
  kill 361
  god 979
  idolatry 991
juggle *deceive* 545
  cunning 702
juggler 548, 599
jugulate 361
juice 333
juiceless 340
juicy 339
jujitsu 718
jujube 396
julep 396
jumble *mixture* 41
  confusion 59
  derange 61
  indiscriminate
    465a
jument 271
jump
  sudden change
    146
  leap 309
  neglect 460

at one – 113
– about 315
– at *willing* 602
  pursue 622
  hasten 684
  consent 762
  seize 789
  desire 865
– to a conclusion
  misjudge 481
  credulous 486
– over 460
– up 307, 309
jumper 225
junction 43
juncture
  circumstance 8
  junction 43
  period 134
jungle *disorder* 59
  vegetation 367
junior 127, 541
– counsel 968
junk 273
junket *dish* 298
  merry-making
  840
Juno 920, 979
junta 696
junto 712
jupe 225
Jupiter 979
jurare in verba ma-
  gistri 481, 486
jurat 967
jure: de – *due* 924
  legal 963
– divino *due* 924
  God 976
juridical 965
jurisconsult 968
jurisdiction 965
  authority 737
Jurisprudence 963
jurist 480, 968
jury 967
  empanel a – 969
– box 966
– mast
  substitute 147
  refuge 666
jus: summum –
  922
– civile
– gentium 963
– nocendi 737
– et norma
  loquendi 567
jussive 741
just *accurate* 494
  right 922

equitable 939
pious 987
– as *similar* 17
  same time 120
– do 639
– now 118
– out 123
– reasoning 476
– so 488
– then 113
– the thing
  agreement 23
  exact 494
– in time 134
juste milieu
  middle 68
  moderation 174
  mid-course 628
justice
  right 922
  honour 939
  magistrate 967
  administration of
  – 965
  bring to – 969
  court of – 966
  do – to *eat* 298
  duty 926
  praise 931
  vindicate 937
  not do – to 483
  retributive – 922,
  972
– seat 966
justifiable 922, 937
justification
  vindication 937
  religious 987
justle *push* 276
  contend 720
jut out 250
jute 205
jutty 250
juvenile 127
– lead 599
juxtaposition 199
j'y suis j'y reste
  141

K

kadi 967
kail 840
kaiser 745
kaleidoscope 149,
  445
καλόν, τὸ – 845
kangaroo 309
κατ᾿ ἐξοχήν
  greatness 31

  superiority 33
  importance 642
Katerfelto 994
kavass 965
K.C. 968
keck 297
kedge *navigate* 267
  anchor 666
keek 527
keel 211
– upwards 21
keelhaul 972
keen *energetic* 171
  sharp 253
  sensible 375
  cold 383
  intelligent 498
  poignant 821
  lament 839
  witty 842
  eager 865
– blast 349
keener 839
keen-eyed 441
keep *do often* 136
  persist 141
  continue 143
  food 298
  store 636
  provision 637
  refuge 666
  preserve 670
  citadel 717
  custody 751
  prison 752
  observe 772
  retain 781
  celebrate 883
– alive 359, 670
– aloof 196, 623
– accounts 811
– an account with
  805
– apart 44
– at it 143
– away 187
– back *late* 133
  conceal 528
  dissuade 616
  not use 678
  restrain 751
  retain 781
– the ball rolling
  143
– one's bed 655
– body and soul
  together *life* 359
  health 654
– within bounds
  304
– close 781

– company 88
– one in counte-
  nance
  conformity 82
  induce 615
  aid 707
  encourage 861
– one's counte-
  nance
  unexcitable 826
  sad 837
– one's course 282
– an eye upon 459
– the field 722
– firm 150
– on foot
  continuance 143
  support 215
  preparation 673
– from *conceal* 528
  refrain 623
  not do 681
  restrain 751
– going
  continue 143
  move 264
– one's ground 141
– one's hand in 613
– one's head above
  water 731, 817
– hold 150
– holy 987
– house 184
– in ignorance 528
– in *restrain* 751
  prohibit 761
– on one's legs 654
– a good look out
  for 507
– in mind 505
– moving 682
– off *avoid* 623
  hinder 706
  defend 717
  resist 719
  prohibition 761
– on *do often* 136
  continue 143
  persevere 604a
– to oneself 528
– in order 693
– out
  - *of the way* 187
  - *of harm's way*
  864
– pace with 27,
  120
– the peace 714
– posted 527
– the pot boiling
  143

– one's promise 772
– quiet 265
– a secret 528
– a shop 625
– in sight 459
– silence 585
– straight 944
– in suspense
  uncertainty 475
  irresolution 605
– in the thoughts 505
– time
  punctual 132
  music 416
– to 604*a*
– together 709
– under
  authority 737
  subjection 749
  restraint 751
– up [*see below*]
– in view
  attend to 457
  remember 505
  expect 507
– waiting 133
– watch 459
– one's word 939
keep up
  continue 143
  preserve 670
  stimulate 824
– appearances 852
– the ball 682, 840
– a correspond-ence 592
– the memory of 505
– one's spirits 836
– with 274
keeper 370, **753**
keeping
  congruity 23
  in – 82
  safe – *safety* 664
  preservation 670
keepsake 505
keg 191
kelpie 979
kelson 211
kempt 652
ken 441, 490
  beyond mortal – 360
kennel
  assemblage 72
  hovel 189
  ditch 259
  conduit 350

Kentish fire 931
képi 225
kérb-stone 233
kerchief 225
  wave a – 550
kern *quern* 330
  low fellow 876
  varlet 949
kernel *heart* 5
  cause 153
  central 222
  important 642
kerosene 356
ketch
  ship 273
Ketch, Jack – 975
kettle *vessel* 191
  caldron 386
  – drum *music* 417
  tea-party 892
  – of fish
  disorder 59
  difficulty 704
key *cause* 153
  opener 260
  music 413
  colour 428
  interpretation 522
  indication 550
  instrument 631, 633
  emblem of au-thority 747
  deliver the –s of the city 725
key-hole 260
key-note *model* 22
  rule 80
  music 413
key-stone
  support 215
  motive 615
  importance 642
  completion 729
khaki 225, 433
khan *inn* 189
  governor 745
khedive 745
kibitka 272
kibitzer 682
kick *impulse* 276
  recoil 277
  assault 716
  thrill 821
  spurn 930
  punish 972
  – against
  oppose 708
  resist 719
  – against the pricks

useless 645
rash 863
unequal 28
superior 33
– up a dust
  active 682
  discord 713
  insolent 885
– a row 900
– one's heels
  kept waiting 133
  nothing to do 681
– off 62
– up a row
  violent 173
  discord 713
– over the traces 742
kicking, alive and – 359
kickshaw *food* 298
  trifle 643
kid *child* 129
  progeny 167
  leather 223
  not to be handled with – gloves
  dirty 653
  difficult 704
kidnap
  deceive 545
  take 789
  steal 791
kidney *class* 75
kilderkin 191
Kilkenny cats 713
kill 361
  – or cure 662
  – the fatted calf 883
  – the goose with golden eggs 699
  – with kindness 902
  – the slain 641
  – time 106
  inactivity 683
  amusement 840
  – two birds with one stone 682
killing **361**
  delightful 829
kill-joy 706
kiln 386
kilowatt 466
kilt 225
kimbo 244
kimono 225
kin 75
kind *class* 75
  benevolent 906

– regards 894
kinder-garten 542
kindle *cause* 153
  produce 161
  quicken 171
  inflame 173
  set fire to 384
  excite 824
  incense 900
kindling wood 388
kindred 9, 11
kine 366
kinematics 264
kinetic energy 157
king 745
  every inch a –
  authority 737
  rank 875
  –maker 694
King –'s Bench 752, 966
  –'s birthday 268
  –'s counsel 968
  – Death 360
  –'s English 560
  –'s evidence 529
  –'s highway 627
  –'s ransom 648
  – of Kings 976
kingcraft 693
kingdom
  region 181
  property 780
  – of heaven 981
kingly 737
king-post 215
kink 248, 378, 608
kiosk 189, 1000
kip 961
kirk 1000
kirtle 225
kismet 601
kiss *touch* 199
  courtesy 894
  endearment 902
  – the book 535
  – the hem of one's garment 928
  – in the ring 840
  – the rod 725
kit *class* 75
  equipment 191
  fiddle 417
  –bag 191
kitcat 556
kitchen 191, 691
  – maid 746
  – range 386
kitchener 386
kitchenette 691
kite *fly* 273

lane 189, 260, 627
langrel 727
lang-syne 122
language **560**
  command of – 582
  strong –
   vigour 574
   malediction 908
languid *weak* 160
  inert 172
  slow 275
  - *style* 575
  inactive 683
  torpid 823
languish
  decrease 36
  ill 655
  inactive 683
  repine 828
 – for 865
languishing
  weak 160
  affected 855
languishment
  lament 839
languor
  [*see* languid]
lank 200
lanky 203, 206
lantern
  window 260
  lamp 423
  magic – 448
  – of Diogenes 461
  – jaws 203
lanterne, à la – 972
lanuginous 256
lanyard 45
Laodicean 822
lap *abode* 189
  support 215
  interior 221
  wrap 225
  encompass 227, 229
  drink 298
  – of luxury
   pleasure 377
  inactivity 683
  voluptuousness 954
lap-dog *animal* 366
  servile 886
lapel 39
lapidary 559
lapidate *kill* 361
  attack 716
  punish 972
lapidescence 323
lapis lazuli
  blue 438

jewel 847
lappet 39, 214
lapse *course* 109
  past 122
  conversion 144
  fall 306
  degeneracy 659
  relapse 661
  loss 776
  vice 945
  guilt 947
  – of memory 506
  – of time 109
lapsus calami 495
lapsus linguæ
  mistake 495
  solecism 568
  stammering 583
Laputa, college of – 538
larboard 239
larceny 791
lard 356
lardaceous 355
larder 636
  contents of the – 298
lares et penates
  home 189
  idols 991
large
  quantity 31
  size 192
  at – *diffuse* 573
  free 748
  become – 194
  – number 102
  – type 642
large-hearted
  liberal 816
  benevolent 906
  disinterested 942
larger 194
largest 784
largest portion 192
larghetto 275, 415
largiloquent 573
largo 275, 415
lariat 45, 247
lark *ascent* 305
  pleasure 827
  spree 840
  with the – 125
larmes:
  fondre en – 839
  – aux yeux 839
larmoyante,
  comédie – 599
larrikin 887, 913
larrup 972
larum 404, 669

larva 129
larynx 351
lascar 269
lasciate ogni spe-
  ranza 859
lascivious 961
lash *tie together* 43
  violence 173
  incite 615
  censure 932
  punish 972
  scourge 975
  under the – *com-
   pelled* 744
  subject 749
  – into fury 909
  – with the tongue 931
  – the waves 645
lass *girl* 129
lassitude 680, 841
lasso 45, 247
last *model* 22
  - *in order* 67
  endure 106
  durable 110
  - in time 122
  continue 141
  at – 133
  breathe one's – 360
  game to the – 604*a*
  never hear the – of 104
  – but one &c. 67
  die in the – ditch 604*a*
  – for ever 112
  at the – extremity 665
  – finish 729
  – gasp 360
  go to one's – home 360
  on – legs *weak* 160
  dying 360
  spoiled 659
  adversity 735
  – resort 666
  – rites 998
  – shift 601
  – sleep 360
  – stage 67
  – straw 153
  – stroke 729
  – touch 729
  – word
   affirmation 535
   obstinacy 606
  – year &c. 122

latch 43, 45
latchet 45
latch-key 631
late *past* 122
  new 123
  tardy 133
  dead 360
  too – 135
lately 122, 123
latency 526
lateness **133**
latent 172, 526
  – organism 153
later 117
laterality **236**
lateritious 434
latest 118
latet anguis in
  herbâ 66
lath 205
  thin as a – 203
lathe
  region 181
  machine 633
lather 332, 353
Latin
  au bout de son – 704
  perdre son – 704
  thieves' – 563
latitancy 528
latitat 969
latitude *extent* 180
  region 181
  breadth 202
  measurement 466
  freedom 748
  – and longitude
   situation 183
latitudinarian 984, 989
latration 412
latria 990
latrines 653
latrociny 791
latter *sequent* 63
  past 122
Latter-day Saint 984
latterly 123
lattice *crossing* 219
  opening 260
laud 931, 990
laudable 944
laudanum 174
laudari a laudato
  viro 931
laudator 935
  – temporis acti
   past 122
   habit 613

– slip
  miss an oppor-
    tunity 135
  neglect 460
  not complete 730
  lose 776
  relinquish 782
– the matter stand
    over 133
– things take their
    course 143
– well alone
  content 831
  caution 864
lethal 361
– chamber 975
lethalis arundo,
    hæret lateri –
    900
lethargy 683, 823
Lethe 982
  waters of – 506
lethiferous 361
letter *mark* 550
  character **561**
  epistle 592
  to the – 494
  – card 524
  – of credit 805
  – of the law 494
  – writer 592
letter-bag 534
letter-carrier 534
lettered 490
letterpress 591
letters
  knowledge 490
  language 560
  description 594
  in large – 642
  man of – 492
  – of marque 791
lettres de cachet
    751
leucophlegmatic
    823
leucorrhea 299
Levant *east* 236
levant *abscond* 623
levanter *wind* 349
  defaulter 808
levée *assemblage* 72
  sociality 892
  – en masse 719
level *uniform* 16
  equal 27
  destroy 162
  horizontal 213
  instrument 213,
    217
  flat 251

smooth 255
lower 308
– at *direct* 278
  intend 620
  attack 716
– best 686
– headed 826
– off 27
– with the ground
    207
lever *cause* 153
  instrument 633
  – de rideau 599
leverage 175
leviathan 192
levigate 255, 330
levitate 320
Levite 996
levity *lightness* **320**
  irresolution 605
  trifle 643
  jocularity 836
  rashness 863
levy *muster* 72
  military 726
  distrain 789
  demand 812
lewd 961
Lewis gun 727
lex – mercatoria
    963
– scripta 697
– scripta et non-
    scripta 963
– talionis
  retaliation 718
  right 922
lexicography 562
lexicology 562
lexicon 86, 562
ley 344
liability **177**
  debt 806
  duty 926
liaison 961
liar 548
libation
  potation 298
  drunkenness 959
  worship 990
libel 934, 938
libelant 989
libeller 936
liberal *ample* 639
  – party 712
  generous 816
  disinterested 942
  over – 818
  – education
    knowledge 490
    teaching 537

liberalism
  freedom 748
liberality
  giving 784
  generosity **816**
liberate 672
liberation 750
liberavi animam
    meam 703
libertinage 961
libertine **962**
libertinism 961
liberty *freedom* 748
  permission 760
  right 924
  exemption 927a
  gain one's – 750
  set at – *free* 750
  exempt 927a
  take a –
  arrogate 739
  make free 748
  insolence 885
  discourtesy 895
libidinous 961
libitum, ad –
  at will 600
  enough 639
  freely 748
librarian 593, 694
library *room* 191,
    593
  books 593
  storehouse 636
librate 314
libretto 593, 599
licence *laxity* 738
  permission 760
  right 924
  exemption 927a
  – to plunder 791
licentiate 492
licentious *lax* 738
  dissolute 954
  debauched 961
lichgate 363
lichen 367
licit 760, 924
lick *lap* 298
  conquer 731
  punish 972
– the dust 933
– into shape 240
lickerish
  savoury 394
  desirous 865
  fastidious 868
  licentious 961
lickpenny 819
lickspittle 886
lictor 965

lid 223
lie *situation* 183
  presence 186
  recline 213
  falsehood 544
  untruth 546
  give the – to 536
  white – 617
  – abed 683
  – in ambush 528
  – by 681
  – at one's door
    926
  – down *flat* 213
  rest 687
  – fallow 674
  – hid 528
  – in *be* 1
  give birth 161
  – low 528
  – under a neces-
    sity 601
  – in a nutshell 32
  – on 215
  – over *defer* 133
  destiny 152
  – in one's power
    157
  – at the root of
    153
  – still 265
  – to
  quiescence 265
  inaction 681
  – under 177
  – in wait for
  expect 507
  inaction 681
lief *pleasant* 829
  as – *willing* 602
  choice 609
liege 745
liegeman 746
lien 771, 805
lienteria 653
lieu 182
  in – of 147
lieutenant 745, 759
  lord – 965
life *essence* 5
  events 151
  vitality **359**
  biography 594
  activity 682
  conduct 692
  cheerful 836
  animal – 364
  battle of – 682
  come to – 660
  infuse into
  excite 824

put – into 359
recall to – 660
see – 840
support – 359
take away – 361
tenant for – 779
– to come 152
– after death 981
– or death
  need 630
  important 642
  contention 720
– and spirit 682
Life, the 976
life-blood 5, 359
life-boat 273, 666
life-giving 168
lifeguards 726
lifeless 172, 360
lifelike 17
lifelong 110
life-preserver 666,
  727
life-size 192
lifetime 108
life-weary 841
lift raise 307
  aid 707
  steal 791
  – cattle 791
  – up the eyes 441
  – a finger 680
  – hand against
    716
  – one's head 734
  – up the heart 990
  – the mask 529
  – the voice
  shout 411
  speak 582
lift-smoke 840
ligament 45
ligation 43
ligature 45
light state 7
  small 32
  window 260
  velocity 274
  arrive 292
  descend 306
  levity 320
  kindle 384
  watch 388
  luminosity 420
  luminary 423
  - in colour 429
  white 430
  aspect 448
  knowledge 490
  interpretation 522
  unimportant 643

easy 705
gay 836
loose 961
blue – signal 550
bring to –
  discover 480a
  manifest 525
  disclose 529
children of – 987
come to – 529
false – 443
foot –s 599
half – 422
make – of
  underrate 483
  easy 705
  inexcitable 826
  despise 930
in one's own – 699
obstruct the – 426
side – 490
see the – life 359
  publication 531
transmit – 425
throw – upon 522
a – breaks in upon
  one 529
– under a bushel
  hide 528
  not hide 878
  modesty 881
  – comedy 599
  – cruiser 726
  – fantastic toe 309
  – upon one's feet
    664
  – heart 836
  – of heel 274
  – horse 726
  – infantry 726
  – purse 804
  – and shade 420
  – of truth 543
  – up illumine 420
  excite 824
  cheer 836
  – upon chance 156
  arrive at 292
  discover 480a
  acquire 775
Light of the World
  976
lighten
  make light 320
  illume 420
  facilitate 705
lighter boat 273
lighterage 812
lighterman 269
light-fingered 791,
  792

light-footed 274,
  682
light-headed 503
lighthouse 550
lightless 421
light-minded 605
lightning
  velocity 274
  flash 420
  spark 423
  like greased – 113
lightsome
  luminous 420
  irresolute 605
  cheerful 836
ligneous 367
lignite 388
lignography 558
ligulate 205
like similar 17
  relish 394
  enjoy 377, 827
  wish 865
  love 897
  do what one –s
    748
  look – 448
  we shall not look
    upon his – again
    33
  – master like man
    19
  – a pin in paper 58
likely 472
  think – 507
likeness 21, 554
  bad – 555
likewise 37
liking 865, 897
  have a – for 827
  to one's – 829
lilac colour 437
Liliputian 193
Lillith 994
lilt 416, 836
lily white 430
  beauty 845
  paint the – 641
lily-livered 862
limæ labor
  improve 658
  toil 686
limature 330, 331
limb member 51
  instrument 633
  scamp 949
  – of the law 968
limber 272, 324
limbo prison 751,
  752
  pain 828

purgatory 982
lime entrap 545
– light 423, 531,
  599
Limehouse 908
limine, in – 66
limit complete 52
  end 67
  circumscribe 229
  boundary 233
  qualify 469
  restrain 751
  prohibit 761
limitarian 984
limitation [see
  limit]
  estate 780, 783
limited
  - in quantity 32
  - in size 393
  to a – extent
  imperfect 651
limitless 105
limitrophe 197
limn 556
limner 559
limousine 272
limp weak 160
  slow 275
  supple 324
  fail 732
limpid 425
lin 343, 348
lincture 662
line fastening 45
  continuous 69
  ancestors 166
  descendants 167
  length 200
  no breadth 203
  string 205
  lining 224
  outline 230
  straight 246
  of steamers 273
  direction 278
  music 413
  appearance 448
  measure 466
  mark 550
  writing 590
  verse 597
  vocation 625
  army and navy
    726
  boundary – 233
  draw the – 465
  drop a – to 526
  in a –
    continuous 69
    straight 246

– face 832, 837	**looby** *fool* 501	*dim sight* 443	*ruler* 745
– for 865	*bungler* 701	*come in sight* 446	*nobleman* 875
–headed *wise* 498	*clown* 876	*weave* 691	*God* 976
– life to *glory* 873	**look** *small degree* 32	– of the land 342	O – *worship* 990
approval 931	*see* 441	– up 31	– Chancellor 967
–lived 110	*appearance* 448	**loon** *fool* 501	– of the creation
– odds *chance* 156	*attend to* 457	*clown* 876	372
improbability 473	– about 459, 461	*rascal* 949	–'s day 687
difficulty 704	– after 459, 693	**loop** 245, 247, 629	–s Justices 966,
– pending 110	– ahead 510	– the loop 245	967
– primer 591	– alive 457, 684	**loop-hole**	the – knows 491
– pull and strong	– another way 442	*opening* 260	– lieutenant 965
pull 285	– back 122	*vista* 441	– of Lords 976
– range 196	– beyond 510	*plea* 617	– of the manor
– robe 968	– black *or* blue	*device* 626	779
– run *average* 29	*feeling* 821	*escape* 671	– it over 737, 885
whole 50	*discontent* 832	*fortification* 717	–'s prayer 990
destiny 152	*dejection* 837	**loose** *detach* 44	–'s supper 998
– sea 348	– down upon 930	*incoherent* 47	–'s table 1000
– and the short	– in the face	*pendent* 214	**lordling** 875
whole 50	*sincerity* 703	*desultory* 279	**lordly** 873, 878
concise 572	*courage* 861	*illogical* 477	**Lord Mayor** 745,
–sighted	*pride* 878	*vague* 519	965
dim-sighted 443	– foolish 874	– *style* 575	–'s show 883
wise 498	– for 461, 507	*lax* 738	**lordship**
foresight 518	– forwards 121,	*free* 748	*authority* 737
– since 122	510	*liberate* 750	*property* 780
– spun 573	– here 457	*debauched* 961	*title* 877
– standing	– into 457, 461	give a – to	*judge* 967
diuturnal 110	– before one leaps	- *imagination* 515	**lore** 490, 539
old 124	864	*laxity* 738	**Lorelei** 980
–suffering	– like 17, 448	*permit* 760	**lorette** 962
lenient 740	– on 186	*indulgence* 954	**lorgnette** 445
inexcitable 826	– out *view* 448	let – 750	**lorication**
pity 914	*attention* 457	on the – 961	*armour* 717
– time 110	*care* 459	screw – 713	**loricated**
–winded 573	*seek* 461	– character 961	*clothed* 223
longanimity	*expect* 507	at a – end 685	**lorn** 893
inexcitable 826	*intention* 620	– fish 949, 962	**lorry** 272
forgiving 918	*business* 625	– morals 945	**lose** *forget* 506
longevity 110, 128	*danger* 665	– rein 738	*unintelligible* 519
longhead 500	*warning* 668	– suggestion 514	*fail* 732
longing 865	*caution* 864	– thread 495	*loss* 776
– lingering look	– over *examine*	leave a – 460	no time to – 684
behind 833	461	take up a – 664	– one's balance
longinquity 196	– round *seek* 461	**loosen** 47, 750	732
longitude	– sharp 682	**loot** 791, 793	– breath 688
situation 183	– to 459, 926	**lop** 201	– caste 874, 940
length 200	– through 461	– and top 371	– the clew 475,
measurement 466	– up *prosper* 734	**lopped**	519
longitudinal 200	*high price* 814	*incomplete* 53	– colour 429
longo intervallo	*hope* 858	**loppet** 699	– one's cunning
discontinuity 70	*visit* 892	**lop-eared** 53	699
diuturnity 110	– up to *repute* 873	**lop-sided** 28	– the day 732
distance 196	*respect* 928	**loquacity** **584**	– flesh 195
interval 198	*approbation* 931	**loquendi**	– ground
longshore-man	– upon as 480, 484	cacoëthes – 584	*slow* 275
waterman 269	**looker-on** 444	jus et norma – 567	*regression* 283
plebeian 876	**looking-glass** 445	usus – 582	*shortcoming* 304
longways 217	**loom** *destiny* 152	**lorcha** 273	– one's head
loo 840	*dim* 422	**Lord, lord**	*bewildered* 475

mitigate 174
silence 403
– to sleep 265
lullaby
moderate 174
song 415
verses 597
inactivity 683
relief 834
lumbago 378
lumbar 235
lumbar *disorder* 59
slow 275
store 636
useless 645
hindrance 706
lumbering 647, 846
lumber-room 191
lumbriciform 249
luminary *star* 318
light **423**
sage 500
luminescence 420
luminous *light* 420
intelligible 518
– *paint* 423
lump *whole* 50
chief part 51
amass 72
mass 192
projection 250
weight 319
density 321
in the – 50
– of affectation
855
– sum 800
– together *join* 43
combine 48
assemble 72
lumpish [*see* lump]
inactive 683
ugly 846
Luna 318
lunacy 503
lunar 318
– *caustic* 384
lunatic 503, 504
luncheon 298
lune avec les dents,
prendre la –
158, 471
lunette 717
lunge 276, 716
lungs *wind* 349
loudness 404
shout 411
voice 580
luniform &c. 245
lupanar 961
lurch *incline* 217

sink 306
oscillation 314
failure 732
leave in the –
outstrip 303
deceive 545
relinquish 624
left in the –
defeated 732
lure *attraction* 288,
865
deceive 545
entice 615
lurid *dark* 421
dim 422
red 434
lurk *unseen* 447
latent 526
hidden 528
lurking-place 530
luscious 394, 829
lush *vegetation* 365
drunkenness 959
lushy 959
lusk 683
lusory 840
lust 865, 961
– *after* 921
lustily 404, 686
cry out – 839
lustless 158
lustration 652, 952
lustre
brightness 420
chandelier 423
glory 873
lustrum 108
lusty 159, 192
lusus naturæ 80
lute *cement* 45, 46
guitar 417
luteous 436
Lutheran 984
luxation 44
luxuriant 168, 639
luxuriate in 377,
827
luxurious
pleasant 377
delightful 829
intemperate 954
luxury
physical - 377
redundance 641
enjoyment 827
sensuality 954
lycanthropy 503
Lyceum 542
Lydford law 964
Lydian measure
415

lyddite 727
lying
decumbent 213
deceptive 544
faithless 986
Ly-king 986
lymph *fluid* 333
water 337
transparent 425
lymphatic 337
lynch 972
– *law* 964
lyncher 975
lynching 361
lynx-eyed 441, 498
lyre 417
lyric 415
– *poetry* 597
lyrist 597

M

Mab 979
macadamize 255,
635
Macaire, Robert –
792
macaroni 854
macaronic
absurdity 497
neology 563
verses 597
Macchiavel [*see*
Machiavelism]
mace
weapon 727
sceptre 747
mace-bearer 965
maceration
saturation 337
atonement 952
asceticism 955
rite 998
Macheath 792
Machiavelism
falsehood 544
cunning 702
dishonesty 940
machicolation 257,
717
machination
trick 545
plan 626
cunning 702
–s of the devil 619
machinator 626
machine 633
like a – 698
– gun 407, 727
be a mere – 749

machinist
theatrical - 599
workman 690
macilent 203
mackerel
mottled 440
procuress 962
– *sky* 349, 353
mackintosh 225
macrobiotic 110
macrocosm 318
macrography 441
macrology 577
mac Sycophant,
Sir Pertinax –
886, 935
mactation 991
macte virtute 931
macula 848
maculate
unclean 653
maculation 440, 848
mad *insane* 503
excited 824
drive one – 900
go – 825
– *after* 865
– with rage 900
madam 374
mad-brained 503
madcap
violent 173
lunatic 504
excitable 825
buffoon 844
rash 863
madder *colour* 434
made
– to one's hand
673
– *man* 734
– to order 673
madefaction 339
madman **504**
Madonna
good 948
angel 977
pious 987
madrigal *music* 415
verses 597
Mæcenas 492, 890
Maelstrom
whirl 312
water 348
pitfall 667
maestro 415
maffick 883
magazine
periodical 53
record 551
book 593

– of 902
– off 623, 671
– off with 791
– out *see* 441
  evidence 467
  demonstrate 478
  discover 480a
  know 490
  intelligible 518
  interpret 522
  due 924
– over 658, 783, 784
– peace 723, 724
– a piece of work 832
– things pleasant 702
– a present 784
– public 531
– a push 682
– ready 673
– a requisition 741, 765
– a speech 582
– a sucker of 853
– sure 150, 673
– terms 769
– time 110
– tracks 293
– towards 278
– up [*see below*]
– use of 677
– way 282
– one's way 302, 734
– way for 147, 623
– a wry face 867
make up
  complete 52
  compose 54
  – accounts 811
  – for 30
  – matters 952
  – one's mind
    judgment 480
    belief 484
    resolve 604
  – a quarrel 723
  – a sum 809
  – to *approach* 286
    address 586
maker *artificer* 690
Maker, the – 976
makeshift 147, 617
make-weight
  inequality 28
  compensation 30
  completeness 52
making of, be the –
  utility 644

goodness 648
aid 707
mal du pays 833
mala fides 940
malachite 435
malacology 368
malade imaginaire 837
maladie du pays 833
maladministration 699
maladroit 699
malady 655
malaise 378, 828
malapert 885, 887
Malaprop, Mrs. – 565
malapropism 495
mal à propos 24, 135
malaria 657, 663
malconformation 243
malcontent 710, 832
male 159, 373
  – animal 373
malediction 908
malefaction 947
malefactor 949
malefic 649
maleficent 907
  – being 913
malevolence 907
malfeasance 647
malformed 241
malformation 243
malgré 179
  – soi 603
malice *hate* 898
  spite 907
  bear – *revenge* 919
  – aforethought 907
  – prepense 907
malign *bad* 649
  malevolent 907
  detract 934
malignant 649, 907
malignity
  violence 173
malinger 544, 655
malison 908
malkin 653
mall *walk* 189
  club 276
malleable 324
mallet 276
malnutrition 655
mal-odour 401

malpractice 947
malt liquor 298
maltreat
  injure 649
  aggrieve 830
  molest 907
malum
  – prohibitum 925
  – in se 923
malversation 818, 947
Mameluke 726
mamelon 250
mamma 166
mammal 366
mammiform 250
mammilla 250
Mammon 803, 978
  serve – 989
mammoth 192
man *adult* 131
  mankind 372
  male **373**
  prepare 673
  workman 690
  servant 746
  courage 861
  husband 903
  make a – of 648, 861
  Son of – 976
  straight – 599
  to a – 488
  –at-arms 726
  one's – of business 758
  –'s estate 131
  – in office 745
  – in the street 876
  –of-war 273, 726
  –of-war's man 269
  – at the wheel 694
  – and wife 903
manacle 751, 752
manage 693
  – to *succeed* 731
manageable 705
management
  conduct 692
  skill 698
manager
  stage - 599
  director 694
managery 693
manche après la cognée, jeter le – 859
mancible 637
mancipation 751
mandamus 741
mandarin 745

mandate 630, 741
mandible 298
mandolin 417
mandragora 174
mandrel 312
manducation 298
mane 256
man-eater 361
manége 266, 370
manes 362
manet: – altâmente
  repostum 505
  – cicatrix 919
manful *strong* 159
  resolute 604
  brave 861
manger 191
manger:
  cela se laisse – 394
  – son blé en herbe 818
mangle
  separate 44
  smooth 255
  injure 659
mangled 53
mangy 655
man-hater 911
manhood 131, 861
mania *insanity* 503
  desire 865
maniac 504
manibus pedibus-que 686
manic 503
manic-depressive 503
manicure 847
manicheism 978
manichord 417
manie 865
maniéré 855
manifest
  list 86
  visible 446
  obvious 525
  disclose 529
manifestation 525
manifesto 531
manifold 81, 102
manikin *dwarf* 193
  image 554
maniple 103
manipulate
  handle 379
  use 677
  conduct 692
manipulator 621
mankind 372
manly
  adolescent 131

above –ed 104	– words 477	meseems 484	– out *give* 784
not worth –ing 643	– wreck 659	mesh 198, 219	metempsychosis
mentis gratissimus	merelles 840	meshes *trap* 545	140
error 481	meretricious	*difficulty* 704	meteor 318, 423
mentor *sage* 500	*false* 495	– of sophistry 477	meteoric 173, 420
teacher 540	*vulgar* 851	meshwork 219	meteorology 338
adviser 695	*licentious* 961	mesial	meteoromancy 466
menu 86, 298	merfolk 980	*middle* 68	meter 466
Mephistopheles	merge *combine* 48	mesmerism 992	metheglin 396
980	*include* 76	mesmerist 994	methylated spirit
Mephistophelian	*insert* 300	mesne lord 779	388
945	*plunge* 337	mess *mixture* 41	methinks 484
mephitic 401, 657	– in 56	*disorder* 59	method *order* 58
mephitis 663	– into *become* 144	*barracks* 191	*way* **627**
meracious 392	merged 228	*meal* 298	want of – 59
mercantile 794	meridian	*difficulty* 704	methodical 60
mercatoria, lex –	*region* 181	*portion* 786	Methodist 984
963	*room* 125	make a –	methodist
mercature 794	*summit* 210	*unskilful* 699	*journalist* 988
mercenary	*light* 420	*fail* 732	methodize 60
soldier 726	– of life 131	message	Methuselah 130
servant 746	merit	*intelligence* 532	old as – 12
price 812	*goodness* 648	*command* 741	since the days of –
parsimonious 819	*due* 924	Messalina 962	124
selfish 943	*virtue* 944	messenger 271	meticulous 772
mercer 225	make a – of 884	*envoy* **534**	métier 625
merchandise **798**	– notice 642	*servant* 746	métis 83
merchant **797**	merito, e – 944	– balloon 463	metonymy 521
merchantman 273	meritorious 931	Messiah 976	metoposcopy
merciful 914	Merlin 994	messianic 976	*front* 234
merciless 914*a*	mermaid 341	messmate 890	*appearance* 44
mercurial	*monster* 83	messuage 189	*interpret* 522
changeable 149	*mythology* 979,	messy 59	metre
mobile 264	980	metabolism 140	*length* 200
quick 274	merman 341	metacentre 222	*poetry* 597
excitable 825	mero motu, ex –	metachronism 115	metrical
Mercury 979	600	metage 466	*measured* 466
traveller 268	merriment	metagenesis 140	*verse* 597
quick 274	*cheerful* 836	metagrammatism	metrology 466
messenger 534	*amusement* 840	561	*moderation* 174
mercy *lenity* 740	merry *cheerful* 836	metal 635	*mid-course* 628
pity 914	*drunk* 959	Brittania – 545	metropolis 189
at the – of	make – *sport* 840	metallic *sound* 410	metropolitan
liable 177	make – *with*	metalepsis 521	*archbishop* 996
subject 749	*wit* 842	metallurgy 358	mettle *spirit* 820
cry you – 766	*ridicule* 856	metamorphosis 140	*courage* 861
have at one's –	wish a – Christmas	metaphor	man of – 861
919	&c. 896	*comparison* 464	on one's –
have no – 914*a*	– and wise 842	*figure* **521**	*resolved* 604
– on us! 870	merry-andrew 844	(*analogy* 17)	put on one's –
for –'s sake 765	merry-go-round	metaphrase 522	*excite* 824
– seat 966	312, 840	metaphrast 524	*encourage* 861
mere *simple* 32	merry-making 827,	metaphrastic 516	mettlesome
lake 343	840, 892	metaphysics 450	*energetic* 171
trifling 643	merry-thought 842	metastasis, meta-	*sensitive* 822
– nothing	mersion 337	thesis	*excitable* 825
small 32	meruit ferat, pal-	*change* 140	*brave* 861
trifle 643	mam qui – 873	*inversion* 218	mettre de l'eau
buy for a – noth-	merveille, à – 731	*displacement* 270	dans son vin 160
ing 815	mesa 344	mete *measure* 466	meum et tuum 780
– pretext 617	mésalliance 24, 903	*distribute* 786	

set one's – upon
604
speak one's – 582,
703
to one's – *taste* 850
love 897
willing – 602
– one's book 539
– one's business
456, 457
– at ease 827
make one's – easy
826
–'s eye 515
– what one is
about 864
minded 602, 620
mindful 457, 505
mindless
inattentive 458
imbecile 499
forgetful 506
insensible 823
mine
sap 162
hollow 252
open 260
snare 545
store 636
abundance 639
damage 659
attack 716
defence 717
explosive 727
dig a – *plan* 626
prepare 673
spring a –
unexpected 508
attack 716
– of information
700
–layer 726
–sweeper 726
–thrower 727
– of wealth 803
miner 252
sapper and – 726
mineral 358
– oil 356
mineralogy 358
Minerva 979
– invita 603, 709
– press 577, 594
mingle 41
miniature *small* 193
portrait 556
– painter 559
Minié rifle 727
minikin 193
minim *small* 32
music 413

minimize 36, 483,
934
minimum *small* 32
inferior 34
minion 899
type 591
minister *instru-
mentality* 631
remedy 662
director 694
aid 707
deputy 759
give 784
clergy 996
rites 998
– to 746
ministerial
clerical 995
ministering spirit
977
ministration
direction 693
aid 707
rite 998
ministry
direction 693
aid 707
church 995
clergy 996
miniver 223
minnesinger 597
minnow 193
minor *inferior* 34
infant 129
– key 413
Minorites 996
minority *few* 103
youth 127
Minos 694
minotaur 83
minster 1000
minstrel 416, 597
minstrelsy 415
mint *mould* 22
workshop 691
wealth 803
– of money 800
minuend 38
minuet 415, 840
minus *less* 34
subtracted 38
absent 187
deficient 304
loss 776
in debt 806
non-payment 808
minusculæ 561
minute
- *in degree* 32
- *of time* 108
instant 113

– *in size* 193
record 551
compendium 596
to the – 132
– account 594
– attention 457
minuteness
care 459
minutiæ 32, 79, 643
minx 887, 962
mirabile
– dictu &c. 870
mirabilis, annus –
872
miracle 83, 872
– play 599
miraculous 870
mirage 443
mire 653
mirror *imitate* 19
reflector 445
perfection 650
glory 873
hold up the – 525
hold the – up to
nature 554
magic – 443
mirth 836
misacceptation 235
misadventure 735
misadvised 699
misanthropy 911
misapply
misinterpret 523
misuse 679
mismanage 699
misapprehend 495,
523
misappropriate 679
misarrange 61
misbecome 925
misbegotten 243,
945
misbehave 851, 945
misbehaviour 895,
947
misbelief 485
misbeliever 487,
984
miscalculate
misjudge 481
err 495
disappoint 509
miscall 565
miscarry 732
miscegenation 41
miscellany
mixture 41
collection 72
generality 78
compendium 596

mischance 619, **735**
mischief 619
do – 649
make – 649
mischief-maker
913, 941
miscible 41
miscite 544
miscompute 481,
495
misconceive 495,
523
misconduct 699,
947
– oneself 945
misconjecture 481
misconstrue 523
miscorrect 538
miscount 495
miscreance 485
miscreant 949
miscreated 945
misdate 115
misdeed 947
misdemean 945
misdemeanant 949
misdemeanour 947
misdevotion 988
misdirect 538, 699
misdo 945
misdoing 947
misdoubt 485, 523
mise en scène
appearance 448
drama 599
display 882
misemploy 679
miser 819
–'s hoard 800
miserabile dictu 839
miserable *small* 32
contemptible 943
unhappy 828
miserably *very* 31
miserere 215
sing – 950
misericordiam,
argumentum ad
– 914
miseries of human
life 828
miseris succurrere
disco 914
miserly 819
misery 828
put out of one's –
914
misestimate
misjudge 481
misfeasance 699,
947

[563]

at – 32
make the – of
  over-estimate 482
  exaggerate 549
  improve 658
  use 677
  skill 698
the – 33
– often 136
for the – part 78,
  613
make the – of
  one's time 682
mot 496
– de l'énigme 522
– du guet 550
– à mot 19
– d'ordre 741
– de passe 550
– pour rire 842
mote *small* 32
  light 320
– in the eye
  dim-sighted 443
  misjudging 481
motet 990
moth *bane* 663
moth-eaten 124,
  653, 659
mother *parent* 166
  mould 653
– country 189
– of-pearl 440
– superior 996
– tongue 560
– wit 498
motherly *love* 897
  kind 906
motif 415, 847
motile 264
motion
  change of place
  264
  topic 454
  plan 626
  proposal 763
  request 765
make a – 763
put in – 284
put oneself in –
  680
set in – 677
– downwards 306
– from
  recession 287
  repulsion 289
– into *ingress* 294
  reception 296
– out of 295
– through 302
– towards

[566]

approach 286
attraction 288
– upwards 305
motionless 265
motive **615**
  absence of – **615a**
  – power 264
motivity 264
motley 81, 440
  wearer of the – 844
motor 153, 266
  vehicle 271, 272
  instrument 633
  –boat 273
  –car &c. 272
  –driver 268
  –man 694
motorist 268
motory 264
mottled 440
motto *maxim* 496
  device 550
  phrase 566
motu: ex mero –
  737
suo – 600
mouchard 527
mould *condition* 7
  matrix 22
  convert 144
  form 240
  structure 329
  earth 342
  vegetation 367
  model 554
  carve 557
  decay 653
  turn to account
    677
moulded 820
– on 19
moulder 653, 659
moulding 847
mouldy 653, 659
moulin:
  se battre contre
    des –s 645
  – à paroles 584
moult 226
mound *large* 192
  hill 206
  defence 717
mount *increase* 35
  hill 206
  horse 271
  ascend 305
  raise 307
  display 882
– guard *care* 459
  safety 664
– up to *money* 800

price 812
mountain *large* 192
  hill 206
  weight 319
– artillery 726
– in labour
  waste 638
make –s of mole-
  hills 482
– brought forth
  mouse
  disappoint 509
mountaineer 268
mountainous 206
mountebank
  quack 548
  drama 599
  buffoon 844
mounted *rifles* 726
mourn 828, 839
mourner 363
mournful
  afflicting 830
  sad 837
  lamentable 839
mourning *dress* 225
in – *black* 431
  lament 839
mouse *little* 193
  search 461
  mountain brought
    forth – 509
  not a – stirring
    265
mouse-coloured
  432
mousehole 260
mouser 366
mousetrap 545
mousseux 353
moustache 256
mouth *entrance* 66
  receptacle 191
  brink 231
  opening 260
  eat 298
  estuary 343
  enunciate 580
  drawl 583
deep –ed
  resonant 408
  bark 412
down in the – 879
make –s 929
open one's – 582
stop one's – 581
word of – 582
– honour
  falsehood 544
  show 882
  flattery 933

pass from – to
  mouth 531
– wash 652
– watering 865
mouthful
  quantity 25
  small 32
  food 298
mouthpiece
  speaker 524
  information 527
  speech 582
mouthy *style* 577
moutonné 250
moutons, revenons
  à nos – 660
movable 264, 270
movables 780
move *begin* 66
  motion 264
  propose 514
  induce 615
  undertake 676
  act 680
  offer 763
  excite 824
get a – on 684
good – 626
on the – 293
– forward 282
– from 287
– in a groove 82
– heaven and
  earth 686
– off 293
– on *progress* 282
  activity 682
– out of 295
– quickly 274
– slowly 275
– to 894
moveless 265
movement
  motion 264
  music 415
  action 680
  activity 682
moved with 821
mover 164
movies 448, 599,
  840
movie star 899
moving
  keep – 682
  self – 266
  – pictures 448
mow *shorten* 201
  smooth 255
  agriculture 371
  store 636
– down

contrary 14
dissimilar 18
– surrender 606,
717
– thank you 764
at – time 107
– wonder 871
Noah's ark 41, 72
nob 210
nobilitate 873
nobility 875
noble *great* 31
important 642
rank 873
peer 875
disinterested 942
virtuous 944
noblesse 875
nobody
unsubstantial 4
zero 101
absence 187
low-born 876
– knows
ignorance 491
– knows where
distance 196
– present 187
– would think 508
noctambulation 266
noctivagant
travel 266
dark 421
noctograph 421
noctuary 421, 551
nocturnal
night 126
dark 421
black 431
nocturne 415
nocuous 649
nod *wag* 314
assent 488
signal 550
sleep 683
command 741
bow 894
– of approbation
931
– of assent 488
nodding to its fall
162, 306
noddle 210, 450
noddy 501
node 250
nodosity 250, 256
**nods and becks and
wreathed smiles**
894
nodule 250
nodular 256

**nodus, dignus vin-
dice** – 704
Noel 998
noggin 191
noise 402, 404
– abroad 531
make a – in the
world 873
noiseless 403
noisome
fetid 401
bad 649
unhealthy 657
nolens volens 601
noli me tangere
defiance 715
excitable 825
fastidious 868
nolition 603
nolle prosequi 624
**nolumus leges
Angliæ mutari**
permanence 141
continuance 143
preservation 670
nom de: – guerre
565
– plume 565
nomad 268
nomadic 266
Nomancy 511
nomenclature 564
nominal
unsubstantial 4
word 562
name 564
– price 815
nomination 564,
755
nominee 758
nominis umbra 4
Nomology 963
non:
– compos mentis
503
– constat 477
– deficit alter 100
– est in ventus 187
– hæc in fœdera
536, 610
– nobis Domine
990
– obstante 707
– placet 489
– possumus
impossible 471
obstinate 606
refusal 764
– nostrum tantas
componere lites
471, 713

lex – scripta 963
– semper erit
æstas 111
– sequitur 477
– sum qualis eram
140, 160'
non-addition 38
non-admission 55
nonage 127
nonagenarian 98
non-appearance
447
non-assemblage 73
non-attendance 187
nonce 118
for the – 118, 134
nonchalance
neglect 460
insensibility 823
indifference 866
non-coincidence 14
non-cohesive 47
non-com. 726
**non-commissioned
officer** 745
non-committal 528,
864
non-completion 730
non-compliance
742, 764
nonconformity
difference 15
exception 83
dissent 489
sectarianism 984
non-content 489
non-cooperation
489, 927
nondescript 83
none 101
– else 87
– to spare 640
– such
superior 33
exceptional 83
very good 648
– in the world 4
– the worse 660
non-endurance 825
nonentity
inexistence 2
unsubstantial 4
unimportant 643
non esse 2
non-essential 6,
643
non-existence 2
non-expectance 508
non-extension 180*a*
non-fulfilment 730,
732

– of one's hopes
509
non-imitation 20
non-interference
inaction 681
freedom 748
nonius 466
non-juror 489, 984
non-naturals 657
nonny 501
non-observance
inattention 458
desuetude 614
infraction **773**
dereliction 927
nonpareil 648
type 591
non-payment 808
non-performance
non-completion
730
dereliction 927
non-plus
uncertain 475
difficulty 704
conquer 731
non-preparation
674
non-prevalence 614
non-residence 187
non-resistance 725,
743
non-resonance
408a
nonsense
absurdity 497
unmeaning 517
trash 643
talk – *folly* 499
non-subsistence 2
non-success 732
nonsuch [*see* none]
nonsuit *defeat* 731
fail 732
condemn 971
**nonum prematur in
annum** 133
non-uniformity 16*a*
noodle 501
nook *place* 182
receptacle 191
corner 244
noology 450
noon *mid-day* 125
noon-day *light* 420
clear as –
intelligible 518
manifest 525
nooscopic 450
noose *ligature* 45
loop 247

snare 545
gallows 975
norma loquendi 567
normal
intrinsic 5
mean 29
regular 82
perpendicular 212
– condition
rule 80
normality 80, 502
**Normand, répon-
dre en** – 544
Norns 601
North 278
– and South 237
Northern 237
– light 423
– star
constant 939
North-west
passage 311
nose *prominence*
250
smell 398
with one's – in
the air 878
lead by the – 615,
737
led by the – 749
not see beyond
one's –
misjudge 481
folly 499
unskilful 699
speak through
the – 583
thrust one's – in
interjacence 228
busy 682
under one's –
present 186
near 197
manifest 525
defy 715
put one's – out of
joint *defeat* 731
disrepute 874
– ring 847
nose-dive 306
nosegay 400, 847
nosey 455
Nosology 655
nostalgia 833
nostril 351
breath of one's –s
359
stink in the –s 401
nostrum 626, 662
not *negation* 536
what is – 546

what ought – 923
– at all 32
– allowed 964
– amiss 618, 651,
845
– any 101
– bad 651
– bargain for 508
– a bit 536
– to be borne 830
– a Chinaman's
chance 471
– come up to 34
– cricket 923
– to be despised
642
it will – do 923
– of the earth 987
– expect 508
– fail 939
– far from 197
– a few 102
– fit to be seen 846
– following 477
– grant 764
– guilty 946
– to be had 471,
640
– having 187, 777a
– hardened 950
– hear of 764
– included 55
– know what to
make of 519
– a leg to stand
on 158
– likely 473
– a little 31
– matter 643
– to mention 37
– mind 823, 930
– often 137
– on your life 489
– one 101
– a particle 4
– particular 831
– pay 808
– a pin to choose
27
– playing the
game 923
– within previous
experience 137
– to be put down
604
– quite 32
– reach 304
– right 503
– sorry 827
– a soul 101
– on speaking

terms 889
– the thing 925
– to be thought of
incogitancy 452
impossible 471
refusal 764
hopeless 859
undue 925
disapprobation
932
– trouble oneself
about 460
– understand 519
– vote 609a
– wonder 871
– for the world
603, 764
– worth
trifling 643
useless 645
nota bene 457
notabilia 642
notabilities 875
notable
manifest 525
important 642
active 682
distinguished 873
notables 875
notably 31
notary 553, 968
notation 85
notch 198, **257**, 550
note *cry* 412
music 413
take *cognizance*
450
remark 457
explanation 522
sign 550
record 551
printing 591
epistle 592
minute 596
money 800
fame 873
change one's – 607
make a – of 551
of – 873
take – of 457
– of admiration
870
– of alarm 669
– of preparation
673
note-book
memorandum 505
record 551
compendium 569
writing 590
noted 490, 873

noteworthy
great 31
exceptional 83
important 642
nothing *nihility* 4
zero 101
trifle 643
come to – 304, 732
do – 681
for – 815
go for – 643
good for – 646
make – of
under-estimate
483
fail 732
take – by 732
think of – 930
worse than – 808
– comes amiss 831
– to do 681
– to do with 764
– doing 681
– to go upon 471
– in it 4
– of the kind 18,
536
– loth 602
– on 226
– more to be said
478
– to signify 643
nothingness 2
notice *intellect* 450
observe 457
review 480
information 527
warning 668
bring into – 525
deserve – 642
give –
manifest 525
inform 527
indicate 550
short – 111
take – of 450
this is to give –
457
worthy of – 642
– is hereby given
publication 531
– to quit 782
noticeable 31
notification 527
notion *idea* 453
notional 515
notoriety 531, 873
notorious
known 490
public 531
famous 873

obdurate
  obstinate 606
  severe 739
  malevolent 907
  graceless 945
  impenitent 951
obedience 743
obeisance *bow* 308
  submission 725
  courtesy 894
  reverence 928
obelisk 206, 551
Oberon 979
obese 194
obesity 192
obey 743
  be subject to 749
  – a call 615
  – the helm 705
  – rules 82
obfuscate 421, 426
obfuscated
  drunk 959
obit 360, 363
  post – 360, 363
obiter dictum
  irrelevant 10
  occasion 134
  interjacent 228
obituary 360, 594
object *thing* 3
  matter 316
  take exception 469
  intention 620
  ugly 846
  disapprove 932
  be an –
  important 642
  – to *dislike* 867
  – lesson 82
objection 706, 932
  no – 762
objectionable
  inexpedient 647
  wrong 923, 947
objective
  extrinsic 6
  material 316
objector
  conscientious –
  710
objurgate 932
oblate 201
  – spheroid 249
oblation *gift* 784
  religious - 990
oblectation 827
obligation
  necessity 601
  promise 768
  conditions 770

  debt 806
  confer an – 648
  feeling of – 916
  under an – 916,
  926
oblige *benefit* 707
  compel 744
  duty 926
oblige, bien –
  refusal 764
obliged
  necessity 601
  grateful 916
  duty 926
obligee 800
obliging
  helping 707
  courteous 894
  kind 906
obliquation 279
obliquity
  slope **217**
  vice 945
  – of judgment 481
  – of vision 443
obliteration 552
  – of the past 506
oblivion 506
  nothingness 2
  pardon 506
  forgiveness 918
  redeem from – 505
  – of benefits 917
  – of time 115
oblivious 506
oblong 200
  – spheroid 249
obloquy
  disrepute 874
  disapprobation
  932
  detraction 934
obmutescence 581,
  585
obnoxious
  pernicious 649
  unpleasing 830
  hateful 898
  – to *liable* 177
obnubilated 422
oboe 417
obreption 528
obscene 653, 961
obscurantist 421,
  519, 710
obscure *dark* 421
  dim 422
  unseen 447
  uncertain 475
  unintelligible 519
  eclipse 874

  ignoble 876
obscurity *style* **571**
obscurum per
  obscurius 519
obsecration 765
obsequies 363
obsequious
  subject 749
  servile 886
  courteous 894
  respectful 928
  flattery 932
observance *rule* 82
  attention 457
  habit 613
  practice 692
  fulfilment **772**
  duty 926
  rite 998
observant
  friar 996
observation
  intellect 450
  idea 453
  attention 457
  assertion 535
  – car 272
observatory 318
observe [see observ-
  ance, observa-
  tion]
  remark 535
  – a duty 926
  – rules 82
observer 444
obsess 860, 992
obsession 716
obsidional 716
obsolete *old* 124
  words 563
  effete 645
obstacle 179, 706
obstant, Fata – 601
obstetrician 631
obstetrics 161, 662
obstinacy 606
  prejudice 481
obstipation 261
obstreperous 173,
  404
obstruct *close* 261
  hinder 706
  – the passage of
  light 426
  – the view 424
obstructive
  opponent 710
obstruent 706
obstupefaction 823
obstupui steterunt-
  que comæ 860

obtain *exist* 1
  prevail 78
  get 775
  – under false
  pretences 791
obtainable 470
obtenebration 421
obtestation 765
obtrectation 934
obtrude
  interfere 228
  insert 300
  meddle 682
obtruncate 201
obtrusion 228, 706
obtrusive
  interfering 228
  vulgar 851
  rude 895
obtund *mitigate* 174
  blunt 254
  deaden 376
  paralyze 823
obturate 261
obturator 263
obtuse *blunt* 253
  insensible 376
  imbecile 499
  dull 823
  – angle 244
obtuseness 456a
obumbrate 421
obverse 234
obviate 706
obvious *visible* 446
  evident 474
  clear 518
  manifest 525
ocarina 417
occasion
  juncture 8
  opportunity **134**
  cause 153
  befit the – 646
  have – for 630
  on the present –
  118
  on the spur of –
  612
occasional 475
occasionally 136
occidental 236, 560
occiput 235
occision 361
occlusion 261
  unintelligible 919
  latent 526
  hidden 528
  – art 992
occultism 984
occultation 449, 528

- to be met with
136
ogee 847
Ogham 590
ogive 215
ogle *look* 441
desire 865
rude 895
endearment 902
ogpu 696
ogre *bugbear* 860
evil-doer 913
demon 980
oil *lubricate* 332
grease 355, **356**
pour - on
relieve 834
- on the troubled
waters 174, 714
- lamp 423
- stove 386
oiled *drunk* 959
oilcloth 223
oilskin 386
oil-painting 556
oily *smooth* 255
greasy 355
servile 886
courteous 894
flattery 933
oinomania 959
ointment
grease 356
remedy 662
O.K. 58
old 124
of - 122
- age 128
die of - age 729
- bachelor 904
- clothes 225
- fashioned 851
- fogey 501, 857
- joke 842
- maid *cards* 840
spinster 904
- man *veteran* 130
husband 903
- man of the sea
706
- Nick 978
- school 124
obstinate 606
habit 613
pay off - scores
718
- song
repetition 104
trifle 643
cheap 815
- stager

veteran 130
actor 599
proficient 700
- story
repetition 104
stale news 532
love 897
- times 122
one's - way 613
- woman *fool* 501
wife 903
Oldbuck 122
olden 124
older 128
oldest inhabitant
not in memory of
- 137
old-fashioned 124,
851
oldness **124**
oleagine 356
oleaginous 355
oleomargarine 356
oleum addere
camino 35, 173
olfactory 398
olid 401
oligarch 745
oligarchy 737
olio 41
olive-branch
infant 129
offspring 167
pacification 723
olive-green 435
olla podrida 41
Olympiad 720
Olympus 981
ombre 840
ombres chinoises
448
omega *end* 67
omelet 298
omen **512**
ominate 511
ominous
predicting 511
indicating 550
danger 665
hopeless 859
omission
incomplete 53
exclusion 55
neglect 460
failure 732
non-observance
773
guilt 947
omitted 2, 187
omne tulit
punctum 731

omnibus 272
omnifarious 81
omnific 168
omniform 81
omnigenous 81
omnipotence 157,
976
omnipresence 186,
976
omniscience 490,
976
omnium gatherum
mixture 41
confusion 59
assemblage 72
omnivorous
eating 298
desire 865
gluttony 957
omphalos 68
on *forwards* 282
- account of 155
- all accounts 52
- that account 155
- approval 463
- an average 29
- the brink of 32
- the cards 152
- foot *duration* 106
event 151
doing 170
- the fire 730
- all fours 13, 23
- the other hand
30
- one's head 218
- the increase 35
- a large scale 31
- these lines 627
- the move 264
- the nail 118
- no account 32
- no occasion 107
- a par 27
- the part of 9
- the point of 111
- the present oc-
casion 118
- trial 463
- the whole 50
on dit 532, 588
once *past* 119, 122
seldom 137
at - 113, 132
- for all *final* 67
infrequency 137
tell one - 527
determine - 604
choose 609
- in a blue moon
137

- more 90, 104
- over 457
- upon a time
time 106
different time 119
formerly 122
- in a way 137
Ondine 979
one *identical* 13
whole 50
unity 87
somebody 372
married 903
all - to 823
at - with *agree* 23
concur 178
concord 714
make - of 186
neither - nor the
other 610
of - accord 488
- and all
whole 50
general 78
unanimous 488
from - to another
transfer 783
- thing with
another 476
- of the best 948
- bone and one
flesh 903
- consent 178, 488
- of these days 121
- fell swoop 113,
173
- fine morning 106
- and a half 87
- horse 643
- idea 481
- jump 113
- leg in the grave
160
as - man 488, 709
- mind 178, 488
- by one
separately 44
respectively 79
unity 87
both the - and
the other 89
the - or the other
609
- over the eight
959
- and the same 13
on - side 217, 236
- step 840
- in ten thousand
648, 948
- at a time 87

parse 461, 567
Parsee 984
parsimony **819**
parson 996
parsonage 1000
part *divide* 44
  portion **51**
  diverge 291
  music 413
  book 593
  rôle 599
  function 625
  duty 926
act a – *action* 680
take an active –
  682
bear – in 709
component – 56
fractional – 100*a*
in – *a little* 32
for my – 79
on the – of 707
play a – in 175
principal – 642
take the – of 709
take – with 709
take a – in 680
take no – in 623
– company
  disjunction 44
  avoid 623
  quarrel 713
– and parcel 56
– by part 51
–song 415
– of speech 567
– with 782, 784
partake 778
– of the sacrament
  998
parte, ex – 481
parterre *level* 213
  cultivation 371
Parthis mendacior
  544
parti pris 611
partial *unequal* 28
  incomplete 51
  special 79
  misjudging 481
  unjust 923
– shadow 422
partiality
  preponderance 33
  desire 865
  friendship 888
  love 897
partially 32, 51
partible 44
particeps criminis
  690, 711

participote 709, 778
– in *be a doer* 680
participation **778**
participator 690
particle 32, 330
parti-coloured 440
particular *item* 51
  event 151
  attentive 457
  careful 459
  exact 494
  capricious 608
  odd 851
  fastidious **868**
in – 79
– account 594
– estate 780
particularize
  special 79
  describe 594
particularly 31, 33
particulars 79, 594
partie carrée 892
parting 44
partisan
  auxiliary 711
  weapon 727
  friend 890
  sympathizer 914
partisanship
  warped judgment
    481
  co-operation 709
  partiality 923
partition *wall* 228
  allot 786
partlet 366
partly 51
partner
  companion 88
  auxiliary 711
  sharer 778
  friend 890
  spouse 903
  sleeping – 683
partnership
  party 712
  join – with 709
parts *intellect* 450
  skill 698
  wisdom 498
parturition 161
parturiunt montes
  482, 509
party *assemblage* 72
  special 79
  person 372
  association **712**
  sociality 892
– spirit
  warped judgment

481
  cooperation 709
  wrong 923
– to *action* 680
  agent 690
  co-operate 709
– to a suit 969
– wall 228
parva componere
  magnis 464
parvenu
  new 123
  successful 734
  vulgar 851
  low-born 876
parvitude 193
pas *precedence* 62
  term 71
  precession 280
  rank 873
– de quatre 840
– seul 840
pas si bête 498
paschal 998
pasha 875
pashalic 737
pashaw 745
pasigraphie 560
pasigraphy 590
pasquinade 934
pass *conjuncture* 8
  be superior 33
  course 109
  lapse 122
  happen 151
  interval 198
  defile 203
  move 264
  transfer 270
  move through 302
  exceed 303
  vanish 449
  way 627
  difficulty 704
  thrust 716
  passport 760
  gratuity 815
  - as *property* 783,
    784
  barely – 651
  let it – 460
  make a – at 716
  pretty – 704
– away
  cease to exist 2
  end 67
  transient 111
  past 122
  cease 142
  die 360
– by *course* 109

inattention 458
neglect 460
disrespectful 929
– comprehension
  519
– current 484
– an examination
  648, 873
– the eyes over
  457
– the fingers over
  379
– into one's hand
  785
– through one's
  hands 625
– into 144
– judgment 480
– a law 963
– in the mind 451
– muster
  conform to 82
  sufficient 639
  good 648
  approbation 931
  barely – muster
    651
– under the name
  of 564
– off *be past* 122
  egress 295
– off for 544
– on 282
– an opinion 480
– to the order of
  the day 624
– out of 295
– over
  exclude 55
  cross 302
  give 784
  forgive 918
  exemption 927*a*
– over to 709
– and repass 302,
  314
– in review 457,
  461
– the Rubicon 609
– sentence on 971
– time *exist* 1
  time 106
  do nothing 681
– one's time in
  625
– to 144
– through
  event 151
  motion 302
– one's word 768
passable *small* 32

Paul Pry
  curious 455
  prattle 588
paulo post futurum
  121
paunch 191, 250
pauper 804
pause
  discontinue 70
  cease 142
  quiescence 265
  doubt 485
  irresolution 605
  repose 687
pauvre diable 804
pavanne 840
pave 223
  – the way 705
pavé, on the – 961
pavement *base* 211
  covering 223
  path 627
pavilion 189
paving 211
paviour 673
pavor 859
paw *touch* 379
  retention 781
  – the ivories 416
pawky 702
pawl 45
pawn 771
pawnbroker 787
pax *hush!* 403
  – in bellow 723
  – vobiscum 894
pay *paint* 223
  profitable 775
  defray 807
  expend 809
  income 810
  punish 972
  remunerate 973
  in one's –
    servant 746
    hired 795
  – in advance 809
  – attention to 457
  – back 718
  – down 807
  – dues 924
  – in full 807
  – homage
    submission 725
    worship 990
  – the debt of
    nature 360
  – no attention &c.
    to 458, 460
  – through the

nose 814
– off 718
– off old scores 919
– old debts 807
– out 200, 972
– in one's own
  coin 718
– the penalty 952
– the piper 707
– regard to 484
– one's respects
  894
– too much 814
– a visit 892, 894
– one's way
  defray 807
  economy 817
paymaster 801
payment 807
  remuneration 973
paynim 984
pays, mal du –
  regret 833
  sociality 892
pea 249
peace
  silence 403
  concord 714
  amity **721**
  at – 714
  commission of
    the – 965
  justice of the –
    967
  keep the –
    moderation 174
    concord 714
  make – 723
  make – with 831
  Prince of – 976
  speak – 831
peaceable
  moderate 174
peaceably, get on –
  736
peaceful
  inexcitable 826
peace-maker 714
  mediator 724
  contented 831
peace-offering
  pacification 723
  mediation 724
  gift 784
  atonement 952
peach 529
peach-coloured 434
peacock
  variegation 440
  beauty 845
  proud 878

vain 880
  gaudy 882
jackdaw in –'s
  feathers 701
pea-green 435
pea-jacket 225
peak *height* 206
  summit 210
  sharp 253
  sicken 655
peaked 253
peaky 203
peal *loud* 404
  roll 407
  music 415
  – of bells 407, 417
  – of laughter 838
pearl *type* 591
  goodness 648
  ornament 847
  glory 873
  mother-of– 440
  cast –s before
    swine 638
pearly
  semitransparent
    427
  colour 428
  white 430
  grey 432
  variegated 440
pear-shape 249
peasant 876
peat 388
pebble *little* 193
  hard 323
  – dash 223
peccability 945
peccable 947
peccadillo 947
peccant *bad* 649
  unclean 653
  diseased 655
  – humour 653, 655
peccavi 950
peck *much* 31
  multitude 102
  eat 298
  – at *censure* 932
  – of troubles
    difficulty 704
    adversity 735
    pain 828
peckish 865
Pecksniff 548
pectinated 253
peculate 791
peculator 792
peculiar 79, 83
peculiarly 31, 33
pecuniary 800

pecunious 803
pedagogic 537
pedagogue
  scholar 492
  teacher 540
  pedantic 855
pedagogy 537
pedal 633
  – note 408
  – point 416
pedant *scholar* 492
pedantic
  half-learned 491
  - *style* 577
  affected 855
pedantry 481
peddle *meddle* 683
  hawk 796
peddler 796, 797
peddling
  trifling 643
  miserly 819
pederero 727
pedestal 215
  place on a – 307,
    931
pedestrian 268
pedicel 215
pedicle 215
pedigree 69, 166
pediment 210, 215
pedlar 797
  –'s French 563
pedometer 200
peduncle 215
peek 441
peel *layer* 204
  skin 223
  uncover 226
  – off *separate* 44
peeler 664
peel-house 717
peep 441
  – behind the cur-
    tain 461
  – of day 125
  – into the future
    510
  – out 446, 529
peep-hole 260
peep-show 448, 840
peer *equal* 27
  pry 441
  inquire 461
  lord 875
  – out 446
peerless *supreme* 33
  first rate 648
  glorious 873
  virtuous 944
peeved 900

vain 880
  insolent 885
  discourteous 895
pertain to
  relate to 9
  included under 76
  power 157
  belong 777
  property 780
  duty 926
perte de vue, à –
  196, 447
pertinacity 604*a*
pertinent 9, 23
pertingent 199
perturbation
  derange 61
  ferment 171
  agitation 315
  emotion 821
  excitation 824,
    825
  fear 860
pertusion 260
peruke 225
peruse 539
pervade
  influence 175
  extend 186
  affect 821
  – the soul 824
pervading spirit 820
perverse
  obstinate 606
  difficult 704
  churlish 895
  sulky 901*a*
perversion
  sophistry 477
  misinterpretation
    523
  misteaching 538
  falsehood 544
  untruth 546
  injury 659
  impiety 988
pervert 144, 607
  [*see* perversion]
perverted 495
pervestigation 461
pervicacious 606
pervigilium 682
pervious 260
pessimism
  overrate 482
  underrate 483
  dejection 837
  hopeless 859
pessimist
  [*see* pessimism]
  coward 862

pessomancy 511
pessoribus orti 876
pest 663, 830
pester 830
pest-house 662
pestiferous 657
pestilence 655
pestle 330
pet *love* 897
  favourite 899
  anger 900
  fondle 902
  flatter 933
  – *lamb* 266
petal 367
petard 727
  hoist on one's own
    – 718, 732
Peter to pay Paul:
  borrow of – 788
  rob – *steal* 791
    wrong 923
  –'s pence 784, 809
  peter out 142
petit-maître 854
petite dame 962
petitio principii 477
petition 765, 969,
    990
petitioner 767
petrel *warning* 668
petrify *dense* 321
  hard 323
  freeze 385
  thrill 824
  affright 860
  astonish 870
petrol 388
petroleum 356
pétroleuse 384
petronel 727
petticoat *dress* 225
  woman 374
  – *government*
    authority 737
pettifogger 968
pettifogging
  sophistry 477
  deception 545
  litigious 713
  dishonourable 940
pettish 901
petto, in –
  mental 450
  thought of 454
  concealed 528
  intention 620
petty *little* 32, 193
  unimportant 643
  – *cash* 800, 811
  – *jury* 967

– *larceny* 791
– *officer* 745
– *sessions* 966
– *treason* 742
petulance 885, 901
petulant
  – *language* 574
peu de chose 643
peu s'en faut 32
pew *cell* 191
  church 1000
pewter 41
phaeton 272
Phaethon 423
phalanx 712, 726
phantasm
  unsubstantiality 4
  illusion 443
  appearance 448
  imagination 515
phantasmagoria
    448
phantasy 453, 515
phantom *unreal* 4
  fallacy of vision
    443
  imaginary 515
pharisaical 544, 988
Pharisee 548, 988
pharmacy 662
pharos 550
phase *aspect* 8
  transition 144
  form 240
  appearance 448
  have many –s 149
  assume a new –
    144
  view in all its –s
    461
phasis 448
phasma 443
phenomenon
  event 151
  appearance 448
  prodigy 872
phial 191
Phidias 559
philander 902
philanthropy 784,
    906, 910
Philip drunk to
    Philip sober,
    appeal from –
    658
philippic 932
Philistine 491, 876
philologist 492
philology 560
philomath 492
philomel 416

philosopher 492,
    500
–'s stone
  impossibility 471
  perfect 650
  remedy 662
  wealth 803
philosophical
  thoughtful 451
  calm 826
philosophy
  calmness 826
  knowledge 490
  Moral – 450
  – of the Mind 450
philtre 993
phiz *face* 234
  look 448
phlebotomy
  ejection 297
  remedy 662
Phlegethon 982
phlegm *viscid* 352
  insensibility 823
phlegmatic
  indifferent 866
phlogiston 382
pho! 497
Phœbus *sun* 318
  luminary 423
phœnix
  exception 83
  reproduction 163
  paragon 650
  restoration 660
phonate 402
phonetic
  sound 402
  voice 580
  speech 582
  – spelling 561
phonics 402
phonograph 417,
    418
phonography
  sound 402
  letter 361
  writing 590
phonology 562
Phosphor 423
phosphorescence
    420, 423
phosphorus 423
photo-engraving
    558
photograph *like* 17
photographer 559
photography 445
  light 420
  representation
    554

highway 627	**pin** *fasten* 43	**pink of** *beauty* 845	turn a – 607
weapon 727	*fastening* 45	– fashion 852	**Pisa, tower of** – 217
pikeman 726	*locate* 184	– perfection 650	**pis-aller** 147
pikestaff *tall* 206	*sharp* 253	– politeness 894	**piscatorial** 366
plain 525	*axis* 312	**pinnace** 273	**pisces natare**
pilaster	*trifle* 643	**pinnacle** 210	**docere** 538, 641
support 215	might hear a –	**pinocle** 840	**pisciculture** 370
projection 250	drop 403	**pin-prick** 180*a*	**piscina** 350, 1000
ornament 847	point of a – 193	**pins** *legs* 266	**pish!** *absurd* 497
pile *stake* 45	not a – to choose	– and needles	*trifling* 643
heap 72	27, 609*a*	*bodily pain* 378	*excitable* 825
edifice 161	– down 744, 751	*numb 381*	*irascible* 901
post 215	– one's faith upon	*mental pain* 828	**piste** 551
velvet 256	484	**pinscher** 366	**Pistol** 887
money 800	– oneself upon	**Pinto, Fernam**	**pistol** 727
funeral – 363	746, 886	**Mendez** – 548	**pistol-shot** 197
– up 549, 641	**pinafore** 225	**pioneer**	**piston** 263
pile-driver 276	**pince-nez** 445	*precursor* 64	**pit** *deep* 208
pilfer *steal* 791	**pincers** 781	*leader* 234	*hole* 252
pilferer 792	**pinch** *emergency* 8	*teacher* 540	*opening* 260
pilgarlic	*contract* 195	*prepare* 673	*extract* 301
outcast 893	*pain* 378	**pious** 987	*grave* 363
pilgrim 268, 996	*chill* 385	– fraud 546, 988	*theatre* 599
pilgrimage 266, 676	*need* 630	**pip** 747	*danger* 667
pill *sphere* 249	*difficulty* 704	**pipe** *tube* 260	bottomless – 982
medicine 662	*adversity* 735	*conduit* 350	– of Acheron 982
bitter – 735	*grudge* 819	*vent* 351	– against 708, 713
pillage 659, 791	*hurt morally* 830	*tobacco* 392	– against one
pillager 792	at a – 630, 704	*sound* 410	another 464
pillar *stable* 150	jack at a – 711	*cry* 411	**pit-a-pat**
lofty 206	where the shoe –s	*music* 416, 417	*agitation* 315
support 215	830	*weep* 839	*rattle* 407
monument 551	– of snuff 643	no – no dance 812	*feeling* 821
tablet 590	**pinchbeck** 545, 847	– one's eye 839	*excitation* 824
–s of Hercules 550	**pinched** [see pinch]	– of peace 721,	**pitch** *degree* 26
– of the state &c.	*thin* 203	723	*term* 71
873	*poor* 804	**pipeclay** *habit* 613	*location* 184
from – to post	– with hunger 865	*strictness* 739	*height* 206
transfer 270	**pinching** 383, 819	**piper** 416	*summit* 210
agitation 315	**Pindaric** 597	pay the – 707, 807	*erect* 212
irresolute 505	**ping-pong** 840	**piping** – hot 382	*throw* 284
circuit 629	**pine** *disease* 655	– time 721, 734	*descent* 306
pillion 215	*dejection* 837	**pipkin** 191	*depression* 308
pillory 975	*suffer in mind*	**piquant**	*reel* 314
pillow	828	*pungent* 392	*resin* 356*a*
support 215	– away 837	- *style* 574	*musical* - 413
soft 324	– for 865	*impressive* 821	*black* 431
consult one's –	**pinery** 371	**piquante, sauce** –	absolute – 416
temporize 133	**pinguid** 355	393, 829	– of one's breath
reflect 451	**pin-hole** 260	**pique** *fly* 267	411
pilot *mariner* 269	**pinion** *fasten* 43	*excite* 824	– dark 421
inform 527	*wing* 267	*pain* 830	– into *attack* 716
guide 693	*instrument* 633	*hate* 898	*contend* 720
director 694	*restrain* 751	*anger* 900	*punish* 972
pilot-balloon 463	*fetter* 752	– oneself	– overboard 782
pilot-boat 273	**pink** *notch* 257	*pride* 878	– one's tent 292
pilot-officer 745	*pierce* 260	**piqueerer** 792	– and toss 621
pilot-jacket 225	*thrust* 276	**piquet** 717, 726	– upon *reach* 292
pilous 256	*colour* 434	**pirate** 773, 791, 792	*discover* 480*a*
pimp 962	*perfection* 650	**piroque** 273	*choose* 609
pimple 250, 848	*glory* 873	**pirouette** 218, 312	*get* 775

pitched battle 720
pitcher 191
pitchfork 273, 284
  rain –s 348
pitch-pipe 417
piteous 830
piteously *much* 31
pitfall 545, **667**
pith *gist* 5
  strength 159
  interior 221
  centre 222
  meaning 516
  important part
  642
pithless 158
pithy *meaning* 516
  concise 572
  vigorous 574
pitiable *bad* 649
  painful 830
  contemptible 930
pitied, to be – 828
pitiful
  unimportant 643
  bad 649
  disrepute 874
  pity 914
pitiless 914a
  revengeful 919
pittance
  quantity 25
  dole 640
  allotment 786
  income 810
pitted 848
pituitous 352
pity 914
  express – 915
  what a –
  regret 833
  lament 839
  for –'s sake 914
pivot *junction* 43
  cause 153
  support 215
  axis 222, 312
pix *box* 191, 998
  assay 463
pixy 980
pizzicato 415
placable 918
placard 531
placate 723, 918
place
  circumstances 8
  order 58
  arrange 60
  term 71
  situation **182**, 183

locate 184
abode 189
office 625
rank 873
give – to 623
have – 1
in – 183
in – of 147
make a – for 184
out of – 185
take – 151
– to one's credit
  805
– itself 58
– in order 60
– upon record 551
– under
  include 76
placebit, decies re-
  petita – 829
placebo 933
place-hunter 767
placeman 758
placet 488, 741
placid 826
placket 260
plagiarism
  imitation 19
  borrowing 788
  theft 791
plagiarist 792
Plagiary, Sir
  Fretful – 901
plagiedral 217
plague *disease* 655
  pain 828
  worry 830
plague-spot 657
plaguy 704, 830
plaid *shawl* 225
  variegation 440
plaidoyer 476
plain
  horizontal 213
  country **344**
  obvious 446
  meaning 518
  manifest 525
  style 576
  artless 703
  ugly 846
  simple 849
speak –ly 576
tell one –ly 527
– English 576
– dealing 543
– interpretation
  522
– question 461
– sailing 705
– sense 498

– speaking 525,
  703
– terms
  intelligible 518
  interpreted 522
  language 576
– truth 494
– words 703
plainness **576**
plainsong 990
plain-spoken 525,
  703
plaint 411, 839
plaintiff 938
plaintive 839
plaisance
  [see pleasance]
plaisanterie 842
plaister 223
plait 219, 258
plan *itinerary* 266
  information 527
  representation
  554
  scheme **626**
  according to – 82
planchette 992
plane *horizontal* 213
  flat 251
  smooth 255
  fly 267
  aeroplane 273
  soar 305
  inclined – 633
planet *world* 318
  luminary 423
  fate 601
planet-struck
  adversity 735
  wonder 870
planimeter 466
planish 255
plank *board* 204
  programme 626
  path 627
  safety 666
plant *place* 184
  insert 300
  vegetable 367
  agriculture 371
  trick 545
  tools 633
  property 780
– a battery 716
– a dagger in the
  breast 830
– oneself 184
– a thorn in the
  side 830
plantation
  location 184

agriculture 371
estate 780
planter 188
planter ses choux,
  aller – 893
plaque 204
plash *lake* 343
  stream 348
  sound 405, 408
plashy 345
plasm 22
plasma 847
plasmic 240
plaster *cement* 45
  covering 223
  remedy 662
– up *repair* 660
plastered 959
plastic *alterable* 149
  form 240
  soft 324
– arts 557
plastron 717
plat *weave* 219
  ground 344
plate *dish* 191
  layer 204
  covering 223
  flat 251
  food 298
  engraving 558
– layer 690
– printing 558,
  591
plateau 213, 344
plated 545
platform
  horizontal 213
  support 215
  stage 542
  scheme 626
  arena 728
– orator 582
platinum-blond 430
platitude 517, 843
Platonic
  contemplative 451
  inexcitable 826
  chaste 960
– bodies 244
Platonism 451
platoon 726
– fire 716
platter 191
  layer 204
  flat 251
clean the outside
  of the – 544
plaudit 931
plausible
  probable 472

commonalty 876	– into sorrow 830	poem 597	*honour* 939
ploughman 371	**plunged**	book of –s 593	nice – 697
ploughshare 253	– in debt 806	**pœnitentiæ, locus –**	on the – of 111,
pluck *cheat* 545	– in grief 828	*pity* 914	121
resolution 604	**plunger** 621	*forgive* 918	to the – 572, 642
persevere 604a	**plurality 100**	*vindicate* 937	– an antithesis 578
reject 610	plus 37	*repent* 950	– at *direction* 278
take 789	plus fours 225	**poesy** 597	*direct attention*
steal 791	plush 256	**poet** 597	457
courage 861	**Pluto** 979, 982	**poetaster** 597, 855	*intend* 620
– up courage 861	realms of – 982	**poetic** *style* 574	*discourtesy* 895
– a crow with 932	**Plutocracy** 803	**poetic frenzy** 515	*disrespect* 929
– out 301	**plutonic** 382	**poetry 597**	*censure* 932
plug 261, 263	**Plutus** 803	**poignancy**	– of attack 716
– along 143	**pluvial** 348	*physical energy*	at the – of the
plum *number* 98	**ply** *layer* 204	171	bayonet 173
sweet 396	*fold* 258	*pain* 378	– of the compass
money 800	*use* 677	*pungency* 392	278
plumage 256	*exert* 686	*feeling* 821	– of convergence
plumb *vertical* 212	*request* 765	**pogrom** 361	74
close 261	– one's task 680	**point** *condition* 8	– of death 360
measure 466	– one's trade 625	*degree* 26	– in dispute 461
plumber 690	– a trade 794	*small* 32	– of etiquette 852
plumb-line 212	**Plymouth Brother**	*end* 67	in – of fact 1
plum-coloured 437	984	*term* 71	– the finger of
plume *feather* 256	**p.m.** 114, 126	*poignancy* 171	scorn 930
ornament 847	**pneumatics** 334,	*no magnitude*	– of honour 939
borrowed –s 788	338	180a	– of land 250
– oneself 878	**pneumatology** 450	*place* 182	– a moral 537
plume	**pneumatoscopic**	*speck* 193	– out 155, 457,
coup de – 590	317	*sharp* 253	527
nom de – 565	**poach** 791, 964	*topic* 454	– to – race 720
plumigerous 256	**poacher** 792	*mark* 550	at the – of the
plummet 208, 212	**poachy** 345	*vigour* 574	sword
plumose 256	**pock** 250	*intention* 620	*violence* 173
plump	**pocket** *place* 184	*wit* 842	*severity* 739
instantaneous 113	*pouch* 191	*punctilio* 939	*compulsion* 744
fat 192	*diminutive* 193	at the – of 197	– to *attribute* 155
plunge 310	*receive* 785	come to the –	*direction* 278
unexpected 508	*take* 789	*special* 79	*probable* 472
– down 306	*money* 800	*attention* 457	*predict* 511
– upon 292	*treasury* 802	*reasoning* 476	*mean* 516
plumper	*brook* 826	*plain language*	– of view 441, 448
expansion 194	button up one's –	576	**point d'appui** 215
vote 609	808	culminating – 210	**point-blank**
plunder 791, 793	out of – 776, 806	disputed – 713	*direct* 278
plunderer 792	touch the – 800	from all –s 180	*plain language*
plunge	– the affront 725,	full of – 574	576
revolution 146	918	give –s to 27	*refusal* 764
insert 300	**pocket-book** 551	go straight to	**point-champain** 874
dive 306, **310**	**pocket-handker-**	the – 278	**pointed**
immerse 337	**chief** 225	in – *relative* 9	*great* 31
hurry 684	**pocket-money** 800	*agreeing* 23	*sharp* 253
– into difficulties	**pocket-pistol**	*conformable* 82	*affirmation* 535
704	*bottle* 191	knotty – 704	*marked* 550
– into dissipation	**pococurante** 823,	make a – of	*concise* 572
954	866	*resolution* 604	*language* 574
– headlong 684	**pocula, inter –** 959	*contention* 720	**pointedly**
– into 676	**pod** 191, 223	*compulsion* 744	*intention* 620
– in medias res	**podestà** 967	*conditions* 770	**pointer** *dog* 366
576, 604	**podgy** 201	*due* 924	*indicator* 550

pointless 843
poise 27, 319, 852
  mental – 498
poison 659, 663
  – gas 722, 727
poisoned 655
  commend the –
    chalice 544
poisonous 657, 665
poke
  pocket 191
  pig in a –
    uncertain 475
    chance 621
    dawdle 683
    rash 863
  – at 276, 716
  – the fire 384
  – fun at 856
  – one's nose in
    682
  – out project 250
poker 386
  cards 840
polacca 273
polacre 273
polar 210
  cold 383
  – co-ordinates 466
polarization 420
polariscope 445
polarity
  duality 89
  counteraction 179
  contraposition
    237
pole measure of
  length 200
  tall 206
  summit 210
  axis 222
  punt 267
  rotation 312
  greasy – 840
  opposite –s 237
  from – to pole 180
pole-axe 727
polecat 401
pole-star 550, 693
polemic
  discussion 476
  discord 713
  contention 720
  combatant 726
polemoscope 445
police 965
  – court 966
  – magistrate 967
policeman 664, 965
policy 626, 692
polish smooth 255

rub 331
furbish 658
beauty 845
ornament 847
taste 850
politeness 894
– off finish 729
Polish bank 840
polished
  – language 578
  fashionable 852
  polite 894
polisson 949
polite 894
  offensive to ears –
    579
  – literature 560
  – society 852
politic wise 498
  cunning 702
  cautious 864
  body –
    mankind 372
    government 737
political economy
  692
politician
  director 694
  proficient 700
politics 702
polity conduct 692
  authority 737
  duty 926
polka 840
poll 85, 609
  – tax 812
pollard 193, 201
  tree 367
Poll-parrot 584
pollute soil 653
  corrupt 659
  disgrace 874
pollution
  disease 655
  vice 945
Pollyanna 858
polo 840
polonaise 840
poltroon 862
polyandry 903
polychord 417
polychromatic 428,
  440
polychrome 440,
  556
polygamy 903
polygastric 191
polyglot 522, 560
polygon
  buildings 189
  figure 244

polygraphy 590
polylogy 573
polymorphic 81
polyphonism 580
polypus 250
polyscope 445
polysyllable 561
polytheism 984
pomade 356
pomatum 356
pommel
  support 215
  round 249
  beat 972
Pomona 369
pomp 882
pom-pom 727
pomposity 882
pompous
  language 577
poncho 225
pond 343, 636
  fish – 370
ponder 451
ponderable 316,
  319
ponderation 319,
  480
ponderous 319
  – style 574, 579
  dull 843
pondus fumo, dare
  – 481
poniard 727
pons asinorum 519,
  704
pontifical 995
pontificals 999
pontificate 995
pontiff 996
pontoon
  vehicle 272
  boat 273
  way 627
pony 271
poodle 366
pooh, pooh!
  unimportance 643
  contempt 930
pool lake 343
  combination 709
  prize 775
  billiards 840
poop 235
poor weak 160
  – reasoning 477
  – style 575
  insufficient 640
  trifling 643
  indigent 804
  unhappy 828

cut a – figure 874
  – hand 701
  – head 499
  – house 189
  – man 804
  – in spirit 881
  – stick 501
  – thing 914
poorly 160, 655
  – off 804
poor-spirited 862
pop noise 406
  unexpected 508
  – at 716
  – in ingress 294
  insertion 300
  – off die 360
  – a question 461
  – the question
    request 765
    endearment 902
  – upon arrive 292
    discover 480a
Pope
  infallibility 474
  priest 996
Popedom 995
Pope Joan 840
Popery 984
pop-gun trifle 643
popinjay 854
poplar tall 206
poppy sedative 174
populace 876
popular
  in demand 865
  celebrated 873
  favourite 897
  approved 931
  – opinion 488
popularis, aura –
  873
popularize
  render intelligible
    518
  facilitate 705
  make pleasant
    829
populate 184
population 188, 372
populi, vox –
  publication 531
  election 609
  authority 737
populous
  crowded 72
  multitude 102
  presence 186
porcelain
  baked 384
  sculpture 557

hope 858	*bruise* 330	*loud* 404	*medical* - 662
potable 298	*imprison* 752	- *of style* 574	*doer* 690
potage 298	- together 41	*authority* 737	præcognita 467
potager 191	poundage 813	do all in one's –	prænomen 564
potation 298, 959	pounds, shillings,	686	prætor 967
pot-bellied 194	and pence 800	give – 760	Pragmatic
pot-companion 890	pour *emerge* 295	in the – of	Sanction 769
potency 157	*stream* 348	*authority* 737	pragmatical 855,
potent 157, 159	*sufficient* 639	*subjection* 749	880
potentate 745	it never rains but	literary – 569	pragmatism 677
potential	it –s 641	– of attorney 755	prahu 273
inexistent 2	– out blood like	– behind the	prairie *space* 180
potentiality 157,	water 361	throne 694	*plain* 344
470	– a broadside into	– of money 800	*vegetation* 367
pother *disorder* 59	716	powerful 159, 171	praise *thanks* 916
feeling 821	– forth *eject* 297	– voice 580	*commendation*
excitement 825	*speak* 582	powerless 158, 160	931
annoyance 830	*loquacity* 584	powers that be 745	*worship* 990
pot-herbs 393	– forth like water	pow-wow 588, 696	praiseworthy 931,
pot-hooks 590	818	pox 655	944
pot-house 189	– in *converge* 290	praam 273	prame 273
pot-hunter 767	*ingress* 294	practicable 470, 644	prance 266, 315
potion	*sufficiency* 639	practical	prandial 298
beverage 298	– on *lavish* 784	*acting* 170	prank *caprice* 608
medicine 662	– with rain 348	*expedient* 646	*amusement* 840
cordial 992	– water into a	*executive* 692	*adorn* 847
pot-luck *eating* 298	sieve 638, 818	– joke	prate 584
chance 621	– out 295, 297	*absurdity* 497	prattle 582, 584
non-preparation	pourboire 784	*deception* 545	pravity 945
674	pourparler	*ridicule* 856	praxis
take – with 892	*interlocution* 588	*disrespect* 929	*grammar* 567
Potosi 803	*advice* 695	– knowledge 698	*action* 680
pot-pourri	*council* 696	practically	Praxiteles 559
mixture 41	pout *project* 250	*intrinsically* 5	pray 765, 990
fragrance 400	*sad* 837	practice	prayer 765, 990
music 415	*discourteous* 895	*arithmetic* 85	house of – 1000
pottage 298	*irate* 900	*training* 537	prayer-book 998
pottering 682, 683	*sulky* 901a	*habit* 613	preach *teach* 537
pottery *baked* 384	poverty	*conduct* 692	*speak* 582
art 557	*insufficiency* 640	in – *prepared* 673	*predication* 998
pottle 191	*unimportance* 643	*skilled* 698	– to the winds 645
potulent 298, 959	*indigence* **804**	put in – *use* 677	– to the wise 538
pot-valiant 959	– of *intellect* 499	*action* 680	preacher
potwalloper 876	powder 330	*conduct* 692	*teacher* 540
pouch 191	*cosmetics* 847	*complete* 729	*priest* 996
poudre:	food for – 726	out of – 699	preachment 998
qui n'a pas	gun– 727	– of medicine 662	preadamite 124,
inventé la –	smell – 722	practise *train* 537	130
501, 701	keep one's – dry	*use* 677	preamble 64
jeter de la – aux	673	*act* 680	preapprehension
yeux 442	– and shot 727	– at the bar 968	481
poultice *pulp* 354	waste – 638	– on one's credu-	prebend 995
remedy 662	not worth – 645	lity 545	prebendary 996
relief 834	powdered	– upon	precarious
poultry 298, 366	*variegated* 440	*experiment* 463	*transient* 111
pounce upon	powdering	*deceive* 545	*uncertain* 475
unexpected 508	*ornament* 847	practised	*dangerous* 665
attack 716	power	*skilled* 698	precatory 765
seize 789	*much* 31, 102	– eye 700	precaution
pound *inclose* 232	*numerical* 84	– hand 700	*care* 459
weight 319	*efficacy* **157**	practitioner	*expedient* 626

safety 664
preparation 673
precede
  superior 33
  - *in order* 62
  - *in time* 116
  - *in motion* 280
precedence 873
precedent
  [*see* precede]
  prototype 22
  precursor 64
  habit 613
  legal decision 969
  follow –s 82
precentor 694, 996
precept *adage* 496
  maxim **697**
  order 641
  permit 760
preceptor 540
precession 62, **280**
précieuse ridicule
  855
precinct *region* 181
  place 182
  environs 227
  boundary 233
precious *great* 31
  excellent 648
  valuable 814
  beloved 897
  – metals 800
  – stone 648, 847
precipice
  vertical 212
  slope 217
  dangerous 667
  on the verge of
  a – 665
precipitancy 684,
  863
precipitate
  early 132
  sink 308
  consolidate 321
  refuse 653
  haste 684
  rash 863
  – oneself 306
precipitous 217
précis 596
precise *exact* 494
preciosity 578
precisely
  literally 19
  assent 488
precisianism
  affectation 855
  heterodoxy 984
  over-religious 988

preclude 55, 706
precocious
  early 132
  immature 674
  pert 885
  rude 895
precognition
  forethought 490
  knowledge 510
preconceived idea
  481
preconception 481
preconcert 611, 626
preconcertation 673
precursor
  - *in order* 62, **64**
  - *in time* 116
  predict 511
predatory 789, 791
predecessor 64
predeliberation
  510, 611
predella 215
predesigned 611
predestination
  fate 152
  necessity 601
  predetermination
  611
  Deity 976
predetermination
  611
predial
  land 342
  agriculture 371
  manorial 780
predicament 8, 75
predicate
  affirm 535
  preach 998
prediction **511**
predilection
  bias 481
  affection 820
  desire 865
predispose 615, 673
predisposed
  willing 602
predisposition 176,
  820
predominant 175,
  737
predominate 33
pre-eminent 33, 873
pre-emption 795
preen 847
pre-engage 132
pre-engagement
  768
pre-establish 626
pre-examine 461

pre-exist 1, 116
preface 62, 64
prefect 745, 759
prefecture 737
prefer *choose* 609
  – a claim 969
  – a petition 765
preference 62
preferment
  improvement 658
  ecclesiastical -
  995
prefigure 511
prefix 62, 64
  letter 561
pre-glacial 124
pregnable 158
pregnant
  producing 161
  productive 168
  predicting 511
  - *style* 572
  important 642
  – with meaning
  516
prehensile 789
prehension 789
pre-historic 124
pre-instruct 537
prejudge 481
prejudicate 481
prejudice
  misjudge 481
  evil 619
  detriment 659
prejudicial 481, 649
prelacy 995
prelate 996
prelation 609
prelection 537, 582
prelector 540
preliminaries:
  settle – 673
  – of peace 723
preliminary 62, 64
prelude 62, 64
  beginning 66
  music 415
premature 132, 674
premeditate 611,
  620
prémices 154
premier 694, 759
  – pas 66
premiership 693
premise *prefix* 62
  precede 116
  announce 511
premises
  precursor 64
  prior 116

ground 182
evidence 467
logic 476
premium
  debt 805
  receipt 810
  reward 783
  at a – 814
premonish 668
premonitory 511,
  668
Premonstratensian
  996
premonstration
  appearance 448
  prediction 511
  manifestation 525
premunire 742, 974
prendre la balle au
  bond 134
prenotion
  misjudgment 481
  foresight 510
prensation 789
prentice 541
prenticeship 539
preoccupancy
  possession 777
preoccupation
  inattention 458
preoption 609
preordain 152, 601
preparation **673**
  music 413
  instruction 537
  in – 730
  in course of – 626
preparatory
  preceding 62
prepare the way
  facilitate 705
prepared *expectant*
  507
  ready 698
preparing
  destined 152
prepense
  spontaneous 600
  predetermined
  611
  intended 620
  malice – 907
prepollence 157
πρέπον, τό – 850,
  926
preponderance
  superiority 33
  influence 175
  dominance 737
prepossessed
  obstinate 606

experience 137
prevision 510
pre-war 116
prewarn 668
prey *food* 298
  quarry 620
  booty 793
  victim 732, 828
fall a — to
  be defeated 732
  subjection 749
  — to grief 828
  — to melancholy
    837
  — on the mind
  excite 824
  regret 833
  fear 860
  — on the spirits
    837
price
  consideration 147
  value 648
  money 812
  reward 973
  at any — 604*a*
  beyond — 814
  cheap at the — 815
  of great —
  good 648
  dear 814
  have one's — 812
price-current 812
priceless
  valueless 645
  dear 814
prick *sharp* 253
  hole 260
  sting 378
  sensation of touch
    380
  incite 615
  mental suffering
    830
  kick against the –s
  useless 645
  resistance 719
  — up one's ears
  hear 418
  curiosity 455
  attention 457
  expect 707
prickle 253, 380
pride
  ornament 847
  loftiness **878**
  take a — in 878
prie-dieu 211
priest 996
priestcraft 995
priesthood 995, 996

priest-ridden 988,
  995
prig *steal* 791
  puppy 854
  affected 855
  blusterer 887
priggish 855, 880
prim *affected* 855
  fastidious 868
  proud 878
prima: — donna
  actress 599
  important 642
  proficient 700
  — facie *sight* 441
  appearance 448
  probable 472
  - *meaning* 516
  manifest 525
primacy
  superiority 33
  celebrity 873
  church 995
primary
  original 20
  cause 153
  important 642
  — colour 428
  — education 537
primarily 66
primate 996
primates 875
prime
  primeval 124
  early 132
  teach 537
  important 642
  excellent 648
  prepare 673
  in one's — 131
  in the — of man-
    hood 159
  — cost *price* 812
  cheap 815
  — of life *youth* 127
  adolescence 131
  — and load 673
  — minister 694
  — of the morning
    125
  — mover 153
  — number 84
prime constituent 1
primed
  skilled 698
  tipsy 959
primer 542
primeval 124
  — forest 367
primigenous 124
primitive 124, 153

— colour 428
primogenial 66
primogeniture
  old 124
  age 128
  posterity 167
primordial 20, 124,
  153
primordinate 124
primrose-coloured
  436
primum:
  — mobile 153, 615
primus inter pares
  33
prince
  perfection 650
  master 745
  nobility 875
  — of darkness 978
princely
  authoritative 737
  liberal 816
  famous 873
  noble 875
  generous 942
princeps
  facile — 33
princess 745, 875
principal
  important 642
  director 694
  — part 31, 50
principality 181,
  780
principally 33
principia 66, 496
principiis obstare
  673
principle
  intrinsic 5
  rule 80
  cause 153
  element 316
  idea 453
  reasoning 476
  tenet 484
  maxim 496
  motive 615
  probity 939
  on — 615
  want of — 945
principled, high-
  939
prink 847, 882
print *copy* 21
  mark 550
  engraving 558
  letter-press 591
  out of — 552
printer 591

printing 531, **591**
  — telegraph 553
prior
  - *in order* 62
  - *in time* 116
  clergy 996
priori reasoning,
  a — 476
priority **116**, 234
priory 1000
Priscian's head,
  break — 568
prism
  angularity 244
  optical 445
  see through a —
    443
prismatic
  colour 428
  variegated 440
prison **752**
  cast into — 751
  in — 754
prisoner **754**, 938
  take — 751, 789
prison-house
  secrets of the —
    529, 533
pristine 20, 122
prithee 765
prittle-prattle 588
private *special* 79
  hidden 528
  secluded 893
  to gain some —
    ends 943
  in — 528
  keep — 881
  talk to in — 586,
    588
  — road 627
  — soldier 726
privateer 726, 792
privateering 791
privately 881
privation 776, 804
privative 789
privilege
  freedom 748
  permission 760
  exemption 777*a*
  due 924
privity 490
privy *hidden* 528
  latrines 653
  — to 490
Privy Council 966
prize *good* 618
  palm 733
  gain 775
  booty 793

receipt 810
love 897
approve 931
reward 973
win the – 731
– open 173
prizer 767
prize-fighter 726
prize-fighting 720
prizeman 700
pro: – and con
  476, 615
– formâ 82
– hâc vice
  special 79
  present time 118
  occasion 134
  seldom 137
– rata 23
– re natâ
  circumstances 8
  relation 9
  special 79
  occasion 134
  conditions 770
– tanto 26, 32
– tempore 111
proa 273
probability 156, **472**
probable 858
probate 771
Probate Court 966
probation
  trial 463
  demonstration
  478
probationary 463,
  675
probationer 541
probative 478
probatum est 478,
  931
probe *depth* 208
  perforator 262
  investigate 461
  measure 466
probity **939**
problem *topic* 454
  question 461
  enigma 533
problematical 475
proboscis 250
procacity
  insolence 885
  rudeness 895
  irascibility 901
procedure
  method 627
  action 680
  conduct 692
proceed *time* 109

advance 282
– from 154
– with 692
proceeding
  incomplete 53
  event 151
  action 680
  not finished 730
  course of – 692
proceedings 551
proceeds *gain* 775
  money 800
  receipts 810
procerity 206
procès-verbal
  record 551
  law proceeding
  969
process
  projection 250
  conduct 692
  legal – 963
  – engraving 558
  – of time 109
  in – of time 117
procession
  continuity 69
  march 266
  ceremony 882
processional
  rite 998
prochronism 115
proclaim 531
proclivity 176, 820
proconsul 759
proconsulship 737
procrastination 133,
  460, 683
procreant 168
procreate 161, 168
procreator 166
procrustean 82
  – law 80
Procrustes:
  stretch on the bed
  of – 27
proctor *teacher* 540
  officer 694, 965
  consignee 758
  lawyer 968
proctorship 693
procumbent 213
procurator 694
procuration 170,
  755
procure *cause* 153
  induce 615
  get 775
  buy 795
procuress 962
procurement 170

prod 276
prodigal 641, 816
prodigality **818**
prodigious 31, 870
prodigy 83, **872**
  – of learning 700
prodition 940
prodrome 64
produce
  increase 35
  cause 153
  effect 154
  create 161
  prolong 200
  show 525
  stage 599
  fru t 775
  merchandise 798
  – itself 446
producer **164**
product
  multiple 85
  effect 154
  harvest 636
  gain 775
  finished – 154
production 54, **161**
  [*and see* pro-
  duce]
productive
  cause 153
  power 157
  inventive 515
  profitable 775
productiveness **168**
proem 64
proemial
  preceding in order
  62
  beginning 66
profane
  desecrate 679
  impious 988
  laical 997
  – swearing 908
profanum vulgus
  876
profession
  assertion 535
  pretence 546
  business 625
  promise 768
  enter a – 625
  – of faith 484, 983
professional 700
  – mourner 363,
  839
professor 492, 540,
  700
professorship 542
proffer 763

proficient
  knowledge 490
  skill 698
  adept **700**
proficuous 644
profile
  outline 230
  side 236
  appearance 448
  portraiture 556
profit
  increase 35
  advantage 618
  utility 644
  acquisition 775
  – by use 677
  – sharing 778
profitable
  useful 644
  good 648
  gainful 775
profitless 646
profligacy 945
profluent
  progressive 282
  stream 348
profound
  great 31
  deep 208
  learned 490
  wise 498
  sagacious 702
  feeling 821
  – attention 457
  – knowledge 490
  – secret 533
profundis, de –
  839, 950
profuse
  diffuse style 573
  redundant 641
  prodigal 818
profusion 102, 639
prog 298
progenerate 161
progenitive 163
progenitor 166
progeny 167
prognosis 510, 511,
  522, 655
prognostic 511, 512
prognosticate 511
prognostication 507
programme
  catalogue 86
  publication 531
  plan 626
progress
  growth 144
  motion 264
  advance 282

in – *incomplete*
53, 730
make – 282
in mid – 270
– of science 490
– of time 109
progression
gradation 58
series 69
numerical – 84
motion **282**
progressive
continuous 69
course 109
advancing 282
improving 658
prohibition 761
exclusion 55
stoppage 706
teetotalism 953,
958
project *bulge* 250
impel 284
intend 620
plan 626
projectile 727
projection *map* 554
projector
lantern 423
film 445
designer 626
prolation 580, 582
prole, sine – 169
prolegomena 64
prolepsis 64, 115
proletarian 876
prolific 168
prolix 573
prolocutor
interpreter 524
teacher 540
speaker 582
prologue
precursor 64
drama 599
prolong
protract 110
late 133
continue 143
lengthen 200
prolongation 63,
143
prolusion 64
prom 892
promenade 266
display 882
on pier 189
Promethean 359
prominent
convex 250
manifest 525

important 642
eminent 873
prominently 31, 33
promiscuous
mixed 41
irregular 59
indiscriminate
465a
casual 621
promise
predict 511
engage **768**
hope 858
keep one's – 939
keep – to ear and
break to hope
545
– oneself 507, 858
promissory 768
– note 771, 800
promontory
height 206
projection 250
land 342
promote 153, 658,
707
promoter 626
promotion 658
prompt *early* 132
remind 505
tell 527
induce 615
active 682
advise 695
– memory 505
prompter
drama 599
motive 615
adviser 695
promptuary 636
promulgate 531
– a decree 741
pronation and
supination 218
prone
horizontal 213
proneness
tendency 176
disposition 820
prôner 882, 931
prôneur 935
prong 91
pronounce
judge 480
assert 535
voice 580
speak 582
pronounced 525
pronouncement 531
pronunciamento
531

pronunciation 580
pronunciative 535
proof *hard* 323
insensible 376
test 463
demonstration
478
printing 591
draft 626
ocular – 446
– against
strong 159
resolute 604
safe 664
defence 717
resistance 719
insensible 823
prop 215, 707
propædeutics 537
propagable 168
propaganda 537,
542
propagandism 537
propagandist 540,
996
propagate
produce 161
be productive 168
publish 531
propel 284
propellant 727
propeller 267, 312
propend 602
propendency
predetermination
611
inclination 820
propense 602
propension 820
propensity 176, 820
proper *special* 79
expedient 646
handsome 845
due 924
– name 564
in its – place 58
show a – spirit
939
the – thing 926
– time 134
properties
theatrical – 225,
599
property *power* 157
possessions **780**
wealth 803
property-man 599
prophecy 511
prophet 513, 996
false –s 986
in the name of the

– figs! 497
prophetic 511, 985
Prophets, the – 985
prophylactic
healthful 656
remedy 662
preservative 670
hindrance 706
prophylaxis 670
propinquity 197
propitiate
pacify 723, 724
calm 826
content 831
love 897
pity 914
forgive 918
atone 952
worship 990
propitious
timely 134
beneficial 648
helping 707
prosperous 734
auspicious 858
proplasm 22
proportion
relation 9
degree 26
mathematical 84
symmetry 242
style 578
allotment 786
proportionate
agreeing 23
proportions 180,
192
proposal *plan* 626
propose
suggest 514
broach 535
intend 620
offer 763
offer marriage
912
– a question 461
proposition
supposition 454
reasoning 476
project 626
suggestion 514
offer 763
propound 514, 535
– a question 461
propriâ personâ
in – *speciality* 79
presence 186
proprietary 779
proprietor 779
proprietorship 780
propriety

proximate
next 63
near 197
– cause 153
proximity *near* 197
adjacent 199
proximo 121
proximus ardet
danger 665, 667
proxy 634, 759
prude *affected* 855
chaste 960
prudent
careful 459
wise 498
economical 817
cautious 864
prudery 855, 868
prudish 739
prune
take away 38
lop 201, 371
repair 658
prunes and prisms
855
prunello, leather
or – 643
prurience 865, 961
Prussian blue 438
Prussic acid 663
pry *look* 441
curiosity 455
inquire 461
– into the future
510
Prytaneum 931
psalm 415, 990
psalm-book 998
psalmody 415, 998
psalter 998
psaltery 417
psephomancy 511
pseudo 17, 545
pseudoblepsis 443
pseudonym 565
pseudo-revelation
986
pseudoscope 445
pshaw
trifling 643
excitement 825
psychiatry 662
psychical 450
psycho-analysis
662
psychological
moment 824
Psychology 450
Psychomancy 511
psycho-therapy 662
ptisan 662

ptomaine poisoning
663
ptyalism 229
puberty 127
pubescent 131
public, general –
372
make – 531
– enemy 891
– good 644
– opinion 488
– press 531
– school 542
– spirit 910
– welfare 910
publican 637
publication **531**
production 161
book 593
public-house 189
go to the – 959
publicist 593, 595,
968
publicity 531
publicly rumoured
532
publico, pro bono –
644, 910
publish 531
– the banns 765
publisher 593
puce 433, 437
pucelage *youth* 127
celibacy 904
purity 960
Puck 980
play – 699
pucker *fold* 258
anger 900
in a – 824
pudder
disorder 59
pudding *food* 298
soft 324
pulpy 354
sweets 396
in – time 132
Pudding, Jack –
599
puddle 343
pudicity 960
pudor, proh –
874
puerile *boyish* 129
foolish 499
feeble 575
trifling 643
puerperal 161
puff *inflate* 194
wind 349
tartlet 396

exaggerate 482
advertisement 531
pant 688
boast 884
praise 931
flatter 933
– of smoke 330
– out 194
– up *vanity* 880
puffed up
exaggerated 482
pride 878
puffer 935
puffery 884
puffy 194
pug *short* 201
dog 366
pugilist 726
pugh! 643
pugilism 720
pugilist 726
pugilistic 720
pugnacity 720, 901
puisné
posterior 117
young 127
puissant 157, 159
puke 297
pukka 494
pulchritude 845
pulcinella 599, 844
pule *cry* 411, 412
weep 839
pull *superiority* 33
influence 175
row 267
draw 285
printing 591
a long and a
strong – 709
strong – 636
– the check string
142
– different ways
713
– down 162, 308
– about one's ears
308
– in 751
– an oar 680
– out 301
– to pieces
separate 44
destroy 162
censure 932
detract 934
– upon the purse
814
– by the sleeve
505
– the strings 631

– through 660,
707
– together 709
– towards 288
– up *stop* 142
rest 265
root out 301
reprimand 932
accuse 969
– the wires 693
pulled down 160,
688
pullet 129
pulley 633
Pullman car 272
pullulate
produce 161
multiply 168
grow 194
pulmonary 349
pulmotor 349
pulp 354
pulpiness **354**
pulpit *rostrum* 542
church 1000
the – 996
pulsate
periodic 138
oscillate 314
agitate 315
pulsation
feeling 821
pulse [*see* pulsate]
vegetable 367
feel the –
inquire 461
test 463
pulsion 276
pultaceous 354
pulverize 330
destroy 162
dust 358
pulverulence **330**
pulvil 400
pummel
[*see* pommel]
pump *shoe* 225
water supply 348
inquire 461
– up 349
pump-room
house 189
remedy 662
pun *similarity* 17
absurdity 497
ambiguity 520
wit 842
punce 276
punch *mould* 22
perforate 260
perforator 262

end 67
stop 142
destroy 162
- *oneself* 361
- in force
complete 729
compel 744
- forth
expand 194
suggest 514
publish 531
assert 535
- *a question* 461
- *strength* 686
- forward
suggest 514
publish 531
ostentation 882
- one's hand to 676
- the horses to 673
- in [*see below*]
- to inconvenience 647
- a mark upon 457
- one's nose out of joint 33
- off *late* 133
divest 226
depart 293
plea 617
- on *clothe* 225
deceive 544
hasten 684
affect 855
- out [*see below*]
- on paper 551
- over 484, 731
- a question 461
- right 660
- the saddle on the right horse 155
- the seal to 729, 769
- to [*see below*]
- together *join* 43
combine 48
assemble 161
- one's trust in 484
- up [*see below*]
- upon 545, 649
put in *arrive* 292
insert 300
- an affidavit 535
- hand 676
- one's head 514
- mind 505
- motion 264
- order 60

- the place of 147
- one's pocket 785
- practice 692
- remembrance 505
- shape 60
- trim 60, 673
- the way of 470
- a word 582, 588
put out
destroy 162
outside 220
extinguish 385
darken 421
distract the attention 458
uncertain 475
difficult 704
discontent 832
- of countenance 874
oneself - of court
sophistry 477
bungling 699
- of gear 158
- of one's head 458
- of joint 61
- of one's misery 914
- to nurse 707
- of order 59
put to *attribute* 155
request 765
- the blush 879
- death 361
- the door 261
- it 704
- one's oath 768
- press 591
- the proof 463
- the question 830
- the rack 830
- rights 60
- sea 293
- shame 874
- silence 581
- the sword 361
- task 677
- use 677
- the vote 609
put up *assemble* 72
locate 184
store 636
- to auction 796
- for 865
- a petition } 765
- a prayer } 990
- for sale 796
- a shutter 424
- the sword 723

- to 615
- with 147, 826
putative
attributed 155
believed 484
supposed 514
putid 643
putrefy 653
putrescence 49
putrid 653
putsch 742
puttee 225
putter 683
putting the weight 840
putty 45
puzzle *uncertain* 475
conceal 528
enigma 533
- out 522
puzzled 475, 533
puzzle-headed 499
puzzling 519
pyæmia 655
pyjamas 225
Pylades and Orestes 890
pylon 206
pyramid *heap* 72
height 206
point 253
pyramids
billiards 840
pyre 363
pyriform 249
pyrology 282
pyromaniac 384, 504, 913
pyromancy 511
pyrometer 389
pyrotechnics 423
pyrotechny 382
Pyrrhic victory 814
pyrrhonism 487, 989
Pythagorean 953
Pythia *oracle* 513
Python, -ess 513
pyx *vessel* 191, 998
temple 1000

Q

Q-boat 726
Q.C. 968
Q.E.D. 478
quack *cry* 412
imposter 548

quackery
falsehood 544
want of skill 699
affectation 855
quacksalver 548
quad 189
quadragesima 956
quadrangle
four-sided 95
precinct 182
house 189
angular 244
quadrant 244, 247
quadrate with 23
quadratic 95
quadrature
four 95
angle 244
quadrennial 95
quadrible 96
quadrifid 97
quadriga 95, 272
quadrilateral
sides 236
angles 244
quadrille 840
quadripartition 97
quadrisection **97**
quadrivalent 95
quadroon 41
quadruped 366
quadruplet 96
quadruplex 96
quadruplication **96**
quære 461
quaff 298
- the bitter cup 828
quaggy 345
quagmire
marsh 345
dirty 653
difficult 704
quail 860, 862
quaint *odd* 83
pretty 845
ridiculous 853
quake *oscillate* 314
shake 315
cold 383
fear 860
quakerish 826, 855
Quakerism 984
qualification
[*see qualify*]
power 157
modification **469**
skill 698
discount 813
qualify *change* 140
modify 469

angry 900
censure 932
punish 972
– out *affirm* 535
voice 580
speak 582
– out oaths 885, 908
rapacity
taking 789
stealing 791
avarice 819
greed 865
rape 791, 961
– oil 356
rapid 274
– slope 217
– strides
progress 282
velocity 274
– succession 136
rapids 348
rapier 727
rapine 791
rapparee 792
rappel 722
rapping, spirit – 992
rapport 9
rapports, sous tous les – 494
rapprochement 714, 888
rapscallion 949
rapt *attention* 457
inattention 458
emotion 821
– in thought 451
raptorial 789, 791
rapture 827, 897
rapturous 827
rara avis
exceptional 83
good 648
famous 873
rare *exceptional* 83
few 103
infrequent 137
light 322
excellent 648
raree show 448, 840
rarefaction 194, 322
rari nantes 103
rarity 322
rasa, tabula – 552
rascal 941, 949
rascality 940
rase *obliterate* 552
rash
skin disease 655
reckless 863

rasher 204
rashness 863
rasp 330, 331
rasper *difficult* 704
rasure 552
rat *recant* 607
smell a –
discover 480a
doubt 485
rataplan 407
rat-a-tat 407
ratchet 253
rate *degree* 26
motion 264
measure 466
estimation 480
price, tax 812
abuse 932
at a great – 274
rath *early* 132
fort 717
rather 32, 643
have – 609
– good 651
have – not 867
ratification
confirm 467
affirm 488
consent 762
compact 769
ratio *relation* 9
degree 26
proportion 84
apportionment 786
ratiocination 476
ration *quantity* 25
food 298
provisions 637
allotment 786
short –s 956
rational
– *quantity* 84
intellectual 450
judicious 498
sane 502
rationale *cause* 153
attribution 155
answer 462
interpretation 322
rationalism 476, 989
rationalization 60
rats in the upper story 503
rattan 975
ratten 158
rattle *noise* 407
music 417
prattle 584
death – 360

watchman's – 669
– on 584
rattle-snake 913
rattle-traps 780
rattling 836
– pace 274
raucity 405, 410
raucous *hoarse* 581
ravage 162, 659
ravages of time 659
rave *madness* 503
excitement 824, 825
– against 932
ravel *untwist* 60
derange 61
entangle 219
difficulty 704
ravelin 717
ravelled 59
raven *black* 431
hoarse 581
gorge 957
– for 865
ravening 173, 865
ravenous 789, 865
raver 504
ravine *interval* 198
narrow 203
dike 259
channel 350
raving *mad* 503
feeling 821
excitement 824, 825
ravish *seize* 789
please 829
ravished
pleased 827
ravishment 824
raw *immature* 123
sensitive 378
cold 383
colour 428
unprepared 674
unskilled 699
– head and bloody bones 860
– levies 726
– material 635
raw-boned 203
ray 420
– of comfort 831
rayah 745
rayless 421
raze 162
– to the ground 308
razor 253
cut a whetstone with a – 638

misuse 679
unskilful 699
keen as a – 821
razzia
destruction 162
attack 716
plunder 791
re, in – 9
reabsorb 296
reach *degree* 26
equal 27
distance 196
fetch 270
arrive at 292
river 348
deceive 545
grasp 737
take 789
within – *near* 197
possible 470
– the ear
hearing 418
information 527
– of thought 498
– to *distance* 196
length 200
reach-me-down 673
reaction
compensation 30
reversion 145
counteraction 179
recoil 277
restoration 660
reactionary 145, 607
reactionist 710
read 522, 539
well – 490
– a lecture 537
readable 578
reader *teacher* 540
printer 591
clergyman 996
readership 542
readily 705
reading
speciality 79
knowledge 490
interpretation 522
learning 539
– glass 445
– in 995
reading-desk 1000
readjust 23, 27
readmit 296
ready
expecting 507
willing 602
useful 644
prepare 673

active 682
skilful 698
cash 800
get – 673
make – 673
– to burst forth
  825
– made 673
– memory 505
– money 800
– pen 569
– to sink 824
– wit 842
reaffirm 535
reagent 463
real *existing* 1
  substantial 3
  - *number* 84
  true 494
– estate 780
– property 780
– security 771
realism 494
realistic 17
realize
  speciality 79
  intellect 450
  think 451
  discover 480a
  believe 484
  conceive 490
  imagine 515
  accomplish 729
  acquire 775
  sell 796
really *wonder* 870
realm *region* 181
  people 372
  government 737
  property 780
realness 1
realty 780
ream 593
reamer 262
reanimate
  reproduce 163
  life 359
  resuscitate 660
reap *shorten* 201
  agriculture 371
  take 789
– the benefit of
  be better for 658
– and carry 775
– the fruits
  succeed 731
  acquire 775
  reward 973
– where one has
  not sown 923
– the whirlwind

product 154
failure 732
reappear
  repetition 104
  reproduce 163
  visible 446
  restore 660
rear *sequel* 65
  end 67
  bring up 161
  erect 212
  back **235**
  elevate 307
  teach 537
  in the – 281
– its head
  manifest 525
– one's head
  pride 878
rear-admiral 745
reason *cause* 153
  intellect 450
  thought 451
  argue 476
  wisdom 498
  motive 615
  by – of 615
  feast of – 588
  in – *moderate* 174
  right 922
  listen to – 498
  stand to –
    certain 474
    proof 478
    manifest 525
  what's the – ? 461
  without rhyme
    or – 615a
– in a circle 477
– why 153, 615
reasonable
  moderate 174
  probable 472
  judicious 498
  sane 502
  cheap 815
  right 922
– prospect 472
reasoner 476
reasoning **476**
reasonless 499
reasons 476
reassemble 72
reassert 535
reassure 858, 861
reasty 401, 653
reave 789
rebate
  subtract 38
  decrement 40a
  moderate 174

discount 813
rebeck 417
rebel 742
rebellion 715
rebellow 412
rebirth 660
reboation 412
rebound 277, 283
rebours, à –
  reversion 145
  regression 283
  difficult 704
rebuff *recoil* 277
  resist 719
  repulse 732
  refuse 764
  discourtesy 895
  censure 932
rebuild 660
rebuke 932
rebus 533
rebut *answer* 462
  counter evidence
    468
  confute 479
  deny 536
rebutter 462, 969
recalcitrant 719,
  742
recalcitrate 277,
  719
recalescence 382
recall
  recollect 505
  recant 607
  cancel 756
– to life 660
recant *deny* 536
  retract 607
  resign 756
recapitulate
  enumerate 85
  repeat 104
  describe 594
  summarize 596
recast
  revolution 146
  scheme 626
recede 283, 287
– into the shade
  874
receipt
  scheme 626
  prescription 662
  precept 697
  security 771
  payment 807
– *of money* **810**
– in full 807
receive *include* 76
  admit 296

belief 484
assent 488
acquire 775
take in 785
take 789
– *money* 810
welcome 892, 894
– Christ 987
received *known* 490
  habitual 613
– maxim 496
receiver
  vessel 191
  treasurer 801
  official – 967
– of stolen goods
  792
receiving **785**
recension 85
recent 122, 123
receptacle **191**
reception
  comprehension 54
  inclusion 76
  arrival 292
  ingestion **296**
  interview 588
  receiving 785
  welcome 892, 894
  warm – 892
reception-room 191
recess
  receptacle 191
  corner 244
  regression 283
  ambush 530
  vacation 687
  retirement 893
recesses
  interior 221
  secret – of one's
    heart 820
recession
  motion from **287**
Rechabite 958
réchauffé *copy* 21
  repetition 104
  food 298
  made hot 384
  restored 660
recherché 648, 852
recidivation
  regression 283
  relapse 607, 661
recipe *remedy* 662
  precept 697
recipient 191, 785
reciprocal 12, 84
reciprocate
  correlation 12
  interchange 148

assent 488
concord 714
retaliate 718
reciprocity 709
recision 38
recital 415
recitativo 415
recite
  enumerate 85
  speak 582
  narrate 594
reck 459
reckless
  careless 460
  defiant 715
  rash 863
recklessly profuse
  818
reckon *count* 85
  – among 76
  – upon 484, 507
  – with 807
  – without one's
    host
  unskilful 699
  fail 732
  rash 863
reckoning
  numeration 85
  measure 466
  expectation 507
  payment 807
  accounts 811
  reward 973
  day of – 919
  out of one's – 704
reclaim *restore* 660
  command 741
  due 924
  atonement 952
reclaimed
  penitent 950
recline *lie flat* 213
  depress 308
  repose 687
  – on 215
recluse 893
recognition
  [*see* recognize]
  courtesy 894
  thanks 916
  means of – 550
recognizable 446,
  518
  – by 550
recognizance 771
recognize *see* 441
  attention 457
  discover 480a
  assent 488
  know 490

remember 505
understand 518
permit 760
recognized
  influential 175
  customary 613
  – maxim 496
recoil *reaction* 179
  repercussion **277**
  reluctance 603
  shun 623
  from which
    reason –s 471
  – at *hate* 898
  – from *dislike* 867
recollect 505
recommence 66
recommend 695,
  931
  – itself
  approbation 931
recompense 790,
  973
reconcile *agree* 23
  pacify 723
  content 831
  forgive 918
  – oneself to 826
recondite 519, 528
recondition 660,
  790
reconnaissance 441
reconnoitre 441,
  461
reconsideration 451
  on – 658
reconstitute 660
reconstruct 660
reconvert 660
record **551**
  break the – 33
  court of – 966
  gramophone – 551
recorder **553**
  judge 967
recount 594
recoup 30, 790
recourse 677
recovery
  improvement 658
  reinstatement 660
  getting back 775
  restitution 790
  – of strength 689
recreant
  coward 862
  base 940
  knave 941
  vicious 945
  bad man 949
recreation 840

recrement 653
recriminate 932
recrimination 938
recrudescence 661
recruit *strength* 159
  learner 541
  provision 637
  health 654
  repair 658
  reinstate 660
  refresh 689
  aid 707
  auxiliary 711
  soldier 726
  beat up for –s
    673, 707
rectangle 244
rectangular 214,
  244
rectify
  straighten 246
  improve 658
  re-establish 660
rectilinear 346
rectitude 939, 944
rector 694, 996
rectorship 995
rectory 1000
rectus in curiâ 946
reculer pour mieux
  sauter 673, 702
reculons, à – 283
recumbent 213, 217
recuperation 790
recuperative 660
recur
  repeat 104
  frequent 136
  periodic 138
  – to the mind 505
  – to 677
recure 660
recursion 292
recurvity 245
recusant
  dissenting 489
  denying 536
  disobedient 742
  refusing 764
  impenitent 951
  heterodox 984
red 434
  paint the town –
    840
  turn – *feeling* 821
  – book *list* 86
  – coat 726
  – cross 662
  – flag 668
  – hot *great* 31
  violent 173

  hot 382
  emotion 821
  excited 824
  – letter 550, 883
  –letter day
  important 642
  rest 687
  amusement 840
  celebration 883
  – light 669
  – rag to a bull 900
  – republican 742
  – tape 613
  – tapist 694
  – and yellow 439
redact 590, 658
redan 717
redargue 479
red cap 271
redden *colour* 434
  humble 879
  angry 900
reddition
  interpretation 522
  restitution 790
redeem
  compensate 30
  substitute 147
  reinstate 660
  deliver 672
  regain 775
  restore 790
  pay 807
  atone 952
  – from oblivion
    505
  – one's pledge
    772, 926
Redeemer 976
redemption
  [*see* redeem]
  liberation 750
  duty 926
  salvation 976
red-handed
  murder 361
  in the act 680
  guilty 947
redict 905
redingote 225
redintegrate 660
redintegratio
  amoris 607
redivivus 660
redness **434**
redolence
  odour 398
  fragrance 400
redouble
  increase 35
  duplication 90

piety 987
regeneration
  divine function 976
  baptismal – 998
regent 745, 759
regicide 361
régime
  circumstances **8**
  conduct 692
  authority 737
  ancien – 875
regimen *diet* 298
  remedy 662
  conduct 692
regiment 72, 726
regimentals 225
region 181
register
  arrange 60
  list 86
  chronicle 114
  record 551, 553
registrar 553
registration 551
registry 114
règle: en – 924
regnant 175, 737
regni, anno – 106
regorge 790
regrade 283
regrate 777
regrater 797
regression 283
regret 833, 950
  express – 952
  regretted, to be – 833
reguerdon 973
regular
  uniform 16
  complete 52
  order 58
  arrangement 60
  rule 80
  conformity 82
  periodic 138
  symmetric 242
  habitual 613
  by – intervals 58
  – return 138
régulars 726
regulate
  adjust 23
  arrange 60
  direct 693
regulated by
  conformity 82
regulation 697, 963
regurgitate
  return 283

flow 348
  restore 790
rehabilitate 660, 790
rehearse
  repeat 104
  try 463
  describe 594
  drama 599
  prepare 673
Reichsrath 696
reign 175, 737
  – of terror 739, 860
reimburse 790, 807
rein 752
  – in 275, 751
reincarnation 163
reindeer 271
re infectâ 304, 681
reinforce
  strengthen 159
  restore 660
  aid 707
reinforced concrete 635
reinforcement
  addition 37
  adjunct 39
  materials 635
  provision 637
  aid 707
reinless 738
reins [*see* rein]
  direction 693
  give the – to
  facilitate 705
  lax 738
  permit 760
  hold the – 693
  take the – 737
  give – to the im-
    agination 515
reinstall 660
reinstate 660, 790
reinvest 790
reinvigorate 658, 689
Reis Effendi 694
reiterate 104
reject
  exclude 55
  eject 297
  refuse 764
rejected
  hateful 898
rejection 610
rejoice *exult* 838
  amuse 840
  – the heart
  gratify 829
  cheer 836

– in 827
– in the name of 564
rejoicing 838
rejoin *assemble* 72
  arrive 292
rejoinder
  answer 462
  law pleadings 969
rejuvenescence 660
rekindle
  ignite 384
  excite 824
relapse
  turn back 145, 283
  fall back **661**
relate *narrate* 594
  – to *refer* 9
related *kin* 11
relation 9
  kin 11
  narrative 594
relationship 9
relative 11, 464
  – *position*
relativity 9
relator
  accuser 938
relax *loose* 47
  weaken 160
  moderate 174
  slacken speed 275
  soften 324
  inactive 683
  repose 687
  misrule 738
  liberate 750
  relent 914
  – one's efforts 681
  – the mind 452
relaxation
  [*see* relax]
  amusement 840
  dereliction 927
relaxed *weak* 160
relay 635, 637
release *death* 360
  deliverance 672
  liberate 750
  exempt 760
  from engagement **768a**
  security 771
  restore 790
  repay 807
  forgive 918
  exempt 927a
  discharge 970
  deed of – 923
relegate *banish* 55

transfer 270
  remove 297
relent *moderate* 174
  soften 324
  pity 914
relentless
  resolute 604
  severe 739
  wrathful 900
  malevolent 907
  revenge 919
  impenitent 951
relessee
  possessor 779
  receiver 785
relevancy 9, 23
relevé 298
reliable 474
reliance
  confidence 484
  hope 858
relic *remainder* 40
  reminiscence 505
  token 551
relics *corpse* 362
  sacred 998
relict 40, 905
relief
  prominence 250
  aid 707
  comfort **834**
  bas – 250, 557
  in strong – 446, 525
relieve *improve* 658
  aid 707
  comfort 834
relievo 250, 557
religieuse 996
religion 983, 987
  under the mask of – 988
religionist 988
religious
  honourable 939
  theological 983
  pious 987
  over– 955
  – education 537
  – persuasion 983
  – sects 984
religiously exact 494
relinquish 757
  – hope 859
  – life 360
  – property 782
  – a purpose 624
  recant 607
relinquishment 624, 782

choose 609
store 636
disuse 678
retain 781
shyness 881
in – destined 152
  prepared 673
– forces 726
– oneself 881
reservoir 636
re-shape 140
resiance 189
resiant 186
reside 1, 186
residence 189
resident
  consignee 758
  present 186
  inhabitant 188
residentiary 186,
  188
  clergy 996
residue 40
residuum
  remainder 40
  dregs 653
  commonalty 876
resign 757, 782
– one's being 364
– one's breath 360
– oneself 725, 826
resignation [see
  resign]
  submission 725
  obedience 743
  abdication 757
  renunciation 782
  endurance 826
  humility 879
resile 277
resilience
  regression 283
  elasticity 325
resin 356a
resipiscence 950
resist oppose 179
  withstand 719
  disobey 742
  refuse 764
resistance 719
résistance, pièce de
  – 298
resister
  passive – 710
resisting
  tenacious 327
resistless 159, 601
resolute 604, 861
resolution
  decomposition 49
  conversion 144

music 413
topic 454
investigation 461
mental energy 604
intention 620
scheme 626
courage 861
resolvable into 27,
  144
resolve change 140
  liquefy 335
  investigate 461
  discover 480a
  interpret 522
  determine 604
  predetermine 611
  intend 620
– into elements 49
– into convert 144
resonance 402, 408
resorb 296
resort assemble 72
  focus 74
  dwelling 189
  converge 290
last – 601
– to be present 186
  travel 266
  employ 677
resound loud 404
  ring 408
– praises 931
resourceful 698
resources
  means 632
  property 780
  wealth 803
respect relation 9
  observe 772
  fame 873
  salutation 894
  deference 928
have – to 9
in no – 536
with – to 9
respectability
  mediocrity 736
  repute 873
  probity 939
respectable
  unimportant 643
respectful 928
– distance 623,
  864
respective 79, 786
respectless 458
respects 894, 928
resperse 73
respicere finem 510
respire breathe 349
  live 359

refresh 689
respite
  intermission 106
  defer 133
  pause 142
  deliver 672
  repose 687
  reprieve 970
resplendent
  luminous 420
  splendid 845
respond accord 23
  answer 462
  feel 821
respondent 462
  accused 938
response
  answer 462, 587
  concord 714
  feeling 821
  friendship 888
  worship 990
responsible 177,
  926
responsibility
  upon one's own –
  600
responsive 375
rest remainder 40
  pause 141
  cessation 142
  support 215
  quiescence 265
  death 360
  silence 403
  music 413
  inaction 681
  repose 687
at – repose 687
  content 831
home of – 189
set at –
  answer 462
  ascertain 474
  complete 729
  compact 769
set one's mind at –
  calm 826
set the question
  at – 478, 480
– assured 484, 858
– on support 215
– on one's oars
  142, 687
– satisfied 831
– and be thankful
  681, 687
– upon
  evidence 467
  confide 484
– with duty 926

restaurant 189
– car 272
restaurateur 637
restful 265
resting place
  support 215
  quiet 265
  arrival 292
restitution 790, 660
restive averse 603
  obstinate 606
  disobedient 742
  refusal 764
  perverse 901a
restless
  changeable 149
  moving 264
  agitated 315
  active 682
  excited 825
  fearful 860
restoration 660
restorative
  salubrious 656
  remedial 662
  relieving 834
restore reinstate
  660
  refresh 689
  return 790
– equilibrium 27
– harmony 723
– to health 654
restrain 616, 706,
  751
restrainable 743
restrained 751
restraint 578, 751
  self – 826, 953
restrict hinder 706
  restrain 751
  prohibit 761
restringency 751
result remainder 40
  follow 117
  effect 154
  conclusion 480
  completion 729
resultant 48, 154
resume begin 66
  repeat 104
  change 140
  restore 660
  take 789
résumé 596
resupination 213
resurgence 163, 660
resurrection
  reproduction 163
  restoration 660
  heaven 981

resuscitate
  reproduce 163
  reinstate 660
retable 215
retail *distribute* 73
  inform 527
  barter 794
  sell 796
retailer 797
retain *stand* 150
  keep 781
  – the memory of
    505
  – one's reason 502
retainer 746
retake 789
retaliation 718, 919
retard *later* 133
  slower 275
  hinder 706
retch 297
retection 529
retention 781
retentive 781
  – *memory* 505
reticence 528
reticle 219
reticulation 219,
  248
reticule 191
retiform 219
retina 441
retinue *followers* 65
  series 69
  servants 746
retire *move back* 283
  recede 287
  resign 757
  modest 881
  seclusion 893
– into the shade
  inferior 34
  decrease 36
  – from sight
  disappear 449
  hide 528
retiring
  concave 252
  – *colour* 438
retold 104
retort
  receptacle 191
  vaporizer 336
  boiler 386
  answer 462
  confutation 479
  retaliation 718
  wit 842
retouch *restore* 660
retoucher 559
retrace 505

– one's steps 607
retract
  recant 607
  annul 756
  abjure 757
  violate 773
retreat
  resort 74
  withdraw 187
  abode 189
  regression 283
  recede 287
  ambush 530
  refuge 666
  escape 671
  give way 725
beat a – 623
retreating
  concave 252
retrench *subduct* 38
  shorten 201
  lose 789
  economize 817
retribution
  retaliation 718
  payment 807
  punishment 972
  reward 973
retrieve *restore* 660
  acquire 775
retriever *dog* 366
retroaction
  counteraction 179
  recoil 277
  regression 283
retroactive
  past 122
retrocession
  regression 283
  recession 287
retrograde
  moving back 283
  deteriorated 659
  relapsing 661
retrogression
  regression 283
  deterioration 659
  relapse 661
retrospection
  past 122
  thought 451
  memory 505
retroussé 245
retroversion 218
retrude 289
return *list* 86
  repeat 104
  periodic 138
  reverse 145
  recoil 277
  regression 283

arrival 292
answer 462
report 551
relapse 661
appoint 755
profit 775
restore 790
proceeds 810
reward 973
in –
  compensation 30
  – the compliment
  interchange 148
  retaliate 718
  – to the original
    state 660
  –ed prodigal 950
  – thanks 916, 990
return game 104
return match 104
reunion *junction* 43
réunion
  assemblage 72
  concord 714
lieu de – 74
point de – 74
social – 892
revamp 140
revanche, en – 718
reveal 529
  – *itself* 446
reveille 550
**réveiller le chat qui
  dort, ne pas** –
  668, 864
revel 840, 954
  – in *enjoy* 377
revelation
  disclosure 480a,
    529
  theological 985
Revelations 985
reveller 840
  drunkard 959
revelling 59, 838
revendicate
  claim 741
  acquisition 775
  due 924
revenge 919
  breathe – 900
**revenons à nos
  moutons** 283,
  660
revenue 632, 810
reverberate 277,
  408
reverberatory 386
revere *love* 897
  respect 928
  piety 987

reverence *title* 877
  respect 928
  piety 987
  clergy 996
reverenced 500
reverend 877, 996
reverent 987, 990
reverential 928
reverie
  train of thought
    451
  inattention 458
  imagination 515
reversal 218, 607
reverse *contrary* 14
  inversion 218
  – *of a medal* 235
  anteposition 237
  adversity 735
  abrogate 756
  cards 840
  – of the shield 468
reverseless 150
reversible 605
reversion
  [*see* reverse]
  posterity 117
  return **145**
  possession 777
  property 780
  succession 783
  remitter 790
reversioner 779
revert *repeat* 104
  return 145
  turn back 283
  revest 790
  – to 457
revest 790
revet 223
reviction 660
review *consider* 457
  inquiry 461
  judge 480
  recall 505
  periodical 531
  dissertation 595
  compendium 596
  entertainment 599
  revise 658
  parade 882
reviewer 480, 595
revile 932, 988
reviler 936
revise *copy* 21
  consider 457
  printing 591
  plan 626
  improve 658
revising barrister
  967

roseate *red* 434
  hopeful 858
rose-coloured
  hope 858
Rosetta stone 522
rosette 847
rose-water
  moderation 174
  flattery 933
  not made with –
  704
Rosicrucian
  sect 984
  sorcerer 994
rosin *rub* 331
  resin 356a
Rosinante 271
roster 86
rostrum *beak* 234
  pulpit 542
rosy 434
  – wine 959
rosy-cheeked 845
rot *decompose* 49
  absurdity 497
  rubbish 517
  putrefy 653
  disease 655
  decay 659
rota 86, 138
Rotarian 892
rotate 138
rotation 312
  periodicity 138
rote, by – 505
  know – 490
  learn – 539
rôti 298
rôtisserie 189
rotogravure 531,
  558
rotten *weak* 160
  bad 649
  foul 653
  decayed 659
  – at the core
  deceptive 545
  diseased 655
  – borough 893
rotulorum, custos –
  553
rotund 249
rotunda 189
rotundity 249
roturier 876
roué 949
rouge 434, 847
rouge-et-noir 621
rough *violent* 173
  shapeless 241
  uneven 256

pungent 392
unsavoury 395
sour 397
sound 410
unprepared 674
fighter 726
ugly 846
low fellow 876
bully 887
churlish 895
evil-doer 913
bad man 949
cut up – 900
– copy *writing* 590
unprepared 674
– diamond
uncouth 241
unprepared 674
artless 703
vulgar 851
commonalty 876
good man 948
– draft 626
– guess 514
– it 686
– sea 348
– side of the
  tongue 932
– and tumble 59
– weather 173, 349
rough-cast 256
  covering 223
  shape 240
  scheme 626
  unpolished 674
rough-hew 240, 673
roughly
  nearly 197
rough-neck 876,
  887
roughness 256
rough-rider 268
roughshod over,
  ride – 739
roulade 415
rouleau
  assemblage 72
  cylinder 249
  money 800
roulette 621, 840
round *series* 69
  revolution 138
  - *of a ladder* 215
  curve 245
  circle 247
  rotund 249
  music 415
  fight 720
all – 227
bring – 660
come –

periodic 138
recant 607
persuade 615
dizzy – 312
get – 660
go – 311
go one's –s 266
go the –
  publication 531
make the – of 311
run the – of 682
go the same – 104
turn – *invert* 218
  retreat 283
  revolve 311
– assertion 535
– a corner 311
– dance 840
– game 840
– hand 590
– like a horse in a
  mill 613
– of the ladder 71
– number 84, 102
in – numbers 29,
  197
– pace 274
– of pleasures
  377, 840
– robin
  information 527
  petition 765
  censure 932
– and round 138,
  312
– sum 800
– terms 566
– trot 274
– up 370
– of visits 892
round about
  circumjacent 227
  deviation 279
  circuit 311
  amusement 840
– phrases 573
– way 729
rounded periods
  577, 578
roundelay 597
rounders 840
round-house 752
roundlet 247
round-shouldered
  243
roup 796
rouse 615, 824
– oneself 682
rousing 171
rout *crowd* 72
  agitation 315

overcome 731
discomfit 732
rabble 876
assembly 892
put to the – 731
– out 652
route 627
  en – 270
  en – for 282
routine
  uniform 16
  order 58
  rule 80
  periodic 138
  custom 613
  business 625
rove *travel* 266
  deviate 279
rover *traveller* 268
  pirate 792
roving commission
  475
row *disorder* 59
  series 69
  violence 173
  street 189
  navigate 267
  discord 713
– in the same
  boat 88
rowdy *vulgar* 851,
  876
  blusterer 887
  bad man 949
rowel 253, 615
rower 269
rowlock 215
royal 737
– blue 438
– highness 877
– road 627, 705
Royal Academician
  559
royalist 737
royaliste que le roi,
  plus 33
royalty 737
Rt. Hon. 877
ruade *impulse* 276
  attack 716
ruat cœlum 908
rub *friction* 331
  touch 379
  difficulty 704
  adversity 735
  painful 830
– off corners 82
– down *lessen* 195
  powder 330
– down with an
  oaken towel 972

- *in the mind* 451
  examine 457
  describe 594
  synopsis 596
  overflow 641
- in pairs 17
- parallel 178
- into port 664
- a race *speed* 274
  conduct 692
  contend 720
- in a race
  act 680
he that –s may
  read 525
- a rig 840
- the rig upon 929
- riot *violent* 173
  exaggerate 549
  redundance 641
  active 682
  disobey 742
  intemperance 954
- a risk 665
- rusty 603
- to seed 128, 659
- smooth 705, 734
- a tilt at 716, 720
- of things 151
- through
  uniform 16
  influence 175
  be present 186
  kill 361
  expend 809
  prodigal 818
- up *increase* 35
  build 161
- up an account
  credit 805
  debt 806
  charge 812
- up bills 808
- upon 630
- upon a bank
  808, 809
- to waste 638
- wild 173
run-about 272
runagate
  fugitive 623
  disobey 742
  bad man 949
runaway 623
rundle *circle* 247
  convolution 248
  rotundity 249
rundlet 191
Runes *writing* 590
  poetry 597
  spell 993

rung 215
runnel 348
runner *branch* 51
  courier 268
  messenger 534
running
  continuous 69
  the mind – upon
    451
  the mind – upon
    other things 458
- account 811
- commentary 595
- fight 720
- hand 590
- over 641
- water 348
runnion 949
runt 193
rupture
  disjunction 44
  quarrel 713
rural 189, 371
- dean 893
ruralist 893
rus in urbe 189, 893
ruse 545, 702
Rush, Friar 980
rush *crowd* 72
  violence 173
  velocity 274
  water 348
  plant 367
  trifle 643
  haste 684
  make a – at 716
- to a conclusion
  481, 486
- on destruction
  863
- in medias res
  604
- into print 591
- upon 622
rushlight *dim* 422
  candle 423
rusk 298
Russe, montagne –
  480
russet
  brown 433
  red 434
Russian
- ballet 840
- bath 386, 652
rust *red* 434
  decay 659
  canker 663
  inaction 683
  moth and – 659
- of antiquity 122

rustic
  village 189
  agricultural 371
  vulgar 851
  clown 876
rusticate
  punish 972
  seclude 893
rusticity
  impolite 895
rusticus expectat
  dum defluat
  amnis 858
rustle 405, 407, 409
rustling 791
rusty *dirty* 653
  decayed 659
  sluggish 683
  unskilful 699
  sulky 901a
  run – *averse* 603
rut *rule* 80
  furrow 259
  habit 613
  in a – 16
ruth 914
ruthless
  savage 907
  pitiless 914a
  revengeful 919
rutilant 420
ruttish 961
ryot *servant* 746
  possessor 779
  commonalty 876

S

sabaoth 726
sabbatarian
  ascetic 955
  sectarian 984
  false piety 988
  ritualistic 998
Sabbath *rest* 687
  rite 998
sabbatism 988
Sabellianism 984
Sabianism 984
sable 223, 431
sabot 225
sabotage 162, 742
sabre 361, 727
sabreur *slayer* 361
  soldier 726
sabulous 330
sac 191
- de nuit 225
sacatra 83
saccharine 396

saccular 191
sacerdotal 995
sacerdotalism 988
sachel 191
sachem 745
sachet 400
sack *bag* 191
  discharge 297,
    756
  gain 775
  take 789
  plunder 791
  give the – to 297
sackbut 297
sackcloth and ashes
  lament 839
  atonement 952
  ascetic 955
  rite 998
sacrament 998
sacrarium 1000
sacred
  dignified 873
  holy 976
  revelation 985
  piety 987
sacrifice
  destroy 162
  gift 784
  atonement 952
  worship 990
  idolatry 991
  at any – 604
  fall a – 828
  make a – 942
  make the supreme
    – 361
  self – 942
sacrificed 732
sacrilege 988
sacring bell 550,
  998
sacristan 996
sacristy 1000
sacrosanct
  honourable 873
  inviolable 924
  holy 976
sad *great* 31
  grey 432
  bad 649
  painful 830
  dejected 837
- disappointment
  509
- dog 949
- times 735
- work 699
sadden 830, 837
sadder and wiser
  man 950

saddle 215
in the – 673
– on 37, 43
– on the right
    horse
    discovery 480a
    skill 698
    right 922
    fair 939
– with *add* 37
    attribute 155
    quarter on 184
    clog 706
    impose a duty
        926
    accuse 938
– on the wrong
    horse 495, 699
– up 293
saddle-bags 191
Sadducee 984
sadness, in – 535
safe *cupboard* 191
    hiding place 530
    secure 664
    treasury 802
    cautious 864
– conduct 631
– conscience 926,
    946
– deposit 636
– keeping 670
– and sound 654
on the – side 864
safety 664
– bicycle 272
– curtain 599
– first 665, 864
– match 388
– valve 666
saffron *colour* 436
sag 214, 217, 245
saga 594
sagacious 498, 510
sage 498, **500**
– maxim 496
saggar 386
sagittal 253
sagittary 83
sagum 225
Sahara 169
sahib 373, 745, 875
saick 273
said *preceding* 62
    repeated 104
    prior 116
it is – 532
thou hast – 488
more easily – than
    done 704
sail *navigate* 267

ship 273
set out 293
easy – 174
full – 274
press of – 274
shorten – 275
take in – 174
take the wind out
    of one's –s 706
too much – 863
under – 267
– before the wind
    734
– near the wind
    698
– too near the
    wind 863
sailing: plain – 705
– vessel 273
sailor 269
    fair weather – 701
saint *angel* 977
    revelation 985
    piety 987
    false piety 988
    tutelary – 664
Saint Monday 840
saintly 944, 987
sais quoi, je ne –
    563
sake:
for the – of 615,
    707
for goodness – 765
salaam
    bow 308
    submit 725
    courtesy 894
    respect 928
salacity 961
salad 41
– oil 356
salade 717
salamander 386
salariat 875
salary 973
sale 796
    bill of – 771
    for – *offer* 763
    barter 794
saleable 796
salebrosity 256
salesman 797
salient
    projecting 250
    sharp 253
    manifest 525
    important 642
– angle 244
– points 642
saline 392

saliva 299, 332
salivate 297
salle-à-manger 191
sallet 717
sallow
    colourless 429
    yellow 436
sally *issue* 293
    attack 716
    wit 842
sally-port 295, 717
salmagundi 41
salmi 298
salmon-coloured
    434
saloon 189, 191
salt *sailor* 269
    pungent 392
    condiment 393
    importance 642
    preserve 670
    money 800
    wit 842
    below the – 876
    worth one's – 644
– of the earth
    648, 948
– water 341
saltation 309
saltatory 315
saltinbanco 548
saltpetre 392, 727
saltum, per – 315
salubrity 656
salutary 656
salutatory 582
salute
    allocution 586
    celebration 883
    courtesy 894
    kiss 902
    respect 928
salutiferous
    [*see* salutary]
salva:
– res est 664
– sit reverentia
    928
salvable 946
salvage
    acquisition 775
    tax 812
    discount 813
    reward 973
salvation
    preservation 670
    deliverance 672
    religious 976
    piety 987
    work out one's –
        990

salve *unguent* 356
    remedy 662
    relieve 834
salver 191
salvo *exception* 83
    explosion 406
    qualification 469
    plea 617
    attack 716
    excuse 937
– of artillery
    celebration 883
Samaritan, good –
    906, 912
same 13
all the – to 823
in the – boat 709
in the – breath
    113, 120
go over the –
    ground 104
of the – mind 488
on the – tack 709
adds up to the –
    thing 27
at the – time 30,
    120
sameness 16
samiel 349
samisen 417
Sammael 978
samovar 191
sampan 273
sample 82, 463
Samson 159
sana, mens – 502
– in corpore sano
    827
sanation 660
sanative 662
sanatorium 662
sanctification 976
sanctify 926, 987
sanctimony 988
sanction
    permission 760
    dueness 924
    approbation 931
sanctitude 987
sanctity 987
sanctuary 666, 1000
sanctum 191
– sanctorum
    abode 189
    privacy 893
    temple 1000
sand *powder* 330
–bag 727
built upon – 665
–dance 840
sow the – 645

sax-horn 417
Saxon
  style 576, 578
saxophone 417
say *nearly* 32
  assert 535
  speak 560, 582
  you don't – so 870
  go without –ing
    525
  have one's – 535,
    582
  that is to – 522
  what do you – to
    that 870
  – by heart 505
  – no 489
  – nothing 585
  – to oneself 589
  – one's prayers
    990
  – what comes up-
    permost 612
saying 496, 535
sbirro 965
scabbard 191
  throw away the –
  resolution 604
  war 722
scabby 940
scabrous 256
scaffold
  support 215
  preparation 673
  execution 975
scagliola 545
scalawag 193
scald *burn* 384
  poet 597
scale *transcend* 31
  portion 51
  series 69
  term 71
  slice 204
  skin 223
  mount 305
  weigh 319
  gamut 413
  measure 466
  hold the –s 480
  turn the –
  reversion 145
  influence 175
  counter evidence
    468
  motive 615
  hold the –s even
    922
  –s of justice 922
  – the heights 305
  – the walls 716

–s falling from the
  eyes 441, 529
scalene 243
scallop 248, 257
scalp 226
scalpel 253
scamble 44
scamp *neglect* 460
  shirk 603
  rascal 949
scamped *sham* 545
scamper *speed* 274
  – off 623
scampish 945
scan *see* 441
  attend to 457
  inquire 461
  know 490
  prosody 597
scandal *news* 532
  obloquy 934
scandaleuse, chro-
  nique – 934
scandalize 932
scandal-monger
  532
scandalous 874, 945
scandalum magna-
  tum
  infamy 874
  detraction 934
  accusation 938
scandent 305
scansion 597
scant *small* 32
  few 103
  little 193
  narrow 203
  insufficient 640
scantling *model* 22
  scrap 32
  dimensions 192
scanty [*see* scant]
scape 671
scapegoat 147, 952
scapegrace 863, 949
Scapin 548, 941
scapulary 999
scar *shore* 342
  record 551
  blemish 848
scarab 993
scaramouch 844
scarce
  few 103, 137, 640
  make oneself –
    187, 623
scarcely 32
  – any 103
  – anything 643
  – ever 137

scarcity 103
scare 860
scarecrow 846, 860
scarf 225, 999
scarfskin 223
scarify *notch* 257
  torment 830
scarlet 434
  – Lady 984
scarp *oblique* 217
  defence 717
scathe 649, 659
scatheless 650
scatter *derange* 61
  disperse 73
  diverge 291
  – to the winds
  destroy 162
  confute 479
scatterbrained 458,
  503
scattering 268
scavenger 652
scenario 594, 626
scene
  appearance 448
  painting 556
  drama 599
  excitement 825
  – of action 728
  look behind the
    –s 461
scene-painter 559
scene-painting 556
scenery 448, 559
scenic 599, 882
  – railway 840
scenography 556
scent *smell* 398
  discovery 480a
  disbelieve 485
  knowledge 490
  sign 550
  trail 551
  get – of 527
  put on a new –
    279
  on the – 622
  throw off the –
    623
  on the right – 462
  – from afar 510
scent-bag 400
scent-bottle 400
scented 400
scentless 399
sceptre 747
  sway the – 737
schedule 86
schematist 626
scheme *draft* 554

plan 626
schemer 626
scherif 745, 875
scherzo 415
schesis 7
schism *dissent* 489
  discord 713
  heterodoxy 984
schismless 983a
schistose 204
scholar 492, 541
scholarly 539
scholarship
  knowledge 490
  learning 539
  distinction 873
scholastic
  knowledge 490
  teaching 537
  learning 539
  school 542
scholiast 496, 522
scholium 496, 522
school
  herd 72
  multitude 102
  system of
    opinions 484
  knowledge 490
  teaching 537
  academy **542**
  painting 556
  go to – 539
  send to – 537
schoolboy 129, 541
  familiar to every –
    490
schooldays 127
schoolfellow 541
schoolgirl 129, 541
schoolman 492, 983
schoolmaster 540
  – abroad 490, 537
schoolroom 191
schooner 273
schottische 840
sciatica 378
science 490, 698
scientific *exact* 494
scientist 476, 492
scimitar 727
scintilla *small* 32
  spark 420, 423
scintillate 446, 873
scintillation
  heat 382
  light 420
  wit 842
scintillula forsan,
  latet – 858
sciolism 491

scroll 86, 551
scrub *rub* 331
  bush 367
  clean 652
  dirty person 653
  commonalty 876
scrubby *small* 193
  trifling 643
  stingy 819
  disreputable 874
  vulgar 876
  shabby 940
scruff 235
scruple
  small quantity 32
  weight 319
  doubt 485
  reluctance 603
  probity 939
scrupulous
  careful 459
  incredulous 487
  exact 494
  reluctant 603
  fastidious 868
  punctilious 939
scrutator 461
scrutiny 457, 461
scrutoire 191
scud *sail* 267
  speed 274
  shower 348
  cloud 353
  – under bare
    poles 704
scuffle 720
scull *row* 267
  brain 450
scull-cap 225
scullery 191
scullion 746
sculpsit 558
sculptor 559
sculpture 240, **557**
scum *dirt* 653
  – of the earth 949
  – of society 876
scupper 350
scurf 653
scurrilous
  ridicule 856
  malediction 908
  disrespect 929
  detraction 934
scurry 274, 684
scurvy
  insufficient 640
  unimportant 643
  base 940
  wicked 945
scut 235

scutcheon
  standard 550
  honour 877
scutiform 251
scuttle *destroy* 162
  receptacle 191
  speed 274
  – along *haste* 684
Scylla and Charyb-
  dis, between –
  danger 665
  difficulty 704
Scyllam, incidit
  in – 699
scythe *pointed* 244
  sharp 253
'sdeath! *wonder* 870
  anger 900
  disapprobation
    932
se non e vero e ben
  trovato 546
sea *multitude* 102
  ocean 341
  at – 341
  uncertain 475
  erroneous 495
  go to – 293
  on the high –s 41
  heavy – 315
  the seven –s 341
  – of doubt 475
  – of troubles
    difficulty 704
    adversity 735
seaboard 342
seafarer 269
seafaring 267, 273
sea-fight 720
sea-girt 346
sea-going 267, 341
sea-green 435
seal
  matrix 22
  close 261
  evidence 467
  mark 550
  resolve 604
  complete 729
  compact 769
  security 771
  break the – 529
  under – 769
  – the doom of 162
  – one's infamy 940
  – the lips 585
  – of secrecy 528
  – up *restrain* 751
sealed:
  one's fate is – 601
  hermetically – 261

– book
  ignorance 491
  unintelligible 519
  secret 533
sealing-wax 747
seals *insignia* 747
sealskin 223
seam 43
sea-maid 979
sea-man 269
seamanship 692,
  698
sea-mark 550
seamless 50
seamstress 225,
  690
seamy side 651
séance 525, 696
sea-piece 556
seaplane 273, 736
sea-port 666
sear *dry* 340
  burn 384
  deaden 823
  – and yellow leaf
    128, 659
search *inquire* 461
searching
  severe 739
  painful 830
searchless 519
searchlight 423,
  726
seared conscience
  951
searing 830
seascape 556
sea-serpent 83
seaside 342
season *mix* 41
  time 106
  pungent 392
  accustom 613
  preserve 670
  prepare 673
seasonable 23, 134
seasoning 393
seasons 138
seat *place* 183
  locate 184
  abode 189
  support 215
  posterior 235
  parliament 693
  country – 189
  judgment – 966
  – of government
    737
  – of war 728
seated, firmly – 150
seaway 180

seaweed 367
seaworthy 273, 664
sebaceous 355
secant 219
secede *dissent* 489
  relinquish 624
  disobey 742
seceder
  heterodox 984
secern 297
seclusion **893**
second
  duplication 90
  – *of time* 108
  instant 113
  – *in music* 413,
    415
  abet 707
  play or sing a –
    416
  – best 651, 732
  – childhood 128,
    499
  – crop 168, 775
  – edition 104
  play – fiddle
  obey 743
  subject 749
  disrepute 874
  – nature 613
  – to none 33
  one's – self 17
  – rate 659
  – sight
  foresight 510
  sorcery 992
  – thoughts
  sequel 65
  thought 451
  improvement 658
  – youth 660
secondary
  inferior 34
  following 63
  imperfect 651
  deputy 759
  – education 537
  – evidence 467
  – school 542
seconder 711
second-hand
  imitation 19
  old 124
  deteriorated 659
  received 785
secondly 90
second-rate 651
secret *key* 522
  latent 526
  hidden 528
  riddle **533**

in the – 490
keep a – 585
– motive 615
– passage 627, 671
– place 530
– writing 590
secrétaire 191
secretary
  recorder 553
  writer 590
  director 694
  auxiliary 711
  servant 746
  consignee 758
  – of state 694
  – of the treasury
    801
secrete *excrete* 297
  conceal 528
secretion 299
secretive 528
sect 75
  religious – 983,
    984
sectarian
  dissent 489
  ally 711
  heterodox 984
sectary 489
section *division* 44
  part 51
  class 75
  chapter 593
  troops 726
sector *part* 51
  circle 247
secula seculorum,
  in – 112
secular
  centenary 98
  periodic 138
  laity 997
  – education 537
secularism 984
secundum artem
  82, 698
secure *fasten* 43
  bespeak 132
  belief 484
  safe 664
  restrain 751
  engage 768
  gain 775
  confident 858
  – an object 731
securities 802–805
security *safety* 664
  pledge **771**
  hope 858
  lend on – 787
Sedan

disaster 162
sedan chair 272
sedate
  thoughtful 451
  calm 826
  grave 837
sedative 174, 662
sedentary 265
sedge 367
sedile 1000
sediment *dregs* 653
sedimentary 40
sedition 742
seduce *entice* 615
  love 897
  debauch 961
seducer 962
seduction 829, 865
sedulous 682, 865
see *view* 441
  look 457
  believe 484
  know 490
  bishopric 995
  we shall – 507
  – after 459
  – daylight 480a
  – double 959
  – fit 600, 602
  – at a glance 498
  – justice done 922
  – life 840
  – the light
  born 359
  published 531
  – service 722
  – sights 455
  – through 480a,
    498
  – to *attention* 457
  care 459
  direction 693
  – one's way
  foresight 510
  intelligible 518
  skill 698
  easy 705
seed *small* 32
  cause 153
  posterity 167
  grain 330
  run to – *age* 128
  lose health 659
  sow the – 673
seedling 129
seed-plot 168, 371
seed-time of life
  127
seedy *weak* 160
  disease 655
  deteriorated 659

exhausted 688
  needy 804
seeing that 8, 476
seek *inquire* 461
  pursue 622
  offer 763
  request 765
  – safety 664
seek-sorrow 837
seel 217
seem 448
  as it –s good to
    600
seeming 488
seemingly 472
seemless 846, 925
seemliness 926
seemly
  expedient 646
  handsome 845
  due 924
seep 295
seer *veteran* 130
  madman 504
  oracle 513
  sorcerer 994
see-saw 12, 314
seethe *wet* 339
  hot 382
  make hot 384
  excitement 824
seething caldron
  386
segar 392
segment 44, 51
segnitude 683
s'égosiller 411
segregate
  not related 10
  separate 44
  exclude 55
segregated
  incoherent 47
seigneur, grand –
  pride 878
  insolence 885
seignior 745, 875
seigniority
  authority 737
  possession 777
  property 780
seigniory 737
seine net 232
seisin 777, 780
seismic 314
seismograph 553
seismometer 276,
  314
seize 789, 791
  – an opportunity
    134

seized with
  disease 655
  feeling 821
seizure 925
sejunction 44
seldom 137
select *choose* 609
  good 648
self 13, 79
 –abasement 879
 –accusing 950
 –admiration 880
 –applause 880
 –appointed task
   602
 –assertion 885
 –called 565
 –command 604,
   864
 –communing 451
 –complacency
   836, 880
 –confidence 880
 –conquest 604
 –conscious 855
 –consultation 451
 –contained 52
 –control 604
 –conviction
  belief 484
  penitent 950
  condemned 971
 –counsel 451
 –deceit *error* 495
 –deception 486
 –defence 717
 –delusion 486
 –denial
  disinterested 942
  temperance 953
  penance 990
 –discipline 990
 –effacement 879,
   942
 –esteem 880
 –evident 474, 525
 –examination 990
 –existing 1
 –government 748
 –help 698
 –immolation 991
 –indulgence
  selfishness 943
  intemperance 954
 –interest 943
 –knowledge 881
 –love 943
 –luminous 423
 –mastery 604
 –opinioned 481
 –possession

serial
 continuous 69
 periodic 183
 book 593
seriatim
 in order 58
 continuously 69
 each to each 79
 slowly 275
series 69, 84
sérieux, take au –
 843
serio-comic 853
serious *great* 31
 resolved 604
 important 642
 dejected 837
seriously 535
serjeant:
 common – 967
 –at-law 968
sermon *lesson* 537
 speech 582
 dissertation 595
 pastoral 998
 funeral – 363
sermonizer 584
seroon 72
serosity 333, 337
serpent
 tortuous 248
 snake 366
 hiss 409
 wind instrument
  417
 wise 498
 deceiver 548
 cunning 702
 evil-doer 913
 knave 941
 demon 949
 the old – 978
 great sea – 515
serpentine 248
serrated 244, 257
serried 72, 321
serum 333, 337
servant *instrumen-*
 tality 631
 help 711
 retainer **746**
 – of all work 690
serve *benefit* 618
 business 625
 utility 644
 aid 707
 warfare 722
 obey 743
 servant 746
 – an apprentice-
  ship 539

– faithfully 743
– loyally 743
– notice 527
– out 972
– one right
 retaliation 718
 right 922
 punish 972
– as a substitute
 147
– one's turn 644
– with a writ 969
service *good* 618
 utility 644
 use 677
 warfare 722
 servitude 749
 worship 990
 rite 998
 hold – 363
 at one's – 763
 press into the –
  677
 render a – 644,
  906
serviceable 644, 648
serviette 652
servile 749, 876, **886**
servitor 746
servitorship 749
servitude 749
 penal – 972
sesame, open – 260
 watchword 550
 spell 993
sesqui- 87
sesquipedalia verba
 577
sesquipedalian 200
sess 812
sessile 46
session *council* 696
sessions *law* 966
sestet 597
set
 condition 7
 join 43
 coherence 46
 group 72
 class 75
 firm 150
 tendency 176
 place 184
 form 240
 sharpen 253
 direction 278
 go down 306
 dense 321
 stage 599
 habit 613
 prepare 673

gang 712
impose 741
make a dead – at
 716
– about 66, 676
– abroach 73
– one's affections
 on 897
– afloat 153, 531
– against
 oppose 708
 quarrel 713
 hate 898
 angry 900
– against one
 another 464
– agoing
 impulse 276
 propulsion 284
 aid 717
– apart
 separate 44
 exclude 55
 select 609
– aside
 displace 185
 disregard 458
 neglect 460
 negative 536
 reject 610
 disuse 678
 annul 756
 refuse 764
 not observe 773
 relinquish 782
 dereliction 927
– one's back up
 878
– before
 inform 527
 choice 609
– before oneself
 620
– by 636
– one's cap at
 897, 902
– on a cast 621
– down [*see below*]
– by the ears 898
– at ease 831
– an example
 model 22
 motive 615
– the eyes on 441
– one's face
 against
 oppose 708
 refuse 764
 disapprove 932
– the fashion
 influence 175

authority 737
fashion 852
– fast 704
– on fire
 ignite 384
 excite 824
– on foot 66
– foot on 294
– forth *show* 525
 assert 535
 describe 594
– forward 293
– free 750
– going
 [*see* – *agoing*]
– one's hand to
 467
– one's heart upon
 604, 865
– at hazard 665
– in *begin* 66
 rain 348
– on its legs 150
– on one's legs 159,
 669
– in motion 264,
 677
– to music 416
– at naught
 make light of 483
 reject 610
 oppose 708
 defy 715
 disobey 742
 not observe 773
 dereliction 927
– no store by 483,
 930
– off
 compensation 30
 depart 293
 improve 658
 discount 813
 adorn 845
 display 882
– on 615
– in order 60
– out *arrange* 60
 begin 66
 depart 293
 decorate 845
 display 882
– over 755
– phrase 566
– a price 85, 812
– purpose 620
– at rest *end* 67
 answer 462
 adjudge 480
 complete 729
 compact 769

under the – of
  one's wing 664
shadowy 4, 447
shady 874
shaft *deep* 208
  frame 215
  pit 260
  missile 284
  axis 312
  air-pipe 351
  handle 633
  weapon 727
shaggy 256
shagreen 223
shah 745
shake *totter* 149
  weak 160
  vibrate 314
  agitation 315
  shiver 383
  trill 407
  music 416
  dissuade 616
  injure 659
  impress 821
  excited 824
  fear 860
– one's faith 485
– hands
  pacification 723
  friendship 888
  courtesy 894
  forgive 918
– the head
  dissent 489
  deny 536
  refuse 764
  disapprove 932
– off 297
– off the yoke 759
– to pieces 162
– one's sides 838
– up 315
shakedown *bed* 215
shakes, no great –
  643, 651
shako 225, 717
shaky *weak* 160
  in danger 665
  fearful 860
shallop 273
shallow
  not deep 32, 209
  ignorant 491
  ignoramus 493
  foolish 499
  trifling 643
– pretext 617
– profundity 855
shallow-brain 501
shallowness **209**

shallow-pated 499
shallows
  danger 667
sham *imitation* 19
  falsehood 544
  deception 545,
  546
– fight 720
shaman 994
shamanism 992
shamble 275, 315
shambles 361
shame
  disrepute 874
  wrong 923
  censure 932
  chastity 960
cry – upon 932
false – 855
for – 874
sense of – 879
– the devil 939
to one's – be it
  spoken 874
shamefaced 881
shameful
  disgraceful 874
  profligate 945
shameless
  bold 525
  impudent 885
  profligate 945
  indecent 961
shampoo 652
shandredhan 272
shanghai 791
shank *support* 215
  instrument 633
Shanks's mare 266
shanty 189
shape 240, 448
– one's course
  direction 278
  pursuit 622
  conduct 692
– out a course 626
shapeless 241, 846
shapely 242, 845
shard 51
share
  part 51
  participate 778
  allotted portion
  786
– and share alike
  778
shareholder 778
shark 792
sharp
  energetic 171
  violent 173

  acute 253
  sensible 375
  pungent 392
– *sound* 410
  musical tone 413
  intelligent 498
  active 682
  clever 698
  cunning 702
  feeling 821
  painful 830
  rude 895
  censorious 932
look – 459, 682
– appetite 865
– contest 720
– ear 418
– eye 441
– fellow 682, 700
– frost 383
– look-out 459,
  507
– pain 378
– practice
  cunning 702
  severity 739
  improbity 940
– set 865
sharpen
  [see sharp]
  excite 824
– one's tools 673
– one's wits 537
sharpener 253
sharper 792
sharpness **253**
sharpshooter 726
sharpshooting 716
Shaster 986
shatter *disjoin* 44
  disperse 73
  render powerless
  158
  destroy 162
shatter-brained 503
shattered 160, 688
shave *reduce* 195
  shorten 201
  layer 204
  smooth 255
  grate 330
  lie 546
close – 671
shaved 226
shaving *small* 32
  layer 204
  filament 205
shave-tail 726, 745
shawl 225
shawm 417
shay 272

she 374
sheaf 72
shear *reduce* 195
  shorten 201
  sheep 370
  take 789
shears 253
sheath 191, 223
sheathe 225
  moderate 174
– the sword 723
sheathing 223
sheave 633
shed *scatter* 73
  building 189
  divest 226
  emit 297
  give 784
– blood 361
– light upon 420
– a lustre on 873
– tears 839
Shedim 980
sheen 420
sheep 366
sheep-dog 366
sheep-fold 232
sheepish 881
sheep's eye, cast a –
  desire 865
  modest 881
  endearment 902
sheer *simple* 42
  complete 52
  deviate 279
– off *avoid* 623
sheet *layer* 204
  covering 223
  paper 593
come down in –s
  rain 348
white – 952
winding – 363
– of fire 382
– of water 343
sheet-anchor
  safety 664, 666
  hope 858
sheet-lightning 423
sheik *ruler* 745, 875
  lover 897
  priest 996
shelf 215, 667
on the –
  powerless 158
  disused 678
  inaction 681
shell *cover* 223
  coffin 363
  bombard 716
  bomb 727

–burst 404
–shock 655
– out 784, 807, 809
shellac 356*a*
shellback 269
shell-fish 366
shelter 664, 666
– oneself under plea of 617
sheltie 271
shelve *defer* 133
  locate 184
  slope 217
  neglect 460
  disuse 678
shelving beach 217
shend 659
shepherd *tender of*
  sheep 370
  director 694
  pastor 996
Shepherd, the Good – 976
shepherd's dog 366
Sheppard, Jack – 792
shere 32
sheriff 745, 965
Shetland pony 271
shew [*see* show]
shibboleth 550
shield
  heraldry 550
  safety 664
  buckler 666
  defend 717
  scutcheon 877
  look only at one side of the – 481
  reverse of the – 235, 468
  under the – of 664
shift *change* 140
  convert 144
  substitute 147
  changeable 149
  chemise 225
  move 264
  transfer 270
  deviate 279
  prevaricate 546
  plea 617
  cunning 702
  last – 601
  make a – with 147, 677
  put to one's –s 704, 804
  – one's ground 607

– off *defer* 133
– for oneself 692, 748
  left to – for oneself 893
– one's quarters 264
– the scene 140
– to and fro 149
shifting [*see* shift]
  transient 111
  – sands 149
  – trust or use 783
shiftless 674, 699
shillelagh 727
shilling 800
  cut off with a – 789
  – shocker 594
shilly-shally 605
shimmer 420
shimmy
  dance 840
shindy 720
shine *light* 420
  beauty 845
  glory 873
  take the – out of 874
  – in conversation 588
  – forth 873
  – upon
    illumine 420
    aid 707
shingle 330
shingled
  hair 53
shingles 223
shining [*see* shine]
  – light *sage* 500
Shintoism 984
shiny 420
ship *lade* 190
  transfer 270
  vessel **273**
  take – 267, 293
  one's – coming in 803
  – of the line 726
shipboard, on – 273
ship-load 31, 190
shipman 269
shipmate 890
shipment
  contents 190
  transfer 270
shippen 189
shipping 273
shipshape *order* 58
  conformity 82

skill 698
shipwreck
  destruction 162
  vanquish 731
  failure 732
shire 181
shirk 603, 623, 742
shirker 862
shirt 225
Shiva 979
shive 22, 204
shiver
  small piece 32
  divide 44
  destroy 162
  filament 205
  shake 315
  brittle 328
  cold 383
  fear 860
  go to –s 162
  – in one's shoes 860
shivery *brittle* 328
  powdery 330
shoal
  assemblage 72
  multitude 102
  shallow 209
shoals *danger* 667
  surrounded by – *difficulty* 704
shoat 366
shock *sheaf* 72
  violence 173
  concussion 276
  agitation 315
  unexpected 508
  disease 655
  discord 713
  affect 821
  move 824
  pain 828
  give pain 830
  dislike 867
  scandalize 932
shocking *bad* 649
  painful 830
  ugly 846
  vulgar 851
  fearful 860
  disreputable 874
  hateful 898
  in a – temper 901*a*
shockingly *much* 31
shod 225
shoddy 645
shoe *support* 215
  dress 225
  hindrance 706
  stand in the –s of

  commission 755
  deputy 759
  where the – pinches
  badness 649
  difficulty 704
  opposition 708
  sensibility 822
  painful 830
shoemaker 225
shofle 272
shoful 792
shog 173
shoneen 855
shoot
  offspring 167
  expand 194
  dart 274
  propel 284
  kill 361
  sprout 365, 367
  pain 378
  execute 972
  teach the young idea to – 537
  – ahead 282
  – ahead of 303
  – at 716
  – out beams 420
  – up *increase* 35
  prominent 250
shooting
  [*see* shoot]
  chase 622
  – pain 378
  – star 318, 423
shooting-coat 225
shop 795, 799
  keep a – 625, 794
  shut up – *end* 67
  cease 142
  relinquish 624
  rest 687
  smell of the – 851
shopkeeper 797
shoplifter 792
shoplifting 791
shopman 797
shopmate 890
shopping 794, 795
shore
  support 215
  border 231
  land 342
  buttress 717
  hug the – 286
  on – 342
  – up 215, 670
shoreless 180
shorn *cut short* 21
  deprived 776

plantation 371	– the gates of	– of *weary* 841	**side-track** 287
shrug *sign* 550	mercy 914*a*	*dislike* 867	**sidewalk** 627
– the shoulders	– in 751	*satiated* 869	**sideways** 217, 236
dissent 489	– oneself up 893	in –ness and in	**side-wind**
submit 725	– out 55, 761	health 604	*oblique* 217
discontent 832	– up shop *end* 67	**sick-chamber** 655	*circuit* 629
dislike 867	*cease* 142	**sicken** *nauseate* 395	*cunning* 702
contempt 930	*silence* 403	*disease* 655	**sidle** *oblique* 217
disapprobation	*relinquish* 624	*pain* 830	*lateral* 236
932	*repose* 687	*weary* 841	*deviate* 279
shrunk 193, 195	– up *close* 261	*disgust* 867	**siege** 716
shudder *cold* 383	*confute* 479	**sickener**	*lay* – to 716
fear 860	*imprison* 751	*too much* 641	state of – 722
make one –	**shutter** 424	**sickle** 244, 253	**siege-train** 727
painful 830	**shuttle** 314	**sickly** *weak* 160	**siesta** 683
– at *aversion* 867	**shuttlecock** 605	**sick-room** 655	**sieve** *sort* 60
hate 898	**shy** *deviate* 279	**side**	*perforate* 260
shuffle *mix* 41	*draw back* 283	*consanguinity* 11	*clean* 652
derange 61	*propel* 284	*edge* 231	memory like a –
change 140	*avoid* 623	*laterality* 236	506
interchange 148	*fearful* 860	*party* 712	pour water into
changeable 149	*cowardly* 862	*ostentation* 882	a – 638, 818
move slowly 275	*modest* 881	at one's – 197	stop one hole in
agitate 315	fight – of 623	on every – 227	a – 819
falsehood 544	have a – at 716	on one – 243	**sift** *simplify* 42
untruth 546	– of belief 487	on one's – 714	*sort* 60
irresolute 605	– cock 862	look only at one –	*inquire* 461
recant 607	– of *doubtful* 485	of the shield 481	*discriminate* 465
dance 840	*unwilling* 603	pass from one – to	*clean* 652
improbity 940	*cautious* 864	another 607	– the chaff from
– the cards	*dislike* 867	take up a – 476	the wheat 609
begin again 66	**Shylock** 787	wrong – up 218	**sigh** 405, 839
change 140	**Siamese twins** 89	– by side	– for 865
chance 621	**sib** 11	*accompaniment*	**sighing like**
prepare 673	**Siberia** 383	88	**furnace** 902
patience and –	**sibi gladio hunc**	*near* 197	**sight** *much* 31
the cards 826	**jugulo, suo** – 718	*laterality* 236	*multitude* 102
– off *run away* 623	**sibilation** *hiss* **409**	*party* 712	*vision* 441
– off this mortal	*disrespect* 929	from – to side 314	*appearance* 448
coil 360	*disapprobation*	– with *aid* 707	*ugly* 846
– on 266	932	*co-operate* 709	*prodigy* 872
shuffler 548	**Sibyl** *oracle* 513	*concord* 714	at – 132, 441
shun 623, 867	*ugly* 846	**side-arms** 727	dim – 443
shunt 270, 279	**Sibylline** 511	**side-blow** 702	in – 446
shunted	– leaves 513	**sideboard** 191	in – of 197, 441
shelved 460	**sic** *imitation* 19	**side-car** 272	in plain – 525
shut 261	*exact* 494	**side-dish** 298	keep in – 457
– the door 761	si – omnes! 948	**side-drum** 417	within – of shore
– the door in one's	– transit gloria	**side-kick** 890	858
face 764	mundi 111	**side issue** 643	**sightless**
– the door upon	– volo sic jubeo	**sideling** 279	*blind* 442
893	600	**sidelong** 236	*invisible* 447
– one's ears 419,	– vos non vobis	**sideration** 158	*ugly* 846
487	791	**sidereal** 318	**sightly** 845
– the eyes 442	**siccity** 340	– time 114	**sights, see** – 455
– one's eyes to	**sick** *ill* 655	**siderite** 288	**sightseeing** 441
not attend to 458	make one – 830,	**Sideromancy** 511	**sightseer** 444, 455
neglect 460	867	**side-saddle** 215	**sigil** *seal* 550
not believe 487	visitation of the –	**side-scene** 599	*evidence* 769
permit 760	998	**sideslip** 267	**sigmoidal** 248
not observe 773	– at heart 837	**sidesman** 996	**sign** *attest* 467

prostitute 962
skittish
　capricious 608
　excitable 825
　timid 862
　bashful 881
skittle sharper 792
skittles 840
skiver 253
skulk 528, 862
skull 450
skull-cap 225
skunk 401
skurry 684
sky *summit* 210
　world 318
　air 338
　necessity 601
sky-aspiring 865
sky-blue 438
sky-lark 305
sky-larking 840
sky-light 260
sky-line 196
sky-pilot 996
sky-rocket 305
sky-scraper 206,
　210
slab *layer* 204
　support 215
　flat 251
　viscous 352
　record 551
slabber *slaver* 297
　unclean 653
slack *loose* 47
　weak 160
　inert 172
　slow 275
　cool 385
　fuel 388
　neglectful 460
　unwilling 603
　insufficient 640
　inactive 683
　lax 738
slacken
　loosen 47
　moderate 174
　repose 687
　hinder 706
　one's pace 275
slacker 460, 603,
　623, 927
slag *embers* 384
　inutility 641
　dirt 653
slake *quench* 174
　gratify 829
　satiate 869
　– one's appetite

intemperance 954
slam 276, 406
　– the door in
　　one's face
　oppose 708
　refuse 764
slammerkin 653
slander 934
slanderer 936
slang 560, 563, 908
slant 217
slap *instantly* 113
　strike 276
　censure 932
　punish 972
　– in the face
　　opposition 708
　attack 716
　anger 900
　disrespect 929
　disapprobation
　　932
　– the forehead 461
slap-dash 684
slash 44, 308
slashing *style* 574
slate
　writing tablet 590
　election 609
　disparage 932
　clean the – 918
　– *loose mad* 503
slate-coloured 432
slates *roof* 223
slattern
　disorder 59
　dirty 653
　bungler 701
　vulgar 851
slatternly 699
slaughter 361
slaughter-house
　361
slave *instrumen-*
　tality 631
　toil 686
　servant 746
　a – to 749
　– trade 795
slaver *ship* 273
　slobber 297
　dirt 653
　flatter 933
slavery 686, 749
slavish 749, 886
slay 361
sleave 59
sled 272
sledge 272
sledge-hammer 276
　with a – 162, 686

sleek 255, 845
sleep 683
　last – 360
　rock to – 174
　send to – 841
　not have a wink
　　of – 825
　– with one eye
　　open 459
　– at one's post 683
　– upon 133, 451
　– walker 268
　– walking 266
sleeper *support* 215
　wake the seven –s
　　404
sleeping partner
　683
sleepless 682
sleepy 683
sleet 383
sleeve *skein* 219
　dress 225
　hang on the – of
　　746
　wear one's heart
　　upon his – 525,
　　703
　in one's – 528
　laugh in one's –
　　838, 856
sleeveless 499, 608
　– *errand* 645, 699
sleigh 272
sleight *skill* 698
　– of hand 545
slender *small* 32
　thin 203
　trifling 643
　– *means* 804
sleuth 527
　– *hound* 913
slew round 312
slice *cut* 44
　piece 51
　layer 204
slick 682, 698
slicker 225
slide *elapse* 109
　smooth 255
　pass 264
　locomotion 266
　descend 306
　– back 661
　– in 228
　– into 144
sliding 840
sliding-panel 545
sliding-rule 85
slight *small* 32
　slender 203

rare 322
　neglect 460
　disparage 483
　feeble 575
　trifle 643
　dereliction 927
　disrespect 929
　contempt 930
slight-made 203
slily
　surreptitiously
　　544
　craftily 702
slim 203
　cunning 702
slime *viscous* 352
　dirt 653
sling *hang* 214
　project 284
　weapon 727
slink *hide* 528
　cowardice 862
　– *away avoid* 623
　disrepute 874
slip *small* 32
　elapse 109
　child 129
　strip 205
　petticoat 225
　descend 306
　error 495
　workshop 691
　fail 732
　false coin 800
　vice 945
　guilt 947
　give one the – 671
　let – *liberate* 750
　lose 776
　relinquish 782
　– *away* 187, 623
　– *cable* 623
　– the collar 671,
　　750
　– 'twixt cup and
　　lip 509
　let – the dogs of
　　war 722
　– in (*or* – into) 294
　– the memory 506
　– on 225
　– out 187
　– over *neglect* 460
　– of the pen 568
　– of the tongue
　　solecism 568
　　stammering 583
　– through the
　　fingers *miss an*
　　opportunity 135
　escape 671

fail 732
slipper 225
  hunt the – 840
slippery
  transient 111
  smooth 255
  greasy 355
  uncertain 475
  vacillating 607
  dangerous 665
  facile 705
  faithless 940
  – ground 667
slipshod 575
slipslop
  absurdity 497
  solecism 568
  weak language 575
slit *divide* 44
  chink 198
  furrow 259
slither 264
sliver 51
slobber *drivel* 297
  slop 337
  dirt 653
sloe *black* 431
slog 143
slogan 722
sloop 273
 –of-war 726
slop *spill* 297
  water 337
  dirt 653
slope *oblique* 217
  run away 623
sloppy *moist* 339
  marsh 345
  - *style* 575
slops *clothes* 225
slosh 337, 653
slot 44, 260
sloth 683
slouch *low* 207
  oblique 217
  move slowly 275
  inactive 683
slouching *ugly* 846
slough
  quagmire 345
  dirt 653
  difficulty 704
  adversity 735
  – of Despond 859
sloven *untidy* 59
  bungler 701
slovenly *untidy* 59
  careless 460
  - *style* 575
  dirty 653

awkward 699
vulgar 851
slow *tardy* 133
  inert 172
  moderate 174
  motion 275
  inactive 683
  wearisome 841
  dull 843
  by – degrees 26
  – movement
  music 415
  march in – time 275
  – as molasses in January 275
  be – to
  unwilling 603
  not finish 730
  refuse 764
slow-coach 701
slowness 275
sloyd 537
slubber 653
slubberdegullion 876
sludge 653
slug *slow* 275
  inaction 681
  inactivity 683
  bullet 727
sluggard 275, 683
sluggish 172, 823, 843
sluice *limit* 233
  egress 295
  river 348
  conduit 350
  open the –s 297
slum 653
slumber 683
slump 304
slur *blemish* 847
  stigma 874
  gloss over 937
  reproach 938
  – over *neglect* 460
  slight 483
slush *marsh* 345
  semiliquid 352
  dirt 653
slut *untidy* 59
  female 374
  dirty 653
  unchaste 962
sly *stealthy* 528
  cunning 702
smack
  small quantity 32
  mixture 41
  boat 273

impulse 276
taste 390
thud 406
kiss 902
strike 972
– the lips
pleasure 377
taste 390
savoury 394
rejoice 838
– of *resemble* 17
small
  – *in degree* 32
  – *in size* 193
  become – 195
  feel – 879
  of – account 643
  esteem of –
  account 930
  – arms 727
  – beer 643, 880, 930
  – coin 800
  – chance 473
  – fry 193, 643, 876
  – matter 643
  – number 103
  – part 51
  – pica 591
  in the – hours 125
  on a – scale 32, 193
  – talk 588
small-bore 727
small-clothes 225
smaller 34, 195
smallness 32
smalls 225
smalt 438
smart *pain* 378
  active 682
  clever 698
  feel 821
  grief 828
  witty 842
  pretty 845
  ornamental 847
  – *pace* 274
  – *saying* 842
  – *under* 821
smarten 847
smart-money 973
smash 162, 732
smasher 792
smatch 390
smatterer 493
smattering 491
smear *cover* 223
  soil 653
  blemish 848
smell 398

bad – 401
– of the lamp
  ornate style 577
  prepared 673
– powder 722
smell-feast 886
smelling-bottle 400
smelt *heat* 384
  prepare 673
smicker 838
smile 836, 838
  raise a – 840
  – at 856
  – of contempt 930
  – of fortune 734
  – upon *aid* 707
  courtesy 894
  endearment 902
smirch 431, 653
smirk 838
smite *maltreat* 649
  excite 824
  afflict 830
  punish 972
smith 690
smithereens 161
smitten *love* 897
  – with *moved* 615
smock 225, 258
smock-faced 862
smock-frock 225
smoke
  dust 330
  vapour 336
  heat 382
  tobacco 392
  discover 480a
  suspect 485
  unimportant 643
  dirt 653
  cure 670
  disrespect 929
  end in –
  shortcoming 304
  failure 732
  – the calumet of peace 723
  –ed glasses 424
  – screen 424
  – stack 260
smoking hot 382
smoking-jacket 225
smoking-room 191
smoky *opaque* 426
  dirty 653
smooth *uniform* 16
  calm 174
  flattery 213, 251
  not rough 255
  easy 705
  – the bed of death

707, 906
- down 174
- over 174
- the ruffled brow
  of care 834
- sailing 705
- water *easy* 705
- the way 705
smooth-bore 727
smoothly, go on -
  prosperous 734
smoothness **255**
smooth-tongued
  544, 933
smother
  repress 174
  kill 361
  stifle sound 581
  restrain 751
smoulder *inert* 172
  burn 382
  latent 526
smous 796, 797
smudge 431, 653,
  848
smug *affected* 855
smuggle
  introduce 228
  steal 791
  illegal 964
smuggler 792
smut
  dirt 653
  impurity 961
smutch 431
snack
  small quantity 32
  food 298
snacks, go - 778
snaffle 752
snag *projection* 250
  sharp 253
  danger 667
  hindrance 706
snail *slow* 275
snake *undulation*
  248
  serpent 366
  hissing 406
  miscreant 913
  scotch the - 640
  - in the grass
  hidden 528
  deceiver 548
  bad 649
  source of danger
  667
  evil-doer 913
  knave 941
snake-like
  convoluted 248

snap *break* 44
  eat 298
  brittle 328
  noise **406**
  rude 895
  - at *seize* 789
  bite 830
  censure 932
  - of the fingers
  trifle 643
  - one's fingers at
  defy 715
  insolence 885
  despise 930
  - the thread 70
  - up *seize* 789
  - one up
  censure 932
  -shot 554
snap-dragon 840
snappish 901
snare *deception* 545
snarl *growl* 412
  rude 895
  angry 900
  threaten 909
snatch
  small quantity 32
  seize 789
  - at *pursue* 622
  seize 789
  - a grace beyond
  the reach of art
  845
  - from one's grasp
  789
  - from the jaws of
  death 662, 672
  - from under
  one's nose 702
  - a verdict 545,
  702
snatches, by - 70
sneak *hide* 528
  coward 862
  servile 886
  base 940
  knave 941
  bad man 949
  - off, - out of 623
sneer *disparage* 929
  contempt 930
  blame 932
sneeze *blow* 349
  snuffle 409
  - at *despise* 930
sneezed at, not to
  be - 642
snick 32, 51
snicker 838
sniff *blow* 349

odour 398
  discovery 480a
sniffle 349
snigger *laugh* 838
  ridicule 856
  disrespect 929
sniggle 545
snip
  small quantity 32
  cut 44
  short 201
  tailor 225
sniping 716
snippet 32
snip-snap 713
snip-snap-snorem
  840
snivel *weep* 839
snivelling
  servile 886
snob *vulgar* 851
  plebeian 876
  servile 886
snobbishness
  flattery 933
snood
  headdress 225
  circle 247
snooker 840
Snooks, Mr. - 876
snooze 683
snozzle 250
snore 411, 683
snort 411, 412
snout 250
snow *ship* 273
  ice 383
  white 430
snow-ball 72
snow-blindness 443
snow-drift 72
snow-shoe 272
snow-storm 383
snub *short* 201
  hinder 706
  cast a slur 874
  humiliate 879
  bluster 885
  censure 932
snub-nosed 243
snuff *blow* 349
  pungent 392
  odour 398
  up to - 698, 702
  go out like the -
  of a candle 360
  - out 162, 421
  - up 296, 398
snuff-colour 433
snuffing, want -
  pert 885

snuffle *blow* 349
  hiss 409
  stammer 583
  hypocrisy 988
snuffy 653
snug *closed* 261
  comfortable 377
  safe 664
  prepared 673
  content 831
  secluded 893
  keep - 528, 893
  make all - 673
snuggery 189
snugness 827
so *similar* 17
  very 31
  therefore 476
  method 627
  - be it 488, 762
  - far so good 618
  - let it be 681
  - much the better
  831, 838
  - much the worse
  832, 835
  - to speak 17, 521
soak *immerse* 300
  water 337
  moist 339
  drunkenness 959
  - up 340
So-and-so, Mr. -
  neology 563
soap *lubricate* 332
  oil 356
  cleanser 652
soapy *unctuous* 355
  servile 886
  flattery 933
soar *great* 31
  height 206
  fly 267
  rise 305
sob 839
sober *moderate* 174
  wise 498
  sane 502
  style 576
  grave 837
  temperate 953
  abstinent 958
  - down 174, 502
  humility 879
  in - sadness
  affirmation 535
  - senses 502
  - truth *fact* 494
sober-minded 502
  calm 826
  humble 879

song *music* 415
  poem 597
  death – 360, 839
  love– 597
  for a mere – 815
  no – no supper 812
  old – 643
songster 416
soniferous 402
sonnet 597
sonneteer 597
sonorous *sound* 402
  loud 404
  language 577
sons of:
  – Belial 988
  – God 977
Soofeeism 984
soon *transient* 111
  future 121
  early 132
  too – for 135
sooner: – or later
  another time 119
  future 121
  – said than done
    704
soot 431, 653
sooth 511
  in good – 543
soothe
  allay 174
  relieve 834
  flatter 933
soothing
  faint sound 405
  – syrup 174
soothsay 511
soothsayer 513, 994
soothsaying 511
sop
  small quantity 32
  food 298
  fool 501
  inducement 615
  reward 973
  – to Cerberus 458
  – in the pan 615
soph 492, 541
Sophi 745, 996
sophism 477, 497
sophist *scholar* 492
  dissembler 548
sophister 492
  student 541
sophistical 477
sophisticate *mix* 41
  debase 659
sophisticated
  spurious 545
sophistry 477

sophomore 541
soporific 683, 841
soporous 683
soprano 410, 416
sorbet 298
sorcerer **994**
sorcery **992**
sordes 653
sordet 417
sordid *stingy* 819
  covetous 865
sordine 417
sore
  bodily pain 378
  disease 655
  mental suffering
    828, 830
  discontent 832
  anger 900
  – as a boil 901*a*
  – place 822
  – subject 830, 900
sorely *very* 31
s'orienter 278
sorites 476
sorority 712
sorrel 433, 434
sorrow 828
  give – words 839
sorry *trifling* 643
  grieved 828
  mean 876
  make a – face 874
  cut a – figure 874
  be – for 750, 914
  in a – plight 732
  – sight 830, 837
sort *degree* 26
  arrange 60
  kind 75
  – with
    sociality 892
sortable
sortance }
  agreement 23
sortes
  chance 156, 621
  – Virgilianæ
    sorcery 992
sortie 716
sortilege
  prediction 511
  sorcery 992
sortilegy 621
sortition 621
sorts, out of –
  ill-health 655
  sulky 901*a*
S.O.S. 669, 707
so-so *small* 32
  trifling 643

imperfect 651
sostenuto 415
sot *fool* 501
  drunkard 959
sot à triple étage
  501
sotto voce
  faint sound 405
  conceal 528
  voiceless 581
sou *money* 800
  qui n'a pas le –
    804
soubrette 599, 746
sough *conduit* 350
  noise 405
  cloaca 653
soul *essence* 5
  person 372
  intellect 450
  genius 498
  affections 820
  cure of –s 995
  flow of – 588
  not a – 187
  not dare to say
    one's – is his
    own *subjection*
    749
  fear 860
  – of wit 572
  have one's whole
    – in his work
    686
soulless 683, 823
soul-mate 905
soul-sick 837
soul-stirring 821,
  824
sound *great* 31
  conformable 82
  stable 150
  strong 159
  fathom 208
  bay 343
  noise **402**
  investigate 461
  measure 466
  true 494
  wise 498
  sane 502
  good 648
  perfect 650
  healthy 654
  solvent 803
  orthodox 983*a*
  catch a – 418
  safe and – 654,
    670
  – the alarm
    indication 550

warning 668
  alarm 669
  fear 860
  – asleep 683
  full of – and fury
    unmeaning 517
  insolent 885
  – the horn 416
  – of limb 654
  – locator 726
  – mind 502
  – the praises of
    931
  – the note of prep-
    aration 673
  – reasoning 476
  – a retreat 283
  – sleep 683
  – a trumpet
    publish 531
    alarm 669
  – of wind 654
sounding: big –
  577
  – brass 517
sounding-board 417
soundings 208
soundless
  unfathomable 208
  silent 403
soup 298, 352
soupçon 32, 41
souplé 298
sour *acid* 397
  discontented 832
  embitter 835
  uncivil 895
  sulky 901
  – grapes
    impossible 471
    excuse 617
  – the temper 830
source *beginning* 66
  cause 153
sourdet 417
sourdine 417
  à la – *noiseless* 405
  concealed 528
sourdough 463
soured 832
sourness **397**
sous tous les
  rapports 52
souse 310, 337
South *direction* 278
  North and –
    opposite 237
Southern
  antipodes 237
  – Cross 318
souvenir 505

sovereign
superior 33
all-powerful 159
authorities 737
ruler 745
– contempt 930
– remedy 662
Soviet 696, 737
sow *scatter* 73
pig 366
agriculture 371
female 374
get the wrong –
by the ear
misjudgment 481
error 495
mismanage 699
fail 732
– broadcast 818
– dissension 713,
898
– the sand 645
– the seed
prepare 673
– the seeds of
cause 153
teach 537
– one's wild oats
improve 658
amusement 840
vice 945
intemperance 954
sozzled 959
spa *town* 189
sanatorium 662
space *distribute* 60
time 106
extension **180**
musical 413
celestial –s 318
wide open –'s 180
spaddle 272
spade 272
call a – a spade
plain language
576
straightforward
703
spade-husbandry
371
spahi 726
span *join* 43
link 45
duality 89
time 106
transient 111
distance 196
near 196
length 200
short 201
measure 466

– new 124
spangle *spark* 420
ornament 847
spaniel *dog* 366
servile 886
spanish fly 171
spank *swift* 274
flog 972
spanking *large* 192
– pace 274
spanner 633
spar *beam* 214
quarrel 713
contend 720
spare *extra* 37
small 193
meagre 203
refrain 623
store 636
scanty 640
redundant 641
disuse 678
inaction 681
relinquish 782
give 784
economy 817
exempt 927a
temperate 953
enough and to –
639
not a moment to –
682
to – 641
– diet 956
– no expense 816
– no pains 686
– room 180
– time 685
spared: be –
live 359
it cannot be – 630
sparge 337
spargefaction
scatter 73
wet 337
sparing [*see* spare]
small 32
economy 817
parsimony 819
temperate 953
with a – hand 819
with no – hand
639
– of praise 932
– of words 585
spark *small* 32
heat 382
light 420
luminary 423
wag 844
fop 854

as the –s fly up-
wards *habit* 613
sparkle
bubble 353
glisten 420
sparkling
vigorous 574
excitement 824
cheerful 836
wit 842
beauty 845
with – eyes 827
sparse 73
sparsity 103
Spartacus 742
spartan 739
spasm
sudden change 146
violence 173
agitation 315
pain 378
spasmodic
discontinuous 70
irregular 139
changeable 149
violent 173
spat 225, 713
spate 348
spathic 204
spatter *dirt* 653
spatterdash 225
spatula 191, 272
spavined 655
spawn *produce* 161
offspring 167
dirt 653
spay 38, 158
speak 560, 580, 582
– one fair 894
– for 937
– ill of 932, 934
– for itself 518,
528
– low 581
– of *meaning* 516
publish 531
speak 582
– out *make*
manifest 525
artless 703
– softly 581
– to 586
– up 411
– up for 937
– volumes 467
– well of 931
speakeasy 189, 964
speaker
interpreter 524
chairman 694
speakie 964

speaking: much –
584
way of – 521
– likeness 554
on – terms 888
speaking-trumpet
418
spear 260, 727
– shaped 253
spearman 726
special 79
– correspondent
593
special pleader 968
special pleading
sophistry 477
speciali gratiâ 760
specialist 662, 700
speciality **79**
specialty
security 771
specie 800
species *kind* 75
appearance 448
human – 372
specific *special* 79
remedy 662
– gravity 321
specification 594
specify
particularize 79
tell 527
name 564
specimen 82
specious
probable 472
sophistical 477
beauty 845
flattering 933
pardonable 937
speck 32
speckle 440, 848
spectacle
appearance 448
prodigy 872
show 882
drama 599
spectacles 445
look through rose
coloured – 523
spectacular 882
spectator **444**
spectral 4, 980
spectre
fallacy of vision
443
ugly 846
ghost 980
spectroscope
light 420
colour 428

spring balance 319	*deceptive* 545	– dance 840	*pain* 378, 649,
springe 545	*illegitimate* 925	– deal 922	828
spring-gun 545	**spurlos versenkt** 2,	– the circle 471	*injure* 659
spring tide	449	– inches 180	**stabilimeter** 150
greatness 31	**spurn** *reject* 55	– peg into a round	**stabilisator** 150
increase 35	*disdain* 930	hole 699	**stability** 16, **150**
completeness 52	**spurred** 253	– up 556	**stable** *firm* 150
youth 127	**spurt**	– with 23	*house* 189
high 206	*transient* 111	– yards 180	lock the – door
low 207	*swift* 274	**square-toes** 857	when the steed
wave' 348	*gush* 348	**squash** *destroy* 162	is stolen
water 337	*impulse* 612	*flatten* 251	*too late* 135
springy 325	*haste* 684	*blow* 276	*useless* 645
sprinkle *add* 37	*exertion* 686	*soft* 324	*bungling* 699
mix 41	**sputa** 299	*marsh* 345	– equilibrium 150
scatter 73	**sputter** *emit* 297	*semiliquid* 352	**staccato** 415
wet 337	*splash* 348	*hiss* 409	**stack** 72, 636
rain 348	*stammer* 583	*game* 840	**staddle** 215
variegate 440	**spy** *see* 441	**squashy** 345, 352	**stade** 252
baptize 998	*spectator* 444	**squat** 308	**stadium** 728, 840
sprinkler 348, 385	*inquire* 461	*locate oneself* 184	**stadtholder** 745
sprinkling	*informer* 527	*little* 193	**staff** *support* 215
small quantity 32	*emissary* 534	*short* 201	*music* 413
sprint 274	*watcher* 664	*thick* 202	*measure* 466
sprit *sprout* 167	*warning* 668	*low* 207	*signal* 550
support 215	**spy-glass** 445	**squatter** 188	*council* 696
sprite 979, 980	**squab** *large* 192	**squaw** *woman* 374	*party* 712
sprout *grow* 35	*short* 201	*wife* 903	*weapon* 727
germinate 161	*broad* 202	**squeak**⎱ 411, 412	*chief* 745
offspring 167	*bench* 215	**squeal**⎰	*retinue* 746
expand 194	**squabble** 713	**squeamish** 655	pastoral – 999
– from *result* 154	**squad** 72, 726	*unwilling* 603	– of life 298
spruce 652, 845	**squadron** 726	*fastidious* 868	– of office 747
– up 847	– leader 745	**squeasy** 868	– officer 745
sprue 653	**squalid** 653, 846	**squeezable** 762	**stag** *deer* 366
sprung 651, 659	**squall** *violent* 173	**squeeze**	*male* 373
spry 682, 836	*wind* 349	*contract* 195	*defaulter* 808
spud 272	*cry* 411	*condense* 321	**stage** *degree* 26
spume 353	*quarrel* 713	*embrace* 894	*term* 71
spun out 110, 573	**squalor** 653	**squeeze out** 301,	*time* 106
spunk 861	**squamous** 204, 223	784	*position* 183
spur	**squander** *waste* 638	**squelch** 162	*layer* 205
pointed 250	*misuse* 679	**squib** *sound* 406	*platform* 215
sharp 253	*lose* 776	*lampoon* 856, 934	*forum* 542
incite 615	*prodigal* 818	**squiffy** 959	*drama* 599
hasten 684	**square**	**squilgee** 652	*arena* 728
win –s *succeed* 731	*congruous* 23	**squint**	come upon the –
glory 873	*compensate* 30	*peephole* 260	446
on the – of the	*four* 95	*look* 441	on the – 525, 599
moment	*limited space* 182	*defective sight* 443	go off the – 293
instantly 113	*houses* 189	**squirarchy** 875	revolving – 599
now 118	*perpendicular* 212	**squire** *aid* 707	– business 599
soon 132	*form* 244	*attendant* 746	– coach 272
opportune 134	*sparring* 720	*gentry* 875	– craft 599
impulse 612	*justice* 924	– of Dames 897	– direction 697
– gearing 633	*honourable* 939	**squirm** 315	– effect 882
the – of necessity	make all – 660	**squirrel** 274, 682	– hand 599
745	on the – 939	**squirt** 297, 348	– manager 599
spurious	– accounts	**S.S.C.** 968	– name 565
erroneous 495	*pay* 807	**stab** *pierce* 260	– play 599
false 544	*account* 811	*kill* 361	– player 599

– struck 599
– whisper 580
stager *player* 599
  doer 690
  old – 130
stagger *slow* 275
  totter 314, 821
  agitate 315
  unexpected 508
  dissuade 616
  affect 824
  astonish 870
  – belief *doubt* 485
  – like a drunken
    man 605
staggers 315
stagirite 850
stagnant 265
stagnation 681
stagy 599, 855
staid *wise* 498
  calm 826
  grave 837
stain *paint* 223
  colour 428
  dirt 653
  spoil 659
  blemish 848
  disgrace 874
  – paper *writing*
    590
stained, travel- 266
stainless *clean* 652
  honourable 939
  innocent 946
stair 305, 627
stake *fastening* 45
  wager 621
  danger 665
  security 771
  property 780
  lay down 807
  execution 975
  at – *intended* 620
  in danger 665
  the – *agony* 828
  burn at the – 384
stalactite 224
stalagmite 224
stale *old* 124
  insipid 391
  deteriorated 659
  – flat and unprof-
    itable 645
  – news 532
stale-mate 27, 731
stalk *stem* 153
  support 215
  walk 266
  – abroad
    generality 78

pursue 622
proud 878
stalking-horse
  ambush 530
  plea 617
stall *cease* 142
  abode 189
  receptacle 191
  support 215
  play-house 599
  mart 799
  churchdom 995
  cathedral 1000
  finger– 223
stallion 271, 373
stalwart 159, 192
stamina 159, 604a
stammel 434
stammering 583
stamp
  character 7
  prototype 22
  kind 75
  form 240
  mark 550
  engraving 558
  complete 729
  security 771
  – the foot
    anger 900
  – in the memory
    505
  – out 162, 385
stampede 860
stanch – *a flow* 348
  persevering 604a
  health 654
  reinstate 660
stanchion 215
stanchless 825
stand *exist* 1
  rank 71
  long time 110
  permanent 141
  support 215
  quiescence 265
  difficulty 704
  resistance 719
  brook 821
  patience 826
  brave 861
  at a – 681
  come to a – 704
  make a – 708, 719
  take one's –
    resolve 604
    resist 719
    due 924
  take one's – upon
    reasoning 476
    affirm 535

plea 617
– aghast 870
– aloof 623, 681
– of arms 727
– at attention 507
– the brunt 717
– by *near* 197
  aid 707
  defend 717
– a chance 470,
  472
– committed 754
– at ease 458
– to one's engage-
  ment 772
– fair for 472
– fire 861
– firm 150, 719
– first 66
– for *indicate* 550
  deputy 759
  candidate 763
– forth 446
– one's ground
  preserved 670
  resist 719
– the hazard of
  the die 621
– one in 812
– in need of 630
– no nonsense 604
– off 287, 623
– on 215
– out *project* 250
  visible 446
  obstinate 606
– over 133
– the proof 648
– to reason
  proof 478
  manifest 525
  right 922
– on one's rights
  748
– in the shoes of
  147
– one in good
  stead 644
– still *remain* 141
  stop 265
  difficulty 704
– the test 494, 648
– up [*see below*]
– upon *pride* 878
– upon one's
  rights 924
– in the way of 706
– well in the
  opinion of 931
stand up 212, 307
– against 719

– fight 720
– for 931, 937
– to 459
standard *model* 22
  degree 26
  mean 29
  rule 80
  measure 466
  flag 550
  good 648
  perfect 650
  gold – 800
standard-bearer
  726
standardize 22, 60,
  466
standing *footing* 8
  degree 26
  long time 110
  permanence 141
  situation 183
  note 873
  – army 726
  – dish *rule* 80
  permanent 141
  – jest *wit* 842
  – order 613, 963
  – type 591
  – water 343
stand-pipe 348, 385
stand-point 183,
  441
Stannary Court 966
stanza 597
staple
  fastening 45
  whole 50
  peg 214
  texture 329
  material 635
  trade 794
  mart 799
  – commodity 798
star *luminary* 423
  actor 599
  destiny 601
  badge 747
  ornament 847
  glory 873
  noble 875
  decoration 877
  – in the ascendant
    success 731
    prosperity 734
  – of fashion 852
  – it *drama* 599
  fame 873
  display 882
  – shell 423
  – trap 599
starboard 238

[651]

starch *stiff* 323
  viscid 352
  affected 855
  proud 878
Star Chamber 966
starched
  ostentatious 882
stare *look* 441
  curiosity 455
  wonder 870
  make one – 870
  – out of counte-
    nance
  humiliate 879
  insolent 885
  discourteous 895
  – one in the face
  destiny 152
  manifest 525
  Death –s one in
    the face 360
stare super anti-
  quas vias
  continue 143
  habit 613
  preservation 670
  inaction 681
star-gazing 318
staring 446
stark *very* 31
  sheer 32
  complete 52
  hard 323
  – blind 442
  – naked 226
stark staring 31
  manifest 525
  – mad 503
starlight 422
starlike
  pointed 253
starry 318
stars [see star]
  worlds 318
  bless one's – 916
  – in the firmament
  multitude 102
  – and stripes 550
start *begin* 66
  sudden change
    146
  arise 151
  impulse 276
  move 284
  depart 293
  leap 309
  unexpected 508
  suggest 514
  crack 659
  offer 763
  fear 860

wonder 870
get the –
  precede 280
  success 731
give a – to 276
have the –
  prior 116
  early 132
  get before 280
  – afresh 66
  – a doubt 485
  – game 622
  – off 293
  – a question 461
  – up *project* 250
  arise 305
  appear 446
starting: – hole
  plea 617
  – point
  departure 293
  reasoning 476
  eyes – out of one's
    head 870
startle *doubt* 485
  unexpected 508
  excite 824
  fear 860
  wonder 870
startling 508
startlish 825
starts, by fits and –
  608
starvation 640, 956
starve *cold* 383, 385
  poverty 804
  parsimony 819
  fast 956
starveling *thin* 203
  insufficient 640
  poor 804
state *condition* **7**
  speciality 79
  nation 372
  inform 527
  affirm 535
  government 737
  realm 780
  ostentation 882
  robes of – 747
  secretary of – 694
  – of affairs 151
  –'s evidence 529
  – of facts
  description 594
  lawsuit 969
  – paper 551
  – room 191
  – of siege 722
statecraft 693
stated periods, at –

138
stately *grand* 873
  proud 878
  pompous 882
statement 535, 594
statemonger 694
state prison 752
states-general 696
statesman 694
statesmanlike 698
statesmanship 692,
  693
static 404
Statics *strength* 159
  gravity 319
station *degree* 26
  term 71
  place 182
  situation 183
  locate 184
  rank 873
stationary
  permanent 141
  quiescent 265
stationery 590
station-house 752
statist 694
statistics 85, 86
statu:
  in – pupillari 127
  in – quo 141, 660
statuary 557, 559
statue 554
  still as a – 265
stature 206
status *position* 8
  term: 71
  situation 183
  repute 873
status quo
  past 122
  unchanged 145
  restoration 660
  – ante bellum 145
statute 697, 963
staunch *health* 654
  reinstate 660
  honest 939
  – belief 484
stave *music* 413,
  415
  contention 720
  – in *concave* 252
  hole 260
  – off 133, 706
stay *remain* 106
  wait 133
  continue 141
  stop 142
  dwell 186
  support 215

not move 265
  prevent 706
  – away 187
  – one's hand
  cease 142
  relinquish 624
  rest 687
  – at home 893
stayed [see staid]
stays *corset* 225
stead 644
  in the – of
  substitution 147
  commission 755
  deputy 759
  stand one in
    good – 644
steadfast *stable* 150
  persevering 604a
  – belief 484
  – thought 457
steady *uniform* 16
  regular 80
  periodic 138
  stable 150
  persevering 604a
  unexcitable 826
  cautious 864
steal 791
  – along 275, 528
  – away 623
  – on the ear 405
  – a march
  prior 116
  early 132
  precede 280
  deceive 545
  active 682
  cunning 702
  – upon one 508
stealing **791**
stealth 528
  do good by – &c.
    881
stealthy 528
  cunning 702
  caution 864
steam *navigate* 267
  gas 334
  vaporize 336
  bubbles 353
  under – 267
  under sail and –
    274
  – car 272
  – up 171
  get the – up 673
steamboat 273
steam-engine to
  crack a nut
  waste 638

long 200
narrow 203
furrow 259
light 420
stripe 440
mark 550
streaked 219, 440
stream *assemble* 72
move 264
– *of fluid* **347**
– *of water* 348
– *of air* 349
– *of light* 420
abundance 639
against the – 708
with the –
conformity 82
progression 282
assent 488
facility 705
concord 714
fashion 852
servility 886
– *of events* 151
– *of time* 109
streamer *flag* 550
streaming 47, 73
streamlet 348
street 189, 627
man in the – 876
streets:
in the open – 525
on the – 961
street-walker 962
strength
quantity 25
degree 26
greatness 31
vigour **159**
energy 171
tenacity 327
animality 364
put all one's –
into 686
lose – 655
tower of – 717
– of mind 604
strengthen 35
strengthless 160
strenuous
persevering 604a
active 682
exertion 686
Strephon and Chloe 902
stress *emphasis* 580
requirement 630
importance 642
strain 686
difficulty 704
by – of 601

lay – on 476
– of circumstances
compulsion 744
– of weather 349
stretch *expanse* 180
expand 194
extend 200
exaggerate 549
exertion 686
encroach 925
at a – 69
mind on the – 451
on the – 686
upon the – 457
– away to 196
– forth one's hand
680, 789
– of the imagina-
tion 515, 549
– the meaning 523
– a point 83, 303
exaggerate 549
severity 739
permit 760
not observe 773
undue 925
exempt 927a
– to *distance* 196
length 200
stretcher 215, 272
strew 73
striæ, striated 259, 440
stricken *pain* 828
terror– 860
be – by 655
– in years 128
strict
in conformity 82
exact 494
severe 739
conscientious 939
orthodox 983a
– inquiry 461
– interpretation
522
– search 461
– settlement 780
strictly speaking
literally 19
exact 494
interpreted 522
stricture
constriction 203
hindrance 706
censure 932
stride *distance* 196
motion 264
walk 266
strident 410
strides: make – 282

rapid – 274
stridor 410
strife 713, 720
strigil 652
strike *operate* 170
hit 276
resist 719
disobey 742
impress 824
beat 972
– at 716
– a balance
equalize 27
mean 29
pay 807
– a bargain 769, 794
– a blow *act* 680
– dumb *dumb* 581
excitement 824
wonder 870
humble 879
– the eye 457
– the first blow
716
– one's flag 725
– hard 171
– all of a heap
824, 860
– home 171
– in with
imitate 19
assent 488
cooperate 709
– the iron while it
is hot 134
– a light 384, 420
– the lyre 416
– the mind 457
– out something
new 146, 515
– off *exclude* 55
– one 451
– out *exclude* 55
destroy 162
invent 515
obliterate 552
scheme 626
– off the roll 756, 972
– at the root of
162
– root 150
– sail 275
– tents 293
– terror 860
– up 416
– with wonder 870
striker 927
striking 525
– *likeness* 554

strikingly
greatly 31
string *tie* 43
ligature 45
continuity 69
filament 205
musical note 413
– together 60, 69
**stringed instru-
ments** 417
stringent
energetic 171
authoritative 737
strict 739
compulsory 744
strings: *music* 417
leading – 541
pull the – 175, 693
two – to one's bow
632
stringy 205, 327
strip *adjunct* 39
narrow 203
filament 205
divest 226
take 780
rob 791
stripe *length* 200
variegation 440
mark 550
badge 747
blow 972
stripling 129
stripped *poor* 804
strive *endeavour*
675
exert 686
contend 720
– against 720
stroke *impulse* 276
touch 379
mark 550
evil 619
expedient 626
disease 655
action 680
success 731
painful 830
at a – 113
good – 626
– of death 360
– of the pen
writing 590
command 741
– of policy 626
– of time 113
– of word 686
– the wrong way
256
stroll 266
strolling player 599

strong *great* 31
  powerful 159
  energetic 171
  tough 327
  taste 390
  pungent 392
  fetid 401
  healthy 654
  feeling 821
  wonderful! 870
  smell − of 398
  − accent 580
  − argument 476
  by a − arm 744
  − box 802
  with a − hand
  resolution 604
  exertion 686
  severity 739
  − language 574
  − pull 686
  − point 476
strong-headed 498
stronghold
  refuge 666
  defence 717
  prison 752
strong-minded 498,
  861
strong-scented 398
strong-willed 604
strop 253
strophe 597
strow 73
struck [*see*
  stricken, strike]
  awe− 860
  − down 732
  − all of a heap
  emotion 821
  wonder 870
  humbled 879
  − with *love* 897
structural *state* 7
structure
  production 161
  form 240
  texture 329
  organization 357
struggle *exert* 686
  difficulty 704
  contend 720
strum 416, 517
strumpet 962
strung
  highly − 825
strut *walk* 266
  pride 878
  parade 882
  boast 884
  − and fret one's

hour upon a
  stage 359, 599
strychnine 663
stub 40, 550
stubbed 201
stubble *remains* 40
  useless 645
stubborn
  strong 159
  hard 323
  obstinate 606
  resistance 719
stubby 201
stucco 45, 223
stuck [*see* stick]
  − fast 150, 704
  be − on 897
stuck-up 878
stud *hanging-peg*
  214
  knob 250
  horses 271
studded *many* 102
  spiked 253
  variegated 440
student 541
stud-farm 370
studied
  predetermined
  611
studio *room* 191
  painting 556
  workshop 691
studious
  thoughtful 451
  docile 539
  intending 620
study *copy* 21
  room 191
  thought 451
  attention 457
  research 461
  learning 539
  painting 556
  intention 620
  retreat 893
  brown − 515
stuff *substance* 3
  contents 190
  expand 194
  line 224
  matter 316
  texture 329
  absurdity 497
  unmeaning 517
  material 635
  trifle 643
  overeat 957
  such − as dreams
  are made of 515
  − gown 968

− in 300
− the memory
  with 505
− and nonsense
  unsubstantial 4
  absurdity 497
  unmeaning 517
− up *close* 261
  hoax 545
stuffed
  redundancy 641
stuffing *contents* 190
  lining 224
  stopper 263
stuffy 321, 382
stultified 732
stultify oneself 699
stultiloquy 497
stumble *fall* 306
  flounder 315
  error 495
  unskilful 699
  failure 732
  − on *chance* 156
  discover 480a
stumbling-block
  difficulty 704
  hindrance 706
stump
  remainder 40
  trunk 51
  walk 266
  drawing 556
  speak 582
  stir your −s
  active 682
  worn to the − 659
  − along *slow* 275
stump orator 582,
  887
stumpy *short* 201
stun *physically*
  insensible 376
  loud 404
  deafen 419
  unexpected 508
  morally insen-
  sible 823
  affect 824
  astonish 870
stung [*see* sting]
  − to the quick 824
stunt *shorten* 201
  performance 680
stunted 193, 195
  insufficient 640
stupe 834
stupefaction 826
stupefy
  - *physically* 376
  - *morally* 823

  astonish 870
stupendous
  great 31
  large 192
  wonderful 870
stupid
  unsubstantial 4
  misjudging 481
  credulous 486
  unintelligent 499
  tiresome 841
  dull 843
stupor
  insensibility 823
  wonder 870
stupration 961
sturdy *strong* 159
  persevering 604a
  − *beggar* 767, 792
stutter 583
sty *house* 189
  enclosure 232
  dirt 653
Stygian *dark* 421
  diabolic 945
  infernal 982
  cross the − *ferry*
  die 360
  − *shore*
  death 360
style *state* 7
  time 114
  painting 556
  graver 558
  name 564
  diction **569**
  writing 590
  beauty 845
  fashion 852
stylet
  awl 262
  dagger 727
stylist 578
Stylites, Simon −
  893
stylographic pen
  590
stylography 590
stylus 590
styptic 397
Styx 982
suasible 602
suasion 615
suave mari magno
  664
suaviter in modo
  826, 894
suavity 894
sub 34
  − spe rati 475
subacid 397

subaction 330
subahdar 745
subalpine 206
subaltern
  inferior 34
  soldier 726
  officer 745
  servant 746
  plebeian 876
subaqueous 208
subastral 318
subaudition 527
subcommittee 696
subconscious 317
subcontrary 237
subcutaneous 221
subdean 996
subdichotomy 91
subdititious 147
subdivide 44
subdivision
  part 51
  class 75
  military 726
  realty 780
subdolous 702
subdominant 413
subdual 731
subduction **38**
subdue *calm* 174
  succeed 731
subdued
  morally 826
sub-editor 593
subitaneous 113
subito 113
subjacent 207
subject *dominate*
  175
  liable 177
  topic 454
  meaning 516
  servant 746
  enthral 749
  - of dispute 713
  - to examination
  461
  - of inquiry 461
  - of thought 454
  - to 469, 475
subjection **749**
subjective
  intrinsic 5
  immaterial 317
  intellectual 450
subjoin 37
subjugate 731, 749
subjugation 732,
  824
subjunctive 37
sublapsarian 984

sublation 38
sublevation 307
sub-lieutenant 745
sublimate
  elevate 307
  lighten 320
  vaporize 336
sublime *high* 206
  language 574
  beauty 845
  glory 873
  magnanimous
  942
from the − to the
  ridiculous 853
subliminal 317
sublineation 550
sublunary 318
submarine
  deep 208
  ship 272
  warship 726
  − chaser 726
  − warfare 722
submediant 413
submerge
  destroy 162
  immerse 300
  plunge 310
  steep 337
submersible 273,
  726
submersion 208
subministration
  707
submission **725**
  obedience 743
submissive
  tractable 705
  enduring 826
  humble 879
submit to arbitra-
  tion 774
submonish 695
submultiple 84
subordinate
  inferior 34
  unimportant 643
  subject 749
subordination 58
suborn 615, 795
subpœna 741, 969
subreption
  falsehood 544
  acquisition 775
subrogation 147
subscribe
  assent 488
  aid 707
  agree to 769
  give 784

subscript 39, 65
subscription
  gift 784
subsequent
  - *in order* 63
  - *in time* 117
subserviency
  servility 886
subservient
  instrumental 631
  aid 707
  subject 749
subside 36, 306
subsidiary *aid* 707
  servant 746
subsidy
  assistance 707
  gift 784
  pay 809
subsist *exist* 1
  continue 141
  live 359
subsistence 298
subsoil 221, 342
substance
  existence 1
  thing 3
  quantity 25
  inside 221
  matter 316
  texture 329
  important part
  642
  wealth 803
  in − 596
  man of − 803
substantial
  existing 1
  hypostatic 3
  material 316
  dense 321
  true 494
  − *meaning* 516
substantiality **3**
substantially
  intrinsically 5
  − *true* 494
substantiate 467,
  924
substantive 1, 3
substitute
  inferior 34
  change 147
  means **634**
  deputy 759
substitution **147**
substratum
  substance 3
  layer 204
  base 211
  support 215

  interior 221
  materiality 316
substructure 211
subsultory 315
subsume 54
subtend 237
subterfuge 617
  sophistry 477
  lie 546
  cunning 702
subterranean 208
subtile *light* 320
  rare 322
  - *texture* 329
subtilize *rarefy* 322
  sophistry 477
subtle *slight* 32
  light 320
  cunning 702
  − *point* 704
  − *reasoning* 476
subtlety 477, 498
subtraction
  subduction 38
  arithmetic 85
  taking 789
subtrahend 38, 84
suburb *town* 189
  near 197
  environs 227
subvention
  support 215
  aid 707
  gift 784
subversion 146
subvert *destroy* 162
  invert 218
  depress 308
subway 627
  − train 272
succedaneum 147
succeed *follow* 63
  posterior 117
  success 731
  transfer 783
  − to *acquire* 775
succès d'estime 873
success **731**
succession
  sequence 63
  continuity 69
  repetition 104
  posteriority 117
  transfer 783
  in quick − 136
  in regular − 138
  − of ideas 451
  − of time 109
successless 732
successor 65, 117
succinct 572

succour 707
succubus 980
succulent
  nutritive 298
  juicy 333
  semiliquid 352
succumb
  fatigue 688
  yield 725
  fail 732
succussion 315
such: – as 17
  – being the case 8
  – like 17
  – a one 372
suchwise 8
suck
  draw off 297
  drink 298
  take 789
  – in 296
  – the blood of 789
sucker 260, 547
suckle 707
suckling *infant* 129
suction *force* 157
  reception 296
sudary 652
sudation 299
sudatory 386
sudden
  transient 111
  instantaneous 113
  soon 132
  unexpected 508
  – burst 508
  – death 360
  – and quick in
    quarrel 901
  – thought 612
sudorific 382
suds *froth* 353
  in the – 704, 837
sue *demand* 765
  go to law 969
suet 356
suffer *physical pain*
  378
  disease 655
  allow 760
  feel 821
  endure 826
  moral pain 828
  – for 972
  – punishment 972
sufferance, tenant
  on – 779
suffice 639
sufficiency 639
suffix *adjunct* 39
  sequence 63

sequel 65
letter 561
suffiation 349
suffocate *kill* 361
  excess 641
suffocating 382, 401
suffocation 361
suffragan 996
suffrage 609
suffragette 742
suffusion
  mixture 41
  feeling 821
  blush 879
sugar 396
sugar-loaf 253
suggest *suppose* 514
  inform 527
  influence 615
  advise 695
  – itself 451, 515
  – a question 461
suggestio falsi 546
suggestion 626, 695
suggestive
  reminder 505
  significant 516
  descriptive 594
  bawdy 961
sui generis 83
suicidal 162
suicide *killing* 361
suisse *beadle* 996
Suisse, point d'ar-
  gent point de –
  812
suit *accord* 23
  series 69
  class 75
  clothes 225
  expedient 646
  petition 765
  courtship 902
  follow – 19
  law– 969
  love– 897
  – the action to the
    word 550
  – the occasion 646
  do – and service
    743
suit case 191
suitable 23, 646
  – season 134
suite *sequel* 65
  series 69
  escort 88
  retinue 746
  – of rooms 189, 191
suitor
  petitioner 767

lover 897
lawsuit 969
sulcated 259
sulky *carriage* 272
  obstinate 606
  discontented 832
  dejected 837
  sullen 901a
sullen
  obstinate 606
  gloomy 837
  discourteous 895
  sulky 901a
sullenness 901a
sully 653, 874
sulphur 388
  – coloured 436
sultan 745
sultry 382
sum *number* 84
  money 800
  – and substance
    meaning 516
  synopsis 596
  important part
    642
  – total 800
  – up *reckon* 85
  description 594
  compendium 596
sumless 105
summation 37, 85
summary
  transient 111
  early 132
  short 201
  concise 572
  compendious 596
  illegal 964
  – of facts 594
summer *season* 125
  support 215
  heat 382
  Indian – 125
  St. Luke's – 125
  St. Martin's – 125
  – lightning 423
  – time 114
summer-house 191
summerset 218
summit *top* **210**
summon 741, 969
  – up 505, 824
  – up courage 861
summum:
  – bonum 618, 827
  – jus 922
sump *base* 211
  pool 343
  slough 345
  store 636

cess 653
sumpter-horse 271
sumptuary 800, 809
sumptuous 882
sum-total 50
sun 318
  luminary 423
  glory 873
  bask in the – 377
  going down of
    the – 126
  farthing candle to
    the – 645
  under the – 180,
    318
  as the – at noon-
    day *bright* 420
  certain 474
  plain 525
  – oneself 384
Sun:
  – of Righteousness
    976
sunbeam 420
  –s from cucumbers
    471
sunburn *heat* 384
sunburnt *brown* 433
Sunday:
  – Monday &c. 138
  –'s best 847, 882
  – school 542
sunder 44
sundial 114
sundown 126
sundry 102
sunk [*see* sink]
  deep 208
  – fence 717
  – in iniquity 945
  – in oblivion 508
sunken rocks 667
sunless 421
sunlight 420
sunny *warm* 382
  luminous 420
  cheerful 836
sunny side 829
  view the – 858
  – of the hedge 734
sun-painting 556
sunrise 125
sunset 126
  at – 133
sunshade 223, 424
sunshine *light* 420
  prosperity 734
  happy 827
  cheerful 836
sunstroke 384, 503
sun-up 125

suo: – periculo 926|
– sibi gladio hunc
jugulo
absurdity 479
retaliation 718
sup *small quantity*
32
feed 298
– full of horrors
828
super *theatrical* 599
superable 470
superabound 641
superadd 37
superannuated 128
superb 845
supercargo 694
supercherie 545
supercilious
proud 878
insolent 885
disrespectful 929
scornful 930
superdreadnought
726
supereminence
648, 873
supererogation 641,
645
superexaltation 873
superexcellence
648
superfetation 37,
168
superficial
shallow 209
outside 220
misjudging 481
ignorant 491
– extent 180
superficies 220
superfine 648
superfluitant 305
superfluity 40, 641
superfluous 645
superhuman 650,
976
superimpose 233
superimposed 206
superincumbent
206, 319
superinduce
change 140
cause 153
produce 161
superintend 693
superintendent 694
superior *greater* 33
– *in size* 194
important 642
good 648

director 694
superiority 33
superjunction 37
superlative 33
superlatively good
648
superman 33
supernal 206, 210,
981
supernatant 206,
305
supernatural 976,
980
– aid 707
supernumerary
adjunct 39
theatrical 599
reserve 636
redundant 641
superpose 37, 223
supersaturate 641
superscription 550,
590
supersede
substitute 147
disuse 678
relinquish 782
supersensible 317
superstition
credulity 486
error 495
religion 984
superstratum 220
superstructure 729
supertax 812
supertonic 413
supervacaneous
641
supervene
extrinsic 6
be added 37
succeed 117
happen 151
supervise 693
supervisor 694
supination 213
supine
horizontal 213
inverted 218
sluggish 683
mentally torpid
823
suppeditate 637
supper 298
supplant 147
supple *soft* 324
servile 886
supplement
addition 37
adjunct 39
completion 52

publication 531
book 593
suppletory 37
suppliant 765, 767
supplicate *beg* 765
pity 914
worship 990
supplies
materials 635
aid 707
money 800
supply *store* 636
provide 637
give 784
– aid 707
– deficiencies 52
– the place of 147
– and transport
726
support *perform* 170
sustain 215
evidence 467
preserve 670
aid 707
feel 821
endure 826
vindicate 937
– life 359
supporter 711
–s *heraldic* 550
suppose 514
supposing 469
supposition 514
supposititious 546
suppress
destroy 162
conceal 528
silent 581
restrain 751
suppression of
truth 544
suppuration 653
suppute 85
supralapsarian 984
supramundane 939
supremacy 33, 737
supreme 33
summit 210
authority 737
in a – degree 31
Supreme Being 976
surbate 659
surbated 688
surcease 142
surcharge 641
– and falsify 811
surcingle 45
surcoat 225
surd *number* 84
deaf 419
silent letter 561

sure *certain* 474
belief 484
safe 664
make – against
673
make – of
inquire 461
take 789
you may be – 535
to be – *assent* 488
on – ground 664
security 771
sure-footed
careful 459
skilful 698
cautious 864
surely 489, 602, 870
sureness 474
surety 474, 664
surf 348, 353
surface *outside* 220
texture 329
below the – 526
lie on the – 518,
525
skim the – 460
Surface, Joseph –
548
surfeit 641, 869
surge *swarm* 72
swell 305
rotation 312
wave 348
surgeon 662
surgery 662
surgit amari
aliquid 651
surly *gruff* 895
sullen 901a
unkind 907
surmise 514
surmount *be*
superior 33
tower 206
transcursion 303
ascent 305
– a difficulty
overcome 731
surmountable 470
surname 564
surpass
be superior 33
grow 194
go beyond 303
outshine 873
surplice 999
surplus 40, 641
surplusage 641
surprint 550
surprise
non-expectation

- wine 396
- words 894
sweeten 396, 829
sweetheart 897
sweetmeat 396
sweetness 396
sweets 298, 396
sweet-scented 400
swell *increase* 35
  expand 194
  wave 348
  sound 404
  emotion 821
  fop 854
  nobility 875
  swagger 885
  extol 931
  ground – 315
  – over 250
  – with rage 900
  – the ranks of 37
  – out
    diffuse style 573
swelling
  expansion 194
  prominence 250
  - *style* 577
  excitement 824
swell-mob 792
swelter 382
swerve *change* 140
  deviate 279
  demur 603
  tergiversation 607
swift 274
swig 298, 959
swill *dirt* 653
  drink 298
  intemperance 954
  drunkenness 959
swim *navigate* 267
  float 305
  light 320
  – against the
    stream 704
  – in *pleasure* 377
  abundance 639
  – with the stream
    82, 683
  – with the tide
    734
swimming 840
  - *eyes* 443
  - *head* 503
  – belt 666
  – pool 652, 840
swimmingly
  easily 705
  success 731
  prosperity 734
swindle 545, 791

swindler 548, 792
swine 366
  cast pearls
    before – 638
  – of Epicurus
    954*a*
swineherd 746
swing
  operation 170
  space 180
  hang 214
  oscillate 314
  freedom 748
  amusement 840
  full – 682, 731
  give full – 705
  have one's – 738
  – the lead 544
swinge 972
swinging *great* 31
swinish 954, 957
  – multitude 876
swink 686
swipe 276
swirl 312
swish 409
switch *shunt* 279
  flog 972
  rod 975
switchback 840
Swithin, reign of
  St. – 348
swivel *hinge* 312
  cannon 727
swivel-eye 443
swollen 194, 878
swoon 158, 688
swoop 274
  descend 306
  seize 789
  at one fell – 173
swop 794
sword *weapon* 727
  draw the – ⎫
  flesh one's– ⎬ 722
  measure –s 720,
    722
  at the point of
    the – 722, 889,
    898
  severity 739
  compulsion 744
  subjection 749
  put to the – 361
  – of Damocles 667
  – in hand
    prepare 673
    war 722
  turn –s into
    ploughshares
    723

– of state 747
swordsman 726
Sybarite 954*a*
sybaritism 954
sycophancy 933
sycophant 886, 935
syenite *blue* 438
syllable 561
  breathe not a –
    528
syllabus 86, 596
syllogism 476
sylph 979
sylvan 367
symbol
  copy 21
  mathematical - 84
  sign 550
symbolize 526, 550
  represent 554
symmetrical 80
symmetry
  equality 27
  order 58
  conformity 82
  centrality 222
  regular form 242
  style 578
  beauty 845
  want of – 846
sympathizer
  partisan 890
sympathy
  concord 714
  friendship 888
  love 897
  kindness 906
  pity 914
  condolence 915
symphonious 413
symphony
  overture 64
  music 415
  concord 714
symphysis 43
symposium 72, 840,
  892
symptom 550, 668
symptomatology
  522
synagogue 1000
synchronism 120
synchysis 218
syncopation 415
syncope
  impotence 158
  musical 413
  rhetoric 572
  fatigue 688
syncretic 61
syncretism 24, 984

syndic 745, 967
syndicate 696, 712
synecdoche 521
synod 696, 995
synonym
  identity 13
  meaning 516
  interpretation 522
  term 564
synonymous 13
synopsis
  arrangement 60
  list 86
  compendium 596
synovia 332, 356
syntagma 60
syntax 567
synthesis
  combination 48
  composition 54
  reasoning 476
synthesize 54
syntony 23, 120
syringe 337, 348
syrup 352, 396
system *order* 58
  rule 79
  plan 626
  – of knowledge
    490
  – of opinions 484
systematize 60, 626
systole 195
syzygy 199

T

T, to a – 494
tab 39, 550, 747
tabard 225
tabby *mottled* 440
  gossip 588
tabefaction 195
tabernacle 189,
  1000
  house 189
  temple 1000
tabid *shrunk* 195
  thin 203
  disease 655
  deteriorated 659
table
  arrangement 60
  list 86
  defer 133
  layer 204
  support 215
  flat 251
  repast 298
  writing 590

tape *string* 205
  measure 466
  – machine 553
taper *contract* 195
  narrow 203
  candle 423
  – to a point 253
tapestry 556, 847
tapinois, en – 528
tapis: on the –
  event 151
  topic 454
  intention 620
  plan 626
tap-root 153
taps 550
tapster 746
tar *cover* 223
  sailor 269
  pitch 356a
  – and feather 929, 972
taradiddle 546
tarantass 272
tarantella 840
tarboosh 225
tardiloquence 583
tardy 133, 275
tare 40a
  – and tret 813
tares 645
targe 717
target 620
  shield 717
tariff 812
tarmac 635
tarn 343
tarnish
  discoloration 429
  soil 653
  deface 848
  disgrace 874
tarpaulin 223
tarry *remain* 110, 265
  later 133
  continue 141
  – for *expect* 507
tart *pastry* 298, 396
  acid 397
  rude 895
  irascible 901
  harlot 962
tartan 440
tartane 273
Tartar *choleric* 901
  catch a – *dupe* 547
  unskilful 699
  retaliation 718
tartar *dirt* 653
  – *emetic* 663

Tartarus 982
Tartufe
  hypocrisy 544
  deceiver 548
  impiety 988
task *lesson* 537
  business 625
  put to use 677
  fatigue 688
  command 741
  hard – 704
  set a – 741
  take to – 932
  – the memory 505
taskmaster 694
tass 191
tassel 847
taste *sapidity* **390**
  experience 821
  good taste **850**
  man of – 850
  to one's – *savoury* 394
  pleasant 829
  love 897
tasteful 850
tasteless *insipid* 391
tasty 394, 850
tâtonner 463
tatter
  small quantity 32
tatterdemalion 876
Tattersalls 799
tatters *garments* 225
  tear to – 162
tatting 847
tattle 588
tattler 532, 588
tattoo
  drumming 407
  mottled 440
  summons 741
taught [*see* teach]
  fastened 43
taunt 929, 938
tauromachy 720
taut 43
tautology 104, 573
tavern 189
tawdry 851
tawny 433, 436
tax *inquire* 461
  employ 677
  fatigue 688
  command 741
  compel 744
  request 765
  accounts 811
  impost 812

  discount 813
  accuse 938
  – one's energies 686
  – the memory 505
taxi 266
taxi-cab 272
taxi-driver 268
taxidermy 368
taxis 60
taxonomy 60
tazza 191
Te Deum 990
te fabula narratur, de – *retaliate* 718
  condemn 971
tea 298
teach 537
  – one's grand-mother 641, 885
  – one his place 879
teachable 539
teacher **540**, 673
teaching **537**
  false – 538
teacup, storm in a –
  overrate 482, 549
  exaggerate 549
teagown 225
team *assemblage* 69, 72
teamster 694
tea-party 892
tea-pot 191
tear *separate* 44
  violence 173
  move rapidly 274
  excite 825
  weeping 839
  – away from 789
  – oneself away 623
  – asunder one's bonds 750
  – one's hair 839
  – out 301
  – to pieces
   separate 44
   destroy 162
  – up *destroy* 162
tear-gas 663, 727
tearful 839
tearing passion 839
tears: draw – 830
  shed – 839
  – in one's eyes
   excited 824
   sad 837
tease *annoy* 830
  spite 907
teaser *difficult* 704

teasing 830
teat 250
tea-table talk 588
technic 698
technica, memoria – 505
technical
  conformable 82
  workmanlike 698
  – college 542
  – education 537
  – knowledge 698
  – school 542
  – term 564
technicality
  special 79
  cant term 563
  formulary 697
technique 556, 698
technocracy 698
technology 698
techy 901
tedious 841
  while away the – hours 681
tedium 841
teem
  produce 161
  productive 168
  abound 639
  – with *multitude* 102
teemful 168
teeming *crowd* 72
teemless 169
'teens 98
  in one's – 127, 129
teeter 314
teeth 330, 781
  armed to the – 673, 717, 722
  between the – 405
  cast in one's – 938
  chattering of – 383
  have cut one's eye – 698
  in the – of 704, 708
  grind one's – 900
  the run of one's – 815
  set one's – 604
  show one's – 900
  in spite of one's – 708, 744
  make one's – chatter 385, 860
  set the – on edge
   scrape 331
   saw 397
   stridor 410
   pain the feelings

830

tee 66

teetotalism 953, 958

teetotum 312, 840

teg 366

tegument 223

teind 99

teinoscope 445

tekel upharsin 668

telautograph 553

telegram 532

telegraph
velocity 274
messenger 534
signal 550
− boy 534
by − haste 684

telegraphone 553

telegraphy
publication 531

teleology 620

telemeter 200

telepathy 992

telephone 418
inform 527
messenger 534

telescope 445
− word 572

telescopic 196

telesis 658

telesm 993

tell count 85
influence 175
evidence 467
inform 527
speak 582
describe 594
succeed 731
let me − you 535
who can − 475
− one's beads 990, 998
− the cause of 522
− fortunes 511
− how 155
− a lie 544
− a piece of one's mind 529
− of 467
− off 85
− one plainly 527
− its own tale 518
− tales
disclose 529
− the truth 543

teller treasurer 801
− of tales 594

telling 175
graphic 518
important 642

exciting 824

with − effect 171, 175

telltale news 532
indicator 550
knave 941

telluric 318

telum imbelle 158

temerity 863

temper nature 5
state 7
moderate 174
elasticity 323
pliability 324
modify 469
prepare 673
affections 820
irascibility 901
command of − 826
lose one's − 900
out of − 901a
trial of − 824
− the wind to the shorn lamb 834

tempera 556

temperament
nature 5
tendency 176
musical 413
affections 820

temperance 174, **953**

temperate
[see temperance]
mild 826

temperature 382
increase of − 384
reduction of − 385

tempest
violence 173
agitation 315
wind 349
excitement 825

tempestivity 134

tempest-tossed 824

tempestuous 59

Templar 996
Good − 958

temple house 189
side 236
church **1000**
− of the Holy Ghost 983a

templet 22

tempora:
O −! O mores!
lament 839
disreputable 874
disapprobation 932
improbity 940

vice 945
− mutantur 140

temporal
transient 111
laical 997
lords − and spiritual 875

temporality 997

temporary 111

temporize
protract 110
defer 133
cunning 702

temporizer 943

tempt entice 615
attempt 675
desire 865
− fortune 621, 675
− Providence 863, 885

tempter 615
Satan 978
voice of the − 615

temulency 959

ten 98
− to one 472
− thousand 98

tenable 664

tenacity
coherence 46
toughness **327**
memory 505
resolution 604
obstinacy 606
retention 781
avarice 819
courage 861
− of life 357
− of purpose 604a

tenaculum 781

tenancy 777

tenant
present 186
occupier 188
possessor 779

tenantless
absence 187
seclusion 893

tenax propositi 204, 939

tend conduce 176
− animals 370
aid 707
serve 631, 746
− towards 278

tendence 749

tendency **176**

tender slight 32
ship 273
soft 324
painful 378

colour 428
war vessel 726
offer 763
susceptible 822
affectionate 897
compassionate 914
− age 127
− conscience 926
− heart
susceptible 822
kind 906
compassionate 914
− mercies [ironical]
badness 649
severity 739
cruelty 907
− passion 897
− one's resignation 757
− to 707

tenderfoot 57, 541

tendon 45

tendril fastening 45
offshoot 51
infant 129
filament 205
convoluted 248
plant 367

tenebrious 421

tenebrosity 421

tenement 189, 780
− of clay 362

tenet belief 484

tenner 800

tennis 840
− ground 213

tenor course 7
degree 26
direction 278
high note 410
singer 416
violin 417
meaning 516
pursue the noiseless − of one's way 881

tense hard 323

tensile 325

tension 159, 200

tensure 200

tent abode 189
covering 223
pitch one's −
locate 184
arrive 292

tentacle 781

tentative 463, 675

tente d'abri 223

tented field 722

Toledo 727
tolerable
  a little 32
  trifling 643
  pretty good 648
  not perfect 651
  satisfactory 831
tolerably, get on –
  736
toleration
  laxity 738
  lenity 740
  permission 760
  feeling 821
  calmness 826
  benevolence 906
toll *sound* 407
  tax 812
  – the knell 363
tollbooth
  prison 752
  market 799
tomahawk 727
tomb 363
  lay in the – 363
  – of the Capulets
    506
tombé des nues 83,
  870
tombola 156
tomboy 129, 851
tombstone 363
tom-cat 373
tome 593
tomentous 256
tomfool 501
tomfoolery
  absurdity 497
  amusement 840
  wit 842
  ostentation 882
Tom Noddy 501
Tommy Atkins 726
tommy-gun 727
to-morrow 121
  – and to-morrow
    104, 109
tompion 263
tomtit 193
Tom Thumb 193
tom-tom 417, 722
ton *weight* 319
  fashion 852
  –s of money 800
tonality 413, 420
tone *state* 7
  strength 159
  tendency 176
  sound 402
  music 413
  colour 428

  blackness 431
  painting 556
  method 627
  disposition 820
  give a – to 852
  – down
    moderate 174
    darken 421
    discolour 429
  – in with 714
  – of voice 580
tone poem 415
toney 852
tongs
  fire-irons 386
  retention 781
tongue
  projection 250
  taste 390
  language 560
  bite the – 392
  bridle one's – 585
  give – 404, 580
  hold one's – 403
  slip of the –
    error 495
    solecism 568
    stammering 583
  on the tip of
    one's –
    near 197
    forget 506
    latent 526
    speech 582
  wag the – 582
  – cleave to the
    roof of one's
    mouth 870
  have a – in one's
    head 582
  – of land 342
  – running loose
    584
  keep one's – be-
    tween one's
    teeth 585
tongueless 581
tongue-tied 581
tonic
  musical note 413
  healthy 656
  medicine 662
  – sol fa 415
tonicity 159
tonnage 192
tonsillectomy 662
tonsils 351
tonsure 999
tonsured 226
tontine 810
tony 501

Tony Lumpkin 876
too
  also 37
  excess 641
  – bad
    disreputable 874
    wrong 923
    censure 932
  – clever by half
    702
  in a – great degree
    31
  – far 641
  – hot to hold one
    830
  – late 133
  – late for 135
  – little 640
  – many 641
  – much [*see below*]
  – soon 132
  – soon for 135
  – true 833 839
too much
  redundance 641
  intemperance 954
  have – of 869
  make – of 482
  – for 471
  – of a good thing
    869
tool *instrument* 633
  steer 693
  catspaw 711
  ornament 847
  servile 886
  edge – 253
  mere – 690
toot 406
tooth *fastening* 45
  projection 250
  sharp 253
  roughness 256
  notch 257
  texture 329
  taste 390
  sweet –
    desire 865
    fastidious 868
  – and nail
    violence 173
    exertion 686
    attack 716
  – paste &c. 652
toothache 378
toothed 253
toothsome 394
top *supreme* 33
  summit 210
  roof 223
  spin 312

  sleep like a – 683
  fool to the – of
    one's bent 545
  go over the – 861
  – to bottom 52
  – coat 225
  – hat 225
  at the – of the
    heap 210
  – of the ladder 873
  at the – of one's
    speed 274
  from – to toe 200
  at the – of the
    tree 210, 873
  at the – of one's
    voice 404, 411
toparchy 737
topaz 436, 847
top-boot 225
tope *tomb* 363
  trees 367
  drink 959
  temple 1000
topee 225
toper 959
top-full 52
top-gallant mast,
  206, 210
top-heavy
  unbalanced 28
  inverted 218
  dangerous 665
  tipsy 959
Tophet 982
topiary 847
topic 454
  – of the day 532
topical 183
top-mast 206
topmost 210
topography 183
topographer 466
topple
  unbalanced 28
  perish 162
  decay 659
  – down *fall* 306
  – over 28, 306
topsail schooner
  273
topsawyer 642, 700
top sergeant 745
topsy-turvy 14, 218
toque 225
tor 206
torch 388, 423
  apply the – 824
  light the – of war
    722
  – of Hymen 903

Tories 712
torment
physical 378
moral 828, 830
place of − 982
Tormes, Lazarillo de − 941
torn [*see* tear]
discord 713
tornado 312, 349
torpedo *bane* 663
sluggish 683
weapon 727
evil-doer 913
− boat 726
− boat destroyer 726
− plane 276
torpid, torpor
inert 172
inactive 683
insensible 823
torque 847
torrefy 384
torrent
violence 173
rapid 274
flow 348
rain in −s 348
torrid 382
torsion 248
torso 50
tort 925, 947
tort et à travers, à −
disagreement 24
absurdity 497
resolution 604
tortious 925
tortile 248
tortive 248
tortoise 275
tortoise-shell 440
tortuous
twisted 248
dishonourable 940
torture
physical 378
moral 828, 830
cruelty 907
punishment 972
− a question 476
torvity 901*a*
toss *derange* 61
throw 284
oscillate 314
agitate 315
− in a blanket 929
− the caber 840
− the head
pride 878
insolence 885

contempt 930
− off *drink* 298
− overboard 610
− on one's pillow 825
− up 156, 621
tosspot 959
tot *child* 129
tot homines, tot sententiæ 15
total 50, 84
sum − 800
− abstinence 953, 955
− eclipse 421
totalisator 621
totality 52
totally 52
totidem verbis 19, 494
totient 84
toties quoties 136
totis viribus 686
totitive 84
toto: in − 52
− cœlo 52
totter
changeable 149
weak 160
limp 275
oscillate 314
agitate 315
decay 659
danger 665
− to its fall 162
touch *relate to* 9
small quantity 32
mixture 41
contact 199
sensation **379, 380**
music 416
test 463
indication 550
act 680
receive 785
excite 824
pity 914
− and go
instant 113
soon 132
changeable 149
easy 705
− the guitar 416
− the hat 894
− the heart 824
− on 516
− to the quick 822
− up 658
− upon 595
in − with 9

touched *crazy* 503
tainted 653
compassion 914
− in the wind 655
− with *feeling* 821
touching 830
touchstone 463
touchwood
fuel 388
irascible 901
touchy 901
tough *coherent* 46
tenacious 327
difficult 704
toujours perdrix
repetition 104
weary 841
satiety 869
toupee 256
tour 266
tour de force
skill 698
stratagem 702
display 882
touring car 272
tourist 268
tournament 720
tourniquet 263
tournure 230, 448
belle − 845
tous les rapports, sous − 494
tousle 61
tout *solicit* 765
tout: − au contraire 14
− court 265
− ensemble 50
− le monde 78
touter *agent* 758
solicitor 767
eulogist 935
tow 285
take in − *aid* 707
towage 812
towardly 705
towards 278
draw − 288
move − 286
towel *clean* 652
flog 972
tower
stability 150
edifice 161
abode 189
height 206
soar 305
defence 717
− of strength
strong 159
influential 175

safety 664
towering *great* 31
furious 173
large 192
high 206
− passion 900
− rage 900
town *city* 189
fashion 852
man about − 854
on the − 961
all over the − 532
talk of the − 873
− council 696
town-hall 189, 966
township 181
townsman 188
fellow − 892
town-talk 532, 588
toxic 657
toxicology 663
toxophilite 284
toy *trifle* 643
amusement 840
fondle 902
toy-dog 366
toy-shop 840
trabant 717
tracasserie 713
trace *inquire* 461
discover 480a
mark 550
record 551
delineate 554
− back 122
− out 480a
− to 155
− up 461
tracery
lattice 219
curve 245
ornament 847
traces *harness* 45
trachea 351
tracing 21
track *trace* 461
record 551
way 627
cover up one's −s 528
in one's −s 113
racing − 840
− meet 840
− racing 728
trackless
space 180
difficult 704
− trolley 272
tract *region* 181
book 593
dissertation 595

– of time 109
tractable
  malleable 324
  willing 602
  easy 705
tractarian 984
tractile
  traction **285**
  soft 324
traction **285**
tractor 271
trade *exchange* 148
  business 625
  traffic 794
  drive a – 625
  learn one's – 539
  tricks of the – 702
  two of a – 708
  – with 794
trader 797
trade-mark 550
tradesman 797
trade-publication 531
trade-union 712
trade-wind 349
tradition *old* 124
  description 594
  custom 613
traduce 934
traducer 936
traffic 794
tragedian 599
tragedy
  drama 599
  evil 619
tragic *drama* 599
tragical 830
tragi-comedy 599
tragi-comic 853
trail *sequel* 65
  pendent 214
  slow 275
  follow 281
  traction 285
  odour 398
  inquiry 461
  record 551
  highway 627
  follow in the – of 281
  – of a red herring 615, 706
train *sequel* 65
  series 69
  pendent 214
  vehicle 272
  sequence 281
  traction 285
  – *animals* 370
  teach 537

[674]

accustom 613
  prepare 673
  bring in its – 615
  in – 673
  in the – of 281, 746
  lay a – 626, 673
  put in – 673
  siege – 727
  – de luxe 272
  – of reasoning 476
  – of thought 451
train-band 726
train-bearer 746
train-ferry 272
trained 698
trainer
  – *of horses* 268
  – *of animals* 370
  teacher 540
training
  education 537
  – *college* 542
train-oil 356
traipse 275
trait *speciality* 79
  appearance 448
  mark 550
  description 594
traitor
  disobedient 742
  knave 941
  enemy 891
trajection 297
trajectory 627
tra-la-la 838
tralatitious 521
tralineate 279
tralucent 425
tram 272
trammel *hinder* 706
  restrain 751
  fetter 752
  cast –s off 750
tramontane
  foreign 57
  distant 196
  wind 349
  outlandish 851
tramp *stroll* 266
  stroller 268
  idler 683
  vagabond 867
  on the – 264
trample
  – in the dust
  destroy 162
  prostrate 308
  – out 162
  – under foot
  vanquish 731

not observe 773
  disrepute 874
  insolence 885
  dereliction 927
  contempt 930
  – upon 649, 739
tramway 627
trance *insensibility* 376
  dream 515
  sleep 683
  lethargy 823
tranquil *calm* 174
  quiet 265
  peaceful 721
  calmness 871
  – *mind* 826
tranquillize
  moderate 174
  pacify 723
  soothe 826
transact *act* 680
  conduct 692
  – *business* 625
  – business with 794
transaction 151, 625, 680, 769
transactions 551
transalpine 196
transanimation 140
transatlantic 196
transcalency 384
transcend *great* 31
  superior 33
  go beyond 303
transcendency 641
transcendent 33, 873
transcendental 78, 519
transcendentalism 450
transcolate 295
transcribe 19, 590
transcript 21, 590
transcursion 303
transept 1000
transfer
  copy 21
  displace 185
  – *of things* 270
  – *of property* **783**
transference **270**
transfiguration
  change 140
  divine – 998
transfix 260
transfixed *firm* 150
transform 140
transformation

scene 599
transfuse 41, 270
  – the sense of 522
transgress
  go beyond 303
  infringe 773
  violate 927
  sin 945
transgression 947
transi de froid 383
transient 111, 149
transientness **111**
transilience 146, 303
transit
  conversion 144
  motion 264
  transference 270
  – *circle* 244
transit gloria mundi, sic – 735, 874
transition 144, 270
transitional 140
transitory 111
transitu, in –
  transient 111
  journey 266
  transference 270
translate
  interpret 522
  promote 955
translator 524
translation
  transference 270
  resurrection 981
translocation 270
translucence 425
transmarine 196
transmigration 140, 144
transmission
  moving 270
  passage 302
  – *of property* 783
transmit light 425
transmogrify 140
transmutation 140, 144
transom 215
transparency **425**
transparent
  transmitting light 425
  obvious 518
transpicuous
  transmitting light 425
  obvious 518
transpierce 260
transpire

evaporate 336
appear 525
be disclosed 529
transplace 270
transplant 270
transplendent 420
transpontine 196
transport
transfer 270
ship 273
war vessel 726
excitement 825
delight 827
please 829
punish 972
– of love 897
– plane 273
transpose
exchange 148
displace 185
invert 218
transfer 270
- *music* 413
transubstantiation
change 140
sacrament 998
transude 295, 302
transume 140
transumption 270
transverse 217, 219
tranter 271
trap *closure* 261
gig 272
snare 545
stage – 599
pitfall 667
fall into a – 547, 699
lay a – for 545
trap bat and ball 840
trap-door
opening 260
snare 545
pitfall 667
trapan 545
trapes 701
trappings
adjunct 39
clothes 225
equipment 633
ornament 847
Trappist 996
traps
clothes 225
baggage 780
trash
unmeaning 517
trifling 643
useless 645
trashy – style 575

traulism 583
traumatic 662
travail 161, 686
trave 215
travel 266
– out of the record 477
traveller **268**
bagman 758
tricks upon –s 545, 702
–'s tale 546, 549
travelling bag 191
traverse *move* 266
pass 302
negative 536
obstruct 706
travesty
imitate 19, 21
misinterpret 523
misrepresent 555
ridicule 856
travis 215
trawl 285, 463
trawler 273
tray 191
treacherous 907, 940
– *memory* 506
treachery 545, 940
treacle 352, 396
tread 264, 266
– the beaten track 82, 613
– the boards 599
– down 739, 879
– on the heels of 281
– a path 266, 622
– the stage 599
– in the steps of 19
– under foot
destroy 162
subjection 749
disrepute 874
insolence 885
contempt 930
– upon 649
treadle 633
treadmill 975
treason 742, 940
treasure *cherish* 897
store 636
goodness 648
money 800
– trove 618
– up in the memory 505
treasurer **801**
treasury **802**
– note 800

treat *physical pleasure* 377
manage 692
bargain 769
delight 827, 829
amusement 840
– of 595
– oneself to 827
– well 906
treatise 593, 595
treatment
painting 556
conduct 692
ill – 649
medical – 662
treaty 769
treble
three 93
shrill 410
childish – 581
tree *pedigree* 166
plant 367
gallows 975
top of the – 210
up a – 704
as the – falls 151
– of knowledge 493
treenail 45
trefoil 92
trek 266
trellis 219
tremble
fluctuate 149
weakness 160
shake 315
cold 383
emotion 821
fear 860
make one – 860
trembling:
– in the balance 475, 665
– to its fall 160
tremblingly alive 822
tremendous 830, 860
tremendously 31
tremolo 415
tremor
agitation 315
emotion 821
fearful 860
tremulous
agitated 315
– *voice* 583
irresolute 605
fear 860
trench *moat* 232
furrow 259

concavity 252
defence 717
– *mortar* 727
– *on near* 197
trespass 303
moral trespass 925
trenchant
energetic 171
assertive 535
concise style 572
vigorous language 574
important 642
emotion 821
discourteous 895
censure 932
trench-coat 225
trencher *plate* 191
layer 204
trenches, open the – 716
trend *tendency* 176
bend 278
deviate 279
trennel 45
trepan 260
snare 545
borer 262
trephine 260, 267
trepidation
agitation 315
emotion 821
excitement 825
fear 860
tres juncta in uno 92
trespass
go beyond 303
vice 945
guilt 947
tress 256
trestle 215
trevet 215
[*and see* trivet]
trews 225
trey 92
triad 92
triagonal 244
trial *inquiry* 461
experiment 463
essay 675
difficulty 704
adversity 735
suffering 828, 830
lawsuit 969
punishment 972
– of temper 824
triality **92**
trialogue 588
triangle 92, 244

adversity 735
pain 828
painful 830
bring into – 649
get into – 649, 732
in – 619, 735
take – 686
– one's head
about 682
– one for 765
– oneself 686
troubled waters,
fish in – 704
troublesome 686,
704, 830
troublous 59, 173
– times 713
trough *hollow* 252
trench 259
conduit 350
trounce 932, 972
troupe 72
trousers 225
trousseau 225
trouvaille 775
trouvère 597
trover 775, 964
trow *think* 451
believe 484
know 490
trowel 191
troy-weight 319
truant *absent* 187
runaway 623
idle 682
apostate 941
truce *cessation* 142
deliverance 672
peace 721
pacification 723
flag of – 724
trucidation 361
truck *summit* 210
vehicle 272
barter 794
truck driver 268
truck farm 371
truckle to
submit 725
servile 886
flatter 933
truckle-bed 215
truck-load 31
truckman 268
truculent 907
trudge 266, 275
truditur dies die
109
true *real* 1
straight 246
assent 488

accurate 494
veracious 543
faithful 772
honourable 939
orthodox 983a
– bill
vindicate 937
accuse 938
lawsuit 969
see in its –
colours 480a
– meaning 516
– to nature 17
– to oneself 604a
– saying 496
– to scale 494
true-hearted 543,
939
true-love 897
true-lover's knot
897, 902
true-penny 939
truism *axiom* 496
unmeaning 517
trull 962
truly *very* 31
assent 488
really 494
indeed 535
trump *perfect* 650
honourable 939
good man 948
turn up –s 731
– card *device* 626
success 731
– up *falsehood* 544
accuse 938
trumped up 468,
545, 546
trumpery 517, 643
trumpet *music* 417
war cry 722
boast 884
flourish of –s
ostentation 882
celebration 883
boasting 884
ear– 418
penny –
skill 410
sound of –
alarm 669
speaking – 418
– blast 404
– call 550, 741
– forth 531
trumpeter
musician 416
messenger 534
boaster 884
trumpet-toned 410

trumpet-tongued
404, 531
truncate 201, 241
truncated 53
truncheon
weapon 727
staff of office 747
*instrument of
punishment* 975
trundle 284, 312
trunk *whole* 50
origin 153
paternity 166
box 191
trunk-hose 225
trunnion
support 215
projection 250
truss *tie* 43
pack, packet 72
support 215
trust
belief 484
combination 709
property 780
credit 805
hope 858
– to a broken reed
699
– to the chapter of
accidents 621
trustee
consignee 758
possessor 779
treasurer 801
trustful 484
trustless 940
trustworthy
certain 474
belief 484
- *memory* 505
veracious 543
honourable 939
truth
exactness **494**
veracity 543
probity 939
arrive at the –
480a
in – *certainly* 474
love of – 543
of a – 535, 543
prove the – of 937
religious – 983a
speak the – 529,
543
in very – 543
Truth, Spirit of –
976
truthless 544
trutination 319

try *experiment* 463
adjudge 480
endeavour 675
use 677
lawsuit 969
– a case 967
– a cause 480
– conclusions
discuss 476
quarrel 713
contend 720
– one's hand 675
– one's luck 621
– one 704
– out 463
– the patience 830
– a prisoner 967
– one's temper 824
– one's utmost 686
trying 688, 704
tryst 892
trysting-place 74
tsar [*see* czar]
tu quoque 718
– argument
counter-evidence
468
confutation 479
accuse 938
tub 191
– thumper 582
– to a whale 545,
617
tuba 417
tùbam trepidat,
ante – 860, 862
tubby 202
tube 260
test – 144
tubercle 250
tuberculous 655
tuberosity 250
tubman 968
tubular 260
tubulated 260
tubule 260
tuck *fold* 258
dagger 727
– in *locate* 184
eat 298
insert 300
tucker 225
tuft *collection* 72
rough 256
tufted 256
tuft-hunter 836,
943
tuft-hunting 886,
933
tug *ship* 273
pull 285

148, 149
- turtle 218
- and twist 248
- under 258
- up [see below]
- upon
  depend upon 154
  retaliate 718
turn over give 784
  invert 218
  entrust 755
- the leaves 457,
  539
- in the mind 451
- a new leaf
  change 140
  improve 658
  repent 950
- to 270
turn up happen 151
  chance 156
  visible 446
  unexpected 508
- one's eyes
  wonder 870
  hypocrisy 988
- one's nose at
  aversion 867
  fastidious 868
  contempt 930
turn-coat 605, 607
turnover 298
turned of 128
turning-point
  crisis 8
  end 67
  occasion 134
  reversion 145
  cause 153
  summit 210
  limit 233
turnkey 753
turnpike 706
- road 627
turnscrew 633
turnspit 366
turnstile 553, 706
turpentine and
  beeswax 255
Turpin, Dick - 792
turpitude 874, 940
turquoise blue 438
  jewel 847
turret 206
turret-ship 726
turtle savoury 394
turtle-doves 897
tush silence 403
  taciturn 585
  trifling 643
tusk 253

tussle 720
tussock 256
tut [see tush]
  censure 932
tutelage
  teaching 537
  learning 539
  safety 664
  subjection 749
tutelary safety 664
- genius
  auxiliary 711
  god 979
- god 664
- saint 890, 912
tutor cultivate 375
  teach 537
  teacher 540
tutus, cavendo -
  664
tuyère 386
twaddle
  absurd 497
  unmeaning 517
  diffuseness 573
  talk 584
twain 89
  in - 44
twang taste 390
  pungency 392
  sound 402
  stridor 410
  music 416
  voice 583
twattle
  [see twaddle]
tweak 378
- the nose 830
tweed 219
tweedle touch 379
  music 416
tweedledum and
  tweedledee 415
tweeny 746
tweezers 781
twelfth 99
twelve 98
twentieth century
  118
twenty &c. 98
- shillings in the
  pound 803
twice 90
twice-told tale 104,
  841
twiddle 379
twig 51
  hop the - 360
twilight
  morning 125
  evening 126

dusk 422
- sleep 376
twill crossing 219
  convolution 248
  fold 258
twin similar 17
  accompanying 88
  two 89
  duplicate 90
twine string 205
  intersect 219
  convolution 248
- round 43, 227
twinge 378, 828
twinkle
  instantaneous 113
  light 420
  dimness 422
twinkling of an eye,
  in the - 113
twins 11
twire 315
twirl convolute 248
  revolve 311
  rotate 312
twist join 43
  thread 205
  oblique 217
  crossing 219
  distort 243
  convolution 248
  deviate 279
  bend 311
  prejudice 481
  insanity 503
  fault 651
  appetite 865
twit deride 856
  disrespect 929
  censure 932
  accuse 938
twitch pull 285
  shake 315
  pain 378
  mental - 828
twitter
  agitation 315
  cry 412
  music 416
  emotion 821
  excitement 824
'twixt 228
two 89
  kill - birds with
    one stone 682
  make - bites of a
    cherry 629, 956
- dozen 98
- meanings 520
in - places at once
  471

game at which -
  can play 718
- score 98
fall between -
  stools 732
- strings to one's
  bow 632
- or three 100
- of a trade 708
unable to put -
  words together
  583
two-bits 800
two-edged 253
two-faced 544
twofold 90
twopenny-haif-
  penny 643
two-sided 90
two-step 840
Tyburn tree 975
tycoon 745
tyg 191
tyke 876
tymbal 417
tympani 417
tympanum 210, 218
tympany 194
type essential 5
  similarity 17
  pattern 22
  class 75
  form 240
  prediction 511
  metaphor 521
  indication 550
  letter 561
  printing 591
  heavy - 550
- script 21
- writing 590
typhoon 349
typical special 79
  conformable 82
  metaphorical 521
  significant 550
typist 590
typify 511
typography 591
tyranny 739
tyrant severe 739
  ruler 745
  evil-doer 913
tyre 230
tyro ignoramus 493
  learner 541

U

uberrima fides 484
uberty 168
ubiety 186

ubiquity 186
U-boat 726
Ucalegon, proxi-
  mus ardet – 667
udder 191
ugh! 867
ugliness **846**
ugly 846
  – customer *source
    of danger* 667
  evil-doer 913
  bad man 949
  – duckling 948
  call by – names
    932
  take an – turn 732
uhlan 726
ukase 741
ukulele 417
ulcer *disease* 655
  care 830
ulema 967, 996
uliginous 352
ullage 53, 190
ulster 225
ulterior
  additional 37
  extraneous 57
  - *in time* 121
  - *in space* 196
  – motive 615
ultima ratio 744
  – regum 722
ultima Thule 196
ultimate 67
ultimately 121, 133,
  151
ultimatum
  definite 474
  intention 620
  requisition 630
  terms 770
ultimo 122
ultra 31, 33
  – vires 925
  ne plus – 729
  – crepidam 471
ultramarine 438
ultramontane
  foreign 57
  distant 196
  heterodox 984
  church 995
ultramundane 196
ultra-violet rays
  420
ululation **412**, 839
Ulysses 702
umbilicus 222
umbra 421
  magni nominis –

659
umbrage *shade* 424
  hatred 898
  take – *anger* 900
umbrageous 421
umbrella
  covering 223
  shade 424
  protection 666
umpire
  judgment 480
  mediator 724
  judge 967
unâ voce 488
unabashed
  bold 861
  vain 880
  insolent 885
unabated 31
unable 158
  – to say 'No' 605
unacceptable 830
unaccommodating
  disagreeing 24
  disagreeable 830
  discourteous 895
  sulky 901a
unaccompanied 87
unaccomplished
  730
unaccountable
  exceptional 83
  unintelligible 519
  irresponsible 927a
  arbitrary 964
unaccustomed
  unusual 83
  unused 614
  unskilful 699
unachievable 471
unacknowledged
  489, 917
unacquainted 491
unacquired 777a
unadmonished 665
unadorned 576, 849
  beauty – 845
unadulterated 42,
  494, 652
unadventurous 864
unadvisable 647
unadvised 665, 699
unaffected
  genuine 494
  sincere 543
  – *style* 578
  obstinate 606
  artless 703
  insensible 823
  simple 849
  taste 850

unafflicted 831
unaided *weak* 160
unalarmed 861
unalienable 924
unallayed 159
unallied 10
unallowable 923
unallowed 925
unalloyed 42
  – happiness 827
  – truth 494
unalluring 866
unalterable 150
unaltered 13, 150
unamazed 871
unambiguous 518
unambitious 866
unamiable 907
unanimated 823
unanimity 23, 488,
  714
unannexed 44
unanswerable
  demonstrative 478
  irresponsible 927a
  arbitrary 964
unanswered 478
unanticipated 508
unappalled 861
unappareled 226
unapparent 526
unappeasable 173
unappetizing 398
unapplied 678
unappreciated 482
unapprehended 491
unapprehensive 861
unapprized 491
unapproachable
  great 31
  infinite 105
  distant 196
unapproached 33
unappropriated 782
unapproved 932
unapt
  incongruous 24
  important 158
  unskilful 699
unarmed 158
unarranged 59, 674
unarrayed 849
unascertained 475,
  491
unasked 602, 766
unaspiring 866, 881
unassailable 664
unassailed 748
unassembled 73
unassisted 160, 706
  – eye 441

unassociated 44
unassuming 881
unatoned 951
unattached 44
unattackable 664
unattainable 471
unattained 732
unattempted 623
unattended 87
  – to 460
unattested 468
unattracted
  indifferent 866
unattractive 866
unauthenticated
  unproved 468
  uncertain 475
  error 495
unauthoritative 475
unauthorized
  prohibited 761
  undue 925
  lawless 964
unavailing 645, 918
unavenged 918
unavoidable 474,
  601
unavowed 489
unawakened 683
unaware 491, 508
  take –s 674
unawed 861
unbalanced 28
unbar 750
unbearable 830
unbeaten 123
unbeauteous 846
unbecoming
  incongruous 24
  disreputable 874
  undue 925
  dishonourable 940
  – a gentleman 895
unbefitting 24, 925,
  940
  [*see* unbecom-
  ing]
unbegotten 2
unbeguile 527, 529
unbegun 67, 674
unbelief **485**, 989
unbeloved 898
unbend
  straighten 246
  repose 687
  – the mind 452
unbending 323
unbenevolent 907
unbenign 907
unbeseeming 851,
  940

unbesought 766
unbetrayed 939
unbewailed 932
unbiassed 498, 748
unbidden 600, 742
unbigoted 498
unbind 44, 750
unblamable 946
unblamed 946
unblemished 650,
  946
unblenching 861
unblended 42
unblest 735, 932
  – with 777a
unblown 674
uncommenced 67
unblushing
  proud 878
  vain 880
  imprudent 885
unboastful 881
unbodied 317
unboiled 674
unbolt 750
unbookish 491
unborn 2, 152
unborrowed 787,
  788
unbosom oneself
  529
unbought
  not bought 796
  honorary 815
  honourable 939
  unselfish 942
unbound 748, 927a
unbounded 105
unbrace 160, 655
unbreathed 526
unbred 895
unbribed 939, 942
unbridled
  violent 173
  lax 738
  free 748
unbroken
  entire 50
  continuous 69
  preserved 670
  unviolated 939
unbruised 50
unbuckle 44
unburden
  – one's mind 529
unburdened 705
unburied 362
unbusinesslike 699
unbuttoned 748
uncalculating 863
uncalled for

redundant 641
useless 645
not used 678
uncandid 544, 907
uncanny 846, 980
uncanonical 984
uncared for
  neglected 460
  indifference 866
  disliked 867
  hated 898
uncase 226
uncaught 748
uncaused 156
unceasing 112
uncensured 931
unceremonious
  880, 895
uncertain
  irregular 139
  not certain 475
  doubtful 485
in an – degree 32
uncertainty 475
unchain 44, 750
unchained 748
unchallenged 488,
  924
unchangeable 150,
  604a
unchanged 16, 141
unchanging 5
uncharitable 907
unchartered 925,
  964
unchaste 961
unchastised 970
unchecked 748
uncheckered 141
uncheerful 837
unchivalric 940
unchristian 984,
  989
uncial 590
uncinated 244
uncircumscribed
  180
uncircumspect 460
uncivil 851, 895
uncivilized 876, 895
unclaimed 748
unclassical 851
uncle kin 11
  my –'s
  pawnshop 787
unclean 653
  – spirit 978, 980
uncleanness 653
unclipped 50
unclog 705, 750
unclose 260, 750

unclothe 226
unclouded 420, 446
unclubbable 893
unclutch 790
uncoif 226
uncoil 313
uncoloured
  achromatic 429
  true 494
uncombed 653, 851
uncombined
  simple 42
  incoherent 47
uncomeatable 471
uncomely 846
uncomfortable 828,
  830
uncommenced 67
uncommendable
  blamable 932
  bad 945
  guilt 947
uncommensurable
  24
uncommon 31, 83,
  137
uncommonly 31
uncommunicated
  781
uncommunicative
  528
uncompact 322
uncompassionate
  914a
uncompelled 748
uncomplaisant 764
uncompleted
  incomplete 53
  unfinished 730
  failure 732
uncomplying 742,
  764
uncompounded 42
uncompressed 320,
  322
uncompromising
  conformable 82
  severe 739
unconcealable 525
unconceived
  uncreated 12
  unintelligible 519
unconcern 823, 866
unconcocted 674
uncondemned 970
unconditional
  complete 52
  free 748
  permission 760
  consent 762
  release 768a

unconducive 175a
unconfined 748
unconfirmed 475
unconformity
  disagreement 24
  irregularity 83
unconfused
  methodical 58
  clear 518
unconfuted 478,
  494
uncongealed 333
uncongenial 24, 657
unconnected
  irrelative 10
  disjointed 44
  discontinuous 70
  illogical 477
unconquerable
  strong 159
  persevering 604a
  – will 604
unconquered 719
unconscientious
  940
unconscionable
  excessive 31
  unprincipled 945
unconscious
  ignorant 491
  insensible 823
unconsenting 603,
  764
unconsidered 452
unconsolable 837
unconsolidated 47
unconsonant 24
unconspicuous 447
unconstitutional
  925, 964
unconstrained 748,
  880
unconsumed 40
uncontested 474
uncontradicted 488
uncontrite 951
uncontrollable
  violent 173
  necessity 601
  emotion 825
uncontrolled
  free 748
  excitability 825
uncontroverted 488
unconventional 83,
  614
unconversant 491,
  699
unconverted
  dissenting 489
  irreligious 989

unforfeited 781	ungranted 764	unhinge 61, 158	uninflammable 385
unforgettable 505	ungrateful 917	unhinged	uninfluenced
unforgiving 919	ungratified 832	*impotent* 158	*obstinate* 606
unforgotten 505	ungrounded	*insane* 503	*unactuated* 616
unformed 241, 674	*unsubstantial* 4	*failure* 732	*free* 768
unfortified	*erroneous* 495	unhitch 44	uninfluential 172,
pure 42	ungrudging 816	unholy 989	175a
powerless 158	unguarded	unhonoured 874	uninformed 491
unfortunate	*neglected* 460	unhook (44)	uningenuous 544
ill-timed 135	*spontaneous* 612	unhoped 508	uninhabit, -able,
failure 732	*unprepared* 674	unhorsed 732	-ed 187, 893
adversity 735	in an − moment	unhostile 888	uninitiated 491, 699
unhappy 828	*unexpectedly* 508	unhouse 297	uninjured
− *woman* 962	unguem, ad − 494,	unhoused 185	*perfect* 650
unfounded 546	650	unhurt 670	*healthy* 654
unfrequent 137	unguent 356	unicorn	*preserved* 670
unfrequented 893	unguibus et rostro	*monster* 83	uninjurious 656
unfriended	686	*carriage* 272	uninquisitive 456
powerless 158	unguided	unideal *existing* 1	uninspired 823
secluded 893	*ignorant* 491	*no thought* 452	uninstructed 491
unfriendly	*impulsive* 612	*true* 494	unintellectual 452,
opposed 708	*unskilled* 699	unification 48, 87	499
hostile 889	unguilty 946	uniform	unintelligent 499
malevolent 907	unhabitable 187	*homogeneous* 16	unintelligibility **519**
unfrock 756, 972	unhabituated 614	*simple* 42	unintelligible 519
unfrozen 382	unhackneyed 614	*orderly* 58	- *style* 571
unfruitful 169	unhallowed 988,	*regular* 80	render − 538
unfulfilled 713, 925	989	*dress* 225	unintentional
unfurl	unhand 750	*symmetry* 242	*necessary* 601
unfold 313	unhandseled 123	*livery* 550	*undesigned* 621
− a flag 525, 550	unhandsome 940	uniformity **16**	uninterested 456,
unfurnished 640,	unhandy 699	unilluminated 421	841, 843
674	unhappy	unimaginable 471,	unintermitting
ungainly 846, 895	*adversity* 735	473	*unbroken* 69
ungallant 895	*pain* 828	*wonderful* 870	*durable* 110
ungarnished 849	*dejected* 837	unimaginative 576,	*continuing* 143
ungathered 678	make − 830	843, 868	*persevering* 604a
ungenerous 819,	unharbored 185	unimagined 1, 494	uninterrupted
943	unhardened	unimitated 20	*continuous* 69
ungenial 657	*tender* 914	unimpaired 670	*perpetual* 112
ungenteel 851, 895	*innocent* 946	unimpassioned 826	*unremitting* 893
ungentle 173, 895	*penitent* 950	unimpeachable	unintroduced 893
ungentlemanly	unharmonious 24,	*certain* 474	uninured 614
vulgar 851	414	*true* 494	uninvented 526
rude 895	unharness 750	*due* 924	uninvestigated 491
dishonourable 940	unhatched 674	*approved* 931	uninvited 893
ungifted 499	unhazarded 664	*innocent* 946	uninviting 830
unglorified 874	unhealthy 655, 657	unimpeached 931,	union
unglue 47	unheard of	946	*agreement* 23
ungodly 989	*exceptional* 83	unimpeded 705, 748	*junction* 43
ungovernable	*improbable* 473	unimportance **643**	*combination* 48
violent 173	*ignorant* 491	unimpressed 838	*concurrence* 178
disobedient 742	*wonderful* 870	unimpressible 823	*workhouse* 189
passionate 825	unheated 383	unimproved 659	*party* 712
ungoverned 748	unheed, -ed 460	unincreased 36	*concord* 714
ungraceful	unheeding 458	unincumbered	*marriage* 903
- *language* 579	unhesitating	*easy* 705	unionist 712
ugly 846	*belief* 484	*exempt* 927a	union-jack 550
vulgar 851	*resolved* 604	uninduced 616	union-pipes 417
ungracious 895, 907	unhewn 241, 674	uninfected 652	unique
ungrammatical 568	unhindered 748	uninfectious 656	*dissimilar* 18

original 20
exceptional 83
alone 87
unirritating 174
unison
  agreement 23
  melody 413
  concord 714
unit 51, 87
Unitarian 984
unite *join* 43
  combine 48
  assemble 72
  concur 178
  converge 290
  party 712
  – one's efforts 709
  – in pairs 89
  – with 709
united 46, 714
unity *identity* 14
  uniformity 16
  whole 50
  complete 52
  single **87**
  concord 714
  – of time 120
Unity, Trinity in –
  976
universal 78
  – Church 983*a*
  – favourite 899
universality 52
universe 318
university 542
  – education 537
  – extension 537
  go to the – 539
unjust *wrong* 923
  impious 988
unjustifiable
  wrong 923
  inexcusable 938
  wicked 945
unjustified 923
  undue 925
unkempt
  unclean 753
  vulgar 851
unkennel *eject* 297
  disclose 529
unkind 907
  –est cut of all 828
unknightly 940
unknit (44)
unknowable 519
unknowing 491
unknown
  ignorant 491
  latent 526
  – to fame

inglorious 874
low-born 876
– quantities 491
unlaboured
  - *style* 578
  unprepared 674
unlace (44)
unlade 297
unladylike
  vulgar 851
  rude 895
unlamented
  hated 898
  disapproved 932
unlatch 44, 750
unlawful
  undue 925
  illegal 964
unlearn 506
unlearned 491
unleavened 674
unless
  circumstances 8
  except 83
  qualification 469
unlettered 491
  – Muse 579
unlicensed 761
unlicked
  unprepared 674
  vulgar 851
  clownish 876
  – cub
  youngster 129
  shapeless 241
  unmannerly 895
unlike 18
unlikely 473
unlikeness 15
unlimber 323
unlimited
  great 31
  infinite 105
  free 748
  – space 180
unliquefied 321
unlively 837, 843
unload
  displaced 185
  eject 297
  disencumber 705
unlock *unfasten* 44
  discover 480*a*
unlooked for 508
unloose
  unfasten 44
  liberate 750
unloved 898
unlovely 846
unlucky
  inopportune 135

bad 649
unfortunate 735
in pain 830
unmade 2
unmaimed 654
unmake 145
unman
  mutilate 38
  render powerless
  158
  madden 837
  frighten 860
unmanly
  effeminate 374
  dishonourable 940
unmanageable
  unwieldy 647
  perverse 704
unmanned
  dejected 837
  cowardly 862
unmannered 895
unmannerly 895
unmarked 460
unmarred 654, 670
unmarried 904
unmask 529
unmatched
  different 15
  dissimilar 18
  unparalleled 20
unmeaningness **517**
unmeant 517
unmeasured
  infinite 105
  undistinguished
  465*a*
  abundant 639
unmeditated 612
unmeet 925
unmellowed 674
unmelodious 414
unmelted 321
unmentionable 874
  –s 225
unmentioned 526
unmerciful 914*a*
unmerited 925
unmethodical 59
unmindful
  inattentive 458
  neglectful 460
  ungrateful 917
unmingled 42
unmissed 460
unmistakable
  certain 474
  intelligible 518
  manifest 525
unmitigable 173
unmitigated

great 31
complete 52
violent 173
unmixed 42
unmolested 664,
  831
unmoneyed 804
unmoral 823
unmourned 898
unmoved
  quiescent 265
  obstinate 606
  insensible 823
unmusical 424
  – voice 581
unmuzzled 748
unnamed 565
unnatural
  exceptional 83
  affected 855
  spiteful 907
unnecessary
  redundant 641
  useless 645
  inexpedient 647
unneeded 645
unneighbourly 895
unnerved
  powerless 158
  weak 160
  dejected 837
unnoted } 460
unnoticed } 874
unnumbered 105
unnurtured 674
uno saltu 113
unobeyed 742
unobjectionable
  good 648
  pretty good 651
  innocent 946
unobnoxious 648
unobscured 420
unobservant 458
unobserved 460
unobstructed 705,
  749
unobtainable 471
unobtained 777*a*
unobtrusive 881
unoccupied
  vacant 187
  unthinking 452
  doing nothing 681
  inactive 683
  untenanted 893
unoffended
  enduring 826
  humble 879
unofficial 964
unoften 137

unopened 261
unopposed 709
unorganized 674
 – matter 358
unornamental 846
unornamented
 - *style* 576
 simple 849
unorthodox 984
unostentatious 881
unowed 807
unowned 782
unpacific 713, 722
unpacified 713
unpack
 unfasten 44
 take out 297
unpaid *debt* 806
 honorary 815
the great –
 magistracy 967
 – *worker* 602
unpalatable 395,
 830
unparagoned
 supreme 33
 best 648
 perfect 650
unparalleled
 unimitated 20
 supreme 33
 exceptional 83
unpardonable 938,
 945
unparliamentary
 language 895,
 908
unpassable 261
unpassionate 826
unpatriotic 911
unpeaceful 720, 722
unpeople
 emigration 297
 banishment 893
unperceived
 neglected 460
 unknown 491
unperformed 730
unperjured 543,
 939
unperplexed 498
unpersuadable 606
unpersuaded 616
unperturbed 826
unphilosophical 499
unpierced 261
unpin (44)
unpitied 932
unpitying 914*a*
unplaced 185
unplagued 831

unpleasant 830
unpleasing 830
unpoetical 598, 703
unpolished
 rough 256
 inelegant 579
 unprepared 674
 vulgar 851, 876
 rude 895
unpolite 895
unpolluted
 good 648
 perfect 650
unpopular 830, 867
unpopularity 898
unportioned 804
unpossessed 777*a*
unpractical 699
unprecedented 83,
 137
unprejudiced 498,
 748
unpremeditated
 impulsive 612
 undesigned 621
 unprepared 674
unprepared 508,
 674
unprepossessed 498
unprepossessing
 846
unpresentable 851
unpretending 881
unprevented 748
unprincipled 945
unprivileged 925
unprized 483
unproclaimed 526
unproduced 2
unproductive 645
unproductiveness
 169
unproficiency 699
unprofitable
 unproductive 169
 useless 645
 inexpedient 647
 bad 649
unprolific 169
unpromising 859
unprompted 612
unpronounceable
 519
unpronounced 526
unpropitious
 ill-timed 135
 opposed 708
 hopeless 859
unproportioned 24
unprosperous 735
unprotected 665

unproved 477
unprovided
 scanty 640
 unprepared 674
unprovoked (616)
unpublished 526
unpunctual
 tardy 133
 untimely 135
 irregular 139
unpunished 970
unpurchased 796
unpurified 653
unpurposed 621
unpursued 624
unqualified
 incomplete 52
 impotent 158
 certain 474
 unprepared 674
 inexpert 699
 unentitled 925
 – *truth* 494
unquelled 173
unquenchable
 strong 159
 desire 865
unquenched
 violence 173
 heat 382
unquestionable 474
unquestionably 488
unquestioned 474,
 488
unquiet
 motion 264
 agitation 315
 excitable 825
unravel *untie* 44
 arrange 60
 straighten 246
 evolve 313
 discover 480*a*
 interpret 522
 disembarrass 705
unreached 304
unread 491
unready 674
unreal
 not existing 2
 erroneous 495
 imaginary 515
unreasonable
 impossible 471
 illogical 477
 misjudging 481
 foolish 499
 exorbitant 814
 unjust 923
unreclaimed 951
unrecognizable 146

unreconciled 713
unrecorded 552
unrecounted 55
unreduced 31
unrefined 851
unreflecting 458
unreformed 951
unrefreshed 688
unrefuted 478, 494
unregarded
 neglected 460
 unrespected 929
unregenerate 988
unregistered 552
unreined 748
unrelated 10
unrelenting 914*a*,
 919
unreliable
 uncertain 475
 irresolute 605
 dangerous 665
unrelieved 835
unremarked 460
unremembered 506
unremitting
 continuous 69
 continuing 110
 unvarying 143
 persevering 604*a*
unremoved 184
unremunerated 808
unrenewed 141
unrepealed 141
unrepeated 87, 103
unrepentant 951
unrepining 831
unreplenished 640
unrepressed 173
unreproached 946
unreproved 946
unrequited 806, 917
unresented 918
unresenting 826
unreserved
 manifest 525
 veracious 543
 artless 703
unresisted 743
unresisting 725
unresolved 605
unrespected 929
unrest 149, 264
unrestored 688
unrestrained
 capricious 608
 unencumbered
 705
 free 748
unrestricted
 undiminished 31

concealment 526, 527
conceal 528
ambush 530
behind the − 360
draw aside the − 529
take the − 893, 995
veiled
　uncertain 475
　invisible 447
　concealed 528
vein temper 5
　tendency 176
　thin 203
　thread 205
　channel 350
　humour 602
　mine 636
　affections 820
　in the − 602
　not in the − 603
veined 440
veld 344
velis et remis 274
velitation 720
velleity 600
vellicate 315
vellicating 392
vellum 590
veloce music 415
velocipede 272
velocity 264, 274
　angular − 244
veluti in speculum 17
velvet 255, 256
　pleasure 377
　on − easy 705
venal price 812
　stingy 819
　dishonest 940
　selfish 943
venation 622
vend 796
vendee 795
vender 796
vendetta 919
vendible 796
venditation 884
vendor 796
veneer 204, 223
venenation 659
venerable old 124
　aged 128
　sage 500
　respected 928
veneration
　respect 928
　piety 987

venereal disease 655
venery killing 361
　hunting 622
　impurity 961
venesection
　ejection 297
　remedy 662
Venetian blinds 351
vengeance 919
　cry to heaven for − 923
　with a − 31, 173
vengeful 919
veni vidi vici 731
venial 937
veniam petimusque damusque vicissim 918
venienti occurrere morbo 673
venison 394
venom 663, 907
venomous bad 649
　poisonous 657
　rude 895
　maleficent 907
vent opening 260
　egress 295
　air-pipe 351
　disclose 529
　escape 671
　sale 796
　find − egress 295
　passage 302
　publish 531
　escape 671
　give − to 297, 529
　− one's rage 900
　− one's spleen 900
venter 191
ventiduct 351
ventilate
　begin 66
　air 338
　wind 349
　discuss 595
　− a question 461, 476
ventilator 349, 351
ventosity 349
vent-peg
　stopper 263
　safety 666
　escape 671
ventre
　− à terre 274
　danse du − 840
ventricle 191
ventriloquism 580

venture
　chance 621
　danger 665
　try 675
　courage 861
　I'll − to say 535
venturesome
　undertaking 677
　brave 861
　rash 863
venue 74, 183
Venus woman 374
　planet 423
　beauty 845
　love 897
　goddess 919
veracity 543
verandah 191
verbal 562
　− intercourse 582, 588
　− quibble 497, 842
verbatim
　imitation 19
　exact 494
　words 562
verbiage
　unmeaning 517
　words 562
　diffuse 573
verbis:
　totidem − 494
　− ad verbera 720
verborum, copia −
　diffuse 573
　eloquence 582
　loquacious 584
verbosity
　words 562
　diffuse 573
　loquacity 584
verboten 761
verbum sapienti 527
verdant 367, 435
verd-antique 435
verdict
　opinion 480
　lawsuit 969
　snatch a − 545, 702
verdigris 435
verditer 435
verdure 367, 435
verecundiam, argumentum ad − 874, 939
verecundity 879, 881
veredical 543
Verein 712

verge
　tendency 176
　near 197
　edge 231
　limit 233
　direction 278
verger 996
veriest 31
verification 463, 771
verify 463
　evidence 467
　demonstrate 478
　find out 480a
verily truly 494
verisimilitude 472
veritable 494
veritas, nuda − 494
vérité, palais de − 703
verity 494
verjuice 397
vermicular
　convoluted 248
　worm 366
vermiform 248
vermilion 434
vermin
　animal 366
　unclean 653
　base 876
vernacular
　native 188
　internal 221
　language 560
　habitual 613
vernal 123, 125
vernier
　minuteness 193
　- scale 466
vero, vitam impendere − 535, 939
verrons, nous − 507
versatile 149
verse division 51
　poetry 597
versed in 490
versicolour 440
versify 597
version change 140
　special 79
　interpretation 522
versus 278, 708
vert 435
vertebral 222
vertebrate 366
vertex 210
verticality 212
verticity 312
vertigo
　rotation 312

find its – 302
gather – 267
get into the – of 613
go one's – 293
go your – 297
let it have its – 681
it must have its – 601
have one's own – 748
in a – 828, 900
in the – *near* 197
in the – of 706, 708
make – 302
make one's –
  journey 266
  progression 282
  passage 302
  prosperity 734
make – for
  substitution 147
  opening 260
  turn aside 279
  avoid 623
  facilitate 705
  courtesy 894
on the – 282
place in one's – 763
put in the – of 470, 537
see one's – 490
show the – 693
under – *move* 264
  sail 267
  progression 282
  depart 293
wing one's – 267
– in 294
long – off 196
have – on 267
– out 295
– of speaking 521
– of thinking 484
not know which – to turn 475
Way, the – 976
wayfarer 268
wayfaring 266
waylay 545, 702
wayless 261
ways 692
in all manner of – 278
– and means 632, 800
wayward
  changeable 149

obstinate 606
capricious 608
sullen 901a
waywode 745
wayworn 266, 688
wayzgoose 840
weak *feeble* 160
  water 337
  insipid 391
  illogical 477
  foolish 499
  – *style* 575
  irresolute 605
  trifling 643
  lax 738
  compassionate 914
  vicious 945
  – point 477, 651
  expose one's – point 479
  – side 499, 945
weaken
  decrease 36, 37
  enfeeble 160
  refute 468
weaker vessel 374
weak-headed 499
weak-hearted 862
weak-kneed 725
weakness 160
  – of the flesh 945
weal 618
  common – 644
weald 367
wealth 780, **803**
wean 484, 614
  – from 616
  – one's thoughts from 506
weanling 129
weapon 727
weaponless 158
wear *decrease* 36
  clothes 225
  deflect 279
  use 677
  – *away cease* 142
  deteriorate 659
  – the breeches 737
  – off 142, 614
  – on 109
  – out 659, 688
  – and tear
  decrease 36
  waste 638
  injury 659
  exertion 686
weariness 841
wearing 841
  – apparel 225

wearisome
  laborious 686
  fatiguing 688
  painful 830
weary *fatigue* 688
  painful 828
  sad 837
  ennuyant 841
  – flat, stale, and unprofitable 843
  – *waste* 344
  – Willie 876
weasand 260, 351
weasel asleep,
  catch a – 471, 682
weather 338
  keep one's – eye open 864
  rough – 173, 349
  – the storm
  stability 150
  recover 660
  safe 664
  succeed 731
weather permitting 469, 470
weather-beaten
  weak 160
  damaged 659
  fatigue 688
weather-bound 751
weathercock
  changeable 149
  wind 349
  indication 550
  fickle 607
weathered 659
weather-gauge 338
weather-glass 338
weather-proof 654, 664
weatherwise 338
  foresight 510
weave *produce* 161
  interlace 219
  – a tangled web 704
weazen 193
web
  complexity 59
  intersection 219
  texture 329
wed 48, 903
wedded: – pair 903
  – to *belief* 484
  habit 613
  loving 897
  – to an opinion
  misjudgment 481
  obstinacy 606
wedding 903

– breakfast 892
– day 883
wedge *join* 43
  angular 244
  sharp 253
  instrument 633
  thin edge of the – *begin* 66
  insinuate 228
  cunning 702
  – in 228
wedged in 751
wedlock 903
wee 193
weed *exclude* 55
  few 103
  plant 367
  agriculture 371
  cigar 392
  trifle 643
  clean 652
  – out 297, 301
weeds *dress* 225
  useless 645
  mourning 839
  widowhood 905
weedy 203, 643
week 108
weekly 138
  – paper 531
ween *judge* 480
  believe 484
  know 490
weeny 32
weep 839, 914
weet 480, 490
weetless 491
weft, warp and – 329
weigh *influence* 175
  lift 307
  heavy 319
  ponder 451
  under – [*see* way]
  – anchor 293
  – carefully 465
  – down 649, 749
  – on the heart 830
  – heavy on 649
  – on the mind
  regret 833
  dejection 837
  fear 860
  – with 615
weighed and found wanting 34, 932
weighing machine 319
weight
  influence 175
  gravity 319